Palgrave Handbook of Econometrics

—

Palgrave Handbook of Econometrics

Volume 1 Econometric Theory

Edited by

Terence C. Mills

and

Kerry Patterson

First published in 2006 by
PALGRAVE MACMILLAN
Houndmills, Basingstoke, Hampshire RG21 6XS and
175 Fifth Avenue, New York, N.Y. 10010
Companies and representatives throughout the world.

PALGRAVE MACMILLAN is the global academic imprint of the Palgrave
Macmillan division of St. Martin's Press, LLC and of Palgrave Macmillan Ltd.
Macmillan® is a registered trademark in the United States, United Kingdom
and other countries. Palgrave is a registered trademark in the European
Union and other countries.

ISBN-13: 978–1–4039–4155–8
ISBN-10: 1–4039–4155–6

This book is printed on paper suitable for recycling and made from fully
managed and sustained forest sources.

A catalogue record for this book is available from the British Library.

Library of Congress Cataloging-in-Publication Data

    Palgrave handbook of econometrics / edited by
  Terence C. Mills and Kerry Patterson.
      p. cm.
    Includes bibliographical references and index.
    Contents: Vol. 1. Econometric theory
    ISBN 1–4039–4155–6 (alk. paper)
      1. Econometrics. I. Mills, Terence C. II. Patterson, K. D.

HB139.P345 2006
330′.01′5195---dc22   2005050049

10 9 8 7 6 5 4 3 2 1
15 14 13 12 11 10 09 08 07 06

Printed and bound in Great Britain by
Antony Rowe Ltd, Chippenham and Eastbourne

Contents

Notes on Contributors	viii
Foreword	xi
Editors' Introduction	xiii

Part I An Overview

1 Econometrics in Retrospect and Prospect	3

Aris Spanos, Virginia Polytechnic Institute and State University

Part II Methodology and History of Econometrics

2 The Methodology of Econometrics	61

Kevin D. Hoover, University of California

3 Early Explorations in Econometrics	88

Richard William Farebrother, University of Manchester

4 The First Fifty Years of Modern Econometrics	117

*Christopher L. Gilbert, Università degli Studi di Trento
and Duo Qin, Queen Mary College, University of London*

Part III Asymptotic Techniques and Theorems

5 Asymptotic Methods and Functional Central Limit Theorems	159

James Davidson, University of Exeter

Part IV Time Series and Regression Methods

6 Stationary Linear Univariate Time Series Models	215

Andrew Tremayne, University of Sydney and University of York

7 Improving Size and Power in Unit Root Testing	252

*Niels Haldrup, University of Aarhus and Michael Jansson,
University of California, Berkeley*

8 Dealing with Structural Breaks	278

Pierre Perron, Boston University

9 Semiparametric Estimation of Long-Memory Models	353

*Carlos Velasco, Department of Economics, Universidad
Carlos III de Madrid*

10 Univariate Nonlinear Time Series Models	396

Timo Teräsvirta, Stockholm School of Economics

Part V Multivariate Models

11 Estimating Functions and Equations: An Essay on Historical
    Developments with Applications to Econometrics   427
    Anil K. Bera, University of Illinois, Yannis Bilias, University of Cyprus
    and Pradosh Simlai, University of Illinois
12 Vector Autoregressive Models   477
    Helmut Lütkepohl, European University Institute
13 Nonstationary Panels   511
    In Choi, Hong Kong University of Science and Technology
14 Cointegration: An Overview   540
    Søren Johansen, University of Copenhagen
15 Threshold Effects in Multivariate Error Correction Models   578
    Jesùs Gonzalo, University of Madrid and Jean-Yves Pitarakis,
    University of Southampton
16 Common Cycles   610
    Farshid Vahid, Australian National University

Part VI Cross-Section and Panel Data Models

17 Panel Data Models   633
    Badi H. Baltagi, Texas A&M University
18 Nonstandard Dependent Variables Models: Some Common
    Structures of Simulated Specification Tests   662
    Lung-fei Lee, Ohio State University
19 Censored Data and Truncated Distributions   695
    William Greene, Leonard N. Stern School of Business, New York
    University

Part VII Stochastic Volatility

20 Modeling Volatility   737
    Richard T. Baillie, Michigan State University
21 Multivariate Volatility Models   765
    Chris Brooks, Cass Business School

Part VIII Computation and Econometrics

22 The Role of Simulation in Econometrics   787
    Jurgen A. Doornik, Nuffield College, Oxford University
23 Bootstrap Methods in Econometrics   812
    Russell Davidson, McGill University and James G. MacKinnon,
    Queen's University, Canada

Part IX Bayesian Analysis of Econometric Models

24 Bayesian Econometrics   841
    Dale J. Poirier, University of California at Irvine and
    Justin L. Tobias, Iowa State University
25 Bayesian Approaches to Cointegration   871
    Gary Koop, University of Strathclyde, Rodney Strachan, University
    of Leicester, Herman van Dijk, Erasmus University and
    Mattias Villani, Sveriges Riksbank and Stockholm University

Part X Special Topics

26 Spatial Econometrics   901
    Luc Anselin, University of Illinois, Urbana-Champaign
27 Signal Extraction   970
    Andrew Harvey and Giuliano De Rossi, University of Cambridge
28 Nonparametric Econometrics   1001
    Jeff Racine, Queen's University, Canada and Aman Ullah, University
    of California at Riverside
29 Performance of Seasonal Adjustment Procedures: Simulation
    and Empirical Results   1035
    Dennis Fok, Philip Hans Franses and Richard Paap, Erasmus
    University Rotterdam

Author Index   1057
Subject Index   1076

Notes on Contributors

Luc Anselin is Director of the Spatial Analysis Laboratory and Professor of Geography, Agriculture and Consumer Economics and Urban and Regional Planning, University of Illinois at Urbana-Champaign, USA.

Richard T. Baillie is A.J. Pasant Professor of Economics and Finance at Michigan State University, USA and part-time Professor at Queen Mary, University of London.

Badi H. Baltagi is Professor of Economics, George Summey Jr. Professor of Liberal Arts, Department of Economics, Texas A&M University, USA.

Anil Bera is Professor of Economics at the University of Illinois, Urbana-Champaign, USA.

Yannis Bilias is Associate Professor at the University of Cyprus, Cyprus.

Chris Brooks is Professor of Finance at Cass Business School, UK.

In Choi is Professor of Economics at Hong Kong University of Science and Technology, Hong Kong.

James Davidson is Professor of Econometrics at University of Exeter, UK.

Russell Davidson is Professor of Econometrics at McGill University, Canada.

Giuliano De Rossi is Fellow and Lecturer at Christ's College, University of Cambridge, UK.

Herman van Dijk is Professor of Econometrics at Erasmus University Rotterdam, The Netherlands.

Jurgen A. Doornik is Research Fellow at Nuffield College, University of Oxford, and Director of OxMetrics Technologies Ltd., UK.

Richard William Farebrother is former Reader and Honorary Reader in Economic Studies at the University of Manchester, UK.

Dennis Fok is Assistant Professor of Economics at the Erasmus University, Rotterdam, the Netherlands.

Philip Hans Franses is Professor of Economics at the Erasmus University, Rotterdam, the Netherlands.

Christopher L. Gilbert is Professor of Economics and Finance at Università degli Studi di Trento, Italy.

Jesùs Gonzalo is Professor of Economics at Universidad Carlos III de Madrid, Spain.

William Greene is Professor of Economics and Faculty Fellow of Entertainment, Media and Technology at Leonard N. Stern School of Business, New York University, USA.

Niels Haldrup is Professor of Economics at University of Aarhus, Denmark.

Andrew Harvey is Professor of Econometrics at University of Cambridge, UK.

Kevin D. Hoover is Professor and Chair of Economics at University of California at Davis, USA.

Michael Jansson is Assistant Professor of Economics at the University of California, Berkeley, USA.

Søren Johansen is Professor of Mathematical Statistics at the University of Copenhagen, Denmark.

Gary Koop is Professor of Economics at the University of Strathclyde, UK.

Lung-fei Lee is Professor of Economics at Ohio State University, USA.

Helmut Lütkepohl is Professor of Econometrics at the European University Institute, Italy.

James G. MacKinnon is Sir Edward Peacock Professor of Econometrics and Head of the Economics Department at Queen's University, Canada.

Richard Paap is Associate Professor of Economics at the Erasmus University, Rotterdam, the Netherlands.

Pierre Perron is Professor of Economics at Boston University, USA.

Jean-Yves Pitarakis is Reader in Economics at the University of Southampton, UK.

Dale J. Poirier is a Professor of Economics at the University of California, Irvine, USA.

Duo Qin is Senior Lecturer in Economics, Queen Mary College, University of London, UK.

Jeff Racine is Senator William McMaster Chair of Econometrics, Queen's University, Canada.

Pradosh Simlai is Lecturer in Economics at the University of Illinois, USA.

Aris Spanos is Wilson Schmidt Professor at Virginia Polytechnic Institute and State University, USA.

Rodney Strachan is Lecturer in Economics at University of Leicester, UK.

Timo Teräsvirta is Professor of Econometrics at Stockholm School of Economics, Sweden.

Justin L. Tobias is Associate Professor of Economics at Iowa State University.

Andrew Tremayne is Professor of Econometrics at the University of Sydney, Australia and the University of York, UK.

Aman Ullah is Professor at the University of California, USA.

Farshid Vahid is Professor of Economics at the Australian National University, Australia.

Carlos Velasco is Associate Professor of Economics at the Universidad Carlos III de Madrid, Spain.

Mattias Villani is at the Research Department at Sveriges Riksbank and a Lecturer in the Department of Statistics of Stockholm University, Sweden.

Foreword

Econometrics began as an offshoot of the classical discipline of Mathematical Statistics because the data found in economics had unusual properties. This data can be in the form of a panel, a cross-section, or a time series. A vector of economic variables can be related simultaneously or dynamically, or both. Further, variables can be constrained in various ways such as being positive, being bounded, or censored, or truncated. The time series can have difficult properties, such as stochastic seasonal components and stochastic trends called integrated terms. Because of the properties of the data involved in our area, special methods of analysis have to be developed.

To do this, econometricians have produced a list of possible models of increasing complexity, some of which have economic interpretations. The list essentially starts with simple linear models such as a low order autoregressive for a single series, and then move to a vector form. Progressively, these simple models were considered in more general and realistic forms to include seasonal terms, deterministic and (later) stochastic trends, breaks, time-varying parameters, and a wide variety of nonlinear models.

To the theoretical econometrician, the resulting set of research topics were clear given a particular model: how to estimate it, what are the small- and large-sample properties of the estimates, how to choose between alternative estimating methods, how to test between alternative forms of the same model – or between competing models having similar properties. To answer all of the possible questions concerning estimation, testing, and model comparison leads to a large research agenda.

The applied econometrician has to ask if the model provides a useful approximation to an actual, or realistic, part of the economy. If no good examples can be found, the model can be considered to be an "empty box," an interesting piece of theory with no actual application. With the use of data comes the question of evaluation of a model and this can take many forms from simplistic data-fitting to being relevant for some purpose. When considering evaluation or any other aspect of the methodology of econometrics, it is vital to concentrate on the purpose of the model, and then to evaluate it accordingly. A model designed to explain the past will not necessarily be any good at looking at the future, for example. A forecasting model will inevitably be based on analysis of past data but its specification will result from evaluation of its ability to forecast.

This handbook has chapters covering all, or certainly most, of the major areas of theoretical econometrics. It surveys the past looking at the standard techniques developed over the past twenty years as well as some of the more recent areas of development.

I forecast that it is a text that will be much referenced and cited in the future and certainly welcome its appearance.

Sir Clive W.J. Granger
San Diego
August, 2005

Editors' Introduction

Terence C. Mills and Kerry Patterson

This volume on theoretical econometrics inaugurates the *Palgrave Handbook of Econometrics*. The motivating idea behind the Handbook is that the pace of econometric development is such that it is difficult for textbooks to do justice to the breadth and depth of the subject. In the face of such development, it is helpful to be able to take stock of where the subject is and where it is going. In so doing we, as econometricians in general and as editors in particular, need guidance through an ever-growing number of articles and journals devoted to econometrics.

To this end, the chapters in this book have been specially commissioned from acknowledged experts in their fields; further, each of the chapters has been reviewed by the editors, one or more of the associate editors and a referee. Thus, the process is akin to submission to a journal; however, whilst ensuring standards in the evaluation process, the chapters have been conceived of as part of a whole, which is to convey major developments in econometrics in a way that is accessible to econometricians who may wish to know about developments outside their particular field of specialization, and to postgraduate students who find that existing textbooks are insufficient for their study needs or who are contemplating possible areas of research. In addition, it is likely that economists in and outside academia will find that the chapters offer a "short cut" into an ever-growing literature. It is possible that even students specializing in econometrics in their final year of undergraduate study will find their appetite for the subject whetted by dipping into the chapters.

This growth in econometrics is to be welcomed, for it indicates the vitality and importance of the subject. Indeed, this growth and, arguably, the dominance over the last ten or twenty years of econometric developments in driving economics forward, is a notable change from the situation faced by the subject some 25 years or so ago. At that time, econometrics was still largely viewed as the "handmaiden" of economics; it provided necessary, but sometimes uncomfortably received, tools for the quantification of theoretical relations, where the latter was a territory rarely ventured into by "homo econometricien." Indeed, often no more was claimed by even the best available econometric texts of the time. Malinvaud, in his textbook, defines the aim of econometrics "to be the empirical determination of economic laws. Econometrics rounds off theory by using numerical data to verify the existence of postulated relationships and to define their precise forms" (Malinvaud, 1970, p. vii). Whilst this is still an aim of econometrics, the history of the influence of econometrics shows that it is now very much more.

Three examples from the last two decades serve to make the point. First, the concepts and practical tools arising from the framework, indeed paradigm, of cointegration have markedly changed the course of econometrics *and* economics; it has been, to borrow a concept from econometrics itself, a permanent change, at least as far as the finiteness of time will allow us to make such a judgement. As it happens, the beginnings of the conceptual development of the cointegration framework were being laid in the 1960s, and a case could be made that embryonic thinking was present much earlier with the ideas of correction mechanisms: see Phillips (1954, 1957) and Sargan (1964).

However, as far as take-off was concerned, the 1980s saw an acceleration of interest in methods of dealing with integrated series, with the article by Nelson and Plosser (1982) changing the way many economists viewed time series data. Other research recognised the importance of integration as causing particular problems in estimation: for example, Granger and Newbold (1974) and Evans and Savin (1981, 1984). In an early recognition of the basic cointegration framework, which was the key, as far as economists were concerned, to unlocking the impact of individually integrated time series, Granger and Weiss (1983) set out a framework that was to be famously developed in Engle and Granger (1987). Almost simultaneously, others had recognised the importance of integrated series and the necessity of bringing into the picture the idea of equilibrium, an essential part of economic model building, where two or more economic variables were linked together. Critical mass had been reached. Important contributions were also made by Stock and Watson (1988), Ahn and Reinsel (1988), Phillips (1991), Phillips and Ouliaris (1990) and Sims, Stock and Watson (1990) and, as far as estimation, and then subsequent application, was concerned, Johansen (1988) has proven to be one of the most influential articles in econometrics and economics of the last two decades.

The second example of the power and importance of econometric ideas is the development of Engle's (1982) ARCH framework for modeling (conditional) volatility.[1] Initially, Engle applied his ideas to estimate the means and variances of inflation in the UK.[2] At the time this was an understandable area for application; in the 1970s the UK had experienced (high and variable) inflation rates that now look like data errors in the historical series! However, this is not where Engle's concepts were to have their greatest impact. It soon became apparent that modelling the conditional variance was a way into explaining the volatility clustering that was a central feature of financial data. Once the idea took hold, its impact was pandemic. As Engle notes in the introduction to his edited collection of ARCH readings (Engle, 1995): "Since the introduction of the Autoregressive Conditional Hetero-skedasticity (ARCH) model over ten years ago, the variations, extensions, and applications have become breathtaking and intimidating." The impact of ARCH and its many extensions has been such that no course in finance can now ignore its influence. Modelling volatility for the rate of return of a financial asset is now de rigueur, with models not only for individual variables but for sets of returns and sets of markets.

The two preceding examples relate to time series econometrics, whereas the third relates to cross-section econometrics and models involving "non-standard" dependent variables: for example, dichotomous random variables. These two are not inherently tied together, but often go hand-in-hand because of the nature of the models that have been developed and the samples that have become available. These topics were not much more than "footnotes," if present at all, in standard econometric textbooks of thirty to forty years ago; for example, cross-section analysis is not indexed in Goldberger (1964), Malinvaud (1970) or Theil (1971); whereas Goldberger includes a small section on qualitative and limited dependent variables in a chapter on extensions of linear regression, Theil includes a subsection on probit and logit analysis, while Malinvaud does not even index this subject. These topics became more important in the early 1980s and, for example, Judge *et al.* (1985) includes a chapter on qualitative or limited dependent variables and a chapter on cross-sectional data. Nevertheless, despite this acknowledgement, these topics did not become centre stage as, for example, cointegration did for time series econometrics. However, more recent developments in data and techniques have led to important advances in the econometrics and economics of "microdata" and "microeconometrics." This was recognised in the joint award of the Nobel Prize in Economics to James Heckman and Daniel McFadden.[3]

We hope that this book helps the reader understand some important developments in econometrics. To this end we have organized the chapters into ten parts. The parts aren't watertight, but serve as a useful initial organization of the central themes. To enable perspective, and to recognise that econometrics has both a methodological and an historical base, the Handbook starts with two related parts: first, an "overview" chapter by Aris Spanos, which offers a view on different approaches in econometrics that should encourage thought, discussion, and perhaps some controversy, on the development of the subject. Kevin Hoover then assesses the methodology of econometrics; this is a topic generally absent from textbooks, which tend to concentrate on developing a set of techniques but leave a broader consideration of the philosophical basis of the nature of econometrics to an implicit interpretation. To illustrate a connection in themes, although one possibility as far as method is concerned is the "probabilistic reduction" approach, a methodological issue is whether the framework of the probability approach is even suitable for the study of economic relationships.

The two remaining chapters in Part II, by Bill Farebrother and Chris Gilbert and Duo Qin, respectively, map out some important landmarks in the history of econometrics; the former considers developments primarily before the twentieth century, whereas the latter continues to chart developments, taking the reader into the later part of the twentieth century and up to vector autoregressive models. Students, particularly undergraduates, often have a very limited sense of the history of econometrics, taking, for example, material on subjects such as OLS, the classical linear regression model and the estimation of simultaneous equations, as if their development was ahistorical. Taken together, the first two parts of this volume are a readable introduction to a subject that now has a maturity of development.

Part III comprises a chapter by James Davidson, entitled "Asymptotic Methods and Functional Central Limit Theorems", which is important in developing an understanding of later chapters, especially those in Parts IV and V. To illustrate, it is impossible to understand the nature of present day time series econometrics without some knowledge of Brownian Motion, the Central Limit Theorem and the Functional Central Limit Theorem. James Davidson takes the reader through these concepts with appropriate developments and extensions.

Part IV comprises five chapters that concern univariate methods and related developments. Andrew Tremayne opens this part with a chapter setting out the familiar ARMA (autoregressive-moving average) framework and its key role in econometrics, together with some interesting extensions, for example the ARAR (autoregressive-autoregressive) model and the development of ARMA models to count data, leading to INAR (integer-autoregressive) and INMA (integer-moving average) models.

Next, Niels Haldrup and Michael Jansson focus on testing for a unit root, a topic that has preoccupied the time series literature following Dickey and Fuller's seminal work (Fuller, 1976; Dickey and Fuller, 1979, 1981) and its application to economic time series by Nelson and Plosser (1982). The last thirty years has seen an almost uncountable number of "unit root" tests being proposed, so that it is time to take stock and provide direction; this chapter considers the properties of unit root tests in respect of size, for example the question of the "fidelity" of actual to nominal size, and power, in addition to other theoretical and practical considerations.

Whilst the question of whether time series are better characterized as being stationary or integrated has been a central theme of the last 25 years, finding a clear answer in respect of candidate economic time series is far from straightforward. Not only is there the question of the fidelity and power of the particular unit root test, there is also the tantalizing prospect that the underlying structure has not been constant, so that nonstationarity in the form of an integrated series is apparent rather than real: the nonstationarity being due to a change in the underlying structure. Just as the unit root literature has grown like a (drifting) integrated series, so has the complementary literature on "structural breaks," with much of the direction being provided by Pierre Perron's (1989) seminal article. We are fortunate, therefore, to have a comprehensive update and extension by this author, who takes the reader through developments applicable to univariate processes, recent extensions to multivariate processes, and structural change in long memory processes.

It is sometimes a convenient fiction that the researcher knows the full parametric specification of the proposed model for a particular application; in practice, there are some uncertainties that are contained in assumptions about, for example, dynamic specification, that may not be regarded as the parameters of interest, at least initially. In this case a different approach may be warranted that concentrates on a less than full parametric specification; a leading example of this approach is the semi-parametric approach to estimating the long-run "memory" parameter, which encompasses the unit root model as a special case. Carlos Velasco provides a critical overview and development of the frequency domain semiparametric approach, which also covers some important extensions to multivariate models. (The later chapter by Jeff Racine and Aman Ullah also deals with some related issues from a nonparametric perspective.)

Another limitation that has attracted sustained research input in the last ten to 15 years is the assumption of linearity, which is so often made in both univariate and multivariate models. This has often led to illogical conclusions, for example that a bounded variable, say a portfolio share or nominal interest rate, is generated by an unconstrained random walk. Recent applications to exchange rates have provided evidence that allowing for nonlinear effects can substantially change previously accepted conclusions. Timo Teräsvirta provides an assessment of a number of leading nonlinear models, together with diagnostic tests against linearity and constructive advice on building, and forecasting with, nonlinear models.

Part V comprises six chapters that focus on multivariate time series models. The opening chapter in this part is by Anil Bera, Yannis Bilias and Pradosh Simlai, who are concerned with estimation methods, general principles (including sufficiency and lower bounds) and comparisons. The essence of their approach is to view the estimation set-up as that of obtaining the roots of certain functions of the parameters and the data, which gives rise to estimating functions and, consequently, to estimating equations (EE). For example, maximum likelihood, least squares and the generalized method of moments can all be viewed (and compared) in this way. The EE approach leads to some interesting developments, such as the role of the score function and the combination of estimating equations, and the generality of the approach enables a range of problems to be solved: for example, dependent observations, ARCH, threshold autoregressive models, spatial regression, quantile regression, panel data models, and much more.

The vector autoregressive model is undoubtedly the baseline for much multivariate modeling, and in Chapter 12 Helmut Lütkepohl provides a tour de force of the key issues, including specification, structural and reduced forms, model specification and checking, forecasting, Granger-causality and impulse response analysis.

An important development of the unit root testing framework has been to recognise that economists often develop models that are applicable to panels of data, which have two dimensions, those of the time series and the cross-section. Economic examples include purchasing power parity applied to a set (or panel) of exchange rates over time, and a panel of interest rates, which might comprise of rates on like instruments of different maturities or rates on like maturities but different instruments. The chapter by In Choi starts with the extension of unit root tests for cross-sectionally independent panels and extends the framework to allow for cross-sectional dependence and cointegration within the panel. The challenge from a distributional point of view is to consider the case where two indices, rather than one, tend to infinity. The placement of this chapter emphasizes the development on nonstationary panel data models from a multivariate modelling perspective; the reader may also like to note that Part VI contains further chapters on panel data models.

A section devoted to multivariate models must have a chapter on cointegration, and Soren Johansen provides rather more than just the overview that is the subtitle of his chapter! The concept of cointegration has transformed modelling with several series and Johansen takes the reader through alternative approaches, Granger's Representation Theorem, hypothesis testing on the long-run coefficients and the adjustment coefficients, test statistics for cointegrating rank, and recent developments, including nonlinear cointegration, explosive roots, and I(2) models.

We noted earlier the importance of nonlinear models for univariate time series as a development and extension of the linear model; one important class contains the threshold-based models, in which different regimes operate in the parameter space defined by a threshold indicator. In Chapter 15, Jesus Gonzalo and Jean-Yves Pitarakis extend threshold models to a multivariate framework that includes cointegration. This is an important line of development given the extent of practical interest in frictions, for example transaction costs, that characterize markets and appear to support sustained periods of disequilibrium. Topics covered in this chapter include estimation of the threshold parameter and testing for regime changes, an extension of the concept of cointegration to nonlinear systems, and the estimation of, and testing for, cointegrating rank.

The chapter by Farshid Vahid complements the emphasis on (common) trend behavior by providing a detailed consideration of the implied cyclical behavior of time series. The context is explicitly multivariate and addresses the idea of common cycles and related concepts. A good starting point is the well-known Beveridge–Nelson (1981) decomposition and its multivariate extension, which can be interpreted within the more general concept of a "common feature" (Engle and Kozicki, 1993). The chapter also covers some important alternative approaches (for example, the "structural time series," or unobserved components, approach) and extends the concept of a cycle to idiosyncratic cycles.

Part VI comprises three chapters that recognise the importance of developments in the past twenty years or so in the variety of data available to econometricians. We have in mind here the importance of panels of data, such as the Panel Study of Income Dynamics (PSID) and the National Longitudinal Survey of Market Experience (NLS) in the US, the British Household Panel Survey, and many panels of survey data. However, note that the problems associated with panel data sets and limited dependent variables are also considered in Part X, in the chapters concerned with spatial econometrics and nonparametric econometrics, where the context of the application or the nature of the techniques makes for particular consideration of panel data.

The chapter by Badi Baltagi provides a critical review of key issues in panel data econometrics. This chapter recognises the importance of panel data sources and the particular challenges and problems raised by pooled (across cross-sectional units) sets of time series data. A natural place to start is the "one-way error component" model, with the alternatives of the "fixed effects" or "random effects" set-ups for the specification of the model for the disturbances. The chapter develops the basic framework to include: testing for the distinction between fixed and random effects; the potential endogeneity of regressors, leading to simultaneous equation models with error components; and dynamic panel data models.

There has been a very close interaction between developments in panel data econometrics and those of "nonstandard" dependent variables, which is partly because of the nature of the "microdata sets" that have become available on a cross-sectional basis. Nonstandard variables include those that are limited by their range, usually referred to as truncated variables, or range of responses, as in the case of censored samples, and variables that are limited by their discrete nature (for example, binary choice variables). Models that are structured for these cases are no different, at least in principle, from those for conventional continuous, unrestricted dependent variables in needing specification or diagnostic type tests to help ensure a statistically adequate model. The chapter by Lung-fei Lee addresses both general principles and the application of these principles to leading cases of practical interest. Amongst the important cases covered are: an omitted variables test and a test for normality in multinormal choice models; tests for omitted variables, serial correlation and state dependence in dynamic discrete choice panel data models and dynamic Tobit models; and a test for GARCH-type heteroskedasticity in the latter. Outwith the usual context of panel data models, these tests are also considered for the economically interesting case of dynamic disequilibrium models.

The chapter by William Greene deals with particular issues arising either from some action that changes the available characteristics of the data, described as "censored data," or from the nature of the sample-generating, or data-gathering, process, resulting in a "truncated distribution." These characteristics usually arise in the context of panel data sets and are sometimes dealt with under the rubric of "limited dependent variables," which might be prefaced by "qualitative" or "discrete choice." The description preferred here is more indicative of the nature of how such particularities arise and leads one to note that they are not features of the data generating process. Censoring arises through the (many-to-one) transformation of one variable, say y^*, into a (usually simpler) variable, say y, such that $y = T(y^*)$; the familiar binary choice model is an example here. Truncation is a different feature of the available data and usually affects the range of responses that are recorded; Greene gives the example of modeling the probabilities of visits to recreation sites based only on individuals who have visited those sites at least once. After setting the scene with detailed consideration of estimation and inference problems, the range of models is extended to models for counts, sample selection, and hazard models for duration data; the chapter concludes with a consideration of some key areas at the frontier of developments.

Part VII comprises two chapters addressing one of the topics mentioned earlier, that of Engle's path-breaking work on modeling conditional volatility. Richard Baillie takes the reader through developments of the family of ARCH/GARCH-type models in the univariate case, whereas Chris Brooks concentrates on the various multivariate extensions to this family. Stochastic volatility (SV) models are considered by both authors. Whilst, in the case of GARCH models, or variants thereof, the conditional variance is a deterministic function of the previous period's information set, models based on the SV concept introduce a stochastic disturbance term directly into the volatility equation. GARCH-type models are much easier to estimate because it is possible to write the likelihood function directly in terms of observables, but in the case of SV models the (heteroskedastic) variances are not directly observed. In both chapters, the weight of econometric advances favors GARCH-type models and this is reflected in the discussion; some interesting recent developments are, however, also included: for example, the realized volatility concept that has arisen in the context of very high frequency data from financial markets is discussed by Baillie, while Brooks considers alternatives to GARCH and SV models.

Another critical development in econometrics, particularly over the last 15 years, has been the increase in readily available computing power. This has meant that newly proposed estimation procedures and tests are, as a matter of course, subject to simulations to determine or illustrate their small sample properties. Since it is generally still the case that most is known about the asymptotic properties of econometric methods, rather than their finite-sample properties, simulation offers an inexpensive way of broadening our understanding of whether promised asymptotic gains are delivered for realistically available sample sizes. Another development, arising from the availability of inexpensive computing power, has been a growing interest in the bootstrap and other resampling techniques. Amongst other benefits, these techniques offer a practical way of avoiding any dependence on possibly inappropriate asymptotic critical values and a method of reducing finite-sample bias. Part VIII comprises two chapters dealing with issues relating to simulation and bootstrapping.

At the heart of a simulation is the ability to generate random numbers, which form the replicated samples in each "draw." The chapter by Jurgen Doornik brings to our attention that, whilst many use simulation software in one form or another, there have been concomitant developments in random number generation of which we should be aware. Econometricians often use Monte Carlo experiments (a particular kind of simulation, although the terms are often used interchangeably), and an important consideration is whether the efficiency of these experiments can be improved through, for example, antithetic variates and control variables. Also of importance is designing the experiments to make the results less specific and presenting the results to enhance intelligibility.

The following chapter by Russell Davidson and James G. MacKinnon clarifies what is meant by a "bootstrap" and, hence, the types of bootstrap. They summarize the uses of bootstrap techniques and alert the reader to some of the potential pitfalls awaiting the design of bootstrap-type simulations. Where the bootstrap is used for inference, for example in testing or confidence interval construction, the importance of a pivotal test statistic is underlined. Two key issues that arise in constructing a bootstrap relate to how to deal with heteroskedasticity and dependent data. A further set of complications arise when considering systems of equations. Of course, as Davidson and MacKinnon explain, a bootstrap may fail in the sense of providing a poor approximation to the true DGP.

The two chapters in Part IX relate to "Bayesian Econometrics." Some might argue that the implied distinction between "classical" (or "frequentist") and "Bayesian" econometrics is somewhat artificial, in that prior views inform the former as much as the latter; however, there is undoubtedly a line of development that has led to a particular set of constructs and methodology that distinguishes the two approaches, at least at a formal level. Dale Poirier and Justin Tobias first set out the basic principles of Bayesian analysis, covering such central issues as point and interval estimation, hypothesis testing and prediction. Key practical issues, such as the choice of prior and model building, are also considered. Just as the ready availability of cheap computing power has transformed classical econometrics, it has had an equally important impact in developing the practical implications of the Bayesian approach. The chapter also includes an example of how the Bayesian approach works in practice.

The second chapter in this part, by Gary Koop, Rodney Strachan, Herman van Dijk and Mattias Vilani, opens up another important contribution from Bayesian econometrics, that of a Bayesian approach to cointegration. A central issue in cointegration analysis is the identification (or separation) of the cointegrating coefficients and the adjustment coefficients (the parameters of interest). It is well known (see, for example, Johansen, 1995), that there is an inherent non-uniqueness in this separation. The problems of global and local (non-)identification are considered from a Bayesian perspective; standard priors are unsuitable for cointegration analysis because the reduced rank of a cointegrated system necessarily implies nonlinearity in the parameters of interest. Thus, the questions of identification and specification of the priors are key issues amongst those considered in this chapter.

Part X of the Handbook comprises four chapters that reflect the diversity of recent developments in econometrics. The first chapter in this part is by Luc Anselin and is entitled "Spatial Econometrics." The spatial dimension of economic decisions has increasingly come to be recognised as an important factor, for example, in household and retail decisions that depend upon location, distance or spatial arrangement. Developments in spatial econometrics were initially motivated by urban and regional economics, environmental economics and real estate economics, as well as aspects of economic geography; however, recent developments have shown a much wider field of application. Spatial effects arise from spatial dependence and spatial heterogeneity; in the former case, the key factor is that the covariance between observations relates to a dimension that is fundamentally about geographic (or network) space; in the latter case, heterogeneity in the component units of analysis is often more likely to be the norm than homogeneity. Some of the tools of analysis will be familiar from other fields of application (for example, estimation by maximum likelihood, the method of moments or instrumental variables), but the context, and the solutions to the problems that arise, reflect the particular nature of spatial data. As the chapter indicates in its coverage, spatial data also arises in the context of time series and panel data sets and models for limited dependent variables.

Andrew Harvey and Giuliano de Rossi address various issues connected with the general topic of signal extraction. In this chapter, the reader is introduced to the framework of unobserved components (UC) and the structural and reduced forms of this class of models. An efficient way of conceptualizing UC models is through their state space form (SSF), which is then amenable to application of the Kalman Filter. Univariate and multivariate models are easily treated in this way, and estimation by maximum likelihood is achieved by means of the prediction error decomposition. An extensive number of developments of this framework are also considered and include: continuous time models, irregular spacing of observations, distinguishing between stocks and flows, nonlinear models, non-Gaussian models, models for count data and qualitative observations, filters and smoothers, and more.

The chapter by Jeff Racine and Aman Ullah, entitled "Nonparametric Econometrics" provides a thought-provoking contrast to assumptions that are conventional in parametric econometrics. "Conventional" econometrics involves a parametric specification of a model, the standard linear regression being the most familiar, which may then be complicated by some relaxation of the standard assumptions, resulting in the estimation of the model by a technique that delivers, at least, a consistent estimator. Often, the parametric form is just a practical approximation to some unknown form; whilst this is acknowledged in principle, attention is soon focused elsewhere and this key underlying assumption is "forgotten." However, it can resurface, as in the case indicated by a failure in one or more of the usual battery of diagnostic tests, implying that the model is not statistically adequate and some "remediable" action is needed. An alternative paradigm is to eschew the, anyway doubtful, assumption that the parametric form of the model is known, in favor of modeling the regression function locally, rather than globally, by nonparametric methods. Racine and Ullah explain the crucial role of nonparametric "kernel" methods, which share the property of "local averaging" and involve choosing a "window width" for the local information. (In the standard parametric approach the window width is infinite.) The chapter includes coverage of combining the parametric and nonparametric approaches, guidance on window width selection, structural nonparametric models, hypothesis testing, discrete variables, censored and truncated regression (see also the chapter by William Greene), and panel data models.

Last, but not least, the final chapter by Denis Fok, Philip Hans Franses and Richard Paap covers another important dimension of economic data, namely their periodicity or seasonality. This is an area that is often understated in its importance in econometrics textbooks, yet is vital to practical applications. Economists often work with seasonally adjusted data, where the adjustment has been undertaken by a separate agency; the data is usually taken on faith that nothing is either fundamentally added or removed, apart from the adjustment due to seasonal variations that are outside the immediate interest of the analysis. A natural question to ask is whether this is a valid assumption. For example, suppose that primary interest centres on the cointegration characteristics of a candidate set of variables, so that key properties relate to the presence or absence of common trends. If seasonally adjusted data is used, are the properties relating to the trends preserved by the use of such adjusted data? Several other related issues are considered in this chapter; for example, changing seasonal patterns, models with periodically varying parameters, seasonality in the variance and much more.

This last chapter indicates how closely linked theoretical and applied econometrics have become, and emphasizes the related importance of simulation methods in providing practical guidance. These are themes that will be taken up and elaborated upon in the second volume (*Palgrave Handbook of Econometrics, Volume II, Applied Econometrics*), which is due to be published in 2008.

Finally, thanks are due to many in enabling this volume to appear on schedule. First, our thanks go collectively to the authors who have cooperated in contributing chapters; they have, without exception, responded positively to our several and sometimes many requests, especially in meeting deadlines and accommodating editorial suggestions. The quality of these chapters we hope will be an evident record of the way the vision of the Handbook has been embraced.

We would also like to record our gratitude to the Advisory Editors, Philip Hans Franses, Lung-fei Lee, Katsuto Tanaka and Jeffrey Wooldridge, who have between them read and commented on all of the chapters, often against increasingly tight deadlines. Their support has been invaluable.

Our commissioning editor at Palgrave Macmillan, Amanda Hamilton, has given us unstinting support and encouragement, which we are pleased to put on record as unrivalled in our experience. Thanks also go the production team at Palgrave Macmillan, only some of whom can we name individually: Katie Button, the editorial assistant on this project, brought the production ends of the project together, and her reminders of what was missing served to coordinate the important final details; the role of the copy-editor, in this case Nick Brock, should not be underrated as anyone who has cursed their own incompetence on a computer key board, and knowledge of grammatical niceties, will know; we are grateful to the marketing team for involving us at crucial stages in the design of the book and accompanying material and to the Web team for creating an authors' website for prepublication of the chapters.

We would like to thank Clive Granger for writing the Foreword to this, the first volume of the Palgrave Handbook. We cannot, however, miss this opportunity to acknowledge Clive's immense contribution to econometrics, for which he was so rightly honoured in 2003 with the award of a Nobel Laureate, jointly with Robert F. Engle. Whilst the citation for Clive Granger's Nobel prize is for "for methods of analyzing economic time series with common trends (cointegration)," this brief description is a shorthand for a lifetime's influence over the direction of econometrics and economics. Whilst not wishing to risk the sin of omission, if modern econometrics has "founding fathers," then Clive Granger is clearly one of them.

Notes

1. Robert Engle and Clive Granger were jointly awarded the Nobel Prize in Economics for the year 2003. Their prize citations are, respectively, as follows: "for methods of analyzing time series with time varying volatility (ARCH)"; and "for methods of analyzing economic time series with common trends (cointegration)".
2. There is another UK connection that links the Nobel prize citations for Granger and Engle. In his acceptance lecture (Granger, 2003), the former acknowledges the role of David

Hendry in putting to him the proposition that a linear combination of integrated series could be stationary; Granger reports that he set out to disprove this statement only to find that it was correct, which led him to develop the "missing" concept of cointegration. Engle reports that it was David Hendry who suggested the ARCH acronym. The importance of "topological" connections in network space (see chapter 26 by Luc Anselin on spatial econometrics) could well be illustrated by these two critical developments in the history of econometrics!

3. James Heckman and Daniel McFadden have done much to advance the study of "microeconometrics" and were awarded the Nobel Prize in Economics for the year 2000. Their prize citations are, respectively, as follows: "for his development of theory and methods for analyzing selective samples"; and "for his development of theory and methods for analyzing discrete choice."

References

Ahn. S.K. and G.C. Reinsel (1988) Nested reduced-rank auto-regressive models for multiple time series. *Biometrika* **80**, 855–68.

Beveridge, S. and C.R. Nelson (1981) A new approach to decomposition of economic time Series into permanent and transitory components with particular attention to measurement of the "business cycle." *Journal of Monetary Economics* **7**, 151–74.

Dickey D.A. and W.A. Fuller (1979) Distribution of the estimators for autoregressive time series with a unit root. *Journal of the American Statistical Association* **74**, 427–31.

Dickey D.A. and W.A. Fuller (1981) Likelihood ratio statistics for autoregressive time series with a unit root. *Econometrica* **49**, 1057–1072.

Engle, R.F. (1982) Autoregressive conditional heteroscedasticity with estimates of the variance of United Kingdom Inflation. *Econometrica* **50**, 987–1007.

Engle, R.F. (1995) *ARCH, Selected Readings*. Oxford: Oxford University Press.

Engle, R.F. and S. Kozicki (1993) Testing for common features. *Journal of Economic and Business Statistics* **11**, 369–80.

Evans, G.B.A. and N.E. Savin (1981) Testing for unit roots: 1. *Econometrica* **49**, 753–79.

Evans, G.B.A. and N.E. Savin (1984) Testing for unit roots: 2. *Econometrica* **52**, 1241–1269.

Fuller, W.A. (1976) *The Statistical Analysis of Time Series*. New York: Wiley.

Goldberger, A.S. (1964) *Econometric Theory*. New York: Wiley.

Granger, C.W.J. (2003) Time Series Analysis, Cointegration and Applications. Nobel Prize Lecture; http://nobelprize.org/economics/laureates/2003/index.html.

Granger, C.W.J. and P. Newbold, (1974) Spurious regressions in econometrics. *Journal of Econometrics* **2**, 111–20.

Granger, C.W.J. and A.A. Weiss (1983) Time series analysis of error-correction models. In S. Karlin, T. Amemiya and L.A. Goodman (eds), *Studies in Econometrics, Time Series and Multivariate Statistics, in Honor of T.W. Anderson*. San Diego: Academic Press, pp. 255–78.

Johansen. S. (1988) Statistical analysis of cointegration vectors. *Journal of Economic Dynamics and Control*, vol. 12, pp. 231–54.

Johansen. S.J. (1995) *Likelihood-Based Inference in Cointegrated Vector Autoregressive Models*. Oxford: Oxford University Press.

Judge, G.G., W.E. Griffiths, R. Carter Hill, H. Lütkepohl and T.-C. Lee (1985) *The Theory and Practice of Econometrics*, 2nd edn. New York: Wiley International.

Malinvaud, E. (1970) *Statistical Methods in Econometrics*, 1st English edn. Amsterdam: North-Holland.

Nelson C.R. and C.I. Plosser (1982) Trends and random walks in macroeconomic time series. *Journal of Monetary Economics* **10**, 139–62.

Perron, P. (1989) The Great Crash, the oil price shock and the unit root hypothesis. *Econometrica* **60**, 119–43.

Phillips, A.W. (1954) Stabilisation policy in a closed economy. *Economic Journal* **64**, 290–323.

Phillips, A.W. (1957) Stabilisation policy and the time form of lagged responses. *Economic Journal* **67**, 265–77.

Phillips, P.C.B. (1991) Optimal inference in co-integrated systems. *Econometrica* **59**, 282–306.

Phillips, P.C.B. and S. Ouliaris (1990) Asymptotic properties of residual based tests of cointegration. *Econometrica* **58**, 165–94.

Sargan, J.D. (1964) Wages and prices in the United Kingdom: a study in econometric methodology. In P.E. Hart, G. Mills and J.K. Whittaker (eds), *Econometric Analysis for National Economic Planning*. London: Butterworth.

Sims, C.A., J.H. Stock and M.W. Watson (1990) Inference in linear time series with some unit roots. *Econometrica* **58**, 113–44.

Stock, J.H. and M.W. Watson (1988) Testing for common trends. *Journal of the American Statistical Association* **83**, 1097–1107.

Theil, H. (1971) *Principles of Econometrics*. New York: Wiley.

Part I
An Overview

1

Econometrics in Retrospect and Prospect

Aris Spanos

Abstract

The objective of this chapter is to undertake a retrospective view of econometrics by revisiting a vision of econometrics, articulated in the early twentieth century, as being the inductive component that could provide economics with pertinent empirical foundations. It is argued that, despite the impressive developments in econometric techniques, this vision remains largely unfulfilled. The "quantification of theoretical relationships" perspective has given rise to a theory-dominated approach to empirical modeling that invariably leads to unreliable empirical evidence. This unreliability of evidence stems from applying statistical techniques for quantification without proper statistical justification, leading to unwarranted inductive inferences. The way to ensure statistical reliability is to allow data to have "a life of their own" by introducing the Fisher–Neyman probabilistic perspective into econometrics, thus separating the statistical from the substantive information at the initial stages of modeling. What is needed is a methodology of error inquiry that explicitly recognises the gap between theory and data, and encourages probing of the different ways an inductive inference could be in error, in order to promote both the reliability and precision of inference. This will create the preconditions for a creative dialogue between theory and data that could give rise to a reciprocating error-corrective interchange and thus establish economics as an empirical science.

1.1   Introduction   4
        1.1.1   Econometrics: the vision of early twentieth-century pioneers   4
        1.1.2   A summary of the current state of affairs in econometrics   5
        1.1.3   A call to arms   8
1.2   The "unreliability" of empirical evidence   8
        1.2.1   A methodology of error inquiry   10
1.3   Econometrics 1900–1930: promising beginnings   13
        1.3.1   Economic methodology at the end of the nineteenth century   13
        1.3.2   Early twentieth-century statistics   15
        1.3.3   The prospect of early twentieth-century econometrics   15
        1.3.4   Henry L. Moore   16
        1.3.5   The "deductive" method re-instated?   19
1.4   Modern statistical inference   19
        1.4.1   R. A. Fisher   19
        1.4.2   Outstanding issues in modern statistics   21
        1.4.3   Time series modeling   23

	1.4.4	Bayesian statistics	23
	1.4.5	Nonparametric statistics	24
1.5	Econometrics 1930–1942: a period of zymosis		24
	1.5.1	Ragnar Frisch	24
	1.5.2	Jan Tinbergen	25
	1.5.3	Tjalling Koopmans	26
1.6	Econometrics 1943–1962: Haavelmo and the Cowles Commission		26
	1.6.1	Haavelmo 1944	26
	1.6.2	The Cowles Commission: 1932–1954	28
1.7	Econometrics 1963–present: the textbook approach		30
	1.7.1	Formulating the textbook approach	30
	1.7.2	The critics of the textbook approach	32
	1.7.3	Whither textbook econometrics?	34
1.8	The prospect of twenty-first-century econometrics		36
	1.8.1	The probabilistic reduction (PR) approach	36
	1.8.2	Addressing the unreliability of evidence conundrum	43
	1.8.3	The Gauss–Markov perspective and reliability/precision	45
	1.8.4	Statistical reliability and structural models	47
	1.8.5	Recent developments	48
1.9	Conclusions		51
1.10	Appendix: Basic Misspecification Tests		52

1.1 Introduction

The vision of econometrics articulated in the early twentieth century was that it would supply economics with genuine empirical foundations by endowing it with an inductive component, based on statistics. The primary purpose of this chapter is to put forward a retrospective view of econometrics by revisiting this vision. The objective is to assess the extent to which this vision has been fulfilled, take stock of what has been accomplished so far, and emphasize what remains to be done. The intention is to elucidate the problems that have posed obstacles to fulfilling this vision, as well as to offer concrete suggestions for making progress in overcoming them.

The viewing angle of this retrospective is one of an academic econometrician who has actively studied, taught, practiced and grappled with the broader issues of empirical modeling for more than a quarter of a century. I undertake this task cognizant of the fact that it exposes me to "two serious charges: that of tedium and that of presumption," as well as offering "the greatest opportunity for internecine strife" (Harrod, 1938, p. 383). Having said that, it is important to emphasize at the outset that the critical stance of this chapter is *not* aimed at individual authors and their contributions, but solely at the current state of econometric modeling and its underlying methodological framework.

1.1.1 Econometrics: the vision of early twentieth-century pioneers

Viewing econometrics broadly as the utilization of statistics to provide empirical foundations to economics, its roots can be traced back to the late nineteenth and early twentieth centuries. During the nineteenth century, there was a general consensus that economic theorizing begins with certain initial postulates, comprising the premises, proceeds to derive deductively certain "economic laws," and then their appropriateness in enhancing our understanding of economic phenomena is assessed. In a certain sense this constitutes a primitive version of what became known as the *hypothetico-deductive* method. The disagreements during the nineteenth century centered on the nature and the method of assessment of the initial postulates and the derived economic laws. Despite the widespread misuse of the terms "deduction" and "induction" in methodological discussions during the nineteenth century (see Redman, 1997), the consensus at the end of that century was that "deductive" and "inductive" methods, broadly defined, were considered complementary and that statistics, viewed as quantitative induction, could help to provide pertinent empirical foundations to economics; see Keynes (1891).

By the late nineteenth century the deductive component was considered to be largely in place (Marshall, 1890, chapters 3 and 4), and the leading economists of that generation (Jevons, Menger, Edgeworth, Walras and Pareto) sought ways to provide empirical foundations to economics. The vision of these early pioneers was articulated by Moore (1908, pp. 1–2) in the following way: "economics will become an empirical science when its deductive component is supplemented with an adequate inductive component based on statistics." Jevons (1871, p. 12) expressed the same vision even earlier: "The deductive science of economics must be verified and rendered useful by the purely empirical science of statistics." A similar vision provided the cornerstone upon which the Econometric Society was founded in 1930 (see Frisch, 1933).

In the next subsection we will summarize the current state of econometrics in respect of this vision, in an attempt to provide the vantage point for the retrospective view undertaken in the sequel.

1.1.2 A summary of the current state of affairs in econometrics

At the dawn of the twenty-first century, econometrics has developed from the humble beginnings of "curve fitting" by least squares in the early twentieth century, into a powerful array of statistical tools for modeling all types of data, from the traditional time series to cross-section and panel data. In view of this, the question that naturally arises is the extent to which the inductive vision of econometrics has been fulfilled.

The main thesis of this chapter is that a century later this vision remains largely unrealized. The impressive developments in econometrics during the twentieth century concern primarily the sophistication and rigor of techniques and methods for "quantifying theory models", but these do not amount to a comprehensive methodology for "learning from data about observable economic phenomena".

In order to provide the background for the current state of affairs in econometrics, it is enlightening to compare Leontief's appraisal of the state of econometrics in 1948 and then in 1971. Leontief (1948), after tracing the development of econometrics from Irving Fisher and Moore, to Cobb and Douglas, Schultz, Roos and Tinbergen, appeared to be very optimistic about its prospects. The reason for his optimism was primarily the new methodological framework, introduced by Haavelmo (1944), based on "the modern theory of statistical inference." "Considerable progress has been achieved in recent years toward the understanding of proper and improper application of statistical procedures to economic analysis" (Leontief, 1948, p. 393). He embraced Haavelmo's view that the new methodological framework was: "... essentially a systematic attempt to develop a method to bridge the commonly recognized gap between abstract theory and the actually observed facts which it is supposed to explain" (ibid., p. 394). Leontief considered the period 1933–1948 as one dominated by methodological concerns (he called it a "reflective stage"), as opposed to actual empirical modeling. Secondary reasons for his optimism were: (i) the formalization of simultaneity and the associated structural models, and (ii) the move away from errors-in-variables toward errors-in-equations (ibid., p. 402). His concluding message called for a constructive dialogue between theorists and econometricians (ibid., p. 393).

Twenty years later his optimism had vaporized: "the weak and all too slowly growing empirical foundation clearly cannot support the proliferating super-structure of pure, or should I say, speculative economic theory" (Leontief, 1971, p. 1). He blamed the "indifferent performance" on the unreliability of empirical evidence arising from non-testable probabilistic assumptions: "the validity of these statistical tools depends itself on the acceptance of certain convenient assumptions pertaining to stochastic properties of the phenomena which the particular models are intended to explain; assumptions that can be seldom verified" (ibid., p. 3). His main conclusion concerning the empirical foundations for economics was that "in no other field of empirical inquiry has so massive and sophisticated a statistical machinery been used with such indifferent results. Nevertheless, theorists continue to turn out model after model and mathematical statisticians to devise complicated procedures one after another" (ibid., p. 3).

More than 30 years later, has the reliability of empirical evidence improved? The situation is arguably worse today. The rapid accumulation of new economic data, together with the widespread use of statistical software on personal computers, have lowered the cost of producing empirical evidence, but has not improved their reliability. Indeed, one can make a case that, at the dawn of the twenty-first century, the applied econometric literature is filled with a disorderly assemblage of "study-specific," "period-specific," and largely unreliable evidence, which collectively provide a completely inadequate empirical foundation for economics. The experience of this author with published empirical evidence has been that very few, if any, empirical studies can even survive a thorough probing of their statistical premises, regardless of any empirical merit the underlying theories might have. It is argued that the unreliability of evidence is symptomatic of an inadequate methodological framework, and thus the critical discourse of this chapter is not directed toward individual authors and their work, but at the methodological framework itself.

As things currently stand, the economic theorist feels no obligation to take account of such "empirical evidence" (and rightly so!), and the development of theoretical models is driven by a variety of motivating factors, such as mathematical sophistication and rigor, fecundity, generality and simplicity, to the exclusion of empirical adequacy. Similarly, the (theoretical) econometrician is content to continue devising sophisticated statistical techniques, unconcerned with the appropriateness of these methods for economic data or the unreliability and imprecision of the ensuing empirical results; "goodness of fit" reigns supreme as the primary criterion for assessing the appropriateness of a new technique. In journal publishing a premium is placed on asymptotically "optimal" procedures based on the weakest set of probabilistic assumptions, such as the Generalized Method of Moments (GMM), proposed by Hansen (1982), as well as nonparametric methods.

Caught in the middle, the applied econometrician stares with esteem at the mathematical dexterity of the other two, but finds himself modeling data from observable economic phenomena which are usually not the result of the "ideal circumstances" envisaged by the theory, but of an ongoing complex data-generation process which shows no respect for ceteris paribus clauses, and tramples over individual agents' intentions with no regard for rationality.

At the start of the twenty-first century econometric modeling has made meager progress towards its primary objective of furnishing apposite empirical foundations to economics. Using empirical evidence has been undermined as a way to test economic theories; see Summers (1991). The primary reason for this is that the current textbook approach to empirical modeling has given rise to mountains of unreliable evidence that amount to nothing more than heaps of statistically meaningless "non-regularities," which, unfortunately, are ascribed "theoretical meaning" (using unwarranted statistical inferences), under the guise of identification. Worse still, these "non-regularities" are often used as the basis of empirical support for theories, as well as for policy analysis and predictions. What is conspicuously missing from current econometric modeling are genuinely reliable methods and procedures that enable one to discriminate between the numerous models and theories that could fit the same data equally well or better.

The primary problem of current econometric modeling is unreliable evidence built upon unwarranted inductive inferences. One of the main contributing factors is that the premises of induction, the probabilistic assumptions comprising the underlying statistical model, are often incompletely specified and are rarely probed thoroughly for departures. This is symptomatic of the current methodological framework, where the emphasis on the "quantification of theoretical relationships" gives rise to a theory-dominated approach to empirical modeling, which invariably fails to take into account: (i) the huge gap between theory and data, (ii) the probabilistic structure of the data, and (iii) the different ways an inference could be in error. By making assumptions about errors, the emphasis is placed on the least restrictive assumptions, irrespective of their verifiability, that would "justify" the quantification method. The idea is that the less restrictive the assumptions, the less susceptible to misspecification the results are likely to be. As argued in section 1.8, this is clearly a deductively motivated argument that forestalls both the reliability and the precision of inference; weak assumptions give rise to imprecise inference, and non-verifiable assumptions render the substantiation of statistical adequacy impossible; see Spanos (2001b).

1.1.3 A call to arms

The above critical summary of the current state of affairs in econometrics is offered in the spirit of constructive self-criticism, and not as an indictment of a field that the author shares in the responsibility for its current plight. It is offered as a "call to arms" to ameliorate the current predicament of econometrics with a view to fulfilling the vision of the early pioneers in providing empirical foundations to economics.

In order to meet this challenge, one needs to take a retrospective of the development of econometrics during the twentieth century with a view to tracing the source of particular weaknesses in current practice. In the next sections a selective summary of some of these developments is given in light of three important influences on the evolution of econometrics.

First, how developments in probability and statistics during the twentieth century influenced the evolution of econometrics. The basic idea is that, even though some of the problems in econometric modeling can be traced to "inveterate" problems in statistics, econometrics has not made judicious use of certain important developments in probability and statistics.

Second, how the underlying methodological framework of empirical modeling in economics has been affected by both its own internal dynamics as well as the broader "currents" in the philosophy of science. The basic idea is to trace the development of econometric methodology from the broad problem of bridging the gap between theory and data, in the early twentieth century, to the current approach of focusing narrowly on the "quantification of theoretical relationships."

Third, how the various twentieth-century developments in econometrics have been distilled into the current textbook approach to econometrics. The demarcation of econometrics in the early 1960s by two popular textbooks has distilled the earlier developments through the Gauss–Markov "curve fitting" perspective to the detriment of empirical modeling in economics.

For a more balanced discussion of the history of econometrics see Stigler (1954, 1962), Christ (1985), Epstein (1987), Fox (1989), Morgan (1990), Heckman (1992), Qin (1993) and Hendry and Morgan (1995).

1.2 The "unreliability" of empirical evidence

The question that naturally arises is "why has econometric modeling made such meager progress toward its primary objective of furnishing apposite empirical foundations to economics?" Making the critical arguments in the constructive way I would like is complicated by the fact that the notions of deduction and induction have been greatly misused in economics since the early nineteenth century (see Redman, 1997), and the idea of "empirical foundations" has shifted greatly since then. Any adequate retrospective must recognize that:

(1) There is unclarity and debate as to what is required of an "inductive component" in order that it supply genuine empirical foundations, and, alongside this,
(2) there are the disagreements and controversies regarding the nature and role of statistics in science in general, and in economics in particular.

It is well known that economists employ data to "quantify theoretical relation-ships," the results of which are often taken as providing "support" for their theories, but it is apparent, given the heaps of unreliable and non-incisive pub-lished evidence, that this does not suffice for pertinent empirical foundations. What is not manifest is the source of the unreliability of this evidence.

A textbook approach econometrician begins with a theory which he uses to derive a theory-model in the form of functional relationships among variables of interest (exclusively determined by the theory in question). The object of the empirical modeling is to "quantify" this theoretical relationship and/or to verify the theory in question. The quantification/verification is guided by both theoretical (sign, size of estimated parameters), as well as statistical considerations, such as R^2 "goodness of fit," t-ratios and F-tests. Typically, a textbook applied econometrician begins with a theory model, more or less precisely specified, and proceeds to transform it into a statistical model in the context of which the quantification will take place. The primary objective of the quantification is to use data to provide empirical evi-dence *for* the theory in question. This is achieved by viewing the theory model as furnishing the systematic error component and a white noise error as appending the non-systematic component. The quantification is driven by a search for an "optimal" estimator (OLS, GLS, FGLS, IV, 2SLS, 3SLS, k-class, LIML, FIML, etc.) for each different set of error assumptions. It is invariably assumed that the data chosen measure the concepts in terms of which the theory in question is articulated.

In a typical scenario, after an unsuccessful first attempt at "quantification" using the Classical Linear Regression (CLR) model $\mathbf{y} = \mathbf{X}\boldsymbol{\beta} + \mathbf{u}$, an applied econometrician finds himself faced with non-white noise residuals, indicating that the OLS estimator $\hat{\boldsymbol{\beta}} = (\mathbf{X}^\top\mathbf{X})^{-1}\mathbf{X}^\top\mathbf{y}$ is no longer optimal. The recommendation from the textbook approach is to retain the original systematic component $\mathbf{X}\boldsymbol{\beta}$, but allow for non-white errors by modifying the assumptions of the error term $\mathbf{u}$. The underlying rationale is that these "error-fixing" corrections are used to get better estimators as well as valid standard errors for the theoretical model under quantification. For instance, if the Durbin–Watson (D–W) statistic indicates a departure from the no-autocorrelation assumption, $E(\mathbf{u}\mathbf{u}^\top) = \mathbf{I}_T$, "correcting" for autocorrelation amounts to adopting the GLS estimator $\tilde{\boldsymbol{\beta}} = (\mathbf{X}^\top\mathbf{V}_T^{-1}\mathbf{X})^{-1}\mathbf{X}^\top\mathbf{V}_T^{-1}\mathbf{y}$, where $\mathbf{V}_T = E(\mathbf{u}\mathbf{u}^\top)$. The formal justification for this move is that $\tilde{\boldsymbol{\beta}}$ is "more" optimal because $Cov(\hat{\boldsymbol{\beta}}) \geq Cov(\tilde{\boldsymbol{\beta}})$. The success of this inference is assessed in terms of the value of the new D–W test statistic, as well as the theoretical validity of the sign and magnitude of the estimated coefficients. As argued in the sequel, the primary problem with the textbook approach is that it invariably leads to unreliable inferences because the inference procedures used to choose the "appropriate" estimator have very limited capacity to uncover the different ways such an inference could be false.

First, by focusing exclusively on the error term, the textbook perspective over-looks the ways in which the systematic component may be misspecified, and sometimes fails to acknowledge other implicit assumptions. Moreover, the "error-fixing" strategy ignores the fact that, by definition, $\mathbf{u} = \mathbf{y} - \mathbf{X}\boldsymbol{\beta}$, and thus "fixing" the error involves modeling the systematic component indirectly: this sometimes leads to internally inconsistent models; see Spanos (1995b).

Second, the "error-fixing" strategy is designed to "save the theory" because, by retaining the systematic component, it ignores alternative theories which might fit the same data equally well or even better. That is, the "error-fixing" strategy misuses data in ways that "appear" to provide empirical (inductive) support for the theory in question, when in fact the inferences are unwarranted.

Third, the "error-fixing" strategies are littered with flawed reasoning (see Spanos, 1986, 2000). For instance, when autocorrelated residuals are interpreted as auto-correlated errors, inference on the new estimator $\tilde{\beta}$ (or, equivalently, the new model based on $\mathbf{V}_T = E(\mathbf{u}\mathbf{u}^\top)$) is unwarranted because the method used to choose it had no chance to uncover the various other forms of departures that could have been responsible for the presence of residual autocorrelation; see Spanos (1986) and McGuirk and Spanos (2003). The general reasoning flaw in this respecification strategy is that adopting the alternative hypothesis in a misspecification test often amounts to committing the fallacy of rejection: in non-exhaustive cases, evidence *against* the null is erroneously interpreted as evidence *for* the alternative. Hence, after such "error-fixing" takes place, by choosing the "optimal" estimator associated with the new set of error assumptions, one often ends up with a misspecified model because these new assumptions have not been tested. This is an instance of a classic inductive fallacious move: infer a claim, or save a model from anomaly, by adjusting a feature to "account for" the data, when in fact the data underdetermines this particular save (see Mayo and Spanos, 2004).

Admittedly, misspecification testing (assessing the validity of the probabilistic assumptions) and respecification (choosing a more appropriate model) raise some fundamental issues concerning inference and evidence in general, such as double use of data, which are neither trivial nor obvious in the case of empirical modeling; see Spanos (1999, 2000, 2001a). Indeed, misspecification testing is often con-sidered as unwarranted data mining; see Kennedy (2003). This might help to explain why these problems persisted for so long in econometrics. Nevertheless, addressing these issues is urgently called for in order to improve the reliability of inference in econometric modeling.

1.2.1 A methodology of error inquiry

A philosophy of science that will help to organize the issues I wish to highlight is the error statistical account articulated by Mayo (1991, 1996). Unlike other philosophical accounts of evidence, whether data $\mathbf{Z} = (z_1, \ldots, z_n)$ provide evidence for a hypothesis H is not a mere matter of logical or probabilistic relationships between $\mathbf{Z}$ and H, but is an empirical issue that requires considering how $\mathbf{Z}$ was generated and how H was selected, in order to determine the overall reliability of the inference. Moreover, the error statistical account deals explicitly with the frequentist statistical methodology which provides the foundation for empirical modeling in economics.

What is missing from economics, when compared to other more successful sciences, is a constructive dialog between theory and data, as a result of which learning can take place. As argued by Mayo (1996), when a theory in a scientific discipline is found wanting after being confronted with data, the rejection should give rise to some form of reliable inquiry into its causes. Inquiries which should lead to some form of learning, however rudimentary: perhaps the data were inappropriate or inaccurate, or the theory needs to be revised. Indeed, she considers "learning from an anomaly" to be a demarcation criterion for scientific inquiry.

It is argued that what is needed for modern econometrics is a methodology of error inquiry that encourages detecting and identifying the different ways an inductive inference could be in error by applying efficacious methods and procedures which would detect such errors when present with very high probability. Learning from error, according to Mayo (1996, p. 7), amounts to deliberate and reliable argument from error based on severe testing: "a testing procedure with an overwhelmingly good chance of revealing the presence of specific error, if it exists – but not otherwise." Mere fit is insufficient for Z to pass H severely, as such a good fit must be very difficult to achieve, and so very improbable, were H to be in error. Nevertheless, the fact that Z were used to arrive at a good fit with H(Z) does not preclude counting Z as good evidence for H(Z) – it all depends on whether the procedure for arriving at H(Z) would find evidence erroneously with very low probability.

Mayo (1996) applies the severe test reasoning to the Neyman–Pearson (N–P) hypothesis testing framework in order to supplement it with a post-data evaluation procedure that addresses most of the criticisms of frequentist testing; see also Mayo and Spanos (2006). In particular, it provides the reasoning to address the question "When do data Z provide evidence for a hypothesis or a claim H?" In this evidential intepretation of tests, one wants to avoid tests which are either too sensitive or not sensitive enough for the inference in question.

Mayo's way of implementing the severe testing reasoning is to localize the error probing by viewing it in the context of compartmentalised, but highly interconnected, pieces (models), comprising the overall theory testing. These interconnected pieces come in the form of a hierarchy of models (primary, experimental and data) devised to link the primary hypothesis to the data; see Mayo (1996, chapter 5). The idea behind the hierarchy of models is to localize errors and apply severe testing in a piece-meal way at a level which enables one to pose questions concerning errors one at a time in an exhaustive fashion and then piece them together to provide an overall testing procedure.

Mayo (1996) proposed a methodology of error inquiry concerned with "learning from experiments" to provide coherent philosophical foundations for new experimentalism (see Chalmers, 1999). Her notion of "experiment," however, is broad enough, "any planned inquiry in which there is a deliberate and reliable argument from error" (ibid., p. 7), to render it appropriate for certain non-experimental situations. The idea is that, in cases where no literal control or manipulation over the phenomena being modeled is possible, one can still ascertain deliberate and reliable argument from error by probing thoroughly the different ways one's claim can be wrong. This renders the error-statistical methodology eminently relevant for empirical modeling in economics. The main difficulty in implementing the severe testing reasoning arises from the fact that, in certain situations, one cannot accomplish the same level of cogency as in cases of carefully controlled experiments. This, however, could serve as a challenge to improve the current procedures and methods used to probe for error, as well as to delineate the limits of empirical modeling using non-experimental data. Indeed, the hope of this author is that severe testing reasoning will help to furnish criteria that alleviate some of the discomforts associated with several methodological problems in econometric modeling, such as pre-test bias, post-designation, data snooping, and other forms of exploratory data analysis. Moreover, the value of ascertaining that one is *not* able to infer that $\mathbf{Z}$ provides good evidence for H is that it provides an important source of guidance as to what to try next.

In direct analogy to Mayo's hierarchy of models, the methodological framework for econometric modeling discussed in section 1.8 consists of a sequence of models ranging from the *theory model* to the *structural model* that links the theory (substantive information) to the data via by the *statistical model* (statistical information), and the synthesis of substantive and statistical information gives rise to the empirical model (see Figure 1.1). The reliability of evidence is assessed at all levels of different models by using severe testing reasoning, quantitative as well as qualitative, to probe the different types of errors that arise in that context.

In the context of a *statistical model* the primary sources of error are:

(I) *Statistical misspecification*: some of the probabilistic assumptions comprising the statistical model (premises of induction) are invalid for data $\mathbf{Z} = (z_1, \ldots, z_n)$.

A misspecified statistical model gives rise to unreliable inferences because the *actual* error probabilities are very different from the *nominal* ones – the ones assumed to hold if the premises are true. Applying a 0.05 significance level t-test, when the actual type I error is 0.95, renders the test highly unreliable; see Mayo (1996) and Spanos (2005c).

(II) *Inaccurate data*: data $\mathbf{Z}$ are marred by systematic errors imbued by the collection/compilation process.

The inaccuracy and inadequacies of economic data as of the late 1950s has been documented by Morgenstern (1950/1963) and Kuznets (1950). Since then the accuracy of economic data has been improving steadily, but not enough attention has been paid to issues concerning how the collection, processing and aggregation

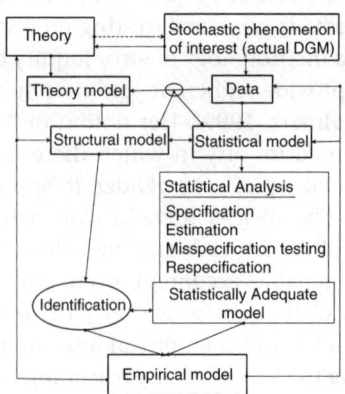

Figure 1.1 A methodological framework for econometric modeling

of data in economics might imbue systematic errors that can undermine their statistical analysis; see Abadir and Talmain (2002) for an illuminating discussion.

In the context of an *structural model* the relevant source of error is:

(III) *Incongruous measurement*: data Z do not measure the concepts ξ envisioned by the theory model (e.g., intentions vs realizations).

This is a fundamental issue because, typically, theory models are built on static intentions, but the available data measure realizations of ongoing convoluted processes. Moreover, the overwhelming majority of economic data are collected by government agencies and private institutions, not the modelers themselves. Measuring economic theory concepts constitutes a form of "experimentation," in the sense used by Mayo in the above quotation, which needs to be recognized as such before the incongruous measurement problem can be adequately addressed.

In the context of *theory and empirical models* the primary source of error is:

(IV) *External invalidity*: the circumstances envisaged by the theory differ "systematically" from the actual Data Generating Mechanism (DGM); *ceteris paribus* clauses, missing confounding factors, causal claims (see Hoover, 2001), etc. External validity concerns the extent to which the inferences based on the estimated structural model are germane to the phenomenon of interest.

This is a most fundamental issue that has been inadequately addressed in econometrics, because external invalidity affects, and is affected by, all the other sources of error; see Guala (2005) on external validity and experimental economics.

The typology of different models is designed to delineate questions concerning different errors and to render their probing much more effective than lumping them together in one overall error term, as the textbook approach practices!

It is unfortunate that the recent methodology of economics literature (see Backhouse, 1994; Maki, 2002, inter alia) has largely ignored the methodology of econometrics in their discussions of the various philosophy of science perspectives in economics; notable exceptions are Stigum (2003) and Hoover (2006).

In summary, the current textbook approach to econometrics does not provide a methodological framework for a reliable/effective error probing inquiry that leads to learning from data. What renders the overwhelming majority of published evidence in econometrics unreliable is that they were produced by methods and procedures which had very limited ability to detect errors if, in fact, they were present.

For the attempt to trace the roots of the current state of econometrics, it will be convenient to divide the twentieth-century developments in econometrics into four broad periods: 1900–1930: the promising beginnings; 1930–1943: the period of zymosis; 1944–1962: the Cowles Commission; 1963–present: the textbook approach.

1.3 Econometrics 1900–1930: promising beginnings

1.3.1 Economic methodology at the end of the nineteenth century

The methodological discussions during the nineteenth century concerning the proper method of economics focused primarily on whether the method of the physical sciences, as initially envisaged by Bacon and exemplified by Newton's work, could or should be applied to the social sciences. There was a widely held consensus that a primitive hypothetico-deductive method was appropriate for economic theorizing; this might explain the appeal of Popper's falsifiability in economics (Blaug, 1992). The disagreements during the nineteenth century centered on the nature, and the method of assessment of the initial postulates (premises) and the (deductively derived) economic laws. In very broad terms, economists like Hume, Smith, McCulloch, and Say advocated that the grounding and method of assessment for both the initial postulates and the economic laws should be empirical (anchored in the observable world), and they are often labeled "inductivists." At the other extreme, economists like Ricardo, Senior, Torrens and Cairnes opposed this and, instead, emphasized the deductive aspects of theorizing from plausible premises, arguing that the plausibility of the premises and the appositeness of the deductions did not necessitate empirical grounding or testing; these economists are often labeled "deductivists."

There was consensus that economics differed from physics in some important respects, such as the inaccessibility of the experimental method, and the presence of innumerable factors in economic phenomena, but there was no agreement as to how the primitive hypothetico-deductive method should be modified to accommodate these differences. Mill (1874, 1884) straddled both camps by arguing for inductively established initial postulates, but put the emphasis on deductively derived (as opposed to experimentally determined) economic laws establishing "tendencies" instead of the exact predictions churned out by physical laws. He construed empirical analysis of economic laws as establishing "empirical uniformities" that provide a way to shed light on the question of delineating the "perturbations" (the less important factors) influencing a particular phenomenon; see Mill (1874, p. 154). Mill's methodology influenced both Marshall (1890) and Keynes (1891) in so far as they both adopted: (i) the empirical grounding of initial postulates, (ii) the importance of deductively derived economic laws, as well as (iii) the view that economic laws only establish "tendencies." Indeed, Marshall (1890, pp. 31–2) adopts, almost verbatim, Mill's thesis that economics is an inexact science (the inherent presence of innumerous pertubations), more like the field of tidology (concerned with sea tides) than the exact science of astronomy (Mill, 1884, pp. 587–8).

Jevons (1871, 1874) redressed the balance between induction and deduction in Mill's discussion by re-stating the hypothetico-deductive nature of the proper method for economics, introducing probability into induction, and reaffirming the role of empirical testing for deductively derived laws.

Keynes (1891) played the role of the master synthesizer of the methodological discussions during the nineteenth century, by couching the consensus view in a way that emphasized economics as a positive science, and not as a normative art, and ascribing to statistics a much greater role than hitherto (pp. 342–6): "The functions of statistics in economic enquiries are:...descriptive,...to suggest empirical laws, which may or may not be capable of subsequent deductive explanation,...to supplement deductive reasoning by checking its results,... enabling the deductive economist to test and, where necessary, modify his premises,...measure the force exerted by disturbing agencies."

1.3.2 Early twentieth-century statistics

The most important development in statistics during the twentieth century is undoubtedly the recasting of statistical induction into its modern form by R. A. Fisher (1922). His modus operandi was the notion of a statistical model in the form of a pre-specified "hypothetical infinite population," with data $x := (x_1, x_2, \ldots, x_n)$ interpreted as a representative sample from that "population."

Before Fisher, the notion of a statistical model was only implicit, and its role was primarily confined to the description of the distributional features of the data in hand using the histogram and the first few sample moments. The problem was that statisticians would use descriptive summaries of the data to claim generality beyond the data in hand. The conventional wisdom at the time is encapsulated by Mills (1924) as "statistical description" vs "statistical induction," where the former is always valid and "may be used to perfect confidence, as accurate descriptions of the given characteristics" (Mills, p. 549), but the validity of the latter depends on the inherent assumptions of (a) "uniformity" for the population, and (b) the "representativeness" of the sample (ibid., pp. 550–2).

The fine line between statistical description and statistical induction was nebulous until the 1920s, for a number of reasons. First, "no distinction was drawn between a sample and the population, and what was calculated from the sample was attributed to the population" (Rao, 1992, p. 35). Second, it was thought that the "inherent assumptions" for the validity of statistical induction were not empirically verifiable; see Mills (1924, p. 551). Third, there was (and, unfortunately, still is) a widespread belief, exemplified in the above quotation from Mills, that statistical description does not require any assumptions because "it's just a summary of the data." The reality is that there are appropriate and inappropriate summaries of the data. For example, the arithmetic average is an inappropriate summary of a trending time series because it measures no feature of that data; the same applies to the sample variance and to higher central moments over the arithmetic mean; see Spanos (2001b). It is, however, an appropriate summary when the data constitute a realization of an Independent and Identically Distributed (IID) process, because it represents a reliable estimate of the mean of the process.

Karl Pearson elevated descriptive statistics to a higher level of sophistication by proposing the "graduation (smoothing) of histograms" into "frequency curves," and introducing a new family of such curves; see Pearson (1895). The problem of statistical induction was understood by Pearson (1920) in terms of being able to ensure the "stability" of empirical results in subsequent samples, by invoking "uniformity" and "representativeness" assumptions. This is a form of induction by enumeration, which attempts to generalize observed events, like "80 percent of A's in this data are B's," beyond the data in hand; see Salmon (1966).

1.3.3 The prospect of early twentieth-century econometrics

In the early twentieth century, pioneers, like Moore, aspiring to provide empirical foundations to economics, had several things going for them. Substantive progress was made in the collection and systematization of economic data; statistical offices, index numbers, etc. Neoclassical economic theory was in the process of complete mathematization, providing them with economic models which were amenable to empirical inquiry. At the end of the nineteenth century there were several developments in statistical methods, like periodogram analysis, correlation and least-squares, multiple correlation (regression) and least-squares curve-fitting, which seemed appropriate for analyzing economic data.

At the same time, however, these pioneers were facing an insuperable obstacle in so far as the inductive component of statistics was lacking. Statistics amounted to a toolkit of descriptive methods for summarizing data, accompanied by ill-defined allusions to inductive inference using probabilistic terms. These descriptive methods, emanating from the works of Graunt, Petty, Quetelet, Galton and Karl Pearson, were largely disjoined from the theory of probability as developed by Bernoulli, Gauss, Poisson, Cournot, Venn, Peirce and Edgeworth; see Stigler (1986). To make matters more confusing, the language of probability, with references to the "law of error," "probable error," and "correlation," abounded in the statistics literature of that time. Proper integration of probability theory with statistical inference did not begin until the 1920s with R. A. Fisher (1922).

1.3.4   Henry L. Moore

In this selective reappraisal of the development of econometrics, Moore is chosen as the quintessential pioneer of the early twentieth century. His empirical studies were instrumental in generating discussions on how the newly developed statistical tools of Galton, Karl Pearson and Yule could be utilized to render economics an empirical science. This early period is important, because some of the crucial weaknesses of the current textbook approach can be traced back to Moore (1911, 1914).

The inductive procedure was seen by Moore at the outset as comprising two intertwining branches. One proceeds from data (and statistical laws established via correlation and regression) to theory, and the other begins with theory and relates that to data, either as theory-quantification or as theory-testing. The basic objective of empirical modeling was seen to involve both explanation as well as prediction. Moore used the data-to-theory inductive process to study business cycles by first establishing "statistical regularities" (using periodogram analysis, correlation and regression), and then relating them to theory. Fitting periodograms to rainfall series observed between 1839 and 1910 from the Ohio Valley, he detected two cycles of 8 and 33 years, and went on to correlate them with cycles of the yield of agricultural products, such as corn, hay, oats and potatoes. He (mis-) interpreted the observed correlation as evidence for a "causal connection" between rainfall and yield of crops, and proceeded to complete the inductive intertwine using the theory-to-data inductive process by evaluating the "law of demand" for these products.

Moore fitted demand curves for a number of agricultural products using the least squares method. For illustrative purposes, let us use Moore's (1914) demand for corn, based on annual observations for the period 1866 to 1911, as a typical example. The reported "interpolated curve" was:

$$y_t = 7.79 - 0.886x_t \qquad (1.1)$$

where $x_t = 100 \, \Delta p_t / p_t$ and $y_t = 100 \, \Delta q_t / q_t$, p_t being the average price per bushel and q_t production in bushels. His criteria for considering (1.1) to be a "statistical law of demand" were: the "simplicity of the formula, its fecundity, its closeness of fit, its ease of calculation, its a priori validity" (Moore, 1908, p. 21).

A priori validity is justified in terms of the sign and magnitude of the estimated coefficients as they relate to a theoretical demand function. Taking the estimates (7.79, -0.886) at face value, without any accompanying measures of uncertainty (e.g., standard errors), Moore's analysis constitutes descriptive statistics with all its limitations. However, that did not stop Moore from drawing inductive inferences of the form "the demand elasticity for corn is -1.129" (Moore, 1914, p. 84), or predicting the price of corn for 1912 using (1) (ibid., p. 78). What could provide the justification for such inferences?

1.3.4.1 *Moore's empirical "non-regularities"*

Taking an anachronistic look at Moore's analysis from today's vantage point, we can say that its primary limitation is that his criteria are inadequate to provide a sound underpinning for his inductive inferences. For Moore, "excellence of fit" is both necessary and sufficient for establishing "statistical laws" (see Moore, 1914, p. 17). What is missing is any discussion of the different ways that these inferences might be in error. As argued in section 1.2, the most rudimentary way that such an inference might be false is statistical misspecification.

From today's vantage point, the implicit statistical model for Moore's curve fitting is the Gauss Linear model (see Spanos, 1986, chapter 18), whose assumptions are:

$$[1] \; u_t \sim N(.,.) \quad [2] \; E(u_t) = 0 \quad [3] \; Var(u_t) = \sigma^2 \quad [4] \; E(u_t u_s) = 0, \quad t \neq s$$

Re-estimating (1.1) using Moore's data yields:

$$y_t = \underset{(2.175)}{7.219} - \underset{(0.083)}{0.699} \, x_t + \underset{(14.447)}{\hat{u}_t} \qquad R^2 = 0.622 \qquad n = 45 \qquad (1.2)$$

where the standard errors are reported in brackets. Before we rush into pronouncements that Moore was right after all, by quoting t-ratios, F-tests and the R^2, it is important to remind ourselves that the reliability of any inductive inference based on (1.2) depends on whether assumptions [1]–[4] are valid for the corn data. Some basic misspecification tests (see appendix) are reported in Table 1.1, with the associated p-values (in square brackets).

The tiny p-values indicate significant departures from assumptions [2]–[4]. Hence, Moore's inferences concerning the sign and the magnitude of the coefficients (β_0, β_1) are unwarranted, since (1.2) constitutes unreliable evidence. This is not intended to be a criticism of Moore's empirical work, but to highlight the fact

Table 1.1 Misspecification Tests

Non-Normality	$D'AP = 3.252 \; [0.197]$
Non-linearity	$F(1,42) = 18.560 \; [0.00095]$
Heteroskedsticity	$F(2,40) = 14.902 \; [0.000015]$
Autocorrelation	$F(2,42) = 18.375 \; [0.000011]$

that the overwhelming majority of published applied papers almost 100 years later
are unlikely to pass this same statistical adequacy test.

1.3.4.2   Moore's "upward-sloping demand curve"

Where does this leave Moore's revolutionary vision of econometrics as the
inductive component of economics? The statistical unreliability in his empirical
work did not help his mission. Without a way to distinguish between genuine
empirical regularities and nonregularities, both forms of inductive inference, from
data-to-theory and vice versa, were inadvertently exposed to disrepute. This came
sooner than later in the form of a "positively sloping statistical demand curve" for
pig iron (Moore, 1914, pp. 110–16). "Goodness of fit" was enough for Moore to
pronounce that an "interpolated line" between the percentage change of the
production of pig iron y_t and the average price x_t was "a new type of demand
curve." Re-estimation of his equation yields:

$$y_t = \underset{(2.800)}{-\,4.575} + \underset{(0.129)}{0.521\,x_t} + \underset{(16.540)}{\hat{u}_t} \qquad R^2 = 0.288 \qquad n = 42 \qquad (1.3)$$

where the estimates of $(\beta_0, \beta_1, \sigma^2)$ are almost identical to Moore's original estimates.
Before one can establish (1.3) as a statistical regularity, never mind "a new type of
demand curve," one needs to ensure its statistical adequacy. It turns out that (1.3) is
misspecified because most of the assumptions [1]–[4] are invalid.

Unfortunately, Moore's (1914) publication of the "new demand curve" gave rise
to fomented discussions which, despite some positive lessons learned, painted
prematurely a rather distorted picture of the issues involved in bridging the gap
between theory and data: a picture that continues to befuddle econometric
modeling to this day. The ensuing discussion by Lenoir, Wright, Working and
Ezekiel (see Stigler, 1962; Christ, 1985; Fox, 1989; Morgan, 1990; Hendry and
Morgan, 1995, inter alia), focused almost exclusively on (a) the wrong sign on
the slope coefficient β_1, and (b) Moore's handling of the *ceteris paribus* clause. The
ensuing econometric literature on what was wrong with Moore's upward-sloping
"statistical demand curve" concluded that Moore committed a blunder, because
he actually estimated a supply curve; see Morgan (1990). In addition, Moore's
attempt to address the issues raised by the *ceteris paribus* clause, using a combination of (i) "data adjustment," such as "trend ratios" (detrended data) and "link
relatives" (x_t/x_{t-1}), and (ii) "model adjustment," by including other potentially
relevant factors, was deemed inadequate.

Viewing this discussion in light of the above classification of the different ways
an inference might be in error, we can say that, given the estimated curve (1.3) is
statistically misspecified, there is no "statistical regularity" to confer theoretical
meaning upon. In addition, Moore's (1914, p. 113) discussion of the data provides
enough hints for the potential presence of certain serious systematic errors; the
distorted dynamics brought out by the misspecification tests attest to that. To
make matters worse, external validity is seriously undermined because Moore's
data did not measure the theoretical concept "demand," defined as representing
"aggregate intentions to buy"; see Spanos (1995a) for an extensive discussion.

Unfortunately, as a result of the discussions in the late 1910s and early 1920s, economic theory was inadvertently granted the authority to bestow theoretical meaning upon statistical "non-regularities" in the name of identification. In their attempt to flesh out the *ceteris paribus* clause in the case of a demand function, the econometric literature of the 1920s focused on how certain omitted factors could have caused shifts in the supply curve, but kept constant the demand curve, so as to identify the latter from data on "quantities transacted" and the corresponding "prices." The end result was that the all-encompassing problem of bridging the gap between theory and data was, in effect, transformed into "story telling" to identify a theory relationship in ways which ignore the probabilistic structure of the data.

1.3.5 The "deductive" method re-instated?

During the first quarter of the twentieth century, economic theory went through a process of mathematization that emphasized the deductive component of the primitive hypothetico-deductive method, and moved away from the empirical grounding of the initial postulates and the testing of the deduced laws using statistics. Robbins (1932/1937) re-instated a radical form of the deductive method, which viewed economic theory as a system of deductions from a set of initial postulates derived from introspection, and not amenable to empirical verification. He poked fun at statistical methods applied to economics because of their dependence on the notion of a random sample, and argued that economic data could never qualify as such (ibid., p. 102). Hutchison (1938) attempted a rebuttal by arguing in favor of importing into economics the "empiricism" of the newly founded "logical positivism" movement in the philosophy of science, known as the Vienna Circle; see Chalmers (1999). His case for confining economic inquiry to empirically testable propositions, however, was undermined by his emphasis on the testability of the initial postulates, rather than the theory's predictions. As a result, his form of "empiricism" did not have any discernible impact on the development of econometrics, but generated some inflamed discussions in economic methodology concerning the nature and testability of the initial postulates in economic theory; see Knight (1940), Friedman (1953) and Machlup (1955).

The gallant efforts of Mitchell (1927) and his co-workers at the National Bureau of Economic Research to restore faith in empirical regularities associated with economic time series, such as trends and cycles, was gravely handicapped by the inadequacy of their probabilistic framework to "model" these regularities in a systematic way. The proper probabilistic framework for modeling time series data, in the form of stochastic processes, was not erected until the mid-1930s by Kolmogorov and Khinchine; see Spanos (1999, chapter 8).

1.4 Modern statistical inference

1.4.1 R. A. Fisher

One of R. A. Fisher's most remarkable, but least recognized, achievements was to pioneer the recasting of statistical induction. Instead of starting with data

$\mathbf{x} := (x_1, x_2, \ldots, x_n)$ in search of a descriptive model, he would interpret the data as a representative sample from a prespecified "hypothetical infinite population": Fisher (1922, 1925). This might seem like a trivial re-arrangement of Karl Pearson's procedure but, in fact, constitutes a complete reformulation of statistical induction from generalizing observed "events" related with the data to modeling the underlying "process" that gave rise to the data.

The modeling process begins with a prespecified parametric statistical model (envisioned in the form of "a hypothetical infinite population"), chosen so as to ensure that the observed data $\mathbf{x}_0$ can be viewed as a random sample from that "population," i.e., a truly "typical realization" of the population $\mathbf{X}$: "The postulate of randomness thus resolves itself into the question, "Of what population is this a random sample?" which must frequently be asked by every practical statistician" (Fisher, 1922, p. 313).

A key concept in Fisher's approach to inference is the likelihood function:

$$L(\theta; \mathbf{x}) = \ell(\mathbf{x}) \cdot f(\mathbf{x}; \theta), \quad \theta \in \Theta,$$

where $\ell(\mathbf{x})$ denotes a proportionality constant, and $\{f(\mathbf{x}; \theta), \mathbf{x} \in \mathbb{R}_X^n\}$ is the distribution of the sample, encapsulating the information in the statistical model. Given that the choice of a statistical model is appropriate when it renders the observed data $\mathbf{x}_0$ a "truly typical" realization, Fisher (1922) defined the "optimal" estimator of θ to be the value $\hat{\theta}(\mathbf{x}_0) \in \Theta$ which attributes to $\mathbf{x}_0$ the highest chance of occurring, calling $\hat{\theta}(\mathbf{X})$ the maximum likelihood estimator. In Karl Pearson's perspective, $\hat{\theta}(\mathbf{X})$ did not exist, and the distinction between θ and $\hat{\theta}(\mathbf{x}_0)$ was blurred by an implicit asymptotic argument, ascribing to both the same logical status. In Fisher's perspective, the estimator $\hat{\theta}(\mathbf{X})$ constitutes an inference procedure aiming at pinpointing the true value θ^* of θ, an unknown parameter, and the estimate $\hat{\theta}(\mathbf{x}_0)$ constitutes an instantiation of a $\hat{\theta}(\mathbf{X})$ corresponding to a particular data set $\mathbf{x}_0$. The reliability of the inference procedure is assessed in terms of the associated error probabilities.

1.4.1.1 Fisher's recasting of statistical induction

Fisher's most enduring contribution is his devising of a general way to "operationalize" errors by embedding the material experiment into a statistical model, thus taming errors via probabilification, i.e., by defining frequentist error probabilities in the context of a statistical model. These error probabilities (a) are deductively derived from the statistical model, and (b) provide a measure of the "trustworthiness" of the inference procedure, i.e., how often a certain method will give rise to reliable inferences concerning the underlying actual Data Generating Mechanism (DGM). The form of induction envisaged by Fisher and Peirce (see Mayo, 1996, chapter 12) is one where the reliability of the inference emanates from the "trustworthiness" of the procedure used to arrive at the inference. As argued by (Fisher, 1935, p. 14): "In order to assert that a natural phenomenon is experimentally demonstrable we need, not an isolated record, but a reliable method of procedure." In the parlance of inductive logic, the inference is reached by an inductive procedure which, with high probability, will reach true conclusions (estimation, testing, prediction) from true (or approximately true) premises (statistical model). This is in contrast to induction by enumeration, where the focus is on observed "events" and not on the "process" generating the data.

Fisher's crucial contributions to the built-in deductive component, known as "sampling theory," in the form of deriving the finite sampling distributions of several estimators and test statistics, initiated the recasting of statistical induction in terms of "reliable procedures" based on "ascertainable error probabilities." Fisher recognized that the trustworthiness of an inference procedure depends crucially on the adequacy of the assumed statistical model vis-à-vis the data x_0. Viewing x_0 as a "truly representative" realization of a stochastic process $\{X_t, t \in T\}$ underlying the prespecified statistical model, Fisher facilitated the recasting of statistical induction and render its premises explicit as well as testable; see Spanos (1999). The soundness of the premises is assessed using misspecification tests and in turn, statistical adequacy ensures the reliability of inference. It is interesting to note that most of the tests proposed by Fisher (1925) were misspecification tests concerned with testing the Normality and IID assumptions.

Fisher's view concerning the relevance of statistics to the social sciences, and economics in particular, was clearly expressed in Fisher (1925, p. 2): "statistical methods are essential to social studies, and it is principally by the aid of such methods that these studies may be raised to the rank of science." Fisher went on to criticize the perspective on "statistics as a branch of economics" expounded by Bowley (1920), calling it an "unfortunate misapprehension." To do justice to Fisher's numerous contributions to modern statistics would require a major digression; see Bartlett (1965), Rao (1992), Spanos (2005a).

1.4.1.2 *Neyman and observational data*

The question that naturally arises at this stage is "to what extent is Fisher's modeling strategy relevant for non-experimental data?" The contention is that the insights and experience gained after three centuries of interaction between experimentation and statistics can be used to shed light on learning from observational data. Fisher focused primarily on modeling data from agricultural experiments, but Neyman had substantial experience in modeling observational data from a variety of fields, including astronomy, biology, epidemiology and economics. His empirical research (see Neyman, 1950, 1952) has effectively extended Fisher's view of the modeling process by viewing statistical models broadly as "chance mechanisms," emphasizing the gap between the phenomenon of interest and the statistical model chosen to "represent" it, and distinguishing between structural and statistical models (Neyman, 1976; Lehmann, 1990). These are important innovations which are of paramount interest to econometrics; see Spanos (2005a) for further discussion.

1.4.2 Outstanding issues in modern statistics

The probabilistic foundations of statistics, as we understand them today, were in place by the 1950s, but the field was still struggling with the proper form of its own inductive reasoning; see Mayo (2005). Fisher was arguing for "inductive inference" spearheaded by his significance testing (see Fisher, 1955, 1956), and Neyman was arguing for "inductive behavior" based on Neyman–Pearson testing (see Neyman, 1956 and Lehmann, 1993). Neither account of inductive reasoning, however, provided an adequate account of how to address the question "when do data Z provide evidence for (or against) a hypothesis or a claim H?" The pre-data error-probabilistic account of inference seemed inadequate for a post-data evaluation of the inference reached; see Hacking (1965, pp. 99–101).

Pre-data error probabilities in estimation (see Fisher, 1922, 1925, 1935) are used to determine the "optimality" of an estimator $\hat{\theta}$ (stemming from its capacity to pinpoint the true value θ^*), using its sampling distribution evaluated under the "true state of nature" (factual reasoning), say $\theta = \theta^*$. This factual reasoning, however, renders these error probabilities impossible to operationalize post-data, because of its dependence on the unknowable θ^*. Symptomatic of this difficulty is the confusion surrounding the use of error probabilities in conjunction with confidence intervals.

In contrast to estimation, error probabilities of type I and II in hypothesis testing are determined by evaluating the sampling distribution of a test statistic using counterfactual reasoning under hypothetical values of $\theta \in \Theta$ (the parameter space) relating to the null as well as alternative hypotheses. Fisher's significance testing utilizes counterfactual reasoning under the null, but Neyman and Pearson (1933) extend that to scenarios under alternative hypotheses. Neyman–Pearson pre-data error probabilities provided a theory for "optimal" tests; based on their capacity to discriminate between true and false hypotheses. The counterfactual reasoning in testing poses sharper questions and elicits more informative answers, whose "trustworthiness" can be assessed using error probabilities, without invoking the true θ^*. It turns out that severe testing reasoning (section 1.2.1) can be used to supplement Neyman–Pearson testing with a post-data evaluation component; see Mayo (1996). This supplement can be utilized to address the problem raised by Hacking (1965), as well as several criticisms leveled against frequentist testing; see Mayo and Spanos (2006).

In addition to the problems of (a) the proper form of its own inductive reasoning, (b) structural vs statistical models, (c) post-data interpretation of Neyman–Pearson testing, (d) the appropriate error probabilities in multiple testing situations, (e) double use of data, and (f) pre-designation vs post-designation, one needs to address the chronic problems of (g) statistical model selection (specification) and (h) validation. According to Rao (2004, p. 2): "The current statistical methodology is mostly model-based, without any specific rules for model selection or validating a specified model." In section 1.8, it is argued that some of these inveterate problems, including statistical model specification and validation, can be addressed in the context of a Fisher–Neyman modeling framework when judiciously adapted/ extended using the error-statistical account based on severe testing reasoning (section 1.2.1).

1.4.3 Time series modeling

Although time series provided the main type of data for statistical modeling from its early beginnings in the seventeenth century, modeling using descriptive statistics techniques was problematic because it ignored the inherent heterogeneity and temporal dependence exhibited by such data. Initially, time series data were treated as if they were realizations of IID processes, but by the late nineteenth century periodogram and correlation analysis was available to capture these inherent features. However, the search for periodicities using periodograms, and the use of temporal correlations, conflated these two features of time series data, and invariably led to unreliable inferences, false periodicities and nonsense correlations (see Morgan, 1990). The first statistical models for time series data were proposed by Yule (1927) and Slutsky (1927) in the form of the Autoregressive (AR(p)) and Moving Average (MA(q)) formulations, respectively. These models, however, were viewed in the context of the curve fitting tradition because the necessary probabilistic perspective was yet to be developed; Kolmogorov and Khinchine did not introduce the notions of stationarity, ergodicity and Markov dependence until the mid 1930s. Using these new concepts, Wold (1938) provided a probabilistic perspective that united the two formulations to form the ARMA(p,q) model; see Spanos (2001a).

1.4.4 Bayesian statistics

The Bayesian approach to the problem of inductive inference is framed in terms of revising one's prior beliefs $\pi(\theta)$ concerning the parameters of interest θ, in view of the data $\mathbf{x}_0$, by evaluating the posterior distribution:

$$\pi(\theta|\mathbf{x}_0) \propto \pi(\theta) \cdot L(\theta; \mathbf{x}_0), \quad \theta \in \Theta$$

where $L(\theta; \mathbf{x}_0)$ denotes the likelihood function; $\pi(\theta|\mathbf{x}_0)$ provides the basis of any inference concerning $\theta \in \Theta$. The Bayesian inductive inference account frames induction in terms of the change in the prior probability for a claim, say $\theta = \theta_0$, in view of $\mathbf{x}_0$, to yield the posterior $\pi(\theta_0|\mathbf{x}_0)$. In particular, $\pi(\theta_0|\mathbf{x}_0) > \pi(\theta_0)$ is interpreted as $\mathbf{x}_0$ providing evidence for $\theta = \theta_0$.

The Bayesian approach to statistical inference was built on a subjective interpretation of probability by Bayes and Laplace, and was criticized by Venn, Boole (see Hald, 1998) and Peirce (1878), as well as by Fisher (1922). Keynes (1921) proposed a subjective "rational degree of belief" interpretation of probability as a "logical property" of propositions conditional on data, which had an important impact on the philosophy of confirmation (Carnap, 1962), but less impact on statistical inference, by influencing Jeffreys with regard to the weaknesses of the frequency interpretation of probability. Jeffreys (1939) proposed a notion of "objective" non-informative priors, which often lead to Bayesian inferences analogous to the frequentist approach but, in addition, enable one to attach probabilities to parameters and thus to hypotheses. Further revival of the Bayesian approach was fervently promoted by Savage (1954) through reviving the work of Ramsey and de Finetti, based on a purely personal/subjective interpretation of probability. Zellner (1971) was instrumental in re-introducing Jeffreys (1939) into both econometrics and statistics.

1.4.5   Nonparametric statistics

In an attempt to reduce the reliance of statistical inference propositions (optimal estimators and test statistics) on the Normal distribution, the statistics literature in the early 1940s initiated an approach to inference designed to replace Normality with more general forms of distributional assumptions, such as continuity and unimodality of the density function; these methods became known as nonparametric or distribution free; see Scheffe (1943) for an early survey. These methods relied mainly on order and rank statistics, leading to inference propositions which are "robust" to departures from Normality; see Lehmann (1975).

Another important line· of development in this literature was initiated by Rosenblatt (1956), who proposed a nonparametric estimator of the density function based on "smoothing" the histogram. This gave rise to kernel smoothing methods, which have been extended to the estimation of multivariate and conditional densities as well as regression and skedastic functions; see Simonoff (1996).

1.5   Econometrics 1930–1942: a period of zymosis

The period of zymosis, 1930–1942, is largely dominated by the efforts of three eminent pioneers: Ragnar Frisch, Jan Tinbergen and Tjalling Koopmans. The prevailing view in the 1920s was that the application of statistical inference tools in economics was questionable because: (i) it is impossible to apply the "experimental method" to the study of economic phenomena, (ii) there is always an unlimited number of potential factors influencing economic phenomena – hence the invocation of *ceteris paribus* clauses, (iii) economic phenomena are intrinsically heterogeneous (spatial and temporal variability), and (iv) economic data are vitiated with errors of measurement.

1.5.1   Ragnar Frisch

Frisch advanced the "curve fitting" perspective of the early statistical efforts on estimating demand/supply functions and analyzing business cycles to a higher level of sophistication, but at the same time he contributed significantly to forestalling the introduction of the probabilistic perspective into econometric modeling.

In relation to estimating demand/supply functions, Frisch (1934) treated all observable random variables, including prices and quantities, $(x_{kt}, k = 1, 2, \ldots, m)$, as a priori symmetrical and comprising two orthogonal components: a systematic (non-random) unobservable (μ_{kt}), and an erratic (random) unobservable ε_{kt}:

$$x_{kt} = \mu_{kt} + \varepsilon_{kt} \quad k = 1, 2, \ldots, m \tag{1.4}$$

He then considered "curve fitting" (which he called confluence analysis) as a problem in vector space geometry, where the number r of "independent" linear relationships among the systematic components:

$$a_{0j}\mu_{0t} + a_{1j}\mu_{1t} + \cdots + a_{mj}\mu_{mt} = 0 \quad j = 1, 2, \ldots, r \tag{1.5}$$

is determined by the singularity of the matrix $[\mu_{kt}]_{k=1,\,...,\,m}^{t=1,\,...,\,t}$. Since this matrix is not observable, these linear relationships can only be determined using the data matrix $[x_{kt}]_{k=1,\,...,\,m}^{t=1,\,...,\,t}$, which includes the errors.

Frisch decided that Fisher's methods were inappropriate for non-experimental data, and consciously disparaged the probabilistic perspective as only applicable to cases where experimental control was possible. His answer to the non-experimental nature of economic data came in the form of a hybrid specification of a deterministic theory (1.5), referred to as structural, combined with erratic errors carrying the probabilistic understructure. It is interesting to note that, in a reply to a question by E. B. Wilson in 1940 concerning Frisch's scheme, Fisher charged economists of perpetuating a major confusion between "statistical" regression coefficients and "coefficients in abstract economic laws"; see Bennett (1990, p. 305).

1.5.2 Jan Tinbergen

Tinbergen's most influential contribution came in the form of two monographs (1939) on "Statistical Testing of Business Cycle Theories," where he proposed the first macroeconometric models for the US economy in the form of a system of dynamic equations (see Morgan, 1990, for an extensive discussion). Despite the title, these monographs had very little to do with statistical testing as such. The emphasis was placed almost exclusively on estimation, with only occasional references to tests of significance for regression coefficients. It was an attempt to combine Fisher's theory of estimation relating to regression with Frisch's confluence analysis by utilizing Koopmans (1937) hybrid formulation (see below).

For our present purposes, Tinbergen's empirical work is interesting because it represents the first version of the methodological framework that was to dominate empirical modeling in econometrics for the rest of the century. Tinbergen extended Moore's combination of statistical "goodness of fit" criteria and "economic validity" as the basis of "empirical reliability" by utilizing more modern statistical techniques to allow some leeway in determining the lags and trends empirically (Tinbergen, 1939, p. 26). Like Moore, Tinbergen raised the issue of "static theory" vs "time series" (dynamic) data, and argued in favor of utilizing "sequence analysis" instead of long-run equilibrium in developing theory models. He went beyond Moore by reporting standard errors of estimators and making extensive use of graphical techniques, which included a plot of the residuals.

In reviewing Tinbergen (1939), Keynes (1939) raised several problems associated with the use of regression in econometrics. Viewed from a current perspective, the issues raised by that debate comprise a mixture of substantive and statistical problems: (i) the inclusion of all relevant factors, (ii) the measurability of certain factors, (iii) the interdependence of these factors, (iv) the use of *ceteris paribus* clauses, (v) the spatial and temporal heterogeneity of economic phenomena, (vi) the functional form of estimated relationships, and (vii) the specification of the dynamics, including lags and trends; see Morgan (1990) and Epstein (1987). The perceived outcome of the debate, which gave Keynes the moral high ground and Tinbergen the success on pragmatic grounds, did very little to restore the reliability of empirical evidence in economics.

1.5.3   Tjalling Koopmans

The tension between the descriptive "curve fitting," as extended by Frisch, and Fisher's probabilistic perspective is best demonstrated in Koopmans (1937). His stated intention was to integrate Frisch's confluence analysis with Fisher's statistical inference (sampling) framework. More than any other econometrician of his time, Koopmans appreciated Fisher's statistical inference framework, and made an impressive effort in his 1937 book to bring into econometrics some of its most important features, including the distinction between unknown "parameters" and their "estimators," the problems of "specification, estimation and distribution," as well as the method of Maximum Likelihood.

Despite his impressive efforts, he could not integrate Frisch's "curve fitting" and Fisher's probabilistic perspectives because there was a fundamental incompatibility between the two perspectives. In light of Wold (1938), one can argue that Frisch's scheme (1.4) was probabilistically inappropriate for time series data, because his orthogonal decomposition $X_t = \mu_t + \varepsilon_t$ would render ε_t non-systematic only if the systematic component is defined by $\mu_t = E(X_t \mid D_t)$, and the conditioning information set D_t includes the past of the process, e.g., $D_t = \sigma(X_{t-1}, X_{t-2}, \ldots, X_0)$, where $\sigma(Z)$ denotes the sigma-field generated by Z; see Stigum (1990). In such a case, μ_t could not be realistically viewed as a deterministic function of t.

1.6   Econometrics 1943–1962: Haavelmo and the Cowles Commission

1.6.1   Haavelmo 1944

Haavelmo was a student and an assistant to Frisch in Oslo, but spent the late 1930s and early 1940s in the USA, where he interacted with two early pioneers in statistics, Neyman and Wald. The single most significant publication in econometrics during the twentieth century is arguably Haavelmo (1944). This appraisal is based not only on its actual influence on the development of econometrics, via the Cowles Commission, but also on its potential impact, which never materialized.

The primary influences of the monograph include: (i) introducing probabilistic foundations as well as methods of modern statistical inference (maximum likelihood and Neyman–Pearson testing) into econometrics, (ii) formalizing the notion of interdependence (simultaneity) in economic phenomena, (iii) emphasizing the importance of autonomous (structural) relationships in empirical modeling (see Christ, 1985; Epstein, 1987; and Morgan, 1990), and (iv) introducing different types of models as the primary tools for empirical modeling. Haavelmo argued convincingly that the probabilistic perspective of stochastic processes provides the proper framework for: (a) modeling time series data which exhibit both dependence as well as heterogeneity, and (b) embedding theory models into statistical (probabilistic) models for the purposes of inference: "For no tool developed in the theory of statistics has any meaning . . . without being referred to some stochastic scheme" (Haavelmo, 1944, p. iii); "economists might get more useful and reliable information (and also fewer spurious results) out of their data by adopting more clearly formulated probabilistic models; and that such formulation might help in suggesting what data to look for and how to collect them" (ibid., p. 114). He emphasized how the joint distribution of the observables can be used, not only for inference, but also as a basis for statistical model specification: "The class of n-dimensional probability laws can, therefore, be considered as a rational classification of all a priori conceivable mechanisms that could rule the behavior of the n observable variables considered" (ibid., p. 49). It is no exaggeration to say that the last quotation reads like an informal stating of Kolmogorov's theorem: Under some general regularity conditions, the probability structure of the stochastic process $\{X_t, t \in \mathbb{T}\}$ is completely specified if one is given the joint probability distribution $F_n(x_{t_1}, x_{t_2}, \ldots, x_{t_n})$ for all $n \geq 1$ and all $(t_1, t_2, \ldots, t_n) \in \mathbb{T}$; see Kolmogorov (1933), Doob (1953). This was formalized and extended to give rise to the Probabilistic Reduction approach (see section 1.8.1).

The potential impact of the monograph derives from Haavelmo's insightful diagnosis of the methodological problems bedeviling empirical modeling in economics in the 1930s. He proposed a broad methodological framework that mapped out clearly the gap between theory and data, and proposed several systematic ways to contemplate how to bridge this gap: "When we set up a system of theoretical relationships and use economic names for the otherwise purely theoretical variables involved, we have in mind some actual experiment, or some design of an experiment, which we could at least imagine arranging, in order to measure those quantities in real economic life that we think might obey the laws imposed on their namesakes" (Haavelmo, 1944, p. 6).

If we return to the different ways (I)–(IV) that an inference can be wrong (see section 1.2.3), we can see that Haavelmo made a serious attempt to map out the issues (III)–(IV) associated with substantive inadequacies. His suggestion for dealing with incongruous measurement was to distinguish between "true," "theoretical," and "observational" variables (ibid., p. 7): "'true' variables represent our ideal as to accurate measurements of reality 'as it is in fact,'" "theoretical" variables "are the true measurements that we should make if reality were actually in accordance with our theoretical model," and "observational" variables are those quantified by the available data (see ibid., pp. 5–7). He argued that, given a theoretical model and its associated design, as well as a set of observations, two questions need to be posed:

(1) Have we actually observed what we meant to observe, i.e., can the given set of observations be considered as a result obtained by following our design of "ideal" experiments?, and

(2) Do the "true" variables actually have the properties of the theoretical variables? "One should study very carefully the actual series considered and the conditions under which they were produced, before identifying them with the variables of a particular theoretical model." (ibid., p. 7)

His suggestion for emphasizing the external invalidity issue was to compare the conditions envisaged by the theory model with those of the "actual DGM," and to bridge the gap by modifying the former so as to "resemble" the latter: "We try to choose a theory and a design of experiments to go with it, in such a way that the resulting data would be those which we get by passive observation of reality" (ibid., p. 14). Unfortunately for econometrics, Haavelmo's suggestions concerning the gap between theory and data were not pursued further by the subsequent literature, perhaps because their implementation is non-trivial; see Spanos (1989) and Hendry *et al.* (1989).

1.6.2   The Cowles Commission: 1932–1954

The research of the Cowles Commission for Research in Economics during the period 1932–9, at Colorado Springs, was dominated by the descriptive statistics, "curve fitting" perspective, as exemplified by the work of Davis (1941), Roos (1934) and Tintner (1940). After the Cowles Commission was moved to Chicago (1939–1954), its main research agenda changed drastically and focused on formalizing and extending the work of Haavelmo (1943, 1944), with a view to improving the macroeconometric modeling exemplified by Tinbergen (1939); see Morgan (1990). The focus of the Cowles Commission group in Chicago narrowed the intended scope of Haavelmo's monograph down to the problem of inference in the context of the Simultaneous Equations Model (SEM), utilizing the modern statistical inference methods developed by Fisher and Neyman–Pearson. Let us summarize their main results.

The Structural Form (SF) of the model often comes in the form of a system of simultaneous linear equations:

$$\Gamma^\top \mathbf{y}_t = \Delta^\top \mathbf{x}_t + \varepsilon_t, \quad \varepsilon_t \sim \mathbf{N}(\mathbf{0}, \Omega), \quad \boldsymbol{\alpha} = \mathbf{h}(\Gamma, \Delta, \Omega) \in \Phi, \quad t \in \mathbb{T}, \qquad (1.6)$$

where $\mathbf{y}_t : m \times 1$ denotes a vector of endogenous variables and $\mathbf{x}_t : k \times 1$ a vector of exogenous variables; let $\boldsymbol{\alpha} : n_1 \times 1$ denote a vector of the (structural) unknown parameters in (Γ, Δ, Ω). The corresponding Reduced Form (RF) is:

$$\mathbf{y}_t = \mathbf{B}^\top \mathbf{x}_t + \mathbf{u}_t, \quad \mathbf{u}_t \sim \mathbf{N}(\mathbf{0}, \Sigma), \quad \theta = \mathbf{g}(\mathbf{B}, \Sigma) \in \Theta, \quad t \in \mathbb{T} \qquad (1.7)$$

where θ denotes a $n_2 \times 1$ $(n_2 \geq n_1)$ vector of the unknown parameters in $(\mathbf{B}, \Sigma)$. The two forms are interrelated parametrically via the system of equations:

$$\text{(i) } \mathbf{B}(\theta)\Gamma(\boldsymbol{\alpha}) = \Delta(\boldsymbol{\alpha}), \quad \text{(ii) } \Omega(\boldsymbol{\alpha}) = \left(\Gamma^\top(\boldsymbol{\alpha})\Sigma(\theta)\Gamma(\boldsymbol{\alpha}) \right).$$

Identification of the structural parameters $\boldsymbol{\alpha}$ takes the parameters θ as given, and poses the question: "can one 'solve' uniquely for $\boldsymbol{\alpha} = \mathbf{H}(\theta)$ the implicit system of equations (i)–(ii)?"

When the SF (1.6) is just identified, the mapping $\boldsymbol{\alpha} = \mathbf{H}(\theta)$, $\theta \in \Theta$, is bijective, defining a reparameterization with $\theta = \mathbf{H}^{-1}(\boldsymbol{\alpha})$, $\boldsymbol{\alpha} \in \Phi$. When the structural model is overidentified the mapping is surjective, defining a reparameterization/restriction, because $\mathbf{H}^-(\cdot)$, the pre-image of the mapping $\mathbf{H}(\cdot)$, imposes restrictions on the statistical parameters:

$$\theta^* = \mathbf{H}^-(\alpha), \qquad \alpha \in \Phi \Rightarrow \theta^* \in \Theta_1 \subset \Theta$$

The test of overidentifying restrictions is based on the implicit hypotheses: H_0 : $\theta^* \in \Theta_0$ vs. $H_1 : \theta^* \in \Theta_1$, where (Θ_0, Θ_1) is a partition of Θ; see Spanos (1986, 2006b).

Using modern statistical inference methods, the Cowles Commission group was commendably successful in addressing the technical problems of identification, estimation, testing and prediction in the context of the SEM; see Koopmans (1950) and Hood and Koopmans (1953). Their crucial influences on the development of econometrics during the second half of the twentieth century come in the form of (a) fortifying the use of modern statistical methods, and (b) focusing attention on estimating "autonomous structure" for empirical modeling purposes in econometrics. A retrospective view of the Cowles Commission's influence reveals that the research agenda of this group was, in some respects, a lot more influential in shaping the research in theoretical econometrics until the 1970s, than in influencing empirical modeling in econometrics. The mainstream theoretical research effort of the 1960s and 1970s was primarily channeled into simplifying and extending the work of the Cowles Commission group, especially in estimation (LIML, FIML, 2SLS, 3SLS, IV, k-class, etc.) and identification of the SEM; see Hendry (1976) for a unifying survey. The narrowing of Haavelmo's blueprint by the Cowles Commission down to the problem of simultaneity bias of the OLS estimator, and the additional rigidity introduced into his methodological framework, contributed to its early perceived failure as a general approach to empirical modeling. Indeed, most of the protagonists turned away from econometrics by the mid-1950s; see Epstein (1987). This rigidity, as well as the restrictiveness of the probabilistic assumptions on the errors, was perceptively criticized by Orcutt (1952). Moreover, the empirical work on macroeconometric modeling that followed the Cowles Commission era by Klein and Goldberger (1955) brought out the inappropriateness of the proposed framework.

As a result of the Cowles Commission methodology, the theory-dominated methodological framework of the 1920s and 1930s was greatly fortified against any predilection towards empirical regularities and the data-to-theory inductive process. Their theory-dominated perspective commences with a fully specified structural model which, in turn, determines the reduced form in conjunction with the probabilistic structure of the error terms. A way to explain this perspective is to see it as an attempt to imitate the "perceived" form of empirical modeling in fields like physics, where the "laws" are clearly known a priori and observation can only help to quantify them; discrepancies between the laws and the data can only arise from measurement and/or sampling errors. Needless to say, this perceived form of empirical modeling in physics is misleading; see Cartwright (1983).

As argued in Spanos (1986, 1990), the reduced form is the (implicit) statistical model in the context of which the structural model is embedded. Hence, the statistical model not only "has no life of its own," but it is totally dominated by the

Table 1.2 The multivariate linear regression (MLR) model

$$\mathbf{y}_t = \boldsymbol{\beta}_0 + \mathbf{B}_1^\top \mathbf{x}_{1t} + \mathbf{u}_t, \ t \in \mathrm{T}$$

[1] Normality:	$D(\mathbf{y}_t \mid \mathbf{x}_{1t}; \boldsymbol{\psi})$ is Normal
[2] Linearity:	$E(\mathbf{y}_t \mid \mathbf{X}_{1t} = \mathbf{x}_{1t}) = \boldsymbol{\beta}_0 + \mathbf{B}_1^\top \mathbf{x}_{1t}$, linear in $\mathbf{x}_{1t}$
[3] Homoskedasticity:	$Cov(\mathbf{y}_t \mid \mathbf{X}_{1t} = \mathbf{x}_{1t}) = \boldsymbol{\Sigma}$, free of $\mathbf{x}_{1t}$
[4] Independence:	$\{(\mathbf{y}_t \mid \mathbf{X}_{1t} = \mathbf{x}_{1t}), t \in \mathrm{T}\}$, independent process
[5] t-homogeneity:	$(\boldsymbol{\beta}_0, \mathbf{B}_1^\top, \boldsymbol{\Sigma})$ are not functions of $t \in \mathbb{T}$

where $\mathbf{B}_1 = Cov(\mathbf{X}_{1t})^{-1} Cov(\mathbf{X}_{1t}, \mathbf{y}_t), \quad \boldsymbol{\beta}_0 := E(\mathbf{y}_t) - \mathbf{B}_1^\top E(\mathbf{X}_{1t})$
$\boldsymbol{\Sigma} := Cov(\mathbf{y}_t) - Cov(\mathbf{y}_t, \mathbf{X}_{1t}) Cov(\mathbf{X}_{1t})^{-1} Cov(\mathbf{X}_{1t}, \mathbf{y}_t)$

theory model in both form and probabilistic structure via the error term assumptions. The fact of the matter is that if any of the assumptions [1]–[5] (see Table 1.2, where $\mathbf{B}^\top = (\boldsymbol{\beta}_0^\top, \mathbf{B}_1^\top)$ and $\mathbf{x}_t := (1, \mathbf{x}_{1t})$) turn out to be invalid for data $\mathbf{Z} := (\mathbf{X}, \mathbf{y})$, any inference based on the estimated structural model (1.6) is likely to be unreliable. It is interesting to note that the limited use of the probabilistic perspective by the Cowles Commission was raised by Vining (1949, p. 85); see Spanos (2005b) for further details.

In conclusion, the Cowles Commission group provided a crucial impetus to the development of econometrics by presenting econometricians with technical problems arising from the SEM, but contributed little to the advancement of the methodology of empirical modeling. Their methodological framework constituted a retrogression from that of Haavelmo (1944), especially as it relates to the error probing inquiries concerning the ways [(I)–(IV)] that an inductive inference might be false. Theirs was a theory-dominated approach to empirical modeling that allowed no real role for the systematic statistical information in the data.

1.7 Econometrics 1963–present: the textbook approach

1.7.1 Formulating the textbook approach

The textbook approach to econometrics was shaped in the early 1960s by Johnston (1963) and Goldberger (1964), by demarcating its intended scope to be the "quantification of theoretical relationships in economics," and formalizing the Gauss–Markov (G–M) perspective; both elements have dominated econometrics to this day. This is both a tribute to the appeal of the edifice built by these two influential pioneers, and an indictment of the uncritical attitude of the subsequent literature. It is argued that the G–M perspective constitutes a return to the earlier "curve fitting" paradigm, where the theory dominates the specification of the statistical model and, in conjunction with "white noise" error terms, decrees the probabilistic structure the available data is alleged to have.

1.7.1.1 The Gauss–Markov blueprint

The key statistical model of the Gauss–Markov perspective is the so-called Classical Linear Regression (CLR), specified in the form of:

$$\mathbf{y} = \mathbf{X}\boldsymbol{\beta} + \mathbf{u}$$

where $\mathbf{y}: T \times 1$ and $\mathbf{X}: T \times k(T > k)$, together with the Gauss–Markov (G–M) assumptions:

(1) $E(\mathbf{u}) = \mathbf{0}$ (3) $\text{rank}(\mathbf{X}) = k$

(2) $E(\mathbf{uu}^\top) = \sigma^2 \mathbf{I}_T$ (4) $\mathbf{X}$ is fixed in repeated samples

The error term is thought to include: (i) approximation errors, (ii) omitted factors, (iii) variability in human behavior, (iv) aggregation errors, and (v) errors of measurement; see Valavanis (1959). A glance at this list of potential errors suggests that one is facing an impossible task in trying to disentangle, not to mention probe thoroughly, all these possible sources of error in the context of one error term.

A caricature of the methodological framework of the textbook approach begins with a theory which one uses to derive a theory-model in the form of functional relationships among variables of interest (exclusively determined by the theory in question). The object of the empirical modeling is to "quantify" this theoretical relationship and/or verify a theory. This quantification/verification is guided by both theoretical (sign, size of estimated parameters) and statistical considerations, such as R^2 goodness of fit measures, t-ratios and F-tests. The textbook perspective shares with the Cowles Commission the predominance of theory in the specification of the statistical model, but it allows for more flexibility in so far as statistical considerations are allowed to influence the final choice of the model. In addition, the error term, which was primarily viewed as relating to autonomous shocks in the Cowles Commission tradition, becomes a "catch-all" component carrying the probabilistic structure of the underlying statistical model. Indeed, the error term in the G–M perspective takes center stage in determining the sampling properties of inference procedures, and is endowed with "a random life of its own"; any departures from assumptions (1)–(2) are addressed by "modeling" the error term! How did this change from the Cowles Commission perspective come about?

A case can be made that Richard Stone played an important role in influencing the forging of the textbook approach to econometrics; see Gilbert (1991). The methodological framework is clearly discernible in Stone (1954a), and the CLR model with assumptions (1)–(4) is clearly specified in that form by Stone (1954b), ch. 19). The roots of the G–M assumptions can be traced back to Aitken (1934) and David and Neyman (1938), and the extension of assumption (2) to the case where $E(\mathbf{uu}^\top) = \Omega_T \neq \sigma^2 \mathbf{I}_T$ can be traced back to the Cambridge tradition of Yule (1926), Cochrane and Orcutt (1949) and Durbin and Watson (D–W) (1950). In particular, the last two papers had a lasting influence on the shaping of the textbook approach, both in terms of testing for the presence, as well as the modeling, of error-autocorrelation. Indeed, the D–W test was the first misspecification test to be widely applied.

This textbook approach blueprint begins with the CLR model with assumptions (1)–(4), and views the other statistical models of interest in econometrics as variations/extensions of this model. The central axis around which the textbook modeling strategy unfolds, however, is not the choice of an appropriate statistical model in view of the data, but the choice of an "optimal" estimator in view of the theory model. Textbook econometrics revolves around the Gauss–Markov theorem as justifying the use of the OLS estimator under assumptions (1)–(4). Whenever any one of these assumptions is violated, the OLS estimator loses its optimality and a better estimator is sought: GLS, FGLS, Ridge, Instrumental Variables (IVs), 2SLS, 3SLS, LIML, FIML, k-class, double-k class, etc.; see Kennedy (2003) for a clear exposition. A bird's eye view of this blueprint is as follows.

Chapter 1: The Gauss–Markov theorem. Under assumptions (1)–(4), the OLS estimator $\hat{\beta} = \left(\mathbf{X}^\top \mathbf{X}\right)^{-1} \mathbf{X}^\top \mathbf{y}$ is the Best, Linear, Unbiased Estimator (BLUE) of β. That is, $\hat{\beta}$ is a relatively efficient estimator (minimum variance) within the class of unbiased estimators, which are also restricted to be linear functions of $\mathbf{y}$. Every subsequent chapter deals with a particular violation of assumptions (1)–(4) and discusses its consequences for $\hat{\beta}$, as well as the remedies that give rise to another "optimal" estimator.

Chapter 2	*Non-zero mean:* $E(\mathbf{u}) = \mathbf{0}$
Chapter 3	*Autocorrelation:* $E(\mathbf{u}\mathbf{u}^\top) = \sigma^2 \mathbf{I}_T.$
Chapter 4	*Heteroskedasticity:* $E(\mathbf{u}\mathbf{u}^\top) = \Lambda_T = \operatorname{diag}(\sigma_1^2, \sigma_2^2, \ldots, \sigma_T^2)$
Chapter 5	*Multicollinearity:* $\operatorname{rank}(\mathbf{X}) < k.$
Chapter 6	*Stochastic regressors:* $E\left(\mathbf{X}^\top \mathbf{u}\right) \neq \mathbf{0}$ (a) Errors-in-variables,
	(b) Simultaneous Equations.

As we can see, the textbook approach replaced the Simultaneous Equations Model (SEM) of the Cowles Commission from center stage with the Classical Linear Regression (CLR) model, viewing the SEM as a variant of the CLR. A comparison between Johnston (1963) and Greene (2003), perhaps the most successful recent graduate textbook in econometrics, reveals that, besides raising the level of mathematical sophistication of statistical inference, the main difference between them is that the latter includes several new statistical models of interest in econometrics, together with their associated statistical inference propositions – primarily estimation. Additional models include discrete dependent, limited dependent and duration models for cross-section data, models for time series data (ARMA, ARIMA, VAR, ARCH), and models for panel data, which were introduced into textbook econometrics during the 1980s and 1990s. There is no doubt that the impressive developments in econometrics came in the form of more and better statistical models and their associated estimation procedures. These additions, however, have the hallmark of the Gauss–Markov "curve fitting" perspective, which has a theory-dominated view of empirical modeling, with the emphasis placed on "the quantification of theory models."

1.7.2   The critics of the textbook approach

In an attempt to remedy the perceived failings of the textbook approach, in this subsection we will briefly mention a number of alternative approaches to empirical modeling in econometrics from the point of view of how they suggest modifying the textbook approach in order to address some of its problems discussed above; for more extensive discussions of some of these approaches see Pagan (1987), Spanos (1988), Hendry *et al.* (1990), Granger (1990) and Hoover (2006). All these critics agree on one thing: the textbook approach often gives rise to unreliable inferences and delivers poor predictive performance, but they disagree on the sources of unreliability and on how to address these problems.

A. The Box–Jenkins (1970) ARIMA time series modeling approach, based on:

$$y_t^* = \alpha_0 + \sum_{k=1}^{p} \alpha_k y_{t-k}^* + \sum_{l=1}^{q} \beta_l \varepsilon_{t-l} + \varepsilon_t, \quad \varepsilon_t \sim \text{NIID}(0, \sigma^2) \tag{1.8}$$

where $y_t^* := \Delta^d y_t$, brought out the statistical inadequacy problem as it relates to the temporal structure and heterogeneity exhibited by economic time series data. The use of "differencing," in order to render the data stationary, was questioned in the late 1970s and that led to the "unit root revolution" in econometric time series modeling; see Dickey and Fuller (1979) and Phillips (1987).

B. The Sims VAR methodology extended the ARIMA model to:

$$Z_t = a_0 + \sum_{k=1}^{p} A_k Z_{t-k} + E_t, \quad E_t \sim \text{NIID}(0, \Omega) \tag{1.9}$$

in order to model both the contemporaneous as well as the temporal structure of economic time series. Sims (1980, 1982) diagnosed the unreliability of the textbook approach to structural models as emanating from two sources: the neglect of the temporal structure of these series and the "implausibility" of the substantive information forced upon the data.

C. The Sargan–Hendry LSE tradition (see Sargan, 1964; Hendry, 2003) was also motivated by the neglect of the temporal structure of the data, but tried to preserve a link between the statistical and substantive information. Hence, the LSE tradition proposed the (AD) model:

$$y_t = \alpha_0 + \sum_{k=1}^{p} \alpha_k y_{t-k} + \sum_{l=0}^{q} \beta_l^\top \mathbf{x}_{t-l} + \varepsilon_t, \quad \mathbf{x}_t : k \times 1 \quad \varepsilon_t \sim \text{NIID}(0, \sigma^2) \tag{1.10}$$

as a data-based formulation capturing the short-run dynamics, with equilibrium economic theory being relevant in determining the long-run solution of this stochastic difference equation. To deal with the "unreliability of evidence" problem, the LSE tradition suggests allowing the data to determine the choice of optimal (p,q) by following a "General to Specific" procedure from large initial values (p,q) and testing downwards for a more parsimonious representation (see Hendry, 1995; Mizon, 1995). To avoid statistically unreliable inferences, the LSE approach recommends diagnostic tests in the spirit of the Box–Jenkins approach.

A particular case of the AD model, known as the error correction model, which, when $p=q=1$ takes the form:

$$\Delta y_t = \gamma_0 + \gamma_1 (y_{t-1} - \gamma_2^\top \mathbf{x}_{t-1}) + \gamma_3^\top \Delta \mathbf{x}_t + v_t, \quad v_t \sim \text{NIID}(0, \sigma_v^2) \tag{1.11}$$

proved to be empirically a very successful specification; see Hendry (1993). It turned out that the empirical success of the error-correction model can be explained in terms of the cointegrating properties of certain nonstationary time series; see Engle and Granger (1987). This provided a connection between the AD and the Sims VAR approach, extending the error-correction model (1.11) to systems of equations; see Johansen (1991, 1995), Boswijk (1995).

D. The Lucas–Sargent tradition (Lucas, 1976; Lucas and Sargent, 1981) attempts to address the problem of unreliable empirical evidence associated with the textbook approach in two interrelated ways. First, by improving economic theory to account for the dynamic structure of economic time series and, second, by basing forecasts and policy evaluations not on empirical regularities but on estimated structural models which are invariant to policy interventions.

E. Leamer's Bayesian-oriented criticism of the practised variant of textbook econometrics was motivated by the great disparity between the formal textbook approach and its practised variant, which he called "cookbook" econometrics; see Leamer (1978). His suggestion is to make honest modelers out of cookbook econometricians by formalizing their ad hoc procedures using informal Bayesian procedures such as extreme bounds analysis (see Leamer and Leonard, 1983). This aims to expose the possible fragility of estimated relationships by testing their robustness to changes in prior information.

1.7.3   Whither textbook econometrics?

Although the various critics of the textbook approach pinpoint the crucial weaknesses of the approach and make constructive suggestions on how to address them, none constitute a comprehensive methodology of econometric modeling that can replace what they are berating; see Pagan (1987). The question that naturally arises is to what extent can one systematize some of the suggestions made by the critics so as to put forward a more comprehensive methodology that can potentially replace that of the textbook.

Taking stock of what the critics *A–C* bequeathed to empirical modeling, one can argue that the Box–Jenkins (B–J) approach offered four primary innovations:

(i) *Predesignated family of statistical models*: the modeling of time series data within such a family of models that was thought to adequately capture their temporal dependence and heterogeneity (including seasonality).

(ii) *Modeling as an iterative process*: empirical modeling is not a one-stage activity, but an iterative process that involves several stages, those of identification, estimation and diagnostic checking, before any prediction is made.

(iii) *Model assessment by diagnostic checks*: diagnostic checks, based on the residuals from the fitted model, provide a way to detect model inadequacies with a view to improving the original model.

(iv) *Warranted Exploratory Data Analysis (EDA)*: exploratory data analysis is not intrinsically sinful or deceptive, but can be legitimately used to select (identify) a model within the predesignated family.

(v) *Model overfitting*: for assessing the adequacy of a selected (identified) model, it is advisable to embed it into a more general specification in order to put the model "in jeopardy" (see Box and Jenkins, 1970, p. 286).

The B–J approach constituted a major departure from the rigid textbook approach, where the model is assumed to be devised in a single step and in advance of any data. The almost algorithmic nature of the B–J iterative modeling process added to its appeal, but it was its predictive success in the early 1970s (see Cooper, 1972, inter alia) that convinced econometricians that they could ignore the temporal dependence and heterogeneity of time series data only to the detriment of the predictive performance of their models (see Granger and Newbold, 1986).

Sims (1980), in an attempt to broaden the intended scope of the B–J approach to include prediction and description, extended the predesignated family of models to the VAR (1.9) in order to capture the joint temporal dependence and heterogeneity of related (via some form of theory) time series data.

The LSE tradition embraced (i)–(v) and broadened the predesignated family of models even further to allow for prediction, description and explanation. The main motivation for introducing the AD family (1.10), which also incorporates the contemporaneous dependence (captured by $\beta_0^\top x_t$) among related time series, was to leave the door open for linking such data-oriented models to economic theory via their long-run solution. In addition, the LSE approach formalized (v) to:

(vi) *General to Specific (G-to-S) procedure:* to secure adequacy, one should commence from a general dynamic model, such as (1.10), and test downwards to a more specific but *congruent* empirical model (Hendry, 1995, p. 365).

The modeling conceptions (i)–(vi) were never integrated into the textbook approach because they cannot be accommodated into its methodological framework without a major overhaul. As a result, the critics A–C have generated their own modeling cultures within applied macroeconomics focusing on time series data. The countercharge by Textbook Econometricians (TE) is that the critics A–C simply ignore, or pay lip service to, economic theory; a return to "measurement without theory"; see Koopmans (1947). Models (1.8)–(1.10) are clearly not theory motivated, and thus ad hoc and arbitrary when viewed in the context of the textbook approach. By the same token, the Lucas–Sargent approach did have some influence on the textbook approach because it called for no changes to its basic methodological framework. The primary lessons from that approach are that:

(vii) The ultimate objective of empirical modeling should be to "unveil" structural models with high degree of invariance to policy changes.

(viii) Static equilibrium economic models need to be extended to dynamic models to be able to account for the temporal structure exhibited by economic data.

The thesis defended in this chapter is that critics A–C brought out certain crucial weaknesses of the textbook approach that invariably lead to unreliable inferences, but their proposals did not go far enough to address the unreliability of inference problem; they raised but did not address adequately the statistical unreliability problem, and they did not provide an adequate link between these predesignated families of data-oriented models and economic theory, thus neglecting the substantive unreliability problem. A TE would ask "where do models (1.8)–(1.10) come from?" and "how does one justify them if not on theory grounds?" The only reply is that these models are justified on pragmatic grounds, because they "capture" the systematic information in some time series data much better than the various structural models in the literature. The TE would reply that, even on pragmatic grounds, not all time series data can be adequately modeled using this Linear/Normal/Homoskedastic family of models, and they are clearly inappropriate for cross-section and panel data. What can one do when models (1.8)–(1.10) are found to be wanting? Moreover, even when these models turn out to be appropriate, they are overly data-specific and could not possibly capture the invariant (structural) features of the phenomena being modeled because they largely ignore the available substantive subject matter information.

To be able to address these questions and the associated methodological concerns, one needs to envisage a methodological framework where the issue of statistical and/or substantive unreliability can be adequately addressed without jeopardizing either form of information.

1.8   The prospect of twenty-first-century econometrics

Summarizing the argument so far, the persistent unreliability of empirical evidence produced by the textbook approach can be traced to three primary sources. The first source of unreliability stems from the fact that data are viewed "in light of a theory," but not "in light of a stochastic process that would render the data a truly typical realization thereof." The perceived outcomes of the Keynes vs Tinbergen and the Koopmans vs Vining debates reinforced this theory-dominated view of inductive inference. The second source of unreliability stems from the way that the gap between theory and data is often glossed over by implicitly assuming that: (i) the available data provide measurements congruous to the concepts envisaged by economic theory, (ii) the circumstances envisaged by theory coincide with the actual DGM, and thus, (iii) the substantive information "encompasses" the statistical, apart from white noise error(s), whatever the data! The third source of unreliability arises from the fact that inductive inferences are often not probed adequately in the different ways they can be in error. One can make a case that little progress has been made in addressing the problems of (I) Statistical misspecification, (II) inaccurate data, (III) incongruous measurement, and (IV) external invalidity, since Moore (1914).

These concerns were instrumental in motivating a methodological framework, called the Probabilistic Reduction (PR) approach, proposed in Spanos (1986).

1.8.1   The probabilistic reduction (PR) approach

The Probabilistic Reduction (PR) approach, as discussed in this subsection, is a methodological framework whose primary objective is to foster a self-reflective meeting ground of the disparate approaches; a framework wherein the strengths and weaknesses of the various approaches can be discussed and compared. It offers a methodological forum in the context of which legitimate methodological concerns, such as the mistrust of data-oriented models and preliminary data analysis, the imperativeness of predesignation, the abuse of substantive information, as well as the neglect of statistical information, can be illuminated and hopefully addressed.

1.8.1.1 Substantive vs statistical information

The starting point of the PR approach is that empirical models constitute a blending of substantive and statistical information, and their primary objective is to enable us to learn about observable phenomena of interest using data. The substantive information derives from the subject matter theory, and the statistical information is reflected in the "chance regularity (recurring) patterns" exhibited by the data. In an attempt to address the problems raised by the textbook approach, and explain when the choice of models such as (1.8)–(1.10) makes sense, the two kinds of information are encapsulated initially by two different models, the theory and statistical models. The former is stipulated in terms of theoretical variables, some of which might be unobservable, but the latter is specified exclusively in terms of the observable random variables underlying the data $\mathbf{Z} := (\mathbf{z}_1, \mathbf{z}_2, \ldots, \mathbf{z}_T)$. The idea is that the Lucas–Sargent call for structural modeling can be accommodated as theory models but, at the same time, the data-oriented models suggested by critics *A–C* can be justified as statistical models. The problem is to find ways to link the two without compromising the integrity of either the substantive or the statistical information.

1.8.1.2 Statistical model specification

Let us focus on statistical models first. A statistical model presupposes the choice of the relevant data $\mathbf{Z}$ (chosen by a theory or theories) and is specified by utilizing the Fisher–Neyman probabilistic perspective, which views $\mathbf{Z}$ as a "realization" of a (vector) stochastic process $\{\mathbf{Z}_t, t \in \mathbb{T}\}$, whose probabilistic structure is such that it would render $\mathbf{Z}$ "truly typical." This probabilistic structure, according to Kolmogorov's theorem, can be fully described, under certain mild regularity conditions, in terms of the joint distribution $D(\mathbf{Z}_1, \mathbf{Z}_2, \ldots, \mathbf{Z}_T; \boldsymbol{\phi})$; see Doob (1953). A statistical model constitutes a parameterization of the assumed probabilistic structure of $\{\mathbf{Z}_t, t \in \mathbb{T}\}$ and can be viewed as a reduction from this joint distribution.

To illustrate how the same $D(\mathbf{Z}_1, \mathbf{Z}_2, \ldots, \mathbf{Z}_T; \boldsymbol{\phi})$ can give rise to different (but related) statistical models, consider the case where $\{\mathbf{Z}_t, t \in \mathbb{T}\}$ is assumed to be a Markov, of order p (M(p)), and Stationary (S) process. On the basis of these assumptions one can deduce:

$$D(\mathbf{Z}_1, \mathbf{Z}_2, \ldots, \mathbf{Z}_T; \boldsymbol{\phi}) \stackrel{\mathrm{M}(p)}{=} D_t(\mathbf{Z}_1; \boldsymbol{\varphi}_1) \prod_{t=2}^{T} (\mathbf{Z}_t | \mathbf{Z}_{t-1}^p; \boldsymbol{\varphi}_t)$$

$$\stackrel{\mathrm{M}(p)\&\mathrm{S}}{=} D(\mathbf{Z}_1; \boldsymbol{\varphi}_1) \prod_{t=2}^{T} (\mathbf{Z}_t | \mathbf{Z}_{t-1}^p; \boldsymbol{\varphi}) \qquad (1.12)$$

where $\mathbf{Z}_{t-1}^p : (\mathbf{Z}_{t-1}, \mathbf{Z}_{t-2}, \ldots, \mathbf{Z}_{t-p})$, i.e., the joint distribution $D(\mathbf{Z}_1, \mathbf{Z}_2, \ldots, \mathbf{Z}_T; \boldsymbol{\phi})$ is reduced to a product of conditional distributions $D(\mathbf{Z}_t | \mathbf{Z}_{t-1}^p; \boldsymbol{\varphi})$. Assuming, in addition, that $\{Z_t, t\in\mathbb{T}\}$ is Normal (N), $D(Z_t|Z_{t-1}^p;\varphi)$ gives rise to the VAR(p) model (1.9). That is, the VAR(p) model provides a particular representation of a (N, M(p), S) process $\{Z_t, t\in\mathbb{T}\}$. However, in view of the fact that:

$$D(Z_t|Z_{t-1}^p;\varphi) = D(y_t|X_t, Z_{t-1}^p;\varphi) \cdot D(X_t|Z_{t-1}^p;\varphi)$$

it can be easily shown that the AD(p, p) (1.10), based on $D(y_t|X_t, Z_{t-1}^p;\varphi)$, provides another parameterization of the same stochastic process $\{Z_t, t\in\mathbb{T}\}$. How does one decide which statistical model to choose? The choice depends entirely on how a particular parameterization would enable one to embed the structural model in its context. This, of course, presupposes that there is a structural model providing a bridge between the theory and the statistical model. How the two sources of information are sythesized will be discussed after a more detailed discussion of how the PR approach addresses some of the statistical issues left open by critics A–C.

This PR reduction provides a justification for the VAR(p) and AD(p, p) as statistical models, but also brings out their most crucial weakness; they do not constitute a panacea for modeling time series data. When any of the probabilistic assumptions (N, M(p), S) are inappropriate, these models are likely to be misspecified. Moreover, the critics A–C did not adequately address the problems of (a) specification (how one initially chooses a statistical model), (b) MisSpecification (M-S) testing (how one proceeds to probe thoroughly the different ways a statistical model can be false), and (c) respecification (how one proceeds when the initial statistical model is found wanting). Indeed, one can argue that there is a lot in common between the critics A–C and the strategy of model selection based on Akaike-type information criteria. All these procedures narrow the problem of statistical model specification down to model selection within a predesignated family of models. As perceptively stated by Lehmann (1990, p. 162): "this view of model selection ignores a preliminary step: the specification of the class of models from which the selection is to be made." If the predesignated family of models turns out to be statistically misspecified, the selection process is likely to lead to misleading choices; the actual error probabilities are likely to be different from the assumed ones. Moreover, once such a family is selected on statistical adequacy grounds, no further model selection is needed, because an integral part of establishing statistical adequacy is the choice of maximum lags/trends needed to capture the systematic (recurring) information in the data see Spanos (2005a, 2006b) for the details.

As argued in Spanos (1986, 2001a), the specification of statistical models in terms of error assumptions, such as those in (1.8)–(1.10), is inadequate because such specifications are often incomplete (they invariably involve hidden assumptions), and because some of the error assumptions seem non-testable, or innocuous, until they are translated in terms of the observable random variables. In the case of the VAR(1) model (to simplify notation), the complete set of probabilistic assumptions in terms of $\{Z_t, t\in\mathbb{T}\}$ are given in Table 1.3. If we compare assumptions [1]–[5] with NIID for the error we can see that assumption [5] is not explicitly stated in the error specification. Indeed, in the textbook specification the t-invariance of Ω is often conflated with homoskedasticity [3]; the distinction

Table 1.3 The VAR(1) model

$$Z_t = a_0 + A_1^\top Z_{t-1} + E_t, \quad t \in \mathbb{T}$$

[1] **Normality:** $D(Z_t | Z_{t-1}^0; \psi)$ is Normal
[2] **Linearity:** $E(Z_t | \sigma(Z_{t-1}^0)) = a_0 + A_1^\top Z_{t-1}$, linear in Z_{t-1}
[3] **Homoskedasticity:** $Cov(Z_t | \sigma(Z_{t-1}^0)) = \Omega$, free of Z_{t-1}^0
[4] **Markov dependence:** $\{Z_t, t \in \mathbb{T}\}$ is a vector Markov Process
[5] **t-homogeneity:** (a_0, A, Ω) are not functions of $t \in \mathbb{T}$

where $A_1 = Cov(Z_{t-1})^{-1} Cov(Z_{t-1}, Z_t)$, $\quad a_0 := E(Z_t) - A_1^\top E(Z_{t-1})$
$\Omega := Cov(Z_t) - Cov(Z_t, Z_{t-1}) Cov(Z_{t-1})^{-1} Cov(Z_{t-1}, Z_t)$

---

becomes clear when the VAR(1) model is seen in the context of the reduction (1.12).

It goes without saying that an incomplete specification will be a major stumbling block to ensuring statistical adequacy. A key element of the PR approach is a complete specification of the probabilistic assumptions in terms of the observable processes involved. The complete set of statistical model assumptions reveals itself when the distribution underlying it, say $D(Z_t | Z_{t-1}^p; \varphi)$, is related to the joint distribution $D(Z_1, Z_2, \ldots, Z_T; \phi)$ via the reduction (1.12) itself. At the same time, this reduction demarcates the model in question relative to all other possible models (P) that could, potentially, have given rise to data $Z := (z_1, z_2, \ldots, z_T)$, because all the potential models in P can be perceived as reductions from the same joint distribution based on different reduction assumptions from three broad categories: (D) Distribution, (M) Dependence, (H) Heterogeneity. For instance, if one were to replace the Normality assumption with that of a Student's t distribution, a whole new family of models corresponding to (1.9)–(1.11) would arise from the reduction in (1.12); see Spanos (1986, 2001a). Viewing the model in question, say M_0, in the context of all potential models P, provides a broad and flexible enough framework to address the issues of M–S testing and respecification left open by the critics *A–C*.

1.8.1.3 Statistical vs structural error terms

An important dimension of the PR approach is that one is able to probe for different types of errors at different levels in the spirit of the error statistical account briefly discussed in section 1.2.1. Although it is important to distinguish clearly between the different types of errors (I)–(IV) and the error terms associated with different models, the two notions are related in so far as it is important to delineate the types of errors to probe for in assessing the non-systematic nature of error terms.

In the context of a statistical model, such as the VAR(1):

$$Z_t = a_0 + A_1^\top Z_{t-1} + E_t, \quad t \in \mathbb{T}$$

the error term E_t represents a particular case of a *martingale difference* process $E_t^* = Z_t - E(Z_t | \sigma(Z_{t-1}^0))$, when $E(Z_t | \sigma(Z_{t-1}^0)) = a_0 + A_1 Z_{t-1}$. What is crucially important in probing for misspecification errors in the context of a statistical model is to realize that the universe of discourse for statistical purposes the relevant information is confined to $\mathcal{F} := \sigma(\mathbf{Z}_1, \mathbf{Z}_2, \dots, \mathbf{Z}_T)$, denoting the sigma-field generated by $(\mathbf{Z}_1, \mathbf{Z}_2, \dots, \mathbf{Z}_T)$. That is, one needs to probe the different ways assumptions [1]–[5] could be false relative to the information set F. In particular, missing factors can only be relevant for statistical (as opposed to substantive) misspecification purposes if they belong to F. This renders the assumptions of the statistical error term empirically testable using the data $(\mathbf{Z}_1, \mathbf{Z}_2, \dots, \mathbf{Z}_T)$; see Spanos (2005b) for further details. In assessing the non-systematic nature of this error term one needs to focus primarily on probing for errors associated with (I) statistical misspecification, and (II) inaccurate data.

In a structural model of the form:

$$y = h(\mathbf{X}; \boldsymbol{\phi}) + \varepsilon(\mathbf{X}, \mathbf{U}) \tag{1.13}$$

where $\mathbf{y} := (y_1, \dots, y_m)$ and $\mathbf{X} := (X_1, \dots, X_k)$, with $\boldsymbol{\phi}$ denoting the unknown structural parameters, $\varepsilon(\mathbf{X}, \mathbf{U}) = \mathbf{y} - h(\mathbf{X})$ represents the structural error term, which is regarded as a function of both $\mathbf{X}$ and $\mathbf{U}$: a set of potentially relevant (observable or unobservable) factors. The structural error term is "autonomous" and represents all unmodeled influences; see Spanos (2005b) for further details. Hence, in assessing the non-systematic nature of this error term one needs to focus primarily on probing for errors associated with (III) incongruent measurement, and (IV) external invalidity; in particular, on probing for missing factors to ensure substantive reliability; see Spanos (2006a).

1.8.1.4 *Misspecification (M-S) testing/respecification*

In the context of the PR approach, the question posed by M-S testing is in the form of the hypotheses:

$$H_0 : f_0(\mathbf{z}) \in M_0 \quad \text{against} \quad H_1 : f_0(\mathbf{z}) \in [P - M_0] \tag{1.14}$$

where $f_0(\mathbf{z})$ denotes the "true" distribution of $\{\mathbf{Z}_t, t \in \mathbb{T}\}$. The real problem is how one can probe $[P - M_0]$ adequately, given that it invariably entails an infinity of models. The answer is provided by the reduction itself, because the specification of the particular model, say M_0, amounts to imposing probabilistic assumptions which partition P. Re-partitioning provides an effective strategy to probe $[P - M_0]$ for the different ways M_0 could be in error, when it is based on information concerning potential departures from M_0; see Spanos (2005a) . The use of graphical techniques, justified as a form of qualitative severe testing reasoning, can be utilized to render re-partitioning deliberatively effective. It should be noted that M-S tests differ from Neyman–Pearson (N–P) tests in so far as the probing in the case of the latter takes place within the boundary of a prespecified model M_0, but the former constitutes probing $[P - M_0]$ without M_0, thus rendering M-S tests a type of Fisherian significance test; see Spanos (1999). An effective M-S testing strategy should take account of the assumptions underlying the tests themselves, as well as avoiding the problem of infinite regress. With that in mind, the use of a combination of parametric and non-parametric M-S tests is often the best strategy to probe $[P - M_0]$ more exhaustively; see Mayo and Spanos (2004).

The above procedure constitutes a more effective M-S testing strategy than the limited scope of error diagnostic checks based on the residuals from the fitted model proposed by the Box–Jenkins approach. Moreover, this view of M-S testing is different from that of the LSE tradition, as explained by Hendry and Richard (1982), in so far as the latter views diagnostic tests as "design criteria" and not as genuine "independent checks" on the validity of the model. It is also important to note that statistical adequacy is not the same as the model congruency propounded by the LSE tradition. Model congruency specifies a set of desirable properties of empirical models in general, which constitute a mixture of statistical and substantive criteria; see Hendry (1995, p. 365). In contrast, statistical adequacy is confined to statistical information and is always defined relative to the probabilistic assumptions comprising the particular statistical model in question. Hence, unlike a congruent model, a statistically adequate model does not have to be homoskedastic, etc. (see Spanos, 1994, 1995a–b). More importantly, it does not have to be consistent with a particular theory; it only needs to provide an embedding framework for the theory or theories under consideration.

The same re-partitioning of P, using reduction assumptions from the three broad categories, can be used to respecify the original statistical model in view of the detected departures from M_0. The details of statistical model respecification, which involves the relationship between reduction and model assumptions, the creative use of M-S test results as a whole, as well as the utilization of graphical techniques, are discussed in Spanos (1999, 2000). The important point to make is that each respecified model is assessed for statistical adequacy by testing its own assumptions and the process ends when such a statistically adequate model is found. This provides a respecification strategy with the emphasis placed on constructing a new statistical model within P that adequately captures the statistical systematic information in the data.

1.8.1.5 Bridging the gap between theory and data

The PR approach highlights the gap between theory and data and proposes generic ways to bridge it using a sequence of interlinked models, emanating from the phenomenon of interest and furcating into models based on the statistical information in the data (statistical model), and models based on the substantive information (theory and structural models). The two families of models are blended at the level of the empirical model. Often economic theory comes in the form of static equilibrium relationships like a demand/supply model, but the available data refer to quantities transacted and the corresponding prices. In such cases, there is a need to construct estimable models, specified in terms of the observables, which could serve as a link between the theory and statistical models; Spanos (1989). The term structural model stands for a theory or an estimable model when the latter is called for. The insistence of the textbook and the Lucas–Sargent approaches on estimating structural models is distinctly desirable, but often its proper implementation requires one to probe theory models for potential errors that can arise from incongruous measurements, as well as external invalidity. Dynamic decision functions might not go far enough to bridge the gap between intentions and the available data, and the devising of estimable models, in the form of quantity and price adjustment equations, is called for; see Spanos (1995a).

A statistically adequate model provides a convenient summary of the statistical information in the data. It might turn out that one can find no such statistical model for a particular data Z, in which case the error-probing should give rise to a re-consideration of either the structural model or the choice of data, or both. The idea is that an adequate statistical model might not have any explanatory power. The structural model, when its restrictions on the statistically adequate model are data-acceptable, contains the substantive information that will supplement the statistical information and bestow upon the statistical model additional explanatory power, giving rise to an empirical model. Hence, the empirical model is likely to be less data-specific and thus more informative than the statistical model. Hopefully, the empirical model will "reflect" the invariance structure of the phenomenon being modeled, and it will be of use for prediction and explanation, as well as policy analysis purposes. We refer to the data-acceptability of a structural model within the context of an embedding adequate statistical model identification. We note that this use of the term is different from that of the Box–Jenkins approach, which refers to the choice of the optimal values of (p,d,q) in an ARIMA(p,d,q) model, or that of the textbook approach which adopted the Cowles Commission use of the term as explained in section 1.6.2.

It goes without saying that the PR approach does not offer a systematic method and a logic on how to "discover" appropriate structural models; it offers a framework to facilitate this process by bringing out the distinctions that help to ask the right questions, even though the answers might be very difficult at times; they often depend crucially on detailed substantive subject matter information as well as on in-depth knowledge of the substantive aspects of the data in question. At the same time, however, the PR approach suggests that the process of structural model choice does not rely exclusively on imagination and inspiration; it interacts in important ways with the statistical information and that interaction can be systematized in ways which can often render the imagination more creative and effective; see Spanos (2005b) for further discussion.

1.8.1.6   *Substantive adequacy*

It is important to emphasize that a statistically adequate model is necessary for the assessment of substantive adequacy. Once this is established one can proceed to pose questions concerning substantive information, including external validity. A missing confounding factor does not necessarily lead to invalid statistical inferences; see Spanos (2006a) for further discussion, but it might lead to invalid substantive inferences. The only way to assess that, however, is in the context of a statistically adequate model which "includes" the confounding factor. Sometimes, statistical misspecification which cannot be rectified by respecifying the statistical model within the same P might be an indication of a missing factor whose systematic effect is left in the residuals of the estimated statistical model. Again, this can only be established in the context of a statistically adequate model that includes that factor. Moreover, strange results in M-S testing often provide good indications of inaccurate data; Moore's (1914) data for pig iron provide an example of distorted dynamics due to imbued systematic errors; see Spanos (2005b) for further discussion.

1.8.1.7 The PR approach and recent developments in statistics

In addition to adopting the Fisher–Neyman probabilistic perspective, the probabilistic reduction (PR) approach integrates a number of different twentieth-century developments in statistics to give rise to a model-based statistical methodology with very specific rules for model specification as well as model validation, thus addressing the issues raised by Rao (2004). Firstly, the PR approach is built squarely on the frequentist foundations laid down by Fisher and extended by Neyman and Pearson. It avoids some of the problems with frequentist testing by using post-data evaluation based on severity; see Mayo (1996), Mayo and Spanos (2006). Secondly, it integrates the various developments associated with nonparametric techniques (Lehmann, 1975; Simonoff, 1996) and Exploratory Data Analysis (see Tukey, 1977; Mosteller and Tukey, 1977) into the PR framework as tools to enhance the effectiveness of the process from statistical model specification to a statistically adequate model. Specification, misspecification testing and respecification rely heavily on the use of graphical techniques, as well as nonparametric methods grounded on both rank statistics and kernel smoothing techniques; see Spanos (1999, 2001b), Mayo and Spanos (2004). However, the statistically adequate model in the context of which the structural model will be embedded is invariably a parametric statistical model, in order to ensure both the embedding as well the precision of inference. Thirdly, the PR approach brings out the important role that bootstrapping (Efron and Tibshirani, 1993) and other resampling techniques (see Politis et al., 1999) can play in evaluating the relevant error probabilities associated with particular inductive inferences.

The severe testing reasoning (section 1.2.1) is used to address a number of issues, such as (i) model selection vs model specification, (ii) misspecification testing vs Neyman–Pearson testing, (iii) respecification vs error-fixing, (iv) statistical vs substantive significance, (v) pre-designation vs post-designation, (vi) what constitutes data-mining, omitted variable bias, pre-test bias, data snooping; see Spanos (2000).

1.8.2 Addressing the unreliability of evidence conundrum

As argued above, the textbook approach to econometrics focuses on "saving the theory" by fashioning confirming empirical evidence, with little concern for assessing the different ways such inferences can be false. The source of the problem is the mistrust for "statistical regularities," accompanied by an undue confidence in theory's ability to weed out such untrustworthy "regularities"; an attitude that can be traced back to the 1920s. The mistrust for "statistical regularities" is based on the belief that they are too easy to contrive, and if one is willing to try hard enough, the data can be molded to "fit" any theory or hypothesis. There is also the lingering mistrust that if the choice of data Z is not theory-motivated, it will lead to a plethora of meaningless "data-based regularities." This was certainly true at the time of Moore, but Fisher's approach to statistical inference changed that drastically to make the fallacious nature of such an argument obvious.

The Fisher–Neyman probabilistic perspective asserts that: (a) Every statistical (inductive) inference is based on certain premises, in the form of a statistical model parameterizing an underlying stochastic process $\{Z_t, \ t \in \mathbb{T}\}$ that would have produced data $Z := (z_1, z_2, \ldots, z_T)$ as "a matter of course." (b) Statistical adequacy is necessary for establishing the reliability of "statistical regularities." Unfortunately, the Fisher–Neyman probabilistic perspective has not as yet permeated empirical modeling in economics because deep-rooted erroneous impressions, such as there is no such thing as statistical information separate from substantive information, are often hard to eliminate.

An estimated regression model with a high R^2 does not constitute a "statistical regularity," unless the probabilistic assumptions [1]–[5] of the statistical model (Table 1.2) have been vigorously probed, using potent misspecification tests, and no misspecification detected, i.e., statistical adequacy has been established. In this author's experience, statistically adequate empirical regularities are rare because assumptions such as [4]–[5] are not easily met in practice. Hence, even though statistical "non-regularities" based on goodness of fit criteria abound, severely probed statistically adequate regularities are very rare indeed. Once statistical adequacy is established, the reliability of the ensuing inductive inference assures the trustworthiness of the assessment of the substantive information (in the form of a structural model). Statistically inadequate premises give rise to non-regularities, and "theoretical meaningfulness" cannot transform it into a regularity of any sort.

The difficulty in establishing statistical adequacy suggests that mindless assemblages of data are unlikely to give rise to any such regularities; but even if they sometimes do, probing for incongruous measurement and external validity assessments will weed them out. Hence, the attitude that the process of establishing statistical regularities cannot even begin unless one has a complete and detailed structural form of the type envisaged by the Cowles Commission group is misplaced in fields like economics. The process might begin with low level theory or theories (conjectures), and use statistical regularities to guide the elaboration/testing of such theories. Indeed, the fleshing out of *ceteris paribus* clauses can reliably be done using statistically adequate models which ensure the trustworthiness of the inferences based upon them. That is, statistically adequate models provide the cornerstone for the process to probe for both incongruous measurement and the external invalidity of theories. Often, the inability to establish statistical adequacy within the chosen information set is a strong signal that important factors effecting the phenomenon of interest might be missing. This suggests that statistically adequate regularities can be of great help in disciplines like economics, where substantive information is not as precise or reliable as in some other fields like physics. Instead of subordinating observation to theory, it might pay to allow observation to play some role in the "discovery" process as well. Once a statistically adequate model is reached, one can assess the extent to which the theory in question accounts for these regularities, as well as contemplate alternative ways inductive inferences based on these regularities might be substantively false due to incongruous measurement and/or external invalidity.

1.8.2.1 Revisiting Moore's "demand" for corn

Let us return to Moore's "demand for corn" and consider the issue of respecifying his "interpolated curve" in order to ensure statistical adequacy. It turns out that using his transformed data $(x_t, y_t, t = 1, \ldots, n)$, no statistically adequate model is possible, suggesting that Moore's "data adjustment" is likely to have introduced systematic errors. However, if one returns to the original data, p_t (average price per bushel) and q_t (production in bushels), the following dynamic linear regression model:

$$\ln q_t = \underset{(0.794)}{0.401} - \underset{(0.078)}{0.679} \ln p_t + \underset{(0.082)}{0.734} \ln p_{t-1} + \underset{(0.082)}{0.960} + \underset{(0.109)}{\hat{u}_t}$$

$$R^2 = 0.909, \quad n = 44 \tag{1.15}$$

turns out to be statistically adequate, using similar misspecification tests as in the appendix. The model (1.15) can now provide the basis for a dialog between theory and data to probe for other errors, including theoretical validity, inaccurate data, incongruous measurements and external invalidity. For instance, it is clear from Moore's own discussion of how these data were compiled that some systematic errors are likely to have crept in. It is also obvious from his discussion of the observed data that they do not measure "demand" as understood in economic theory; intentions to buy corresponding to hypothetical prices. In view of the fact that the data measure actual production and average observed prices, the estimated equation could not be a demand schedule, but it could be a quantity adjustment equation; see Spanos (1995a). Can economic theory shed further light by providing a rationalization for (1.15) as an adjustment equation? To what extent is such an adjustment equation appropriate for the US market? These are questions that need to be addressed by the modeler.

1.8.3 The Gauss–Markov perspective and reliability/precision

One of the important elements of the PR approach summarized above is that the specification of statistical models, based on the probabilistic structure of the vector stochastic process $\{Z_t, t \in \mathbb{T}\}$, should be as specific and complete as possible. The rationale is that the narrower the premises, the more precise the inferences – assuming that the postulated structure is valid for the data in question – hence the important role ascribed to statistical adequacy. The weaker (less specific) the postulated probabilistic structure, the less precise and incisive the inferences. Moreover, weaker probabilistic assumptions do not necessarily render the inference more reliable, but they inevitably contribute to the imprecision of inference; see Spanos (2000).

This goes against the textbook conventional wisdom which emphasizes the weakest probabilistic structure that would "justify" a method yielding "consistent" estimators of the parameters of interest. In particular, the Gauss–Markov (G–M) theorem, as well as analogous theorems concerning the "optimality" of IV, GMM and nonparametric methods, distance themselves from strong probabilistic assumptions, such as Normality, in an attempt to claim greater generality and less susceptibility to misspecification. Indeed, these methods are often motivated by claims of weak probabilistic assumptions as a way to overcome unreliability; Matyas (1999, p. 1).

The rationale underlying this argument is that the reliance on weaker probabilistic assumptions will render OLS, IV and GMM-based inferences less prone to statistical misspecifications and thus more reliable. The cornerstone of this rationale is the G–M theorem. Minimum variance within the class of unbiased estimators of β, which are also linear in $\mathbf{y}$, of course, amounts to relative efficiency within a very narrow and not so interesting class of estimators. For Gauss in 1809 linearity might have been an attractive property, but now it has no value for inference purposes beyond its historical context. This is a mathematically interesting result, but it does not serve well the reliability and precision of inference. To see this let us consider how an econometrician using this theorem can proceed to draw inferences on the basis of $\hat{\beta}$.

A. Finite sample inference. The sampling distribution D(.) of $\hat{\beta}$ is:

$$\hat{\beta} = \left(\mathbf{X}^\top\mathbf{X}\right)^{-1}\mathbf{X}^\top\mathbf{y} \overset{?}{\sim} \mathrm{D}\left(\beta, \sigma^2\left(\mathbf{X}^\top\mathbf{X}\right)^{-1}\right)$$

When testing hypotheses, such as $H_0 : \beta = \bar{\beta}$ versus $H_1 : \beta \neq \bar{\beta}$, the type I and II error probabilities cannot be evaluated directly because D(.) is unknown. Hence, the only way finite sample inference is possible is to use its first two moments, in conjunction with inequalities such as Chebyshev's or Liapunov's, to provide upper/lower bounds for such error probabilities. It is well known, however, that these upper/lower bounds can be very crude in practice (see Spanos, 1999, chapter 10), leading to very imprecise inferences.

B. Asymptotic inference. One hopes that as $T \to \infty$ the crudeness of finite sample inferences will be ameliorated via the asymptotic sampling distribution: $\sqrt{T}\left(\hat{\beta} - \beta\right) \underset{a}{\sim} N(0, \sigma^2 \mathbf{Q}_X^{-1})$, where $\mathbf{Q}_X = \lim_{T \to \infty} T^{-1}(\mathbf{X}^\top\mathbf{X})$. The main problem with all asymptotic inferences is that its approximation error cannot be evaluated for a given T. One can, however, contemplate a number of scenarios where the approximation might be good, bad or uncertain.

(*a*) *Good.* When assumptions [1]–[5] (see Table 1.2) are valid, the approximation:

$$\hat{\beta} \cong N\left(\beta, \sigma^2\left(\mathbf{X}^\top\mathbf{X}\right)^{-1}\right) \tag{1.16}$$

will be excellent because it is true for any T.

(*b*) *Bad.* When any of the assumptions [2]–[5] (see Table 1.2) are invalid, the approximation (1.16) is likely to be bad. Even small deviations from these assumptions can have a sizeable distorting affect on error probabilities see Spanos (2005c). It is important to note that the distorting affect of certain forms of misspecification, such as trending data, does not decrease with the sample size, it increases; see Spanos and McGuirk (2001). Moreover, we know that when $D(\mathbf{y}_t|\mathbf{X}_t; \psi)$ is skewed, the reliability of inference concerning H_0 is also adversely affected by the 'non-Normality' of the $\{X_t, t \in \mathbb{T}\}$ process; see Ali and Sharma (1996).

(c) *Uncertain*. When only assumption [1] is invalid, the approximation (1.16) might or might not be bad. For instance, if the true distribution is highly non-Normal, say highly skewed, the approximation is not very good even for moderate sample sizes; see Spanos and McGuirk (2001).

The real problem in practice is that a G–M modeler has no idea which of the above scenarios applies to a particular situation unless thorough misspecification testing is applied to assess the validity of [1]–[5] (see Table 1.2) with data $Z := (y, X)$. Unfortunately, the G–M theorem discourages probing for departures from these assumptions (especially Normality), which could shed light on how good the asymptotic approximation might be for a given T. Hence, the modeler would be considerably more informed about the potential reliability of any inferences based on the CLR model if assumptions [1]–[5] (see Table 1.2) were probatively assessed, even in the case where some of them are rejected by the data, rather than invoke the G–M theorem and be oblivious of the appropriateness of assumptions [1]–[5] for data Z.

In addition to the reliability problem, the textbook modeler has to face the imprecision of inference issue because weaker assumptions give rise to less precise inference. Hence, the textbook strategy to address the problem of potential unreliability emanating from statistical misspecification leads inevitably to imprecision of inference, rendering empirical evidence non-decisive! The apparent trade-off between reliability and precision of inference, created by the G–M perspective, can be effectively addressed by thorough misspecification testing before any inference is made.

1.8.4 Statistical reliability and structural models

The statistical unreliability problem becomes much worse when the structural model is "framing" the inference with the statistical model *not* even specified explicitly. This can be best illustrated by the textbook discussion of Instrumental Variables (IVs) as providing a way to tackle the problems of bias and inconsistency for the OLS estimator $\hat{\alpha} = \left(X^\top X\right)^{-1} X^\top y$, arising from the dependence between the stochastic regressors X_t and the error term ε_t:

$$y_t = \alpha^\top X_t + \varepsilon_t \quad E(X_t \varepsilon_t) \neq 0, \quad t = 1, \ldots, T \tag{1.17}$$

where X_t: $m \times 1$. How does one decide that condition (a) $E(X_t \varepsilon_t) \neq 0$ holds? One is supposed to tell an economic theory "story" on how some of the omitted variables (that one can think of) included in ε_t are likely to be correlated with X_t. Is the story sufficient to render (a) operational? Clearly not statistically operational, because ε_t is never observable, and for every story one can tell, somebody else can tell another claiming the opposite.

How does the textbook narrative solve the bias and inconsistency problems? By finding another vector of observable variables Z_t : $p \times 1$, $p \geq m$, such that (b) $E(Z_t \varepsilon_t) = 0$. How is this an operational solution? One is supposed to tell another economic theory "story" on how the omitted variables included in ε_t (that one can think of) are unlikely to be correlated with $\mathbf{Z}_t$, but they are correlated with $(y_t, \mathbf{X}_t)$, i.e., (c) $E(\mathbf{Z}_t\, y_t) = \sigma_{31} \neq \mathbf{0}$, (d) $E(\mathbf{Z}_t\, \mathbf{X}^\top) = \Sigma_{32} \neq \mathbf{0}$, (e) $E(\mathbf{Z}_t\mathbf{Z}_t^\top) = \Sigma_{33} > \mathbf{0}$. What about the omitted factors in ε_t that one cannot think of, some of which are not even measurable? Condition (b) is clearly non-operational in the same sense that (a) is not, and the "solution" boils down to verifying (c)–(e) by calculating their sample analogues, say (c′) $T^{-1}\mathbf{Z}^\top\mathbf{y} \neq \mathbf{0}$, (d′) $T^{-1}\mathbf{Z}^\top\mathbf{X} \neq \mathbf{0}$, and (e′) $T^{-1}\mathbf{Z}^\top\mathbf{Z} \neq \mathbf{0}$. This, of course, is pitiably inadequate from the statistical viewpoint because there will be thousands of instruments whose sample second moments would seem to satisfy (c′)–(e′), and statistical reliability cannot be based on who can tell the "best story"; it's like playing tennis with the net down! The reliability of inference always depends on the adequacy of the underlying statistical model. However, one will be hard pressed to find the implicit statistical model mentioned in the traditional textbook discussion.

Viewing this argument in light of the discussion in section 1.8.4, (1.17) is a structural model whose "embedding" statistical model is the Multivariate Linear Regression (MLR) in Table 1.2, with $\mathbf{y}_t := (y_t, \mathbf{X}_t)$ and $\mathbf{x}_{1t} := \mathbf{z}_t$. As shown in Spanos (1986), (1.17) constitutes a reparameterization/restriction of the MLR model, and the reliability of any inference based on the IV estimator $\hat{\alpha} = (\mathbf{X}^\top\mathbf{P}_Z\mathbf{X})^{-1}\mathbf{X}^\top\mathbf{P}_Z\mathbf{y}$, where $\mathbf{P}_Z = \mathbf{Z}(\mathbf{Z}^\top\mathbf{Z})^{-1}\mathbf{Z}^\top$, depends crucially on (i) testing thoroughly assumptions [1]–[5] (Table 1.2), detecting no departures, and then (ii) testing and accepting the overidentifying restrictions. This author is unaware of any empirical studies using IVs which have passed these tests. In conclusion, if the substantive information concerning the potentially relevant factors is not assessed in relation to a statistically adequate (implicit) statistical model, IV-based inference is likely to be unreliable; see Spanos (2006c).

1.8.5   Recent developments[1]

The above criticisms of the Gauss–Markov (G–M) perspective apply equally well to its more recent extensions such as Generalized Method of Moments (see Matyas, 1999; Hayashi, 2000) as well as certain nonparametric (see Pagan and Ullah, 1999) and semi-parametric methods (see Horowitz, 1998), when used as a basis for substantive inference. The specification of statistical models relying exclusively on substantive information, the absence of specific distributional assumptions, and the presence of non-testable assumptions, as well as the use of statistical models with "broad" premises, are not conducive to reliable/precise inferences. As argued above, nonparametric procedures can be of great value, not for imbedding structural models and/or as a basis of substantive inferences, but for exploratory data analysis purposes. Such models can contribute decisively to the specification, misspecification testing and respecification facets of modeling, as expounded in the context of the PR approach; see Spanos (1999).

The dominating influence of the G–M perspective is clearly apparent in the textbook discussion of the statistical models introduced into econometrics since the 1960s, including discrete and limited dependent and duration models for cross-section data (see Wooldridge, 2002) and models for panel data (see Baltagi,

2001; Arellano, 2003). The discussion of these statistical models: (i) views the probabilistic structure of statistical models almost exclusively in terms of assumptions concerning error terms, (ii) these specifications are often incomplete, and invariably involve non-testable assumptions, (iii) the statistical analysis focuses primarily on estimation, and (iv) respecification is often confined to "error-fixing." As argued above, when framing the structural model the error terms plays a crucial role, but thinking in terms of an autonomous error term carrying the probabilistic structure of a statistical model can lead to numerous confusions.

Over the last 20 years or so, certain significant developments have taken place in time series econometrics, beginning with Granger and Newbold (1974) revisiting the spurious regression problem raised initially by Yule (1926). By simulating two uncorrelated Normal random walks ($x_t = x_{t-1} + \varepsilon_{1t}$, $y_t = y_{t-1} + \varepsilon_{2t}$, $E(\varepsilon_{1t}\varepsilon_{2t}) = 0$), they showed that inferences based on the regression model $y_t = \beta_0 + \beta_1 x_t + u_t$ are seriously unreliable; the actual error probabilities are very different from the nominal ones. Phillips (1986) explained these results using non-standard inference propositions associated with unit roots in AR(p) models; see Dickey and Fuller (1979). Unfortunately, the literature missed the crucial lesson that misspecification is the real source of spurious regression, and instead focused on how the traditional inference propositions (sampling distributions of estimators and test statistics) need to be modified when modeling unit root processes; Phillips (1987). As a result, the empirical evidence accumulated by the unit root testing literature is largely unreliable, and needs to be reconsidered in light of statistically adequate models; see Andreou and Spanos (2003). Moreover, the inadequate attention paid to the probabilistic prespective of unit root (UR) processes has misled this literature into the false premise that one can test for the presence of a unit root in the context of an AR(p) model, when in fact the AR and UR processes are non-nested; see Spanos and McGuirk (2002). On the positive side, the focus on unit roots has led to important theoretical developments in time series econometrics, such as cointegration and error-correction models; Engle and Granger (1987), Johansen (1991), Boswijk (1995), Hendry (1995) inter alia.

Despite these important developments, the dominating influence of the G–M perspective is still apparent in the textbook discussion of statistical models for time series data (see Hamilton, 1994, Greene, 2003), but there are some encouraging signs that this literature is moving towards the probabilistic perspective propounded above. The first sign is that the Sims VAR and the Sargan-Hendry AD models seem to have influenced the literature enough for more attention to be paid to the probabilistic structure of the data. Related to this, there has been growing interest in model evaluation and diagnostic checking, not only in the research literature (Newey, 1985; Tauchen, 1985, inter alia), but also at the textbook level; see Hendry (1995), Mills (1999) and Patterson (2000). Despite these encouraging signs, the current focus of statistical model specification is still on probabilistic assumptions for the error term, often leading to incomplete and sometimes internally inconsistent specifications; see Spanos (1995b). This renders misspecification testing and respecification a much less systematic activity than the PR approach envisages. In

Table 1.4 The logit/probit model

$$Y_k = F(\alpha^\top \mathbf{x}_k) + \mathbf{u}_k, \ k \in \mathbb{N}$$

[1] Bernoulli:	$D(y_k \mid \mathbf{x}_k; \theta_k)$ is Bernoulli distributed
[2] Logit/Probit:	$E(Y_k \mid \mathbf{X}_k = \mathbf{x}_k) = F(\alpha^\top \mathbf{x}_k)$
[3] Heteroskedasticity:	$Var(Y_k \mid \mathbf{X}_k = \mathbf{x}_k) = F(\alpha^\top \mathbf{x}_k)[1 - F(\alpha^\top \mathbf{x}_k)]$
[4] Independence:	$\{(Y_k \mid \mathbf{X}_k = \mathbf{x}_k), k \in \mathbb{N}\}$, independent process
[5] k-homogeneity:	the parameters α are not functions of $k \in \mathbb{N}$

where $F(z_k) = \exp(z_k)/1 + \exp(z_k)$ for the Logit model
and $F(z_k) = \frac{1}{\sqrt{2\pi}} \int_{-\infty}^{z_k} \exp(-u^2/2)du$ for the Probit model; $z_k := \alpha^\top \mathbf{x}_k$.

this sense the probabilistic perspective proposed in Spanos (1986) has had very little impact on traditional econometric textbooks. Having said that, the discussion concerning "model evaluation and diagnostic testing" in the last edition of the Johnston textbook (see Johnston and DiNardo, 1997) is very encouraging.

One can make a case that what is currently needed is to extend the Fisher–Neyman probabilistic perspective, as utilized in the case of time series models (see Spanos, 2001a), to the other statistical models for cross-section and panel data, as well as developing methods and procedures for specification, misspecification testing and respecification for these models. Such a probabilistic perspective will provide a complete and internally consistent set of testable probabilistic assumptions (in terms of observables) for these models, which is a necessary first step for ascertaining statistical adequacy. For instance, such a specification for the Logit/Probit "regression-like" models (see Wooldridge, 2002, chapter 13) will look like Table1.4: the Poisson and duration "regression-like" models are specified similarly. This makes it clear that the choice between the logit and probit models should be based on statistical adequacy grounds (testing thoroughly [2]–[5]), and not on some "goodness of fit" and/or "theoretical meaningfulness" criteria.

Another example of how the probabilistic perspective can shed light on the structure of the panel data models concerns the standard question of "fixed versus random effects". This question is posed as a choice between the following models:

(a) fixed effects $y_{it} = \alpha_i + \mathbf{x}_{it}^\top \boldsymbol{\beta} + \varepsilon_{it}, \qquad i \in \mathbb{N}, \quad t \in \mathbb{T}$

(b) random effects $y_{it} = \alpha_i + \mathbf{x}_{it}^\top \boldsymbol{\beta} + (u_i + \varepsilon_{it}) \quad i \in \mathbb{N}, \quad t \in \mathbb{T}$

accompanied by several assumptions (most of them non-testable) concerning the "white noise" error terms (u_i, ε_{it}), the most crucial being:

$$E(\varepsilon_{it} \mid \mathbf{X}) = 0, \qquad E(u_i \mid \mathbf{X}) = 0, \qquad E(\varepsilon_{it} u_j) = 0, \quad \text{for all } i, j, \text{ and } t$$

$$E(\varepsilon_{it}^2 \mid \mathbf{X}) = \sigma_\varepsilon^2, \quad E(u_i^2 \mid \mathbf{X}) = \sigma_u^2, \quad E(\varepsilon_{it} \varepsilon_{jt} \mid \mathbf{X}) = 0, \quad E(u_i u_j \mid \mathbf{X}) = 0, \quad i \neq j$$

see Greene (2003, chapter 13). Transforming these assumptions in terms of the observables, via $E(y_{it} \mid \mathbf{X}_{it} = \mathbf{x}_{it})$ and $Var(y_{it} \mid \mathbf{X}_{it} = \mathbf{x}_{it})$ reveals that the fixed effects term captures first moment heterogeneity, since in (a) $\alpha_i = E(y_{it}) - E(\mathbf{X}_{it})^\top \boldsymbol{\beta}$. By contrast, the random effects model imposes first order homogeneity (in (b), $\alpha = E(y_{it}) - E(\mathbf{X}_{it})^\top \boldsymbol{\beta}$ and u_i can only capture second moment "ephemeral" heterogeneity, since it relates to the conditional variance $Var(y_{it} \mid \mathbf{X}_{it} = \mathbf{x}_{it}) = (\sigma_u^2 + \sigma_\varepsilon^2)$.

Hence, the view that these two models are substitutes is misleading. Additional insight will be gained when all the probabilistic assumptions concerning the error terms are transformed into assumptions relating to the conditional distribution $D(y_{it} \,|\, X_{it};\ \theta)$, and the parameters $\left(\alpha_i, \alpha, \beta, \sigma_\varepsilon^2, \sigma_u^2\right)$ are given explicit statistical parameterizations stemming from the joint distribution $D(y_{it},\ X_{it};\ \phi)$ analogous to those of the parameters in Tables 1.2–1.3.

Although a detailed discussion of Bayesian methods in econometrics (see Zellner, 1971; and Bauwens *et al.*, 1999) is beyond the scope of this chapter, it is important to emphasize that the G–M perspective also permeates these methods, and they are equally susceptible to the unreliability and imprecision of inference problems discussed above. While a more explicit specification of the probabilistic assumptions of the model helps, the use of priors cannot address the issues raised by a misspecified statistical model. Equally ineffective for addressing statistical misspecification is Leamer's call for a Bayesian formalization of "cookbook econometrics," because the formalization of fallacious "error-fixing" strategies would create "honest" but misguided modelers; it would not deal with the reliability and precision of inference problems.

1.9   Conclusions

The above assessment of twentieth-century developments in econometrics suggests that, despite the impressive developments in econometric methods and techniques, the vision of furnishing apposite empirical foundations to economics remains largely unfulfilled. The current methodological framework, based on the Gauss–Markov "curve fitting" perspective, has given rise to a theory-dominated approach to empirical modeling that invariably leads to unreliable empirical evidence. The unreliability of evidence stems primarily from applying statistical techniques for quantification without proper justification, i.e. they are produced by methods and procedures which have very limited ability to detect errors if, in fact, they were present. Inductive inferences which concern the sign and magnitude of the coefficients in a regression can only be justified in terms of the validity of the premises; the probabilistic assumptions underlying the statistical model are approximately true for the data in question. That requires thorough misspecification testing, not "goodness of fit."

It is argued that what is needed is a methodological framework which: (a) brings out the gap between theory and data, (b) encourages error probing inquiries at all stages of modeling, (c) affords the data "a life of their own" by adopting the Fisher–Neyman probabilistic perspective, (d) specifies statistical models in terms of the observable processes, and (e) separates the statistical and structural model specification; the former is built upon the statistical information contained in the data, and the latter on the substantive information emanating from the theory. The probabilistic perspective views the statistical model in the context of all possible such models that could have given rise to data **Z**, and provides the foundation and overarching framework for establishing statistical adequacy: specification, misspecification, respecification. Reliable theory testing takes place only when the structural model is confronted with a statistically adequate description of the systematic statistical information in the data. In addition to statistical mis-specification, this methodological framework should emphasize probing for errors concerning the accuracy of the data, whether they measure what they are sup-posed to (congruous measurement), as well as whether the inductive inferences reached can be extended to the phenomenon of interest (external validity). This methodological framework would also guide the practitioner through the maze of technical results currently available, and indicate how such an impressive armory of techniques can be appropriately applied in order to produce reliable and incisive evidence.

This methodological framework will create the preconditions for a constructive dialogue between theory and data, revolving around the question "When do data Z provide evidence for a theory or a claim H?" The form of inductive reasoning that best addresses this question is based on the notion of severe testing (see Mayo, 1996), which strongly encourages the probing of the different ways an inference might be in error. The severe testing reasoning can also shed light on several important methodological issues which concern the nature, interpretation, and justification of methods and models that are relied upon to learn from observational data. Only then can "learning from data" contribute significantly towards establishing economics as an empirical science.

1.10   Appendix: Basic Misspecification Tests

Normality: D'Agostino and Pearson (1973) test.

Linearity: H_0: $\gamma_2 = \gamma_3 = 0$, using the artificial regression:

$$\hat{u}_t = \gamma_0 + \gamma_1 x_t + \gamma_2 x_t^2 + \gamma_3 x_t^3 + v_t$$

Homoskedasticity: H_0: $\delta_1 = \delta_2 = 0$, using the artificial regression:

$$\hat{u}_t^2 = \delta_0 + \delta_1 x_t^2 + \delta_2 x_t^3 + v_t$$

Independence: H_0 : $\alpha_2 = \alpha_3 = 0$, using the artificial regression:

$$\hat{u}_t = \alpha_0 + \alpha_1 x_t + \alpha_2 y_{t-1} + \alpha_3 x_{t-1} + v_t$$

For details, see Spanos (1986, 1999).

Acknowledgments

I'm most grateful to Deborah Mayo for some invaluable suggestions and comments on an earlier draft of the chapter. Thanks are also due to Karim Abadir, Bernt Stigum, Terence Mills and an associate editor for several useful comments and suggestions.

Note

1. It is important to reiterate that the criticisms in this section are not directed toward the authors of the textbooks referenced, whom I regard with esteem, but towards the Gauss–Markov perspective that dominates current econometrics.

References

Abadir, K. and G. Talmain (2002) Aggregation, persistence and volatility in a macro model. *Review of Economic Studies* **69**, 749–79.

Aitken, A.C. (1934) On least squares and linear combinations of observations. *Proceedings of the Royal Society of Edinburgh* **55**, 42–8.

Ali, M.M. and S.C. Sharma (1996) "Robustness to Nonnormality of Regression F-tests," *Journal of Econometrics* **71**, 175–205.

Andreou, E. and A. Spanos (2003) Statistical adequacy and the testing of trend versus difference stationarity. *Econometric Reviews* **22**, 217–52 (with discussion).

Arellano, M. (2003) *Panel Data Econometrics*. Oxford: Oxford University Press.

Backhouse, R.E. (1994) *New Directions in Economic Methodology*. London: Routledge.

Baltagi, B.H. (2001) *Econometric Analysis of Panel Data*, 2nd edtion. New York: Wiley.

Bartlett, M.S. (1965) R. A. Fisher and the last fifty years of statistical methodology. *Journal of the American Statistical Association* **60**, 395–409.

Bauwens, L., M. Lubrano and J.-F. Richard (1999) *Bayesian Inference in Dynamic Econometric Models*. Oxford: Oxford University Press.

Bennett, J.H. (ed.) (1990) *Statistical Inference and Analysis: Selected Correspondence of R. A. Fisher*. Oxford: Clarendon Press.

Blaug, M. (1992) *The Methodology of Economics*. Cambridge: Cambridge University Press.

Boswijk, P.H. (1995) Efficient inference on cointegration parameters in structural error correction models. *Journal of Econometrics* **69**, 133–58.

Bowley, A.L. (1920) *Elements of Statistics*, 4th edtion. London: P.S. King and Son.

Box, G.E.P. and G.M. Jenkins (1970/1976) *Time Series Analysis: Forecasting and Control*, revised edition. San Francisco: Holden-Day.

Carnap, R. (1962) *Logical Foundations of Probability*, 2nd edtion. Chicago: The University of Chicago Press.

Cartwright, N. (1983) *How the Laws of Physics Lie*. Oxford: Clarendon Press.

Chalmers, A.F. (1999) *What is this Thing called Science?*, 3rd edtion. Indianapolis: Hackett.

Christ, C.F. (1985) Early progress in estimating quantitative economic relationships in America. *American Economic Review* **75**, 39–52.

Cochrane, D. and G.H. Orcutt (1949) Application of least squares regression to relationships containing auto-correlated error terms. *Journal of the American Statistical Association* **44**, 32–61.

Cooper, R.L. (1972) The predictive performance of quarterly econometric models of the United States. In B.G. Hickman (ed.), *Econometric Models of Cyclical Behavior*. New York: Columbia University Press, NY.

D'Agostino, R.B. and E.S. Pearson (1973) Tests for departure from normality. Empirical results for the distributions of $b2$ and $\sqrt{b1}$. *Biometrika* **60**, 613–22.

David, F.N. and J. Neyman (1938) Extension of the Markoff theorem on least squares. *Statistical Research Memoirs* **II**, 105–16.

Davis, H.T. (1941) *The Theory of Econometrics*. Indiana: Principia Press Inc.

Dickey, D.A. and W.A. Fuller (1979) Distribution of the estimators for autoregressive time series with a unit root. *Journal of the American Statistical Association* **74**, 427–31.

Doob, J.L. (1953) *Stochastic Processes*. New York: Wiley.

Durbin, J. and G.S. Watson (1950) Testing for serial correlation in least squares regression I. *Biometrika*, **37**, 409–28.

Efron, B. and R. Tibshirani (1993) *An Introduction to the Bootstrap*. London: Chapman and Hall.

Engle, R.F. and C.W.J. Granger (1987) Co-integration and Error-correction: representation, estimation and testing. *Econometrica* **55**, 251–76.

Epstein, R.J. (1987) *A History of Econometrics*. Amsterdam: North-Holland.

Fisher, R.A. (1922) On the mathematical foundations of theoretical statistics. *Philosophical Transactions of the Royal Society A*, **222**, 309–68.

Fisher, R.A. (1925) *Statistical Methods for Research Workers*. Edinburgh: Oliver and Boyd.

Fisher, R.A. (1935) *The Design of Experiments*. Edinburgh: Oliver and Boyd.

Fisher, R.A. (1955) Statistical methods and scientific induction. *Journal of the Royal Statistical Society* **B**, **17**, 69–78.

Fisher, R.A. (1956) *Statistical Methods and Scientific Inference*. Edinburgh: Oliver and Boyd.

Fox, K.A. (1989) Agricultural economists in the econometric revolution: institutional background, literature and leading figures. *Oxford Economic Papers* **41**, 53–70.

Friedman, M. (1953) *Essays in Positive Economics*. Chicago: University of Chicago Press.

Frisch, R. (1933) Editorial. *Econometrica* **1**, 1–4.

Frisch, R. (1934) *Statistical Confluence Analysis by Means of Complete Regression Systems*. Oslo: Univeritetets Okonomiske Institutt.

Gilbert, C.L. (1991) Richard Stone, demand theory and the emergence of modern econometrics. *Economic Journal* **101**, 288–302.

Goldberger, A.S. (1964) *Econometric Theory*. New York: John Wiley & Sons.

Granger, C.W.J. (ed.) (1990) *Modelling Economic Series*. Oxford: Clarendon Press.

Granger, C.W.J. and P. Newbold (1974) Spurious regressions in econometrics. *Journal of Econometrics* **2**, 111–20.

Granger, C.W.J. and P. Newbold (1986) *Forecasting Economic Time Series*, 2nd edtion. London: Academic Press.

Greene, W.H. (2003) *Econometric Analysis*, 5th edition. New Jersey: Prentice Hall.

Guala, F. (2005) *The Methodology of Experimental Economics*. Cambridge: Cambridge University Press.

Haavelmo, T. (1943) The statistical implications of a system of simultaneous equations. *Econometrica* **11**, 1–12.

Haavelmo, T. (1944) The probability approach to econometrics. *Econometrica* **12**, suppl., 1–115.

Hacking, I. (1965) *Logic of Statistical Inference*. Cambridge: Cambridge University Press.

Hald, A. (1998) *A History of Mathematical Statistics from 1750 to 1930*. New York: Wiley.

Hamilton, J.D. (1994) *Time Series Analysis*. Princeton, NJ: Princeton University Press.

Hansen, L.P. (1982) Large sample properties of generalized method of moments estimators. *Econometrica* **97**, 93–115.

Harrod, R.F. (1938) Scope and method of economics. *Economic Journal* **48**, 383–412.

Hayashi, F. (2000) *Econometrics*. Princeton, NJ: Princeton University Press.

Heckman, J.J. (1992) Haavelmo and the birth of modern econometrics: a review of *The History of Econometric Ideas* by Mary Morgan. *Journal of Economic Literature*, **XXX**, 876–86.

Hendry, D.F. (1976) The structure of simultaneous equations estimators. *Journal of Econometrics* **4**, 51–88.

Hendry, D.F. (1993) *Econometrics: Alchemy or Science?* Oxford: Blackwell.

Hendry, D.F. (1995) *Dynamic Econometrics*. Oxford: Oxford University Press.

Hendry, D.F., E.E. Leamer and D.J. Poirier (1990) The ET dialogue: a conversation on econometric methodology. *Econometric Theory* **6**, 171–261.

Hendry, D.F. and M.S. Morgan (ed.) (1995) *The Foundations of Econometric Analysis*. Cambridge: Cambridge University Press.

Hendry, D.F., A. Spanos and N. Ericsson (1989) Trygve Haavelmo's contributions to econometrics. *Socialokonomen* **11**, 12–17.

Hood, W.C. and Koopmans, T.C. (eds) (1953) *Studies in Econometric Method*, Cowles Commission Monograph, No. 14. New York: John Wiley and Sons.

Hoover, K.D. (2001) *Causality in Macroeconomics*. Cambridge: Cambridge University Press.

Hoover, K.D. (2006) *The Methodology of Econometrics*. ch. 2, this volume.

Horowitz, J.L. (1998) *Semiparametric Methods in Econometrics*. New York: Springer-Verlag.

Hutchison, T.W. (1938) *The Significance and Basic Postulates of Economic Theory*, Augustus M. Kelly reprints, 1965, New York.

Jeffreys, H. (1939) *Theory of Probability*. Oxford: Oxford University Press.

Jevons, W.S. (1871) *The Theory of Political Economy*. London: Macmillan.

Jevons, W.S. (1874) *The Principles of Science*. London: Macmillan.

Johansen, S. (1991) Estimation and hypothesis testing of cointegrating vectors in Gaussian vector autoregressive models. *Econometrica* 59, 1551–1580.

Johansen, S. (1995) *Likelihood-based Inference in Cointegrated Vector Autoregressive Models.* Oxford: Oxford University Press.

Johnston, J. (1963) *Econometric Methods*, 4th edtion. New York: McGraw-Hill.

Johnston, J. and J. DiNardo (1997) *Econometric Methods.* New York: McGraw-Hill.

Judge, G.G., C.R. Hill, W.E. Griffiths, H. Lütkepohl and T.-C. Lee (1988) *Introduction to the Theory and Practice of Econometrics.* New York: Wiley.

Kennedy, P. (2003) *A Guide to Econometrics*, 5th edtion. Cambridge: MIT Press.

Keynes, J.M. (1921) *A Treatise on Probability.* London: Macmillan.

Keynes, J.M. and Tinbergen, J. (1939–40) Professor's Tinbergen's Method, *Economic Journal* 49, 558–68; A Reply, by J. Tinbergen, and Comment, by Keynes 50, 141–56.

Keynes, J.N. (1891) *The Scope and Method of Political Economy.* London: Macmillan.

Klein, L.R. and A.S. Goldberger (1955) *An Econometric Model of the United States, 1929–1952.* Amsterdam: North-Holland.

Knight, F.H. (1940) "'What is Truth' in Economics?," *Journal of Political Economy* 48, 1–32.

Kolmogorov, A.N. (1933) *Foundations of the Theory of Probability*, 2nd English edition. New York: Chelsea Publishing Co.

Koopmans, T.C. (1939) *Linear Regression Analysis of Economic Time Series*, Netherlands Economic Institute, Publication No. 20. Haarlem: F. Bohn.

Koopmans, T.C. (1947) Measurement without theory. *Review of Economics and Statistics* 17, 161–72.

Koopmans, T.C. (ed.) (1950) *Statistical Inference in Dynamic Economic Models*, Cowles Commission Monograph, No. 10. New York: John Wiley & Sons.

Kuznets, S. (1950) Book review of *On the accuracy of economic observations*, by O. Morgenstern (1950). *Journal of the American Statistical Association* 45, 576–9.

Leamer, E.E. (1978) *Specification Searches: Ad Hoc Inference with Nonexperimental Data.* New York: Wiley.

Leamer, E.E. and H.B. Leonard (1983) Reporting the fragility of regression estimates. *Review of Economics and Statistics* 65, 306–17.

Lehmann, E.L. (1975) *Nonparametrics: Statistical Methods Based on Ranks.* San Francisco: Holden-Day.

Lehmann, E.L. (1990) Model specification: the views of Fisher and Neyman, and later developments. *Statistical Science* 5, 160–8.

Lehmann, E.L. (1993) The Fisher and Neyman–Pearson theories of testing hypotheses: one theory or two? *Journal of the American Statistical Association* 88, 1242–9.

Leontief, W.W. (1948) Econometrics. In H.S. Ellis (ed.), *A Survey of Contemporary Economics.* Homewood, IL: Irwin.

Leontief, W.W. (1971) Theoretical assumptions and nonobserved facts. *American Economic Review* 1–7.

Lucas, R.E. (1976) Econometric policy evaluation: a critique. In K. Brunner and A.M. Meltzer (eds), *The Phillips Curve and Labour Markets*, Carnegie-Rochester Conference on Public Policy. Amsterdam: North-Holland, pp. 19–46.

Lucas, R.E. and T.J. Sargent (1981) *Rational Expectations and Econometric Practice.* London: George Allen & Unwin.

Maki, U. (2002) *Fact and Fiction in Economics.* Cambridge: Cambridge University Press.

Marshall, A. (1890) *Principles of Economics.* London: Macmillan.

Matchlup, F. (1955) The problem of verification in economics. *Southern Economic Journal* 22, 1–21.

Matyas, L. (ed.) (1999) *Generalized Method of Moments Estimation.* Cambridge: Cambridge University Press.

Mayo, D.G. (1991) Novel evidence and severe tests. *Philosophy of Science* 58, 523–52.

Mayo, D.G. (1996) *Error and the Growth of Experimental Knowledge.* Chicago: The University of Chicago Press.

Mayo, D.G. (2005) "Statistics, Philosophy of." In S. Sarkar and J. Pfeifer (eds), *The Philosophy of Science: An Encyclopedia*. London: Routledge, pp. 802–14.

Mayo, D.G. and A. Spanos (2004) "Methodology in Practice: Statistical Misspecification Testing," *Philosophy of Science*, **71**, 1007–1025.

Mayo, D.G. and A. Spanos (2006) "Severe Testing as a Basic Concept in a Neyman–Pearson Philosophy of Induction," forthcoming, *The British Journal for the Philosophy of Science*.

McGuirk, A. and A. Spanos (2003) Revisiting error autocorrelation correction: common factor restrictions and Granger non-causality, Virginia Tech working paper.

Mill, J.S. (1874) *Essays on Some Unsettled Questions of Political Economy*, 2nd edition. London: Longmans.

Mill, J.S. (1884) *A System of Logic*, 8th edition. New York: Harper and Brothers.

Mills, F.C. (1924/1938) *Statistical Methods*. New York: Henry Holt and Co.

Mills, T.C. (1999) *The Econometric Modelling of Financial Time Series*, 2nd edition. Cambridge: Cambridge University Press.

Mitchell, W.C. (1927) *Business Cycles: The Problems and its Setting*. New York: National Bureau of Economic Research.

Mizon, G.E. (1995) Progressive modelling of macroeconomic time series: the LSE methodology. In K.D. Hoover (ed.), *Macroeconometrics: Developments, Tensions and Prospects*. Dordrecht: Kluwer.

Moore, H.L. (1908) The statistical complement of pure economics. *Quarterly Journal of Economics* **23**, 1–33.

Moore, H.L. (1911) *The Law of Wages*. New York: Macmillan.

Moore, H.L. (1914) *Economic Cycles – Their Laws and Cause*. New York: Macmillan.

Morgan, M.S. (1990) *The History of Econometric Ideas*. Cambridge: Cambridge University Press.

Morgenstern, O. (1950/1963) *On the Accuracy of Economic Observations*, 2nd edition. Princeton, NJ: Princeton University Press.

Mosteller, F. and J.W. Tukey (1977) *Data Analysis and Regression*. Reading: Addison-Wesley.

Newey, W.K. (1985) Maximum likelihood specification testing and conditional moment tests. *Econometrica* **53**, 1047–70.

Neyman, J. (1950) *First Course in Probability and Statistics*. New York: Henry Holt.

Neyman, J. (1952) *Lectures and Conferences on Mathematical Statistics and Probability*, 2nd edition. Washington, DC: US Department of Agriculture.

Neyman, J. (1956) Note on an article by Sir Ronald Fisher. *Journal of the Royal Statistical Society* B, **18**, 288–94.

Neyman, J. (1976) Tests of statistical hypotheses and their use in studies of natural phenomena. *Communications in Statistics – Theory and Methods* 5, 737–51.

Neyman, J. and E.S. Pearson (1933) On the problem of the most efficient tests of statistical hypotheses. *Phil. Trans. of the Royal Society, A*, **231**, 289–337.

Orcutt G.H. (1952) Book review of *Statistical Inference in Dynamic Economic Models*, ed. by Koopmans, T.C. (1950). *The American Economic Review* **42**, 165–9.

Pagan, A.R. (1987) Three econometric methodologies: a critical appraisal. *Journal of Economic Surveys* 1, 3–24. Reprinted in C.W.J. Granger (1990).

Pagan, A.R. and A. Ullah (1999) *Nonparametric Econometrics*. Cambridge: Cambridge University Press.

Patterson, K. (2000) *Introduction to Applied Econometrics: A Time Series Approach*. London: Macmillan.

Pearson, K. (1895) Contributions to the mathematical theory of evolution II. Skew variation in homogeneous material. *Philosophical Transactions of the Royal Society of London, Series A*, **186**, 343–414.

Pearson, K. (1920) The fundamental problem of practical statistics. *Biometrika* **XIII**, 1–16.

Peirce, C.S. (1878) The probability of induction. *Popular Science Monthly* **12**, 705–18.

Phillips, P.C.B. (1986) Understanding spurious regression in econometrics. *Journal of Econometrics* **33**, 311–40.

Phillips, P.C.B. (1987) Time series regressions with a unit root. *Econometrica* **55**, 227–301.

Politis, D.N., J.P. Romano and M. Wolf (1999) *Subsampling*. New York: Springer.

Qin, D. (1993) *The Formation of Econometrics: a Historical Perspective*. Oxford: Clarendon Press.

Rao, C.R. (1992) R. A. Fisher: the founder of modern statistics. *Statistical Science* **7**, 34–48.

Rao, C.R. (2004) Statistics: reflections on the past and visions for the future. *Amstat News* **327**, 2–3.

Redman, D.A. (1997) *The Rise of Political Economy as a Science*. Cambridge, MA: The MIT Press.

Robbins, L. (1932/1937) *An Essay on the Nature and Significance of Economic Science*. London: Macmillan.

Roos, C.F. (1934) *Dynamic Economics*, Cowles Commission Monograph 1. Indiana: Principia Press Inc.

Rosenblatt, M. (1956) Remarks on some nonparametric estimates of a density function. *Annals of Mathematical Statistics* **27**, 832–5.

Salmon, W. (1966) *The Foundations of Scientific Inference*. Pittsburgh: University of Pittsburgh Press.

Sargan, J.D. (1964) Wages and prices in the U.K.: a study in Econometric Methodology. In P.E. Hart, G. Mills and J.K. Whitaker (eds), *Econometric Analysis for National Economic Planning*. London: Butterworths.

Savage, L.J. (1954) *The Foundations of Statistics*. New York: Wiley.

Scheffe, H. (1943) Statistical inference in the non-parametric case. *Annals of Mathematical Statistics* **14**, 305–32.

Simonoff, J.S. (1996) *Smoothing Methods in Statistics*. New York: Springer-Verlag.

Sims, C.A. (1980) Macroeconomics and reality. *Econometrica* **48**, 1–48.

Sims, C.A. (1982) Policy analysis with econometric models. *Brookings Papers on Economic Activity* 107–64.

Slutsky, E. (1927) The summation of random causes as the source of cyclic processes (in Russian); English translation in *Econometrica* **5**, 1937.

Spanos, A. (1986) *Statistical Foundations of Econometric Modelling*. Cambridge: Cambridge University Press.

Spanos, A. (1988) Towards a unifying methodological framework for econometric modelling. *Economic Notes*, 107–34. Reprinted in Granger (1990).

Spanos, A. (1989) On re-reading Haavelmo: a retrospective view of econometric modeling. *Econometric Theory* **5**, 405–29.

Spanos, A. (1990) The Simultaneous Equations Model revisited: statistical adequacy and identification. *Journal of Econometrics* **44**, 87–108.

Spanos, A. (1994) On modeling heteroskedasticity: the student's t and elliptical regression models. *Econometric Theory* **10**, 286–315.

Spanos, A. (1995a) On theory testing in econometrics: modeling with nonexperimental data. *Journal of Econometrics* **67**, 189–226.

Spanos, A. (1995b) On normality and the linear regression model. *Econometric Reviews* **14**, 195–203.

Spanos, A. (1999) *Probability Theory and Statistical Inference: Econometric Modeling with Observational Data*. Cambridge: Cambridge University Press.

Spanos, A. (2000) Revisiting data mining: "hunting" with or without a license. *The Journal of Economic Methodology* **7**, 231–64.

Spanos, A. (2001a) Time series and dynamic models. In B. Baltagi (ed.), *A Companion to Theoretical Econometrics*. Oxford: Blackwell Publishers, pp. 585–609.

Spanos, A. (2001b) Parametric versus non-parametric inference: statistical models and simplicity. In A. Zellner, H. A. Keuzenkamp and M. McAleer (eds), *Simplicity, Inference and Modelling*. Cambridge University Press, pp. 181–206.

Spanos, A. (2005a) Where Do Statistical Models Come From? Revisiting the Problem of Specification, forthcoming in the *2nd Erich Lehmann symposium volume ##*, Institute of Mathematical Statistics.

Spanos, A. (2005b) Structural vs. Statistical Models in Econometric Modeling, Virginia Tech discussion paper.

Spanos, A. (2005c) Misspecification and the reliability of inference: the t-test in the presence of Markov dependence, Virginia Tech working paper.

Spanos, A. (2005d) Structural Equation Modeling, Causal Inference and Statistical Adequacy, pp. 639–61, *Logic, Methodology and Philosophy of Science: Proceedings of the Twelfth International Congress*, Editors, P. Hajek, L. Valdes-Villanueva and D. Westerstahl, King's College, London.

Spanos, A. (2006a) Revisiting the Omitted Variables Argument: Substantive vs. Statistical Adequacy, forthcoming in the *Journal of Economic Methodology*.

Spanos, A. (2006b) The Curve-Fitting Problem, Akaike-type information criteria, and the error statistical approach, Virginia Tech working paper.

Spanos, A. (2006c) The Instrumental Variables Method revisited: On the Nature and Choice of Optimal Instruments, forthcoming in G.D.A. Phillips (ed.), *Essays in Memory of Michael Magdalinos*. Cambridge: Cambridge University Press.

Spanos, A. and A. McGuirk (2001) The model specification problem from a probabilistic reduction perspective. *Journal of the American Agricultural Association* 83, 1168–1176.

Spanos, A. and A. McGuirk (2002) Revisiting the foundations of unit root testing: statistical parameterizations and implicit restrictions, Virginia Tech working paper.

Stigler, G.J. (1954) The early history of the empirical studies of consumer behavior. *The Journal of Political Economy* 62, 95–113. Reprinted in G.J. Stigler (1962).

Stigler, G.J. (1962) Henry L. Moore and statistical economics. *Econometrica* 30, 1–21.

Stigler, S.M. (1986) *The History of Statistics: the Measurement of Uncertainty before 1900*. Cambridge, MA: Harvard University Press.

Stigum, B.P. (1990) *Toward a Formal Science of Economics*. Cambridge, MA: MIT Press.

Stigum, B.P. (2003) *Econometrics and the Philosophy of Economics*. Princeton, NJ: Princeton University Press.

Stone, J.R.N. (1954a) Linear expenditure systems and demand analysis: an application to the pattern of British demand. *Economic Journal* 64, 511–21.

Stone, J.R.N. (1954b) *The Measurement of Consumers' Expenditure and Behaviour in the United Kingdom, 1920–1938*. Cambridge: Cambridge University Press.

Summers, L. (1991) The scientific illusion in empirical macroeconomics. *Scandinavian Journal of Economics* 93, 129–43.

Tauchen, G.E. (1985) Diagnostic testing and evaluation of maximum likelihood models. *Journal of Econometrics* 30, 415–43.

Tinbergen, J. (1939) *Statistical Testing of Business Cycle Research*, 2 vols. Geneva: League of Nations.

Tintner, G. (1940) *The Variate Difference Method*, Cowles Commission Monograph 5, Indiana: Principia Press Inc.

Tukey, J.W. (1977) *Exploratory Data Analysis*. Addison-Wesley.

Valavanis, S. (1959) *Econometrics*. New York: McGraw-Hill.

Vining, R. and Koopmans, T.C. (1949) Methodological issues in quantitative economics. *Review of Economics and Statistics* 31, 77–94.

Wold, H.O. (1938) *A Study in the Analysis of Stationary Time Series*. Uppsala: Almquist and Wicksell.

Wooldridge, J.M. (2002) *Econometric Analysis of Cross-Section and Panel Data*. Cambridge, MA: The MIT Press.

Yule, G.U. (1926) Why do we sometimes get nonsense correlations between time series – a study in sampling and the nature of time series. *Journal of the Royal Statistical Society* 89, 1–64.

Yule, G.U. (1927) On a method of investigating periodicities in disturbed series, with special reference to Wolfer's sunspot numbers. *Philosophical Transactions of the Royal Society, A,* 226, 267–98.

Zellner, A. (1971) *Introduction to Bayesian Inference in Econometrics*. New York: Wiley.

Part II

Methodology and History of Econometrics

2
The Methodology of Econometrics

Kevin D. Hoover

Abstract

The methodology of econometrics is not the study of particular econometric techniques, but a meta-study of how econometrics contributes to economic science. As such it is part of the philosophy of science. The essay begins by reviewing the salient points of the main approaches to the philosophy of science – particularly, logical positivism, Popper's falsificationism, Lakatos's methodology of scientific research programs, and the semantic approach – and orients econometrics within them. The principal methodological issues for econometrics are the application of probability theory to economics and the mapping between economic theory and probability models. Both are raised in Haavelmo's (1944) seminal essay. Using that essay as a touchstone, the various recent approaches to econometrics are surveyed – those of the Cowles Commission, the vector autoregression program, the LSE approach, calibration, and a set of common, but heterogeneous approaches encapsulated as "textbook econometrics." Finally, the essay considers the light shed by econometric methodology on the main epistemological and ontological questions raised in the philosophy of science.

2.1	What is methodology?	62
	2.1.1 Methods vs methodology	62
	2.1.2 What is econometrics?	63
	2.1.3 Econometric themes	64
2.2	The place of econometrics in a scientific methodology	65
	2.2.1 What can econometrics do?	65
	2.2.2 The main approaches to scientific methodology	66
2.3	Do probability models apply to economic data?	71
	2.3.1 The probability approach to econometrics	71
	2.3.2 Responses to Haavelmo	72
2.4	The main econometric methodologies	73
	2.4.1 The Cowles Commission	74
	2.4.2 Vector autoregressions	74
	2.4.3 The LSE approach	75
	2.4.4 Calibration	78
	2.4.5 Textbook econometrics	79
2.5	Some key issues in econometric methodology	80
2.6	Wither econometric methodology?	82

2.1   What is methodology?

2.1.1   Methods vs methodology

The etymology of *methodology* implies that it is the study of methods. Taken narrowly, it would neatly describe the typical econometrics textbook or the subject matter of most econometrics journals. And, of course, it is not infrequently used this way, as when an article on an applied topic has an "econometric-methodology" section. Yet, "methodology" has come to have a broader meaning in the philosophy of science – both in the physical and life sciences and in economics and the social sciences. Methodology is not the study of particular methods, but a meta-study of the ways in which particular methods contribute to the overall scientific enterprise.

Mark Blaug (1992, p. xii) defines the *methodology of economics* as

> ...a study of the relationship between theoretical concepts and warranted conclusions about the real world; in particular, methodology is that branch of economics where we examine the ways in which economists justify their theories and the reasons they offer for preferring one theory over another; methodology is both a descriptive discipline – "this *is* what most economists do" – and a prescriptive one – "this is what economists *should* do to advance economics"...

Recent economic methodology has taken a "naturalistic turn"; it stresses the descriptive rather than the prescriptive function. (The subtitle to Blaug's book is the thoroughly descriptive "Or How Economists Explain," despite its frequently prescriptive content.)

The naturalistic turn is partly a reaction to a long-standing charge from economists that those who cannot do economics turn to methodology (e.g., Fisher, 1933; Hahn, 1992a, b). The examples of methodological work by great practitioners – John Stuart Mill, Lionel Robbins, Milton Friedman, and Paul Samuelson, among others – exposes the charge as a canard (see Hoover, 1995b).

Nevertheless, until very recently much methodology has been concerned with questions, such as what is the line of demarcation between science and non-science, that seem distant to the quotidian concerns of economists. The place of methodology is to address the larger conceptual and philosophical questions that arise in the everyday practice of economics. The naturalistic turn is partly an attempt to realign methodological thinking with that practice.

The naturalistic turn arises out of the humility of methodologists, who are unwilling to prescribe to economists. Ironically, the greater attention to the fine details of a field that followed in the wake of the naturalistic turn provides a sounder basis for prescription than previously. The philosopher Alexander Rosenberg asserts what might be called the "continuity thesis": the practice and methodology of economics or other sciences are not different fields but the same field addressed from different levels of generality:

> If theory adjudicates the rules of science, then so does philosophy [methodology]. In the absence of demarcation, philosophy is just very general, very abstract science and has the same kind of prescriptive force for the practice of science as any scientific theory. Because of its generality and abstractness it will have less detailed bearing on day-to-day science than, say, prescriptions about the calibration of pH meters, but it must have the same kind of bearing. (Rosenberg, 1992, p. 11)

This history of econometrics in the twentieth century (see Epstein, 1987; Morgan, 1990; Hendry and Morgan, 1995) is full of methodological discussions. The key documents of the systematization of the field in the 1940s and early 1950s, Haavelmo (1944) and the Cowles Commission volumes (Koopmans, 1950; and Hood and Koopmans, 1953), are particularly rich. From the 1950s to about 1980 econometricians tended to focus on technical developments (methods) rather than larger conceptual issues (methodology). Interest in econometric methodology has been reborn in the subsequent period in a variety of articles (e.g., Hendry, 1980; Sims, 1980; Leamer, 1983; McAleer, Pagan, and Volcker, 1985; Pagan, 1987; Aldrich, 1989; Hoover, 1990, 1994a,b, 1995a,b; Kydland and Prescott, 1991; and Spanos, 1995) and books (e.g., Spanos, 1986, 1999; Darnell and Evans, 1990; Lawson, 1997; Cartwright, 1999; Magnus and Morgan, 1999; Granger, 1999; Keuzenkamp, 2000; Stigum, 2003; and Zellner, Keuzenkamp, and McAleer, 2001).

2.1.2 What is econometrics?

While econometrics may go back as far as the work of Davenant and King in the seventeenth century, it did not come into self-consciousness as a separate field until the founding of the Econometric Society in 1933. The society defined econometrics as "economic theory in its relation to statistics and mathematics" and its object as the "unification of the theoretical-quantitative and the empirical-quantitative approach to economic problems" (cited by Frisch, 1933, p. 1). The central problem for the field over the next seven decades has been just how to combine economic theory, mathematics, and statistics.

The term *econometrics* has come to refer mainly to the statistical apex of the economic theory–mathematics–statistics triangle, but it is a statistics that is centrally conditioned by economic theory. Econometric methodology could mean merely the methodology of the statistics that happens to be used in economics; yet it typically means something beyond that.

Perhaps the number one concern of a methodology of statistics is the proper interpretation of probability and how it applies to data. Here, the debate between classical and Bayesian interpretations of probability is central. This is, of course, also an important issue for econometric methodology, yet we will largely ignore it here. First, it predates econometrics as a separate field, and so belongs to a larger methodological or philosophical discussion. Secondly, it is addressed in the chapters on Bayesianism elsewhere in this volume. And thirdly, it is not the issue that distinguishes econometrics from other uses of statistics in non-economic contexts.

So how does econometrics differ from statistics applied to economic subjects? There are at least two answers, each controversial in its own way. The philosopher Nancy Cartwright gives a clear statement of the first. Econometrics, she believes, provides a uniquely revealing application of statistics because, unlike, say, sociology, "economics is a discipline with a theory" (Cartwright 1989, p. 14). Cartwright (1999, ch. 7) argues that probabilities are not there for the taking, but are characteristics of quite particular set-ups (e.g., of roulette tables or particular configurations of unstable atoms). Only in such designed set-ups do objects display well-behaved probabilities. The role of economic theory (and of quantum-mechanical theory) is to provide the conditions that articulate such a well-defined set-up: a *nomological* (or law-generating) *machine*. Cartwright's views resonate with those of many econometricians, who believe that economic theory must provide the identification needed to render statistics economically interpretable. They also suffer from the problem of all *a priori* approaches: we must have the *right* theory to define the nomological machine or to identify the model, but if the inferential direction runs only from theory to data, how could we ever use empirical evidence to determine which theory is right? (see Hoover 2001a, ch. 4; 2001b, lecture 2; 2002 for critical accounts of Cartwright's views).

The economist James Heckman provides a second answer for what distinguishes econometrics from statistics: econometrics focuses on establishing causation, while statistics is content with correlation. Heckman writes:

> Most econometric theory adapts methods originally developed in statistics. The major exception to this rule is the econometric analysis of the identification problem and the companion analyses of structural equations, causality, and economic policy evaluation. (Heckman, 2000, p. 45)
>
> *The major contributions* of twentieth century econometrics to knowledge were the definition of causal parameters ... the analysis of what is required to recover causal parameters from data ... and clarification of the role of causal parameters in policy evaluation ... (Heckman, 2000, p. 45, abstract, emphasis added)

The idea that econometrics is a science of causes is attractive (see Hoover, 1990, 2001a), but it is almost certainly unhistorical (Hoover, 2004). Most econometricians through most of the post-World-War-II period have subscribed to a vision closer to Cartwright's than to Heckman's. Still, in the last twenty years, there has been a causal revival among both micro- and macroeconometricians.

2.1.3 Econometric themes
The different approaches to distinguishing econometrics from statistics suggest two thematic questions that will help to organize our discussion. First, do social sciences generally, and economics particularly, provide suitable material for the application of probability?

A long tradition in economics – clearly expressed in Mill (see Hausman 1992, ch. 6), Marshall (see Stigler 1999, ch. 1), and Robbins (1937) – holds that social relationships are too complex, too multifarious, and too infected with capricious human choice to generate enduring, stable relationships that could be modeled by tractable probability distributions. These views were an important element of Keynes' (1939) criticism of Tinbergen's (1939) early econometric business-cycle model.

Although these views did not put a stop to the statistical analysis of economic data in the pre-World-War-II period, they were reinforced by developments within statistics itself, such as Yule's (1926) analysis of nonsense regressions. Although we now view Yule as having laid the groundwork for later developments in cointegration analysis, the discovery that high correlations in time series were frequently artifacts appeared at the time to undercut the goal of applying probability theory to economic data.

The theory of probability, especially in the work of R.A. Fisher (1930, 1935), had come to be seen as intimately tied to the design of experiments. Stigler (1999, ch. 10), for example, attributes the early adoption (relative to economics) of probabilistic statistics in psychology, especially by the polymath philosopher C.S. Peirce in the 1880s, to the development of a well-defined program of psychological experimentation. Although experimental economics is *now* a flourishing field, economics – of its very nature – provides a more restricted scope for experimentation than many other human, life, and physical sciences. The dominant place of *a priori* theory in economics is partly a reflection of the paucity of experimental opportunities.

The second thematic question then concerns theory: how do econometric procedures applied to empirical data relate to economic theory? We will postpone further consideration of the first thematic question until section 2.3. This question, however, ties directly into broader issues in the methodology and philosophy of science. It is to these that we turn next.

2.2 The place of econometrics in a scientific methodology

2.2.1 What can econometrics do?

One of the central questions in the philosophy of science concerns the relationship of empirical evidence to theoretical understanding. Econometrics naturally stands on the evidential end of this relationship. There are at least four roles for econometrics:

First, the most obvious is that econometrics is used to *test* an implication of a theory.

Secondly, econometrics may be used to *measure* unknown values of theoretically defined parameters or unobservable variables. In the extreme case, we might think of econometrics as giving flesh to a phenomenal law – that is, directly measuring a basic relationship posited by economic theory.

These two roles place theory ahead of evidence. In the first case theory proposes, evidence disposes. In the second, theory is essential to define or identify the object of measurement.

Thirdly, econometrics may be used to *predict* the value of a variable. Prediction may be based directly on a prior economic theory or it may be an atheoretical statistical exercise. Prediction presumes a background uniformity that warrants projection of a relationship out of sample. This is, in itself, a weak assumption. Still, a theoretical account is frequently offered to buttress the distinction between accidental and genuine regularities. Without it, econometricians might be seen as little removed from stock-market chartists.

Finally, econometrics may be used to *characterize* a relationship or phenomenon. It packages the data in a way that reveals relationships that, in turn, become the fodder for theory.

2.2.2   The main approaches to scientific methodology

However econometrics may be used as a source of evidence, the question of the relationship of evidence to theory is one that applies broadly to science, not simply to economics. (Excellent general discussions of the philosophy of science are found in Newton-Smith 1981, Caldwell 1982, Blaug 1992, and Hausman 1992.)

The approaches to scientific methodology that appear most relevant to econometrics are variants of, or successors to, *logical positivism*, a philosophical school that grew out of the Vienna Circle in the 1920s, a group of philosophers and physical and social scientists, including Otto Neurath, Herbert Feigl, Karl Menger, Kurt Gödel and Rudolph Carnap, among others. Positivists viewed scientific knowledge as having two sources: deductive inference from indisputable axioms and inductive inference from empirical data. Following David Hume (1777), they dismissed beliefs not founded on these two bases as unscientific metaphysics.

Hacking identifies six instincts that characterize logical positivist methodologies:

> (1) An emphasis upon *verification* (or some variant such as *falsification*): Significant propositions are those whose truth or falsehood can be settled in some way. (2) *Pro-observation*: What we can see, feel, touch, and the like, provides the best content or foundation for all the rest of our non-mathematical knowledge. (3) *Anti-cause*: There is no causality in nature, over and above the constancy with which events of one kind are followed by events of another kind. (4) *Downplaying explanations*: Explanations may help to organize phenomena, but do not provide any deeper answers to *Why* questions except to say that the phenomena regularly occur in such and such a way. (5) *Anti-theoretical entities*: Positivists tend to be non-realists, not only because they restrict reality to the observable but also because they are against causes and are dubious about explanations … (6) Positivists sum up items (1) to (5) by being *against metaphysics*. (Hacking, 1983, pp. 41–2)

By the 1960s, variants on logical positivism came to dominate Anglo-American philosophy of science. Although it has been the object of substantial criticism and revision, especially since Thomas Kuhn's *The Structure of Scientific Revolutions* (1962), the sensibility of logical positivism provides the implicit philosophical background to most empirical economics. We now consider some of the main variants and descendants of logical positivism.

A   The received view

Sometimes known as the *covering-law model of explanation* or as the *hypothetical-deductive method*, the *received view* understands scientific theories as networks of scientific laws, which are themselves understood as true, universal generalizations (Hoover, 2001b, lecture 2). Explanations then take a *deductive-nomological form*: the relevant (or "covering") set of laws, taken with a set of initial conditions, allows us to deduce an empirically relevant conclusion. If the conclusion is yet to be observed, the deduction provides a prediction; if it is already known, an explanation. Explanation and prediction are symmetrical: explanation is just prediction directed to the past.

The received view agrees with Hacking's six logical-positivist instincts nearly perfectly. It nonetheless is not suitable in its pure form for many sciences, including economics. Actual economic behavior is influenced by more factors than theory can typically account for. We often say, then, that the theory holds *ceteris paribus*. Too often, however, *ceteris paribus* clauses act as unfulfilled promissory notes: not knowing just what to hold constant, theoretical conclusions are conditional on factors that are not only unspecified, but unimagined.

To avoid the pitfalls of *ceteris paribus*, advocates of the received view propose a weaker, but more applicable, desideratum: the *inductive-statistical explanation*, in which laws hold only probabilistically and the inferences are not to what happens, but to the probability that it happens. The role for econometrics in such explanations is obvious.

B   Popper's falsificationism

Advocates of the received view typically used evidence positively: a theory predicts an outcome; if the outcome occurs, the theory gains support; the more support, the more warranted our belief in the theory. Such verificationism, however, falls foul of one of the oldest problems in epistemology – Hume's (1739, book II, part III) riddle of induction: on what grounds can we justify a universal generalization from a collection of particular cases (e.g., how can we legitimately infer that the demand curve slopes down just because, when $price_i$ rose, demand for $good_i$ fell, for a large number of j's).

Numerous solutions to Hume's riddle rely on auxiliary universal generalizations, such as the uniformity of nature, that themselves stand in need of justification. Economists are inclined to view the downward-sloping demand curve (accounting separately for income effects) as a theorem, based on axioms that are known more or less intuitively. But unless we are willing to accept the subjectivist approach of the extreme Austrians (e.g., Mises, 1966) that places the main principles of economics on a par with the axioms of mathematics – that is, unless we are willing to regard economics as a non-empirical science – then Hume's riddle is not easily dismissed.

Hume's objection to induction has an analogue in deductive logic. The following invalid syllogism illustrates the *fallacy of affirming the consequent*: A implies B; B is true; therefore A is true. The philosopher Karl Popper (1959) sees all induction as an application of this fallacy. Hume's riddle, he believes, cannot be solved; it can only be dissolved by adopting another strategy. In place of the invalid syllogism, Popper proposes a valid one – *modus tollens*: A implies B; B is false; therefore A is false. Evidence, no matter how many positive cases are collected, cannot establish the truth of a theory; it can only establish its falsehood. We should not adopt theories because they enjoy a high level of affirmative support, but instead reject those that are falsified. Science proceeds not through generalization from data but through a series of theoretical conjectures, tests, and empirical rejections.

Popper's strategy is clearest when the deductions from a theory are deterministic. Yet, as we already saw in the case of the received view, economics almost certainly requires statistical rather than deterministic conclusions. But, in that case, what counts as a falsifying instance? Very quickly we must appeal to the conventions of statistical testing, such as the critical value. We can now see that the question of which convention to adopt (should we use the ubiquitous 5 percent test? or 1 percent? or 10 percent? or X percent?) is no longer a merely technical question but one that lies near the heart of a key methodological issue. Popper does not resolve it.

Even if we could agree practically on what to count as falsification, a number of commentators have observed that economists rarely play the test-and-reject game consistently. Blaug (1992, p. 241) likens the research strategy of the typical economist to "playing tennis with the net down." Summers (1991) and Keuzenkamp and Magnus (1995) claim that no scientifically significant proposition has every been decided on the basis of a statistical test. Where Blaug (1992, p. 244) calls for a redoubled commitment to serious, as opposed to innocuous, falsificationism, Summers, and Keuzenkamp and Magnus reject the falsificationist strategy altogether.

Another key problem with falsificationism is that it rules theories out without giving guidance on which theories to use. Suppose we entertain two theories with some importantly different implications and neither have been rejected. Popper's view is that all theories are conjectural and never proven, but which should we use in the meantime? Popper argues that the theory with the richest content, in the sense that it rules out the most possible states of the world and is, therefore, easiest to reject, ought to be taken up for testing. Intuitively, the theory that survives the most rigorous tests is the best corroborated and, as a methodological rule, ought to be used even while we continue to try to reject it. Popper's (1959, appendix *ix) attempts to provide a formal measure of the degree of corroboration suffered from apparently insoluble technical problems that cast the whole strategy into doubt (Newton-Smith, 1981, pp. 59–65; Keuzenkamp, 2000, pp. 60–2).

The problem is worse than even this perhaps technical failing. Theories are generally incomplete, and testing cannot proceed without auxiliary hypotheses. The failure of a test cannot be directed to the core theory (or some particular proposition within it), but acts on the whole complex of theory and auxiliary propositions. As Duhem (1906) and Quine (1951) have famously pointed out, there is considerable latitude in how the whole complex is adjusted in the face of contrary evidence. If all the adjustments are made to auxiliary hypotheses, then the core theory may never be threatened, even by an unambiguous falsification. Popper gives us little useful guidance on how to proceed constructively.

C Lakatos's methodology of scientific research programs

A measure of the degree of corroboration is intended to guide the choice among conjectured theories. But how do we come to these conjectures? Popper's methodology offers no guidance and relegates theory construction to the realms of psychology, aesthetics, and unstructured imagination. In general, falsificationism does little to connect empirical evidence to the positive development of theoretical understanding.

In part to address these issues, Popper's student Imré Lakatos (1970) proposed the *methodology of scientific research programs*. Lakatos viewed science not as a set of competing theories but as a set of competing programs, each defined by a set of essential propositions, known as the *hard core*. Every theory within a program consists of this hard core, a set of *negative* and *positive heuristics* for theory development, and a set of propositions that extend the hard core into a complete theory known as the *protective belt*.

In Lakatos's view, Popper's methodological rule to reject a theory that is falsified is useless because every theory is falsified on some dimension. Instead, he proposes to judge the success of a research program both by what it explains (novel facts predicted, anomalies resolved) and by what it fails to explain (anomalies discovered or reinstated). Programs develop by adjusting the protective belt according to the methodological guidance provided by the positive and negative heuristics, always leaving the hard core intact.

One program is superior to another when it explains the anomalies of the other program and successfully predicts more novel facts. Importantly, the standard is not static. A program is *progressive* and ought to receive support (for example, in the form of funding and professional esteem) when it shows an ever-increasing ability to predict novel facts. A program that fails to keep up or one that becomes mired in constructing accounts of its own anomalies without sufficient payoff in novel predictions ought to lose ground relative to more progressive programs.

More than was the case with falsificationism, the methodology of scientific research programs employs all four of the possible uses of econometrics cited earlier: testing; measurement or instantiation of a phenomenal law; prediction; characterization or discovery of empirical relationships or phenomena. Yet Lakatos's methodology was only briefly popular in economics, starting in the mid-1970s (Latsis, 1976). It has proved too difficult to fit the activities of economists into a set of competing programs with clearly differentiated hard cores: Is all neoclassical economics a single program? Or do we count general equilibrium theory, game theory, and macroeconomic theory as separate programs? If so, how do we account for cross-fertilization among programs that appears to suggest that no proposition is really immune from revision? (See Hoover 1991a.) Equally, an uncontroversial definition of the key notion of the "novel fact" has proved problematic (Hands, 1993a). In the end, Lakatos's methodology has provided a useful vision of the scientific process while failing to offer a secure basis for prescription on how to advance the field (see particularly the variety of assessments in Blaug and De Marchi, 1991).

D   The semantic approach to scientific theory

Although Lakatos's methodology is prescriptive, it is also naturalistic in the sense that it attempts to provide a positive account for the constructive activities of scientists. An increasingly popular methodological account is provided by the *semantic approach to scientific theories*. The received view was a *syntactic* account in that the central action concerned the deductive relationship between theories as formal systems and their implications. Once one agreed to certain theoretical axioms, the deductive work could be done algebraically, as it were, without reference to the meanings of the key terms. Advocates of the semantic approach reject such a content-neutral approach to science.

The key notion in the semantic approach is the *model*, in the sense of the content of a formalization. For example, a formal system might involve the minimization of an objective function subject to a constraint. A model for that system might involve identifying its terms with factor inputs, output, and various prices. A formal system might have more than one model. In the classic accounts of the semantic approach, a theory is a formal system plus the set of models with which it is consistent (Suppes, 1962; Suppe, 1989).

Recently, Davis (2000, 2005) and Chao (2002, 2005) have explored the role of econometrics in a semantic approach to economics. Perhaps the most thorough account is given by Stigum (2003), who emphasizes that modeling takes place on two levels, which he regards as separate "worlds."

The world of theory deals with theoretical models with crisp concepts. Theoretical deductions generate only theoretical conclusions.

The world of data is the realm of econometrics and statistics. Data are what they are, but the interesting properties of data are the relationships among them, which are not immediately evident but must themselves be modeled. Ideally, one would want to know the true probability distribution that governs the data. In practice, a particular probability model may be more or less successful as an approximation; but its success must be judged on grounds other than correspondence to the truth, since that yardstick is not directly accessible.

The world of theory and the world of data are not immediately commensurable. Stigum and other advocates of the semantic approach argue that they must be connected by bridge principles that stipulate the mapping between theoretical variables, such as national output, unemployment, or money supply, and their statistical counterparts, such as GDP as reported in the national income and product accounts, the official unemployment rate, or M1. Bridge principles will not always be as straightforward as mere assignment of a data category to a theoretical concept. A theoretical concept such as the natural rate of unemployment, for instance, can be tied to data only through commitment to a model-dependent measuring strategy.

The object of the semantic approach is neither exclusively the falsification nor the verification of competing theories – although each may play a role; rather, it is the construction of richer models, more complete at both the theoretical and data levels and more consistent between the levels. This is not a mechanical enterprise, since the failures of the program may be remedied by adjustments to either the theoretical or data models or to the bridge principles that connect them.

Stigum's account belongs to the tradition that embeds models into detailed logical formalisms and relies on logical theory to check consistency. A "softer" model-theoretical account is provided in the work of Giere (2000), Cartwright (1999), and the contributors to Morgan and Morrison (1999) (Boumans, 1999, in particular, addresses economics directly). One of the primary advantages of such a softer account is that it is more naturalistic, drawing more immediately on, and more immediately applicable to, the practices of workaday scientists, economists, and econometricians.

2.3 Do probability models apply to economic data?

A model-theoretic methodology makes it easier to cast the question of the applicability of the theory of probability to economic data into high relief. The ordinary practices of econometrics assume, with little reflection, that probability models apply quite naturally to econometric data. It is hard to recapture the once-widespread resistance to accepting this as natural. The issues at stake in the earlier debates are, however, by no means settled and account for some of the continuing methodological differences.

2.3.1 The probability approach to econometrics

Trygve Haavelmo's "Probability Approach to Econometrics" (1944) is the *locus crucis* of econometrics and can be seen as marking the beginning of its modern period. Before Haavelmo, a long tradition questioned the applicability of probability models to economic data. Histograms of raw economic data rarely displayed a bell curve, and many economists doubted that economic behavior was sufficiently uniform to be beat into the mould of any standard probability model. Economics was not, of course, unique in this respect. But in other fields controlled experimentation was used to generate data that could be suitably described using probability models. Fisher's work on experimental design, especially for agricultural applications, dominated statistical thinking in the first half of the twentieth century (e.g., Fisher, 1935). Fisher's view was that, without a controlled experiment, a probability model was simply inappropriate.

Econometricians nonetheless plowed ahead, conducting ever more statistical investigations. Still, the absence of an acceptable methodological foundation for their activities undermined confidence in their results. Haavelmo's insight was that properly accounting for the naturally occurring variations in economically important factors could act as a surrogate for the missing explicit experimental controls. If a regression equation were properly specified, then the residual errors would necessarily conform to a well-defined probability distribution. Such conformity, then, provides a test of proper specification.

Economic theory ideally explains which factors are the appropriate ones in an econometric specification. If the articulation of the theory and the data are compatible, then the observed data can be seen as independent realizations of the actual, complicated underlying process that generates the data – what econometricians refer to as the data-generating process and what Cartwright (1999, ch. 3) calls a nomological machine. When statistical account is taken of the appropriate observed factors, repeated, controlled experiments are not necessary, even in a time-series context.

Regression, rather than, say, correlation or analysis of variance, is the natural statistical technique in Haavelmo's program, because its coefficient estimates assign values to the importance of each factor that corresponds to the relationships implied by economic theory. The correspondences are, of course, not necessarily straightforward. Haavelmo saw the data-generating process (to use the modern term) as a complex system, so that measurement of the influence of individual factors (e.g., a price elasticity or the marginal propensity to consume) demanded that attention be paid to the system characteristics of the data-generating process. This *identification problem* had already been addressed by a variety of economists, including Haavelmo (1943) himself (Morgan 1990, ch. 6; Hendry and Morgan 1995, part III). Now, however, he had exposed its conceptual roots.

Haavelmo clearly believed that a complex economic system truly lay behind observed economic data. He nonetheless insisted that econometric work does not treat reality directly but, instead, involves our own constructions (models) that may vary in scope. The scope of our model depends, in part, on our particular interests and, in part, on the need to identify autonomous relationships – that is, ones that remain stable in the face of natural or intentional interventions (Aldrich, 1989). Haavelmo's implicit orientation of viewing theory and statistics in terms of models places his work in substantial sympathy with the semantic approach to scientific theories.

2.3.2   Responses to Haavelmo

Before Haavelmo, linear regression models had been developed in the context of several distinct traditions. In Fisher's approach to experimental design, regressions were used to sort out the effects of independently varying factors in controlled and randomized experiments. The emphasis was on testing whether or not each of these factors had a hypothesized effect. Data mining was taboo because it violated the assumptions of randomness and independence. An experiment might be redesigned and rerun, but the data should be analyzed only in accordance with its original design. Information gathered from experimentation could test particular hypotheses, and the results of the tests could be used to inform the construction of theories. A clear route existed from data to theory.

In contrast, the theory-of-errors approach, traceable to Gauss and Legendre, took regression to be a tool of approximation of known theoretical relationships applied to empirical data, such as observations of planetary motions (Stigler 1986, chs. 1 and 4; 1999, ch. 17). In astronomical work, the underlying theory was presumed to be true; the role of the regression was not to test but to measure in the face of unavoidable observational errors. Data mining is acceptable as a means of obtaining better approximations.

Both the experimental-design and the theory-of-errors approaches have informed econometricians' reactions to Haavelmo. On the one hand, "textbook" econometrics takes theory as a surrogate for experimentation, which bows considerably to Fisher. On the other hand, if theory is to stand in the place of experimental controls, it must be the right theory. Where Fisher was free to redesign and rerun experiments that failed on some statistical criteria, theory cannot easily be redesigned, as the evidence presupposed its truth in the first place (what Leamer, 1978, p. 4, refers to as the "axiom of correct specification").

Spanos (1995) argues that, as a result of this commitment to prior theory, "textbook" econometrics has adopted the strategy of reacting to the failure of errors to reflect statistical assumptions by modifying those assumptions rather than by modifying theory. The use of Cochrane–Orcutt transformations of error terms in the face of serially correlated errors provides one of many examples of the "robust-estimation" approach. This approach treats all violations of the statistical assumptions that one would expect to see from a well-designed experiment as failures to model the error terms correctly, rather than, as Fisher would have it, a failure to institute adequate controls.

Paradoxically, such a strategy tends to enshrine a one-way relationship from theory to data more appropriate to the theory-of-errors approach than to the experimental-design approach. Hoover (1994b) refers to this strategy as "econometrics as measurement."

Another approach, which Spanos (1995) refers to as "probabilistic reduction" and Hoover (1994b) as "econometrics as observation," reacts differently to Haavelmo (also see Spanos, chapter 1, in the current volume). (Spanos traces this approach to the biometric tradition of Galton and Pearson.) A complete, true theory necessarily induces desirable statistical properties in data: independent, serially uncorrelated, white noise. The object of econometrics, therefore, should be to find compact representations of the data that deliver these properties without loss of information. These representations are the statistical regularities that theory must explain. Again, as with the experimental-design approach, a clear path is opened from data to theory. Where the robust-estimation approach seeks to mitigate the effect of any deviations from desirable statistical properties, the probabilistic-reduction approach seeks to characterize the systematic elements of the statistical model in such a way that the desirable properties arise naturally. Such an approach is not only compatible with data mining; it requires it.

2.4 The main econometric methodologies

Haavelmo's probability approach emphasizes the relationship between economic theory and the statistical modeling of data. Different econometric methodologies can be classified according to the different roles that they assign to theory and to the degree of independence from theory that they assign to characterizations of data.

2.4.1   The Cowles Commission

The work of the Cowles Commission in the late 1940s and early 1950s was an outgrowth of Haavelmo's seminal monograph (Koopmans, 1950; Hood and Koopmans, 1953). The Cowles Commission was particularly concerned with the mapping between theory and data – that is, with the *identification problem*. It worked out the theory of identification to a high degree of completeness. The general problem is illustrated by the example used in most econometrics textbooks: given that we have only realized data on prices and quantities and both supply and demand relate prices to quantities, how can we separately identify the supply and demand curve? The Cowles Commission solution relies on economic theory to propose restrictions on the form of estimated regressions that permit us to break down the observational equivalence between supply and demand curves. Most commonly, these restrictions take the form of exogenous variables that appear in one equation but not in another.

As with Haavelmo, the Cowles Commission methodology was subject to alternative interpretations. In the "measurement-without-theory" debate with Vining, Koopmans, for instance, strongly maintained that theory must be prior to data (Hendry and Morgan, 1995, ch. 43). Data could not be interpreted without theoretical presuppositions. Such an approach implied that the object of econometrics was purely one of measurement and not one of exploration and discovery. Koopmans' position places the empiricist in a vicious circle: how do we obtain empirically justified theory if empirical observation can only take place on the supposition of a true background theory?

Not all members of the Cowles Commission group adopted Koopmans' hard line. Simon (1953), for instance, in a paper showing the equivalence of the identified system with a causally ordered system, argued that experiments (natural or otherwise) could be used to distinguish between otherwise observationally equivalent systems (Hoover, 1990, 1991b, 2001a).

The profession was more influenced by Koopmans than by Simon on this point. From the 1950s through the 1970s, the estimation of models consisting of theoretically identified systems of equations was the gold standard of applied econometrics. Much of the work in theoretical econometrics focused on developing appropriate systems estimators.

2.4.2   Vector autoregressions

Some critics, notably Liu (1960), noticed early on that the number of restrictions needed to identify large-scale macroeconomic models far exceeded the number that economic theory could be confidently relied upon to provide. The point was driven home in Christopher Sims' "Macroeconomics and Reality" (1980), in which Sims referred to the restrictions typically employed by macromodelers as "incredible."

Sims' proposal was to remove the pretence of applying theoretical structure to the data and, instead, to use unrestricted systems of reduced form equations (or *vector autoregressions* or *VARs*) to model the responses of variables to shocks. Each equation in a VAR system regresses one variable on its own lags and the lags of all the other variables. Such a procedure still requires a form of identification. The reduced-form errors are generally intercorrelated; distinct shocks for each equation require that they be orthogonalized. Sims proposed to "identify" the shocks using a Choleski decomposition to normalize the system. Such a transformation renders the covariance matrix of the error terms diagonal and establishes a hierarchy (a triangular or Wold-causal order) among the variables such that contemporaneous shocks to higher ordered variables feed through to lower ordered variables but not vice versa. Such orderings are arbitrary, in the sense that there are as many triangular orders as there are permutations of the variables (i.e., if there are n variables, there are $n!$ possible orders). What is more, orthogonalized shocks can be achieved in orderings that are overidentified (or non-triangular) – that is that have more restrictions than the $n(n-1)/2$ needed to establish a just-identified Wold-causal order.

Initially, Sims regarded the choice of causal order as unproblematic. But under criticism from Cooley and LeRoy (1985) and Leamer (1985), among others, Sims (1986) came to accept that different causal orders had different implications for impulse-response functions and for innovation accounting and were, therefore, analytically significant. Once the need to commit to a particular causal order was accepted, the VAR transformed to reflect a particular contemporaneous causal order became known as a *structural* VAR (*SVAR*).

The same issue arises, then, for Sims' SVAR methodology as for the Cowles Commission's structural-modeling methodology: what restrictions are to be imposed and what makes them credible? Standard economic theory rarely implies Wold-causal, or other recursive, orderings among variables – simultaneity is the norm. VAR practitioners have typically appealed to very informal, casual arguments to justify particular orderings.

2.4.3 The LSE approach

The London School of Economics (LSE) methodology originated in the work of Denis Sargan and is now strongly associated with David Hendry and various colleagues and students widely dispersed among academic institutions, mainly in Britain and Europe (see Mizon, 1995 for a systematic discussion). The LSE methodology is closely related to a wider range of work on integrated and cointegrated systems, originating in the work of Engle and Granger at the University of California, San Diego, and of Johansen and Juselius at the University of Copenhagen (Juselius, 1999). Where Koopmans' strongly apriorist version of the Cowles Commission's methodology and Sims' SVAR methodology belong more to the theory-of-errors approach, the LSE program is a species of the probabilistic-reduction genus. As with the VAR methodology, the LSE methodology stresses dynamic specification with special attention to the lag structures. There are, however, some key differences: it pays particular attention to stationarity and cointegration; and it is not content with profligate parameterizations, but seeks parsimonious specifications that nevertheless deliver errors with good statistical properties (white-noise innovations).

The leading principle of the LSE approach is consistently to apply the theory of encompassing (Mizon, 1984; Hendry, 1988). Roughly, one specification encompasses another if it carries all of the information of the other specification in a more parsimonious form. An easy way to think about encompassing is to consider two competing specifications for the same dependent variable. Both can be nested in a joint model formed from the nonredundant set of regressors found in the two specifications. If one of the specifications is a valid restriction of this joint model and the other not, then the one *encompasses* the other. The LSE approach proceeds in a series of horse-races. Any specification is maintained only tentatively. Any proposed alternative specification is judged on its ability to encompass the reigning specification.

While encompassing is the key idea of the LSE methodology, most attention has been paid to Hendry's *general-to-specific modeling strategy*. The general-to-specific strategy derives in large measure from Hendry's vision of the economy as governed by a true data-generating process – the complex probability distribution that actually governs the realizations of economic variables. From this starting point, Hendry develops a theory of data reduction (Hendry, 1995, ch. 9). The origins of the theory of reduction are found in the analysis of exogeneity in the seminal article of Engle, Hendry, and Richard (1983). The central question is always: how can the data be characterized in a way that is partial or simpler than the true data-generating process without loss of information relative to the questions of interest? The theory defines the conditions under which the key steps in the reduction would be legitimate.

Practically, the general-to-specific approach involves starting with as broad a general specification as possible and then searching over the space of possible restrictions to find the most parsimonious specification. At each step in a sequential reduction (usually along multiple paths), the statistical properties of the errors are tested, the validity of the reduction is tested statistically both against the immediate predecessor and the general specification, and encompassing is tested against all otherwise satisfactory alternative specifications.

Despite strong advocacy among econometricians of the LSE school, the general-to-specific strategy is not an essential element of the methodology. The data-generating process assumed at the start of any search is "local" and not the true one. Its specification is based on common sense, the availability of data (both the particular variables and the number of observations, which dictates the degrees of freedom), and exploratory data analysis. Since there is no direct access to the true data-generating process, there is no way to demonstrate that the local data-generating process is itself a legitimate reduction of the true one.

It is always possible that an alternative specification exists that is not, in fact, nested in the local data-generating process. In this case, the local process is supplemented with the alternative specification to form a new local data-generating process, and the search is run again. But this is a specific-to-general strategy.

Although not essential, the general-to-specific strategy retains a strong heuristic justification. It ensures that the space of alternative specifications is fully explored, minimizing the danger that relevant competing specifications are ignored, and ensures that no information is lost relative to the general specification.

Critics of the LSE approach (Faust and Whiteman, 1995, 1997) argue, among other things, that the general-to-specific approach is vitiated because it is a form of data mining in which the large number of sequential tests render the reported test statistics uninterpretable. This objection is supported by studies of data-mining algorithms that show large size distortions (e.g., Lovell, 1983). The LSE response is to note that there are two sources of error that need to be taken into account: (i) size distortions (the cost of search); and (ii) statistics based on a misspecified regression are not likely to reflect those of a correct specification (the cost of misspecification). Critics of data mining tend to stress the first and ignore the second. Yet Monte Carlo studies of the efficacy of general-to-specific search show that the costs of search are small: size tends to be close to the nominal size of the exclusion tests used in the search; power achieves a high fraction of the power given knowledge of the correct specification; and the ability to recover the true specification is high (Hoover and Perez, 1999, 2004; Hendry and Krolzig, 1999; and Krolzig and Hendry, 2001).

The different conclusions reached about the effectiveness of data-mining appear to arise because of differences between the general-to-specific algorithm and the relatively simpler algorithms tested by Lovell and others (e.g., maximum R^2, step-wise regression, maxi-min $|t|$). These simpler search algorithms do not enforce any requirement that particular specifications pass reasonable tests of statistical adequacy. They are thus more susceptible to specification error.

A theorem due to White (1990, pp. 379–80) states that, for a fixed set of specifications and a battery of specification tests, as the sample size grows toward infinity and increasingly smaller test sizes are employed, the test battery will – with a probability approaching unity – select the correct specification from the set. White's theorem implies that type I and type II error both fall asymptotically to zero. White's theorem says that, given enough data, only the true specification will survive a stringent enough set of tests. The true specification survives precisely because the true specification is necessarily, in the long run, the fittest specification (see Hoover and Perez, 2000 for further discussion). The theorem suggests that a stringent battery of tests should help to reduce the costs of misspecification; in practice, the Monte Carlo studies indicate that costs of misspecification dominate the costs of search.

Hendry refers to the LSE methodology and the general-to-specific strategy as a "progressive research strategy" with an explicit reference to Lakatos (Hendry, 2000, pp. 116, 117, 363–4, and 440; cf. Mizon, 1995). The methodology is Lakatosian in spirit in that it applies the encompassing principle repeatedly, so that the appropriate unit of appraisal is not, say, an individual regression model but a family of models incorporating the relevant information as it becomes available. Hendry stresses that the true test of a specification that has been constructed to meet statistical design criteria is its success on new data – much like

Lakatos's requirement of successful prediction of novel facts. Though Lakatosian in spirit, the LSE approach has no particular commitment to the details of Lakatos's methodology, with its emphasis on hard core propositions, protective belts, and heuristics for development of suitable theories.

Like the VAR approach in its initial formulation, the LSE approach stands on the side of probabilistic reduction rather than the theory of errors. Theory plays a part in helping to define the range of variables that should be included in the local data-generating process and in choosing interpretable transformations of those variables (that is, as a bridge principle), but Koopmans' notion that a complete, *a priori* theoretical articulation must precede statistical investigation is rejected. Although data may be packaged in more or less illuminating ways, it is the job of theory in the LSE view to conform to, and explain, the facts of the data, not of data to conform to the presuppositions of theory.

2.4.4 Calibration

The calibration methodology is the polar opposite of the LSE methodology: it maintains a commitment to prior core economic theory above all. Calibration is largely associated with Finn Kydland and Edward Prescott's (1991) program of quantifying dynamic general-equilibrium macroeconomic models, though it is closely related to the methodology of computable general-equilibrium models common in the trade, development, and taxation literatures (Mansur and Whalley, 1984).

A calibrated model starts with a theoretical model – for Kydland and Prescott generally a representative-agent rational-expectations model of the business cycle or growth – and completes it by assigning numerical values to the key parameters. These values are not estimated through systems-equations methods according to the Cowles Commission program (as, for example, in Hansen and Sargent, 1980). Instead, they are drawn from considerations of national accounting, the "great ratios," unrelated statistical estimations, common sense, experience, and other informal sources. Once parameterized, the calibrated model is validated through simulation. Do the simulated data display patterns of covariances that adequately mimic the patterns found in the actual data? Once validated, calibrated models are used to explain historical economic performance and for policy analysis. (See Hartley, Hoover, and Salyer, 1997; 1998, chapters 1 and 2, for a detailed critical description of the calibration methodology.)

Many econometricians question whether calibration, with its rejection of statistical estimation, can be counted as an econometric methodology. Kydland and Prescott (1991) vigorously defend its standing as *bona fide* econometrics, arguing that it fits clearly into the original vision of the Econometric Society of econometrics as "economic theory in its relation to statistics and mathematics." Some econometricians have attempted to recast calibration into a form more in keeping with mainstream understandings of the term (e.g., Gregory and Smith, 1991, 1993).

A calibration methodology is superior to econometric alternatives in Kydland and Prescott's view. First, they regard basic economic theory as established, secure knowledge that need not be tested. Second, they believe that the goal for quantitative economics should be the construction of artificial economies or models that sufficiently well mimic key dimensions of the actual economy that can be used as a test bed for counterfactual experiments. Third, they acknowledge that such models are only approximations to complex reality that will successfully mimic the actual economy only along a limited set of chosen dimensions. This limited focus, however, rules out standard likelihood-based statistical estimates of model parameters, since those methods penalize the models for failing to fit on dimensions irrelevant to the intended use of the models.

Although the notion that models built for one purpose may be inadequate for others is a sound one (Hoover, 1995a), the calibration methodology raises some significant doubts. Kydland and Prescott reject the application of standard methods of statistical estimation to their models because they see them as an application of the Koopmans' variant of the Cowles Commission methodology, which seeks to estimate directly completely articulated theoretical models. The purpose-built models that they advance are necessarily incompletely articulated and are, therefore, necessarily easy to reject according to Cowles Commission standards.[1] But this raises a key question never clearly answered by calibrationists: what is the standard for assessing the adequacy of the values assigned to the parameters of a calibrated model?

The second doubt is similar. Models are assessed by a comparison of descriptive statistics between simulated and actual data. The standard implicit in most calibration exercises is "looks good to Ed." The question of a non-subjective standard for judging, or even of guidance for assessing, the quality of the output of calibrated models has rarely – if ever – been addressed in the literature. A corollary is that there is no established method for adjudicating between the claims of competing calibrated models.

It is surprising that advocates of calibration methodologies have not noticed that their objections to the Cowles Commission methodology do not apply to the LSE methodology or to any probabilistic-reduction approach. An adequate statistical characterization of data may help to supply robust parameterizations for calibrated models. And Hoover (1994a) has proposed the application of the encompassing principle in a manner that would help to adjudicate among competing calibrated model while preserving Kydland and Prescott's insight that a theoretical model may be a valuable tool of historical assessment and policy guidance even though incompletely articulated.

2.4.5 Textbook econometrics

By the middle of the 1950s, the Cowles Commission program had seized the methodological high ground. The focus of econometric research shifted away from high-level conceptual questions to ground-level concerns with the development of particular estimators and tests. Still, Cowles Commission attitudes continued to dominate econometric thought, even in the face of the failure of systems estimation of macroeconomic models or of microeconomic demand systems to live up to the promise of the Cowles Commission methodology.

Econometrics textbooks and many of the applications of econometrics to applied problems reverted to single-equation regression models. Much of the applied work was atheoretical or – at best – weakly theoretically justified. The robust-estimation approaches that were part of the post-Cowles Commission developments dominated textbook econometrics (Spanos, 1995).

Other applied econometricians took the notion that a single equation was always embedded in a larger system more seriously, addressing it through the application of instrumental-variables estimators to obtain consistent estimates. In most such applications, Koopmans' notion that theory must be prior to data dominates: the choice of instruments was guided by *a priori* considerations; the goal continued to be estimation in the theory-of-errors tradition.

Recently – especially in the applied labor economics literature – a data-first approach has captured substantial support. The goal is to use "natural experiments" – e.g., changes in institutional arrangements – as instruments to help identify causal effects (Angrist and Krueger, 2001). Here, contrary to Koopmans, the information obtained from statistical processing of the data restricts the class of acceptable explanatory theories.[2]

2.5   Some key issues in econometric methodology

The main philosophical approaches to science discussed in section 2.2 are variants (or, at least, descendants) of logical positivism. Most econometricians are positivists in the very broad sense of finding the source of scientific knowledge either in logical deductions from secure premises or in empirical observation. Yet few are logical positivists in the sense of subscribing to all of Hacking's six characteristics cited in section 2.2. Considering how econometrics and its different methodologies relate to Hacking's list provides a way of tying together the somewhat separate discussions of the main philosophical approaches to science with the main econometric methodologies.

1 *Emphasis on verification or falsification.* Essentially, logical positivism is characterized as mainly concerned with the testing of theories. But econometrics has many goals that involve little or no testing of theories. Even an econometrician such as Hendry (1980, pp. 27–8), who says that the three golden rules of econometrics are "test, test, test," is not concerned so much with the direct test of theories as with achieving statistical adequacy. Econometrics in the Cowles Commission program is mainly concerned with the measurement of theoretically articulated parameters. And other approaches often seek to establish the best statistical models for data reduction or forecasting. The criticism of Summers (1991) that no econometric test ever decided an economic question, or the challenge of Keuzenkamp and Magnus (1995) to produce an example of a case in which a statistical test was decisive for an economic question, miss the point: neither verification nor falsification is typically the sharp result of single tests; rather, empirical research is gradually redirected from lines less consonant to lines more consonant with the accumulated weight of evidence. Econometrics thus operates

in a Lakatosian spirit, albeit with no commitment to the fine details of Lakatos's methodology.

2 *Pro-observation.* Virtually all econometricians could be described as pro-observation, but the important methodological question is what exactly counts as an observation. Raw data, such as that collected by national statistical agencies, are not observations in the relevant sense; for what economic theory predicts is typically relationships among these raw data, although forecasting along the lines of the covering-law model is also possible.

The Cowles Commission program (at least in Koopmans' variant) sees true observations only when adequately identified by *a priori* theory. Calibrationists, who are otherwise skeptical of the Cowles Commission methodology, share this understanding, which is what justifies the title of Prescott's paper, "Theory Ahead of Business Cycle Measurement" (1986).

The data-mining procedures of the LSE school can be seen as an effort to get good observations, to focus the telescope as it were (Hoover, 1994b). Leamer's book, *Specification Searches* (1978), proceeds in a similar spirit. Leamer's (1983) *extreme-bounds analysis* tries to find observations that are robust, in the sense that parameters of interest maintain the direction of their influence however their magnitude may change. Despite similar motivations, there remains a substantive argument over the relative efficacy of extreme-bounds analysis relative to the LSE methodology (McAleer, Pagan and Volcker, 1985; Pagan, 1987; Hoover and Perez, 2004).

3 *Anti-cause.* Causality is principally about the structure of influence of one variable over another (Hoover, 2001a). Up to the heyday of the Cowles Commission in the early 1950s, conceptual discussions of causes were commonplace and causal talk was ubiquitous (Hoover, 2004). In the subsequent period, causal language nearly dropped out of econometric discussion. It revived somewhat with the development of Granger-causality tests. But "causality," as Granger uses it, is not closely related to structural notions (Granger, 1980). The absence of causal language does not imply an abandonment of causality. Cause is a diagnostic notion: when we flip a switch we would not normally say "I caused the light to come on"; but if the light failed to come on we would say "I wondered what caused that?" At the theoretical extreme, the calibrationist methodology is fundamentally about a commitment to models that reflect particular structures of economic influence. Though the word "cause" rarely turns up in calibrationist discourse, it takes a deeply causal view of the world and is in no sense anti-cause.

Zellner (1979) has advocated using the philosopher Feigl's (1953, p. 408) notion that cause as a shorthand for "predictability according to law" (also see Keuzenkamp, 2000, p. 240). Unfortunately, such a proposal begs the question; for it assumes that there is a clear concept of a law – applicable to economics – that can stand as surrogate for causal structure and that prediction is the sole goal of econometrics, neither of which is the case (Hoover 2001a, chapter 4; 2001b, lecture 2).

4 *Downplaying explanations.* The received view starts with universal laws and deduces predictions from them. The symmetry thesis holds that there is no

fundamental difference between explanation and prediction. Yet if prediction is not the principal objective of applied econometric investigation, then some of the same problems arise here as they did in the discussion of causality: are there economic laws? And, if so, where do they come from? The view that economic theory is given *a priori* to the econometrician, far from downplaying explanation, places emphasis on it. Elster (1994) argues that there are few, if any, universal empirical regularities, but that we can come to understand economic mechanisms that explain rather than predict. Such a view is compatible with the LSE and other probabilistic-reduction approaches. Their object is not to seek universal regularities, but regularities that arise in particular institutional and temporal contexts, which may in turn become the object of theoretical explanation. The same general strategy underlies the natural-experiment approach in applied microeconomics, as well as the strategy of behavioral finance, which seeks to construct an account of financial behavior from experimental and other empirical observations, rather than from *a priori* assumptions of economic rationality.

5 *Anti-theoretical entities.* To the true anti-realist or instrumentalist, theory is a convenient summary of the relationships among empirical data. Some econometricians entertain such positions. Keuzenkamp (2000, p. 216), for instance, maintains that the object of econometrics is not discovery, but intervention leading to predictable outcomes. He deeply opposes the LSE methodology with the slogan, "the Data Generation Process does not exist" (Keuzenkamp 2000, p. 214). Others, such as Lawson (1997), are extreme realists who believe that the complexity of the economy renders even locally stable regularities a virtual impossibility. Most econometricians appear to fall somewhere in between these extremes. Once again, those who insist on the primacy of *a priori* theory can hardly think of that theory as an instrumental data summary without a real referent; while those who seek probabilistic reductions generally do so on the assumption that the data-generating process does, in fact, exist. The two camps differ over how knowledge is to be made secure, but not over the ontological status of economic entities.

2.6   Wither econometric methodology?

Hacking's sixth point merely states that the first five taken together amount to a rejection of metaphysics on the part of logical positivists. Of the five, econometricians can be reliably expected to agree with one: the attitude of being pro-observation. It would be unreasonable, then, to deduce that econometricians are typically against metaphysics. Nonetheless, metaphysical questions rarely arise explicitly in econometric discourse. In fact, econometric methodology is a largely underdeveloped field in which practicing econometricians address methodological issues at best implicitly. That the field is ripe for substantial development is clear from two points that have arisen in this survey.

First, the main approaches to the philosophy of science, with the exception of the semantic approach broadly conceived, do not square well with the failure of the main econometric methodologies to conform to a broadly logical positivist program. One key research program, then, is to develop a methodology of economics which clarifies the role of econometrics in a larger philosophy of science.

Second, while there are connections and continuities among the different econometric methodologies, there are also deep divisions that do not turn on merely technical matters. These divisions cry out for conceptual resolution – a task better suited to explicit methodological thought than to the tacit methodology found in the pages of *Econometrica*.

Notes

1. "Purpose-built" is the literal meaning of *ad hoc*, but this latter term has become such a term of abuse among economists that it is doubtful that Kydland and Prescott would willingly describe their theory-based models as *ad hoc* (see Hands, 1993b).
2. Time, space, and ignorance compel me to omit detailed discussion of another approach to econometrics: *simplicity*. See Keuzenkamp (2000, ch. 5) and Zellner, Keuzenkamp, and McAleer (2001) for detailed discussion.

References

Aldrich, John (1989) Autonomy. *Oxford Economic Papers* **41**(1), 15–34.

Angrist, J. and A. Krueger (2001) Instrumental variables and the search for identification: from supply and demand to natural experiments. *Journal of Economic Perspectives* **15**(4), pp. 69–85.

Blaug, Mark. (1992). *The Methodology of Economics: Or How Economists Explain,* 2nd edition. Cambridge: Cambridge University Press.

Blaug Mark and Neil de Marchi (eds) (1991) *Appraising Economic Theories: Studies in the Application of the Methodology of Research Programs.* Aldershot: Edward Elgar.

Boumans, Marcel (1999) Built-in Justification. In Morgan and Morrison (eds), *Models and Mediators*, pp. 66–96.

Caldwell, Bruce J. (1982) *Beyond Positivism: Economic Methodology in the Twentieth Century.* London: Allen & Unwin.

Cartwright, Nancy (1989) *Nature's Capacities and Their Measurement.* Oxford: Clarendon Press.

Cartwright, Nancy (1999) *The Dappled World.* Cambridge: Cambridge University Press.

Chao, Hsiang-Ke (2002) Representation and structure: the methodology of econometric models of consumption. PhD dissertation, University of Amsterdam.

Chao, Hsiang-Ke (2005) A misconception of Semantic Conception of Econometrics? *Journal of Economic Methodology,* **12**(1), 125–35.

Cooley, Thomas F. and Stephen F. LeRoy (1985) Atheoretical macroeconometrics: a critique. *Journal of Monetary Economics* **16**(3), 283–308.

Darnell, Adrian C. and J. Lynne Evans (1990) *The Limits of Econometrics.* Aldershot: Edward Elgar.

Davis, George C. (2000) A semantic conception of Haavelmo's structure of econometrics. *Economics and Philosophy* **16**(2), 205–28.

Davis, George (2005) Clarifying the "Puzzle" between textbook and LSE approaches to econometrics: a comment on Cook's Kuhnian perspective on econometric modelling. *Journal of Economic Methodology,* **12**(1), 93–115.

Duhem, Pierre (1906) *The Aim and Structure of Physical Theory,* trans. Louis de Broglie. Princeton: Princeton University Press, 1954.

Elster, Jon (1994) A plea for mechanisms. Unpublished manuscript, Oslo; cited in Stigum (2003).

Engle, Robert F., David F. Hendry and Jean-François Richard (1983) "Exogeneity," *Econometrica* 51(2), 277–304.

Epstein, Roy J. (1987) *A History of Econometrics*. Amsterdam: North-Holland.

Faust, Jon and Charles H. Whiteman (1995) Commentary [on Grayham E. Mizon 'Progressive Modeling of Macroeconomic Times Series: The LSE Methodology']. In Hoover (1995c), pp. 171–80.

Faust, Jon and Charles H. Whiteman (1997) General-to specific procedures for fitting a data-admissible, theory-inspired, congruent, parsimonious, encompassing, weakly-exogenous, identified, structural model to the DGP: a translation and critique. *Carnegie-Rochester Conference Series on Economic Policy*, 47, December.

Feigl, Herbert (1953) Notes on causality. In Herbert Feigl and Mary Brodbeck (eds), *Readings in the Philosophy of Science*. New York: Appleton-Century-Crofts, pp. 408–18.

Fisher, I. (1933) "Statistics in the Service of Economics," *Journal of the American Statistical Association* 28(181), 1–13.

Fisher, Ronald A. (1930) *Statistical Methods for Research Workers*. Edinburgh: Oliver and Boyd.

Fisher, Ronald A. (1935) *The Design of Experiments*. Edinburgh: Oliver and Boyd.

Frisch, Ragnar (1933) Editor's note. *Econometrica* 1(1), 1–4.

Giere, Ronald N. (2000) Theories. In W. H. Newton-Smith (ed.), *A Companion to the Philosophy of Science*. Oxford: Blackwell.

Granger, C.W.J. (1980) Testing for causality: a personal viewpoint. *Journal of Economic Dynamics and Control* 2(4), 329–52.

Granger, C.W.J. (1999) *Empirical Modelling in Economics: Specification and Evaluation*. Cambridge: Cambridge University Press.

Gregory, Allan W. and Gregor W. Smith (1991) Calibration as testing: inference in simulated macroeconomic models. *Journal of Business and Economic Statistics* 9(3), 297–303.

Gregory, Allan W. and Gregor W. Smith (1993) Statistical aspects of calibration in macroeconomics. In G.S. Maddala, C.R. Rao and H.D. Vinod (eds), *Handbook of Statistics*, vol. 11. Amsterdam: North-Holland, pp. 703–19.

Haavelmo, Trgyve (1943) The statistical implications of a system of simultaneous equations. *Econometrica* 11(1), 1–12.

Haavelmo, Trgyve (1944) The probability approach in econometrics. *Econometrica* 12 (supplement), July.

Hacking, Ian (1983) *Representing and Intervening*. Cambridge: Cambridge University Press.

Hahn, Frank (1992a) Reflections. *Royal Economic Society Newsletter*, no. 77, April.

Hahn, F. (1992b) Answer to Backhouse: Yes. *Royal Economic Society Newsletter*, no. 78, July.

Hands, D. Wade. (1993a) The problem of excess content: economics, novelty, and a long Popperian tale. In *Testing, Rationality, and Progress: Essays on the Popperian Tradition in Economic Methodology*. Lanham, MD: Rowman and Littlefield, pp. 125–41.

Hands, D. Wade. (1993b) Ad hocness in economics and the Popperian tradition. In *Testing, Rationality, and Progress: Essays on the Popperian Tradition in Economic Methodology*. Lanham, MD: Rowman and Littlefield, pp. 83–99.

Hansen, Lars Peter and Thomas J. Sargent (1980) Formulating and estimating dynamic linear rational expectations models. In Robert E. Lucas, Jr. and Thomas J. Sargent (eds), *Rational Expectations and Econometric Practice*. London: George Allen & Unwin, 1981.

Hartley, James E., Kevin D. Hoover and Kevin D. Salyer (1997) The limits of business cycle research: assessing the real business cycle model. *Oxford Review of Economic Policy* 13(3), 34–54.

Hartley, James E., Kevin D. Hoover and Kevin D. Salyer (eds) (1998) *Real Business Cycles: A Reader*. London: Routledge.

Hausman, D.M. (1992). *The Inexact and Separate Science of Economics*. Cambridge: Cambridge University Press.

Heckman, James J. (2000) Causal parameters and policy analysis in economics: a twentieth century retrospective. *Quarterly Journal of Economics* 115(1), 45–97.

Hendry, David F. (1980) Econometrics: alchemy or science? In Hendry (2000), pp. 1–28.

Hendry, David F. (1988) Encompassing. *National Institute Economic Review* (August), 88–92.

Hendry, David F. (1995) *Dynamic Econometrics*. Oxford: Oxford University Press.

Hendry, David F. (2000) *Econometrics: Alchemy or Science*, 2nd edition. Oxford: Blackwell.

Hendry, David F. and Hans-Martin Krolzig (1999) Improving on "Data Mining Reconsidered" by K.D. Hoover and S.J. Perez. *Econometrics Journal* 2(2), 202–18.

Hendry, David F. and Mary S. Morgan (eds) (1995) *The Foundations of Econometric Analysis*. Cambridge: Cambridge University Press.

Hood, W.C. and T.C. Koopmans (eds) (1953) *Studies in Econometric Method*, Cowles Commission Monograph 14. New York: Wiley.

Hoover, Kevin D. (1990) The logic of causal inference: econometrics and the conditional analysis of causation. *Economics and Philosophy* 6(2), 207–34.

Hoover, Kevin D. (1991a) Scientific research program or tribe? A joint appraisal of Lakatos and the New Classical macroeconomics. In Blaug and De Marchi (1991).

Hoover, Kevin D. (1991b) The causal direction between money and prices: an alternative approach. *Journal of Monetary Economics* 27(3), 381–423.

Hoover, Kevin D. (1994a) Six queries about idealization in an empirical context. *Poznan Studies in the Philosophy of the Sciences and the Humanities* 38, 43–53.

Hoover, Kevin D. (1994b) Econometrics as observation: the Lucas critique and the nature of econometric inference. *Journal of Economic Methodology* 1(1), 65–80.

Hoover, Kevin D. (1995a) Facts and artifacts: calibration and the empirical assessment of real-business-cycle models. *Oxford Economic Papers* 47(1), 24–44.

Hoover, Kevin D. (1995b) Why does methodology matter for economics? *Economic Journal* 105(430), 715–34.

Hoover, Kevin D. (ed.) (1995c) *Macroeconometrics: Developments, Tensions, and Prospects*. Dordrecht: Kluwer.

Hoover, Kevin D. (2001a) *Causality in Macroeconomics*. Cambridge: Cambridge University Press.

Hoover, Kevin D. (2001b) *The Methodology of Empirical Macroeconomics*. Cambridge: Cambridge University Press.

Hoover, Kevin D. (2002) Econometrics and reality. In Uskali Mäki (ed.), *Fact and Fiction in Economics: Models, Realism, and Social Construction*. Cambridge: Cambridge University Press.

Hoover, Kevin D. (2004) Lost causes. *Journal of the History of Economic Thought* 26(2), 149–64.

Hoover, Kevin D. and Stephen J. Perez (1999) Data mining reconsidered: encompassing and the general-to-specific approach to specification search. *Econometrics Journal* 2(2), 167–91.

Hoover, Kevin D. and Stephen J. Perez (2000) Three attitudes towards data mining. *Journal of Economic Methodology* 7(2), 195–210.

Hoover, Kevin D. and Stephen J. Perez (2004) Truth and robustness in cross country growth regressions. *Oxford Bulletin of Economics and Statistics* 66(5), 765–98.

Hume, David (1739) *A Treatise of Human Nature*. Page numbers refer to the edition edited by L.A. Selby-Bigge. Oxford: Clarendon Press, 1888.

Hume, David (1777) *An Enquiry Concerning Human Understanding*. Page numbers refer to L.A. Selby-Bigge (ed.), *Enquiries Concerning Human Understanding and Concerning the Principles of Morals*, 2nd edition. Oxford: Clarendon Press, 1902.

Juselius, Katarina (1999) Models and relations in economics and econometrics. *Journal of Economic Methodology* 6(2), 259–90.

Keuzenkamp, Hugo A. (2000) *Probability, Econometrics, and Truth: The Methodology of Econometrics*. Cambridge: Cambridge University Press.

Keuzenkamp, Hugo A. and Jan R. Magnus (1995) On tests and significance in economics. *Journal of Econometrics* 67(1), 5–24.

Keynes, John Maynard. (1939) Professor Tinbergen's method. *Economic Journal* 49(195), 558–68.

Koopmans, T.C. (1950) *Statistical Inference in Dynamic Economic Models*, Cowles Commission Monograph 10. New York: Wiley.

Krolzig, Hans-Martin and David F. Hendry. (2001) Computer automation of general-to-specific model selection procedures. *Journal of Economic Dynamics and Control* 25(6–7), 831–66.

Kuhn, Thomas (1962) *The Structure of Scientific Revolutions*, 2nd edn. Chicago: University of Chicago Press, 1970.

Kydland, Finn E. and Edward C. Prescott (1991) The econometrics of the general equilibrium approach to business cycles. *Scandinavian Journal of Economics* 93(2), 161–78.

Lakatos, Imré (1970) Falsification and the methodology of scientific research programmes. In Lakatos and Alan Musgrave (eds), *Criticism and the Growth of Knowledge*. Cambridge: Cambridge University Press, 1970.

Latsis, S. J. (1976) *Method and Appraisal in Economics*. Cambridge: Cambridge University Press.

Lawson, Tony (1997) *Economics and Reality*. London: Routledge.

Leamer, Edward E. (1978) *Specification Searches: Ad Hoc Inference with Nonexperimental Data*. Boston: John Wiley.

Leamer, Edward E. (1983) Let's take the con out of econometrics. *American Economic Review* 73(1), 31–43.

Leamer, Edward E. (1985) Vector autoregressions for causal inference? *Carnegie Rochester Conference Series on Public Policy* 22, 255–303.

Liu, T. (1960) Underidentification, structural estimation, and forecasting. *Econometrica* 28(4), 855–65.

Lovell, Michael C. (1983) Data mining. *The Review of Economics and Statistics* 65(1), 1–12.

Magnus, Jan R. and Mary S. Morgan (eds) (1999) *Methodology and Tacit Knowledge*. New York: Wiley.

Mansur, Ahsan and John Whalley (1984) Numerical specification of applied general-equilibrium models: estimation, calibration, and data. In Herbert E. Scarf and John B. Shoven (eds), *Applied General Equilibrium Analysis*. Cambridge: Cambridge University Press.

McAleer, Michael, Adrian R. Pagan, and Paul A. Volcker (1985) What will take the con out of econometrics. *American Economic Review* 75(3), 293–307.

Mises, Ludwig von (1966) *Human Action: A Treatise on Economics*, 3rd edn. Chicago: Henry Regnery.

Mizon, Grayham E. (1984) The encompassing approach in econometrics. In D.F. Hendry and K.F. Wallis (eds), *Econometrics and Quantitative Economics*. Oxford: Basil Blackwell, pp. 135–72.

Mizon, Grayham E. (1995) Progressive modelling of economic time series: The LSE methodology. In Hoover (1995c), pp. 107–70.

Morgan, Mary S. (1990) *The History of Econometric Ideas*. Cambridge: Cambridge University Press.

Morgan, Mary S. and Margaret Morrison (eds) (1999) *Models as Mediators*. Cambridge: Cambridge University Press.

Newton-Smith, William (1981) *The Rationality of Science*. Boston: Routledge & Kegan Paul.

Pagan, Adrian (1987) Three econometric methodologies: a critical appraisal. *Journal of Economic Surveys* 1(1), 3–24.

Popper, Karl (1959) *The Logic of Scientific Discovery*. London: Hutchinson.

Prescott, Edward C. (1986) Theory ahead of business cycle measurement. *Federal Reserve Bank of Minneapolis Quarterly Review* 10(4), 9–22.

Quine, Willard V.O. (1951) Two dogmas of empiricism. In *From a Logical Point of View*, 2nd edn. Cambridge: Harvard University Press, 1961.

Robbins, L. (1937) *An Essay on the Nature and Significance of Economic Science*. London: Macmillan.

Rosenberg, A. (1992) *Economics: Mathematical Politics or Science of Diminishing Returns?* Chicago: Chicago University Press.

Simon, Herbert A. (1953) Causal ordering and identifiability. In Herbert A. Simon, *Models of Man*. New York: Wiley, 1957, ch. 1.

Sims, Christopher A. (1980) Macroeconomics and reality. *Econometrica* 48(1), 1–48.

Sims, Christopher A. (1986) Are forecasting models usable for policy analysis? *Federal Reserve Bank of Minneapolis Quarterly Review* **10**(1), 2–15.

Spanos, Aris (1986) *Statistical Foundations of Econometric Modelling*. Cambridge: Cambridge University Press.

Spanos, Aris (1995) On theory testing in econometrics: modeling with nonexperimental data. *Journal of Econometrics* **67**(1), 189–226.

Spanos, Aris (1999) *Probability Theory and Statistical Inference: Econometric Modeling with Observational Data*. Cambridge: Cambridge University Press.

Stigler, Stephen M. (1986) *The History of Statistics: Measurement of Uncertainty Before 1900*. Cambridge, MA: Belknap Press.

Stigler, Stephen M. (1999) *Statistics on the Table*. Cambridge, MA: Harvard University Press.

Stigum, Bernt P. (2003) *Econometrics and the Philosophy of Economics: Theory–Data Confrontations in Economics*. Princeton: Princeton University Press.

Summers, Lawrence H. (1991) The scientific illusion in empirical macroeconomics. *Scandinavian Journal of Economics* **93**(2), 129–48.

Suppe, Frederick (1989) *The Semantic Conception of Theories and Scientific Realism*. Urbana: University of Illinois Press.

Suppes, Patrick (1962) Models of data. In Ernest Nagel, Patrick Suppes and Alfred Tarski (eds), *Logic, Methodology and Philosophy of Science: Proceedings of the 1960 International Congress*. Stanford: Stanford University Press, pp. 252–61.

Tinbergen, Jan. (1939) *Statistical Testing of Business-Cycle Theories*, Vol. II: *Business Cycles in the United States of America, 1919–1932*. Geneva: League of Nations.

White, Halbert (1990) A consistent model selection procedure based on *m*-testing. In C.W.J. Granger (ed.), *Modelling Economic Series: Readings in Econometric Methodology*. Oxford: Clarendon Press, pp. 369–83.

Yule, George U. (1926) Why do we sometimes get nonsense correlations between time series? A study of sampling and the nature of time series (with discussion). *Journal of the Royal Statistical Society* **89**(1), 1–64.

Zellner, Arnold A. (1979) Causality and econometrics. In Karl Brunner and Allan H. Meltzer (eds), *Three Aspects of Policy Making: Knowledge, Data and Institutions*, Carnegie-Rochester Conference Series on Public Policy, vol. 10. Amsterdam: North-Holland, pp. 9–54.

Zellner, Arnold, Hugo A. Keuzenkamp, and Michael McAleer (eds) (2001) *Simplicity, Inference, and Modeling: Keeping It Sophisticatedly Simple*. Cambridge: Cambridge University Press.

3
Early Explorations in Econometrics

Richard William Farebrother

Abstract

This chapter focuses on some aspects of the early history of econometric theory that has not been covered in texts such as those by Mary Morgan (1990) and Morgan and David Hendry (1995). It begins by considering the various algebraic procedures that have been suggested as possible solutions to the problem of fitting a given mathematical relationship to a set of observations on the variable quantities of this relationship. Emphasis is placed on the fitting of a nonlinear function, so that these algebraic methods may be interpreted from a modern perspective as ways of obtaining initial values for iterative solution procedures, and as approximations to the algorithm originally provided by Gauss in 1809 as a solution to this problem. It is emphasized that Gauss' "true" method of least squares only became widely used after the advent of modern computers from the late 1960s. Indeed, other procedures, most notably the method of averages, retained their popularity over least squares until this time. The analysis is then generalized to the simultaneous equations model, within the framework of fitting a demand curve to data on the price and quantity of an agricultural good. Various approaches are considered, including orthogonal, indirect and two-stage least squares, instrumental variables and path analysis. Early attempts to incorporate determinants and matrices are also identified, and the chapter ends by dating the advent of "modern econometrics" as 1944, after the publication of Haavelmo's seminal paper.

3.1	Introduction	89
3.2	Introduction to single equation methods	91
3.3	Traditional curve-fitting methods	92
	3.3.1 Least sum of powers of absolute errors	92
	3.3.2 The method of selected points	92
	3.3.3 The method of averages	92
	3.3.4 The method of moments	92
	3.3.5 Preliminary transformations of the functional form	93
3.4	Applications to nonlinear problems	93
	3.4.1 The logistic and related nonlinear functions	93
	3.4.2 Elementary fitting procedures	94
	3.4.3 The method of moments	95
	3.4.4 The least squares fitting of transformed relationships	96
3.5	The true method of least squares	98
	3.5.1 Criticism of Pearl and Reed's method	98
	3.5.2 Practical objections to the true method of least squares	98
	3.5.3 Discussion	99

3.6	Computational difficulties in the linear case	99
3.7	Least absolute deviations and minimax fitting procedures	100
3.8	Optimality results for the method of averages	101
	3.8.1 The linear statistical model	101
	3.8.2 The simple linear model	102
	3.8.3 Two-dimensional results	102
	3.8.4 Durbin's procedure	103
	3.8.5 Three-dimensional results	103
	3.8.6 Errors-in-variables models	103
3.9	The simultaneous equations model	104
	3.9.1 Introduction to the simultaneous equations model	104
	3.9.2 Method of averages	105
	3.9.3 Orthogonal least squares	107
3.10	Data adjustment techniques	107
	3.10.1 Data adjustment by link relatives and trend ratios	107
	3.10.2 Frisch and Waugh's results	107
3.11.	More advanced estimation techniques	108
	3.11.1 Instrumental variable estimation	108
	3.11.2 Indirect and two-stage least squares	108
	3.11.3 Path analysis	109
3.12	Determinants and matrices in econometrics	110
3.13	Origins of modern econometrics	110
3.14	Concluding remarks	111

3.1 Introduction

The analysis of statistical data has a long history in economics. Many authors begin their history of the subject with the work of John Graunt and William Petty in the middle of the seventeenth century. Indeed, some early members of the Cowles Commission even traced some aspects of their work to Girolamo (or Geronimo) Cardano, as noted by Harold Davis in his *The Adventures of an Ultra-Crepidarian* (1962, pp. 368–9):

> There is no doubt that Cardano was one of the most important scientific figures in the sixteenth century. But there is also no doubt that he was a gambler, a thief, a caster of horoscopes, a medicine man – in fact, a glorified charlatan . . . And Cardano it was who led the great procession in the hall of the Cowles Commission. It was fitting, however, that this should be so, for in 1933 Mr. Cowles had published a paper under the title: "Can Stock Market Forecasters Forecast?" In this monograph which has since become a classic, Mr. Cowles showed that the forecasting ability of the best business analysts of that day was no better than random chance. In other words, the "casters" of market advice in the twentieth century were scarcely better in their results than the old Italian "caster" of horoscopes . . .

In this chapter, we shall not be concerned with the analysis of economic time series or with the problem of forecasting from them. We may therefore delete

Girolamo Cardano, John Graunt and William Petty from further consideration. Readers interested in this aspect of the subject are referred to Davis (1941a) and Morgan (1990, chapters 1–4). Instead, we shall attempt to provide an insight into some aspects of the early history of econometric theory which has not already been covered by Morgan (1990) and Hendry and Morgan (1995).

The method of maximum likelihood had been developed by Johann Heinrich Lambert and Daniel Bernoulli in the second half of the eighteenth century. Similar ideas were presented in a Bayesian framework by Pierre Simon Laplace and Carl Friedrich Gauss between 1774 and 1816. Indeed, Bayesian techniques were in common use throughout the nineteenth century, notably in Gauss' (1809) first derivation of the normal law of errors and the associated method of least squares, and in what Aldrich (1998, p. 67) is pleased to call the "corruption of Bayesian analysis" in the studies by Pearson (1896) and Pearson and Filon (1898). For further details, see the historical texts by Dale (1991), Farebrother (1999), Hald (1990, 1998), and Stigler (1986, 1999).

In view of the long history of Bayesian and non-Bayesian variants of the method of maximum likelihood, it is somewhat surprising to find that these methods seem to have been little employed in econometric work in the first half of the twentieth century, but had to wait until the reintroduction of likelihood techniques by R.A. Fisher between 1912 and 1922 and the probabilistic revolution fomented some while later in econometrics by Trygve Haavelmo (1944): see Aldrich (1997), Morgan (1987, 1990, chapter 8), and Qin (1996).

The reasons for this late introduction of likelihood and Bayesian techniques have been analysed in some detail by Morgan (1987, 1990, chapter 8). The principal reason why economists were reluctant to adopt statistical procedures is that they thought that the stochastic elements in their observations were serially related. Although they correctly deduced that these observations should be analysed by time series methods, they then failed to make much effort to adjust their fitting techniques to the needs of practical economics. A second, more practical, reason was the computational difficulties which procedures such as maximum likelihood and Bayesian inference imposed on practitioners. Thus, the lack of computing power and the absence of appropriate computational procedures mitigated against the use of these techniques. In practice, economists were constrained to use less rigorous fitting procedures and, in the present chapter, we shall explore what techniques were actually employed in econometric work in the first half of the twentieth century.

This chapter can be divided into two parts; in sections 3.2–3.8 we shall be concerned with the fitting of a single (generally nonlinear) relationship in isolation, and in sections 3.9–3.13 with the fitting of a single equation embedded in a system of simultaneous equations. The analysis in sections 3.2–3.6 is very closely related to an earlier work by Farebrother (1998) and that in sections 3.9–3.13 is much indebted to Morgan's (1990) historical study. The paucity of explicit references in econometric work to the fitting procedures discussed in sections 3.2–3.6 has obliged the author to substitute some examples taken from the literature of biometrics and demography.

3.2 Introduction to single equation methods

A fundamental problem in the theory of errors, which seems to have first attracted the attention of leading scientists in the middle of the eighteenth century, was that of fitting a given mathematical relationship (whose precise form is defined by a system of two or more unknown constants) to a set of discordant observations on the variable quantities of this relationship. This problem is still of interest today, but would now be expressed in a statistical form. In sections 3.2–3.8 we shall discuss the various algebraic procedures which have been suggested as possible solutions to this problem over the last two hundred years. These algebraic procedures would now be regarded as little more than satisfactory methods for obtaining initial values for iterative solution procedures. However, a study of these methods offers valuable insights into the nature of the problems faced by practising econometricians before the advent of modern computing equipment in the late 1960s.

For simplicity, in sections 3.2–3.8 we shall restrict our discussion to the case of functions determined by two or more unknown constants. This fundamental problem takes the following mathematical form. We are given a linear or nonlinear function, $f(\cdot)$, which is characterized by a system of p observed variable quantities $x, w, z, \ldots$, and a system of q unobserved fixed quantities $a, b, c, \ldots$. If the quantities $x, w, z, \ldots$ and the corresponding value of the function $f(\cdot)$ were observed without error, then we would have a system of n equations of the form

$$y_t = f(x_t, w_t, z_t, \ldots; a, b, c, \ldots) \quad t = 1, 2, \ldots, n$$

relating the tth observed value of the function y_t to the tth observed values of its variable arguments $x_t, w_t, z_t, \ldots$. However, this situation rarely occurs in practice, and our problem becomes one of choosing values for the unknown quantities $a, b, c, \ldots$ in such a way that the errors of observation $v_1, v_2, \ldots, v_n$ are as small as possible in some sense, where v_t is given by

$$v_t = y_t - f(x_t, w_t, z_t, \ldots; a, b, c, \ldots) \quad t = 1, 2, \ldots, n$$

The most familiar solution to this problem is the method of least squares, which chooses values for the unknown constants $a, b, c, \ldots$ in such a way as to minimize the sum of the squared errors of observation $\sum_t v_t^2$. This method was first proposed as an algebraic procedure by Gauss and Legendre between 1795 and 1809 and later justified on a variety of statistical grounds by Gauss, Laplace, Gauss again, Cauchy, and Thiele: see Farebrother (1999) for details.

Despite the fact that Gauss (1809) had provided a simple computational algorithm for use in the nonlinear case, this "true" method of least squares was often replaced by a variant which applied the least squares procedure to the given equations after they had been transformed to a linear or a more linear form, or had been reduced in number by aggregation. These simpler variants of the method of least squares need to be distinguished from the original untransformed method and, following Schultz (1930), we shall refer to the unmodified procedure as the "true" method of least squares.

Between 1750 and 1805 five distinct algebraic methods for linear or nonlinear curve fitting were clearly enunciated, namely the method of selected points, the method of averages, the method of least sum of squared errors, the method of least sum of absolute errors, and the method of least maximum absolute error. A sixth, the method of moments, was suggested at a later date. It is our purpose in sections 3.3–3.8 to demonstrate that these six alternatives to the true procedure continued in common use until high-speed electronic computers became readily available in the late 1960s.

For ease of exposition, we shall restrict our discussion of the nonlinear problem to the case of functions with a single explanatory variable. In this context, our problem is that of choosing values for the q unknown constants $a, b, c, \ldots$ in such a way that the n equations

$$y_t = f(x_t; a, b, c, \ldots) \quad t = 1, 2, \ldots, n$$

fit the observed values of x_t and y_t as closely as possible for a given function $f(\cdot)$ of known form.

3.3 Traditional curve-fitting methods

3.3.1 Least sum of powers of absolute errors

Our first task is to describe the six traditional curve fitting procedures enumerated in section 3.2. Three closely related methods are easily described. Given the definition of the errors of observation $v_1, v_2, \ldots, v_n$, the method of least squares chooses values for $a, b, c, \ldots$ to minimize the sum of the squared errors $\sum_t v_t^2$; the method of least absolute errors chooses $a, b, c, \ldots$ to minimize the sum of the absolute errors $\sum_t |v_t|$; and the minimax procedure chooses $a, b, c, \ldots$ to minimize the largest absolute error $\max_t |v_t|$.

3.3.2 The method of selected points

The most obvious solution to the problem of section 3.2 is to discard $n - q$ of the equations and solve the remaining q equations for the q unknowns. This fitting procedure is variously known as the method of selected points, the method of subsets, or the method of elemental sets.

3.3.3 The method of averages

An alternative method of reducing the n given equations to a set of q equations is to partition the observations into q groups of roughly equal size. These observations are aggregated within groups to yield a system of equations which are then solved for the q unknowns of the problem.

3.3.4 The method of moments

The method of moments discussed in Pearson (1902) represents an extension of the method presented in his 1895 paper to data which are not necessarily the abscissas and ordinates of a frequency curve. Thus, given that

$$y = f(x; a, b, c, \ldots) + v$$

represents the fitted relationship between x and y, Pearson suggests that the q unknown coefficients should be determined by setting

$$\int_l^u x^j f(x; a, b, c, \ldots) dx = \int_l^u x^j y \, dx$$

for $j = 0, 1, \ldots, q-1$ and where, for some suitable range of values $l \leq x \leq u$, the expression on the left of this equation is to be evaluated algebraically and that on the right by numerical quadrature (say by Simpson's rule). This procedure, and an alternative based on the equations

$$\sum_{t=1}^n x_t^j f(x_t; a, b, c, \ldots) = \sum_{t=1}^n x_t^j y \, dx \qquad j = 0, 1, \ldots, q-1$$

were subsequently described by Huntington (1924). This procedure is clearly closely related to Hansen's (1982) generalized method of moments.

3.3.5 Preliminary transformations of the functional form

Each of these six curve-fitting procedures may be formally modified by a preliminary transformation of the given equations. In our statement of the nonlinear curve-fitting problem at the end of section 3.2, we followed tradition and failed to specify an explicit error term. In this context, the practitioner may attempt to simplify the structure of the fitted equation before embarking on the fitting process itself, without regard to the nature of the postulated error term: see Huntington (1924, p. 62) for a very full list of possible transformations. Nor was the use of such preliminary transformations restricted to the work of applied economists with little training in statistics, as these techniques were employed by Harold Davis, Harold Hotelling, Karl Pearson, Gerhard Tintner and George Udny Yule, amongst others.

3.4 Applications to nonlinear problems

3.4.1 The logistic and related nonlinear functions

In this section we shall describe the fitting of equations of the form outlined in section 3.2 by the methods discussed in section 3.3. For simplicity, we shall restrict our attention to the logistic function

$$y_t = k/(1 + b \exp(-at))$$

and the Gompertz function

$$y_t = k b^{c^t}$$

which are readily transformed to the modified exponential function by taking reciprocals

$$\frac{1}{y_t} = \frac{1}{k} + \left(\frac{b}{k}\right) \exp(-at)$$

and logarithms

$$\log y_t = \log k + (\log b)c^t$$

respectively.

Our primary interest in this section is in the logistic function, which Davis (1941b, p. 210) describes in the following terms:

> The logistic curve appears to have been employed in population studies as early as 1845 by P.F. Verhulst [see Yule (1925, pp. 41–5)], but its application in economics is subsequent to the work of Pearl and Reed [1920]. The most extensive use of this curve as a trend for production data has been made by S.S. Kuznets [1930], who fitted logistics to some 50 or more series such as the production of wheat, corn, potatoes, cotton, pig iron, Portland cement, coal, copper, lead, etc. He also studied by this means the growth of bank clearings in New York City, Boston, Chicago, and Philadelphia, the growth of railroads, and the tonnage cleared from various countries... The logistic curve seems to be especially well-designed for the description of new industries, for population studies and for production series which depend on the growth of population itself...

The logistic function is no longer so widely used as it was in the 1930s, but a series of recent papers suggest that it still has a role in studies of human populations, market innovations, and technological change, if only in the modified form of the displaced logistic function

$$y_t = f + k/(1 + b\exp(-at))$$

proposed by Pearl (1924) and Oliver (1969).

3.4.2   Elementary fitting procedures

In view of the widespread use of the method of least squares for linear curve fitting problems, and of the prominent publication of the corresponding iterative procedure for nonlinear problems, it seems reasonable to anticipate that the iterative procedure would have been widely used well before the mid 1960s. In fact this was not the case, as practitioners seem to have preferred to transform their given equations to linear form before applying the method of least squares, or to employ a nonlinear variant of the method of averages when this was not possible. Thus, in his practical account of the logistic function, Yule (1925, pp. 49–53) describes three elementary methods for determining the unknown coefficients k, $\alpha = 1/a$ and $\beta = \log b/a$ from the n equations

$$\frac{1}{y_t} = \frac{1}{k} + \frac{1}{k}\exp((\beta - t)/\alpha) \quad t = 1, 2, \ldots, n$$

Yule's first method (1925, pp. 49–50), which we recognise as an application of the method of selected points, obtains the required coefficients from the equations associated with three equally spaced values of t. He notes that "with populations that run fairly smoothly it is quite adequate." By contrast with his first method,

Yule's second method (1925, pp. 51–52) is a variant of the method of averages which "brings all the data into account, provided the number of censuses available is a multiple of 3." In this context, with $n = 3r$, he sums the first r equations, the next r equations, and the last r equations to obtain

$$S_1 = \frac{r}{k} + \frac{C}{k}\exp\left(\frac{\beta}{\alpha}\right), \quad S_2 = \frac{r}{k} + \frac{C}{k}\exp\left(\frac{\beta - r}{\alpha}\right), \quad S_3 = \frac{r}{k} + \frac{C}{k}\exp\left(\frac{\beta - 2r}{\alpha}\right)$$

which may be solved for k, α and β, where

$$S_1 = \frac{1}{y_1} + \frac{1}{y_2} + \cdots + \frac{1}{y_r}$$

$$S_2 = \frac{1}{y_{r+1}} + \frac{1}{y_{r+2}} + \cdots + \frac{1}{y_{2r}}$$

$$S_3 = \frac{1}{y_{2r+1}} + \frac{1}{y_{2r+2}} + \cdots + \frac{1}{y_{3r}}$$

$$C = \frac{1 - \exp(-r/\beta)}{1 - \exp(-1/\beta)}$$

Yule's third method (1925, pp. 52–53) is based on a least squares fit of the linear relationship

$$\frac{y_{t+h} - y_t}{y_t} = \left(1 - \frac{y_{t+h}}{k}\right)(\exp(h/\alpha) - 1)$$

for a fixed value of h. However, he observes that "I do not think this is a very good method of fitting, but it is rather an interesting one."

3.4.3   The method of moments

Some 23 years earlier, Yule's teacher Karl Pearson (1902, p. 298) had considered a closely related problem in the following terms:

> Given a mortality table – i.e., a table which gives the number of survivors out of n people born in the same year at each year of age of the group – then if l_x denotes the number who attain the age of x, the table will be closely represented between the ages 20–25 to 85–90 by Makeham's formula, i.e.
>
> $$l_x = k s^x g^{c^x}$$
>
> where k, s, g and c are constants to be determined from the data of the table. Now there will be some 60 to 70 corresponding values of x and l_x and it is a quite hopeless task to think of discovering the values of k, s, g and c from the equation as it stands. If we take logarithms the equations may be written:
>
> $$L_x = K + xS + Gc^x$$
>
> where the capitals are the logarithms of the small letter quantities. The determination of K, S, G and c by the method of least squares is still impracticable.

Of course four corresponding values of L_x and x would give K, S, G and c, but such a selection of four arbitrary values out of 60 or 70 is unsatisfactory in the extreme. Accordingly Messrs G. King and G.F. Hardy have determined values of these constants by a process of averaging series of corresponding values of L_x and x, so that the final values of the constants shall depend on as much of the table as possible. [Footnote: *Journal of Institute of Actuaries*, vol. XXII, p. 200 or G. King: *Institute of Actuaries' Text-Book*, vol. II, p. 79 et seq., especially p. 82.] The values reached for the constants are good, but no doubt better ones could be found, and the process from the standpoint of systematic curve fitting is unsatisfactory. It involves empirical trials – e.g. "various groupings were tried and the best was found to be, four groups of eighteen years of life each" (*Text-Book*, p. 82) and therefore follows no general rule for curve fitting.

Having dismissed the claims of the method of least squares, the method of selected points, and the method of averages in this way, Pearson (1902, p. 298) embarked on a detailed account of "how the method of moments can be applied to Makeham's formula." Despite the fact that Pearson (1902) strongly endorsed this method for use when the method of least squares was impractical, and despite the fact that he provided a worked example for Makeham's formula which could easily have been adjusted for use with the logistic function by setting $S = 0$, Yule (1925) did not discuss this approach to the problem. Instead, as we have seen, he developed an alternative procedure based on the method of averages, which was still being taught as a suitable method for fitting the logistic, modified exponential, and Gompertz functions some forty years later, see Croxton and Cowden (1939, 1955, pp. 298–311) and Mills (1938, pp. 667–80, 1965, pp. 751–65).

3.4.4   The least squares fitting of transformed relationships

Yule's renewed interest in this area had been stimulated by the publication of the paper by Raymond Pearl and Lowell Reed in 1920. In this paper, Pearl and Reed had used the first of Yule's curve-fitting methods to obtain preliminary estimates, a_0, b_0 and k_0, of the unknown constants a, b and k. Later, Pearl (1924, pp. 575–9) developed a more complicated estimation procedure which makes use of the preliminary estimate of a, but not those of b or k. We define $c = 1/b$, $d = k/b$ and $h = a - a_0$, so that the logistic function may be rewritten as

$$y_t = \frac{d}{\exp(-a_0 t)\exp(-ht) + c}$$

Now, approximating $\exp(-ht)$ by $1 - ht$, we have

$$y_t = \frac{d}{\exp(-a_0 t)(1 - ht) + c}$$

or

$$d - cy_t + hty_t\exp(-a_0 t) = y_t\exp(-a_0 t)$$

and we may obtain estimates of c, d and h for a given value of a_0 by applying the method of least squares to the second expression.

Although Yule (1925) did mention the publication of Pearl's (1924) book, he did not discuss the new method of estimation developed in it. Instead, as we have seen, he proposed an alternative which, in the special case of interest here, is based on the least squares fitting of the equation

$$\frac{y_{t+1} - y_t}{y_t} = (\exp(a) - 1)\left(1 - \frac{y_{t+1}}{k}\right)$$

Variants of this procedure were subsequently proposed by Rhodes (1940) and Nair (1954), based on the transformed equations

$$\frac{1}{y_{t+1}} = \frac{\exp(-a)}{y_t} + \frac{(1 - \exp(-a))}{k}$$

and

$$\frac{1}{y_{t+1}} - \frac{1}{y_t} = \left(\frac{\exp(a) - 1}{\exp(a) + 1}\right)\left[\frac{2}{k} - \left(\frac{1}{y_t} + \frac{1}{y_{t+1}}\right)\right]$$

respectively. Further expressions of this type may be obtained as approximations to the derivative of the logistic function

$$\frac{dy_t}{dt} = ay_t - \frac{a}{k}y_t^2$$

For example, Davis (1941b, p. 222) and Tintner (1952, p. 210) discussed the expression

$$\frac{y_{t+1} - y_t}{y_t} = a - \frac{a}{k}y_t$$

which they attributed to Hotelling (1927). Again, further examples of this approach are to be found in Nair (1954). All variants of this procedure determine values for a and k but none for b. However, such values may readily be obtained from any one of the following three equations by summing the chosen equation over a suitable range of values of t:

$$\frac{k}{y_t} - 1 = b\exp(-at) \qquad \left(\frac{k}{y_t} - 1\right)\exp(at) = b$$

$$\log\left(\frac{k}{y_t} - 1\right) = \log b - at$$

Alternatively, if it is known that y_t takes the value $k/2$ when $t = t_0$, then the appropriate value of b is given by $b = \exp(at_0)$: see Davis (1941b, p. 223).

3.5   The true method of least squares

3.5.1   Criticism of Pearl and Reed's method

Pearl and Reed's method of curve fitting was criticized by Henry Schultz (1930, pp. 163–4):

> The fact that the Pearl–Reed procedure is not a true least square procedure does not necessarily mean that it will not give a good fit. It cannot be used, however, to determine the weights [reciprocal variances] of the parameters. We are restricted therefore, to the standard least squares procedure for fitting a non-linear function which gives corrections to all the parameters [if we also wish to know their weights].

The same criticism may also be lodged against Hotelling's method, but Schultz does not seem to have persuaded any of his contemporaries to adopt this iterative method in preference to the simpler methods described in section 3.3, even though his paper was read by some of the leading applied statisticians of the day.

3.5.2   Practical objections to the true method of least squares

In each of his two worked examples, Schultz (1930) took the Pearl–Reed estimates of a, d and c as his initial values, expanded the logistic equation in a Taylor series about these values, and obtained corrections δa, δd and δc by fitting the linear equation

$$y_t = \frac{d_0}{\exp(-a_0 t) + c_0} + \frac{d_0 t \exp(-a_0 t)}{(\exp(-a_0 t) + c_0)^2} \delta a + \frac{1}{\exp(-a_0 t) + c_0} \delta d$$
$$- \frac{d_0}{(\exp(-a_0 t) + c_0)^2} \delta c$$

by the method of least squares. This technique provided a satisfactory fit for census data on the population of the US between 1790 and 1910 but, when he applied it to data on the growth of a yeast culture, Schultz found that the quadratic terms omitted from the linear equation were not negligible, so that the fit obtained by his one-step procedure "is still not good from a strict least squares point of view." This observation provided Davis (1941b, p. 221) with his

> principal objection to this adjustment [procedure which is to be] found in the fact that k may be so large that differences of second order cannot be neglected. Hence the correction must be made successively several times before an approximation better than that of the Pearl–Reed method is attained.

Unlike Davis, Tintner (1952, p. 209) does not discuss the methods proposed by Pearl and Reed (1920) and Schultz (1930), but merely notes that

> the constants in [the logistic] equation enter in a non-linear fashion. Hence the application of the method of least squares is difficult ... As Hotelling has shown,

however, this difficulty can be overcome by considering the differential equation of the logistic function...

Thus, in their influential econometrics textbooks, Davis (1941b) and Tintner (1952) each recommended that the parameters of the logistic function should be estimated by the arbitrary procedures developed by Pearl and Reed (1920) or Hotelling (1927), rather than by the "true" least squares procedure championed by Schultz (1930). Both authors give several worked examples drawn from a wide range of disciplines.

3.5.3 Discussion

This rejection of the true method of least squares by Davis (1941b) and Tintner (1952) was so final that it does not seem to have been restored to favor, at least not in this context, until after the publication of the papers by Oliver (1964, 1966) in the mid-1960s. For a procedure that was proposed by Gauss in 1809 and illustrated by worked examples drawn from astronomy and geodesy, this conclusion may seem extraordinary. However, it should be noted that Gauss was concerned with the problem of fitting nonlinear functions suggested by celestial mechanics and spherical geometry to data which closely followed these functions, whereas his successors were concerned with the fitting of empirical laws to data which only followed these laws approximately: see Stigler (1981, 1999, chapter 17). Thus, while Gauss was able to obtain satisfactory results after a single iteration, his successors often needed several iterations before satisfactory results could be obtained. And, in an era before the advent of modern computers, it is not surprising to find that Davis (1941b) and Tintner (1952) preferred to avoid this additional computational burden by adopting alternative procedures which appeared to produce satisfactory results without iteration.

3.6 Computational difficulties in the linear case

In sections 3.4 and 3.5 we have shown that practitioners seldom employed the "true" method of least squares to solve their nonlinear curve fitting problems. Instead, they seem to have preferred to use variants of the method of averages and the method of least squares which yield satisfactory results in a single noniterative computation. Nor was this reluctance to use the true method of least squares restricted to nonlinear problems, as the availability of large data sets made the method impractical for all but the most important linear problems. For, as Guest (1951, p. 537) notes in the context of polynomial curve-fitting problems:

An appreciable shortening in the time required to fit a curve to a series of equally spaced observations $y(x)$ is effected by the use of tables of the orthogonal polynomials $T_j(x)$.... However the process is still tedious if the number of observations is at all large. A considerable time is spent in the calculation of the orthogonal moments and a mistake in these calculations can easily be made.

Or again, [Guest (1954, p. 62)]:

> The fitting of polynomials to equally spaced observations by the method of least squares is carried out by means of power moments...or orthogonal moments...; tables of orthogonal polynomials and related functions being used. When the number of observations is large (greater than 104) such tables are no longer available and it becomes necessary to group the observations before performing the calculations. Even if the number of observations is less than 104 it may be considered advisable to group the observations in order to reduce the time spent on the calculations...

This variant of the method of least squares, which Thiele had named the "method of normal places" in (1897, pp. 92–6, 1903, pp. 106–11), is to be distinguished from the method of averages. Indeed, the method of averages may be regarded as a special case of the method of normal places in which the number of retained groups is the same as the number of unknown constants.

Towards the middle of the twentieth century, several papers were published on variants of the method of averages for which some of the observations may be excluded from the final computations and the retained groups may be unequal in size. Nowadays, this literature is usually associated with the work of Wald (1940), Bartlett (1949) and Durbin (1954) on methods for fitting linear relationships when the explanatory variables are not directly observed. However, there was a parallel literature (particularly favoured in physics) stemming from the work of Bose (1938) and Nair and Shrivastava (1942) on the use of the method of averages in the conventional statistical framework.

Apparently working in a continuation of this physical tradition, the numerical analysts Dahlquist, Sjoberg, and Svenssen (1968, p. 843) compared the method of least squares and the method of averages (MA) in the following terms:

> We do not advocate the application of MA for polynomial approximation. The fact that the efficiency can be as high as it is in this test example indicates that MA deserves to be considered as a method for data reduction, in particular when small computers without built-in multiplication are used.

Thus it cannot be much more than thirty years since the method of least squares was admitted as standard by leading statisticians and numerical analysts for all linear fitting problems. The corresponding adoption of the method for nonlinear curve fitting problems occurred at about the same time and for the same reason; and both events were conditioned by the ready availability of sufficiently accurate numerical procedures and sufficiently robust computing equipment.

3.7 Least absolute deviations and minimax fitting procedures

It remains to give some account of the least absolute deviations (or L_1-norm) and the minimax (or L_∞-norm) line fitting procedures briefly defined in section 3.3.1.

The least absolute deviations procedure was developed by Boscovich, Laplace and Gauss between 1757 and 1809, but it was not until the period between 1887 and 1930 that improved schemes for implementing this procedure were presented by Edgeworth (1923), Bowley (1928) and Rhodes (1930). Each presented worked examples of the least absolute deviations fitting procedure applied to economic data. Nevertheless, it is only recently that this fitting procedure has attracted any attention in applied economic work. Indeed, it was still regarded as lying on the frontiers of econometrics when Taylor (1974) prepared his contribution to the volume edited by Zarembka.

It is perhaps unfortunate that applied economists failed to follow the lead offered by Edgeworth, Bowley and Rhodes in the early years of the twentieth century, as the computational difficulties that practitioners then experienced with the method of least squares may have persuaded more economists of the viability of the method of least absolute deviations long before it was reintroduced to management scientists in the guise of a linear programming problem by Charnes, Cooper and Ferguson (1955).

By contrast with the pivotal role of the minimax or Chebyshev criterion in game theory and approximation theory, the corresponding fitting procedure does not seem to have featured in any recent economic or econometric work. However, it does survive, in a modified form, in the numerous variants of Rousseeuw's (1984) least median of squared errors procedure.

For a detailed account of a class of fitting procedures based on elemental set estimators prior to Theil's (1950) nonparametric procedure, see Farebrother (1997). For other historical details relating to the least absolute deviations and minimax procedures, see Farebrother (1999), Hald (1998) or Stigler (1986).

3.8 Optimality results for the method of averages

3.8.1 The linear statistical model

The method of averages described in section 3.3.3 has been employed as a fitting procedure by leading practical scientists since the middle of the eighteenth century. In this section we outline some of the optimality results established in respect of this and related procedures since 1938. We consider the problem of estimating the $q - 1$ slope parameters $\beta_2, \beta_3, \ldots, \beta_q$ in the standard linear statistical model

$$y_t = \beta_1 + x_{t2}\beta_2 + \cdots + x_{tq}\beta_q + \varepsilon_t \qquad t = 1, 2, \ldots, n$$

where y_t is the tth observation on the dependant variable, x_{tk} is the tth observation on the kth explanatory variable, and ε_t is the tth observation on the disturbance term. These n disturbance terms are independently distributed with zero means and constant variance:

$$E(\varepsilon_t) = 0 \quad E(\varepsilon_t^2) = \sigma^2 \qquad t = 1, 2, \ldots, n$$
$$E(\varepsilon_s \varepsilon_t) = 0 \quad s \neq t = 1, 2, \ldots, n$$

where, for simplicity, we assume that the $n \times q$ matrix $X = \langle x_{tk} \rangle$ has full column rank q.

3.8.2   The simple linear model

We begin by supposing that $q = 2$ and that we are interested in estimating the slope parameter β_2 in the simple model:

$$y_t = \beta_1 + x_{t2}\beta_2 + \varepsilon_t \quad t = 1, 2, \ldots, n$$

Again, for simplicity, we restrict our discussion to the class of unbiased linear estimators of the form

$$\tilde{\beta}_2 = \frac{\sum_t (z_{t2} - \bar{z}_2)y_t}{\sum_t (z_{t2} - \bar{z}_2)x_{t2}}$$

where $z_{12}, z_{22}, \ldots, z_{n2}$ are either a set of fixed numbers or a set of variable numbers whose values are determined by those of $x_{12}, x_{22}, \ldots, x_{n2}$, and where the means of these two series are given by $\bar{x}_2 = n^{-1} \sum_t x_{t2}$ and $\bar{z}_2 = n^{-1} \sum_t z_{t2}$, respectively.

It is well known that the method of averages estimator $\tilde{\beta}_2$, defined above, is dominated within the class of all linear unbiased estimators of the slope parameter β_2 by the least squares estimator

$$\hat{\beta}_2 = \frac{\sum_t (x_{t2} - \bar{x}_2)y_t}{\sum_t (x_{t2} - \bar{x}_2)x_{t2}}$$

according to a wide class of optimality criteria. Nevertheless, it is still worth considering estimators defined by the method of averages as they are computationally far simpler than the method of least squares and the necessary increase in variance may be relatively slight.

3.8.3   Two-dimensional results

If the elements $x_{12}, x_{22}, \ldots, x_{n2}$ are arranged in increasing order, then Nair and Shrivastava (1942) and Bartlett (1949), building on the work of Bose (1938) and Wald (1940), respectively, have shown that the variance of the estimator $\tilde{\beta}_2$ is minimised by setting the first n_1 elements of $z_{12}, z_{22}, \ldots, z_{n2}$ equal to $-1/n_1$, followed by $n_2 = n - n_1 - n_3$ zero elements, and n_3 elements of size $1/n_3$.

If the values of n_1 and n_3 are not fixed, but are at our disposal, then Bose (1938) and Wald (1940) have shown that, when $n_2 = 0$ and the elements $x_{12}, x_{22}, \ldots, x_{n2}$ are fixed and evenly spaced, say $x_{t2} = t$, then we should set $n_1 = n_3 = 0.5n$. Similarly, if $x_{t2} = t$, and we are permitted to omit some of the observations from the expression defining the estimator $\tilde{\beta}_2$, then Nair and Shrivastava (1942) and Bartlett (1949) have shown that we should set $n_1 = n_3 = 0.33n$. On the other hand, if the x_{t2} are not fixed but are stochastic, then Theil and van Yzeren (1956) and Gibson and Jowett (1957a) have shown that we should set $n_1 = n_3 = 0.33n$

when x_{t2} is uniformly distributed and $n_1 = n_3 = 0.27n$ when x_{t2} is normally distributed.

For completeness, we note that the estimators proposed by Nair and Shrivastava (1942) and Bartlett (1949) are formally distinct as Nair and Shrivastava, in accordance with the strict tenets of the method of averages, entirely discard the middle n_2 observations from all their calculations, whereas Bartlett retains them for use in the estimation of the intercept parameter β_1.

3.8.4 Durbin's procedure

In general, Durbin's (1954) algebraic procedure partitions the data on each of the $q - 1$ nonconstant variables into r groups of equal size $(2 \leq r \leq n)$ and sets $z_{tk} = 1, 2, \ldots, r$ accordingly as x_{tk} is placed in the first, second, ..., or rth group. For $q = 2$ and $r = 2$, Durbin's prescription defines Wald's (1940) procedure, for $q = 2$ and $r = 3$, it defines Bartlett's (1949) procedure, and for $q = 2$ and $r = 3$ it defines the 'nine-group' procedure discussed by Gibson and Jowett (1957b).

3.8.5 Three-dimensional results

Nair and Shrivastava (1942) also generalized their procedure to the case of $q = 3$ unknowns with $x_{t3} = x_{t2}^2$, say $x_{t2} = t$ and $x_{t3} = t^2$. In this context, they suggested that the data should be partitioned into five contiguous groups, the second and fourth of these groups entirely omitted, and the slope parameters estimated from the equations given by the remaining three groups. Assuming that the three retained groups are of equal size, Nair and Shrivastava found that the variance of the method of averages estimator of the highest order slope parameter $\tilde{\beta}_3$ is minimized when $0.2n$ observations are placed in each of the five groups. If this restriction is removed, then Guest (1954, p. 72) found that the efficiency of estimation could be increased to 0.896 by placing $0.132n$ observations in the first and fifth groups and $0.441n$ observations in the middle group. On the other hand, if no observations are to be deleted, then Dahlquist, Sjoberg and Svensson (1968) found that the expected sum of the squared residuals is minimized when $0.2n$ observations are placed in the first and last groups and $0.6n$ observations are placed in the middle group.

Hooper and Theil (1958) considered a more exotic case in which the data on x_{t2} and x_{t3} is uniformly distributed over the surface of an equilateral triangle, but found that their supposedly optimal "four-group" partition of the data between four contiguous equilateral triangles (each half the size of the original triangle) was, in fact, less efficient than the "nine-group" estimator discussed by Gibson and Jowett (1957b).

3.8.6 Errors-in-variables models

It should perhaps be pointed out at this stage that none of the results described above are relevant in the errors-in-variables model, as the assumption that the x_{tk} are observed is not satisfied. Indeed, in the case of $q = 2$ unknowns, our problem is to estimate the parameter β_2 in the model

$$y_t = \beta_1 + \xi_{t2}\beta_2 + \varepsilon_t$$
$$t = 1, 2, \ldots, n$$
$$x_{t2} = \xi_{t2} + \delta_{t2}$$

In this context, Farebrother (1985–87), following Pakes (1982), has shown that all these estimators have exactly the same small-sample expectation as the ordinary least squares estimator when ξ_{t2}, δ_{t2}, and ε_t are independently normally distributed with zero means and fixed variances.

Clearly, the familiar observation that the order of the observed x_{t2} will be close to that of the unobserved ξ_{t2} when the errors δ_{t2} are small is not sufficient to guarantee the consistency of members of this class of estimators in the context of the errors-in-variables model. Fortunately, these adverse results were not available some forty years earlier, or continuing research in this area might have foundered: see Morgan (1990, p. 224).

3.9   The simultaneous equations model

3.9.1   Introduction to the simultaneous equations model

Thus far in this chapter, we have been concerned with linear or nonlinear fitting problems in which the explanatory variables are either fixed or are treated as though they were fixed. In section 3.8, we mentioned an alternative (measurement errors or errors-in-variables) model in which the explanatory variables are not directly observed. In the present section, we shall be concerned with a third model, the simultaneous equations or errors-in-equations model, in which the explanatory variables are observed but are stochastic.

The concept of a demand or supply schedule was already familiar at the beginning of the twentieth century. Thus, the additional problem which faced the econometricians of the period was that of attempting to relate these abstract concepts to the available data. In section 3.4 we had no trouble identifying time as the independent variable of the logistic function as there is no way in which an increase in population could cause time to pass! By contrast, in early demand studies it was not clear whether the price of a good should be regarded as a function of the corresponding quantity or vice versa.

In the remainder of this chapter, we shall restrict our discussion to the problem of fitting a demand curve to data on the price and quantity of selected agricultural goods. Although it is not clear at first sight which of these two variables should be regarded as determining the other, we arbitrarily suppose that the quantity demanded or supplied should serve as the dependent variable. Further, since the supply of agricultural goods varies dramatically from year to year whilst demand remains relatively constant, it is clear that the demand function will be traced out by movements in supply (this outline solution to the identification problem is due to Lenoir, 1913, and Lehfeldt, 1915).

Besides the (endogenous) variables p_t and q_t determined within the model, we suppose that our simple demand and supply model contains a set of pre-determined variables $x_t, w_t, z_t, \ldots$, which are either determined outside the model (exogenous) or are lagged values of the endogenous variables. Thus our model consists of a demand function:

$$q_t^D = f(p_t, x_t, w_t, z_t, \ldots; a_0, a_1, a_2, \ldots) \quad t = 1, 2, \ldots, n$$

and a supply function:

$$q_t^S = g(p_t, x_t, w_t, z_t, \ldots; b_0, b_1, b_2, \ldots) \quad t = 1, 2, \ldots, n$$

where, as in section 3.2, $f(\cdot)$ and $g(\cdot)$ are linear or nonlinear functions whose precise form is determined by the values of the unknown constants $a_0, a_1, a_2, \ldots$ and $b_0, b_1, b_2, \ldots$. It should be pointed out that we have again not included error terms in the specification of our model, for, as Morgan (1990, p. 182n) notes in respect of Tinbergen's work in the early 1930s:

> Tinbergen..., like all other econometricians of the period, wrote down his econometric models without error terms and made no explicit probabilistic statements about his estimation...

3.9.2 Method of averages

After suitable linearization, the demand equation in the simultaneous equations model was usually estimated in early studies by the method of ordinary least squares; although some authors preferred to use the method of averages and some the method of orthogonal least squares. We shall address the first of these alternative procedures here and the second in section 3.9.3. In his survey of early studies of consumer behaviour, George Stigler mentions two statistical demand curves obtained by two variants of the method of averages. In Stigler (1954, 1965, p. 219n), he notes that Rudolfo Benini (1907) estimated the demand for coffee using a straightforward application of the method of averages:

> Benini estimated the demand function for coffee in Italy, using data for 1880–81 to 1905–06. He ranked the years by price and then divided the data into a number of classes equal to the number of constants to be estimated and selected constants such that their function passed through the averages for the classes.

Three years later, Corrado Gini (1910) estimated demand functions for a number of goods, including that for tea in Great Britain, using a semi-log function borrowed from psychophysics: $q = a + b \log p$. Again, Stigler (1954; 1965, p. 220n) notes:

> The procedure was as follows: (i) Group the annual data into three to six classes to eliminate minor fluctuations; (ii) average the logarithms of price for each

class and average the corresponding quantities; (iii) calculate the mean deviations of the quantities and logarithms of prices; and (iv) determine the regression coefficient as

$$\frac{\textit{Mean deviation in consumption}}{\textit{Mean deviation of logarithms of price}}$$

Gini's procedure is clearly a generalization of the method of averages that is distinct from Thiele's (1897, 1903) method of normal places, which would have employed the method of least squares to obtain the regression coefficient from the grouped averages. Further, as both mean deviations would have taken zero values, it is presumed that the third stage of Gini's procedure must have been preceded by an intermediate step in which all equations with negative logarithm price deviations were negated. In connection with this, Morgan (1990, pp. 139–40) observes:

> Applied work carried out using these simple models and methods was generally thought successful. But the criteria for success in applied work were rather weak, economic-theoretic, rules rather than statistical ones. These rules involved some idea of "reasonableness." Initially this meant simply: is the estimated demand parameter negative and does it have a reasonable value? If the answers were yes, then the inference was that the "true" demand curve had been found. The problem of measuring demand curves was actually more complex, as quickly emerged in work by [Henry Ludwell] Moore, Marcel Lenoir and Robert Lehfeldt in the years 1913–14.
>
> Along with his "successful" ... work on agricultural goods, Moore (1914) estimated the demand curve for pig-iron (raw steel). He claimed to have found a brand new type of demand curve, namely the positively sloped demand curve applicable to all producer goods ... But his contemporaries thought the positive demand curve sufficiently "unreasonable" to reject it. A critical review by Lehfeldt (1915) suggested that Moore had estimated a supply curve for pig-iron because the data indicated a moving demand curve ... and a relatively stable supply curve; and P.G. Wright (1915) demonstrated the same point using a graph. Judged by the economic criteria, Moore's positive demand curve was unacceptable ...

Morgan (1990, pp. 153–7) has traced the gradual development of these early ideas on model specification and testing, culminating in the mid-1930s with the work of Ezekiel (1933), Gilboy (1932) and Whitman (1934). In particular, Morgan (1990, p. 157) remarks:

> With its primary emphasis on model specification and testing using statistical and model stability criteria, Whitman's [1934] article exemplifies the best of the 1930s' applied work. Although statistical tests were being gradually adopted in econometrics throughout the 1930s, there was variation in the tests carried out and no ground rules for reporting the results.

3.9.3 Orthogonal least squares

The two-variable orthogonal least squares problem was hardly new in the 1920s when Gini (1921), Schultz (1925), Ezekiel (1928) and, later, Gilboy (1932) had recommended it as a partial solution to the problem of simultaneity. Indeed, this fitting procedure had been proposed and solved in 1877–79 by R.J. Adcock and Charles Kummell, who are otherwise unknown to statistics. Furthermore, a multivariate version of this procedure was formulated and solved by Karl Pearson in 1901 and later developed as the basis of principal components analysis by Harold Hotelling in 1933. As Morgan (1990, p. 199) observes:

> The idea that inexact results were obtained because of the presence of mea-surement errors in the data was formally introduced into econometrics by Gini (1921) and more forcefully by Schultz (1925). Both writers also suggested using the orthogonal regression, ... Schultz (1928) noted that it made particular assumptions about the measurement errors which might not be correct. He also noted the problem of scale dependency and thought it made the orthogonal regression unreliable to use.

Despite these reservations regarding its practical utility, the orthogonal least squares procedure survived to appear in some of the leading econometrics texts of the 1960s and 1970s.

3.10   Data adjustment techniques

3.10.1   Data adjustment by link relatives and trend ratios

The econometricians of the early twentieth century did not simply apply their preferred fitting procedure to the data as given. Instead, they first attempted to sta-bilize the fitted relationship by correcting the data for any obvious trend. For example, Moore (1914) took first differences (which he called "link relatives") and ratios of prices and quantities to their trend values ("trend ratios"), before attempting to fit the relationship of interest. In this connection, Morgan (1990, p. 145) notes:

> Moore's work in this area proved influential. His data adjustment methods (link relatives and trend ratios) were naturally used by his disciple Henry Schultz, but they were adopted by many other econometricians, particularly in agricultural economics.

3.10.2   Frisch and Waugh's results

Schultz (1933) examined the three alternatives approaches to the estimation of the parameters of the demand equation of including a time trend, taking link relatives, or taking trend ratios. In a simulation study of the problem, he found that the three methods often gave similar results, although the link relative results some-times differed significantly from the other two. The same problem was examined theoretically by Frisch and Waugh (1933); their results are summarized by Aldrich 1998, p. 67) in the following terms:

> Frisch & Waugh (1933, p. 396)... remarked that the Gaussian algorithm is founded on successive bivariate regressions with residuals as variables... [so] there is no conflict between regression with de-trended data (least squares residuals) and regression with unadjusted data and time as an explicit regressor

Later in the same work, Aldrich (1998, p. 78) denigrates Davidson and MacKinnon's (1993, pp. 19–24) use of the phrase "Frisch–Waugh–Lovell theorem" to identify a generalization of Frisch and Waugh's results as it overemphasizes the contribution of Lovell (1963) to the total exclusion of those of Gauss, Laplace, Cauchy, Bienaymé and Yule. In this connection, see also Farebrother (1988, 1999).

3.11 More advanced estimation techniques

3.11.1 Instrumental variable estimation

A series of papers published in the early 1940s relate to the estimation of the parameters of the errors-in-equations and the errors-in-variables models. Working within the context of Frisch's concept of "confluence analysis" (see Frisch, 1934, or Hendry and Morgan, 1989), Reiersøl (1941) developed the idea of an estimator which incorporates observations on a set of additional "instrumental" variables. A similar idea was developed independently by Geary (1942, 1943) and, subsequently, the method of averages estimator proposed by Wald (1940) was identified as a type of instrumental variables estimator. In view of this familiar history, it is rather surprising to find that Morgan (1990, p. 178) has identified the concept of an instrumental variable estimator in Wright (1928):

> Wright's proposed alternative to data adjustment methods was to make direct use of additional factors in the estimation process... He demonstrated... how the additional factor (A), uncorrelated with supply but correlated with demand... could be used to find the elasticity of supply (and similarly how a supply factor (B), uncorrelated with shifts in demand, could be used to find the demand elasticity)... Wright... also showed that the method of path analysis,... developed by his son Sewall Wright, would give the same result as his instrumental variable method.

However, with the exception of Schultz (1928) and Wright (1928), path analysis was rarely applied in econometrics: see section 3.11.3 below.

3.11.2 Indirect and two-stage least squares

Nowadays, the fitting problems associated with the simultaneous equations model are usually solved by means of Reiersøl's (1941) method of instrumental variables or Hansen's (1982) generalized method of moments. The most familiar examples of these techniques include the two-stage least squares procedure of Basmann

(1957) and Theil (1961) and the indirect least squares procedure of Tinbergen (1930). In this connection, it is somewhat surprising to find that Tinbergen employed the "indirect least squares" procedure in the identification phase of his 1930 study, but reverted to ordinary ("direct") least squares to estimate the parameters of the structural model. Indeed, indirect least squares was not formally introduced into econometrics until after the probabilistic revolution of the 1940s.

In this context, the numerous variants of the method of averages proposed by Benini (1907), Yule (1925), Wald (1940), Bartlett (1949), Durbin (1954) and others, and the method of moments proposed by Pearson (1902), may be regarded as particular cases of the indirect least squares procedure. Similarly, the method of normal places discussed by Theile (1897, 1903) and Guest (1951, 1954) may be interpreted as early examples of the two-stage least squares procedure. However, it should be noted that all these identifications suffer from the formal defect that the instruments employed by the method of averages, the method of moments, and the method of normal places are fixed mathematical constants, whereas most present-day econometricians would reserve this term for instances in which at least some of the instruments are economic variables. But this consideration does not seem to have worried the econometricians of the early 1940s: see Morgan (1990, pp. 226–8).

3.11.3 Path analysis

In his biographical essay on Sewall Wright, Provine (2001, p. 16616), notes that:

> his major statistical contribution was developing the method of path analysis. This is a way of measuring the relative contribution of different causal paths to a quantity of interest, such as size or performance. This was presented in a diagram in which causal paths were designated by arrows and correlations by curved, two-headed arrows (Wright, 1921). A path coefficient, measuring the influence of a path, is a standardized partial regression coefficient. Wright formulated a set of simple rules that made the analysis easy to apply. This method enjoyed great popularity among livestock breeders, although recently it has been largely replaced by more sophisticated, computer-driven techniques that permit analysis of large bodies of data, and measurement of the precision of the estimates. The technique is most useful for nonexperimental situations and in recent years has found its greatest use in the social sciences [see Goldberger (1972)]. Wright himself used the method in the late [1910s] to analyse 510 correlations of 42 variables involving corn yields and prices and hog production. He could not get this monumental paper published because an animal husbandryman was not supposed to know about economics. It was not published until several years later [1925], and only after the intervention of Henry A. Wallace, son of the then [US] Secretary of Agriculture.

In passing, we note that Wallace was an early aficionado of machine computations. In 1925 he and George W. Snedecor published an article describing a variant of the Gauss–Doolittle procedure: see Grier (1999) for details.

3.12   Determinants and matrices in econometrics

Farebrother (1996, 1999) has identified several early statistical applications of the theory of determinants in papers published during the nineteenth century. For example, in 1841 Jacobi used the theory of determinants to obtain an explicit characterization of the solution to the linear least squares problem as a weighted sum of elemental set determinations. Aldrich (1998, p. 74) has supplied some more recent references:

> Determinants were used in other important work on least squares and corre-lation – including Pearson (1896), Fisher (1922), Frisch & Waugh (1933) and David & Neyman (1938). Yule [1907] did not use them but Pearson (1916) went on to obtain Yule's [correlation] results by "direct determinantal analysis," a task that required new results on determinants.

Thus, before the mid-1930s, statisticians seem to have employed determinants rather than matrices in their theoretical work. This statement would seem to be at variance with Magnello's (2001, p. 252) assertion that: "In this seminal paper on 'Regression, Heredity and Panmixia' in 1896, Pearson introduced matrix algebra into statistical theory," and again, Magnello (2001, p. 253): "The methodology incorporated in the Drapers' Biometric Laboratory [set up by Pearson in 1903]...included the use of Pearson's statistical methods, matrix algebra and analytical solid geometry..." Without checking the original source material, the books by Stigler (1986) and Hald (1998) do not seem to contain any evidence in support of Magnello's thesis. However, a passage from Hald (1998, p. 621) suggests that she may have used the phrase "matrix algebra" to refer to the determinantal analysis performed by Edgeworth (1893) and Pearson (1896) in their description of the multivariate normal distribution.

Thus, however near to the surface the elements of matrix algebra may seem to be in the work of Gauss, Cauchy, and Thiele (see Farebrother, 1999), it is evident that matrix theory did not feature in any statistical work published before 1930. The most familiar examples of such applications occur in the monograph by Turnbull and Aitken (1932) and in Aitken (1935) on the generalized least squares problem. Econometric applications followed some 15 years later in connection with work on the estimation of the simultaneous equations model: see Koopmans (1950) or Hood and Koopmans (1953) for details. From this substantial bridgehead, the role of matrix theory in econometrics and statistics rapidly increased as the mathe-matical requirements of the simultaneous equations model and multivariate analysis became apparent in the second half of the twentieth century.

3.13   Origins of modern econometrics

Finally, we must address the problem of identifying a possible starting date for "Modern Econometrics." Preliminary investigations suggest a date between the publication of the first volume of *Econometrica* in 1933 and that of the Cowles

Commission Monograph 10 in 1950. It is difficult to maintain the earlier date if we accept S.M. Stigler's (1999, chapter 8) use of the same date for the foundation of (modern) Mathematical Statistics. Particularly so, when we discover that Stigler's thesis is, in part, based on an analysis of an extensive econometric study by Secrist (1933) that is vitiated by his misunderstanding of the nature of regression analysis when this technique is applied to grouped data. For further information on the so-called "regression fallacy," see Friedman (1992) and Stigler (1999, chapter 9).

Moving the trial date forward to 1941 (when Haavelmo's (1944) paper was first distributed) is of no avail, as we recollect that this year also saw the publication of Davis' (1941b) textbook, which is hardly representative of "Modern Econometrics."

In view of these considerations, it seems appropriate to defer our proposed date for the foundation of modern econometrics until after the publication of Haavelmo's seminal paper in 1944. This is the date implicitly adopted by Morgan (1990) in her historical studies. A later date of, say, 1950 could still be justified as Tintner's (1952) textbook discusses both the old curve fitting methods and the maximum likelihood procedures characteristic of the early stages of "Modern Econometrics."

3.14 Concluding remarks

In this chapter, we have largely been concerned with the prehistory of the subject matter of chapters 6, 10, and 11. However, it should be pointed out that our principal historical references also contain material relevant to the contents of chapters 5, 16 and 27: for the early history of asymptotic methods and functional central limit theorems (particularly the early theory due to Laplace and Cauchy), see Hald (1998) and Stigler (1986); for an account of Jevons' sunspot theory and Moore's Venus theory, see Morgan (1990, chapter 1); and, for a description of the early techniques employed in the analysis of economic time series, see Morgan (1990, chapters 2–4) and Davis (1941a).

References

Aitken, A.C. (1935) On least squares and linear combination of observations. *Proceedings of the Royal Society of Edinburgh, Part A*, **55**, 42–7.

Aldrich, J. (1997) R.A. Fisher and the making of maximum likelihood 1912–22. *Statistical Science* **12**, 162–76.

Aldrich, J. (1998) Doing least squares: perspectives from Gauss and Yule. *International Statistical Review* **66**, 61–81.

Bartlett, M.S. (1949) Fitting a straight line when both variables are subject to error. *Biometrics* **5**, 207–12.

Basmann, R.L. (1957) A generalized classical method of linear estimation of coefficients in a structural equation. *Econometrica* **25**, 77–83.

Benini, R. (1907) Sull'uso delle formole empiriche nell'economia applicata. *Giornale degli Economisti, Series 2*, 35, 1053–1063.

Bose, S.S. (1938) Relative efficiencies of regression coefficients estimated by the method of finite differences. *Sankhyā* **3**, 339–46.

Bowley, A.L. (1902) Methods of representing the statistics of wages and other groups not fulfilling the normal law of error II: applications to wage statistics and other groups. *Journal of the Royal Statistical Society* **65**, 331–54.

Bowley, A.L. (1928) *F.Y. Edgeworth's Contributions to Mathematical Statistics*. London: The Royal Statistical Society. Reprinted by Augustus M. Kelley, Clifton, New Jersey, 1972.

Charnes, A., Cooper, W.W., Ferguson, R.O. (1955) Optimal estimation of executive compensation by linear programming. *Management Science* **1**, 138–51.

Cowles, A. (1933) Can stock market forecasters forecast? *Econometrica* **1**, 309–24.

Croxton, F.E., Cowden, D.J. (1939) *Applied General Statistics*. Englewood Cliffs, NJ: Prentice-Hall. (Second edition, Pitman, London, 1955.)

Dahlquist, G., Sjöberg, B., Svenssen, S. (1968) Comparison of the method of averages with the method of least squares. *Mathematics of Computation* **22**, 833–46.

Dale, A.I. (1991) *A History of Inverse Probability from Thomas Bayes to Karl Pearson*. New York: Springer-Verlag.

David, F.N. and J. Neyman (1938) Extension of the Markoff theorem on least squares. *Statistical Research Memoirs*, University College London, **2**, 105–16.

Davidson, R. and J.G. MacKinnon (1993) *Estimation and Inference in Econometrics*. Oxford: Oxford University Press.

Davis, H.T. (1941a) *The Analysis of Economic Time Series*. Bloomington, IN: Principia Press. Reprinted by Trinity University Press, San Antonio, Texas.

Davis, H.T. (1941b) *The Theory of Econometrics*. Bloomington, IN: Principia Press.

Davis, H.T. (1962) *The Adventures of an Ultra-Crepidarian*. San Antonio, Texas.

Durbin, J. (1954) Errors in variables. *Revue de l'Institut Internationale de Statistique* **22**, 23–32.

Edgeworth, F.Y. (1893) Note on the calculation of correlation between organs. *Philosophical Magazine, Series 5*, **36**, 350–1.

Edgeworth, F.Y. (1902) Methods of representing statistics of wages and other groups not fulfilling the normal law of error I: Mathematical considerations. *Journal of the Royal Statistical Society* **65**, 325–31.

Edgeworth, F.Y. (1923) On the use of medians for reducing observations relating to several quantities. *Philosophical Magazine, Series 6*, 46, 1074–1088.

Ezekiel, M. (1928) Statistical analyses and the "laws" of price. *Quarterly Journal of Economics* **42**, 199–227.

Ezekiel, M. (1933) Some considerations on the analysis of the prices of competing or substitute commodities. *Econometrica* **1**, 172–80.

Farebrother, R.W. (1985–87) The exact bias of Wald's estimator: problem and solution. *Econometric Theory* **1**, 419 and 3, 162.

Farebrother, R.W. (1988) *Linear Least Squares Computations*. New York: Marcel Dekker.

Farebrother, R.W. (1996) Some early statistical contributions to the theory and practice of linear algebra. *Linear Algebra and Its Applications* **237**, 205–24.

Farebrother, R.W. (1997) Notes on the early history of elemental set methods. In Y. Dodge (ed.), *L_1-Statistical Procedures and Related Topics*. Hayward, CA: Institute of Mathematical Statistics, pp. 161–70.

Farebrother, R.W. (1998) Nonlinear curve fitting and the true method of least squares. *The Statistician* **47**, 137–47.

Farebrother, R.W. (1999) *Fitting Linear Relationships: A History of the Calculus of Observations 1750–1900*. New York: Springer-Verlag.

Fisher, R.A. (1922) The goodness of fit of regression formulae, and the distribution of regression coefficients. *Journal of the Royal Statistical Society* **85**, 597–612.

Friedman, M. (1992) Do old fallacies ever die? *Journal of Economic Literature* **30**, 2129–2132.

Frisch, R. (1934) *Statistical Confluence Analysis by Means of Complete Regression Systems*. Oslo: Universitetets Okonomiske Institutt.

Frisch, R. and F.V. Waugh (1933) Partial time regressions as compared with individual trends. *Econometrica* **1**, 387–401.

Gauss, C.F. (1809) *Theoria Motus Corporum Coelestium in Sectionibus Conicis' Solem Ambientium.* Hamburg: F. Perthes and I.H. Besser. Reprinted in his *Werke,* vol. 7, F Perthes, Gotha. 1871. English translation by C.H. Davis, Little, Brown and Company, Boston, 1857. Reprinted by Dover, New York, 1963.

Geary, R.C. (1942) Inherent relations between random variables. *Proceedings of the Royal Irish Academy, Section A* **47**, 63–76.

Geary, R.C. (1943) Relations between statistics: The general and the sampling problem when the samples are large. *Proceedings of the Royal Irish Academy, Section A,* **49**, 177–96.

Gibson, W.M. and G.H. Jowett (1957a) Three-group regression analysis, 1: simple regression analysis. *Applied Statistics* **6**, 114–22.

Gibson, W.M. and G.H. Jowett (1957b) Three-group regression analysis, II: multiple regression analysis. *Applied Statistics* **6**, 189–97.

Gilboy, E.W. (1932) Studies in demand: milk and butter. *Quarterly Journal of Economics* **46**, 671–97.

Gini, C. (1910) Prezzi e consumi. *Giornale degli Economisti, Series 3,* **40**, 99–114 and 235–49.

Gini, C. (1921) Sull' interpolazione di una retta quando i valori della variabile indipendente so no affetti da errori accidentali. *Metron* **1**, 63–81.

Goldberger, A.S. (1972) Structural equation methods in the social sciences. *Econometrica* **40**, 979–1001.

Grier, D.A. (1999) Statistical laboratories and the origins of statistical computing. *Chance* **12**(2), 14–20.

Guest, P.G. (1951) The fitting of polynomials by the method of weighted grouping. *Annals of Mathematical Statistics* **22**, 537–48.

Guest, P.G. (1954) Group methods in the fitting of polynomials to equally spaced observations. *Biometrika* **41**, 62–76.

Haavelmo, T. (1944) The probability approach in econometrics. *Econometrica* **12**, Supplement, 1–118.

Hald, A. (1990) *A History of Probability and Statistics and Their Applications' Before 1750.* New York: Wiley.

Hald, A. (1998) *A History of Mathematical Statistics 1750–1930.* New York: Wiley.

Hansen, L.P. (1982) Large sample properties of generalized method of moments estimators. *Econometrica* **50**, 1029–1054.

Hendry, D.F. and M.S. Morgan (1989) A re-analysis of confluence analysis. *Oxford Economic Papers* **41**, 35–52.

Hendry, D.F. and M.S. Morgan (eds) (1995) *Foundations of Econometric Analysis.* Cambridge: Cambridge University Press. (Contains (English translations of) excerpts from Frisch (1934), Haavelmo (1944), Lenoir (1913), Tinbergen (1930), and a preview of Reiersøl (1945).)

Hood, W.C. and T.C. Koopmans (eds) (1953) *Studies in Econometric Methods.* New York: Wiley.

Hooper, J.W. and H. Theil (1958) The extension of Wald's method of fitting straight lines to multiple regression. *Revue de l'Institut Internationale de Statistique* **26**, 37–47.

Hotelling, H. (1927) Differential equations subject to error and population estimates. *Journal of the American Statistical Association* **22**, 283–314.

Hotelling, H. (1933) Analysis of a complex of statistical variables into principal components. *Journal of Educational Psychology* **24**, 417–41 and 498–520.

Huntington, E.V. (1924) Curve fitting by least squares and the method of moments. In Rietz, H.L. (ed.), *Handbook of Mathematical Statistics.* New York: Houghton Mifflin Company, pp. 62–70.

Koopmans, T.C. (ed.) (1950) *Statistical Inference in Dynamic Economic Models.* New York: Wiley.

Kuznets, S.S. (1930) *Secular Movements in Production and Prices.* Boston. Houghton Mifflin.

Lehfeldt, R. (1915) Review of Moore (1914). *Economic Journal* 25, 409–11.

Lenoir, M. (1913) *Etudes sur la Formation et le Mouvenent des Prix*. Paris: M. Giard et E. Brière.

Lovell, M.C. (1963) Seasonal adjustment of economic time series and multiple regression analysis. *Journal of the American Statistical Association* 58, 993–1010.

Magnello, M.E. (2001) Karl Pearson. In C.C. Heyde and E. Senata (eds), *Statisticians of the Centuries*. New York: Springer-Verlag, pp. 248–56.

Mills, F.C. (1938) *Statistical Methods Applied to Economic and Business*, revised edition. New York: Henry Holt and Company. (Third edition, Pitman, London, 1965.)

Moore, H.L. (1914) *Economic Cycles: Their Law and Cause*. New York: Macmillan.

Morgan, M.S. (1987) Statistics without probability and Haavelmo's revolution in econometrics. In L. Krüger, G. Gigerenzer and M.S. Morgan (eds), *The Probabilistic Revolution*, vol. II: Ideas in the Sciences. Cambridge, MA: MIT Press.

Morgan, M.S. (1990) *The History of Econometric Ideas*. Cambridge: Cambridge University Press.

Nair, K.R. (1954) The fitting of growth curves. In O. Kempthorne, T.A. Bancroft, J.W. Cowen and J.L. Lush (eds), *Statistics and Mathematics in Biology*. Ames, IA: Iowa State College Press.

Nair, K.R. and K.S. Bannerjee (1943) A note on fitting straight lines if both variables are subject to error. *Sankhyā* 6, 331.

Nair, K.R. and Shrivastava, M.P. (1942) On a simple method of curve fitting. *Sankhyā* 6, 121–32.

Oliver, F.R. (1964) Methods of estimating the logistic growth function. *Applied Statistics* 13, 57–66.

Oliver, F.R. (1966) Aspects of maximum likelihood estimation of the logistic growth function. *Journal of the American Statistical Association* 61, 697–705.

Oliver, F.R. (1969) Another generalisation of logistic growth functions. *Econometrica* 37, 144–7.

Oliver, F.R. (1982) Notes on the logistic curve for human populations. *Journal of the Royal Statistical Society, Series A*, 145, 359–63.

Pakes, A. (1982) On the asymptotic bias of Wald-type estimators of a straight line when both variables are subject to error. *International Economic Review* 23, 491–7.

Pearl, R. (1924) *Studies in Human Biology*. Baltimore: Williams and Wilkins.

Pearl, R. and L.J. Reed (1920) On the rate of growth of the population of the United States since 1790 and its mathematical representation. *Proceedings of the National Academy of Sciences* 6, 275–88.

Pearson, K. (1895) Contributions to the mathematical theory of evolution I: Skew variation in homogenous material. *Philosophical Transactions of the Royal Society* [of London], *Series A*, 186, 343–71.

Pearson, K. (1896) Mathematical contributions to the theory of evolution III: Regression, heredity and panmixia. *Philosophical Transactions of the Royal Society* [of London], *Series A*, 187, 253–318.

Pearson, K. (1901) On lines and planes of closest fit. *Philosophical Magazine, Series 6*, 2, 559–72.

Pearson, K. (1902) On the systematic fitting of curves to observations and measurements. *Biometrika* 1, 265–303.

Pearson, K. (1916) On some novel properties of partial and multiple correlation in a universe of manifold characteristics. *Biometrika* 11, 231–8.

Pearson, K. and L.N.G. Filon (1898) Mathematical contributions to the theory of evolution IV: On the probable errors of frequency constants and on the influence of random selection on variation and correlation. *Philosophical Transactions of the Royal Society* [of London], *Series A*, 191, 229–311.

Provine, W.B. (2001) Sewall Wright (1889–1988). In N.J. Smelser and P.B. Baltes (eds), *International Encyclopedia of the Social and Behavioral Sciences*. New York: Pergamon Press, pp. 16615–18.

Qin, D. (1996) Bayesian econometrics: the first twenty years. *Econometric Theory* 12, 500–16.

Reiersøl, O. (1941) Confluence analysis by means of lag moments and other methods of confluence analysis. *Econometrica* 9, 1–24.

Reiersøl, O. (1945) Confluence analysis by means of instrumental sets of variables. *Arkiv for Matematik, Astronomi och Fysik* **32A**(4), 1–119.

Rhodes, E.C. (1930) Reducing observations by the method of minimum deviations. *Philosophical Magazine, Series 7*, **9**, 974–92.

Rhodes, E.C. (1940) Population mathematics III. *Journal of the Royal Statistical Society* **103**, 362–87.

Rousseeuw, P.J. (1984) Least median of squares regression. *Journal of the American Statistical Association* **79**, 871–80.

Schultz, H. (1925) The statistical law of demand. *Journal of Political Economy* **33**, 481–504 and 577–637.

Schultz, H. (1928) *Statistical Laws of Demand and Supply with Special Application to Sugar.* Chicago: University of Chicago Press.

Schultz, H. (1930) The standard error of forecast from a curve. *Journal of the American Statistical Association* **25**, 139–85.

Schultz, H. (1933) A comparison of elasticities of demand obtained by different methods. *Econometrica* **1**, 274–308.

Schultz, H. (1938) *The Theory of Measurement of Demand.* Chicago: University of Chicago Press.

Secrist, H. (1933) *The Triumph of Mediocrity in Business.* Evanston, IL: Bureau of Business Research, Northwestern University.

Stigler, G.J. (1954) The early history of empirical studies of consumer behaviour. *Journal of Political Economy* **62**, 95–113. Reprinted in his *Essays in the History of Economics.* Chicago: University of Chicago Press, 1965, pp. 198–233.

Stigler, S.M. (1981) Gauss and the method of least squares. *Annals of Statistics* **9**, 465–74.

Stigler, S.M. (1986) *The History of Statistics: The Measurement of Uncertainty before 1900.* Cambridge, MA: Harvard University Press.

Stigler, S.M. (1999) *Statistics on the Table: The History of Statistical Concepts and Methods.* Cambridge, MA: Harvard University Press.

Taylor, L.D. (1974) Estimating by minimizing the sum of absolute errors. In P. Zarembka (ed.), *Frontiers of Econometrics.* New York: Wiley, pp. 169–90.

Theil, H. (1950) A rank-invariant method for linear and polynomial regression analysis. *Koninklijke Nederlands Akademie van Wetenschappen Proceedings, Part A*, **53**, 386–92, 521–5, 1397–1412.

Theil, H. (1961) *Economic Forecasts and Policy*, 2nd edition. Amsterdam: North-Holland.

Theil, H. and J. van Yzeren (1956) The efficiency of Wald's method of fitting straight lines. *Revue de l'Institut Internationale de Statistique* **24**, 17–26.

Theile, T.N. (1897) *Elementær Iagttagelseslære.* Copenhagen: Gyldendal.

Theile, T.N. (1903) *The Theory of Observations.* London: Layton. Reprinted in *Annals of Mathematical Statistics* **2** (1931), 165–308.

Tinbergen, J. (1930) Bestimmung und Deutung von Angebotskurven. *Zeitschrift für Nationalökonomie* **1**, 669–79. (English summary 798–99.)

Tintner, G. (1952) *Econometrics*, New York: Wiley.

Turnbull, H.W. and Aitken, A.C. (1932) *An Introduction to the Theory of Canonical Matrices.* Glasgow: Blackie. Reprinted by Dover, New York, 1961.

Verhulst, P.F. (1845) Rechérches mathématiques sur la loi d'accroissement de la population. *Nouveaux Mémoires de l'Académie Royale des Sciences et Belles Lettres de Bruxelles* **18**, 1–38.

Wald, A. (1940) The fitting of straight lines if both variables are subject to error. *Annals of Mathematical Statistics* **11**, 284–300.

Whitman, R.H. (1934) The problem of statistical demand techniques for producers' goods: An application to steel. *Journal of Political Economy* **42**, 577–94.

Wright, P.G. (1915) Review of Moore (1914). *Quarterly Journal of Economics* **29**, 631–41.

Wright, P.G. (1928) *The Tariff on Animal and Vegetable Oils.* New York: Macmillan.

Wright, S. (1921) Correlation and causation. *Journal of Agricultural Research* **20**, 557–85.

Wright, S. (1925) Corn and hog correlations. Bulletin No. 1300, Washington, DC: US Department of Agriculture.

Yule, G.U. (1907) On the theory of correlation for any number of variables, treated by a new system of notation. *Proceedings of the Royal Society* [of London], *Series A*, **79**, 182–93.

Yule, G.U. (1925) The growth of population and the factors which control it. *Journal of the Royal Statistical Society* **88**, 1–62.

4

The First Fifty Years of Modern Econometrics

Christopher L. Gilbert and Duo Qin

Abstract

We characterize modern econometrics in terms of the emergence of a widely accepted analytical framework. A major theme which dominated much of the debate through the century was whether and how econometric models can reflect theory-generated economic structures. In the period prior to World War II, economists adopted a wide variety of analytical methods, some *ad hoc* but others reflecting advances in statistical methodology. Business cycle analysis and demand analysis were the two major areas in which statistical theory was employed. Methods became increasingly formalized, but problems of data adequacy, estimation and identification were not always well distinguished. During and immediately after the war, Cowles Commission research sought to base econometrics on autonomous probabilistic models specified in terms of underlying structural parameters. Least squares would not normally be consistent in such models and maximum likelihood estimation was to be preferred. Subsequently, however, the pendulum swung back towards least squares-based methods and this was reflected in the textbook expositions of what was accepted as standard econometrics in the late 1960s and early 1970s. Later, the paradigm was undermined by the challenges imposed by rational expectations modeling, which challenged standard identification assumptions, and by the poor forecasting performance of many macroeconomic models by comparison with black box time series competitors. The result was a revival of non-structural modeling, particularly in the analysis of macroeconomic data.

4.1	Introduction	118
4.2	The rise of modern econometrics: the pre-1940 period	118
	4.2.1 Data-instigated analyses	119
	4.2.2 Theory-based investigations	120
	4.2.3 Exploration of statistical methods	121
	4.2.4 Theoretical innovations	122
	4.2.5 Methodological debates	124
	4.2.6 Summary	126
4.3	The formalization of econometrics: the 1940s	126
	4.3.1 Estimation	127
	4.3.2 Identification	129
	4.3.3 Model specification and the probability approach	130

4.3.4	Hypothesis testing	132
4.3.5	Summary	132
4.4	The emergence of standard regression-based econometrics	133
4.4.1	The fall and rise of least squares	133
4.4.2	Residual serial correlation and equation dynamics	136
4.4.3	Consolidation and dissemination	137
4.5	Paradigm lost	139
4.5.1	The rise of Bayesian econometrics	140
4.5.2	The rise of theory-led dynamic models	141
4.5.3	Microeconometrics	142
4.5.4	Data-based modeling again	143
4.6	Final comment	145

4.1 Introduction

In this chapter, we characterize modern econometrics in terms of the emergence of a widely accepted standard framework in which economic data can be analyzed and on the basis of which subsequent methodological developments would take place. We argue that it was only in the mid-1960s that this framework came into existence. On that basis, the first fifty years of modern econometrics, interpreted as the period in which the framework was being generated, starts around the time of World War I. This seems right – it is possible to find precursors of modern methods prior to 1914, but they were isolated, had relatively little influence and did not constitute a movement.

From the mid-1960s onwards, econometrics was established and accepted as a discipline in its own right. Advances in computer technology and software, together with the availability of larger and higher quality data sets, eliminated most computational constraints and permitted real advances. These produced solid dividends in microeconometrics, but less so in the analysis of aggregate macroeconomic time series. The greater diversity apparent over the final three decades of the century demonstrates a new maturity in the discipline.

4.2 The rise of modern econometrics: the pre-1940 period

At the start of the twentieth century, there were no generally accepted and established paradigms for synthesizing data evidence and theory. Various mathematical and statistical methods were employed, economic postulates were rearticulated in mathematical equations, different approaches were tried and debated, and new concepts and new schemes were proposed. However, all of these activities took place in a relatively unstructured environment, both conceptually and geographically. For these reasons, it is difficult to discuss the literature from this period in a systematic and comprehensive manner.[1] In what follows, we consider a selected group of influential works from this period under five interrelated topics: data-instigated analyses, theory-based investigations, theoretical inventions, pursuit of new statistical methods, and methodological debates.

4.2.1 Data-instigated analyses

A major area where data-instigated attempts thrived was business cycle analysis. However, these undertakings adopted different perspectives and served different purposes. This contrast is evident in a comparison of the contemporaneous analyses of Moore (1914) and Persons (1916, 1919), which come right at the start of our fifty-year period.

Moore (1914) was interested in the question of whether there was a regular length to business cycles. He related the observed cyclical patterns in grain yields and price data to cyclical climatic conditions, such as those observed in rainfall data. The methods that he used were periodograms and Fourier frequency analysis. These helped Moore to arrive at a general causal explanation of business cycles and to an estimate of an eight-year per cycle average length; but such a partial explanation was obviously too naïve to capture the distinct irregularities in business fluctuations. Persons (1916, 1919) was both more ambitious and more practical. His attempts to forecast short-run business cycle movements entailed more intensive data analysis. Persons classified the forces he saw as the causes of economic data fluctuations into four types: secular (long-term) forces, seasonal forces, cyclical forces and accidental (irregular) forces. He first attempted to filter out the trend (secular) element from time series data by the methods of moving averages and curve fitting. He then used seasonal median values to remove any obvious seasonal patterns. The remaining cyclical and irregular patterns in the filtered data were the focus of Persons' attention. He found it very difficult to distinguish between these two types of forces. Instead, he attempted to construct, out of numerous detrended and seasonally adjusted time series, a few composite indices which would "epitomize," and even lead, the general business situation. These indices formed the basis of what became known as Harvard ABC barometers (e.g., Samuelson, 1987). However, the barometers did not correspond to any economic causes of the cycles in spite of their practical appeal. Clearly, Persons was much more interested in how economic time series behave than in testing or measuring theories.

Data-instigated investigations also emerged in other areas of economics. For example, Bowley (1933) examined the statistical distributions of a number of very different economic time series, including changes in wholesale and retail prices and in household income. He attempted to relate departures from normality to specific economic factors. Around the same time, Working (1935) examined wholesale wheat prices with the objective of learning how commodity futures prices respond to the impact of multiple factors under "laws of dynamic equilibrium." He related spot-futures differentials (premia or backwardations) in the Chicago wheat market to inventories and storage availability. He also showed how Chicago spot prices reacted to shocks from the US wheat market, to shocks originating in other US markets and to shocks originating from abroad (specifically from the Liverpool market). Working's research anticipates methods which have since become standard in financial econometrics.

The mid-1930s saw the impact of newly formed statistical inference procedures, specifically deriving from the work of R.A. Fisher, but also from J. Neyman and

E.S. Pearson. The result was a subtle translation from a search for economic "laws" or regularities to a framework based on hypothesis testing.

Coase and Fowler's (1937) study of the pig cycle serves as an interesting illustration. They set out to test whether the widely used cobweb model adequately described pig cycles by positing the model as the null hypothesis, but their data analyses generated results that rejected the model. In an effort to provide an alternative hypothesis, they discovered that expectations of future pork prices "must be considered as independent variables determining the demand in the same way as actual prices." As well as constituting a pioneering economic application of the new Neyman–Pearson methodology, this was a clear precursor of more recent expectations-based modeling.

Perhaps the most ambitious attempt to use data evidence to test theories, treated as hypotheses rather than laws, was carried out by J. Tinbergen for the League of Nations in the late 1930s. Haberler (1937) had already undertaken an extensive survey of various business-cycle theories. At Haberler's request, Tinbergen's task was to carry out statistical tests of these theories. This resulted in Tinbergen's (1939) monumental business-cycle volume (see also Morgan, 1990, chapter 4), in which state of the art econometrics was used and which showed a clear move of econometric practice away from a data-led to a theory-led approach (see subsection 4.2.5).

In summary, the interwar period saw an exploration of new methods and a gradual move toward theory-driven explanations in what remained an applied (forecasting and policy) orientated environment.

4.2.2 Theory-based investigations

Turning now to theory-based studies, most of these are clustered in consumption and demand analyses, where theory was well-developed and widely accepted. Applied work was therefore able to focus on parameter measurement. The main obstacle encountered in these studies was the *ceteris paribus* gap between theory and data.

An early pioneer of statistical demand studies using price (p) and quantity (q) time series data was H.L. Moore. For each commodity, Moore (1914, 1925) used ordinary least squares to estimate two regressions: $p_t = \alpha_0 + \alpha_1 q_t$, which he interpreted as the demand relation, and $q_t = \beta_0 + \beta_1 p_{t-1}$, which he interpreted as the supply relation.[2] Implicitly, the *ceteris paribus* condition is supposed to be satisfied through prior detrending of price and quantity data. Moore was led to believe that he had discovered a new type of demand curve when he obtained positive parameter estimates from his demand regression for some producer goods. His claim prompted discussions on how to empirically distinguish a demand curve from a supply curve using time series data sets: see subsection 4.2.5 below.

Lehfeldt (1914) focused explicitly on the *ceteris paribus* requirements in his estimate of the price elasticity of demand for wheat. He adjusted his data to make them as consistent as possible with the theoretical definition of the elasticity. The quantity series was standardized by population to remove population growth effects and the price series was adjusted to remove the impact of possible supply-side dynamic shocks. The elasticity estimate was finally obtained not by regression, but by taking the ratio of standard deviations of the logs of the pre-adjusted quantity to price series.

These two cases define the extremes. The bulk of demand studies combined adjusted data with interpretations of theory adapted according to the purposes of the studies. This is best seen from Tinbergen's (1930) ingenious study of supply curves. He tackled the problem of differentiating between supply and demand curves by adding different explanatory variables to the demand and supply equations respectively, e.g., a variable measuring the domestic stock of the commodity was added to the demand equation and the quantity supplied from abroad to the supply equation. He also used a time dummy to detrend the price series, rather than detrending prior to regression. Finally, he derived and estimated the reduced form before inferring the demand and supply coefficients indirectly, a technique which subsequently came to be known as Indirect Least Squares (ILS).

Flexible adaptation of theories, data and regression functional forms is quite commonly seen with early practitioners. For example, Staehle (1937, 1938) experimented with a consumption function, estimated on German quarterly time series data, which explained retail sales by real labor income both with and without an additional variable measuring income inequality. Dirks (1938) proposed an alternative, nonlinear, regression explaining the change of retail sales by the lagged change of income. Clark (1938) used both current and lagged income variables to estimate the UK consumption function, again on quarterly data. Stone and Stone (1938) experimented with a variety of functional forms, including log-linear, log-quadratic and with additional time trends when regressing aggregate consumption on income using both time series and cross-section data sets.[3]

To summarize, the *ceteris paribus* gap between received theory and data was often too wide for empirical studies to be anchored directly in theory. This posed the question of whether theory was to be regarded as immutable, indicative or inadequate? Furthermore, what criteria should one use to judge the empirical results: economic or statistical? Although the main purpose of demand and consumption studies was the measurement of elasticities and multipliers, these studies threw up new methods of data and inference, in particular in relation to the issues of identification and multicollinearity.

4.2.3 Exploration of statistical methods

At the start of the twentieth century, simple correlation, basic descriptive statistics and regression were known and widely used by the small number of quantitatively-oriented economists. The need for new statistical methods gradually arose from a number of empirical attempts to fill the gaps between data and theory. Early innovations were proposed as *ad hoc* methods to handle particular problems. For example, Wright (1928) came up with the idea of the instrumental variable (IV) method for the purpose of circumventing the simultaneity problem between demand and supply. Wright saw the need for using extra information and demonstrated how to get both demand and supply curves by using an additional factor uncorrelated with supply but correlated with demand, and vice versa. Handling the same simultaneity problem, Tinbergen (1930) derived the ILS method for estimating his simultaneous equations supply and demand model: see section 4.2.2.

Concerns over measurement errors in variables were a dominant theme in the interwar period and these often motivated questions about the appropriate direction for regression. Both Gini (1921) and Schultz (1925) proposed orthogonal regression to estimate what are now referred to as errors-in-variables models. Similarly, Frisch (1929) developed diagonal mean regression as a solution for choosing the bivariate regression direction. The 1930s saw more concerted attempts to devise universally applicable statistical tools for economic data analysis. Frisch (1934b) invented the method of bunch map analysis in an attempt to resolve the problem of non-unique relationships holding simultaneously among a set of variables all subject to measurement errors (see Hendry and Morgan, 1989). Roos (1937) and Koopmans (1937)[4] advocated the explicit use of statistical optimality criteria in choosing estimation methods and devised general forms of weighted regression as the best estimators for error-in-variables regression models. Koopmans based his derivation on the maximum likelihood (ML) principle (see Qin, 1993, chapter 3). His analysis paved the way for the systematic adoption of formal statistical criteria in what would become known as econometric inference.

Active interchanges between pioneering econometricians and statisticians, as well as applied researchers in other disciplines, resulted in recently invented statistical methods becoming known and used in economic analyses. For example, Philip Wright (1928) introduced path analysis, which had been invented by his son, Sewall, for use in genetics, for causal chain determination of prices and quantities of agricultural products.[5] The early econometricians also quickly became aware of the new methods of principle components and canonical correlation invented by Hotelling (1933, 1936) in the context of factor analysis models applied to psychological data (see Koopmans, 1937), though applications were not reported until the 1940s: see Waugh (1942) and Stone (1947). Interestingly, these methods subsequently faded from econometric practice, although they have now re-emerged in the context of cointegration analysis and leading indicator models.

In summary, we can see a steady process of formalization gathering place over the interwar period such that econometric methods were becoming more obviously based on clear statistical foundations while, at the same time, there was an openness to comparable developments taking place in other disciplines.

4.2.4 Theoretical innovations

The need for a general and appropriate mathematical apparatus to help conceptualize and describe economic dynamics, together with the difficulty of constructing such an apparatus, became increasingly clear in the initial decades of the century. The initial approach was to describe business cycles in terms of Fourier series based on periodic analyses of time series data, as in Moore (1914).

The apparatus quickly came to be regarded as unhelpful due to its lack of foundation in economic theory and the difficulties in adapting it to account for the erratic features of economic data.[6] The method was further discredited by Yule's (1927) investigation of the impact of random shocks on time series, which showed that cycles might be the result of sizeable shocks (or errors), rather than regular cyclical factors, which, on this view, would no longer be identifiable from the data.

Subsequent attempts mainly used difference equations or mixed difference and differential equations. This could be traced to the influential works of Yule (1927) and Slutsky (English translation 1937).[7] Yule argued that it was more straightforward to represent random time series by autoregressive equations in the time domain than in the frequency domain. Slutsky postulated that the observed cyclical time series data were generated by a summation of random shocks and hence could be represented by a moving average model of random errors. These ideas were combined in Frisch's (1933a) macrodynamic model. Frisch deplored the absence of any element of structural explanation in Yule and Slutsky's time series models. He rejected the decomposition of economic time series into trend, cyclical, seasonal and erratic shock components as "mechanical." In his view, the macrodynamics of economic time series could be characterized by the combination of a *propagation* mechanism and *impulse* shocks. To establish the propagation mechanism, one should start from a dynamically formulated economic model, i.e., a model which contains economically interpretable lagged (or leading) variables in the form of mixed difference and differential equations and then augment this by random shocks.[8] Frisch's programme evolved into a fuller agenda for econometric research which later became known as the structural approach: see Frisch (1937) and Bjerkholt (2005). His approach was tried out and popularised by Tinbergen's practical modeling work, first in the Dutch model (see Tinbergen, 1936, English translation 1959, and Morgan, 1990, chapter 4), and then in the US model for the League of Nations (Tinbergen, 1939).

The problems of how to characterize economic time series were discussed from a somewhat different angle by Wald (1936).[9] Wald refers to as "internal" the definition of components of time series in terms of "unequivocal functions of the original data," e.g., trend, cycle, seasonal and erratic shocks, as opposed to the "external definition," which relates the time series to a set of *a priori* postulated economic causes. After pondering over various difficulties in starting the analysis from the theory-led "external" definitions, Wald concluded that the only fruitful approach is to start from the data-led "internal" definitions and to try to establish how "the internal components correspond with the equivalent external components." Technically, Wald's internal definition was strengthened by Wold's (1938) rigorous formulation of random time series decomposition on the basis of probability theory and stochastic distribution theorems.[10] Methodologically, however, Wald's ideas were overshadowed by Frisch's (1937, 1938) persuasive argument for the structural approach,[11] until they were subsequently incorporated into Burns' and Mitchell's (1946) methods for measuring business cycles (e.g., Morgenstern, 1961) and, much later, in the general-to-specific dynamic modeling approach (e.g., Hendry, 1995).

Toward the late 1930s, concerns over the economic foundation of applied econometric modeling had already come to dominate those relating to the dynamic characterization of time series decompositions: see Qin (1993, chapter 2). Empirical examination of time series properties were reduced to an intermediate step prior to the derivation and estimation of structural time series models, known as the "final equations" following Tinbergen (1939). Theoretical studies of the economic dynamics of Frisch's (1933a) model were pursued by James and Belz (1936, 1938) and Koopmans (1940), who used periodic analysis to examine the cyclical and dynamic features of the estimated final equations. However, this approach faded in importance as a consequence of the probability revolution associated with the publication of Haavelmo (1944) (see section 4.3), which advocated a complete reformulation of structural models in terms of stochastic variables instead of a deterministic system of differential/difference equations augmented by random errors. The frequency domain method largely disappeared in econometrics until the 1960s: see section 4.5.4.

In summary, the interwar period provides evidence of an increasing separation between the macroeconomic and econometric approaches to business cycle analysis. Theory formulation came to be delegated to economists, leaving econometricians with the task of specifying and estimating the structural model. Data-led considerations of economic dynamics became marginalized by theoretical worries about simultaneity and static equilibrium.

4.2.5   Methodological debates

Methodological debates promote and enliven the development of science and econometrics is no exception in this regard. As illustrated in the previous sections, the early econometricians adopted different approaches and methods in exploring ways of theorizing and modeling data evidence. Arguments and debates over the relative merits of these different choices were unavoidable.

An early and important issue for debate originated from regression-based demand analysis. The methodological issue is whether and how one can be sure that the regression results correspond to demand curves. Lehfeldt and Wright immediately noted that the positive curve estimated by Moore (1914) was much more likely to be a supply curve than a demand curve: see Morgan (1990, chapter 5) and Hendry and Morgan (1995, part 3). This raised awareness of the substantial data–theory gap. Different opinions were put forward as to the main causes of the gap. For example, Working (1927) believed that lack of information was the main culprit in preventing modelers from identifying the theoretical curves of demand and supply, whereas Ezekiel (1928) argued that the bivariate static demand equation was only part of the correct theoretical model of demand (i.e., the correct model should contain other economic factors). Correspondingly, different solutions were proposed: either by pre-adjusting data to bring them closer to theory, by augmenting theory to bring it closer to data, or by choosing statistical concepts or tools thought to be appropriate to theoretical requirements.

The famous "pitfalls" debate between Leontief and Frisch, published in the *Quarterly Journal of Economics* in the early 1930s,[12] largely turns on the validity of

Leontief's identification of economic theory with the statistical assumption of independence between the error terms of the demand and supply equations: see Hendry and Morgan (1995, introduction and chapter 22). For Frisch, this identification was misleading, as the two error terms were unlikely to correspond purely to independent demand and supply shocks. The debate was closely related to the issue of how applied modelers should conceptualize the error terms: whether they were measurement errors or errors in equations and, if the latter, whether they were not further decomposable to allow for augmented theoretical models.[13] The issue was also related to the appropriate choice of estimation method, e.g., whether OLS was adequate rather than, say, weighted least squares.

Pre-adjustment of data was a commonly used practice to try and bring data closer to a controlled experiment environment where theories were normally postulated, i.e., under the *ceteris paribus* condition. For example, Moore and his student, Schultz, insisted that modelers should use detrended data to ensure sufficient dynamic variation to capture the underlying static demand and/or supply curves: see Schultz (1925, 1928). Prior detrending of the data was opposed by Smith (1925) and Ferger (1932): see Morgan (1990, chapter 5). However, Frisch and Waugh (1933) pointed out that the regression coefficients of a model of two level variables plus a linear time trend and a model of the two variables pre-adjusted by removing from each a linear trend were actually identical. They argued that what was crucial was to have an explicit *a priori* "structural" model to enable applied modelers to interpret their statistical results in as close a correspondence as possible to the structural model.

Frisch (1937) elaborated on the idea of starting empirical modeling from a structural model in an "ideal program" that he sketched at the European Meeting of the Econometric Society in 1936 (see also Frisch, 1938). It took a certain amount of persuasion before his program became the accepted econometric approach. As shown in previous sections, the early econometricians chose various ways of bridging data and theory, some following a more theory-led approach while others were more data oriented. Tinbergen (1935), for example, favored the data-led approach, which he referred to as the "historical" method and which he contrasted to the theory-led "structural" method. At that time, his view was that available theories were generally inadequate to explain the data to hand. However, he reversed his position in the late 1930s and endorsed Frisch's structural approach (see Qin, 1993, chapter 2).

A major factor that helped to unite Tinbergen and other econometricians under Frisch's structural approach was the skepticism of non-econometric economists in relation to the scientific validity of the nascent econometric methods. This scepticism was powerfully expressed by Keynes (1939, 1940) in his critique of Tinbergen's approach to testing business cycle theories: see also Tinbergen (1940). The issues of the debate were so fundamentally important for econometricians that Frisch (1938) and Marschak and Lange (1940) joined ranks with Tinbergen in vehemently defending the new discipline.[14] The debate was also a motivation for Haavelmo's comprehensive exposition of the foundations of econometrics (see section 4.5).

4.2.6   Summary

By the end of the 1930s, econometrics had already grown into a vibrant enterprise. A great deal of the available raw material had been studied and tried out. What remained absent was a coherent and unified view of the econometric program which could be accepted by practitioners and understood by the rest of the economics profession. The Keynes–Tinbergen debates emphasized this requirement. Moreover, there was an impetus to standardize econometric practice with a strong reliance on economics and to get econometrics recognised as a subdiscipline of economics. From a practical standpoint, and aside from the impact of Keynes' criticism, there were worries in relation to the dangers of nonsense and spurious regressions, illustrated by Yule (1926, 1927). Further, Tinbergen's (1939, 1940) modeling highlighted the potential role of models in policy analysis, as distinct from just out-of-sample forecasting. Policy analysis entails the construction of autonomous structural models, e.g., see Frisch (1938) and Marschak and Lange (1940). However, the type of macrodynamic model explored by Frisch and Tinbergen was criticized for not being sufficiently theoretical by comparison with the approach of the dynamically extended Walrasian system advocated by Hicks.[15] These and other considerations reinforced the perceived need to strengthen Frisch's structural approach to modeling.

4.3   The formalization of econometrics: the 1940s[16]

The formalization of Frisch's structural approach took place during World War II, largely in the US. The war itself was important for the development of econometrics in two distinct respects. First, and paradoxically, it served to bring many of the early econometricians together. As the Nazi onslaught closed down normal academic discourse in Continental Europe, many active European econometricians sought refuge in the United States. The effect was to bring together the European scholars, coming from different traditions, both with other European econometricians and also with American statisticians and econometricians. For example, Haavelmo, who came to Harvard from occupied Norway, where he had studied under Frisch, was apparently converted to probabilistic reasoning by contact with Neyman, who was of Romanian origin and who had arrived at Columbia via Vienna (Morgan, 1990, p. 242).

The Cowles Commission (henceforth, CC) played an important role in this process (see Epstein, 1987). Founded in Colorado Springs in 1932, it moved to Chicago in 1939. US entry into the war in 1942 resulted in many key staff leaving. Marschak, who came via Oxford from the Marxist school of German economics, was appointed director the same year. Hurwicz (Polish origin), Lange (Polish) and Koopmans (Dutch, director of the CC from 1948) were among other Europeans recruited to the CC by Marschak. Haavelmo was invited as a consultant. Prominent Americans who joined the CC included Anderson, Arrow, Christ, Mosak, Klein and Simon (see Christ, 1952).

The second respect in which the war facilitated econometrics is that it established an economic policy environment which favored and even required active government. This was true at the macroeconomic level, where there was now general acceptance of the need for fiscal activism to maintain full employment, but also in the wartime and postwar regimes of regulated prices. As Epstein (1987) observes, price controls required knowledge of industry cost curves and even demand elasticities. Marschak saw econometrics as an instrument for "social engineering," a phrase which was later softened to the analysis of "rational eco-nomic policy," where rational was taken to imply statistically-based (see Epstein, 1987, pp. 61–2). Those European econometric refugees to the United States who came from socialist or social democratic backgrounds made an easy transition to working on the technocratic implementation of the New Deal policies.

The formalization of econometrics was mainly carried out at the CC under the leadership of, first, Marschak and, subsequently, Koopmans, with much of the work undertaken by Haavelmo and Koopmans. Under Frisch's dominating influ-ence (see, e.g., Bjerkholt, 2005), Haavelmo laid the groundwork for shaping econometrics into a more systematic discipline within economics (see, especially, Haavelmo, 1944). His work was further elaborated and standardized by the CC, culminating in the famous monographs 10 (Koopmans, 1950) and 14 (Hood and Koopmans, 1953). The formalization involved systematizing econometric procedures in model specification, estimation, identification and testing within the paradigm of a stochastic framework. The baseline economic model was the dynamic Walrasian general equilibrium system, i.e., a dynamic, simultaneous-equations model (SEM):

$$A_0 x_t + A_1 x_{t-1} + \cdots + A_m x_{t-m} = u_t \qquad (4.3.1)$$

where x_t is a vector of all the relevant variables of an economy, u_t a vector of random disturbances, and the As are structural parameter matrices to be estimated, with A_0 a non-diagonal matrix, thus allowing the possibility of simultaneity.

4.3.1 Estimation

The early econometricians were already aware that the least squares estimation method had to be adapted in accordance with the assumptions made about the error terms in a regression model (see section 4.2.3 above). For example, when the two variables in a bivariate regression were both subject to errors, weighted least squares should be used instead of OLS. Statistical optimality criteria were also brought in during the late 1930s (e.g., by Koopmans, 1937) as explicit yardsticks for choosing estimators. Research on estimation methods during the 1940s emphasized the importance of combining these two concerns in choosing esti-mators, i.e., estimators should be contingent on model formulation, especially on the error term specification, as well as on statistical optimality. As nonlinear estimators became the principal choice, this research opened up a new dimension: how to adapt the estimation procedure to ease the computational burden.

Haavelmo (1943) was influential in the development of estimation methods for the SEM.[17] Haavelmo demonstrated that the OLS parameter estimates of an SEM, when extended with error terms in equations, are inconsistent. Such systematic inconsistency became known as the "Haavelmo bias." Haavelmo showed that, if this inconsistency is to be corrected, it is necessary to consider the joint distributions of the variables in the stochastic SEM, a direction which would lead to the maximum likelihood principle.

Haavelmo's advocacy of ML estimators in the SEM context raised questions about the statistical properties of these estimators. A significant statistical extension of Haavelmo's work was carried out by Mann and Wald (1943), who provided proofs of the consistency and asymptotic normality of the ML estimators of a linear, stochastic difference equation system with normally distributed errors. Mann and Wald also showed that certain *a priori* restrictions would be required on the closed SEM system (4.3.1) to achieve unique estimates, a condition linked to the issue of identification. They demonstrated this point by transforming the SEM into what they called the "reduced form" of the model (a term which is now commonly accepted):

$$x_t = (-A_0^{-1}A_1)x_{t-1} + \cdots + (-A_0^{-1}A_m)x_{t-m} + (-A_0^{-1})u_t$$
$$= \Pi_1 x_{t-1} + \cdots + \Pi_m x_{t-m} + \varepsilon_t \qquad (4.3.2)$$

Their derivation provides a formalization of Tinbergen's (1930) ILS procedure.

Mann and Wald's work was pursued further by Koopmans and the CC group in three directions (see Koopmans, 1950).[18] The first was to extend the closed SEM to an open SEM and thus allow the presence of exogenous variables. Business cycle research during the 1930s had encouraged the extension of the closed system (4.3.2) to an open one in this way, with the vector of variables x_t being classified into a subset of endogenous variables y_t and a second subset of exogenous variables z_t:

$$B_0 y_t + B_1 y_{t-1} + \cdots + B_m y_{t-m} = \Gamma_0 z_t + \Gamma_1 z_{t-1} + \cdots + \Gamma_m z_{t-m} + u_t \qquad (4.3.3)$$

with its reduced form:

$$y_t = P_1 y_{t-1} + \cdots + P_m y_{t-m} + Q_0 z_t + \cdots + Q_m z_{t-m} + \varepsilon_t \qquad (4.3.4)$$

The second extension was to separate the issue of whether a set of structural parameters is uniquely estimable from that of the choice of estimator (see section 4.3.2).

The third extension was to search for a simpler calculation procedure, as the ML estimator was nonlinear and entailed a high computational burden for any reasonably sized SEM at a time when only hand calculators were available. This led to the development of limited information ML (LIML) estimators, which concentrated the likelihood function with respect to parameters in other equations to allow estimation of only those parameters in the equation of interest. The original system ML estimator was now termed full information ML (FIML).

The discovery of the LIML method was apparently initiated by Girshick, who sent a letter to the CC in 1945 proposing to estimate, for simplicity, an SEM from its reduced form first and then solve back for the structural estimates: see Epstein (1987, 1989). This idea was quickly extended and formalized by Anderson and Rubin (1949) in the form of the LIML estimator. It is possible that LIML is the "black magic" estimator hinted at by Girshick in his 1945 letter (see Malinvaud, 1983, and Epstein, 1989).

To summarize, work under the leadership of the CC established a new paradigm in terms of estimation methods and statistical rigour, explicitly linked on the one hand to model specification and identification conditions and, on the other, to practical concerns about computability.

4.3.2 Identification

The formalization of identification conditions, as taught in present-day econometrics textbooks, plays an essential role in the formalisation of econometrics as a subdiscipline of economics. Although the early econometricians developed *ad hoc* methods for tackling the identification problem in the 1920s and 1930s, it was not until the beginning of the 1940s that the problem was separated from estimation issues and clearly formulated in mathematical and statistical terms.

In Frisch's initial attempt to formalize the structural approach (see, e.g., Frisch, 1938), the correspondence issue stood out, i.e., how a modeler could get the appropriate statistical econometric model which corresponds to an *a priori* formulated structural model. Frisch saw the correspondence problem as arising out of limited data information. In practical terms, Frisch proposed checking the rank condition of the data matrix relating to the structural variables. However, from a modern viewpoint, Frisch's discussion of the correspondence problem muddles issues of identification with those of multicollinearity and estimability.

Identification became more clearly isolated from these other issues through discussion of the general conditions under which the structural parameters of an SEM can be uniquely determined. For example, Marschak (1942; written in 1940) distinguished two aspects of identification: one of "variate parameters," i.e., the issue of deciding which equation in an SEM possesses relatively stable parameters, and the other of "lost dimensions," i.e., the condition under which those stable parameters are estimable. He also represented the condition in terms of a rank check, via a non-vanishing Jacobian determinant.[19] Haavelmo (1940, 1944) provided a more focused representation. He described identification as one of the two key issues in structural parameter estimation, namely that of how to establish sufficient conditions for the unique estimability of structural parameters using the available data (the other being the issue of how to choose the "best" estimators). Technically, he also followed the idea of rank checking using Jacobian determinants.

The clear demonstration of the relationship between the SEM and its reduced form in Mann and Wald (1943) demonstrated that the classic identification problem was generic to the SEM type of model. This led to subsequent formalization work by the CC. The group separated out identification as a logically independent step lying between model specification and estimation. They introduced two additional clarifications: the requirement for additional restrictions to allow the determination of structural parameters in the SEM and the need for data variability to guarantee that these parameters can, in fact, be determined from a given sample. These two aspects were represented by the now familiar rank (necessity) and order (sufficiency) conditions in terms of the Bs and Γs of (4.3.3): see the paper by Koopmans, Rubin and Leipnik in Koopmans (1950).

The rank condition also helped the group to classify three types of state: unique identification, over-identification and under-identification (see the paper by Hurwicz in Koopmans, 1950), and to the design of over-identification tests (see Anderson and Rubin, 1950). Subsequently, Koopmans and Reiersøl (1950) extended the identification conditions to errors-in-variables models. The CC research programme on identification provided the paradigm for later research on parameter identifiability for models of other classes.

Technical clarification of the identification conditions as a separate modeling step also stimulated further conceptual explication of this step in relation to structural model formulation, specifically to the issues of exogeneity and causality. Koopmans explored the link between identifying conditions and the need for exogenous variables under the question "When is an equation system complete for statistical purposes?" (Koopmans, 1950, chapter 17).[20] His discussion drew on issues of how to test the validity of an assumed exogenous conditioning and on the limits to the statistical testability of certain causal implications of a structural SEM. It also touched on the weakness of statistical methods in helping model choice.

The link between identifiability and causality was exhaustively examined by Simon (1953, 1955), who attempted to formalize the idea of causal ordering to justify asymmetric static relationships, in particular exogeneity in the context of an SEM, as distinct from causal asymmetry in the time dimension (such as lagged input causing current output). This conceptual aspect of identification has aroused recurrent controversy. Wold challenged the clarity of the causal formulation of a general, unidentifiable SEM, preferring to rationalize exogeneity in terms of a causal chain (see Wold and Juréen, 1953). Orcutt (1952), and later Liu (1960), criticized the arbitrariness of exogeneity specifications, which they argued were made with the sole objective of obtaining unique estimates of *a priori* assumed structural parameters, but which might have little or no correspondence with reality.

4.3.3   Model specification and the probability approach

The concept of "specification" was introduced into econometrics by Koopmans (1937). In an attempt to rigorously generalize Frisch's statistical analysis of the errors-in-variables model, Koopmans advocated the full adoption of R.A. Fisher's model specification procedures (see Qin, 1993, chapter 2). This entailed an explicit distinction between sample and population. Concurrently, Wold (1938) developed a more ambitious argument for the adoption of sampling theory, probability, and stochastic process concepts into time series analysis, in particular in conjunction with the business cycle modeling work of Frisch and Tinbergen.

The stimulus of the Keynes–Tinbergen debates led Koopmans (1941) to further clarify the logic of model specification procedures. He adapted these procedures to Frisch's structural approach by making the formulation of structural models the starting point of econometric research. He maintained that the structural model should be regarded as a "general working hypothesis" for causal relationships deduced from economic theory. Specification should then cover all the additional information required to allow conditional statistical inferences to be drawn. He listed five specification principles for the model formulation and specification steps, principally to make the model as explicit, precise, plausible and simple as possible.

Thorough foundational work on the structural model approach was carried out by Haavelmo (1944) in his well-known manifesto for the probability approach. More than Koopmans and his mentor Frisch, Haavelmo offered a forceful justification of probability theory and the stochastic specification of structural models from both the conceptual and operational aspects. His argument for the probability approach has three connected components, which start out from the data and move to the theory. First, economic time series data should be viewed as realizations of stochastically generated series and thus should obey certain probability distributions; second, sampling theory is applicable to the analysis of such data and to conducting statistical inference; and third, economic theories should be formulated explicitly as stochastic, testable hypothetical models. Operationally, he demonstrated, using the case of an SEM, how important it was to have an explicit stochastic specification of an *a priori* structural model in order to avoid inconsistent estimation methods (see also Haavelmo, 1943). His probability approach bridged economic and econometric models by extending the Walrasian deterministic system of general equilibrium to a stochastic and dynamic system.

Haavelmo's pathbreaking program was pursued and extended by the CC. The CC's research was focused on the statistical formalization of the modeling procedures, starting from a general structural model of the SEM type. The problem of how to make selections among "multiple hypotheses" in structural model construction was tentatively left aside (see Marschak, 1946, and Koopmans, 1950, pp. 44–5). The CC's achievements amplified the operational aspects of Haavelmo's probability arguments. Indeed, his probability legacy became mostly known through Haavelmo bias and Haavelmo distribution. His conceptual argument for the necessity of forming structural models as stochastic and testable hypotheses had little influence during this period.

The formalized structural modeling approach of the CC lacked an operational procedure for posing theories as testable hypotheses and for allowing data-based selection among the various tentative postulates. The approach met immediate criticism from the NBER (National Bureau of Economic Research) business cycle researchers for disregarding what is now known as "specification search" in probability theory (see Vining, 1949). While Koopmans (1947) made a successful counter argument by criticizing the NBER data-led approach as "measurement without theory," the problem of how applied econometric modelers should handle the lack of sufficiently general specified structural models remained unsolved. They were obliged to rely on *ad hoc* rules in applied modeling for years to come.[21]

4.3.4   Hypothesis testing

The desire to test economic theories using data evidence was a major impetus behind the rise of econometrics. However, this desire remained incoherent and vaguely defined among the early practitioners, for example in Tinbergen's (1939, 1940) ambitious modeling work. The statistical concept and apparatus of hypothesis testing came into econometrics in the late 1930s with Neyman–Pearson methodology (see, e.g., Brown, 1937). Although the Neyman–Pearson approach was not rejected, econometricians at the time were more preoccupied with concerns over solving various problems in relating the results of economic data analysis to available economic theories than in adopting rigorous statistical testing.

The Neyman–Pearson approach inspired Haavelmo in his reformulation of Frisch's structural modeling program within the framework of probability theory.[22] In his 1944 monograph, Haavelmo emphasized two key aspects of the hypothesis testing scheme: one was the formulation of *a priori* theories into a set of "admissible hypotheses," and the other was the choice of the optimal critical regions underlying statistical tests. The former aspect appears to have particularly appealed to Haavelmo. He used it as an essential argument for the justification of the probability approach, for the paramount importance of stochastic specification of economic models prior to econometric analysis, and for the importance of spelling out the identification conditions in order to make structural models estimable.

Haavelmo (1944) devoted one chapter to the Neyman–Pearson hypothesis testing approach. However, his discussion was largely in terms of adoption rather than adaptation. Unlike his research on the joint distribution specification and least squares simultaneity bias, Haavelmo fell short of offering an operational route which would combine the Neyman–Pearson hypothesis testing apparatus with the structural modeling approach so as to utilize the test tools to discriminate statistically between valid and invalid hypotheses to assist in the model choice problem. Rather, he considered the choice of the set of admissible hypotheses "a matter of general knowledge and intuition."

The CC also bypassed the issue of model choice, as mentioned above. Development of testing tools enjoyed very low priority in their research agenda. Classical tests, such as *t*- and *F*-tests, were adopted but not adapted. Since the structural SEM was assumed correct, there was little perceived need to develop diagnostic tests. The only in-house test invention that the group made was the over-identification test (see Anderson and Rubin, 1949, 1950). It was nearly a decade later that a set of diagnostic tests was conscientiously assembled for the purpose of misspecification analysis (see Theil, 1957a). The importance of model testing did not become widely acknowledged until the 1970s, see section 4.5.4.

4.3.5   Summary

The Cowles Commission motto was "science is measurement" (see Christ, 1952, 1994). Their approach to research may be characterized as that of making all assumptions explicit so that problems could be discovered and assumptions revised in the light of these problems. The assumptions should be as consistent as possible with knowledge of human behavior and may be classified into two types: the first are those assumptions which are statistically testable and the second are provisional working hypotheses. The objective was to produce results which would ultimately be useful for economic policy analyses.

Haavelmo's pioneering work on the probability approach has become recognized as a crucial landmark in the building of econometrics. It was the first systematic attempt to bridge empirical research and theory in a logically rigorous manner. This process would facilitate cross-fertilization between theory and data. The legacy in terms of a methodology for identifying and estimating structural models remains strong, especially in microeconometrics: see, e.g., Heckman (2000a, 2000b).

4.4 The emergence of standard regression-based econometrics

The two decades up to and including World War II were a period in which, exaggerating only slightly, a thousand econometric flowers bloomed. Less metaphorically, by 1945 many of the foundations for modern econometrics had been laid. The process of methodological innovation continued through the postwar period but, simultaneously, a process of consolidation took place. This consolidation was mainly around the linear regression model, which became the dominant tool in econometrics. The consolidation occurred though applied practice, as well as through the spread of government sponsored macroeconometric model building and the growth of econometrics teaching in universities.

4.4.1 The fall and rise of least squares

Least squares regression had been widely used by applied researchers throughout the interwar period, particularly by agricultural economists (see Fox, 1986, 1989). Nevertheless, it was only in the postwar period that it was to become accepted as the principal tool in the economist's toolbox. Before that, however, the identification and bias issues discussed by the CC led to a temporary decline in its acceptance.

The implication of the identification problem discussed in section 4.3.2, and the subsequent discovery of the Haavelmo bias, was that least squares estimates would generally result in biased estimates of the parameters of structural models. The discovery of the LIML estimator promised a viable alternative approach and resulted in what Epstein (1989) has called "the fall of OLS." The consequence was that, under the influence of the CC, least squares regression appeared to be a flawed technique. Reviewing Haavelmo (1944), Stone (1946) summarized this position in stating that "except in very special cases, unbiased estimates...cannot be obtained by considering each equation in isolation." New estimation methods were required, and LIML was to become the most prominent candidate.

It is difficult to know to what extent LIML was actually employed, as distinct from being discussed, but the Klein–Goldberger (1955) model, an annual Keynesian model of the US economy over the period 1929–52 (omitting 1942–45), was one prominent implementation. One reason for the failure of LIML to supplant OLS is that some of the early implementations failed to show much practical difference between the two estimators. Fox (1956) re-estimated the Klein–Goldberger model by OLS and found the Haavelmo bias to be smaller than expected, while Christ (1960) used Monte Carlo experiments to compare ML and least squares in finite samples. He also found that the results differed little. These results contributed to the widespread view that the Klein–Goldberger LIML estimates of the parameters of the 14 behavioral equations in their model offered few improvements over OLS estimates: see Epstein (1987, pp. 118–21) for discussion.

LIML is computationally much more burdensome than OLS, and this was important at a time when computations were undertaken on hand calculators.[23] Two-stage least squares (2SLS), due independently to Theil (1953) and Basmann (1957), simplified these computations and, with electronic calculators now more widely available, facilitated comparison with OLS. This technical innovation played an important role in the return to favor of least squares. For example, 2SLS was the main estimation method in the large scale macroeconometric models, such as the Wharton model.[24] Further developments of least squares and related methods also helped, in particular SURE, 3SLS and IV. The final verdict in favor of least squares was pronounced by Waugh (1961).

Another important debate between least squares and ML was led by Wold (1943–44), who had defended least squares from a very different angle: see also Bentzel and Wold (1946). He saw the SEM as a poorly specified causal model and advocated clearly specified causal chain models. With no simultaneity in the model, LS becomes legitimate (see Qin, 1993, chapter 6.3). Wold's argument was fully adopted later by Liu (1969) in his experimental monthly model of the US.[25]

A second reason relates to the foundations for inference in relation to estimated least squares equations. R.A. Fisher's (1925) formulation of the "classical" errors-in-equations regression model and the Neyman–Pearson hypothesis testing apparatus became known to economists in the late 1930s: see section 4.3.4, where we also noted Haavelmo's (1944) arguments for the formal statistical testing of hypotheses. It is exactly the probabilistic formulation of models that allowed the regression model to rise above the "statistics without probability" paradigm that had kept it at the level of one of a number of available statistical tools (Morgan, 1990, pp. 230–8). Morgan attributes the formulation of this approach to Koopmans (1937). However, Koopmans was not able to define a clear sampling framework for economic time series. Instead, it was left to Wold (1938) and Haavelmo (1944) to argue that classical methods could be applied to economic time series by regarding the data set (y, X) as a single realization (sample) from the infinite number of possible realizations (the population) that "Nature" might have chosen. This approach to regression formed the basis of what was to become the standard treatment in the 1950s and 1960s.

The probabilistic basis for the classical errors-in-equations regression model was important in this, rather than the errors-in-variables model, becoming the standard for applied research. The errors-in-variables model underlay Frisch's (1934b) confluence analysis approach (see Hendry and Morgan, 1989). However, Frisch was not able to provide probabilistic foundations for the bunch map techniques used to implement confluence analysis.[26] Instead, bunch maps were regarded as visual devices for discriminating between alternative model specifications (e.g., direction of regression, variables to be included and excluded). Because specification analysis was the major gap in the CC program, it might be thought that confluence analysis would complement regression modeling but, instead, lacking probabilistic foundations, it was unclear how it could be related to the errors-in-equations model, or explained to the newer generation of economists brought up to model in probabilistic terms.

A good example of this process is the evolution of the (pre-demand system) research on demand analysis carried out at the Cambridge (UK) Department of Applied Economics (DAE) over the immediate postwar decade by Stone and his co-workers (see Gilbert, 1991). There were four important contributions: Stone (1945), Prest (1949) and Stone (1951, 1954). Stone (1945) was based entirely on bunch maps (in conjunction with a general theoretical structure) and reports only point estimates of coefficients ("fiducial limits" being regarded as possibly misleading). In effect, Stone used bunch maps as a form of equation diagnostic: with short samples, the number of variables suggested by theory exceeded the number of accurately estimable coefficients. An "exploding" bunch map indicated that simplification was required.

Prest (1949) discusses bunch maps in relation to methodology but not in relation to the estimated equations, while Stone (1951) is entirely based on the errors-in-equations regression model. Stone (1954) contains bunch maps but does not discuss them.[27] The most important criterion for equation specification in all three of these later DAE papers is the R^2 statistic. While confluence analysis is also discussed at length, Stone (1954) provides a thorough and modern discussion of estimation and inference in the errors-in-equations regression model.[28] Once "fiducial limits" (confidence bands) had become accepted as the appropriate way to judge how well individual parameters were determined, confluence analysis became redundant. Both it and its associated bunch maps simply faded away over the first postwar decade.

Although the problems of OLS when applied to an SEM was recognised by Stone (1946) almost immediately after Haavelmo and the CC's contribution, Stone (1954) soon considered that the CC had over-emphasized the importance of simultaneity in the estimation of consumer demand equations and believed that OLS estimates were likely to be more accurate than their LIML counterparts (see Gilbert, 1991). Residual serial correlation and the need to model lagged responses, emphasized in Prest (1949), were more serious practical issues.

Haavelmo's methodology was correct in principle, but problems other than simultaneity were likely to be more important in practice. So, whereas in 1950 the CC researchers were able to look forward to a future in which structural estimators such as LIML would provide the basis for future econometric research, by 1960, when it was becoming feasible to estimate sizeable models, it was less clear that LIML or other "sophisticated" estimators offered any advantage over least squares estimators such as 2SLS (see Epstein, 1987, pp. 118–21). Simultaneous equations bias and possible lack of identification came to be seen as just one of a number of problems that might arise in applications and, where simultaneity was a problem, 2SLS appeared to cope adequately.

4.4.2   Residual serial correlation and equation dynamics

Insufficient variation in short time series, manifesting itself as collinearity, was one of the major problems faced by practicing econometricians in the postwar period. A second set of problems which came to dominate research were those related to dynamic specification and residual serial correlation.

Much of this work on serial correlation took place at the DAE in Cambridge, possibly as a consequence of Yule, who had argued that (in modern terminology) integrated time series with either random or conjunct (correlated) differences can show spurious correlations (Yule, 1926).[29] There were two strands to the research on residual serial correlation: diagnosis and treatment. Champernowne (1945) had noted that the demand equations reported in Stone (1945) might suffer from residual serial correlation. At that time, the standard test for serial correlation was the von Neumann ratio (von Neumann, 1941, 1942), but this was appropriate only for observed time series, not for series of regression residuals. The statistic which has become known as the Durbin–Watson statistic was one of a number of diagnostics suggested by Anderson (1948), who lectured on this problem in Cambridge in 1948 (Gilbert, 1991). Durbin and Watson (1950) developed the theory for bounding the critical values of the statistic. Turning to treatment, Cochrane and Orcutt (1949) showed that, when the errors in an equation follow a first order autoregressive process, Aitken's (1934) generalized least squares estimator can be implemented by quasi-differencing the equation prior to estimation. This suggested the "fairly obvious" two stage procedure which bears their name (Cochrane and Orcutt, 1949, p. 58). However, based on Monte Carlo evidence, which followed Yule (1926) in using integrated series, they recommended differencing in preference to quasi-differencing. This was the procedure followed in the time series estimates in Stone (1954).[30] The emphasis on integrated series subsequently faded, possibly as the consequence of textbook treatments of what had become known as the Cochrane–Orcutt (CORC) estimator, as in Johnston (1963).[31]

While the British approach to dynamics focused on patching up the estimation to take into account residual correlation, US researchers tended to look for specifications for dynamic models implied by economic theory. Koyck, who was part of the Dutch school, had utilized the distributed lag model, initially introduced by Irving Fisher in the 1920s, to describe the investment process (Koyck, 1954).[32] Klein (1958) and Solow (1960) further developed distributed lag methods. The adaptive expectations formulation of the Permanent Income Hypothesis for time series data was due to Friedman (1956). The partial adjustment hypothesis was initially developed by Nerlove (1958) in relation to agricultural supply response. We take up these themes in section 4.5.2.

The London School of Economics (LSE), which had not hitherto featured in the history of econometrics, assumed an important role from the mid-1950s, initially under the influence of A.W. Phillips, a New Zealander with a background in sociology and engineering. His reputation was made by his hydraulic models of the circular flow of income, often known as "Phillips machines" (see Gilbert, 1989). He is now best known for the Phillips Curve (Phillips, 1958), a nonlinear proportional feedback relationship from the level of unemployment to nominal wages. Phillips devised an idiosyncratic but effective estimation procedure for the nonlinear Phillips Curve which is reminiscent of *ad hoc* pre-CC statistical methods: see Gilbert (1976) and Wulwick (1987, 1989). The feedback concept was incorporated by Sargan (1964) in his model of real wage determination, which follows Phillips (1957) in including proportional and also derivative controls, but with the proportional control relating to the real wage level.[33] This anticipated the error correction mechanism which was made explicit in Davidson *et al.* (1978).

Although the LSE tradition is often seen as being data-based rather than theory-driven, a number of the contributions from that group embodied the implication that dynamic specification should be more closely related to theory, in line with the dominant US approach. In particular, an implication of the common factor approach to equation dynamics (Sargan, 1980; Hendry and Mizon, 1978) is that the autoregressive error specification which underlies the Cochrane–Orcutt procedure entails a particular set of testable restrictions on the coefficients of a more general model. If these restrictions are rejected, the autoregressive model is misspecified and the modeler is required to reconsider the specification.

These developments in dynamic modeling all served to move econometric discussion away from the simultaneity and identification issues which had dominated the CC's discussions although without explicitly detracting from the propositions that the CC had advanced. Unlike the CC concerns, they were motivated by practical concerns with modeling and policy design, rather than intellectual preoccupations with how econometrics should be undertaken. Simultaneity remained a subject for discussion and research but assumed a lower priority than previously.

4.4.3 Consolidation and dissemination

For the pioneering generation of econometricians, econometrics was simply what they chose to do. There was no need to think of econometrics as a separate discipline so much as a way of doing applied economics. Similarly, there was no sharp demarcation between economic statistics, econometrics and mathematical economics. For their students, the structure of the discipline and its demarcation from other aspects of applied economics and statistics was defined by the courses they followed and the textbooks they used. Demarcation between the content of different courses was reflected in the textbooks which derived from these courses. Faculty were required to cover these more specifically defined courses and these persons could allow themselves to become more specialized than the earlier generation who had developed the tools that they now taught. Whereas the development of econometrics was driven by research and policy imperatives, teaching imperatives may have been responsible for the process by which it became standardized into a coherent body of knowledge and techniques, with accepted boundaries separating it from related areas of economics.

In the immediate postwar decades, econometrics was generally identified with empirical economics, with emphasis on the measurability of economic relationships. Hence Klein (1974, p. 1) commences the second edition of his textbook (Klein, 1952) by "Measurement in economics is the subject matter of this volume," and in Klein (1962, p. 1) he states "the main objective of econometrics is to give empirical content to *a priori* reasoning in economics." This view of econometrics encompassed specification issues and issues of measurement and national income accounting, as well as statistical estimation. In many universities, econometrics teaching concentrated on these broader issues well into the 1970s.

This wide conception was narrowed down to the subset of "statistical methods of econometrics," the title of Malinvaud (1964). Malinvaud is quite explicit about this focus. He states (1964, p. vii) "Econometrics may be broadly interpreted to include every application of mathematics or of statistical methods to the study of economic phenomena...we shall adopt a narrower interpretation and define the aim of econometrics to be the empirical determination of economic laws." Johnston (1960, p. 3) provides an even clearer demarcation: "Economic theory consists of the study of...relations which are supposed to describe the functioning of...an economic system. The task of econometric work is to estimate these relationships *statistically*,..." (italics in original).

The new generation of textbooks also had a more or less standard menu of contents and, increasingly, adopted the standard notation which endures today. After a discussion of the linear regression model and an introduction to matrix algebra, Johnston (1963) considers errors in variables, autocorrelation and simultaneous equations methods (in that order). Goldberger (1964) follows a similar order but discusses autocorrelation more briefly in a chapter on extensions of linear regression, and errors in variables equally briefly in a chapter on regression with stochastic regressors. Malinvaud (1964) is the most comprehensive and longest of this generation of texts and was based on a course given from 1954 (Holly and Phillips, 1987). Autocorrelation is discussed in the context of time series models and the final five chapters of the book are devoted to simultaneity and identification issues.

Johnston (1963) and Goldberger (1964) share the standard $y = X\beta + \varepsilon$ regression model notation, or close variants of this. The similarities between the two texts arise out of Johnston's tenure of a visiting position at the University of Wisconsin, Madison, in 1958–59, at the invitation of Orcutt. Johnston delivered the graduate lectures in econometrics to a class which included Orcutt himself (Johnston, 1979). These lectures formed the basis for Johnston (1963). In the preface, Johnston (1963, p. ix) thanks Goldberger, also a member of the Wisconsin faculty, for the loan of the mimeographed lecture notes which would form the basis for Goldberger (1964), while Goldberger (1964, p. viii) himself acknowledges a partial draft of Johnston (1963).

The standardization of econometric notation therefore appears to have taken place in Madison. How it arrived there is more conjectural. Gilbert (1991) notes the similarities between the notation in chapter XIX of Stone (1954) and Johnston (1963) and it is possible that Orcutt was the vehicle for this transmission. Stone himself thanked Durbin and Watson for assistance with that chapter, and Durbin himself noted that "we were probably the first people to use the $y = X\beta + \varepsilon$ notation that later became standard in econometrics" (Gilbert, 1991).

Malinvaud has remarked that the period following the 1940s was one of consolidation for econometrics, and that his textbook (1964) was "a kind of witness to this consolidation process" (Holly and Phillips, 1987, p. 292). This is not to say that important innovations were absent, but only that part of the activities of what was now becoming seen as a distinct econometric profession were devoted to synthesis of the work that had gone before. Econometrics was defined more narrowly than previously on problems of estimation, inference and policy. This synthesis was built upon the foundations of probabilistic modeling advocated by Haavelmo (1944), but at the same time tended to relegate simultaneity problems to the role of advanced techniques. Linear regression had reassumed centre stage, but often with allowance for serially correlated errors.

A further important element in the dissemination of econometric practice was the development of fast computers. In the interwar period, regression was often performed by hand or by a mixture of calculating machines (used for moment calculations) and manual solution. In the early postwar years, econometricians would sometimes thank the "computors" (the people, almost invariably young ladies, who operated the computing machines) for their assistance. Rapid progress in computer technology during the 1960s greatly facilitated macromodelers' work, as appreciated by Klein (1971), "A single development stands out as a breakthrough, namely, the development of the computer...We no longer shun nonlinearity, high dimensionality, covariance calculations, etc. This is all due to the development of computer technology" (p. 134). This is despite the fact that it was only in the late 1970s that software became available which gave access to econometric methods to the wider economics profession.

4.5 Paradigm lost

While the 1960s saw the consolidation of standard econometrics through textbooks, there were growing signs in research, of deviations from, as well as dissatisfaction with, the standard approach. These occurred as researchers were trying to strengthen the bridge between theory and data following the paradigm laid down by Haavelmo and the CC. The SEM framework built by the CC was intended as an econometric interface with economic theories of the most general kind (both simultaneous and dynamic). But its execution in practice was apparently hampered by paucity of both data and testable theories.

The bridge-mending job was tackled from several directions: developing more informative theories by those who held a strong faith in the theory-led approach; devising better means to process and enhance data evidence by those who gave primacy to data-based judgments; and through the better adaptation of statistical theory to economic applications by those who viewed it as most important to strengthen the internal consistency of the link between theory and data. During the 1970s and 1980s, these diverse research strategies came to pose an increasing challenge to SEM-based standard econometrics. This final section briefly sketches how a number of these strands originated.

4.5.1   The rise of Bayesian econometrics[34]

The key attraction of the Bayesian approach lies in its statistical coherence in combining *a priori* beliefs with *a posteriori* data evidence. This attraction was appealing to econometricians of the 1960s for several reasons. Most importantly, the issue of specification choice was perceived as a serious challenge facing applied modeling. The Bayesian method appeared to offer a coherent framework in which this problem could be tackled. In particular, the Bayesian principle was felt to relate more easily to the problem of decision-making by applied modelers, who faced uncertainty in both their economic theory and in the sample data to hand, and felt obliged to compromise in combining the two in their statistical inference.[35] A second consideration related to the use of structural models for policy analysis. Under the influence of research led by the Netherlands Central Planning Bureau (CPB), model-based policy analysis became a central research topic.[36] Policy analysis poses a decision issue in which government chooses the policy mix to maximize an explicit welfare function. In this context, the Bayesian approach appeared more natural than classical methods since the welfare outcomes are more or less satisfactory rather than correct or incorrect. Further, the Bayesian approach to public policy appeared to closely mirror the manner in which individual agents make choices under uncertainty.

The potential use of Bayesian methods was discussed in econometric circles as early as the mid-1950s: see, for example, Marschak (1954). Serious adaptation of the method for econometric usage occurred in the 1960s, pioneered mainly by Drèze, Rothenberg and Zellner. Drèze (1962) attempted to reformulate the identification conditions of an SEM by the Bayesian approach to better incorporate the uncertain nature of the prior information. Zellner worked mainly on applying Bayesian estimation methods to economic data in collaboration with the statistician George Tiao: see Tiao and Zellner (1964) and Zellner and Tiao (1964). Rothenberg resorted to the Bayesian route to combine a classical SEM with a loss function representing policy decisions so as to be able to evaluate the effect of different priors on the posterior parameter estimates (Rothenberg, 1963).

These early Bayesian works aimed to strengthen, rather than displace, the CC's SEM paradigm. They resulted in a systematic reformulation of the CC structural modeling paradigm by Bayesian techniques, as embodied in the first Bayesian econometrics textbook by Zellner (1971a). The key point of contention was largely on the statistical side, specifically with regard to the use of classical versus Bayesian statistical methods. The epistemological foundations of the competing methods were also an issue: see, for example, Zellner (1971b) and Rothenberg (1971).

The Bayesian movement set out to enhance the internal consistency of the CC paradigm. However, early results showed that "for many (perhaps most) statistical problems which arise in practice the difference between Bayesian methods and traditional methods is too small to worry about and that when the two methods differ it is usually a result of making strongly different assumptions about the problem" (Rothenberg, 1971, p. 195). This may be crudely parsed as "economic specification is more important than statistical estimation," or, within a Bayesian framework, that results are highly sensitive to the choice of priors. These disappointments fermented a gradual change in direction on the part of the Bayesian camp which culminated in Leamer's (1978) influential book *Specification Searches*. This book led Bayesian econometrics into a new phase in which it became an independent approach to econometric methodology, running in opposition to the CC paradigm in which specification is taken as known: see Pagan (1987) and Qin (1996, 1998).

4.5.2 The rise of theory-led dynamic models

The need for better theoretical models, especially dynamic ones, was recognised by the CC researchers soon after their foundational work on econometrics (see, for example, Koopmans, 1957). In fact, a substantial part of the CC group, including Arrow, Debreu, Hurwicz, and Koopmans himself, moved into theoretical model building and led the way to the rise of dynamic equilibrium models and growth theories. This line of research, however, contains a shift of agenda: the key task of characterizing economic dynamics was recast as that of establishing conditions of stability or equilibrium of dynamic systems (see Weintraub, 1991). Theoretical analysis of the time paths of economic variables in the form of testable structural models was, for the most part, shelved for possible later attention.

Meanwhile, characterization of these time paths was left to the *ad hoc* treatment of applied modelers. As described in section 4.4.2, various modelers, particularly those working on consumption and investment behavior, managed to incorporate a dynamic behavioral component in *a priori* structural models. These dynamic behavioral models carry empirically testable implications and may be seen as a natural extension of the SEM framework. Indeed, many of these single-equation-based dynamic "theories" were assimilated into large-scale macroeconometric models during the 1960s (see Bodkin *et al.*, 1991). However, systematic reformation of macroeconomics into dynamically testable structural models did not occur until almost the post-1973 oil crisis era.

The reformation is now widely known as the Rational Expectations (RE) revolution. The introduction of the RE hypothesis emerged originally from research at Carnegie-Mellon University in the early 1960s. Two strands of research apparently fostered the introduction. One was Simon's (1957) game theoretical research on "rational choice" and the implications of this model for describing human behavior. The second was the joint empirical work by Holt, Modigliani, Muth and Simon (1960) on deriving operational models for inventory control. Their approach led to dynamic regression models which could be rationalised in terms of the expectations underlying business decision making. The ideas of rational behavior and dynamic expectations were amalgamated into the RE hypothesis proposed by Muth (1961) in the context of generalising dynamic models for price movements. In Muth's RE model, expectations are formed as unbiased predictors and interpreted as agents' "rational expectations" of the variables in question.

It is now widely acknowledged that Lucas's (1972) rediscovery of Muth's model marked the beginning of the RE movement in macroeconomics, although his work is preceded by Walters's (1971) application of Muth's RE hypothesis to macro-monetary analysis.[37] Somewhat similarly to the Bayesian reformation of econometrics, the RE movement started with the intention of strengthening the CC approach by making systematic improvements to the theory side. However, this initiative rapidly resulted in two discoveries which would severely undermine the SEM approach. The first was the well-known Lucas Critique which argued that, under the RE hypothesis, certain structural parameters are not invariant to policy shifts (Lucas, 1976). As Lucas immediately noted, this would seem to invalidate the use of SEMs in policy analysis. The second was the observational equivalence of RE models with Vector Autoregressive (VAR) models, noticed by Sargent (1976) when he tried to work out a general test for the rationality of expectations. This discovery, together with a revival of Liu's (1960) concerns over identification by Sims (1980), eventually led to Sims' advocacy of the abandonment of the SEM approach and its replacement by the data-based VAR approach.

4.5.3   Microeconometrics

Although the distinction between microeconometrics and macroeconometrics (or time series econometrics) is relatively new, the analysis of microeconomic data, i.e., data measured at the level of the individual agent, household or firm, extends back to the earliest decades of the discipline. Data could come in the form of either cross-sections or time series, but few practical distinctions were drawn at that time between the methods appropriate to the analysis of the two types of data.

A number of precursors to modern microeconometrics may be identified in the first two postwar decades, although in the main these did not attract widespread attention from contemporaries. According to Cramer (1991, p. 41), the first economic application of the probit model was due to Farrell (1954), who was a member of Stone's DAE group. Aitchison and Brown (1957), also in the DAE, compared the logit and probit models. From the CC group, the Tobit ("Tobin's probit") estimator was devised by Tobin (1958). This was the final contribution of the original CC (strictly now the Cowles Foundation) researchers to econometric methodology, and the only application specifically to microeconomic data. It vividly illustrated the power of the Haavelmo methodology of building economic models on secure distributional foundations (see Epstein, 1987, p. 112).

Among the CC group, Orcutt had despaired of any resolution of the identification problem by the analysis of aggregate time series and advocated the collection of data at the individual level (Orcutt, 1952). He was ahead of his time – neither were the individual data available nor was there the computing power to analyze the data, had they been available. These concerns were reinforced by research on aggregation. Klein (1946a,b) and Nataf (1948, 1953) had emphasized that exact ("perfect") aggregation from individual to aggregate relations was only possible under implausibly strong assumptions. Theil (1965) reached only marginally more optimistic conclusions in looking at approximate aggregation.

This research was primarily motivated by the desire to provide solid structural foundations for macroeconometric models. In the 1960s and 1970s, attention shifted to the analysis of tax reform and, in particular, to the negative income tax proposal. The aggregation literature was now taken as demonstrating the importance of heterogeneity across individuals in the manner anticipated by Orcutt 25 years previously. This view implied that policy discussions should relate to individuals in the full diversity of their economic and social situations, instead of to supposedly representative agents. In the 1970s, interest in these microeconomic issues coincided with the increased availability of survey data, which allowed the questions to be tackled, and the increase in computing power which facilitated the implied data-processing exercise.

The US income maintenance experiments,[38] which were motivated by interest in tax reform issues, generated some of the most extensive datasets, which gave rise to novel problems, particularly those of sample selection bias, censoring and attrition bias. Research on labor supply decisions gave rise to the issue of systematically missing data, since persons not in employment do not report wage levels (Gronau, 1973; Lewis, 1974; Heckman, 1974). Choice over multiple, mutually exclusive, alternatives provided a focus in transportation studies (see Domencich and McFadden, 1975).

The specification issues, particularly those of dynamics, which dominated much of the macroeconometric debate, were absent from microeconometrics. Identification issues, which were present, took a different form. Above all, microeconometric research still remains grounded in the broad CC structural tradition (see Heckman, 2000b, for an eloquent statement of this view), while macroeconometrics was moving towards a more data-based approach.

4.5.4 Data-based modeling again

Several factors fostered the gradual revival of the data-led modeling approach in macroeconometrics. In addition to the factors already mentioned (the revival of least squares-based regression, dissatisfaction with what were becoming seen as the arbitrary identification conditions of the SEM approach, and the increased popularity of the VAR approach), two further developments had been important: the development of hypothesis testing as a tool for model selection and increased attention to forecasting methodology.

Commercial and governmental demands for economic forecasts provided a major stimulus for large macroeconometric model building. There was visible optimism that forecast accuracy would improve with the increase of model size and structural complexity (see, for example, Klein, 1971). However, this optimism was dampened by poor forecast results, including conditional forecasts/policy simulations,[39] especially by comparison with the forecasts from simple time series models following the strategy proposed by Box and Jenkins (1970).[40] The Box–Jenkins strategy introduced a number of concepts which were either missing or neglected in the CC approach: in particular, the principle of "parsimony" in model formation, the need for rigorous diagnostic checks on model adequacy, and a data-led "identification" procedure, which essentially connotes model specification search rather than the CC sense of the terminology. The Box–Jenkins procedure offered a formal methodology for tackling the model selection issue which had been set aside by the CC but, at the same time, its "black box" conceptualization stood in stark contrast to the CC structural approach.

Single-equation modeling was the most favored testbed for comparing rival macroeconomic theories, although Griliches (1968) had advised the large macromodels to subject their experience to autopsy. In the most prominent debate, Friedman and Meiselman (1963) confronted monetary and fiscal approaches to macroeconomic policy (see also McCallum, 1986). This gave renewed exposure to a number of old econometric problems: estimated regressions gave poor forecasts; parameter estimates lacked constancy; and the single explanatory variable approach proved too primitive for theory evaluation. However, in retrospect, the most evident deficiency in this debate was the *ad hoc* nature of the procedure for handling empirically testable hypotheses, in particular when these failed to exhibit a nested structure (see also Dhrymes *et al.*, 1972). A fallout of the debate was the development of the St Louis model, built primarily for purposes of policy simulation at the Federal Reserve Bank of St Louis, and which ran counter to the structural tradition in adopting a reduced-form approach, based upon a small number of equations with long lag lengths in each equation (see Andersen and Carlson, 1974).

Continued cross-fertilization from progress in statistics also played an important part in the revival of the data-led approach to modeling, in particular with regard to hypothesis testing. Pesaran (1974) was possibly the first econometrician to apply the Cox (1961, 1962) methodology for non-nested tests. Similarly, Ramsey's (1969) RESET model specification test became widely implemented.

One particular example of cross-fertilization from the statistics literature was the revival of frequency domain analysis, discarded as useless forty years previously (see section 4.2.4). Thanks to John Tukey's extension of frequency analysis from univariate to multivariate cases, the method was soon adopted in econometrics by Granger and Hatanaka (1964).[41] The research led Granger to become aware of the lack of an adequate statistical characterization of causality, a concern which eventually resulted in what is now known as "Granger causality" (Granger, 1969), which was extensively used by the RE movement (see also Phillips, 1997). Not only does Granger causality rely on posterior data information as the criterion of causal judgement, it also abandons the possibility of contemporaneous causality.

Post-estimation diagnostic testing, which became routine as batteries of tests were implemented in standard econometric packages, tended to undermine structural models because these invariably turned out to be overly simple. Models needed to be adapted, often in apparently arbitrary ways, if they were to survive confrontation with the data. Data-instigated adaptation of model specifications led to the charge of "data-mining," articulated most clearly in Leamer (1978, 1983). Some of these issues were subsequently clarified through the development of cointegration analysis (Johansen, 1988) within the VAR framework, since this permits the interpretation of dynamic adjustment coefficients as nuisance parameters. Others followed Leamer in concluding that poor test results often reflected more on the inadequacies of classical inferential procedures than on the economic theories being tested.

4.6 Final comment

At the start of the twentieth century, the term "econometrics" did not exist. By the end of the century, econometrics had a clear connotation and had become a separate discipline within economics, with its own journals and with dedicated faculty teaching a range of specialized courses. The process of becoming a discipline involved the formation of a standard paradigm. While not everyone agreed with the entire paradigm, dissident positions were defined with reference to it. This was a process which took place between 1950 and 1980, building on the foundations laid in the interwar period and their consolidation over the wartime period, when European econometricians from different backgrounds were brought together in the United States as they fled the Nazis.

Many of the advances in econometrics were in statistical theory relating to the linear regression model (including multivariate versions of the model), developed in response to the specific problems faced in analyzing non-experimental data, often generated with error processes correlated over time and over variables. These advances were progressive in the sense that, once discovered, this knowledge was not forgotten. After the mid-century, these advances were matched by advances in computing which, over time, eliminated a most serious constraint on applied econometric analysis.

A major theme which dominated much of the debate throughout the century was how, and indeed whether, econometric models can reflect theory-generated economic structures. These debates were less progressive in the sense that old, and even apparently vanquished, themes re-emerged over time. Haavelmo's probabilistic claims, fostered by the Cowles Commission, gained the high ground at the mid-century, but the assumptions required for the specific Cowles models to retain their validity were questioned in subsequent decades and, empirically, structural macroeconometric models were found to perform less well than their non-structural data-based counterparts. Over the last quarter of the century, the paradigm became looser as econometricians moved to defining their positions relative to each other rather than, as earlier, relative to their non-econometric colleagues. The result was a greater diversity in both theory and practice, but with a shared language and a common history. Paradoxically, the Cowles structural tradition, which had emerged at a time when the vast majority of applications were to macroeconomics, has survived most effectively in microeconometrics.

Notes

1. See Morgan (1990) and Hendry and Morgan (1995) for a comprehensive discussion.
2. He also investigated polynomial regressions by adding quadratic and cubic regressors.
3. For a detailed study of the history of the consumption function, see Thomas (1989).
4. This was his 1936 doctoral thesis.

5. Goldberger (1972) gives a detailed description of Wright's path analysis; Farebrother (1986) describes the very early history of IV, which goes back to the 1750s.
6. Crum (1923) tried to use periodic analysis on cyclical patterns in commercial paper rates and found the results unsatisfactory. Greenstein (1935) used the method on business failures in the US, but came to partially negative conclusions about the method.
7. This was originally published in Russian in 1927.
8. Frisch illustrated this by an investment demand equation. Dynamically formulated mathematical models of economic "laws" were increasingly used both in macro and micro studies during this period, e.g., Roos's (1934) dynamic demand model and the well-known cobweb model: see Ezekiel (1938) for a survey.
9. This work was undertaken at the request of Oscar Morgenstern of the Vienna Business Cycle Research Institute: see Hendry and Morgan (1995, Introduction).
10. Wold (1938) referred to the works of Yule, Slutsky, Frisch and Tinbergen. However, despite some citations, this work had little impact on econometricians.
11. "External" factors were used to refer to non-structural random shocks in Haavelmo (1940).
12. See Frisch (1933b, 1934a) and Leontief (1934a, 1934b).
13. See Qin and Gilbert (2001) for further discussion on the history of the error term.
14. Neither Frisch's memorandum (1938) nor Marschak and Lange's paper (1940) was published at the time. Marschak and Lange acknowledged that their paper benefited from discussions with Haavelmo, and the Chicago economists J.L. Mosak and T.O. Yntema.
15. See Tintner's comment in the report of the Econometric Society Meeting at Philadelphia in 1939 (Leaven, 1940).
16. There is a relatively rich literature on this period of history: see, e.g., Christ (1952, 1994), Hildreth (1986), Epstein (1987), Morgan (1990) and Qin (1993). This section is a summary of the literature and builds heavily on Qin (1993).
17. The main result of this paper was already available in his 1941 mimeograph and known to Marschak, Wald, Koopmans and others well before 1943.
18. The work was mostly complete by the mid-1940s: see Epstein (1987).
19. Both Frisch (1938) and Marschak (1942) are included in Hendry and Morgan (1995); cf. Hendry and Morgan (1995, introduction).
20. The two aspects of model formulation discussed by Koopmans (1950) – causal formulation in terms of endogenous and exogenous variables and completeness – were originally distinguished by Tinbergen (1939).
21. How to conduct specification search remains a recurring topic of methodological debates. The arbitrary practice of applied econometric model specification was referred to as "sinning in the basement" by Leamer (1978) in his advocacy for the Bayesian approach: see section 4.5.1. The issue was recently discussed again by Kennedy (2002), Hendry (2002) and Magnus (2002).
22. Haavelmo had a very high respect of Neyman: see Bjerkholt (2005).
23. Electronic calculators started to become available around 1945 (Goldberger, 2002).
24. The Wharton model used quarterly time series, whereas the Klein–Goldberger model had used annual data. This allowed Wharton to give greater focus to short-run forecasts. To better capture dynamics, it employed Almon distributed lags (Almon, 1965) in investment equations and first differences (growth rates) in some other equations (see Bodkin *et al.*, 1991).
25. Liu had become disillusioned by the SEM approach when he tried to build a quarterly model (1960). In essence, he attempted to achieve identification through the use of higher frequency data.
26. Reiersøl (1945) and Geary (1949) subsequently provided this framework through the development of instrumental variables, but this approach was not widely understood until the same methods were applied to the simultaneity problem: see also Epstein (1987, p. 165, fn 10).

27. The Stone (1951) estimates are the food sector subset of those subsequently reported in Stone (1954).
28. A summary of this had appeared in Prest (1949).
29. Stone (1951) refers to Yule's (1926) "picturesque examples" and Orcutt (1948) regarded nonstationarity as the norm in economics.
30. Stone (1954) imposed income elasticities from cross-section estimates.
31. Although Johnston does not provide an attribution.
32. According to Alt (1942), the concept of distributed lags was first introduced in I. Fisher (1925) and soon used by G.C. Evans and C.F. Roos repeatedly. Distributed lag equations were also used extensively in Tinbergen's macroeconometric models, e.g., Tinbergen (1939).
33. Despite the fact that both Phillips and Sargan were members of the LSE Economics Department, there is no evidence for any direct link between the two specifications: see Gilbert (1989).
34. This subsection draws heavily from Qin (1996), which contains a far more detailed description.
35. This problem had already been tackled by Theil (1963) using a classical approach.
36. Much of this research is embodied in Tinbergen (1952, 1956), which formalized the distinction between instruments and targets, and subsequently in Theil (1954, 1957b, 1964), which extended Tinbergen's analysis (see also Hughes Hallett, 1989).
37. There are numerous studies on the history and methodology of the rational expectations movement: see, e.g., Maddock (1984), Pesaran (1987), Sent (1998), Sheffrin (1983) and Miller (1994).
38. This literature is discussed in Munnell (1987).
39. In a number of model reviews, unsatisfactory forecasts were found to be widely present in various macroeconometric models and were believed to serve as a strong sign of internal model weakness: see, e.g., Evan (1966), Griliches (1968), Gordon (1970) and Hickman (1972).
40. For example, Nelson (1972) used simple ARIMA models of the Box–Jenkins type to compare with the forecasting performance of the structural model jointly developed by the Federal Reserve Board, MIT and the University of Pennsylvania. The ARIMA time series models performed better.
41. Morgenstern was pursuing this research on the recommendation of von Neumann. He delegated the work to Granger (see Morgenstern, 1961, and Granger and Morgenstern, 1963).

References

Aitchison, J. and J.A.C. Brown (1957) *The Lognormal Distribution.* Cambridge: Cambridge University Press.

Aitken, A.C. (1934) On least squares and linear combinations of observations. *Proceedings of the Royal Society of Edinburgh* 55, 42–8.

Almon, S. (1965) The distributed lag between capital appropriations and expenditures. *Econometrica* 33, 178–96.

Alt, P.L. (1942) Distributed lags. *Econometrica* 10, 113–28.

Andersen, L.C. and K.M. Carlson (1974) St. Louis model revisited. *International Economic Review* 15, 305–25.

Anderson, T.W. (1948) On the theory of testing serial correlation. *Scandinavisk Aktuar-ietidskrift* 31, 88–116.

Anderson, T.W. and H. Rubin (1949) Estimation of the parameters of a single equation in a complete system of stochastic equations. *Annals of Mathematical Statistics* 20, 46–63.

Anderson, T.W. and H. Rubin (1950) The asymptotic properties of estimates of the parameters of a single equation in a complete system of stochastic equations. *Annals of Mathematical Statistics* 21, 570–82.

Basmann, R.L. (1957) A generalized classical method of linear estimation of coefficients in a structural equation. *Econometrica* **25**, 77–83.

Bentzel, R. and H.O.A. Wold (1946) On statistical demand analysis from the viewpoint of simultaneous equations. *Skandinavisk Aktuarietidskrift* **29**, 95–114.

Birk, K.N. (1987) Effective microcomputer statistical software. *American Statistician* **41**, 222–8.

Bjerkholt, O. (2005) Frisch's econometric laboratory and the rise of Trygve Haavelmo's probability approach. *Econometric Theory* **21**, 491–533.

Bodkin, R.G., L.R. Klein and K. Marwah (1991) *A History of Macroeconometric Model-Building*. Aldershot: Edward Elgar Publishing.

Bowley, A.L. (1933) The action of economic forces in producing frequency distributions of income, prices and other phenomena: A suggestion for study. *Econometrica* **1**, 358–72.

Brown, E.H.P. (1937) Report of the Oxford Meeting, September 25–9, 1936. *Econometrica* **5**, 361–83.

Burns, A.F. and W.C. Mitchell (1946) *Measuring Business Cycles*. New York: NBER.

Champernowne, D.A. (1945) Comment on Stone (1945). *Journal of the Royal Statistical Society* **108**, 385–7.

Christ, C.F. (1952) History of the Cowles Commission, 1932–1952. In *Economic Theory and Measurement: A Twenty Year Research Report 1932–1952*. Chicago: Cowles Commission for Research in Economics, pp. 3–65.

Christ, C.F. (1960) Simultaneous equations estimation: Any verdict yet? *Econometrica* **28**, 835–45.

Christ, C.F. (1994) The Cowles Commission's contributions to econometrics at Chicago, 1939–1955. *Journal of Economic Literature* **32**, 30–59.

Clark, C. (1938) Determination of the multiplier from national income statistics. *Economic Journal* **48**, 435–48.

Coase, R.H. and R.F. Fowler (1937) The pig-cycle in Great Britain: An explanation. *Economica* **4**, 55–82.

Cochrane, D. and G.H. Orcutt (1949) Application of least squares regression to relationships containing autocorrelated error terms. *Journal of the American Statistical Association* **44**, 32–61.

Cox, D.R. (1961) Tests of separate families of hypotheses. *Proceedings of the Fourth Berkeley Symposium* **1**, 105–23.

Cox, D.R. (1962) Further results on tests of separate families of hypotheses. *Journal of the Royal Statistical Society* B, **24**, 406–24.

Cramer, J.S. (1991) *An Introduction to the Logit Model for Economists*. London: Edward Arnold.

Crum, W.L. (1923) Cycles of rates on commercial paper. *Review of Economic Statistics* **5**, 17–29.

Davidson, J.E.H., D.F. Hendry, F. Srba and S. Yeo (1978) Econometric modelling of the aggregate time series relationship between consumers' expenditure and income in the United Kingdom. *Economic Journal* **88**, 661–92.

Dhrymes, P., E.P. Howrey, S.H Hymans, J. Kmenta, E.E. Leamer, R.E. Quandt, J.B. Ramsey, H.T. Shapiro and V. Zarnowitz (1972) Criteria for the evaluation of econometric models. *Annals of Economic and Social Measurement* **1**, 259–90.

Dirks, F.C. (1938) Retail sales and labor income. *Review of Economic Statistics* **20**, 128–34.

Domencich, T.A. and D. McFadden (1975) *Urban Travel Demand*. Amsterdam: North-Holland.

Drèze, J. (1962) The Bayesian approach to simultaneous equations estimation, O.N.R. Research Memorandum 67, Northwestern University.

Durbin, J. and G.S. Watson (1950) Testing for serial correlation in least squares regression I. *Biometrika* **37**, 409–28.

Engle, R.F. and C.W.J. Granger (1987) Cointegration and error correction: representation, estimation and testing. *Econometrica* **55**, 251–76.

Epstein, R. (1987) *A History of Econometrics*. Amsterdam: North-Holland.

Epstein, R. (1989) The fall of OLS in structural estimation. *Oxford Economic Papers* **41**, 94–107.

Evans, M. (1966) Multiplier analysis of a post-war quarterly US model and a comparison with several other models. *Review of Economic Studies* **33**, 337–60.

Ezekiel, M. (1928) Statistical analysis and the "laws" of price. *Quarterly Journal of Economics* **42**, 199–227.

Ezekiel, M. (1938) The cobweb theorem. *Quarterly Journal of Economics* **52**, 255–80.

Farebrother, R. (1986) The early history of instrumental variable estimation. *Department of Econometrics and Social Statistics Discussion Paper* **175**, University of Manchester.

Farrell, M.J. (1954) The demand for motorcars in the United State, *Journal of the Royal Statistical Society* A, **117**, 171–200.

Ferger, W.F. (1932) The static and the dynamic in statistical demand curves. *Quarterly Journal of Economics* **47**, 36–62.

Fisher, I. (1925) Our unstable dollar and the so-called business cycle. *Journal of the American Statistical Association* **20**, 179–202.

Fisher, R.A. (1925) *Statistical Methods for Research Workers*. Edinburgh: Oliver and Boyd.

Fox, K.A. (1956) Econometric models of the United States. *Journal of Political Economy* **64**, 128–42.

Fox, K.A. (1986) Agricultural economists as world leaders in applied econometrics, 1917–33. *American Journal of Agricultural Economics* **68**, 381–86.

Fox, K.A. (1989) Some contributions of US agricultural economists and their close associates to statistics and econometrics. *Oxford Economic Papers* **41**, 53–70.

Friedman, M. (1956) *A Theory of the Consumption Function*. Princeton, NJ: Princeton University Press.

Friedman, M. and D. Meiselman (1963) The relative stability of monetary velocity and the investment multiplier in the United States, 1897–1958. In *Stabilization Policies*, prepared for the Commission on Money and Credit. Englewood Cliffs, NJ: Prentice-Hall, pp. 165–268.

Frisch, R. (1929) Correlation and scatter in statistical variables. *Nordic Statistical Journal* **8**, 36–102.

Frisch, R. (1933a) Propagation problems and impulse problems in dynamic economics, in *Economic Essays in Honour of Gustav Cassel*. London: Allen and Unwin.

Frisch, R. (1933b) Pitfalls in the construction of demand and supply curves. *Veröffentlichungen der Frankfurter Gesellschaft für Konjunkturforschung*, **V**. Leipzig: Hans Buske.

Frisch, R. (1934a) More pitfalls in demand and supply curve analysis. *Quarterly Journal of Economics* **48**, 749–55.

Frisch, R. (1934b) *Statistical Confluence Analysis by Means of Complete Regression Systems*. Oslo: Universitetets Økonomiske Institutt.

Frisch, R. (1937) An ideal programme for macrodynamic studies. *Econometrica* **5**, 365–6.

Frisch, R. (1938) Autonomy of economic relations, unpublished until inclusion in D.F. Hendry and M.S. Morgan (eds) (1995), *The Foundations of Economic Analysis*. Cambridge: Cambridge University Press, pp. 407–19.

Frisch, R. and F.V. Waugh (1933) Partial time regressions as compared with individual trends. *Econometrica* **1**, 387–401.

Geary, R.C. (1949) Determination of linear relations between systematic parts of variables with errors of observation the variances of which are not known. *Econometrica* **17**, 30–58.

Gilbert, C.L. (1976) The original Phillips Curve estimates. *Economica* **43**, 51–7.

Gilbert, C.L. (1989) LSE and the British approach to time series econometrics. *Oxford Economic Papers* **41**, 108–28.

Gilbert, C.L. (1991) Richard Stone, demand theory and the emergence of modern econometrics. *Economic Journal* **101**, 288–302.

Gini, C. (1921) Sull'interpolazione di una retta quando i valori della variabile independente sono affetti da errori accidentali. *Metro* **1**, 63–82.

Goldberger, A.S. (1964) *Econometric Theory*. New York: Wiley.

Goldberger, A.S. (1972) Structural equation methods in the social sciences. *Econometrica* **40**, 979–1001.

Goldberger, A.S. (2002) Structural equation models in human behavior genetics. *Wisconsin Madison – Social Systems Working Paper* 22.

Gordon, R.J. (1970) The Brookings model in action: A review article. *Journal of Political Economy* **78**, 489–525.

Granger, C.W.J. (1969) Investigating causal relations by econometric models and cross-spectral methods. *Econometrica* **37**, 424–38.

Granger, C.W.J. and M. Hatanaka (1964) *Spectral Analysis of Economic Time Series*. Princeton, NJ: Princeton University Press.

Granger, C.W.J. and O. Morgenstern (1963) Spectral analysis of stock market prices. *Kyklos* **16**, 1–27.

Greenstein, B. (1935) Periodogram analysis with special application to business failures in the United States, 1867–1932. *Econometrica* **3**, 170–98.

Griliches, Z. (1968) The Brookings model volume: A review article. *Review of Economics and Statistics* **50**, 215–34.

Gronau, R. (1973) The effects of children on the housewife's value of time. *Journal of Political Economy* **81**, 169–99.

Haberler, G. von (1937) *Prosperity and Depression*. Geneva: League of Nations.

Haavelmo, T. (1940) The inadequacy of testing dynamic theory by comparing theoretical solutions and observed cycles. *Econometrica* **8**, 312–21.

Haavelmo, T. (1943) The statistical implications of a system of simultaneous equations. *Econometrica* **11**, 1–12.

Haavelmo, T. (1944) The Probability Approach in Econometrics. *Econometrica* **12**, supplement; mimeograph (1941) at Harvard University.

Heckman, J.J. (1974) Shadow prices, market wages and labor supply. *Econometrica* **42**, 679–94.

Heckman, J.J. (2000a) Causal parameters and policy analysis in economics: A twentieth century retrospective. *Quarterly Journal of Economics* **115**, 47–97.

Heckman, J.J. (2000b) Microdata, heterogeneity and the evaluation of public policy. *Bank of Sweden Nobel Memorial Lecture in Economic Sciences*.

Hendry, D.F. (1995) *Dynamic Econometrics*. Oxford: Oxford University Press.

Hendry, D.F. (2002) Applied econometrics without sinning. *Journal of Economic Surveys* **16**, 591–604.

Hendry, D.G. and G.E. Mizon (1978) Serial correlation as a convenient simplification, not a nuisance: A comment on a study of the demand for money by the Bank of England. *Economic Journal* **88**, 549–63.

Hendry, D.F. and M.S. Morgan (1989) A re-analysis of confluence analysis. *Oxford Economic Papers* **41**, 35–52.

Hendry, D.F. and M.S. Morgan (eds) (1995) *The Foundations of Econometric Analysis*. Cambridge: Cambridge University Press.

Hickman, B.G. (ed.) (1972) *Econometric Models of Cyclical Behavior*. New York: NBER, Columbia University Press.

Hildreth, C. (1986) *The Cowles Commission in Chicago 1939–1955*. Berlin: Springer-Verlag.

Holly, A. and P.C.B. Phillips (1987) The ET interview: Professor Edmund Malinvaud. *Econometric Theory* **3**, 273–95.

Holt, C.C., F. Modigliani, J.F. Muth and H.A. Simon (1960) *Planning Production, Inventories and Work Force*. New York: Prentice-Hall.

Hood, W.C. and T.C. Koopmans (eds) (1953) *Studies in Econometric Methods*, Cowles Commission Monograph 14. New York: Wiley.

Hotelling, H. (1933) Analysis of a complex of statistical variables into principal components. *Journal of Educational Psychology* **24**, 417–41 and 498–520.

Hotelling, H. (1936) Relations between two sets of variables. *Biometrica* **28**, 321–77.

Hughes Hallett, A. (1989) Econometrics and the theory of economic policy: the Tinbergen-Theil contributions 40 years on. *Oxford Economic Papers* **41**, 189–214.

Hurwicz, L. (1950) Generalization of the concept of identification. In T.C. Koopmans (ed.), *Statistical Inference in Dynamic Economic Models*, Cowles Commission Monograph 10. New York: Wiley, pp. 245–57.

James, R.W. and M.H. Belz (1936) On mixed difference and differential equations. *Econometrica* **4**, 157–60.

James, R.W. and M.H. Belz (1938) The significance of the characteristic solutions of mixed difference and differential equations. *Econometrica* **6**, 326–43.

Johansen, S. (1988) Statistical analysis of cointegration vectors. *Journal of Economic Dynamics and Control* **12**, 231–54.

Johnston, J. (1960) *Statistical Cost Analysis*. New York: McGraw-Hill.

Johnston, J. (1963) *Econometric Methods*. New York: McGraw-Hill.

Johnston, J. (1979) *This Week's Classic Citation* **16**, 16 April.

Kennedy, P.E. (2002) Sinning in the basement: What are the rules? The ten commandments of applied econometrics. *Journal of Economic Surveys* **16**, 569–89.

Keuzenkamp, H.A. (2000) *Probability, Econometrics and Truth: The Methodology of Econometrics*. Cambridge: Cambridge University Press.

Keynes, J.M. (1939) Professor Tinbergen's method. *Economic Journal* **49**, 556–68.

Keynes, J.M. (1940) Reply. *Economic Journal* **50**, 154–6.

Klein, L.R. (1946a) Macroeconomics and the theory of rational behavior. *Econometrica* **14**, 93–108.

Klein, L.R. (1946b) Remarks on the theory of aggregation. *Econometrica* **14**, 303–12.

Klein, L.R. (1952) (second edition 1974) *A Textbook in Econometrics*. Englewood Cliffs, NJ: Prentice-Hall.

Klein, L.R. (1958) The estimation of distributed lags. *Econometrica* **26**, 553–65.

Klein, L.R. (1962) *An Introduction to Econometrics*. Englewood Cliffs, NJ: Prentice-Hall.

Klein, L.R. (1971) Forecasting and policy evaluation using large scale econometric models: the state of the art. In M.D. Intriligator (ed.), *Frontiers of Quantitative Economics*, Amsterdam: North-Holland, pp. 133–63.

Klein, L.R. and A.S. Goldberger (1955) An Econometric Model of the United States 1929–1952. Amsterdam: North-Holland.

Koopmans, T.C. (1937) *Linear Regression Analysis of Economic Time Series*. Haarlem: De Erven F. Bohn.

Koopmans, T.C. (1940) The degree of damping in business cycles. *Econometrica* **8**, 79–89.

Koopmans, T.C. (1941) The logic of econometric business-cycle research. *Journal of Political Economy* **49**, 157–81.

Koopmans, T.C. (1947) Measurement without theory. *Review of Economic Studies* **29**, 161–72.

Koopmans, T.C. (ed.) (1950) *Statistical Inference in Dynamic Economic Models*, Cowles Commission Monograph 10. New York: Wiley.

Koopmans, T.C. (1957) *Three Essays on the State of Economic Science*. New York: McGraw-Hill.

Koopmans, T.C. and O. Reiersøl (1950) The identification of structural characteristics. *The Annals of Mathematical Statistics* **21**, 165–81.

Koyck, L.M. (1954) *Distributed Lags and Investment Analysis*. Amsterdam: North-Holland.

Leamer, E.E. (1978) *Specification Searches*. New York: Wiley.

Leamer, E.E. (1983). Let's take the con out of econometrics. *American Economic Review* **73**, 31–43.

Leaven, D.H. (1940) Report of the Philadelphia Meeting, December 27–29, 1939. *Econometrica* **8**, 176–92.

Lehfeldt, R.A. (1914) The elasticity of demand for wheat. *Economic Journal* **24**, 212–17.

Leontief, W.W. (1934a) More pitfalls in demand and supply curve analysis: a reply. *Quarterly Journal of Economics* **48**, 355–61.

Leontief, W.W. (1934b) More pitfalls... – a final word. *Quarterly Journal of Economics* **48**, 755–9.

Lewis, H.G. (1974) Comments on selectivity biases in wage comparisons. *Journal of Political Economy* **82**, 1145–55.

Liu, T.C. (1960) Underidentification, structural estimation, and forecasting. *Econometrica* **28**, 855–65.

Liu, T.C. (1969) A monthly recursive econometric model of the United States: a test of feasibility. *Review of Economics and Statistics* **51**, 1–13.

Lucas, R.E. (1972) Expectations and the neutrality of money. *Journal of Economic Theory* **4**, 103–24.

Lucas, R.E. (1976) Econometric policy evaluation: a critique. In K. Brunner and A.H. Meltzer (eds), *The Phillips Curve and Labor Markets*, Carnegie-Rochester Conference Series on Public Policy, vol. 1. Amsterdam: North-Holland.

McCallum, B.T. (1986) Monetary vs. fiscal policy effects: a review of the debate, *NBER Working Paper* W1556.

Maddock, R. (1984) Rational expectations macro theory: a Lakatosian case study in program adjustment. *History of Political Economy* **16**, 291–309.

Magnus, J.R. (2002) The missing tablet: comment on Peter Kennedy's ten commandments. *Journal of Economic Surveys* **16**, 605–10.

Malinvaud, E. (1964) (English edition 1968) *Statistical Methods in Econometrics*. Amsterdam: North-Holland.

Malinvaud, E. (1983) Econometric methodology: rise and maturity. Paper presented at the 50th anniversary of the Cowles Commission for Research in Econometrics, Yale University.

Mann, H.B. and A. Wald (1943) On the statistical treatment of linear stochastic difference equations. *Econometrica* **11**, 173–220.

Marschak, J. (1942) Economic interdependence and statistical analysis. In O. Lange, F. McIntyre and T.O. Yntema (eds), *Studies in Mathematical Economic and Econometrics – In Memory of Henry Schultz*. Chicago: University of Chicago Press, pp. 135–50.

Marschak, J. (1946) Quantitative studies in economic behaviour (Foundations of rational economic policy), Report to the Rockefeller Foundation, Rockefeller Archive Centre.

Marschak, J. (1954) Probability in the social sciences. *Cowles Commission Papers*, New Series 82.

Marschak, J. and O. Lange (1940) Mr. Keynes and the statistical verification of business cycle theories. Unpublished until inclusion in D.F. Hendry and M.S. Morgan (eds) (1995), *The Foundations of Economic Analysis*. Cambridge: Cambridge University Press, pp. 390–8.

Miller, P.J. (ed.) (1994) *The Rational Expectations Revolution: Readings from the Front Line.* Boston: Massachusetts Institute of Technology.

Moore, H.L. (1914) *Economic Cycles – Their Law and Cause.* New York: Macmillan.

Moore, H.L. (1925) A moving equilibrium of demand and supply. *Quarterly Journal of Economics* **39**, 357–71.

Morgan, M.S. (1990) *The History of Econometric Ideas.* Cambridge: Cambridge University Press.

Morgenstern, O. (1961) A new look at economic time series analysis. In H. Hegeland (ed.), *Money, Growth, and Methodology and Other Essays in Economics: In Honor of Johan Akerman.* Lund: CWK Gleerup Publishers, pp. 261–72.

Munnell, A.H. (ed.) (1987) *Lessons from the Income Maintenance Experiments*, Federal Reserve Bank of Boston, Conference Series, **30**.

Muth, J.F. (1961) Rational expectations and the theory of price movements. *Econometrica* **29**, 315–35.

Nataf, A. (1948) Sur la possibilité de construction de certains macro-modèles, *Econometrica* **16**, 232–44.

Nataf, A. (1953) Sur des questions d'agrégation en économétrie, *Publications de l'Institut de Statistique de l'Université de Paris*, **2**.

Nelson, C.R. (1972) The prediction performance of the FRB–MIT–PENN model of the U.S. economy. *American Economic Review* **62**, 902–17.

Nerlove, M. (1958) *The Dynamics of Supply: Estimation of Farmers' Response to Price.* Baltimore: John Hopkins Press.

Orcutt, G.H. (1948) A study of the autoregressive nature of time series used for Tinbergen's model of the economic system of the United States 1919–32. *Journal of the Royal Statistical Society* B, **10**, 1–53.

Orcutt, G.H. (1952) Toward partial redirection of econometrics. *Review of Economics and Statistics* **34**, 195–200.

Pagan, A. (1987) Three econometric methodologies: a critical appraisal. *Journal of Economic Surveys* **1**, 3–24.

Persons, W.M. (1916) Construction of a business barometer based upon annual data. *American Economic Review* **6**, 739–69.

Persons, W.M. (1919) Indices of business conditions. *Review of Economic Statistics* **1**, 5–110.

Pesaran, M.H. (1974) On the general problem of model specification. *Review of Economic Studies* **41**, 153–71.

Pesaran, M.H. (1987) *The Limits to Rational Expectations*. Oxford: Basil Blackwell.

Phillips, A.W. (1954) Stabilisation policy in a closed economy. *Economic Journal* **64**, 290–323.

Phillips, A.W. (1957) Stabilisation policy and the time form of lagged responses. *Economic Journal* **67**, 265–77.

Phillips, A.W. (1958) The relationship between unemployment and the rate of change of money wages in the United Kingdom, 1861–1957. *Economica* **25**, 283–99.

Phillips, P.C.B. (1997) The ET interview: Professor Clive Granger. *Econometric Theory* **13**, 253–303.

Prest, A.R. (1949) Some experiments in demand analysis. *Review of Economics and Statistics* **31**, 33–49.

Qin, D. (1993) *The Formation of Econometrics: A Historical Perspective*. Oxford: Oxford University Press.

Qin, D. (1996) Bayesian econometrics: the first twenty years. *Econometric Theory* **12**, 500–16.

Qin, D. (1998) Bayesian econometric methodology. In J.B. Davis, D.W. Hands and U. Maki (eds), *The Handbook of Economic Methodology*. Cheltenham: Edward Elgar, pp. 33–6.

Qin, D. and C.L. Gilbert (2001) The error term in the history of time series econometrics. *Econometric Theory* **17**, 424–50.

Ramsey, J.B. (1969) Tests for specification errors in classical linear least-squares regression analysis. *Journal of the Royal Statistical Society* B, **31**, 350–71.

Reiersøl, O. (1945) Confluence analysis by means of instrumental sets of variables. *Arkiv for Matematik, Astronomi och Fysik* **32**, 1–119.

Roos, C.F. (1934) *Dynamic Economics*, Cowles Commission Monograph 1. Bloomington, IN: Cowles Commission.

Roos, C.F. (1937) A general invariant criterion of fit for lines and planes where all variates are subjected to error. *Metron* **13**, 3–20.

Rothenberg, T.J. (1963) A Bayesian analysis of simultaneous equations systems, *Econometric Institute Report 6315*, Netherlands School of Economics.

Rothenberg, T.J. (1971) The Bayesian approach and alternatives in econometrics. In M.D. Intriligator (ed.), *Frontiers of Quantitative Economics*. Amsterdam: North-Holland, pp. 194–207.

Samuelson, P.A. (1987) Paradise lost and refound: the Harvard ABC barometers. *Journal of Portfolio Management* Spring, 4–9.

Sargan, J.D. (1964) Wages and prices in the United Kingdom: a study in econometric methodology. In R.E. Hart, G. Mills and J.K. Whittaker (eds), *Econometric Analysis for National Economic Planning*. London: Butterworth, pp. 25–63.

Sargan, J.D. (1980) Some tests of dynamic specification for a single equation. *Econometrica* **48**, 879–97.

Sargent, T.J. (1976) The observational equivalence of natural and unnatural rate theories of macroeconomics. *Journal of Political Economy* **84**, 207–37.

Schultz, H. (1925) The statistical law of demand as illustrated by the demand for sugar. *Journal of Political Economy* **33**, 481–504 and 577–637.

Schultz, H. (1928) *The Statistical Laws of Demand and Supply with Special Application to Sugar*. Chicago: University of Chicago Press.

Sent, E.-M. (1998) *The Evolving Rationality of Rational Expectations: An Assessment of Thomas Sargent's Achievements*. Cambridge: Cambridge University Press.

Sent, E.-M. (2002) How (not) to influence people: the contrary tale of John F. Muth. *History of Political Economy* **34**, 291–319.

Sheffrin, S.M. (1983) *Rational Expectations*. Cambridge: Cambridge University Press.

Simon, H.A. (1953) Causal ordering and identifiability. In W.C. Hood and T.C. Koopmans (eds), *Studies in Econometric Methods*, Cowles Commission Monograph 14. New York: Wiley, pp. 49–74.

Simon, H.A. (1955) Causality and econometrics: comment. *Econometrica* **23**, 193–5.

Simon, H.A. (1957) A behavioural model of rational choice. *Quarterly Journal of Economics* **69**, 99–118.

Sims, C.A. (1980) Macroeconomics and reality. *Econometrica* **48**, 1–48.

Smith, B.B. (1925) The error in eliminating secular trend and seasonal variation before correlating time series. *Journal of the American Statistical Association* **20**, 543–5.

Slutsky, E. (1937) The summation of random causes as the source of cyclic processes. *Econometrica* **5**, 105–46.

Solow, R.W. (1960) On a family of lag distributions. *Econometrica* **28**, 393–406.

Staehle, H. (1937) Short-period variations in the distribution of income. *Review of Economic Statistics* **19**, 133–43.

Staehle, H. (1938) New considerations on the distribution of incomes and the propensity to consume. *Review of Economic Statistics* **20**, 134–41.

Stone, J.R.N. (1945) The analysis of market demand. *Journal of the Royal Statistical Society* **108**, 286–382.

Stone, J.R.N. (1946) Review of Haavelmo (1944). *Economic Journal* **56**, 265–9.

Stone, J.R.N. (1947) On the interdependence of blocks of transactions. *Journal of the Royal Statistical Society* **9 (suppl)**, 1–45.

Stone, J.R.N. (1951) The demand for food in the United Kingdom before the war. *Metroeconomica* **3**, 8–27.

Stone, J.R.N. (1954) *The Measurement of Consumers' Expenditure and Behaviour in the United Kingdom, 1920–38*, Volume 1. Cambridge: Cambridge University Press.

Stone, J.R.N. and W.M. Stone (1938) The marginal propensity to consume and the multiplier: A statistical investigation. *Review of Economic Studies* **6**, 1–24.

Theil, H. (1953) Repeated least squares applied to complete equations systems, Central Planning Bureau, The Hague, mimeo.

Theil, H. (1954) Economic policy and welfare maximisation. *Weltwirtschaftsliches Archiv* **72**, 60–83.

Theil, H. (1957a) Specification errors and the estimation of economic relationships. *Review of International Statistical Institute* **25**, 41–51.

Theil, H. (1957b) A note on certainty equivalence in dynamic planning. *Econometrica* **25**, 246–9.

Theil, H. (1963) On the use of incomplete prior information in regression analysis. *Journal of the American Statistical Association* **58**, 401–14.

Theil, H. (1964) *Optimal Decision Rules for Government and Industry*. Amsterdam: North-Holland.

Theil, H. (1965) *Linear Aggregation of Economic Relations*. North-Holland: Amsterdam.

Thomas, J.J. (1989) Early economic history of consumption function. In N. de Marchi and C.L. Gilbert (eds), *History and Methodology of Econometrics*. Oxford: Oxford University Press, pp. 131–49.

Tiao, G.C. and A. Zellner (1964) On the Bayesian estimation of multivariate regression. *Journal of the Royal Statistical Society* **26**, 277–85.

Tinbergen, J. (1930) Determination and interpretation of supply curves: an example [Bestimmung und deutung von angebotskurven. Ein beispiel]. *Zeitschrift für Nationalökonomie* **1**,

669–79; English translation in D.F. Hendry and M.S. Morgan (eds) (1995), *The Foundations of Econometric Analysis*. Cambridge: Cambridge University Press, pp. 233–45.

Tinbergen, J. (1935) Annual survey: Suggestions on quantitative business cycle theory. *Econometrica* **3**, 241–308.

Tinbergen, J. (1936) Preadvies voor de Vereniging voor Staathuishoudkunde, The Hague.

Tinbergen, J. (1939) *Statistical Testing of Business-Cycle Theories*. Geneva: League of Nations.

Tinbergen, J. (1940) On a method of statistical business research: a reply. *Economic Journal* **40**, 141–54.

Tinbergen, J. (1952) *On the Theory of Economic Policy*. Amsterdam: North-Holland.

Tinbergen, J. (1956) *Economic Policy: Principles and Design*. Amsterdam: North-Holland.

Tobin, J. (1958) Estimation of relationships for limited dependent variables, *Econometrica* **26**, 24–36.

Vining, R. (1949) Koopmans on the choice of variables to be studied and of methods of measurement, A rejoinder. *Review of Economics and Statistics* **31**, 77–86, 91–4.

Von Neumann, J. (1941) Distribution of the ratio of the mean square successive difference to the variance. *Annals of Mathematical Statistics* **12**, 367–95.

Von Neumann, J. (1942) A further remark on the distribution of the ratio of the mean square successive difference to the variance. *Annals of Mathematical Statistics* **13**, 86–8.

Wald, A. (1936) Calculation and elimination of seasonal fluctuations [Berechnung und ausschaltung von saisonschwankungen], Vienna: Julius Springer, chapter 1; English translation in D.F. Hendry and M.S. Morgan (eds) (1995), *The Foundations of Econometric Analysis*. Cambridge: Cambridge University Press, pp. 175–9.

Walters, A.A. (1971) Consistent expectations, distributed lags, and the quantity theory. *Economic Journal* **81**, 273–81.

Waugh, F.V. (1942) Regression between two sets of variables. *Econometrica* **10**, 290–310.

Waugh, F.V. (1961) The place of Least Squares in econometrics. *Econometrica* **29**, 386–96.

Weintraub, R.E. (1991) *Stabilizing Dynamics*. Cambridge: Cambridge University Press.

Wold, H.O.A. (1938) *A Study in the Analysis of Stationary Time Series*. Stockholm: Almqvist and Wiksell.

Wold, H.O.A. (1943–44) A synthesis of pure demand analysis, I-III. *Skandinavisk Aktuarietidskrigft* **26**, 84–119, 220–63; **27**, 69–120.

Wold, H.O.A. and L. Juréen (1953) *Demand Analysis: A Study in Econometrics*. New York: Wiley and Sons.

Working, E.J. (1927) What do statistical demand curves show? *Quarterly Journal of Economics* **41**, 212–35.

Working, H. (1935) Differential price behavior as a subject for commodity price analysis. *Econometrica* **3**, 416–27.

Wright, P.G. (1928) *The Tariff on Animal and Vegetable Oils*. New York: Macmillan.

Wulwick, N.J. (1987) The Phillips Curve: Which? Whose? To do what? How? *Southern Economic Journal* **53**, 834–57.

Wulwick, N.J. (1989) Phillips' approximate regression. *Oxford Economic Papers* **41**, 170–88.

Young, W. and W. Darity Jr. (2001) The early history of rational and implicit expectations. *History of Political Economy* **33**, 773–813.

Yule, G.U. (1926) Why do we sometimes get nonsense correlations between time series? A study in the sampling and nature of time series. *Journal of the Royal Statistical Society* **89**, 1–64.

Yule, G.U. (1927) On a method of investigating periodicities in disturbed series, with special reference to Wolfer's sunspot numbers. *Philosophical Transactions of the Royal Society of London* Series A **226**, 267–98.

Zellner, A. (1971a) *An Introduction to Bayesian Inference in Econometrics*. New York: Wiley.

Zellner, A. (1971b) The Bayesian approach and alternatives in econometrics. In M.D. Intriligator (ed.), *Frontiers of Quantitative Economics*. Amsterdam: North-Holland, pp. 178–93.

Zellner, A. and G.C. Tiao (1964) Bayesian analysis of the regression model with autocorrelated errors. *Journal of the American Statistical Association* **59**, 763–78.

Part III
Asymptotic Techniques and Theorems

5

Asymptotic Methods and Functional Central Limit Theorems

James Davidson

Abstract

This chapter sketches the fundamentals of asymptotic distribution theory, and applies these specifically to questions relating to weak convergence on function spaces. These results have important applications in the analysis of nonstationary time series models. A simple case of the functional central limit theorem for processes with independent increments is stated and proved, after detailing the necessary results relating to the topology of spaces of functions and of probability measures. The concepts of weak convergence, tightness and stochastic equicontinuity, and their roles in the derivation of functional central limit theorems, are defined and reviewed. It is also shown how to extend the analysis to the vector case, and to various functionals of Brownian motion arising in nonstationary regression theory. The analysis is then widened to consider the problem of dependent increments, contrasting linear and nonparametric representations of dependence. The properties of Brownian motion and related Gaussian processes are examined, including variance-transformed processes, the Ornstein–Uhlenbeck process and fractional Brownian motion. Next, the case of functionals whose limits are characterized by stochastic integrals is considered. This theory is essential to (for example) the analysis of multiple regression in integrated processes. The derivation of the Itô integral is summarized, followed by application to the weak convergence of covariances. The final section of the chapter considers increment distributions with infinite variance, and shows how weak convergence to a Lévy process generalizes the usual case of the FCLT, having a Gaussian limit.

5.1	Naïve distribution theory	160
5.2	Asymptotic theory	161
	5.2.1 Stochastic convergence	163
	5.2.2 Application to regression	166
	5.2.3 Autoregressive and unit root processes	168
5.3	Distributions on a function space	170
	5.3.1 Random sequences	170
	5.3.2 Spaces of functions	171
	5.3.3 The space $C_{[0,1]}$	173
	5.3.4 The space $D_{[0,1]}$	174
	5.3.5 Brownian motion	176
5.4	The functional central limit theorem	177
	5.4.1 Weak convergence	177
	5.4.2 Tightness	178

	5.4.3	Stochastic equicontinuity	179
	5.4.4	Convergence of probability measures	181
	5.4.5	Proof of the FCLT	182
	5.4.6	The multivariate case	184
	5.4.7	Functionals of B	185
5.5	Dependent increments		188
	5.5.1	Martingale differences	188
	5.5.2	General dependence	189
	5.5.3	Linear processes	190
	5.5.4	Mixing	191
	5.5.5	Near-epoch dependence	192
	5.5.6	More on linear forms	193
5.6	Processes related to Brownian motion		194
	5.6.1	Variance-Transformed BM	194
	5.6.2	Ornstein–Uhlenbeck process	195
	5.6.3	Fractional Brownian motion	196
5.7	Stochastic integrals		199
	5.7.1	Derivation of the Itô integral	199
	5.7.2	Weak convergence of covariances	201
	5.7.3	Application to regression	203
5.8	The infinite variance case		205
	5.8.1	α-stable distributions	205
	5.8.2	Lévy motion	207

5.1   Naïve distribution theory

We begin this chapter with a brief explanation of why its subject matter is important to econometricians. To make inferences about econometric models and their parameters, something must be known about the distributions of estimates and test statistics. What range will these random variables typically fall into when a certain hypothesis is true? How far outside this range should the statistic fall before the chance of its realization is so small that we should conclude that the hypothesis is false?

At the elementary level, these difficult questions are often handled by postulating an idealized and simplified world satisfying the assumptions of the Classical Regression Model (CRM). In the CRM world, all the observed economic variables except one (the dependent variable) can be treated as fixed. That is to say, more precisely, "fixed in repeated samples." For illustration, consider the regression model

$$y = X\beta + u \tag{5.1.1}$$

Were we to have the opportunity to observe this phenomenon (the pair y, X) repeatedly, the variables X should assume the same sample values in successive drawings, and only the dependent variable y should vary. In addition, it is usually assumed that the dependent variable is normally and independently distributed with fixed variance, as $y \sim N(X\beta, \sigma^2 I)$. It would then follow that the least squares estimator $\hat{\beta} = (X'X)^{-1}X'y$ has the property

$$\hat{\beta} \sim N(\beta, \sigma^2(X'X)^{-1})$$

and the regression "t ratios" and "F statistics" would exactly follow the Student's t and F distributions when the null hypotheses are true. Our questions are then simply answered with reference to the t and F tables.

Popular as it is, this justification of inference procedures is, of course, dishonest. In economics (an essentially non-experimental discipline), cases in which a repeated sampling exercise will throw up the same pattern of explanatory variables are almost unheard of. When a new sample of firms or households is drawn, all the variables are randomly replaced, not just the dependent. However, notwithstanding that the CRM world is a fiction, the theory still yields generally valid results provided two assumptions hold. First, the sample observations must be independently distributed. Second, it is required that $u \,|\, X \sim N(0, \sigma^2 I)$, where $u \,|\, X$ denotes the conditional distribution of u, holding X fixed. It is sometimes thought that all that is required is for u_t to be serially independent, implying no more than a notion of correct specification, but this is incorrect. The rows of X also need to be independent of each other, a condition virtually never attained in time series data. In time series it is rarely possible to assume that x_{t+j} for $j > 0$ does not depend on u_t, a shock preceding it in time, and this would invalidate the conditioning exercise.

If the sample were truly independent, as in a randomly drawn cross-section for example, conditioning u on X is merely equivalent to conditioning u_t on x_t for each $t = 1, \ldots, T$ (T denoting sample size). In this case, while the CRM does not hold and $\hat{\beta}$ is not normally distributed (unconditionally), it is still the case that $\hat{\beta} \,|\, X$ is normal. The t and F statistics for the regression follow the t and F distributions exactly, since their conditional distributions are free of dependence on X, and hence equivalent to their unconditional distributions. We may "act as if" the CRM assumptions hold. However, when either the conditional normality assumption fails, or the sample is in any way dependent (both conditions endemic in econometric data sets), the only recourse available is to large-sample (asymptotic) approximations.

5.2 Asymptotic theory

The asymptotic approach to econometric inference is to derive approximate distributions under weaker assumptions than in the CRM setup, where the approximation improves with sample size. These arguments invoke a collection of theorems on stochastic convergence. In this section the scene is set with a brief resume of the fundamental ideas, starting with the axiomatic probability model. For further reading on these topics, see, for example, Davidson (1994). Another accessible text aimed at nonspecialists is Pollard (2002).

The standard representation of a probability space (a mathematical model of a random experiment) is the triple $(\Omega, \mathcal{F}, P)$, where Ω is the sample space (the collection of all random objects under consideration), $\mathcal{F}$ is a σ-field, being the collection of random events (subsets of Ω) to which probabilities are to be assigned, and P is the probability measure, such that $P(A) \in [0,1]$ is the probability of the event A, for each $A \in \mathcal{F}$. Recall that a σ-field is a class of subsets of Ω having the properties

(a) $\Omega \in \mathcal{F}$.
(b) if $A \in \mathcal{F}$ then $A^c \in \mathcal{F}$ where $A^c = \Omega - A$.
(c) if $A_1, A_2, A_3, \ldots \in \mathcal{F}$ (an infinite collection) then $\bigcup_{i=1}^{\infty} A_i \in \mathcal{F}$.

If C is any class of subsets of Ω the notation $\sigma(C)$ represents the smallest σ-field containing C. This is called the "σ-field generated by C." A probability measure (p.m.) $P : \mathcal{F} \mapsto [0, 1]$ is then a set function having the properties $P(\Omega) = 1$, and

$$P\left(\bigcup_{i=1}^{\infty} A_i\right) = \sum_{i=1}^{\infty} P(A_i)$$

for disjoint collections $A_1, A_2, A_3, \ldots \in \mathcal{F}$.

It is worth being reminded of why a probability space is defined in this manner. We need a way to assign probabilities to all sets of interest, but these are usually too numerous to allow a rule to assign each one individually. Hence, we assign probabilities to a class C of "basic" events, and then extend these probabilities to elements of $\sigma(C)$ using the rules of set algebra. The *extension theorem* is the fundamental result in probability, stating that if the class C is rich enough, probabilities can be uniquely assigned to all the members of $\sigma(C)$. C is called a *determining class* for P. However, to go beyond $\sigma(C)$ is to run the risk of encountering so-called "non-measurable" sets. In infinite spaces it is not feasible to simply let $\mathcal{F}$ be the power set of Ω without running into contradictions.

Often, $(\Omega, \mathcal{F}, P)$ is to be thought of as the "fundamental" probability space for a particular random experiment, where the outcomes are not necessarily numerical magnitudes. The outcomes are then mapped into a "derived" space, by the act of measurement. The best known example of a derived probability space, on which random variables live, is $(\mathbb{R}, \mathcal{B}, \mu)$, where $\mathbb{R}$ denotes the real line, and $\mathcal{B}$, called the *Borel field* of $\mathbb{R}$, is the σ-field generated by the set of the half-lines $(-\infty, x]$ for $x \in \mathbb{R}$. The fact that this is a rich enough collection is evidenced by the fact that $\mathcal{B}$ is also the σ-field generated by the open sets of $\mathbb{R}$, containing also the intervals, the closed sets, and much more besides. A random variable (r.v.) can be thought of as a measurable mapping $X : \Omega \mapsto \mathbb{R}$ where "measurable" means that $X^{-1}(A) \in \mathcal{F}$ for every $A \in \mathcal{B}$, and the probabilities are assigned by the rule $\mu(A) = P(X^{-1}(A))$ for each $A \in \mathcal{B}$. A fundamental result, since the half-lines form a determining class for this space, is that specifying a cumulative distribution function (c.d.f.) $F(x) = \mu((-\infty, x])$ is sufficient to define $\mu(A)$ uniquely for every $A \in \mathcal{B}$.

5.2.1 Stochastic convergence

Given this background, we can now describe the basic toolbox of results for asymptotic analysis. The essential idea is that of a random sequence, $X_1, X_2, \ldots, X_T, \ldots = \{X_t\}_{t=1}^{\infty}$, and the essential problem whether, and how, such a sequence might converge as T increases. The more familiar case is the sequence of constants $\{a_t\}_{t=1}^{\infty}$; say, $a_t = t$, or $a_t = 1/t$. If for every $\varepsilon > 0$ there exists an integer N_ε such that $|a_T - a| < \varepsilon$ for all $T > N_\varepsilon$, then we say "a_T converges to a," and write $a_T \to a$. The first of our examples does not converge, on this criterion, but the second one converges to 0.

By contrast, there are several different ways to capture the notion of the convergence of a sequence of r.v.s. The basic approach is to define certain associated nonstochastic sequences, and consider whether these converge. Let μ_T represent the probability measure associated with X_T, such that $\mu_T(A) = P(X_T \in A)$, where A is any set of real numbers to which probabilities are to be assigned. Here are four contrasting convergence concepts:

1. *Almost sure convergence*

$$X_T(\omega) \to X(\omega) \text{ for every } \omega \in C, \text{ where } C \in \mathcal{F} \text{ and } P(C) = 1. \text{ Write } X_T \overset{a.s.}{\to} X.$$

2. *Convergence in mean square*

$$E(X_T - X)^2 \to 0. \text{ Write } X_T \overset{ms}{\to} X.$$

3. *Convergence in probability*

$$P(|X_T - X| < \varepsilon) \to 1 \text{ for all } \varepsilon > 0. \text{ Write } X_T \overset{pr}{\to} X.$$

4. *Convergence in distribution* (weak convergence of probability measures)
   $\mu_T(A) \to \mu(A)$ for every $A \in \mathcal{F}$ such that $\mu(\delta A) = 0$, where δA denotes the boundary points of A. Equivalently, $F_T(x) \to F(x)$ at all continuity points of F. Write $\mu_T \Rightarrow \mu$ or $X_T \overset{d}{\to} X$, where $X \sim \mu$.

Almost sure convergence and convergence in mean square both imply convergence in probability, and convergence in probability implies weak convergence, and is equivalent to weak convergence when the limit is a constant. Otherwise, none of the reverse implications hold. There is an important distinction to be made between weak convergence and the other modes, since this specifies a limiting distribution but not a limiting r.v. In other words, if $X_T \overset{pr}{\to} X$ this implies that (say) $|X_{2T} - X_T| \overset{pr}{\to} 0$ such that when the sample is large enough, the effect of doubling it is negligible. However, it is *not* the case that $X_T \overset{d}{\to} X$ implies $|X_{2T} - X_T| \overset{d}{\to} 0$. What converges in this case is the sequence of probability measures, not a sequence of random variables. The conventional, rather imprecise, notation implies that the limit is the distribution of a specified r.v. X, and sometimes this is written in the more explicit form "$X_T \xrightarrow{d} N(0, \sigma^2)$" or similar.

The sequence with typical index T that satisfies these convergence criteria is usually a sequence of sample statistics or estimators, hence functions of T data points. The data points themselves also constitute real sequences, which we often distinguish with the typical index t. The following are the most important asymptotic results concerning the sequences generated by constructing averages of data sequences $\{U_1, U_2, \ldots, U_T\}$ as T increases. Let

$$\bar{U}_T = \frac{1}{T}\sum_{t=1}^{T} U_t.$$

1. *The weak (strong) law of large numbers* (W(S)LLN)
   If $E|U_t| < \infty$ for each $t \geq 1$, then under suitable additional regularity conditions

$$\bar{U}_T - E(\bar{U}_T) \xrightarrow{pr} 0 \;(\xrightarrow{a.s.} 0) \tag{5.2.1}$$

2. *The central limit theorem* (CLT)
   If $EU_t^2 < \infty$ for each $t \geq 1$, then under suitable additional regularity conditions

$$\frac{\bar{U}_T - E(\bar{U}_T)}{\sqrt{E(\bar{U}_T - E(\bar{U}_T))^2}} \xrightarrow{d} N(0, 1) \tag{5.2.2}$$

Two points to note. First, (5.2.1) does not imply that $E(\bar{U}_T)$ must be a constant independent of T, or even that it is a convergent sequence, although of course this is often the case. Second, it is often the case that

$$E(\bar{U}_T - E(\bar{U}_T))^2 = \sigma^2/T$$

where σ^2 is the common variance of the data points, and then (5.2.2) can be restated with the customary "$\sqrt{T}$" normalization. Our version simply emphasizes that it is the sample average, re-normalized to have zero mean and unit variance, that is the sequence of interest here.

The laws of large numbers are rather straightforward and intuitive. Few would doubt that a sample average usually approaches a limiting value as the sample increases, simply because the marginal contribution of the last term is inevitably getting smaller relative to the whole. It is perhaps of more interest to note those situations where the convergence fails, primarily when $E|U_t| = \infty$. The Cauchy distribution is a well-known counter-example, in which new sample drawings can be large enough, with high enough probability, that the average never settles down to a fixed value – and is, in fact, just another Cauchy variate.

On the other hand, many people find the fact that the normal (or Gaussian) "bell curve" arises by aggregating many independent zero-mean shocks to be mysterious at an intuitive level, even though the mathematics is quite simple and transparent. One way to appreciate the mechanism at work is through the fact that, among those possessing a variance, the Gaussian is the unique distribution to be invariant under the summation of independent drawings. As is well known, the *characteristic function* (ch.f.) of any random variable U, defined as

$$\phi_U(\lambda) = E(e^{i\lambda U}) \qquad (5.2.3)$$

is an equivalent representation of the distribution. If $U_1, \ldots, U_T$ are independent drawings from this distribution, and $S_T = (U_1 + \cdots + U_T)/a_T$ for some $a_T > 0$, then

$$\begin{aligned} \phi_{S_T}(\lambda) &= E(e^{i\lambda U_1/a_T}) \cdots E(e^{i\lambda U_T/a_T}) \\ &= [\phi_{U_1}(\lambda) \cdots \phi_{U_T}(\lambda)]^{1/a_T}. \end{aligned} \qquad (5.2.4)$$

This identity raises the interesting question of whether, for some sequence a_T, the functional forms of $\phi_{S_T}(\lambda)$ and $\phi_U(\lambda)$ are the same. As is well known, the Gaussian distribution with mean 0 and variance σ^2 has ch.f. $\phi_U(\lambda) = e^{-\sigma^2\lambda^2/2}$, and in this case it is easily seen that setting $a_T = \sqrt{T}$ yields the desired result:

$$\phi_{S_T}(\lambda) = (e^{-(\sigma/\sqrt{T})^2\lambda^2/2})^T = e^{-\sigma^2\lambda^2/2}. \qquad (5.2.5)$$

This fact helps us to appreciate how the Gaussian distribution acts as an "attractor" for sums of independent r.v.s, normalized by the square root of the sample size. A formal proof of the CLT may be obtained by considering the Taylor's expansion of $\phi_{S_T}(\lambda)$ and showing that the first and second order terms match those of (5.2.5), while the higher order terms are of small order in T. Note that the variances of the r.v.s must be finite and, of course the "$\sqrt{T}$" normalization corresponds to the familiar summation rule for variances of independent sums.

We will avoid specifying regularity conditions for the LLN and CLT in detail here, since there are so many different ways to formulate them. Various specific cases are cited in the sequel. Let it suffice to say two things at this point. First, if the sequence elements are identically and independently distributed, then no extra conditions are required. However, if the sequence elements are either heterogeneously distributed, or serially dependent, or both, then a range of different sufficient restrictions can be demonstrated. A condition that frustrates the CLT is where a finite number of terms of the sum are influential enough to affect the whole. The well-known *Lindeberg condition* for the CLT rules out this possibility. *Uniform integrability* is a distinct but related restriction relevant to the LLN, ruling out certain pathological cases where the absolute moments depend excessively on extreme values in the limit. However, requiring that the order of existing moments be slightly larger than 1 in the LLNs, or larger than 2 in the CLT, is a simple way to avoid a failure of either of these weaker but more subtle conditions.

Standard treatments of the CLT assume stationary process increments, but it is an important fact that this is not a necessary restriction. In particular, conditions of the form

$$E(U_t^2) = t^\alpha \sigma^2 \tag{5.2.6}$$

can be accommodated, for any $\alpha > -1$. In other words, the variances may diverge to infinity, and even converge to 0, provided the variance sequence is not actually summable. This form of CLT is especially useful for deriving certain forms of the functional CLT, as explained in section 5.6.

Regularity conditions restricting the dependence are of many sorts. Some involve assuming the process is *linear* (i.e., has an infinite-order MA representation with independent shocks) and placing restrictions on the coefficients. Others, such as mixing and near-epoch dependence, are purely non-parametric conditions imposing "short memory." The martingale difference assumption is a sufficient restriction on dependence for all these results, a very useful fact for econometric applications in particular. We say more about these cases in the discussion of the FCLT, see section 5.5.

Certain supplementary results, the handmaidens of the LLN and CLT so to speak, are constantly invoked in asymptotic analysis.

1. *Slutsky's Theorem* If $X_T \overset{\text{pr}}{\to} a$, and $g(\cdot)$ is continuous at a, then plim $g(X_T) = g(a)$.
2. *Cramér's Theorem* If $Y_T \overset{\text{d}}{\longrightarrow} Y$ and $X_T \overset{\text{pr}}{\longrightarrow} a$ then
   (i) $X_T + Y_T \overset{\text{d}}{\longrightarrow} a + Y$
   (ii) $X_T Y_T \overset{\text{d}}{\longrightarrow} aY$
   (iii) $\frac{Y_T}{X_T} \overset{\text{d}}{\longrightarrow} \frac{Y}{a}$ when $a \neq 0$.
3. *Continuous Mapping Theorem* (CMT) If $X_T \overset{\text{d}}{\longrightarrow} X$ and $g(\cdot)$ is continuous, then $g(X_T) \overset{\text{d}}{\longrightarrow} g(X)$.

Versions of these results for random vectors are easy extensions, using the following result in particular.

4. *Cramér–Wold Theorem* Let $\mathbf{X}_T$ be a sequence of random vectors. Then $\mathbf{X}_T \overset{\text{d}}{\longrightarrow} \mathbf{X}$ if and only if for all conformable fixed vectors λ, $\lambda' \mathbf{X}_T \overset{\text{d}}{\longrightarrow} \lambda' \mathbf{X}$.

Additional background on all these results, including formal statements, proofs and mathematical details, can be found in a number of specialist texts with an econometric emphasis and motivation such as McCabe and Tremayne (1993), Davidson (1994) and White (1999).

5.2.2 Application to regression

Now, to return to the problem posed in Section 5.1. Letting T denote sample size, and $\hat{\boldsymbol{\beta}}$ the least squares estimator as before, write

$$\sqrt{T}(\hat{\boldsymbol{\beta}} - \boldsymbol{\beta}) = \left(\frac{\mathbf{X}'\mathbf{X}}{T}\right)^{-1} \frac{\mathbf{X}'u}{\sqrt{T}}. \tag{5.2.7}$$

Subject to regularity conditions, the matrix $T^{-1}X'X$ converges in probability to its mean, M_{xx}, thanks to the WLLN. This matrix must be nonsingular. Subject to further regularity conditions, the vector $X'u/\sqrt{T}$ is jointly normally distributed in the limit according to the vector generalization of the CLT, making use of the Cramér–Wold theorem. The variance matrix of this vector under the limiting distribution is shown to equal $\sigma^2 M_{xx}$, making use of the assumed uncorrelatedness of x_t and u_t and the result (using the consistency of $\hat{\beta}$ and the Slutsky theorem) that $s^2 \overset{\text{pr}}{\to} \sigma^2$.

The Slutsky Theorem (the result that the plim of the inverse matrix is the inverse of the plim) and the Cramér Theorem (the result that $T(X'X)^{-1}$ can be replaced by M_{xx}^{-1} in the limiting distribution) can now be combined with the CLT and WLLN to yield the conclusion

$$\sqrt{T}(\hat{\beta} - \beta) \overset{\text{d}}{\to} N(0, \sigma^2 M_{xx}^{-1}).$$

Since the limiting covariance matrix $\sigma^2 M_{xx}^{-1}$ is consistently estimated by $Ts^2 (X'X)^{-1}$, as just indicated, and since the Student's t family approaches the normal as the degrees of freedom increase, the spurious "Student's t" result can therefore be justified as an approximation to the distribution actually attained by the "t-ratios" in large samples. The discussion must then focus on the variety of regularity conditions required for this large-sample result to hold.

In independent samples, these conditions are comparatively simple to express. Letting x_t' denote the tth row of X, and u_t the corresponding element of u, two basic requirements are

$$E(x_t u_t) = 0$$

and

$$E(x_t x_t' u_t^2) = \sigma^2 M_{xx} < \infty.$$

If it is possible to assume that the data are identically distributed, then both $E(u_t^2)$ and $E(x_t x_t')$, if they exist, are finite constants not depending on t. If the data are heterogeneously distributed, a conveniently stated sufficient condition for the CLT is

$$E|\lambda' x_t u_t|^{2+\delta} \leq B$$

for all conformable vectors λ of unit length, some $\delta > 0$, and all $t = 1, \ldots T$, $T \geq 1$, where B is a finite bound (see Davidson, 2000, 3.5.1).

In time series, matters are always more complicated, because serial independence of (x_t, u_t) is an improbable restriction, as noted above. We are forced to introduce asymptotic results for dependent processes. One might do this by assuming that the independent variables follow some well-known model such as the VAR, so that the amount of dependence depends in a fairly simple way on the autoregressive root closest to the unit circle. However, such assumptions would often be heroic, requiring much more detailed knowledge of the generation mechanism of the sample than we would ever need under serial independence. It is also possible to cite mixing and/or near-epoch dependence conditions (see Sections 5.5.4 and 5.5.5), although when this is done the conditions are not easily verified without specifying an explicit model. Asymptotics can therefore be problematic in time series, and there is also the rarely cited fact that dependence must slow the rate of convergence in the CLT, reducing the effective sample size. Subject to these caveats, asymptotic theory may provide a workable if imperfect solution to the inference problem.

5.2.3 Autoregressive and unit root processes

We now examine a particularly well-known example of a time series model in a bit more detail. We focus on the simple case,

$$x_t = \lambda x_{t-1} + u_t, \qquad u_t \sim iid(0, \sigma_u^2)$$

where $x_0 = 0$; generalizations with more lags and more variables will not contribute much to the important insights we seek. If $|\lambda| < 1$, it is well-known that the autoregressive series is asymptotically stationary with a finite variance $E(x_t^2) = \sigma_u^2/(1 - \lambda^2)$, and that its dependence (serial correlation) declines exponentially. Applying the arguments in the previous section yields the result

$$\sqrt{T}(\hat{\lambda} - \lambda) = \frac{T^{-1/2} \sum_{t=2}^{T} x_{t-1} u_t}{T^{-1} \sum_{t=2}^{T} x_{t-1}^2} \underset{asy}{\sim} N(0, 1 - \lambda^2). \tag{5.2.8}$$

However, it is evident that this formula is tending to break down as λ approaches 1. It appears that at that point, $\sqrt{T}(\hat{\lambda} - \lambda)$ is approaching 0 in probability, since the variance is tending to zero.

To analyze the problem in more detail, consider first the denominator of (5.2.8). With $\lambda = 1$ we have

$$x_t = x_{t-1} + u_t = \sum_{s=1}^{t} u_t. \tag{5.2.9}$$

This is called an *integrated* or *partial sum* process. Under the other stated assumptions,

$$E(x_{t-1}^2) = (t - 1)\sigma_u^2. \tag{5.2.10}$$

The sample average of these terms is therefore likely to be diverging, not tending to a constant. The obvious thing is to consider instead

$$T^{-2} \sum_{t=2}^{T} x_{t-1}^2. \tag{5.2.11}$$

Since it is well-known that

$$\sum_{t=2}^{T}(t-1)=\frac{T(T-1)}{2}$$

it is evident from (5.2.10) that (5.2.11) has a finite mean in the limit, equal to $\sigma_u^2/2$. So far, so good. However, is there a law of large numbers with this normalization, such that (5.2.11) converges to a constant? This is where the conventional arguments start to come unstuck, for the sequence $\{x_1^2, \ldots, x_T^2\}$ does not satisfy a LLN. Since the mean (and also variance) of these terms grows with T, at most a finite number of them at the end of the sequence must dominate the average. The variable represented in (5.2.11) is accordingly random even in the limit. Moreover, while we can show that $T^{-1}\sum_{t=2}^{T}x_{t-1}u_t$ converges to a limiting distribution, this is both non-normal and also correlated with (5.2.11). Therefore, the limiting distribution of the appropriately normalized error of the estimate $T(\hat{\lambda}-\lambda)$ is not normal. The "naïve" distribution theory for least squares estimates therefore fails, even as an approximation.

The strategy for tackling the problem involves two steps. First, we have to recognize that the integrated time series $\{x_1, \ldots, x_T\}$ has a limiting distribution itself, after suitable normalization. Second, we make use of this distribution, and of the CMT and some related tools, to derive the limiting distribution of the sample statistic. To illustrate these developments we continue with the simple partial-sum process (5.2.9). Since the time series is a cumulation of independent shocks, it is immediate from the CLT that

$$\frac{1}{\sqrt{T}}x_T \xrightarrow{d} N(0, \sigma_u^2). \tag{5.2.12}$$

However, if T is an even number then

$$\frac{1}{\sqrt{T/2}}x_{T/2} \xrightarrow{d} N(0, \sigma_u^2) \tag{5.2.13}$$

is equally true. Indeed, any fixed fraction of the sample, such that its size increases with T, can be held to obey the corresponding rule. Therefore, let r denote any point of the interval $[0,1]$, and use this to select a part of the sample by defining the notation $[Tr]$ to mean the largest integer not exceeding Tr. Then (5.2.12) can be generalized to

$$\frac{1}{\sqrt{T}}x_{[Tr]} \xrightarrow{d} N(0, r\sigma_u^2).$$

The next key step is to observe that (for any particular realization $\{u_1, \ldots, u_T\}$) the equations

$$X_T(r) = \frac{1}{\sigma_u\sqrt{T}}x_{[Tr]}, \quad 0 \leq r \leq 1 \tag{5.2.14}$$

define a function on the real line. This function is discontinuous, having little jumps at the points where $Tr = [Tr]$, but it has the interesting property that, regarded as a drawing from the underlying joint distribution of shocks, its values in the intervals $(t-1)/T \leq r < t/T$, for $t = 1, \ldots, T$, are tending to become Gaussian with variance r. Of course, at the same time, the intervals are getting narrower as T increases. The variance of the random "jumps" shrinks by a factor $1/T$ as the intervals shrink by a factor of $1/T$. It appears that the limiting case is a continuous "Gaussian function." In the following section we review the properties of this limiting function in detail, and then go on to consider the manner of convergence to the limit.

5.3 Distributions on a function space

The first major hurdle is to extend distribution theory from comparatively simply objects like random variables to very complex objects such as random functions. When we say "complex," the point to bear in mind is that a function on a real-valued domain, say $x(r)$ for $0 \leq r \leq 1$, represents an uncountable infinity of real numbers. To each of these points, in principle, a distribution has to be assigned. We are familiar with the idea of a joint distribution of two, three, or several random variables, that has to specify not just the distribution of each one standing alone (the marginal distributions), but also the nature of their interactions and the dependence between them. The extension of these ideas to the case of functions is evidently fairly heroic, and as we shall see, a number of interesting mathematical problems arise along the way. The acknowledged primary source for many of the results is Billingsley (1968). Although a fundamental under-pinning of modern asymptotic theory, the material of this section has yet to make its way into mainstream econometrics texts. The most accessible reference is probably Davidson (1994). Other useful sources include Pollard (1984) and Jacod and Shiryaev (1987), and many probability texts devote sections to stochastic processes: see, for example, Feller (1971), Billingsley (1986) or Dudley (1989).

5.3.1 Random sequences

The sequences considered in this section are not, as a rule, assumed to be con-verging like the sequences discussed in section 5.2.1. They are typically collections of sequential observations, with equally spaced dates attached (the indices t). Being an ordered, countably infinite collection of real numbers, one may also conveniently think of a sequence as a point in the space $\mathbb{R}^{\infty}$.

Given the probability space $(\Omega, \mathcal{F}, P)$, a random sequence may be defined as a measurable mapping from Ω to $\mathbb{R}^{\infty}$. Note the significance of this definition; *one* drawing $\omega \in \Omega$ maps into an *infinite* sequence

$$x(\omega) = \{X_1(\omega), X_2(\omega), \ldots, X_t(\omega), \ldots\}.$$

Our next task is to construct this derived probability space in which the random elements are infinite sequences. For obvious reasons, this is not a trivial undertaking.

Let $\mathcal{C}$ denote the collection of *finite-dimensional cylinder sets* of $\mathbb{R}^\infty$, that is, the sets of $\mathbb{R}^\infty$ of which at most a finite number of sequence coordinates are restricted to sets of $\mathcal{B}$ (the Borel field of of $\mathbb{R}$). Thus, the elements of $\mathcal{C}$ can be thought of as mapping one-for-one into random vectors, points in $\mathbb{R}^k$ for some k, representing the number of restricted sequence coordinates. Recall that a Borel field of any space is the σ-field generated by the open sets. In this case, it is possible to show that $\mathcal{B}^\infty$, the Borel field of sets of $\mathbb{R}^\infty$, is identical with $\sigma(\mathcal{C})$, the smallest σ-field containing $\mathcal{C}$. It remains to show that distributions can be constructed on the pair $(\mathbb{R}^\infty, \mathcal{B}^\infty)$.

The fundamental result is *Kolmogorov's consistency theorem*. It is difficult to give a formal statement of the theorem without resorting to technical language, but an informal explanation goes as follows. First, the distribution of any k coordinates of the sequence can be represented as a distribution of a random k-vector in the space $(\mathbb{R}^k, \mathcal{B}^k, \mu_k)$, which is a reasonably straightforward extension of the one-dimensional case. Even with an infinite sequence, marginalizing with respect to all but k coordinates yields such a distribution. These are called the *finite dimensional distributions* (or *fidis*) of the sequence. Note that, for any choice of k coordinates, the largest of them is still a finite number, and so the fidis can always be represented in this way. The consistency theorem then states that, given a family of distributions $\{\mu_k\}$ specified for every finite k, subject to the consistency condition

$$\mu_k(E) = \mu_m(E \times \mathbb{R}^{m-k}) \text{ for } E \in B^k \quad \text{and} \quad m > k > 0$$

there exists a unique infinite random sequence distributed on $(\mathbb{R}^\infty, \mathcal{B}^\infty, \mu_\infty)$ such that the collections of the μ_k, for $k = 1, 2, 3, \ldots$, are the fidis of the sequence. In other words, to specify a unique distribution for x it is sufficient to specify the fidis in a suitable manner. This overcomes the practical problem of specifying how an infinite sequence of coordinates is distributed. The consistency condition says that, if μ_m is a fidi, then the distributions μ_k for $k < m$ are obtained in the usual way, by marginalizing with respect to the $m - k$ extra coordinates. Another way to express the same result is to say that the cylinder sets $\mathcal{C}$ form a determining class for x. If probabilities are assigned to each member of $\mathcal{C}$ (a feasible project by standard methods), the whole distribution of x is given uniquely.

5.3.2 Spaces of functions

The number of coordinates of a sequence is countably infinite. The number of coordinates of a function is uncountable, which is to say, equipotent with the real continuum, and not capable of being labelled using the integers as an index set.

Let $R_{[0,1]}$, also denoted as just R when the context is clear, denote the set of all possible real-valued functions x: $[0,1] \mapsto \mathbb{R}$, an element of which associates every point $r \in [0,1]$ with a unique value $x(r)$. If the domain represents time, as it usually does, we call this a *process*, and if x is a random drawing from a specified distribution, a *stochastic* process. To construct such a distribution, the first question to be considered is whether a Borel field can be constructed for R, by analogy with $\mathbb{R}$ and $\mathbb{R}^\infty$. Since a Borel field is generated by the open sets of a space, this means being able to define an open set or, equivalently, to define a topology on the space.[1] This is usually done by defining a metric, a measure of "closeness" of two elements of the space, and so making the space into a metric space. The usual metric adopted for $\mathbb{R}$ is, of course, the *Euclidean distance* $|x - y|$, for real numbers x and y, although the metric

$$d_0(x, y) = \frac{|x - y|}{1 + |x - y|}$$

is topologically equivalent to $|x - y|$, while being bounded by 1.[2] Constructing a topology for $\mathbb{R}^\infty$ is a formalization that could be avoided, and so was left implicit in the discussion of random sequences, although note that a valid metric for this purpose (also bounded) is provided by

$$d_\infty(x, y) = \sum_{k=1}^{\infty} 2^{-k} d_0(x_k, y_k).$$

In the case of a space of functions, however, the topological properties of the space are a central issue. Since we can no longer enumerate the coordinates, a natural alternative is to adopt the *uniform metric*, defining the distance between elements $x, y \in R$ as

$$d_U(x, y) = \sup_{0 \le t \le 1} |x(t) - y(t)|.$$

Armed with this definition, we can define the Borel field $\mathcal{B}_R$ of the metric space (R, d_U) as the smallest σ-field containing the *open spheres* of the space, which are defined as

$$B(x, r) = \{y \in R : d_U(x, y) < r\} \quad \text{for all } x \in R, \ r > 0.$$

How, then, to assign probabilities to sets of $(R, \mathcal{B}_R)$? One place we might start is with the finite dimensional cylinder sets; in other words, sets of functions that are unrestricted except at a finite number of coordinates, $t_1, \ldots, t_k$. For example, consider a case with $k = 2$; the open set $A = \{x \in R : x(1/2) < 0, 0 < x(3/4) < 2\}$. Let $\mathcal{H}$ denote the set of all such finite-dimensional sets, and let $\mathcal{P} = \sigma(\mathcal{H})$. $\mathcal{P}$ is called the *projection* σ-field, since we can think of $\mathcal{H}$ as the set of projections of the function onto finite sets of coordinates. If this case were to be comparable to the sequence case, then we should have $\mathcal{P} = (\mathcal{B}_R)$. Alas, it turns out that $\mathcal{P} \subset \mathcal{B}_R$. In other words, $\mathcal{B}_R$ contains sets that are not countable unions of $\mathcal{H}$ sets. The non-countability of the domain presents a problem.

As a first approach to the measurability problem, we might attempt to construct a probability measure on $(R, \mathcal{P})$. Assuming the fundamental space $(\Omega, \mathcal{F}, P)$, let $x : \Omega \mapsto R$ denote an $\mathcal{F}/\mathcal{P}$-measurable mapping, and so generate a probability measure (p.m.) derived from P. The fidis associated with this distribution are the joint distributions of finite sets of coordinates $(x_{t_1}, \ldots, x_{t_k})$. The consistency theorem can be extended to identify this p.m. uniquely with the fidis, provided a second consistency condition is satisfied. This is as follows:

> Permuting the coordinates $t_1, \ldots, t_k$ changes the p.m. according to the same rule as permuting the integers $1, \ldots, k$.

There is no way to represent this distribution by a simple device such as the c.d.f. or characteristic function. However, the expected values $E(f(x))$, for all bounded continuous functionals[3] $f: R \mapsto \mathbb{R}$, are always defined uniquely and these values can be used to fingerprint the distribution.

So far, so good, and if this approach serves, it is the simplest available. However, the problem is that $\mathcal{P}$ may not contain all the cases we are interested in. Our goal should be to assign probabilities to all the Borel sets. This has proved impossible because the space (R, d_U) is really too big to handle. It is not a *separable* space, which means, as we shall see, that it contains Borel sets that cannot have measures assigned to them without running into inconsistencies. There are two ways we can attempt to overcome this difficulty, both of which, separately or in combination, have been exploited in the literature. The first is to consider a suitable subset of R containing most of the functions of interest. The second is to adopt a different topology, so that open sets can be defined in a more tractable way. The first of these methods involves fewer technicalities, but is mathematically rather clumsy. The second – or, strictly, a combination of both approaches – has been the most favoured technique in recent research.

5.3.3   The space $C_{[0,1]}$

One way to view the problem of applying distribution theory to functions is to find generalizations of the commonplace relations between real numbers that we use, often unconsciously, to construct distributions of random variables on the line. One way to achieve this is by working in the space of *continuous* functions on the unit interval, equipped with the uniform metric. This is denoted $C_{[0,1]}$, properly $(C_{[0,1]}, d_U)$ when it is necessary to specify the choice of metric, but also sometimes just C, when the context is clear.

The main virtue of $C_{[0,1]}$ is that it is a separable space, which means that it contains a countable, dense subset.[4] The space $\mathbb{R}$ is separable, since the rational numbers are countable, and also dense in the space. To show that $C_{[0,1]}$ is separable, one can exhibit the set of *piecewise-linear* functions, which consists of functions constructed from a countable set of points of the domain joined up with straight lines – the type of construction commonly used to plot discrete time series on a graph. If the points are assigned rational ordinates, then a countable collection of numbers defines each member of the set, and accordingly the set itself is countable – yet we can show that every continuous function is arbitrarily close, in d_U, to a member of this set.

The second important property of $C_{[0,1]}$ is *completeness*. This means that every Cauchy sequence of elements has a limit lying in the set. Recall that a Cauchy sequence is one in which the successive points are getting arbitrarily close together as we move down it. Although it is not hard to define sequences in $C_{[0,1]}$ having discontinuous limits, in the uniform metric such sequences cannot be Cauchy, because going from continuous to discontinuous must involve a positive jump at some point – and remember that all the points of the sequence must lie in $C_{[0,1]}$. Completeness is another property shared with $\mathbb{R}$, for Cauchy sequences of real numbers all have a real number as the limit.

The cash value of these properties, from the present point of view, is very simply that they imply $\mathcal{P}_C = \mathcal{B}_C$, where these are the restrictions to $C_{[0,1]}$ of the projection σ-field and Borel field of functions respectively.[5] The space $C_{[0,1]}$ equipped with d_U is from the topological viewpoint sufficiently like $\mathbb{R}$ that the construction of a probability space on $(C_{[0,1]}, \mathcal{B}_C)$ can follow similar lines. The actual procedure is the same as was described in the last section, constructing fidis on the cylinder sets, and then extending, using the consistency theorem. The difference is that the extension takes us to $\mathcal{B}_C$, while it failed to take us to $\mathcal{B}_R$.

The chief difficulty with working in $C_{[0,1]}$ to derive FCLTs is that the functions of chief interest do not belong to it! These are, of course, of the form X_T as defined in (5.2.14). Note that this function is constant except at points r that satisfy $r = [Tr]/T$, at which it jumps a distance $u_{[Tr]}$. A slightly clumsy fix to this problem is provided by the following trick. Define

$$X_T^*(r) = X_T(r) + \frac{u_{[Tr]+1}(Tr - [Tr])}{\sigma_u \sqrt{T}}. \tag{5.3.1}$$

This is a piecewise linear function of the type just described. X_T^* is an element of $C_{[0,1]}$ for any T, and as we shall see subsequently, the extra term can be shown to be negligible, and hence ignored in convergence arguments. This is how the simplest proofs of the FCLT are set up, and is the approach we adopt below. However, recent research has tended to adopt a different approach, somewhat more technically advanced, but also more flexible and easy to generalize. We next look briefly at the arguments invoked in this approach.

5.3.4   The space $D_{[0,1]}$

We found in Section 5.3.2 that the space R was "too large," when endowed with the uniform metric, to allow construction of a probability distribution without running into problems. Then we showed that the space $C_{[0,1]}$ was a feasible case, but unfortunately too small for our needs, without invoking awkward constructions. A compromise is provided by the space $D_{[0,1]}$ of *cadlag* functions on $[0,1]$. Cadlag is a French acronym standing for "continue à droit, limites à gauche," in other words, functions that may contain jumps, but not isolated points, such as to be discontinuous in both directions. Cadlag functions are right-continuous, and every point has a limit-point to its left. X_T in (5.2.14) is a good example. Its value at any point of discontinuity can be represented as the limit of a decreasing sequence of points to the right of it.

$D_{[0,1]}$ turns out to contain all the functions we are interested in, and there is no loss in excluding those cases featuring isolated discontinuities. However, $D_{[0,1]}$ is not separable under the uniform metric. The problem is that functions with discontinuities can have positive *uniform* distance from each other in spite of being equal at all but a single point. Consider, for example, the set of functions $\{x_\theta : \theta \in [0,1]\}$, where

$$x_\theta(t) = \begin{cases} 0, & t < \theta \\ 1, & t \geq \theta \end{cases}. \tag{5.3.2}$$

There are an uncountable number of these functions, one for each point of the unit interval, and yet in the uniform metric they are all at a distance $d_U = 1$ from each other. Thus, no subset of $(D_{[0,1]}, d_U)$ can be dense in $(D_{[0,1]}, d_U)$ yet also be countable.

What this means in practice is that $\mathcal{B}_D$ with the uniform metric still contains too many sets to define a probability space. Some of its elements are nonmeasurable. As already mentioned, one possible solution is to work with the projection σ-field.[6] However, probably the most commonly adopted solution in practice is to work with a different metric, such that $D_{[0,1]}$ becomes separable. What is popularly called the *Skorokhod metric* (actually, what Skorokhod (1956) dubbed the J1 metric) is

$$d_S = \inf_{\lambda \in \Lambda} \left\{ \varepsilon > 0 : \sup_t |\lambda(t) - t| \leq \varepsilon, \ \sup_t |x(t) - y(\lambda(t))| \leq \varepsilon \right\}$$

where Λ denotes the set of all increasing continuous functions $\lambda : [0,1] \mapsto [0,1]$. When functions have discontinuities, this is a more natural distance measure than d_U, because it allows functions to be compared by moving them "sideways" as well as vertically. The functions Λ can be thought of as representing a choice of little distortions of the time domain, and we choose the one that makes the distance between x and y as small as possible in both directions. Functions, x_θ and $x_{\theta+\delta}$, jumping a distance 1 at times θ and $\theta + \delta$ respectively and otherwise constant, can now be considered at a distance δ from each other, not 1, which is what the uniform metric would give.

The Skorokhod metric defines a topology on $D_{[0,1]}$, and it is this that matters from the point of view of defining the Borel field. The key property is that the metric space $(D_{[0,1]}, d_S)$ is separable. Unfortunately, though, it is not a complete space. Consider, for given $\delta > 0$, the function $z_{\theta\delta} = x_\theta - x_{\theta+\delta}$. This function is equal to 0 on the intervals $[0,\theta)$ and $[\theta+\delta, 1]$, and to 1 on the interval $[\theta, \theta+\delta)$. Thus, consider the Cauchy sequence of functions $z_{\theta,1/n}$, for $n = 1, 2, 3, \ldots$ The limit of this sequence is equal to 1 at point θ and zero everywhere else. It has an isolated discontinuity, and so is not an element of $D_{[0,1]}$.

However, this problem can be remedied by a modification that preserves the same topology. Billingsley (1968) shows that $(D_{[0,1]}, d_B)$ is a separable complete metric space, where

$$d_B = \inf_{\lambda \in \Lambda} \left\{ \varepsilon > 0 : \|\lambda\| \leq \varepsilon, \ \sup_t |x(t) - y(\lambda(t))| \leq \varepsilon \right\}$$

with

$$\|\lambda\| = \sup_{t \neq s} \left| \log \frac{\lambda(t) - \lambda(s)}{t - s} \right|$$

and Λ is the set of increasing continuous functions λ such that $\|\lambda\| < \infty$. Note how Billingsley's definition imposes some smoothness on the choice of possible transformations of the time domain, since its slope must be kept as near 1 as possible at each point, to prevent $\|\lambda\|$ becoming large. d_B also generates the Skorokhod topology. The key consequence is, of course, that the Borel field $\mathcal{B}_D$ is equal to the projection σ-field of $(D_{[0,1]}, d_B)$. Finite dimensional projections are a determining class for distributions on $(D_{[0,1]}, \mathcal{B}_D)$ with this metric.

5.3.5 Brownian motion

To conclude this discussion of function spaces and distributions defined on them, we exhibit the most important and best-known example. As is well-known, the botanist Robert Brown first noted the irregular motion of pollen particles suspended in water in 1827. As we now also know, thanks to Einstein's famous 1905 paper,[7] these are due to thermal agitation of the water molecules. The mathematical model of Brownian motion was developed by Norbert Wiener (1923) and it is sometimes called *Wiener measure*.

Formally, the standard real-valued Brownian motion (BM) process on the unit interval, denoted B, is defined by the following three properties:

1. $B(r) \sim N(0, r)$, $0 \leq r \leq 1$.
2. Increments $B(r_1) - B(0)$, $B(r_2) - B(r_1), \ldots, B(r_N) - B(r_{N-1})$ are totally independent of each other, for any collection $0 < r_1 < \cdots < r_N$.
3. Realizations of B are continuous, with $B(0) = 0$, with probability 1.

This is the natural extension to function spaces of the ordinary Gaussian distribution specified in the CLT. According to property 3, we may consider it as an element of $C_{[0,1]}$ almost surely. However, since exceptions of probability zero should not be ruled out in a formal statement, even if they have no practical consequences, we should strictly treat it as an element of $D_{[0,1]}$.

BM has a number of well-known attributes following from the definition. Independence of the increments means that $E(B(t)B(s)) = \min(t,s)$ and $E[(B(t) - B(s))B(s)] = 0$ for $t > s$. BM is *self-similar*, meaning that B has the same distribution as B^* defined by

$$B^*(t) = k^{-1/2}(B(s + kt) - B(s)), \quad 0 \leq t \leq 1$$

for any s and k such that $0 \leq s < 1$ and $0 < k \leq 1 - s$. As such, realizations of BM belong to the class of curves known as *fractals* (Mandelbrot, 1983). While it is almost surely continuous, observe that for any $t \in [0,1)$ and $0 < h < 1 - t$,

$B(t+h) - B(t) \sim N(0, h)$ implying

$$\frac{B(t+h) - B(t)}{h} \sim N(0, h^{-1}). \tag{5.3.3}$$

Letting $h \downarrow 0$ results in distributions with infinite variance. In other words, BM is nowhere differentiable, with probability 1. Moreover, realizations are almost surely of unbounded variation. Observe that $E|B(t+h) - B(t)| = O(T^{-1/2})$, and hence we can show

$$\sum_{j=0}^{T-1} |B((j+1)/T) - B(j/T)| \to \infty \text{ as } T \to \infty, \text{ with probability 1.}$$

5.4 The functional central limit theorem

The object of this section is to show that empirical processes such as X_T in (5.2.14) converge "weakly" to BM, under suitable regularity conditions. The result to be ultimately proved, under rather simple assumptions, is the following, originally due to Donsker (1951).

Theorem 5.4.1 *Suppose that $u_t \sim iid(0, \sigma_u^2)$, and the stochastic process X_T is defined by*

$$X_T(r) = \frac{1}{\sigma_u \sqrt{T}} \sum_{t=1}^{[Tr]} u_t, \quad 0 \le r \le 1$$

Then $X_T \xrightarrow{d} B$.

Before proceeding to an actual demonstration, we must first define some terms and deal with various technical preliminaries.

5.4.1 Weak convergence

The term "weak convergence of distributions" is probably widely misunderstood. The term "weak" here has a wholly different connotation from that in (say) "weak law of large numbers," and derives from concepts in topology.

The fundamental problem, worth digressing into briefly at this point, is to consider what it means to say that one p.m. is close to another. In the preceding section, we have been addressing this question in respect of functions on the unit interval. The problem we now consider, while obviously related, is distinct and somewhat more abstract. We must be careful not to confuse them. Since a p.m. is, in essence, just a set of rules for assigning probabilities to sets of random objects (in the present case functions on [0,1], but they could be completely arbitrary), it is not at all obvious how to answer this question, and how to impose a topological structure on the problem. This is essential, however, if we are to know what we mean by "convergence."

For a random variable, it turns out that the characteristic function (see (5.2.3)) acts as a reliable "fingerprint" for the distribution, and has a central role in proofs of the CLT. We watch what happens to the ch.f. as T increases, and see if it approaches the known normal case as in (5.2.5). For more general distributions, this neat trick unfortunately does not work. Instead, we can consider a *class* of functions, for example, the set $\mathbb{U}$ of bounded, uniformly continuous functions whose domain is the set of random objects in question, and whose range is the real line. Note that, regardless of the underlying probability space, the expectations $E(f) = \int f d\mu$, for $f \in \mathbb{U}$, are always just finite real numbers.

Now, let $\mathbb{M}$ denote the space (i.e., the collection) of all the p.m.s μ under consideration. Given $f \in \mathbb{U}$, note that $\int f d\mu$, $\mu \in \mathbb{M}$, defines a real-valued function with domain $\mathbb{M}$. We can work with the idea that two p.m.s are close to each other if these expectations are close (in the usual Euclidean norm on $\mathbb{R}$) for a number of different $f \in \mathbb{U}$. They are considered closer, as the distances are smaller, and the number of different f for which they are close is greater. This trick can be used to show that the p.m.s inhabit a metric space on which standard notions of convergence are defined. The "weak topology" on $\mathbb{M}$, defined by these functions, is simply the minimal collection of subsets of $\mathbb{M}$ whose images under the mappings $\int f d\mu : \mathbb{M} \mapsto \mathbb{R}$, for all $f \in \mathbb{U}$, are open sets of $\mathbb{R}$. When we speak of weak convergence, we simply mean that the definition of closeness implied by the weak topology is used as a criterion for the convergence of a sequence of p.m.s, such as that defined by increasing the sample size for partial sums, in the standard application.

In practice, weak convergence of a sequence of probability measures $\{\mu_T, T = 1, 2, 3, \cdots\}$ to a limit μ, written $\mu_T \Rightarrow \mu$, is equivalent to the condition that $\mu_T(A) \to \mu(A)$ for every set A of random objects in the probability space, such that $\mu(\delta A) = 0$, where δA denotes the boundary points of A. This is the definition already given in section 5.2.1 for the case of real random variables.

5.4.2 Tightness

Now, it might appear that, in an informal way, we have already proved the FCLT. That parts 1 and 2 of the definition of Brownian motion are satisfied is immediate from the CLT, and the construction of the process, and we have even made a good informal case for part 3. In fact, the CLT alone is sufficient to establish *pointwise* convergence to B. However, this by itself is not sufficient for all the applications of these results. For example, it is not sufficient to establish such results as

$$\sup_{0 \le r \le 1} |X_T(r)| \xrightarrow{d} \sup_{0 \le r \le 1} |B(r)| \tag{5.4.1}$$

whereas this does follow from the FCLT, which establishes convergence of the function as a whole, not just finite-dimensional projections of it.

Thus, the question to be considered is whether a given sequence of p.m.s on the spaces $C_{[0,1]}$ or $D_{[0,1]}$ converges weakly to a limit in the same space. This is not a foregone conclusion. There are familiar examples of sequences within a certain space whose limits lie outside the space. Consider a sequence of rational numbers (terminating decimals) whose limit is a real number (a non-terminating decimal).

In the present case, the question is whether a sequence of p.m.s defined on a space of functions ($C_{[0,1]}$ or $D_{[0,1]}$, as the case may be) has as a limit a p.m. on the same space. This is, in its essence, the issue of uniform tightness of the sequence.

In the CLT, the random elements under consideration (normalized sums) are real-valued random variables with probability 1, and the fact that the limit random variable is also distributed on the real line is something that we take as implicit. However, it is possible to construct sequences of distributions on the real line, depending on an index T, that are well defined for every finite T, yet break down in the limit. A simple example is where X_T is uniformly distributed on the interval $[-T,T]$. The c.d.f. of this distribution is

$$F_T(x) = \begin{cases} 0 & x < -T \\ (1 + x/T)/2 & -T \le x \le T \\ 1 & x > T \end{cases}$$

However, as $T \to \infty$, $F_T(x) \to \frac{1}{2}$ for every $x \in \mathbb{R}$, which does not define a distribution. This is a distribution that is getting "smeared out" over the whole line and, in the limit, appearing to assign positive probability mass to infinite values. Such distributions lack the attribute known as *tightness*.[8] A distribution on the line is tight if there exists, for every $\varepsilon > 0$, a finite interval having a probability exceeding $1 - \varepsilon$. Non-tight distributions are regarded as "improper," and are not well-defined distributions according to the mathematical criteria. Here we have a case of sequences of distributions that are not *uniformly* tight, even though tight for all finite T.

While the only examples of non-tight distributions on the line are obviously pathological examples like the above, in the world of continuous or cadlag functions on the unit interval the uniform tightness property is a real concern. In $C_{[0,1]}$ the issue becomes, in effect, one of whether the limit distribution assigns a probability arbitrarily close to 1 to some set in $C_{[0,1]}$, such that discontinuities arise with probability zero. It is not at all difficult to construct examples where the sample processes are a.s. continuous for all finite T (like X_T^* in (5.3.1)), yet are almost surely discontinuous in the limit. Even if the sequences we consider lie in $D_{[0,1]}$ for all finite T, like X_T in (5.2.14), we still need to establish that the limit lies in the same space, and is also continuous a.s., such as to correspond to BM. Proving uniform tightness of the sequence of p.m.s is what converts the pointwise convergence implied by the CLT to the FCLT proper, allowing conclusions such as (5.4.1).

5.4.3 Stochastic equicontinuity

To set conditions ensuring that a sequence of distributions on $C_{[0,1]}$, or $D_{[0,1]}$ is uniformly tight, the natural step is to characterize compact sets of functions in these spaces, the analogues of the finite interval of the line. One can then impose tightness by ensuring a high enough probability is assigned to these compact sets in the limit. In $\mathbb{R}$, a compact set is one that is closed and bounded, and a finite interval can contain any such set. Compactness in a general topological space is a more primitive and abstract concept, but the basic idea is the same; a point cannot be the limit of a sequence of points of a compact space without itself belonging to the space. Compactness is not the same thing as completeness, which is the property that Cauchy sequences always converge in the space. Compactness implies, rather, that all sequences contain convergent subsequences with limits contained in the space.

To characterize compactness, we conventionally appeal to a well-known result on the topology of function spaces, the *Arzelà–Ascoli theorem*. For a function $x: [0,1] \mapsto \mathbb{R}$, the *modulus of continuity* is defined as

$$w_x(\delta) = \sup_{|s-t| < \delta} |x(s) - x(t)|. \tag{5.4.2}$$

In other words, it is the largest change in the function over an interval of width less than δ. In a uniformly continuous function, we must have that $w_x(\delta) \to 0$ as $\delta \to 0$. According to the Arzelà–Ascoli theorem, a set of functions $A \subset C_{[0,1]}$ is relatively compact (i.e., its closure is compact) if the following two conditions hold:

(a) $\sup_{x \in A} |x(0)| < \infty$

(b) $\lim_{\delta \to 0} \sup_{x \in A} w_x(\delta) = 0$.

The space $C_{[0,1]}$ of continuous functions inevitably contains elements that are arbitrarily close to discontinuous functions, which would therefore violate condition (b), but if we confine attention to a set A satisfying the Arzelà–Ascoli conditions, we know that it is relatively compact, and therefore that its closure contains the cluster points of all sequences in the set.

In the case of $D_{[0,1]}$, the modulus of continuity has to be defined differently. It can be shown that a cadlag function on $[0,1]$ can have at most a countable set of discontinuity points. Let Π_δ denote a partition $\{t_1, \ldots, t_r\}$ of the unit interval with $r \leq [1/\delta]$ and $\min_i\{t_i - t_{i-1}\} > \delta$. Then define

$$w'_x(\delta) = \inf_{\Pi_\delta} \left\{ \max_{1 \leq i \leq r} \left\{ \sup_{s, t \in [t_{i-1}, t_i)} |x(t) - x(s)| \right\} \right\}$$

This definition modifies (5.4.2) by allowing the function to jump at up to r points $t_1, \ldots, t_r$, so that $w'_x(\delta) \to 0$ as $\delta \to 0$ when x is cadlag. However, note that right continuity is required for this to happen, so arbitrary discontinuities are ruled out.

A sequence of functions in $C_{[0,1]}$ or $D_{[0,1]}$ that is contained in a relatively compact set is said to be *uniformly equicontinuous*, where "uniformly" refers to uniformity with respect to the domain of the functions, and "equicontinuous" means continuous in the limit. The Arzelà–Ascoli conditions ensure functions are uniformly equicontinuous. *Stochastic equicontinuity* (the "uniform" qualifier being generally taken as implicit here) is a concept applying to random functions, and refers to the probability that a particular sequence of functions is relatively compact. There are several possible definitions, but it is typically sufficient to specify that this probability approaches 1 "in the tail," beyond some finite point in the sequence.

5.4.4 Convergence of probability measures

The next step in the argument is to make the formal link between compactness of sets of continuous (or cadlag) functions, and uniform tightness of probability measures on $C_{[0,1]}$ (or $D_{[0,1]}$). For reasons of space we examine these arguments, and then go on to give a proof of the FCLT, only for the case $C_{[0,1]}$. This means working with version (5.3.1) of the partial sum function, rather than (5.2.14). With certain technical modifications, the parallel arguments for $D_{[0,1]}$ are broadly similar, once stochastic equicontinuity has been defined appropriately. For details see Billingsley (1968) and also Davidson (1994, Chapter 28).

Think of a discontinuous function as having a relationship to $C_{[0,1]}$ analogous to that of the points $\pm\infty$ in relation to $\mathbb{R}$. A p.m. on $C_{[0,1]}$ that assigned positive probability to functions with discontinuities would fail to be tight, in just the same way as measures on the line that assigned probabilities exceeding $\varepsilon > 0$ to sets outside some specified finite interval, depending on ε. It will be sufficient for tightness if we can show, using the Arzelà–Ascoli conditions, that the p.m.s in question assign probabilities arbitrarily close to 1 to a compact set in $C_{[0,1]}$. This is the object of a collection of theorems due to Billingsley (1968). Letting $\{\mu_T, T = 1, 2, 3, \ldots\}$ denote a sequence of probability measures on $C_{[0,1]}$, Billingsley's results for this case can be summarized as follows:

Theorem 4.2 *The sequence* $\{\mu_T\}$ *is uniformly tight if there exists* $T^* \geq 1$ *such that, for all* $T > T^*$ *and all* $\eta > 0$,

(a) *$\exists\, M > 0$, such that* $\mu_T(\{x : |x(0)| > M\}) \leq \eta$,
(b) *for each* $\varepsilon > 0$, $\exists\, \delta \in (0,1)$ *such that*

$$\mu_T(\{x : w_x(\delta) \geq \varepsilon\}) \leq \eta. \tag{5.4.3}$$

Moreover, (5.4.3) holds if

$$\sup_{0 \leq t \leq 1-\delta} \mu_T\left(\left\{x : \sup_{t \leq s \leq t+\delta} |x(s) - x(t)| \geq \frac{\varepsilon}{2}\right\}\right) \leq \frac{\eta\delta}{2}. \tag{5.4.4}$$

This result formalizes, in the "ε-δ" style of analysis, the finiteness and equicontinuity requirements needed to ensure that the limiting measure assigns probabilities at most arbitrarily close to zero, to sets containing discontinuous functions.

The fact that this is a non-trivial requirement can be appreciated by returning to the example of X_T^* in (5.3.1). We are depending on the random variables $u_{[Tr]+1}/\sqrt{T}$, for every $r \in [0,1]$, becoming negligible with arbitrarily high probability as T increases. The problem is that even if the probability of an extreme value of order T is very small, the number of potential "jumps" increases with the sample size. While it may be the case that $u_{[Tr]+1}/\sqrt{T} \to 0$ in probability, for any r, there can still be circumstances in which $\sup_{0 \le r \le 1}(u_{[Tr]+1}/\sqrt{T})$ vanishes with probability less than 1. This would lead to a failure of condition (b) in Billingsley's theorem. However, as we now show, a condition sufficient to avoid this outcome is the existence of the variance or, in other words, that $\sigma^2 < \infty$. Since this is required in any case for the pointwise convergence via the CLT, no additional restrictions on the setup are necessary.

5.4.5   Proof of the FCLT

To prove Theorem 5.4.1, there are broadly two steps involved. The first, which we take as already done, is to prove the CLT for $X_T(1)$, and hence also for $X_T(r)$ for each r. Since the increments are independent by assumption, it is an elementary application of the CLT to show that the fidis of the process – the joint distributions of all the finite collections of process coordinates $r = r_1, r_2, \ldots, r_M$, for any finite M – are multivariate Gaussian, with covariance matrix defined according to

$$E(X(r_i)X(r_j)) = \min(r_i, r_j).$$

If the limiting process has these finite dimensional distributions, *and* is almost surely continuous, it fulfils the definition of BM. Note that there is no issue of uniqueness of the limit to worry about here. If the sequence converges in the space at all, it can only be to BM given the facts noted above, so it suffices to ensure this happens with probability 1.

Hence, the second step is just to prove uniform tightness of the sequence of p.m.s in $C_{[0,1]}$. It is sufficient that the processes X_T^* satisfy the conditions of Theorem 5.4.2, being finite at the origin (trivial in this case since $X_T^*(0) = 0$ a.s.) and uniformly equicontinuous. This result depends on a well known maximal inequality for partial sums, which for sums of independent processes is known as *Kolmogorov's inequality*:

Lemma 5.4.1.   *If $S_T = x_1 + \cdots + x_T$, where $x_1, \ldots, x_T$ are i.i.d. random variables, then for $\lambda > 0$ and $p \ge 1$,*

$$P(\max_{1 \le k \le T} |S_k| > \lambda) \le \frac{E|S_T|^p}{\lambda^p}$$

Clearly, we may use this result to deduce that

$$P(\sup_{r \le s \le r+\delta} |X_T(s) - X_T(r)| > \lambda) \le \frac{1}{\lambda^p} E|X_T(r+\delta) - X_T(r)|^p$$

for any chosen r and δ. Note that, since the number of terms in this partial sum is increasing with T, the pointwise CLT allows us to deduce that, for any $r \in [0, 1-\delta)$,

$$E|X_T(r+\delta) - X_T(r)|^p \to \delta^{p/2}\mu_p \tag{5.4.5}$$

as $T \to \infty$, where $\mu_p < \infty$ is the pth absolute moment of the standard normal distribution. Given Lemma 5.4.1, there is therefore a sample size T large enough (say T_1^*) that

$$P(\sup_{r \le s \le r+\delta} |X_T(s) - X_T(r)| > \lambda) \le \frac{\delta^{p/2}\mu_p}{\lambda^p}, T > T_1^*. \tag{5.4.6}$$

Now, given arbitrary $\varepsilon > 0$ and $\eta > 0$, choose λ, $p > 2$ and $0 < \delta < 1$ to satisfy the inequalities

$$0 < \lambda \le \varepsilon/4, \quad \frac{\delta^{p/2}\mu_p}{\lambda^p} \le \frac{\eta\delta}{4}. \tag{5.4.7}$$

With $p = 3$, for example, the requirement is fulfilled by setting $\lambda = \varepsilon/4$ and

$$\delta < \min\left\{1, \left(\frac{\varepsilon^3\eta}{64\mu_3}\right)^2\right\}.$$

Since the same argument holds for every $r \in [0, 1-\delta]$, (5.4.6) and (5.4.7) imply that

$$\sup_{0 \le r \le 1-\delta} P\left(\sup_{r \le s \le r+\delta} |X_T(s) - X_T(r)| > \frac{\varepsilon}{4}\right) \le \frac{\eta\delta}{4}, T > T_1^*. \tag{5.4.8}$$

Comparing with (5.4.4), it can be seen that we are on the way to fulfilling the equicontinuity requirement for X_T^*.

To complete the argument, refer to (5.3.1) and note that, for all $0 \le r < s \le 1$,

$$|X_T^*(s) - X_T(s) - X_T^*(r) + X_T(r)| \le \frac{|u_{[Tr]+1}| + |u_{[Ts]+1}|}{\sigma\sqrt{T}} = O_p(1/\sqrt{T}).$$

Therefore, it is certainly true that there exists a T large enough (say T_2^*) that

$$P\left(|X_T^*(s) - X_T(s) - X_T^*(r) + X_T(r)| \ge \frac{\varepsilon}{4}\right) \le \frac{\eta\delta}{4}, T > T_2^*. \tag{5.4.9}$$

For any random variables x and y, we have

$$P(|x+y| > \varepsilon/2) \le P(\{|x| > \varepsilon/4\} \cup \{|y| > \varepsilon/4\})$$
$$\le P(|x| > \varepsilon/4) + P(|y| > \varepsilon/4)$$

where the first inequality holds because the one event is implied by the other, and the second is the sub-additive property of probabilities. Therefore, from (5.4.8) and (5.4.9) there exists $T^* = \max(T_1^*, T_2^*)$ such that, for $T > T^*$,

$$\sup_{0 \leq r \leq 1-\delta} P\left(\sup_{r \leq s \leq r+\delta} |X_T^*(s) - X_T^*(r)| > \frac{\varepsilon}{2} \right) \leq \frac{\eta \delta}{2}.$$

Here, P implicitly denotes the probability measure relating to X_T^*, and hence inequality (5.4.4) is established. The sequence of distributions of the X_T^* processes is uniformly tight, and the functional central limit theorem follows.

Let's reiterate that this is only one of several possible approaches to proving Donsker's theorem. The alternative of working directly in $D_{[0,1]}$ is illustrated by the approach of Theorem 5.8.2 below, among others. Billingsley (1968, Section 16), gives details.

5.4.6   The multivariate case

For practical applications in econometrics, the basic FCLT for scalar processes will generally need to be extended to cover convergence of the joint distributions of sequences of vectors $x_t = (x_{1t}, \ldots, x_{mt})'$. For this purpose, it is necessary to consider the topology of the space $C_{[0,1]}^m$, which can be thought of as the Cartesian product of m copies of $C_{[0,1]}$. $C_{[0,1]}^m$ can be endowed with a metric such as

$$d_U^m(x, y) = \max_{1 \leq j \leq m} \{d_U(x_j, y_j)\}$$

and it can be shown that d_U^m induces the *product topology* – that is to say, the weak topology induced by the coordinate projections. Under the product topology, the coordinate projections are continuous. For any set $A \in C_{[0,1]}^m$, let $\pi_j(A) \in C_{[0,1]}$ be the set containing the jth coordinates of the elements of A, for $1 \leq j \leq m$. If $\pi_j(A)$ is open, continuity implies that A is open. The important implication of this for the present purpose is that $(C_{[0,1]}^m, d_U^m)$ is a separable space, inheriting the property from $(C_{[0,1]}, d_U)$.

It follows that the arguments deployed above for distributions on $C_{[0,1]}$ can be generalized in quite a straightforward way to deal with the vector case. The Cramér-Wold Theorem from section 5.2.1 is applied to generate the fidis of the multivariate distributions, wherever required. Under suitably generalized regularity conditions for the FCLT, the limit processes are vector Brownian motions B. These constitute a family of distributions with multivariate Gaussian fidis, having covariance matrices Ω such that $E(B(r)B(r)') = r\Omega$. Essentially, the approach is to show that $X_T \to_d B$ if $\lambda' X_T \to_d \lambda' B$ for each fixed λ ($m \times 1$) of unit length. Note that if each of the elements of the vector X_T is in $C_{[0,1]}$, then $\lambda' X_T \in C_{[0,1]}$ too, and under the FCLT the limits $\lambda' B$ are scalar BMs with variances $\lambda' \Omega \lambda$.

One very important feature of the multivariate FCLT is the fact that, because the limit process is Gaussian, dependence between the coordinates is completely represented by Ω in the limit. This means that even if the distribution of x_t features arbitrary forms of dependence between the coordinates, linear projections will nonetheless suffice to induce independence in large samples. Thus, if $x_t = (y_t, z_t')'$ with corresponding limit process $B_x = (B_y, B_z')'$, then $B_z(m-1 \times 1)$ and $B_{y|z} = B_y - B_z' \Omega_{zz}^{-1} \Omega_{zy}$ (defining the obvious partition of Ω) are independent BMs, a property invariant to the joint distribution of y_t and z_t in finite samples.

In principle, the same type of arguments can be adapted to vectors of cadlag processes. Referring to the definitions in section 5.3.4, consider the metric space $(D_{[0,1]}^m, d_B^m)$ where

$$d_B^m(x,y) = \max_{1 \leq j \leq m} \{d_B(x_j, y_j)\}.$$

This metric induces the Skorokhod topology in suitably generalized form, and the space is separable and complete. There is just one potential pitfall deserving mention in this case. In the case of continuous functions, we noted that linear combinations of continuous functions are continuous, and further that a sequence $\{\lambda'X_T\}$ has its limit in C provided this is true of each coordinate of X_T. However, the analogous property does not hold for elements of $(D_{[0,1]}^m, d_B^m)$. Consider for example a vector $(X_{1T}, X_{2T})'$ where $X_{1T} = x_\theta$ as defined in (5.3.2), for every T, whereas $X_{2T} = x_{\theta + 1/T}$. Both $\{X_{1T}\}$ and $\{X_{2T}\}$ converge in $(D_{[0,1]}, d_B)$ (the former, trivially) but the limit of the sequence $\{X_{2T} - X_{1T}\}$ is not in $D_{[0,1]}$, featuring an isolated discontinuity at θ. Under the d_B metric, this is not a Cauchy sequence. Hence, convergence of the marginal distributions of individual functions in $D_{[0,1]}$ does not imply their joint convergence, without further restrictions. However, it suffices for the limit vector to lie in $C_{[0,1]}^m$ with probability 1. Therefore, proofs of the multivariate FCLT can be set in the cadlag framework, just like their scalar counterparts. More details on all these issues can be found in Davidson (1994, chapters 6.5, 27.7 and 29.5).

5.4.7 Functionals of B

The functional central limit theorem has to be supplemented by the continuous mapping theorem (CMT) to have useful applications in statistical inference. The CMT was stated for real r.v.s in section 5.2.1, but this is just a case of a much more general result. For present purposes, the required variant is as follows.

Continuous mapping theorem for random functions
Let $h : D_{[0,1]} \mapsto \mathbb{R}$ be a measurable mapping from elements of $D_{[0,1]}$ to points of the real line. If the mapping is continuous except at points of the domain with zero probability under the distribution of B, and $X_T \overset{d}{\to} B$, then $h(X_T) \overset{d}{\to} h(B)$.

For example, consider the integral

$$\int_0^1 X_T(r)dr = \frac{1}{T}\sum_{t=1}^{T}\frac{1}{\sigma_u\sqrt{T}}x_t = \frac{1}{\sigma_u T^{3/2}}\sum_{t=1}^{T}\sum_{s=1}^{t}u_s \qquad (5.4.10)$$

The FCLT and CMT allow us to conclude that this random variable has a Gaussian limit. One can easily show (apply the ordinary CLT for heterogeneous sequences after re-arranging the double sum) that it is distributed as $N(0,1/3)$. However, the foregoing argument shows that it can also be written as $\int_0^1 B(r)dr$.

The same approach allows us to establish that

$$\int_0^1 X_T(r)^2 dr = \frac{1}{\sigma_u^2 T^2} \sum_{t=1}^T x_t^2 \xrightarrow{d} \int_0^1 B(r)^2 dr$$

which is, however, a random variable without a representation in terms of known distributions. The FCLT and CMT simply assure us that all squared partial sum processes with increments satisfying the regularity conditions converge in distribution to the same limit. This is what we call an *invariance principle*, because the limit is invariant to the distribution of the statistic in finite samples.

Returning to the original problem of model (5.2.9), we can now consider the distribution of $T(\hat\lambda - 1)$, which is better known as the Dickey–Fuller statistic of the first type. A further result required is the distribution of

$$\frac{1}{T} \sum_{t=1}^T x_{t-1} u_t \tag{5.4.11}$$

but this can be obtained by a neat trick. Note that

$$2x_{t-1}u_t = x_t^2 - x_{t-1}^2 - u_t^2 \tag{5.4.12}$$

and hence, if $u_t \sim iid(0, \sigma_u^2)$ and $x_0 = 0$, then

$$\frac{1}{\sigma_u^2 T} \sum_{t=1}^T x_{t-1} u_t = \frac{1}{2\sigma_u^2 T}\left(x_T^2 - \sum_{t=1}^T u_t^2\right)$$

$$\xrightarrow{d} \frac{1}{2}(B(1)^2 - 1)$$

$$\sim \frac{1}{2}(\chi^2(1) - 1). \tag{5.4.13}$$

Since the variance cancels in the ratio, the CMT now allows us to conclude that

$$T(\hat\lambda - 1) \xrightarrow{d} \frac{B(1)^2 - 1}{2 \int_0^1 B(r)^2 dr}$$

which is the well-known formula for the limiting distribution of the Dickey–Fuller statistic without mean or trend correction. However, it is important to note that the steps in (5.4.13) do *not* generalize to other models, in particular to where the u_t are not identical with the increments of x_t. There is no useful vector generalization of (5.4.12). The problem of general stochastic integrals is treated in section 5.7.

Using the FCLT and CMT, a number of other important processes related to BM are easily shown to be the weak limits of sample processes. We consider just two simple examples. Defining

$$S_t = \sum_{t=1}^{t} u_t$$

consider the mean deviation process

$$x_t = S_t - \bar{S} \tag{5.4.14}$$

where $\bar{S} = T^{-1} \sum_{s=1}^{T} S_s$. If $X_T(r) = x_{[Tr]}/(\sigma\sqrt{T})$, it is easily shown using (5.4.10) that

$$X_T \overset{d}{\to} B - \int_0^1 B ds$$

where the limit process is called a *de-meaned* BM.

However, be careful to note that de-meaning is not the appropriate way to account for an intercept in the generating equation. Suppose that, instead of (5.2.9), we have

$$\begin{aligned} x_t &= \alpha + x_{t-1} + u_t. \\ &= S_t + t\alpha. \end{aligned} \tag{5.4.15}$$

The intercept induces a deterministic trend that dominates the stochastic trend in the limit, and the normalization of $T^{-1/2}$ is not appropriate. Instead, divide by T to obtain the limit

$$X_T(r) = T^{-1} x_{[Tr]} \overset{pr}{\to} \alpha r.$$

However, the stochastic component can be isolated by regressing x_t onto the trend dummy. Let the residuals from this regression (including an intercept) be represented as

$$x_t^* = x_t - \bar{x} - (t - \bar{t}) \frac{\sum_{s=1}^{T}(s - \bar{t})x_s}{\sum_{s=1}^{T}(s - \bar{t})^2}$$

$$= S_t - \bar{S} - (t - \bar{t}) \frac{\sum_{s=1}^{T}(s - \bar{t})S_s}{\sum_{s=1}^{T}(s - \bar{t})^2}$$

where $\bar{t} = T^{-1} \sum_{t=1}^{T} t = (T+1)/2$, and the second equality follows directly on substitution from (5.4.15). Noting that $([Tr] - \bar{t})/T \to r - \frac{1}{2}$ and that $T^{-3} \sum_{t=1}^{T}(t - \bar{t})^2 \to 1/12$, we can therefore use the CMT to show that

$$X_T(r) = x_{[Tr]}^*/(\sigma_u\sqrt{T})$$

$$\overset{d}{\to} B(r) - \int_0^1 B(s)ds - 12\left(r - \frac{1}{2}\right)\int_0^1 \left(s - \frac{1}{2}\right)B(s)ds.$$

This process is called a de-trended BM.

Whereas (5.4.14) puts the partial sum process into mean deviation form, putting the increments of the partial sums into mean deviation form yields a quite different limit. Consider the array

$$x_{Tt} = \sum_{s=1}^{t} (u_s - \bar{u}), \quad t = 1, \dots, T$$

where $\bar{u} = T^{-1} \sum_{s=1}^{T} u_t$. This process has the property that $x_{TT} = 0$ identically. If $X_T(r) = x_{T,[Tr]}/(\sigma_u \sqrt{T})$, it is again easy to see using the FCLT and CMT that $X_T \overset{d}{\to} B^o$, where

$$B^o(r) = B(r) - rB(1), \quad 0 \le r \le 1$$

B^o is called a *Brownian bridge*, having the property $B^o(1) = B^o(0) = 0$. It does not have independent increments, and $E(B^o(t)B^o(s)) = \min\{t, s\} - ts$.

5.5 Dependent increments

5.5.1 Martingale differences

We have assumed for simplicity up to now that the driving sequence $\{u_t\}$ is independent and identically distributed. In practice, the same results can be obtained under a variety of weaker assumptions about the dependence. One easy extension is to allow $\{u_t\}$ to be a stationary martingale difference (m.d.) sequence; in other words, an integrable process having the property

$$E(u_t | \mathcal{F}_{t-1}) = 0 \text{ a.s.}$$

where $\{\mathcal{F}_t\}$ is a nested sequence of σ-fields such that u_t is $\mathcal{F}_t$-measurable (the pairs $\{u_t, \mathcal{F}_t\}$ are said to form an *adapted* sequence). Intuitively, an m.d. is a process that is unpredictable in mean, one step ahead.

The two main planks in our FCLT proof that used the independence assumption, the CLT and the Kolmogorov maximal inequality, can both be extended to the m.d. case without additional assumptions.[9] To verify that the fidis are converging to those of BM, we use the martingale CLT and the fact that m.d.s are uncorrelated sequences. The key assumption that $E(X_T(r)^2) = r$ for $0 \le r \le 1$ follows from this property, and the increments of X_T are uncorrelated. They are not independent in finite samples, in general, but because uncorrelated *Gaussian* increments are independent of each other, the increments are *asymptotically* independent. Hence, the fidis match all the requirements. With the modified maximal inequality for m.d.s, the FCLT proof given above goes through otherwise unchanged.

This result is of particular importance in econometrics, since the assumption of independence is strong, and much less likely to hold in economic data than the m.d. assumption. For example, considering the case where $u_t = y_t - \boldsymbol{\beta}' x_t$, the disturbances in a regression model, the only assumption needed to make u_t an m.d. is that $E(y_t | \mathcal{I}_t) = \boldsymbol{\beta}' x_t$ where $\mathcal{F}_{t-1} \subset \mathcal{I}_t \subset \mathcal{F}_t$ and x_t is $\mathcal{I}_t$-measurable. These assumptions are plausibly fulfilled in a correctly specified regression model, and they do not rule out such phenomena as stationary ARCH or GARCH (predictability in variance), provided there is no predictability in mean. By contrast, there are rarely firm grounds to assume that the disturbances in a time series regression are truly independent. Moreover, the m.d. property is inherited by $x_t u_t$ under the assumption given, which is very useful for establishing asymptotic normality in the general setup described in section 5.2.2.

5.5.2 General dependence

Of course, we would like the FCLT to hold in more general cases still, where the increments are autocorrelated and generally dependent. The reason this is especially important is that the FCLT is used to construct the distributions of statistics involving observed integrated processes. In stationary data, it is sufficient for the asymptotic normality of regression coefficients if the disturbances satisfy the m.d. assumption, as detailed in the previous section, since only a LLN is needed to hold for the regressor variables. By contrast, the FCLT must hold for all the regressors in an I(1) modeling setup. To illustrate with a familiar case, the Dickey–Fuller test is customarily used to test whether measured time series are I(1) or I(0). While there is an "augmented" variant of the test for data with correlated increments, the sole function of the augmenting correction is to estimate the increment variance consistently. The FCLT is required to hold with correlated increments, in this case.

In essence the sufficient conditions are twofold. First, it is necessary that the increments have at least finite variances, with a slightly stronger moment condition in cases when the marginal distributions are heterogeneous. Second, the processes must satisfy a short-memory condition. Memory conditions are, first and foremost, conditions on the autocorrelation function of the process. When the increments are covariance stationary, note that

$$\lim_{t \to \infty} \frac{1}{T} E \left(\sum_{t=1}^{T} u_t \right)^2 = \sum_{j=-\infty}^{\infty} E(u_1 u_{1-j})$$

$$= \sigma_u^2 + 2\lambda_{uu} = \omega_{uu} \tag{5.5.1}$$

where $\lambda_{uu} = \sum_{j=1}^{\infty} E(u_1 u_{1-j})$. Accordingly, $\omega_{uu}^{1/2}$ has to replace σ_u as the normalization to make the limit process a standard BM, and ω_{uu} must be both finite and positive. As is well known, this is equivalent to the condition that the spectral density is bounded away from both infinity and zero at the origin. Summability of the autocovariances is the property sometimes called weak dependence.[10]

However, limited autocorrelations cannot supply a sufficient condition for the CLT and FCLT to hold unless the process in question is jointly Gaussian, such that the dependence is fully represented by the autocorrelation function. In non-Gaussian and nonlinear processes (the best-known examples of the latter are probably ARCH/GARCH processes), there has to be some limitation on the nonlinear dependence as well. The term 'I(0)'[11] is sometimes defined loosely to mean a stationary process (such that $E(u_t u_{t-j})$ is both finite and independent of t, for every j) and also, more properly, to mean a stationary weakly dependent process (such that the covariances are summable). It would both be more consistent, and avoid complications arising with nonlinear dependence, to use "I(0)" to refer simply to processes whose normalized partial sums converge weakly to BM. Then, we should note that nonstationarity (of a local variety) is not necessary, but also that "weak dependence" is a sufficient condition only in Gaussian and linear cases.

5.5.3 Linear processes

Linear processes, including ARMA processes of finite or infinite order, are a common assumption in time series modeling. The one-sided moving average form, which includes (possibly after solving out) all the cases of interest, is

$$u_t = \sum_{j=0}^{\infty} \theta_j \varepsilon_{t-j} = \theta(L)\varepsilon_t \qquad (5.5.2)$$

where $\{\varepsilon_t\}$ is the driving process, often assumed i.i.d.$(0,\sigma^2)$, $\{\theta_j\}_{j=0}^{\infty}$ is a sequence of constant coefficients with $\theta_0 = 1$, and $\theta(L) = \sum_{j=0}^{\infty} \theta_j L^j$, where L denotes the lag operator. A weaker assumption that will often serve as well as serial independence is that $\{\varepsilon_t\}$ is a stationary m.d. The convenience of linear models is that stationarity of u_t then holds by construction and, in effect, the dependence is solely a property of the coefficients θ_j. The scheme is sometimes justified by an appeal to Wold's Theorem (Wold, 1938), which states that every stationary nondeterministic process can be put in the form of (5.5.2), where the process $\{\varepsilon_t\}$ is stationary and *uncorrelated*. However, this uncorrelatedness is equivalent to neither the i.i.d. nor the stationary m.d. assumptions, unless the process is also Gaussian. This is itself a rather strong assumption that fails in many economic and financial data sets.

If the dependence is linear, there is a technically easy way to modify the application of the FCLT using the *Beveridge–Nelson* (1981) *decomposition*. This idea is examined in Phillips and Solo (1992). Considering again the model $x_t = x_{t-1} + u_t$, where now u_t is given by (5.5.2), the easily verified identity

$$\theta(L) = \theta(1) + \theta^*(L)(1 - L)$$

where $\theta_j^* = -\sum_{i=j+1}^{\infty} \theta_i$, may be used to re-order the summation as

$$u_t = \theta(1)\varepsilon_t + \theta^*(L)\Delta\varepsilon_t.$$

Hence, letting $z_t = \sum_{s=1}^{t} \varepsilon_s$,

$$x_t = \sum_{s=1}^{t} u_t = \theta(1)z_t + \theta^*(L)(\varepsilon_t - \varepsilon_0).$$

Now write the normalized partial sum process as

$$X_T(r) = \theta(1)Z_T(r) + \frac{\theta^*(L)(\varepsilon_{[Tr]} - \varepsilon_0)}{\sigma_u\sqrt{T}}.$$

Provided the second right-hand side term is of small order, it can be neglected in calculations involving the limit distribution. A sufficient condition is that the sequence $\{\theta_j^*\}$ be absolutely summable, implying that the sequence $\{\theta^*(L)\varepsilon_t\}$ is "short memory." Using elementary results on summability,[12] this is true if $\theta_j^* = O(j^{-1-\mu})$ for $\mu > 0$, and hence if $\theta_j = O(j^{-2-\mu})$. Sequences with the latter property are sometimes said to be "1-summable," since $\sum_{j=1}^{\infty} j|\theta_j| < \infty$.

5.5.4 Mixing

When the linear process assumption does not serve, mixing conditions are probably the best-known type of restriction for limiting serial dependence. There are several variants, of which the most often cited are probably strong mixing (α-mixing) and uniform mixing (ϕ-mixing). To define the mixing concept, begin by introducing the notation $\mathcal{F}_{t_1}^{t_2} \subset \mathcal{F}$ for $t_1 \leq t_2$, for a σ-field representing "information dated $s \in [t_1, t_2]$." If $\mathcal{F}$ represents the collection of events relating to the complete history of a stochastic sequence $\{x_t, -\infty < t < +\infty\}$, we also sometimes write $\mathcal{F}_{t_1}^{t_2} = \sigma(x_{t_1}, \ldots, x_{t_2})$ to show that this is the σ-field "generated by" this segment of the sequence, although it is also possible for the set to contain additional information relating to these dates. Then, $\mathcal{F}_{-\infty}^{t}$ represents "history up to date t," and $\mathcal{F}_{t+m}^{+\infty}$ "events from date $t+m$ onwards." With this notation, the mixing coefficients are defined respectively as

$$\alpha_m = \sup_t \sup_{A \in \mathcal{F}_{-\infty}^t, B \in \mathcal{F}_{t+m}^{+\infty}} |P(A \cap B) - P(A)P(B)|$$

$$\phi_m = \sup_t \sup_{A \in \mathcal{F}_{-\infty}^t, B \in \mathcal{F}_{t+m}^{+\infty}, P(B) > 0} |P(A|B) - P(A)|$$

for $m = 1, 2, 3, \ldots$ The sequences $\{\alpha_m\}_0^{\infty}$ and $\{\phi_m\}_0^{\infty}$ are alternative measures of the rate at which remote parts of the sequence are becoming independent of each other as the gap increases. A random sequence is said to be strong (respectively uniform) mixing of size $-\lambda_0$ if $\alpha_m = O(m^{-\lambda})$ (respectively $\phi_m = O(m - \lambda)$) for $\lambda > \lambda_0$. It is not difficult to show that $\phi_m \geq \alpha_m$, so that "strong" mixing is actually the weaker of the two concepts.

This approach to quantifying dependence has the advantage of being completely nonparametric, and well defined whatever the actual dynamic generation mechanism of the data. However, it has some drawbacks. An obvious one is to be able to actually verify from the structure of a model that the condition is satisfied, rather than just assuming it. However, the chief problem is that, because we are "sup"ing over all possible pairs of remote events, this necessarily embraces any odd and pathological cases that may exist. It is well-known (Andrews, 1984) that even a stable autoregression (which depends on the whole history of past shocks, albeit with weights converging to zero exponentially fast) can violate the strong mixing condition. Andrews' counter-example involves an AR(1) with a discrete (Bernoulli) innovation sequence, but to derive mild sufficient conditions for mixing in linear processes is nonetheless surprisingly difficult (see Davidson 1994, section 14.5). Not merely a continuous shock distribution, but some kind of smoothness condition on the density, appears unavoidable.

5.5.5 Near-epoch dependence

Because of the limitations of mixing assumptions they can, with advantage, be combined with or substituted by another condition called near-epoch dependence. This one has slightly more structure, in that it explicitly represents a random sequence as depending on past and/or future values of some underlying sequence (that could be mixing, or possibly independent) and also calls for the existence of moments up to some order such as 2. For a chosen $p > 0$, the condition takes the general form

$$\sqrt[p]{E|u_t - E(u_t|\mathcal{F}_{t-m}^{t+m})|^p} \leq d_t v_m \tag{5.5.3}$$

where d_t is a sequence representing scale factors in a heterogeneous sequence (e.g. $d_t = (E|u_t|^p)^{1/p}$). We say that the sequence is L_p-NED of size $-\mu_0$ if $v_m = O(m^{-\mu})$ for $\mu > \mu_0$.

$E(u_t|\mathcal{F}_{t-m}^{t+m})$ represents the best prediction of u_t based on information from the "near epoch." If u_t is a short-memory process, then it is mainly determined by the near epoch, and v_m should diminish rapidly with m. Note that NED is not a restriction on the process memory as such, but rather a condition on the mapping from the underlying driving process generating $\{\mathcal{F}_s^t\}$ to the observed process. In practice, it is applied by specifying that the underlying process is mixing, or possibly independent. Its advantage is that it avoids the odd counter-examples that make the mixing condition over-sensitive in many situations. For example, the AR(1) case with Bernoulli innovations cited in section 5.5.4 is certainly L_2-NED on the independent shock process. For additional background, see Gallant and White (1988) and Davidson (1994).

The way these conditions can be applied is illustrated by the following FCLT for processes with dependent increments, taken from Davidson (2002). This result also departs from the stationarity assumption to show how, in particular, processes with heterogeneous variances might be handled. We might, for example, have a situation where the variances changed according to a seasonal pattern. Most situations except trending variances (dealt with in section 5.6.1) can be handled in this way. Similarly, it is not assumed that $E(u_t) = 0$ for every t, only that a suitable mean correction is made to each observation.

Theorem 5.1 *Let* $X_T : [0, 1] \mapsto \mathbb{R}$ *be defined by*

$$X_T(r) = \omega_T^{-1/2} \sum_{t=1}^{[Tr]} (u_t - Eu_t) \quad 0 < r \leq 1 \tag{5.5.4}$$

where $\omega_T = \mathrm{Var}(\sum_{t=1}^{T} u_t)$. *Let the following assumptions hold:*

(a) u_t *is* L_2-*NED of size* $-\frac{1}{2}$ *on a process* $\{v_s\}$ *with respect to constants* $d_t \leq E(|u_t|^r)^{1/r}$, *where* v_s *is either* α-*mixing of size* $-r/(r-2)$ *for* $r > 2$ *or* ϕ-*mixing of size* $-r/(2r-2)$, *for* $r \geq 2$.
(b) $\sup_t E|u_t - Eu_t|^r < \infty$ *for* r *defined in (a), and if* $r = 2$ *then* $\{(u_t - Eu_t)^2\}$ *is uniformly integrable.*
(c) $\frac{\omega_T}{T} \to \omega_u > 0$, *as* $T \to \infty$.

Then, $X_T \overset{d}{\to} B$.

Note that being able to assert ϕ-mixing allows more relaxed size and moment conditions than otherwise. The special feature of this result, which distinguishes it from sufficient conditions for the CLT, is condition (c). This is sufficient to ensure that $E(X_T(r)^2) \to r$ as $T \to \infty$ for $0 < r \leq 1$, as is required for BM to be the limit process. By contrast, the ordinary CLT specifies only the conditions for convergence for $r = 1$. Various kinds of heterogeneity of the variance sequence are compatible with this case, including trending variances as in (5.2.6), but not with condition (c).

5.5.6 More on linear forms

It is of interest to contrast linearity with the property of near-epoch dependence on an independent shock process. It is easy to show direct from (5.5.3) (see Davidson 1994, Example 17.3) that, if (5.5.2) describes the relationship between u_t and a driving process $\{\varepsilon_t\}$, then

$$v_m = O\left(\sum_{j=m+1}^{\infty} |\theta_j|\right)$$

in (5.5.3). The usual summability arguments yield the requirement $\theta_j = O(j^{-3/2 - \mu})$ for $\mu > 0$, in order for the L_p-NED size of a linear process to be $-\frac{1}{2}$, and so satisfy the condition of Theorem 5.1. Note that this is a weaker condition than that obtained for the FCLT using the Beveridge–Nelson decomposition, without even taking into account that the driving process can itself be generally dependent in this case. The i.i.d. or m.d. assumptions imposed in (5.5.2) can be replaced by a mixing assumption. For example, with Gaussian increments (letting $r \to \infty$) the α-mixing size of $-\frac{1}{2}$ is permitted, and ϕ-mixing size of -1 is compatible with no moments beyond the variance.

However, the virtue of linear forms, in a more general context, is that the amount of dependence compatible with weak convergence to Brownian motion can be significantly greater than in the purely nonparametric setting. Moving averages of processes satisfying the conditions of Theorem 5.1 yield the same limit result, under quite weak restrictions on the coefficients. This result, from Davidson (2002), goes as follows.

Theorem 5.2 *Let $X_T : [0, 1] \mapsto \mathbb{R}$ be defined by*

$$X_T(\xi) = \sigma_T^{-1} \sum_{t=1}^{[T\xi]} (u_t - Eu_t) \quad 0 < \xi \leq 1$$

where $\sigma_T^2 = \mathrm{Var}(\sum_{t=1}^{T} u_t)$, and let

$$u_t = \sum_{j=0}^{\infty} \theta_j v_{t-j}$$

where
(a) v_t satisfies conditions (a), (b) and (c) of Theorem 5.1,
(b) the sequence $\{\theta_j\}$ is regularly varying at ∞ and satisfies the conditions

$$0 < \left| \sum_{j=0}^{\infty} \theta_j \right| < \infty, \tag{5.5.5}$$

$$\sum_{k=0}^{\infty} \left(\sum_{j=1+k}^{T+k} \theta_j \right)^2 = o(T). \tag{5.5.6}$$

Then, $X_T \overset{d}{\to} B$.

The first striking thing about this result is that the summability specified in condition (b) is weaker than absolute summability. If the coefficients change sign, they can take substantially longer to decay absolutely than if they are all (say) positive. In fact, the only restriction placed on their absolute rate of decay is (5.5.6), which enforces square summability. The second striking feature, as we show in section 5.6.3, is that these come close to being necessary conditions. We exhibit a case where (b) is violated, and show (under supplementary assumptions) that a limit distribution different from B is obtained.

5.6 Processes related to Brownian motion

5.6.1 Variance-Transformed BM

The results given in sections 5.5.5 and 5.5.6 allowed some nonstationarity of the distributions of the $\{u_t\}$ sequence, provided this was of a local sort that would be averaged out in the limit. Cases where the nonstationarity is not averaged out, and therefore affects the limit distribution, are said to be globally nonstationary.

Thus, suppose the variance of the driving process is growing, or shrinking, with time. Specifically, suppose that $E(u_t^2) = (1 + \alpha)t^\alpha \sigma_u^2$ as in (5.2.6), where $\alpha > -1$.

Assume serial independence, so that $\omega_T = \text{Var}(\sum_{t=1}^{T} u_t) \approx T^{1+\alpha}\sigma_u^2$. Then, defining

$$X_T(r) = \frac{1}{\sqrt{\omega_T}} \sum_{t=1}^{[Tr]} u_t$$

note that

$$E(X_T(r)^2) \to r^{1+\alpha}. \tag{5.6.1}$$

Using a version of the CLT for trending-variance processes, as in (5.2.6), it is possible to show that the fidis of the limit process are those of

$$B_\alpha(r) = B(r^{1+\alpha}).$$

Stochastic equicontinuity holds for processes of this type, leading to an FCLT. More generally, if $\omega_{[Tr]}/\omega_T \to \eta(r)$, where $\eta(\cdot)$ is any increasing homeomorphism on $[0, 1]$ and the other FCLT assumptions hold, the limit process takes the form

$$B_\eta(r) = B(\eta(r)).$$

For these results see White and Wooldridge (1988), Davidson (1994) and de Jong and Davidson (2000). Note that these processes are not BM, although they are still a.s. continuous Gaussian processes having independent increments. They can be thought of as BMs that have been subjected to some lateral distortion, through stretching or squeezing of the time domain.

5.6.2 Ornstein–Uhlenbeck process

Consider a process X defined by

$$X(r) = \frac{B(e^{2\beta r})}{\sqrt{2\beta}e^{\beta r}}, \quad 0 \le r \le 1 \tag{5.6.2}$$

for $\beta > 0$, where if the domain of X is $[0, 1]$ as we have assumed, then the domain of B must in this case be $[0, e^{2\beta}]$. It can be verified that $E(X(r)X(s)) = 1/(2\beta e^{\beta|r-s|})$ depending only on $|r-s|$, and hence the process is stationary. It is also easily verified that the increments are negatively correlated.

Considering a time interval $[r, r+\delta]$, observe that

$$\frac{E[B(e^{2\beta(r+\delta)}) - B(e^{2\beta r})]^2}{2\beta e^{2\beta r}} = \frac{e^{2\beta\delta} - 1}{2\beta}$$

$$= E[B(r+\delta) - B(r)]^2 + o(\delta).$$

Letting $B(r+d) - B(r)$ approach $dB(r)$ as $\delta \to 0$, $X(r)$ can evidently be viewed, for r large enough, as a solution of the stochastic differential equation

$$dX(r) = -\beta X(r)dr + dB(r).$$

The conventional solution of this equation yields the alternative representations

$$X(r) = \int_0^r e^{-\beta(r-s)} dB = B(r) - \beta \int_0^r e^{-\beta(r-s)} B(s) ds \qquad (5.6.3)$$

where the second version of the formula is obtained by integration by parts. This is the Ornstein–Uhlenbeck (OU) process. Letting β tend to 0 yields ordinary BM in the limit according to the last formula, although note that the stationary representation of (5.6.2) is accordingly breaking down as $\beta \downarrow 0$.

The OU process is the weak limit of an autoregressive process with a root local to unity, that is,

$$x_t = (1 - \beta/T)x_{t-1} + u_t.$$

To show this, write for brevity $\lambda_T = 1 - \beta/T$, and using the identity

$$\lambda_T^k - 1 = (\lambda_T - 1) \sum_{j=0}^{k-1} \lambda_T^j$$

note that

$$x_t = \sum_{j=1}^t \lambda_T^{t-j} u_j$$

$$= \sum_{j=1}^{t-1} \left[\lambda_T^{t-j} - 1 \right] u_j + \sum_{j=1}^t u_j$$

$$= (\lambda_T - 1) \sum_{j=1}^{t-1} \sum_{k=0}^{t-j-1} \lambda_T^k u_j + \sum_{j=1}^t u_j$$

$$= (\lambda_T - 1) \sum_{k=1}^{t-1} \lambda_T^{t-k-1} \sum_{j=1}^k u_j + \sum_{j=1}^t u_j.$$

Substituting for λ_T and also noting that $(1 - \beta/T)^{[T\delta]} = e^{-\beta\delta} + o(1)$, the Brownian FCLT and CMT then yield

$$\frac{1}{\sqrt{T}} x_{[Tr]} = \frac{1}{\sqrt{T}} \sum_{j=1}^{[Tr]} u_j - \beta \frac{1}{T} \sum_{j=1}^{[Tr]-1} e^{-\beta([Tr]-j)} \frac{1}{\sqrt{T}} \sum_{k=1}^j u_j$$

$$\xrightarrow{d} B(r) - \beta \int_0^r e^{-\beta(r-s)} B(s) ds$$

5.6.3 Fractional Brownian motion

Consider the *fractionally integrated* process defined by $x_t = x_{t-1} + (1-L)^{-d} u_t$ for $-\frac{1}{2} < d < \frac{1}{2}$, where

$$(1-L)^{-d} = \sum_{j=0}^{\infty} b_j L^j \qquad (5.6.4)$$

in which

$$b_j = \frac{\Gamma(j+d)}{\Gamma(d)\Gamma(j+1)}.$$

The justification for the notation $(1-L)^{-d}$ follows from calculating the infinite order binomial expansion and verifying that the coefficients match the b_j. For the case $d > 0$, these increment processes are called "long memory" because the MA lag weights (and hence the autocorrelations) are nonsummable. In the case $d < 0$, the increments are called "anti-persistent" and feature the special property that the MA lag weights sum to 0, indicating a generalized form of over-differencing.

The summations may be rearranged to obtain

$$x_t = \sum_{k=1}^{t} \sum_{j=0}^{\infty} b_j u_{k-j} = \sum_{s=-\infty}^{t} a_{ts} u_s \tag{5.6.5}$$

where

$$a_{ts} = \sum_{j=\max\{0,\,1-s\}}^{t-s} b_j.$$

From this representation, it can be shown by direct calculation that $T^{-1-2d} E(x_T^2) \to \omega_{uu} V_d$, where V_d is a scale constant to be defined. This suggests defining the empirical process

$$X_T(r) = \frac{x_{[Tr]}}{\omega_{uu}^{1/2} \sqrt{V_d} T^{1/2+d}}.$$

It can then be further verified that

$$E(X_T(r))^2 \to r^{1+2d}$$

and

$$E(X_T(r+\delta) - X_T(r))(X_T(r)) \to \tfrac{1}{2}[(r+\delta)^{1+2d} - r^{1+2d} - \delta^{1+2d}]$$

Thus, this process has a different convergence rate, similar to the trending variance case in (5.6.1), but, unlike that case, it has dependent increments, even in the limit. It can be verified that the serial correlation is positive when $d > 0$ and negative when $d < 0$.

To establish a weak limit for X_T, the first step is to identify a candidate limit process. One sharing the same correlation structure is *fractional* Brownian motion (fBM) defined by Mandelbrot and Van Ness (1968). Denote fBM by X, where

$$X(r) = \frac{1}{\Gamma(d+1)} \left(\int_{-\infty}^{r} (r-s)^d dB - \int_{-\infty}^{0} (-s)^d dB \right), \quad r \geq 0 \tag{5.6.6}$$

and B is regular BM. It can be verified that

$$E(X(1)^2) = \frac{1}{\Gamma(d+1)^2}\left(\frac{1}{2d+1} + \int_0^\infty [(1+\tau)^d - \tau^d)]^2 d\tau\right)$$

$$= \frac{\Gamma(1-2d)}{(2d+1)\Gamma(1-d)\Gamma(1+d)}$$

and this constant[13] is equated with V_d defined above. To complete the proof that fBM is the weak limit of the fractionally integrated process, it remains to show that the fidis of X_T are Gaussian, and that the distributions are uniformly tight. These results can be established using the approach of Davydov (1970). The basic step is to note that the fidis are those of weighted sums of the driving process $\{u_t\}$ as in (5.6.5). The re-ordered summation converts an issue of long memory into one of heteroscedasticity. The trending variances of the terms of the form $a_{ts}u_s$ in (5.6.5) can be handled using variants of the techniques cited in section 5.6.1. The stochastic equicontinuity of the increments is established similarly. Essentially, a result is available for the case where $\{u_t\}$ satisfies the assumptions of Theorem 5.1; see Davidson and de Jong (2000) for the details. However, it may be noted that the conditions on $\{\theta_j\}$ specified in Theorem 5.2 are violated by the coefficients in (5.6.4), and the same argument can be used to show that the limit is an fBM in that case. Theorem 5.2 can be viewed as giving a necessary memory condition for the linear case.

Sometimes (5.6.6) is referred to as Type 1 fBM, terminology coined by Marinucci and Robinson (1999). Type 2 fBM is the case

$$X(r) = \frac{1}{\Gamma(d+1)} \int_0^t (r-s)^d dB \tag{5.6.7}$$

with the integral over the range $(-\infty, 0]$ omitted. This formula is obtained as the limit of the process derived from

$$x_t = \sum_{k=1}^t \sum_{j=0}^{k-1} b_j u_{k-j} = \sum_{s=1}^t a_{ts} u_s$$

(compare (5.6.5)) or, in other words, the process generated from the sequence $\{I(t \geq 1)u_t\}$, where $I(\cdot)$ is the indicator function of its argument). A number of studies have used the Type 2 representation of fBM, although arguably the setup is somewhat artificial, and it is perhaps worrying that this model yields different asymptotics. However, one virtue of formula (5.6.7) is that it may be compared directly with the OU process (5.6.3), in which the hyperbolic weight function is replaced by an exponential weight function. The two models represent alternative ways of introducing autocorrelation into a stochastic process.

5.7 Stochastic integrals

There is one result required for asymptotic inference for which the FCLT and CMT do not provide a general solution. This is the limiting distribution of normalized sums of the form

$$G_T = \frac{1}{T\sqrt{\omega_{uu}\omega_{ww}}} \sum_{t=1}^{T-1} \sum_{s=1}^{t} u_s w_{t+1} \tag{5.7.1}$$

where ω_t and u_t are I(0) processes. The weak limits of expressions of this type, involving both integrated processes and their increments, are known as Itô integrals.

5.7.1 Derivation of the Itô integral

Let f be a random element of the space $D_{[0,1]}$, and let B be a BM. The Itô integral of f with respect to B (respectively, integrand and integrator functions) is a random process written

$$I(t) = \int_0^t f dB$$

and satisfying the property

$$E(I(t)^2) = E\left(\int_0^t f^2 ds\right). \tag{5.7.2}$$

Itô's rule is the generalization of the integration-by-parts formula to objects of this kind. It states that, if g is a twice-differentiable function of a real variable and $g(0) = 0$, then

$$g(B(t)) = \int_0^t g'(B) dB + \frac{1}{2} \int_0^t g''(B) ds, \quad \text{a.s.}$$

For example, the case $g(B) = B^2$ yields

$$\int_0^t B dB = \frac{1}{2}(B(t)^2 - t) \tag{5.7.3}$$

which may be noted to correspond to (5.4.13) with $t = 1$.

We sketch here the derivation of these processes by a limit argument, omitting many details and technical excursions. For a fuller account see, for example, Karatzas and Shreve (1988) among numerous good texts on stochastic calculus, many with applications to financial modelling. A *filtration* $\{\mathcal{F}(r), r \in [0, 1]\}$ is a collection of nested σ-fields indexed by points of the line, and we assume that f and B are adapted processes, such that $f(r)$ and $B(r)$ are $\mathcal{F}(r)$-measurable. Choose a partition $\Pi_k = \{r_0, r_1, \dots r_k\}$ of $[0, 1]$, where $r_0 = 0$, $r_k = 1$ and $r_j < r_{j+1}$, and consider

$$I_k = \sum_{j=0}^{k-1} f(r_j)(B(r_{j+1}) - B(r_j)). \tag{5.7.4}$$

Notwithstanding that B is of unbounded variation, we may show that I_k converges to the limit $\int_0^1 f dB$ in mean square, as $k \to \infty$, such that $\max_j |r_{j+1} - r_j| \to 0$ (for example, let $r_j - j/k$).

It is easiest to show this result initially for the case of *simple* functions having the form

$$f_k(r) = f(r_j), \quad r_j \leq r < r_{j+1}, \quad j = 0, \dots, k-1. \tag{5.7.5}$$

In these cases, the Itô integral with respect to BM is defined by (5.7.4), since

$$I_k = \int_0^1 f_k dB = \sum_{j=0}^{k-1} f(r_j) \int_{r_j}^{r_{j+1}} dB(r).$$

Note the special property that the increments of the integrator function are dated to lead the integrand, and hence are unpredictable with respect to $\mathcal{F}(r_j)$, by definition of BM.

Now define an increasing sequence $\{k(n), n = 1, 2, 3, \dots\}$ with a corresponding sequence of partitions satisfying $\Pi_{k(1)} \subset \Pi_{k(2)} \subset \Pi_{k(3)} \subset \cdots$. For example, take $k(n) = 2^n$. Note that for $m > 0$,

$$I_{k(n+m)} - I_{k(n)} = \sum_{j=0}^{k(n+m)-1} [f_{k(n+m)}(r_j) - f_{k(n)}(r_j)](B(r_{j+1}) - B(r_j))$$

Also, applying the law of iterated expectations and the fact that $f(r_j)$ is measurable with respect to $\mathcal{F}(r_j)$, we have the properties

$$E[f(r_j)(B(r_{j+1}) - B(r_j))]^2 = E[f(r_j)^2 E[(B(r_{j+1}) - B(r_j))^2 | \mathcal{F}(r_j)]$$
$$= E[f(r_j)^2](r_{j+1} - r_j)$$

and

$$E[f(r_j)(B(r_{j+1}) - B(r_j))f(r_{j'})(B(r_{j'+1}) - B(r_{j'}))] = 0$$

whenever $r_j \neq r_{j'}$. Hence,

$$E(I_k^2) = \sum_{j=0}^{k-1} E f(r_j)^2 (r_{j+1} - r_j) = E\left(\int_0^1 f(r)^2 dr \right).$$

Now, every function f on $[0,1]$ can be associated with a sequence $\{f_{k(n)}\}$ of simple functions, by applying definition (5.7.5) for a suitable class of partitions. For the class of square-integrable, 'progressively measurable' functions f on $[0,1]$,[14] it can be shown that there exists a sequence of simple functions such that, for each $m > 0$,

$$E(I_{k(m+n)} - I_{k(n)})^2 = E\left(\int_0^1 (f_{k(n+m)}(r) - f_{k(n)}(r))^2 dr\right) \to 0$$

as $n \to \infty$. It follows that

$$E(I_{k(n)} - I)^2 \to 0$$

where $I = \int_0^1 f dB$ is defined in this mean-square limiting sense. BM is, of course, a candidate case of f under this definition, leading to the class of random variables with the property in (5.7.3).

5.7.2 Weak convergence of covariances

In functional limit theory, the role of the Itô integral is to characterize the weak limits of random sequences of type (5.7.1). The arguments needing to be deployed to show convergence are again quite involved and technical,[15] and it is not possible to do more than just sketch an outline of the main steps. Let $X_T(r)$ be defined as in (5.2.14) and $Y_T(r)$ defined similarly with respect to the partial sum process $y_t = \sum_{s=1}^t w_s$, where $w_t \sim iid(0, \sigma_w^2)$. We assume that $(X_T, Y_T) \overset{d}{\to} (B_X, B_Y)$, where the notation is intended to indicate *joint* convergence of the sequence of pairs, and we don't rule out the possibility that x_t and y_t are contemporaneously correlated or, indeed, identical. Let

$$G_T^* = \sum_{j=0}^{k(T)-1} X_T(r_j)(Y_T(r_{j+1}) - Y_T(r_j))$$

where $\{r_0, \ldots, r_{k(T)}\} = \Pi_T$ is a nested sequence of partitions as defined previously, and $k(T) \to \infty$ as $T \to \infty$, although more slowly, such that $k(T)/T \to 0$, and

$$\min_{0 \le j < k(T)} |Tr_{j+1} - Tr_j| \to \infty$$

whereas the condition

$$\max_{0 \le j < k(T)} |r_{j+1} - r_j| \to 0 \qquad (5.7.6)$$

still holds. G_T^* is an approximation to G_T, constructed from time-aggregated components that approach independent segments of Brownian motions as T increases, by the FCLT. We accordingly attempt to show that

$$G_T^* \overset{d}{\to} \int_0^1 B_X dB_Y. \qquad (5.7.7)$$

The FCLT is not sufficient alone to let us deduce (5.7.7). However, a clever result known as the *Skorokhod representation theorem* supplies the required step. Roughly speaking, this asserts that (in the present case), whenever the joint distribution of a sequence (X_T, Y_T) converges weakly to (B_X, B_Y), there exists a sequence of random processes (X^T, Y^T) converging almost surely to limit processes that are jointly distributed as (B_X, B_Y). (Since these processes are elements of $D_{[0,1]}$, the relevant concept of convergence has, in practice, to be carefully specified in terms of the Skorokhod topology.) It therefore suffices to show that, if a random variable G^{*T} is constructed like G_T^* except in terms of the Skorokhod processes (X^T, Y^T), then

$$\left| G^{*T} - \int_0^1 B_X dB_Y \right| \xrightarrow{\text{pr}} 0.$$

Since convergence in probability implies convergence in distribution, and G^{*T} and G_T^* have the same distribution by construction, this line of argument suffices to establish (5.7.7).

It then remains to consider $G_T - G_T^*$. Defining $T_j = [Tr_j]$, we have

$$Y_T(r_{j+1}) - Y_T(r_j) = \frac{1}{\sigma_w T^{1/2}} \sum_{t=T_j}^{T_{j+1}-1} w_{t+1}$$

and

$$X_T(r_j) = \frac{1}{\sigma_u T^{1/2}} \sum_{m=0}^{T_j-1} u_{T_j-m}.$$

Therefore,

$$G_T - G_T^* = \frac{1}{\sigma_u \sigma_w T} \sum_{j=1}^{k(T)} \left(\sum_{t=T_{j-1}}^{T_j-1} \sum_{m=0}^{T_j-1} u_{t-m} w_{t+1} - \sum_{m=0}^{T_j-1} u_{T_j-m} \sum_{t=T_{j-1}}^{T_j-1} w_{t+1} \right)$$

$$= \frac{1}{\sigma_u \sigma_w T} \sum_{j=1}^{k(T)} \sum_{t=T_{j-1}+1}^{T_j-1} \left(\sum_{m=0}^{t-T_{j-1}-1} u_{t-m} \right) w_{t+1}$$

Recall our assumption that the processes $\{u_t, w_t\}$ are serially independent. In this case we may show convergence in mean square as follows:

$$E(G_T - G_T^*)^2 = \frac{1}{\sigma_u^2 \sigma_w^2 T^2} \sum_{j=1}^{k(T)} \sum_{t=T_{j-1}+1}^{T_j-1} E\left(\sum_{m=0}^{t-T_{j-1}-1} u_{t-m} \right)^2 E(w_{t+1})^2$$

$$= \frac{1}{T^2} \sum_{j=1}^{k(T)} \sum_{t=T_{j-1}+1}^{T_j-1} (t - T_{j-1})$$

$$\leq \frac{1}{T^2} \sum_{j=1}^{k(T)} (T_j - T_{j-1})^2$$

$$= O\left(\max_{1 \leq j \leq k(T)} |r_j - r_{j-1}| \right) = o(1)$$

where the final order of magnitude holds in view of (5.7.6). This implies convergence in probability, as noted.

Showing this convergence in probability for the general case where $\{u_t, w_t\}$ are serially correlated is generally more difficult, and will not be attempted here, although the assumptions required are comparable with those needed for the FCLT to hold. The main thing to note is that in these cases the probability limit is not zero, and

$$\operatorname{plim}(G_T - G_T^*) = \lambda_{uw} = \frac{1}{\sqrt{\omega_{uu}\omega_{ww}}} \sum_{m=1}^{\infty} E(u_{1-m}w_1).$$

It goes without saying that the cross-autocorrelations need to form a summable series, under the assumptions validating these results. The full convergence result that is commonly cited in arguments relating to convergence of regression statistics, for example, is

$$G_T \xrightarrow{d} \int_0^1 B_X dB_Y + \lambda_{uw}.$$

For reference, let us state here a fairly general stochastic integral convergence theorem (SICT), adapted from De Jong and Davidson (2000). This is a companion result to Theorem 5.1 with essentially the same set of assumptions.

Theorem 5.7.1 *Let (X_T, Y_T) be defined as in (5.5.4) with respect to increment processes $\{u_t, w_t\}$. Let these processes satisfy conditions (a)–(c) of Theorem 5.1, with long-run variances ω_{uu} and ω_{ww} and long-run covariance*

$$\omega_{uw} = \sigma_{vw}^2 + \lambda_{uw} + \lambda_{wu}'$$

where $\lambda_{uw} = \sum_{m=1}^{\infty} E(u_{1-m}w_1)$ and $\lambda_{wu}' = \sum_{m=1}^{\infty} E(w_{1-m}u_1)$. If

$$G_T = \sum_{t=1}^{T} X_T(t/T)(Y_T((t+1)/T) - Y_T(t/T))$$

then

$$(X_T, Y_T, G_T) \xrightarrow{d} (B_X, B_Y, \int_0^1 B_X dB_Y + \lambda_{uw})$$

Note the importance of specifying the *joint* convergence of the three components in this result. This is mainly a formality as far as the proof is concerned, but it is required to be able to apply the CMT to functionals of the components.

5.7.3 Application to regression

A standard case is a cointegrating regression. In a simplified setup in which there are no deterministic components such as intercepts, consider the model

$$y_t = \beta x_t + \varepsilon_t$$
$$\Delta x_t = u_t$$

where $\{u_t, \varepsilon_t\}$ are (at worst) stationary short memory processes, such that their normalized partial sums converge to BM. Let $\hat{\beta}$ represent the OLS estimator. Combining the FCLT and SICT with the CMT, it can be shown that

$$T(\hat{\beta} - \beta) = \frac{T^{-1}\sum_{t=1}^{T} x_t\varepsilon_t}{T^{-2}\sum_{t=1}^{T} x_t^2} \xrightarrow{d} \frac{\sqrt{\omega_{uu}\omega_{\varepsilon\varepsilon}} \int_0^1 B_x dB_\varepsilon + \sigma_{u\varepsilon} + \lambda_{u\varepsilon}}{\omega_{uu} \int_0^1 B_x^2 dr} \tag{5.7.8}$$

where the quantities $\omega_{\varepsilon\varepsilon}$, $\sigma_{u\varepsilon}$ and $\lambda_{u\varepsilon}$ are defined by analogy with Theorem 7.1, although be careful to note that the increments ε_t are not those of the y_t process.

This result embodies all the known asymptotic properties of the cointegrating regression. First, "superconsistency," or convergence at the rate T^{-1}. Second, median bias of order $O(T^{-1})$.[16] Third, the limiting distribution is certainly not Gaussian, noting that the numerator and denominator in (5.7.8) are dependent in general.

However, it is also possible to appreciate the special properties of OLS in the case where the regressor is *strongly exogenous*. This is the case when the pairs (u_{t-j}, ε_t) are independent, for all j and all t. This is not an easy assumption to validate in most economic contexts, but if it holds, much more useful results emerge. Firstly, we can put $\sigma_{u\varepsilon} = \lambda_{u\varepsilon} = 0$, removing this source of bias. More importantly, however, it is now valid to consider the limiting distribution of $T(\hat{\beta} - \beta)$ *conditional* on B_X, which in the context of the conditional distribution can be treated as a deterministic process – effectively, as though it were a type of trend function. It is straightforward to show that

$$\sqrt{\omega_{uu}\omega_{\varepsilon\varepsilon}} \int_0^1 B_x dB_\varepsilon | B_x \sim N\left(0, \omega_{uu}\omega_{\varepsilon\varepsilon} \int_0^1 B_x^2 dr\right)$$

and hence that

$$T(\hat{\beta} - \beta)|B_x \sim N\left(0, \omega_{\varepsilon\varepsilon}\left(\omega_{uu} \int_0^1 B_x^2 dr\right)^{-1}\right).$$

Here the unconditional distribution is *mixed Gaussian*. This means that it is distributed like a drawing from a two-stage sampling procedure in which first a positive random variable V is drawn from the distribution of $\omega_{\varepsilon\varepsilon}\left(\omega_{uu} \int_0^1 B_x^2 dr\right)^{-1}$, and then a drawing from the $N(0, V)$ distribution yields the observed variable. This distribution is distinguished by excess kurtosis, but this is less important than the fact that the t ratio for the regression, being normalized by an "estimate" of the random variance, is asymptotically standard normal. Hence, standard asymptotic inference is available in this model, and the same arguments generalize in a natural way to the multiple regression case. However, in the case of non-strongly endogenous regressors, different procedures are necessary to achieve standard inference. See, for example, Phillips and Hansen (1990) and Phillips and Loretan (1991) for further discussion of these methods.

5.8 The infinite variance case

5.8.1 α-stable distributions

An essential property of the driving process in all the foregoing results has been a finite variance. Without this, there is no CLT in the usual sense. To understand what might happen instead, we must define the class of *stable* distributions. If X has a stable distribution, then for any T, there exist identically distributed r.v.s $U_1, \ldots, U_T$ and real sequences $\{a_T, b_T\}$, where $a_T > 0$, such that $S_T = U_1 + \cdots + U_T$ has the same distribution as $a_T U + b_T$. The distribution is sometimes called *strictly stable* when this is true for the case $b_T = 0$. A stable distribution is, by construction, *infinitely divisible*, meaning that it can be represented as the distribution of a T-fold sum of i.i.d. r.v.s, for any T. The leading example is the $N(\mu, \sigma^2)$ distribution, being the stable case in which S_T has the same distribution as $\sqrt{T}U + (T - \sqrt{T})\mu$. It is clear that, if it is to act as an attractor for the distribution of a normalized partial sum, a distribution must be stable.

The normal is the unique stable distribution possessing a variance. However, there exists an extensive class of stable distributions with infinite variance, identified by the form of their characteristic functions. (Except for the normal, the density functions are not generally available in closed form.) In general, members of the stable class can be positively or negatively skewed around a point of central tendency. Confining attention, for simplicity, to symmetric distributions centered on zero, the ch.f.s have the form.

$$\phi_U(\lambda) = e^{-\delta|\lambda|^\alpha} \tag{5.8.1}$$

for $0 < \alpha \leq 2$ (stability parameter) and $\delta > 0$ (scale parameter). The $N(0, \sigma^2)$ distribution is the case where $\alpha = 2$ and $\delta = \sigma^2/2$. When $\alpha < 2$, distributions with ch.f. shown in (5.8.1), having no variance, are characterized by "fat tails" with a relatively high probability of outlying values.

Considering again identity (5.2.4), we find that, in this case,

$$[\phi_U(\lambda)]^T = \phi_U(\lambda T^{1/\alpha})$$

and the stability property is obtained with $b_T = 0$ and $a_T = T^{1/\alpha}$. Distributions having this property for a_T (not necessarily with $b_T = 0$) are called stable with exponent α, or α-stable. If the ch.f. takes the special form of (5.8.1) they are called *symmetric α-stable* or $S\alpha S$. Another leading $S\alpha S$ case is the Cauchy distribution, corresponding to $\alpha = 1$. Since $e^{-|\lambda|^\alpha} = E(e^{i\lambda\delta^{-1/\alpha}U})$, one might think by analogy with the standard normal of the "standard" $S\alpha S$, having $\delta = 1$, obtained by dividing the r.v. by $\delta^{-1/\alpha}$. Useful references on the properties of stable distributions include Breiman (1968), Feller (1971), Ibragimov and Linnik (1971) and Samorodnitsky and Taqqu (1994).

Every distribution with finite variance lies in the "domain of attraction of the normal law." However, there evidently exists a whole family of stable convergence laws of which the CLT is only the leading case. The most important question, of course, is what distributions may fall within the domain of attraction of a stable law associated with given α? The answer to this more general question relates to the tail behavior of the distributions in question, and can be stated in terms of the distribution function F. Breiman (1968, Th. 9.34) gives the necessary and sufficient conditions as follows: that there exist nonnegative constants M^+ and M^-, of which at least one is positive, such that

$$\frac{F(-x)}{1-F(x)} \to \frac{M^-}{M^+} \text{ as } x \to \infty$$

and, for every $\xi > 0$, as $x \to \infty$,

$$\text{if } M^+ > 0 \quad \text{then} \quad \frac{1-F(\xi x)}{1-F(x)} \to \xi^{-\alpha} \tag{5.8.2}$$

$$\text{if } M^- > 0 \quad \text{then} \quad \frac{F(-\xi x)}{F(-x)} \to \xi^{-\alpha}. \tag{5.8.3}$$

Note that stable laws can be skewed although, of course, $M^+ = M^-$ in symmetric cases. This is one point of difference from the normal CLT, in which normalized sums of skewed r.v.s are nonetheless symmetric in the limit.

In the symmetric case, properties (5.8.2) and (5.8.3) are satisfied if

$$P(|U| > x) = x^{-\alpha}L(x)$$

where L is a *slowly varying* function, having the property that $L(ax)/L(x) \to 1$ as $x \to \infty$ for any $a > 0$. For example, $\log x$ is slowly varying. The key property is that there exists $B > 0$ such that $x^{-\alpha} < L(x) < x^{\alpha}$ for all $x > B$. We say in this case that the tails of the distribution obey a power law with exponent α. Note the implication, if the distribution is continuous and f_U denotes the p.d.f., that

$$f_U(x) = O(|x|^{-\alpha-1}L(x))$$

as $x \to \pm\infty$, such that the tail integrals are of the specified order of magnitude. By contrast, to ensure that

$$E(U^2) = \int_{-\infty}^{\infty} x^2 f_U(x)dx < \infty$$

note that the tails of the p.d.f. must be of $O(|x|^{-3-\varepsilon})$ for $\varepsilon > 0$, and hence need $\alpha > 2$. In this case, the attractor p.d.f. has exponentially vanishing tails according to the CLT, regardless of α, whereas for $\alpha < 2$ the tail behavior is shared by the limit distribution, under the stable law.

We summarize these points by noting that there exists a generalization of the CLT of the following sort.

Theorem 5.8.1 *If* $S_T = \sum_{t=1}^{T} U_t$, *and* $U_1, \ldots, U_T$ *are i.i.d. random variables in the domain of attraction of a symmetric stable law with parameter* α, *there exists a slowly varying function L such that* $S_T/(T^{1/\alpha}L(T))$ *converges weakly to SαS.*

Little research appears to have been done to date on the case of dependent increments, one obvious difficulty being that the autocorrelation function is undefined. However, it appears a reasonable conjecture that suitable variants of the arguments deployed for the dependent CLT, such as Theorem 5.1, might yield generalizations for L_p-NED functions of mixing processes with $p < \alpha$.

5.8.2 Lévy motion

If convergence to an α-stable law takes the place of the usual CLT, the existence of a corresponding FCLT must be our next concern. Consider, as before, the normalized partial sum process $X_T \in D_{[0,1]}$ such that

$$X_T(r) = \frac{1}{T^{1/\alpha}L(T)} \sum_{t=1}^{[Tr]} U_t. \tag{5.8.4}$$

Consider the behavior of this process as T increases. Note first of all that

$$P(T^{-1/\alpha}L(T)^{-1}|U_t| > x) = O(T^{-1}L(T))$$

and, therefore, the normalization ensures that the probability that the process jumps by a positive amount is converging to zero. However, note too how the proof of tightness in $C_{[0,1]}$, given in Section 5.4.5, now fails. With $p < 2$, the inequality in (5.4.7) cannot be satisfied for arbitrary $\varepsilon, \eta > 0$ under the stated conditions. In fact, the limit process does *not* lie in $C_{[0,1]}$ almost surely.

A more general class of processes in $D_{[0,1]}$ containing these limits is defined as follows. A random function $X : [0,1] \mapsto \mathbb{R}$ is called a *Lévy process* if

(a) it is cadlag, a.s.
(b) it has independent increments,
(c) it is continuous in probability: $P(X(r+s) - X(r)) \to 0$ as $s \to 0$,
(d) it is time-homogeneous: the distribution of $X(s+r) - X(r)$ does not depend on r,
(e) $X(0) = 0$ a.s.

BM is a Lévy process on this definition, although one enjoying additional continuity properties. On the other hand, if the fidis of a Lévy process are strictly stable distributions with parameter α, such that $X(s+r) - X(r)$ is distributed as $s^{1/\alpha}X(1)$ for all $0 < s < 1$ and $0 \le r < 1-s$, it is called an α-stable motion, or a *Lévy motion*, denoted Λ_a.

In addition to the fidis converging to those of Lévy motion, the counterpart of the FCLT for these processes must establish that the sequence of p.m.s associated with X_T is uniformly tight, and the limit process lies in $D_{[0,1]}$ almost surely. The tightness conditions are less stringent than for the Gaussian case, since it is only necessary to rule out realizations with isolated discontinuities arising with positive probability. Billingsley (1968, Theorem 15.6) gives a sufficient condition for tightness for processes in $D_{[0,1]}$. The weak convergence specified in the following result is defined as before with respect to the Skorokhod topology on $D_{[0,1]}$.

Theorem 5.8.2   *If X and $\{X_T, T = 1,2,3,\ldots\}$ are random elements of $D_{[0,1]}$ and*

(a) *the fidis of X_T converge to those of X;*
(b) *there exist $\gamma \ge 0$, $\mu > 1$ and a continuous nondecreasing function F on $[0,1]$ such that*

$$P(\min\{|X_T(r) - X_T(r_1)|, |X_T(r_2) - X_T(r)|\} \ge \lambda) \le \frac{[F(r_2) - F(r_1)]^\mu}{\lambda^{2\gamma}}$$

for all $T \ge 1$, and $r_1 \le r \le r_2$ whenever $r_1, r_2 \in K_X$, where $K_X \subseteq [0,1]$ is the set of points r at which $P(X(r) \ne X(r-)) = 0$, including 0 and 1;

then $X_T \xrightarrow{d} X$.

For the case of a Lévy motion we can take $K_X = [0,1]$. Condition (b) sets the probability of isolated discontinuities sufficiently low to ensure uniform tightness. A sufficient condition for (b) is

$$E(|X_T(r) - X_T(r_1)|^\gamma |X_T(r_2) - X_T(r)|^\gamma) \le [F(r_2) - F(r_1)]^\mu. \qquad (5.8.5)$$

Suppose the fidis are tending to $S\alpha S$ limits, and that the increments are independent. Then, choosing $\gamma < \alpha$ such that the moments exist, note that the left-hand side of (5.8.5) equals

$$E|X_T(r) - X_T(r_1)|^\gamma E|X_T(r_2) - X_T(r)|^\gamma \le M \frac{([Tr_2] - [Tr])^{\gamma/\alpha}([Tr] - [Tr_1])^{\gamma/\alpha}}{T^{2\gamma/\alpha}} \qquad (5.8.6)$$

for some $M < \infty$. If $\min(r_2 - r, r - r_1) < T^{-1}$ then note that the left-hand side of (5.8.6) vanishes. Otherwise, the right-hand side is bounded by

$$M \frac{([Tr_2] - [Tr_1])^{2\gamma/\alpha}}{T^{2\gamma/\alpha}} \le 4M(r_2 - r_1)^{2\gamma/\alpha}.$$

Choosing $\gamma > 0$ to satisfy $\gamma < \alpha < 2\gamma$ shows that condition (b) of Theorem 5.8.2 is satisfied, and the weak limit of such a process is a Lévy motion.

More research remains to be done before the infinite variance case is understood as thoroughly as convergence to Brownian motion, especially under dependence. There are various new issues to be treated, such as the restrictions on joint convergence to limits in D^m, as described in section 5.4.6. However, the prevalence of fat-tailed distributions in economic data, especially in finance, is not in doubt. See Barndorff-Nielsen and Shephard (2001), among many recent references, on the importance of these processes in econometric inference.

Notes

1. A *topology* on a space is a collection of subsets that includes the whole space and the empty set, and is closed under arbitrary unions and finite intersections. Such sets are called *open*. This defines an open set, and the usual characterization of openness in $\mathbb{R}$ and other metric spaces derives from this fundamental definition.
2. A metric on a space $\mathbb{S}$ is a distance measure for pairs of points of the space, having the following properties for all $x, y \in \mathbb{S}$:

    1. $d(x,y) = d(y,x)$
    2. $d(x,y) = 0$ if and only if $x = y$
    3. $d(x,y) \le d(x,z) + d(y,z)$, $z \in \mathbb{S}$.

3. A functional is a function whose argument is another function. Integrals are well-known examples.
4. A set A is dense in a space $\mathbb{S}$ if every point of $\mathbb{S}$ lies arbitrarily close to a point of A.
5. Thus, for example, $\mathcal{B}_C = \{A \cap C : A \in \mathcal{B}_R\}$.
6. See Pollard (1984) for an account of this approach.
7. This is not the 1905 paper on special relativity, nor the Nobel-prize winning contribution of the same year on the photoelectric effect, but the third original product of Einstein's *annus mirabilis*.
8. For another example, consider (5.3.3).
9. See Davidson (1994), respectively Theorem 24.3 and Theorem 15.14, for these results.
10. This is (unfortunately) the third distinct usage of the word "weak" in this literature, with a different connotation from both "weak LLN" and "weak convergence."
11. This is in the familiar context in which I(1) denotes an integrated process, where the argument represents the order of difference necessary to get I(0).
12. If $\theta_j = O(j^{-1-\mu})$ for $\mu > 0$, then $\sum_{j=0}^{\infty} |\theta_i| < \infty$ and $\sum_{i=j+1}^{\infty} |\theta_i| = O(j^{-\mu})$.
13. The first formula appears in Mandelbrot and van Ness (1968) and other references. I am grateful to a referee for pointing out that the second formula is equivalent.
14. See, e.g., Davidson (1994 Chapter 30.2) for the definition of progressive measurability.
15. Chan and Wei (1988) and Kurtz and Protter (1991) are important references here, and see also Hansen (1992), Davidson (1994, section 30.4) and de Jong and Davidson (2000).
16. It is evident that the numerator does not have a mean of zero, but since it is not straightforward to compute the moments of the limiting ratio, it is better to comment on its distribution directly without invoking integrability.

References

Andrews, D. W. K. (1984) Non-strong mixing autoregressive processes. *Journal of Applied Probability* **21**, 930–4.

Barndorff-Nielsen, O. E., and N. Shephard (2001) Modelling by Lévy processess for financial Econometrics. In Ole E. Barndorff-Nielsen, T. Mikosch and S. Resnick (eds), *Lévy Processes – Theory and Application*. New York: Birkhauser, pp. 283–318.

Beveridge, S., and Nelson, C. R. (1981) A new approach to the decomposition of economic time series into permanent and transitory components with particular attention to measurement of the "business cycle." *Journal of Monetary Economics* **7**, 151–74.

Billingsley, P. (1968) *Convergence of Probability Measures*. New York: John Wiley.

Billingsley, P. (1986) *Probability and Measure*, 2nd edn. New York: John Wiley.

Breiman, L. (1992) *Probability*. Philadelphia: Society for Industrial and Applied Mathematics.

Chan, N. H. and Wei, C. Z. (1988) Limiting distributions of least squares estimates of unstable autoregressive processes. *Annals of Statistics* **16**, 367–401.

Davidson, J. (1994) *Stochastic Limit Theory*. Oxford: Oxford University Press.

Davidson, J. (2000) Establishing conditions for the functional central limit theorem in nonlinear and semiparametric time series processes. *Journal of Econometrics* **106**, 243–69.

Davidson, J. (2004) Convergence to stochastic integrals with fractionally integrated integrator processes: theory, and applications to fractional cointegration analysis. Working paper at http://www.ex.ac.uk/~jehd201.

Davidson, J. and R. M. de Jong (2000) The functional central limit theorem and weak convergence to stochastic integrals II: fractionally integrated processes. *Econometric Theory* **16**(5), 643–66.

Davydov, Yu. A. (1970) The invariance principle for stationary processes. *Theory of Probability and its Applications* **XV**(3), 487–98.

De Jong, R. M. and J. Davidson (2000) The functional central limit theorem and weak convergence to stochastic integrals I: weakly dependent processes. *Econometric Theory* **16**(5), 621–42.

Donsker, M. D. (1951) An invariance principle for certain probability limit theorems. *Memoirs of the American Mathematical Society* **6**, 1–12.

Dudley, R. M. (1989) *Real Analysis and Probability*. Pacific Grove, CA: Wadsworth and Brooks/Cole.

Embrechts, P., C. Kluppelberg and T. Mikosch (1997) *Modelling Extremal Events*. Berlin: Springer-Verlag.

Feller, W. (1971) *An Introduction to Probability Theory and its Applications*, vol. II. New York: John Wiley.

Gallant, A. R. (1997) *An Introduction to Econometric Theory*. Princeton, NJ: Princeton University Press.

Gallant, A. R. and H. White (1988) *A Unified Theory of Estimation and Inference for Nonlinear Dynamic Models*. Oxford: Basil Blackwell.

Hansen, B. E. (1992) Converence to stochastic integrals for dependent heterogeneous processes. *Econometric Theory* **8**, 489–500.

Ibragimov, I.A., and Linnik, Y. (1971) *Independent and Stationary Sequences of Random Variables*. Groningen: Wolters-Noordhoff.

Jacod, J. and A. N. Shiryaev (1987) *Limit Theorems for Stochastic Processes*. Berlin: Springer-Verlag.

Karatzas, I. and Shreve, S. E. (1988) *Brownian Motion and Stochastic Calculus*. New York: Springer-Verlag.

Kurtz, T. G. and Protter, P. (1991) Weak limit theorems for stochastic integrals and stochastic differential equations. *Annals of Probability* **19**, 1035–70.

Mandelbrot, B. B. (1983) *The Fractal Geometry of Nature*. New York: W.H. Freeman.

Mandelbrot, B. B. and J. W. van Ness (1968) Fractional Brownian motions, fractional noises and applications. *SIAM Review* **10**(4), 422–37.

Marinucci, D. and P. M. Robinson (1999) Alternative forms of fractional Brownian motion. *Journal of Statistical Inference and Planning* **80**, 111–22.

McCabe, B. and A. Tremayne (1993) *Elements of Modern Asymptotic Theory with Statistical Applications*. Manchester: Manchester University Press.

Phillips, P. C. B. (1988) Weak convergence of sample covariance matrices to stochastic integrals via martingale approximations. *Econometric Theory* **4**, 528–33.

Phillips, P. C. B. and B. E. Hansen (1990) Statistical inference in instrumental variables regression with I(1) processes. *Review of Economic Studies* **57**, 99–125.

Phillips, P. C. B. and M. Loretan (1991) Estimating long-run economic equilibria. *Review of Economic Studies* **58**, 407–37.

Phillips, P. C. B. and V. Solo (1992) Asymptotics for linear processes. *Annals of Statistics* **20**, 971–1001.

Pollard, D. (1984) *Convergence of Stochastic Processes*. New York: Springer-Verlag.

Pollard, D. (2002) *A User's Guide to Measure Theoretic Probability*. Cambridge: Cambridge University Press.

Samorodnitsky, G. and M. Taqqu (1994) *Stable Non-Gaussian Random Processes*. Boca Raton: Chapman and Hall.

Skorokhod, A. V. (1956) Limit theorems for stochastic processes. *Theory of Probability and its Applications* **1**, 261–90.

White, H. (1984) *Asymptotic Theory for Econometricians*. Orlando: Academic Press.

Wiener, N. (1923) Differential space. *Journal of Mathematical Physics* **2**, 131–74.

Wold, H. (1938) *A Study in the Analysis of Stationary Time Series*. Uppsala: Almqvist and Wiksell.

Woolridge, J. M. and White, H. (1988) Some invariance principles and central limit theorems for dependent heterogeneous processes. *Econometric Theory* **4**, 210–30.

Part IV

Time Series and
Regression Methods

6

Stationary Linear Univariate Time Series Models

Andrew Tremayne

Abstract

Linear time series models of the autoregressive-moving average class have been a handmaiden of econometric methods for time series data for nigh on two generations, and have their origins many years before that. Although designed for use with stationary data, they can be adapted to handle data with stochastic trends that often arise in macroeconomics by using the differencing operation. The two basic forms of model, viz. finite order autoregressive and finite order moving average models, can be thought of as economically atheoretical approximations to a true, but unknown, transfer function for a stationary linear process. The generalization of the former of these, in particular, to the multivariate case as a stationary vector autoregression has found widespread application in economics. So, although the basic models are extensively used by practitioners in the field, their importance also clearly lies in the fact that they have been fundamental as the basis of a wide range of subsequent developments. Many of these continue to form a mainstay of modern econometric analysis. The hybrid autoregressive-moving model sometimes provides a parsimoniously parameterized model for series that may require quite a large number of parameters in either of the two basic (pure) forms to obtain a satisfactory representation of the true data-generating mechanism. For this reason, it may be attractive in applications. The range of topics encountered in this chapter is, perforce, selective but includes the central ones of: model determination; parameter estimation; and diagnostic checking. In addition, there is discussion of model selection procedures and other, perhaps more peripheral and less frequently encountered, issues.

6.1	Introduction		216
6.2	The three prototypical models		218
	6.2.1	Autoregressive (AR) models	219
	6.2.2	Moving average models	222
	6.2.3	Mixed autoregressive-moving average models	224
6.3	Model determination		225
6.4	Parameter estimation		229
	6.4.1	Method of moments	229
	6.4.2	Conditional least squares methods	230
	6.4.3	Estimation by maximum likelihood	231

6.5	Checking model adequacy	235
	6.5.1 Portmanteau tests	237
	6.5.2 Tests based on the score (Lagrange multiplier) principle	238
	6.5.3 Likelihood ratio tests	239
6.6	Model selection procedures	239
6.7	Some further issues	242
	6.7.1 Hannan–Rissanen search procedure	243
	6.7.2 Parameter redundancy	243
	6.7.3 Indirect inference and ARAR models	244
	6.7.4 Time series models for counts	245
6.8	Conclusions	247

6.1   Introduction

Linear models have a long history in econometrics and time series analysis. The use of explicit statistical modeling techniques for time series dates from around the time of Yule's (1927) classic paper that proposed autoregressive (AR) models. The equally well-known moving average (MA) model was introduced in the same year by Slutsky (1927). Wold (1938) also has an extensive early discussion of these two models. The hybrid autoregressive-moving average (ARMA) was subsequently considered, arising from work in the frequency domain on rational spectral functions.

The probabilistic foundations needed to use such models in the context of observed series were laid down largely by Kolmogorov (1933), and Cramér (1937) was able to link the time series literature with that on stochastic processes. In the late 1930s, Wold was working on his doctoral thesis under the direction of Cramér and it was he who provided a unifying statistical framework for stationary time series in his seminal work (Wold, 1938). The great contribution made there was the celebrated Wold Decomposition Theorem which shows that, under suitable regularity conditions, any stationary stochastic process can be written as a sum of a purely deterministic component (i.e., one that is perfectly predictable from its own past) and a purely non-deterministic component that may be expressed as an infinite moving average of current and past white noise errors. This will be called a linear process (LP), a term employed by Bartlett (1946).

A contribution of this length can perforce seek only to offer a broad brush in its account and a selective one at that. For an in-depth treatment, the reader must look elsewhere. The intention is to provide an overview of some topics that are central to the modeling of stationary time series in econometrics and other fields and, along the way, to provide pointers to the literature. The body of relevant work is truly voluminous, as the remarkably comprehensive bibliography of almost 750 papers, books and monographs compiled by Choi (1992) attests. Pride of place amongst the available texts on time series methods must go to the work of Box and Jenkins (1970), which can reasonably be argued to constitute a cornerstone of modern methods of time series analysis. Other excellent texts that provide comprehensive accounts include Hamilton (1994), Brockwell and Davis (1996), Harvey (1993), Fuller (1996) and Granger and Newbold (1986). Davidson and MacKinnon (2004, chapter 13) gives a concise and clear account while Spanos (2001) has a chapter of similar length to this on time series and dynamic models.

The pioneering work of Box and Jenkins is now in its third edition as Box, Jenkins and Reinsel (1994). This book popularized the use of linear time series methods and introduced a three-step approach to modeling stationary series, viz. model: identification; estimation; and diagnostic checking. More than 30 years on, this approach endures in a wide range of empirical contexts. Box and Jenkins (1970) also showed how it will often be possible to model nonstationary series by using the difference operator to reduce series with a stochastic trend to stationarity. The analysis of series which may have unit roots has, of course, proved very popular in the field of time series econometrics for many years, perhaps first impacting seriously on the econometrics fraternity through the striking evidence for unit roots found by Nelson and Plosser (1982) in their work on US macroeconomic time series. These authors used the methodology of Dickey (1975) and Fuller (1976) in their analysis. Chapter 7 of this volume considers the topic in detail.

The main ideas of statistical analysis of time series and econometric methodology overlap in many ways, despite their distinctive aspects. For instance, notions like data coherency of models – as discussed, for example, by Hendry and Richard (1982) – are relevant to the problem of choosing suitable time series models. It seems appropriate to regard time series analysis and econometric analysis of time series as being complementary disciplines. Pagan (1985, p. 2000) explicitly contends that "the interpretation and formulation of dynamic specification is inextricably bound up with the nature of the time series used in the modelling exercise." Of course, it is important that time series methods used in econometrics should be fit for purpose and this explains why time series analysts have expended much energy on the task of obtaining and refining tests of model adequacy, the last stage in the Box–Jenkins paradigm. This problem is closely allied to those of model determination and selection. Chow (1981) has an extensive discussion of these matters from the standpoint of econometrics, whilst Hannan (1980) offers an interesting treatment from the point of view of a pure time series analyst.

The plan of the chapter is as follows. Section 6.2 provides a brief review of the three main models of stationary linear time series analysis, viz. the: autoregressive; moving average; and mixed ARMA models. Standard methods for model determination are discussed in section 6.3 and parameter estimation in section 6.4. The next section is devoted to a review of tests for model adequacy, with section 6.6 considering the problem of model selection procedures. The remaining main section discusses what might be regarded as less central issues. It deals with the problem of parameter redundancy that can arise with ARMA models, together with some less used, but nevertheless important, time series concepts, including indirect inference. Most univariate time series methods have been developed on the assumption that the variable to be modeled can be regarded as continuous, often driven by Gaussian innovations. Section 6.7 also provides a brief treatment of models for (low) counts data when such an assumption is unsustainable. There follow some concluding remarks.

6.2   The three prototypical models

Consider modeling a univariate process $y_t = \{y_t\}_{-\infty}^{\infty}$ on which observations $\mathbf{y} = (y_1, y_2, \ldots, y_n)' = \{y_t\}_1^n$ are available. Throughout the chapter it is assumed that the series is covariance, weakly or wide-sense stationary. This implies that $E(y_t) = \mu_y$ for all t and that $E(y_t - \mu_y)(y_{t-s} - \mu_y) = \gamma(s) = \gamma(-s)$ for all t and s, so that the mean and covariance structure are constant at all times and that the autocovariance at lag s depends upon that lag, but not on t. The variance of the process is, of course, $\gamma(0)$. For a fuller treatment see, for example, Hamilton (1994, section 3.1). All coefficients of any parametric model are assumed to be time invariant. A basic building block for all the models to be considered is a sequence of random variables $\{\varepsilon_t\}_{-\infty}^{\infty}$, known as a white noise (WN) process, satisfying $E(\varepsilon_t) = 0, E(\varepsilon_t^2) = \sigma^2$ with zero autocovariance at all leads and lags. An example of a WN process is, of course, given by specifying that $\varepsilon_t \sim NID(0, \sigma^2)$ (where *NID* stands for normal, independent and identically distributed), though this is a stronger requirement than WN which does not require either independence or normality (Gaussianity).

All of the linear models to be exposited can be thought of as stemming from Wold's (1938, theorem 7) famous Decomposition Theorem. This provides a way of representing any covariance stationary process as

$$y_t = \delta_t + \sum_{j=0}^{\infty} \theta_j \varepsilon_{t-j}, \tag{6.1}$$

where $\{\varepsilon_t\}_{-\infty}^{\infty}$ is zero-mean WN with variance σ^2, δ_t is a deterministic component (uncorrelated with ε_{t-j} for all j) that is perfectly predictable from its past history and the $\{\theta_j\}_0^{\infty}$ are square summable, $\sum_{j=0}^{\infty} \theta_j^2 < \infty$, with $\theta_0 = 1$. The purely nondeterministic component $\sum_{j=0}^{\infty} \theta_j \varepsilon_{t-j}$ is a LP. For our purposes it is sufficient to take $\delta_t = \mu_y$ and omit further consideration of the deterministic component. Introduce the lag operator L which, when applied to any series x_t, is such that $L^j x_t \equiv x_{t-j}$. Then (6.1) may be written as $y_t = \delta_t + \theta(L)\varepsilon_t$, where $\theta(L) = \sum_{j=0}^{\infty} \theta_j L^j$. The time-invariant linear filter $\theta(L)$ is sometimes called the transfer function of the process. It can be shown that the autocovariance structure of a stationary stochastic process with Wold decomposition as in (6.1) with mean μ_y is given by

$$\gamma(k) = E(y_t - \mu_y)(y_{t-k} - \mu_y) = \sigma^2 \sum_{j=0}^{\infty} \theta_j \theta_{j+|k|}, \quad k = 0, \pm 1, \pm 2, \ldots. \tag{6.2}$$

The details of this and many of the other issues discussed are available in the admirable text by Brockwell and Davis (1996).

Clearly, finding the Wold decomposition for any stationary stochastic process would require an infinite number of parameters to be determined, viz. ($\sigma^2, \theta_1, \theta_2, \ldots$) and this will not be possible with finite realizations of data. What has to be done to make progress on a practical analysis of stationary time series data is, therefore, to make some additional assumptions about the coefficients $\theta_1, \theta_2, \ldots$ of the Wold decomposition, i.e. about the transfer function in (6.1). The next three subsections introduce the main ways in which this is done in time domain analysis. The models to be discussed are members of the ARMA class. For this class of models, the covariance (used to characterize the dependence) between y_t and y_{t-k} decreases quite rapidly as k increases; these processes are examples of short memory processes. The autocovariances of any process y_t will be measured in the squares of the units in which the process itself is measured. It is, therefore, convenient to define a standardized version of the autocovariance function via

$$\rho(k) = \gamma(k)/\gamma(0). \tag{6.3}$$

By virtue of the symmetry, we usually only consider $\rho(k), k = 1, 2, \ldots$ and note that $\rho(0) = 1$. Yule (1926) introduced the name serial correlations for the $\rho(k), k = 1, 2, \ldots$, but the terminology autocorrelations is also widely used. We shall call the $\{\rho(k)\}_1^\infty$ the autocorrelation function (ACF) of the process. For members of the ARMA class, the ACF is geometrically bounded, that is for some positive c and $r \in (0,1)$

$$|\rho(k)| \leq cr^{-k}, \quad k = 1, 2, \ldots. \tag{6.4}$$

See, for example, Brockwell and Davis (1996, section 13.2).

6.2.1 Autoregressive (AR) models

Suppose that the linear filter $\theta(L)$ is approximated by specifying that y_t is generated in terms solely of p lagged values of itself plus a WN error term. Then (6.1) becomes

$$y_t = \mu + \sum_{j=1}^{p} \alpha_j y_{t-j} + \varepsilon_t \tag{6.5}$$

and the model is known as an autoregressive model of order p, $AR(p)$. It is assumed that $\alpha_p \neq 0$ as an identifiability condition. The constant term μ allows for the fact that most economic time series do not have a zero mean.

The coefficient μ in (6.5) is not the unconditional mean of y_t, μ_y. It can be shown that the unconditional mean and variance of y_t are given by: $\mu/(1 - \sum_{j=1}^{p} \alpha_j)$; and a fairly complicated, but time-invariant, function of $\{\alpha_j\}_1^p$, σ^2 and the first

p autocovariances of y_t, respectively (the method suggested below near (6.7) will accomplish the latter, for example). The fact that these (unconditional) moments are constant through time is, of course, a requirement for weak stationarity to hold. The conditional moments of an $AR(p)$ process are: $E(y_t|\mathcal{F}_{t-1}) = \mu + \sum_{j=1}^{p} \alpha_j y_{t-j}$; and $Var(y_t|\mathcal{F}_{t-1}) = \sigma^2$, where $\mathcal{F}_{t-1}$ indicates the past history of y_t, i.e. $y_{t-1}, y_{t-2}, \dots$. Hence the conditional mean is time varying, but the conditional variance is not. This highlights the basis of the ground-breaking work of Engle (1982) and the many succeeding authors who have written about autoregressive conditional heteroskedasticity and its extensions, since they model the conditional variance as a time varying quantity. This material is discussed in detail in Chapter 22 on volatility modeling. Note also that the conditional mean of y_t is linear in its past. Grunwald, Hyndman, Tedesco and Tweedie (2000) (writing explicitly about the first-order case) employ the acronym CLAR for a conditionally linear autoregressive process; processes other than linear, constant coefficient continuous AR processes belong to this class and another (nonlinear) example will arise in section 6.7.4.

The simplest autoregressive model when $p = 1$, has been in use in econometrics for many years, certainly dating back to Frisch (1933), to model the dynamic evolution of series. In this case the polynomial in the lag operator of the Wold decomposition is approximated in the following way. Rearranging (6.5) for $p = 1$, we have

$$y_t - \alpha_1 y_{t-1} = (1 - \alpha_1 L)y_t = \alpha(L)y_t = \mu + \varepsilon_t. \tag{6.6}$$

Provided that the polynomial $\alpha(L)$ can be inverted, it is immediately clear that $\alpha^{-1}(L) \approx \theta(L)$. The relevant polynomial inversion can be performed when the root of the characteristic equation $\alpha(z) = 0$ (where z is an algebraic indeterminate) satisfies $|z| > 1$. This is, of course, the condition that must be satisfied for stationarity of the process. Extending to the pth order case, the characteristic equation is $\alpha(z) = 1 - \sum_{j=1}^{p} \alpha_j z^j = 0$ and the process is stationary provided the solutions $\{z_j\}_1^p$ lie outside the unit circle, i.e. $|z_j| > 1$, $j = 1, \dots, p$, where the roots are either real or complex conjugate pairs, since the coefficients of (6.5) are real. Hereafter, these stationarity conditions are assumed to be satisfied.

It follows from (6.6) that

$$\mu_y = E(y_t) = \mu + \alpha_1 E(y_{t-1}) = \mu + \alpha_1 \mu_y,$$

and thus that $\mu_y = \mu/(1 - \alpha_1)$. Generalizing this argument to the pth order case, it can be seen that $\mu_y = \mu/(1 - \sum_{j=1}^{p} \alpha_j)$, as stated above. To simplify the notation in what follows, we shall redefine $y_t^* = y_t - \mu_y$ for the demeaned process and henceforth omit the superscript asterisk in order to avoid confusion. Thus y_t now denotes a zero mean process with autocovariance structure as before.

For the stationary case with $p = 1$, it can be seen that the coefficients of the Wold decomposition are approximated by $\alpha^{-1}(L) = 1/(1 - \alpha_1 L) = 1 + \alpha_1 L + \alpha_1^2 L^2 + \dots$, i.e. θ_j is approximated by α_1^j. Assuming an infinite past, the $AR(1)$

model can equivalently be represented by

$$y_t = \varepsilon_t + \alpha_1 \varepsilon_{t-1} + \alpha_1^2 \varepsilon_{t-2} + \cdots .$$

This is the simplest expression to use to work out the autocovariance structure of the model, since the ε_t are uncorrelated. Multiplying through by y_{t-k} and taking expectations gives

$$\gamma(k) = E(y_t y_{t-k}) = E\left(\sum_{i=0}^{\infty} \alpha_1^i \varepsilon_{t-i} \right) \left(\sum_{j=0}^{\infty} \alpha_1^j \varepsilon_{t-j-k} \right). \tag{6.7}$$

The variance of y_t is $\gamma(0) = \sigma^2/(1 - \alpha_1^2)$ and $\gamma(k) = \alpha_1^k \gamma(0)$. These autocovariances can also be obtained by use of an autocovariance-generating function $\gamma_y(z) = \sigma^2/\alpha(z)\alpha(z^{-1}) = \sigma^2[\ldots + \gamma(2)z^{-2} + \gamma(1)z^{-1} + \gamma(0) + \gamma(1)z^1 + \gamma(2)z^2 + \ldots]$. That is, the coefficient of z^k (resp. z^{-k}) generates the kth autocovariance. Notice that the symmetry property of the autocovariances of stationary processes ($\gamma(k) = \gamma(-k)$) has been used here. Of course, the same approach can be used to generate the autocovariance structure of any Wold decomposition (6.1) via $\gamma_y(z) = \sigma^2\theta(z)\theta(z^{-1})$; see Brockwell and Davis (1996, chapter 3) for further details.

For the $AR(1)$ process, $\rho(j) = \alpha_1^j$, so that the ACF declines geometrically to zero, as expected. This dampening occurs in oscillatory fashion if $\alpha_1 \in (-1, 0)$. More generally, in $AR(p)$ models the actual rate of the decline of the ACF depends on the zeros of the characteristic equation that are closest to the unit circle. If $\alpha(z) = 0$ has one or more roots close to the unit circle, the rate of decay may be quite slow, even though the process is a short memory one.

The same general principles are used to analyze the dependence structure of higher order AR models. We only consider explicitly the extension to the $AR(2)$ model

$$y_t = \alpha_1 y_{t-1} + \alpha_2 y_{t-2} + \varepsilon_t. \tag{6.8}$$

The process (6.8) will be stationary provided that the equation $\alpha(z) = 1 - \alpha_1 z - \alpha_2 z^2 = 0$ has both its roots outside the unit circle. This leads to a triangular area of the α_1/α_2 parameter space for stationary $AR(2)$ models that will be familiar to practitioners. The appropriate parametric restrictions are: $\alpha_1 + \alpha_2 < 1$; $\alpha_2 - \alpha_1 < 1$; and $\alpha_2 \in (-1, 1)$. A diagram of the stationarity region is widely available, see for example, Box, Jenkins and Reinsel (1994, figure 3.3), which also provides the admissible region for the first two autocorrelations for a stationary $AR(2)$ process. Box, Jenkins and Reinsel (1994, figure 3.2) show the generic shapes of the ACF and partial autocorrelation function (introduced directly below) for various regions of the admissible parameter space.

The partial autocorrelation function (PACF) also contains vital information about the dependence structure of time series processes; like the ACF it, too, depends only on the second order properties of the process. The partial autocorrelation at lag k, denoted $\rho_k(k)$, may be regarded as the correlation between y_t and y_{t-k} when the dependence of the intervening observations $y_{t-1}, \ldots, y_{t-k+1}$ has been accounted for. In this sense it plays an analogous role to that of a partial regression coefficient in multiple regression. There the kth regression coefficient measures the marginal effect on the conditional mean of the response variable to a unit change in the kth design variable once the effect of other variables in the model have been taken into account. Put another way, $\rho_k(k)$ is the true value of the last coefficient in the linear regression of y_t on the first k lagged values of itself

$$y_t = \rho_k(1)y_{t-1} + \rho_k(2)y_{t-2} + \cdots + \rho_k(k)y_{t-k} + \eta_t, \tag{6.9}$$

where η_t is a regression error. The subscript k appears on all the coefficients in (6.9) to make it clear that the values thereof do depend upon k; it is the last one that measures the (population) partial autocorrelation at lag k.

Consider the $AR(1)$ model and (6.9) with $k=1$. Then clearly we can set $\rho_1(1) = \alpha_1$ and $\eta_t = \varepsilon_t$, so that the first order partial autocorrelation in an $AR(1)$ model is just the coefficient α_1. Setting $k=2$, it is evident that choosing $\rho_2(1) = \alpha_1$ and $\rho_2(2) = 0$ (with $\eta_t = \varepsilon_t$ as before) satisfies (6.9), so that the second (and higher order) ordinate(s) of the PACF of an $AR(1)$ model are identically zero. Moving on to the $AR(2)$ model, for $k=1$ it is necessary to choose a value for $\rho_2(1)$ so as to minimize a suitable criterion function. Whatever value is chosen, there will still be serial dependence in the resulting $\{\eta_t\}$ and the value of $\rho_2(1)$ will typically be nonzero. When $k=2$ it can immediately be seen that (6.9) will be satisfied by setting $\rho_2(1) = \alpha_1$, $\rho_2(2) = \alpha_2$ and $\eta_t = \varepsilon_t$; the second order partial autocorrelation is equal to the last coefficient in the $AR(2)$ model (and is, of course, nonzero by hypothesis). For the case $k=3$, it is evident that (6.9) will be satisfied by choosing $\rho_3(1) = \alpha_1$, $\rho_3(2) = \alpha_2$, $\rho_3(3) = 0$ and $\eta_t = \varepsilon_t$, so that the third order partial autocorrelation of an $AR(2)$ process is zero in truth. This feature generalizes to any stationary $AR(p)$ model for which $\rho_p(p) = \alpha_p$ and $\rho_{p+k}(p+k) = 0$ for all $k \geq 1$.

6.2.2 Moving average models

A moving average representation for a process y_t is one that expresses the process as a sum of current and past white noise terms, so the Wold Decomposition (6.1) is a moving average process of infinite order, $MA(\infty)$. Clearly, such a specification can represent any stationary stochastic process, since such processes always have a Wold Decomposition. From an empirical modeling perspective, it is expedient to consider finite MA models of order q as a second means of approximating the transfer function of a process. Nicholls, Pagan and Terrell (1975) present three examples showing how time series models can exhibit moving average disturbances. A nonzero mean can be accommodated as before, but this is set to zero here (since other values are easily allowed for) and the upper limit of summation to q, viz.

$$y_t = \varepsilon_t + \sum_{j=1}^{q} \beta_j \varepsilon_{t-j} = \beta(L)\varepsilon_t, \tag{6.10}$$

where $\beta_q \neq 0$. The notation $\{\beta_j\}$ is used to emphasize that these are generally not the coefficients of the true Wold decomposition and β_0 is normalized to unity as an identifiability condition. The innovation $\varepsilon_t \sim WN(0, \sigma^2)$ as usual.

Evidently, the unconditional mean of the process given by (6.10) is zero and its unconditional variance is readily seen to be $\sigma^2(1 + \sum_{j=1}^{q} \beta_j^2)$. The autocovariance-generating function of the $MA(q)$ model is $\gamma_y(z) = \sigma^2 \beta(z)\beta(z^{-1})$. Since q is finite, it is seen that all autocovariances of finite moving averages are time-invariant which, together with the unconditional mean and variance, indicates that all $MA(q)$ processes are weakly stationary. Thus the roots of the equation $\beta(z) = 0$ can take any values without compromizing stationarity. Nevertheless, there may be utility in being able to invert the polynomial $\beta(z)$, because this permits a finite order MA to be expressed as an $AR(\infty)$ model. This inversion is possible provided a counterpart to the stationarity condition for autoregressive operators is satisfied, to whit that the characteristic equation $\beta(z) = 0$ should have all its roots outside the unit circle. This is called the invertibility condition and any $MA(q)$ process whose coefficients satisfy it is said to be invertible. The infinite AR representation is naturally $\beta^{-1}(L)y_t = \varepsilon_t$. This provides a duality between pure autoregressions and pure moving averages, i.e., all stationary $AR(p)$ processes have an $MA(\infty)$ representation and all invertible $MA(q)$ processes have an $AR(\infty)$ representation.

The invertibility condition serves a further purpose since, in the absence of unit roots in the equation $\beta(z) = 0$ with distinct roots, there are, in fact, 2^q different moving average polynomials $\beta(L)$ that give rise to the same autocorrelation structure, but only one of these is invertible. Invoking the criterion of invertibility, therefore, confers uniqueness on the parameterization of a moving average with given autocorrelation structure. Unless otherwise stated, it will be assumed henceforth that invertible moving average representations are being used.

Setting q to unity in (6.10) gives the first order moving average, $MA(1)$, model

$$y_t = \varepsilon_t + \beta_1 \varepsilon_{t-1}. \tag{6.11}$$

The autocovariances from $\gamma_y(z) = \sigma^2 \beta(z)\beta(z^{-1}) = \sigma^2(1 + \beta_1 z)(1 + \beta_1 z^{-1})$ are seen to be: $\gamma(0) = \sigma^2(1 + \beta_1^2)$; $\gamma(1) = \gamma(-1) = \sigma^2 \beta_1$; and $\gamma(k) = 0$ for all $|k| > 1$. It is now straightforward to show that the ACF obeys $\rho(1) = \beta_1/(1 + \beta_1^2)$ with $\rho(k) = 0$ for $k \geqslant 2$. Notice that the 2^1 values $\beta_1 = \beta^*$ and $\beta_1 = 1/\beta^*$ will yield the same value of $\rho(1)$, thereby providing an exemplar of the issue raised in the previous paragraph. In contradistinction to $AR(p)$ models, therefore, the ACF of an $MA(1)$ "cuts off" to zero after the first nonnormalized ordinate. It is also the case that $|\rho(1)| \leqslant 0.5$, so a value of $|\rho(1)| > 0.5$ is prima facie evidence against a process being $MA(1)$.

Generalizing to an $MA(q)$ specificiation, the autocovariance structure is available from the coefficients in the autocovariance-generating function

$$\gamma_y(z) = \sigma^2 \beta(z)\beta(z^{-1}) = \sigma^2 \left(1 + \sum_{j=1}^{q} \beta_j z^j\right)\left(1 + \sum_{j=1}^{q} \beta_j z^{-j}\right). \tag{6.12}$$

Since the powers of z in (6.12) cannot go outside the bounds $-q$ and q inclusive, it follows that $\rho(k) = 0$ for $k \geqslant q + 1$, so that the ACF has the property of "cutting off" after lag q.

The PACF for an MA process is also available from (6.9). It is clear that (6.9) will never be satisfied exactly for finite k (so that η_t will always retain some serial dependence), since the AR representation of an invertible finite qth order moving average is $AR(\infty)$. This provides a way of discriminating finite order AR from MA processes: the former has an ACF that does not "cut off" and a PACF that does, with the reverse holding for the latter.

6.2.3 Mixed autoregressive-moving average models

In practice, it is sometimes the case that, to obtain a satisfactory approximation to the true but unknown transfer function of a stationary process, the finite order p of a pure autoregression, or q of a pure moving average, may need to be large. A natural next step is to specify a mixed $ARMA(p, q)$ model given by

$$y_t = \sum_{j=1}^{p} \alpha_j y_{t-j} + \varepsilon_t + \sum_{j=1}^{q} \beta_j \varepsilon_{t-j} \tag{6.13}$$

or, upon rearrangement, $\alpha(L)y_t = \beta(L)\varepsilon_t$. The model first appeared in the literature in section 1.4 in Appendix 2 of the second edition of Wold (1938) (published as Wold, 1954) which was written by Peter Whittle. It approximates the true transfer function $\theta(L)$ by the rational function $\beta(L)/\alpha(L)$. It is assumed that (6.13) is stationary and invertible, unless otherwise indicated, and the approximation to the true transfer function $\theta(L)$ is $\alpha^{-1}(L)\beta(L)$. The autocovariance-generating function of such a process, from which the ACF is obtainable, is $\gamma_y(z) = \sigma^2 \beta(z)\beta(z^{-1}) / [\alpha(z)\alpha(z^{-1})]$. McLeod (1975) gives an algorithm for evaluating the autocovariances in terms of the parameters $\alpha_1, \ldots, \alpha_p$ and $\beta_1, \ldots, \beta_q$ and Karanasos (1998) provides a novel way of obtaining the theoretical autocovariance function of a mixed ARMA process from the roots of $\alpha(z) = 0$ and the coefficients of $\beta(z)$.

It is the case that a rich range of autocovariance structures can be adequately modeled with ARMA models using small values of p and q. Indeed, the most commonly encountered model in this class is the $ARMA(1,1)$ given by

$$y = \alpha_1 y_{t-1} + \varepsilon_t + \beta_1 \varepsilon_{t-1},$$

for which the stationarity and invertibility conditions are, respectively, $|\alpha_1| < 1$ and $|\beta_1| < 1$. The autocovariance-generating function is then $\gamma_y(z) = \sigma^2(1 + \beta_1 z)$ $(1 + \beta_1 z^{-1})/[(1 - \alpha_1 z)(1 - \alpha_1 z^{-1})] = \sigma^2(1 + \beta_1^2 + \beta_1 z + \beta_1 z^{-1})(1 + \alpha_1 z + \alpha_1^2 z^2 + \cdots)$ $(1 + \alpha_1 z^{-1} + \alpha_1^2 z^{-2} + \cdots)$. From this it can be deduced, among other things, that: $\gamma(0) = \sigma^2(1 + \beta_1^2 + 2\alpha_1\beta_1)/(1 - \alpha_1^2); \gamma(1) = \sigma^2[(1 + \alpha_1\beta_1)(\alpha_1 + \beta_1)]/(1 - \alpha_1^2);$ and $\gamma(k) = \alpha_1\gamma(k-1), k = 2, 3, \ldots$. It, therefore, follows that the first ordinate of the ACF is $\rho(1) = (1 + \alpha_1\beta_1)(\alpha_1 + \beta_1)/(1 + \beta_1^2 + 2\alpha_1\beta_1)$ and that subsequent values of $\rho(k)$ decline geometrically as in the $AR(1)$ case.

This feature carries over to the general $ARMA(p,q)$ specification, in that the first q autocorrelations will be quite complex functions of $\{\alpha_j\}_1^p$ and $\{\beta_j\}_1^q$ and the ACF ordinates thereafter will decline according to the pattern associated with an $AR(p)$ specification. This behavior is mirrored by the PACF, for which the first p ordinates are governed by the AR coefficients. After this they decline in similar fashion to those of an $MA(q)$ without ever exhibiting the "cut-off" property.

6.3 Model determination

In practice, the task of a modeler or forecaster using stationary linear time series methods is to use available data to justify the approximation of $\theta(L)$ by $\beta(L)/\alpha(L)$ and to estimate the parameters of this rational polynomial as $\hat{\beta}(L)/\hat{\alpha}(L)$, where the caret represents a value estimated by some means such as those to be discussed in section 6.4. Many time series modelers would seek to invoke the principle of Occam's Razor which offers, according to *Encyclopaedia Britannica*, that "entities should not be multiplied beyond what is necessary" and "[in] science, the simplest theory that fits the facts of a problem is the one that should be selected." In other words, models that are parsimoniously parameterized are preferable to those that are profligate, if they adequately model the data.

Box and Jenkins (1970) espouse such a modeling approach based on four steps, of which we shall consider the last three in this and the succeeding two sections. The steps are, slightly paraphrasing Hamilton (1994, p. 110): (1) transform the data, if necessary, so that the assumption of stationarity is a reasonable one; (2) make an initial guess of (small) values for p and q for an $ARMA(p,q)$ model for the (possibly transformed) data; (3) estimate the parameters in $\alpha(L)$ and $\beta(L)$ (and σ^2); and (4) perform diagnostic analysis to check if the model is coherent with respect to the data. If step (4) is answered in the negative, steps (2)–(4) are repeated until it is satisfied.

The problem of model determination is interpreted as being one of choosing appropriate integer parameters p and q. These are assumed constant, no matter what the sample size. Some authors have suggested that an alternative to classical methods might involve $p=p(n)$ and $q=q(n)$ with $p(n),q(n) \to \infty$ and $p(n)/n$, $q(n)/n \to 0$ as $n \to \infty$; see, for example, Geweke (1984, section 5). Phillips (1996) also considers parameterizations whose dimensionality increases with sample size.

Before suggesting methods for determining appropriate values for p and q, a set of theoretical relations that link the coefficients and autocovariance structure of an $AR(p)$ process are introduced; they bear a marked similarity to, though they are different from, (6.9) used in computing PACFs. Given a covariance stationary $AR(p)$ as in (6.5) with $\mu=0$

$$y_t = \sum_{j=1}^{p} \alpha_j y_{t-j} + \varepsilon_t,$$

take the model and multiply it successively by the p lagged values $y_{t-1}, y_{t-2}, \ldots, y_{t-p}$. Then take expectations to yield a system of p simultaneous equations linking the p coefficients $\alpha_1, \ldots, \alpha_p$ and the first p autocovariances (not counting $\gamma(0)$), which may be written in terms of autocorrelations as

$$\rho(k) = \sum_{j=1}^{p} \alpha_j \rho(|j-k|), \quad k=1, \ldots, p. \tag{6.14}$$

This set of p equations can be written together compactly in matrix-vector notation as

$$\boldsymbol{\rho} = \boldsymbol{\varrho}\boldsymbol{\alpha}, \tag{6.15}$$

where $\boldsymbol{\rho} = (\rho(1),\dots,\rho(p))'$, $\boldsymbol{\alpha} = (\alpha_1,\dots,\alpha_p)'$ and $\boldsymbol{\varrho}$ is a $p \times p$ Toeplitz matrix with unity on the main diagonal and $\rho(1)$ in the principal off-diagonals, $\rho(2)$ in the next up to $\rho(p-1)$ in the north east and south west corner elements. Equations (6.14) (and (6.15)) are known as the Yule–Walker equations (the nomenclature stemming from the work of Yule, 1927 and Walker, 1931) and provide an explicit link between the coefficients of an $AR(p)$ model and its autocorrelations.

The matrix $\boldsymbol{\varrho}$ in (6.15) is nonsingular and so the relations between the elements of $\boldsymbol{\rho}$ and $\boldsymbol{\alpha}$ can be solved to provide a unique closed form solution for $\boldsymbol{\alpha}$ given by

$$\boldsymbol{\alpha} = \boldsymbol{\varrho}^{-1}\boldsymbol{\rho} \tag{6.16}$$

from which it is clear that the coefficients of a pth order autoregression can be determined from a knowledge of the first p (non-normalized) ordinates of the ACF.

In similar vein, consider the set of k equations (6.9) multiplied through by $y_{t-1}, y_{t-2}, \dots, y_{t-k}$, take expectations and standardize by $\gamma(0)$ to give the following equations relating the ACF to the PACF and, in particular, $\rho_k(k)$ with $\rho(1)$ through $\rho(k)$

$$\rho(1) = \rho_k(1) + \rho_k(2)\rho(1) + \rho_k(3)\rho(2) + \cdots + \rho_k(k)\rho(k-1)$$
$$\rho(2) = \rho_k(1)\rho(1) + \rho_k(2) + \rho_k(3)\rho(1) + \cdots + \rho_k(k)\rho(k-2)$$
$$\vdots$$
$$\rho(k) = \rho_k(1)\rho(k-1) + \rho_k(2)\rho(k-2) + \cdots + \rho_k(k)\rho(1)$$

or

$$\boldsymbol{\rho} = \boldsymbol{\varrho}\boldsymbol{\rho}_k, \tag{6.17}$$

where $\boldsymbol{\rho}_k = (\rho_k(1), \dots, \rho_k(k))'$. The vector $\boldsymbol{\rho}$ and matrix $\boldsymbol{\varrho}$ are as in (6.15), but it should be emphasized that (6.17) applies for any stationary process, not just an autoregressive one. From (6.17) and use of Cramér's rule, it can be seen that the kth partial autocorrelation is given by

$$\rho_k(k) = \det \boldsymbol{\varrho}_k / \det \boldsymbol{\varrho}, \tag{6.18}$$

where det stands for determinant and $\boldsymbol{\varrho}_k$ is the matrix $\boldsymbol{\varrho}$ with k'th column replaced by $\boldsymbol{\rho}$. From (6.18), it is evident that $\rho_1(1) = \rho(1)$ and $\rho_2(2) = (\rho(2) - \rho(1)^2)/(1 - \rho(1)^2)$ are the first two partial autocorrelations of a stationary process. It is, perhaps, worth pointing out that this last expression indicates explicitly that $\rho_2(2) = 0$ for an $AR(1)$ process, since for such a process $\rho(1) = \alpha_1$ and $\rho(2) = \alpha_1^2$.

Standard means of determining potential values for p and q are based on sample analogs of the ordinates of the ACF and PACF. To obtain these it is necessary to estimate the autocorrelations. The resultant sample ACF and PACF will be labeled SACF and SPACF, respectively. Setting $\bar{y} = n^{-1} \sum_{t=1}^{n} y_t$ as the natural estimator of μ_y, the kth-order sample autocovariance can be estimated by

$$c(k) = \sum_{t=k+1}^{n} (y_t - \bar{y})(y_{t-k} - \bar{y})/(n - k), \ k = 0, 1, 2, \ldots . \tag{6.19}$$

From (6.19) the SACF can be obtained from the estimator of ρ having typical element

$$r(k) = c(k)/c(0), \ k = 1, 2, \ldots . \tag{6.20}$$

A graph of $r(k)$ against k for $k = 1,2,\ldots$ is typically known as the (sample) corre-logram. The SPACF can be calculated from the sample counterpart of (6.18) with, for example, ρ replaced with $r = (r(1),\ldots,r(k))'$. Thus, $r_1(1) = r(1)$, $r_2(2) = (r(2) - r(1)^2)/(1 - r(1)^2)$ and so forth.

Graphs of the SACF and SPACF form the basis of simple model determination devices and may be especially useful in the context of pure AR or pure MA models because of the "cut off" properties obeyed by their theoretical counterparts and summarized at the end of section 6.2.2. An $AR(p)$ process will usually have nonzero ordinates at all lags but there are, of course, exceptions to this, like the special fourth-order autocorrelation model popularized in the context of serial correlation testing in the errors of regression equations by Wallis (1972). He proposes a quarterly analog of the Durbin–Watson test where the null of serial independence is tested against the scheme with a coefficient α_4 parameterizing the fourth lag in the error structure and for which $\rho(4k) = \alpha_4^k, k = 1, 2, \ldots$, with $\rho(j) = 0$ otherwise. Even here, of course, the ACF never "cuts off," although it exhibits gaps. So, if a SACF appears to die away to zero for good, this may be an indication that a pure MA may be appropriate for the data, especially if this happens after a small value of k. Similarly, the PACF for an $AR(p)$ is zero for $k \geqslant p + 1$, whereas this is not the case for an MA process. Hence a SPACF that appears to 'cut off' after lag p can be suggestive of the appropriateness of an $AR(p)$ model. Therefore, it is generally good practice at the outset of any modeling exercise to graph the correlogram and SPACF of any series and to inspect it for these features. Of course, the attempt to eyeball situa-tions where the relevant graphs appear to die away to zero must be tempered by noting that this is likely to happen fairly rapidly to both graphs because of the fact that the (stationary) series being modeled is assumed to be short memory.

The procedures suggested in the last paragraph are essentially ones of explora-tory data analysis, but asymptotic theory can help to put such devices onto a more formal basis. Anderson (1942) shows that the serial correlation coefficients have limiting Gaussian distributions in stationary models, so that they can be treated as asymptotically normal for the purposes of inference in finite samples. Quenouille (1949) demonstrates that, for an $AR(p)$ process, $r_k(k) \overset{a}{\sim} N(0, n^{-1})$

for $k > p$, where $\overset{a}{\sim}$ indicates "is asymptotically distributed as." Bartlett (1946) proves that in an $MA(q)$ process $r(k) \overset{a}{\sim} N(0, (1 + 2\sum_{j=1}^{q} \rho_j^2)/n)$ for $k > q$. Davies and Newbold (1980) show that this approximation is improved if n is replaced by

$$n^* = n(n+2)/(n-k). \tag{6.21}$$

The finite sample adjustment given in (6.21) will be seen to arise again in section 6.5 in the context of portmanteau tests of model adequacy.

The asymptotic results outlined in the last paragraph can be used to help in the model determination stage of model building, but are not directly applicable with mixed ARMA processes. The ideas that the SACF of an $ARMA(p,q)$ model can be expected to decay like those of a pth-order AR after lag q and that the SPACF will mimic that of a qth-order MA after lag p may sometimes be of help, but more sophisticated methods are usually employed if an ARMA model is to be identified. One of the most regularly used techniques in this case is one due to Hannan and Rissanen (1982), although a less popular one is introduced in the final paragraphs of this section. Discussion of the more ubiquitous method is deferred until section 6.7. Parameter estimation and some finite sample properties of the statistics discussed above in relation to the SACF and SPACF are considered in section 6.4.

A further method that can be used for model identification is based on the inverse autocorrelation function (IACF), originally due to Cleveland (1972). The idea was introduced in the frequency domain as the autocorrelations associated with the reciprocal of the spectrum of a series. It is discussed in the time domain by Chatfield (1979), for example, but has never been widely used in practice. It is, however, an attractive idea theoretically that merits attention. Consider a LP with autocovariance-generating function $\gamma_y(z) = \sigma^2 \theta(z)\theta(z^{-1})$. Then the inverse auto-covariance-generating function is given by $\gamma i_y(z)$ satisfying

$$\gamma_y(z)\gamma i_y(z) = 1 \tag{6.22}$$

and the coefficient of z^k in $\gamma i_y(z)$ satisfying (6.22), $\gamma^i(k)$, is the inverse auto-covariance at lag k. The ordinates of the IACF are obtained from $\rho i(k) = \gamma i(k)/\gamma i(0)$. Observe that $\gamma i(0) \neq 1/\gamma(0)$ in general; see Chatfield (1979) below his (3.6) for an example.

Suppose we have an $ARMA(p,q)$ model (6.13). Then the IACF of the model is the same as the ACF of the inverse model

$$\beta(L)y_t = \alpha(L)\varepsilon_t. \tag{6.23}$$

The device may be useful when attempting to identify a pure AR or pure MA model in a fairly simple way. An $AR(p)$ model arises if $\beta(L) = 1$ in (6.13) and an $MA(q)$ if $\alpha(L) = 1$. In the former case, the IACF is the ACF of the model $y_t = \alpha(L)\varepsilon_t$, while in the latter it is the ACF of $\beta(L)y_t = \varepsilon_t$. Taking the simple $p = 1$ $(q = 0)$ case, it is easily shown that: $\rho i(0) = 1$; $\rho i(1) = \rho i(-1) = -\alpha_1/(1 + \alpha_1^2)$; and $\rho i(k) = 0, |k| \geqslant 2$. This is symptomatic of the IACF for all pure $AR(p)$ processes; their IACF "cuts off" after lag p. The corresponding property for $MA(q)$ is that the IACF does not have this "cut off" property, rather it declines geometrically to zero. In this sense, the properties of the IACF mimic those of the PACF. Chatfield (1979) also considers the technique in the context of mixed models. Godfrey and Tremayne (1988) discuss the proposal from the point of view of checking model adequacy and Bhansali (1980) examines the consistency of estimators of the inverse auto-correlations, though this matter is not pursued here.

6.4 Parameter estimation

There are a variety of ways that the parameters of an ARMA model can be estimated, but they can mainly be classified into one of three groups, discussed in turn in sections 6.4.1–6.4.3. Naturally, there is a close overlap between them and, in many situations, estimators will be asymptotically equivalent to one another. This may often be because they only differ one from another by transient end effects. Nevertheless, it seems worthwhile, from an organizational point of view at least, to treat them separately. Apart from the white noise error variance, σ^2, the degrees of the polynomials $\alpha(L)$ (of degree p) and $\beta(L)$ (q) and their associated structural parameters $(\alpha_1, \ldots, \alpha_p)$ and $(\beta_1, \ldots, \beta_q)$ (if any) must be estimated. In the introductory paragraph of section 6.3 the generic notation $\hat{}$ was introduced to indicate an estimated value. This section provides only a cursory treatment; considerably fuller accounts are provided by Hamilton (1994), Brockwell and Davis (1996) and Box, Jenkins and Reinsel (1994).

6.4.1 Method of moments

Some of the simplest estimators available for the parameters of interest are based on a method of moments approach. This has already been introduced in section 6.3 as a means of estimating μ_y using $\bar{y}$ and $\gamma(k)$ and $\rho(k)$ by $c(k)$ and $r(k)$ respectively. In an $AR(p)$ model it is straightforward to suggest estimates of $\boldsymbol{\alpha} = (\alpha_1, \ldots, \alpha_p)'$ from the sample counterparts of the Yule–Walker equations (6.14) (or (6.15)) and their solution (6.16) using these sample quantities, i.e., from computing

$$\hat{\alpha} = \mathbf{R}^{-1}\mathbf{r}, \tag{6.24}$$

where $\mathbf{R}$ is the sample counterpart of $\boldsymbol{\varrho}$ using the method of moments estimators $\{r(k)\}$. The estimators in (6.24) are known as Yule–Walker estimators. In the $AR(1)$ case this yields an estimator

$$\hat{\alpha}_{1,YW} = r(1)/r(0) = c(1)/c(0) = \sum_{t=2}^{n}(y_t - \bar{y})(y_{t-1} - \bar{y}) \Big/ \sum_{t=1}^{n}(y_t - \bar{y})^2. \tag{6.25}$$

Take the $AR(p)$ model (6.5) (with $\mu = 0$), multiply by y_t and take expectations to give

$$\gamma(0) = \sum_{j=1}^{p}\alpha_j\gamma(j) + \gamma_{y\varepsilon}(0). \tag{6.26}$$

Since the contemporaneous cross-covariance of y_t and ε_t, $\gamma_{y\varepsilon}(0)$, is easily shown to be equal to σ^2, (6.26) can be rearranged and expressed in terms of sample moment quantities as

$$\hat{\sigma}^2 = c(0) - \sum_{j=1}^{p} \hat{\alpha}_j c(j) \qquad (6.27)$$

to give an estimator of σ^2.

Other means using the SACF and SPACF exist for estimating the parameters of an $AR(p)$ model. For instance, the SPACF could be estimated by successive application of the sample counterpart of (6.18) for $k = 1, 2, \ldots, p$. Box, Jenkins and Reinsel (1994, Appendix A.3.2) provides a recursive method for estimating α originally due to Durbin (1960); this procedure obviates the need for matrix inversion inherent in using (6.16) directly. Box, Jenkins and Reinsel (1994, section 6.3.3) note that the resultant estimators are approximately full maximum likelihood estimators (MLE). The sampling properties of these estimators will be discussed in a little more detail presently.

Initial estimators for the coefficients of an $MA(q)$ based on the moment estimators $r(1)$ through $r(q)$ can be based on the nonlinear equations obtainable by considering (6.12) further. From (6.12) it follows that:

$$\gamma(0) = \sigma^2 \left(1 + \sum_{j=1}^{q} \beta_j^2 \right);$$

$$\gamma(k) = \sigma^2 (\beta_k + \beta_1 \beta_{k+1} + \cdots + \beta_{q-k} \beta_q), \quad k = 1, \ldots, q$$

$$\gamma(k) = 0, \ k > q.$$

Sample analogs of these equations for $k = 1, \ldots, q$ divided by $\gamma(0)$ may be used to solve for method of moments estimators $\hat{\beta}_1, \cdots, \hat{\beta}_q$ based on $r(1), \ldots, r(q)$, but, in contradistinction to the AR case, these equations are nonlinear and must be solved by iterative means. An estimator of σ^2 can then be found from $\hat{\sigma}^2 = c(0)/(1 + \sum_{j=1}^{q} \hat{\beta}_j^2)$. However, it turns out that the resultant estimators are less efficient than others based on a likelihood approach. They are, however, consistent estimators and one of their uses might be as first-stage consistent estimators in a procedure to obtain asymptotically efficient estimators based on MLE.

6.4.2   Conditional least squares methods

Simple means of estimating the coefficients of AR processes can also be based upon a (conditional) least squares approach. If an $AR(p)$ model has been identified for data, then model (6.5) can be fitted. Supposing $\{y_t\}_1^n$ are available, a regression is fitted to the last $(n - p)$ observations. The relevant parameter estimators are obtained by application of Ordinary Least Squares (OLS).

In the case $p = 1$, it is easy to see that

$$\hat{\alpha}_{1, LS} = \sum_{t=2}^{n} (y_t - \bar{y})(y_{t-1} - \bar{y}) \bigg/ \sum_{t=2}^{n} (y_t - \bar{y})^2 \qquad (6.28)$$

and $\hat{\sigma}^2 = \sum_{t=2}^{n} (y_t - \hat{\mu} - \hat{\alpha}_{1,LS} y_{t-1})^2 / (n-3)$ (with $\hat{\mu}$ the usual OLS estimator of μ). (Of course, the value of $\bar{y}$ will also be marginally influenced by end effects, but these are ignored for clarity of exposition.) A comparison of (6.25) and (6.28) shows that the two differ only by the extra $(y_1 - \bar{y})^2$ term in the denominator of (6.25), which is asymptotically irrelevant since the probability limit of the ratio of the two denominators is unity. Hence the Yule–Walker (YW) and conditional least squares (CLS) estimators in the stationary $AR(1)$ model are asymptotically equivalent. A similar argument applies for the more general $AR(p)$ model.

It is pertinent to ask at this stage whether the evidence suggests that these two methods provide estimators with desirable properties. Since the work of Marriott and Pope (1954), it has been known that the YW and CLS estimators, whilst consistent, are biased in finite samples. Tjøstheim and Paulsen (1983) and Paulsen and Tjøstheim (1985) shed light on the question of bias. These authors show in their two papers that the YW estimators are inferior to their CLS counterparts and that, when the roots of $\alpha(z) = 0$ are close to the unit circle, the former can be severely biased, even with fairly large samples. They further indicate that Burg-type estimators (see Paulsen and Tjøstheim, 1985, and references therein, for details) are also superior to YW and that the bias in YW carries over to the variance parameter σ^2 as well.

6.4.3 Estimation by maximum likelihood

Maximum likelihood methods can be used to estimate the parameters of pure AR or MA models and mixed ARMA specifications. Consider the causal $ARMA(p,q)$ model as in (6.13) and assume, for the purposes of evaluating the joint distribution of $\mathbf{y} = (y_1, \ldots, y_n)'$, that $\varepsilon_t \sim NID(0,\sigma^2)$. The likelihood function for the parameters given the random variable $\mathbf{y}$ is given by

$$L(\boldsymbol{\alpha}, \boldsymbol{\beta}, \sigma^2; \mathbf{y}) \propto f(\mathbf{y}; \boldsymbol{\alpha}, \boldsymbol{\beta}, \sigma^2),$$

where $f(\mathbf{y}; \cdot)$ denotes the joint distribution of $\mathbf{y}$. The constant of proportionality is taken to be unity without loss of generality and $\boldsymbol{\alpha} = (\alpha_1, \ldots, \alpha_p)'$, $\boldsymbol{\beta} = (\beta_1, \ldots, \beta_q)'$. The normal (Gaussian) assumption for the innovations $\{\varepsilon_t\}$ implies that the joint distribution of $\mathbf{y}$ is multivariate normal. This multivariate distribution has zero mean vector and, to keep notation simple, we shall write the variance covariance matrix of $\mathbf{y}$ as $\boldsymbol{\Omega}(\boldsymbol{\alpha}, \boldsymbol{\beta}, \sigma^2) = \boldsymbol{\Omega}$ for short. That is to say, $\mathbf{y} \sim N_n(\mathbf{0}, \boldsymbol{\Omega})$, with the subscript n obviously indicating the dimensionality of the multivariate Gaussian random variable. Thus the (natural) logarithm of this joint density gives the loglikelihood function as

$$\ell(\boldsymbol{\alpha}, \boldsymbol{\beta}, \sigma^2; \mathbf{y}) = \log[L(\boldsymbol{\alpha}, \boldsymbol{\beta}, \sigma^2; \mathbf{y})]$$
$$= -(n/2) \log 2\pi - 0.5 \log \det \boldsymbol{\Omega} - 0.5 \mathbf{y}' \boldsymbol{\Omega}^{-1} \mathbf{y}. \tag{6.29}$$

The function given by (6.29) is difficult to work with in general because of the presence of the $n \times n$ matrix $\boldsymbol{\Omega}$. This can be circumvented by writing the matrix as the product of an upper triangular matrix times its transpose. The paper by

Ansley (1979) describes one algorithm for evaluation of the loglikelihood. The Kalman filter is often used for the purpose and Hamilton (1994, chapter 13) provides an accessible introduction. It is, essentially, the MA component of ARMA models that renders MLE difficult and consideration turns back to the simpler AR specification before returning to the MA and mixed models.

The MLE in an $AR(p)$ model can be written down fairly easily using the prediction error decomposition. This permits the log of the joint density of the observations to be factored into two parts, basically using the multiplication rule of probability, to write the log of the joint probability of two events as the sum of the logs of a conditional and a marginal probability. The technique is described in detail by Harvey (1993). The joint density

$$f(\mathbf{y}; \boldsymbol{\alpha}, \sigma^2) = f(y_1, \ldots, y_{n-1}; \boldsymbol{\alpha}, \sigma^2) \cdot f(y_n | y_{n-1}, \ldots, y_1; \boldsymbol{\alpha}, \sigma^2).$$

By successive application of this rule we obtain

$$f(\mathbf{y}; \boldsymbol{\alpha}, \sigma^2) = \prod_{j=p+1}^{n} f(y_j | \mathbf{y}_{j-1}; \boldsymbol{\alpha}, \sigma^2) \cdot f(y_1, \ldots, y_p; \boldsymbol{\alpha}, \sigma^2),$$

where $\mathbf{y}_{j-1} = (y_1, \ldots, y_{j-1})'$. Now, in an AR model, each of the conditional distributions is just $N(\sum_{j=1}^{p} \alpha_j y_{t-j}, \sigma^2)$ and the term $f(y_1, \ldots, y_p; \boldsymbol{\alpha}, \sigma^2)$ is the marginal distribution of the first p observations. Hence the exact loglikelihood for the $AR(p)$ model is given by

$$\ell(\boldsymbol{\alpha}, \sigma^2; \mathbf{y}) = \log[L(\boldsymbol{\alpha}, \sigma^2; \mathbf{y})]$$
$$= -[(n-p)/2]\log(2\pi\sigma^2) - 0.5 \sum_{t=p+1}^{n} \left(y_t - \sum_{j=1}^{p} \alpha_j y_{t-j}\right)^2 / \sigma^2$$
$$+ \log[f(y_1, \ldots, y_p; \boldsymbol{\alpha}, \sigma^2)]. \tag{6.30}$$

The conditional MLE (CMLE) arises from ignoring the joint marginal of the first p observations represented by the last term in (6.30) and the exact MLE (EMLE) obtains when this transient term is fully taken into account. Hamilton (1994, sections 5.2–5.3) has a full discussion. Notice that the criterion function to be maximized for the CMLE under a Gaussian assumption is essentially just the negative of that for CLS in this problem, so the two estimators will coincide. When the innovations are not Gaussian, but a loglikelihood function (6.30) is used, the relevant estimators are, of course, quasi-MLE.

Assuming stationarity, the variances in these marginal distributions for the initial observations in (6.30) must be treated carefully. Take the $AR(1)$ case as an example, where the relevant marginal distribution is $f(y_1; \boldsymbol{\alpha}, \sigma^2)$ and $y_1 \sim N(0, \sigma^2/(1 - \alpha_1^2))$. Hence the contribution of this term to (6.30) in the $AR(1)$ case will be

$$\log\left[f(y_1; \alpha_1, \sigma^2)\right] = -0.5\left\{\log(2\pi) + \log\left[\sigma^2/(1 - \alpha_1^2)\right] + y_1^2(1 - \alpha_1^2)/\sigma^2\right\}.$$

For a treatment of second and higher order AR models, the reader is again referred to Hamilton (1994, section 5.3) and, in particular, his expression (5.3.4).

It is only necessary to consider the simple $MA(1)$ model to gain an appreciation of why MA and mixed models are harder to estimate than pure AR ones. Suppose, as before, that $\varepsilon_t \sim NID(0,\sigma^2)$ and that presample values such as ε_0 are known to take their expected value of zero, so that, for example, $y_1 \sim N(0,\sigma^2)$. This transient conditioning permits evaluation of the conditional likelihood function. From (6.11), if ε_{t-1} is known,

$$f(y_t|\varepsilon_{t-1}; \beta_1, \sigma^2) = (2\pi\sigma^2)^{-0.5} \exp[-0.5(y_t - \beta_1\varepsilon_{t-1})^2/\sigma^2].$$

By virtue of the conditioning $y_1 = \varepsilon_1$, the value of ε_1 is known. Thus the conditional distribution of y_2, given y_1 and $\varepsilon_0 = 0$, is

$$f(y_2|\varepsilon_1, \varepsilon_0 = 0; \beta_1, \sigma^2) = (2\pi\sigma^2)^{-0.5} \exp[-0.5(y_2 - \beta_1\varepsilon_1)^2/\sigma^2].$$

Since y_2 and ε_1 are known, it follows that $\varepsilon_2 = y_2 - \beta_1\varepsilon_1 = y_2 - \beta_1 y_1$ is known. By repeated application of this procedure, it can be seen that the single condition $\varepsilon_0 = 0$ permits the full sequence of epsilons to be evaluated from the y's, given the parameters. The conditional loglikelihood for the $MA(1)$ model is thus

$$\ell(\beta_1, \sigma^2; \mathbf{y}) = -0.5\left\{ n\log(2\pi) + n\log\sigma^2 + \sum_{t=1}^{n} \varepsilon_t^2/\sigma^2 \right\}. \tag{6.31}$$

Given a value of β_1 the sequence of implied $\{\varepsilon_t\}_1^n$ can be calculated recursively. However, (6.31) is quite a complicated function of β_1 and there is no closed form solution for the CMLE, so numerical optimization techniques must be used in models with MA components. There is also the question of what starting value to use in any iterative numerical procedure. The iterations should be started from first-stage consistent estimates of the model coefficients. Since the same issue arises with ARMA models, further discussion is postponed. To obtain the EMLE in MA models requires methods like those referenced below (6.29); see the latter part of Hamilton (1994, section 5.5) for further details.

As a caveat to the use of moving average components, it should be pointed out that their estimation, even with low orders like $q = 1$ or 2, can be problematical whenever any of the roots of the characteristic equation are close to the unit circle (e.g. in an $MA(1)$ when, say, $\beta_1 > 0.9$ or so) and users should exercise extreme caution in using and interpreting such models. See also the related work by Newbold, Agiakloglou and Miller (1994). Davis and Dunsmuir (1996) consider the matter explicitly. They note that, in practice, economic time series are often differenced to attain stationarity and that (Davis and Dunsmuir, 1996, p. 3) "Often after differencing by the correct amount, the moving average estimate is at or near 1." This provides a strong motivation for their development of a suitable asymptotic theory.

A unique invertible MA lag operator polynomial can be specified unless there are unit roots to the characteristic equation $\beta(z)=0$. However, should $z=1$ satisfy $\beta(z)=0$, the MA operator is not invertible, though the data generating mechanism is still stationary as long as the AR operator has solutions of $\alpha(z)=0$ that all lie outside the unit circle. The estimation of MA models with roots actually on the unit circle (rather than close to it as in the last paragraph) by maximum likelihood has attracted the attention of a number of researchers, including Davidson (1981), Anderson and Takemura (1986), McCabe and Leybourne (1998) and Shephard (1993), who provides a method for accurately approximating the distribution of the MLE in MA models when the process is strictly noninvertible. McCabe and Leybourne (1998) point out that standard $\sqrt{n}$-consistency asymptotics are not applicable to unit root MA processes any more than they are to unit root AR processes and observe that this feature is not widely acknowledged in the profession.

The correct asymptotics for the MA unit root parameter in the stationary, noninvertible case is nonstandard (Sargan and Bhargava, 1983). Davis and Dunsmuir (1996) provide a comprehensive analysis for the *MA*(1) case based upon considering the distribution of the local maximizer of the likelihood function closest to the unit circle. The asymptotic distribution of the (global) MLE is also derived and shown to differ slightly from that of the local maximizer. They state that their analysis can be extended along similar lines to handle maximum likelihood in mixed models with MA components on, or close to, the unit circle. The results mentioned emphasize that care needs to be taken with (AR)MA models close to the nonivertibility boundary.

Estimation of the parameters of mixed ARMA models is largely effected by combining the arguments relating to the pure AR and MA models outlined above, with similar numerical complexities arising via the MA terms. For the present, assume that the *ARMA*(p,q) model $\alpha(L)y_t=\beta(L)\varepsilon_t$ is such that $\alpha(L)$ and $\beta(L)$ have no common factors, for failure of this results in parameter redundancy. To see this, suppose instead that $\alpha(L)=\alpha^*(L)\delta(L)$ and $\beta(L)=\beta^*(L)\delta(L)$ with $\delta(L)=1+\sum_{j=1}^r \delta_j L^j$. The *ARMA*($p,q$) model then has an identical transfer function to the *ARMA*(p^*,q^*) model $\alpha^*(L)y_t=\beta^*(L)\varepsilon_t$ with $p^*=p-r$ and $q^*=q-r$. The latter model is known as the one of minimal degree (assuming, of course, that there are no further common factors) and the parameters of $\delta(L)$ are redundant. A quest for parsimony alone is likely to mitigate in favor of models of minimal degrees, but the implications for identification and estimation of models with parameter redundancy are examined briefly in section 6.7.2. Unless needed, the superscript asterisk is not further used.

A CMLE can be found by using the approach described for the MA case above by noting first that

$$\varepsilon_t = y_t - \sum_{j=1}^{p} \alpha_j y_{t-j} - \sum_{j=1}^{q} \beta_j \varepsilon_{t-j}$$

and then obtaining a (conditional) loglikelihood like the right-hand side of (6.31) (compare Hamilton, 1994, equation 5.6.3), having set the start-up first p y's and first q ε's to their expected values, for example. To obtain the EMLE, one may again use the Kalman filter. An extensive literature exists on the topic; a starting point containing many references is provided by Choi (1992, p. 27).

In stationary linear time series models, the likelihood surface to be searched for its maximum can be very irregular and it is quite important for the convergence of algorithms that, amongst other things, sensible starting values are used in iterations. As a practical matter, Newbold, Agiakloglou and Miller (1994) point out that different methods employed by different computer packages can yield different estimates, so that care must be taken. Moreover, it can sometimes be the case that, even if two programs provide the same coefficient estimates, they provide estimated standard errors that do not conform to one another!

The issue of first-stage estimators for the coefficients of (AR)MA models was mentioned above. A simple means for doing this can be based on a modification of the method of Durbin (1960), which involves fitting a long $AR(P)$ to the data at hand and using the residuals from this as consistent estimates of the innovation process. There remains the question of just how long this fitted autoregression should be. Using the results of An, Chen and Hannan (1982), Poskitt and Tremayne (1984) employ $P = \max\{(p + q), \sqrt{n/\log n}\}$.

Once appropriate parameter estimates have been obtained for ARMA models, it is necessary to have suitable inference procedures. Most results in the field are based on asymptotic theory and, except when MA roots on the unit circle are considered, the relevant asymptotics are $\sqrt{n}$-consistency asymptotics. Setting $\boldsymbol{\phi} = (\boldsymbol{\alpha}', \boldsymbol{\beta}')'$, this implies that $\hat{\boldsymbol{\phi}}$ satisfies a suitable central limit theorem and that

$$\sqrt{n}(\hat{\boldsymbol{\phi}} - \boldsymbol{\phi}) \xrightarrow{d} N_{p+q}(0, \mathbf{V}), \tag{6.32}$$

where $\mathbf{V}$ is the variance–covariance matrix of the limit distribution and $\xrightarrow{d}$ indicates convergence in distribution. Since the problem is a standard one in maximum likelihood, it follows that ML is asymptotically efficient, so that $\mathbf{V}$ is equal to the inverse of the Fisher information matrix in the sample divided by n. There is more than one way in which $\mathbf{V}$ can be estimated; Hamilton (1994, section 5.8) provides a concise account of inference procedures and alternative means of obtaining estimated standard errors.

6.5 Checking model adequacy

The modeling approach of Box and Jenkins (1970) implies that the smallest satisfactory values for integer parameters like p and q should be chosen. However, these linear time series models are of the "black box" type. That is, the transfer function describes the mechanism by which the unobservable WN input is transformed to yield the observable output process $\{y_t\}$, but the model is not usually founded in economic or some other theory for non-econometric applications. For this and other reasons, users of ARMA models must entertain the possibility that inadequate values of p and/or q were identified at the model determination stage of the model-building process. This calls for statistical tests that can help to assess the adequacy of a fitted specification. To evidence the fact that checks of model adequacy, or diagnostic checks, retain a high profile in contemporary time series analysis, it should be noted that Li (2004) has recently published an entire book on the topic, to which interested readers are referred.

The prevailing practice, stemming from the use of Box–Jenkins techniques, has led many model adequacy tests to be based on a simple-to-general philosophy. This contrasts with the general-to-specific approach that is frequently encountered in econometrics. The work of Box and Pierce (1970) represents one of the first substantial attempts to structure tests of model adequacy in time series.

If the values of p and q are the (minimal) correct degrees and the true parameter values are used to compute the true time series innovations $\{\varepsilon_t\}_1^n$, then the associated autocorrelations are uncorrelated with zero mean and $\sqrt{n}\rho_\varepsilon(k) \overset{d}{\to} NID(0, 1)$. Then, if $\boldsymbol{\rho}_\varepsilon = (\rho_\varepsilon(1), \ldots, \rho_\varepsilon(m))'$, it follows that $\sqrt{n}\boldsymbol{\rho}_\varepsilon \overset{d}{\to} N_m(0, \mathbf{I}_m)$, where $\mathbf{I}_m$ represents an identity matrix of order m. In fact, Box and Pierce (1970, equation 1.4) indicate that in finite samples an adjustment equivalent to (6.21) improves the approximation.

The basic idea underlying tests of model adequacy is that, once an appropriate *ARMA(p,q)* model has been fitted to data, the resultant residuals

$$\hat{\varepsilon}_t = [\hat{\alpha}(L)/\hat{\beta}(L)]y_t$$

should be approximately white noise. These residuals are calculated from the fitted time series model and they are not true time series variables. This has an effect on their sampling properties, so that sample statistics constructed using them do not have the same behavior as parallel statistics based on the true time series innovations, a situation not uncommon in statistics and econometrics.

Descriptive statistical devices to assess the behavior of the $\{\hat{\varepsilon}_t\}$ are the residual SACF and residual SPACF. The former will be based on a graph of statistics like

$$r_\varepsilon(k) = c_\varepsilon(k)/c_\varepsilon(0) = \sum \hat{\varepsilon}_t \hat{\varepsilon}_{t-k} \Big/ \sum \hat{\varepsilon}_t^2,$$

where the lower limits of summation depend upon k and the model orders (the upper limits are n). Both numerator and denominator may be normalized by slightly different functions of n to reflect a desire to make finite sample adjustment for the fact that there will be more terms in the denominator than the numerator, but the precise details need not detain us here. Durbin (1970) proves that the replacement of $\rho_\varepsilon(k)$ by $r_\varepsilon(k)$ is not innocuous. The limiting distribution of the vector $\mathbf{r}_\varepsilon = (r_\varepsilon(1), \ldots, r_\varepsilon(m))'$ is shown by Box and Pierce (1970), under the null hypothesis of correct specification of p and q, to be

$$\sqrt{n}\mathbf{r}_\varepsilon \overset{d}{\to} N_m[0, (\mathbf{I}_m - \mathbf{X})]. \tag{6.33}$$

In (6.33) the $m \times m$ matrix $\mathbf{X}$ is an idempotent matrix whose elements are functions of the coefficients of the Wold Decomposition (6.1). Full details are provided in Box and Pierce (1970, section 2) for AR processes, with the generalization needed to accomodate MA components appearing in section 5 of their paper.

6.5.1   Portmanteau tests

Result (6.33) forms the basis of the so-called portmanteau diagnostic check for time series model adequacy that is used in many commercial software packages. The variance–covariance matrix of the scaled (by $\sqrt{n}$) residual autocorrelation vector $\mathbf{r}_\varepsilon$ is, of course, singular. When an *ARMA(p,q)* model has been (correctly) fitted to data, the rank of this variance matrix is $m - p - q$. Moreover, the theoretical developments of Box and Pierce require that $m \to \infty$, though at a slower rate than n, to hold for the validity of the asymptotic distribution theory. The portmanteau statistic Q is based on the sum of squares of residual autocorrelations from the fitted specification and is given by

$$Q = n\mathbf{r}_\varepsilon'\mathbf{r}_\varepsilon = n\sum_{j=1}^{m} r_\varepsilon^2(j). \tag{6.34}$$

For simplicity of notation here and subsequently, it is assumed that the available number of observations for model fitting is n (so presample values are presumed available, where needed, or are dealt with in some other suitable way). On the null hypothesis of correct specification of p and q, Q follows a chi-squared distribution with $m - p - q$ degrees of freedom $(\chi^2(m - p - q))$ asymptotically. The null hypothesis of correctly specified values for p and q is rejected for sufficiently large values of Q.

Many authors have observed that the finite sample behavior of this statistic can be unsatisfactory and a culprit has often been suspected to be the use of n in (6.34). The efficacy of using n^* of (6.21) in place of n is considered by Ljung and Box (1978) who propose a modified portmanteau test

$$Q^* = n(n+2)\sum_{j=1}^{m} r_\varepsilon^2(j) \Big/ (n - j). \tag{6.35}$$

The Q^* statistic of (6.35) is widely computed by software packages. However, care needs to be taken with its use for various reasons. In the first place, the power properties of these portmanteau procedures are often less than impressive, see, for example, Davies and Newbold (1979). Moreover, the default value used for m by some packages may be rather higher than is to be recommended if empirical power properties are to be satisfactory; values like $m = 20$ are commonplace. Das Gupta and Perlman (1974) draw attention to the fact that the power of tests is often a declining function of the degrees of freedom index and their arguments can be adapted to the current context. This last point is also noted in Kwan, Sim and Wu (2005), a paper that evidences the continuing interest in tests such as these. The authors discuss the results of a wide-ranging Monte Carlo analysis; see their paper and references therein for details of this and other recent work on portmanteau tests.

Some authors, e.g., Ljung (1986), have suggested that statistics like (6.35) should be used in conjunction with small values of m, but even then care must be taken that the spirit of the original asymptotic theory of Box and Pierce (1970) is not breached. However the score, or Lagrange multiplier (LM), tests of section 6.5.2 afford another way of implementing these tests, for there are equivalence results linking the two approaches. Godfrey and Tremayne (1988, section 2.1) have further discussion on the issues raised in this and the previous paragraph.

6.5.2   Tests based on the score (Lagrange multiplier) principle

Godfrey (1979) provides a useful addition to the range of diagnostic checks of the null hypothesis of a fitted $ARMA(p,q)$ model to be tested against $ARMA(p+r, q)$, or $ARMA(p,q+s)$ alternatives using the score (Rao, 1948), or LM (Silvey, 1959), procedure. The approach is particularly attractive when deriving misspecification tests, as here. The test shares the asymptotic properties of a likelihood ratio test but only requires estimation of the null model. Newbold (1980) demonstrates that the LM test is equivalent to one based on residual autocorrelations and Poskitt and Tremayne (1980) show that testing the null against $ARMA(p+r,q)$ is equivalent to testing against $ARMA(p,q+r)$, so that a significant value of the test statistic does not indicate whether it is the AR polynomial or the MA polynomial that should be augmented with a view to determining a more satisfactory model. In the light of the equivalence between LM and portmanteau procedures found by Newbold (1980), the same argument applies to the statistics of section 6.5.1. One difference between the two approaches is that the LM procedure does not require that the degrees of freedom of the test increase without bound with n as portmanteau procedures do (albeit at a slower rate than sample size), so r is not to be interpreted in the same way that m in section 6.5.1 is.

Godfrey (1979) shows that the LM test can be implemented by use of an auxiliary regression, where the residual from the null model is regressed on the $p+q+r$ derivative processes $\partial \varepsilon_t / \partial \alpha_j, j = 1, \ldots, p+r$ and $\partial \varepsilon_t / \partial \beta_j, j = 1, \ldots, q$, to test the need to augment a fitted $ARMA(p,q)$ by r terms. Assuming an additive alternative, so that the $(p+r)$th order AR polynomial of the alternative is $\alpha(L) = 1 - \sum_{j=1}^{p+r} \alpha_j L^j$, the derivative processes are: $\partial \varepsilon_t / \partial \alpha_j = -y_{t-j} / (1 + \beta_1 L + \cdots + \beta_q L^q)$; and $\partial \varepsilon_t / \partial \beta_j = -\varepsilon_{t-j} / (1 + \beta_1 L + \cdots + \beta_q L^q)$. These can be evaluated recursively. When there are fitted MA components, construction of the test regressors is not immediately straightforward, though when an $AR(p)$ is fitted as the null model, the test regressors are just lagged values of y_t, or of the residuals $\hat{\varepsilon}_t$ if the perceived alternative is $ARMA(p,r)$ It would be easy to amend popular computer packages to carry out the auxiliary regression and then compute the test statistic

$$LM = nR^2, \tag{6.36}$$

where R^2 is the coefficient of multiple determination from the regression, although typically they currently do not offer this statistic routinely. Under the null hypothesis of an adequate specification for the null model, $LM \overset{a}{\sim} \chi^2(r)$. The tests may also be asymptotically equivalently computed as *F*-tests, following the proposal of Kiviet (1986).

In practical situations, Monte Carlo evidence (see, for example, Godfrey, 1979, and Godfrey and Tremayne, 1988, for a more general discussion) suggests that the LM test is likely to outperform all variants of the portmanteau test in terms of both size and power. The arguments of Das Gupta and Perlman (1974) again suggest that the value of r should remain small in applications wherever possible.

6.5.3 Likelihood ratio tests

Of course, with modern software, it is perfectly feasible to base tests of model adequacy on the likelihood ratio (LR) approach, though caveats relating to para-meter redundancy and difficulties with MA components with roots close to the unit circle may mitigate against this. One approach, as in section 6.5.2, is to utilize the arguments of Poskitt and Tremayne (1980) relating to locally equivalent alternatives (i.e., that testing *ARMA(p,q)* against *ARMA(p + r,q)* is asymptotically equivalent to testing the null against an *ARMA(p,q + r)* alternative) and base model checks on entertaining an extension of the AR operator of the null model. Again, as with LM tests, it will generally be preferable in any such exercise to keep r small.

The recent work of Canepa and Godfrey (2005) adopts bootstrap methods to improve the performance of LR tests in time series. They do find particular problems with the empirical size properties of a test based on conventional asymptotic theory in data-generating mechanisms with certain types of MA components. These may stem in part, at least, from the flatness of the likelihood function, but the bootstrap approach is seen to offer a substantial improvement over asymptotic theory.

6.6 Model selection procedures

Since the mid-1980s the use of model selection devices has become very popular for selecting from a range of potential statistical models in many areas of inves-tigation. Linear time series analysis is no exception. Such procedures often involve the estimation of many, or even all, members of some model choice set and then application of some criterion to select one, or more, preferred models from amongst that choice set.

Before proceeding to introduce a range of so-called information criteria (IC), a procedure due to Anderson (1971) that can be used with pure AR models is worth describing. Suppose that a researcher believes their data can be satisfactorily modeled by an AR process and is prepared to assert that the upper bound to the order of $\alpha(L)$ is p_{max}. Then they wish to determine a preferred *AR(p)* model, where $p \in [0,[1],p_{max}]$. Selecting the preferred order is a multiple decision problem and Anderson (1971, chapter 6) provides a very full discussion of how this can be done with hypothesis testing techniques with a Gaussian distributional assumption for the random variables of interest. The selection of the appropriate order of an AR model is also discussed in section 5.7 of Anderson's book. The procedure he suggests is, effectively, based on a sequence of t-tests on the final coefficient, α_p, of an $AR(p)$ model for p taking successive values p_{max}, $p_{max} - 1, \ldots$ the testing sequence proceeds from one stage to the next for as long as the hypothesis that the last coefficient is zero cannot be rejected and the selected order $\hat{p}$ is determined as being that corresponding to the first significant coefficient in this sequence of nested hypothesis tests. Under the assumptions made, the members of the sequence of tests are independent of one another; the properties of completeness and sufficiency needed for this independence do require that the test sequence be conducted from general-to-specific and not the other way round. Of course, the preferred $AR(p)$ model should be checked to ensure its residuals are free from serial correlation using, for example, a score test as described in section 6.5.2.

An alternative means of order determination is to devise a criterion that penalizes overfitting by assigning a cost to additional model parameters. Akaike (1969) suggested a suitable one for use with autoregressions called the forward prediction error, based, as its name suggests, on predicted mean squared error considerations. This was the first step toward the development of model selection criteria that are very common in contemporary modeling.

When the model choice set involves both AR and MA components, the decision problem becomes one of selecting between nonnested alternatives and no obvious procedure based on formal hypothesis testing procedures is available. The important contribution of Akaike (1977), based on Kullback–Liebler concepts from information theory, extended the use of model selection criteria in time series analysis. The work that this has spawned in the ensuing 25 years or so is truly voluminous and the coverage here highlights only some major points. The methodology has been extensively developed and used in both the classical and Bayesian time series literatures.

Suppose that a model choice set has been determined such that the data to hand is believed to be satisfactorily modeled by some $ARMA(p,q)$ model with $p \in [0,[1]$, $p_{max}]$ and $q \in [0,[1],q_{max}]$, with the preferred $\hat{p}$ and $\hat{q}$ to be determined. On a Gaussian assumption for the innovations, apart possibly from transient errors, the MLE of all models in the choice set is obtained by minimizing the criterion function

$$S(\boldsymbol{\alpha}, \boldsymbol{\beta}) = \sum_{t=1}^{n} \varepsilon_t^2 / n. \qquad (6.37)$$

The proposal of Akaike (1977) is to compute the information criterion

$$AIC = \log S(\hat{\alpha}_1, \hat{\alpha}_2, \ldots, \hat{\alpha}_p, \hat{\beta}_1, \hat{\beta}_2, \ldots, \hat{\beta}_q) + 2(p+q)/n \qquad (6.38)$$

for all values of p and q in the choice set and then to choose the integer parameters $\hat{p}$ and $\hat{q}$ that minimize (6.38) across that choice set. The first term reflects the (negative of) the maximized loglikelihood and the second is a parameter penalty adjustment to mitigate against the choice of more profligate models unless the first term is reduced by a suitable amount by adding additional parameters. Brockwell and Davis (1996, section 9.3) have a discussion of AIC and related concepts.

AIC of (6.38) is by no means the only information criterion in use. It was observed at an early stage that: AIC shows some empirical tendency to select quite profligate models; and that the 'one size fits all' parameter penalty adjustment based on twice the number of fitted parameters in $\alpha(L)$ and $\beta(L)$ may not always be desirable. Bhansali and Downham (1977), for example, experiment with allowing the integer 2 in the second term of (6.38) to increase gradually up to 5 as n rises to 1000.

Suppose that there are true degrees of the polynomials $\alpha(L)$ and $\beta(L)$, call them p^* and q^*. Then it can be shown for AIC that, as n increases, $P(\hat{p} \geq p^*) = 1$ and $P(\hat{q} \geq q^*) = 1$ (where $P(\cdot)$ indicates probability of), but that $P(\hat{p} = p^*) \neq 1$ and similarly for $\hat{q}$. Should an information criterion satisfy $P(\hat{p} = p^*) = 1$ and $P(\hat{q} = q^*) = 1$, it is said to be consistent, so AIC is seen to be an inconsistent model selection criterion. Of course, there may be no true degrees, in which case this may not be of concern. Shibata (1980) examines this issue in the context of forecasting with AR models for which there are no true degrees.

To obtain information criteria that do satisfy the consistency property requires a parameter penalty adjustment that formalizes the type of adjustment suggested by Bhansali and Downham (1977) and which specifies the term as a suitable increasing function of n. The best known and most widely used such criterion is the Bayesian Information Criterion, BIC, due to Schwarz (1978). It replaces the constant 2 in AIC by $\log n$, an increasing function of n, to give

$$BIC = \log S(\hat{\alpha}_1, \hat{\alpha}_2, \ldots, \hat{\alpha}_p, \hat{\beta}_1, \hat{\beta}_2, \ldots, \hat{\beta}_q) + [(p+q)\log n]/n. \qquad (6.39)$$

Since $\log n > 2$ for all realistic sample sizes, a greater penalty is imposed on parameter profligacy by BIC than AIC. It is reasonable to enquire just what is the slowest rate of increase of the parameter penalty adjustment that will lead to a consistent model selection criterion. This question is answered in Hannan and Quinn (1979), who propose

$$HQIC = \log S(\hat{\alpha}_1, \hat{\alpha}_2, \ldots, \hat{\alpha}_p, \hat{\beta}_1, \hat{\beta}_2, \ldots, \hat{\beta}_q) + [c(p+q)\log\log n]/n, \ c > 2. \quad (6.40)$$

Although the original authors perhaps thought that (6.40) was of theoretical interest only, the present author has often found with moderate sample sizes (actually using a value of c near the bottom of the required range) that a model selected by minimizing it across the model choice set can provide a useful compromise between minimizing AIC and BIC. Other information criteria for model selection have been proposed; see, e.g., Rissanen (1978) for an important contribution.

Whichever IC is used for model selection, it will often be the case that the values of IC for more than one specification will be (very) close to one another.

Poskitt and Tremayne (1987) develop the notion of a portfolio of models based on Bayesian posterior odds considerations. It represents, in essence, an example of model averaging, which has become very popular in the Bayesian statistics literature. The use of such a weighted average of models may be of value in forecasting, where a combination of forecasts is often used to provide an improvement in accuracy over one based on a single model; Marriott and Tremayne (1988) use this approach in an application.

Phillips (1996) provides an extremely elegant account of central considerations in model determination. Although his methods are essentially Bayesian in flavour and based on posterior information criteria, they can also be justified on classical grounds. In Phillips (1996, p. 773) he observes "Obviously, there are many . . . ways of modelling the data. Without divine intervention or extraordinary sample coincidence we cannot expect any empirically feasible alternative procedure to hit upon the true probability measure . . . of the data." He continues by pointing out that the most reasonable question that can be posed relates to how well a fitted model does in characterizing the true data-generating mechanism. Even if there is a "true model" in the class under consideration, he shows that there is a (random) bound (dependent on the dimensionality of the parameter space) to how close we can hope to get to that true probability mechanism. Further, in Phillips (1996, section 2.4) there is a discussion of recursive model determination and acknowledgement that one is likely to consider more complicated models as the information available to the statistician increases. For a full coverage of these important considerations, the reader is referred to the original paper and references therein.

6.7   Some further issues

The obtaining of first-stage consistent estimators of the coefficients of ARMA models via a long autoregression to approximate the transfer function is discussed in section 6.4.3. If one wishes to use the model selection devices of section 6.6 to choose a preferred model, then the model choice set consists of $(p_{max}+1)(q_{max}+1)$ models, of which all but $(p_{max}+1)$ include MA terms. Evidently, there will be a substantial computational burden if all models are to be fitted by maximum likelihood. However, there are various ways in which this computational burden can be eased. In the first place, the obtaining of first-stage consistent estimators for all specifications with MA components can be based on the results of a single long autoregression fitted as the basis of them. Suppose that the residuals from this (long) $AR(P)$ for suitably chosen P are $\{e_t\}_{P+1}^n$. Then first stage consistent estimators of $\alpha_1, \ldots, \alpha_p, \beta_1, \ldots, \beta_q$ for any model in the choice set are available by fitting the regression

$$y_t = \sum_{j=1}^{p} \alpha_j y_{t-j} + \sum_{j=1}^{q} \beta_j e_{t-j} + \eta_t,$$

where η_t is a regression error. The estimated values can then be used as input to a suitable ML routine and all members of the model choice set can be treated in a similar way using the one set of e_t.

6.7.1 Hannan–Rissanen search procedure

The procedure of the opening paragraph of this section does not, of itself, obviate the need to fit a potentially large number of models by maximum likelihood. A recursive model selection strategy due to Hannan and Rissanen (1982) may often be helpful in this respect. There are various ways that their ideas can be implemented, but a particularly simple way of proceeding is provided in what follows. As above, it is assumed that the true (minimal) degrees of $\alpha(L)$ and $\beta(L)$ are, respectively, p^* and q^* (and that at least one of them is nonzero). A model choice set should be proposed in which $p_{max} = q_{max}$. Now use the residuals from the long autoregression, following Durbin (1960), to fit the p_{max} models

$$y_t = \sum_{j=1}^{p} \alpha_j y_{t-j} + \sum_{j=1}^{p} \beta_j e_{t-j} + \eta_t, \quad p = 1, \ldots, p_{max}, \tag{6.41}$$

i.e., the set of p_{max} $ARMA(p,p)$ models. The models in (6.41) may be fitted by OLS to yield consistent, though not asymptotically efficient, estimates (Saikkonen, 1986, provides relevant discussion of asymptotic properties). See Brockwell and Davis (2002, section 5.1.4) for an accessible account of the whole procedure. Hannan and Rissanen (1982) show that the chosen value, $\hat{p}$, arrived at by determining the minimum of some consistent model selection criterion like *BIC*, converges to $\max(p^*, q^*)$, almost surely. Some care needs to be taken for increasing values of $p = q$ because the parameter redundancy issue discussed later in this section can prove problematic. Hannan and Rissanen (1982, section 1) suggest how this might be monitored in practice.

At this stage, a consistent estimate of the degree of the higher order of the two polynomials $\alpha(L)$ and $\beta(L)$ has been determined. An investigator may then continue to search for a preferred specification amongst the remaining $2\hat{p}$ $ARMA(p,q)$ models for which one of p or q is equal to $\hat{p}$ and the other is less than that. These $2\hat{p}$ models can be fitted by OLS and the preferred $ARMA(\hat{p}, \tilde{q})$ or $ARMA(\tilde{p}, \hat{p})$ chosen using a consistent model selection criterion. Alternatively, the latter part of the selection strategy could be carried out using MLE to fit the relevant set of $(2\hat{p} + 1)$ models so that the estimators of the parameters of the one chosen are asymptotically efficient.

6.7.2 Parameter redundancy

As in section 6.4.3, consider an $ARMA(p+r, q+r)$ model

$$y_t = \sum_{j=1}^{p+r} \alpha_j y_{t-j} + \varepsilon_t + \sum_{j-1}^{q+r} \beta_j \varepsilon_{t-j},$$

or $\alpha(L)y_t = \beta(L)\varepsilon_t$, where $\alpha(L)$ may be written as $\alpha^*(L)\delta(L)$ and $\beta(L) = \beta^*(L)\delta(L)$ with $\delta(L) = 1 + \sum_{j=1}^{r} \delta_j L^j$, so that there are common factors in the lag operator polynomials; this is the parameter redundancy problem. Brockwell and Davis (1996, p. 86) remark that any factors common to the AR and MA operators can be cancelled, thereby leaving the model of minimal degrees, and thus such models are

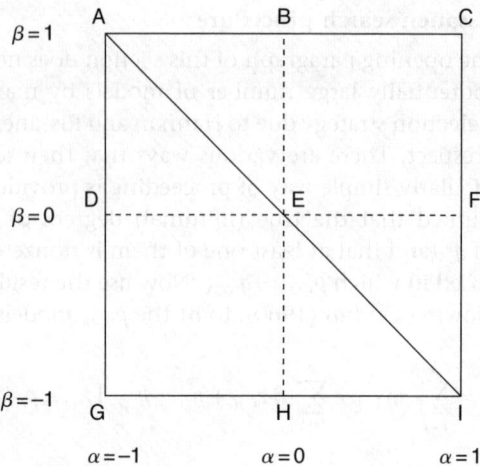

Figure 6.1   The α–β parameter space for stationary and invertible $ARMA(1,1)$ models

rarely considered. In applications it will, of course, likely not be known that such cancellation is available and considerable difficulties can arise when attempting to fit models that are overspecified in this way. The problems stem in part from the fact that the overspecified model will have a singular Fisher information matrix and estimation problems arise because of the existence of an equivalence class of likelihood maximizing parameter points in the admissible space.

Figure 6.1 provides a simple example in depicting the parameter space for stationary and invertible $ARMA(1,1)$ specifications. The lines AG and CI on the figure represent the closure of the parameter space, along which all values represent nonstationary autoregressive behavior (i.e., the unit root problem of Chapter 7), whilst AC and GI represent noninvertible MA processes. The equivalence class is given by AEI with all parameter pairs along this line having the transfer function of a white noise process (i.e., identical to that of point E). Pure $AR(1)$ and $MA(1)$ models lie on the dashed lines.

One of the main consequences of this problem is that it is almost always advisable when contemplating models from the ARMA class for data to adopt a specific-to-general search procedure for a preferred specification. Karanasos (1998, section 4) provides a sufficient condition for the absence of parameter redundancy in an $ARMA(p,q)$. He then continues to discuss the matter and provides an example of redundancy in the context of a special $ARMA$ (2, 2) model that is expressible as $ARMA(1, 1)$. Of course, problems of this type do not arise if a specification search is confined to AR specifications with p_{max} set sufficiently large (and q_{max} set to zero), which some researchers may find attractive.

6.7.3   Indirect inference and ARAR models

The problems of model determination, estimation and inference inherent in the use of ARMA models have led authors to investigate a number of avenues for attenuating the difficulties associated with the practical use of mixed models. Two such approaches are briefly discussed. The first is the use of indirect inference. This is developed in Smith (1993) and Gourieroux, Monfort and Renault (1993) (the latter appear in their paper to acknowledge that the former author first introduced the idea into the literature). A clear summary of the method is provided by Davidson and MacKinnon (2004, section 13.3). As Davidson and MacKinnon opine, it may be unlikely that the approach will be made available in statistical software, but it is nevertheless of interest.

The fundamental idea in a univariate linear time series context is to eschew an (AR)MA specification that may be hard to estimate in favor of an auxiliary model whose transfer function is quite similar to that of (6.13). This auxiliary model is chosen so that its parameters are linked to those of (6.13) by what are called linking functions, but which is easier to estimate. When there are as many parameters in the auxiliary model as in the original specification, a unique solution via the linking functions is often available; Davidson and MacKinnon (2004, p. 571) discuss the example where the former is $AR(1)$ and is used to estimate an $MA(1)$ model's parameters. It is, however, commonplace that the number of parameters in the auxiliary model exceeds that of the true model and then a Generalized Method of Moments (GMM) type criterion must be minimized. The method uses computer-intensive techniques and seems to work well when: (a) it is feasible to draw simulated samples from the data generating process of interest; and (b) the parameters of the auxiliary model can be readily estimated. See the original references given earlier in the previous paragraph for full details.

In a somewhat similar vein, Carter and Zellner (2003, 2004) introduce an autoregressive model with autoregressive errors, the so-called ARAR model. They argue, following Nicholls, Pagan and Terrell (1975) and others, that there is no inevitability about the occurrence of MA disturbances. The ARAR specification replaces the moving average part of (6.13) with $\varepsilon_t/\omega(L)$, where $\omega(L) = 1 - \sum_{j=1}^{m} \omega_j L^j$, such that the characteristic equation $\omega(z) = 0$ has all its roots outside the unit circle and they label such a specification $ARAR(p,m)$. The basic idea is to simplify inference and Carter and Zellner observe that rich behavior in the autocovariance structure of the unobserved component on the right-hand side of the ARAR model $\alpha(L)y_t = \varepsilon_t/\omega(L)$ can be found for values of m as small as 2. They also maintain that the specification is in the spirit of Wold's Decomposition, since no truncation is implied in the $MA(\infty)$ representation of a covariance stationary process. The interested reader is left to consult the original references for further details.

6.7.4 Time series models for counts

Many time series are observed as counts. Examples of data where the models to be introduced in this subsection might be useful include a count of numbers of: workers' compensation claims at an insurance company for a particular industry; strikes in a society involving 500 people or more; number of absentees from the workforce of a firm; and sell orders for a financial stock in a trading system. All counts would be observed for a sequence of time intervals to provide a series. When counts are quite large, it may be reasonable to use the kinds of continuous models assumed in the foregoing. On occasion this may not be appropriate, particularly if counts are small. With count data and a linear model, the very operation of multiplying integer values by non-integer parameters on the right-hand side of a model is almost certain to compromise the counts on the left-hand side to which it is to be equated. This can limit the usefulness of linear models.

There is now an extensive literature in stationary time series models for counts data. Some of these models are observation-driven and bear close resemblance to models in the ARMA class. McKenzie (1985, 1988) and Al-Osh and Alzaid in a series of papers including Al-Osh and Alzaid (1987, 1988) and Alzaid and Al-Osh (1990) introduce integer autoregressive (INAR) and moving average (INMA) models. McKenzie (1988) introduces a mixed specification by coupling two processes with a common innovation. From this a general *INARMA(p,q)* model would be given by

$$y_t = \sum_{j=1}^{p} \alpha_j \circ x_{t-j-q} + \varepsilon_{t-q} + \sum_{j=1}^{q} \beta_j \circ \varepsilon_{t+1-j}, \tag{6.42}$$

where the latent process x_t provides the autoregressive component. In (6.42) $\circ$ denotes the binomial thinning operator (Steutel and van Harn, 1979), which serves to retain the integer aspect of the data, and ε_t is an independent, non-negative integer innovation term. No consideration of the case $p > 1$ with $q > 0$ appears to be in the literature.

However, in retaining the integer structure of the data, the intrinsic property of linearity of the model is lost. Nevertheless, the similarity of structure of these models to what has gone before affords the licence to consider them here. The basic questions to be answered in using such models are similar to those with ARMA models, viz. determination of a suitable model for data, estimation of its parameters and tests for the adequacy of the model. It is most common to consider an INAR model where the moving average component is absent. However, Brännäs and Hall (2001) and Al-Osh and Alzaid (1988) are two examples where INMA specifications have been employed. See also Al-Osh and Alzaid (1991) for a discussion of the mixed *INARMA*(1, *q*) model, which also arises in the recent review by McKenzie (2003). Other interesting references include, inter alia, Brännäs (1994), Brännäs and Hellström (2001) and Freeland (1998). Jung and Tremayne (2003) discuss tests for establishing the existence of dependence structure in data.

Many papers and most of the applications focus on the relatively simple *INAR*(1) model, i.e., the model with $p = 1$ and $q = 0$, and often assume a Poisson distribution for the innovations. Although not a linear model, the *INAR*(1) model is a member of the CLAR class, which acronym was used in section 6.2.1. Jung, Ronning and Tremayne (2005) compare estimation methods in *INAR*(1) models and refer to earlier papers where this has been considered. Extensions to higher-order integer autoregression are available, but the requisite generalizations are neither straightforward, nor unique. There are at least three approaches (all of which are equivalent in an *INAR*(1) model with Poisson innovations), two of which are discussed by Jung and Tremayne (2006) in the context of the *INAR*(2) model. One of these extensions is a CLAR model and the other is not. Although in principle feasible, extension to higher orders becomes still more cumbersome and may not prove fruitful.

One aspect of time series modeling where it may be useful to preserve the integer structure of the data is forecasting, particularly if the counts are low. Freeland and McCabe (2004) and Jung and Tremayne (2006) consider the problem of what they call coherent forecasting in the context of the *INAR*(1) and *INAR*(2) models, respectively.

This short subsection provides little detail, but serves to alert readers to the existence of this class of models which do not enjoy widespread exposure in econometrics and time series texts.

6.8 Conclusions

Time series data, whether economic or other, stationary or not, have particular features that require special methods to be used. Methods for univariate stationary time series constitute a subset of the vast literature and this chapter has not attempted a comprehensive coverage, since one could not be provided in a contribution of this length. Certain features that it would be of interest to discuss have been omitted entirely. These might include: the influence of heteroskedasticity in time series models; the use of nonnested testing methods; and long memory models, to name but three. Rather, some of the main issues of model specification, estimation and testing are reviewed, together with brief accounts of important topics such as model selection. A fairly lengthy bibliography is provided so that the interested reader can trace back ideas in considerably more detail, should they so wish. At this point it seems worthwhile to draw attention again to the phenomenal list of relevant references assembled by Choi (1992).

Research on stationary univariate models for time series was an active research area for most of the last century and promises to be so for much of the present one. Although such models may be considered a workhorse of time series econometrics, many of the other models used in contemporary analysis of nonstationary and nonlinear models often require a sound underpinning of methodology provided by the models discussed here. For that reason alone, it is important for practitioners in the field to have a sound working knowledge of them.

Acknowledgments

Much of this work was completed whilst the author was visiting the Department of Economics, University of Otago, Dunedin, New Zealand. I am very grateful for the generous hospitality I received there, especially from Carlyn Ramlogan and Steve Dobson. I also thank Steph de Silva and Robert Jung for helpful comments and suggestions but, alas, I cannot shift the blame for errors of omission or commission onto any of them.

References

Akaike, H. (1969) Fitting autoregressions for predictions. *Annals of the Institute of Statistical Mathematics* **21**, 243–7.

Akaike, H. (1977) On entropy maximisation principle. In P.R. Krishnaiah (ed.), *Applications of Statistics*. Amsterdam: North-Holland, pp. 27–41.

Al-Osh, M.A., and A.A. Alzaid (1987) First order integer-valued autoregressive (INAR(1)) process. *Journal of Time Series Analysis* **8**, 261–75.

Al-Osh, M.A., and A.A. Alzaid (1988) Integer-valued moving average (INMA) process. *Statistical Papers* **29**, 281–300.

Al-Osh, M.A., and A.A. Alzaid (1991) Binomial autoregressive moving average models. *Communications in Statistics: Stochastic Models* **7**, 261–82.

Alzaid, A.A. and M.A. Al-Osh (1990) An integer-valued p-th order autoregressive structure (INAR(p)) process. *Journal of Applied Probability* **27**, 314–24.

An, H.-Z., Z.-G. Chen and E.J. Hannan (1982) Autocorrelation, autoregression and auto-regressive approximation. *Annals of Statistics* **10**, 926–36.

Anderson, R.L. (1942) Distribution of the serial correlation coefficient. *Annals of Mathematical Statistics* **13**, 1–13.

Anderson, T.W. (1971) *The Statistical Analysis of Time Series*. New York: Wiley.

Anderson, T.W. and A. Takemura (1986) Why do noninvertible estimated moving averages occur? *Journal of Time Series Analysis* **7**, 235–54.

Ansley, C.F. (1979) An algorithm for the exact likelihood of a mixed autoregressive-moving average process. *Biometrika* **66**, 59–65.

Bartlett, M.S. (1946) On the theoretical specification of sampling properties of autocorrelated time series. Supplement to *The Journal of the Royal Statistical Society* **8**, 27–41.

Bhansali, R.J. (1980) Autoregressive and window estimates of the inverse autocorrelation function. *Biometrika* **67**, 551–65.

Bhansali, R.J. and D.Y. Downham (1977) Some properties of the order of an autoregressive model selected by a generalization of Akaike's FPE criterion, *Biometrika* **64**, 547–51.

Box, G.E.P. and G.M. Jenkins (1970) *Time Series Analysis: Forecasting and Control*. San Francisco: Holden-Day.

Box, G.E.P., G.M. Jenkins and G.C. Reinsel (1994) *Time Series Analysis: Forecasting and Control*. 3rd edn. Englewood Cliffs, NJ: Prentice Hall.

Box, G.E.P., and D.A. Pierce (1970) Distribution of residual autocorrelations in autoregressive-integrated moving average time series models. *Journal of the American Statistical Association* **65**, 1509–1526.

Brännäs, K. (1994) Estimation and testing in integer-valued AR(1) models, unpublished Umea Economic Studies paper 335.

Brännäs, K. and A. Hall (2001) Estimation in integer-valued moving average models. *Applied Stochastic Models in Business and Industry* **17**, 277–91.

Brännäs, K. and J. Hellström (2001) Generalized integer-valued autoregression. *Econometric Reviews* **20**, 425–43.

Brockwell, P.J. and R.A. Davis (1996) *Time Series: Theory And Methods*, 2nd edn. New York: Springer-Verlag.

Brockwell, P.J. and R.A. Davis (2002) *Introduction to Time Series and Forecasting*, 2nd edn. New York: Springer-Verlag.

Canepa, A. and L.G. Godfrey (2005) Improvement of the likelihood ratio test in ARMA models: some results on the use of the bootstrap, unpublished University of York paper.

Carter, R.A.L. and A. Zellner (2003) AR versus MA disturbance terms. *Economics Bulletin* **3**(21), 1–3.

Carter, R.A.L. and A. Zellner (2004) The ARAR error model for univariate time series and distributed lag. *Studies in Nonlinear Dynamics and Control* **8**, issue 1, article 2.

Chatfield, C. (1979) Inverse autocorrelations. *Journal of the Royal Statistical Society* Series A **142**, 363–77.

Choi, B.S. (1992) *ARMA Model Identification*. Berlin: Springer-Verlag.

Chow, G.C. (1981) Selection of econometric models by the information criteria. In: E.G. Charatsis (ed.) *Proceedings of the European Econometric Society Meeting, 1979*. Amsterdam: North-Holland.

Cleveland, W.S. (1972) The inverse autocorrelations of a time series and their applications, *Technometrics* **14**, 277–98.

Cramér, H. (1937) *Random Variables and Probability Distributions.* Cambridge: Cambridge University Press.

Das Gupta, S. and M.D. Perlman (1974) Power of the noncentral F-test: effects of additional variates on Hotelling's T^2-test. *Journal of the American Statistical Association* **69**, 174–80.

Davidson, J. (1981) Problems with the estimation of moving average processes. *Journal of Econometrics* **16**, 295–310.

Davidson, R. and J.G. MacKinnon (2004) *Econometric Theory and Methods.* Oxford: Oxford University Press.

Davies, N. and P. Newbold (1979) Some power studies of a portmanteau test of time series model specification. *Biometrika* **66**, 153–5.

Davies, N. and P. Newbold (1980) Sample moments of the autocorrelations of moving average processes and a modification to Bartlett's asymptotic variance formula. *Communications in Statistics* A **9**, 1473–1481.

Davis, R.A. and W.T.M. Dunsmuir (1996) Maximum-likelihood estimation for MA(1) processes with a root on or near the unit circle. *Econometric Theory* **12**, 1–29.

Dickey, D.A. (1975) Hypothesis testing for nonstationary time series. Unpublished manuscript, Iowa State University.

Durbin, J. (1960) The fitting of time series models. *Review of the International Statistical Institute* **28**, 233–44.

Durbin, J. (1970) Testing for serial correlation in least-squares regression when some of the regressors are lagged dependent variables. *Econometrica* **38**, 410–21.

Engle, R.F. (1982) Autoregressive conditional heteroskedasticity with estimates of the variance of United Kingdom inflation. *Econometrica* **50**, 987–1007.

Freeland, K. (1998) Statistical analysis of discrete time series with applications to the analysis of workers compensation claims data. Unpublished University of British Columbia PhD thesis.

Freeland, K. and B.P.M. McCabe (2004) Forecasting discrete valued low count time series. *International Journal of Forecasting* **20**, 427–34.

Frisch, R. (1933) Propagation problems and impulse problems in dynamic economics. In *Economic essays in honour of Gustav Cassel.* London: Allen and Unwin, pp. 171–205.

Fuller, W. (1976) *Introduction to Statistical Time Series.* New York: Wiley.

Fuller, W. (1996) *Introduction to Statistical Time Series*, 2nd edn. New York: Wiley.

Geweke, J. (1984) Inference and causality in economic time series models. In Z. Griliches and M.D. Intriligator (eds), *Handbook of Econometrics*, vol. 2. Amsterdam: North-Holland.

Godfrey, L.G. (1979) Testing the adequacy of a time series model. *Biometrika* **66**, 67–72.

Godfrey, L.G. and A.R. Tremayne (1988) Checks of model adequacy for univariate time series models and their application to econometric relationships. *Econometric Reviews* **7**, 1–42.

Gourieroux, C., A. Monfort and E. Renault (1993) Indirect inference. *Journal of Applied Econometrics* **8**, S85–S118.

Granger, C.W.J. and P. Newbold 1986 *Forecasting Economic Time Series*, 2nd edn. Orlando: Academic Press.

Grunwald, G.K., R.J. Hyndman, L. Tedesco and R.L. Tweedie (2000) Non-Gaussian conditional linear AR(1) models. *Australian and New Zealand Journal of Statistics* **42**, 479–95.

Hamilton, J.D. (1994) *Time Series Analysis.* Princeton, NJ: Princeton University Press.

Hannan, E.J. (1980) The estimation of the order of an ARMA model. *Annals of Statistics* **8**, 1071–1081.

Hannan, E.J. and B.G. Quinn (1979) The determination of the order of an autoregression. *Journal of the Royal Statistical Society*, Series B **41**, 190–5.

Hannan, E.J. and J. Rissanen (1982) Recursive estimation of mixed autoregressive-moving average order. *Biometrika* **69**, 81–94.

Harvey, A.C. (1993) *Time Series Models*, 2nd edn. Cambridge MA: MIT Press.

Hendry, D.F. and J.-F. Richard (1982) On the formulation of empirical models in dynamic econometrics. *Journal of Econometrics* 20, 3–34.

Jung, R.C., G. Ronning and A.R. Tremayne (2005) Estimation in conditional first order autoregression with discrete support. *Statistical Papers* 46, 195–224.

Jung, R.C. and A.R. Tremayne (2003) Testing for serial dependence in time series of counts. *Journal of Time Series Analysis* 25, 65–84.

Jung, R.C. and A.R. Tremayne (2006) Coherent forecasting in integer time series models. *International Journal of Forecasting*, forthcoming.

Karanasos, M. (1998) A new method for obtaining the autocovariance of an ARMA model: an exact form solution. *Econometric Theory* 14, 622–40.

Kiviet, J.F. (1986) On the rigour of some misspecification tests for modelling dynamic relationships. *Review of Economic Studies* 53, 241–61.

Kolmogorov, A.N. (1933) Grundbegriffe der Wahrscheinlichkeitrechnung, Berlin. *Foundations of the Theory of Probability*, 2nd English edn. New York: Chelsea.

Kwan, A.C.C., A.-B. Sim and Y. Wu (2005) A comparative study of the finite-sample performance of some portmanteau tests for randomness of a time series. *Computational Statistics and Data Analysis* 48, 391–413.

Li, W.K. (2004) *Diagnostic Checks in Time Series.* Monographs on statistics and applied probability 102. Boca Raton, FL: Chapman and Hall/CRC.

Ljung, G.M. (1986) Diagnostic testing of univariate time series models. *Biometrika* 73, 725–30.

Ljung, G.M. and G.E.P. Box (1978) On a measure of lack of fit in time series models. *Biometrika* 65, 297–303.

McCabe, B.P.M. and S.J. Leybourne (1998) On estimating an ARMA model with an MA unit root. *Econometric Theory* 14, 326–38.

McKenzie, E. (1985) Some simple models for discrete variate time series. *Water Resources Bulletin* 21, 645–50.

McKenzie, E. (1988) Some ARMA models for dependent sequences of counts. *Advances in Applied Probability* 20, 822–35.

McKenzie, E. (2003) Discrete variate time series. In D. Shanbhag and C. Rao (eds), *Handbook of Statistics*, vol. 21. Amsterdam: Elsevier Science.

McLeod, A.I. (1975) Derivation of the theoretical autocovariance function of an autoregressive-moving average time series. *Journal of the Royal Statistical Society*, Series C Applied Statistics 24, 255–6.

Marriott, F.H.C. and J.A. Pope (1954) Bias in the estimation of autocorrelation. *Biometrika* 41, 390–402.

Marriott, J.M. and A.R. Tremayne (1988) Alternative statistical approaches to time series modelling for forecasting purposes. *The Statistician* 37, 187–97.

Nelson, C.R. and C.I. Plosser (1982) Trends and random walks in macroeconomic time series: some evidence and implications. *Journal of Monetary Economics* 10, 139–62.

Newbold, P. (1980) The equivalence of two tests of time series model adequacy. *Biometrika* 67, 463–5.

Newbold, P., C. Agiakloglou and J. Miller (1994) Adventures with ARIMA software. *International Journal of Forecasting* 10, 573–81.

Nicholls, D., A.R. Pagan and R.D. Terrell (1975) The estimation and use of models with moving average disturbance terms; a survey. *International Economic Review* 16, 113–34.

Pagan, A.R. (1985) Time series behaviour and dynamic specification. *Oxford Bulletin of Economics and Statistics* 47, 199–211.

Paulsen, J. and D. Tjøstheim (1985) On the estimation of residual variance and order in autoregressive time series. *Journal of the Royal Statistical Society*, Series B 47, 216–28.

Phillips, P.C.B. (1996) Econometric model determination. *Econometrica* 64, 763–812.

Poskitt, D.S. and A.R. Tremayne (1980) Testing the specification of a fitted autoregressive-moving average model. *Biometrika* 67, 359–63.

Poskitt, D.S. and A.R. Tremayne (1984) Model selection and diagnostic checking in univariate time series analysis. In O.D. Anderson (ed.) *Time Series Analysis: Theory and Practice* 5. Amsterdam: North-Holland.

Poskitt, D.S. and A.R. Tremayne (1987) Determining a portfolio of linear time series models. *Biometrika* **74**, 125–37.

Quenouille, M.H. (1949) Approximate tests of correlation in time series. *Journal of the Royal Statistical Society*, Series B **11**, 68–84.

Rao, C.R. (1948) Large sample tests of statistical hypotheses concerning several parameters with applications in problems of estimation. *Proceedings of the Cambridge Philosophical Society* **44**, 50–7.

Rissanen, J. (1978) Modeling by shortest data description. *Automatica* **14**, 465–71.

Saikkonen, P. (1986) Asymptotic properties of some preliminary estimates for autoregressive moving average time series models. *Journal of Time Series Analysis* **7**, 133–55.

Sargan, J.D. and A. Bhargava (1983) Maximum likelihood estimation of regression models with first order moving average errors when the root lies on the unit circle. *Econometrica* **51**, 799–820.

Schwarz, G. (1978) Estimating the dimension of a model. *Annals of Statistics* **6**, 461–4.

Shephard, N. (1993) Distribution of the ML estimator of an MA(1) and a local level model. *Econometric Theory* **9**, 377–401.

Shibata, R. (1980) Asymptotically efficient selection of the order of the model for estimating parameters of a linear process. *Annals of Statistics* **8**, 147–64.

Silvey, S.D. (1959) The Lagrangian multiplier test. *Annals of Mathematical Statistics* **30**, 389–407.

Slutsky, E. (1927) The summation of random causes as the source of cyclical processes (in Russian), English translation 1937, published in *Econometrica* **5**, 105–46.

Smith, A.A. Jr. (1993) Estimating nonlinear time-series models using simulated vector auto-regressions. *Journal of Applied Econometrics* **8**, S63–S84.

Spanos, A. (2001) Time series and dynamic models. In B. Baltagi (ed.) *A Companion to Theoretical Econometrics*. Oxford: Blackwell. pp. 585–609.

Steutel, F.W. and K. van Harn (1979) Discrete analogues of self-decomposability and stability. *Annals of Probability* **7**, 893–9.

Tjøstheim, D. and J. Paulsen (1983) Bias of some commonly-used time series estimates. *Biometrika* **70**, 389–99.

Wallis, K.F. (1972) Testing for fourth order autocorrelation in quarterly regression equations. *Econometrica* **40**, 617–36.

Walker, G. (1931) On periodicity in series of related terms. *Proceedings of the Royal Society*, Series A **131**, 518–32.

Wold, H. (1938) *A Study in the Analysis of Stationary Time Series* (2nd edn, 1954). Uppsala: Almqvist and Wiksell.

Yule, G.U. (1926) Why do we sometimes get nonsense correlations between time series? – A study in sampling and the nature of time-series. *Journal of the Royal Statistical Society* **89**, 1–63.

Yule, G.U. (1927) On a method of investigating periodicities in disturbed series, with special reference to Wolfer's sunspot numbers. *Philosophical Transactions of the Royal Society*, Series A **226**, 267–98.

7
Improving Size and Power in Unit Root Testing

Niels Haldrup and Michael Jansson

Abstract

A frequent criticism of unit root tests concerns the poor power and size properties that many such tests exhibit. However, during the past decade or so intensive research has been conducted to alleviate these problems and great advances have been made. The present chapter provides a selective survey of recent contributions to improve upon both the size and power of unit root tests and, in so doing, the approach of using rigorous statistical optimality criteria in the development of such tests is stressed. In addition to presenting tests where improved size can be achieved by modifying the standard Dickey–Fuller class of tests, the chapter presents the theory of optimal testing and the construction of power envelopes for unit root tests under different conditions allowing for serial correlation, deterministic components, assumptions regarding the initial condition, non-Gaussian errors, and the use of covariates.

7.1	Introduction		252
7.2	Unit root testing		254
	7.2.1	The augmented Dickey–Fuller and Phillips–Perron classes of tests	255
	7.2.2	Size distortions of unit root tests	257
	7.2.3	Modified unit root tests with good size	259
	7.2.4	Deterministics	260
7.3	Power envelopes for unit root tests		262
	7.3.1	The leading special case	262
	7.3.2	Serial correlation	265
	7.3.3	Deterministics	266
	7.3.4	The initial condition	267
	7.3.5	Non-Gaussian errors	269
	7.3.6	Covariates	271
7.4	Conclusion		272

7.1 Introduction

Since the mid-1980s there has been a veritable explosion of research on the importance of unit roots in the analysis of economic and other time series data.

The reasons for this are manifold, but perhaps the most important motivation for this work is the fact that the development of the notion of cointegration by Granger (1981) and Engle and Granger (1987) has stressed the significance of unit roots and the importance of making valid statistical inference in the presence of nonstationary time series data. There is a vast literature on developing statistical theory for unit root (integrated) processes and the list of empirical applications using unit root testing is even more impressive. There is also a tremendous literature examining the power and size of unit root tests, not least by adopting numerical simulation (Monte Carlo) techniques under a multitude of different designs of the underlying process. Referring to exhaustive lists of contributions to the theoretical, numerical and empirical literature in this field goes far beyond the space limitation we have here, but surveys referring to many of these contributions can be found in, inter alia, Stock (1994), Maddala and Kim (1998), and Phillips and Xiao (1998).

The present chapter reviews some of the results and findings in the unit roots literature that we believe are the most important contributions made over the past decade or so. The review is deliberately chosen to be selective and focuses on those contributions we believe are most likely to be fruitful for future developments of theory as well as in applications. Historically, the criticisms of unit root testing have concerned both the power and size properties of conventional unit root tests (e.g., Schwert, 1989; Agiakloglou and Newbold, 1992; and DeJong, Nankervis, Savin, and Whiteman, 1992a, 1992b). Stimulated in part by these influential Monte Carlo studies, a considerable amount of effort has been devoted to improving the size and/or power properties of unit root tests and much progress has been made. Most of these advances have been made with the help of rigorous statistical theory and are therefore potentially of general methodological interest. Here we survey (a subset of) these recent contributions.

We focus narrowly on the problem of testing for the presence of autoregressive unit roots, partly for concreteness and partly because this branch of nonstationary time series analysis appears to be the one in which the pertinent problems are best understood at this point. Consequently, several important recent advances in the analysis of nonstationary data are abstracted from in the present exposition. These advances include models of higher orders of integration (e.g., Dickey and Pantula, 1987; Haldrup, 1998), tests of seasonally integrated processes (e.g., Hylleberg, Engle, Granger, and Yoo, 1990; Franses, 1996; Ghysels and Osborn, 2001), tests of unit roots against structural breaks (e.g., Perron, 1989, 2005), fractionally integrated processes (e.g., Granger and Joyeux, 1980; Baillie, 1996; Velasco, 2005), testing stationarity against nonstationarity (e.g., Kwiatkowski, Phillips, Schmidt, and Shin, 1992; Saikkonen and Luukkonen, 1993a, 1993b; Jansson, 2004), and panel data unit root tests (e.g., Levin, Lin, and Chu, 2002; Im, Pesaran, and Shin, 2003; and Choi, 2005). Also, a recent literature has developed bootstrap methods for unit root tests (e.g., Park, 2002, 2003; Paparoditis and Politis, 2003; Davidson and MacKinnon, 2005).

The chapter proceeds as follows. Section 7.2 is concerned with the Dickey–Fuller class of tests (Dickey and Fuller, 1979) and the modifications of this testing framework that have been suggested in order to accommodate (particularly) serially dependent processes and the size distortions that this complication generally implies. The modifications discussed herein include the proposal of Said and Dickey (1984) to use long autoregressions to approximate general dependent processes and the nonparametric corrections of Phillips (1987a) and Phillips and Perron (1988). Special emphasis will be put on the further improvements towards alleviating size distortions made in a series of papers by Ng and Perron, culminating in Ng and Perron (2001). The focus of this recent work is on the importance of appropriately estimating the long-run variance by use of an autoregressive-based spectral density estimator, whilst simultaneously accounting for the serious bias that the estimate of the least squares estimator of the autoregressive coefficient implies even in large samples. Extending the approach to allow for deterministic components by exploiting the GLS detrending procedure of Elliott, Rothenberg, and Stock (1996), the class of tests suggested by Ng and Perron (2001) are argued to exhibit excellent power and size performance. In fact, the tests of Ng and Perron are "nearly efficient," in the sense that they almost achieve the asymptotic power envelope for unit root tests.

The concepts of test efficiency and power envelopes in the construction of tests for unit roots are discussed in depth in section 7.3. To highlight the nonstandard aspects of the unit root testing problem, the discussion of efficiency starts from the benchmark case of a zero mean Gaussian AR(1) model, a fully parametric model in which there are no nuisance parameters. Subsequent subsections discuss how Elliott, Rothenberg, and Stock's (1996) efficiency results for the benchmark change under modifications of that model. The discussion emphasizes the role of nuisance parameters caused by the accommodation of serial correlation (Elliott, Rothenberg, and Stock, 1996), deterministic components (Elliott, Rothenberg, and Stock, 1996), and/or a nonzero initial condition (Müller and Elliott, 2003), but also touches upon two sources of potentially important power gains in unit root testing, namely non-Gaussian errors and stationary covariates.

7.2 Unit root testing

Suppose the observed data $\{y_t : t = 1, \ldots, T\}$ is generated by the AR(1) model

$$y_t = \rho y_{t-1} + \varepsilon_t, \tag{7.1}$$

where $y_0 = 0$ and the $\varepsilon_t \sim i.i.d.(0, \sigma_\varepsilon^2)$ are unobserved errors. In this model, the unit root testing problem is that of testing

$$H_0 : \rho = 1 \quad \text{vs} \quad H_1 : \rho < 1.$$

Let

$$\hat{\rho} = \frac{\sum_{t=2}^{T} y_{t-1} y_t}{\sum_{t=2}^{T} y_{t-1}^2}$$

denote the OLS estimator of ρ and let

$$t_{\hat{\rho}} = \frac{\hat{\rho} - 1}{s / \sqrt{\sum_{t=2}^{T} y_{t-1}^2}}, \quad s^2 = T^{-1} \sum_{t=2}^{T} (y_t - \hat{\rho} y_{t-1})^2,$$

be the t-statistic associated with the unit root hypothesis. As is well known, $\hat{\rho}$ and $t_{\hat{\rho}}$ exhibit nonstandard large sample behavior under the unit root hypothesis. Indeed, when $\rho = 1$,

$$T(\hat{\rho} - 1) \rightarrow_d \frac{\int_0^1 W(r) dW(r)}{\int_0^1 W(r)^2 dr} \tag{7.2}$$

and

$$t_{\hat{\rho}} \rightarrow_d \frac{\int_0^1 W(r) dW(r)}{\sqrt{\int_0^1 W(r)^2 dr}} \tag{7.3}$$

where W is a standard Brownian motion (i.e., a Wiener process) and " $\rightarrow_d$ " signifies convergence in distribution. Although the results in the preceding equations can be traced back to White (1958), the limiting distributions in (7.2) and (7.3) are frequently referred to as the Dickey–Fuller distributions, in recognition of the contribution of Dickey and Fuller (1979).

7.2.1 The augmented Dickey–Fuller and Phillips–Perron classes of tests

An important implication of (7.2) and (7.3) is that both $T(\hat{\rho} - 1)$ and $t_{\hat{\rho}}$ are asymptotically pivotal under the null hypothesis; that is, the limiting null distributions of these statistics do not depend on unknown nuisance parameters. However, the practical usefulness of these results is limited by the implausibility of the assumptions regarding the errors ε_t. The impact of serially correlated errors can be illustrated by means of the model

$$y_t = \rho y_{t-1} + u_t, \quad u_t = \psi(L)\varepsilon_t, \tag{7.4}$$

where $y_0 = 0$, $\varepsilon_t \sim i.i.d.(0, \sigma_\varepsilon^2)$, and $\psi(L) = \sum_{j=0}^{\infty} \psi_j L^j$ is a lag polynomial whose coefficients $\{\psi_j\}$ satisfy $\sum_{j=1}^{\infty} j |\psi_j| < \infty$.

The model (7.4) imposes more general assumptions on the serial correlation pattern of $y_t - \rho y_{t-1}$ than does the AR(1) model in (7.1). As in the AR(1) model, the parameter of interest is ρ, the unit root testing problem being $H_0 : \rho = 1$ vs $H_1 : \rho < 1$.

Relative to the AR(1) model (7.1), the unit root testing problem in model (7.4) is complicated by the presence of the nuisance parameters $\{\psi_j\}$.

Phillips (1987a) shows that in this case (7.2) and (7.3) are modified as follows:

$$T(\hat{\rho} - 1) \to_d \frac{\int_0^1 W(r)dW(r) + \lambda}{\int_0^1 W(r)^2 dr} \tag{7.5}$$

and

$$t_{\hat{\rho}} \to_d \frac{\omega}{\sigma} \frac{\int_0^1 W(r)dW(r) + \lambda}{\sqrt{\int_0^1 W(r)^2 dr}}, \tag{7.6}$$

where $\lambda = (\omega^2 - \sigma^2)/(2\omega^2)$, $\sigma^2 = E[u_t^2] = \sigma_\varepsilon^2 \left(\sum_{j=0}^\infty \psi_j^2 \right)$ is the variance of u_t, and $\omega^2 = \lim_{T\to\infty} T^{-1}E\left[\left(\sum_{t=1}^T u_t \right)^2 \right] = \sigma_\varepsilon^2 \left(\sum_{j=0}^\infty \psi_j \right)^2$ is the long-run variance of u_t.[1] When the innovations u_t are *i.i.d.* (i.e., when $\psi_j = 0$ for $j \geq 1$), $\omega^2 = \sigma^2$ and the limiting distributions in (7.5) and (7.6) simplify to the nuisance parameter free limiting distributions in (7.2) and (7.3).

Different routes have been followed in the literature to account for the presence of nuisance parameters in the limiting distributions of $T(\hat{\rho} - 1)$ and $t_{\hat{\rho}}$. It was shown by Dickey and Fuller (1979) that when u_t is an AR process of (finite) order k, $T(\tilde{\rho} - 1)$ and $t_{\tilde{\rho}}$ calculated from the regression

$$y_t = \tilde{\rho}y_{t-1} + \sum_{j=1}^{k-1} \tilde{\gamma}_j \Delta y_{t-j} + \tilde{v}_{tk} \quad (t = k+1, \dots, T) \tag{7.7}$$

will indeed have the limiting null distributions in (7.2) and (7.3). However, if u_t is an ARMA(p, q) process (with $q \geq 1$), then the auxiliary regression model (7.7) will inadequately solve the nuisance parameter problem, at least if k is held fixed. On the other hand, utilizing results of the Berk (1974) variety and generalizing the celebrated results of Said and Dickey (1984), it has been shown by Chang and Park (2002) that, if u_t is an ARMA(p,q) process, then the limiting null distributions of $T(\tilde{\rho} - 1)$ and $t_{\tilde{\rho}}$ coincide with the limiting distributions in (7.2) and (7.3) provided $E(\varepsilon_t^4) < \infty$, $k \to \infty$, and $k = o(T^{1/2-\delta})$ for some $\delta > 0$.[2]

Rather than solving the nuisance parameter problem by employing an autoregressive sieve, Phillips (1987a) and Phillips and Perron (1988) use consistent estimators of ω^2 and σ^2 to transform the statistics $T(\hat{\rho} - 1)$ and $t_{\hat{\rho}}$ in a manner that eliminates the influence of nuisance parameters. More specifically, they suggest the statistics

$$Z_\rho = T(\hat{\rho} - 1) - \frac{\hat{\omega}^2 - \hat{\sigma}^2}{2T^{-2} \sum_{t=2}^T y_{t-1}^2} \tag{7.8}$$

and

$$Z_t = \frac{\hat{\sigma}}{\hat{\omega}} t_{\hat{\rho}} - \frac{\hat{\omega}^2 - \hat{\sigma}^2}{2\sqrt{\hat{\omega}^2 T^{-2} \sum_{t=2}^{T} y_{t-1}^2}}, \qquad (7.9)$$

where $\hat{\omega}^2$ and $\hat{\sigma}^2$ are consistent estimators of ω^2 and σ^2. The limiting null distributions of Z_ρ and Z_t coincide with the limiting distributions in (7.2) and (7.3).

7.2.2   Size distortions of unit root tests

Several studies (for example, Schwert, 1989; Agiakloglou and Newbold, 1992) have documented that the tests discussed in the previous subsection generally exhibit significant size distortions in finite samples when errors are serially correlated, especially when the errors are of the moving average type with a root approaching minus one. Because a near cancellation of roots occurs when the MA root is very close to minus one, it is not surprising that any unit root test will suffer from severe size distortions in that case. However, it has been found that size can be seriously inflated even for negative roots of moderate magnitude. Schwert (1989) found that the test with the least size distortion is the (Said–Dickey) t-test based on $t_{\hat{\rho}}$ obtained from a high order autoregression, but even for this test the size problem is not negligible. Moreover, even though long autoregressions may moderate the size problems, the use of a long autoregression typically leads to a nontrivial loss of power (for example, DeJong, Nankervis, Savin, and Whiteman, 1992a, 1992b).

Ng and Perron (1995, 2001) further scrutinized rules for truncating long autoregressions when performing unit root tests based on (7.7). Consider the information criterion

$$IC(k) = \log \tilde{\sigma}_k^2 + k C_T / T, \quad \tilde{\sigma}_k^2 = (T - k)^1 \sum_{t=k+1}^{T} \tilde{v}_{tk}^2, \qquad (7.10)$$

where $\{C_T\}$ is a positive sequence satisfying $C_T = o(T)$. The Akaike Information Criterion (AIC) sets $C_T = 2$, whereas the Schwartz or Bayesian Information Criterion (BIC) puts $C_T = \log T$. Ng and Perron (1995) found that, although these information criteria satisfy the requirement that $k = o(T^{1/3})$, generally models with too low a value of k are selected, with size distortions as a consequence. Ng and Perron (1995) also demonstrate that using a sequential data dependent procedure, where the significance of coefficients on additional lags are sequentially tested, will yield a test with improved size. However, a problem with the latter procedure is that in other cases the sequential test procedure tends to overparameterize, thereby resulting in a loss of power. More recently, Ng and Perron (2001) have developed an information criterion with a penalty function adequate for integrated time series. The idea is to select some lag order k in the interval between 0 and a preselected value k_{max}, where the upper bound k_{max} satisfies $k_{max} = o(T)$. Their preferred criterion, which can be interpreted as a modified form of the AIC, is given by

$$MAIC(k) = \log \breve{\sigma}_k^2 + 2(\tau_T(k) + k)/(T - k_{max}), \qquad (7.11)$$

where $\breve{\sigma}_k^2 = (T - k_{max})^{-1} \sum_{t=k_{max}+1}^{T} \tilde{v}_{tk}^2$ and $\tau_T(k) = \breve{\sigma}_k^2(\tilde{\rho} - 1)^2 \sum_{t=k_{max}+1}^{T} y_{t-1}^2$.[3]

It is interesting to observe that the penalty function of the modified criteria is data dependent, which is a way to account for the fact that the bias in the sum of the autoregressive coefficients (i.e., $\tilde{\rho} - 1$) is highly dependent upon the selected k. Even though Ng and Perron (2001) did not examine directly the effect on the size of the Said–Dickey test by using the above rules, simulation results in other contexts demonstrate that modified information criteria are superior to conventional information criteria in truncating long autoregressions with integrated variables when moving average errors are present.

In the implementation of the (Phillips–Perron) tests based on Z_ρ and Z_t, the estimator

$$\hat{\sigma}^2 = T^{-1} \sum_{t=2}^{T} \hat{u}_t^2, \quad \hat{u}_t = y_t - \hat{\rho} y_{t-1},$$

serves as a consistent estimator of σ^2. With respect to estimation of ω^2, a wide range of kernel estimators have considered. These kernel estimators are of the form

$$\hat{\omega}_{KER}^2 = T^{-1} \sum_{t=2}^{T} \hat{u}_t^2 + 2 \sum_{j=1}^{T-1} w(j/M_T) \left(T^{-1} \sum_{t=j+2}^{T} \hat{u}_t \hat{u}_{t-j} \right), \qquad (7.12)$$

where $w(\cdot)$ is some kernel (weight) function and M_T is a bandwidth parameter (see for example, Newey and West, 1987; Andrews, 1991).[4] The vast majority of unit root tests proposed in the literature use such kernel estimators of the long-run variance ω^2 to remove the influence of nuisance parameters in the asymptotic distributions. Notwithstanding, it has been shown by Perron and Ng (1996) that no spectral density estimator can completely eliminate size distortions and, in fact, kernel-based estimators tend to aggravate the size distortions.[5] This finding is due to the fact that estimation of ρ and ω^2 are coupled, in the sense that the least squares estimator $\hat{\rho}$ is used in constructing $\hat{u}_t$ and hence affects $\hat{\omega}_{KER}^2$. Because the least squares estimator $\hat{\rho}$ is well known to be seriously biased in finite (and even in large) samples when u_t exhibits strong serial correlation, the nuisance parameter estimator $\hat{\omega}_{KER}^2$ is expected to be very imprecise in critical regions of the serial correlation parameter space. A seemingly obvious way to alleviate this problem is to construct an estimator where residuals are calculated under the null hypothesis, i.e., by using Δ_{y_t} instead of $\hat{u}_t$ in (7.12), but it has been shown by Phillips and Ouliaris (1990) that this leads to inconsistent unit root tests.

To produce an estimator that is consistent under the unit root null whilst attenuating the dependence on $\hat{\rho}$, Perron and Ng (1996, 1998), following earlier work by Berk (1974) and Stock (1999), suggested using an autoregressive spectral density estimator based on estimation of the long autoregression (7.7):

$$\hat{\omega}_{AR}^2 = \frac{\tilde{\sigma}_k^2}{\left(1 - \sum_{j=1}^{k-1} \tilde{\gamma}_j\right)^2}, \tag{7.13}$$

where k is chosen according to one of the information criteria discussed above. The motivation for using the regression (7.7) to estimate $\sum_{j=1}^{k-1} \tilde{\gamma}_j$, rather than basing estimation on an autoregressive model in first differences (i.e., the model under the null), is that this ensures a consistent unit root test (e.g., Stock, 1999). The construction (7.13) decouples estimation of ω^2 from the estimation of ρ and, therefore, helps avoid the problems caused by the bias of ρ. In particular, $\hat{\omega}_{AR}^2$ is immune to potentially severe biases in $\hat{\rho}$ that are caused by the presence of serial correlation in the errors.

In a comparison of the size properties of the Phillips–Perron tests using the estimator $\hat{\omega}_{AR}^2$ and the tests using a Bartlett kernel estimator of ω^2, it was found that significant size improvements can be achieved in the most critical parameter space. Nevertheless, size distortions are still severe and remain so even if $\hat{\omega}_{AR}^2$ is replaced by the (unknown) true value ω^2 (Perron and Ng, 1996), a finding which indicates that biases in $\hat{\rho}$ are an important source of size distortions. The next subsection discusses developments that seek to obtain further improvements by addressing this issue.

7.2.3   Modified unit root tests with good size

Perron and Ng (1996) consider modified Phillips–Perron tests (referred to as M-tests in the following) that appear to have much improved size properties compared to any other unit root test. Moreover, the tests can be designed such that they satisfy desirable optimality criteria in terms of power; a topic which we will later return to. The tests belong to a class originally suggested by Stock (1999), which exploits the fact that a series converges at different rates under the null and the alternative hypotheses.

The first statistic reads

$$MZ_\rho = \frac{T^{-1} y_T^2 - \hat{\omega}_{AR}^2}{2T^{-2} \sum_{t=2}^{T} y_{t-1}^2}, \tag{7.14}$$

which can also be written in terms of Z_ρ as

$$MZ_\rho = Z_\rho + \frac{T}{2}(\hat{\rho} - 1)^2. \tag{7.15}$$

Because $\hat{\rho} - 1 = O_p(T^{-1})$ under the null (super consistency), it is seen that Z_ρ and MZ_ρ will be asymptotically equivalent (under the null), implying in particular that the limiting null distribution of MZ_ρ is the one given in (7.2).

The next statistic reads

$$MSB = \sqrt{\hat{\omega}_{AR}^{-2} T^{-2} \sum_{t=2}^{T} y_{t-1}^2},$$
(7.16)

which is stochastically bounded under the null and is $O_p(T^{-1})$ (and thus tends to zero) under fixed alternatives. This test is related to the Sargan and Bhargava (1983) test, hence the name, and critical values are reported by Stock (1999). Finally, because $Z_t = MSB \cdot Z_\rho$, a modified Phillips–Perron t test can be defined as

$$MZ_t = Z_t + \frac{1}{2} MSB \cdot (\hat{\rho} - 1)^2.$$
(7.17)

Even though $\hat{\rho}$ is superconsistent (under the null), implying that the correction terms associated with Z_ρ and Z_t are asymptotically negligible, it is still the case that the correction factors can be important even in moderately large samples, the reason being that $\hat{\rho}$ is severely biased in the presence of strong serial correlation. Simulation experiments reported in Perron and Ng (1996) show that the M-tests have impressively lower size distortion compared to other unit root tests that are available in the literature. However, it is essential that the autoregressive spectral density estimator $\hat{\omega}_{AR}^2$ is used as an estimator of ω^2 to decouple estimation of the unit root and the long-run variance for the tests to have good size properties. For instance, for an MA root of, e.g., -0.8, the actual size of the MZ_t test is about 6% at a nominal 5% level, whereas Phillips–Perron tests or modified Phillips–Perron tests using kernel estimates of ω^2 have size close to 100%.

The M-tests also appear to be robust to, e.g., measurement errors and additive outliers in the observed series. Franses and Haldrup (1994) and Haldrup, Montanés, and Sanso (2005) show that in these cases with data contamination, unit root inference using standard tests become seriously size affected. Vogelsang (1999) shows that the M-tests effectively solve these problems in terms of test size.[6]

7.2.4 Deterministics

In practical applications the underlying model will also contain deterministic components. These can be accommodated by generalizing (7.4) to a components representation of the form

$$y_t = \mu_t + z_t, \quad z_t = \rho z_{t-1} + u_t,$$
(7.18)

where $z_0 = 0$, u_t is as in (7.4), and μ_t is a deterministic component. Most of the specifications of μ_t used in applications are linear-in-parameters specifications of the form

$$\mu_t = d_t' \beta,$$
(7.19)

where d_t are known k-vectors of deterministic terms (for some $k \geq 1$), while β are k-vectors of unknown parameters. The leading special cases of linear-in-parameters specifications are the constant mean and linear trend specifications, in which $d_t = 1$ and $d_t = (1,t)'$, respectively.[7]

Appropriate detrending of the data is needed if one tests the unit root hypothesis against a trend stationary alternative (i.e., $\rho < 1$ in (7.18) and $d_t = (1,t)'$ in (7.19)). Specifically, the Dickey–Fuller (or Said–Dickey) regressions should take the alternative form

$$y_t = \tilde{\mu}_t + \tilde{\rho}y_{t-1} + \sum_{j=1}^{k-1} \tilde{\gamma}_j \Delta y_{t-j} + \tilde{v}_{tk}. \tag{7.20}$$

Appropriate treatment of deterministics is extremely important. For instance, failure to include a time trend regressor in the auxiliary regression when power against the trend stationary alternative is wanted will lead to a test with zero asymptotic power. Similarly, the Phillips–Perron class of tests allow inclusion of deterministic components or, alternatively, detrending of the series prior to unit root testing can be done. For all cases where the model is augmented with deterministics the relevant distributions change accordingly, as Brownian motion processes are replaced with demeaned and detrended Brownian motions of the form

$$W^d(r) = W(r) - D(r)' \left(\int_0^1 D(s)D(s)'ds \right)^{-1} \left(\int_0^1 D(s)W(s)ds \right), \tag{7.21}$$

where $D(r) = 1$ when $d_t = 1$ and $D(r) = (1,r)$ when $d_t = (1,t)'$.

With respect to the M-tests of the previous subsection, Ng and Perron (2001) suggest an alternative way of dealing with deterministics. The alternative detrending method, local *GLS* detrending, is in the spirit of Elliott, Rothenberg, Stock (1996) and has the advantage of yielding tests that are "nearly" efficient, in the sense that they nearly achieve the asymptotic power envelopes for unit root tests. (A discussion of these power envelopes will be provided in section 7.3.) The *GLS* detrending method can be described as follows. For any series $\{x_t\}_{t=1}^T$ of length T and any constant $\bar{c}$, define $x^{\bar{c}} = (x_1, \Delta x_2 - \bar{c}, T^{-1}x_1 \ldots, \Delta x_T - \bar{c}T^{-1}x_{T-1})'$. The *GLS* detrended series $\{\tilde{y}_t\}$ is given by

$$\tilde{y}_t = y_t - d_t'\tilde{\beta}, \quad \tilde{\beta} = \arg \min_{\beta} (y^{\bar{c}} - d^{\bar{c}'}\beta)'(y^{\bar{c}} - d^{\bar{c}'}\beta).$$

Elliott, Rothenberg, Stock (1996) suggested $\bar{c} = -7$ and $\bar{c} = -13.5$ for $d_t = 1$ and $d_t = (1,t)'$, respectively, as these values of $\bar{c}$ correspond to the local alternatives against which the local asymptotic power envelope for 5 percent tests equals 50 percent. The M-tests constructed using *GLS* detrended data (and using $\hat{\omega}_{AR}^2$ together with the modified information criteria of Section 7.2.2) are denoted, respectively, MZ_ρ^{GLS}, MSB^{GLS}, and MZ_t^{GLS}. These tests are shown by Ng and Perron (2001) to have excellent size and local asymptotic power.

In conclusion, unit root tests can be constructed with both excellent size and local asymptotic power properties, but to achieve these dual objectives it is necessary to use *GLS* detrended data.

7.3 Power envelopes for unit root tests

This section discusses power envelopes (efficiency bounds) for tests of the unit root hypothesis. Power envelopes for unit root tests have proven to be useful for two reasons. First, being attainable upper bounds on power, they give an objective standard against which the power properties of any feasible unit root test can be compared. For instance, the fact that the M-tests discussed in the previous section have local asymptotic power "close" to the appropriate power envelopes (Ng and Perron, 2001) implies that these are "nearly" efficient. Second, the derivation of power envelopes is useful because it suggests how admissible unit root tests with good overall power properties can be constructed. Indeed, the GLS detrending method, which is the key to accommodating deterministic components without sacrificing efficiency, is a natural by-product of the derivation of the power envelope in the presence of deterministic components (Elliott, Rothenberg, and Stock, 1996).

7.3.1 The leading special case

A natural starting point for the discussion of power envelopes for unit root tests is the known-variance, zero-mean Gaussian AR(1) model.[8] In this model, the observed data $\{y_t : t = 1, \ldots, T\}$ is generated as

$$y_t = \rho y_{t-1} + \varepsilon_t, \tag{7.22}$$

where $y_0 = 0$ and $\varepsilon_t \sim i.i.d.\ \mathcal{N}(0, 1)$.

Any (possibly randomized) unit root test can be represented by means of a test function $\phi_T : \mathbb{R}^T \to [0, 1]$, such that H_0, the unit root hypothesis, is rejected with probability $\phi_T(Y)$ if $Y_T = (y_1, \ldots, y_T)' = Y$. The power (function) associated with $\phi_T(\cdot)$ is given by $E_\rho \phi_T (Y_T)$, where the subscript on "E" indicates the distribution with respect to which the expectation is taken (i.e., the argument of the power function).

When evaluating the power properties of a unit root test, a power envelope is very useful. By definition, a power envelope for a class of unit root tests gives an attainable upper bound on $E_\rho \phi_T (Y_T)$ for tests in the class. Throughout this section, the class of tests under consideration will be the class of tests of (asymptotic) size α or some subset thereof. The power envelope for size α tests is the function $\Pi_T^\alpha(\cdot)$ given by[9]

$$\Pi_T^\alpha(\rho) = \max_{\phi_T(\cdot):E_1\phi_T(Y_T)=\alpha} E_\rho \phi_T(Y_T). \tag{7.23}$$

By construction, $\Pi_T^\alpha(\rho)$ is an upper bound on $E_\rho \phi_T(Y_T)$ for test functions $\phi_T(\cdot)$ associated with tests of size α. Moreover, the power envelope is attainable (pointwise) in the sense that, for every ρ, $E_\rho \phi_T(Y_T) = \Pi_T^\alpha(\rho)$ for some $\phi_T(\cdot)$ corresponding to a test of size α.

There is a simple and constructive way to derive the power envelope. For the known-variance, zero-mean Gaussian AR (1) model, the log likelihood function, $L_T(\cdot)$, satisfies the relation

$$L_T(\rho) - L_T(1) = T(\rho - 1)S_T - \frac{1}{2}[T(\rho - 1)]^2 H_T, \qquad (7.24)$$

where $S_T = T^{-1}\sum_{t=2}^{T} y_{t-1}\Delta y_t$ and $H_T = T^{-2}\sum_{t=2}^{T} y_{t-1}^2$. An application of the Neyman–Pearson lemma (e.g., Lehmann, 1994, Theorem 3.1) therefore yields

$$\Pi_T^\alpha(\rho) = \mathrm{Pr}_\rho\left[T(\rho - 1)S_T - \frac{1}{2}[T(\rho - 1)]^2 H_T > k_T^\alpha(\rho)\right], \qquad (7.25)$$

where $k_T^\alpha(\rho)$ satisfies $\mathrm{Pr}_1\left[T(\rho - 1)S_T - \frac{1}{2}[T(\rho - 1)]^2 H_T > k_T^\alpha(\rho)\right] = \alpha$ and the subscript on "Pr" indicates the distribution with respect to which the probability is evaluated.

In addition to providing a formula for computing the power envelope, expression (7.25) delivers a characterization of the test that attains the power envelope at any given value of ρ. Specifically, it follows from (7.25) that the power envelope $\Pi_T^\alpha(\rho)$ is attained by the test which rejects for large values of $T(\rho - 1)S_T - \frac{1}{2}[T(\rho - 1)]^2 H_T$. Because the functional form of the optimal test against any specific alternative $\rho < 1$ depends on ρ, the unit root testing problem does not admit a uniformly most powerful (UMP) size α test, in spite of the fact that it is a one-sided testing problem without any nuisance parameters.

Applying the preceding arguments to other simple hypotheses on ρ, it can be verified that non-existence of a UMP size α test is a property shared by all one-sided hypothesis tests on the autoregressive coefficient ρ in (7.22). In other words, the nonexistence of a UMP size α test is not specific to the unit root hypothesis. What is somewhat special about the unit root hypothesis is the fact that non-existence of a UMP size α test holds even asymptotically.[10]

By analogy with the finite sample situation, the asymptotic power envelope for a class of (sequences of) unit root tests gives an attainable upper bound on local asymptotic power for (sequences of) tests in the class. Assuming the limit exists, the local asymptotic power function of a sequence $\{\phi_T(\cdot)\}$ of unit root tests is the function (with argument $c \leq 0$) $\lim_{T\to\infty} E_{1+T^{-1}c}\phi_T(Y_T)$.[11] A sequence $\{\phi_T(\cdot)\}$ of unit root tests is said to have asymptotic size α if $\lim_{T\to\infty} E_1\phi_T(Y_T) = \alpha$. The asymptotic power envelope for tests asymptotically of size α is the function $\Pi_\infty^\alpha(\cdot)$ given by

$$\Pi_\infty^\alpha(c) = \max_{\{\phi_T(\cdot):\lim_{T\to\infty} E_1\phi_T(Y_T)=\alpha\}} \overline{\lim}_{T\to\infty} E_{1+T^{-1}c}\phi_T(Y_T). \qquad (7.26)$$

An explicit formula for the asymptotic power envelope is available. Because the optimal unit root test against the alternative $\rho = 1 + T^{-1}c$ rejects for large values of $cS_T - \frac{1}{2}c^2 H_T$, it stands to reason that the asymptotic power envelope $\Phi_\infty^\alpha(c)$ is attained by the sequence of tests with rejection regions of the form $\{cS_T - \frac{1}{2}c^2 H_T > k_\infty^\alpha(c)\}$, where $k_\infty^\alpha(c)$ is such that the sequence has asymptotic size α.

Indeed, it can be shown that

$$\Pi_\infty^\alpha(c) = \lim_{T\to\infty} \Pr_{1+T^{-1}c}\left[cS_T - \frac{1}{2}c^2H_T > k_\infty^\alpha(c)\right]$$

$$= \Pr\left[c\int_0^1 W_c(r)dW(r) + \frac{1}{2}c^2\int_0^1 W_c(r)^2dr > k_\infty^\alpha(c)\right],$$

(7.27)

where $k_\infty^\alpha(c)$ satisfies $\Pr\left[c\int_0^1 W(r)dW(r) - \frac{1}{2}c^2\int_0^1 W(r)^2dr > k_\infty^\alpha(c)\right] = \alpha$, W is a Wiener process, and W_c is an Ornstein–Uhlenbeck process satisfying the stochastic differential equation $dW_c(r) = cW_c(r)dr + dW(r)$ with initial condition $W_c(0) = 0$.[12]

As is true of its finite sample counterpart, the asymptotic power envelope can only be attained pointwise. In other words, there does not exist a sequence of tests (asymptotically of size α) which attains $\Pi_\infty^\alpha(c)$ for all values of c. In the absence of a UMP test, it seems natural to try to derive tests enjoying weaker optimality properties in the hope that these tests will have good overall power properties. Two complementary notions of optimality, local optimality and point optimality, have been employed to derive unit root tests with demonstrable optimality properties. The notion of local optimality leads to a test which maximizes (the scaled limit of) the derivative of the power function under the null hypothesis. For the unit root testing problem, the locally most powerful test rejects for small values of S_T.[13] Although admissible, the locally most powerful unit root test turns out to have pretty poor local asymptotic power properties (Stock, 1994). In contrast, the notion of point optimality has been found to deliver (admissible) unit root tests with excellent power properties.

By definition, a point optimal unit root test maximizes power against a specific (point) alternative (e.g., King, 1988).[14] The family of point optimal unit root tests is obtained as a by-product of the power envelope. It consists of all tests with rejection regions of the form $\{cS_T - \frac{1}{2}c^2H_T > k_\infty^\alpha(c)\}$ where c indexes the local alternative against which optimal power is desired. Elliott, Rothenberg, and Stock (1996) found that point optimal unit root tests have local asymptotic power functions essentially identical to the power envelope for a wide range of values of the index c. A popular choice, advocated in the unit root context by Elliott, Rothenberg, and Stock (1996), is the value of c such that the asymptotic power envelope for 5 percent tests equals 50 percent when evaluated at c; that is, the recommended value of c solves the equation $\Pi_\infty^{0.05}(c) = 0.5$.

Numerous other unit root tests have been proposed (for a review, see Stock, 1994). The most well-known examples are probably the Dickey–Fuller (1979) tests (i.e., the tests based on $T(\hat{\rho}-1)$ and $t_{\hat{\rho}}$) and their asymptotic equivalents (e.g., the tests based on Z_ρ and Z_t discussed in section 7.2.1). In the case where the error variance is known to equal unity, a Dickey–Fuller type t-test rejects for small values of

$$\frac{\hat{\rho}-1}{1/\sqrt{\sum_{t=2}^T y_{t-1}^2}} = \frac{S_T}{\sqrt{H_T}}.$$

This test can be interpreted as a (signed) likelihood ratio test.[15] Moreover, the test has excellent local asymptotic power properties (Elliott, Rothenberg, and Stock, 1996). In spite of this, the test does not seem to enjoy any conventional optimality properties.[16] On the other hand, the Dickey–Fuller estimator test, which rejects for small values of $T(\hat{\rho} - 1) = S_T/H_T$, is a member of the class of point optimal tests and is therefore admissible (Stock, 1994).

Power envelopes have been derived for a variety of extensions of the basic model (7.22). The remainder of this section discusses five such extensions. These are all of practical and theoretical interest, the practical interest being due to the empirical relevance of the extensions. To simplify the exposition, we discuss each of the extensions in isolation, in each case studying a model which departs as little as possible from the known-variance, zero-mean Gaussian AR(1) model.

7.3.2 Serial correlation

This subsection discusses the impact of serial correlation on the form of the asymptotic power envelope. As was explained in section 7.2, the presence of serial correlation introduces nontrivial complications for practitioners wanting to employ unit root tests. In contrast, the presence of serial correlation has no impact on the asymptotic properties of the unit root testing problem, because the asymptotic power envelope (7.27) remains valid under rather general assumptions on the short-run temporal dependence properties of the quasi-difference process $\{y_t - \rho y_{t-1}\}$.

Consider the Gaussian variant of (7.4) in which

$$y_t = \rho y_{t-1} + u_t, \quad u_t = \psi(L)\varepsilon_t, \tag{7.28}$$

where $y_0 = 0$, $\varepsilon_t \sim i.i.d.\ \mathcal{N}(0, 1)$, and $\psi(L) = \sum_{j=0}^{\infty} \psi_j L^j$ is a lag polynomial whose (unknown) coefficients $\{\psi_j\}$ satisfy $\sum_{j=0}^{\infty} |\psi_j| < \infty$ and $\psi(e^{ir}) = \sum_{j=0}^{\infty} \psi_j e^{ir} \neq 0$ for all $r \in \mathbb{R}$

The construction of the asymptotic power envelope proceeds in two steps. In the first step, the Neyman–Pearson lemma is used to derive the asymptotic power envelope under the (counterfactual) assumption that $\{\psi_j\}$ is known. The second step then shows that this envelope is indeed the asymptotic power envelope for unit root tests in the model (7.28) by showing that the bound can be attained (pointwise) without knowledge of $\{\psi_j\}$.

For now, suppose the parameters $\{\psi_j\}$ are known. In that case, the derivation of an asymptotic power envelope is conceptually straightforward because ρ is the only parameter of the model. By the Neyman–Pearson lemma, the unit root test with optimal power against the local alternative $\rho = 1 + T^{-1}c$ rejects for large values of the log likelihood ratio $L_T^{\psi}(1 + T^{-1}c) - L_T^{\psi}(1)$, where $L_T^{\psi}(\cdot)$ is the log likelihood function. A slick derivation of the asymptotic power envelope can be based on the fact that

$$L_T^{\psi}(1 + T^{-1}c) - L_T^{\psi}(1) = cS_T^{\psi} - \frac{1}{2}c^2 H_T^{\psi} + o_p(1) \tag{7.29}$$

under the null hypothesis, where $S_T^\psi = \frac{1}{2}(\omega^{-2}T^{-1}y_T^2 - 1)$, $H_T^\psi = \omega^{-2}T^{-2}\sum_{t=2}^T y_{t-1}^2$, and $\omega^2 = \psi(1)^2$ is the long-run variance of $\psi(L)\varepsilon_t$.[17] Using the quadratic expansion (7.29) and the theory of limits of experiments (see, for example, Le Cam and Yang, 2000; van der Vaart, 1998), it can be shown that the asymptotic power envelope for size α tests is attained (at the point c) by the sequence of tests with rejection regions of the form $\{cS_T^\psi - \frac{1}{2}c^2H_T^\psi > k_\infty^{\alpha,\psi}(c)\}$, where $k_\infty^{\alpha,\psi}(c)$ is such that the sequence has asymptotic size α. Under the null and contiguous alternatives, the limiting distribution of (S_T^ψ, H_T^ψ) does not depend on $\{\psi_j\}$. By implication, the critical value function $k_\infty^{\alpha,\psi}(c)$ does not depend on $\{\psi_j\}$. More importantly, the asymptotic power envelope is invariant with respect to $\{\psi_j\}$ and is given by the function $\Pi_\infty^\alpha(\cdot)$ defined in (7.27).

To show that the upper bound $\Pi_\infty^\alpha(\cdot)$ constitutes the asymptotic power envelope for the model (7.28), it must be shown that $\Pi_\infty^\alpha(\cdot)$ is attainable without knowledge of $\{\psi_j\}$. To do so, it suffices to exhibit a pair $(\hat{S}_T^\psi, \hat{H}_T^\psi)$, computable without knowledge of $\{\psi_j\}$, such that $(\hat{S}_T^\psi, \hat{H}_T^\psi) = (S_T^\psi, H_T^\psi) + o_p(1)$ under the unit root hypothesis (irrespective of the value of $\{\psi_j\}$). (Assuming such a pair can be found, the test which rejects for large values of $c\hat{S}_T^\psi - \frac{1}{2}c^2\hat{H}_T^\psi$ will attain the asymptotic power envelope.) The asymptotic equivalence requirement is met by $\hat{S}_T^\psi = \frac{1}{2}(\hat{\omega}^{-2}T^{-1}y_T^2 - 1)$ and $\hat{H}_T^\psi = \hat{\omega}^{-2}T^{-2}\sum_{t=2}^T y_{t-1}^2$, where $\hat{\omega}^2$ is any consistent (under the unit root hypothesis) estimator of ω^2.[18]

7.3.3 Deterministics

Proceeding as in section 7.2.4, deterministic terms can be accommodated by extending the basic model (7.22) as follows:

$$y_t = \mu_t + z_t, \quad z_t = \rho z_{t-1} + \varepsilon_t, \tag{7.30}$$

where μ_t is an unknown deterministic component, $z_0 = 0$, and $\varepsilon_t \sim i.i.d.\ \mathcal{N}(0,1)$.

In this model, $\{\mu_t\}$ is a nuisance feature in the unit root testing problem. When deriving an asymptotic power envelope in the presence of $\{\mu_t\}$, it is tempting to try to employ the same strategy as in the previous subsection; that is, it is tempting to first derive the asymptotic power envelope assuming $\{\mu_t\}$ is known and then attempt to find a feasible test which attains the bound obtained under the assumption that $\{\mu_t\}$ is known. That method of construction breaks down in general, however. On the one hand, because $z_t = y_t - \mu_t$ is generated by the model of section 7.3.1, it is obvious that the asymptotic power envelope is given by the function $\Pi_\infty^\alpha(\cdot)$ (defined in (7.27)) when $\{\mu_t\}$ is known. On the other hand, for many specifications of $\{\mu_t\}$ used in practice, it turns out to be impossible to find tests that attain $\Pi_\infty^\alpha(\cdot)$ without knowledge of $\{\mu_t\}$.

When $\mu_t = d_t'\beta$ (i.e., μ_t is of the linear-in-parameters form (7.19)), the principle of invariance (e.g., Lehmann, 1994, chapter 6) can be employed to eliminate the deterministic component from the unit root testing problem. Any testing problem regarding ρ is invariant under transformations of the form $g_b(y_1, \ldots, y_T) = (y_1 + d_1'b, \ldots, y_T + d_T'b)$ (where $b \in \mathbb{R}^k$), the induced transformation in the parameter space being $\bar{g}_b(\rho, \beta) = (\rho, \beta + b)$. When β is treated as an unknown nuisance parameter, it therefore seems natural to restrict attention to unit root tests that are invariant in the sense that their test functions $\phi_T(\cdot)$ satisfy $\phi_T(y_1 + d_1'b, \ldots, y_T + d_T'b) = \phi_T(y_1, \ldots, y_T)$ for every $b \in \mathbb{R}^k$. In other words, a test is invariant if the conclusion drawn by the test depends on the observed data $\{y_t\}$ only through the unobserved series $\{z_t\}$. As a consequence, an invariant test has a test function whose distribution depends only on ρ.[19] Therefore, reduction by invariance eliminates the nuisance parameter β from the unit root testing problem, thereby making it possible to obtain power envelopes by means of the Neyman–Pearson lemma. Drawing on the work of King (1980) and King and Hillier (1985), Dufour and King (1991) used this insight to obtain point optimal invariant tests of simple hypotheses on ρ in the AR(1) model (7.30). Asymptotic power envelopes were obtained (in a model accommodating serial correlation) for the unit root testing problem by Elliott, Rothenberg, and Stock (1996) in the case where d_t is a polynomial trend term. The functional form of the asymptotic power envelope depends on the order of the polynomial trend. It is given by $\Pi_\infty^z(\cdot)$ in the constant mean case, but not otherwise.

As was true in the model without deterministic components, the derivation of the asymptotic power envelopes in model (7.30) is constructive in the sense that tests attaining the asymptotic power envelope are obtained as a by-product. The optimal invariant test against the local alternative $\rho = 1 + T^{-1}c$ rejects for large values of the profile log likelihood ratio $\max_\beta L_T(1 + T^{-1}c, \beta) - \max_\beta L_T(1, \beta)$, where $L_T(\cdot)$ is the log likelihood function. As in the model without deterministic components, no test attains the power envelope uniformly but appropriately chosen point optimal invariant tests are "nearly efficient" in the sense that their local asymptotic power functions are "close" to the asymptotic power envelopes (Elliott, Rothenberg, and Stock, 1996). This "near-efficiency" property is not shared by the popular Dickey–Fuller (1979) tests, whose local asymptotic power functions fall well short of the asymptotic power envelope. Nevertheless, the class of "nearly efficient" invariant unit root tests contains tests other than the point optimal tests obtained in the derivation of the asymptotic power envelope. Examples include the DF-GLS test of Elliott, Rothenberg, and Stock (1996) and Ng and Perron's (2001) M^{GLS} tests discussed in section 7.2.4. Consequently, the M^{GLS} tests have both excellent size properties and "nearly" optimal power properties.

In view of the inferiority of the Dickey–Fuller (1979) tests in the model (7.30), it would appear that practitioners ought to abandon the use of these tests. More recent research, examining the role of the initial condition y_0, has arrived at a slightly less drastic conclusion. A brief discussion of that literature is provided in the next subsection.

7.3.4 The initial condition

In the known-variance, zero-mean Gaussian AR (1) model of section 7.3.1, the (unobserved) initial observation y_0 is assumed to be equal to zero. Analogous assumptions are made in the models of sections 7.3.2 and 7.3.3. At first sight, these would appear to be innocuous normalizations because it is easy to show that the initial observation is asymptotically negligible whenever $T^{-1/2}y_0 = o_p(1)$, a condition that is also satisfied if y_0 is treated as a nuisance parameter (i.e., modeled as a constant) or modeled as a random variable with a fixed distribution. Now, if $\{y_t : 0 \leq t \leq T\}$ is generated by a stationary Gaussian AR(1) model with auto-regressive coefficient ρ and innovation variance equal to unity, the initial obser-vation will satisfy $y_0 \sim \mathcal{N}[0, 1/(1 - \rho^2)]$. In that case, the initial observation is not asymptotically negligible, the limiting distribution $T^{-1/2}y_0$ being $\mathcal{N}[0, 1/(-2c)]$ under local-to-unity asymptotics with $\rho = 1 + T^{-1}c$ for some $c < 0$. To the extent that stationarity is a plausible alternative to the unit root hypothesis, these con-siderations suggest that the role of the initial condition is worth investigating.

The role of the initial condition can be explored by means of the following stripped-down version of the model studied by Müller and Elliott (2003):

$$y_t = \mu + z_t, \quad z_t = \rho z_{t-1} + \varepsilon_t \tag{7.31}$$

where $\varepsilon_t \sim i.i.d.\ \mathcal{N}(0, 1)$ and $z_0 \sim \mathcal{N}(0, \kappa\sigma_0^2(\rho))$, where $\kappa \geq 0$ is a known constant, $\sigma_0^2(\rho) := 1(|\rho| < 1)/(1 - \rho^2)$, $1(\cdot)$ is the indicator function, and z_0 is independent of $\{\varepsilon_t\}$. The model (7.31) reduces to the model of section 7.3.3 when $\kappa = 0$. When $\kappa = 1$, in contrast, $\{z_t\}$ is generated by a stationary AR(1) whenever $|\rho| < 1$ and the model reduces to a special case of the model studied by Elliott (1999). Irrespective of the value of κ, the initial condition is $z_0 = 0$ under the unit root hypothesis. Due to the inclusion of the constant term μ, this assumption is simply a normalization.

The derivation of the asymptotic power envelope for the unit-root testing problem proceeds as in section 7.3.3. First, the principle of invariance can be employed to remove the nuisance parameter μ. Then, the Neyman–Pearson lemma can be used to characterize the functional form of point optimal invariant tests. The optimal invariant test against the local alternative $\rho = 1 + T^{-1}c$ rejects for large values of the profile log likelihood ratio $\max_\beta L_T^\kappa(1 + T^{-1}c, \beta) - \max_\beta L_T^\kappa(1, \beta)$, where $L_T^\kappa(\cdot)$ is the log likelihood function. The functional form of the point opti-mal tests and the shape of the asymptotic power envelope both depend on the value of the constant κ. Moreover, although the tests discussed in section 7.3.3 ("nearly efficient" when $\kappa = 0$ in the model considered here) are asymptotically similar for any value of κ, these tests have power well below the power envelopes corresponding to moderately large values of κ (Müller and Elliott, 2003).[20]

Müller and Elliott (2003) emphasize an alternative interpretation of the power envelopes discussed in the previous paragraph. If the initial condition z_0 is treated as an unknown nuisance parameter (as opposed to a random variable with a known distribution), the unit root testing problem is complicated by the presence of an unidentified nuisance parameter under the null hypothesis, the parameters μ and z_0 appearing in the likelihood only through their sum. Müller and Elliott (2003) deal with this problem by applying a weighted average power criterion in the spirit of Andrews and Ploberger (1994) when deriving asymptotic power envelopes. The weighting functions employed by Müller and Elliott (2003) cor-respond to the distributional assumption on z_0 made in (7.31) and give rise to the same asymptotic power envelopes.

In addition to deriving asymptotic power envelopes for the model (7.31), Müller and Elliott (2003) explore the extent to which existing unit root tests can be "rationalized" as being point optimal tests in model (7.31) for appropriately selected values of the constant κ and the local-to-unity parameter c. They find that the tests proposed by Bhargava (1986) can be interpreted as (limiting versions of) point optimal tests in the model (7.31), as can the locally best invariant tests derived by Dufour and King (1991) and Nabeya and Tanaka (1990). Moreover, Müller and Elliott (2003) argue that, although the popular Dickey–Fuller (1979) tests cannot be "rationalized" in this way, there is a sense in which the Dickey–Fuller tests are well approximated by certain members of the class of point optimal tests in the model (7.31), albeit with rather large values of κ.

7.3.5 Non-Gaussian errors

All of the power envelopes discussed so far have been derived under the assumption that the latent errors $\{\varepsilon_t\}$ are (standard) normally distributed. Because the normality assumption is implausible in most empirical applications of unit root tests, it is of interest to develop asymptotic power envelopes for unit roots in (possibly) non-Gaussian environments.

Consider the model[21]

$$y_t = \rho y_{t-1} + \varepsilon_t, \tag{7.32}$$

where $y_0 = 0$ and $\{\varepsilon_t\}$ are *i.i.d.* errors from an unknown (possibly non-Gaussian) distribution with mean zero and variance one. The derivation of the asymptotic power envelope in section 7.3.1 made use of two results, the Neyman–Pearson lemma and the fact that

$$(S_T - cH_T, H_T) \to d_c\left(\int_0^1 W_c(r)dW(r), \int_0^1 W_c(r)^2 dr\right), \quad c \le 0.$$

The displayed convergence result, which was used to characterize the local asymptotic power of point optimal tests (derived by means of the Neyman–Pearson lemma), remains valid in the model (7.32). In other words, the limiting representation of (S_T, H_T), the minimal sufficient statistic under the assumption of normality, is invariant with respect to the distribution of $\{\varepsilon_t\}$ as long as $E(\varepsilon_t) = 0$ and $E(\varepsilon_t^2) = 1$.[22] By implication, the local asymptotic power function of the point optimal tests from section 7.3.1 does not depend on the distribution of $\{\varepsilon_t\}$ in the model (7.32). The Gaussian asymptotic power envelope of section 7.3.1 therefore gives a lower bound on maximal attainable local asymptotic power in the model (7.32).

An upper bound on the magnitude of the power gains available when the errors in the model (7.32) are non-Gaussian can be obtained by deriving the asymptotic power envelope under the (counterfactual) assumption that the underlying error distribution is known. Assuming the errors are generated by a continuous distribution with density $f(\cdot)$, it follows from the Neyman–Pearson lemma that the point optimal unit root test against the local alternative $\rho = 1 + T^{-1}c$ rejects for large values of the log likelihood ratio $L_T^f(1 + T^{-1}c) - L_T^f(1)$, where $L_T^f(\cdot)$ is the log likelihood function. Under appropriate smoothness conditions on $f(\cdot)$, the Neyman–Pearson test admits the following quadratic expansion under the unit root hypothesis:

$$L_T^f(1 + T^{-1}c) - L_T^f(1) = \sum_{t=2}^{T} \log f(\Delta y_t - cT^{-1}y_{t-1}) - \sum_{t=2}^{T} \log f(\Delta y_t) \qquad (7.33)$$

$$= cS_T^f - \tfrac{1}{2}c^2 H_T^f + o_p(1)$$

where $S_T^f = T^{-1}\sum_{t=2}^{T} y_{t-1}\ell_f(\Delta y_t)$, $H_T^f = \mathcal{I}_{ff}T^{-2}\sum_{t=2}^{T} y_{t-1}^2$, and $\ell_f(\cdot)$ is a function satisfying $E[\ell_f(\varepsilon_t)] = 0$, $E[\varepsilon_t\ell_f(\varepsilon_t)] = 1$, and $1 \leq \mathcal{I}_{ff} = E[\ell_f(\varepsilon_t)^2] < \infty$.

As the notation suggests, the function $\ell_f(\cdot)$ can be interpreted as a score function and $\mathcal{I}_{ff}$ is the associated Fisher information for location.[23] Jeganathan (1995) gives (absolute continuity and moment) conditions on $f(\cdot)$ under which (7.33) holds with $\ell_f(\varepsilon) = \partial \log f(\varepsilon - \theta)/\partial\theta|_{\theta=0}$, while Jansson (2005) shows that differentiability in quadratic mean, an even weaker condition, is sufficient. By implication, the expansion (7.33) is valid for a wide range of error distributions.

Using (7.33) and the theory of limits of experiments (e.g., Le Cam and Yang, 2000; van der Vaart, 1998), it can be shown that an upper bound on the local asymptotic power of a unit root test (asymptotically of size α) in the model (7.32) is given by the function (of $c \leq 0$)

$$\lim_{T\to\infty} \Pr_{1+T^{-1}c}\left[\mathcal{I}_{ff}^{-1}\left(cS_T^f - \frac{1}{2}c^2 H_T^f\right) > k_\infty^{\alpha,f}(c)\right]$$

$$= \Pr\left[c\mathcal{I}_{ff}^{-1/2}\int_0^1 W_c(r)dB_f(r) + \frac{1}{2}c^2 \int_0^1 W_c(r)^2 dr > k_\infty^{\alpha,f}(c)\right] \qquad (7.34)$$

where $k_\infty^{\alpha,f}(c)$ satisfies $\Pr\left[c\mathcal{I}_{ff}^{-1/2}\int_0^1 W(r)dB_f(r) - \frac{1}{2}c^2\int_0^1 W(r)^2 dr > k_\infty^{\alpha,f}(c)\right] = \alpha$, W and B_f are correlated Wiener processes with coefficient of correlation $\mathcal{I}_{ff}^{-1/2}$, and W_c satisfies the stochastic differential equation $dW_c(r) = cW_c(r)dr + dW(r)$ with initial condition $W_c(0) = 0$.

The upper bound (7.34) depends on the density $f(\cdot)$ through $\mathcal{I}_{ff}$, which equals one when the error ε_t is perfectly correlated with $\ell_f(\varepsilon_t)$ and is strictly greater than one otherwise.[24] Rothenberg and Stock (1997) evaluated (7.34) for various values of $\mathcal{I}_{ff}$ and found large increases in power as $\mathcal{I}_{ff}$ increased. Although this result suggests that non-normality may be an important source of power in unit root testing, a potential problem with the result is that it is derived under the counterfactual assumption the $f(\cdot)$ is known. The upper bound (7.34) is attained by the test which rejects for large values of $cS_T^f - \frac{1}{2}c^2 H_T^f$. Following Jansson (2005), adaptation is said to be possible if there exists a pair $(\hat{S}_T^f, \hat{H}_T^f)$, computable without knowledge of $f(\cdot)$, such that $(\hat{S}_T^f, \hat{H}_T^f) = (S_T^f, H_T^f) + o_p(1)$ under the unit root hypothesis. (If adaptation is possible, then the power envelope (7.34) is attained by the test which rejects for large values of $c\hat{S}_T^f - \frac{1}{2}c^2\hat{H}_T^f$.) Jansson (2005) shows that adaptation is possible when $f(\cdot)$ is known to be symmetric, but not in general.

Section 7.3.6, the final subsection of this section, discusses a source of nontrivial power gains which is available in many cases.

7.3.6   Covariates

In most applications of unit root tests, the series $\{y_t\}$ being tested for a unit root is not observed in isolation. Instead, one typically observes at least one time series, say $\{x_t\}$, in addition to the time series $\{y_t\}$ of interest. As observed by Hansen (1995), the additional time series $\{x_t\}$ contains exploitable information about $\{y_t\}$ whenever its order of integration is known.[25]

As in section 7.3.1, suppose $\{y_t\}$ is generated by the model

$$y_t = \rho y_{t-1} + \varepsilon_t, \tag{7.35}$$

where $y_0 = 0$ and $\varepsilon_t \sim i.i.d.\ \mathcal{N}(0, 1)$. To accommodate a covariate with a known order of integration, suppose an additional time series $\{x_t : 1 \leq t \leq T\}$ is observed whose generating mechanism is

$$\begin{pmatrix} \varepsilon_t \\ x_t \end{pmatrix} \sim i.i.d.\ \mathcal{N}\left(\begin{pmatrix} 0 \\ 0 \end{pmatrix}, \begin{pmatrix} 1 & \delta \\ \delta & 1 \end{pmatrix} \right), \tag{7.36}$$

where δ is known (and satisfies $|\delta| < 1$).

The log likelihood function $L_T^\delta(\cdot)$ associated with the model (7.35)–(7.36) satisfies the relation

$$L_T^\delta(1 + T^{-1}c) - L_T^\delta(1) = cS_T^\delta - \frac{1}{2}c^2 H_T^\delta, \tag{7.37}$$

where $S_T^\delta = T^{-1}\sum_{t=2}^{T} y_{t-1}(\Delta y_t - \delta x_t)$ and $H_T^\delta = T^{-2}\sum_{t=2}^{T} y_{t-1}^2$. By the Neyman–Pearson lemma, the test which rejects for large values of $cS_T^\delta - \frac{1}{2}c^2 H_T^\delta$ is the point optimal unit root test against the local alternative $\rho = 1 + T^{-1}c$. Unless $\{x_t\}$ is independent of $\{y_t\}$ (in which case δ equals zero), this point optimal test makes use of the information in $\{x_t\}$. By implication, the stationary covariate $\{x_t\}$ contains exploitable information about ρ unless it is independent of $\{y_t\}$.

The magnitude of the gains in local asymptotic power achievable by exploiting the information in the covariate $\{x_t\}$ can be evaluated by deriving the asymptotic power envelope for the model (7.35)–(7.36). The asymptotic power envelope (for unit root tests asymptotically of size α) is given by the function

$$\lim_{T \to \infty} \Pr_{1+T^{-1}c}\left[cS_T^\delta - \frac{1}{2}c^2 H_T^\delta > \kappa_\infty^{\alpha,\,\delta}(c) \right]$$

$$= \Pr\left[c\sqrt{1-\delta^2} \int_0^1 W_c(r)dV(r) + \frac{1}{2}c^2 \int_0^1 W_c(r)^2 dr > \kappa_\infty^{\alpha,\,\delta}(c) \right], \tag{7.38}$$

where $\kappa_\infty^{\alpha,\,\delta}(c)$ satisfies $\Pr[c\sqrt{1-\delta^2}\int_0^1 W(r)dV(r) - \frac{1}{2}c^2 \int_0^1 W(r)^2 dr > \kappa_\infty^{\alpha,\,\delta}(c)] = \alpha$ W and V are correlated Wiener processes with coefficient of correlation $\sqrt{1-\delta^2}$, and W_c satisfies the stochastic differential equation $dW_c(r) = cW_c(r)dr + dW(r)$ with initial condition $W_c(0) = 0$. The functional form of the power envelope (7.38) is exactly the same as the functional form of the (infeasible) power envelope (7.34) associated with (known) non-Gaussian error distributions, the quantity $\sqrt{1 - \delta^2}$ playing the same role here as $\mathcal{I}_{ff}^{-1/2}$ did there. As a consequence, appreciable power gains are available whenever "good" covariates (having δ^2 moderately large) can be found.

The asymptotic power envelope (7.38) was derived by Hansen (1995). In addition to (implicitly) proposing a family of point optimal tests, Hansen (1995) proposed a regression-based unit root test, the covariate augmented Dickey–Fuller (CADF) test. The CADF test is "nearly efficient" in the model (7.35)–(7.36). If the model is extended to include deterministic components, however, the local asymptotic power of the CADF test is well below the asymptotic power envelope for invariant tests (Elliott and Jansson, 2003). In contrast, the point optimal tests of Elliott and Jansson (2003) are "nearly efficient" in the presence of deterministic components.

7.4 Conclusion

This chapter has reviewed recent advances in the literature on unit root testing, emphasizing developments aimed at reducing size distortions and/or boosting the power of unit root tests. As should be apparent from the discussion herein, significant advances in both directions have been made during the decade since the publication of Stock (1994). The literature now seems to have reached a relatively mature state and it is difficult to predict if any major advances will occur over the next decade. Nevertheless, it seems worth pointing out two potential shortcomings of the existing body of knowledge. In relation to the first of the two main themes of the present survey, size distortions, it remains an open question whether the use of refined asymptotic approximations can enhance the theoretical understanding of the properties of the bootstrap and/or guide the choice among asymptotically equivalent testing procedures. On the power front, it would appear to be useful to further investigate the extent to which non-Gaussianity and/or extraneous information (other than information about the integration properties of observed covariates, as in section 7.3.6) can be an exploitable source of power in unit root testing applications.

Acknowledgments

The authors thank Terence Mills, Serena Ng, Pierre Perron and Rob Taylor for comments and suggestions.

Notes

1. Under the stated assumptions regarding u_t, the long-run variance ω^2 equals $2\pi f_u(0)$, where $f_u(\cdot)$ is the spectral density of u_t.

2. As shown by Chang and Park (2002), the ARMA (p, q) assumption on u_t can actually be replaced by the weaker assumption that $\sum_{j=0}^{\infty} \psi_j z^j \neq 0$ for every $|z| \leq 1$ (and $\sum_{j=0}^{\infty} j |\psi_j| < \infty$).

3. A similarly modified form of the BIC is

$$MBIC(k) = \log \tilde{\sigma}_k^2 + \log(T - k_{\max})(\tau_T(k) + k)/(T - k_{\max}).$$

4. When $\{y_t\}$ is generated by (7.4), the estimator $\hat{\omega}_{KER}^2$ is consistent if $M_T^{-1} + T^{-1/2} M_T = o(1)$ and $\omega(\cdot)$ satisfies the conditions of Jansson (2002).

5. Also, Kim and Schmidt (1990) demonstrate, by means of Monte Carlo simulations, that a range of different kernel estimators and different ways of selecting the bandwidth parameter seem to deliver unit root tests with fairly similar finite sample properties.

6. Haldrup, Montanés, and Sanso (2005) show that the presence of additive and other types of outliers (as well as measurement errors) has implications for the (moving average) serial correlation structure of the data, so Vogelsangs's (1996) results are consistent with Perron and Ng's (1996) Monte Carlo results on the behavior of the M-tests in the presence of MA errors.

7. The class of linear-in-parameters specifications also includes structural break models with a known break date. In contrast, structural break models with an unknown break date do not belong to the class of linear-in-parameters specifications. For a survey of structural break models, see Perron (2005).

8. The following discussion draws on Stock (1994).

9. More generally, the power envelope for a class Φ_T of tests functions is given by $\sup_{\phi_T \in \Phi_T} E_\rho \phi_T(Y_T)$. In (7.23), "sup" has been replaced with "max" in recognition of the fact that the sup is attained.

10. It follows from (7.24) and the properties of exponential families (e.g., Lehmann, 1994) that the model admits a two-dimensional minimal sufficient statistic whose distribution belongs to a curved exponential family (Efron, 1975). Therefore, the functional form of a most powerful test of a simple null against a simple alternative in the known-variance, zero-mean Gaussian AR(1) model depends on the alternative, implying in that one-sided testing problems do not admit UMP size α tests. The limiting experiment associated with a simple null hypothesis on ρ with $|\rho| < 1$ corresponds to a full exponential family model (the log likelihood ratios are locally asymptotically normal (Le Cam, 1960) and therefore admits a UMP size α test. In contrast, the limiting experiment associated with the unit root hypothesis corresponds to a curved exponential family model (the log likelihood ratios are locally asymptotically quadratic (Jeganathan, 1995), but not locally asymptotically (mixed) normal) and does not admit a UMP size α test.

11. For details on local asymptotic power and local-to-unity asymptotics, see Stock (1994) and the references therein [e.g., Chan Wei (1987) and Phillips (1987b)].

12. A proof of (7.27) can be based on the inequality

$$E_{1+T^{-1}c} \phi_T(Y_T) \leq \Pr\left[cS_T - \frac{1}{2} c^2 H_T > k_T^{\alpha T}(1 + T^{-1}c)\right], \quad \alpha_T = E_1 \phi_T(Y_T),$$

and the fact that $(S_T - cH_T, H_T) \to_{d_c} (\int_0^1 W_c(r) dW(r), \int_0^1 W_c(r)^2 dr)$, where $\to_{d_c}$ signifies convergence in distribution when $\rho = 1 + T^{-1}c$.

13. Local optimality of S_T follows from a Neyman–Pearson argument and the fact that

$$\frac{d}{dc} E_{1+T^{-1}c} \phi_T(Y_T)\Big|_{c=0} = T^{-1} \frac{d}{d\rho} E_\rho \phi_T(Y_T)\Big|_{\rho=1} = E_1[S_T \phi_T(Y_T)]$$

for any test function $\phi_T(\cdot)$.

14. Following Davies (1969), point optimal testing procedures are sometimes referred to as beta-optimal testing procedures.
15. The (signed) likelihood ratio test rejects for large values of

$$\max_{\rho \leq 1} L_T(\rho) - L_T(1) = \frac{\min(S_T, 0)^2}{2H_T},$$

a decreasing function of $S_T/\sqrt{H_T}$.
16. In fact, it appears to be unknown if the Dickey–Fuller (1979) t-test is even admissible, in the sense that there does not exists a unit root test with uniformly superior local asymptotic power. Studying a general class of models with locally asymptotically quadratic log likelihood ratios, Ploberger (2004) gives a complete class result for a two-sided testing problem and shows that the likelihood ratio test is not a member of his (essentially) complete class of tests.
17. Elliott, Rothenberg, and Stock (1992) obtained the expansion (7.29) under the assumption that $\{y_t\}$ is generated by a Gaussian AR model of finite order. Using ingenious arguments, Elliott Rothenberg Stock (1996) established (7.29) for model (7.28) under the additional assumption that $\sum_{j=1}^{\infty} j|\psi_j| < \infty$. The latter assumption can be removed by using a slightly modified version of the proof employed by Elliott, Rothenberg, and Stock (1996).
18. The existence of such estimators follows from Jansson (2002) who shows that standard kernel estimators of ω^2 [e.g., Newey West (1987), Andrews (1991)] are consistent under the assumptions of this subsection.
19. A formal proof of this claim can be based on Lehmann (1994, Theorem 6.3) and the fact that ρ is a maximal invariant under the group of transformations of the form $\bar{g}_b(\rho, \beta)$, where $b \in \mathbb{R}^k$.
20. Asymptotic similarity of the tests discussed in section 7.3.3 follows from the fact that the null distribution of $\{y_t\}$ does not depend on κ. The same fact implies that the test which rejects for large values of $\max_{\beta} L_T^{\kappa}(1 + T^{-1}c, \beta) - \max_{\beta} L_T^{\kappa}(1, \beta)$ is a point optimal unit root test even if κ is treated as an unknown nuisance parameter. By implication, the power envelope for the model in which κ is treated as an unknown nuisance parameter coincides with the family (indexed by κ) of power envelopes derived under the assumption that κ is a known constant.
21. The following discussion draws on Jansson (2005).
22. This invariance result follows from Donsker's theorem (e.g., Billingsley, 1999) and the continuous mapping theorem.
23. Indeed, $\ell_f(\cdot)$ is the score function, evaluated at $\theta = 0$, of the location model $X_i = \theta + \varepsilon_i$, where the errors $\{\varepsilon_i\}$ are *i.i.d.* with density function $f(\cdot)$.
24. The correlation between ε_t and $\ell_f(\varepsilon_t)$ is unity when the underlying distribution is Gaussian, the score function of the standard normal location model being $\ell_f(\varepsilon) = \varepsilon$.
25. An important example of a unit root testing problem in which a covariate with a known order of integration is observed is the problem of testing for absence of cointegration when the (potentially) cointegrating vector is prespecified (Elliott, Jansson, and Pesavento, 2005; Zivot, 2000).

References

Agiakloglou, C. and P. Newbold (1992) Empirical evidence on Dickey–Fuller type tests. *Journal of Time Series Analysis* **13**, 471–83.

Andrews, D.W.K. (1991) Heteroskedasticity and autocorrelation consistent covariance matrix estimation. *Econometrica* **59**, 817–58.

Andrews D.W.K. and W. Ploberger (1994) Optimal tests when a nuisance parameter is present only under the alternative. *Econometrica* **62**, 1383–1414.

Baillie, R. (1996) Long memory processes and fractional integration in econometrics. *Journal of Econometrics* **73**, 6–59.

Berk, K.N. (1974) Consistent autoregressive spectral estimates. *Annals of Statistics* **2**, 489–502.

Bhargava, A. (1986) On the theory of testing for unit roots in observed time series. *Review of Economic Studies* **53**, 369–84.

Billingsley, P. (1999) *Convergence of Probability Measures*, 2nd edn. New York: Wiley.

Chan, N.H. and C.Z. Wei (1987) Asymptotic inference for nearly nonstationary AR(1) processes. *Annals of Statistics* **15**, 1050–1063.

Chang, Y. and J.Y. Park (2002) On the asymptotics of ADF tests for unit roots. *Econometric Reviews* **21**, 431–47.

Choi, I. (2006) Nonstationary panels. *Palgrave Handbooks of Econometrics*, vol. 1. Basingstoke: Palgrave Macmillan.

Davidson, R. and J. MacKinnon (2006) Bootstrap methods in econometrics. *Palgrave Handbooks of Econometrics*, vol. 1. Basingstoke: Palgrave Macmillan.

Davies, R.B. (1969) Beta-optimal tests and an application to the summary evaluation of experiments. *Journal of the Royal Statistical Society, Series B* **31**, 524–38.

DeJong, D., J. Nankervis, N. Savin and C. Whiteman (1992a) Integration versus trend-stationarity in macroeconomic time series. *Econometrica* **60**, 423–34.

DeJong, D., J. Nankervis, N. Savin and C. Whiteman (1992b) The power problems of unit root tests for time series with autoregressive errors. *Journal of Econometrics* **53**, 323–43.

Dickey, D.A. and W.A. Fuller (1979) Distribution of the estimators for autoregressive time series with a unit root. *Journal of the American Statistical Association* **74**, 427–31.

Dickey, D.A. and S.G. Pantula (1987) Determining the order of differencing in autoregressive processes. *Journal of Business and Economic Statistics* **5**, 455–61.

Dufour, J.-M. and M.L. King (1991) Optimal invariant tests for the autocorrelation coefficient in linear regressions with stationary or nonstationary AR(1) errors. *Journal of Econometrics* **47**, 115–43.

Efron, B. (1975) Defining the curvature of a statistical problem (with applications to second order efficiency). *Annals of Statistics* **3**, 1189–1242.

Elliott, G. (1999) Efficient tests for a unit root when the initial observation is drawn from its unconditional distribution. *International Economic Review* **40**, 767–83.

Elliott, G. and M. Jansson (2003) Testing for unit roots with stationary covariates. *Journal of Econometrics* **115**, 75–89.

Elliott, G., M. Jansson and E. Pesavento (2005) Optimal power for testing potential cointegrating vectors with known parameters for nonstationarity. *Journal of Business and Economic Statistics* **23**, 34–48.

Elliott, G., T.J. Rothenberg and J.H. Stock (1992) Efficient tests for an autoregressive unit root. NBER Technical Working Paper No. 130.

Elliott, G., T.J. Rothenberg and J.H. Stock (1996) Efficient tests for an autoregressive unit root. *Econometrica* **64**, 813–36.

Engle, R.F. and C.W.J. Granger (1987) Cointegration and error correction: representation, estimation, and testing. *Econometrica* **55**, 251–76.

Franses, P. (1996) *Periodicity and Stochastic Trends in Economic Time Series*. Oxford: Oxford University Press.

Franses, P.H. and N. Haldrup (1994) The effects of additive outliers on tests for unit roots and cointegration. *Journal of Business and Economic Statistics* **12**, 471–8.

Ghysels, E. and D. Osborn (2001) *The Econometric Analysis of Seasonal Time Series*. Cambridge, UK: Cambridge University Press.

Granger, C.W.J. (1981) Some properties of time series data and their use in econometric model specification. *Journal of Econometrics* **16**, 121–30.

Granger, C.W.J. and R. Joyeux (1980) An introduction to long memory time series models and fractional differencing. *Journal of Time Series Analysis* **1**, 15–29.

Haldrup, N. (1998) An econometric analysis of I(2) variables. *Journal of Economic Surveys* **12**, 595–650.

Haldrup, N., A. Montanés and A. Sanso (2005) Measurement errors and outliers in seasonal unit root testing. *Journal of Econometrics* **127**, 103–28.

Hansen, B.E. (1995) Rethinking the univariate approach to unit root testing: using covariates to increase power. *Econometric Theory* **11**, 1148–1171.

Hylleberg, S., R.F. Engle, C.W.J. Granger and B. Yoo (1990) Seasonal integration and cointegration. *Journal of Econometrics* **44**, 215–38.

Im, K.S., M.H. Pesaran and Y. Shin (2003) Testing for unit roots in heterogeneous panels. *Journal of Econometrics* **115**, 53–74.

Jansson, M. (2002) Consistent covariance matrix estimation for linear processes. *Econometric Theory* **18**, 1449–1459.

Jansson, M. (2004) Stationarity testing with covariates. *Econometric Theory* **20**, 56–94.

Jansson, M. (2005) Semiparametric power envelopes for tests of the unit root hypothesis. Manuscript, UC Berkeley.

Jeganathan, P. (1995) Some aspects of asymptotic theory with applications to time series models. *Econometric Theory* **11**, 818–87.

Kim, K. and P. Schmidt (1990) Some evidence on the accuracy of Phillips–Perron tests using alternative estimates of nuisance parameters. *Economics Letters* **34**, 345–50.

King, M.L. (1980) Robust tests for spherical symmetry and their application to least squares regression. *Annals of Statistics* **8**, 1265–1271.

King, M.L. (1988) Towards a theory of point optimal testing. *Econometric Reviews* **6**, 169–218.

King, M.L. and G.H. Hillier (1985) Locally best invariant tests of the error covariance matrix of the linear regression model. *Journal of the Royal Statistical Society, Series B*, **47**, 98–102.

Kwiatkowski D., P.C.B. Phillips, P. Schmidt and Y. Shin (1992) Testing the null hypothesis of stationarity against the alternative of a unit root: how sure are we that economic time series have a unit root? *Journal of Econometrics* **54**, 159–78.

Le Cam, L. (1960) Locally asymptotically normal families of distributions. *University of California Publications in Statistics* **3**, 37–98.

Le Cam, L. and G.L. Yang (2000) *Asymptotics in Statistics: Some Basic Concepts*, 2nd edn. New York: Springer-Verlag.

Lehmann, E.L. (1994) *Testing Statistical Hypotheses*, 2nd edn. New York: Chapman and Hall.

Levin, A., C.-F. Lin and C.-S.J. Chu (2002) Unit root tests in panel data: asymptotic and finite-sample properties. *Journal of Econometrics* **108**, 1–25.

Maddala, G. and I.M. Kim (1998) *Unit Roots, Cointegration and Structural Change*. Cambridge: Cambridge University Press.

Müller, U.K. and G. Elliott (2003) Tests for unit root and the initial condition. *Econometrica* **71**, 1269–1286.

Nabeya, S. and K. Tanaka (1990) Limiting power of unit-root tests in time-series regression. *Journal of Econometrics* **46**, 247–71.

Newey, W.K. and K.D. West (1987) A simple, positive semi-definite, heteroskedasticity and autocorrelation consistent covariance matrix. *Econometrica* **55**, 703–8.

Ng, S. and P. Perron (1995) Unit root tests is ARMA models with data-dependent methods for the selection of the truncation lag. *Journal of the American Statistical Association* **90**, 268–81.

Ng, S. and P. Perron (2001) Lag length selection and the construction of unit root tests with good size and power. *Econometrica* **69**, 1519–1554.

Paparoditis, E. and D.N. Politis (2003) Residual-based block bootstrap for unit root testing. *Econometrica* **71**, 813–55.

Park, J.Y. (2002) An invariance principle for sieve bootstrap in time series. *Econometric Theory* **18**, 469–90.

Park, J.Y. (2003) Bootstrap unit root tests. *Econometrica* **71**, 1845–1895.

Perron, P. (1989) The great crash, the oil price shock and the unit root hypothesis. *Econometrica* **57**, 1361–1401.

Perron, P. (2006) Dealing with structural breaks. *Palgrave Handbooks of Econometrics,* vol. 1. Basingstoke: Palgrave Macmillan.

Perron P. and S. Ng (1996) Useful modifications to unit root tests with dependent errors and their local asymptotic properties. *Review of Economic Studies* 63, 435–65.

Perron, P. and S. Ng (1998) An autoregressive spectral density estimator at frequency zero for nonstationarity tests. *Econometric Theory* 14, 560–603.

Phillips, P.C.B. (1987a) Time series regression with a unit root. *Econometrica* 55, 277–301.

Phillips, P.C.B. (1987b) Towards a unified asymptotic theory for autoregression. *Biometrika* 74, 535–47.

Phillips, P.C.B. and S. Ouliaris (1990) Asymptotic properties of residual based tests for cointegration. *Econometrica* 58, 165–93.

Phillips, P.C.B. and P. Perron (1988) Testing for a unit root in time series regression. *Biometrika* 75, 335–46.

Phillips, P.C.B. and Z. Xiao (1998) A primer on unit root testing. *Journal of Economic Surveys* 12, 423–69.

Ploberger, W. (2004) A complete class of tests when the likelihood is locally asymptotically quadratic. *Journal of Econometrics* 118, 67–94.

Rothenberg, T.J. and J.H. Stock (1997) Inference in a Nearly Integrated Autoregressive Model with Nonnormal Innovations. *Journal of Econometrics* 80, 269–86.

Said, S.E. and D.A. Dickey (1984) Testing for unit roots in autoregressive-moving average models of unknown order. *Biometrika* 71, 599–607.

Saikkonen, P. and R. Luukkonen (1993a) Point optimal tests for testing the order of differencing in ARIMA models. *Econometric Theory* 9, 343–62.

Saikkonen, P. and R. Luukkonen (1993b) Testing for a moving average unit root in autoregressive integrated moving average models. *Journal of the American Statistical Association* 88, 596–601.

Sargan, J. and A. Bhargava (1983) Testing for residuals from least squares regression being generated by Gaussian random walk. *Econometrica* 51, 153–74.

Schwert, G.W. (1989) Test for unit roots: a Monte Carlo investigation. *Journal of Business and Economic Statistics*, 7, 147–60.

Stock, J.H. (1994) Unit roots, structural breaks and trends. In R.F. Engle and D.L. McFadden (eds), *Handbook of Econometrics, Volume IV*. New York: North Holland, pp. 2739–2841.

Stock, J.H. (1999) A class of tests for integration and cointegration. In *Cointegration, Causality, and Forecasting: A Festschrift for Clive W.J. Granger*. Oxford: Oxford University Press, pp. 135–67.

van der Vaart, A.W. (1998) *Asymptotic Statistics*. Cambridge: Cambridge University Press.

Velasco, C. (2006) Semi-parametric estimation of long memory models. *Palgrave Handbooks of Econometrics*, vol. 1. Basingstoke: Palgrave Macmillan.

Vogelsang, T.J. (1999) Two simple procedures for testing for a unit root when there are additive outliers. *Journal of Time Series Analysis* 20, 237–52.

White, J.S. (1958) The limiting distribution of the serial correlation coefficient in the explosive case. *Annals of Mathematical Statistics* 29, 1188–1197.

Zivot, E. (2000) The power of single equation tests for cointegration when the cointegrating vector is prespecified. *Econometric Theory* 16, 407–39.

8
Dealing with Structural Breaks

Pierre Perron

Abstract

This chapter is concerned with methodological issues related to estimation, testing and computation in the context of structural changes in the linear model. A central theme of the review is the interplay between structural change and unit roots and on methods to distinguish between the two. The topics covered are: methods related to estimation and inference about break dates for single equations with or without restrictions, with extensions to multi-equations systems where allowance is also made for changes in the variability of the shocks; tests for structural changes including tests for a single or multiple changes and tests valid with unit root or trending regressors, and tests for changes in the trend function of a series that can be integrated or trend-stationary; testing for a unit root versus trend-stationarity in the presence of structural changes in the trend function; testing for cointegration in the presence of structural changes; and issues related to long memory and level shifts. Our focus is on the conceptual issues about the frameworks adopted and the assumptions imposed as they relate to potential applicability. We also highlight the potential problems that can occur with methods that are commonly used and recent work that has been done to overcome them.

8.1	Introduction	279
8.2	Introductory historical notes	281
8.3	Estimation and inference about break dates	285
	8.3.1 The assumptions and their relevance	286
	8.3.2 Allowing for restrictions on the parameters	289
	8.3.3 Methods to compute global minimizers	290
	8.3.4 The limit distribution of the estimates of the break dates	290
	8.3.5 Estimating breaks one at a time	293
	8.3.6 Estimation in a system of regressions	294
8.4	Testing for structural change	296
	8.4.1 Tests for a single change without modeling the break	296
	8.4.2 Non-monotonic power functions in finite samples	298
	8.4.3 Tests that allow for a single break	299
	8.4.4 Tests for multiple structural changes	304
	8.4.5 Tests for restricted structural changes	308
	8.4.6 Tests for structural changes in multivariate systems	309
	8.4.7 Tests valid with $I(1)$ regressors	310
	8.4.8 Tests valid whether the errors are $I(1)$ or $I(0)$	313
	8.4.9 Testing for changes in persistence	317

8.5 Unit root versus trend stationarity in the presence of structural
change in the trend function   320
   8.5.1 The motivation, issues and framework   320
   8.5.2 The effect of structural change in trend on standard unit root tests   323
   8.5.3 Testing for a unit root allowing for changes at known dates   324
   8.5.4 Testing for a unit root allowing for changes at unknown dates   326
8.6 Testing for cointegration allowing for structural changes   333
   8.6.1 Single-equation methods   333
   8.6.2 Methods based on a multivariate framework   336
8.7 Conclusions   340

8.1 Introduction

This chapter is concerned with methodological issues related to estimation, testing and computation for models involving structural changes. The amount of work on this subject over the last 50 years is truly voluminous in both the statistics and econometrics literature. Accordingly, any survey article is bound by the need to focus on specific aspects. Our aim is to review developments in the last fifteen years as they relate to econometric applications based on linear models, with appropriate mention of prior work to better understand the historical context and important antecedents. During this recent period, substantial advances have been made to cover models at a level of generality that allows a host of interesting practical applications. These include models with general stationary regressors and errors that can exhibit temporal dependence and heteroskedasticity, models with trending variables and possible unit roots, cointegrated models and long memory processes, among others. Advances in these contexts have been made pertaining to the following topics: computational aspects of constructing estimates, their limit distributions, tests for structural changes, and methods to determine the number of changes present.

These recent developments related to structural changes have paralleled developments in the analysis of unit root models. One reason is that many of the tools used are similar. In particular, heavy use is made in both literatures of functional central limit theorems or invariance principles, which have fruitfully been used in many areas of econometrics. At the same time, a large literature has addressed the interplay between structural changes and unit roots, in particular the fact that both classes of processes contain similar qualitative features. For example, most tests that attempt to distinguish between a unit root and a (trend) stationary process will favor the unit root model when the true process is subject to structural changes but is otherwise (trend) stationary within regimes specified by the break dates. Also, most tests trying to assess whether structural change is present will reject the null hypothesis of no structural change when the process has a unit root component but with constant model parameters. As we can see, there is an intricate interplay between unit root and structural changes. This creates particular difficulties in applied work, since both are of definite practical importance in economic applications. A central theme of this review relates to this interplay and to methods of distinguishing between the two.

The topics addressed in this review are the following. Section 8.2 provides interesting historical notes on structural change, unit root and long memory tests which illustrate the intricate interplay involved when trying to distinguish between these three features. Section 8.3 reviews methods related to estimation and inference about break dates. We start with a general linear regression model that allows multiple structural changes in a subset of the coefficients (a partial change model) with the estimates obtained by minimizing the sum of squared residuals. Special attention is given to the set of assumptions used to obtain the relevant results and their relevance for practical applications (section 8.3.1). We also include a discussion of results applicable when linear restrictions are imposed (8.3.2), methods to obtain estimates of the break dates that correspond to global minimizers of the objective function (8.3.3), the limit distributions of such estimates, including a discussion of benefits and potential drawbacks that arise from the adoption of a special asymptotic framework that considers shifts of shrinking magnitudes (8.3.4). Section 8.3.5 briefly discusses an alternative estimation strategy based on estimating the break dates sequentially, and section 8.3.6 discusses extensions of most of these issues to a general multi-equation system, which also allows changes in the covariance matrix of the errors.

Section 8.4 considers tests for structural changes. We start in section 8.4.1 with methods based on scaled functions of partial sums of appropriate residuals. The CUSUM test is probably the best known example, but the class includes basically all methods available for general models prior to the early 1990s. Despite their wide appeal, these tests suffer from an important drawback, namely that power is non-monotonic, in the sense that the power can decrease and even go to zero as the magnitude of the change increases (8.4.2). Section 8.4.3 discusses tests that directly allow for a single break in the regression underlying their construction, including a class of optimal tests that have found wide appeal in practice (8.4.3.1), but which are also subject to non-monotonic power when two changes affect the system (8.4.3.2), a result which points to the usefulness of tests for multiple structural changes discussed in section 8.4.4. Tests for structural changes in the linear model subject to restrictions on the parameters are discussed in section 8.4.5 and extensions of the methods to multivariate systems are presented in section 8.4.6. Tests valid when the regressors are unit root processes and the errors are stationary, i.e., cointegrated systems, are reviewed in section 8.4.7, while section 8.4.8 considers recent developments with respect to tests for changes in a trend function when the noise component of the series is either a stationary or a unit root process. Section 8.4.9 discusses issues related to changes in persistence when a time series can switch from being stationary to having a unit root, or vice-versa.

Section 8.5 addresses the topic of testing for a unit root versus trend-stationarity in the presence of structural changes in the trend function. The motivation, issues and frameworks are presented in section 8.5.1, while section 8.5.2 discusses results related to the effect of changes in the trend on standard unit root tests. Methods to test for a unit root allowing for a change at a known date are reviewed in section 8.5.3, while section 8.5.4 considers the case of breaks occurring at unknown dates, including problems with commonly used methods and recent proposals to overcome them (section 8.5.4.2).

Section 8.6 tackles the problem of testing for cointegration in the presence of structural changes in the constant and/or the cointegrating vector. We review first single equation methods (section 8.6.1) and then, in section 8.6.2, methods based on multi-equation systems, where the object of interest is to determine the number of cointegrating vectors. Finally, section 8.7 presents concluding remarks outlining a few important topics for future research and briefly reviews similar issues that arise in the context of long memory processes, an area where issues of structural change (in particular level shifts) have played an important role recently, especially in light of the characterization of the time series properties of stock return volatility.

Our focus is on conceptual issues about the frameworks adopted and the assumptions imposed as they relate to potential applicability. We also highlight problems that can occur with methods that are commonly used and recent work that has been done to overcome them. Space constraints are such that a detailed elicitation of all procedures discussed is not possible and the reader should consult the original work for details needed to implement them in practice.

Even with a rich agenda, this review inevitably has to leave out a wide range of important work. The choice of topic is clearly closely related to the author's own past and current work, and it is, accordingly, not an unbiased review, though we hope that a balanced treatment has been achieved to provide a comprehensive picture of how to deal with breaks in linear models.

Important parts of the literature on structural change that are not covered include, among others, the following: methods related to the so-called on-line approach, where the issue is to detect whether a change has occurred in real time; results pertaining to non-linear models, in particular to tests for structural changes in a Generalized Method of Moments framework; smooth transition changes and threshold models; non-parametric methods to estimate and detect changes; Bayesian methods; issues related to forecasting in the presence of structural changes; theoretical results and methods related to specialized cases that are not of general interest in economics; structural change in seasonal models; and bootstrap methods. The reader interested in further historical developments and methods not covered in this survey can consult the books by Clements and Hendry (1999), Csörgö and Horváth (1997), Krämer and Sonnberger (1986), Hackl and Westlund (1991), Hall (2005), Hatanaka and Yamada (2003), Maddala and Kim (1998), and Tong (1990) and the following review articles: Bhattacharya (1994), Deshayes and Picard (1986), Hackl and Westlund (1989), Krishnaiah and Miao (1988), Perron (1994), Pesaran *et al.* (1985), Shaban (1980), Stock (1994), van Dijk *et al.* (2002) and Zacks (1983).

8.2 Introductory historical notes

It will be instructive to start with some interesting historical notes concerning early tests for structural change. Consider a univariate time series, $\{y_t; t = 1, \ldots, T\}$, which under the null hypothesis is independently and identically distributed with mean μ and finite variance. Under the alternative hypothesis, y_t is subject to a one time change in mean at some unknown date T_b, i.e.,

$$y_t = \mu_1 + \mu_2 1(t > T_b) + e_t \tag{8.1}$$

where $e_t \sim i.i.d. (0, \sigma_e^2)$ and $1(\cdot)$ denotes the indicator function. Quandt (1958, 1960) had introduced what is now known as the *Sup F* test (assuming normally distributed errors), i.e., the likelihood ratio test for a change in parameters evaluated at the break date that maximizes the likelihood function. However, the limit distribution was then unknown. Quandt (1960) had shown that it was far from being a chi-square distribution and resorted to tabulating finite sample critical values for selected cases. Following earlier work by Chernoff and Zacks (1964) and Kander and Zacks (1966), an alternative approach was advocated by Gardner (1969), stemming from a suggestion by Page (1955, 1957) to use partial sums of demeaned data to analyze structural changes (see more on this below). The test considered is Bayesian in nature and, under the alternative, assigns weights p_t as the prior probability that a change occurs at date t $(t = 1, \ldots, T)$. Assuming Normal errors and an unknown value of σ_e^2, this strategy leads to the test

$$Q = \hat{\sigma}_e^{-2} T^{-1} \sum_{t=1}^{T} p_t \left[\sum_{j=t+1}^{T} (y_j - \bar{y}) \right]^2$$

where $\bar{y} = T^{-1} \sum_{t=1}^{T} y_t$ is the sample average, and $\hat{\sigma}_e^2 = T^{-1} \sum_{t=1}^{T} (y_t - \bar{y})^2$ is the sample variance of the data. With a prior that assigns equal weight to all observations, i.e., $p_t = 1/T$, the test reduces to

$$Q = \hat{\sigma}_e^{-2} T^{-2} \sum_{t=1}^{T} \left[\sum_{j=t+1}^{T} (y_j - \bar{y}) \right]^2 .$$

Under the null hypothesis, the test can be expressed as a ratio of quadratic forms in Normal variates and standard numerical methods can be used to evaluate its distribution (e.g., Imhof, 1961, though Gardner originally analyzed the case with σ_e^2 known). The limit distribution of the statistic Q was analyzed by MacNeill (1974). He showed that

$$Q \Rightarrow \int_0^1 B_0(r)^2 dr$$

where $B_0(r) = W(r) - rW(1)$ is a Brownian bridge, and noted that percentage points had already been derived by Anderson and Darling (1952) in the context of goodness of fit tests. MacNeill (1978) extended the procedure to test for a change in a polynomial trend function of the form

$$y_t = \sum_{i=0}^{p} \beta_{i,t} t^i + e_t$$

where

$$\beta_{i,t} = \beta_i + \delta_i 1(t > T_b).$$

The test of no change ($\delta_i = 0$ for all i) is then

$$Q_p = \hat{\sigma}_e^{-2} T^{-2} \sum_{t=1}^{T} \left[\sum_{j=t+1}^{T} \hat{e}_j \right]^2$$

with $\hat{\sigma}_e^{-2} = T^{-1} \sum_{t=1}^{T} \hat{e}_t^2$ and $\hat{e}_t$ are the residuals from a regression of y_t on $\{1, t, \ldots, t^p\}$. The limit distribution is given by

$$Q \Rightarrow \int_0^1 B_p(r)^2 dr$$

where $B_p(r)$ is a generalized Brownian bridge. MacNeill (1978) computed the critical values by exact numerical methods up to six decimals accuracy (showing, for $p=0$, the critical values of Anderson and Darling (1952) to be very accurate). The test was extended to allow dependence in the errors e_t by Perron (1991) and Tang and MacNeill (1993) (see also Kulperger, 1987a,b; Jandhyala and MacNeill, 1989; Jandhyala and Minogue, 1993; and Antoch *et al.*, 1997). In particular, Perron (1991) shows that, under general conditions, the same limit distribution obtains using the statistic

$$Q_p^* = \hat{h}_e(0)^{-1} T^{-2} \sum_{t=1}^{T} \left[\sum_{j=t+1}^{T} \hat{e}_j \right]^2$$

where $\hat{h}_e(0)$ is a consistent estimate of (2π times) the spectral density function at frequency zero of e_t.

Even though little of this filtered through the econometrics literature, the statistic Q_p^* is well known to applied economists. It is the so-called KPSS test for testing the null hypothesis of stationarity versus the alternative of a unit root, see Kwiatkowski *et al.* (1992). More precisely, Q_p is the Lagrange Multiplier (LM) and locally best invariant (LBI) test for testing the null hypothesis that $\sigma_u^2 = 0$ in the model

$$y_t = \sum_{i=0}^{p} \beta_{i,t} t^i + r_t + e_t$$

$$r_t = r_{t-1} + u_t$$

with $u_t \sim i.i.d.$ $N(0, \sigma_u^2)$ and $e_t \sim i.i.d.$ $N(0, \sigma_e^2)$. Q_p^* is then the corresponding large sample counterpart that allows correlation. Kwiatkowski *et al.* (1992) provided critical values for $p = 0$ and 1 using simulations (which are less precise than the critical values of Anderson and Darling, 1952, and MacNeill, 1978). In the econometrics literature, several extensions of this test have been proposed; in particular for testing the null hypothesis of cointegration versus the alternative of no cointegration (Nyblom and Harvey, 2000) and testing whether any part of a sample shows a vector of series to be cointegrated (Qu, 2004). Note also that the same test can be given the interpretation of a LBI for parameter constancy versus the alternative that the parameters follow a random walk (e.g., Nyblom and Mäkeläinen, 1983; Nyblom, 1989; Nabeya and Tanaka, 1988; Jandhyala and MacNeill, 1992; Hansen, 1992b). The same statistic is also the basis for a test of the null hypothesis of no-cointegration when considering functionals of its reciprocal (Breitung, 2002).

So what are we to make of all of this? The important message to learn from the fact that the same statistic can be applied to tests for stationarity versus either unit root or structural change is that the two issues are linked in important ways. Evidence in favor of unit roots can be a manifestation of structural changes and vice versa. This was indeed an important message of Perron (1989, 1990); see also Rappoport and Reichlin (1989). In this survey, we shall return to this problem and see how it introduces severe complications when dealing with structural changes and unit roots.

It is also of interest to go back to the work by Page (1955, 1957), who had proposed using partial sums of demeaned data to test for structural change. Letting $S_r = \sum_{j=1}^{r} (y_j - \bar{y})$, his procedure for a two-sided test for change in the mean is based on the quantities

$$\max_{0 \leq r \leq T} \left[S_r - \min_{0 \leq i < r} S_i \right] \quad \text{and} \quad \max_{0 \leq r \leq T} \left[\min_{0 \leq i < r} S_i - S_r \right]$$

and looks at whether either exceeds a threshold (which, in the symmetric case, is the same). So we reject the null hypothesis if the partial sum rises enough from its previous minimum or falls enough from its previous maximum. Nadler and Robbins (1971) showed that this procedure is equivalent to looking at the statistic

$$RS = \left[\max_{0 \leq r \leq T} S_r - \min_{0 \leq r \leq T} S_r \right]$$

i.e., to assessing whether the range of the sequence of partial sums is large enough. But this is also exactly the basis of the popular rescaled range procedure used to test the null hypothesis of short-memory versus the alternative of long memory (see, in particular, Hurst, 1951; Mandelbrot and Taqqu, 1979; Bhattacharya *et al.*, 1983; and Lo, 1991).

This is symptomatic of the same problem discussed above from a slightly different angle; structural change and long memory imply similar features in the data and, accordingly, are hard to distinguish. In particular, evidence for long memory can be caused by the presence of structural changes, and vice versa. The intuition is basically the same as the message in Perron (1990), i.e., level shifts induce persistent features in the data. This problem has recently received a lot of attention, especially in the finance literature concerning the characteristics of stock return volatility (see, in particular, Diebold and Inoue, 2001; Gourieroux and Jasiak, 2001; Granger and Hyung, 2004; Lobato and Savin, 1998; and Perron and Qu, 2004).

8.3 Estimation and inference about break dates

In this section we discuss issues related to estimation and inference about the break dates in a linear regression framework. The emphasis is on describing methods that are most useful in applied econometrics, explaining the relevance of the conditions imposed and sketching some important theoretical steps that help to understand the particular assumptions made.

Following Bai (1997a) and Bai and Perron (1998), the main framework of analysis can be described by the following multiple linear regression with m breaks (or $m + 1$ regimes):

$$y_t = x_t'\beta + z_t'\delta_j + u_t, \quad t = T_{j-1} + 1, \ \ldots, T_j, \tag{8.2}$$

for $j = 1, \ldots m + 1$. In this model, y_t is the observed dependent variable at time t; both x_t ($p \times 1$) and z_t ($q \times 1$) are vectors of covariates and β and δ_j ($j = 1, \ldots, m + 1$) are the corresponding vectors of coefficients; u_t is the disturbance at time t. The indices $(T_1, \ldots, T_m)$, or the break points, are explicitly treated as unknown (the convention that $T_0 = 0$ and $T_{m+1} = T$ is used). The purpose is to estimate the unknown regression coefficients together with the break points when T observations on (y_t, x_t, z_t) are available. This is a partial structural change model since the parameter vector β is not subject to shifts and is estimated using the entire sample. When $p = 0$, we obtain a pure structural change model where all the model's coefficients are subject to change. Note that using a partial structural change models where only some coefficients are allowed to change can be beneficial both in terms of obtaining more precise estimates and also in having more powerful tests.

The multiple linear regression system (8.2) may be expressed in matrix form as

$$Y = X\beta + \bar{Z}\delta + U,$$

where $Y = (y_1, \ldots, y_T)'$, $X = (x_1, \ldots x_T)'$, $U = (u_1, \ldots, u_T)'$, $\delta = (\delta_1', \delta_2', \ldots, \delta_{m+1}')'$, and $\bar{Z}$ is the matrix which diagonally partitions Z at $(T_1, \ldots, T_m)$, i.e., $\bar{Z} = diag(Z_1, \ldots, Z_{m+1})$ with $Z_i = (z_{T_{i-1}} + 1, \ldots, z_{T_i})'$. We denote the true value of a parameter with a 0 superscript. In particular, $\delta^0 = (\delta_1^{0'}, \ldots, \delta_{m+1}^{0'})'$ and $(T_1^0, \ldots, T_m^0)$ are used to denote, respectively, the true values of the parameters δ and the true break points. The matrix $\bar{Z}^0$ is the one which diagonally partitions Z at $(T_1^0, \ldots, T_m^0)$. Hence, the data-generating process is assumed to be

$$Y = X\beta^0 + \bar{Z}^0\delta^0 + U. \tag{8.3}$$

The method of estimation considered is based on the least-squares principle. For each m-partition $(T_1, \ldots, T_m)$, the associated least-squares estimates of β and δ_j are obtained by minimizing the sum of squared residuals

$$(Y - X\beta - \bar{Z}\delta)'(Y - X\beta - \bar{Z}\delta) = \sum_{i=1}^{m+1} \sum_{t=T_{i-1}+1}^{T_i} [y_t - x_t'\beta - z_t'\delta_i]^2.$$

Let $\hat{\beta}(\{T_j\})$ and $\hat{\delta}(\{T_j\})$ denote the estimates based on the given m-partition $(T_1, \ldots, T_m)$ denoted $\{T_j\}$. Substituting these in the objective function and denoting the resulting sum of squared residuals as $S_T(T_1, \ldots, T_m)$, the estimated break points $(\hat{T}_1, \ldots, \hat{T}_m)$ are such that

$$(\hat{T}_1, \ldots, \hat{T}_m) = \mathrm{argmin}_{(T_1, \ldots, T_m)} S_T(T_1, \ldots, T_m), \tag{8.4}$$

where the minimization is taken over some set of admissible partitions (see below). Thus the break-point estimators are global minimizers of the objective function. The regression parameter estimates are the estimates associated with the m-partition $\{\hat{T}_j\}$, i.e., $\hat{\beta} = \hat{\beta}(\{\hat{T}_j\})$, $\hat{\delta} = \hat{\delta}(\{\hat{T}_j\})$.

This framework includes many contributions made in the literature as special cases depending on the assumptions imposed; e.g., a single change, changes in the mean of a stationary process, etc. However, the fact that the method of estimation is based on the least-squares principle implies that, even if changes in the variance of u_t are allowed, provided they occur at the same dates as the breaks in the parameters of the regression, such changes are not exploited to increase the precision of the break date estimators. This is due to the fact that the least-squares method imposes equal weights on all residuals. Allowing different weights, as needed when accounting for changes in variance, requires adopting a quasi-likelihood framework, see below.

8.3.1   The assumptions and their relevance

To obtain theoretical results about the consistency and limit distribution of the break dates, some conditions need to be imposed on the regressors, the errors, the set of admissible partitions and the break dates. To our knowledge, the most general set of assumptions, as far as applications are concerned, are those in Perron and Qu (2005). Some are simply technical (e.g., invertibility requirements), while others restrict the potential applicability of the results. Hence, it is useful to discuss the latter.

- Assumption on the regressors: Let $w_t = (x_t', z_t')'$. For $i = 0, \ldots, m$, $(1/l_i)\sum_{t=T_i^0+1}^{T_i^0+[l_i v]} w_t w_t' \to_p Q_i(v)$, a non-random positive definite matrix uniformly in $v \in [0, 1]$.

This assumption allows the distribution of the regressors to vary across regimes. However, it requires the data to be weakly stationary stochastic processes. It can, however, be relaxed substantially, though the technical proofs then depend on the nature of the relaxation. For instance, the scaling used forbids trending regressors, unless they are of the form $\{1, (t/T), \ldots, (t/T)^p\}$, say, for a polynomial trend of order p. Casting trend functions in this form can deliver useful results in many cases. However, there are instances where specifying trends in unscaled form, i.e. $\{1, t, \ldots, t^p\}$, can deliver much better results, especially if level and trend slope changes occur jointly. Results using unscaled trends with $p = 1$ are presented in Perron and Zhu (2005). A comparison of their results with other trend specifications is presented in Deng and Perron (2005).

Another important restriction is implied by the requirement that the limit be a fixed matrix, as opposed to permitting it to be stochastic. This, along with the scaling, precludes integrated processes as regressors (i.e., unit roots). In the single break case, this has been relaxed by Bai, Lumsdaine and Stock (1998), who considered, among other things, structural changes in cointegrated relationships. Consistency still applies, but the rate of convergence and limit distributions of the estimates are diferent. Another context in which integrated regressors play a role is the case of changes in persistence. Chong (2001) considered an AR(1) model where the autoregressive coeffcient takes a value less than one before some break date and the value one after, or vice versa. He showed consistency of the estimate of the break date and derived the limit distribution. When the move is from stationarity to unit root, the rate of convergence is the same as in the stationary case (though the limit distribution is different), but interestingly, the rate of convergence is faster when the change is from a unit root to a stationary process. No results are yet available for multiple structural changes in regressions involving integrated regressors, though work is in progress on this issue.

The sequence $\{w_t u_t\}$ satisfies the following set of conditions:

- Assumptions on the errors: Let the L_r-norm of a random matrix X be defined by $\|X\|_r = (\sum_i \sum_j E|X_{ij}|^r)^{1/r}$ for $r \geq 1$. (Note that $\|X\|$ is the usual matrix norm or the Euclidean norm of a vector.) With $\{\mathcal{F}_i : i = 1, 2, \ldots$ a sequence of increasing σ-fields, it is assumed that $\{w_i u_i, \mathcal{F}_i\}$ forms a L^r-mixingale sequence with $r = 2 + \delta$ for some $\delta > 0$. That is, there exist nonnegative constants $\{c_i : i \geq 1\}$ and $\{\psi_j : j \geq 0\}$ such that $\psi_j \downarrow 0$ as $j \to \infty$ and, for all $i \geq 1$ and $j \geq 0$, we have: (a) $\|E(w_i u_i | \mathcal{F}_{i-j})\|_r \leq c_i \psi_j$, (b) $\|w_i u_i - E(w_i u_i | \mathcal{F}_{i+j})\|_r \leq c_i \psi_{j+1}$. Also assume (c) $\max_i c_i \leq K < \infty$, (d) $\sum_{j=0}^{\infty} j^{1+k} \psi_j < \infty$, (e) $\|z_i\|_{2r} < M < \infty$ and $\|u_i\|_{2r} < N < \infty$ for some $K, M, N > 0$.

This imposes mild restrictions on the vector $w_t u_t$ and permits a wide class of potential correlation and heterogeneity (including conditional heteroskedasticity) and also allows lagged dependent variables. It rules out errors that have unit roots. In this latter case, if the regressors are stationary (or satisfy the Assumption on the regressors stated above), the estimates of the break dates are inconsistent (see Nunes *et al.*, 1995). However, unit root errors can be of interest; for example, when testing for a change in the deterministic component of the trend function for an integrated series, in which case the estimates are consistent (see Perron and Zhu, 2005). The set of conditions listed above are not the weakest possible. For example, Lavielle and Moulines (2000) allow the errors to be strongly dependent, i.e., long memory processes such as fractionally integrated ones are permitted. They, how-ever, consider only the case of multiple changes in the mean. Technically, what is important is to be able to establish a generalized Hájek-Rényi (1955) type inequality for the zero mean variables $z_t u_t$, as well as a Functional Central Limit Theorem and a Law of Large Numbers.

- Assumption on the minimization problem: The minimization problem defined by (8.4) is taken over all possible partitions such that $T_i - T_{i-1} \geq \varepsilon T$ for some $\varepsilon > 0$.

This requirement was introduced in Bai and Perron (1998) only for the case where lagged dependent variables were allowed. When serial correlation in the errors was allowed they introduced the requirement that the errors be independent of the regressors at all leads and lags. This is obviously a strong assumption which is often violated in practice. The assumptions on the errors listed above are much weaker, in particular concerning the relation between the errors and regressors. This weakening comes at the cost of a mild strengthening of the assumption about the regressors and the introduction of the restriction on the minimization pro-blem. Note that the latter is also imposed in Lavielle and Moulines (2000), though they note that it can be relaxed with stronger conditions on $z_t u_t$ or by constraining the estimates to lie in a compact set.

- Assumption on the break dates: $T_i^0 = [T\lambda_i^0]$, where $0 < \lambda_1^0 < \cdots < \lambda_m^0 < 1$.

This assumption specifies that the break dates are asymptotically distinct. While it is standard, it is surprisingly the most controversial for some. The reason is that it dictates the asymptotic framework adopted. With this condition, when the sample size T increases, all segments increase in length in the same proportions to each other. Oftentimes, an asymptotic analysis is viewed as a thought experiment about what would happen if we were able to collect more and more data in the future. If one adheres to this view, then the last regime should increase in length (assuming no other break will occur in the future) and all other segments then become a negligible proportion of the total sample. Hence, as T increases, we would find ourselves with a single segment, in which case the framework becomes useless. The fact is that any asymptotic analysis is simply a device to enable us to get useful information about the structure, which can help us understand the finite sample distributions, and hopefully to deliver good approximations. The adoption of any asymptotic framework should only be evaluated on this basis, no matter how ad hoc it may seem at first sight. Here, with say a sample of size 100 and 3 breaks occurring at dates 25, 50 and 75, all segments are a fourth of the total sample. It therefore makes sense to use an asymptotic framework whereby this feature is preserved. The same comments apply to contexts in which some parameters are made local to some boundary as the sample size increases. No claim whatsoever is made that the parameter would actually change if more data were collected, yet such a device has been found to be of great use and to provide very useful approximations. This applies to local asymptotic power functions, roots local to unity, or shrinking size of shifts, as we will discuss later. Having said that, it does not mean that the asymptotic framework that is adopted in this literature is the only useful one or even the best. For example, it is conceivable that an asymptotic theory whereby more and more data are added but keeping a fixed span of data would be useful as well. However, such a continuous time limit distribution has not yet appeared in the structural change context.

Under these conditions, the main theoretical results are that the break fractions λ_i^0 are consistently estimated, i.e., $\hat{\lambda}_i \equiv (\hat{T}_i/T) \to_p \lambda_i^0$, and that the rate of convergence is T. More precisely, for every $\varepsilon > 0$, there exists a $C < \infty$, such that for large T,

$$P(|T(\hat{\lambda}_i - \lambda_i^0)| > C\Delta_i^{-2}) < \varepsilon \tag{8.5}$$

for every $i = 1, \dots, m$, where $\Delta_i = \delta_{i+1} - \delta_i$. Note that the estimates of the break dates are not consistent themselves, but the diferences between the estimates and the true values are bounded by some constant, in probability. Also, this implies that the estimates of the other parameters have the same distribution as would prevail if the break dates were known. Kurozumi and Arai (2004) obtain a similar result with $I(1)$ regressors for a cointegrated model subject to a change in some parameters of the cointegrating vector. They show that the estimate of the break fraction obtained by minimizing the sum of squared residuals from the static regression converges at a fast enough rate for the estimates of the parameters of the model to be asymptotically unaffected by the estimation of the break date.

8.3.2 Allowing for restrictions on the parameters

Perron and Qu (2005) approach the issues of multiple structural changes in a broader framework whereby arbitrary linear restrictions on the parameters of the conditional mean can be imposed in the estimation. The class of models considered is

$$y = \bar{Z}\delta + u$$

where

$$R\delta = r$$

with R a k by $(m + 1)q$ matrix with rank k and r a k-dimensional vector of constants. The assumptions are the same as discussed above. Note first that there is no need for a distinction between variables whose coefficients are allowed to change and those whose coefficients are not allowed to change. A partial structural change model can be obtained as a special case by specifying restrictions that impose some coefficients to be identical across all regimes. This is a useful generalization since it permits a wider class of models of practical interest; for example, a model which specifies a number of states less than the number of regimes (with two states, the coefficients would be the same in odd and even regimes). Or it could be the case that the values of the parameters in a specific segment are known. Also, a subset of coefficients may be allowed to change over only a limited number of regimes.

Perron and Qu (2005) show that the same consistency and rate of convergence results hold. Moreover, an interesting result is that the limit distribution (to be discussed below) of the estimates of the break dates are unaffected by the imposition of valid restrictions. They document, however, that improvements can be obtained in finite samples. But the main advantage of imposing restrictions is that much more powerful tests are possible.

8.3.3   Methods to compute global minimizers

We now briefly discuss issues related to the estimation of such models, in particular when multiple breaks are allowed. What are needed are global minimizers of the objective function (8.4). A standard grid search procedure would require least squares operations of order $O(T^m)$ and becomes prohibitive when the number of breaks is greater than 2, even for relatively small samples. Bai and Perron (2003a) discuss a method based on a dynamic programming algorithm that is very efficient. Indeed, the additional computing time needed to estimate more than two break dates is marginal compared to the time needed to estimate a two break model. The basis of the method, for specialized cases, is not new and was considered by Guthery (1974), Bellman and Roth (1969) and Fisher (1958). A comprehensive treatment was also presented in Hawkins (1976).

Consider the case of a pure structural change model. The basic idea of the approach becomes fairly intuitive once it is realized that, with a sample of size T, the total number of possible segments is at most $T(T+1)/2$ and is therefore of order $O(T^2)$. One then needs a method to select which combination of segments (i.e., which partition of the sample) yields a minimal value of the objective function. This is achieved efficiently using a dynamic programming algorithm. For models with restrictions (including the partial structural change model), an iterative procedure is available, which in most cases requires very few iterations (see Bai and Perron, 2003, and Perron and Qu, 2005, who make available Gauss codes to perform these and other tasks). Hence, even with large samples, the computing cost to estimate models with multiple structural changes should be considered minimal.

8.3.4   The limit distribution of the estimates of the break dates

With the assumptions on the regressors and the errors, and given the asymptotic framework adopted, the limit distributions of the estimates of the break dates are independent of each other. Hence, for each break date, the analysis becomes exactly the same as if a single break has occurred. The intuition behind this is that the distance between each break increases at rate T as the sample size increases. Also, the mixing conditions on the regressors and errors impose a short memory property so that events that occur a long enough time apart are independent.

We shall not reproduce the results in detail but simply describe the main qualitative features and the practical relevance of the required assumptions. The reader is referred to Bai (1997a) and Bai and Perron (1998, 2003a), in particular. Also, confidence intervals for the break dates need not be based on the limit distributions of the estimates. Other approaches are possible, for example by inverting a suitable test (e.g., Elliott and Müller, 2004, for an application in the linear model using a locally best invariant test). For a review of alternative methods, see Siegmund (1988).

The limit distribution of the estimates of the break dates depends on: (a) the magnitude of the change in coefficients (with larger changes leading to higher precision, as expected); (b) the (limit) sample moment matrices of the regressors for the segments prior to and after the true break date (which are allowed to be different); (c) the so-called "long-run" variance of $\{w_t u_t\}$, which involves potential serial correlation in the errors (and which again is allowed to be different prior to and after the break); (d) whether the regressors are trending or not. In all cases, all relevant nuisance parameters can be consistently estimated and the appropriate confidence intervals constructed. A feature of interest is that the confidence intervals need not be symmetric given that the data and errors can have different properties before and after the break.

To get an idea of the importance of particular assumptions needed to derive the limit distribution, it is instructive to look at a simple case with *i.i.d.* errors u_t and a single break (for details, see Bai, 1997a). Then the estimate of the break satisfies,

$$\hat{T}_1 = \arg \min SSR(T_1) = \arg \max [SSR(T_1^0) - SSR(T_1)]$$

Given the rate of convergence result (8.5), the inequality $|\hat{T}_1 - T_1^0| < C\Delta^{-2}$ is satisfied with probability one in large samples (here, $\Delta = \delta_2 - \delta_1$). Hence, we can restrict the search over the compact set $C(\Delta) = \{T_1 : |T_1 - T_1^0| < C\Delta^{-2}\}$. Then, for $T_1 < T_1^0$,

$$SSR(T_1^0) - SSR(T_1) = -\Delta' \sum_{t=T_1+1}^{T_1^0} z_t z_t' \Delta + 2\Delta' \sum_{t=T_1+1}^{T_1^0} z_t u_t + o_p(1) \qquad (8.6)$$

and, for $T_1 \geq T_1^0$,

$$SSR(T_1^0) - SSR(T_1) = -\Delta' \sum_{t=T_1^0+1}^{T_1} z_t z_t' \Delta + 2\Delta' \sum_{t=T_1^0+1}^{T_1} z_t u_t + o_p(1) \qquad (8.7)$$

The problem is that, with $|T_1 - T_1^0|$ bounded, we cannot apply a Law of Large Numbers or a Central Limit Theorem to approximate the sums above with something that does not depend on the exact distributions of z_t and u_t. Furthermore, the distributions of these sums depend on the exact location of the break. Now let

$$W_1(m) = -\Delta' \sum_{t=m+1}^{0} z_t z_t' \Delta + 2\Delta' \sum_{t=m+1}^{0} z_t u_t$$

for $m < 0$ and

$$W_2(m) = -\Delta' \sum_{t=1}^{m} z_t z_t' \Delta + 2\Delta' \sum_{t=1}^{m} z_t u_t$$

for $m > 0$. Finally, let $W(m) = W_1(m)$ if $m < 0$, and $W(m) = W_2(m)$ if $m > 0$ (with $W(0) = 0$). Now, assuming a strictly stationary distribution for the pair $\{z_t, u_t\}$, we have that

$$SSR(T_1^0) - SSR(T_1) = W(T_1 - T_1^0) + o_p(1)$$

i.e., the assumption of strict stationarity allows us to get rid of the dependence of the distribution on the exact location of the break. Assuming further that $(\Delta' z_t)^2 \pm (\Delta' z_t) u_t$ has a continuous distribution ensures that $W(m)$ has a unique maximum, so that

$$\hat{T}_1 - T_1^0 \rightarrow^d \arg \max_m W(m).$$

An important early treatment of this result for a sequence of i.i.d. random variables is Hinkley (1970). See also Feder (1975) for segmented regressions that are continuous at the time of break, Bhattacharya (1987) for maximum likelihood estimates in a multi-parameter case, and Bai (1994) for linear processes.

Now the issue is that of getting rid of the dependence of this limit distribution on the exact distribution of the pair (z_t, u_t). Looking at (8.6) and (8.7), what we need is for the difference $T_1 - T_1^0$ to increase as the sample size increases, so that a Law of Large Numbers and a Functional Central Limit Theorem can be applied. The trick is to realize that, from the convergence rate result (8.5), the rate of convergence of the estimate will be slower if the change in the parameters Δ_i gets smaller as the sample size increases, but does so slowly enough for the estimated break fraction to remain consistent. Early applications of this framework are Yao (1987), in the context of a change in distribution for a sequence of i.i.d. random variables, and Picard (1985) for a change in an autoregressive process.

Denoting $\Delta = \Delta_T$ to highlight the fact that the change in the parameters depends on the sample size, this leads to the specification $\Delta_T = \Delta_0 v_T$, where v_T is such that $v_T \rightarrow 0$ and $T^{(1/2) - \alpha} v_T \rightarrow \infty$ for some $\alpha \in (0, 1/2)$. Under these specifications, we have from (8.5) that $\hat{T}_1 - T_1^0 = O_p(T^{1-2\alpha})$. Hence, we can restrict the search to those values T_1 such that $T_1 = T_1^0 + [s v_T^{-2}]$ for some fixed s. We can write (8.6) as

$$SSR(T_1^0) - SSR(T_1) = \Delta_0' v_T^2 \sum_{t=T_1+1}^{T_1^0} z_t z_t' \Delta + 2\Delta_0' v_T \sum_{t=T_1+1}^{T_1^0} z_t u_t + o_p(1).$$

The next steps depend on whether the z_t includes trending regressors. Without trending regressors, the following assumptions are imposed (in the case where u_t is i.i.d.)

- Assumptions for limit distribution: Let $\Delta T_i^0 = T_i^0 - T_{i-1}^0$ then as $\Delta T_i^0 \rightarrow \infty$: (a) $(\Delta T_i^0)^{-1} \sum_{t=T_{i-1}^0+1}^{T_{i-1}^0 + [s\Delta T_i^0]} z_t z_t' \rightarrow_p s Q_i$, (b) $(\Delta T_i^0)^{-1} \sum_{t=T_{i-1}^0+1}^{T_{i-1}^0 + [s\Delta T_i^0]} u_t^2 \rightarrow_p s \sigma_i^2$

These imply that

$$(\Delta T_i^0)^{-1/2} \sum_{t=T_{i-1}^0+1}^{T_{i-1}^0+[s\Delta T_i^0]} z_t u_t \Rightarrow B_i(s)$$

where $B_i(s)$ is a multivariate Gaussian process on $[0, 1]$ with mean zero and covariance $E[B_i(s)B_i(u)] = \min\{s, u\}\sigma_i^2 Q_i$. Hence, for $s < 0$,

$$SSR(T_1^0) - SSR(T_1^0 + [sv_T^{-2}]) = -|s|\Delta_0'Q_1\Delta_0 + 2(\Delta_0'Q_1\Delta_0)^{1/2}W_1(-s) + o_p(1)$$

where $W_1(-s)$ is a Weiner process defined on $(0, \infty)$. A similar analysis holds for the case $s > 0$ and for more general assumptions on u_t. But this suffices to make clear that, under these assumptions, the limit distribution of the estimate of the break date no longer depends on the exact distribution of z_t and u_t but only on quantities that can be consistently estimated. For details, see Bai (1997) and Bai and Perron (1998, 2003a). With trending regressors, the assumption stated above is violated but a similar result is still possible (assuming trends of the form (t/T)) and the reader is referred to Bai (1997a) for the case where z_t is a polynomial time trend.

So, what do we learn from these asymptotic results? First, for large shifts, the distributions of the estimates of the break dates depend on the exact distributions of the regressors and errors even if the sample is large. When shifts are small, we can expect the distributions of the estimates of the break dates to be insensitive to the exact nature of the distributions of the regressors and errors. The question is then, how small do the changes have to be? There is no clear-cut solution to this problem and the answer is case specific. The simulations in Bai and Perron (2005) show that the shrinking shifts asymptotic framework provides useful approximations to the finite sample distribution of the estimated break dates, but their simulation design uses normally distributed errors and regressors. The coverage rates are adequate, in general, unless the shifts are quite small, in which case the confidence interval is too narrow. The method of Elliott and Müller (2004), based on inverting a test, works better in that case. However, with such small breaks, tests for structural change will most likely fail to detect a change, in which case most practitioners would not pursue the analysis further and consider the construction of confidence intervals. On the other hand, Deng and Perron (2005a) show that the shrinking shift asymptotic framework leads to a poor approximation in the context of changes in a linear trend function and that the limit distribution based on a fixed magnitude of shift is highly preferable.

8.3.5   Estimating breaks one at a time

Bai (1997b) and Bai and Perron (1998) showed that it is possible to consistently estimate all break fractions sequentially, i.e., one at a time. This is due to the following result. When estimating a single break model in the presence of multiple breaks, the estimate of the break fraction will converge to one of the true break fractions, the one that is dominant in the sense that taking it into account allows the greatest reduction in the sum of squared residuals. Then, allowing for a break at the estimated value, a second one-break model can be applied which will consistently estimate the second dominating break, and so on (in the case of two breaks that are equally dominant, the estimate will converge with probability 1/2 to either break). Fu and Cornow (1990) presented an early account of this property for a sequence of Bernoulli random variables when the probability of obtaining a 0 or a 1 is subject to multiple structural changes (see also, Chong, 1995).

Bai (1997b) considered the limit distribution of the estimates and showed that they are not the same as those obtained when estimating all break dates simultaneously. In particular, except for the last estimated break date, the limit distributions of the estimates of the break dates depend on the parameters in all segments of the sample (when the break dates are estimated simultaneously, the limit distribution of a particular break date depends on the parameters of the adjacent regimes only). To remedy this problem, Bai (1997b) suggested a procedure called "repartition." This amounts to re-estimating each break date conditional on the adjacent break dates. For example, let the initial estimates of the break dates be denoted by $(\hat{T}_1^a, \ldots, \hat{T}_m^a)$. The second round estimate for the *ith* break date is obtained by fitting a one break model to the segment starting at date $\hat{T}_{i-1}^a + 1$ and ending at date $\hat{T}_{i+1}^a$ (with the convention that $\hat{T}_0^a = 0$ and $\hat{T}_{m+1}^a = T$). The estimates obtained from this repartition procedure have the same limit distributions as those obtained simultaneously, as discussed above.

8.3.6 Estimation in a system of regressions

The problem of estimating structural changes in a system of regressions is relatively recent. Bai *et al.* (1998) considered asymptotically valid inference for the estimate of a single break date in multivariate time series allowing stationary or integrated regressors as well as trends. They show that the width of the confidence interval decreases in an important way when series having a common break are treated as a group and estimation is carried out using a quasi-maximum likelihood (QML) procedure. Also, Bai (2000) considers the consistency, rate of convergence and limiting distribution of estimated break dates in a segmented stationary VAR model, estimated again by QML, when the breaks can occur in the parameters of the conditional mean, the covariance matrix of the error term, or both. Hansen (2003) considers multiple structural changes in a cointegrated system, though his analysis is restricted to the case of known break dates.

To our knowledge, the most general framework is that of Qu and Perron (2005), who consider models of the form

$$y_t = (I \otimes z_t')S\beta_j + u_t$$

for $T_{j-1}+1 \leq t \leq T_j$ ($j = 1, \ldots, m+1$), where y_t is an n-vector of dependent variables and z_t is a q-vector that includes the regressors from all equations. The vector of errors u_t has mean 0 and covariance matrix Σ_j. The matrix S is of dimension nq by p with full column rank. Although in principle it is allowed to have entries that are arbitrary constants, S is usually a selection matrix involving elements that are 0 or 1 and, hence, specifies which regressors appear in each equation. The set of basic parameters in regime j consists of the p vector β_j and of Σ_j. They also allow for the imposition of a set of r restrictions of the form $g(\beta, vec(\Sigma)) = 0$, where $\beta = (\beta_1', \ldots, \beta_{m+1}')'$, $\Sigma = (\Sigma_1, \ldots, \Sigma_{m+1})$ and $g(\cdot)$ is an r-dimensional vector. Both within- and cross-equation restrictions are allowed, in each case within or across regimes. The assumptions on the regressors z_t and the errors u_t are similar to those discussed in section 8.3.1 (properly extended for the multivariate nature of the problem). Hence, the framework permits a wide class of models, including VAR, SUR, linear panel data, change in means of a vector of stationary processes, etc. Models with integrated regressors (i.e., models with cointegration) are not permitted.

Allowing for general restrictions on the parameters β_j and Σ_j permits a very wide range of special cases that are of practical interest: (a) partial structural change models where only a subset of the parameters are subject to change; (b) block partial structural change models where only a subset of the equations are subject to change; (c) changes in only some elements of the covariance matrix Σ_j (e.g., only variances in a subset of equations); (d) changes in only the covariance matrix Σ_j, while β_j is the same for all segments; (e) ordered break models where one can impose the breaks to occur in a particular order across subsets of equations; etc.

The method of estimation is again QML (based on Normal errors) subject to the restrictions. Qu and Perron (2005) derive the consistency, rate of convergence and limit distribution of the estimated break dates. They obtain a general result stating that, in large samples, the restricted likelihood function can be separated into two parts: one that involves only the break dates and the true values of the coefficients, so that the estimates of the break dates are not affected by the restrictions imposed on the coefficients, the other involving the parameters of the model, the true values of the break dates and the restrictions; showing that the limiting distributions of these estimates are influenced by the restrictions, but not by the estimation of the break dates. The limit distribution results for the estimates of the break dates are qualitatively similar to those discussed above, in particular they depend on the true parameters of the model. Although only root-T consistent estimates of (β, Σ) are needed to construct asymptotically valid confidence intervals, it is likely that more precise estimates of these parameters will lead to better finite sample coverage rates. Hence, it is recommended to use the estimates obtained by imposing the restrictions, even though imposing restrictions does not have a first-order effect on the limiting distributions of the estimates of the break dates. To make estimation possible in practice, for any number of breaks, they present an algorithm which extends the one discussed in Bai and Perron (2003a) using, in particular, an iterative GLS procedure to construct the likelihood function for all possible segments.

The theoretical analysis shows how substantial efficiency gains can be obtained by casting the analysis into a system of regressions. In addition, the result of Bai *et al.* (1998), that when a break is common across equations the precision increases in proportion to the number of equations, is extended to the multiple break case. More importantly, the precision of the estimate of a particular break date in one equation can increase when the system includes other equations, even if the parameters of the latter are invariant across regimes. All that is needed is that the correlation between the errors be non-zero. While surprising, this result is ex-post fairly intuitive, since a poorly estimated break in one regression affects the likelihood function through both the residual variance of that equation and the correlation with the rest of the regressions. Hence, by including ancillary equations without breaks, additional forces are in play to better pinpoint the break dates.

Qu and Perron (2005) also consider a novel (to our knowledge) aspect to the problem of multiple structural changes, labeled "locally ordered breaks." Suppose one equation is a policy-reaction function and the other is some market-clearing equation whose parameters are related to the policy function. According to the Lucas critique, if a change in policy occurs, it is expected to induce a change in the market equation, but the change may not be simultaneous and may occur with a lag, say because of some adjustments due to frictions or incomplete information. However, it is expected to take place soon after the break in the policy function. Here, the breaks across the two equations, are "ordered" in the sense that we have the prior knowledge that the break in one equation occurs after the break in the other. The breaks are also "local" in the sense that the time span between their occurrence is expected to be short. Hence, the breaks cannot be viewed as occurring simultaneously nor can the break fractions be viewed as asymptotically distinct. An algorithm to estimate such models is presented. Also, a framework to analyze the limit distribution of the estimates is introduced. Unlike the case with asymptotically distinct breaks, here the distributions of the estimates of the break dates need to be considered jointly.

8.4 Testing for structural change

In this section, we review testing procedures related to structural changes. The following issues are covered: tests obtained without modeling any break, tests for a single structural change obtained by explicitly modeling a break, the problem of non-monotonic power functions, tests for multiple structural changes, tests that are valid with $I(1)$ regressors, and tests for a change in slope that allow the noise component to be either $I(0)$ or $I(1)$.

8.4.1 Tests for a single change without modeling the break

Historically, tests for structural change were first devised based on procedures that did not estimate a break point explicitly. The main reason is that the distribution theory for the estimates of the break dates (obtained using a least-squares or likelihood principle) was not available and the problem was solved only for a few special cases (see, e.g., Hawkins, 1977; Kim and Siegmund, 1989). Most tests proposed were of the form of partial sums of residuals. We have already discussed in section 8.2 the Q test based on the average of partial sums of residuals (e.g., demeaned data for a change in mean) and the rescaled range test based on the range of partial sums of similarly demeaned data.

Another statistic which has played an important role in theory and applications is the CUSUM test proposed by Brown, Durbin and Evans (1975). This test is based on the maximum of partial sums of recursive residuals. More precisely, for a linear regression with k regressors

$$y_t = x_t'\beta + u_t$$

it is defined by

$$CUSUM = \max_{k+1<r<T} \left| \frac{\sum_{t=k+1}^{r} \tilde{v}_t}{\hat{\sigma}\sqrt{T-K}} \right| \bigg/ \left(1 + 2\frac{r-k}{T-k}\right)$$

where $\hat{\sigma}^2$ is a consistent estimate of the variance of u_t (usually the sum of squared OLS residuals although, to increase power, one can use the sum of squared demeaned recursive residuals, as suggested by Harvey, 1975) and $\tilde{v}_t$ are the recursive residuals defined by

$$\tilde{v}_t = (y_t - x_t'\hat{\beta}_{t-1})/f_t$$
$$f_t = (1 + x_t'(X_{t-1}'X_{t-1})x_t)^{1/2}$$

where X_{t-1} contains the observations on the regressors up to time $t-1$ and $\hat{\beta}_{t-1}$ is the OLS estimate of β using data up to time $t-1$. For an extensive review of the use of recursive methods in the analysis of structural change, see Dufour (1982) (see also Dufour and Kiviet, 1996, for finite sample inference in a regression model with a lagged dependent variable).

The limit distribution of the CUSUM test can be expressed in terms of the maximum of a weighted Wiener process, i.e.,

$$CUSUM \Rightarrow \sup_{0 \leq r \leq 1} \left| \frac{W(r)}{1+2r} \right|$$

where $W(r)$ is a unit Wiener process defined on $(0,1)$, see Sen (1982). Also, it was shown by Kramer, Ploberger and Alt (1988) that the limit distribution remains valid even if lagged dependent variables are present as regressors. Furthermore, Ploberger and Kramer (1992) showed that using OLS residuals instead of recursive residuals yields a valid test, though the limit distribution under the null hypothesis is diferent (expressed in terms of a Brownian bridge, $W(r) - rW(1)$, instead of a Wiener process). Their simulations showed the OLS based CUSUM test to have higher power except for shifts that occur early in the sample (the standard CUSUM tests having small power for late shifts).

An alternative, also suggested by Brown, Durbin and Evans (1975), is the CUSUM of squares test. It takes the form:

$$CUSSQ = \max_{k+1<r<T} \left| S_T^{(r)} - \frac{r-k}{T-k} \right|$$

where

$$S_T^{(r)} = \left(\sum_{t=k+1}^{r} \tilde{v}_t^2 \right) \Bigg/ \left(\sum_{t=k+1}^{T} \tilde{v}_t^2 \right)$$

Ploberger and Kramer (1990) considered the local power functions of the CUSUM and CUSUM of squares. The former has non-trivial local asymptotic power unless the mean regressor is orthogonal to all structural changes. On the other hand, the latter has only trivial local power (i.e., power equal to size) for local changes that specify a one-time change in the coefficients (see also Deshayes and Picard, 1986). This suggests that the CUSUM test should be preferred, a conclusion we shall revisit below.

Another variant using partial sums is the fluctuations test of Ploberger, Kramer and Kontrus (1989), which looks at the maximum difference between the OLS estimate of β using the full sample and the OLS estimates using subsets of the sample from the first observation to some date t, ranging from $t=k$ to T. A similar test for a change in the slope of a linear trend function is analyzed in Chu and White (1992). Also, Chu, Hornik and Kuan (1995) looked at the maximum of moving sums of recursive and least-squares residuals.

8.4.2   Non-monotonic power functions in finite samples

All tests discussed above are consistent for given fixed values in the relevant set of alternative hypotheses. Many are, however, subject to the following problem. For a given sample size, the power function can be non-monotonic, in the sense that it can decrease and even reach a zero value as the alternative considered becomes further away from the null value. This was shown by Perron (1991) for the Q statistic and extended to a wide range of tests in a comprehensive analysis by Vogelsang (1999).

This was illustrated using a basic shift in mean process or a shift in the slope of a linear trend (for some statistics designed for that alternative). In the change in mean case, with a single shift occurring, it was shown that the power of many tests discussed above eventually decreases as the magnitude of the shift increases and can reach zero. This decrease in power can be especially pronounced and effective with smaller mean shifts when a lagged dependent variable is included as a regressor to account for potential serial correlation in the errors.

The basic reason for this feature is the need to estimate the variance of the errors (or the spectral density function at frequency zero when correlation in the errors is allowed) to properly scale the statistics. Since no break is directly modeled, one needs to estimate this variance using least-squares or recursive residuals that are "contaminated" by the shift under the alternative. As the shift gets larger, the estimate of the scale gets inflated with a resulting loss in power. With a lagged dependent variable, the problem is exacerbated because the shift induces a bias of the autoregressive coefficient towards one (Perron, 1989, 1990). See Vogelsang (1999) for a detailed treatment that explains how each test is differently affected, and which also provides empirical illustrations of this problem showing its practical relevance. Crainiceanu and Vogelsang (2001) also show how the problem is exacerbated when using estimates of the scale factor that allow for correlation, e.g., weighted sums of the autocovariance function. The usual methods to select the bandwidth (e.g., Andrews, 1991) will choose a value that is severely biased upward and lead to a decrease in power. With changes in slope, the bandwidth increases at rate T and the tests become inconsistent.

This is a troubling feature since tests that are consistent and have good local asymptotic properties can perform rather badly globally. In simulations reported in Deng and Perron (2005c), this feature does not occur for the CUSUM of squares test. This leads us to the curious conclusion that the test with the worst local asymptotic property (see above) has the better global behavior.

Methods to overcome this problem have been suggested by Altissimo and Corradi (2003) and Juhl and Xiao (2005). They suggest using non-parametric or local averaging methods, where the mean is estimated using data in a neighborhood of a particular data point. The resulting estimates and tests are, however, very sensitive to the bandwidth used. A large bandwidth leads to properly sized tests in finite samples but with low power, while a small bandwidth leads to better power but large size distortions. There is currently no reliable method to appropriately choose this parameter in the context of structural change.

8.4.3 Tests that allow for a single break

The discussion above suggests that, to have better tests for the null hypothesis of no structural change versus the alternative hypothesis that changes are present, one should consider statistics that are based on a regression that allows for a break. As discussed in the introduction, the suggestion by Quandt (1958, 1960) was to use the likelihood ratio test evaluated at the break date that maximizes this likelihood function. This is a non-standard problem since one parameter is only identified under the alternative hypothesis, namely the break date (see Davies, 1977, 1987; King and Shively, 1993; Andrews and Ploberger, 1994; and Hansen, 1996).

The problem raised by Quandt was treated under various degrees of specificity by Deshayes and Picard (1984b), Worsley (1986), James, James and Siegmund (1987), Hawkins (1987), Kim and Siegmund (1989), and Horvath (1995) and was generalized by Andrews (1993a). The basic method, advocated by Davies (1977), for the case in which a nuisance parameter is present only under the alternative, is to use the maximum of the likelihood ratio test over all possible values of the parameter in some pre-specified set as a test statistic. In the case of a single structural change occurring at some unknown date, this translates into the following statistic

$$\sup_{\lambda_1 \in \Lambda_\varepsilon} LR_T(\lambda_1)$$

where $LR(\lambda_1)$ denotes the value of the likelihood ratio evaluated at some break point $T_1 = [T\lambda_1]$ and the maximization is restricted over break fractions that are in $\Lambda_\varepsilon = [\varepsilon_1, 1 - \varepsilon_2]$, some subset of the unit interval $[0,1]$ with ε_1 being the lower bound and $1 - \varepsilon_2$ the upper bound. The limit distribution of the statistic is given by

$$\sup_{\lambda_1 \in \Lambda_\varepsilon} LR_T(\lambda_1) \;\Rightarrow\; \sup_{\lambda_1 \in \Lambda_\varepsilon} G_q(\lambda_1)$$

where

$$G_q(\lambda_1) = \frac{[\lambda_1 W_q(1) - W_q(\lambda_1)]'[\lambda_1 W_q(1) - W_q(\lambda_1)]}{\lambda_1(1 - \lambda_1)} \tag{8.8}$$

with $W_q(\lambda)$ a vector of independent Wiener processes of dimension q, the number of coefficients that are allowed to change (this result holds with non-trending data). Not surprisingly, the limit distribution depends on q but it also depends on Λ_ε. This is important since the restriction that the search for a maximum value be restricted is not simply a technical requirement. It influences the properties of the test in an important way. In particular, Andrews (1993a) shows that if $\varepsilon_1 = \varepsilon_2 = 0$, so that no restrictions are imposed, the test diverges to infinity under the null hypothesis (an earlier statement of this result in a more specialized context can be found in Deshayes and Picard, 1984a). This means that critical values grow and the power of the test decreases as ε_1 and ε_2 get smaller. Hence, the range over which we search for a maximum must be small enough for the critical values not to be too large and for the test to retain decent power, yet large enough to include break dates that are potential candidates. In the single break case, a popular choice is $\varepsilon_1 = \varepsilon_2 = .15$. Andrews (1993a) tabulates critical values for a range of dimensions q and for intervals of the form $[\varepsilon, 1 - \varepsilon]$. This does not imply, however, that one is restricted to imposing equal trimming at both ends of the sample. This is because the limit distribution depends on ε_1 and ε_2 only through the parameter $\gamma = \varepsilon_2(1 - \varepsilon_1)/(\varepsilon_1(1 - \varepsilon_2))$. Hence, the critical values for a symmetric trimming are also valid for some asymmetric trimmings.

To better understand these results, it is useful to look at the simple one-time shift in mean of some variable y_t specified by (8.1). For a given break date $T_1 = [T\lambda_1]$, the Wald test is asymptotically equivalent to the LR test and is given by

$$W_T(\lambda_1) = \frac{SSR(1, T) - SSR(1, T_1) - SSR(T_1 + 1, T)}{[SSR(1, T_1) + SSR(T_1 + 1, T)]/T}$$

where $SSR(i,j)$ is the sum of squared residuals from regressing y_t on a constant using data from date i to date j, i.e.,

$$SSR(i, j) = \sum_{t=i}^{j}\left(y_t - \frac{1}{j - i}\sum_{t=i}^{i} y_t\right) = \sum_{t=i}^{j}\left(e_t - \frac{1}{j - i}\sum_{t=i}^{k} e_t\right)$$

Note that the denominator converges to σ^2 and the numerator is given by

$$\sum_{t=1}^{T}\left(e_t - \frac{1}{T}\sum_{t=1}^{T}e_t\right)^2 - \sum_{t=1}^{T_1}\left(e_t - \frac{1}{T_1}\sum_{t=1}^{T_1}e_t\right)^2 - \sum_{t=T_1+1}^{T}\left(e_t - \frac{1}{T-T_1}\sum_{t=T_1}^{T}e_t\right)^2$$

$$= \left[\frac{T_1}{T}\left(1 - \frac{T_1}{T}\right)\right]^{-1}\left(\frac{T_1}{T}T^{-1/2}\sum_{t=T_1+1}^{T}e_t - \frac{T-T_1}{T}T^{-1/2}\sum_{t=1}^{T_1}e_t\right)^2$$

after some algebra. If $T_1/T \to \lambda_1 \in (0,1)$, we have $T^{-1/2}\sum_{t=1}^{T_1}e_t \Rightarrow \sigma W(\lambda_1)$, $T^{-1/2}\sum_{t=T_1+1}^{T}e_t = T^{-1/2}\sum_{t=1}^{T}e_t - T^{-1/2}\sum_{t=1}^{T_1}e_t \Rightarrow \sigma[W(1) - W(\lambda_1)]$ and the limit of the Wald test is

$$W_T(\lambda_1) \Rightarrow \frac{1}{\lambda_1(1-\lambda_1)}[\lambda_1 W(1) - \lambda_1 W(\lambda_1) - (1-\lambda)W(\lambda_1)]^2$$

$$= \frac{1}{\lambda_1(1-\lambda_1)} [\lambda_1 W(1) - W(\lambda_1)]^2$$

which is equivalent to (8.8) for $q = 1$.

Andrews (1993a) also considered tests based on the maximal value of the Wald and LM tests and shows that they are asymptotically equivalent, i.e., they have the same limit distribution under the null hypothesis and under a sequence of local alternatives. All tests are also consistent and have non-trivial local asymptotic power against a wide range of alternatives, namely those for which the parameters of interest are not constant over the interval specified by Λ_ε. This does not mean, however, that they all have the same behavior in finite samples. Indeed, the simulations of Vogelsang (1999), for the special case of a change in mean, showed the LM_T test to be seriously affected by the problem of non-monotonic power, in the sense that, for a fixed sample size, the power of the test can rapidly decrease to zero as the change in mean increases.[1] Hence, we shall not discuss it any further.

In the context of Model (8.2) with *i.i.d.* errors, the LR and Wald tests have similar properties, so we shall discuss the Wald test. For a single change, it is defined by (up to a scaling by q):

$$\sup_{\lambda_1 \in \Lambda_\varepsilon} W_T(\lambda_1;q) = \sup_{\lambda_1 \in \Lambda_\varepsilon} \left(\frac{T - 2q - p}{k}\right)\frac{\hat{\delta}'H'(H(\bar{Z}'M_X\bar{Z})^{-1}H')^{-1}R\hat{\delta}}{SSR_k} \tag{8.9}$$

where H is the conventional matrix such that $(H\delta)' = (\delta'_1 - \delta'_2)$ and $M_X = I - X(X'X)^{-1}X'$. Here SSR_k is the sum of squared residuals under the alternative hypothesis, which depends on the break date T_1. One thing that is very useful with the sup W_T test is that the break point that maximizes the Wald test is the same as the estimate of the break point, $\hat{T}_1 \equiv [T\hat{\lambda}_1]$, obtained by minimizing the sum of squared residuals provided the minimization problem (8.4) is restricted to the set Λ_ε, i.e.,

$$\sup_{\lambda_1 \in \Lambda_\varepsilon} W_T(\lambda_1;q) = W_T(\hat{\lambda}_1;q)$$

When serial correlation and/or heteroskedasticity in the errors is permitted, things are different since the Wald test must be adjusted to account for this. In this case, it is defined by

$$W_T^*(\lambda_1; q) = \frac{1}{T}\left(\frac{T - 2q - p}{k}\right)\hat{\delta}'H'(H\hat{V}(\hat{\delta})H')^{-1}H\hat{\delta}, \tag{8.10}$$

where $\hat{V}(\hat{\delta})$ is an estimate of the variance–covariance matrix of $\hat{\delta}$ that is robust to serial correlation and heteroskedasticity; i.e., a consistent estimate of

$$V(\hat{\delta}) = \text{plim}_{T\to\infty} T(\bar{Z}'M_X\bar{Z})^{-1}\bar{Z}'M_X\Omega M_X\bar{Z}(\bar{Z}'M_X\bar{Z})^{-1} \tag{8.11}$$

For example, one could use the method of Andrews (1991) based on weighted sums of autocovariances. Note that it can be constructed allowing identical or different distributions for the regressors and the errors across segments. This is important because, if a variance shift occurs at the same time and is not taken into account, inference can be distorted (see, e.g., Pitarakis, 2004).

In some instances, the form of the statistic reduces in an interesting way. For example, consider a pure structural change model where the explanatory variables are such that $\text{plim}T^{-1}\bar{Z}'\Omega\bar{Z} = h_u(0)\text{plim}T^{-1}\bar{Z}'\bar{Z}$, with $h_u(0)$ the spectral density function of the errors u_t evaluated at the zero frequency. In that case, we have the asymptotically equivalent test $(\hat{\sigma}^2/\hat{h}_u(0))W_T(\lambda_1; q)$, with $\hat{\sigma}^2 = T^{-1}\sum_{t=1}^{T}\hat{u}_t^2$ and $\hat{h}_u(0)$ a consistent estimate of $h_u(0)$. Hence, the robust version of the test is simply a scaled version of the original statistic. This is the case, for instance, when testing for a change in mean as in Garcia and Perron (1996).

The computation of the robust version of the Wald test (8.10) can be involved, especially if a data-dependent method is used to construct the robust asymptotic covariance matrix of $\hat{\delta}$. Since the break fractions are T-consistent even with correlated errors, an asymptotically equivalent version is to first use the supremum of the original Wald test, as in (8.9), to obtain the break points, i.e., imposing $\Omega = \sigma^2 I$. The robust version of the test is obtained by evaluating (8.10) and (8.11) at these estimated break dates, i.e., using $W_T^*(\hat{\lambda}_1; q)$ instead of $\sup_{\lambda_1\in\Lambda_\varepsilon} W_T^*(\hat{\lambda}_1; q)$, where $\hat{\lambda}_1$ is obtained by minimizing the sum of squared residuals over the set Λ_ε. This will be especially helpful in the context of testing for multiple structural changes.

8.4.3.1   Optimal tests

The sup-*LR* or sup-Wald tests are not optimal, except in a very restrictive sense. Andrews and Ploberger (1994) consider a class of tests that are optimal, in the sense that they maximize a weighted average power. Two types of weights are involved. The first applies to the parameter that is only identified under the alternative. It assigns a weight function $J(\lambda_1)$ that can be given the interpretation of a prior distribution over the possible break dates or break fractions. The other is related to how far the alternative value is from the null hypothesis within an asymptotic framework that treats alternative values as being local to the null hypothesis. The dependence of a given statistic on this weight function occurs only through a single scalar parameter c. The higher the value of c, the more distant is the alternative value from the null value, and vice versa. The optimal test is then a weighted function of the standard Wald, LM or LR statistics for all permissible fixed break dates. Using either of the three basic statistics leads to tests that are asymptotically equivalent. Here, we shall proceed with the version based on the Wald test (and comment briefly on the version based on the LM test).

The class of optimal statistics is of the following exponential form:

$$Exp\text{-}W_T(c) = (1+c)^{-q/2} \int \exp\left\{\frac{1}{2}\frac{c}{1+c}W_T(\lambda_1)\right\}dJ(\lambda_1)$$

where we recall that q is the number of parameters that are subject to change, and $W_T(\lambda_1)$ is the standard Wald test defined in our context as in (8.9). To implement this test in practice, one needs to specify $J(\lambda_1)$ and c. A natural choice for $J(\lambda_1)$ is to specify it so that equal weights are given to all break fractions in some trimmed interval $[\varepsilon_1, 1-\varepsilon_2]$. For the parameter c, one version sets $c=0$ and puts greatest weight on alternatives close to the null value, i.e., on small shifts; the other version specifies $c=\infty$, in which case greatest weight is put on large changes. This leads to two statistics that have found wide appeal. When $c=\infty$, the test is of an exponential form, viz.

$$Exp\text{-}W_T(\infty) = \log\left(T^{-1}\sum_{T_1=[T\varepsilon_1]+1}^{T-[T\varepsilon_2]}\exp\left(\frac{1}{2}W_T\left(\frac{T_1}{T}\right)\right)\right)$$

When $c=0$, the test takes the form of an average of the Wald tests and is often referred to as the *Mean-W_T* test. It is given by

$$Mean\text{-}W_T = Exp\text{-}W_T(0) = T^{-1}\sum_{T_1=[T\varepsilon_1]+1}^{T-[T\varepsilon_2]}W_T\left(\frac{T_1}{T}\right).$$

The limit distributions of the tests are

$$Exp\text{-}W_T(\infty) \Rightarrow \log\left(\int_{\varepsilon_1}^{1-\varepsilon_2}\exp\left(\frac{1}{2}G_q(\lambda_1)\right)d\lambda_1\right)$$

$$Mean\text{-}W_T \Rightarrow \int_{\varepsilon_1}^{1-\varepsilon_2}G_q(\lambda_1)d\lambda_1$$

where $G_q(\lambda_1)$ is defined in (8.8).

Andrews and Ploberger (1994) presented critical values for both tests for a range of values for symmetric trimmings $\varepsilon_1 = \varepsilon_2$, although, as stated above, they can be used for some non-symmetric trimmings as well. Simulations reported in Andrews, Lee and Ploberger (1996) show that the tests perform well in practice. Relative to other tests discussed above, the *Mean-W_T* has highest power for small shifts, though the test *Exp-$W_T(\infty)$* performs better for moderate to large shifts. None of them uniformly dominates the *Sup-W_T* test and they recommend the use of the *Exp-$W_T(\infty)$* form of the test, referred to as the Exp-Wald test below.

As mentioned above, both tests can equally be implemented (with the same asymptotic critical values) with the LM or LR tests replacing the Wald test. As noted by Andrews and Ploberger (1994), the Mean-LM test is closely related to Gardner's (1969) test (discussed in section 8.2). This is because, in the change in mean case, the LM test takes the form of scaled partial sums. Given the poor properties of this test, especially with respect to large shifts when the power can reach zero, we do not recommend the asymptotically optimal tests based on the *LM* version. In our context, tests based on the Wald or LR statistics have similar properties.

Elliott and Müller (2003) consider optimal tests for a class of models involving non-constant coefficients which, however, rule out one-time abrupt changes. The optimality criterion relates to changes that are in a local neighborhood of the null values, i.e., for small changes. Their procedure is accordingly akin to locally best invariant tests for random variations in the parameters. The suggested procedure does not explicitly model breaks and the test is then of the "function of partial sums type." It has not been documented if the test suffers from non-monotonic power. They show via simulations, with small breaks, that their test also has power against a one-time change. The simulations can also be interpreted as providing support for the conclusion that the Sup, Mean and Exp tests, tailored to a one-time change, also have power nearly as good as the optimal test for random variation in the parameter. For optimal tests in a Generalized Method of Moments framework, see Sowell (1996).

8.4.3.2   *Non-monotonicity in power*

The Sup-Wald and Exp-Wald tests have monotonic power when only one break occurs under the alternative. As shown in Vogelsang (1999), the Mean-Wald test can exhibit a non-monotonic power function, though the problem has not been shown to be severe. All of these, however, suffer from some important power problems when the alternative is one that involves two breaks. Simulations to that effect are presented in Vogelsang (1997) in the context of testing for a shift in trend. This suggests a general principle, which remains, however, just a conjecture at this point. The principle is that any (or most) tests will exhibit non-monotonic power functions if the number of breaks present under the alternative hypothesis is greater than the number of breaks explicitly accounted for in the construction of the tests. This suggests that, even though a single break test is consistent against multiple breaks, substantial power gains can result from using tests for multiple structural changes. These are discussed below.

8.4.4   Tests for multiple structural changes

The literature on tests for multiple structural changes is relatively scarce. Andrews, Lee and Ploberger (1996) studied a class of optimal tests. The *Avg-W* and *Exp-W* tests remain asymptotically optimal in the sense defined above. The test *Exp-W$_T(c)$* is optimal in finite samples with fixed regressors and known variance of the residuals. Their simulations, which pertain to a single change, show the test constructed with an estimate of the variance of the residuals to have power close to the known variance case. The problem, however, with these tests in the case of multiple structural changes is practical implementation. The *Avg-W* and *Exp-W* tests require the computation of the *W*-test over all permissible partitions of the sample, hence the number of tests that need to be evaluated is of the order $O(T^m)$, which is already very large with $m=2$ and prohibitively large when $m>2$. Consider instead the Sup-*W* test. With *i.i.d.* errors, maximizing the Wald statistic with respect to admissible break points is equivalent to minimizing the sum of squared residuals when the search is restricted to the same possible partitions of the sample. As discussed in section 8.3.3, this maximization problem can be solved with a very efficient algorithm. This is the approach taken by Bai and Perron (1998) (an earlier analysis with two breaks was given in Garcia and Perron, 1996). To this date, no one knows the extent of the power loss, if any, in using the sup-*W* type test compared with the *Avg-W* and *Exp-W* tests. To the author's knowledge, no simulations have been presented, presumably because of the prohibitive cost of constructing the *Avg-W* and *Exp-W* tests.

In the context of model (8.2) with *i.i.d.* errors, the Wald test for testing the null hypothesis of no change versus the alternative hypothesis of k changes is given by

$$W_T(\lambda_1, \ldots, \lambda_k; q) = \left(\frac{T - (k+1)q - p}{k}\right) \frac{\hat{\delta}' H'(H(\bar{Z}' M_X \bar{Z})^{-1} H')^{-1} H\hat{\delta}}{SSR_k}$$

where H now is the matrix such that $(H\delta)' = (\delta'_1 - \delta'_2, \ldots, \delta'_k - \delta'_{k+1})$ and $M_X = I - X(X'X)^{-1}X'$. Here, SSR_k is the sum of squared residuals under the alternative hypothesis, which depends on $(T_1, \ldots, T_k)$. Note that one can allow different variances across segments when constructing SSR_k; see Bai and Perron (2003a) for details. The sup-*W* test is defined by

$$\sup_{(\lambda_1, \ldots, \lambda_k) \in \Lambda_\varepsilon} W_T(\lambda_1, \ldots, \lambda_k; q) = W_T(\hat{\lambda}_1, \ldots, \hat{\lambda}_k; q)$$

where

$$\Lambda_\varepsilon = \{(\lambda_1, \ldots, \lambda_k); |\lambda_{i+1} - \lambda_i| \geq \varepsilon, \lambda_1 \geq \varepsilon, \lambda_k \leq 1 - \varepsilon\}$$

and $(\hat{\lambda}_1, \ldots, \hat{\lambda}_k) = (\hat{T}_1/T, \ldots, \hat{T}_k/T)$, with $(\hat{T}_1, \ldots, \hat{T}_k)$ the estimates of the break dates obtained by minimizing the sum of squared residuals by searching over partitions defined by the set Λ_ε. This set dictates the minimal length of a segment. In principle, this minimal length could be different across the sample but then critical values would need to be computed on a case by case basis.

When serial correlation and/or heteroskedasticity in the residuals is allowed, the test is

$$W_T^*(\lambda_1, \ldots, \lambda_k; q) = \frac{1}{T}\left(\frac{T - (k+1)q - p}{k}\right) \hat{\delta}' H'(H\hat{V}(\hat{\delta})H')^{-1} H\hat{\delta},$$

with $\hat{V}(\hat{\delta})$ as defined by (8.11). Again, the asymptotically equivalent version with the Wald test evaluated at the estimates $(\hat{\lambda}_1, \ldots, \hat{\lambda}_k)$ is used to make the problem tractable.

The limit distribution of the tests under the null hypothesis is the same in both cases, namely,

$$\sup W_T(k; q) \; \Rightarrow \; \sup W_{k,q} \stackrel{def}{=} \sup_{(\lambda_1, \ldots, \lambda_k) \in \Lambda_\varepsilon} W(\lambda_1, \ldots, \lambda_k; q)$$

with

$$W(\lambda_1, \ldots, \lambda_k; q) \stackrel{def}{=} \frac{1}{k} \sum_{i=1}^{k} \frac{[\lambda_i W_q(\lambda_{i+1}) - \lambda_{i+1} W_q(\lambda_i)]'[\lambda_i W_q(\lambda_{i+1}) - \lambda_{i+1} W_q(\lambda_i)]}{\lambda_i \lambda_{i+1}(\lambda_{i+1} - \lambda_i)}$$

again assuming non-trending data. Critical values for $\varepsilon = 0.05$, k ranging from 1 to 9 and for q ranging from 1 to 10, are presented in Bai and Perron (1998). Bai and Perron (2003b) present response surfaces to get critical values, based on simulations for this and the following additional cases (all with q ranging from 1 to 10): $\varepsilon = .10$ $(k = 1, \ldots, 8)$, $\varepsilon = .15$ $(k = 1, \ldots, 5)$, $\varepsilon = .20$ $(k = 1, 2, 3)$ and $\varepsilon = .25$ $(k = 1, 2)$. The full set of tabulated critical values is available on the author's web page (the same sources also contain critical values for other tests discussed below). The importance of the choice of ε for the size and power of the test is discussed in Bai and Perron (2003a, 2005). Also discussed in Bai and Perron (2003a) are variations in the exact construction of the test that allow one to impose various restrictions on the nature of the errors and regressors, which can help improve power.

8.4.4.1 *Double maximum tests*

Often, one may not wish to pre-specify a particular number of breaks to make inference. For such instances, a test of the null hypothesis of no structural break against an unknown number of breaks given some upper bound M can be used. These are called the "double maximum tests." The first is an equal-weight version defined by UD max $W_T(M, q) = \max_{1 \le m \le M} W_T(\hat{\lambda}_1, \ldots, \hat{\lambda}_m; q)$, where $\hat{\lambda}_j = \hat{T}_j/T$ $(j = 1, \ldots, m)$ are the estimates of the break points obtained using the global minimization of the sum of squared residuals. This UD max test can be given a Bayesian interpretation in which the prior assigns equal weights to the possible number of changes (see, e.g., Andrews, Lee and Ploberger, 1996). The second test applies weights to the individual tests such that the marginal p-values are equal across values of m and is denoted WD max $F_T(M, q)$ (see Bai and Perron, 1998, for details). The choice $M = 5$ should be sufficient for most applications. In any event, the critical values vary little as M is increased beyond 5.

Double maximum tests can play a significant role in testing for structural changes and they are arguably the most useful tests to apply when trying to determine if structural changes are present. While the test for one break is consistent against alternatives involving multiple changes, its power in finite samples can be rather poor. First, there are types of multiple structural changes that are difficult to detect with a test for a single change (for example, two breaks with the first and third regimes the same). Second, as discussed above, tests for a particular number of changes may have non-monotonic power when the number of changes is greater than specified. Third, the simulations of Bai and Perron (2005) show that the power of the double maximum tests is almost as high as the best power that can be achieved using the test that accounts for the correct number of breaks. All these elements strongly point to their usefulness.

8.4.4.2 Sequential tests

Bai and Perron (1998) also discuss a test of ℓ versus $\ell + 1$ breaks, which can be used as the basis of a sequential testing procedure. For the model with ℓ breaks, the estimated break points, denoted by $(\hat{T}_1, \ldots, \hat{T}_\ell)$, are obtained by a global minimization of the sum of squared residuals. The strategy proceeds by testing for the presence of an additional break in each of the $(\ell + 1)$ segments (obtained using the estimated partition $\hat{T}_1, \ldots, \hat{T}_\ell$). The test amounts to the application of $(\ell + 1)$ tests of the null hypothesis of no structural change versus the alternative hypothesis of a single change. It is applied to each segment containing the observations $\hat{T}_{i-1} + 1$ to $\hat{T}_i$ $(i = 1, \ldots, \ell + 1)$. We reject in favor of a model with $(\ell + 1)$ breaks if the overall minimal value of the sum of squared residuals (over all segments where an additional break is included) is sufficiently smaller than the sum of squared residuals from the ℓ breaks model. The break date thus selected is the one associated with this overall minimum. More precisely, the test is defined by:

$$W_T(\ell + 1|\ell) = \{S_T(\hat{T}_1, \ldots, \hat{T}_\ell) - \min_{1 \le i \le \ell + 1} \inf_{\tau \in \Lambda_{i,\varepsilon}} S_T(\hat{T}_1, \ldots, \hat{T}_{i-1}, \tau, \hat{T}_i, \ldots, \hat{T}_\ell)\}/\hat{\sigma}^2,$$

(8.12)

where $S_T(\cdot)$ denotes the sum of squared residuals,

$$\Lambda_{i,\varepsilon} = \{\tau; \hat{T}_{i-1} + (\hat{T}_i - \hat{T}_{i-1})\varepsilon \le \tau \le \hat{T}_i - (\hat{T}_i - \hat{T}_{i-1})\varepsilon\},$$

(8.13)

and $\hat{\sigma}^2$ is a consistent estimate of σ^2 under the null hypothesis and also, preferably, under the alternative. Note that for $i = 1$, $S_T(\hat{T}_1, \ldots, \hat{T}_{i-1}, \tau, \hat{T}_i, \ldots, \hat{T}_\ell)$ is understood as $S_T(\tau, \hat{T}_1, \ldots, \hat{T}_\ell)$ and for $i = \ell + 1$ as $S_T(\hat{T}_1, \ldots, \hat{T}_\ell, \tau)$. It is important to note that one can allow different distributions across segments for the regressors and the errors. The limit distribution of the test is related to the limit distribution of a test for a single change.

Bai (1999) considers the same problem of testing for ℓ versus $\ell + 1$ breaks while allowing the breaks to be global minimizers of the sum of squared residuals under both the null and alternative hypotheses. This leads to the likelihood ratio test defined by:

$$\sup LR_T(\ell + 1|\ell) = \frac{S_T(\hat{T}_1, \ldots, \hat{T}_\ell) - S_T(\hat{T}_1^*, \ldots, \hat{T}_{\ell+1}^*)}{S_T(\hat{T}_1^*, \ldots, \hat{T}_{\ell+1}^*)/T}$$

where $\{\hat{T}_1, \ldots, \hat{T}_\ell\}$ and $\{\hat{T}_1^*, \ldots, \hat{T}_{\ell+1}^*\}$ are the sets of ℓ and $\ell+1$ breaks obtained by minimizing the sum of squared residuals using ℓ and $\ell+1$ break models, respectively. The limit distribution of the test is different and is given by:

$$\sup LR_T(\ell+1|\ell) \Rightarrow \max\{\xi_1, \ldots, \xi_{\ell+1}\}$$

where $\xi_1, \ldots, \xi_{\ell+1}$ are independent random variables with the following distribution

$$\xi_i = \sup_{\eta_i \leq s \leq 1 - \eta_i} \sum_{j=1}^{q} \frac{B_{i,j}(s)}{s(1-s)}$$

with the $B_{i,j}(s)$ being independent standard Brownian bridges on $[0,1]$ and $\eta_i = \varepsilon/(\lambda_i^0 - \lambda_{i-1}^0)$. Bai (1999) discusses a method of computing the asymptotic critical values and also extends the results to the case of trending regressors.

These tests can form the basis of a sequential testing procedure. One simply needs to apply the tests successively, starting from $\ell = 0$, until a non-rejection occurs. The estimate of the number of breaks thus selected will be consistent provided the significance level used decreases at an appropriate rate. The simulation results of Bai and Perron (2005) show that such an estimate of the number of breaks is much better than those obtained using information criteria as suggested by, among others, Liu *et al.* (1997) and Yao (1998) (see also, Perron, 1997b). But for the reasons discussed above (concerning the problems with tests that allow a number of breaks smaller than the true value), such a sequential procedure should not be applied mechanically. It is easy to have cases where the procedure stops too early. The recommendation is to first use a double maximum test to ascertain if any break is at all present. The sequential tests can then be used, starting at some value greater than 0, to determine the number of breaks. An alternative sequential method is provided by Altissimo and Corradi (2003) for the case of multiple changes in mean. It consists of testing for a single break using the maximum of the absolute value of the partial sums of demeaned data. One then estimates the break date by minimizing the sum of squared residuals and continues the procedure, conditional on the break date previously found, until a non-rejection occurs. They derive an appropriate bound to use as critical values for the procedure to yield a strongly consistent estimate of the number of breaks. It is unclear, however, how the procedure can be extended to the more general case with general regressors.

8.4.5 Tests for restricted structural changes

As discussed in section 8.3.2, Perron and Qu (2005) consider the estimation of structural change models subject to restrictions. Consider testing the null hypothesis of no breaks versus an alternative with k breaks. Recall that the restrictions are $R\delta = r$. Define

$$W_T(\lambda_1, \ldots, \lambda_k; q) = \tilde{\delta}'H'(H\tilde{V}(\tilde{\delta})H')^- H\tilde{\delta}, \tag{8.14}$$

where $\tilde{\delta}$ is the restricted estimate of δ obtained using the partition $\{\lambda_1, \ldots, \lambda_k\}$, and $\tilde{V}(\tilde{\delta})$ is an estimate of the variance covariance matrix of $\tilde{\delta}$ that may be constructed to be robust to heteroskedasticity and serial correlation in the errors. As usual, for a matrix A, A^- denotes the generalized inverse of A. Such a generalized inverse is needed since, in general, the covariance matrix of $\tilde{\delta}$ will be singular given that restrictions are imposed. Again, instead of using the sup $W_T(\lambda_1, \ldots, \lambda_k; q)$ statistic, where the supremum is taken over all possible partitions in the set Λ_ε, we consider the asymptotically equivalent test that evaluates the Wald test at the restricted estimate, i.e., $W_T(\tilde{\lambda}_1, \ldots, \tilde{\lambda}_k; q)$.

The restrictions can alternatively be parameterized by the relation

$$\delta = S\theta + s$$

where S is a $q(k+1)$ by d matrix, with d the number of basic parameters in the column vector θ, and s is a $q(k+1)$ vector of constants. Then

$$W_T(\hat{\lambda}_1, \ldots, \hat{\lambda}_k; q, S) \Rightarrow \sup_{|\lambda_i - \lambda_{i-1}| > \varepsilon} W(\lambda_1, \ldots, \lambda_k; q, S)$$

with

$$W_T(\lambda_1, \ldots, \lambda_k; q, S)$$
$$= W^{*'}S[S'(\Lambda \otimes I_q)S]^{-1}S'H'[HS(S'(\Lambda \otimes I_q)S')^{-1}H'S']^- HS[S'(\Lambda \otimes I_q)S]^{-1}S'W^*$$

where $\Lambda = diag(\lambda_1, \lambda_2 - \lambda_1, \ldots, 1 - \lambda_k)$, I_q is the standard identity matrix of dimension q and the $q(k+1)$ vector W^* is defined by

$$W^* = [W_q(\lambda_1), W_q(\lambda_2) - W_q(\lambda_1), \ldots, W_q(1) - W_q(\lambda_k)]$$

with $W_q(r)$ a q vector of independent unit Wiener processes. The limit distribution depends on the exact nature of the restrictions so that it is not possible to tabulate critical values that are valid in general. Perron and Qu (2005) discuss a simulation algorithm to compute the relevant critical values given some restrictions. Imposing valid restrictions results in tests with much improved power.

8.4.6 Tests for structural changes in multivariate systems

Bai *et al.* (1998) considered a sup Wald test for a single change in a multivariate system. Bai (2000) and Qu and Perron (2005) extend the analysis to the context of multiple structural changes. They consider the case where only a subset of the coefficients is allowed to change, whether it be the parameters of the conditional mean, the covariance matrix of the errors, or both. The tests are based on the maximized value of the likelihood ratio over permissible partitions assuming uncorrelated and homoskedastic errors. As above, the tests can be corrected to allow for serial correlation and heteroskedasticity when testing for changes in the parameters of the conditional mean assuming no change in the covariance matrix of the errors.

The results are similar to those obtained in Bai and Perron (1998). The limit distributions are identical and depend only on the number of coefficients allowed to change, and the number of times that they are allowed to do so. However, when the tests involve potential changes in the covariance matrix of the errors, the limit distributions are only valid assuming a normal distribution for these errors. This is because, in this case, the limit distributions of the tests depend on the higher-order moments of the errors' distribution. Without the assumption of normality, additional parameters are present which take different forms for different distributions. Hence, testing becomes case specific even in large samples. It is not yet known how assuming normality affects the size of the tests when it is not valid.

An important advantage of the general framework analyzed by Qu and Perron (2005) is that it allows changes in the variance of the errors to be studied in the presence of simultaneous changes in the parameters of the conditional mean, thereby avoiding inference problems when changes in variance are studied in isolation. Also, it allows for the two types of changes to occur at different dates, thereby avoiding problems related to tests for changes in the paremeters when, for example, a change in variance occurs at some other date (see, e.g., Pitarakis, 2004).

Tests using the quasi-likelihood based method of Qu and Perron (2005) are especially important in light of Hansen's (2000) analysis. First, note that the limit distribution of the Sup, Mean and Exp type tests in a single equation system have the stated limit distribution under the assumption that the regressors and the variance of the errors have distributions that are stable across the sample. For example, the mean of the regressors or the variance of the errors cannot undergo a change at some date. Hansen (2000) shows that when this condition is not satisfied the limit distribution changes and the test can be distorted. His asymptotic results pertaining to the local asymptotic analysis show, however, the sup-Wald test to be little affected in terms of size and power. The finite sample simulations show that if the errors are homoskedastic, the size distortions are quite mild (over and above that applying with *i.i.d.* regressors, given that he uses a very small sample of $T = 50$). The distortions are, however, quite severe when a change in variance occurs. But both problems of changes in the distribution of the regressors and the variance of the errors can easily be handled using the framework of Qu and Perron (2005). If a change in the variance of the residuals is a concern, one can perform a test for no change in some parameters of the conditional model allowing for a change in variance, since the tests are based on a likelihood ratio approach. If changes in the marginal distribution of some regressors is a concern, one can use a multi-equation system with equations for these regressors. Whether this is preferable to Hansen's (2000) bootstrap method remains an open question. Note, however, that in the context of multiple changes it is not clear if that method is computationally feasible, especially for the heteroskedastic case.

8.4.7   Tests valid with $I(1)$ regressors

With $I(1)$ regressors, the case of interest is that of a system of cointegrated variables. The goal is then to test whether the cointegrating relationship has changed and to estimate the break dates and form confidence intervals for them.

Consider, for simplicity, the following case with an intercept and m $I(1)$ regressors y_{2t}:

$$y_{1t} = a + \beta y_{2t} + u_t \tag{8.15}$$

where u_t is $I(0)$ so that y_{1t} and y_{2t} are cointegrated with cointegrating vector $(1, -\beta)$. To our knowledge, the only contribution concerning the consistency and limit distribution of the estimates of the break dates is that of Bai *et al.* (1998). They consider a single break in a multi-equation system and show the estimates obtained by maximizing the likelihood function to be consistent. They also obtain a limit distribution under a shrinking shifts scenario, with the shift in the constant a decreasing at rate T^{b_1} for some $b_1 \in (0, 1/2)$ and the shift in β decreasing at rate T^{b_2} for some $b_2 \in (1/2, 1)$. Under this scenario the rate of convergence is the same as in the stationary case (since the coefficients on the $I(1)$ variables are assumed to shrink at a faster rate).

For testing, an early contribution in this area is Hansen (1992a). He considers tests of the null hypothesis of no change in both coefficients (for an extension to partial changes, see Kuo, 1998, who considers tests for changes in intercept only and tests for changes in all coefficients of the cointegrating vector). The tests considered are the sup and Mean LM tests directed against an alternative of a one time change in the coefficients. He also considers a version of the LM test directed against the alternative that the coefficients are random walk processes, denoted L_c. The latter is an extension of Gardner's (1969) Q-test to the multivariate cointegration context, which is based on the average of the partial sums of the scores and the use of a full sample estimate of the conditional variance of these scores. For related results with respect to LM tests for parameter constancy in cointegrated regressions, see Quintos and Phillips (1993).

Gregory *et al.* (1996) study the finite sample properties of Hansen's (1992a) tests in the context of a linear quadratic model with costs of adjustments. They show that power can be low when the cost of adjustment is high and suggest a simple transformation of the dependent variable that can increase power. They also consider the behavior of standard residuals based tests of the null hypothesis of no cointegration and show that their power reduces considerably when structural breaks are present in the cointegrating relation. Again, this is simply a manifestation of the fact that unit root tests have little power when the process is stationary around a trend function that changes. Moreover, since Hansen's (1992a) tests can also be viewed as a test for the null hypothesis of stationarity, in this context it can also be viewed as a test of the null hypothesis of cointegration versus the alternative of no cointegration. Note, however, that the sup and Mean Wald test will also reject when no structural change is present and the system is not cointegrated. Hence, the application of such tests should be interpreted with caution. No tests are available for the null hypothesis of no change in the coefficients a and β allowing the errors to be $I(0)$ or $I(1)$. This is because, when the errors are $I(1)$, we have a spurious regression and the parameters are not identified. To be able to properly interpret the tests, they should be used in conjunction with tests for the presence or absence of cointegration allowing shifts in the coefficients (see section 6). The same comments apply to other tests discussed below.

Consider now a cointegrated VAR system written in the following error correction format with $y'_t = (y_{1t}, y'_{2t})'$ of dimension $n = m + 1$,

$$\Delta y_t = \mu + \alpha B' y_{t-1} + \sum_{i=1}^{p} \Gamma_i \Delta y_{t-i} + u_t \tag{8.16}$$

where B $(n \times r)$ is the cointegrating matrix and α $(n \times r)$ the adjustment matrix (hence, there are r cointegrating vectors). Under the null hypothesis, both are assumed constant, while under the alternative either one or both are assumed to exhibit a one-time change at some unknown date T_1. For the case of a triangular system with the restriction that $B' = [I_r, B^*]$, Seo (1998) considers the Sup, Mean and Exp versions of the LM test for the following three cases: (1) the constant vector μ is excluded (and the data are assumed non-trending); (2) the constant μ is included but the data are not trending; (3) the constant μ is included and the data are trending. The Sup and Mean LM tests in this cointegrated VAR setup are shown to have a similar asymptotic distribution as the Sup and Mean LM tests of Hansen (1992a) for the case of a change in all coefficients. See also Hao (1996), who also considers the L_c tests for no cointegration allowing for a one-time change in intercept at some unknown date using the maximal value over all possible break dates.

Hansen and Johansen (1999) also consider a VAR process.[2] Then the MLE (based on normal errors) of the cointegrating matrix B are the eigenvectors corresponding to the r largest eigenvalues of the system

$$|\lambda S_{11} - S_{10} S_{00}^{-1} S_{01}| = 0$$

where

$$S_{ij} = T^{-1} \sum_{j=1}^{T} R_{it} B_{jt} \tag{8.17}$$

with R_{0t} (resp., R_{1t}) being the residuals from a regression of Δy_t (resp., y_{t-1}) on a constant and lags of Δy_t. Hansen and Johansen (1999) show that instability in α and/or B will manifest themselves in the form of unstable eigenvalue estimates when evaluated using different samples. They therefore suggest the use of recursive estimates of λ. Their test takes the form of the fluctuations test of Ploberger *et al.* (1989) and will have power when either α or B change (see also Quintos, 1997). They also suggest a test that allows the detection of changes in β, an extension of the L_c test of Hansen (1992a) that can be constructed using recursive estimates of λ. Interestingly, Quintos (1997) documents that such tests over-reject the null hypothesis of no structural change when the cointegrating rank is over specified, i.e., when the number of stochastic trends, or unit root components, is under specified. This is the multivariate equivalent of the problem discussed in section 8.2, namely that structural change and unit roots can easily be confounded. She proposes a test for the stability of the cointegrating rank. However, when the alternative hypothesis is of a greater rank (less unit roots), the tests will not have power if structural change is present. This is the dilemma faced when trying to assess jointly the correct rank of a cointegrating system and whether structural change is present in the cointegrating vectors. Another contribution, again based on functions of partial sums, is Hao and Inder (1996), who consider the CUSUM test based on OLS residuals from a cointegrating regression.

From this brief review, most tests available are seen to be of the LM type. Given our earlier discussion, these can be expected to have non-monotonic power since they do not explicitly allow for any break. However, no simulation study is available to substantiate this claim and show its relevance in practice. More work is needed in that direction and in considering Wald or LR type tests in a multiple structural change context. Also, these tests are valid if the cointegrating rank is well specified. As discussed above, a rejection can be due to an over specification of this rank. The problem of jointly determining whether the cointegrating rank is appropriate and whether the system is structurally stable is an important avenue of further research.

A potential, yet speculative, approach to determining if the data suggest structural changes in a cointegrating relationship or a spurious regression is the following. Suppose that one is willing to put an upper bound M (say 5) on the possible number of breaks. One can then use a multiple structural change test as discussed in section 8.4.4. The reason is that if the system is cointegrated with less than M breaks, the tests can be used to consistently estimate the number of breaks. However, if the regression is spurious, the number of breaks selected will always (in large enough samples) be the maximum number of breaks allowed. The same occurs when an information criterion is used to select the number of breaks (see Nunes *et al.*, 1996; Perron, 1997b). Hence, selecting the maximum permissible number of breaks can be symptomatic of the presence of $I(1)$ errors. Of course, more work is needed to turn this argument into a rigorous procedure.

8.4.8 Tests valid whether the errors are $I(1)$ or $I(0)$

We now consider the issue of testing for structural change when the errors in (8.2) may have a unit root. In the general case with arbitrary regressors, this question is of little interest. If the regressors are $I(0)$ and the errors $I(1)$, the estimates of the break dates will be inconsistent and so will the tests. This is simply due to the fact that the variability in the errors masks any potential shifts. With $I(1)$ regressors, we have a cointegrated system when the errors are $I(0)$, and a spurious regression with $I(1)$ errors. In general, only the former is of interest.

The problem of testing for structural changes in a linear model with errors that are either $I(0)$ or $I(1)$ is, however, of substantial interest when the regression is on a polynomial time trend. The leading case is testing for changes in the mean or slope of a linear trend, a question of substantial interest with economic data. We shall use this example to illustrate the main issues involved.

Consider the following structure for some variable y_t $(t = 1, \ldots, T)$

$$y_t = \beta_0 + \beta_1 t + u_t \tag{8.18}$$

where the errors follow a (possibly nonstationary) $AR(k)$ process

$$A(L)u_t = e_t$$

with $A(L) = (1 - \alpha L)A^*(L)$ and the roots of $A^*(L)$ all outside the unit circle. If $\alpha = 1$ the series contains an autoregressive unit root, while if $|\alpha| < 1$, it is trend-stationary. The Q statistic is defined by

$$Q_1^* = \hat{h}_e(0)^{-1} T^{-2} \sum_{t=1}^{T} \left[\sum_{j=t+1}^{T} \hat{u}_j \right]^2$$

where $\hat{h}_u(0) = \sum_{\tau=-m}^{m} w(m, \tau) \hat{R}_u(\tau)$ with $\hat{R}_u(\tau) = T^{-1} \sum_{t=\tau+1}^{T} \hat{u}_t \hat{u}_{t-r}$, $w(m, \tau)$ is some weight function with $m/T \rightarrow 0$ (e.g., $w(m, \tau) = 1 - |\tau|/m$ if $|\tau| < m$ and 0 otherwise), and $\hat{u}_t$ are the least-squares residuals from estimating (8.18) by OLS. Then if $|\alpha| < 1$,

$$Q_1^* \Rightarrow \int_0^1 B_1(r)^2 dr \tag{8.19}$$

where

$$B_1(r) = W(r) + 2 \left[W(1) - 3 \int_0^1 W(s)ds \right] r - 3 \left[W(1) - 2 \int_0^1 W(s)ds \right] r^2.$$

On the other hand, if $\alpha = 1$,

$$(m/T) Q_1^* \Rightarrow \int_0^1 \left[\int_0^T W_1^*(s)ds \right]^2 dr/\kappa \int_0^1 W_1^*(r)^2 dr$$

with

$$W_1^*(r) = W(r) - 4 \left[\int_0^1 W(s) \, ds - (3/2) \int_0^1 sW(s) \, ds \right]$$
$$+ 6r \left[\int_0^1 W(s)ds - 2 \int_0^1 sW(s) \, ds \right]$$

and $\kappa = \int_{-1}^1 K(s)ds$, where $K(\tau/m) = \omega(m, \tau)$ (see Perron, 1991). Hence, the limit distribution is not only different under both the $I(1)$ and $I(0)$ cases, but the scaling needed is different. If one does not have prior knowledge about whether the series is integrated or not, one would need to use the statistic $(m/T) Q_1^*$ and reject using the critical values in the $I(1)$ case in order to have a test that has asymptotic size no greater than some prespecified level in all cases. But this would entail a test with zero asymptotic size whenever the series is stationary. As suggested by Perron (1991), a solution is to base the test on a regression that parametrically accounts for the serial correlation in u_t, namely

$$y_t = \beta_0 + \beta_1 t + \sum_{j=1}^{k} \alpha_j y_{t-j} + e_t \qquad (8.20)$$

Since the errors are uncorrelated, one uses the statistic

$$QD_1 = \hat{\sigma}_e^{-2} T^{-2} \sum_{t=k+1}^{k} \left[\sum_{j=t+1}^{T} \hat{e}_j \right]^2$$

where $\sigma_e^2 = T^{-1} \sum_{t=k+1}^{T} \hat{e}_t^2$, with $\hat{e}_t$ the residuals from estimating (8.20) by OLS (since the dynamics is taken into account parametrically, there is no need to scale with an estimate of the "long-run" variance). When $|\alpha| < 1$, result (8.19) still holds, while when $\alpha = 1$ we have

$$QD_1 \Rightarrow \int_0^1 \left[B_1(r) + H(1) \int_0^r W_1^*(s)ds \right]^2 dr$$

where $H(1) = \int_0^1 W_1^*(s)dW(s) / \int_0^1 W_1^*(s)^2 ds$. The limit distributions are different but now the scaling for the convergence is the same. Hence, a conservative procedure is to use the largest of the two sets of critical values, which correspond to those from the limit distribution that applies to the $I(1)$ case. The test is then somewhat asymptotically conservative in the $I(0)$ case but power is still non-trivial. Perron (1991) discusses the power function in detail and shows that it is non-monotonic, in that the test has zero power for large shifts (of course, when testing for a shift in level, the test has little power, if any, when the errors are $I(1)$).

A natural extension is to explicitly model breaks and consider a regression of the form

$$y_t = \beta_0 + \beta_1 t + \gamma_1 DU_t + \gamma_2 DT_t + u_t \qquad (8.21)$$

where $DU_t = 1(t > T_1)$ and $DT_t = 1(t > T_1)(t - T_1)$. One can then use any of the tests advocated by Andrews and Ploberger (1996), though they may not be optimal with $I(1)$ errors. These tests, however, also have different rates of convergence under the null hypothesis for $I(0)$ and $I(1)$ errors when based on regression (8.21). To remedy this problem, one can use a dynamic regression of the form

$$y_t = \beta_0 + \beta_1 t + \gamma_1 DU_t + \gamma_2 DT_t + \sum_{j=1}^{k} \alpha_j y_{t-j} + e_t$$

This is the approach taken by Vogelsang (1997). He considers the Sup, Mean and Exp Wald tests and shows that they have well-defined limit distributions under both $I(0)$ and $I(1)$ errors, which are, however, different. Again, at any significance level, the critical values are larger in the $I(1)$ case and these are to be used to ensure tests with an asymptotic size no greater than pre-specified in both cases.

Interestingly, Vogelsang's results show that the Sup and Exp Wald tests have monotonic power functions but that the Mean-Wald test does not, the decrease in power being especially severe in the case of a level shift (this is due to the fact that the Sup and Exp tests assign most weight to the correct date, unlike the Mean test). Banerjee *et al.* (1992) also consider a Sup Wald test for a change in any one or more coefficients in a regression of y_t on $\{1, t, y_{t-1}, \Delta y_{t-1}, \ldots, \Delta y_{t-k}\}$ assuming y_t to be $I(1)$.

Vogelsang (2001) takes a different approach to obtain a statistic that has the same rate of convergence under both the $I(0)$ and $I(1)$ cases (see also Vogelsang, 1998a,b). Let $W_T(\lambda_1)$ be the Wald statistic for testing that $\gamma_1 = \gamma_2 = 0$ in (8.21). The statistic considered is

$$PSW_T(\lambda_1) = W_T(\lambda_1)\left[s_u^2/(100T^{-1}s_z^2)\right]\exp(-bJ_T(m))$$

where $s_u^2 = T^{-1}\sum_{t=1}^{T}\hat{u}_t^2$, with $\hat{u}_t$ the OLS residuals from regression (8.21), $s_z^2 = T^{-1}\sum_{t=1}^{T}\hat{v}_t^2$, where $\hat{v}_t$ are the OLS residuals from the following partial sum regression version of (8.21)

$$y_t^p = \beta_0 t + \beta_1((t^2 + t)/2) + \gamma_1 DT_t + \gamma_2\left[DT_t^2 + DT_t\right]/2 + v_t \tag{8.22}$$

where $y_t^p = \sum_{j=1}^{t} y_j$ and $J_T(m)$ is a unit root test that has a non-degenerate limit distribution in the $I(1)$ case and converges to 0 in the $I(0)$ case. Consider first the case with $I(0)$ errors. We have $W_T(\lambda_1)$, s_u^2 and $T^{-1}s_z^2$ all $O_p(1)$, hence $PSW_T(\lambda_1) = O_p(1)$, which does not depend on b. If the errors are $I(1)$, $W_T(\lambda_1) = O_p(T)$, $T^{-1}s_u^2 = O_p(T)$ and $T^{-1}s_z^2 = O_p(1)$, hence $PSW_T(\lambda_1) = O_p(1)$ again. The trick is then to set b at the value which makes the critical values the same in both cases for any prescribed significance level. One can then use the Sup, Mean or Exponential version of the Wald test, though neither of the three have any optimal property in this context (another version based directly on the partial sums regression (8.22) is also discussed).

Perron and Yabu (2005) consider an alternative approach which leads to more powerful tests. Consider the following special case of (8.21) for illustration

$$y_t = \beta_0 + \beta_1 t + \gamma_2 DT_t + u_t \tag{8.23}$$

so that the goal is to test for a shift in the slope of the trend function with both segments joined at the time of break. Assume that the errors are generated by an AR(1) process of the form

$$u_t = \alpha u_{t-1} + e_t \tag{8.24}$$

(an extension to the more general case is also discussed). If $\alpha = 1$, the errors are $I(1)$ and if $|\alpha| < 1$, the errors are $I(0)$. Consider the infeasible GLS regression

$$y_t^* = \beta_0^* + \beta_1 t^* + \gamma_2 DT_t^* + e_t$$

where for any variable, a* indicates the quasi-differenced data, e.g., $y_t^* = (1 - \alpha L)y_t$. For a fixed break point T_1, the Wald test would be the best test to use and the limit distribution would be chi-square in both the $I(1)$ and $I(0)$ cases. However, if one used a standard estimate of α to construct a test based on the feasible GLS regression (e.g., $\hat{\alpha}$ obtained by estimating (8.24) with u_t replaced by $\hat{u}_t$, the OLS residuals from (8.23)), the limit distribution would be different in both cases. Perron and Yabu (2005) show, however, that the same chi-square distribution prevails if one replaces $\hat{\alpha}$ by a truncated version given by

$$\hat{\alpha}_s = \begin{cases} \hat{\alpha} & \text{if } T^\delta |\hat{\alpha} - 1| > d \\ 1 & \text{if } T^\delta |\hat{\alpha} - 1| \leq d \end{cases}$$

for some $\delta \in (0,1)$ and some $d > 0$. Theoretical arguments presented in Perron and Yabu (2004) show that $\delta = 1/2$ is the preferred choice. Also, finite sample improvements are possible if one replaces $\hat{\alpha}$ by a median unbiased estimate (e.g., Andrews, 1993b) or the estimate proposed by Roy and Fuller (2001; see also Roy et al., 2004). When the break date is unknown, the limit distributions of the Sup, Mean or Exp Wald tests are no longer the same for the $I(0)$ and $I(1)$ cases. However, for the Exp version, the asymptotic critical values are very close (for all common significance levels). Hence, with this version, there is no need for an adjustment. Simulations show that for this case, a value $d = 1$ leads to tests with good finite sample properties and a power function that is close to that which could be obtained using the infeasible GLS regression, unless the value of α is close to but not equal to one.

The issue of testing for structural changes in the trend function of a time series without having to take a stand on whether the series is $I(1)$ or $I(0)$ is of substantial practical importance. As discussed above, some useful recent developments have been made. Much remains to be done, however. First, none of the procedures proposed have been shown to have some optimality property. Second, there is still a need to extend the analysis to the multiple structural change case with unknown break dates.

8.4.9 Testing for changes in persistence

A problem involving structural change and the presence of $I(0)$ and $I(1)$ processes relates to the quite recent literature on changes in persistence. What is meant, in most cases, by this is that a process can switch at some date from being $I(0)$ to being $I(1)$, or vice versa. This has been an issue of substantial empirical interest, especially concerning inflation series (e.g., Barsky, 1987; Burdekin and Siklos, 1999), short-term interest rates (e.g., Mankiw et al., 1987), government budget deficits (e.g., Hakkio and Rush, 1991) and real output (e.g., Delong and Summers, 1988). As discussed in section 8.3.1, Chong (2001) derived the limit distribution of the estimate of the break date obtained by minimizing the sum of squared residuals from a regression that allows the coefficient on the lagged dependent variable to change at some unknown date. However, he provided no procedure to test whether a change has occurred and in which direction.

As discussed in this review, tests for structural change started with statistics based on partial sums of the data (or some appropriate residuals, in general), as in the Q test of Gardner (1969), and tests of the null hypothesis of stationarity versus a unit root process started with the same statistic. Interestingly, we are again back to Gardner (1969) when devising procedures to test for a change in persistence.

Kim (2000) and Busetti and Taylor (2001) consider testing the null hypothesis that the series is $I(0)$ throughout the sample versus the alternative that it switches from $I(0)$ to $I(1)$ or vice versa. The statistic used is the ratio of the unscaled Gardner's (1969) Q test over the post and pre-break samples. With the partial sums $S_{i,t} = \sum_{j=i+1}^{t} \hat{u}_j$, where $\hat{u}_t$ are the residuals from a regression of the data y_t on a constant (non-trending series) or on a constant and time trend (for trending series), it is defined by

$$\Xi_T(T_1) = \frac{(T - T_1)^{-2} \sum_{t=T_1+1}^{T} S_{T_1,t}^2}{T_1^{-2} \sum_{t=1}^{T_1} S_{1,t}^2} \tag{8.25}$$

Under the null hypothesis of $I(0)$ throughout the sample, both the numerator and denominator are $O_p(1)$. Consider an alternative with the process being $I(0)$ in the first sample and $I(1)$ is the second; the numerator is then $O_p(T^2)$ and one rejects for large values. If the alternative is reversed, the denominator is $O_p(T^2)$ and one rejects for small values. Hence, with a known break date, a two-sided test provides a consistent test against both alternatives. For the case with an unknown break date, Kim (2001) considers the sup, Mean or Exp functionals of the sequence $\Xi_T(T_1)$ with, as usual, a set specifying a range for permissible values of T_1/T (he suggests $[0.2, 0.8]$). The test is then consistent for a change from $I(0)$ to $I(1)$ but inconsistent for a change from $I(1)$ to $I(0)$. Busetti and Taylor (2005) note that maximizing the reciprocal of the test $\Xi_T(T_1)$ provides a consistent test against the alternative of a change from $I(1)$ to $I(0)$. Hence, their suggestion is to use the maximum of the test based on $\Xi_T(T_1)$ and its reciprocal (whether the sup, Mean of Exp functional is used). Interestingly, Leybourne and Taylor (2004) suggest scaling both the numerator and denominator of (25) by an estimate of the long-run variance constructed from the respective sub-samples, in which case the test is then exactly the ratio of the Q tests applied to each sub-sample. No version of the test will deliver a consistent estimate of the break date and they suggest using the ratio of the post-break to pre-break sample variances of the residuals $\hat{u}_t$. They show consistency of the estimate but no limit distribution is obtained, thereby preventing making inference about the break date.

Another issue related to this class of tests is the fact that they reject the null hypothesis often when the process is actually $I(1)$ throughout the sample. This is due to the fact that, though the statistic $\Xi_T(T_1)$ is $O_p(1)$ in this case, the limit distribution is quite different from that prevailing in the constant $I(0)$ case, with quantiles that are greater. Harvey et al. (2004) use the same device suggested by Vogelsang (1998, 2001) to solve the problem by multiplying the test by $\exp(-bJ_T)$, with J_T a unit root test that has a non-degenerate limit distribution in the constant $I(1)$ case and that converges to zero in the constant $I(0)$ case. For a given size of the test, one can then select b so that the critical values are the same in both cases (see section 8.4.8).

Busetti and Taylor (2005) also consider locally best invariant (LBI) tests. As discussed in this review, this class of tests has important problems (e.g., non-monotonic power) and here is no exception. Consider the LBI test for a change from $I(0)$ to $I(1)$. The form of the statistic is then given by

$$\hat{\sigma}^{-2}(T - T_1)^{-2} \sum_{t=T_1+1}^{T} S_{t,T}^2 \tag{8.26}$$

where $\hat{\sigma}^2 = T^{-1}\sum_{t=1}^{T} \hat{u}_t^2$ is the estimate of the variance of the residuals using the full sample. Under the alternative, $\hat{\sigma}^2$ is $O_p(T)$ and, hence, the test is $O_p(T)$ under the alternative. Busetti and Harvey (2005) also consider using the sup, Mean or Exp functionals of the original Q test applied to the post-break data only. It is similar to the test (8.26) but with a scaling based on $\hat{\sigma}_1^2(T_1) = (T - T_1)^{-1}\sum_{t=T_1+1}^{T} \hat{u}_t^2$, an estimate of the variance based on the post-break data. This test has similar properties. In fact, using the Q test itself applied to the whole sample would be consistent against a change from $I(0)$ to $I(1)$, showing that this class of tests will reject the null hypothesis with probability one in large samples if the process is $I(1)$ throughout the sample. Both the LBI and the post-break Q tests have a scaling that is $O_p(T)$ when the alternative is true whatever break date is used. Consider now the statistic (8.26) scaled by $\hat{\sigma}_0^2(T_1) = T_1^{-1}\sum_{t=1}^{T_1} \hat{u}_t^2$. The test would then have the same limit distribution under the constant $I(0)$ null hypothesis but would be $O_p(T^2)$ under the alternative and, hence, more powerful. This illustrates, once again, a central problem with LBI or LM type tests in the context of structural changes. The scaling factor is evaluated under the null hypothesis, which implies an inflated estimate when the alternative is true and a consequent loss of power.

Leybourne *et al.* (2003) consider instead the null hypothesis that the process is $I(1)$ throughout the sample, with the same alternatives that it can switch from $I(1)$ to $I(0)$, or vice versa. Their test for a change from $I(0)$ to $I(1)$ is based on the minimal value of the unit root test $ADF^{GLS}(T_1)$, the ADF test proposed by Elliott *et al.* (1996) constructed using observations up to time T_1 (labeled recursive test). Since this test does not use all information in the data for any given particular break date, they also consider using a similar unit root test from a full sample regression in which the coefficient on the lagged level is constrained to be zero in the post-break sample (labeled sequential). To test against the alternative hypothesis of a change from $I(1)$ to $I(0)$, the same procedures are applied to the data arranged in reverse order. When the direction of the change is unknown, they consider the minimal value of the pair of statistics for each case. These tests will, however, reject when the process has no change and is $I(0)$ throughout the sample. To remedy this problem, Leybourne *et al.* (2003) consider an alternative procedure when the null hypothesis is $I(1)$ throughout the sample. It is the ratio of the minimal value of the pre-break sample variance of the residuals constructed from the original series relative to the minimal value of the same statistic constructed using time reversed data. The test has a well-defined limit distribution under the null hypothesis of constant $I(1)$, rejects when there is a shift and has a limit value of 1 when the process is $I(0)$ throughout, which implies a non-rejection asymptotically in the latter case. Kurozumi (2005) considers a test constructed upon the LM principle. He shows that the test is asymptotically equivalent to the sum of the t-statistics on α_1 and α_2 in the regression

$$\Delta \tilde{y}_t = \alpha_1 1(t \le T_1)\tilde{y}_{t-1} + \alpha_2 1(t \le T_1)\tilde{y}_{t-1} + \sum_{i=1}^{k} c_i \Delta \tilde{y}_{t-i} + e_t$$

where $\tilde{y}_t$ are OLS detrended data (he also considers a version with GLS detrended data, but his simulations show no power improvement). This test performs rather poorly and he recommends using a regression with a fitted mean that is allowed to change at the break date, even though this results in a test with lower local asymptotic power. With an unknown break date, one takes the minimal value of the tests over the range of permissible break dates.

Deng and Perron (2005b) take the null hypothesis to be $I(1)$ throughout and they follow the approach suggested by Elliott *et al.* (1996) in specifying the null hypothesis as involving an autoregressive parameter (in the $I(0)$ subsample) that is local to unity. They consider the case of a known break date and derive the Gaussian local power envelope and a feasible test that achieves this power envelope. It is shown that the test has in general higher power than those of Leybourne *et al.* (2003) and Kurozumi (2005), according to both the local power function and to the finite sample power (via simulations). But they also find a curious feature. The test is consistent when only a constant is included but inconsistent when a constant and a time trend are included. This is really a theoretical artifact that has little impact on finite sample power but is interesting nevertheless. Under the null hypothesis, the support of the test is the positive real line and one reject for small values. When a fitted trend is included, the limit distribution of the test under the alternative is not exactly zero. Most of the mass is at zero but there is a very small tail to the right, so that the probability of rejecting does not go to one for all possible significance levels.

8.5   Unit root versus trend stationarity in the presence of structural change in the trend function

As discussed throughout this review, structural changes and unit root non-stationarity share similar features in the sense that most tests for structural changes will reject in the presence of a unit root in the errors and, vice versa, tests of stationarity versus unit root will reject in the presence of structural changes. We now discuss methods to test the null hypothesis of a unit root in the presence of structural changes in the trend function.

8.5.1   The motivation, issues and framework

To motivate the problem addressed, it is useful to step back and look at some basic properties of unit root and trend-stationary processes. Consider a trending series generated by

$$y_t = \mu + \beta t + u_t \tag{8.27}$$

where

$$\Delta u_t = C(L)e_t \tag{8.28}$$

with $e_t \sim i.i.d.$ $(0, \sigma_e^2)$ and $C(L) = \sum_{j=0}^{\infty} c_j L^j$ such that $\sum_{j=1}^{\infty} j|c_j| < \infty$ and $c_0 = 1$. A popular trend-cycle decomposition is that suggested by Beveridge and Nelson (1981). The trend is specified as the long-run forecast of the series conditional on current information, which results in the following

$$\tau_t = \mu + \beta t + C(1) \sum_{j=1}^{t} e_j$$

while the cycle is given by $c_t = \tilde{C}(L)e_t$ with $\tilde{C}(L) = \sum_{j=0}^{\infty} \tilde{c}_j L^j$, where $\tilde{c}_j = \sum_{i=j+1}^{\infty} c_i$. Here the trend has two components, a deterministic one (a linear trend) and a stochastic one specified by a random walk weighted by $C(1)$. Hence, the trend exhibits changes every period in the form of level shifts. Note that if one considered a process which is potentially integrated of order 2, the trend would exhibit changes in both level and slope every period. When the process has no unit root, $C(1) = 0$ and the trend is a linear deterministic function of time.

Within this framework, one can view the unit root versus trend-stationary problem as addressing the following question: do the data support the view that the trend is changing every period or never? The empirical analysis of Nelson and Plosser (1982) provided strong evidence that, if the comparison is restricted to these polar cases, the data support the view that a trend which "always" changes is a better description than a trend that "never" changes (using a variety of US macroeconomic variables; furthermore many other studies have reached similar conclusions for other series and other countries).

The question is then why restrict the comparison to "never" or "always"? Would it not be preferable to make a comparison between "always" and "sometimes"? Ideally, then, the proper question to ask would be "what is the frequency of permanent shocks?" This is a question for which no satisfactory framework has been provided and, as such, still remains a very important item for further research.

The basic motivation for the work initiated by Perron (1989, 1990) is to take a stand on what is "sometimes" (see also Rappoport and Reichlin, 1989). The specific number chosen then becomes case-specific. His argument was that in many cases of interest, especially with historical macroeconomic time series (including those analyzed by Nelson and Plosser, 1982), the relevant number of changes is relatively small, in many cases only one. These changes are then associated with important historical events: the Great Crash (US and Canada, 1929, change in level), the oil price shock (G7 countries, 1973, change in slope); World War II (European countries, change in level and slope), World War I (United Kingdom, 1917, change in level), and so on. As far as statistical modeling is concerned, the main conceptual issue is to view such changes as possibly stochastic but of a different nature than shocks that occur every period, i.e., drawn from a different distribution. However, the argument that such large changes are infrequent makes it difficult to specify and estimate a probability distribution for them. The approach is then to model these infrequent large changes in the trend as structural changes. The question asked by unit root tests is then: "do the data favor a view that the trend is 'always' changing or is changing at most occasionally?" or "if allowance is made for the possibility of some few large permanent changes in the trend function, is a unit root present in the structure of the stochastic component?" Note that two important qualifications need to be made. First, the setup allows but does not impose such large changes. Second, by "permanent" what should be understood is not that it will last forever but that, given a sample of data, the change is still in effect. For instance, the decrease in the slope of the trend function after 1973 for US real GDP is still in effect (see Perron and Wada, 2005).

When allowance is made for a one-time change in the trend function, Perron (1989, 1990) specified two versions of four different structures: (1) a change in level for a non-trending series; and for trending series, (2) a change in level, (3) a change in slope, and (4) a change in both level and slope. For each of the four cases, two different versions allow for different transition effects. Following the terminology in Box and Tiao (1975), the first is labeled the "additive outlier model" and specifies that the change to the new trend function occurs instantaneously. The second is labeled the "innovational outlier model" and specifies that the change to the new trend function is gradual. Of course, in principle, there is an infinity of ways to model gradual changes following the occurrence of a "big shock." One way out of this difficulty is to suppose that the variables respond to the "big shocks" the same way as they respond to so-called "regular shocks" (shocks associated with the stationary noise component of the series). This is the approach taken in the modelization of the "innovational outlier model," following the treatment of intervention analyses in Box and Tiao (1975). The distinction between the additive and innovational outlier models is important not only because the assumed transition paths are different but also because the statistical procedures to test for unit roots are different.

The additive outlier models for each of the four specifications for the types of changes occurring at a break date T_1 are specified as follows:

Model (AO-0)　$y_t = \mu_1 + (\mu_2 - \mu_1)DU_t + u_t$

Model (AO-A)　$y_t = \mu_1 + \beta t + (\mu_2 - \mu_1)DU_t + u_t$

Model (AO-B)　$y_t = \mu_1 + \beta_1 t + (\beta_2 - \beta_1)DT_t^* + u_t$

Model (AO-C)　$y_t = \mu_1 + \beta_1 t + (\mu_2 - \mu_1)DU_t + (\beta_2 - \beta_1)DT_t^* + u_t$

where $DU_t = 1, DT_t^* = t - T_1$ if $t > T_1$ and 0 otherwise, and u_t is specified by (8.28). Under the null hypothesis, $C(1) \neq 0$, while under the alternative hypothesis, $C(1) = 0$. Alternatively, one can define the autoregressive polynomial $A(L) = (1 - L) C(L)^{-1}$. The null hypothesis then specifies that a root of the autoregressive polynomial is one, i.e., that we can write $A(L) = (1 - L) A^*(L)$, where all the roots of $A^*(L)$ are outside the unit circle. Under the alternative hypothesis of stationary fluctuations around the trend function, all the roots of $A(L)$ are strictly outside the unit circle. Model (AO-B) was found to be useful for the analysis of postwar quarterly real GNP for the G7 countries and Model (AO-0) for some exchange rate series as well as the US real interest rate, among others. It is important to note that changes in the trend function are allowed to occur under both the null and alternative hypotheses.

The innovational outlier models are easier to characterize by describing them separately under the null and alternative hypotheses. Note also that the innovational outlier versions have been considered only for Models (A) and (C) in the case of trending series. The basic reason is that the innovational outlier version of Model (B) does not lend itself easily to empirical applications using linear estimation methods. Under the null hypothesis, we have:

Model (IO-0-UR) $y_t = y_{t-1} + C(L)\,(e_t + \delta D(T_1)_t)$

Model (IO-A-UR) $y_t = y_{t-1} + b + C(L)\,(e_t + \delta D(T_1)_t)$

Model (IO-C-UR) $y_t = y_{t-1} + b + C(L)\,(e_t + \delta D(T_1)_t + \eta DU_t)$

where $D(T_1)_t = 1$ if $t = T_1 + 1$ and 0 otherwise. Under this specification, the immediate impact of the change in the intercept is δ while the long-run impact is $C(1)\delta$. Similarly, under Model (IO-C), the immediate impact of the change in slope is η while the long-run impact is $C(1)\eta$. Under the alternative hypothesis of stationary fluctuations, the specifications are:

Model (IO-0-TS) $y_t = \mu + C(L)^*(e_t + \theta DU_t)$

Model (IO-A-TS) $y_t = \mu + \beta t + C(L)^*\,(e_t + \theta DU_t)$

Model (IO-C-TS) $y_t = \mu + \beta t + C(L)^*\,(e_t + \theta DU_t + \gamma DT_t^*)$

where $C(L)^* = (1 - L)^{-1}C(L)$. The immediate impact of the change in the intercept of the trend function is θ while the long-run impact is $C(1)^*\theta$, and the immediate impact of the change in slope is γ while the long-run impact is $C(1)^*\gamma$.

8.5.2 The effect of structural change in trend on standard unit root tests

A standard unit root test used in applied research is the so-called augmented Dickey–Fuller (1979) test, which is based on the t-statistic for testing that $\alpha = 1$ in the following regression

$$y_t = \mu + \beta t + \alpha y_{t-1} + \sum_{i=1}^{k} c_i \Delta y_{t-i} + e_t$$

with the trend regressor excluded when dealing with non-trending series. A central message of the work by Perron (1989, 1990) is that, when the true process involves structural changes in the trend function, the power of such unit root tests can dramatically be reduced. In particular, it was shown that if a level shift is present, the estimate of the autoregressive coefficient (α when $k = 0$) is asymptotically biased toward 1. If a change in slope is present, its limit value is 1. It was shown that this translates into substantial power losses. Simulations presented in Perron (1994) show the power reduction to increase as k is increased (see also the theoretical analysis of Montañés and Reyes, 2000, who also show that the power problem remains with the Phillips–Perron (1988) type unit root test). For a more precise and complete theoretical analysis, see Montañés and Reyes (1998, 1999). Under the null hypothesis, the large sample distribution is unaffected by the presence of a level shift (Montañés and Reyes, 1999) and the test is asymptotically conservative in the presence of a change in slope. It can, however, have a liberal size if the break occurs very early in the sample ($\lambda_1 < .15$), as documented by Leybourne *et al.* (1998) and Leybourne and Newbold (2000). Intuitively, the latter result can be understood by thinking about the early observations as outliers such that the series reverts back to the mean in effect for the rest of the sample. The latter problem is, however, specific to the Dickey–Fuller (1979) type unit root test, which is based on the conditional likelihood function, discarding the first observations (see Lee, 2000).[3] It has also been documented that the presence of stuctural breaks in trend affects tests of the null hypothesis of stationarity (e.g., the Q or KPSS tests) by inducing size distortions toward rejecting the null hypothesis too often (e.g., Lee *et al.*, 1997). This is consistent with the effect on unit root tests in the sense that, when trying to distinguish the two hypotheses, the presence of structural changes induces a bias in favor of the unit root representation.

It is important to discuss these results in relation to the proper way to specify alternative unit root tests. The main result is that large enough changes in level and/or slope will induce a reduction in the power of standard unit root tests. Small shifts, especially in level, are likely to reduce power only slightly. Hence, what is important is to account for the large shifts, not all of them if the others are small. Consider analyzing US real GDP over, say, the period 1900–1980. Within this sample, one can identify two shifts related to the 1929 crash (change in level) and the post-1973 productivity slowdown (change in slope). However, the post-73 sample consists of only a small proportion of the total sample and the shift in slope in this period is unlikely to induce a bias and need not be accounted for. Hence, the testing strategy discussed below need not make a statement about the precise number of changes. It should rather be viewed as a device to remove biases induced by shifts large enough to cause an important reduction in power.

8.5.3   Testing for a unit root allowing for changes at known dates

The IO models under the null and alternative hypotheses can be nested in a way which specifies the regression, from which the statistics will be constructed, as follows:

$$y_t = \mu + \theta DU_t + \beta t + \gamma DT_t^* + \delta D(T_1)_t + \alpha y_{t-1} + \sum_{i=1}^{k} c_i \Delta y_{t-i} + e_t \qquad (8.29)$$

for a value of the truncation lag parameter k chosen to be large enough as to provide a good approximation (for methods on how to choose k, see Ng and Perron, 1995, 2001). For Model (IO-0), the regressors (t, DT_t^*) are not present, while for Model (IO-A), the regressor (DT_t^*) is not present. The null hypothesis imposes the following restrictions on the coefficients. For Model (IO-0), these are $\alpha = 1$, $\theta = \mu = 0$ and, in general, $\delta \neq 0$ (if there is a change in the intercept). For Model (IO-A), the restrictions are $\alpha = 1$, $\beta = \theta = 0$ and again, in general, $\delta \neq 0$ while for Model (IO-C), $\alpha = 1$, $\beta = \gamma = 0$. Under the alternative hypothesis, we have the following specifications: $|\alpha| < 1$ and, in general, $\delta = 0$. These restrictions are, however, not imposed by most testing procedures. The test statistic used is the t-statistic for testing the null hypothesis that $\alpha = 1$ versus the alternative hypothesis that $|\alpha| < 1$, denoted $t_\alpha(\lambda_1)$ with $\lambda_1 = T_1/T$. It is important to note that, provided the specified break date corresponds to the true break date, the statistic is invariant to the parameters of the trend-function, including those related to the changes in level and slope (for an analysis of the case when the break date is mis-specified, see Hecq and Urbain, 1993, Montañés, 1997, Montañés and Olloqui, 1999, and Montañés *et al.*, 2005, who also consider the effect of choosing the wrong specification for the type of break). The limit distribution of the test under the null hypothesis is

$$t_\alpha(\lambda_1) \Rightarrow \frac{\int_0^1 W^*(r, \lambda_1)dW(r)}{\left[\int_0^1 W^*(r, \lambda_1)^2 dr\right]^{1/2}} \tag{8.30}$$

where $W^*(r, \lambda_1)$ is the residual function from a projection of a Wiener process $W(r)$ on the relevant continuous time versions of the deterministic components ({1, 1 $(r > \lambda_1)$} for Model (IO-0) and {1, 1$(r > \lambda_1)$, r} for Model (IO-A) {1, 1$(r > \lambda_1)$, r, 1$(r > \lambda_1)(r - \lambda_1)$} for Model (IO-C)). Tabulated critical values can be found in Perron (1989, 1990). See also Carrion-i-Silvestre *et al.* (1999).

For the additive outlier models, the procedures are different and consist of a two-step approach. In the first step, the trend function of the series is estimated and removed from the original series via the following regressions estimated by OLS for Model (AO-0) to (AO-C), respectively:

$$y_t = \tilde{\mu} + \tilde{\gamma}DU_t + \tilde{y}_t$$
$$y_t = \tilde{\mu} + \tilde{\beta}t + \tilde{\gamma}DU_t + \tilde{y}_t$$
$$y_t = \tilde{\mu} + \tilde{\beta}t + \tilde{\gamma}DT_t^* + \tilde{y}_t$$
$$y_t = \tilde{\mu} + \tilde{\beta}t + \tilde{\theta}DU_t + \tilde{\gamma}DT_t^* + \tilde{y}_t$$

where $\tilde{y}_t$ is accordingly defined as the detrended series. The next step differs according to whether or not the first step involves DU_t, the dummy associated with a change in intercept. For Models (AO-0), (AO-A) and (AO-C), the test is based on the value of the t-statistic for testing that $\alpha = 1$ in the following autoregression:

$$\tilde{y}_t = \alpha\tilde{y}_{t-1} + \sum_{j=0}^{k} d_j D(T_1)_{t-j} + \sum_{i=1}^{k} a_i\Delta\tilde{y}_{t-i} + e_t$$

Details about the need to introduce the current value and lags of the dummies $D(T_b)_t$ can be found in Perron and Vogelsang (1992b). The limit distributions of the tests are then the same as for the IO case. There is no need to introduce the dummies in the second step regression for Model (AO-B), where no change in level is involved and the two segments of the trend are joined at the time of the break.

The limit distribution is, however, different; see Perron and Vogelsang (1993a, 1993b). Again, in all cases, the tests are invariant to the change in level or slope provided the break date is correctly specified.

These unit root tests with known break dates have been extended in the following directions. Kunitomo and Sato (1995) derive the limit distribution of the likelihood ratio tests for multiple structural changes in the AO case. Amsler and Lee (1995) consider a LM type test in the context of a shift in level of the AO type. Saikkonen and Lütkepohl (2001) also consider cases with a level shift of the AO type, though they allow for general forms of shifts which can be indexed by some unknown parameter to be estimated. Following Elliott *et al.* (1996), they propose a GLS-type detrending procedure, which is, however, based on an $AR(p)$ process for the noise. On the basis of simulation results, they recommend using GLS detrending under the null hypothesis instead of a local alternative as is done in Elliott *et al.* (1996). Lanne *et al.* (2002) propose a finite sample modification which is akin to a pre-whitening device. Let the detrended series be

$$y_t^{GLS} = y_t - \tilde{\mu} - \tilde{\gamma}DU_t - \tilde{\beta}t$$

and the estimate of the autoregressive polynomial of the first difference Δu_t be $\tilde{b}(L)$ (all estimates being obtained from the GLS procedure). With the filtered series defined as $\tilde{\omega}_t = \tilde{b}(L)y_t^{GLS}$, the test is then the t-statistic for testing that $\alpha = 1$ in the regression

$$\tilde{\omega}_t = \mu + \alpha\tilde{\omega}_{t-1} + \pi\tilde{b}(L)D(T_1)_t + \sum_{i=1}^{k} a_i\Delta y_{t-i}^{GLS} + e_t.$$

Note that the limit distribution does not depend on the break date. This is because the data are detrended using a GLS approach under the null hypothesis of a unit root (or more generally under a sequence of alternatives that are local to a unit root) and the level shift regressor is, in the terminology of Elliott *et al.* (1996), a slowly evolving trend, in which case the limit distribution is the same as it would be if it was excluded (loosely speaking, the level shift becomes a one-time dummy). Hence, the limit distribution of the test is the same as that of Elliott *et al.* (1996) for their unit root test when only a constant is included as a deterministic regressor. Lanne and Lütkepohl (2002) show that this test has better size and power than the test proposed in Perron (1990) and the LM test of Amsler and Lee (1995). A similar procedure for level shifts of the IO type is presented in Lütkepohl, Müller and Saikkonen (2001).

8.5.4 Testing for a unit root allowing for changes at unknown dates

The methodology adopted by Perron (1989, 1990) was criticized by, among others, Christiano (1992), on the grounds that using a framework whereby the break is treated as fixed is inappropriate. The argument is that the choice of the break date is inevitably linked to the historical record and, hence, involves an element of data-mining. He showed that if one did a systematic search for a break when the series is actually a unit root process without break, using fixed break critical values would entail a test with substantial size distortions. While the argument is correct, it is difficult to quantify the extent of the "data-mining" problem in Perron's (1989) study. Indeed, no systematic search was done, the break dates were selected as obvious candidates (the Crash of 1929 and the productivity slowdown after 1973) and the same break date was used for all series. Given the intractability of correctly assessing the right p-values for the tests reported, the ensuing literature addressed the problem by adopting a completely agnostic approach where a complete and systematic search was done. While this leads to tests with the correct asymptotic size (under some conditions to be discussed), it obviously implies a reduction in power. We shall return to the practical importance of this point.

An avenue taken by Banerjee *et al.* (1992) was to consider rolling and recursive tests. Both perform standard unit root tests without breaks, the former using a sample of fixed length (much smaller than the full sample) that moves sequentially from some starting date to the end of the sample. The latter considers a fixed starting date for all tests and increases the sample used (from some minimal value to the full sample). In each case, one then considers the minimal value of the unit root test and rejects the null hypothesis of a unit root if this minimal value is small enough. Asymptotically, such procedures will correctly reject the null hypothesis if the alternative is true but the fact that all tests are based on sub-samples means that not all information in the data is used and consequently one can expect a loss of power.

An alternative strategy, more closely related to the methodology of Perron (1989), was adopted by Zivot and Andrews (1992) as well as Banerjee *et al.* (1992). They consider the IO type specification and a slightly different regression that does not involve the one-time dummy when a shift in level is allowed under the alternative hypothesis. For example, for Model C, the regression is

$$y_t = \mu + \theta DU_t + \beta_t + \gamma DT_t^* + \alpha y_{t-1} + \sum_{i=1}^{k} c_i \Delta y_{t-i} + e_t \tag{8.31}$$

and the test considered is the minimal value of the t-statistic for testing that $\alpha = 1$ over all possible break dates in some pre-specified range for the break fraction $[\varepsilon, 1 - \varepsilon]$, where a popular choice for ε is 0.15. Denote the resulting test by $t_\alpha^* = \inf_{\lambda_1 \in [\varepsilon, 1-\varepsilon]} t_\alpha(\lambda_1)$, where $t_\alpha(\lambda_1)$ is the t-statistic for testing $\alpha = 1$ in (8.31) when the break date $T_1 = [T\lambda_1]$ is used. The limit distribution of the test is

$$t_\alpha^* \Rightarrow \inf_{\lambda_1 \in [\varepsilon, 1-\varepsilon]} \frac{\int_0^1 W^*(r, \lambda_1) dW(r)}{\left[\int_0^1 W^*(r, \lambda_1)^2 dr \right]^{1/2}} \tag{8.32}$$

with $W^*(r, \lambda_1)$ as defined in (8.30). Perron (1997a) extended their theoretical results by showing, using projection arguments, that trimming for the possible values of λ_1 was unnecessary and that one could minimize over all possible break dates.[4] For the Nelson–Plosser (1982) data set, Zivot and Andrews (1992) reported fewer rejections compared to what was reported in Perron (1989) using a known break date assumption. These rejections should be viewed as providing stronger evidence against the unit root but a failure to reject does not imply a reversal of Perron's (1989) conclusions. This is a commonly found misconception in the literature, which overlooks the fact that a failure to reject may simply be due to tests with low power.

Zivot and Andrews' (1992) extension involves, however, a substantial methodological difference. The null hypothesis considered is that of a unit root process with no break while the alternative hypothesis is a stationary process with a break. Hence, there is an asymmetric treatment of the specification of the trend under the null and alternative hypotheses. In particular, the limit result (8.32) is not valid if a break is present under the null hypothesis. Vogelsang and Perron (1998) show that, in this case, t_α^* diverges to $-\infty$ when a shift in slope is present. This implies that a rejection can be due to the presence of a unit root process with a breaking trend. The reason for this is the following. With a fixed break date, the statistic $t_\alpha(\lambda_1)$ from regression (8.29) is invariant to the values of the parameters of the trend function under both the null and alternative hypotheses. When searching over a range of values for the break date (only one of which corresponds to the true value), this invariance no longer holds. In the case of Model A with only a level shift and for non-trending series with a change in mean considered by Perron and Vogelsang (1992a), the statistic t_α^* is asymptotically invariant to the value of the level shift but not in finite samples. Simulations reported by Perron and Vogelsang (1992b) show size distortions that increase with the magnitude of the level shift. They argue, however, that substantial size distortions are in effect only when implausibly large shifts occur and that the problem is not important in practice. Vogelsang and Perron (1998) make the same arguments for the case of a shift in slope. Even though in practice the distortions may be small, it nevertheless remains a problematic feature of this approach and we consider recent attempts below which do not have this problem.

Perron and Vogelsang (1992a), for the non-trending case, and Perron (1997a), for the trending case, extend the analysis of Zivot and Andrews (1992). They consider tests for both the IO and AO cases based on the minimal value of the t-statistic for testing that $\alpha = 1$, and also tests based on $t_\alpha(\lambda_1)$ with T_1 selected by maximizing the absolute value of the t-statistic on the coefficient of the appropriate shift dummy, DU_t, if only a level shift is present, and DT_t^* if a slope change is present (see also Christiano, 1992; Banerjee *et al.*, 1992). For the IO case, they also suggest using regression (8.29) instead of (8.31), which includes the one-time dummy $D (T_b)_t$, since that would be the right regression to use with a known break date. They derive the limit distribution under the null hypothesis of a unit root and no break (in which case it does not matter if the one-time dummy $D(T_b)_t$ is incorporated). Perron (1997a) also considers tests where the break date is selected by minimizing or maximizing the value of the t-statistic on the slope dummy, which allows one to impose a priori the restriction of a direction for the change in slope and provides a more powerful test. Carrion-i-Silvestre *et al.* (2004) consider statistics which jointly test the null hypothesis and the zero value of appropriate deterministic regressors, extending the likelihood ratio test of Dickey and Fuller (1981).

8.5.4.1 Extensions and other approaches

We now briefly review some extensions and alternative approaches and return below to an assessment of the various methods discussed above. Unless stated otherwise, all work described below specifies the null hypothesis as a unit root process with no break in trend.

Perron and Rodríguez (2003) consider tests for trending series with a shift in slope in the AO framework. Following Elliott *et al.* (1996), they derive the asymptotic local power envelope and show that using GLS detrended series (based on a local alternative) yields tests with power close to the envelope. For the non-trending case, Clemente, Montañés and Reyes (1998) extend the results of Perron and Vogelsang (1992a) to the case with two breaks. A similar extension is provided by Lumsdaine and Papell (1997) for the case of trending series.

Generalizations to multiple breaks include the following. Ohara (1999) extends the Zivot and Andrews (1992) approach to the general case with m breaks, though only critical values for the two-break case are presented. Ohara (1999) also proves an interesting generalization of a result in Perron (1989) to the effect that, if a unit root test allowing for m_1 changes in slope is performed on a series having m_0 changes with $m_0 > m_1$, then the least-squares estimate of α converges to one. This provides theoretical support for Rule 6 stated in Campbell and Perron (1991), which states that "a non-rejection of the unit root hypothesis may be due to misspecification of the deterministic components included as regressors."

Kapetanios (2005) also deals with the multiple break case, but considers the following strategy, based on the sequential method of Bai (1997b) and Bai and Perron (1998) (see section 8.3.5). First, denote the set of t-statistics for a unit root over all possible one break partitions by τ^1. Choose the break date that minimizes the sum of squared residuals. Then impose that break and insert an additional break over all permissible values (given some imposed trimming) and store the associated unit root tests in the set τ^2, then choose the additional break that minimizes the sum of squared residuals. Continue in this fashion until an m break model is fitted and m sets of unit root tests are obtained. The unit root test selected is then the one that is minimal over all m sets. The limit distribution is, however, not derived, and the critical values are obtained through simulation with $T = 250$.

Saikonnen and Lütkepohl (2002) extend their tests for a level shift with a known break date (of a general form possibly indexed by some unknown parameter) to the case of a shift occurring at an unknown date. It can be performed in both the AO and IO frameworks and the resulting procedure is basically the same as discussed in section 8.5.3 for the known break date case. This is because, with a GLS detrending procedure based on a specification that is local to a unit root, the limit distribution of the test is the same whatever the break point is selected to be. Hence, one can substitute any estimate of the break date without affecting the limit null distribution of the test. They recommend using a unit root specification for the detrending (as opposed to using a local alternative as in Elliott *et al.*, 1996), since it leads to tests with finite sample sizes that are robust to departures of the estimate of the break date from its true value. Of course, power is highly sensitive to an incorrectly estimated break date. Lanne *et al.* (2003) assess the properties of the tests when different estimates of the break date are used. A substantial drawback of their approach is that they found the test to have non-monotonic power, in the sense that the larger the shift in level, the lower the power in rejecting the unit root. Also, the power is sensitive to departures from the exact specification for the type of change, and power can be reduced substantially if allowance is made for a general shift indexed by some parameter when the shift is actually an abrupt one.

Consider now testing the null hypothesis of stationarity. Tests of the type proposed by Kwiatkowski *et al.* (1992) will reject the null hypothesis with probability one in large enough samples if the process is affected by structural changes in mean and/or slope but is otherwise stationary within regimes. This follows in an obvious way once one realizes that the KPSS test is also a consistent test for structural change (see, nevertheless, simulations in Lee *et al.*, 1997). In order not to incorrectly reject the null hypothesis of stationarity, modifications are therefore necessary. Kurozumi (2002), Lee and Strazicich (2001b) and Busetti and Harvey (2001, 2003) consider testing the null hypothesis of stationarity versus the alternative of a unit root in the presence of a single break for the specifications described above (see also Harvey and Mills, 2003). Their test is an extension of the Q-statistic of Gardner (1969) or, equivalently, the KPSS test as discussed in section 8.2. The test is constructed using least-squares residuals from a regression incorporating the appropriate dummy variables. They provide critical values for the known break date case. When the break date is unknown, things are less satisfactory. To ensure the consistency of the test, Lee and Strazicich (2001b) and Busetti and Harvey (2001, 2003) consider the minimal value (as opposed to the maximal value) of the statistics over all permissible break dates. Since the test rejects for large values, this implies the need to resort to the value of the statistic at the break point that permits the least-favorable outcome against the alternative. Hence, it results in a procedure with low power. Kurozumi (2002), as well as Busetti and Harvey (2001, 2003), also considers using the estimate of the break date that minimizes the sum of squared residuals from the relevant regression under the null hypothesis. Since the estimate of the break fraction is then consistent, one can use critical values corresponding to the known break date case. They show, however, that the need to estimate the break date induces substantial power losses. Busetti (2002) extended this approach to a multivariate setting, where the null hypothesis is that a set of series all share a common trend subject to a change and a stationary noise function, the alternative being that one or more series have unit root noise components.

Also of related interest is the study by Kim *et al.* (2002), who study unit root tests with a break in innovation variance following the work by Hamori and Tokihisa (1997). The issue of unit roots and trend breaks has also been addressed using a Bayesian framework, with results that are generally in agreement with those of Perron (1989): see Zivot and Phillips (1994), Wang and Zivot (2000) and Marriott and Newbold (2000).

8.5.4.2 *Problems and recent proposals*

Theoretical results by Vogelsang and Perron (1998) and simulation results reported in Perron and Vogelsang (1992a), Lee and Strazicich (2001a), Harvey *et al.* (2001) and Nunes *et al.* (1997) yield the following conclusions about the tests when a break is present under the null hypothesis. For the IO case when a slope shift is present, both versions using the break date selected by minimizing the unit root test or maximizing the absolute value of the t-statistic on the coefficient of the slope dummy, yield tests with similar features, namely an asymptotic size of 100%. In the presence of a level shift, the asymptotic size is correct but liberal distortions occur when the level shift is large. When the one-time dummy $D(T_1)_t$ is included in the regression, the source of the problem is that the break point selected with highest probability (which increases as the magnitude of the break increases) is $T_1^0 - 1$, i.e., one period before the true break; and it is for this choice of the break date that the tests have most size distortions. Lee and Strazicich (2001a) show that the problem is the same as if the one-time dummy $D(T_1)_t$ was excluded when considering the known break date case. Their result also implies that, when unit root tests are performed using a regression of the form (8.31) without the one-time dummy $D(T_1)_t$, the correct break date is selected but the tests are still affected by size distortions (which was also documented by simulations). In cases with only a level shift, Harvey *et al.* (2001) suggest evaluating the unit root *t*-statistic at the break date selected by maximizing the absolute value of the *t*-statistic on the coefficient of the level shift plus one, and show that the tests then have correct size even for large breaks.

For the AO-type models, the following features apply. When the break date is selected by minimizing the unit root test, similar size distortions apply. However, when the break date is selected by maximizing the absolute value of the *t*-statistic on the relevant shift dummy, the tests have the correct size even for large breaks, and the correct break date is selected in large samples. Vogelsang and Perron (1998) argue that the limit distribution of the unit root tests is then that corresponding to the known break date case. They suggest, nevertheless, using the asymptotic critical values corresponding to the no break case, since this leads to a test having asymptotic size no greater than that specified for all magnitudes of the break, even though this implies a conservative procedure when a break is present.

An alternative testing procedure, which naturally follows from the structural change literature reviewed in section 8.3, is to evaluate the unit root test at the break date selected by minimizing the sum of squared residuals from the appropriate regression. Interesting simulations pertaining to the IO case are presented in Lee and Strazicich (2001). They show that if one uses the usual asymptotic critical values that apply for the no break case under the null hypothesis, the tests are conservative when a break is present (provided the one time dummy $D(T_1)_t$ is included in the regression). They correctly note, however, that the limit null distribution when no break is present depends on the limit distribution of the estimated break date, which may depend on nuisance parameters. Hatanaka and Yamada (1999) present useful theoretical results for the IO regression (though they specify the data generating process to be of the AO type). They show that, when a change in slope is present, the estimate of the break fraction λ_1, obtained by minimizing the sum of squared residuals, is consistent and that the rate of convergence is T in both the $I(1)$ and $I(0)$ cases. They also show that this rate of convergence is sufficient to ensure that the null limit distribution of the unit root test is the same as when the break date is known. Hence, one need only use the critical values for the known break date case that pertains to the estimated break date. The test has accordingly more power since the critical values are smaller in absolute value (they also consider a two break model and show the estimates of the break dates to be asymptotically independent). The problem, however, is that the results will only apply as long as there is a break in the slope under the null hypothesis. Indeed, if no break is present, the known break date limit distribution no longer applies; and if the break is small, it is likely to provide a poor approximation to the finite sample distribution. Hatanaka and Yamada (1999) present simulation results calibrated to slope changes in Japanese real GDP that show the estimates of the break dates to have a distribution with fat tails and the unit root test accordingly shows size distortions.

For the AO case, the work of Kim and Perron (2005) leads to the following results based on prior work by Perron and Zhu (2005). Under the null hypothesis of a unit root, if a slope change is present, the rate of convergence of the estimate of the break date obtained by minimizing the sum of squared residuals is not fast enough to lead to a limit distribution for the unit root tests (evaluated at this estimate of the break date) that is the same as in the known break date case. They, however, show that a simple modification yields a result similar to the IO case. It involves performing the unit root test by trimming or eliminating data points in a neighborhood of the estimated break date. This again leads to unit root tests with higher power.

Let us summarize the above discussion. First, in the unknown break date case, the invariance properties with respect to the parameters of the trend no longer apply as in the known break date case. Popular methods based on evaluating the unit root test at the value of the break date that minimizes it, or maximizes the absolute value of the t-statistic on the coefficient of the relevant dummy variable, suffer from problems of liberal size distortions when a large break is present (except with the latter method to select the break date in the IO case) and little if any when the break is small. When the break is large, evaluating the unit root test at the break date that minimizes the sum of squared residuals leads to a procedure with correct size and better power. So this suggests a two-step procedure that requires, in the first step, a test for a change in the trend function that is valid whether a unit root is present or not, i.e., under both the null and alternative hypotheses. In this context, the work of Perron and Yabu (2005) becomes especially relevant. This is the approach taken by Kim and Perron (2005). They use a pre-test for a change in trend valid whether the series is $I(1)$ or $I(0)$. Upon a rejection, the unit root test is evaluated at the estimate of the break date that minimizes the sum of squared residuals from the relevant regression. If the test does not reject, a standard Dickey–Fuller test is applied. This is shown to yield unit root tests with good size properties overall and better power. In cases where only level shifts are present, similar improvements are possible even though, with a fixed magnitude of shift, the estimate of the break date is not consistent under the null hypothesis of a unit root.

8.6 Testing for cointegration allowing for structural changes

We now discuss issues related to testing for cointegration when allowing for structural changes. We first consider, in section 8.6.1, single equation methods involving systems with one cointegrating vector. Here tests have been considered with the null hypothesis as no-cointegration and the alternative as cointegration, and vice versa. In section 8.6.2, we consider the multivariate case, where the issue is mainly determining the correct number of cointegrating vectors. Since many of the issues are similar to the case of testing for unit roots allowing structural breaks, our discussion will be brief and outline only the main results and procedures suggested.

8.6.1 Single-equation methods

Consider an n-dimensional vector of variables $y_t = (y_{1t}, y_{2t})$, with y_{1t} a scalar, and y_{2t} an $n-1$ vector. We suppose that the sub-system y_{2t} is not cointegrated. Then the issue is to determine whether or not there exists a cointegrating vector for the full system y_t. Consider the following static regression

$$y_{1t} = \alpha + \beta y_{2t} + u_t \tag{8.33}$$

The system is cointegrated if there exists a β such that the errors u_t are $I(0)$. Hence, a popular method is to estimate this static regression by OLS and perform a unit root test on the estimated residuals (see Phillips and Ouliaris, 1990). Here the null hypothesis is no-cointegration and the alternative is cointegration. Another approach is to use the Error Correction Model (ECM) representation, given by:

$$\Delta y_{1t} = b z_{t-1} + \sum_{i=1}^{k} d_i \Delta y_{2t} + e_t$$

where $z_t = y_{1t} - \beta y_{2t}$ is the equilibrium error. In practice, one needs to replace β by an estimate that is consistent when there is cointegration. The test can then be carried out using the t-statistic for testing that $b = 0$ (see, e.g., Banerjee *et al.*, 1986).

When adopting the reverse null and alternative hypotheses, a statistic that has been suggested is, again, Gardner's (1969) Q test (see Shin, 1994). It can be constructed using the OLS residuals from the static regression when the regressors are strictly exogenous, or, more generally, the residuals from a regression augmented with leads and lags of the first-differences of the regressors, as suggested by Saikkonen (1991) and Stock and Watson (1993). Of course, many other procedures are possible.

Here, structural changes can manifest themselves in several ways. First, there can be structural changes in the trend functions of the series without a change in the cointegrating relationship (i.e., a change in the marginal distributions of the series). Campos *et al.* (1996) have documented that shifts in levels do not affect the size of tests of the null hypothesis of no cointegration, for both the ECM-based test and the test based on the residuals from the static regression. However, they affect the power of the latter, though not of the former. If all regressors have a common break in the slope of their trend function, the tests can be liberal and reject the null hypothesis of no-cointegration too often, though different tests are affected differently (Leybourne and Newbold, 2003). This is related to what has been labelled as co-breaking processes. Changes in the variance of the errors u_t can also induce size distortions if they occur early enough in the sample (e.g., Noh and Kim, 2003).

Second, structural changes can manifest themselves through changes in the long-run relationship (8.33), either in the form of a change in the intercept, or a change in the cointegrating vector. Here, the power of standard tests for the null hypothesis of no-cointegration can have substantially reduced power, as documented by Gregory *et al.* (1996) and Gregory and Hansen (1996a).

An early contribution that proposed tests for the null hypothesis of no-cointegration allowing for the possibility of a change in the long-run relation is that of Gregory and Hansen (1996a). They extend the residual-based tests by incorporating appropriate dummies in regression (8.33) and taking as the resulting test-statistic the minimal value over all possible break dates. Cases covered are: (1) allowing a change in the level α; (2) allowing for a similar change in level when regression (8.33) includes a time trend; (3) allowing for changes in both the level α and the cointegrating vector β (with no trend); (4) the case allowing for a change in the level and slope of an included trend and of the cointegrating vector is analyzed in Gregory and Hansen (1996b). The limit distributions of the various tests are derived under the null hypothesis that the series are not cointegrated and are individually $I(1)$ processes with a stable deterministic trend component. As in the case of tests for unit roots, the value of the break date associated with the minimal value of a given statistic is not, in general, a consistent estimate of the break date if a change is present. Cook (2004) shows the size of the tests to be affected (toward excessive rejections) when the series are not cointegrated and are individually $I(1)$ processes with a change in trend.

The issue of allowing the possible change in trend under both the null and alternative hypotheses does arise in the context of testing the null hypothesis of no-cointegration. Indeed, under the null hypothesis, the model is a spurious one and the parameters of the cointegrating vector are not identified. It might be possible to identify a change in the slope of a trend under the null hypothesis, but this case is seldom of empirical interest. This means that no further gains in power are possible by trying to exploit the fact that a change in specification occurs under both the null and alternative hypotheses, as was done for unit root tests. Such gains are, however, possible when adopting cointegration as the null hypothesis.

Concerning tests that takes the null hypothesis to be cointegration, the contributions include Bartley *et al.* (2001), Carrion-i-Silvestre and Sanso (2004) and Arai and Kurozumi (2005). All are based on various modifications of Gardner's

(1969) Q statistic as used by Shin (1994) without structural breaks. The general framework used is to specify the cointegrating relationship by

$$y_{1t} = \alpha_1 + \alpha_2 1(t > T_1) + \gamma_1 t + \gamma_2(t - T_1)1(t > T_1) \\ + \beta_1 y_{2t} + \beta_1 y_{2t} 1(t > T_1) + u_t.$$

(8.34)

The required residuals to construct the Q test are based on transformed regressions that allow the construction of asymptotically optimal estimates of the cointegrating vector. Bartley *et al.* (2001) consider only a change in the level and slope of the trend and use the canonical cointegrating regression approach suggested by Park (1992) to estimate the cointegrating vector β. The break date is selected by minimizing the sum of squared residuals from the canonical cointegrating regression. They argue that the resulting estimate of the break fraction is consistent and that the limit distribution of the test corresponds to that applying in the known break date case. The simulations supports this assertion. Carrion-i-Silvestre and Sanso (2004) and Arai and Kurozumi (2005) extend the analysis to cover more cases, in particular allowing for a change in the cointegrating vector. In the case of strictly exogenous regressors, they construct the Q test using residuals from the static regression (8.34) (scaled appropriately with an estimate of the long-run variance of the errors, which allows for serial correlation). In the general case without strictly exogenous regressors, both recommend using the residuals from regression (8.34) augmented with leads and lags of the first-differences of y_{2t} (Carrion-i-Silvestre and Sanso (2004) show that the use of the Fully Modified estimator of Phillips and Hansen (1990) leads to tests with very poor finite sample properties). Both select the break date by minimizing the sum of squared residuals from the appropriate regression, following the work of Kurozumi and Arai (2004), who show that the estimate of the break fraction in this model converges at least at rate $T^{1/2}$. This permits limit critical values corresponding to the known break date case. They also consider selecting the break date as the value which minimizes the Q statistic, but do not recommend its use given that the resulting tests then suffers from large size distortions in finite samples.

A caveat about the approach discussed above is the fact that, for the suggested methods to be valid, there must be a change in the cointegrating relationship, if cointegration actually holds. This is because the search for the potential break date is restricted to break fractions that are bounded, in large samples, from the boundaries 0 and 1. Hence, when there is no change the limit value cannot be 0 or 1, the estimate is inconsistent and has a non-degenerate limit distribution, which in turn affects the limit distribution of the test (i.e., it does not correspond to the one that would prevail if no break was present). But to ascertain whether a break is present, one needs to know if there is cointegration, which is actually the object of the test. Tests of whether a change in structure has occurred (as reviewed in section 8.4.7) will reject the null hypothesis of no change when a change actually occurs in a cointegrating relationship, and will also reject if the system is simply not cointegrated. Hence, we are led to a circular argument. The test procedure needs to allow for the possibility of a change and not impose it. It may be possible to relax the restriction on the search for the break date by allowing all possible values. In the context of cointegrated $I(1)$ regressors, it is, however, unknown at this point if the estimate of the break fraction would converge to 0 or 1 when no change is present.

8.6.2 Methods based on a multivariate framework

We now consider tests that have been proposed when the variables are analyzed jointly as a system. Here, the results available in the literature are quite fragmentary and much of it pertains to a single break at a known date. Also, different treatments are possible by allowing for a change in the trend function of the original series (i.e., the marginal processes), or in allowing for a change in the cointegrating relation.

One of the early contributions is that of Inoue (1999). It allows for a one-time shift in the trend function of the series at some unknown date, either in level for non-trending series and for both level and slope in trending series. He considers an AO-type framework and also an IO type regression when only a shift in intercept is allowed in the VAR. The specification of the null and alternative hypotheses follows Zivot and Andrews (1992) and Gregory and Hansen (1996a,b), in that the shifts are allowed only under the alternative hypothesis. Hence, the null hypothesis is that the system contains no break and no more than r cointegrating vectors, and the alternative hypothesis is that the data can exhibit a change in trend and that the cointegrating rank is $r+1$, or greater than r. The breaks are assumed to occur at the same date for all series. Under the alternative hypothesis, the series are not assumed to be co-breaking, in the sense that the cointegrating vector that reduces the nonstationarity in the stochastic component also eliminates the nonstationarity in the deterministic trend. He considers the trace and maximal eigenvalue tests of Johansen (1988, 1991) with data appropriately detrended allowing for a shift in trend, and the resulting statistic is based on the maximal values over all permissible break dates. It is unclear what the properties of the tests are when the null hypothesis is true with data that have broken trends. Also, although the parameter r can be selected arbitrarily, the procedures cannot be applied sequentially to determine the cointegrating rank of the system. This is because the breaks are not allowed under the null hypothesis, only under the alternative. So if one starts with, say, $r=0$, breaks are allowed for alternatives such that the cointegrating rank is greater than 0. But, upon a rejection, if one then wants to test the null of rank 1 versus an alternative with rank greater than 1, one needs to impose no break under the null hypothesis of rank 1, a contradiction from what was specified in the earlier step.

Saikkonen and Lütkepohl (2000a) also consider a test of the null hypothesis of r cointegrating vectors versus the alternative that this number is greater than r, allowing for a break in the trend function of the individual series under both the null and alternative hypotheses. They, however, only consider a level shift (in trending or non-trending series) occurring at some known date. To estimate the coefficients of the trend component of the series, they use a similar GLS procedure, as discussed in section 8.5.3, appropriately extended for the multivariate nature of the problem. This detrending method imposes the null hypothesis. Hence, the effect of level shifts is negligible in large samples and the limit distribution of the test is the same as the standard (no-break) cointegration test of Lütkepohl and Saikkonen (2000) and Saikkonen and Lütkepohl (2000b). Once the detrended data is obtained, the test is based on the eigenvalues of a reduced rank problem where restrictions implied by the process and the breaks are not imposed.

Johansen *et al.* (2000) consider a more general problem but still with known break dates. They consider multiple structural changes in the following VAR of order k,

$$\Delta_{yt} = (\Pi, \Pi_j)\binom{y_{t-1}}{t} + \mu_j + \sum_{i=1}^{k-1} \Gamma_i \Delta y_{t-i} + e_t$$

for $T_{j-1}+k<t\leq T_j$ ($j=1,\ldots,m$). Hence, there are m breaks which can affect the constant and the coefficients of the trend. Various tests for the rank of the cointegrating matrix are proposed (imposing or not various restrictions on the deterministic components). Since the estimates of the coefficients of the trend are estimated from a maximum-likelihood type approach (following Johansen, 1988, 1991), the limit distribution depends on the exact specification of the deterministic components and on the true break dates. Asymptotic critical values are presented via a response surface analysis.

For the special case of a single shift in level, Lütkepohl *et al.* (2003) compare the two approaches of Saikkonen and Lütkepohl (2000a) and Johansen *et al.* (2000). They show that the former has higher local asymptotic power. However, the finite sample size-adjusted power is very similar. They recommend using the method of Saikkonen and Lütkepohl (2000a) on the basis of better size properties in finite samples and also on the fact that they view having a limit distribution free of the break dates to be advantageous. A problem with this argument is that the non-dependence of the limit distribution on the break date with the procedure of Saikkonen and Lütkepohl (2000a) no longer holds in more general models, especially when slope shifts are involved. Indeed, no result is yet available for this approach with a GLS type detrending procedure when slope shifts are present.

Lütkepohl *et al.* (2004) extend the analysis of Saikkonen and Lütkepohl (2002), which pertained to testing for a unit root allowing for a change in the level of a series occurring at an unknown date (see section 8.5.4.1). The GLS-type procedure discussed above is used to estimate the coefficients of the deterministic components. Once the series are detrended, the cointegration tests of Johansen (1988) can be used. In the unit root case, with a GLS detrending procedure that imposes the null hypothesis, the change in mean reduces to an outlier in the first-differenced series. Here, things are more complex and a consistent estimate of the break date is preferable. Estimating the break date has, however, no effect on the limit null distribution of the test statistic since, here again, it does not depend on the true value of the break date.

It is useful to consider in more detail the issue of estimating the break date. The n vector of data y_t is assumed to be generated by

$$y_t = \mu + \theta DU_t + \delta_t + x_t$$

where $DU_t = 1(t > T_1)$ and x_t is a noise component generated by a VAR, with the following ECM representation,

$$\Delta x_t = \Pi x_{t-1} + \sum_{i=1}^{k} \Gamma_i \Delta x_{t-i} + e_t$$

Here, the presence of cointegration implies the decomposition $\Pi = \alpha\beta'$, with β the $n \times r$ matrix of cointegrating vectors. Hence, we also have the following ECM representation for y_t

$$\Delta y_t = v + \alpha\beta'(y_{t-1} - \delta(t-1) - \theta DU_{t-1}) + \sum_{i=1}^{k} \Gamma_i \Delta y_{t-i} + \sum_{i=1}^{k} \gamma_i \Delta DU_{t-i} + e_t \qquad (8.35)$$

This ECM representation will be affected by a level shift if $\beta'\theta \neq 0$, otherwise only the impulse dummies ΔDU_{t-i} are present. In most cases of interest, we have $\beta'\delta = 0$, which specifies that the same linear combinations that eliminate the stochastic nonstationarity also eliminate the nonstationarity induced by the trend. The condition $\beta'\theta = 0$ can be interpreted in the same way, i.e., if some variables are affected by changes in trend, the linear combination of the data specified by the cointegrating vectors will be free of structural breaks. This is often referred to as "co-breaking." Hence, the condition $\beta'\theta \neq 0$ requires that the series be non co-breaking, which may be unappealing in many cases. Lütkepohl *et al.* (2004) estimate the break date by minimizing the determinant of the sample covariance matrix of the estimates of the errors e_t. They show the estimate of the break fraction to converge at rate T, though no limit distribution is given since this rate is enough to guarantee that the limit distribution of the test be independent of the break date. Note that the search for the break date is restricted to an interval that excludes a break fraction occurring near the beginning or end of the sample. This is important, since it makes the procedure valid conditional on shifts in level occurring. Without shifts, the true break fraction is 0 or 1, which are excluded from the search. Hence, in this case the estimated break fractions will converge to some random variable. But given that a GLS type detrending is done, this has no impact on the limit distribution of the rank test. A similar result holds when co-breaking shifts are present, though Lütkepohl *et al.* (2004) argue that, if the shifts are large enough, they can be captured by the impulse dummies ΔDU_{t-i} (for more details on estimation of break dates in this framework, see Saikkonen *et al.*, 2004).

All contributions discussed above do not address the problem of a potential shift in the cointegrating vector. A recent analysis by Andrade *et al.* (2005) deals with this in the context of a one-time change. The object is to test the null hypothesis of r cointegrating vectors versus the alternative that this value is greater than r. They allow the change in the cointegrating relationship to occur under both the null and alternative hypotheses and the number of cointegrating vectors is the same in both regimes. This allows a sequential procedure to determine the rank. The issues are addressed using the following generalized ECM

$$\Delta y_t = 1(t \le T_1)[\alpha_0\beta_0'y_{t-1} - \delta_0 d_t] + 1(t > T_1)[\alpha_1\beta_1'(y_{t-1} - y_{T_1}) - \delta_1 d_t]$$
$$+ \sum_{i=1}^{k}\Gamma_i\Delta y_{t-i} + e_t$$

where d_t is a vector of deterministic components (usually the null set or a constant). Note that the data is re-normalized after the break to start again at 0. This is done since otherwise the variance of $\beta_1'y_{t-1}$ would increase after the break given that it depends on the value of $\beta_1'y_{T_1}$. They note that the estimation of this model by maximum likelihood is quite involved and suggest a simpler principle components analysis. Let $\beta_{i\perp}$ be a matrix such that $\beta_i'\beta_{i\perp} = 0$, and suppose that the loading factors (or adjustment matrices) are constant, i.e., $\alpha_0 = \alpha_1$. The test of the null hypothesis that the cointegrating rank is r is based on testing that $\gamma_0 = \gamma_1 = 0$ in the following system

$$\Delta y_t = 1(t \le T_1)\left[\gamma_0\hat{\beta}_{0\perp}'y_{t-1} + \alpha\hat{\beta}_0'y_{t-1}\right] + 1(t > T_1)\left[\gamma_1\hat{\beta}_{1\perp}'y_{t-1} + \alpha\hat{\beta}_1'(y_{t-1} - yT_1)\right]$$
$$+ \sum_{i=1}^{k}\Gamma_i\Delta y_{t-i} + e_t$$

where $\hat{\beta}_1'$ and $\hat{\beta}_{i\perp}'$ are estimates obtained from the principle components analysis. The statistic is based on a multivariate Fisher-type statistic modified to eliminate the effect of nuisance parameters on the limit distribution under the null hypothesis. They also consider a version that is valid when the break date is unknown, based on the maximal values over a specified range for the break date, and present a test to evaluate how many cointegrating vectors are subject to change across regimes. When both the cointegrating matrix β and the loading factors α are allowed to change, a more involved testing procedure is offered, which applies, however, only to the known break date case.

An interesting recent contribution is that of Qu (2004). It proposes a procedure to detect whether cointegration (or stationarity in the scalar case) is present in any part of the sample, more precisely whether there is evidence in any part of the sample that a system is cointegrated with a higher cointegrating rank than the rest of the sample. The test procedure is based on a multivariate generalization of Gardner's (1969) Q test as used in Breitung (2002). The main device used is that if one or more sub-samples have a different cointegrating rank, one can find them by searching, in an iterative fashion, over all possible partitions of the sample with three segments or two breaks. The relevant limit distributions are derived allowing the possibility of imposing some structure if desired (e.g., that the change occurs at the beginning or end of the sample). He also discusses how to consistently estimate the break dates or the boundaries of the regimes when a change has been detected. A modification is also suggested to improve the finite sample performance of the test. This approach also permits testing for changes in persistence with the null hypothesis specified as an $I(1)$ process throughout the sample.

It also permits detecting whether cointegration is present when the cointegrating vector changes at some unknown, possibly multiple, dates.

8.7   Conclusions

This review has discussed a large amount of research that has been done in the last fifteen years or so pertaining to issues related to structural changes and to try to distinguish between structural changes and unit roots. But some important questions remain to be addressed: limit distributions of estimates of break dates in a cointegrated system with multiple structural changes, issues of non-monotonic power functions for tests of structural change and how to alleviate the problems, evaluating the frequency of permanent shocks; just to name a few. Research currently under progress is trying to address these and other issues.

One recent area of research where similar tools have been applied is related to distinguishing between long-memory processes and short-memory processes with structural changes, in particular, level shifts. This is especially important in financial economics, where it is widely documented that various measures of stock return volatility exhibit properties similar to those of a long-memory process (e.g., Ding *et al.*, 1993; Granger and Ding, 1995; and Lobato and Savin, 1998). For reviews of the literature on purely long-memory processes, see Robinson (1994a), Beran (1994) and Baillie (1996). As mentioned in section 8.2, a popular test for long-memory is the rescaled-range test. Yet, interestingly, Gardner's (1969) Q test makes yet another appearance. Indeed, it was, along with a slight modification, also proposed as a test for this problem by Giraitis *et al.* (2003). So we have the same test acting with the null hypothesis of a stable short-run memory process versus an alternative that is either structural change, a unit root or long-memory. This goes a long way towards showing how the three problems are interrelated.

One of the most convincing demonstrations that stock market volatility may be better characterized by a short-memory process affected by occasional level shifts is that of Perron and Qu (2004). They show that the behavior of the log-periodogram estimate of the long-memory parameter (the fractional differencing coefficient), as a function of the number of frequencies used in the regression, is very different for the two types of processes. The pattern found with data on daily SP500 return series (absolute or square root returns) is very close to what is expected with a short-memory process with level shifts. They also present a test which rejects the null hypothesis of long memory.

Given that unit root and long memory processes share similar features, it is not surprising that many of the same problems are being addressed with similar findings. Along the lines of Perron (1989) for unit roots, it has been documented that short-memory processes with level shifts will exhibit properties that make standard tools conclude that long memory is present (see, for example, Diebold and Inoue, 2001; Engle and Smith, 1999; Gourieroux and Jasiak, 2001; Granger and Ding, 1996; Granger and Hyung, 2004; Lobato and Savin, 1998; and Teverosovky and Taqqu, 1997). Some papers have also documented the fact that long-memory processes will induce, similar to unit root processes, a rejection of the null hypothesis of no-structural change when using standard structural change tests; for the CUSUM and the Sup-Wald test applied to a change in a polynomial trend, see Wright (1998) and Krämer and Sibbertsen (2002).

Results about the rate of convergence of the estimated break fraction in a single mean shift model can be found in Kuan and Hsu (1998). When there is structural change, the estimate is consistent but the rate of convergence depends on d. When $d \in (0, 1/2)$ and there is no change, the limit value is not 0 or 1, but rather the estimate of the break fraction converges to a random variable, suggesting a spurious change, exactly as in the unit root case (see Nunes *et al.*, 1995; Bai, 1998). For results related to multiple structural changes in mean, see Lavielle and Moulines (2000). A test for a single structural change occurring at some known date in the linear regression model is discussed in Hidalgo and Robinson (1996). It is essentially a Wald test for testing that the coefficients are the same in both regimes, which accounts for the long-memory correlation pattern in the residuals. Lazarová (2005) presents a test for the case of a single change in the parameters of a linear regression model occurring at an unknown date. The test follows the "fluctuations tests" approach of Ploberger *et al.* (1989) with different metrics used to weight the differences in the estimates for each permissible break date (giving special attention to the Sup and Mean functionals). The limit distribution depends on nuisance parameters and a bootstrap procedure is suggested to obtain the relevant critical values.

Related to the problem of change in persistence (see section 8.4.9), Beran and Terrin (1996) present a test for a change in the long-memory parameter, based on the maximal difference, across potential break dates, of appropriately weighted sums of autocovariances. Related to unit root tests allowing for a change in the trend function, Gil-Alana (2004) extends Robinson's (1994b) test to allow for a one-time change occurring at a known date. For a review of some related results, see Sibbertsen (2004).

The literature on structural changes in the context of long memory processes is quite new and few results are available. Still, there is a large demand for empirical applications. Given the nature of the problems and series analyzed, it is important to have procedures that are valid for multiple structural changes. For example, with many financial time series, it is the case that allowing for structural breaks reduces considerably the estimates of the long-memory parameters within regimes (e.g., Granger and Hyung, 2004, for stock return volatility). Are the reductions statistically significant? Are the reductions big enough that one can consider the process as being of a short-memory nature within regimes? Is there significant evidence of structural changes? Is the long-memory parameter stable across regimes? The econometrics and statistics literatures have a long way to go to provide reliable tools to answer these questions. Given that the issues are similar to the structural change versus unit root problem, our hope is that this survey will provide a valuable benchmark to direct research in specific directions and to alert researchers of the potential merits and drawbacks of the various approaches.

Acknowledgments

For useful comments on an earlier draft, I wish to thank Jushan Bai, Songjun Chun, Ai Deng, Mohitosh Kejriwal, Dukpa Kim, Eiji Kurozumi, Zhongjun Qu, Jonathan Treussard, Tim Vogelsang, Tatsuma Wada, Tomoyoshi Yabu, Yunpeng Zhang, Jing Zhou.

Notes

1. Note that what Vogelsang (1998b) actually refers to as the sup Wald test for the static case is actually the sup LM test. For the dynamic case, it does correspond to the Wald test.
2. A contribution related to multiple structural changes occurring at known dates in the context of cointegrated VAR processes is Hansen (2003), in which case all tests have the usual chi-square distribution.
3. Kim *et al.* (2004) study what happens when the trend regressor is absent and the series has a broken trend with the coefficients on the trend and shift in slope shrinking to zero as the sample size increases.
4. Perron (1997a) also showed how the weak convergence result could be obtained using the usual sup metric instead of the hybrid metric adopted in Zivot and Andrews (1992).

References

Altissimo, F. and V. Corradi (2003) Strong rules for detecting the number of breaks in a time series. *Journal of Econometrics* **117**, 207–44.

Amsler, C. and J. Lee (1995) An LM test for a unit root in the presence of a structural change. *Econometric Theory* **11**, 359–68.

Anderson, T.W. and D.A. Darling (1952) Asymptotic theory of certain "goodness of fit" criteria based on stochastic processes. *The Annals of Mathematical Statistics* **23**, 193–212.

Andrade, P., C. Bruneau and S. Gregoir (2005) Testing for the cointegration rank when some cointegrating directions are changing. *Journal of Econometrics* **124**, 269–310.

Andrews, D.W.K. (1991) Heteroskedasticity and autocorrelation consistent covariance matrix estimation. *Econometrica* **59**, 817–58.

Andrews, D.W.K. (1993a) Tests for parameter instability and structural change with unknown change point. *Econometrica* **61**, 821–56 (Corrigendum, **71**, 395–7).

Andrews, D.W.K. (1993b) Exactly median-unbiased estimation of first-order autoregressive/ unit root models. *Econometrica* **61**, 139–65.

Andrews, D.W.K., I. Lee and W. Ploberger (1996) Optimal change point tests for normal linear regression. *Journal of Econometrics* **70**, 9–38.

Andrews, D.W.K. and W. Ploberger (1994) Optimal tests when a nuisance parameter is present only under the alternative. *Econometrica* **62**, 1383–1414.

Antoch, J., M. Hušková and Z. Prášková (1997) Effect of dependence on statistics for determination of change. *Journal of Statistical Planning and Inference* **60**, 291–310.

Arai, Y. and E. Kurozumi (2005) Testing the null hypothesis of cointegration with structural breaks. Unpublished manuscript, Hitotsubashi University.

Bai, J. (1994) Least squares estimation of a shift in linear processes. *Journal of Time Series Analysis* **15**, 453–72.

Bai, J. (1997a) Estimation of a change point in multiple regression models. *Review of Economic and Statistics* **79**, 551–63.

Bai, J. (1997b) Estimating multiple breaks one at a time. *Econometric Theory* **13**, 315–52.

Bai, J. (1998) A note on spurious break. *Econometric Theory* **14**, 663–9.

Bai., J. (1999) Likelihood ratio tests for multiple structural changes. *Journal of Econometrics* **91**, 299–323.

Bai, J. (2000) Vector autoregressive models with structural changes in regression coefficients and in variance–covariance matrices. *Annals of Economics and Finance* **1**, 303–39.

Bai, J., R.L. Lumsdaine and J.H. Stock (1998) Testing for and dating breaks in multivariate time series. *Review of Economic Studies* **65**, 395–432.

Bai, J. and P. Perron (1998) Estimating and testing linear models with multiple structural changes. *Econometrica* **66**, 47–78.

Bai, J. and P. Perron (2003a) Computation and analysis of multiple structural change models. *Journal of Applied Econometrics* **18**, 1–22.

Bai, J. and P. Perron (2003b) Critical values for multiple structural change tests. *Econometrics Journal* 6, 72–8.

Bai, J. and P. Perron (2005) Multiple structural change models: a simulation analysis. Forthcoming in D. Corbea, S. Durlauf and B.E. Hansen (eds), *Econometric Essays*. Cambridge University Press.

Baillie, R.T. (1996) Long memory processes and fractional integration in econometrics. *Journal of Econometrics* 73, 5–59.

Banerjee, A., J.J. Dolado, D.F. Hendry and G.W. Smith (1986) Exploring equlibrium relationships in econometrics through static models: some Monte Carlo evidence. *Oxford Bulletin of Economics and Statistics* 48, 253–77.

Banerjee, A., R.L. Lumsdaine and J.H. Stock (1992) Recursive and sequential tests of the unit-root and trend-break hypotheses: theory and international evidence. *Journal of Business and Economic Statistics* 10, 271–87.

Barsky, R.B. (1987) The Fisher hypothesis and the forecastibility and persistence of inflation. *Journal of Monetary Economics* 19, 3–24.

Bartley, W.A., J. Lee and M.C. Strazicich (2001) Testing the null of cointegration in the presence of a structural break. *Economics Letters* 73, 315–23.

Bellman, R. and R. Roth (1969) Curve fitting by segmented straight lines. *Journal of the American Statistical Association* 64, 1079–1084.

Beran, J. (1994) *Statistics for Long Memory Processes*. New York: Chapman & Hall.

Beran, J. and N. Terrin (1996) Testing for a change of the long-memory parameter. *Biometrika* 83, 627–38.

Beveridge, S. and C.R. Nelson (1981) A new approach to decomposition of economic time series into permanent and transitory components with particular attention to measurement of the "Business Cycle." *Journal of Monetary Economics* 7, 151–74.

Bhattacharya, P.K. (1987) Maximum likelihood estimation of a change-point in the distribution of independent random variables, general multiparameter case. *Journal of Multivariate Analysis* 23, 183–208.

Bhattacharya, P.K. (1994) Some aspects of change-point analysis. In E. Carlstein, H.-G. Müller and D. Siegmund (eds), *Change Point Problems*, IMS Lecture Notes – Monograph Series, 23, 28–56.

Bhattacharya, R.N., V.K. Gupta and E. Waymire (1983) The Hurst effect under trends. *Journal of Applied Probability* 20, 649–62.

Box, G.E.P. and Tiao, G.C. (1975) Intervention analysis with applications to economic and environmental problems. *Journal of the American Statistical Association* 70, 70–9.

Breitung, J. (2002) Nonparametric tests for unit roots and cointegration. *Journal of Econometrics* 108, 343–63.

Brown, R.L., J. Durbin and J.M. Evans (1975) Techniques for testing the constancy of regression relationships over time. *Journal of the Royal Statistical Society* B 37, 149–63.

Burdekin, R.C.K. and P.L. Siklos (1999) Exchange rate regimes and shifts in inflation persistence: does nothing else matter? *Journal of Money, Credit and Banking* 31, 235–47.

Busetti, F. (2002) Testing for (common) stochastic trends in the presence of structural breaks. *Journal of Forecasting* 21, 81–105.

Busetti, F. and A.C. Harvey (2001) Testing for the presence of a random walk in series with structural breaks. *Journal of Time Series Analysis* 22, 127–150.

Busetti, F. and A.C. Harvey (2003) Further comments on stationarity tests in series with structural breaks at unknown points. *Journal of Time Series Analysis* 24, 137–40.

Busetti, F. and A.M.R. Taylor (2001) Tests stationarity against a change in persistence. Discussion Paper 01–13, Department of Economics, University of Birmingham.

Busetti, F. and A.M.R. Taylor (2005) Tests stationarity against a change in persistence. *Journal of Econometrics*. Forthcoming.

Campbell, J.Y. and P. Perron (1991) Pitfalls and opportunities: what macroeconomists should know about unit roots. *NBER Macroeconomics Annual*, vol. 6, Blanchard, O.J., Fisher, S. (eds.), 141–201.

Campos, J., N.R. Ericsson and D.F. Hendry (1996) Cointegration tests in the presence of structural breaks. *Journal of Econometrics* **70**, 187–220.

Carrion-i-Silvestre, J.L. and A.S. Sansó-i-Rosselló (2004) Testing the null hypothesis of cointegration with structural breaks. Unpublished manuscript, Departament d'Econometria, Estadística i Economia Espanyola, Universitat de Barcelona.

Carrion-i-Silvestre, J.L., A.S. Sansó-i-Rosselló and M. Artis (2004) Joint hypothesis specification for unit root tests with a structural break. Unpublished manuscript, Departament d'Econometria, Estadística i Economia Espanyola, Universitat de Barcelona.

Carrion-i-Silvestre, J.L. and A.S. Sansó-i-Rosselló and M.A. Ortuño (1999) Response surface estimates for the Dickey–Fuller test with structural breaks. *Economics Letters* **63**, 279–83.

Chernoff, H. and S. Zacks (1964) Estimating the current mean of a normal distribution which is subject to changes in time. *The Annals of Mathematical Statistics* **35**, 999–1018.

Chong, T.T.L. (1995) Partial parameter consistency in a misspecified structural change model. *Economics Letters* **49**, 351–7.

Chong, T.T.L. (2001) Structural change in AR(1) models. *Econometric Theory* **17**, 87–155.

Christiano, L.J. (1992) Searching for breaks in GNP. *Journal of Business and Economic Statistics* **10**, 237–50.

Chu, C.-S.J., K. Hornik and C.-M. Kuan (1995) MOSUM tests for parameter constancy. *Biometrika* **82**, 603–17.

Chu, C.-S.J. and H. White (1992) A direct test for changing trend. *Journal of Business and Economic Statistics* **10**, 289–99.

Clemente, J., A. Montañés and M. Reyes (1998) Testing for a unit root in variables with a double change in the mean. Economics Letters **59**, 175–82.

Clements, M.P. and D.F. Hendry (1999) *Forecasting Non-stationary Economic Time Series*. Cambridge, MA: MIT Press.

Cook, S. (2004) Spurious rejection by cointegration tests incorporating structural change in the cointegrating relationship. Unpublished manuscript, Department of Economics, University of Wales Swansea.

Crainiceanu, C.M. and T.J. Vogelsang (2001) Spectral density bandwidth choice: source of nonmonotonic power for tests of a mean shift in a time series. Unpublished manuscript, Department of Economics, Cornell University.

Csörgö, M. and L. Horváth (1997) *Limit Theorems in Change-Point Analysis*, Wiley Series in Probability and Statistics. New York: John Wiley.

Davies, R.B. (1977) Hypothesis testing when a nuisance parameter is present only under the alternative. *Biometrika* **64**, 247–54.

Davies, R.B. (1987) Hypothesis testing when a nuisance parameter is present only under the alternative. *Biometrika* **74**, 33–43.

DeLong, J.B. and L.H. Summers (1988) How does macroeconomic policy affect output? *Brookings Papers on Economic Activity* **2**, 433–94.

Deng, A. and P. Perron (2005a) A comparison of alternative asymptotic frameworks to analyze a structural change in a linear time trend. Unpublished manuscript, Department of Economics, Boston University.

Deng, A. and P. Perron (2005b) A locally asymptotic point optimal test that is inconsistent: the case of a change in persistence. Unpublished manuscript, Department of Economics, Boston University.

Deng, A. and P. Perron (2005c) On the finite sample power function of the dynamic cusum and cusum of squares tests. Unpublished manuscript, Department of Economics, Boston.

Deshayes, J. and D. Picard (1984a) Principe d'invariance sur le processus de vraisemblance. *Annales de l'Institut Henri Poincaré, Probabilités et Statistiques* **20**, 1–20.

Deshayes, J. and D. Picard (1984b) Lois asymptotiques des tests et estimateurs de rupture dans un modèle statistique classique. *Annales de l'Institut Henri Poincaré, Probabilités et Statistiques* **20**, 309–27.

Deshayes, J. and D. Picard (1986) Off-line statistical analysis of change point models using non-parametric and likelihood methods. In M. Basseville and A. Beneviste (eds), *Detection of Abrupt Changes in Signals and Dynamical Systems* (Lecture Notes in Control and Information Sciences 77). Berlin: Springer, pp. 103–68.

Dickey, D.A. and W.A. Fuller (1979) Distribution of the estimators for autoregressive time Series with a unit Root. *Journal of the American Statistical Association* **74**, 427–31.

Dickey, D.A. and W.A. Fuller (1981) Likelihood ratio statistics for autoregressive time series with a unit root. *Econometrica* **49**, 1057–1072.

Diebold, F. and A. Inoue (2001) Long memory and regime switching. *Journal of Econometrics* **105**, 131–59.

Ding, Z., R.F. Engle and C.W.J. Granger (1993) A long memory property of stock market returns and a new model. *Journal of Empirical Finance* **1**, 83–106.

Dufour, J.M. (1982) Recursive stability analysis of linear regression relationships: an exploratory methodology. *Journal of Econometrics* **19**, 31–76.

Dufour, J.-M. and J.F. Kiviet (1996) Exact tests for structural change in first-order dynamic models. *Journal of Econometrics* **70**, 39–68.

Elliott, G. and U.K. Müller (2003) Optimally testing general breaking processes in linear time series models. Unpublished manuscript. Department of Economics, University of California at San Diego.

Elliott, G. and U.K. Müller (2004) Confidence sets for the date of a single break in linear time series regressions. Unpublished manuscript, Department of Economics, University of California at San Diego.

Elliott, G., T.J. Rothenberg and J.H. Stock (1996) Efficient tests for an autoregressive unit root. *Econometrica* **64**, 813–36.

Engle, R.F. and A.D. Smith (1999) Stochastic permanent breaks. *Review of Economics and Statistics* **81**, 533–74.

Feder, P.I. (1975) On asymptotic distribution theory in segmented regression problems: identified case. *Annals of Statistics* **3**, 49–83.

Fisher, W.D. (1958) On grouping for maximum homogeneity. *Journal of the American Statistical Association* **53**, 789–98.

Fu, Y.-X. and R.N. Curnow (1990) Maximum likelihood estimation of multiple change points. *Biometrika* **77**, 563–73.

Garcia, R. and P. Perron (1996) An analysis of the real interest rate under regime shifts. *Review of Economics and Statistics* **78**, 111–25.

Gardner, L.A. (1969) On detecting changes in the mean of normal variates. *The Annals of Mathematical Statistics* **40**, 116–26.

Giraitis, L., P. Kokoszka, R. Leipus and G. Teyssière (2003) Rescaled variance and related tests for long memory in volatility and level. *Journal of Econometrics* **112**, 265–94 (Corrigendum, **126**, 571–2).

Gil-Alana, L.A. (2004) A joint test of fractional integration and structural breaks at a known period of time. *Journal of Time Series Analysis* **25**, 691–700.

Gourieroux, C. and J. Jasiak (2001) Memory and infrequent breaks. *Economics Letters* **70**, 29–41.

Granger, C.W.J. and Z. Ding (1996) Varieties of long memory models. *Journal of Econometrics* **73**, 61–77.

Granger, C.W.J. and N. Hyung (2004) Occasional structural breaks and long memory with an application to the S&P 500 absolute stock returns. *Journal of Empirical Finance* **11**, 399–421.

Gregory, A.W. and B.E. Hansen (1996a). Residual-based tests for cointegration in models with regime shifts. *Journal of Econometrics* **70**, 99–126.

Gregory, A.W. and B.E. Hansen (1996b) Tests for cointegration in models with regime and trend shifts. *Oxford Bulletin of Economics and Statistics* **58**, 555–60.

Gregory, A.W., J.M. Nason and D.G. Watt (1996) Testing for structural breaks in cointegrated relationships. *Journal of Econometrics* **71**, 321–41.

Guthery, S.B. (1974) Partition regression. *Journal of the American Statistical Association* **69**, 945–7.

Hackl, P. and A.H. Westlund (1989) Statistical analysis of "structural change": an annotated bibliography. *Empirical Economics* 14, 167–92.

Hackl, P. and A.H. Westlund (eds) (1991) *Economic Structural Change: Analysis and Forecasting.* Berlin: Springer-Verlag.

Hakkio, C.S. and M. Rush (1991) Is the budget deficit too large? *Economic Inquiry* 29, 429–45.

Hall, A.R. (2005) *Generalized Methods of Moments.* Oxford: Oxford University Press.

Hamori, S. and A. Tokihisa (1997) Testing for a unit root in the presence of a variance shift. *Economics Letters* 57, 245–53.

Hansen, B.E. (1992a) Tests for parameter instability in regressions with I(1) processes. *Journal of Business and Economic Statistics* 10, 321–35.

Hansen, B.E. (1992b) Testing for parameter instability in linear models. *Journal of Policy Modeling* 14, 517–33.

Hansen, B.E. (1996) Inference when a nuisance parameter is not identified under the null hypothesis. *Econometrica* 64, 413–30.

Hansen, B.E. (2000) Testing for structural change in conditional models. *Journal of Econometrics* 97, 93–115.

Hansen, H. and S. Johansen (1999) Some tests for parameter constancy in cointegrated VAR-models. *Econometrics Journal* 2, 306–33.

Hansen, P.R. (2003) Structural changes in the cointegrated vector autoregressive model. *Journal of Econometrics* 114, 261–95.

Harvey, D.I., S.J. Leybourne and A.M.R. Taylor (2004) Modified tests for a change in persistence. Unpublished manuscript, Department of Economics, University of Birmingham.

Hájek, J. and A. Rényi (1955) Generalization of an inequality of Kolmogorov. *Acta Mathematica Academiae Scientiarum Hungaricae* 6, 281–3.

Hao, K. (1996) Testing for structural change in cointegrated regression models: some comparisons and generalizations. *Econometric Reviews* 15, 401–29.

Hao, K. and B. Inder (1996) Diagnostic test for structural change in cointegrated regression models. *Economics Letters* 50, 179–87.

Harvey, A.C. (1975) Comment on the paper by Brown, Durbin and Evans. *Journal of the Royal Statistical Society B* 37, 179–80.

Harvey, D.I., S.J. Leybourne and P. Newbold (2001) Innovational outlier unit root tests with an endogenously determined break in level. *Oxford Bulletin of Economics and Statistics* 63, 559–75.

Harvey, D.I. and T.C. Mills (2003) A note on Busetti–Harvey tests for stationarity in series with structural breaks. *Journal of Time Series Analysis* 24, 159–64.

Hatanaka, M. and K. Yamada (1999) A unit root test in the presence of structural changes in I(1) and I(0) Models. In R.F. Engle and H. White (eds), *Cointegration, Causality, and Forecasting: A Festschrift in Honour of Clive W.J. Granger.* Oxford: Oxford University Press.

Hatanaka, M. and K. Yamada (2003) *Co-trending: A Statistical System Analysis of Economic Trends.* Tokyo: Springer-Verlag.

Hawkins, D.L. (1987) A test for a change point in a parametric model based on a maximal Wald-type statistic. *Sankhya* 49, 368–76.

Hawkins, D.M. (1976) Point estimation of the parameters of piecewise regression models. *Applied Statistics* 25, 51–7.

Hawkins, D.M. (1977) Testing a sequence of observations for a shift in location. *Journal of the American Stastistical Association* 72, 180–6.

Hecq, A. and J.P. Urbain (1993) Misspecification tests, unit roots and level shifts. *Economics Letters* 43, 129–35.

Hidalgo, J. and P.M. Robinson (1996) Testing for structural change in a long-memory environment. *Journal of Econometrics* 70, 159–74.

Hinkley, D.V. (1970) Inference about the change-point in a sequence of random variables. *Biometrika* 57, 1–17.

Horváth, L. (1995) Detecting changes in linear regression. *Statistics* 26, 189–208.

Hurst, H. (1951) Long term storage capacity of reservoirs. *Transactions of the American Society of Civil Engineers* 116, 770–99.

Imhof, J.P. (1961) Computing the distribution of quadratic forms in normal variables. *Biometrika* 48, 419–26.

Inoue, A. (1999) Tests of cointegrating rank with a trend-break. *Journal of Econometrics* 90, 215–37.

James, B., K.L. James and D. Siegmund (1987) Test for a change-point. *Biometrika* 74, 71–83.

Jandhyala, V.K. and I.B. MacNeill (1989) Residual partial sum limit process for regression models with applications to detecting parameter changes at unknown times. *Stochastic Processes and their Applications* 33, 309–23.

Jandhyala, V.K. and I.B. MacNeill (1992) On testing for the constancy of regression coefficients under random walk and change-point alternatives. *Econometric Theory* 8, 501–17.

Jandhyala, V.K. and C.D. Minogue (1993) Distributions of Bayes-type change-point statistics under polynomial regression. *Journal of Statistical Planning and Inference* 37, 271–90.

Johansen, S. (1988) Statistical analysis of cointegrating vectors. *Journal of Economic Dynamics and Control* 12, 231–54.

Johansen, S. (1991) Estimation and hypothesis testing of cointegration vectors in Gaussian vector autoregressive models. *Econometrica* 59, 1551–1580.

Johansen, S., R. Mosconi and B. Nielsen (2000) Cointegration analysis in the presence of structural breaks in the deterministic trend. *Econometrics Journal* 3, 216–49.

Juhl, T. and Z. Xiao (2005) Tests for changing mean with monotonic power. Unpublished manuscript, Department of Economics, Boston College.

Kander, Z. and S. Zacks (1966) Test procedures for possible changes in parameters of statistical distributions occurring at unknown time points. *The Annals of Mathematical Statistics* 37, 1196–1210.

Kapetanios, G. (2005) Unit-root testing against the alternative hypothesis of up to *m* structural breaks. *Journal of Time Series Analysis* 26, 123–33.

Kim, D. and P. Perron (2005) Unit root tests with a consistent break fraction estimator. Manuscript, Department of Economics, Boston University.

Kim, H.-J. and D. Siegmund (1989) The likelihood ratio test for a change-point in simple linear regression. *Biometrika* 76, 409–23.

Kim, J.Y. (2000) Detection of change in persistence of a linear time series. *Journal of Econometrics* 95, 97–116 (corrigendum, 2002, 109, 389–92).

Kim, T.-H., S.J. Leybourne and P. Newbold (2002) Unit root tests with a break in innovation variance. *Journal of Econometrics* 109, 365–87.

Kim, T.-H., S.J. Leybourne and P. Newbold (2004) Behavior of Dickey–Fuller unit root tests under trend misspecification. *Journal of Time Series Analysis* 25, 755–64.

King, M.L. and T.S. Shiveley (1993) Locally optimal testing when a nuisance parameter is present only under the alternative. *Review of Economics and Statistics* 75, 1–7.

Krämer, W., W. Ploberger and R. Alt (1988) Testing for structural change in dynamic models. *Econometrica* 56, 1355–1369.

Krämer, W. and H. Sonnberger (1986) *The Linear Regression Model Under Test*. Heidelberg: Physica-Verlag.

Krämer, W. and P. Sibbertsen (2002) Testing for structural changes in the presence of long memory. *International Journal of Business and Economics* 1, 235–42.

Krishnaiah, P.R. and B.Q. Miao (1988) Review about estimation of change points. In P.R. Krishnaiah and C.R. Rao (eds), *Handbook of Statistics*, vol. 7. New York: Elsevier.

Kuan, C.-M. and C.-C. Hsu (1998) Change-point estimation of fractionally integrated processes. *Journal of Time Series Analysis* 19, 693–708.

Kulperger, R.J. (1987a) On the residuals of autoregressive processes and polynomial regression. *Stochastic Processes and their Applications* 21, 107–18.

Kulperger, R.J. (1987b) Some remarks on regression residuals with autoregressive errors and their residual processes. *Journal of Applied Probability* 24, 668–78.

Kunitomo, N. and S. Sato (1995) Tables of limiting distributions useful for testing unit roots and co-integration with multiple structural changes. Manuscript, Department of Economics, University of Tokyo.

Kuo, B.-S. (1998) Test for partial parameter stability in regressions with $I(1)$ processes. *Journal of Econometrics* **86**, 337–68.

Kurozumi, E. (2002) Testing for stationarity with a break. *Journal of Econometrics* **108**,63–99.

Kurozumi, E. (2005) Detection of structural change in the long-run persistence in a univariate time series. *Oxford Bulletin of Economics and Statistics* **67**, 181–206.

Kurozumi, E. and Y. Arai (2004) Efficient estimation and inference in cointegrating regressions with structural breaks. Unpublished manuscript, Department of Economics, Hitotsubashi University.

Kwiatkowski, D., P.C.B. Phillips, P. Schmidt and Y. Shin (1992) Testing the null hypothesis of stationarity against the alternative of a unit root: how sure are we that economic time series have a unit root. *Journal of Econometrics* **54**, 159–78.

Lanne, M. and H. Lütkepohl (2002) Unit root tests for time series with level shifts: a comparison of different proposals. *Economics Letters* **75**, 109–14.

Lanne, M., H. Lütkepohl and P. Saikkonen (2002) Comparison of unit root tests for time series with level shifts. *Journal of Time Series Analysis* **23**, 667–85.

Lanne, M., H. Lütkepohl and P. Saikkonen (2003) Test procedures for unit roots in time series with level shifts at unknown time. *Oxford Bulletin of Economics and Statistics* **65**, 91–115.

Lavielle, M. and E. Moulines (2000) Least-squares estimation of an unknown number of shifts in a time series. *Journal of Time Series Analysis* **21**, 33–59.

Lazarová, Š. (2005) Testing for structural change in regression with long memory errors. Forthcoming in the *Journal of Econometrics*.

Lee, J. (2000) On the end-point issue in unit root tests in the presence of a structural break. *Economics Letters* **68**, 7–11.

Lee, J., C.J. Huang and Y. Shin (1997) On stationary tests in the presence of structural breaks. *Economics Letters* **55**, 165–72.

Lee, J. and M.C. Strazicich (2001a) Break point estimation and spurious rejections with endogenous unit root tests. *Oxford Bulletin of Economics and Statistics* **63**, 535–58.

Lee, J. and M.C. Strazicich (2001b) Testing the null of stationarity in the presence of a structural break. *Applied Economics Letters* **8**, 377–82.

Leybourne, S., T.-H. Kim, V. Smith and P. Newbold (2003) Tests for a change in persistence against the null of difference-stationarity. *Econometrics Journal* **6**, 291–311.

Leybourne, S.J., T.C. Mills and P. Newbold (1998) Spurious rejections by Dickey–Fuller tests in the presence of a break under the null. *Journal of Econometrics* **87**, 191–203.

Leybourne, S.J. and P. Newbold (2000) Behavior of the standard and symmetric Dickey–Fuller type tests when there is a break under the null hypothesis. *Econometrics Journal* **3**, 1–15.

Leybourne, S.J. and P. Newbold (2003) Spurious rejections by cointegration tests induced by structural breaks. *Applied Economics* **35**, 1117–1121.

Leybourne, S.J. and A.M.R. Taylor (2004) On tests for changes in persistence. *Economics Letters* **84**, 107–15.

Leybourne, S.J., A.M.R. Taylor and T.-H. Kim (2003) An unbiased test for a change in persistence. Unpublished manuscript, Department of Economics, University of Birmingham.

Liu, J., S. Wu and J.V. Zidek (1997) On segmented multivariate regressions. *Statistica Sinica* **7**, 497–525.

Lo, A. (1991) Long-term memory in stock market prices. *Econometrica* **59**, 1279–1313.

Lobato, I.N. and N.E. Savin (1998) Real and spurious long-memory properties of stock-market data. *Journal of Business and Economics Statistics* **16**, 261–8.

Lumsdaine, R.L. and D.H. Papell (1997) Multiple trend breaks and the unit root hypothesis. *Review of Economics and Statistics* **79**, 212–18.

Lütkepohl, H. and P. Saikkonen (2000) Testing for the cointegrating rank of a VAR process with a time trend. *Journal of Econometrics* **95**, 177–98.

Lütkepohl, H., P. Saikkonen and C. Trenkler (2003) Comparison of tests for cointegrating rank of a VAR process with a structural shift. *Journal of Econometrics* **113**, 201–29.

Lütkepohl, H., C. Muller and P. Saikkonen (2001) Unit root tests for time series with a structural break when the break point is known. In C. Hsiao, K. Morimune and J. Powell (eds), *Nonlinear Statistical Modelling: Essays in Honor of Takeshi Amemiya*. Cambridge: Cambridge University Press, pp. 327–48.

Lütkepohl, H., P. Saikkonen and C. Trenkler (2004) Testing for the cointegrating rank of a VAR process with level shift at unknown time. *Econometrica* **72**, 647–62.

MacNeill, I.B. (1974) Tests for change of parameter at unknown time and distributions on some related functionals of Brownian motion. *Annals of Statistics* **2**, 950–62.

MacNeill, I.B. (1978) Properties of sequences of partial sums of polynomial regression residuals with applications to tests for change of regression at unknown times. *The Annals of Statistics* **6**, 422–33.

Maddala, G.S. and I.M. Kim (1998) *Unit Roots, Cointegration and Structural Change*. Cambridge: Cambridge University Press.

Mandelbrot, B.B. and M.S. Taqqu (1979) Robust R/S analysis of long run serial correlation. In *Proceedings of the 42nd Session of the International Statistical Institute*, vol. 2, pp. 69–99.

Mankiw, N.G., J.A. Miron and D.N. Weil (1987) The adjustment of expectations to change in regime: a study of the founding of the federal reserve. *American Economic Review* **77**, 358–74.

Marriott, J. and P. Newbold (2000) The strength of evidence for unit autoregressive roots and structural breaks: a Bayesian perspective. *Journal of Econometrics* **98**, 1–25.

Montañés, A. (1997) Level shifts, unit roots and misspecification of the breaking date. *Economics Letters* **54**, 7–13.

Montañés, A. and I. Olloqui (1999) Misspecification of the breaking date in segmented trend variables: effect on the unit root tests. *Economics Letters* **65**, 301–7.

Montañés, A., I. Olloqui and E. Calvo (2005) Selection of the break in the Perron-type tests. Forthcoming in the *Journal of Econometrics*.

Montañés, A. and M. Reyes (1998) Effect of a shift in the trend function on Dickey–Fuller unit root tests. *Econometric Theory* **14**, 355–63.

Montañés, A. and M. Reyes (1999) The asymptotic behavior of the Dickey–Fuller tests under the crash hypothesis. *Statistics and Probability Letters* **42**, 81–9.

Montañés, A. and M. Reyes (2000) Structural breaks, unit roots and methods for removing the autocorrelation pattern. *Statistics and Probablity Letters* **48**, 401–9.

Nabeya, S. and K. Tanaka (1988) Asymptotic theory of a test for the constancy of regression coefficients against the random walk alternative. *Annals of Statistics* **16**, 218–35.

Nadler, J. and N.B. Robbins (1971) Some characteristics of Page's two-sided procedure for detecting a change in a location parameter. *The Annals of Mathematical Statistics* **42**, 538–51.

Nelson, C.R. and C.I. Plosser (1982) Trends and random walks in macroeconomics time series: some evidence and implications. *Journal of Monetary Economics* **10**, 139–62.

Ng, S. and P. Perron (1995) Unit root tests in ARMA models with data dependent methods for selection of the truncation lag. *Journal of the American Statistical Association* **90**, 268–81.

Ng, S. and P. Perron (2001) Lag length selection and the construction of unit root tests with good size and power. *Econometrica* **69**, 1519–1554.

Noh, J. and T.-H. Kim (2003) Behavior of cointegration tests in the presence of structural breaks in variance. *Applied Economics Letters* **10**, 999–1002.

Nunes, L.C., C.-M. Kuan and P. Newbold (1995) Spurious break. *Econometric Theory* **11**, 736–49.

Nunes, L.C., P. Newbold and C.-M. Kuan (1996) Spurious number of breaks. *Economics Letters* **50**, 175–8.

Nunes, L.C., P. Newbold and C.-M. Kuan (1997) Testing for unit roots with breaks: evidence on the great crash and the unit root hypothesis reconsidered. *Oxford Bulletin of Economics and Statistics* **59**, 435–48.

Nyblom, J. (1989) Testing the constancy of parameters over time. *Journal of the American Statistical Association* **84**, 223–30.

Nyblom, J. and A.C. Harvey (2000) Tests of common stochastic trends. *Econometric Theory* **16**, 176–99.

Nyblom, J. and T. Mäkeläinen (1983) Comparisons of tests for the presence of random walk coefficients in a simple linear model. *Journal of the American Statistical Association* **78**, 856–64.

Ohara, H.I. (1999) A unit root test with multiple trend breaks: a theory and application to US and Japanese macroeconomic time-series. *The Japanese Economic Review* **50**, 266–90.

Page, E.S. (1955) A test for a change in a parameter occurring at an unknown point. *Biometrika* **42**, 523–7.

Page, E.S. (1957) On problems in which a change in a parameter occurs at an unknown point. *Biometrika* **44**, 248–52.

Park, J.Y. Canonical cointegrating regressions. *Econometrica* **60**, 119–43.

Perron, P. (1989) The great crash, the oil price shock and the unit root hypothesis. *Econometrica* **57**, 1361–1401.

Perron, P. (1990) Testing for a unit root in a time series with a changing mean. *Journal of Business and Economic Statistics* **8**, 153–62.

Perron, P. (1991) A test for changes in a polynomial trend function for a dynamic time series. *Research Memorandum No. 363.* Econometric Research Program, Princeton University.

Perron, P. (1994) Trend, unit root and structural change in macroeconomic time series. In B.B. Rao (ed.), *Cointegration for the Applied Economist.* Basingstoke: Macmillan Press, pp. 113–46.

Perron, P. (1997a) Further evidence from breaking trend functions in macroeconomic variables. *Journal of Econometrics* **80**, 355–85.

Perron, P. (1997b) L'estimation de modèles avec changements structurels multiples. *Actualité Économique* **73**, 457–505.

Perron, P. and Z. Qu (2004) An analytical evaluation of the log-periodogram estimate in the presence of level shifts and its implications for stock return volatility. Manuscript, Department of Economics, Boston University.

Perron, P. and Z. Qu (2005) Estimating restricted structural change models. Forthcoming in *Journal of Econometrics.*

Perron, P. and G.H. Rodríguez (2003) GLS detrending, efficient unit root tests and structural change. *Journal of Econometrics* **115**, 1–27.

Perron, P. and T.J. Vogelsang (1992a) Nonstationarity and level shifts with an application to purchasing power parity. *Journal of Business and Economic Statistics* **10**, 301–20.

Perron, P. and T.J. Vogelsang (1992b) Testing for a unit root in a time series with a changing mean: corrections and extensions. *Journal of Business and Economic Statistics* **10**, 467–70.

Perron, P. and T.J. Vogelsang (1993a) The great crash, the oil price shock and the unit root hypothesis: erratum. *Econometrica* **61**, 248–9.

Perron, P. and T.J. Vogelsang (1993b) A note on the additive outlier model with breaks. *Revista de Econometria* **13**, 181–201.

Perron, P. and T. Wada (2005) Trends and cycles: a new approach and explanations of some old puzzles. Manuscript, Department of Economics, Boston University.

Perron, P. and T. Yabu (2004) Estimating deterministic trends with an integrated or stationary noise component. Manuscript, Department of Economics, Boston University.

Perron, P. and T. Yabu (2005) Testing for shifts in trend with an integrated or stationary noise component. Unpublished manuscript, Department of Economics, Boston University.

Perron, P. and X. Zhu (2005) Structural breaks with stochastic and deterministic trends. Forthcoming in the *Journal of Econometrics.*

Pesaran, H.M., R.P. Smith and J.S. Yeo (1985) Testing for structural stability and predictive failure: a review. *The Manchester School of Economic & Social Studies* **53**, 281–95.

Phillips, P.C.B. and S. Ouliaris (1990) Asymptotic properties of residual based tests for cointegration. *Econometrica* **58**, 165–93.

Phillips, P.C.B. and P. Perron (1988) Testing for a unit root in time series regression. *Biometrika* **75**, 335–46.

Picard, D. (1985) Testing and estimating change-points in time series. *Journal of Applied Probability* **17**, 841–67.

Pitarakis, J.-Y. (2004) Least squares estimation and tests of breaks in mean and variance under misspecification. *Econometrics Journal* 7, 32–54.

Ploberger, W. and W. Krämer (1990) The local power of the cusum and cusum of squares tests. *Econometric Theory* 6, 335–47.

Ploberger, W. and W. Krämer (1992) The CUSUM test with OLS residuals. *Econometrica* 60, 271–85.

Ploberger, W., W. Krämer and K. Kontrus (1989) A new test for structural stability in the linear regression model. *Journal of Econometrics* 40, 307–18.

Qu, Z. (2004) Searching for cointegration in a dynamic system. Manuscript, Department of Economics, Boston University.

Qu, Z. and P. Perron (2005) Estimating and testing multiple structural changes in multivariate regressions. Manuscript, Department of Economics, Boston University.

Quandt, R.E. (1958) The estimation of the parameters of a linear regression system obeying two separate regimes. *Journal of the American Statistical Association* 53, 873–80.

Quandt, R.E. (1960) Tests of the hypothesis that a linear regression system obeys two separate regimes. *Journal of the American Statistical Association* 55, 324–30.

Quintos, C.E. (1997) Stability tests in error correction models. *Journal of Econometrics* 82, 289–315.

Qunitos, C.E. and P.C.B. Phillips (1993) Parameter constancy in cointegrated regressions. *Empirical Economics* 18, 675–706.

Rappoport, P. and L. Reichlin (1989) Segmented trends and non-stationary time series. *Economic Journal* 99, 168–77.

Robinson, P.M. (1994a) Time series with strong dependence. In C. Sims (ed.), *Advances in Econometrics, 6th World Congress*. Cambridge: Cambridge University Press, pp. 47–95.

Robinson, P.M. (1994b). Efficient tests of nonstationary hypotheses. *Journal of the American Statistical Association* 89, 1420–1437.

Roy, A., B. Falk and W.A. Fuller (2004) Testing for trend in the presence of autoregressive errors. *Journal of the American Statistical Association* 99, 1082–1091.

Roy, A. and W.A. Fuller (2001) Estimation for autoregressive time series with a root near 1. *Journal of Business and Economic Statistics* 19, 482–93.

Saikkonen, P. (1991) Asymptotically efficient estimation of cointegrated regressions. *Econometric Theory* 7, 1–21.

Saikkonen, P. and H. Lütkepohl (2000a) Testing for the cointegrating rank of a VAR process with structural shifts. *Journal of Business and Economic Statistics* 18, 451–64.

Saikkonen, P. and H. Lütkepohl (2000b) Trend adjustment prior to testing for the cointegrating rank of a vector autoregressive process. *Journal of Time Series Analysis* 21, 435–56.

Saikkonen, P. and H. Lütkepohl (2001) Testing for unit roots in time series with level shifts. *Allgemeines Statistisches Archiv* 85, 1–25.

Saikkonen, P. and H. Lütkepohl (2002) Testing for a unit root in a time series with a level shift at unknown time. *Econometric Theory* 18, 313–48.

Saikkonen, P., H. Lütkepohl and C. Trenkler (2004) Break date estimation and cointegration testing in VAR processes with level shift. Manuscript, Humboldt University Berlin and University of Helsinki.

Sen, P.K. (1980) Asymptotic theory of some tests for a possible change in the regression slope occurring at an unknown time point. *Zeitschrift für Wahrscheinlichkeitstheorie und verwandte Gebiete* 52, 203–18.

Sen, P.K. (1982) Invariance principles for recursive residuals. *The Annals of Statistics* 10, 307–12.

Seo, B. (1998) Tests for structural change in cointegrated systems. *Econometric Theory* 14, 222–59.

Shaban, S.A. (1980) Change point problem and two-phase regression: an annotated bibliography. *International Statistical Review* 48, 83–93.

Shin, Y. (1994) A residual-based test of the null of cointegration against the alternative of no cointegration. *Econometric Theory* 10, 91–115.

Sibbertsen, P. (2004) Long memory versus structural breaks: an overview. *Statistical Papers* **45**, 465–515.

Siegmund, D. (1988) Confidence sets in change-point problems. *International Statistical Review* **56**, 31–48.

Sowell, F. (1996) Optimal tests for parameter instability in the generalized method of moments framework. *Econometrica* **64**, 1085–1107.

Stock, J.H. (1994) Unit roots, structural breaks and trends. In R.F. Engle and D. MacFadden (eds), *Handbook of Econometrics*, vol. 4. Amsterdam: Elsevier, pp. 2740–2841.

Stock, J.H. and M.W. Watson (1993) A simple estimator of cointegrating vectors in higher order integrated systems. *Econometrica* **64**, 783–820.

Tang, S. M. and I.B. MacNeill (1993) The effect of serial correlation on tests for parameter change at unknown time. *Annals of Statistics* **21**, 552–75.

Teverovsky, V. and M. Taqqu (1997) Testing for long-range dependence in the presence of shifting means or a slowly declining trend, using a variance-type estimator. *Journal of Time Series Analysis* **18**, 279–304.

Tong, H. (1990) *Non-linear Time Series: A Dynamical System Approach*. Oxford: Oxford University Press.

van Dijk, D., T. Terasvirta and P.H. Franses (2002) Smooth transition autoregressive models–a survey of recent developments. *Econometric Reviews* **21**, 1–47.

Vogelsang, T.J. (1997) Wald-type tests for detecting breaks in the trend function of a dynamic time series. *Econometric Theory* **13**, 818–49.

Vogelsang, T.J. (1998a) Trend function hypothesis testing in the presence of serial correlation. *Econometrica* **66**, 123–48.

Vogelsang, T.J. (1998b) Testing for a shift in mean without having to estimate serial-correlation parameters. *Journal of Business and Economic Statistics* **16**, 73–80.

Vogelsang, T.J. (1999) Sources of nonmonotonic power when testing for a shift in mean of a dynamic time series. *Journal of Econometrics* **88**, 283–99.

Vogelsang, T.J. (2001) Testing for a shift in trend when serial correlation is of unknown form. Manuscript, Department of Economics, Cornell University.

Vogelsang, T.J. and P. Perron (1998) Additional tests for a unit root allowing the possibility of breaks in the trend function. *International Economic Review* **39**, 1073–1100.

Wang, J. and E. Zivot (2000) A Bayesian time series model of multiple structural change in level, trend and variance. *Journal of Business and Economic Statistics* **18**, 374–86.

Worsley, K.J. (1986) Confidence regions and test for a change-point in a sequence of exponential family random variables. *Biometrika* **73**, 91–104.

Wright, J.H. (1998) Testing for a structural break at unknown date with long-memory disturbances. *Journal of Time Series Analysis* **19**, 369–76.

Yao, Y.-C. (1987) Approximating the distribution of the maximum likelihood estimate of the change-point in a sequence of independent random variables. *Annals of Statistics* **15**, 1321–1328.

Yao, Y.-C. (1988) Estimating the number of change-points via Schwarz' criterion. *Statistics and Probability Letters* **6**, 181–9.

Zacks, S. (1983) Survey of classical and Bayesian approaches to the change-point problem: fixed and sequential procedures of testing and estimation. In M.H. Rivzi, J.S. Rustagi and D. Siegmund (eds), *Recent Advances in Statistics*. New York: Academic Press.

Zivot, E. and D.W.K. Andrews (1992) Further evidence on the great crash, the oil price shock and the unit root hypothesis. *Journal of Business and Economic Statistics* **10**, 251–70.

Zivot, E. and P.B.C. Phillips (1994) A Bayesian analysis of trend determination in economic time series. *Econometric Reviews* **13**, 291–336.

9
Semiparametric Estimation of Long-Memory Models

Carlos Velasco

Abstract

This chapter reviews semiparametric methods of inference on different aspects of long memory time series. The main focus is on estimation of the memory parameter of linear models, analyzing bandwidth choice, bias reduction techniques and robustness properties of different estimates, with some emphasis on nonstationarity and trending behaviors. These techniques extend naturally to multivariate series, where the important issues are the estimation of the long-run relationship and testing for fractional cointegration. Specific techniques for the estimation of the degree of persistence of volatility for nonlinear time series are also considered.

9.1	Introduction	354
9.2	Memory estimation	356
	9.2.1 Log-periodogram estimation	357
	9.2.2 Local Whittle estimation	360
	9.2.3 Averaged periodogram estimation	363
	9.2.4 Bias reduction and bandwidth choice	364
	9.2.5 Global methods: FEXP and FAR estimates	369
9.3	Extensions	370
	9.3.1 Nonstationary long memory	370
	9.3.2 Tapering	371
	9.3.3 Alternative nonstationary fractional processes	374
	9.3.4 Cyclical and seasonal long memory	376
9.4	Developments	378
	9.4.1 Fractional cointegration	378
	9.4.2 Nonlinear models	385
	9.4.3 Other areas of application	388
9.5	Conclusion	388

9.1   Introduction

The concepts of long memory and long range dependence describe the property that many time series models exhibit, despite being stationary, higher persistence than that predicted by usual short-run linear models, such as ARMA processes. The same type of persistence, with a slow decay in the autocorrelation function, has been observed in many economic series, such as the increments of trending data, measures of volatility, and errors in long-run equilibrium relationships; see Henry and Zaffaroni (2003) for a review of applications of long memory time series in economics.

Although several long memory parametric models can be found in the literature, such as Fractionally Integrated ARMA (ARFIMA) models (Hosking, 1981; Granger and Joyeaux, 1980) or fractional Gaussian noise (e.g. Sinai, 1976), there has long been an interest in modeling the long- and short-run features of time series separately. Since parametric models and the weak limit of partial sums of a large class of long memory processes describe the degree of persistence by means of a memory parameter, usually denoted as d in the econometrics literature, much attention has been paid to stating alternative, semiparametric definitions of long-range dependent behavior and, based upon them, providing corresponding estimates of d that avoid the specification of short memory properties.

If X_t is a covariance stationary sequence, long memory is described in the time domain by means of the asymptotic relation

$$\gamma_X(j) = \text{Cov}(X_t, X_{t+j}) \sim c_X j^{2d-1}, \quad \text{as } j \to \infty, \tag{9.1}$$

where $a \sim b$ means that the limit of a/b is 1. The constant $|c_X| > 0$ can be replaced by a slowly varying function at infinity to achieve greater generality. Equation (9.1) states that the autocovariance function $\gamma_X(j)$ decays to zero as a power function of the lag j, where the decay rate is determined by the long memory parameter d, so that when $d > 0$ we have:

$$\sum_{j=-\infty}^{\infty} \gamma_X(j) = \infty, \tag{9.2}$$

and it is required that $d < 0.5$ for covariance stationarity.

Alternatively, long-range dependence is reflected in the spectral density $f_X(\lambda)$ of X_t, defined by

$$\gamma_X(j) = \int_{-\pi}^{\pi} f_X(\lambda) \exp(ij\lambda) d\lambda, \quad j = 0, \pm 1, \dots,$$

through its behavior at low frequencies,

$$f_X(\lambda) \sim G_X |\lambda|^{-2d} \quad \text{as } \lambda \to 0, \tag{9.3}$$

for some finite constant $G_X > 0$. Therefore, the spectral density has a pole at zero frequency when $d > 0$, agreeing with (9.2) and reflecting the increasing contribution of low frequency components to the variance decomposition of X_t. Negative values of d can be allowed, although they are not likely to occur in practice unless some differencing has first been applied to X_t. In this case (9.3) indicates that there is no contribution from the zero frequency to the variance of X_t, as would happen after first differencing a stationary time series, and such a property is termed negative memory or 'antipersistence'. However, as long as $d > -0.5$, the series remains invertible. When $d = 0$, $f_X(0)$ is bounded and positive, and we say that the series is weakly dependent. Note that (9.1) does not specify the behavior of γ_X for short lags nor does (9.3) gives the properties of f_X for cyclical, seasonal or short-run frequencies.

Long memory behavior is reflected also in the fact that the sample mean converges to the true expectation of X_t at the rate $T^{d-1/2}$, slower than the usual root-T rate for uncorrelated and weakly dependent sequences, where T is the sample size (Adentstedt, 1974). Similarly, the asymptotic properties of other basic statistics, such as partial sums (Mandelbrot and Van Ness, 1968), autocovariances (Hosking, 1996) or least squares (LS) regression coefficients (Yajima, 1988, 1991), depend primarily on the value of d.

The long memory concept can also cross the stationarity border $d = 1/2$ and it can be useful to characterize the long-run behavior of nonstationary time series by means of the class of integrated $I(d)$ processes. This class nests the unit root $I(1)$ processes as well as the $I(0)$ weakly dependent processes. Here the concept of integration refers to the application of fractional difference/integration filters, defined by the formal binomial expansion of $(1 - L)^d$ in terms of the lag operator L, such that for any real $d \neq 1, 2, \ldots$

$$(1 - L)^d = \sum_{j=0}^{\infty} \psi_j(d) L^j, \quad \psi_j(d) = \frac{\Gamma(j - d)}{\Gamma(j + 1)\Gamma(-d)}, \quad j = 0, 1, \ldots, \quad (9.4)$$

where $\Gamma(z) = \int_0^\infty x^{z-1} e^{-x} dx$ is the gamma function and $\Gamma(0)/\Gamma(0) = 1$. Thus $\psi_0(d) = 1, \psi_j(d) = \psi_{j-1}(d)(j - d - 1)/j, j \geq 1$, and, using Stirling's formula, the coefficients $\psi_j(d)$ behave as $\Gamma(-d)^{-1} j^{-d-1}$ for $j \to \infty$. When d is a positive integer, only the first $d + 1$ terms are nonzero and we obtain the usual definition of the d-th difference operator. Then X_t is $I(d)$, i.e., integrated of order d, if $(1 - L)^d X_t$ is weakly dependent. Note that the transfer function associated with the fractional filter $(1 - L)^d$ is

$$|1 - e^{i\lambda}|^{2d} = (2 \sin |\lambda/2|)^{2d} \sim |\lambda|^{2d} \quad \text{as } \lambda \to 0, \quad (9.5)$$

giving a simple intuition of the effect of fractional differencing in the frequency domain by means of annihilating the contribution at zero frequency.

Under this framework, the concept of long memory and fractional integration are key to the modeling of long-run relationships among nonstationary trending time series. As proposed by Granger (1981), the series are (fractionally) cointegrated if a linear combination has reduced memory compared with the original series, reflecting a long-run equilibrium (at least when the linear combination is stationary). When the memory levels are no longer an a priori assumption, as under the CI(1,0) paradigm stressed since Engle and Granger (1987) with $I(1)$ levels and $I(0)$ errors, the inference problems complicate because of the unknown degree of cointegration.

We will first focus in section 9.2 on semiparametric methods of estimating d in the frequency domain. These are the most frequently used in practice and many extensions, including studies of volatility and subsequent refinements, have appeared. We also provide a guide to the choice of the range of frequencies over which the relationship (9.3) holds approximately for a particular problem with a given sample size, trying to balance bias and variability. In this vein we present several proposals for bias reduction, borrowing ideas from nonparametric statistics, as well as methods that consider all frequencies but are semiparametric in essence. In section 9.3 we consider the extension of the methods to nonstationary fractionally integrated series and discuss the possibility of long memory at other nonzero frequencies, such as cyclical and seasonal ones. Section 9.4 describes applications of semiparametric methods to the analysis of economic series, stressing those applications to cointegrated multivariate nonstationary time series and to white noise series with persistence in their volatility.

9.2 Memory estimation

Each of the different asymptotic characterizations of long memory can lead to alternative estimates of the memory parameter, where population quantities are replaced by sample equivalents. The rate of convergence of partial sums was exploited by the rescaled range (or R/S) analysis introduced by Hurst (1951) and Mandelbrot and Wallis (1968). Time domain estimates proposed by Robinson (1994c) were analyzed by Hall, Koul and Turlach (1997), while Geweke and Porter-Hudak (1983), GPH henceforth, proposed using frequency domain estimates.

Frequency domain semiparametric methods exploit the asymptotic relationship (9.3) as a valid (semiparametric) model for the spectral density at low frequencies: in particular, the first m Fourier frequencies, $\lambda_j = 2\pi j/T, j = 1, \ldots, m$, where

$$\frac{1}{m} + \frac{m}{T} \to 0 \text{ as } T \to \infty, \tag{9.6}$$

so that m is increasing with the sample size T in the asymptotics, but at a slower rate. These local methods are also termed narrow band estimates, because only a degenerating band of the spectrum around $\lambda = 0$ is modeled, basically in terms of the long memory parameter d. The idea behind all of the estimates in the frequency domain is to compare the spectral density f_x with its sample counterpart, the periodogram, across this range of frequencies and to find the value of d that best suits the data by alternative criteria. Define the discrete Fourier transform (DFT) of X_t, for a sample of T observations, $t = 1, \ldots, T$, as

$$w_X(\lambda) = \frac{1}{\sqrt{2\pi T}} \sum_{t=1}^{T} X_t \exp(i\lambda t),$$

and the periodogram of X_t as

$$I_X(\lambda) = |w_X(\lambda)|^2.$$

Note that $w_X(\lambda_j), 0 < j < T$, is invariant to shifts in mean, rendering periodogram based methods independent of mean estimation by dropping the zero frequency.

9.2.1 Log-periodogram estimation

GPH observed that by taking logs of both sides of (9.3) we obtain

$$\log f_X(\lambda_j) \sim \log G_X - 2d \log \lambda_j, \quad j = 1, \ldots, m$$

and on substituting by $\log f_X(\lambda_j)$ by $\log I_X(\lambda_j)$, we obtain the linear regression model on the log-periodogram,

$$\log I_X(\lambda_j) = \alpha + dz_j + u_j, \quad j = 1, \ldots, m \tag{9.7}$$

with regressor $z_j = -2 \log \lambda_j$ and $\alpha = \log G_X - \eta, \eta = 0.5772\ldots$ being Euler's constant. The error term $u_j = \log I_X(\lambda_j)/G_X\lambda_j^{-2d} + \eta$ is expected to be asymptotically homoskedastic with zero mean since, at least for weakly dependent Gaussian time series, each $\log I_X(\lambda_j)/f_X(\lambda_j)$ is approximately an independent and identically distributed (iid) $\log \chi_2^2/2$ random variate, with expectation $-\eta$. Based on this fact, GPH proposed running an ordinary least squares (OLS) regression to estimate d in (9.7). Robinson (1995a) justified such a procedure for multivariate Gaussian time series with possibly different memory parameters in the interval $(-0.5, 0.5)$ by trimming the first ℓ Fourier frequencies, since for fixed $j, I_X(\lambda_j)$ is asymptotically biased for $f_X(\lambda_j)$ when $d \neq 0$. Later, Hurvich, Deo and Brodsky (1998) showed that such trimming is not necessary for the log-periodogram (LP) estimate to have nice asymptotic properties. It is also possible to replace the regressor z_j in the LP regression by some asymptotically equivalent sequence, such as $-2 \log(2 \sin \lambda_j/2)$, which arises naturally if X_t is fractionally integrated, cf. (9.5), as proposed by GPH.

Robinson (1995a) proposed pooling a finite number of adjacent periodogram ordinates to improve efficiency. For $K = 1, 2, \ldots$, fixed, (assuming m/K is integer), define

$$Y_{X,j}^{(K)} = \log \left(\sum_{k=1}^{K} I_X(\lambda_{j+k-K}) \right), \quad j = K, 2K, \ldots, m,$$

so the (pooled) LP estimate considered in Robinson (1995a) for a stationary and invertible time series is

$$\hat{d}_m^{LP} = \left(\sum_j \Lambda_j^2 \right)^{-1} \left(\sum_j \Lambda_j Y_{X,j}^{(K)} \right).$$

In this section all summations in j run for $j = k, 2K, \ldots, m$ and $\Lambda_j = z_j - \bar{z}_m$, $\bar{z}_m = (K/m)^{-1} \sum_j z_j$. Obviously, for $K = 1, \hat{d}_m^{LP}$ is the OLS coefficient in (9.7). Shimotsu and Phillips (2002) considered the case where K is allowed to grow in the asymptotics with T.

The asymptotic distribution of $\hat{d}_m^{LP}$ is given by

$$2m^{1/2}\left(\hat{d}_m^{LP} - d\right) \xrightarrow{d} \mathcal{N}\left(0, K\dot{\psi}(K)\right) \tag{9.8}$$

where $\psi(z) = (d/dz)\log\Gamma(z)$ is the digamma function, and the upper dot denotes first derivative. Under (9.6), semiparametric estimates with root-m convergence as in (9.8) are infinitely inefficient compared to usual parametric estimates which are standardized by $T^{1/2}$, but, by contrast, are more robust to misspecification. Note that the variance of the log of a $\chi^2_{2K}/2$ random variable (which is the weak limit of the centered $Y_{X,j}^{(K)}$) is equal to $\dot{\psi}(K)$ and $\sum_j \Lambda_j^2 \sim 4m/K$ as $m \to \infty$. For $K = 1$ we find that $K\dot{\psi}(K) = \pi^2/6$ and, using $\dot{\psi}(K+1) = \dot{\psi}(K) - K^{-2}$, it can be shown that $K\dot{\psi}(K)$ decreases with K, so choosing K large increases the (asymptotic) efficiency. In regular cases for which (9.3) is a good approximation, including ARFIMA processes, m can be chosen to just satisfy

$$\frac{\log^2 T}{m} + \frac{m^5}{T^4} \to 0 \tag{9.9}$$

as $T \to \infty$ (see Robinson, 1995a, assumption 6 and Hurvich *et al.*, 1998, theorem 2). A consistent estimate of G_X can be obtained as $\hat{G}_m^{LP} = \exp(\hat{\alpha}_m - \psi(K))$, where $\hat{\alpha}_m$ is the OLS intercept and noting that the expectation of a $\log(\chi^2_{2K}/2)$ variate is $\psi(K)$.

A multivariate $N \times 1$ time series $\mathbf{X}_t$, with possibly different memory parameters, can be considered if we assume that (9.3) holds for the spectral density of each of the components of $\mathbf{X}_t$, that is, the diagonal elements of the spectral density matrix $\mathbf{f}_X(\lambda)$, defined implicitly by

$$\Gamma_X(j) = \text{Cov}(\mathbf{X}_t, \mathbf{X}_{t+j}) = \int_{-\pi}^{\pi} \mathbf{f}_X(\lambda)e^{ij\lambda}d\lambda,$$

satisfy $f_{nn}(\lambda) \sim G_{nn}|\lambda|^{-2d_n}, n = 1, \ldots, N$, as $\lambda \to \infty$. Defining the coherence between the r-th and s-th components of $\mathbf{X}_t$ by

$$R_{rs}(\lambda) = \frac{f_{rs}(\lambda)}{(f_{rr}(\lambda)f_{ss}(\lambda))^{1/2}}, \quad r, s, = 1, \ldots, N,$$

Robinson (1995a) justified the LP regression when the coherence matrix at zero frequency is nonsingular, so the long-run variance matrix of $\mathbf{X}_t$ is full rank, and the elements of $\mathbf{f}_X(\lambda)$ satisfy $(d/d\lambda)\log f_{rs}(\lambda) = O(|\lambda|^{-1})$ as $\lambda \to \infty$.

The simultaneous estimation of $\mathbf{d} = (d_1, \ldots d_N)'$ and the intercept coefficients $\boldsymbol{\alpha} = (\alpha_1, \ldots, \alpha_N)'$ is obtained by means of a multivariate regression with dependent vector $\mathbf{Y}_j^{(K)} = \left(Y_{1,j}^{(K)}, \ldots, Y_{N,j}^{(K)} \right)'$,

$$\begin{pmatrix} \hat{\boldsymbol{\alpha}}_m \\ \hat{\mathbf{d}}_m^{LP} \end{pmatrix} = \mathrm{vec} \left[\sum_j \mathbf{Y}_j^{(K)} \mathbf{Z}_j \left(\sum_j \mathbf{Z}_j \mathbf{Z}_j' \right)^{-1} \right].$$

where $\mathbf{Z}_j = (1, z_j)'$. Then $\hat{G}_{n,m}^{LP} = \exp(\hat{\alpha}_{n,m} - \psi(K))$, $n = 1, \ldots, N$, and the asymptotic properties of the LP regression coefficients are described by

$$\begin{bmatrix} \frac{m^{1/2}}{\log T} (\hat{\boldsymbol{\alpha}}_m - \boldsymbol{\alpha}) \\ 2m^{1/2} \left(\hat{\mathbf{d}}_m^{LP} - \mathbf{d} \right) \end{bmatrix} \xrightarrow{d} \mathcal{N} \left(0, K \begin{bmatrix} 1 & -1 \\ -1 & 1 \end{bmatrix} \otimes \Omega^{(K)} \right),$$

where, paralleling standard OLS theory, $\Omega^{(K)}$ can be estimated consistently by

$$\tilde{\Omega}_m^{(K)} = \frac{K}{m} \sum_j \tilde{\mathbf{u}}_j \tilde{\mathbf{u}}_j',$$

using the OLS residual vector $\tilde{\mathbf{u}}_j$. The factor $K/(4m)$ in the approximate variance of $\hat{\mathbf{d}}_m^{LP}$, $\Omega^{(K)} K/(4m)$, can be replaced in finite samples by $(\sum_j \Lambda_j^2)^{-1}$ to match the standard computation of standard errors in linear regression. Velasco (2000) and Hurvich, Moulines and Soulier (2002) show the robustness of these results to some non-Gaussian linear processes.

Following Robinson (1995a), we can define a Wald-type test of the hypothesis $H_0 : \mathbf{Pd} = \boldsymbol{\varrho}$, where $\mathbf{P}$ is a given $q \times N$ matrix and $\boldsymbol{\varrho}$ is a $q \times 1$ vector. This rejects the null if

$$W_m = \frac{4m}{K} \left(\mathbf{P} \hat{\mathbf{d}}_m^{LP} - \boldsymbol{\varrho} \right)' \left(\mathbf{P} \tilde{\Omega}_m^{(K)} \mathbf{P}' \right)^{-1} \left(\mathbf{P} \hat{\mathbf{d}}_m^{LP} - \boldsymbol{\varrho} \right)$$

is significantly large compared to the χ_q^2 distribution. If some restrictions on $\mathbf{d}$ are assumed, we can obtain more efficient estimates by using this information. Thus, if it is known that $d_1 = \cdots = d_N = d$, so that $\mathbf{d} = d\mathbf{1}_N$, $\mathbf{1}_N$ being the $N \times 1$ vector of ones, the following generalized LS (GLS) type of estimate is proposed,

$$\hat{d}_m^{GLS} = -\frac{\sum_j \Lambda_j \mathbf{1}_N' \tilde{\Omega}_m^{(K)-1} \mathbf{Y}_j^{(K)}}{2 \mathbf{1}_N' \tilde{\Omega}_m^{(K)-1} \mathbf{1}_N \sum_j \Lambda_j^2},$$

whose asymptotic variance can be consistently estimated by $(K/4)(\mathbf{1}_N' \tilde{\Omega}_m^{(K)-1} \mathbf{1}_N)^{-1}$.

The idea of the LP regression has been extended to variance decompositions other than the frequency domain one given by the periodogram. The tapered periodogram provides a first possibility, which is analyzed in section 9.3.1 in the context of memory estimation of nonstationary processes. A second proposal is related to wavelet analysis in the context of self-similar processes, which are characterized by a scale invariant property and whose increments display long-range dependence (Taqqu, 2003). The sample wavelet coefficients are the counterpart of the DFT, giving a decomposition of the variance of X_t at different scales. The wavelet coefficients possess some fundamental characteristics similar to those of the DFT, i.e., they reproduce in the wavelet domain the power laws defining the scale invariance of self-similar and long memory processes, being weakly correlated (see, e.g., Twefik and Kim, 1992; and Bardet, Lang, Moulines and Soulier, 2000). This has been exploited in the design of estimates similar to the LP regression by Jensen (1999) and Bardet *et al.* (2000), among others. Furthermore, the wavelet coefficients, under appropriate choices of the mother wavelet function, can satisfy some higher order properties (zero moments) which guarantee robustness to deterministic trends, similar to those that can be obtained through tapering (see equation (9.30) below). These properties, together with computationally efficient multiresolution algorithms, make wavelets amenable for the analysis of long-range dependent series with possible trending or nonstationary behaviors.

9.2.2 Local Whittle estimation

Based on a proposal of Künsch (1987), Robinson (1995b) studied the Gaussian semiparametric estimate of d based on the minimization of a local Whittle frequency domain (minus) log-likelihood,

$$\mathcal{L}_m(d, G) = \frac{1}{m} \sum_{j=1}^{m} \left\{ \log G\lambda_j^{-2d} + \frac{I_X(\lambda_j)}{G\lambda_j^{-2d}} \right\},$$

using the semiparametric model (9.3), which is valid for such frequencies. Denoting the interval of admissible estimates of d by $D = [\nabla_1, \nabla_2]$, where ∇_1 and ∇_2 are numbers such that $-\frac{1}{2} < \nabla_1 < \nabla_2 < \frac{1}{2}$, the local Whittle (LW) estimates are defined by

$$(\hat{d}_m^{LW}, \hat{G}_m^{LW}) = \arg \min_{d \in D, 0 < G < \infty} \mathcal{L}_m(d, G).$$

Concentrating out $\hat{G}_m^{LW}$, we obtain

$$\hat{d}_m^{LW} = \arg \min_{d \in D} R_m(d),$$

where

$$R_m(d) = \log \hat{G}_m^{LW}(d) - 2d \frac{1}{m} \sum_{j=1}^{m} \log \lambda_j, \quad \hat{G}_m^{LW}(d) = \frac{1}{m} \sum_{j=1}^{m} \lambda_j^{2d} I_X(\lambda_j). \tag{9.10}$$

For linear time series with homoskedastic martingale difference innovations, and with spectral density satisfying the same regularity conditions as for LP estimation, Robinson (1994b) found that $\hat{d}_m^{LW}$ is consistent and its asymptotic normal distribution is

$$2m^{1/2}\left(\hat{d}_m^{LW} - d\right) \xrightarrow{d} \mathcal{N}(0, 1), \tag{9.11}$$

so its asymptotic variance is free of nuisance parameters and smaller than that of the LP estimate. Therefore, when using the same number of frequencies, LW estimation is more efficient than the LP regression. The bandwidth m has to satisfy

$$\frac{1}{m} + \frac{m^5 \log^2 m}{T^4} \to 0 \tag{9.12}$$

if the approximation (3) has error $O(|\lambda|^{2-2d})$ as $\lambda \to 0$.

Following Lobato and Robinson (1998) and Lobato (1999), we can propose a joint estimate of the memory parameters of a vector X_t based on the semiparametric multivariate model for the spectral density matrix $\mathbf{f}_X(\lambda)$, such as

$$\mathbf{f}_X(\lambda) \sim \Lambda(\mathbf{d})\Xi_X\Lambda(\mathbf{d}) \quad \text{as} \quad \lambda \to +0, \tag{9.13}$$

where Ξ_X is a positive definite (complex) hermitian matrix and $\Lambda(\mathbf{d}) = \text{diag}\,(\lambda^{-d_1}, \ldots, \lambda^{-d_N})$. For fractional models with long-run variance matrix G_X, we have that $\Xi_X = \Xi_X(\mathbf{d}) = \Phi(\mathbf{d})G_X\Phi^*(\mathbf{d})$, where $G_X = \{g_{ab}\}$ is a real positive definite matrix, $\Phi(\mathbf{d}) = \text{diag}\,(e^{i\pi d_1/2}, \ldots, e^{i\pi d_N/2})$, and $*$ means simultaneous transposition and complex conjugation. Therefore (9.13) ignores some information about how the real and imaginary parts of $\Xi_X(\mathbf{d})$ relate in terms of $\mathbf{d}$.

The local Whittle likelihood, as a function of the memory parameters $\mathbf{d}$ and the scale matrix Ξ, is given by

$$\mathcal{L}_m(\mathbf{d}, \Xi) = \frac{1}{m}\sum_{j=1}^{m}\left\{\log\det\left[\Lambda_j(\mathbf{d})\Xi\Lambda_j(\mathbf{d})\right] + tr\left[(\Lambda_j(\mathbf{d})\Xi\Lambda_j(\mathbf{d}))^{-1}\mathbf{I}_X(\lambda_j)\right]\right\}, \tag{9.14}$$

where $\Lambda_j(\mathbf{d}) = \text{diag}\,\{\lambda_j^{-d_1}, \ldots, \lambda_j^{-d_N}\}$ and $\mathbf{I}_X(\lambda_j) = \mathbf{w}_X(\lambda_j)\mathbf{w}_X(\lambda_j)^*$ is the periodogram matrix of X_t. Since

$$\mathcal{L}_m(\mathbf{d}, \Xi) = \frac{1}{m}\sum_{j=1}^{m}\{2\log\det[\Lambda_j(\mathbf{d})] + \log\det[\Xi] + tr[\Xi^{-1}\Lambda_j^{-1}(\mathbf{d})\mathbf{I}_X(\lambda_j)\Lambda_j^{-1}(\mathbf{d})]\}$$

we find that

$$\frac{\partial}{\partial\Xi} = \mathcal{L}_m(\mathbf{d}, G) = \frac{1}{m}\sum_{j=1}^{m}\{\Xi^{-1} - \Xi^{-1}[\Lambda_j^{-1}(\mathbf{d})\mathbf{I}_X(\lambda_j)\Lambda_j^{-1}(\mathbf{d})]\Xi^{-1}\},$$

and, on setting,

$$\hat{\Xi}_m(\mathbf{d}) = \frac{1}{m}\sum_{j=1}^{m}\Lambda_j^{-1}(\mathbf{d})\mathbf{I}_X(\lambda_j)\Lambda_j^{-1}(\mathbf{d}), \tag{9.15}$$

we obtain from (9.14) the following concentrated objective function (Lobato, 1999)

$$\Upsilon_m(\mathbf{d}) = -\frac{2}{m}\sum_{i=1}^{N} d_i \sum_{j=1}^{m} \log(\lambda_j) + \log \det[\hat{\Xi}_m(\mathbf{d})],$$

because $\log \det[\Lambda_j(\mathbf{d})] = -\log(\lambda_j)\sum_{i=1}^{N} d_i$.

The estimation procedure proposed by Lobato (1999) is a two-step estimator based on this objective function. The first step is to compute the univariate local Whittle estimate for every series (denote that vector by $\hat{\mathbf{d}}_m^{(1)}$) and the second step is obtained through the following expression

$$\hat{\mathbf{d}}_m^{(2)} = \hat{\mathbf{d}}_m^{(1)} - \left(\frac{\partial^2 \Upsilon_m(\mathbf{d})}{\partial \mathbf{d}\partial \mathbf{d}'}\bigg|_{\hat{\mathbf{d}}_m^{(1)}}\right)^{-1}\left(\frac{\partial \Upsilon_m(\mathbf{d})}{\partial \mathbf{d}}\bigg|_{\hat{\mathbf{d}}_m^{(1)}}\right). \tag{9.16}$$

Further iterations could be considered, e.g., $\hat{\mathbf{d}}_m^{(s)}, s = 2, 3, \ldots$, having the same first order efficiency. An estimator of the long run variance $\mathbf{G}_X$ can be constructed as

$$\hat{\mathbf{G}}_{X,m} = \hat{\mathbf{G}}_{X,m}(\hat{\mathbf{d}}_m^{(2)}) = \text{Re}\{\hat{\Phi}_m^* \hat{\Xi}_{X,m} \hat{\Phi}_m\} \tag{9.17}$$

where $\hat{\Xi}_{X,m} = \hat{\Xi}_m(\hat{\mathbf{d}}_m^{(2)})$, $\hat{\Phi}_m = \Phi(\hat{\mathbf{d}}_m^{(2)})$ and Re stands for real part.

Extending Robinson's (1995b) analysis, Lobato (1999) showed that

$$m^{1/2}\left(\hat{\mathbf{d}}_m^{(2)} - \mathbf{d}\right) \xrightarrow{d} \mathcal{N}(0, \mathbf{E}^{-1}),$$

where $\mathbf{E} = 2(I_N + \Xi_X \circ \Xi_X^{*-1})$ and $\circ$ denotes the element by element Hadamard matrix product. He assumed that X_t is a linear process given by

$$X_t = \mu + \sum_{j=0}^{\infty} A_j \varepsilon_{t-j}$$

where ε_t is a martingale difference sequence with constant first four conditional moments, and the transfer function $A(\lambda) = \sum_{j=0}^{\infty} A_j e^{ij\lambda}$ is differentiable around $\lambda = 0$. The asymptotic variance can be estimated by using the previous estimate of Ξ_X, obtaining $\hat{\mathbf{E}}_m = 2\left(I_N + \hat{\Xi}_{X,m} \circ \hat{\Xi}_{X,m}^{*-1}\right)$.

In order to achieve more efficient estimation of the vector $\mathbf{d}$, we could consider explicitly that Ξ_X is a function of $\mathbf{d}$, $\Xi_X(\mathbf{d}) = \Phi(\mathbf{d})\mathbf{G}_X\Phi(\mathbf{d})^*$, see Shimotsu (2003). Furthermore, if we want to impose a rate for the semiparametric approximation (9.13) that is valid for fractional time series, we could consider

$$\mathbf{f}_X(\lambda) = \bar{\Lambda}(\mathbf{d})\mathbf{G}_X\bar{\Lambda}^*(\mathbf{d})(1 + O(\lambda^2)) \quad \text{as } \lambda \to +0, \tag{9.18}$$

where now $\bar{\Lambda}(\mathbf{d}) = \text{diag}\,(\lambda^{-d_1}e^{i(\pi-\lambda)d_1/2}, \ldots, \lambda^{-d_N}e^{i(\pi-\lambda)d_N/2})$, so we can obtain $\bar{\Lambda}(\mathbf{d})\mathbf{G}_X\bar{\Lambda}^*(\mathbf{d}) \sim \Lambda(\mathbf{d})\Xi_X(\mathbf{d})\Lambda(\mathbf{d})$ as $\lambda \to +0$.

As with LP estimates, efficient improvements are possible if a valid restriction on the vector $\mathbf{d}$ is used. If $d_1 = \cdots = d_N = d$, then we can set

$$\tilde{\mathbf{d}}_m^{LW} = \arg\min_{d \in D} \tilde{\Upsilon}_m(d) \tag{9.19}$$

where

$$\tilde{\Upsilon}_m(d) = -\frac{2N}{m} d \sum_{j=1}^{m} \log(\lambda_j) + \log\det[\hat{\mathbf{G}}_{X,m}(d\mathbf{1}_N)],$$

and now $\hat{\mathbf{G}}_{X,m}(d\mathbf{1}_N) = \mathrm{Re}\,(\hat{\Xi}_{X,m})$, given the restriction of a unique d. The asymptotic variance of $\tilde{\mathbf{d}}_m^{LW}$, $1/4N$, reflects the extra information used.

Wald tests are easily implemented as with LP estimates, but with the objective function $\Upsilon_m(\mathbf{d})$ we can also employ the Lagrange Multiplier and Likelihood Ratio principles. An LM-type test of $d_1 = \cdots = d_N = 0$ was proposed by Lobato and Robinson (1998). The LM test for $H_0 : \mathbf{Pd} = \varrho$ uses the statistic

$$LM_m = m \frac{\partial \Upsilon_m(\tilde{\mathbf{d}}_m^{LW})}{\partial \mathbf{d}'} [\mathbf{P}\hat{\mathbf{E}}_m \mathbf{P}'] \frac{\partial \Upsilon_m(\tilde{\mathbf{d}}_m^{LW})}{\partial \mathbf{d}},$$

compared to a χ_q^2 distribution, where $\tilde{\mathbf{d}}_m^{LW}$ minimizes $\Upsilon_m(\mathbf{d})$ subject to $\mathbf{Pd} = \varrho$ and $\hat{\mathbf{E}}_m$ can be computed also under this restriction. For the test of $d_1 = \cdots = d_N = d_0$, the LM statistic reduces to

$$LM_m = \frac{m}{4N} \left[\frac{\partial \tilde{\Upsilon}_m(d_0)}{\partial d} \right]^2$$

with $q = 1$.

9.2.3 Averaged periodogram estimation

Many alternative semiparametric estimates have been proposed, both in the time and frequency domain. In this section we describe briefly the proposal of Robinson (1994a), the averaged periodogram estimate of d,

$$\hat{d}_{m,q}^{AP} = \frac{1}{2} - \frac{\log\{F_{X,T}(q\lambda_m)/F_{X,T}(\lambda_m)\}}{2\log q}$$

where $q \in (0,1)$ is a user-chosen tuning parameter and $F_{X,T}$ is the averaged periodogram (AP),

$$F_{X,T}(\lambda) = \frac{2\pi}{T} \sum_{j=1}^{[T\lambda/2\pi]} I_X(\lambda_j).$$

The AP will be important in the discussion of narrow band estimates of long-run relationships.

Note that $\hat{d}^{AP}_{m,q} \in (-\infty, 0.5]$, so it cannot estimate nonstationary values of d. Robinson (1994a) showed that $F_{X,T}(\lambda_m)$ is a consistent estimate of $F_X(\lambda_m) = \int_0^{\lambda_m} f_X(z)dz$ if $m^{-1} + mT^{-1} \to 0$ with the sample size when X_t is a linear process with martingale innovations. Thus it is easy to show that, under (3), $\hat{d}^{AP}_{m,q}$ is also consistent for d.

Lobato and Robinson (1996) analyzed the asymptotic distribution of the AP estimate. This is only normal for $d < 0.25$, for which $f_X(\lambda)$ is square integrable around $\lambda = 0$. In particular, if $d \in (0, 0.25)$,

$$m^{1/2}\left(d^{AP}_{m,q} - d\right) \xrightarrow{d} \mathcal{N}\left(0, \frac{(1 + q^{-1} - 2q^{-2d})}{\log^2 q}\frac{(0.5 - d)^2}{1 - 4d}\right).$$

For $d \in (0.25, 0.5)$ the asymptotic distribution of $d^{AP}_{m,q}$ is a functional of a Rosenblatt variate. The asymptotic variance of $d^{AP}_{m,q}$ when $d < 0.25$ depends on q and d, and by its minimization Lobato and Robinson (1996) find that for each d there is an optimal value of q. Lobato (1997) extends some of these results to a multivariate time series framework and Robinson and Marinucci (2000) to nonstationary vectors, see section 9.3.

9.2.4 Bias reduction and bandwidth choice

The most important issue when applying any semiparametric memory estimate is the decision on the number of Fourier frequencies m to be used. For these frequencies we regard the model (9.3) as approximately valid, but increasing m leads to a reduction of the variance of estimates at the cost of an increment in bias due to the consideration of too high frequencies where the semiparametric model is not appropriate. We concentrate in this section on univariate and no pooled ($K = 1$) estimates.

Under the assumption that

$$f_X(\lambda) = |2\sin(\lambda/2)|^{-2d}f^*(\lambda) \tag{9.20}$$

where $f^*(\lambda)$ is nonnegative, even, integrable, twice continuously differentiable and positive at $\lambda = 0$, Hurvich *et al.* (1998) obtained the Mean Square Error (MSE) of the LP estimate and derived the expression for the MSE-optimal bandwidth,

$$m^{opt}_{LP} = T^{4/5}\left[\frac{27}{128\pi^2}\left(\frac{f^*(0)}{\ddot{f}^*(0)}\right)^2\right]^{1/5},$$

assuming for the second derivative $\ddot{f}^*$ of f^* that $\ddot{f}^*(0) \neq 0$. This expression gives the MSE-optimal rate for m, $T^{4/5}$, but depends on the short-run dynamics of X_t described by $\ddot{f}^*$. Based on this formula, Hurvich and Deo (1999) devised a plug-in estimate of the optimal constant in m^{opt}_{LP} by means of an augmented LP regression,

$$\log I_X(\lambda_j) = \alpha + dw_j + \rho\frac{\lambda_j^2}{2} + u_j, \quad j = 1, \ldots, m_\rho, \tag{9.21}$$

where now $w_j = -2\log(2\sin(\lambda_j/2))$. Noting that $\dot{f}^*(0) = 0$ by the evenness of $f^*(\lambda)$, the OLS estimate of ρ in the regression (9.21) is consistent for $b_2 = \ddot{f}^*(0)/f^*(0)$, since we can write

$$\log f^*(\lambda) = \log f^*(0) + b_2 \frac{\lambda^2}{2} + O(\lambda^3)$$

if $f^*(\lambda)$ is smooth enough. The initial choice of the auxiliary bandwidth m_ρ is given by $m_\rho = AT^a$ for some $a > 3/4$ and some positive constant A. Note that when m is proportional to $T^{4/5}$, $m = BT^{4/5}$ say, the bandwidth conditions for the asymptotic normality (9.8), e.g. (9.9), are no longer valid, so asymptotic inference has to be adapted to take into account the asymptotic bias. Thus, on introducing a bias correction, it is the case that

$$2m^{1/2}\left(\hat{d}_m^{LP} - d\right) - \frac{4}{9}\pi^2 b_2 B^{4/5} \xrightarrow{d} \mathcal{N}\left(0, \frac{\pi^2}{6}\right),$$

leading to bias-corrected versions of $\hat{d}_m^{LP}$ when using MSE-optimal bandwidths.

Andrews and Guggenberger (2003) generalize this idea to obtain LP estimates with reduced bias in augmented regressions. To that end, it is assumed that

$$\log f^*(\lambda) = \log f^*(0) + \sum_{k=1}^{r} b_{2k}\frac{\lambda^{2k}}{(2k)!} + o(\lambda^{2r}) \quad \text{as } \lambda \to 0+, \tag{9.22}$$

where

$$b_k = \left(\frac{\mathrm{d}}{\mathrm{d}\lambda}\right)^k \log f^*(\lambda)\Bigg|_{\lambda=0},$$

and the polynomial LP (PLP) estimate $\hat{d}_{r,m}^{PLP}$ of order r is given by the corresponding OLS coefficient in the linear regression

$$\log I_X(\lambda_j) = \alpha + dz_j + \sum_{k=1}^{r} \rho_k \lambda_j^{2k} + u_j. \tag{9.23}$$

Andrews and Guggenberger (2003) show that the OLS estimate of this regression satisfies

$$2m^{1/2}(\hat{d}_{r,m}^{PLP} - d) - v_T(r) \xrightarrow{d} \mathcal{N}\left(0, c_r\frac{\pi^2}{6}\right) \tag{9.24}$$

if $m = O(T^{2\phi/(2\phi+1)})$, $\phi = 2 + 2r$, $v_T(r)$ is the asymptotic bias, $c_0 = 1$ and $c_r = (1 - \mu_r'\Gamma_r^{-1}\mu_r)^{-1}$, $r \geq 1$, with

$$\mu_{r,k} = \frac{2k}{(2k+1)^2}, \quad k = 1, \ldots, r$$

$$\Gamma_{r,ik} = \frac{4ik}{(2k+2i+1)(2i+1)(2k+1)}, \quad i, k = 1, \ldots, r.$$

Assuming enough smoothness of $\log \log f^*$ in (9.22) so that the error term is $O(\lambda^{2r+2})$, the asymptotic bias $v_T(r)$ is given by

$$v_T(r) = m^{(5/2)+2r} T^{-(2+2r)} b_{2+2r} \tau_r,$$

where

$$\tau_r = \frac{\kappa_r c_r}{2}(1 - \mu_r' \Gamma_r^{-1} \xi_r),$$

$$\kappa_r = \frac{(2\pi)^{2+2r}(2+2r)}{(3+2r)!(3+2r)}$$

and $\xi_r = (\xi_{r,1}, \ldots, \xi_{r,r})'$ with

$$\xi_{r,k} = \frac{2k(3+2r)}{(2r+2k+3)(2k+1)}, \quad k = 1, \ldots, r.$$

The bias term $v_T(r)$ disappears in the asymptotic distribution (9.24) when a slower bandwidth $m = o(T^{2\phi/(2\phi+1)})$ is used instead of the MSE-optimal one. This analysis also allows calculation of the asymptotic MSE of the PLP estimate, generalizing the expression for the optimal bandwidth,

$$m_{PLP}^{opt} = T^{(4+4r)/(5+4r)} \left[\frac{\pi^2 c_r}{24(4+4r)\tau_r^2 b_{2+2r}^2} \right]^{1/(5+4r)}.$$

The unknown b_{2+2r} can be estimated by means of an augmented regression similar to (9.21).

Similar studies have been conducted for other semiparametric estimates. Thus, for spectral densities satisfying

$$f(\lambda) = G\lambda^{-2d}(1 + E_\gamma \lambda^\gamma + o(\lambda^\gamma)), \quad \text{as } \lambda \to 0, \tag{9.25}$$

for some $\gamma \in (0, 2]$ and $E_\gamma \neq 0$, Henry and Robinson (1996) approximate the MSE of the LW estimate, for which the optimal bandwidth is given by

$$m_{LW}^{opt} = T^{2\gamma/(1+2\gamma)} \left[\frac{(1+\gamma)^4}{2\gamma^3 E_\gamma^2 (2\pi)^{2\gamma}} \right]^{1/(1+2\gamma)}, \tag{9.26}$$

and propose an iterative method to estimate the unknown constant $E\gamma$ in m_{LW}^{opt}.

For spectral densities satisfying (9.20), Andrews and Sun (2004) investigate the MSE, optimal bandwidth and asymptotic properties of a generalization of the LW estimate similar to the PLP. They consider the local polynomial Whittle likelihood

$$\mathcal{L}_{r,m}(d, G, \theta) = \frac{1}{m}\sum_{j=1}^{m}\left\{ \log[G\lambda_j^{-2d}\exp(-p_r(\lambda_j; \theta))] + \frac{I_X(\lambda_j)}{G\lambda_j^{-2d}\exp(-p_r(\lambda_j; \theta))} \right\}, \tag{9.27}$$

for $r \geq 0$, where

$$p_r(\lambda_j; \boldsymbol{\theta}) = \sum_{k=1}^{r} \theta_k \lambda_j^{2k}, \quad \boldsymbol{\theta} = (\theta_1, \dots, \theta_k)'.$$

This likelihood includes higher-order terms from expanding $\log f^*(\lambda)$ around $\lambda = 0$ up to order $2r$, as in (9.22). Concentrating out G we obtain that

$$(\hat{d}_{r,m}^{PLW}, \boldsymbol{\theta}_{r,m}^{PLW}) = \arg \min_{d,\theta \in D} R_{r,m}(d, \boldsymbol{\theta}),$$

where

$$R_{r,m}(d, \boldsymbol{\theta}) = \log \hat{G}_{r,m}^{PLW}(d, \boldsymbol{\theta}) - \frac{1}{m}\sum_{j=1}^{m} p_r(\lambda_j; \boldsymbol{\theta}) - 2d\frac{1}{m}\sum_{j=1}^{m} \log \lambda_j + 1,$$

$$\hat{G}_{r,m}^{PLW}(d, \boldsymbol{\theta}) = \frac{1}{m}\sum_{j=1}^{m} \lambda_j^{2d} \exp(-p_r(\lambda_j; \boldsymbol{\theta}))I_X(\lambda_j).$$

Andrews and Sun (2004) show the consistency and asymptotic normality of when $(\hat{d}_{r,m}^{PLW}, \boldsymbol{\theta}_{r,m}^{PLW})$ when $m^{4r+1}/T^{4r} \to \infty$ and $m^{2\phi+1}/T^{2\phi} = O(1), \phi = 2 + 2r$, under similar regularity assumptions to Robinson (1995b) together with (9.22). In particular,

$$2m^{1/2}(\hat{d}_{r,m}^{PLW} - d) - v_T(r) \xrightarrow{d} \mathcal{N}(0, c_r).$$

Therefore, the PLW estimate has the same asymptotic bias as the PLP estimate, but retains its efficiency even if we consider r correcting terms. Similarly, it is possible to generalize the expression for the optimal bandwidth of the LW estimate,

$$m_{PLW}^{opt} = T^{(4+4r)/(5+4r)} \left[\frac{c_r}{16(1+r)\tau_r^2 b_{2+2r}^2} \right]^{1/(5+4r)}.$$

Note that for $r = 0$ and $\gamma = 2$ this gives the same expression (9.26) for m_{LW}^{opt} given by Henry and Robinson (1996), noting that $E_2 = b_2/2$, which is the only unknown in the optimal bandwidth.

Robinson and Henry (2003) provide a different approach to the problem of bias reduction. They propose M-estimates based on higher-order kernels that are able to nest different classes of semiparametric estimates of d, such as versions of the LP and LW estimates. This class of M-estimates is based on a kernel function $k_q(u)$ with the property that

$$\int_0^1 k_q(u)du = 1,$$

and setting $U_{iq} = \int_0^1 (1 + \log u)u^{2i}k_q(u)du$, it is required that $U_{iq} = 0, i = 1, \ldots, q - 1,$ and $U_{qq} \neq 0$ for some $q \geq 1$. Other important ingredients are a real valued monotonic function ψ, which is particularized to the Box–Cox transformation, $\psi_\alpha(z) = (z^\alpha - 1)/\alpha$ for $\alpha > 0$, and $\psi_0(z) = \log z$, and a function $g(\lambda)$ which is asymptotically equivalent to λ, in the sense that

$$g(\lambda) = \lambda + G\lambda^3 + o(\lambda^3) \quad \text{as } \lambda \to 0+,$$

such as $g(\lambda) = 2\sin(\lambda/2)$.. Then the q-order kernel M-estimate of d, $\hat{d}_m^{Mq}$ is given as a solution of the equation

$$\sum_j k_q\left(\frac{j}{m}\right)v_{qj}(g)\psi_\alpha\left(\bar{I}_X^{(K)}(\lambda_j)g(\lambda_j)^{2\hat{d}_m^{Mq}}\right) = 0$$

where

$$v_{qj}(g) = \log g(\lambda_j) - \frac{\sum_j k_q\left(\frac{j}{m}\right)\log g(\lambda_j)}{\sum_j k_q\left(\frac{j}{m}\right)}$$

and

$$\bar{I}_X^{(K)}(\lambda_j) = \sum_{k=1}^K I_X(\lambda_{j+k-K}), \quad j = K, 2K, \ldots, m.$$

Thus, when $K = 1, q = 1$ and $\alpha = 0$ we obtain the LP estimate, whereas with $\alpha = 1$ we get the LW estimate, and with values of $\alpha \in (0, 1)$ we interpolate between both methods. The asymptotic variance also varies with α between those found for $\alpha = 0, 1$. On the other hand, for a particular ψ, choosing a higher-order kernel with $q \geq 2$ allows room for potential bias and MSE reduction, under the assumption that $f^*(\lambda) = f(\lambda)g(\lambda)^{2d}$ is $2q + 1$ times differentiable, cf. (9.22). Finally, the choice of g does not affect the asymptotic variance, but may have important effects on bias given this previous assumption.

The reviewed bias reduction and estimation of optimal bandwidth techniques rely on a priori assumptions on the smoothness of the spectral density, given by the value of the parameter γ or the number of derivatives of $\log f^*$. In practice, it is not easy to obtain information about such restrictions, so adaptive techniques have been developed. Giraitis, Robinson and Samarov (1997) showed that the LP estimate is rate optimal among a class of semiparametric estimates for processes with spectral density of γ degree of smoothness, cf. (9.25), whereas Giraitis, Robinson and Samarov (2000) propose an adaptive estimate to the unknown degree of smoothness based on a modified LP regression, whose asymptotic risk is larger than the optimal risk only by a logarithmic factor. Related results have been obtained for the polynomial LP estimate by Andrews and Guggenberger (2003) and for the LW estimate by Andrews and Sun (2004). Alternatively,

Hurvich and Beltrao (1994) propose a cross-validation method to estimate the integrated local MSE of any estimate of d around zero frequency and base a bandwidth choice on the minimization of such an estimate. For the AP estimate, Robinson (1994a) provides expressions for the MSE and the optimal bandwidth, which Delgado and Robinson (1996a) estimate by means of a plug-in iterative method, and Delgado and Robinson (1996b) find optimal kernels for the averaging.

9.2.5 Global methods: FEXP and FAR estimates

The fractional exponential (FEXP) estimate, proposed by Robinson (1994c), consists of a LP regression similar to (9.23), but expanding $\log f^*$ on a cosine basis, so that the coefficients $\theta_k = \int_{-\pi}^{\pi} \log f^*(\lambda) \cos k\lambda d\lambda$ define the cepstrum of f^*. The FEXP estimate $\hat{d}_r^{FEXP}$ of d is given by the corresponding coefficient in the OLS estimation of

$$Y_{X,j}^{(K)} = dz_j + \sum_{k=0}^{r} \theta_k \cos k\lambda_j + u_j, \quad j = K, 2K, \ldots, m,$$

allowing for periodogram pooling, $K \geq 1$. If we let $r \to \infty$ with T, then we can approximate nonparametrically the whole of f^*, so these methods are called global, in contrast with local methods, such as the LP or LW estimates. The asymptotic properties of the FEXP estimate have been analyzed by Moulines and Soulier (1999) for Gaussian series and by Hurvich, Moulines and Soulier (2002) for non-Gaussian series, see also Hurvich and Brodsky (2001). The analysis relies on the smoothness of f^*, so that the θ_k are square summable, and on a related restriction on r,

$$\frac{1}{r} + \frac{r \log^5 T}{T} + \left(\frac{T}{r}\right)^{1/2} \sum_{k=r}^{\infty} |\theta_k| \to 0.$$

Then

$$\left(\frac{T}{r}\right)^{1/2} \left(\hat{d}_r^{FEXP} - d\right) \xrightarrow{d} \mathcal{N}\left(0, K\Omega^{(K)}\right),$$

showing that the convergence rate of $\hat{d}_r^{FEXP}$ can be very close to the parametric rate of $T^{1/2}$ if r can be chosen very small so that it approximates f^* with fidelity. Iouditsky, Moulines and Soulier (2002) investigate an adaptive FEXP estimate, extending results of Hurvich (2001), who had proposed a local version of Mallow's C_L criterion to select a FEXP model by minimizing the asymptotic MSE.

   Another global estimate in a similar spirit is the Fractional AutoRegressive (FAR) estimate, which is based on fitting an ARFIMA$(r, d, 0)$ model with r increasing with sample size T. Bhansali and Kokoszka (2001) have showed the consistency of this estimate when based on a full-band Whittle estimate.

9.3 Extensions

We consider in this section two natural extensions of the semiparametric model (9.3). The first relaxes the assumption of stationarity, $d < 0.5$, so that it is possible to check the robustness of the previous methods to the trending nonstationary of fractionally integrated series for large d. In this case, special modifications of semiparametric memory estimates might be necessary to robustify inference against possible nonstationarity of unknown degree. The second extension considers the possibility of persistence at frequencies different from zero, which poses new problems and requires some extra care when applying semiparametric methods.

9.3.1 Nonstationary long memory

There are alternative ways of defining possibly nonstationary trending processes with persistence characterized by a long memory parameter d which can take values larger than 0.5, nesting in this way $I(1)$ unit root processes. Following Hurvich and Ray (1995), we can say that the nonstationary process $\{X_t\}$ has memory parameter $d \in [\frac{1}{2}, \frac{3}{2})$ if the zero mean covariance stationary process $\Delta X_t = (1 - L)X_t$ has spectral density

$$f_{\Delta X}(\lambda) = |1 - \exp(i\lambda)|^{-2(d-1)} f^*(\lambda),$$

where $f^*(\lambda)$ is as in (9.20). Then, we can write, for any $t \geq 1$,

$$X_t = X_0 + \sum_{k=1}^{t} v_k, \qquad (9.28)$$

where $v_t = \Delta X_t$ and X_0 is a random variable not depending on time t. We also need now to define a generalized spectral density function, which should be equal to the usual spectral density function for stationary X_t, but without restrictions on the value of d when not. From (9.5), the natural option is to extend the definition of f_X to

$$f_X(\lambda) = |1 - \exp(i\lambda)|^{-2} f_{\Delta X}(\lambda) = |1 - \exp(i\lambda)|^{-2d} f^*(\lambda),$$

when $d > 0.5$, so that $f_X(\lambda)$ satisfies (9.3) for some $d < 1.5$, irrespective of X_t being stationary or not. Note that for nonstationary $X_t(d \geq 0.5)$, f_X is not integrable in $[-\pi, \pi]$ and is not a proper spectral density. We do not assume that f^* is the spectral density of a stationary and invertible ARMA process, as would be the case if v_t followed a fractional ARIMA model. For example, f^* may have (integrable) poles or zeros at frequencies beyond the origin.

When estimating the memory of nonstationary series, the above definition of nonstationarity based on the increments leads to the so called 'differencing and adding back' method. This consists of taking first differences when it is known that $d \in (0.5, 1.5)$, estimating the memory of the increments by $\hat{d}_m^{\Delta X}$, say, and then setting $\hat{d}_m = \hat{d}_m^{\Delta X} + 1$. Similarly, series with higher degrees of nonstationarity, $d \geq 1.5$, can be defined in terms of successive partial sums, and the actual memory estimated with successive differencing to guarantee that the true d is in $(-0.5, 0.5)$. However, such a method requires some a priori knowledge on the degree of nonstationarity of the observed series, which in many cases is difficult to obtain, such as when we suspect that $d \approx 0.5$. A first approach to this problem is the analysis of the previous semiparametric methods, designed for covariance stationary series, under this more general nonstationary framework without assumptions on whether $d < 0.5$ or $d \geq 0.5$. This study is based on some robustness properties of the periodogram.

For short memory processes, the periodogram is an inconsistent but asymptotically unbiased estimate of f_X at continuity points of the spectral density and is approximately independent across frequencies λ_j. Robinson (1995a) extended such results for stationary long-range dependent series. Interestingly, the normalized periodogram $I_X(\lambda_j)/f_X(\lambda_j)$ still has a limit expectation equal to one (and the DFTs at different frequencies are asymptotically uncorrelated) for nonstationary integrated time series at Fourier frequencies moving slowly away from the origin (Hurvich and Ray, 1995; Velasco, 1999b). Note also that the DFT is invariant to X_0 at nonzero Fourier frequencies. In fact, it is possible to show the consistency of the LP estimate when $d < 1$, while the asymptotic distribution remains the same, cf. (9.8), but only when $d < 0.75$ (Velasco, 1999b). Velasco (1999a) obtained related results for the LW estimate, which is also asymptotically normal with an asymptotic variance of 0.25 when $d < 0.75$.

9.3.2 Tapering

The limitations of the applicability of usual semiparametric inference for large d when there is no a priori assumption on the degree of nonstationarity is due to the periodogram bias caused by the leakage from the nonstationary zero frequency. To alleviate this problem, the traditional remedy in time series analysis is tapering. Define the tapered DFT of X_t, for $t = 1, \ldots, T$ and a taper sequence $\{h_t\}_{t=1}^T$, as

$$w_X^{(h)}(\lambda) = \left(2\pi \sum_{t=1}^T h_t^2\right)^{-1/2} \sum_{t=1}^T h_t X_t \exp(i\lambda t),$$

and the tapered periodogram as $I_X^{(h)}(\lambda) = |w_X^{(h)}(\lambda)|^2$. The usual DFT has $h_t \equiv 1$. Typically, h_t downweights the observations at both extremes of the sequence, leaving largely unchanged the central part of the data. The improved bias properties of the tapered periodogram also have an immediate counterpart in terms of the DFT. Thus, if h_t is differentiable and vanishes at the boundaries, we obtain by summation by parts that

$$w_X^{(h)}(\lambda) \approx \frac{e^{i\lambda}}{1 - e^{i\lambda}}\left[w_{\Delta X}^{(h)}(\lambda) + \frac{w_X^{(\dot{h})}(\lambda)}{T}\right] \tag{9.29}$$

for $\lambda \neq 0$, explaining why a sufficiently smooth taper can reproduce the usual properties of the DFT with difference-stationary series. Furthermore, if for some positive integer p, the tapered DFT of integer powers of time t satisfies

$$w_{t^\ell}^{(h)}(\lambda_{jp}) = 0, \quad \ell = 0, 1, \ldots, p - 1, \tag{9.30}$$

then the taper scheme h_t is able to remove polynomial trends in the observed sequence when concentrating on the restricted set of frequencies $\lambda_{jp}, jp \neq 0$. This property generalizes the shift invariant property of the usual DFT and helps to define a class of tapers of order p. Lobato and Velasco (2000) provide an application of this property to avoid the effect of nonlinear trends in the traded volume of stocks when estimating its persistence.

There are several alternative tapering schemes having desirable properties to control leakage from remote frequencies. Following Velasco (1999a,b), we may consider a general class of so-called tapers of type-I and orders $p = 1, 2, \ldots$, denoted as $\{h_t^{(1,p)}\}$, whose non-scaled DFT satisfies

$$\sum_{t=1}^{T} h_t^{(1,p)} e^{it\lambda} = \frac{a(\lambda)}{T^{p-1}} \left(\frac{\sin[T\lambda/2p]}{\sin[\lambda/2]} \right)^p, \tag{9.31}$$

where $a(\lambda)$ is a complex function whose modulus is positive and bounded. Some examples of tapers which satisfy (9.31) are the triangular Bartlett window ($p=2$), the Parzen window ($p=4$) or Zhurbenko's (1979) class for integer p. Zhurbenko's tapers are obtained by increasingly smooth convolutions of the uniform density, and when $p=1$ give the nontapered DFT weights, $h_t \equiv 1$; when $p=3$ they are similar to the full cosine bell $h_t = (1 - \cos \lambda_t)/2$; while for $p=4$ they are very close to Parzen's, given when $T=4N$ by

$$h_t = \begin{cases} 1 - 6[\{(2t - T)/T\}^2 - |(2t - T)/T|^3], & N < t < 3N; \\ 2\{1 - |(2t - T)/T|\}^3, & 1 \leq t \leq N \text{ or } 3N \leq t \leq 4N. \end{cases}$$

Type-I tapers provide interesting insights into the behavior of the periodogram of time series with spectral densities displaying peaks or troughs, but have the undesirable property of introducing some extra dependence among adjacent periodogram ordinates. This leads to some restrictions in the design and inference of frequency domain memory estimates. The use of a restricted set of Fourier frequencies, such as in (9.30), to guarantee orthogonality generally leads to an efficiency loss (Velasco, 1999b). To reduce the size of such sets of omitted frequencies, Hurvich, Moulines and Soulier (2002) and Hurvich and Chen (2000) propose alternative type-II complex data tapers,

$$h_t^{(2,p)} = h_{t,T}^{(2,p)} = (1 - \exp(i\lambda_t))^{p-1}, \quad p = 1, 2 \ldots, \tag{9.32}$$

so the tapered periodogram and DFT are obtained by

$$I_X^{(2,p)}(\lambda) = |w_X^{(2,p)}(\lambda)|^2 = \left(2\pi \sum_{t=1}^{T} |h_t^{(2,p)}|^2 \right)^{-1} \left| \sum_{t=1}^{T} h_t^{(2,p)} X_t e^{it\lambda} \right|^2.$$

It can be shown that $\sum_{t=1}^{T} |h_t^{(2,p)}|^2 = Ta_p$, where $a_p = \binom{2(p-1)}{p-1}$. Here the order p is equivalent to $p-1$ as set by Hurvich *et al.* (2002), but is equivalent to the order p of Velasco (1999a,b) or Hurvich and Chen (2000), so both tapers of order $p=1$ give the usual DFT and periodogram. However, for higher order tapers, tapered DFTs at Fourier frequencies are correlated, though type-II tapers are not asymptotically correlated as $T \to \infty$ if $|j - k| \geq p$.

This correlation between tapered periodogram ordinates can be taken into account in different ways when the LP regression is designed. One alternative is to use only asymptotically uncorrelated periodograms. For type-II tapers, such an approach would imply neglecting $p-1$ frequencies of every p in the LP regression. To alleviate the efficiency loss incurred following this policy, Hurvich *et al.* (2002) use a pooling of periodogram ordinates as proposed by Robinson (1995a). However, as the correlation dies out very fast in $|j - k|$ for both types of tapered DFT, we can consider the use of all frequencies in the LP regression as in the nontapered case, that is, use all

$$\bar{I}_X^{(v,p)}(\lambda_j) = \sum_{k=1}^{K} I_X^{(v,p)}(\lambda_{j+k-K}), \quad j = K, 2K, \ldots, m,$$

and let that the correlation among adjacent $\log \bar{I}_X^{(v,p)}$ appear in the asymptotic variance of the LP estimates. For type-II tapers the correlation affects at most a fixed number of adjacent periodograms, but for type-I tapers all periodograms display correlation.

Robinson (1995a), for $p = 1$ and all K, and Hurvich *et al.* (2002), for $p > 1$ and large K, give explicit expressions for the expectation and variance of the pooled LP, $\log \bar{I}_X^{(2,p)}(\lambda_j)$, which can be used to estimate the asymptotic variance of the LP regression memory estimate. Alternatively, we can use a consistent estimate of the asymptotic variance based on the LP residuals, which takes into account the LP correlation across Fourier frequencies,

$$\sigma_{K,v,p}^2(k) = \lim_{T \to \infty} \mathrm{Cov}\left[\log \bar{I}_X^{(v,p)}(\lambda_j), \log \bar{I}_X^{(v,p)}(\lambda_{j+k})\right], \quad k = 0, \pm K, \pm 2K, \ldots .$$

Note that in the nontapered case, $\sigma_{K,v,p}^2(k) = 0$ for $k \neq 0, v = 1, 2$. This correlation appears in the asymptotic variance of the LP estimates, i.e., under standard conditions,

$$2m^{1/2}\left(\hat{d}_K^{(v,p)} - d\right) \xrightarrow{d} \mathcal{N}\left(0, K\Omega_K^{(v,p)}\right)$$

where

$$\Omega_K^{(v,p)} = \lim_{T \to \infty} \frac{4m}{K}\left(\sum_j \Lambda_j^2\right)^{-2} \sum_j \sum_k \Lambda_j \Lambda_k \sigma_{K,v,p}^2(j - k).$$

A feasible estimate of $\hat{\Omega}_K^{(v,p)}$, proposed by Arteche and Velasco (2004) along the lines of Robinson (1995a), is

$$\hat{\Omega}_K^{(v,p)} = \frac{4m}{K} \left(\sum_j \Lambda_j^2 \right)^{-2} \sum_j \sum_{|k| \leq \ell} \Lambda_j \Lambda_{j+k} \hat{\sigma}_{K,v,p}^2(k),$$

where ℓ is a fixed integer such that $\ell \geq K[1 + (p-1)/K]$ when $v = 2$, and $\hat{\sigma}_{K,v,p}^2$ are the sample residual autocovariances

$$\hat{\sigma}_{K,v,p}^2(k) = \frac{K}{m} \sum_j \hat{u}_{m,j}^{(v,p)} \hat{u}_{m,j+|k|}^{(v,p)}, \quad k = 0, \pm K, \pm 2K, \ldots,$$

based on the observed residuals $\hat{u}_{m,j}^{(v,p)}$ of the LP regression. Arteche and Velasco (2004) show the consistency of such estimates for type-II tapers in a related context. For type-I tapers, $v = 1$ and the lag number ℓ should be chosen to increase with T such that $\ell^{-1} + \ell m^{-1} \to 0$ as $T \to \infty$, to account asymptotically for the correlation among all the tapered periodograms, as in usual HAC asymptotic variance estimation.

Asymptotics of tapered LW estimates are considerably simpler than those of LP estimates and, using all Fourier frequencies, $j = 1, 2, \ldots, m$, inference can be conducted according to

$$2m^{1/2} \left(\tilde{d}_{LW}^{(v,p)} - d \right) \xrightarrow{d} \mathcal{N}(0, \Phi^{(v,p)})$$

where

$$\Phi^{(v,p)} = \lim_{T \to \infty} T \left(\sum_{t=1}^{T} \left| h_t^{(v,p)} \right|^2 \right)^{-2} \sum_{t=1}^{T} \left| h_t^{(v,p)} \right|^4 \quad (9.33)$$

is a well-known tapering inflation factor, $\Phi^{(v,p)} \geq 1$: see Velasco (1999a) for more details.

These asymptotic results on tapered semiparametric memory estimates go through for nonstationary series if enough tapering is applied, i.e., if p is large enough compared to d. In particular, for series with stationary increments ($d < 1.5$), any of the previous tapering schemes with $p > 1$ provide consistent and asymptotically normal LP and LW estimates, where the asymptotic variances are not affected by the possible nonstationarity, only by the tapering employed.

9.3.3 Alternative nonstationary fractional processes

There are other ways to define nonstationary long memory or fractionally nonstationary processes. Thus, it is possible to consider (e.g. Robinson and Marinucci, 2001; Phillips, 1999) processes ζ_t of memory α generated by a truncated fractional filter as

$$\zeta_t = (1 - L)^{-\alpha} \{ \eta_t 1_{t>0}(t) \} = \sum_{j=0}^{t-1} \psi_j(-\alpha) \eta_{t-j}, \quad t = 1, 2, \ldots, \quad (9.34)$$

where $1_A(\cdot)$ is the indicator function of the set A, so all the past weakly dependent stationary innovations $\eta_t, t \le 0$, are ignored. Truncation in the definition of ζ_t is necessary because the coefficients $\psi_j(-\alpha)$ are not square-summable for $\alpha \ge \frac{1}{2}$. This convention makes essential the date of the start of the observations. However, this framework can easily be generalized by allowing a warming-up period where the inflow of information can begin before we actually observe the process. The filtered process ζ_t, though with finite variance for fixed t, is nonstationary for any value of $\alpha \ne 0$. However, if $\alpha < 0.5$, it converges in mean square as $t \to \infty$ to the covariance stationary X_t obtained by

$$X_t = (1-L)^{-\alpha}\eta_t = \sum_{j=0}^{\infty} \psi_j(-\alpha)\eta_{t-j}, \quad \alpha < 0.5, \tag{9.35}$$

cf. (9.4), for the same sequence of innovations $\eta_j, j = 1, \ldots, t$. As $\Gamma(\alpha)\psi_j(-\alpha) \sim j^{\alpha-1}$ as $j \to \infty$, when $\alpha \ge 0.5$ the variance of ζ_t grows without limit with t and ζ_t is nonstationary long-range dependent in the sense of Heyde and Yang (1997). The long-range properties of the processes (9.34) and (9.35) are described by the memory parameter α, and under regularity conditions and appropriately normalized, such processes converge to different versions of fractional Brownian motion with parameter $\alpha > 0.5$ respectively (see Marinucci and Robinson, 2000, for a discussion). This reflects the fact that alternative definitions of nonstationary fractional processes differ in the treatment of initial conditions, which are transmitted through a long-range dependent process v_t in (9.28), while the stationary dynamics depend on the weakly dependent process η_t in (9.34).

Sufficient conditions for valid large-sample LP inference on α for Gaussian processes defined by (9.34) are investigated in Velasco (2004) using local conditions on the spectral density of η_t. Several extensions of model (9.34) are considered, such as series with negative memory ($\alpha < 0$), which are relevant for statistical inference on fractionally differenced data; processes with filters initialized at a remote point in the past; and fractional differencing and integration of stationary long memory time series with η_t satisfying (9.3) with $0 < |d| < 0.5$ (see Marinucci and Robinson, 2001). Robinson (2004) considered bounds for the moments of the difference between the DFT of both types of nonstationary processes, useful to investigate the asymptotic behavior of a large class of estimates linear in the periodogram. The consistency of the LW estimate for asymptotically stationary processes given by (9.34), $|\alpha| < 0.5$, is studied in Marmol and Velasco (2004) for linear η_t. Also Shimotsu and Phillips (2004) have studied the behavior of the LW estimate for series generated by (9.34) for the nonstationary and unit root cases, showing similar results to when the series is given by a partial sum process, cf. (9.28).

However, the knowledge that ζ_t is given by (9.34) can be used directly in the estimation of α, either through numerical properties of the DFT (similar to (9.29) but taking into account end effects) or by using directly the time-domain truncated fractional differencing structure of ζ_t. The first route is followed in Phillips (1999) and Kim and Phillips (2000) for the LP estimates and in Shimotsu and

Phillips (2000) for the LW estimates. The second option is pursued in Shimotsu and Phillips (2005a), where the following *exact LW* log-likelihood is analyzed,

$$\mathcal{L}_m^E(a, G) = \frac{1}{m} \sum_{j=1}^m \left\{ \log G \lambda_j^{-2a} + \frac{I_{\Delta^a \zeta}(\lambda_j)}{G} \right\},$$

where $I_{\Delta^a \zeta}$ denotes the periodogram of the series

$$\Delta^a \zeta_t = \sum_{j=0}^{t-1} \psi_j(a) \zeta_{t-j}, \quad t = 1, 2, \ldots, T.$$

The normalization of the periodogram by λ_j^{2d} used in $\mathcal{L}_m$ is replaced in $\mathcal{L}_m^E$ by the fractional differencing of the original data, allowing in principle any value of α to be considered. The ELW estimates are defined by minimization of $\mathcal{L}_m^E(a, G)$ and, as usual, concentrating out G we obtain

$$\hat{\alpha}_m^{ELW} = \arg \min_{a \in D} R_m^E(a),$$

where

$$R_m^E(a) = \log \hat{G}_m^{ELW}(a) - 2a \frac{1}{m} \sum_{j=1}^m \log \lambda_j, \quad \hat{G}_m^{ELW}(a) = \frac{1}{m} \sum_{j=1}^m I_{\Delta^a \zeta}(\lambda_j).$$

Under conditions slightly more restrictive than those of Robinson (1995b), Shimotsu and Phillips (2005a) found that $\hat{\alpha}_m^{ELW}$ is consistent and asymptotically normal with the usual 1/4 asymptotic variance when

$$\frac{1}{m} + \frac{m^{1+2\gamma} \log^2 m}{T^{2\gamma}} + \frac{\log T}{m^\varepsilon} \to 0, \quad \text{as } T \to \infty,$$

for some $\varepsilon > 0$, where the parameter γ is equivalent to that given in (9.25) but for the spectral density of η_t in (9.34). The interest in this procedure, which is somewhat more cumbersome than that of the usual LW, is based on the fact that nonstationary values of α can be included in D, with the only restriction being that $\nabla_2 - \nabla_1 < 9/2$, which requires limited prior information on the value of α, avoiding in this way the efficiency loss of tapering. The relationship between these variants and the traditional version of the LW estimator is discussed by Shimotsu and Phillips (2005b).

9.3.4 Cyclical and seasonal long memory

It is possible to conceive of stochastic processes X_t that show strong persistence at some frequency $\omega \in (0, \pi]$ different from the origin, such that their spectral density satisfies

$$f_X(\omega + \lambda) \sim G_X |\lambda|^{-2d} \quad \text{as } \lambda \to 0. \tag{9.36}$$

A time series with such a spectral density displays cycles of period $2\pi/\omega$, which are more persistent the larger d is. The condition $d < \frac{1}{2}$ entails stationarity by the integrability of f_X. The autocovariances of such processes show an asymptotic slow decay typical of long memory, but with oscillations that depend on the frequency ω where the spectral pole or zero occurs, so that

$$\gamma_j \sim c_X \cos(j\omega) j^{2d-1} \quad \text{as } j \to \infty$$

(see, for example, Chung, 1996; Andel, 1986, who introduced the Gegenbauer ARMA (GARMA) processes; or Gray, Zhang and Woodward, 1989). Oppenheim, Ould Haye and Viano (2000) and Lindholdt (2002) show that the seasonal long memory that has been found in many macroeconomic time series can be explained by cross-sectional aggregation and structural changes, providing ways of generating parametric seasonal long memory models. Arteche and Robinson (1999) called this property Seasonal or Cyclical Long Memory (SCLM) and investigated semiparametric inference for SCLM processes based on versions of the LP and LW estimates. When two-sided estimates are used, the asymptotic variance should be adapted since, in fact, we are using $2m$ different periodograms, instead of the usual m, when considering the zero frequency long memory. Arteche (2002) addresses the issue of testing for equal memory parameters when more than one seasonal frequency is considered.

Arteche and Robinson (2000) have further introduced Seasonal or Cyclical Asymmetric Long Memory (SCALM), for which

$$f_X(\omega + \lambda) \sim G_{X1} \lambda^{-2d_1} \quad \text{as } \lambda \to 0^+$$
$$f_X(\omega - \lambda) \sim G_{X2} \lambda^{-2d_2} \quad \text{as } \lambda \to 0^+,$$

where $\omega \in (0, \pi), 0 < G_{Xi} < \infty, |d_i| < \frac{1}{2}, i = 1, 2,$ and it is permitted that $d_1 \neq d_2$ and/or $G_{X1} \neq G_{X2}$. This (semi)parameterization shows that the extension of the concept of long memory from $\omega = 0$ to any ω between 0 and π broadens the scope for modeling, since the spectrum is symmetric about zero and π. The spectral asymmetry involves a different persistence for cycles of period just shorter and just larger than $2\pi/\omega$. Arteche and Robinson (2000) have discussed semiparametric inference based on one-sided LP and LW estimates for both memory parameters d_1 and d_2. When d_1 and d_2 have opposite signs there is very strong leakage from the peak, which indicates strong persistence, to the zero at the other side of the singularity, affecting noticeably semiparametric inference in finite samples. To alleviate this problem, Arteche and Velasco (2005) find similar benefits of tapering as those for treating symmetric nonstationary singularities in f_X.

A related problem in some applications is the estimation of the location ω of the pole when $d > 0$. Hidalgo and Soulier (2004) employed a semiparametric model for f_X around ω,

$$f_X(\lambda) = |1 - e^{i(\lambda-\omega)}|^{-d} |1 - e^{i(\lambda+\omega)}|^{-d} f^*(\lambda),$$

to generate behavior such as (9.36). If f^* is smooth this model allows for poles where the exponent of the singularity is defined as $\alpha = d$ if $\omega \in (0, \pi)$ and as $\alpha = 2d$ if $\omega \in \{0, \pi\}$. The estimate of ω they propose is the maximum of the periodogram,

$$\hat{\omega}_T = \frac{2\pi}{T} \arg \max_{1 \leq j \leq \tilde{T}} I_X(\lambda_j),$$

where $\tilde{T} = [(T - 1)/2]$. This estimate is consistent for Gaussian time series and its convergence rate is close to the parametric rate T obtained by Giraitis, Hidalgo and Robinson (2001), but its asymptotic distribution is unknown. Hidalgo (2005) investigates the asymptotic distribution of an alternative estimate of ω which also has a rate of convergence close to the parametric rate T, provided the process X_t has enough finite moments. Furthermore, Hidalgo and Soulier (2004) show that the LP estimate of d when we plug in the estimate $\hat{\omega}_T$ is robust to estimation of the location of the pole, with the usual asymptotic properties. This result relies on the symmetry of the peak $f_X(\lambda)$ around ω and on the use of both sides of the periodogram around ω when $\omega \in (0, \pi)$.

9.4   Developments

In this section we consider two fields where the semiparametric methodology of memory estimation has been widely developed and applied to solve inference problems on economic time series where parametric models are often difficult to justify. These are fractionally cointegrated systems and nonlinear models of conditional heteroskedasticity for time series with persistent volatility. In the first case, the new challenges are related to the treatment of nonstationary series of unknown degree of integration, together with the analysis of vector time series with degenerate long-run dynamics in the case of cointegration. In the second problem, the nonlinearity produces difficulties in applying usual semiparametric methods, so ad hoc modifications have been developed.

9.4.1   Fractional cointegration

We consider a $P \times 1$ fractionally integrated vector

$$Z_t = \mu + diag\left\{(1 - L)^{-d_1}, \ldots, (1 - L)^{-d_p}\right\} u_t 1_{t>0}(t), \quad t = 0, 1, 2, \ldots,$$

with memory parameters $\mathbf{d} = (d_1, \ldots, d_P)'$, where $\mathbf{u}_t$ is a zero mean weakly dependent vector process. The concept of (fractional) cointegration establishes that a certain (non-null) linear combination $\mathbf{b}'Z_t$ has less memory than the vector Z_t in some sense. When we allow for different memory parameters there are many ways to make precise such a definition (see, e.g., the review in Robinson and Yajima, 2002). If we partition the original vector as $Z_t' = (X_t', Y_t)$, then one of the simplest possibilities is to state that Z_t is fractionally cointegrated if there exists an $M \times 1$ vector $\beta, M = P - 1$, such that $e_t = Y_t - \boldsymbol{\beta}'X_t$ is $I(\delta)$ with $\delta < d_Y$. This definition implies that $d_i = d_Y$ for at least one $i = 1, \ldots, M$, since we impose the restriction that the coefficient of Y_t in **b** is not null, and leads to the linear regression representation

$$Y_t = \beta'X_t + e_t, \tag{9.37}$$

where β could be estimated by standard methods, such as OLS.

To develop this line of argument, define a version of the AP statistic introduced in section 9.2.3,

$$\mathbf{F}_{ab}(n) = 2\frac{2\pi}{T}\sum_{j=1}^{n} \mathrm{Re}\{\mathbf{I}_{ab}(\lambda_j)\} - \frac{2\pi}{T}\mathbf{I}_{ab}(\pi)1\{n = T/2\}, \quad 1 \le n \le T/2.$$

Note that $\mathbf{F}_{ab}([T/2])$ is equal to the usual covariance matrix between a_t and b_t, $t = 1, \ldots, T$, so $\mathbf{F}_{ab}(n)$ reflects the contribution to that covariance from frequencies up to λ_n. Omitting the zero frequency implies mean correction as usual. Robinson (1994a), for stationary series, and Robinson and Marinucci (2001), for nonstationary processes, proposed the narrow band or frequency domain least squares (FDLS) coefficients

$$\beta_n = \mathbf{F}_{XX}(n)^{-1}\mathbf{F}_{XY}(n)$$

to estimate the cointegrating vector β in the representation (9.37) under the assumption of rank one cointegration (so β is the only direction which reduces the memory of Z_t). See also Robinson and Marinucci (2000), Chen and Hurvich (2003a) and Robinson and Iacone (2005) for related results in the presence of deterministic trends and Marinucci (2000) for alternative estimates using continuous periodogram averages.

When $n = [T/2]$, β_n is the OLS estimate with intercept, but $n < [T/2]$ may be desirable. When a nondegenerating band of frequencies is considered, $n \sim CT$, $C \in (0, 0.5)$ this corresponds to the band-spectrum regression introduced by Hannan (1963). However, when the convergence condition (9.6) holds, β_n still uses an increasing number of frequencies, but in a degenerating band around the origin. This option solves the consistency problem of OLS estimates in stationary frameworks due to simultaneity bias, and in the nonstationary case also avoids some asymptotic bias terms and focuses on the relevant frequencies for the analysis of long-run relationships. The improvements depend basically on the degree of nonstationarity of the observed series. The more interesting cases analyzed in Robinson and Marinucci (2001) are the so-called "less than unit root nonstationarity," with $d_i > 0.5, \delta \ge 0$ and $d_i + \delta < 1$, for which

$$T^{d_i+d_{\min}-1}(\beta_{i,[T/2]} - \beta_i) \quad \text{and} \quad T^{d_i-\delta}n^{\delta+d_{\min}-1}(\beta_{i,n} - \beta_i) \tag{9.38}$$

converge to well-defined nondegenerate random variables under (9.6), and the "greater than unit root nonstationarity," with $d_1 = \cdots = d_M > 0.5$ and $\delta > 0$, $d_i + \delta > 1$, when

$$T^{d_i - \delta}(\beta_{i,[T/2]} - \beta_i) \quad \text{and} \quad T^{d_i - \delta}(\beta_{i,n} - \beta_i) \tag{9.39}$$

both converge weakly. In the well-studied case of unit root cointegration, $d_1 = \cdots = d_M = 1$ and $\delta = 0$, the rate of convergence of both estimates is also $T^{d_i - \delta} = T$. The limits are functionals of fractional Brownian motions. The standardizations in (9.38) show that FDLS may achieve a great superiority over OLS given (9.6) holds, although some benefits can also be found in the unit root case.

For these results to be useful requires, on the one hand, that there exists cointegration of rank one (up to scale, only one cointegration vector exists) and, on the other hand, that the orders of integration are known or can be estimated consistently. The existence of cointegration can be deduced from the values of the memory parameters d_i, d_y and δ, so we first concentrate on this problem.

The memory of observables X_t can be estimated semiparametrically by any of the methods discussed in section 9.2. For the cointegrating errors e_t we could use similar ideas, but two further problems arise, namely the use of the residuals $\hat{e}_t = Y_t - \hat{\beta}'_n X_t$, and the ignorance of whether these are stationary or not. Dittmann (2000) studies the finite-sample performance of several residual-based tests for fractional cointegration. The effects of the use of residuals depend fundamentally on the rates of convergence (9.38)–(9.39) of the estimates of the cointegrating vectors, which can be very fast, but also arbitrarily slow when $d_{\min}$ is close to δ, even if it is assumed from the outset that cointegration exists with stationary errors. Hassler, Marmol and Velasco (2003) and Velasco (2003a) have studied the estimation of the memory parameters of the vector $(X'_t, e_t)'$ with the LP and LW estimates respectively, both using (FD)LS residuals $\hat{e}_t$ or their increments, $\Delta \hat{e}_t$. LW memory estimation with (nonparametric) residuals was first studied by Robinson (1997). The main conclusion is that asymptotic semiparametric inference for δ based on cointegrating residuals is not affected by β estimation as far as the $\hat{\beta}_n$ are superconsistent, i.e., $d_i - \delta > 0.5$, all i. If $d_i - \delta \leq 0.5$ for some i, the semiparametric estimates of δ may remain consistent (LP estimates seem to require further pooling or tapering), but with a slower rate. In the "greater than unit root nonstationarity" case, original residuals or increments of the residuals have to be used depending on whether $\delta < 0.5$ or $\delta > 0.5$. However, tapering renders semiparametric inference robust to the decision of which input is used. In the "less than unit root nonstationarity" case, only original residuals should be used since $\delta > 0.5$ necessarily and there can be additional restrictions on the range of allowed bandwidths m depending on the values of d and δ.

Using the theory reviewed in section 9.2, we could test hypotheses on the values of the parameters d_i and δ, but the previous restrictions under the assumption of cointegration lead to some caution in constructing a direct test of the null of no cointegration, $\delta = d$, against $\delta < d$, assuming $d_1 = \cdots = d_M$. Alternatively, Marinucci and Robinson (2001) propose a Hausman (1978)-type test based on alternative LW estimates of d when $M = 1$,

$$H_m = 8m\left(\hat{d}_m^{LW} - \tilde{d}_m^{LW}\right)^2,$$

where the univariate $\hat{d}_m^{LW}$ can be based on either ΔX_t or ΔY_t, and $\tilde{d}_m^{LW}$ is the efficient restricted estimate of the memory $d_Y = d_1$ with input $(\Delta X_t, \Delta Y_t)'$, cf. (9.19). Then $\tilde{d}_m^{LW}$ and $\hat{d}_m^{LW}$ have asymptotic variances of $1/8$ and $1/4$ respectively, so their difference is expected to have asymptotic variance $1/4 - 1/8 = 1/8$ under the null of no cointegration. Note that, under this null hypothesis, the long-run variance matrix $\mathbf{G}_Z$ of Z_t is non-singular, and that $d = \delta$, so the distribution of H_m can be approximated by that of a χ_1^2 variable, but under the alternative $\mathbf{G}_Z$ is singular and $\hat{d}_m^{LW}$ will not be consistent for d.

Velasco (2003b) considers an alternative semiparametric method of estimating the degree of cointegration $\alpha = d - \delta \geq 0$ of a vector Z_t that avoids the use of residuals that depend on initial slope estimates. For this it is assumed that the (pseudo) spectral density matrix $\mathbf{f}_Z$ of the bivariate vector $Z_t = (X_t, e_t)'$ satisfies

$$\mathbf{f}_Z(\lambda) = \lambda^{-2d}\begin{pmatrix} \Xi_{XX} & \Xi_{Xe}\lambda^\alpha \\ \Xi_{eX}\lambda^\alpha & \Xi_{ee}\lambda^{2\alpha} \end{pmatrix}(1 + o(1)) \quad \text{as } \lambda \to 0^+, \tag{9.40}$$

where the matrix $\Xi = \{\Xi_{ab}\}$, $a, b \in \{X, e\}$, is hermitian and nonsingular (see also Levy (2003)). Then, using (9.37) and (9.40), it is possible to show that the squared coherence between Y_t and X_t satisfies

$$|R_{XY}(\lambda)|^2 \sim 1 - \Xi_H\lambda^{2\alpha} \quad \text{as } \lambda \to 0^+, \tag{9.41}$$

for a real constant $0 < \Xi_H < \infty$,

$$\Xi_H = \frac{\Xi_e}{\Xi_X}\left[1 - \frac{|\Xi_{eX}|^2}{\Xi_e\Xi_X}\right] = \frac{G_e}{G_X}\left[1 - \frac{G_{eX}^2}{G_eG_X}\right],$$

that depends on the (normalized) noise to signal ratio and on the coherence at zero between X_t and e_t using the long run variance $\mathbf{G}_Z$. Rearranging and taking logs in (9.41) we have that

$$\log(1 - |R_{XY}(\lambda)|^2) \sim \log \Xi_H + 2\alpha \log \lambda \quad \text{as } \lambda \to 0^+, \tag{9.42}$$

which suggests the log-coherence regression estimate of α, analogous to GPH LP regression,

$$\hat{\alpha}_m = -\left(\sum_{j=\ell}^m \Lambda_j^2\right)^{-1}\sum_{j=\ell}^m \Lambda_j \log(1 - |\hat{R}_{XY,n}(\lambda_j)|^2).$$

$\hat{\alpha}_m$ uses consistent estimates of $|R_{XY}(\lambda)|^2$ at frequencies λ_j in a degenerating band around the origin,

$$|\hat{R}_{XY,n}(\lambda_j)|^2 = \frac{|\hat{f}_{XY,n}(\lambda_j)|^2}{\hat{f}_{X,n}(\lambda_j)\hat{f}_{Y,n}(\lambda_j)},$$

where $\hat{f}_{XY,n}, \hat{f}_{X,n}, \hat{f}_{Y,n}$ are nonparametric estimates of the corresponding (pseudo) spectral densities with bandwidth n (see also Hidalgo, 1996). As in Robinson (1995a), a trimming of the very first $\ell - 1$ coherence estimates is allowed. This approach is valid for both stationary and nonstationary series (tapering might be used to eliminate an intercept or polynomial trend in (9.37) or to cover very nonstationary situations, $d \geq 1$) and it is not affected asymptotically by the endogeneity of the residuals ($\Xi_{eX} \neq 0$). However, if X_t and e_t are incoherent at zero frequency, the semiparametric model (9.42) provides a better approximation.

The analysis of $\hat{\alpha}_m$ is complicated with respect to the LP memory estimate due to the nonlinear and nonparametric nature of the sample coherences $|\hat{R}_{XY,n}(\lambda_j)|^2$. Velasco (2003b) showed the consistency of $\hat{\alpha}_m$ and suggested approximating its sample variability by

$$\text{Var}\left[\hat{\alpha}_m\right] \approx \left(\sum_j \Lambda_j^2\right)^{-2} 4\sum_j \sum_k \Lambda_j \Lambda_k \text{Cov}\left[\tanh^{-1}(|\hat{R}_{XY,n}(\lambda_j)|), \tanh^{-1}(|\hat{R}_{XY,n}(\lambda_k)|)\right].$$

$$(9.43)$$

Here the transformation $\tanh^{-1}$ is variance-stabilizing because $\hat{R}_{XY,n}$ is a sort of correlation coefficient in the frequency domain and, when $\hat{R}_{XY,n}$ uses spectral estimates with uniform weights over $2q + 1$ Fourier frequencies, we can approximate the covariance in (9.43) by

$$\text{Cov}\left[\tanh^{-1}(|\hat{R}_{XY,n}(\lambda_j)|), \tanh^{-1}(|\hat{R}_{XY,n}(\lambda_{j+p})|)\right] \approx \frac{2q + 1 - |p|}{2(2q + 1)^2},$$
$$p = 0, \pm 1, \ldots, \pm 2q,$$

and assume that estimates of $\hat{R}_{XY,n}$ evaluated at frequencies sufficiently far apart are asymptotically uncorrelated. For tapered series this approximation has to be adjusted by $\Phi^{(v,p)}$ as for the LW memory estimates in (9.33).

Robinson and Yajima (2002) have investigated semiparametric methods of inference on the cointegration rank of a stationary vector. The methods proposed depend, first, on obtaining subsets of Z_t with the same memory by sequential testing, using modified Wald tests based on (univariate) LW semiparametric estimates to account for the degeneracy of the asymptotic distribution in case of cointegration (because G_Z is singular). The cointegration rank is then determined by analyzing the eigenvalues of the estimate of G_Z, given by $\hat{G}_{Z,m} = \hat{G}_{Z,m}(\tilde{d}_m)$ defined in (9.17), where $\tilde{d}_m$ is the vector containing the univariate LW estimates of the memory of each of the components of Z_t. A similar procedure using ELW estimation is pursued by Nielsen and Shimotsu (2004).

Following a parallel route, Chen and Hurvich (2003b) study the properties of eigenvectors of an AP matrix of differenced, tapered observations, where the bandwidth m is fixed in asymptotics. They show that the eigenvectors corresponding to the smallest eigenvalues (as many as the cointegrating rank) lie close to the space of true cointegrating vectors with high probability. An implicit assumption is that all cointegration relationships have the same memory, so Chen and Hurvich (2004) propose to separate the space of cointegrating vectors into subspaces that might yield different memory parameters. The rate of convergence for the estimated cointegrating vectors depends only on the difference between the memory parameters in the given and adjacent subspaces, and residual-based LW estimation of the memory parameters is proposed to consistently identify the cointegrating subspaces and to test for fractional cointegration.

In a related, but nonstationary, framework, Marmol and Velasco (2004) propose a test for fractional cointegration in a $P \times 1$ nonstationary fractionally integrated (*NFI*) vector

$$Z_t = (1 - L)^{-d}\{\mathbf{u}_t 1_{t>0}(t)\}, \quad t = 0, 1, 2, \ldots,$$

where $\mathbf{u}_t = \sum_{j=-\infty}^{\infty} \mathbf{A}_{t-j}\varepsilon_j$ is a linear process with iid innovations ε_t and long-run covariance matrix $\mathbf{\Omega} = \mathbf{A}(1)\mathbf{A}(1)'$, $\mathbf{A}(1) = \sum_{j=-\infty}^{\infty} \mathbf{A}_j$. With the partition $Z'_t = (Y_t, X'_t)$, the matrix $\mathbf{A}(1)$ is parameterized as

$$\mathbf{A}(1) = \begin{pmatrix} \omega_{YY}^{1/2}(1 - \rho^2)^{1/2} & \rho\overline{\omega}'_{XY}\Omega_{XX}^{-1/2} \\ 0 & \Omega_{XX}^{1/2} \end{pmatrix}, \quad \Omega_{ZZ} = \begin{pmatrix} \omega_{YY} & \omega'_{XY} \\ \omega_{XY} & \Omega_{XX} \end{pmatrix}$$

where Ω_{XX} is positive definite, $\omega_{YY} > 0, \overline{\omega}'_{XY}$ is an $M \times 1$ vector satisfying $\overline{\omega}'_{XY}\Omega_{XX}^{-1}\overline{\omega}_{XY} = \omega_{YY}$, and $\rho^2 = \omega'_{XY}\Omega_{XX}^{-1}\omega_{XY}/\omega_{YY}$ is the squared coefficient of multiple correlation computed from Ω_{ZZ}, so that $0 \leq \rho^2 \leq 1$. The long-run covariance ω_{XY} is given by $\rho\overline{\omega}_{XY}$, where $\overline{\omega}_{XY}$ expresses the direction of the covariance, while $\beta_0 = \Omega_{XX}^{-1}\omega_{XY}$ is the projection vector of Y_t on X_t. The parameter ρ measures the strength of the covariance and the type of long-run relationship among the elements of the nonstationary Z_t. When $\rho^2 < 1, \Omega_{ZZ}$ is nonsingular and we say that Z_t is spuriously related. This model is completed when $\rho^2 = 1$, so that Ω_{ZZ} is singular and the model is disturbed to produce a (fractionally) cointegrated vector Z_t with $\beta'_0 Z_t$ of memory $\delta \in [d - 1, d)$.

As is well known, in the spurious case, the usual OLS statistics of a regression of Y_t on X_t may lead to the conclusion that there is a meaningless linear relationship between the elements of Z_t. This result is, in part, a consequence of standardization by the residual sample variance, which ignores any serial correlation (or nonstationarity) in the residual series. A first step toward a feasible cointegration test is an alternative studentization of the OLS coefficients that uses all frequencies by means of the matrix

$$\hat{V}_T = \left(\sum_{j=-\tilde{T}}^{\tilde{T}} I_X(\lambda_j)\right)^{-1} \sum_{j=-\tilde{T}}^{\tilde{T}} I_X(\lambda_j) I_{\hat{e}}(\lambda_j) \left(\sum_{j=-\tilde{T}}^{\tilde{T}} I_X(\lambda_j)\right)^{-1},$$

where $I_{\hat{e}}(\lambda_j)$ stands for the residual periodogram computed with the observed residuals $\hat{e}_t = Y_t - \hat{\beta}_T' X_t$, $\hat{\beta}_T$ is the OLS coefficient in (9.37) and $\tilde{T} = [T/2]$. The test statistic proposed by Marmol and Velasco (2004) is given by the following Wald or adjusted F statistic

$$\mathcal{W}_T = \mathcal{W}_T(\hat{\beta}_T, \hat{\beta}_{0,n}) = \frac{1}{M} \left(\hat{\beta}_T - \hat{\beta}_{0,n}\right)' \hat{V}_T^{-1} \left(\hat{\beta}_T - \hat{\beta}_{0,n}\right),$$

where the OLS estimate $\hat{\beta}_T$ is inconsistent under no cointegration and $\hat{\beta}_{0,n}$ is an alternative semiparametric GLS-type estimate, which is consistent under this hypothesis,

$$\hat{\beta}_{0,n} = \hat{\beta}_{0,n}(\hat{d}_m, \hat{\delta}_m) = \hat{\Omega}_{XX,n}^{-1}(\hat{d}_m)\hat{\omega}_{XY,n}(\hat{\delta}_m). \tag{9.44}$$

Here $\hat{\Omega}_{XX,n}$ is similar to $\hat{G}_{X,m}$ in (9.17) up to a constant, but using a common d and the periodogram of the increments of X_t,

$$\hat{\Omega}_{XX,n}(d) = \frac{2\pi}{n} \sum_{j=1}^{n} \lambda_j^{2(d-1)} \text{Re}\{I_{\Delta X}(\lambda_j)\},$$

in the same way that

$$\hat{\omega}_{XY,n}(\delta) = \frac{2\pi}{n} \sum_{j=1}^{n} \lambda_j^{2(\delta-1)} \text{Re}\{I_{\Delta X \Delta Y}(\lambda_j)\}$$

uses the cross periodogram of the increments ΔX_t and ΔY_t. In (9.44), $\hat{d}_m$ is a $\log T$-consistent semiparametric estimate of d, as given in sections 9.2.1–9.2.2, based on any subset of ΔX_t, but $\hat{\delta}_m$ is a consistent estimate of δ based on OLS residuals. By contrast with the customary F-statistic, constructed using the usual (time-domain) residual sum of squares, the Wald statistic $\mathcal{W}_T$ has a well-defined limiting distribution under the null of a spurious relationship.

Under the null of no cointegration $\delta = d$, both semiparametric memory estimates in $\hat{\beta}_{0,n}$ have the same probabilistic limit and the periodograms in $\hat{\Omega}_{XX,n}(\hat{d}_m)$ and $\hat{\omega}_{XY,n}(\hat{\delta}_m)$ are (asymptotically) properly normalized, so $\hat{\beta}_{0,n}$ is consistent for β_0 if $\{q^{d-2} + q^{\varepsilon-1} \log T\} \log^2 T + qT^{-1} \to 0$, for $q = n, m$ and some $\varepsilon > 0$, together with the usual regularity conditions on the spectral density of u_t. However, under the alternative of fractional cointegration, $\delta < d$, $\hat{\omega}_{XY,n}(\hat{\delta}_m)$ does not have an adequate normalization, and it can be shown to diverge as $T, n \to \infty$, whereas $\hat{\Omega}_{XX,n}(\hat{d}_m)$ remains consistent for Ω_{XX}. Therefore, the Wald statistic diverges with

T when $0 < d - \delta < 0.5$, leading to the consistency of the test, which rejects the null of no cointegration for large values of $\mathcal{W}_T$.

9.4.2 Nonlinear models

Many economic time series display conditional heteroskedasticity, this being the main feature of the dynamics of many asset prices, whose levels are assumed generally to form a martingale sequence. Robinson and Henry (1999) and Henry (2001) illustrate the robustness of LW and AP estimation of the memory of the levels in the presence of conditional heteroskedasticity. Recent interest has been focused on the estimation of the degree of persistency of volatility itself through a long memory parameter that describes the slowly decaying autocorrelation of nonlinear transformations of the returns of the corresponding asset. The availability of long records of high-frequency returns of many financial assets calls for the intensive use of the semiparametric methodology in the investigation of the long-range properties of these time series.

Robinson (1991) proposed that the conditional volatility $\sigma_t^2 = \text{Var}[X_t|I_{t-1}]$, where I_s is the σ-field of events generated by $X_k, k \leq s$, may display long-range dependence in an ARCH(∞) specification,

$$\sigma_t^2 = \sigma^2 + \sum_{j=1}^{\infty} \theta_j X_{t-j}^2,$$

where the θ_j decay slowly as the weights $\psi_j(-d)$ in (9.4) for $d > 0$, and propose LM testing of this possibility. This has also been an issue in applied work; see, e.g., Ding, Granger and Engle (1993).

Considerable effort has been put into studying parametric generalized autoregressive conditional heteroskedasticity (GARCH) specifications which actually produce long-range dependence in σ_t^2 and valid inference procedures (see, e.g., the fractionally integrated GARCH (FIGARCH) model of Baillie, Bollerslev and Mikkelsen (1996), the fractionally integrated exponential GARCH (FIEGARCH) of Bollerslev and Mikkelsen (1996) or Giraitis, Robinson and Surgailis (2000)), and also semiparametric proposals (Giraitis, Kokoszka, Leipus and Teyssière, 2000). However, stochastic volatility (SV) specifications have been more amenable to semiparametric analysis. Harvey (1998) and Breidt, Crato and de Lima (1998) studied a Long Memory SV (LMSV) model for asset returns defined by

$$X_t = \sigma_t \xi_t, \quad \sigma_t = \sigma \exp(v_t/2),$$

where v_t is a stationary long memory process independent of ξ_t, which is itself iid with zero mean and unit variance. The persistence in the volatility of X_t depends on the persistence of v_t. Breidt *et al.* (1998) proposed its estimation by a global Whittle estimate, using the linearization

$$\begin{aligned}
\log X_t^2 &= \log \sigma_t^2 + \log \xi_t^2 \\
&= \log \sigma^2 + E[\log \xi_t^2] + v_t + \{\log \xi_t^2 - E[\log \xi_t^2]\} \\
&= \mu + v_t + u_t,
\end{aligned} \tag{9.45}$$

say, where u_t is a zero mean iid random sequence and independent of v_t, whose spectral density depends on some parameters. Note that the autocovariances of $\log X_t^2$ are the same as those of v_t except at lag zero, for which it is $\sigma_v^2 + \sigma_u^2$. A justification of such procedures can be found in Hosoya (1997).

However, semiparametric methods are also natural in this context if we assume that f_v satisfies (9.3), especially given the difficulty of properly specifying all short-run dynamics and the availability of long data sets at different sampling frequencies. Breidt *et al.* (1998) and Andersen and Bollerslev (1997) propose LP estimation on some nonlinear transformation of X_t, such as $\log X_t^2$ or $|X_t|$, but this violates the usual Gaussianity assumption. In the case of a LMSV, note that if v_t follows a fractional model with spectral density $|2 \sin \lambda/2|^{-2d} g_v^*(\lambda)$, then $f_{\log X^2}(\lambda) = |2 \sin \lambda/2|^{-2d} f^*(\lambda)$, where now

$$f^*(\lambda) = g_v^*(\lambda) + |2 \sin \lambda/2|^{2d} \frac{\sigma_u^2}{2\pi} = g_v^*(0)\left\{1 + O(\lambda^{2d})\right\} \quad \text{as } \lambda \to 0+, \qquad (9.46)$$

for smooth g^*. This justifies the use of customary semiparametric models, since f^* is bounded above and away from zero (if $g_v^*(\lambda)$ is bounded for all λ and positive at $\lambda = 0$) and $f_{\log X^2}(\lambda)/f_v(\lambda) \to 1$ as $\lambda \to 0$. Deo and Hurvich (2001) show that the central limit theorem (9.8) for the LP estimate holds for Gaussian v_t when we replace I_X by $I_{\log X^2}$, and m is chosen to satisfy

$$\frac{\log^2 T}{m} + \frac{m^{4d+1} \log^2 m}{T^{4d}} \to 0 \quad \text{as } T \to \infty, \qquad (9.47)$$

with f^* twice differentiable. This condition corresponds to that of Robinson (1995a, Assumption 6) when $\gamma = 2d$ in (9.25), cf. (9.46). Note that this result implies that $d > 0$ (and $\gamma > 0$), so long memory in v_t is assumed. Hurvich and Soulier (2002) have extended the previous result to the case $d = 0$ for volatility persistence testing, whereas Arteche (2004) gives a similar analysis for the LW estimate leading to (9.11) under the usual conditions and (9.46)–(9.47).

The additive structure of f^* in (9.46) suggests a bias problem in the selection of the bandwidth m, much restricted when d is small. To control this problem, Sun and Phillips (2003), in the spirit of the bias reduction techniques of section 9.2.4, propose enlarging the LP regression with a term in λ^{2d}, cf. (9.21), thus leading to the so called nonlinear LP (NLP) regression estimate, which now has no explicit expression. It is shown that the NLP estimate is consistent under (9.6), allowing for $\sigma_u^2 = 0$, but $d > 0$. If further

$$\frac{T^{4d(1+\varepsilon)}}{m^{4d(1+\varepsilon)+1}} + \frac{m^{8d+1}}{T^{8d}} \to 0 \quad \text{as } T \to \infty,$$

for some $\varepsilon > 0$, which allows for much larger choices of m than (9.47), and so faster converging estimates, then

$$2m^{1/2}\left(\hat{d}_m^{NLP} - d\right) \xrightarrow{d} \mathcal{N}\left(0, \frac{\pi^2}{6} \frac{(2d+1)^2}{4d^2}\right).$$

This limit, by contrast, reflects the increase in asymptotic variance due to the use of additional (nonlinear) regressors.

Hurvich and Ray (2003) exploit the same idea for the PLW estimate, introducing the term in λ^{2d} in (9.27), with $\exp(-p_r(\lambda_j; \boldsymbol{\theta}))$ replaced by $1 + \theta\lambda_j^{2d}$, and consider possibly nonstationary time series. Denoting this estimate as $\hat{d}_m^{NLW}$, Hurvich and Ray show that

$$2m^{1/2}\left(\hat{d}_m^{NLW} - d\right) \xrightarrow{d} \mathcal{N}\left(0, \frac{(2d+1)^2}{4d^2}\right),$$

for $d \in (0, 0.75)$ if

$$\frac{T^{4d}}{m^{4d+1}} + \frac{m^{2\gamma+1}\log^2 m}{T^{2\gamma}} \to 0 \quad \text{as } T \to \infty, \tag{9.48}$$

under (9.25), for linear v_t and $\gamma > 2d$. Note that typically $\gamma = 2$ for regular cases, cf. (9.25).

Building on this research, Hurvich, Moulines and Soulier (2005) consider a semiparametric specification for the spectral density of $\log X_t^2$ that nests both the LMSV and the FIEGARCH models, allowing for possible correlation between the signal and noise processes in (9.45) by means of the augmented correction factor

$$1 + \theta_1\lambda_j^{2d} \operatorname{Re}\left((1 - e^{i\lambda_j})^{-d}\right) + \theta_2\lambda_j^{2d}, \tag{9.49}$$

which replaces $\exp(-p_r(\lambda_j; \boldsymbol{\theta}))$ in the nonlinear PLW criterion (9.27). In this way they nest the usual LW estimate and the NLW estimate of Hurvich and Ray (2003) by setting $\theta_1 = \theta_2 = 0$ or $\theta_1 = 0$, respectively. The NLW estimate defined using the correcting factor (9.49), $\hat{d}_m^{N2LW}$ say, recovers basically the optimal semiparametric rate of convergence implied by (9.48), and its additional bias control properties have the counterpart of an increased asymptotic variance, since

$$2m^{1/2}\left(\hat{d}_m^{N2LW} - d\right) \xrightarrow{d} \mathcal{N}\left(0, (d+1)^2\frac{(2d+1)^2}{4d^2}\right),$$

for $d \in (0, 0.75)$ if, additionally to (9.48), $T^{4d}m^{\varepsilon-4d-1} \to 0$ for some $\varepsilon > 0$.

Apart from the problems of bias and bandwidth choice, other difficulties arise in semiparametric estimation of the persistence of financial time series. These include the choice of volatility measures and the role of aggregation (Bollerslev and Wright, 2000), the treatment of smooth trends and cointegration (Lobato and Velasco, 2000; Christensen and Nielsen, 2002), or seasonality and efficient estimation, (see, e.g., Deo, Hurvich and Lu, 2005). In particular, Deo *et al.* (2005) investigate the choice of power transformations to make the distribution of $\log X_t^2$ closer to Gaussian to enhance the properties of a Whittle estimate of a LMSV model, noting that this procedure might affect the persistence of the volatility series (Dittmann and Granger, 2002).

9.4.3   Other areas of application

Semiparametric inference on the persistence properties of time series has been applied to many other fields of empirical economics. Apart from descriptive and exploratory analysis, semiparametric estimation and testing for the degree of integration are key features in the modeling of many macroeconomic series, especially in the presence of complex cyclical, seasonal or short run dynamics. These have been applied to series of output (Diebold and Rudebush, 1989; Michelacci and Zaffaroni, 2000), consumption (Diebold and Rudebush, 1991), exchange rates (Cheung, 1993) and inflation (Hassler and Wolters, 1995). Following the application of a modified R/S analysis by Lo (1991), frequency and time domain semiparametric methods have also been used to document long memory in stock prices (Lee and Robinson, 1996; Lobato and Savin, 1997) and the relationship of volatility with other time series, such as traded volume (Bollerslev and Jubinski, 1999).

Semiparametric estimates, despite their inefficiency, can also be used in optimization routines or in plug-in methods which do not require a fast converging, but a robust, initial estimate of the long-run memory parameter. This is important in (fractional) cointegration analysis (see, e.g., Robinson and Hualde, 2003; or Marmol and Velasco, 2004). A major field of application of semiparametric methods is in the studentization of other parameter estimates, possibly of a parametric nature, or in testing problems, as pursued in a general setting by Robinson (2005). A related problem is the design of efficient semiparametric estimates of regression coefficients in the presence of long memory time series, as in Hidalgo and Robinson (2002) or Hualde and Robinson (2004).

9.5   Conclusion

There is a growing menu of semiparametric methods offered to the practitioner to analyze long memory properties of economic time series. Despite initial analyses having focused on LP estimation, mainly because of its computational appeal and the availability of approximate inference rules, LW methodology has become more popular as it is more efficient, flexible and robust to the presence of non-Gaussian characteristics or changing conditional higher moments. However, the overall performance of the semiparametric methodology depends dramatically on the bandwidth choice, especially when nonstationarity, trending or cyclical behavior may affect the dynamics of the series under investigation. In these cases, we recommend using appropriate modifications to robustify semiparametric memory estimation. Tapering provides a simple solution but, due to the loss of efficiency implied, it might only be appropriate if long enough records are available. In the presence of substantial ignorance on the degree of integration, ELW methods can provide more efficient solutions, but these might be more sensitive to the presence of unknown means or trends (Shimotsu, 2004). Volatility analysis based on nonlinear transformations of returns should account for the bias problem that otherwise may severely affect semiparametric inference for a wide range of bandwidths. In all cases, automatic bandwidth choices must be supplemented with knowledge about cyclical and seasonal patterns which otherwise would restrict the empirical validity of the basic long memory semiparametric model.

As in many other inference problems, semiparametric methods in time series analysis are of general application and apparently require a limited degree of previous knowledge or experience. However, some care must be taken when employing these methods. Following some justifications for the presence of long memory in observed time series by aggregation mechanisms of different types, possibly involving heavy tailed innovations (see the review in Diebold and Inoue, 2001), several simple models which are able to reproduce some long-range dependence properties have been investigated. Many of the models developed are not properly long memory, as defined in the Introduction, but with an appropriate choice of key parameters can generate long memory features in finite samples, as described, for example, by the convergence rate of partial sums or correlograms (see, e.g., Granger and Teräsvirta, 1999). GPH's LP regression estimate is one of the benchmarks used by Gourieroux and Jasiak (2001), Diebold and Inoue (2001) and Granger and Hyung (2004) to evaluate different models, including stochastic permanent breaks, regime switching and occasional structural break models. It turns out that this semiparametric estimate is highly biased for the estimation and testing of the true degree of integration of the process, thus issuing a serious warning that routine application of these methods may lead to the finding of spurious long memory if the data contain some of these features. Remedies can consist of applying structural break tests robust to long memory (see the revision in Banerjee and Urga, 2005) or allowing for possible breaks in memory estimation (e.g., Bos, Franses and Ooms, 1999; Choi and Zivot, 2005).

Despite these potential drawbacks, which may affect even more seriously the specification and estimation of parametric models, semiparametric inference for long memory processes have increasing potential for the analysis of economic time series. Future developments can be expected in the derivation of (semi)automatic methods of inference, procedures for the study of multivariate and possibly nonstationary and cointegrated time series, and specific techniques for the analysis of nonlinear and financial time series.

References

Adentstedt, R. (1974) On large sample estimation for the mean of a stationary random sequence. *Annals of Statistics* 2, 1095–1107.

Andel, J. (1986) Long-memory time series models. *Kybernetika* 22, 105–23.

Andersen, T. and T. Bollerslev (1997) Intraday periodicity and volatility persistence in financial markets. *Journal of Empirical Finance* 4, 115–58.

Andrews, D.W.K. and P. Guggenberger (2003) A bias-reduced log-periodogram regression estimator for the long-memory parameter. *Econometrica* 71, 675–712.

Andrews, D.W.K and Y.X. Sun (2004) Adaptive local polynomial Whittle estimation of long-range dependence. *Econometrica* 72, 569–614.

Arteche, J. (2002) Semiparametric robust tests on seasonal or cyclical long memory time series. *Journal of Time Series Analysis* 23, 251–86.

Arteche, J. (2004) Gaussian semiparametric estimation in long memory in stochastic volatility and signal plus noise models. *Journal of Econometrics* **119**, 131–54.

Arteche, J. and P.M. Robinson (1999) Seasonal and cyclic long memory. In S. Ghosh (ed.), *Asymptotics, Nonparametrics and Time Series: A Tribute to Madan Lal Puri*. New York: Marcel Dekker, pp. 115–45.

Arteche, J. and P.M. Robinson (2000) Semiparametric inference in seasonal and cyclical long memory processes. *Journal of Time Series Analysis* **21**, 1–25.

Arteche, J. and C. Velasco (2005) Trimming and tapering semiparametric estimates in asymmetric long memory time series. *Journal of Time Series Analysis*, **29**, 581–611.

Baillie, R.T., T. Bollerslev and H.O. Mikkelsen (1996) Fractionally integrated generalized autoregressive conditional heteroskedasticity. *Journal of Econometrics* **74**, 3–30.

Banerjee, A. and G. Urga (2005) Modelling structural breaks, long memory and stock market volatility: an overview. *Journal of Econometrics*, forthcoming.

Bardet, J.-M., G. Lang, E. Moulines and P. Soulier (2000) Wavelet estimator of long-range dependent processes. *Statistical Inference for Stochastic Processes* **3**, 85–99.

Bhansali, R.J. and P.S. Kokoszka (2001) Estimation of the long-memory parameter: a review of recent developments and an extension. In I.V. Basawa, C.C. Heyde and R.L. Taylor (eds), *Proceedings of the Symposium on Inference for Stochastic Processes*, IMS Lecture Notes, pp. 125–50.

Bollerslev, T. and P.D. Jubinski (1999) Equity trading volume and volatility: latent information arrivals and common long-run dependencies. *Journal of Business and Economic Statistics* **17**, 9–21.

Bollerslev, T. and H.O. Mikkelsen (1996) Modeling and pricing long memory in stock market volatility. *Journal of Econometrics* **73**, 151–84.

Bollerslev, T. and J.W. Wright (2000) Semiparametric estimation of long-memory volatility dependencies: the role of high-frequency data. *Journal of Econometrics* **98**, 81–106.

Bos, C., S.P.H. Franses and M. Ooms (1999) Long-memory and level shifts: re-analyzing in inflation rates. *Empirical Economics* **24**, 427–49.

Breidt, F.J., N. Crato and P. de Lima (1998) The detection and estimation of long memory in stochastic volatility. *Journal of Econometrics* **83**, 32–348.

Chen, W.W. and C.M. Hurvich (2003a) Estimating fractional cointegration in the presence of polynomial trends. *Journal of Econometrics* **117**, 95–121.

Chen, W.W. and C.M. Hurvich (2003b) Semiparametric estimation of multivariate fractional cointegration. *Journal of the American Statistical Association* **463**, 629–42.

Chen, W.W. and C.M. Hurvich (2004) Semiparametric estimation of fractional cointegrating subspaces. Preprint, Texas A&M University.

Cheung, Y.-W. (1993) Long memory in foreign exchange rates. *Journal of Business and Economic Statistics* **11**, 93–101.

Choi, K. and E. Zivot (2005) Long Memory and structural breaks in the forward discount: An empirical investigation. Preprint Ohio University.

Chung, C.F. (1996) Estimating a generalized long memory process. *Journal of Econometrics* **73**, 237–59.

Christensen, B.J. and M.O. Nielsen (2002) Semiparametric analysis of stationary fractional cointegration and the implied-realized volatility relation. University of Aarhus Working Paper No. 2001–4.

Delgado, M.A. and P.M. Robinson (1996a) Optimal spectral bandwidth for long memory. *Statistica Sinica* **6**, 97–112.

Delgado, M.A. and P.M. Robinson (1996b) Optimal spectral kernel for long-range dependent time series. *Statistics and Probability Letters* **30**, 37–43.

Deo, R.S. and C.M. Hurvich (2001) On the log periodogram regression estimator of the long memory parameter in the long memory stochastic volatility models. *Econometric Theory* **17**, 686–710.

Deo, R.S., C.M. Hurvich and Y. Lu (2005) Forecasting realized volatility using a long-memory stochastic volatility model: estimation, prediction and seasonal adjustment. *Journal of Econometrics*, forthcoming.

Diebold, F.X. and A. Inoue (2001) Long memory and regime switching. *Journal of Econometrics* 105, 131–59.

Diebold, F.X. and G. Rudebush (1989) Long memory and persistence in aggregate output. *Journal of Monetary Economics* 24, 189–209.

Diebold, F.X. and G. Rudebush (1991) Is consumption too smooth? long memory and the Deaton paradox. *Review of Economics and Statistics* 73, 1–9.

Ding, Z., C.W.J. Granger and R. Engle (1993) A long memory property of stock market returns and a new model. *Journal of Empirical Finance* 1, 83–106.

Dittmann, I. (2000) Residual-based tests for fractional cointegration: a Monte Carlo study. *Journal of Time Series Analysis* 21, 614–47.

Dittmann, I. and C.W.J. Granger (2002) Properties of nonlinear transformations of fractionally integrated processes. *Journal of Econometrics* 110, 113–33.

Engle, R. and C.W.J. Granger (1987) Co-integration and error correction: representation, estimation, and testing. *Econometrica* 55, 251–77.

Geweke, J. and S. Porter-Hudak (1983) The estimation and application of long memory time series models. *Journal of Time Series Analysis* 4, 221–38.

Giraitis, L., J. Hidalgo and P.M. Robinson (2001) Gaussian estimation of parametric spectral density with unknown pole. *Annals of Statistics* 29, 987–1023.

Giraitis, L., P. Kokoszka, R. Leipus and G. Teyssière (2000) Semiparametric estimation of the intensity of long memory in conditional heteroskedasticity. *Statistical Inference for Stochastic Processes* 3, 113–28.

Giraitis, L., P.M. Robinson and A. Samarov (1997) Rate optimal semiparametric estimation of the memory parameter of the Gaussian time series with long range dependence. *Journal of Time Series Analysis* 18, 49–60.

Giraitis, L., P.M. Robinson and A. Samarov (2000) Adaptive semiparametric estimation of the memory parameter. *Journal of Multivariate Analysis* 72, 183–207.

Giraitis, L., P.M. Robinson and D. Surgailis (2000) A model for long memory conditional heteroscedasticity. *The Annals of Applied Probability* 10, 1002–1024.

Gourieroux, C. and J. Jasiak (2001) Memory and infrequent breaks. *Economics Letters* 70, 29–41.

Granger, C.W.J. (1981) Some properties of time series data and their use in econometric model specification. *Journal of Econometrics* 16, 121–30.

Granger, C.W.J. and N. Hyung (2004) Occasional structural breaks and long memory with an application to the S&P 500 absolute stock returns. *Journal of Empirical Finance* 11, 399–421.

Granger, C.W.J. and R. Joyeux (1980) An introduction to long-memory time series models and fractional differencing. *Journal of Time Series Analysis* 1, 15–29.

Granger, C.W.J. and T. Teräsvirta (1999). A simple nonlinear time series model with misleading linear properties. *Economics Letters* 62, 161–5.

Gray, H.L., N.F. Zhang and W.A. Woodward (1989) On generalized fractional processes. *Journal of Time Series Analysis* 10, 233–57.

Hall, P., H.L. Koul and B.A. Turlach (1997) Note on convergence rates of semiparametric estimators of dependence index. *Annals of Statistics* 25, 1725–1739.

Hannan, E.J. (1963) Regression for time series with errors of measurement. *Biometrika* 50, 293–302.

Harvey, A.C. (1998) Long memory in stochastic volatility. In J. Knight and S. Satchell (eds), *Forecasting Volatility in the Financial Markets*. London: Butterworth-Heinemann, pp. 307–20.

Hassler, U., F. Marmol and C. Velasco (2003) Residual log-periodogram inference for long run relationships. *Journal of Econometrics*, forthcoming.

Hassler, U. and J. Wolters (1995) Long memory in inflation rates: international evidence. *Journal of Business and Economic Statistics* 13, 37–45.

Hausman, J. (1978) Misspecification tests in econometrics. *Econometrica* **46**, 1251–1271.

Henry, M. (2001) Robust automatic bandwidth for long memory. *Journal of Time Series Analysis* **22**, 293–316.

Henry, M. and P.M. Robinson (1996) Bandwidth choice in Gaussian semiparametric estimation of long range dependence. In P.M. Robinson and M. Rosenblatt (eds), *Athens Conference on Applied Probability and Time Series in Memory of E. J. Hannan*, Volume II. New York: Springer-Verlag.

Henry, M. and P. Zaffaroni (2003) The long range dependence paradigm for macroeconomics and finance. In P. Doukhan, G. Oppenheim and M.S. Taqqu (eds), *Theory and Applications of Long-Range Dependence*. Boston: Birkhäuser.

Heyde, C.C. and Y. Yang. (1997) On defining long-range dependence. *Journal of Applied Probability* **34**, 939–44.

Hidalgo, F.J. (1996) Spectral analysis for bivariate long-memory time series. *Econometric Theory* **12**, 773–92.

Hidalgo, F.J. (2005) Semiparametric estimation for stationary processes whose spectra have an unknown pole. *Annals of Statistics* **33**, 1843–1889.

Hidalgo, F.J. and P.M. Robinson (2002) Adapting to unknown disturbance autocorrelation with long memory. *Econometrica* **70**, 1545–1581.

Hidalgo, J. and P. Soulier (2004) Estimation of the location and exponent of the spectral singularity of a long memory process. *Journal of Time Series Analysis* **25**, 55–81.

Hosking, J.R.M. (1981) Fractional differencing. *Biometrika* **68**, 165–76.

Hosking, J.R.M. (1996) Asymptotic distributions of the sample mean, autocovariances and autocorrelations of long-memory time series. *Journal of Econometrics* **73**, 261–84.

Hosoya, Y. (1997) A limit theory for long-range dependence and statistical inference on related models. *Annals of Statistics* **25**, 105–37.

Hualde, J. and P.M. Robinson (2004) Semiparametric estimation of fractional cointegration. Preprint, Universidad de Navarra.

Hurst, H. (1951) Long term storage capacity of reservoirs. *Transactions of the American Society of Civil Engineers* **116**, 770–99.

Hurvich, C.M. (2001) Model selection for broadband semiparametric estimation of long memory in time series. *Journal of Time Series Analysis* **22**, 679–709.

Hurvich, C.M. and K.I. Beltrao (1994) Automatic semiparametric estimation of the memory parameter of a long memory time series. *Journal of Time Series Analysis* **15**, 285–302.

Hurvich, C.M. and J. Brodsky (2001) Broadband semiparametric estimation of the memory parameter of a long-memory time series using fractional exponential models. *Journal of Time Series Analysis* **22**, 221–49.

Hurvich, C.M. and W. Chen (2000) An efficient taper for potentially overdifferenced long-memory time series. *Journal of Time Series Analysis* **21**, 155–80.

Hurvich, C.M. and R.S. Deo (1999) Plug-in selection of the number of frequencies in regression estimates of the memory parameter of a long memory time series. *Journal of Time Series Analysis* **20**, 331–41.

Hurvich, C.M. and B.K. Ray (1995) Estimation of the memory parameter for nonstationary or noninvertible fractionally integrated processes. *Journal of Time Series Analysis* **16**, 17–41.

Hurvich, C.M. and B. Ray (2003) The local Whittle estimator of long-memory stochastic volatility. *Journal of Financial Econometrics* **1**, 445–70.

Hurvich, C.M. and P. Soulier (2002) Testing for long memory in volatility. *Econometric Theory* **18**, 1291–1308.

Hurvich, C.M., R.S. Deo and J. Brodsky (1998) The mean squared error of Geweke and Porter–Hudak's estimator of the memory parameter of a long-memory time series. *Journal of Time Series Analysis* **19**, 19–46.

Hurvich, C.M., E. Moulines and P. Soulier (2002) The FEXP estimator for potentially non-stationary linear time series. *Stochastic Processes and Their Applications* **97**, 307–40.

Hurvich, C.M., E. Moulines and P. Soulier (2005) Estimating long memory in volatility. *Econometrica*, forthcoming.

Iouditsky, A., E. Moulines and P. Soulier (2002) Adaptive estimation of the fractional differencing coefficient. *Bernoulli* 7, 699–731.

Jensen, M.J. (1999) Using wavelets to obtain a consisten ordinary least squares estimator of the long-memory parameter. *Journal of Forecasting* 18, 17–32.

Kim, C. and P.C.B. Phillips (2000) Modified log periodogram regression. Preprint Department of Economics, Yale University.

Künsch, H.R. (1987) Statistical aspects of self-similar processes. In Y. Prohorov and V.V. Sazarov (eds), *Proceedings of the First World Congress of the Bernoulli Society*, vol. 1. Utrecht: VNU Science Press, pp. 67–74.

Lee, D. and P.M. Robinson (1996) Semiparametric exploration of long memory in stock prices. *Journal of Statistical Planning and Inference* 50, 155–74.

Levy, D. (2003) Cointegration in the frequency domain. *Journal of Time Series Analysis* 23, 333–9.

Lindholdt, P.M. (2002) Sources of seasonal fractional integration in macroeconomic time series. CAF Working Paper 125.

Lo, A. (1991) Long term memory in stock market prices. *Econometrica* 59, 1279–1313.

Lobato, I.N. (1997) Consistency of the averaged cross-periodogram in long memory series. *Journal of Time Series Analysis* 18, 137–55.

Lobato, I.N. (1999) A semiparametric two-step estimator for a multivariate long memory model. *Journal of Econometrics* 90, 129–53.

Lobato, I.N. and P.M. Robinson (1996) Averaged periodogram estimation of long memory. *Journal of Econometrics* 73, 303–24.

Lobato, I.N. and P.M. Robinson (1998) A nonparametric test for I(0). *Review of Economic Studies* 65, 475–95.

Lobato, I.N. and N.E. Savin (1997) Real and spurious long memory in stock market data. *Journal of Business and Economic Statistics* 16, 261–8.

Lobato, I.N. and C. Velasco (2000) Long memory in stock market trading volume. *Journal of Business and Economic Statistics* 18, 410–27.

Mandelbrot, B.B. and J.W. Van Ness (1968) Fractional Brownian motion, fractional noises and applications. *SIAM Review* 10, 422–37.

Mandelbrot, B.B. and J.R. Wallis (1968) Noah, Joseph and operational hydrology. *Water Resources Research* 4, 909–18.

Marinucci, D. (2000) Spectral regression for cointegrated time series with long memory innovations. *Journal of Time Series Analysis* 21, 685–705.

Marinucci, D. and P.M. Robinson (2000) Weak convergence of multivariate fractional processes. *Stochastic Processes and their Applications* 86, 103–120.

Marinucci, D. and P.M. Robinson (2001) Semiparametric fractional cointegration analysis. *Journal of Econometrics* 105, 225–47.

Marmol, F. and C. Velasco (2004) Consistent testing of cointegration relationships. *Econometrica* 72, 1809–1844.

Michelacci, C. and P. Zaffaroni (2000) (Fractional) beta convergence. *Journal of Monetary Economics* 45, 129–53.

Moulines, E. and P. Soulier (1999) Broadband log-periodogram regression of time series with long-range dependence. *Annals of Statistics* 27, 1415–1439.

Nielsen, M.Ø. and K. Shimotsu (2004) Determining the cointegrating rank in non-stationary fractional systems by the exact local Whittle approach. Preprint, Cornell University.

Oppenheim, G., M. Ould Haye and M.C. Viano (2000) Long memory with seasonal effects. *Statistical Inference for Stochastic Processes* 3, 53–68.

Phillips, P.C.B. (1999) Discrete Fourier transforms of fractional processes. Cowles Foundation Discussion Paper no. 1243, Yale University.

Robinson, P.M. (1991) Testing for strong serial-correlation and dynamic conditional heteroskedasticity in multiple-regression. *Journal of Econometrics* **47**, 67–84.

Robinson, P.M. (1994a) Semiparametric analysis of long-memory time series. *Annals of Statistics* **22**, 515–39.

Robinson, P.M. (1994b) Rates of convergence and optimal spectral bandwidth for long range dependence. *Probability Theory and Related Fields* **99**, 443–73.

Robinson, P.M. (1994c) Time series with strong dependence. In C.A. Sims (ed.), *Advances in Econometrics: Sixth World Congress*, vol. 1. Cambridge: Cambridge University Press, pp. 47–96.

Robinson, P.M. (1995a) Log-periodogram regression of time series with long range dependence. *Annals of Statistics* **23**, 1048–1072.

Robinson, P.M. (1995b) Gaussian semiparametric estimation of long range dependence. *Annals of Statistics* **23**, 1630–1661.

Robinson, P.M. (1997) Large sample inference for nonparametric regression with dependent errors. *Annals of Statistics* **25**, 2054–2083.

Robinson, P.M. (2004) The distance between rival nonstationary fractional processes. *Journal of Econometrics*, forthcoming.

Robinson, P.M. (2005) Robust covariance matrix estimation: 'HAC' estimates with long memory/antipersistence correction. *Econometric Theory*, forthcoming.

Robinson, P.M. and M. Henry (1999) Long and short memory conditional heteroscedasticity in estimating the memory parameter of levels. *Econometric Theory* **15**, 299–336.

Robinson, P.M. and M. Henry (2003) Higher-order kernel semiparametric M-estimation of long memory. *Journal of Econometrics* **114**, 1–27.

Robinson, P.M. and J. Hualde (2003) Cointegration in fractional systems with unknown integration orders. *Econometrica* **71**, 1727–1766.

Robinson, P.M. and F. Iacone (2005) Cointegration in fractional systems with deterministic trends. *Journal of Econometrics*, forthcoming.

Robinson, P.M. and D. Marinucci (2000) The averaged periodogram for nonstationary vector time series. *Statistical Inference for Stochastic Processes* **3**, 149–60.

Robinson, P.M. and D. Marinucci (2001) Narrow-band analysis of nonstationary processes. *Annals of Statistics* **29**, 947–86.

Robinson, P.M. and Y. Yajima (2002) Determination of cointegrating rank in fractional systems. *Journal of Econometrics* **106**, 217–41.

Shimotsu, K. (2003) Gaussian semiparametric estimation of multivariate fractionally integrated processes. No. 571, Economics Discussion Papers from University of Essex, Department of Economics.

Shimotsu, K. (2004) Exact local Whittle estimation of fractional integration with unknown mean and time trend. Preprint, Queen's University.

Shimotsu, K. and P.C.B. Phillips (2000) Modified local Whittle estimation of the memory parameter in the nonstationary case. Cowles Foundation Discussion Paper No. 1265, Yale University.

Shimotsu, K. and P.C.B. Phillips (2002) Pooled log-periodogram regression. *Journal of Time Series Analysis* **23**, 57–93.

Shimotsu, K. and P.C.B. Phillips (2004) Local Whittle estimation in nonstationary and unit root cases. *Annals of Statistics* **32**, 656–92.

Shimotsu, K. and P.C.B. Phillips (2005a) Exact local Whittle estimation of fractional integration. *Annals of Statistics* **33**, 1890–1933.

Shimotsu, K. and P.C.B. Phillips (2005b) Local Whittle estimation of fractional integration and some of its variants. *Journal of Econometrics*, forthcoming.

Sinai, Y. G. (1976) Self-similar probability distributions. *Theory of Probability and its Applications* **21**, 64–80.

Sun Y.X. and P.C.B. Phillips (2003) Nonlinear log-periodogram regression for perturbed fractional processes. *Journal of Econometrics* **115**, 355–89.

Taqqu, M.S. (2003) Fractional Brownian motion and long-range dependence. In P. Doukhan, G. Oppenheim and M.S. Taqqu (eds), *Theory and Applications of Long-Range Dependence*. Boston: Birkhäuser.

Twefik, A.H. and M. Kim (1992) Correlation structure of the discrete wavelet coefficients of fractional Brownian motions. *IEEE Transmission on Information Theory* IT-38, 904–9.

Velasco, C. (1999a) Semiparametric Gaussian estimation of non-stationary time series. *Journal of Time Series Analysis* 20, 87–127.

Velasco, C. (1999b) Non-stationary log-periodogram regression. *Journal of Econometrics* 91, 325–71.

Velasco, C. (2000) Non-Gaussian log-periodogram regression. *Econometric Theory* 16, 44–79.

Velasco, C. (2003a) Gaussian semiparametric estimation of fractional cointegration. *Journal of Time Series Analysis* 24, 345–78.

Velasco, C. (2003b) Nonparametric frequency domain analysis of non-stationary multi-variate time series. *Journal of Statistical Planning and Inference* 116, 209–47.

Velasco, C. (2004) The periodogram of fractional processes. Preprint, Universidad Carlos III de Madrid.

Yajima, Y. (1988) On estimation of a regression model with long-memory stationary errors. *Annals of Statistics* 16, 791–807.

Yajima, Y. (1991) Asymptotic properties of the LSE in a regression model with long-memory stationary errors. *Annals of Statistics* 19, 158–77.

Zhurbenko, I.G. (1979) On the efficiency of estimates of a spectral density. *Scandinavian Journal of Statistics* 6, 49–56.

10
Univariate Nonlinear Time Series Models

Timo Teräsvirta

Abstract

In this essay developments in the analysis of univariate nonlinear time series are considered. First a number of commonly used nonlinear models are presented. The next section is devoted to methods of testing linearity, which is an important part of nonlinear model building. Techniques of modeling nonlinear series within a predetermined family of models are discussed thereafter. Forecasting with nonlinear models also has its own section. A brief set of final remarks closes the chapter.

10.1	Introduction	397
10.2	Commonly used nonlinear models	397
	10.2.1 Threshold autoregressive model	398
	10.2.2 Smooth transition autoregressive model	400
	10.2.3 Hidden Markov or Markov-switching autoregressive model	402
	10.2.4 Artificial neural network models	403
	10.2.5 Other models	406
10.3	Testing linearity	408
	10.3.1 Testing linearity against parametric alternatives	408
	10.3.2 Testing linearity against unspecified alternatives	414
10.4	Modeling nonlinear series	415
	10.4.1 Building threshold autoregressive models	416
	10.4.2 Building smooth transition autoregressive models	416
	10.4.3 Building Markov-switching autoregressive models	417
	10.4.4 Building autoregressive single hidden-layer neural network models	417
10.5	Forecasting with nonlinear models	418
	10.5.1 Numerically obtained forecasts	418
	10.5.2 Analytic forecasts	419
10.6	Final remarks	419

10.1 Introduction

Univariate nonlinear time series models do not have a long history in economic analysis. In fact, early nonlinear models applied to economic problems have been multivariate. Switching and Markov-switching regression models may serve as an example. Disequilibrium models constitute another example. Perhaps the first univariate model introduced with economists in mind was the bilinear model that Granger and Andersen (1978) considered in a monograph. The first economic applications of some popular nonlinear models, such as the threshold autoregressive model, smooth transition autoregressive model or the Markov-switching autoregressive model, appeared only after the models had been developed by statisticians and applied to non-economic data. The number of economic applications has been growing steadily, and nonlinear models have been fitted to many macroeconomic and financial time series, both for forecasting and for testing implications of economic theories.

Several surveys of nonlinear time series models exist. Monographs and texts written on the topic include Tong (1990), Granger and Teräsvirta (1993), Guégan (1994) and Franses and van Dijk (2000). Shorter surveys, highlighting different sections of the field, include Brock and Potter (1993), Teräsvirta, Tjøstheim and Granger (1994), Potter (1999), Swanson and Franses (1999), Granger (2001), van Dijk, Teräsvirta and Franses (2002), and Tsay (2002, Chapter 4). This survey is restricted to parametric models. For a recent treatment of nonparametric models, see Fan and Yao (2003). Deterministic processes are another area beyond the scope of consideration here. For more information on deterministic time series and their properties, see, for example, Chatterjee and Yilmaz (1992), Guégan (1994, Chapter 6) or Tong (1995).

This chapter is organized as follows. Some commonly used nonlinear models are presented in section 10.2. Section 10.3 is devoted to methods of testing linearity, which is an important part of nonlinear model building. Techniques of modeling nonlinear series are discussed in Section 10.4 and forecasting with nonlinear models in section 10.5. Section 10.6 contains final remarks.

10.2 Commonly used nonlinear models

There exist a large number of univariate nonlinear models. In this chapter only a few of them that have found application in the analysis of economic time series will be discussed. A popular idea in economic applications has been some form of regime-switching. This means that the data-generating process to be modeled is viewed as a linear process that switches between a number of regimes according to some rule. For example, changes in government policy may instigate a change in regime. As another example, it may be argued that the dynamic properties of the volume of industrial production or gross national product are different in recessions and expansions. In both cases, explaining the behavior of observed series with models with switching regimes would be a possibility. It may also be assumed that there is a continuum of switches, that is, there is a smooth transition from one extreme regime to the other. Some models of this type will be considered as well.

10.2.1   Threshold autoregressive model

10.2.1.1   Definition

The standard self-exciting threshold autoregressive (SETAR) model is defined as follows:

$$y_t = \sum_{j=1}^{r} (\boldsymbol{\alpha}'_j \mathbf{z}_t + \sigma_j \varepsilon_t) I(c_{j-1} < y_{t-d} \le c_j) \tag{10.1}$$

where $\mathbf{z}_t = (1, \mathbf{y}'_{t-1})'$ with $\mathbf{y}_t = (y_t, \ldots, y_{t-p+1})'$, $d > 0$ is the delay parameter (integer), $\boldsymbol{\alpha}_j = (\alpha_{j1}, \ldots, \alpha_{jp})'$, $j = 1, \ldots, r$, are parameter vectors, $c_0, c_1, \ldots, c_r$ are threshold parameters, $c_0 = -\infty$, $c_r = M < \infty$, and $I(A)$ is an indicator function: $I(A) = 1$ when event A occurs; zero otherwise. Furthermore, $\varepsilon_t \sim \text{iid}(0,1)$, and $\sigma_j > 0$, $j = 1, \ldots, r$. It is seen that (10.1) is a piecewise autoregressive model whose switch-points or thresholds are generally unknown. A popular alternative in practice is the two-regime TAR model

$$y_t = (\boldsymbol{\alpha}'_1 \mathbf{z}_t + \sigma_1 \varepsilon_t) I(y_{t-d} \le c_1) + (\boldsymbol{\alpha}'_2 \mathbf{z}_t + \sigma_2 \varepsilon_t)\{1 - I(y_{t-d} \le c_1)\}. \tag{10.2}$$

The SETAR model has been widely applied in economics. A comprehensive account of the model and its statistical properties can be found in Tong (1990). One of the features of this model, as emphasized by Tong, is that at some parameter values it can generate limit cycles. This means that when one takes equation (10.1) and extrapolates assuming that the error terms equal zero, the extrapolated series display oscillations of a given length that do not die out. This feature, however, may be less interesting in economic applications than it is in science. The first applications of the model were to ecological time series and the famous annual sunspot series (see Tong and Lim, 1980), but it has also found wide application in economics.

A special case of the SETAR model, suggested by Enders and Granger (1998) and called the momentum-TAR model, is one with two regimes and where the threshold variable y_{t-d} is replaced by its first difference Δy_{t-d}. This model may be used to characterize processes in which the asymmetry lies in growth rates: as an example, the growth of the series when it occurs may be rapid but the return to a lower level slow. Yet another model of interest is the three-regime model in which the mid-regime describes random walk behavior whereas the outer regimes are stationary in such a way that the whole TAR process is stationary. In the simple first-order form,

$$y_t = \alpha_j y_{t-1} + \varepsilon_t \tag{10.3}$$

where the mid-regime is defined by $c_1 < y_{t-1} < c_2$; typically $c_1 < 0$ and $c_2 = -c_1$. In this regime the autoregressive parameter $\alpha_2 = 1$, whereas $\alpha_j < 1$, $j = 1, 3$. For more discussion see Balke and Fomby (1997), who use this model to define *threshold cointegration*. In this context it is often assumed, as is done in (10.3), that the error variance is constant across regimes.

The SETAR model with two regimes (one threshold) is capable of characterizing asymmetric behavior. As an example, suppose that y_{t-d} measures the phase of the business cycle. Then the SETAR model can describe processes whose dynamic properties are different in expansions from what they are in recessions; see Potter (1995) and Peel and Speight (1998). A further refinement would be a model with more than two regimes to describe different phases of the business cycle; see Tiao and Tsay (1994) for a four-regime model. These authors assume, however, that the threshold parameters in this model are known.

As a historical note, it may be interesting to observe that the switching regression model, a multivariate single-equation counterpart of the SETAR model, had already been considered before the appearance of the SETAR model in the time series literature. The reader may consult Quandt (1958) or Goldfeld and Quandt (1973a) for more information.

There is a related model that has become popular in time series econometrics. It is obtained from the standard SETAR model by replacing the transition variable y_{t-d} by time t or standardized time t/T, where T is the number of observations. This model is an autoregression with $r-1$ breaks. There is a growing literature on determining the number of breaks and estimating the break-points $c_1, \ldots, c_r$; see, for example, Bai (1997).

10.2.1.2 Estimation

The SETAR model is piecewise linear and can therefore be estimated using ordinary least squares as follows. First arrange the values of the threshold variable in ascending order and remove the k smallest and largest values such that k/T is small, say 0.15. Denote the sequence of these values $\{y_{t-d}^{(k+1)}, \ldots, y_{t-d}^{(T-k)}\}$. Then estimate the regimes using an arbitrary value between $y_{t-d}^{(k+j)}$ and $y_{t-d}^{(k+j+1)}, j=1, \ldots, T-2k-1$, as the value of the threshold variable and compute the sum of squared residuals. The estimates minimizing the residual sum of squares over $j=1, \ldots, T-2k-1$ are the final least squares estimates.

Consistent estimation of the parameters of the SETAR model requires weak stationarity and ergodicity of y_t. Necessary and sufficient conditions for weak stationarity and ergodicity of SETAR models exist for the first-order SETAR model (10.2); see Tong (1990) for discussion. Chan (1993) proved the consistency of the least squares estimator of the parameters of (10.2) under the assumption of stationarity and ergodicity. He showed that assuming $\max_i \sum_{j=1}^{p} |\alpha_{ij}| < 1$ and that ε_t is absolutely continuous with a positive probability density everywhere is sufficient for this result to hold. It is seen that the condition on the coefficients of the model is quite restrictive for $p > 1$, and many obviously stable models do not satisfy it. Chan also showed that, under certain regularity conditions, the least squares estimator of the parameters $\boldsymbol{\alpha}_1$ and $\boldsymbol{\alpha}_2$ is consistent and the estimator of c_1 super-consistent. There is an exception, the continuous two-regime SETAR model. Chan and Tsay (1998) proved that in this model, $\hat{c}_1$ is only root-T consistent for c_1.

10.2.2　Smooth transition autoregressive model

10.2.2.1　*Exponential autoregressive model*

An early example of a nonlinear model that can be interpreted as a model with a continuum of switches is the exponential autoregressive (EAR) model that Haggan and Ozaki (1981) introduced. It has the form

$$
\begin{aligned}
y_t &= \boldsymbol{\phi}' \mathbf{z}_t + \boldsymbol{\theta}' \mathbf{z}_t G_E(\gamma, \ y_{t-1}) + \varepsilon_t \\
&= \{\boldsymbol{\phi} + \boldsymbol{\theta} G_E(\gamma, \ y_{t-1})\}' \mathbf{z}_t + \varepsilon_t
\end{aligned}
\tag{10.4}
$$

where $\mathbf{z}_t$ is defined as in (10.1), $\boldsymbol{\phi} = (\phi_0, \ \phi_1, \ \ldots, \ \phi_p)'$ and $\boldsymbol{\theta} = (\theta_0, \ \theta_1, \ldots, \ \theta_p)'$ are parameter vectors such that $\phi_0 = \theta_0 = 0$, so the model does not contain an intercept, and $\varepsilon_t \sim \mathrm{iid}(0, \ \sigma^2)$. Furthermore, the transition function is

$$
G_E(\gamma, \ y_{t-1}) = \exp\{-\gamma y_{t-1}^2\}, \ \gamma > 0.
\tag{10.5}
$$

The function (10.5) is symmetric around zero, where it obtains the value one, and $G_E(\gamma, \ y_{t-1}) \to 0$ as $|y_{t-1}| \to \infty$. The last expression in (10.4) indicates that the model can be interpreted as a linear autoregressive model with stochastic time-varying coefficients $\boldsymbol{\phi} + \boldsymbol{\theta} G_E(\gamma, \ y_{t-d})$. The idea of the authors was to construct a model that could generate nonlinear random vibrations. The EAR model is also capable of generating limit cycles. When $\gamma \to 0$, the model becomes linear, but note that the same also happens when $\gamma \to \infty$. In that case, $G_E(\gamma, \ y_{t-1}) = 0$ except for $y_{t-1} = 0$. Haggan and Ozaki (1981) fitted the EAR model to one of the classic nonlinear time series, the annual series of furs of Canadian lynx auctioned in London. Tong (1990) contains a thorough discussion of this series and the nonlinear models fitted to it.

The EAR model may be generalized by allowing an intercept: $\phi_0 \neq 0$ or $\theta_0 \neq 0$ or both. Another generalization is to drop the requirement of symmetry of the transition function (10.5) around zero by adding a location parameter c and to allow the delay $d \geq 1$:

$$
G(\gamma, \ c, \ y_{t-d}) = 1 - \exp\{-\gamma(y_{t-d} - c)^2\}, \quad \gamma > 0.
\tag{10.6}
$$

Teräsvirta (1994) called the generalized EAR model the exponential smooth transition autoregressive (ESTAR) model. The ESTAR model has been a popular tool in investigating the validity of the purchasing power parity hypothesis; see, for example, the survey by Taylor and Sarno (2002). It has also been successfully used to model macroeconomic series such as strongly fluctuating inflation series; see Arango and González (2001).

10.2.2.2　*Logistic smooth transition autoregressive model*

The smooth transition model originated in the work of Bacon and Watts (1971). These authors considered two regression lines and devised a model in which the transition from one line to the other is smooth. Their model was not a time series model, but a pure regression model with independent observations. Bacon and Watts (1971) used the hyperbolic tangent function to characterize the transition. This function is close to both the cumulative distribution function of the standard normal variable and the logistic function. Maddala (1977, p. 396) in fact recommended the use of the logistic as a transition function, and this has become the standard choice.

The smooth transition autoregressive (STAR) model was introduced into the time series literature by Chan and Tong (1986), who used the cumulative distribution function of the standard normal variable as the transition function. Replacing this function by the (possibly generalized) logistic results in the logistic smooth transition autoregressive (LSTAR) model. It is defined by equation (10.4), where the transition function is now the (generalized) logistic function

$$G(\gamma, \mathbf{c}, y_{t-d}) = \left(1 + \exp\left\{-\gamma \prod_{k=1}^{K}(y_{t-d} - c_k)\right\}\right)^{-1}, \quad \gamma > 0 \qquad (10.7)$$

In (10.7), parameter γ is the slope parameter and $\mathbf{c} = (c_1, \ldots, c_K)'$ is a vector of location parameters, $c_1 \leq \cdots \leq c_K$. These restrictions, as well as restricting γ to be positive, are needed to identify the model. The transition function is a bounded function of y_{t-d}, continuous everywhere in the parameter space for any value of y_{t-d}. The most common choices for K in (10.7) are $K = 1$ and $K = 2$. Setting $K = 1$ yields the standard logistic function. In this case the parameters $\phi + \theta G(\gamma, \mathbf{c}, y_{t-d})$ change monotonically as a function of y_{t-d} from ϕ to $\phi + \theta$. For $K = 2$, they change symmetrically around the mid-point $(c_1 + c_2)/2$ where this logistic function attains its minimum value. The minimum lies between zero and $\frac{1}{2}$. It reaches zero when $\gamma \to \infty$ and equals $\frac{1}{2}$ when $c_1 = c_2$ and $\gamma < \infty$.

When $\gamma = 0$, the transition function $G(\gamma, \mathbf{c}, y_{t-d}) \equiv 1/2$, in which case the LSTAR model becomes a linear model. When $K = 1$ and $\gamma \to \infty$ the LSTAR model approaches the SETAR model (10.2) with $\sigma_1 = \sigma_2$. When $K = 2$, $c_1 \neq c_2$, and $\gamma \to \infty$, the LSTAR model approaches the SETAR model with three regimes such that the outer regimes are identical and the mid-regime is different from the other two.

Teräsvirta (1994) defined a family of STAR models that included both the LSTAR and the ESTAR model and devised a data-driven modeling strategy with the aim of, among other things, helping the user to choose between these two alternatives. Alternatively, the same strategy applies to choosing between the LSTAR models with $K = 1$ and $K = 2$.

Substituting time for y_{t-d} in (10.7) yields a smooth transition model that is called the time-varying autoregressive (TV-AR) model. Analogous to the corresponding modification of the SETAR model, the TV-AR model has a role to play, among other things, in testing parameter constancy in linear autoregressive models; see Lin and Teräsvirta (1994). In this case, smoothly changing parameters form the alternative to the null hypothesis. The piecewise linear model with breaks is nested in this more general alternative.

The LSTAR model has been applied to macroeconomic series with asymmetric behavior, such as industrial production and unemployment. For examples of the former see, for instance, Öcal and Osborn (2000) and Teräsvirta, and Anderson (1992) and for the latter, Skalin and Teräsvirta (2002).

10.2.2.3   *Estimation of STAR models*

Both ESTAR and LSTAR models can be estimated by (conditional) maximum likelihood. The log-likelihood function satisfies the standard regularity conditions. The properties of the maximum likelihood estimators, such as consistency, how-ever, are not generally known because useful necessary and sufficient conditions of geometric ergodicity do not exist. Sufficient conditions exist, see Chen and Tsay (1993), but, as in the case of the SETAR model, they are not satisfied for all models that seem stable and are uninteresting from the practical point of view.

Estimation of STAR models is straightforward but numerical problems may occur when the slope parameter γ is large. The problem is that when the transition is rapid, accurate estimation of γ requires a lot of observations in a small neigh-borhood of c, the location parameter. Furthermore, having γ of much higher order of magnitude than the other parameters slows down the rate of convergence of the optimization algorithm. See Bates and Watts (1988, p. 87), Seber and Wild (1989, pp. 480–1) and Teräsvirta (1994) for discussion.

Leybourne, Newbold and Vougas (1998) pointed out that estimation may be made more efficient by making use of the fact that, when γ and c are fixed, the model is linear in parameters. In that case, parameters ϕ and θ can be estimated by linear least squares. Conditioning on these estimates, one can obtain the next estimates for γ and c. Splitting each iteration into these two steps considerably reduces the dimension of the nonlinear estimation problem and speeds up convergence.

10.2.3   Hidden Markov or Markov-switching autoregressive model

10.2.3.1   *Definitions*

In the SETAR model (10.4) the threshold variable is an observable continuous variable. It may also be an unobservable variable that obtains a finite number of discrete values and is independent of y_t at all lags, as in Goldfeld and Quandt (1973b) and Lindgren (1978). A univariate variant of such a model may be called the autoregressive Markov-switching (AR-MS), or hidden Markov, model. Tyssedal and Tjøstheim (1988) called it the suddenly changing autoregressive (SCAR) model. The AR-MS model is defined by the following equation:

$$y_t = \sum_{j=1}^{r} \alpha'_j \mathbf{z}_t I(s_t = j) + \varepsilon_t \qquad (10.8)$$

where $\{s_t\}$ is a Markov chain with a finite state space consisting of r states, often of order one. If the order equals one, the conditional probability of the event $s_t = i$ given s_{t-k}, $k \geq 1$, equals

$$\Pr\{s_t = i | s_{t-1} = j\} = p_{ij}, \qquad i, j = 1, \ldots, r \qquad (10.9)$$

such that $\sum_{i=1}^{r} p_{ij} = 1$. The transition probabilities p_{ij} are unknown and have to be estimated from the data. The error process ε_t is usually assumed not to be dependent on the "regime" or the value of s_t, but the model may be generalized to incorporate that possibility.

There exists another autoregressive Markov-switching model, proposed by Hamilton (1989), that is more common in econometric applications than the SCAR model. In this model, the intercept is time-varying and determined by the value of the latent variable s_t and its lags. It has the form

$$y_t = \mu_{s_t} + \sum_{j=1}^{p} \alpha_j(y_{t-j} - \mu_{s_{t-j}}) + \varepsilon_t \qquad (10.10)$$

where the behavior of s_t is defined by (10.9), and μ_{s_t} can obtain r discrete values $\mu^{(1)}, \ldots, \mu^{(r)}$. For identification reasons, y_{t-j} and $\mu_{s_{t-j}}$ in (10.10) share the same coefficient. The intercept of this model, $\mu_{s_t} - \sum_{j=1}^{p} \alpha_j \mu_{s_{t-j}}$, can thus obtain r^{p+1} different values, and this gives the model the desired flexibility. A comprehensive discussion of Markov-switching models can be found in Hamilton (1994, chapter 22). They may be applied when the data can be conveniently thought of as having been generated by a model with different regimes such that the regime changes do not have an observable or quantifiable cause. They may also be used when data on the switching variable is not available and no suitable proxy can be found.

The MS-AR model defined in (10.10) has been fitted to many macroeconomic series. Hamilton (1989) considered quarterly post-World War II US GNP, but monthly interest rates have also been a popular application. The model has been generalized to the situation where the transition probabilities are functions of observable quantitites and are thus time-varying. This generalization has been used in modeling US GNP when the time-varying transition probabilities are functions of the NBER business cycle indicator; see Filardo (1994).

10.2.3.2 Estimation

Estimation of Markov-switching models is more complicated than estimation of SETAR or STAR models. This is because the model contains two unobservable processes: the regime indicator that follows a Markov chain and the iid error process ε_t. Hamilton (1993, 1994, chapter 22), among others, discusses maximum likelihood estimation of parameters in this framework. The estimation of the AR-MS model can be carried out by applying the EM algorithm (see Dempster, Laird and Rubin, 1977), that switches between the estimation of transition probabilities p_{ij} and the other parameters. For details, see, for example, Hamilton (1993).

10.2.4 Artificial neural network models

Another nonlinear model that has been frequently applied in practice is the artificial neural network (ANN) model. Many textbooks have been written about these models: see, for example, Fine (1999) or Haykin (1999). For a compact presentation, see White (1989). The discussion here is restricted to the auto-regressive "single hidden-layer" model. It has the following form

$$y_t = f_q(z_t; \theta) + \varepsilon_t = \beta_0' z_t + \sum_{j=1}^{q} \beta_j G(\gamma_j' z_t) + \varepsilon_t \qquad (10.11)$$

where z_t is defined as before, $\theta = (\beta_0', \beta_1, \ldots, \beta_q, \gamma_1', \ldots, \gamma_q')'$, $\beta_0' z_t$ is a linear unit, and β_j, $j = 1, \ldots, q$, are parameters, called "connection strengths" in the neural network literature. Many neural network modelers exclude the linear unit alto-gether, but it is a useful component in time series applications. Furthermore, $G(.)$ is a bounded function called the "squashing function" and γ_j, $j = 1, \ldots, q$, are parameter vectors. Typical squashing functions are monotonically increasing ones, such as the logistic and the hyperbolic tangent functions, and thus have the same form as the transition functions of STAR models. The so-called radial basis functions that resemble density functions are another possibility. The errors ε_t are most often assumed iid$(0, \sigma^2)$. The term "hidden layer" refers to the structure of (10.11). While the output y_t and the input vector z_t are observed, the linear combination $\sum_{j=1}^{q} \beta_j G(\gamma_j' z_t)$ is not. It thus forms a hidden layer between the "output layer" y_t and "input layer" z_t.

A theoretical argument motivating the use of neural network models is that they are universal approximators. Suppose that $y_t = H(z_t)$, that is, there exists a func-tional relationship between y_t and z_t. Then, under mild regularity conditions for H, for any given $\delta > 0$ there exists a positive integer q_0 such that, for any integer $q > q_0$, $|H(z_t) - \sum_{j=1}^{q} \beta_j G(\gamma_j' z_t)| < \delta$. The importance of this result lies in the fact that q is finite, whereby any unknown function H can be approximated arbitrarily accurately by a linear combination of squashing functions $G(\gamma_j' z_t)$. This has been discussed in several papers, including Cybenko (1989), Funahashi (1989), Hornik, Stinchombe and White (1989) and White (1990). The autoregressive neural net-work (AR-NN) model thus has the same flavor as nonparametric models that lie outside the scope of this chapter.

A statistical property separating the artificial neural network (10.11) from other nonlinear time series models, and which is due to its flexibility, is that it is only locally identified. It is seen from equation (10.11) that the hidden units are exchangeable. For example, letting any $(\beta_i, \gamma_i')'$ and $(\beta_j, \gamma_j')'$, $i \neq j$, change places in the equation does not affect the value of the likelihood function. Thus for $q > 1$ there always exists more than one observationally equivalent parameterization, which means that additional parameter restrictions are required for global identification. Furthermore, the sign of one element in each γ_j the first one, say, has to be fixed in advance to exclude observationally equivalent parameteri-zations. The identification restrictions are discussed, for example, in Hwang and Ding (1997).

Stationarity of the AR-NN model is only dependent on the parameters of the linear unit. If and only if the roots of the lag polynomial $1 - \sum_{j=1}^{p} \beta_{0j} L^j$ are outside the unit circle, (10.11) is stationary; see Trapletti, Leisch and Hornik (2000).

The most successful applications of neural networks have not been to economic time series, although they have been applied to both macroeconomic and financial series. The AR-NN model has been used for economic forecasting, however, and its performance has been investigated in large forecasting comparisons such as Stock and Watson (1999) and Teräsvirta, van Dijk and Medeiros (2005).

10.2.4.1 Estimation

The rich parameterization of ANN models makes the estimation of parameters by maximum likelihood difficult. The log-likelihood function typically has many local maxima, and finding good starting-values for the estimation algorithm is essential. Even then, convergence problems are likely to occur. Finding computationally feasible shortcuts has been important. One such shortcut has been back-propagation. In this algorithm, the *i*th iteration yields the following value of θ:

$$\hat{\theta}_i = \hat{\theta}_{i-1} + \lambda \sum_{t=1}^{T} \varepsilon_t(\hat{\theta}_{i-1}) \frac{\partial f(z_t; \hat{\theta}_{i-1})}{\partial \theta} \tag{10.12}$$

where $\hat{\theta}_{i-1}$ is the previous value, $\varepsilon_t(\hat{\theta}_{i-1}) = y_t - f(z_t; \hat{\theta}_{i-1})$ and λ is the steplength; in this context it is called the learning rate. The back-propagation step (10.12) bears some resemblance to the steepest descent, the difference being that the *t*th element in the sum forming the gradient is weighted according to how $f(z_t; \hat{\theta}_{i-1})$ predicts y_t. White (1989) showed that, under certain regularity conditions, it yields consistent and asymptotically normal estimates.

Recently, White (in press) suggested a pragmatic method of estimating AR-NN models. The idea is that, to save computations, the parameters γ_j, $j = 1, \ldots, q$, are assumed fixed so that the model is only linear in variables, not in parameters. Suppose one has estimated model (10.11) with q hidden units. If

$$E\{y_t | Z_t\} - f_q(z_t; \theta) \neq 0$$

with a positive probability, then for almost every $\gamma \in \Gamma$, where Γ is a compact set, one has

$$EG(\gamma' z_t)\varepsilon_t \neq 0.$$

As Γ is compact, one can choose $\hat{\gamma}_{q+1}$ such that

$$|\text{corr}(G(\hat{\gamma}'_{q+1}z_t), \varepsilon_t)| \geq |\text{corr}(G(\gamma' z_t), \varepsilon_t)|$$

for all $\gamma \in \Gamma$. The trick that saves computations is to select $\hat{\gamma}_{q+1}$ from a subset $\Gamma_m \subset \Gamma$ where m is large. Full optimization is avoided by maximizing the correlation over Γ_m instead of Γ and adding the hidden unit to the AR-NN model if $|\text{corr}(G(\hat{\gamma}'_{q+1}z_t), \varepsilon_t)|$ exceeds a predetermined bound. White has developed an algorithm called QuickNet that operates on this principle; see White (in press) for details.

10.2.5   Other models

10.2.5.1   *Bilinear model*

The models hitherto discussed are pure autoregressive models. A model with a moving average component that has attracted some attention is the bilinear model

$$y_t = \phi_0 + \sum_{j=1}^{p} \phi_j y_{t-j} + \sum_{j=1}^{r} \sum_{k=1}^{s} \gamma_{jk} y_{t-j} \varepsilon_{t-k} + \varepsilon_t \tag{10.13}$$

where $\varepsilon_t \sim$ iid$(0, \sigma^2)$. Properties of this model have been studied extensively. Due to the moving average terms, invertibility of the model is an issue. Invertibility conditions for (10.13) have only been derived in a few special cases. Granger and Andersen (1978) and Subba Rao and Gabr (1984) give detailed treatments of bilinear models, including estimation and invertibility conditions. The bilinear model generates realizations that display occasional deviating observations that would be difficult to distinguish from outliers.

The bilinear model has not turned out to be very successful in economic applications. The only application perhaps worth mentioning is Maravall (1983), who fitted a bilinear model to a Spanish 10-day time series of currency in circulation, appropriately differenced, and reported improved forecasting performance over a linear ARMA model. The interpretation of Maravall is that the bilinear model smooths out a couple of outliers in the series, but otherwise does not contribute anything extra compared to linear models.

10.2.5.2   *Random coefficient autoregressive models*

One way of generalizing linear models is to replace the assumption that the parameters of the model be constant by assuming that they are stochastic. The simplest alternative is that the parameters form a sequence of independent identically distributed random variables. This yields the following model:

$$y_t = \alpha_0 + \boldsymbol{\alpha}_t' \mathbf{y}_{t-1} + \varepsilon_t \tag{10.14}$$

where $\mathbf{y}_t = (y_t, \ldots, y_{t-p+1})'$, $\{\boldsymbol{\alpha}_t\} \sim$ iid $(\boldsymbol{\alpha}, \ )$ with   a positive definite matrix and $\varepsilon_t \sim$ iid$(0, \sigma^2)$. Furthermore, cov$(\boldsymbol{\alpha}_t, \varepsilon_s) = 0$ for all t and s. Equation (10.14) defines a random coefficient autoregressive model of order p. Writing $\boldsymbol{\alpha}_t = \boldsymbol{\alpha} + \boldsymbol{\phi}_t$, where $\mathsf{E}\boldsymbol{\phi}_t = 0$, this equation can be reformulated as

$$y_t = \alpha_0 + \boldsymbol{\alpha}' \mathbf{y}_{t-1} + v_t \tag{10.15}$$

where $v_t = \varepsilon_t + \phi_t' z_t$. Equation (10.15) is often called a "linear model with conditional heteroskedasticity," as $E(v_t | z_t) = 0$ and

$$\text{var}(v_t | z_t) = \sigma^2 + z_t' z_t = \sigma^2 + \sigma' s_t$$

where $\sigma = (\sigma_1, \ldots, \sigma_{m(m+1)/2})'$ and $s_t = \text{vech}(z_t z_t')$. The Lagrange multiplier test of the hypothesis $\sigma = 0$ is the well-known White (1980) heteroskedasticity test. It can also be interpreted as a test of constant coefficients in (10.14)

Another random coefficient model occasionally appearing in economic applications is one where the stochastic coefficients follow a vector random walk process. This model belongs to the set of alternative hypotheses in the parameter constancy test of Nyblom (1989). For an example, see Marcellino (2004), who includes this model in his comparison of forecasting methods. A detailed treatment of random coefficient autoregressive models can be found in Nicholls and Quinn (1982).

10.2.5.3 Nonlinear moving average models

Nonlinear autoregressive models have been quite popular among practitioners, but nonlinear moving average models have also been proposed in the literature. A rather general nonlinear moving average model of order q may be defined as follows:

$$y_t = f(\varepsilon_{t-1}, \varepsilon_{t-2}, \ldots, \varepsilon_{t-q}; \theta) + \varepsilon_t$$

where $\{\varepsilon_t\} \sim \text{iid}(0, \sigma^2)$. A problem with these models is that their invertibility conditions may not be known, in which case the models cannot be used for forecasting. A common property of moving average models is that, if the model is invertible, forecasts from it for more than q steps ahead equal the unconditional mean of y_t. Some nonlinear moving average models are linear in parameters, which makes forecasting with them easy, in the sense that no numerical techniques are required when forecasting several steps ahead. As an example of a nonlinear moving average model, consider the asymmetric moving average (asMA) model of Wecker (1981). It has the form

$$y_t = \mu + \sum_{j=1}^{q} \theta_j \varepsilon_{t-j} + \sum_{j=1}^{q} \psi_j I(\varepsilon_{t-j} > 0)\varepsilon_{t-j} + \varepsilon_t \qquad (10.16)$$

when $I(\varepsilon_{t-j} > 0) = 1$ when $\varepsilon_{t-j} > 0$ and zero otherwise, and $\{\varepsilon_t\} \sim \text{nid}(0, \sigma^2)$. This model has the property that the effects of a positive shock and a negative shock of the same size on y_t are not symmetric when $\psi_j \neq 0$ for at least one j, $j = 1, \ldots, q$. Brännäs and De Gooijer (1994) extended (10.16) to contain a linear autoregressive part and called the model an autoregressive asymmetric moving average (ARasMA) model. They applied the model to a set of quarterly industrial production series and found asymmetry in a number of them.

10.3   Testing linearity

Testing linearity is important as a preliminary stage of modeling with nonlinear models. It is important because, if the null hypothesis is not rejected, a linear autoregressive model may be fitted to the series. This often implies a considerable simplification compared to fitting a fully-fledged nonlinear model. Besides, many nonlinear models, including the TAR, STAR and MS-AR models, are only identified when the alternative hypothesis holds (the model is genuinely nonlinear), but not when the null hypothesis is valid. Since the parameters of an unidentified model cannot be estimated consistently, testing linearity before fitting any of these models is an unavoidable step in nonlinear modeling.

There exists a vast literature on testing linearity in time series, and it is not possible to highlight all developments in this chapter. In the following it is assumed that the nonlinear model nests a linear one; tests of nonnested hypotheses will not be considered. Linearity tests may be divided into two main categories. The first category contains tests against a well-specified parametric nonlinear model such as a TAR or STAR model. The second category contains tests that have been developed without a parametric nonlinear alternative in mind. Only a few examples of commonly applied tests in each category will be discussed here.

10.3.1   Testing linearity against parametric alternatives

10.3.1.1   *Standard case*

Consider the following additive autoregressive nonlinear model

$$y_t = \boldsymbol{\beta}' \mathbf{z}_t + G(\mathbf{z}_t; \gamma) + \varepsilon_t, \quad t = 1, \ldots, T \tag{10.17}$$

where $\mathbf{z}_t = (1, y_{t-1}, \ldots, y_{t-p})'$ as before, $\boldsymbol{\beta} = (\beta_0, \beta_1, \ldots, \beta_p)'$ is a $(p+1) \times 1$ parameter vector, and $\varepsilon_t \sim \mathrm{nid}(0, \sigma^2)$. Furthermore, $G(\mathbf{z}_t; \gamma)$ is at least twice continuously differentiable for all $\mathbf{z}_t \in \mathcal{Z}$ (sample space) and all values of the $m \times 1$ parameter vector γ. For example, $G(\mathbf{z}_t; \gamma) = \exp\{\gamma' \mathbf{z}_t\} - 1$. Assume, for notational simplicity, that $G(\mathbf{z}_t; 0) = 0$ and $G(\mathbf{z}_t; \gamma) \neq 0$ for any $\gamma \neq 0$. The linearity hypothesis is thus $\gamma = 0$. From (10.17) it appears that the best way of testing the hypothesis is to apply the Lagrange multiplier (LM) or score principle because that only requires the estimation of the linear model. The first paper to point this out and to develop LM linearity tests was Pagan (1978).

In order to derive the test we need the log-likelihood function of (10.17). Setting $\theta = (\boldsymbol{\beta}', \gamma')'$, it can be written as

$$L_T(\theta) = c - (T/2) \ln \sigma^2 - (1/2\sigma^2) \sum_{t=1}^{T} (y_t - \boldsymbol{\beta}' \mathbf{z}_t - G(\mathbf{z}_t; \gamma))^2.$$

The average score evaluated at $\gamma = 0$ equals

$$s_T(\theta) = [\partial L_T/\partial\beta' \quad \partial L_T/\partial\gamma']' = (\tilde{\sigma}^2 T)^{-1} \sum_{t=1}^{T} \tilde{\varepsilon}_t (0'_{k+1}, \ (h_t^0)')'$$

where $\tilde{\varepsilon}_t = y_t - \tilde{\beta}' z_t$, $\tilde{\beta}$ is the maximum likelihood estimator of β under H_0, $\tilde{\sigma}^2 = T^{-1} \sum_{t=1}^{T} \tilde{\varepsilon}_t^2$ and $h_t^0 = \partial G(z_t; \gamma)/\partial\gamma|_{\gamma=0}$. The second partial derivatives of the likelihood function are

$$\frac{\partial^2 L_T(\theta)}{\partial\beta\partial\beta'} = -(1/\sigma^2) \sum_{t=1}^{T} z_t z_t'$$

$$\frac{\partial^2 L_T(\theta)}{\partial\gamma\partial\gamma'} = -(1/\sigma^2) \sum_{t=1}^{T} \left(h_t h_t' + \varepsilon_t \frac{\partial^2 G(z_t; \gamma)}{\partial\gamma\partial\gamma'} \right)$$

$$\frac{\partial^2 L_T(\theta)}{\partial\beta\partial\gamma'} = -(1/\sigma^2) \sum_{t=1}^{T} z_t h_t'$$

where $h_t = \partial G(z_t; \gamma)/\partial\gamma$. This suggests the following consistent estimator for the population information matrix $I(\theta)$:

$$\tilde{I}_T(\tilde{\theta}) = (1/\tilde{\sigma}^2) \begin{bmatrix} T^{-1}\sum_{t=1}^{T} z_t z_t' & T^{-1}\sum_{t=1}^{T} z_t (h_t^0)' \\ T^{-1}\sum_{t=1}^{T} h_t^0 z_t' & T^{-1}\sum_{t=1}^{T} h_t^0 (h_t^0)' \end{bmatrix}.$$

In matrix form, the LM statistic can thus be written as

$$LM = (1/\tilde{\sigma}^2)\tilde{\varepsilon}' H (H'H - H'Z(Z'Z)^{-1}Z'H)^{-1} H'\tilde{\varepsilon} \qquad (10.18)$$

where $Z = (z_1', \ldots, z_T')'$, $H = ((h_1^0)', \ldots, (h_T^0)')'$ and $\tilde{\varepsilon} = (\tilde{\varepsilon}_1, \ldots, \tilde{\varepsilon}_T)'$. Under H_0, statistic (10.18) has an asymptotic χ^2 distribution with m degrees of freedom. It is exactly the same statistic as the one obtained for testing the null hypothesis $=0$ in the linear model

$$y = Z\beta + H\delta + \varepsilon \qquad (10.19)$$

where $y = (y_1, \ldots, y_T)'$. Another way of viewing the test is that it has been obtained after linearization of (10.17) by a first-order Taylor expansion around the null hypothesis. This suggests that there may be several models leading to the same LM test.

The LM approach does not work in situations where $h_t = z_t$ or a subvector of z_t. As an example, consider model (10.17) such that $G(\cdot)$ is an exponential function:

$$y_t = \beta' z_t + (\exp\{\gamma' z_t\} - 1) + \varepsilon_t, \quad t = 1, \ldots, T. \qquad (10.20)$$

Linearization around the null hypothesis $\gamma = 0$ leads to (10.19) with $H = Z$. In this situation one must estimate the maintained model and apply the Wald or likelihood ratio principle to carry out the test.

It is well-known that the LM test can also be carried out by two regressions. This form of the test is often called the TR^2 form; see Engle (1982) for details. Following Wooldridge (1990), this test can easily be robustified against heteroskedasticity of unspecified form.

10.3.1.2 Identification problem

A common characteristic in nonlinear models, such as the TAR, STAR or MS-AR model, is that they nest a linear model and are not identified if linearity holds. Consider the following additive nonlinear autoregressive model

$$y_t = \boldsymbol{\beta}_0' \mathbf{z}_t + \boldsymbol{\beta}_1' \mathbf{z}_t G(\boldsymbol{\gamma}; \mathbf{s}_t) + \varepsilon_t = (\boldsymbol{\beta}_0 + \boldsymbol{\beta}_1 G(\boldsymbol{\gamma}; \mathbf{s}_t))' \mathbf{z}_t + \varepsilon_t \tag{10.21}$$

where $\{\varepsilon_t\} \sim \text{iid}(0, \sigma^2)$, $\boldsymbol{\beta}_0$ and $\boldsymbol{\beta}_1$ are $(p+1) \times 1$ parameter vectors and $\boldsymbol{\gamma}$ is an $r \times 1$ parameter vector. Function $G(\boldsymbol{\gamma}; \mathbf{s}_t)$ is a bounded scalar function of another set of variables $\mathbf{s}_t$ that can be either stochastic or deterministic. Often $\mathbf{s}_t$ is a scalar and is simply an element of $\mathbf{z}_t$ other than the intercept. Special cases of (10.21) include the TAR model with two regimes, the STAR model and the two-regime MS-AR model. It also includes a linear AR model with a single structural break. The model is linear when $\boldsymbol{\beta}_1 = 0$. When this is the case, the parameter vector $\boldsymbol{\gamma}$ is not identified and is a nuisance parameter. It can take any value without the value of the likelihood of the process being affected. Thus, estimating $\boldsymbol{\beta}_0$, $\boldsymbol{\beta}_1$ and $\boldsymbol{\gamma}$ consistently from (10.21) is not possible. The main consequence of this is that the standard asymptotic theory is not available because it requires consistent estimation of the parameters of the model.

10.3.1.3 Nuisance parameter-free statistics

The problem of testing a null hypothesis when the model is only identified under the alternative was first considered by Davies (1977). The general idea is the following. As discussed above, the model is identified when $\boldsymbol{\gamma}$ is known, and testing linearity of (10.21) is straightforward. Let $S_T(\boldsymbol{\gamma})$ be the corresponding test statistic whose large values are critical and define $\Gamma = \{\boldsymbol{\gamma} : \boldsymbol{\gamma} \in \Gamma\}$, the set of admissible values of $\boldsymbol{\gamma}$. When $\boldsymbol{\gamma}$ is unknown, the statistic is not operational because it is a function of $\boldsymbol{\gamma}$. Davies (1977) suggested that the problem be solved by defining another statistic $S_T = \sup_{\boldsymbol{\gamma} \in \Gamma} S_T(\boldsymbol{\gamma})$ that is no longer a function of $\boldsymbol{\gamma}$. This is a conservative choice as the underlying question is: how large can the value of the test statistic $S_T(\boldsymbol{\gamma})$ be for $\boldsymbol{\gamma} \in \Gamma$ such that the null hypothesis still holds? The asymptotic null distribution of S_T under the null hypothesis provides the answer. It does not generally have an analytic form, but Davies (1977) gives an approximation to it that holds under certain conditions, including the assumption that $S(\boldsymbol{\gamma}) = \text{plim}_{T \to \infty} S_T(\boldsymbol{\gamma})$ has a derivative; for another solution, see Davies (1987).

Other choices of test statistic include the average:

$$S_T = \text{ave } S_T(\gamma) = \int_\Gamma S_T(\gamma) dW(\gamma) \tag{10.22}$$

where $W(\gamma)$ is a weight function defined by the user such that $\int_\Gamma W(\gamma) d\gamma = 1$, and the exponential

$$\exp S_T = \ln \left(\int_\Gamma \exp\{(1/2) S_T(\gamma)\} dW(\gamma) \right). \tag{10.23}$$

Andrews and Ploberger (1994) have recommended these tests and demonstrated their local asymptotic optimality properties. The statistics (10.22) and (10.23) are two special cases in the family of average exponential tests: for definitions and details, see Andrews and Ploberger (1994).

10.3.1.4 Obtaining critical values

Hansen (1996) provides a thorough discussion of the identification problem and shows how to obtain asymptotic critical values for these statistics by simulation under rather general conditions. Given the observations (y_t, z_t'), $t = 1, \ldots, T$, the log-likelihood of (10.21) has the form

$$L_T(\theta, \gamma) = c - (T/2) \ln \sigma^2 - (1/2\sigma^2) \sum_{t=1}^{T} \{y_t - \beta_0' z_t - \beta_1' z_t G(\gamma; s_t)\}^2$$

where $\theta = (\beta_0', \beta_1', \sigma^2)'$. Assuming γ known, the average score for the parameters in the conditional mean equals

$$s_T(\theta, \gamma) = (\sigma^2 T)^{-1} \sum_{t=1}^{T} (z_t \otimes [1 \ G(\gamma; s_t)]') \varepsilon_t. \tag{10.24}$$

Lagrange multiplier and Wald tests can be defined using (10.24) in the usual way. The LM test statistic equals

$$S_T^{LM}(\gamma) = T s_T(\tilde{\theta})' \tilde{I}_T(\tilde{\theta})^{-1} s_T(\tilde{\theta})$$

where $\tilde{\theta}$ is the maximum likelihood estimator of θ under H_0 and $\tilde{I}_T(\tilde{\theta}) = T^{-1} \sum_{t=1}^{T} s_T(\tilde{\theta}) s_T(\tilde{\theta})'$ is a consistent estimator of the population information matrix $I(\theta)$. Accordingly, the Wald statistic equals

$$S_T^W(\gamma) = \hat{\beta}' R' (R \hat{I}_T(\hat{\theta}) R')^{-1} R \hat{\beta}$$

where $\hat{\beta} = (\hat{\beta}_0', \hat{\beta}_1')'$ and $R = [0_m \ I_m]$. A hat indicates that the parameter vector has been estimated under the alternative hypothesis $\beta_1 \neq 0$. An empirical distribution of the supremum or average statistics can be obtained by simulation. If the parameter space Γ is continuous, as is often the case, then in practice it has to be approximated by a discrete space $\Gamma^* = \{\gamma_1, \gamma_2, \ldots, \gamma_A\}$, say. As an example, consider the Lagrange multiplier statistic $S_T^{LM}(\gamma)$. The empirical distribution of S_T is obtained as follows:

1. Generate T observations u_t^j, $t = 1, \ldots, T$, for each $j = 1, \ldots, J$, from a normal $(0, \bar{\sigma}^2)$ distribution, JT observations in all.
2. Compute $\mathbf{s}_T^{(j)}(\boldsymbol{\theta}) = T^{-1} \sum_{t=1}^{T} (\mathbf{z}_t \otimes [1 \ G(\gamma_a; s_t)]')u_t^{(j)}$.
3. Set $S_T^{LM(j)}(\gamma_a) = T\mathbf{s}_T^{(j)}(\tilde{\boldsymbol{\theta}})'\tilde{\mathbf{I}}_T^{(j)}(\tilde{\boldsymbol{\theta}})^{-1}\mathbf{s}_T^{(j)}(\tilde{\boldsymbol{\theta}})$.
4. Compute $S_T^{LM(j)}$ from $S_T^{LM(j)}(\gamma_a)$, $a = 1, \ldots, A$.

Carrying out these steps once gives a simulated value of the statistic. By repeating them J times one generates a random sample $\{S_T^{LM(1)}, \ldots, S_T^{LM(J)}\}$ from the distribution of S_T^{LM}. If the value of S_T^{LM} obtained directly from the sample exceeds the $100(1 - \alpha)\%$ quantile of the empirical distribution, the null hypothesis is rejected at (approximately) significance level α. The power of the test depends on the quality of the approximation Λ^*. If Λ^* is not sufficiently dense, the power may remain weak.

This potential weakness may be remedied by replacing Step 4 by Step 4a:

4a. Compute $S_T^{LM(j)}$ by maximizing $S_T^{LM(j)}(\gamma)$ by simulated annealing.

Simulated annealing is a function optimization technique with the property that it avoids local maxima (if optimization means maximization as in this example) and is likely to find the global maximum; see, for example, Brooks and Morgan (1995), who discuss rules for setting up a simulated annealing algorithm. González and Teräsvirta (2005) show how it can be applied to the present situation.

Hansen (1996) applied steps 1–4 to testing linearity against the two-regime threshold autoregressive model. If the threshold variable is known, the parameter space is one-dimensional. Suppose it is only known that the threshold variable belongs to a predetermined set of variables, which in the TAR case is a set of lags, for example the first p ones $\{y_{t-1}, \ldots, y_{t-p}\}$. This means that the dimension of Λ^* increases from 1 to $p+1$, but the technique itself is still available. The extra ignorance just amounts to an increased computational burden. It should also be mentioned that Hansen (1999) suggested a likelihood ratio test for this purpose and showed how its empirical null distribution may be obtained by a parametric bootstrap. Finally, Caner and Hansen (2001) extended the asymptotic theory of inference to the SETAR model with an autoregressive unit root. Their results make it possible to test the unit root and linearity hypotheses jointly in the SETAR framework.

10.3.1.5   *Lagrange multiplier type tests*

The tests presented in the preceding section have been made applicable by the idea of constructing their distributions by simulation. In this section, another way of handling the identification problem is considered. Instead of approximating the unknown distribution of a test statistic, it is possible to approximate the conditional log-likelihood or the nonlinear model in such a way that the identification problem is circumvented. Saikkonen and Luukkonen (1988) were the first authors to discuss this idea; see also Luukkonen, Saikkonen and Teräsvirta (1988), Granger and Teräsvirta (1993) and Teräsvirta (1994).

Consider again the additive nonlinear model (21), define $\boldsymbol{\gamma} = (\gamma_1, \boldsymbol{\gamma}_2')'$ and assume, furthermore, that $G(\gamma_1, \boldsymbol{\gamma}_2; s_t) \equiv 0$ for $\gamma_1 = 0$. We make the following assumption:

Assumption 1. The transition function $G(\gamma_1, \boldsymbol{\gamma}_2; s_t)$ is at least k times continuously differentiable for all values of s_t in a positive neighborhood of $\gamma_1 = 0$.

Assumption 1 makes it possible to approximate the transition function by a Taylor expansion and circumvent the identification problem that way. Note that the linearity hypothesis can be expressed as $H_0 : \gamma_1 = 0$. A local approximation to G around the null hypothesis has the form

$$G(\gamma_1, \boldsymbol{\gamma}_2; s_t) = \sum_{j=1}^{k} (\gamma_1^j/j!)\delta_j(s_t) + R_k(\gamma_1, \boldsymbol{\gamma}_2; s_t) \tag{10.25}$$

where $\delta_j(s_t) = (\partial^j/\partial\gamma_1^j)G(\gamma_1, \boldsymbol{\gamma}_2; s_t)|_{\gamma_1=0}, j = 1, \ldots, k$. Replacing G in (10.21) by (10.25) yields, after reparameterization,

$$y_t = \boldsymbol{\beta}_0' z_t + \sum_{j=1}^{k} \boldsymbol{\beta}_j(\gamma_1)' z_t \delta_j(s_t) + \varepsilon_t^* \tag{10.26}$$

where the parameter vectors $\boldsymbol{\beta}_j(\gamma_1) = 0$ for $\gamma_1 = 0$, and the error term $\varepsilon_t^* = \varepsilon_t + \boldsymbol{\beta}_1' z_t R_k(\gamma_1, \gamma_2; s_t)$. The original null hypothesis can now be restated as $H_0' : \boldsymbol{\beta}_j(\gamma_1) = 0, j = 1, \ldots, k$. It is a linear hypothesis in a linear model and can thus, in principle, be tested using standard asymptotic theory. Note, however, that this requires the existence of $E\delta_j(s_t)^2 z_t z_t'$. Furthermore, under the null hypothesis, $\varepsilon_t^* = \varepsilon_t$, so that standard asymptotic theory is available. The auxiliary regression (10.26) can be viewed as a result of a trade-off in which information about the structural form of the alternative model is exchanged for a larger null hypothesis and standard asymptotic theory.

As an example, consider the LSTAR model (10.4) with transition function

$$G(\gamma_1, c; s_t) = (1 + \exp\{-\gamma_1(s_t - c)\})^{-1}, \quad \gamma_1 > 0. \tag{10.27}$$

When $\gamma_1 = 0$, $G(\gamma_1, c; s_t) = 1/2$. The first-order Taylor expansion of the transition function around $\gamma_1 = 0$ is

$$T(\gamma_1, c; s_t) = (1/2) - (\gamma_1/4)(s_t - c) + R_1(\gamma_1, c; s_t). \tag{10.28}$$

Substituting (10.28) for (10.27) in (10.21) yields, after reparameterization,

$$y_t = (\boldsymbol{\beta}_0^*)' \mathbf{z}_t + (\boldsymbol{\beta}_1^*)' \mathbf{z}_t s_t + \varepsilon_t^* \qquad (10.29)$$

where $\boldsymbol{\beta}_1^* = \gamma_1 \tilde{\boldsymbol{\beta}}_1^*$ such that $\tilde{\boldsymbol{\beta}}_1^* \neq 0$. The transformed null hypothesis is thus $H_0' : \boldsymbol{\beta}_1^* = 0$. Under this hypothesis and assuming that $\mathrm{E}s_t^2 \mathbf{z}_t \mathbf{z}_t'$ exists, the resulting LM statistic has an asymptotic χ^2 distribution with m degrees of freedom. Kiliç (2004) recently derived the (nonstandard) asymptotic distribution of the LM-type linearity test under the assumption that the autoregressive process is no longer stationary but contains a unit root.

As already mentioned, Hansen's test against threshold autoregression applies in the situation where the threshold variable is unknown but belongs to a predetermined set of lags of y_t. It is also possible to modify the test against STAR in the same way, as discussed in Luukkonen *et al.* (1988). Another observation worth making is that the test based on (10.29) does not work if only the intercept in (10.21) is affected by the transition function, that is, if $\boldsymbol{\beta}_1 = (\beta_{11}, 0, \ldots, 0)'$ in (10.21), and if, at the same time, s_t is an element in $\mathbf{z}_t$. In that case $\boldsymbol{\beta}_1^* = 0$, and the test thus has no power. This problem can be remedied by using a higher-order Taylor approximation, a third-order suffices. This guarantees that the auxiliary regression contains terms such that the test has power; see again Luukkonen *et al.* (1988).

In practice, the LM type tests may be carried out in the TR^2 form. In small and moderate samples, the F-version of the test is preferable to the χ^2-test based on the asymptotic distribution theory. Robustifying the LM type tests against hetero-skedastic errors, following Wooldridge (1990), is possible here as well. They can also be made robust against outliers, as van Dijk, Franses and Lucas (1999) suggested.

The solution to the identification problem presented here is, in theory, not applicable to testing linearity against a threshold autoregressive model (10.1). This is because the transition function $G(\gamma; s_t)$ does not satisfy Assumption 1. In practice, however, the LM type test based on the auxiliary regression (10.29) has power against a threshold autoregressive model with two regimes. The power cannot be as high as it is for the supremum test, because the alternative in the latter is the threshold autoregressive model. On the other hand, the STAR model contains the threshold autoregressive model as a special case, so that the alternative is larger and the power of the test against threshold autoregression thus weaker than the power of the supremum test. A small simulation study in Hansen (1996) illustrates this point.

10.3.2   Testing linearity against unspecified alternatives

There also exists a wide selection of linearity tests against an unspecified alternative. Keenan (1985) derived a one degree of freedom test for testing linearity in the univariate case where the null hypothesis is a stationary autoregressive model. His test is simply the well-known Regression Specification Error Test (RESET) of Ramsey (1969) applied to linear autoregressions. Tsay (1986) argued that Keenan's test may not always have sufficient power and suggested another test with a larger alternative hypothesis. The test consists of testing the null hypothesis $\psi_{ij} = 0, i = 1, \ldots, p; j = i, \ldots, p$, within the following auxiliary autoregression:

$$y_t = \boldsymbol{\phi}'z_t + \sum_{i=1}^{p} \sum_{j=i}^{p} \psi_{ij} y_{t-i} y_{t-j} + \varepsilon_t \tag{10.30}$$

where $\boldsymbol{\phi} = (\phi_0, \phi_1, \ldots, \phi_p)'$, $Ey_t^4 < \infty$ and $\varepsilon_t \sim IN(0, \sigma^2)$. The asymptotic theory is standard, and Tsay recommends an F-test for testing the null hypothesis. The degrees of freedom of the F-statistic are $p(p+1)/2$ and $T - (p+1)(p+2)/2$. Note that equation (10.30) is an artificial construct for carrying out the test. It cannot be interpreted as a data-generating process.

Tsay's test may be regarded as a special case of a more general test based on the 'dual' of the Volterra expansion of a stationary model; see Priestley (1980), also called the Kolmogorov–Gabor polynomial. The auxiliary autoregression based on the k-th order expansion is simply

$$y_t = \boldsymbol{\phi}'z_t + \sum_{i_1=1}^{p} \sum_{i_2=i_1}^{p} \psi_{i_1 i_2} y_{t-i_1} y_{t-i_2} + \cdots + \sum_{i_1=1}^{p} \cdots \sum_{i_k=i_{k-1}}^{p} \psi_{i_1 \ldots i_k} y_{t-i_1} \cdots y_{t-i_k} + \varepsilon_t \tag{10.31}$$

where the null hypothesis of linearity is that the coefficients of all higher-order terms in (10.31) equal zero. A necessary condition for the standard asymptotic theory to work is that $Ey_t^{2k} < \infty$. Thus, the higher the order of the polynomial, the stricter the moment condition required. Choosing $k = 3$ in (10.31) yields the linearity test of Teräsvirta, Lin and Granger (1993) against an AR-NN model. It was derived following the ideas discussed in section 3.1.5.

There also exist nonparametric tests of linearity. They may be based on higher-order spectra; see Brockett, Hinich and Patterson (1988) and references therein. Hjellvik and Tjøstheim (1995) have worked out tests based on a nonparametric comparison of the best nonlinear and linear predictor of y_t. Because the emphasis in this chapter is on parametric nonlinear models, these tests are not discussed in detail here.

10.4   Modeling nonlinear series

A researcher interested in the possibility of fitting a nonlinear model to a time series can choose from a very large number of nonlinear models. It seems very difficult to devise a data-driven specification strategy for selecting a nonlinear model from a large set of alternative functional forms. One possibility that has not been emphasized here is to estimate the functional form itself nonparametrically. Even in that case, model selection problems remain. It may not be clear which lags of the variable of interest should be included in the model, and data-based model selection techniques are required for that purpose; see, for example, Tjøstheim and

Auestad (1994). This is a real problem because nonparametric models typically cannot contain too many lags because of the curse of dimensionality.

10.4.1   Building threshold autoregressive models

If the investigator narrows the choice down to a family of models, there do exist modeling strategies for selecting models within that family and evaluating them. A well-known example is the modeling strategy devised by Box and Jenkins (1970) for linear ARIMA models. Similar strategies exist for nonlinear modeling. Tsay (1989) presents one for SETAR models. The first step, as indicated in section 10.3, consists of testing linearity. If the null hypothesis is rejected, the next problem is to choose the delay parameter d, which is done using the same linearity test. After determining the delay, scatterplots of various statistics are used to locate the thresholds and thus the number of regimes in the model.

It may be noted that the linearity test of Hansen (1999), discussed in section 10.3.1.4, solves the specification problem in the case where the alternative to the linear AR model is a SETAR model with two regimes. This is because the delay may be included as another nuisance parameter in the test. In theory, the test could be used sequentially to take the SETAR model with a single threshold as the null model to be tested against a threshold model with three regimes. Strikholm and Teräsvirta (2005) found, however, that this approach may not work in practice if the true model contains at least three regimes. The reason is that a large number of realizations generated by the parametric bootstrap may be explosive and have to be discarded. Another approach, advocated by Gonzalo and Pitarakis (2002), is to use model selection criteria such as AIC or BIC to sequentially select the number of thresholds. Yet another suggestion is to approximate the SETAR model by an LSTAR model with the location parameter γ fixed to a high value. This makes it possible to use tests developed for STAR model building in the SETAR framework; for details, see Strikholm and Teräsvirta (2005).

Evaluating an estimated model is an integral part of model building, as in the approach of Box and Jenkins (1970). Evaluation of SETAR models will be touched upon in the next subsection.

10.4.2   Building smooth transition autoregressive models

Smooth transition models can be built following the same principles as in the previous subsection. Linearity is tested first and, if rejected, the transition variable and the type of model are determined next. The estimated model is evaluated using a number of misspecification tests. Linearity may, in principle, be tested using Hansen's approach. There would, however, be one nuisance parameter more than in the SETAR case, the slope parameter γ. This would increase the computational effort. Heavy computations can be avoided by adopting the Taylor series expansion idea discussed in section 10.3.1.5. The resulting modeling strategy based on LM-type tests is described in Teräsvirta (1998). The specification stage includes, besides determining the transition variable (lag), also choosing between the LSTAR model with $K = 1$ in (10.7) and the ESTAR model (or the LSTAR model with $K = 2$). Details on how this choice is made are explained in Teräsvirta (1994). A slightly different suggestion can be found in Escribano and Jordá (1999).

There exist several misspecification tests for STAR models. They include tests of no error autocorrelation, no remaining nonlinearity, and parameter constancy. The last two tests are LM-type tests; the details can be found in Teräsvirta (1998). This stands in contrast to SETAR models, for which there are few, if any, misspecification tests. However, tests designed for STAR models may be used as approximate evaluation devices in SETAR modeling. This is possible by approximating the estimated SETAR model by a STAR model with a large slope parameter. The misspecification tests for STAR models may then be applied to this model. When the true null model is the SETAR model, the asymptotic distributions of the STAR-based statistics are unknown. In finite samples, however, they can be applied as indicators of model misspecification.

10.4.3 Building Markov-switching autoregressive models

Testing linearity against MS-AR models can be carried out using Hansen's idea of constructing the empirical distribution of the likelihood ratio statistic by parametric bootstrap; see Hansen (1992). In the Markov-switching framework, this idea leads to a computationally intensive procedure, as one has to estimate both the linear and the MS-AR model and repeat this a number of times. Consequently, the test is rarely applied in practice, and the same is true for Garcia's approach (Garcia, 1998), which is based on deriving the nonstandard asymptotic distribution of the likelihood ratio statistic. Typically, MS-AR modelers simply assume the number of regimes known and proceed from there.

The misspecication tests of STAR models are based on the residuals of the model. The situation in the MS-AR case is different in the sense that no residuals are available. Misspecification testing is still possible following Hamilton (1996), who shows how the score function of the log-likelihood of the MS-AR model can be used for this purpose and presents several tests, including tests of dynamic misspecication and autocorrelation. Unfortunately, it seems that none of them is commonly used in applications.

Breunig, Najarian and Pagan (2003) consider other types of tests, including consistency tests for finding out whether assumptions made in constructing the Markov-switching model are compatible with the data. Furthermore, they discuss encompassing tests that are used to check whether a parameter of some auxiliary model can be encompassed by the estimated Markov-switching model. The authors also emphasize the use of informal graphical methods in checking the validity of the specification. Their techniques can be applied to other nonlinear models as well.

10.4.4 Building autoregressive single hidden-layer neural network models

Building AR-NN models involves two problems. The first is the selection of lags in the model and the second is choosing the number of hidden units. There are two main approaches to AR-NN modeling. One may specify a model with a large number of lags and hidden units and then reduce the size of the model or prune it using an appropriate algorithm. There exist many methods for pruning a network: see, for example, Fine (1999, chapter 6) for an informative account. The opposite strategy is to begin with a small (linear) model and extend it: "grow the network." Swanson and White (1995, 1997a,b) grow the network (11) using the model selection criterion BIC to decide both the number of lags in each hidden unit as well as the number of hidden units. Sequential selection of hidden units may also be carried out by significance tests; see Anders and Korn (1999) and Medeiros, Teräsvirta and Rech (in press) for this approach.

10.5   Forecasting with nonlinear models

10.5.1   Numerically obtained forecasts

Forecasting for more than one period ahead with nonlinear models such as the STAR or AR-NN requires numerical techniques. They can also be applied to forecasting from SETAR models, whereas they are not necessary for MS-AR forecasts. Granger and Teräsvirta (1993), Franses and van Dijk (2000), Fan and Yao (2003) and Teräsvirta (in press), among others, discuss this problem. To illustrate, consider the simple nonlinear model

$$y_t = g(z_{t-1}; \boldsymbol{\theta}) + \varepsilon_t \tag{10.32}$$

where $\varepsilon_t \sim \text{iid}(0, \sigma^2)$ and z_t is defined as before. Forecasting one period ahead does not pose any problem, for the forecast has the form

$$y_{t+1|t} = \mathsf{E}(y_{t+1}|\mathbf{z}_t) = g(\mathbf{z}_t; \theta).$$

For simplicity it is assumed that θ is known, which means that the uncertainty from the estimation of parameters is ignored. Forecasting two steps ahead is already a more complicated affair because one has to work out $\mathsf{E}(y_{t+2}|\mathbf{z}_t)$. This yields

$$
\begin{aligned}
y_{t+2|t} &= \mathsf{E}(y_{t+2}|\mathbf{z}_t) = \mathsf{E}g(g(\mathbf{z}_t; \boldsymbol{\theta}) + \varepsilon_{t+1}, y_t, \dots, y_{t-p+1}; \boldsymbol{\theta}) \\
&= \int_\varepsilon g(g(\mathbf{z}_t; \boldsymbol{\theta}) + \varepsilon_{t+1}, y_t, \dots, y_{t-p+1}; \boldsymbol{\theta}) \mathrm{d}F(\varepsilon)
\end{aligned}
\tag{10.33}
$$

where $F(\varepsilon)$ is the cumulative distribution function of ε_t. One may, however, ignore the error term and just use

$$y_{t+2|t}^s = g(\mathbf{z}_{t+1|t}; \boldsymbol{\theta})$$

which Tong (1990) calls the 'skeleton' forecast. This alternative, while easy to apply, yields a biased forecast for y_{t+2}. It may also lead to substantial losses of efficiency; see Lin and Granger (1994) for simulation evidence of this.

On the other hand, numerical integration of (10.33) may not be tedious either, but will become so when the forecast horizon increases. Granger and Teräsvirta (1993) call this method of obtaining the forecast the exact method, as opposed to two numerical techniques that can be used to approximate the integral in (10.33). One of them is based on simulation, the other on bootstrapping the residuals $\{\hat{\varepsilon}_t\}$ of the estimated nonlinear model.

The simulation approach requires that a distributional assumption is made about the errors ε_t. One draws a sample of N independent error vectors $\{\varepsilon_{t+1}^{(1)}, \ldots, \varepsilon_{t+1}^{(N)}\}$ from this distribution and computes the Monte Carlo forecast

$$y_{t+2|t}^{MC} = (1/N) \sum_{i=1}^{N} g\left(z_{t+1|t} + \varepsilon_{t+1}^{(i)}; \boldsymbol{\theta}\right). \tag{10.34}$$

This method yields an approximately unbiased forecast of y_{t+2}. The bootstrap technique also has this property. The forecast has the form

$$y_{t+2|t}^{B} = (1/N_B) \sum_{i=1}^{N_B} g\left(z_{t+1|t} + \hat{\varepsilon}_{t+1}^{(i)}; \boldsymbol{\theta}\right) \tag{10.35}$$

when the errors $\{\hat{\varepsilon}_{t+1}^{(1)}, \ldots, \hat{\varepsilon}_{t+1}^{(N_B)}\}$ have been obtained by drawing them from the set of estimated residuals of model (10.32) with replacement. Forecasts from (10.35) do not make use of distributional assumptions and are robust against unconditional heteroskedasticity of unknown form in the error process.

This generalizes to longer forecast horizons. In forecasting h periods ahead, $h \geq 2$, one has to draw sequences of errors $\{\varepsilon_{t+1}^{(i)}, \ldots, \varepsilon_{t+h-1}^{(i)}\}$, or construct bootstrap-based sequences $\{\hat{\varepsilon}_{t+1}^{(i)}, \ldots, \hat{\varepsilon}_{t+h-1}^{(i)}\}$, and use those in computing the forecasts. An application of this technique to forecasting with STAR models is discussed in Lundbergh and Teräsvirta (2002), whose empirical example consists of forecasting Australian and Danish quarterly unemployment series.

10.5.2 Analytic forecasts

For some nonlinear models, multi-step forecasts may be obtained analytically. The MS-AR model is perhaps the most prominent example of this. The reason is that the regimes are linear and that the regime indicator variable s_t is independent of the error process. This is not the case in the SETAR model. For details, see, for example, Hamilton (1994) or Teräsvirta (in press).

Another way of cutting down the amount of computation in forecasting y_{t+h} given z_t is to build a separate (nonlinear) model for each of the h forecast horizons. This amounts to building models for y_{t+h} without using the lags $y_{t+h-1}, \ldots, y_{t+1}$. Flexible nonlinear forms, such as the AR-NN model, may be feasible for this type of nonlinear forecasting. At the moment there do not seem to exist studies showing whether this approach would lead to more or less accurate nonlinear forecasts than the ones obtained numerically from standard nonlinear specifications.

10.6 Final remarks

The main considerations in this chapter have been restricted to a number of well-known nonlinear models that have frequently been fitted to economic as well as other time series. The emphasis has been on autoregressive models. There exist, however, many other interesting nonlinear models, some of which have been designed with a particular application in mind. For example, modeling the dynamic behavior of an exchange rate fluctuating in a target zone requires a model that explicitly takes into account the nonlinearity due to the boundaries of the zone. For space reasons, examples of such special models have not been included in the discussion.

The models presented in this chapter have been univariate. Some of them, such as the SETAR and STAR models, also have multivariate single-equation counterparts that have often been fitted to economic series. Extending the considerations to cover them as well would, in many respects, be rather straightforward. Granger (2001) contains a survey of nonlinear macroeconometric models. The present chapter does not cover vector time series models. It may be mentioned, however, that Tsay (1998) has extended his SETAR model selection strategy (Tsay, 1989) to vector threshold autoregressive models. The reader is referred to that paper for details. Vector smooth transition autoregressive (VSTAR) models have also been fitted to economic time series. Camacho (2004) has recently developed a modeling strategy for these models; for another economic application of the VSTAR model, see Rothman, van Dijk and Franses (2001).

References

Anders, U. and O. Korn (1999) Model selection in neural networks. *Neural Networks* **12**, 309–23.

Andrews, D.W.K. and W. Ploberger (1994) Optimal tests when a nuisance parameter is present only under the alternative. *Econometrica* **62**, 1383–1414.

Arango, L.E. and A. González (2001) Some evidence of smooth transition nonlinearity in Colombian inflatation. *Applied Economics* **33**, 155–62.

Bacon, D.W. and Watts D.G. (1971) Estimating the transition between two intersecting straight lines. *Biometrika* **58**, 525–34.

Bai, J. (1997) Estimating multiple breaks one at a time. *Econometric Theory* **13**, 315–52.

Balke, N.S. and T.B. Fomby (1997) Threshold cointegration. *International Economic Review* **38**, 627–45.

Bates, D.M. and D.G. Watts (1988) *Nonlinear Regression Analysis and its Applications*. New York: Wiley.

Box, G.E.P. and G.M. Jenkins (1970) *Time Series Analysis: Forecasting and Control*. San Francisco: Holden-Day.

Brännäs, K. and J.G. De Gooijer (1994) Autoregressive–asymmetric moving average model for business cycle data, *Journal of Forecasting* **13**, 529–44.

Breunig, R., S. Najarian and A. Pagan (2003) Specification testing of Markov switching models. *Oxford Bulletin of Economics and Statistics* **65**, 703–25.

Brock, W.A. and S.M. Potter (1993) Nonlinear time series and macroeconometrics. In G.S. Maddala, C.R. Rao and H.D. Vinod (eds), *Handbook of Statistics*, vol. 11. Amsterdam: North-Holland, pp. 195–229.

Brockett, P.L., M.J. Hinich and D. Patterson (1988) Bispectral-based tests for detection of Gaussianity and linearity in time series. *Journal of the American Statistical Association* **83**, 657–64.

Brooks, S.P. and B.J.T. Morgan (1995) Optimization using simulated annealing. *The Statistician* **44**, 241–57.

Camacho, M. (2004) Vector smooth transition regression models for US GDP and the composite index of leading indicators. *Journal of Forecasting* **23**, 173–96.

Caner, M. and B.E. Hansen (2001) Threshold autoregression with unit root. *Econometrica* **69**, 1555–1586.

Chan, K.S. (1993) Consistency and limiting distribution of the least squares estimator of a threshold autoregressive model. *Annals of Statistics* **21**, 521–33.

Chan, K.S. and H. Tong (1986) On estimating thresholds in autoregressive models. *Journal of Time Series Analysis* **7**, 178–90.

Chan, K.S. and R.S. Tsay (1998) Limiting properties of the least squares estimator of a continuous threshold autoregressive model. *Biometrika* **85**, 413–25.

Chatterjee, S. and M.R. Yilmaz (1992) Chaos, fractals and statistics. *Statistical Science* **7**, 49–68.

Chen, R. and R.S. Tsay (1993) Functional-coefficient autoregressive models, *Journal of the American Statistical Association* **88**, 298–308.

Cybenko, G. (1989) Approximation by superposition of sigmoidal functions. *Mathematics of Control, Signals, and Systems* **2**, 303–14.

Davies, R.B. (1977) Hypothesis testing when a nuisance parameter is present only under the alternative. *Biometrika* **64**, 247–54.

Davies, R.B. (1987) Hypothesis testing when a nuisance parameter is present only under the alternative. *Biometrika* **74**, 33–43.

Dempster, A.P., N.M. Laird and D.B. Rubin (1977) Maximum likelihood from incomplete data via the EM algorithm. *Journal of the Royal Statistical Society B* **39**, 1–38.

Enders, W. and C.W.J. Granger (1998) Unit-root tests and asymmetric adjustment with an example using the term structure of interest rates. *Journal of Business and Economic Statistics* **16**, 304–11.

Engle, R.F. (1982) A general approach to Lagrange multiplier model diagnostics. *Journal of Econometrics* **20**, 83–104.

Escribano, A. and O. Jordá (1999) Improved testing and specification of smooth transition regression models. In P. Rothman (ed.), *Nonlinear Time Series Analysis of Economic and Financial Data*. Dordrecht: Kluwer Academic Publishers, pp. 289–319.

Fan, J. and Q. Yao (2003) *Nonlinear Time Series: Nonparametric and Parametric Methods*. New York: Springer.

Filardo, A.J. (1994) Business cycle phases and their transitional dynamics. *Journal of Business and Economic Statistics* **12**, 299–308.

Fine, T.L. (1999) *Feedforward Neural Network Methodology*. Berlin: Springer-Verlag.

Franses, P.H. and van Dijk, D. (2000) *Non-Linear Time Series Models in Empirical Finance*. Cambridge: Cambridge University Press.

Funahashi, K. (1989) On the approximate realization of continuous mappings by neural networks. *Neural Networks* **2**, 183–92.

Garcia, R. (1998) Asymptotic null distribution of the likelihood ratio test in Markov switching models. *International Economic Review* **39**, 763–88.

Goldfeld, S.M. and R.E. Quandt (1973a) The estimation of structural shifts by switching regressions. *Annals of Economic and Social Measurement* **2**, 475–85.

Goldfeld, S.M. and R.E. Quandt (1973b) A Markov model for switching regressions. *Journal of Econometrics* **1**, 3–16.

González, A. and T. Teräsvirta (2005) Simulation-based finite-sample linearity test against smooth transition models, *SSE/EFI Working Papers in Economics and Finance*, no. 603. Stockholm: Stockholm School of Economics.

Gonzalo, J. and J.-Y. Pitarakis (2002) Estimation and model selection based inference in single and multiple threshold models. *Journal of Econometrics* **110**, 319–52.

Granger, C.W.J. (2001) Overview of nonlinear macroeconometric models. *Macroeconomic Dynamics* **5**, 466–81.

Granger, C.W.J. and A.P. Andersen (1978) *An Introduction to Bilinear Time Series*. Göttingen: Vandenhoeck and Ruprecht.

Granger, C.W.J. and T. Teräsvirta (1993) *Modelling Nonlinear Economic Relationships*. Oxford: Oxford University Press.

Guégan, D. (1994) *Séries chronologiques non linéaires à temps discret*. Paris: Economica.

Haggan, V. and T. Ozaki (1981) Modelling non-linear random vibrations using an amplitude-dependent autoregressive time series model. *Biometrika* **68**, 189–96.

Hamilton, J.D. (1989) A new approach to the economic analysis of nonstationary time series and the business cycle. *Econometrica* **57**, 357–84.

Hamilton, J.D. (1993) Estimation, inference and forecasting of time series subject to changes in regime. In G.S. Maddala, C.R. Rao and H.R. Vinod (eds), *Handbook of Statistics*, vol. 11. Amsterdam: Elsevier, pp. 231–60.

Hamilton, J.D. (1994) *Time Series Analysis*. Princeton, NJ: Princeton University Press.

Hamilton, J.D. (1996) Specification testing in Markov-switching time-series models. *Journal of Econometrics* **70**, 127–57.

Hansen, B.E. (1992) The likelihood ratio test under nonstandard conditions: testing the Markov switching model of GNP. *Journal of Applied Econometrics* **7**, 61–82.

Hansen, B.E. (1996) Inference when a nuisance parameter is not identified under the null hypothesis. *Econometrica* **64**, 413–30.

Hansen, B.E. (1999) Testing for linearity. *Journal of Economic Surveys* **13**, 551–76.

Haykin, S. (1999) *Neural Networks: A Comprehensive Foundation*, 2nd edn. Upper Saddle River, NJ: Prentice Hall.

Hjellvik, V. and D. Tjøstheim (1995) Nonparametric tests of linearity for time series. *Biometrika* **82**, 351–68.

Hornik, K., M. Stinchombe and H. White (1989) Multi-layer feedforward networks are universal approximators. *Neural Networks* **2**, 359–66.

Hwang, J.T.G. and A.A. Ding (1997) Prediction intervals for artificial neural networks. *Journal of the American Statistical Association* **92**, 109–25.

Keenan, J.M. (1985) A Tukey nonadditivity-type test for time series nonlinearity. *Biometrika* **72**, 39–44.

Kiliç, R. (2004) Linearity tests and stationarity. *Econometrics Journal* **7**, 55–62.

Leybourne, S., P. Newbold and D. Vougas (1998) Unit roots and smooth transitions. *Journal of Time Series Analysis* **19**, 83–97.

Lin, C.-F. J. and T. Teräsvirta (1994) Testing the constancy of regression parameters against continuous structural change. *Journal of Econometrics* **62**, 211–28.

Lin, J.-L. and C.W.J. Granger (1994) Forecasting from non-linear models in practice. *Journal of Forecasting* **13**, 1–9.

Lindgren, G. (1978) Markov regime models for mixed distributions and switching regressions. *Scandinavian Journal of Statistics* **5**, 81–91.

Lundbergh, S. and T. Teräsvirta (2002) Forecasting with smooth transition autoregressive models. In M.P. Clements and D.F. Hendry (eds), *A Companion to Economic Forecasting*. Oxford: Blackwell, pp. 485–509.

Luukkonen, R., P. Saikkonen and T. Teräsvirta (1988) Testing linearity against smooth transition autoregressive models. *Biometrika* **75**, 491–9.

Maddala, D.S. (1977) *Econometrics*. New York: McGraw-Hill.

Maravall, A. (1983) An application of nonlinear time series forecasting. *Journal of Business and Economic Statistics* **1**, 66–74.

Marcellino, M. (2004) Forecasting EMU macroeconomic variables *International Journal of Forecasting* **20**, 359–72.

Medeiros, M.C., T. Teräsvirta and G. Rech (in press) Building neural network models for time series: a statistical approach. *Journal of Forecasting*.

Nicholls, D.F. and B.G. Quinn (1982) *Random Coefficient Autoregressive Models: An Introduction*. New York: Springer.

Nyblom, J. (1989) Testing for the constancy of parameters over time. *Journal of the American Statistical Association* **84**, 223–30.

Öcal, N. and D.R. Osborn (2000) Business cycle nonlinearities in UK consumption and production. *Journal of Applied Econometrics* 15, 27–43.

Pagan, A.R. (1978) Some simple tests for non-linear time series models. *CORE Discussion Paper 7810.*

Peel, D.A. and A.E.H. Speight (1998) Threshold nonlinearities in output: Some international evidence. *Applied Economics* 30, 323–33.

Potter, S.M. (1995) A nonlinear approach to US GNP. *Journal of Applied Econometrics* 10, 109–25.

Potter, S.M. (1999) Nonlinear time series modelling: An introduction. *Journal of Economic Surveys* 13, 505–28.

Priestley, M.B. (1980) State-dependent models: A general approach to non-linear time series analysis. *Journal of Time Series Analysis* 1, 47–71.

Quandt, R.E. (1958) The estimation of parameters of a linear regression system obeying two separate regimes. *Journal of the American Statistical Association* 53, 873–80.

Ramsey, J.B. (1969) Tests for specification errors in classical least-squares regression analysis. *Journal of the Royal Statistical Society, Series B*, 31, 350–71.

Rothman, P., D. van Dijk and P.H. Franses (2001) A multivariate STAR analysis of the relationship between money and output. *Macroeconomic Dynamics* 5, 506–32.

Saikkonen, P. and R. Luukkonen (1988) Lagrange multiplier tests for testing nonlinearities in time series models. *Scandinavian Journal of Statistics* 15, 55–68.

Seber, G.A.F. and C.J. Wild (1989) *Nonlinear Regression.* New York: Wiley.

Skalin, J. and Teräsvirta, T. (2002) Modeling asymmetries and moving equilibria in unemployment rates. *Macroeconomic Dynamics* 6, 202–41.

Stock, J.H. and M.W. Watson (1999) A comparison of linear and nonlinear univariate models for forecasting macroeconomic time series. In R.F. Engle and H. White (eds), *Cointegration, Causality and Forecasting: A Festschrift in Honour of Clive W.J. Granger.* Oxford: Oxford University Press, pp. 1–44.

Strikholm, B. and T. Teräsvirta (2005) Determining the number of regimes in a threshold autoregressive model using smooth transition autoregressions. *SSE/EFI Working Papers in Economics and Finance 578.* Stockholm: Stockholm School of Economics.

Subba Rao, T. and M.M. Gabr (1984) *An Introduction to Bispectral Analysis and Bilinear Time Series Models.* New York: Springer.

Swanson, N.R. and P.H. Franses (1999) Nonlinear econometric modelling: a selective review. In P. Rothman (ed.), *Nonlinear Time Series Analysis of Economic and Financial Data.* Amsterdam: Kluwer, pp. 87–109.

Swanson, N.R. and H. White (1995) A model-selection approach to assessing the information in the term structure using linear models and artificial neural networks. *Journal of the Business and Economic Statistics* 13, 265–75.

Swanson, N.R. and H. White (1997a) Forecasting economic time series using flexible versus fixed specification and linear versus nonlinear econometric models. *International Journal of Forecasting* 13, 439–61.

Swanson, N.R. and H. White (1997b) A model selection approach to real-time macroeconomic forecasting using linear models and artificial neural networks. *Review of Economic and Statistics* 79, 540–50.

Taylor, M.P. and L. Sarno (2002) Purchasing power parity and the real exchange rate. *International Monetary Fund Staff Papers* 49, 65–105.

Teräsvirta, T. (1994) Specification, estimation, and evaluation of smooth transition autoregressive models. *Journal of the American Statistical Association* 89, 208–18.

Teräsvirta, T. (1998) Modeling economic relationships with smooth transition regressions. In A. Ullah and D.E. Giles (eds), *Handbook of Applied Economic Statistics.* New York: Dekker, pp. 507–52.

Teräsvirta, T. (in press) Forecasting economic variables with nonlinear models. In G. Elliott, C.W.J. Granger and A. Timmermann (eds), *Handbook of Economic Forecasting.* Amsterdam: Elsevier.

Teräsvirta, T. and H.M. Anderson (1992) Characterizing nonlinearities in business cycles using smooth transition autoregressive models. *Journal of Applied Econometrics* **7**, S119–S136.

Teräsvirta, T., C.-F. Lin and C.W.J. Granger (1993) Power of the neural network linearity test. *Journal of Time Series Analysis* **14**, 309–23.

Teräsvirta, T., D. Tjøstheim and C.W.J. Granger (1994) Aspects of modelling nonlinear time series. In R.F. Engle and D.L. McFadden (eds), *Handbook of Econometrics*, vol. 4. Amsterdam: Elsevier, pp. 2919–2957.

Teräsvirta, T., D. van Dijk and M.C. Medeiros (2005). Smooth transition autoregressions, neural networks, and linear models in forecasting macroeconomic time series: a re-examination. *International Journal of Forecasting* **21**, 755–74.

Tiao, G.C. and R.S. Tsay (1994) Some advances in non-linear and adaptive modelling in time-series. *Journal of Forecasting* **13**, 109–40.

Tjøstheim, D. and B.H. Auestad (1994) Nonparametric identification of nonlinear time series: Selecting significant lags. *Journal of the American Statistical Association* **89**, 1410–1419.

Tong, H. (1990) *Non-Linear Time Series: A Dynamical System Approach.* Oxford: Oxford University Press.

Tong, H. (1995) A personal overview of non-linear time series analysis from a chaos perspective. *Scandinavian Journal of Statistics* **22**, 399–445.

Tong, H. and K.S. Lim (1980) Threshold autoregression, limit cycles and cyclical data. *Journal of the Royal Statistical Society B* **42**, 245–92.

Trapletti, A., F. Leisch and K. Hornik (2000) Stationary and integrated autoregressive neural network processes. *Neural Computation* **12**, 2427–2450.

Tsay, R.S. (1986) Nonlinearity tests for time series. *Biometrika* **73**, 461–6.

Tsay, R.S. (1989) Testing and modeling threshold autoregressive processes. *Journal of the American Statistical Association* **84**, 231–40.

Tsay, R.S. (1998) Testing and modeling multivariate threshold models. *Journal of the American Statistical Association* **93**, 1188–1202.

Tsay, R.S. (2002) *Analysis of Financial Time Series.* New York: Wiley.

Tyssedal, J.S. and D. Tjøstheim (1988) An autoregressive model with suddenly changing parameters. *Applied Statistics* **37**, 353–69.

van Dijk, D., P.H. Franses and A. Lucas (1999) Testing for smooth transition nonlinearity in the presence of outliers. *Journal of Business and Economic Statistics* **17**, 217–35.

van Dijk, D., T. Teräsvirta and P.H. Franses (2002) Smooth transition autoregressive models – a survey of recent developments. *Econometric Reviews* **21**, 1–47.

Wecker, W.E. (1981) Asymmetric time series. *Journal of the American Statistical Association* **76**, 16–21.

White, H. (1980) A heteroskedasticity-consistent covariance matrix estimator and a direct test for heteroskedasticity. *Econometrica* **48**, 817–38.

White, H. (1989) Some asymptotic results for learning in single hidden layer feedforward network models. *Journal of the American Statistical Association* **84**, 1003–1013.

White, H. (1990) Connectionist nonparametric regression: Multilayer feed-forward networks can learn arbitrary mappings. *Neural Networks* **3**, 535–50.

White, H. (in press) Approximate nonlinear forecasting methods. In G. Elliott, C.W.J. Granger and A. Timmermann (eds), *Handbook of Economic Forecasting.* Amsterdam: Elsevier.

Wooldridge, J.M. (1990) A unified approach to robust, regression-based tests. *Econometric Theory* **6**, 17–43.

Part V
Multivariate Models

11

Estimating Functions and Equations: An Essay on Historical Developments with Applications to Econometrics

Anil K. Bera, Yannis Bilias, and Pradosh Simlai

Abstract

The idea of using estimating functions goes back a long way, at least to Karl Pearson's introduction to the method of moments in 1894. It is now a very active area of research in the statistics literature. One aim of this chapter is to provide an account of the developments relating to the theory of estimating functions. Starting from the simple case of a single parameter under independence, we cover the multiparameter, presence of nuisance parameters and dependent data cases. Applications of the estimating function technique to econometrics is still at its infancy. However, we illustrate how this estimation approach could be used in a number of time series models, such as the random coefficient, threshold, bilinear, and autoregressive conditional heteroskedasticity models, in models of spatial and longitudinal data, and median regression analysis. The chapter concludes with some remarks on the place of estimating functions in the history of statistical estimation techniques.

11.1   Prologue: early appearances of the concept of the
estimating function in statistics   428
     11.1.1   A defining moment in the history of statistics   428
     11.1.2   Estimating function approach: a short introduction   429
     11.1.3   The origin of the (optimal) estimating equation/
               function and some surprising findings   430
     11.1.4   Asymptotically shortest confidence interval
               using optimal estimating function   435
     11.1.5   Sufficient statistical estimating function   436
11.2   Basic theory of estimating functions   439
     11.2.1   The fundamental result: Godambe (1960) and Durbin (1960)   439
     11.2.2   Generalization to the multiparameter case   448
     11.2.3   Estimating function in the presence of nuisance parameters   449

    11.2.4   The dependent case and optimal combination
             of (elementary) estimating functions   454
    11.2.5   Estimating functions and generalized method of moments   458
11.3   Applications   459
    11.3.1   Random coefficient autoregressive model   460
    11.3.2   Threshold autoregressive model   462
    11.3.3   Bilinear model   463
    11.3.4   ARCH and GARCH models   464
    11.3.5   Spatial regression model   466
    11.3.6   Longitudinal data analysis   468
    11.3.7   Median regression model   469
11.4   Epilogue   470

11.1   Prologue: early appearances of the concept of the estimating function in statistics

11.1.1   A defining moment in the history of statistics

In the history of any scientific field there is always a defining moment – a moment that arrives with some maturity and when an authoritative figure clearly states the purpose, progress and problems of the field. For statistics, it can safely be argued that the defining moment arrived in 1922 with the appearance of Fisher's epochal article, "On the Mathematical Foundations of Theoretical Statistics." After discussing the purpose of statistical methods, Fisher (1922, p. 313) proclaimed the three fundamental problems in statistics as:

(1) Problems of Specification. These arise in the choice of the mathematical form of the population.
(2) Problems of Estimation. These involve the choice of methods of calculating from a sample statistical derivates, or as we shall call them statistics, which are designed to estimate the values of the parameters of the hypothetical population.
(3) Problems of Distribution. These include discussions of the distribution of statistics derived from samples, or in general any functions of quantities whose distribution is known.

Fisher did not dwell much on the Problem of Specification, and quickly stated, "The discussion of theoretical statistics may be regarded as alternating between problems of estimation and problems of distribution" (p. 315). He occupied himself mostly with the problems of estimation and distribution. In terms of estimation he went on to introduce some of the fundamental concepts, such as consistency, efficiency and sufficiency. These concepts solely focused on estimators which are functions of the observations alone. Fisher demonstrated that his suggested method of estimation, namely, the maximum likelihood

(ML) method (Fisher, 1912) is "superior" to Karl Pearson's method of moments (Pearson, 1894, 1902) in terms of efficiency.

11.1.2 Estimating function approach: a short introduction

In the estimating function (EF) approach to estimation, the focus is on a function that involves both the parameters and the sample, such as $g(y, \theta)$, where $y = (y_1, y_2, \ldots, y_n)$ represent the data and θ the parameter. We obtain the estimator say $\hat{\theta}$, by solving $g(y, \theta) = 0$, which we will call the estimating equation (EE). We can impose certain desirable properties on the function $g(y, \theta)$ rather than on the resulting estimator $\hat{\theta}$. For example, $g(.)$ is unbiased if $E[g(y, \theta)] = 0; g(.)$ is a minimum variance unbiased (MVU) EF if $Var[g(y, \theta)]$ is minimum among all unbiased estimating functions (EFs). At the outset, the benefits of focusing on the EFs rather than on the estimators are not so immediate. Following Durbin (1960), let us consider the first-order autoregressive (*AR*) model:

$$y_t = \theta y_{t-1} + u_t; \quad u_t \sim IID(0, \sigma^2), \quad t = 1, \ldots, n. \tag{11.1}$$

In the context of least squares (LS) estimation, we can focus our attention on three quantities. First, the objective function to be minimized with respect to θ, namely

$$\min_{\theta} \sum_{t=2}^{n} (y_t - \theta y_{t-1})^2. \tag{11.2}$$

Second, the equation for solving the optimization problem,

$$g(y, \theta) = \sum_{t=2}^{n} y_t y_{t-1} - \theta \sum_{t=2}^{n} y_{t-1}^2 = 0, \tag{11.3}$$

and, finally, the estimator $\hat{\theta}$ itself,

$$\hat{\theta} = \frac{\sum_{t=2}^{n} y_t y_{t-1}}{\sum_{t=2}^{n} y_{t-1}^2}. \tag{11.4}$$

A major part of the estimation literature is concerned with the properties of estimators like $\hat{\theta}$, such as unbiasedness, consistency and efficiency. The robust approaches to estimation emphasize the objective function; for example, another legitimate function that we can minimize is $\sum_{t=2}^{n} |y_t - \theta y_{t-1}|$. However, the function (11.2) has the extra appeal of being the same objective function under the ML framework with normality assumptions on the errors u_t. Durbin (1960) observed that viewing the LS estimators as roots of certain equations such as (11.3), i.e., working with the first order conditions directly, is much more convenient than studying the objective function like (11.2) or the estimator $\hat{\theta}$ in (11.4). The function $g(y, \theta)$ in (11.3) is linear in the parameter θ and $E[g(y, \theta)] = 0$. Durbin (1960) termed $g(y, \hat{\theta}) = 0$ as a *linear unbiased estimating equation*. This is a *finite sample* characterization of the EF $g(y, \theta)$, and it is clear that we cannot attach desirable properties, such as linearity and unbiasedness, to the resulting estimator $\hat{\theta}$ in (11.4). Also, as we know, the standard ML estimator (MLE) emphasizes *asymptotic* efficiency rather than finite-sample properties. This simple example illustrates the benefits of focussing on the EFs rather than on the estimators. As we will see later, many of the standard methods of estimation, such as LS, ML, minimum χ^2 and M-estimation, can be considered as special cases of the EF approach.

The literature on estimating functions and equations is indeed very vast. There are quite a few survey articles, such as Desmond (1989), Heyde (1989), Bhat (1990), Godambe and Kale (1991), Liang and Zeger (1995), Naik-Nimbalkar (1996), Vinod (1998) and Kale (2001–2002). Several books and edited volumes are also devoted to this subject; for example, see Godambe (1991a), Chen (1992), Basawa, Godambe and Taylor (1997), McLeish and Small (1998), Heyde (1997) and Mukhopadhyay (2004). However, these papers and books do not cover the very early developments on estimating functions and equations, as discussed below. Also, apart from describing the formal theoretical progress, as is done in this and the following sections, another aim of this chapter is to explore the usefulness of this estimation technique to econometrics. We attempt to do that in section 11.3. While providing the narrative details on some key theoretical developments, we also try to offer some personal perspectives by adding a human element to our narration. It is our experience that students take a greater interest in a subject when they clearly see the historical progress and know more about the personalities involved. The overall aim of this chapter is quite modest; our main purpose is to provide an easy-to-access description of the EF approach and its potential applications in econometrics, so as to attract students' attention to this fascinating research area.

11.1.3   The origin of the (optimal) estimating equation/function and some surprising findings

The idea of using EFs or equations goes back a long way, at least to Karl Pearson's (1894) introduction of the method of moments. To the best of our knowledge, the term "estimating equation" was first used by Yule (1902, p. 197). This, however, referred to estimated linear regressions like $\hat{y}_i = x_i'\beta$, using the popular notation. Therefore, it is quite different from our notion of an EE or EF. When one reads the literature on EF, the presented history appears to be very unambiguous. With minor reference to Fisher (1935a) and Kimball (1946) in terms of terminology and concepts, the whole development appears to start from Durbin (1960) and Godambe (1960). However, this temporal clarity veils some of the much earlier, though disconnected developments. Here we make an attempt to record those historical developments. Of course, it is quite possible that we still miss certain important works.

Although, quite justifiably, R.A. Fisher (Fisher, 1912) is credited with inventing the ML method of estimation, as we all know, nothing under the sun is completely new. ML estimation prefigured many times in earlier works, such as Edgeworth (1908, 1909) (see Bera and Bilias, 2002, fn 9). Edgeworth (1909) is a continuation of Edgeworth (1908), where he attempts to prove a Cramér–Rao-type inequality, more specifically to show that the posterior mode has the smallest variance. The treatment in the 1909 article is more ambitious and the set up is quite general [for an illuminating exposition, that we follow, see Hald (1998, pp. 703–5)]. Edgeworth

(1909, p. 82) stated his objective as, to "determine that function of which the several values, each formed from a large set of observations, hover with minimum dispersion about the true value of some constant represented by a symmetrical function of the observations." He considered the location model with "law of frequency" (probability density function) $f(y - \theta)$ and a class of function defined by the equation

$$\sum_{i=1}^{n} h(y_i - \hat{\theta}) = 0, \tag{11.5}$$

where h is an arbitrary function satisfying $E[h(y - \theta)] = 0$ and where the derivative of h at zero, $h'(0)$, is non zero. To approximate the "error" in estimation $e = \hat{\theta} - \theta$, let us write $h(y_i - \hat{\theta}) = h(z_i - e)$, where $z_i = y_i - \theta$. Now a Taylor expansion gives

$$0 = \sum_{i=1}^{n} h(y_i - \hat{\theta}) = \sum_{i=1}^{n} h(z_i - e) = \sum_{i=1}^{n} h(z_i) - e \sum_{i=1}^{n} h'(z_i) + \cdots, \tag{11.6}$$

and hence a first approximation to the error term e is

$$e = \frac{\sum_{i=1}^{n} h(z_i)}{\sum_{i=1}^{n} h'(z_i)}. \tag{11.7}$$

Replacing sums by integrals, Edgeworth obtained the asymptotic fluctuations (variance) of e as

$$Var(e) = \frac{1}{n} \frac{\int h^2(y)f(z)dz}{[\int h'(y)f(z)dz]^2} = \frac{1}{n} \frac{P^2}{Q^2}, \quad \text{say}, \tag{11.8}$$

where $f(z)$ denotes the probability density function. His objective was to find the function "h" such that P^2/Q^2 is minimised. A minimum is secured if h is such that, when it receives an arbitrary variation (δh), the first term of variation vanishes and the second term is positive. Using Schwartz's inequality, Edgeworth (1909, p. 84) proved the positivity of the second term. Let us concentrate only on the first term of the variation obtained by putting $h + (\delta h)$ in place of h. Using a simplified notation, we have

$$\frac{\int [h + (\delta h)]^2 f dz}{[\int [h' + (\delta h')]f dz]^2} = \frac{\int h^2 f dz + 2 \int (\delta h)h f dz + \int (\delta h)^2 f dz}{[\int h' f dz]^2 + 2 \int h' f dz \int (\delta h')f dz + [\int (\delta h')f dz]^2}$$
$$= \frac{P^2[1 + 2P^{-2} \int (\delta h)h f dz + \cdots]}{Q^2[1 + 2Q^{-1} \int (\delta h')f dz + \cdots]}$$
$$= \frac{P^2}{Q^2} \left[1 + 2P^{-2} \int (\delta h)h f dz + \cdots \right] \left[1 + 2Q^{-1} \int (\delta h')f dz + \cdots \right]^{-1}. \tag{11.9}$$

Since $\int (\delta h') f dz = (\delta h) f]_{-\infty}^{\infty} - \int (\delta h) f' dz = - \int (\delta h) f' dz$, an approximation to (11.9) is given by

$$\frac{P^2}{Q^2} \left[1 + 2P^{-2} \int (\delta h) hf dz + 2Q^{-1} \int (\delta h) f' dz \right]$$

$$= \frac{P^2}{Q^2} \left[1 + 2 \int (\delta h) \{ P^{-2} hf + Q^{-1} f' \} \, dz \right]. \tag{11.10}$$

Therefore, a necessary condition for minimizing *Var(e)* in (11.8) is that the expression in (11.10) is zero, or equivalently,

$$P^{-2} hf + Q^{-1} f' = 0$$

$$\text{i.e.,} \quad h(z) = -\frac{P^2}{Q} \cdot \frac{f'(z)}{f(z)} = c \frac{f'(z)}{f(z)} = c \frac{d \log f(z)}{dz}, \tag{11.11}$$

where c is a constant. In other words, for minimum variance $h(z)$ should be proportional to the score function. At this optimum $h(z)$,

$$P^2 = \int c^2 \left(\frac{f'}{f} \right)^2 f dz = c^2 \int \left(\frac{f'}{f} \right)^2 f dz = c^2 \mathcal{I},$$

$$Q = \int h' f dz = hf]_{-\infty}^{\infty} - \int f' h dz = 0 - \int f' c \frac{f'}{f} dz = -c \int \left(\frac{f'}{f} \right)^2 f dz = -c \mathcal{I},$$

$$\tag{11.12}$$

where $\mathcal{I} = \int (f'/f)^2 f dz = E\left[(f'/f)^2 \right]$ is the standard Fisher's information on each observation. From (11.8) *Var(e)* reduces to

$$\frac{1}{n} \frac{P^2}{Q^2} = (n \mathcal{I})^{-1}. \tag{11.13}$$

Therefore, the asymptotic variance of $\hat{\theta}$, obtained from the optimal EF, reaches the Cramér-Rao lower bound (CRLB).

Edgeworth did not proceed further with his optimal "estimating function" approach. He was more interested in proving that the posterior mode (which is the same function of the observations as the ML estimate) has the smallest asymptotic sample variance. Historically, Edgeworth's work has been treated as a precursor to Fisher's (1912, 1922) work on the ML method. However, we can now see that it is much more than that, for it has the fundamental result of the EF approach. Of course, Edgeworth did not grasp the far reaching implication of his result, but neither did R. A. Fisher (a rare occasion), in the context of Fisher (1935a). As noted by several researchers (see, for example, Desmond, 1989, p. 57), the term "equation of estimation," with its current meaning, first appeared in Fisher (1935a, p. 45). What is overlooked in the EF literature is another of Fisher's pathbreaking results. The result is the same as Edgeworth's, but Fisher did it quite elegantly and under a more general set up.

To maintain a chronological order, we now present yet another result by Fisher that may be regarded as the first substantial illustration on the use of EEs. Fisher (1924) wanted to compare ML and minimum χ^2 as methods of estimation. He simply showed that they are asymptotically equivalent by comparing the first order conditions of the two estimation procedures. For him, it was much easier to analyze properties of estimators when focusing on the corresponding EEs rather than on the objective functions or estimators themselves. The same is possibly true even after eight decades.

To illustrate, let us consider the minimum χ^2 objective function,

$$\chi^2(\theta) = \sum_{j=1}^{k} \frac{[n_j - nq_j(\theta)]^2}{nq_j(\theta)}, \tag{11.14}$$

where n_j is the observed frequency, and $q_j(\theta)$ is the probability of being in the j-th class, $j = 1, 2, \ldots, k$ with $\theta = (\theta_1, \theta_2, \ldots, \theta_p)'$ as the unknown parameter vector. Let $n = \sum_{j=1}^{n} n_j$; thus $nq_j(\theta)$ is the expected frequency of the j-th class. We can write

$$\chi^2(\theta) = \sum_{j=1}^{k} \frac{n_j^2}{nq_j(\theta)} - n.$$

Therefore, the minimum χ^2 estimates will be obtained by solving $\partial \chi^2(\theta)/\partial \theta = 0$, i.e., from

$$\sum_{j=1}^{k} \frac{n_j^2}{[nq_j(\theta)]^2} \frac{\partial q_j(\theta)}{\partial \theta_l} = 0, \quad l = 1, 2, \ldots, p. \tag{11.15}$$

To connect these equations to those from Fisher's (1912) ML equations, we note that, since $\sum_{j=1}^{k} q_j(\theta) = 1$, we have $\sum_{j=1}^{k} \partial q_j(\theta)/\partial \theta_l = 0$. Therefore, from (11.15), the minimum χ^2 EEs are

$$\sum_{j=1}^{k} \frac{n_j^2 - [nq_j(\theta)]^2}{[nq_j(\theta)]^2} \frac{\partial q_j(\theta)}{\partial \theta_l} = 0, \quad l = 1, 2, \ldots, p. \tag{11.16}$$

Under the multinomial framework, Fisher's likelihood function, denoted as $L(\theta)$, is

$$L(\theta) = n! \prod_{j=1}^{k} [(n_j!)^{-1}] \prod_{j=1}^{k} [q_j(\theta)]^{n_j}.$$

Therefore, the log-likelihood function, denoted by $\ell(\theta)$, can be written as

$$\log L(\theta) = \ell(\theta) = \text{constant} + \sum_{j=1}^{k} n_j \log q_j(\theta).$$

The corresponding ML EEs are $\partial \ell(\theta)/\partial\theta = 0$, i.e.,

$$\sum_{j=1}^{k} \frac{n_j}{q_j(\theta)} \frac{\partial q_j(\theta)}{\partial\theta_l} = 0,$$

or, equivalently,

$$\sum_{j=1}^{k} \frac{[n_j - nq_j(\theta)]}{nq_j(\theta)} \cdot \frac{\partial q_j(\theta)}{\partial\theta_l} = 0, \quad l = 1, 2, \ldots, p. \tag{11.17}$$

Fisher (1924) argued that the difference between (11.16) and (11.17) is the factor $[n_j + nq_j(\theta)]/nq_j(\theta)$, which tends to the value 2 for large values of n and, therefore, these two methods are asymptotically equivalent. The point we want to emphasize is that to compare estimates from two different methods, Fisher (1924) used the "estimating equations" rather than the estimates themselves. Here let us mention that, although the two EEs (11.16) and (11.17) are asymptotically equivalent, there is a fundamental difference. Since $E(n_j) = nq_j(\theta)$ and $E(n_j^2) = nq_j(\theta)[1 - q_j(\theta)] + [nq_j(\theta)]^2$, the EFs corresponding to the minimum χ^2 method are not unbiased, while the EFs for the ML method are. As we will discuss later, unbiasedness of the EF is a very important requirement. Of course, an unbiased EF may not lead to an unbiased estimator.

Now getting back to Fisher (1935a), for ease of exposition, we replace Fisher's "summation" sign by an integral. Fisher (1935a, p. 45) started with an unbiased EF $k(y, \theta)$. Differentiating

$$E[k(y, \theta)] = \int k(y, \theta) f(y, \theta) dy = 0, \tag{11.18}$$

where $f(y, \theta)$ denotes the density function, Fisher obtained

$$\int \frac{dk(y, \theta)}{d\theta} f(y, \theta) dy = -\int k(y, \theta) \frac{df(y, \theta)}{d\theta} dy. \tag{11.19}$$

A Taylor series expansion of the sample equation of estimation $\sum_{i=1}^{n} k(y_i, \hat{\theta}) = 0$ around θ gives

$$0 = \sum_{i=1}^{n} k(y_i, \theta) + (\hat{\theta} - \theta) \sum_{i=1}^{n} \frac{dk(y_i, \theta)}{d\theta} + \cdots, \tag{11.20}$$

i.e., approximately,

$$(\hat{\theta} - \theta) = \frac{\sum_{i=1}^{n} k(y_i, \theta)}{\sum_{i=1}^{n} \frac{dk(y_i, \theta)}{d\theta}}. \tag{11.21}$$

Hence, using (11.19), the asymptotic variance of $\hat{\theta}$ is given by

$$
\begin{aligned}
Var(\hat{\theta}) &= \frac{\int k^2(y, \theta)f(y, \theta)dy}{n\left[\int (dk(y, \theta)/d\theta)f(y, \theta)dy\right]^2} \\
&= \frac{\int k^2(y, \theta)f(y, \theta)dy}{n\left[\int k(y, \theta)(df(y, \theta)/d\theta)dy\right]^2} .
\end{aligned}
\tag{11.22}
$$

This is the same as Edgeworth's equation as given in (11.8). After obtaining the expression (11.22), Fisher (1935a, p. 46) stated, "We may now apply the calculus of variations or simple differentiation to find the functions of k, which will minimize the sampling variance. Since the variance must be stationary for variations of each several values of k, the differential coefficients of the numerator and the denominator with respect to k, must be proportional for all classes." Thus for the "optimal values of k," he obtained

$$
k(y, \theta)f(y, \theta) \propto \frac{df(y, \theta)}{d\theta},
\tag{11.23}
$$

which is satisifed by putting

$$
k(y, \theta) = \frac{1}{f(y, \theta)}\frac{df(y, \theta)}{d\theta} = \frac{dlogf(y, \theta)}{d\theta}.
\tag{11.24}
$$

Fisher then noted that $E[k(y, \theta)] = 0$ is the ML equation, and at the optimum value of $k(y, \theta)$ in (11.24), the asymptotic variance in (11.22) reduces to

$$
Var(\hat{\theta}) = \frac{1}{n\left[\int \left(\frac{dlogf(y, \theta)}{d\theta}\right)^2 f(y, \theta)dy\right]} = \frac{1}{n\mathcal{I}(\theta)}, \quad \text{say.}
\tag{11.25}
$$

Fisher (1935a, p. 44) defined $\mathcal{I}(\theta)$ as the amount of information supplied by each observation.

11.1.4 Asymptotically shortest confidence interval using optimal estimating function

Fisher (1935b) developed a theory of fiducial inference by considering a function, say $g(y, \theta)$, which is pivotal, i.e., its distribution is free of θ. Wilks (1938) utilized this approach for interval estimation (see also Wilks, 1962, pp. 371–6). He considered the pivotal function

$$
\sqrt{n}p(y, \theta) = \frac{\sum_{i=1}^{n} S(y_i, \theta)}{\left[\frac{1}{n}\sum_{i=1}^{n} S^2(y_i, \theta)\right]^{1/2}}
\tag{11.26}
$$

where $S(y_i, \theta) = d\log f(y, \theta)/d\theta$. Under certain regularity conditions, $\sqrt{n}p(y, \theta) \rightarrow^D N(0, 1)$, and, hence, asymptotically it is pivotal. Now, denoting $\hat{\theta}$ as the MLE,

$$0 = p(y, \hat{\theta}) = p(y, \theta) + p'(y, \theta)(\hat{\theta} - \theta) + \cdots, \tag{11.27}$$

where $p'(y, \theta) = dp(y, \theta)/d\theta$. Therefore, $\sqrt{n}(\theta - \hat{\theta})p'(y, \theta)$ is asymptotically equivalent to $\sqrt{n}p(y, \theta)$ and hence distributed as $N(0, 1)$ for large enough n. Utilizing this result, Wilks (1938) obtained the $(1 - \alpha)100\%$ confidence interval for θ as

$$\lim_{n \rightarrow \infty} Pr\left[-Z_{\alpha/2} \leq \sqrt{n}(\theta - \hat{\theta})p'(y, \theta) \leq Z_{\alpha/2}\right] = 1 - \alpha, \tag{11.28}$$

where $Z_{\alpha/2}$ is the upper $\alpha/2$-quantile of the standard normal distribution. Thus we have

$$\lim_{n \rightarrow \infty} Pr\left[\hat{\theta} - \frac{Z_{\alpha/2}}{\sqrt{n}p'(y, \theta)} \leq \theta \leq \hat{\theta} + \frac{Z_{\alpha/2}}{\sqrt{n}p'(y, \theta)}\right] = 1 - \alpha. \tag{11.29}$$

Wilks (1938) further showed that, under certain regularity conditions, the ratio of the squared length of this interval to that of a similar interval using any arbitrary EF, converges in probability to a number that cannot exceed 1. In other words the asymptotically shortest confidence interval results when the pivotal function is constructed from the score function $S(y, \theta)$ as in (11.26). Wald (1942) obtained the same result under a more general framework. Barnard (1973) further explored the advantages of Fisher's approach of formulating the parameter estimation problem in terms of pivotal quantities.

11.1.5 Sufficient statistical estimating function

We mentioned in section 11.1.1 that Fisher (1922) suggested three important criteria of estimation, namely, consistency, efficiency and sufficiency; and of these three, he found the concept of "sufficiency" to be most powerful to advance his ideas on ML estimation. He defined "sufficiency" as (p. 310): "A statistic satisfies the criterion of sufficiency when no other statistic which can be calculated from the same sample provides any additional information as to the value of the parameter to be estimated." However, as is now well known, there are certain distributions for which it is not possible to find nontrivial sufficient statistic(s) for the underlying parameter(s).

Kimball (1946) worked with the extreme-value distribution with density function

$$f(y; \theta) = \alpha e^{-\alpha(y-u)} e^{-e^{-\alpha(y-u)}}, \tag{11.30}$$

where α and u denote parameters. Kimball found the ordinary definition of sufficiency to be inadequate for this distribution; however, he (p. 299) "was struck by the fact that certain functions of the data involving one of the parameters could be used to play a very similar role to a set of *sufficient statistics* for determining α and u, in spite of the fact that one function involved the value of α, and hence was not directly determined by the data, – and hence not a 'statistic'." He argued for a broader definition of sufficiency and introduced a new terminology (p. 300), that of the "statistical estimating function." Possibly, this was the first occurrence of the term in the sense currently used in the literature. Kimball (1946), however, acknowledged Wald (1940), who stated (p. 290, fn 13), "An 'estimate' is usually a function of the observations not involving any unknown parameters. We designate here as estimates also some functions involving the parameter α."

Rao (1945, p. 81) also used the term "estimating function" as: "The validity of this (ML) principle arises from the fact that out of a large class of unbiased estimating functions following the normal distribution the function given by maximizing the probability density has the least variance." We see from the context that he essentially meant the "estimating function" of a sample $y = (y_1, y_2, \ldots, y_n)$ only. However, if we consider Rao's sentence "out of context," he might as well be stating that the ML method is based on an optimal EF! Kimball (1946) also introduced the concept of a "stable" EF as the one whose *expectation* is constant in the parameter. In the context of errors-in-variables models, Kendall (1951) introduced an "unbiased" EE that led to a biased estimator. Kendall's concept of unbiasedness is very close to that of stability used by Kimball (1946). Kendall (1951, p. 21) emphasized, "We must draw a distinction between an unbiased estimator and an unbiased estimating equation."

Suppose the density function involves p parameters $\theta = (\theta_1, \theta_2, \ldots, \theta_p)'$, and we have a sample $y = (y_1, y_2, \ldots, y_n)$. Kimball (1946, p. 302) defined a set of statistical functions $g_1(y, \theta), \ldots, g_p(y, \theta)$ to be sufficient estimating functions (SEFs) if

(i) There is a one-to-one correspondence between $(g_1, g_2, \ldots, g_p)$ and $(\theta_1, \theta_2, \ldots, \theta_p)$.

(ii) It is possible to express the joint distribution (likelihood function) $f(y_1, y_2, \ldots, y_n; \theta)$ as:

$$f(y; \theta) = f(y_1, y_2, \ldots, y_n; \theta) = f_1(g_1, g_2, \ldots, g_p; \theta) f_2(y_1, y_2, \ldots, y_n),$$

where the first factor is purely a function of the EFs and parameters, and the second factor is free of the parameters.

Clearly, the requirement (ii) is along the lines of the Neyman–Fisher factorization. To illustrate his approach, Kimball considered a distribution with two parameters θ_1 and θ_2, and claimed that the score functions

$$S_{\theta_1}(y; \theta_1, \theta_2) = \frac{\partial \log f(y; \theta_1, \theta_2)}{\partial \theta_1} \tag{11.31}$$

and

$$S_{\theta_2}(y; \theta_1, \theta_2) = \frac{\partial \log f(y; \theta_1, \theta_2)}{\partial \theta_2} \tag{11.32}$$

are SEFs according to the above definition. To see this, note that $\log f(y; \theta_1, \theta_2)$ can be expressed as

$$\log f(y; \theta_1, \theta_2) = \int_{\theta_1^0}^{\theta_1} S_{\theta_1}(y; \theta_1, \theta_2)d\theta_1 + \int_{\theta_2^0}^{\theta_2} S_{\theta_2}(y; \theta_1, \theta_2)d\theta_2 + \log f(y; \theta_1^0, \theta_2^0), \tag{11.33}$$

where θ_1^0 and θ_2^0 are arbitrarily chosen from the parameter space. The first two terms in (11.33) entirely depend on the scores $S_{\theta_1}, S_{\theta_2}$ (along with the parameters), while the third term is free of θ_1 and θ_2.

For the extreme value distribution in (11.30), Kimball (1946, p. 304) showed that

$$g_1(y; \theta) = [\alpha(\bar{y} - u) - C], \tag{11.34}$$

$$g_2(y; \theta) = \left[\frac{\bar{z}}{z_0} - 1\right], \tag{11.35}$$

are SEFs, where $C = E[\alpha(\bar{y} - u)], z_i = \exp[-\alpha y_i]$ with mean $\bar{z}$, and $z_0 = \exp[-\alpha u]$. Using 57 years of maximum flood data, Kimball (1946) estimated the parameters α and u based on EFs $g_1(y; \theta)$ and $g_2(y; \theta)$ and compared them with the ML estimates. Although Kimball's approach was very novel, it was not followed up much in the later literature on EFs, though Kale (1962) connected sufficiency to the extended CRLB, and Bhapkar (1991) argued that, for any given EF, a sufficient statistic can be used to derive a more informative EF. McLeish and Small (1988, ch. 2) discussed ancillarity, sufficiency and projection in the context of EFs and advocated that sufficiency for EFs should be developed in its own right.

To summarize, in the first half of the last century, we notice some very important but rather sporadic and disconnected progress in the EF approach. Though the criteria of unbiasedness and sufficiency have been thought of as requirements for an EF, what was missing from all these developments is any notion of *optimality* for the EF. The topic was almost forgotten for several years. It was then rekindled with the appearance of V. P. Godambe's seminal article in 1960, and the essence of Godambe (1960) was the introduction of an "optimality" criterion in addition to unbiasedness. This is very much akin to Neyman and Pearson's (1933) theory of hypothesis testing, where they introduced the concept of optimality (through maximization of power) to the earlier somewhat ad hoc significance and likelihood ratio tests. Godambe (1960) introduced optimality through the minimization of the variance of "unbiased estimating functions" for independent samples, while Durbin (1960) did it mainly for the linear unbiased EF for dependent data in the context of the AR time series model.

11.2   Basic theory of estimating functions

Fisher (1935a) noted a basic fact of estimation: that any procedure for obtaining an estimate of a parameter θ can be regarded as a solution to an equation like

$$g(y; \theta) = 0, \tag{11.36}$$

where $g(y; \theta)$ is a function of the observation vector $y = (y_1, y_2, \ldots, y_n)'$ and parameter θ. The traditional approach to estimation imposes conditions on the resulting estimator $\hat{\theta}$, such as linearity, unbiasedness, consistency, invariance, minimum variance, etc. The EF approach shifts the attention from the estimator $\hat{\theta}$ to the properties of the EF. For example, we will consider an *unbiased* EF instead of an unbiased $\hat{\theta}$, i.e., we will require

$$E[g(y; \theta)] = 0. \tag{11.37}$$

The notion of unbiasedness of an EF is an extension of that of an estimator, and it ensures that the root of the equation (11.36) is close to the true value of the parameter θ when little random variation is present. When $g(y; \theta)$ has a special form, for instance, $g(y; \theta) = g(y) - \theta$, then $\hat{\theta} = g(y)$ and an unbiased EF leads to an unbiased estimator. However, in general, the requirement (11.37) does not necessarily imply unbiasedness of the resulting estimator, though under certain regularity conditions it does imply consistency of the estimator (see Desmond, 1997, p. 80). For more on the role and importance of unbiasedness in EFs, see Yanagimoto and Yamamoto (1991, 1993).

   As we discussed in section 11.1, the importance of the role of unbiasedness and sufficiency (as in Kimball, 1946) was well recognized. The missing element was a criterion of optimality. Durbin (1960, p. 146) stated, "it seems reasonable to develop the idea of unbiased estimating equations with minimum variance" and exploited this idea to derive optimal linear unbiased EFs, reminiscent of the Gauss–Markov theorem. Around the same time, Godambe (1960) started with a class of EFs satisfying certain conditions, which he called regular EFs and devised a procedure to select an optimal EF.

11.2.1   The fundamental result: Godambe (1960) and Durbin (1960)

Godambe's (1960) regular EF $g(y; \theta)$ satisfies the following conditions:

   (i) $E[g(y; \theta)] = \int g(y; \theta) f(y; \theta) dy = 0$,
  (ii) $dg(y; \theta)/d\theta$ exists for all $\theta \in \Theta$, where Θ is the parameter space,
 (iii) $\int g(y; \theta) f(y; \theta) dy$ is differentiable under the sign of integration,
  (iv) $E[dg(y; \theta)/d\theta]^2 > 0$, for all $\theta \in \Theta$,
   (v) $Var[g(y; \theta)] = E[g^2(y; \theta)] < \infty$.

Godambe (1960) also assumed that the likelihood function $f(y; \theta) = \Pi_{i=1}^{n} f(y_i; \theta)$ satisfies the regularity conditions required for establishing the CRLB. For ease of exposition, we now consider the *scalar* parameter case; the EF for the multi-parameter case and the presence of nuisance parameters will be discussed in sections 11.2.2 and 11.2.3, respectively. Let $\mathcal{G}$ denote the class of all regular EFs.

Definition 2.1 *A $g^* \in \mathcal{G}$ is said to be optimal if*

$$\frac{E[g^{*2}(y;\theta)]}{\{E[dg^*(y;\theta)/d\theta]\}^2} \leq \frac{E[g^2(y;\theta)]}{\{E[dg(y;\theta)/d\theta]\}^2}, \tag{11.38}$$

for all $g \in \mathcal{G}$ and $\theta \in \Theta$.

Godambe's (1960) justification for this criterion is as follows. First, it is desirable that $g(y;\theta)$ is as close as possible to zero when evaluated at the true value of θ, i.e., we should minimize $Var[g(y;\theta)] = E[g^2(y;\theta)]$, and hence we should have

$$E[g^{*2}(y;\theta)] \leq E[g^2(y;\theta)]. \tag{11.39}$$

Second, $g(y;\theta + \delta\theta)$ should differ from $E[g(y,\theta)] = 0$ by as large a quantity as possible. This is a kind of "sensitivity" requirement, which can also be viewed as an "identification" condition. This translates as $\{E[dg(y;\theta)/d\theta]\}^2$ should be as large as possible, i.e.,

$$\{E[dg^*(y;\theta)/d\theta]\}^2 \geq \{E[dg(y;\theta)/d\theta]\}^2. \tag{11.40}$$

These two goals (11.39) and (11.40) can be accomplished simultaneously by Godambe's criterion in (11.38). Now we can state and prove Godambe's celebrated result.

Theorem 2.1 *For all $g \in \mathcal{G}$,*

$$\frac{E[g^2(y;\theta)]}{\{E[dg(y;\theta)/d\theta]\}^2} \geq \frac{1}{E[dlogf(y;\theta)/d\theta]^2}, \tag{11.41}$$

and the equality is attained by the EF $g^*(y;\theta) = dlogf(y;\theta)/d\theta$.

Here, with a slight change of notation, we denote $E[dlogf(y;\theta)/d\theta]^2 = n\mathcal{I}(\theta)$ as the Fisher's information contained in the whole sample $y = (y_1, y_2, \dots, y_n)$. The proof of Theorem 2.1 is very similar to that of the CRLB.

Proof. Differentiating the unbiasedness condition (11.37) with respect to θ, we obtain

$$\int \frac{dg}{d\theta} f dy + \int g \frac{dlogf}{d\theta} f dy = 0,$$

i.e.,

$$E\left[\frac{dg}{d\theta}\right] = -Cov\left[g, \frac{dlogf}{d\theta}\right]. \qquad (11.42)$$

Here we suppress the arguments of the functions $g(y; \theta)$ and $f(y; \theta)$ for ease of notation. Since

$$\left\{Cov\left[g, \frac{dlogf}{d\theta}\right]\right\}^2 \le Var[g] \quad Var\left[\frac{dlogf}{d\theta}\right],$$

using (11.42) we have,

$$\left\{E\left[\frac{dg}{d\theta}\right]\right\}^2 \le Var[g]E\left[\frac{dlogf}{d\theta}\right]^2,$$

and the result follows immediately.

This result was also mentioned by Durbin (1960, p. 145), and he acknowledged G.A. Barnard for suggesting the "extension to non-linear estimating equations" from his linear EFs. Godambe (1960) was also aware of this, as he stated (p. 1210): "The author acknowledges with pleasure that G.A. Barnard communicated to the Royal Statistical Society, London, a result similar to the preceding theorem, independently and at nearly the same time when the paper was written," and he made a reference to Durbin (1960, p. 415). Godambe's manuscript was received by the *Annals of Mathematical Statistics* on July 28, 1959, and the revised version on May 17, 1960. Durbin's paper, most possibly the final version, was received by the *Journal of the Royal Statistical Society* on August 1959. It is quite a coincidence that Godambe and Durbin reported "similar" (in fact the same) results "at nearly the same time." To put this result in an historical context, let us recall that Rao (1945) and Crámer (1946) provided the *finite-sample* version of Fisher's result that the *asymptotic* variance of a consistent estimator is bounded below by the reciprocal of Fisher's information measure. We can view the Godambe–Durbin result as the finite-sample version of the Edgeworth (1909) and Fisher (1935a) result [noted in equation (11.11) and (11.24)] that asymptotically the score function $dlogf(y; \theta)/d\theta$ is the optimum EF. Therefore, from the Godambe–Durbin result, for the first time we have a *finite-sample justification* of the ML method of estimation.

Durbin is well known among econometricians, starting from his celebrated Durbin–Watson test statistics for serial correlation. An account of Durbin's life and work is also available from the ET interview (see Phillips, 1988). However, Godambe (and his work) is somewhat unfamiliar to econometricians. The only references to his work on EF that we find in econometric textbooks are in Mittelhammer, Judge and Miller (2000, ch. 11) and Davidson and MacKinnon (2004, pp. 369–72). It would not, therefore, be out of place to add a few sentences on V.P. Godambe. Bellhouse (1992) provides a short but illuminating discussion of his life and time. The *Statistical Science* interview (Thompson, 2002) gives further insights on his work and views on statistical methodologies. Vidyadhar (which means "bearer of wisdom") Godambe was born on June 1, 1926 at Poona, India. He studied sanskrit, philosophy, theoretical physics and mathematics during his undergraduate years. After obtaining his MSc degree (the first batch) from the University of Bombay in 1950, he joined the Bureau of Economics and Statistics in the Government of Bombay (the current state of Maharastra, India). He received his PhD from the Imperial College, University of London, under the supervision of George Barnard. He spent a year (1958–59) as Senior Research Fellow at the Indian Statistical Institute, Calcutta, and the seminal 1960 paper was written there. In 1967, just as the Department of Statistics and Actuarial Science at the University of Waterloo, Canada, was being formed, he joined that department. Upon his retirement in 1991, he was awarded the title of Distinguished Professor Emeritus at the same University.

Godambe's 1960 paper, which is just a little over three pages, appears to be well ahead of its time (though in historical context it can be argued to be long overdue given the results of Edgeworth (1909), Fisher (1935a) and CRLB). In Thompson (2002, p. 460), Godambe traced his idea on EF way back to 1948, as he recounted: "When the conventional theory of unbiased minimum variance estimation was introduced to me in 1948, my immediate reaction was that 'modal unbiasedness' rather than 'mean unbiasedness,' was a desirable property for an estimate. And from among all the modally unbiased estimates, one should choose the estimate whose distribution has maximum probability at the mode for all parameter values." Godambe (1960) was not "noticed" by others for a long time; it had only *two* citations (excluding Godambe's own) during the period 1961–75, 37 citations during 1976–90 and around 165 during the last 15 years. This paper played a central role in introducing and crystallizing newer concepts and advancing the EF approach to a fully fledged area of research in its own right. It also foretold what to expect from Godambe in terms of his own contribution. Godambe confined his research to survey sampling during much of the 1960s; then in the 1970s, he began a fruitful research collaboration on EF with his colleague (Mary) Thompson and, as we will see later, that resulted in a series of important papers. There was also an external factor – (George) Barnard delivered a series of lectures at the University of Waterloo during the academic year 1972–73. As Bellhouse noted (1992, p. 4): "For Godambe the lectures stimulated him to return to the problems of inference using estimating functions or estimating equations. His first results on the theory of optimal estimating functions in the presence of nuisance parameters were obtained with Mary Thompson in an Annals paper in 1974." (James) Durbin did not continue his research on EF that vigorously, and we are aware of only one more published paper on EF by him (see Durbin, 1997).

After this somewhat long digression on some personal narration, let us now return to the Godambe–Durbin optimality result. One of the attractive properties of the MLE is that it is invariant under a one-to-one transformation of the parameter, i.e., if $\hat{\theta}$ is the MLE of θ, then the MLE of $\varphi \equiv \alpha(\theta)$, with $J = d\alpha/d\theta \neq 0$, is given by $\hat{\varphi} \equiv \alpha(\hat{\theta})$. This is due to the fact that

$$\frac{dlogf(y;\theta)}{d\theta} = \frac{dlogf(y;\alpha^{-1}(\varphi))}{d\varphi}J. \tag{11.43}$$

The optimal EF shares this property of invariance. To see this, note that if $g(y;\theta)$ is an unbiased EF for θ, then $g(y;\alpha^{-1}(\varphi)) = g_1(y;\varphi)$ is an unbiased EF for φ. Let $\hat{\theta}_g$ and $\hat{\varphi}_{g_1}$ be the estimates from $g=0$ and $g_1=0$, respectively. Then we have the invariance $\hat{\varphi}_{g_1} = \alpha(\hat{\theta}_g)$. Many good estimators, such as the MVU estimator, do not possess the property of invariance. Okuma (1976) provides a useful discussion on invariance of the EF from a different perspective.

There are several ways to represent and interpret the inequality (11.38). The equations $g(y;\theta) = 0$ and $\tilde{g}(y;\theta) = cg(y;\theta) = 0$, where $c \neq 0$ is a constant, will lead to the same estimator, say $\hat{\theta}$. $Var[\tilde{g}(y;\theta)] = c^2 Var[g(y;\theta)]$ can, however, be made arbitrarily small and thus the comparison of two EFs based on their variances alone is not meaningful without some standardization. The standardized version of $g \equiv g(y;\theta)$ is defined as

$$g_s = \frac{g}{E[dg/d\theta]}. \tag{11.44}$$

Thus we have,

$$Var[g_s] = Var[\tilde{g}_s] = \frac{E[g^2]}{\{E[dg/d\theta]\}^2}. \tag{11.45}$$

The Godambe–Durbin optimality result can now be stated as: g^* is optimal in class $\mathcal{G}$ if $g^* \in \mathcal{G}$ and if

$$Var[g_s^*] \leq Var[g_s], \quad \forall g \in \mathcal{G}. \tag{11.46}$$

The asymptotic properties of an estimator are inherited from the statistical behavior (e.g., variance) of the corresponding EF. A first-order Taylor series expansion of $g(\hat{\theta}) = 0$ around θ [as in equation (11.20) in the context of Fisher (1935a)] gives us

$$n^{1/2}(\hat{\theta} - \theta) \approx -n^{-1/2}g(\theta) \times \left(n^{-1}\frac{\partial g}{\partial \theta}\right)^{-1}$$
$$\approx -n^{1/2}g(\theta) \times \left[E\left(\frac{\partial g}{\partial \theta}\right)\right]^{-1}, \tag{11.47}$$

i.e., the estimator $\hat{\theta}$ and the standardized EF g_s in (11.44) are statistically equivalent asymptotically. Also, a measure of the finite sample performance of $g(y;\theta)$ should not conflict with the asymptotic properties of $\hat{\theta}$. Therefore, in order to obtain an estimator with minimum limiting variance, the EF g has to be chosen with minimum variance of its standardized form g_s.

Using the variance minimization criterion (11.46) as a basis for selecting the optimal EF g^*, has some further implications (see, for instance, Bera and Bilias, 2001a). First, consider the correlation between an unbiased EF g for the parameter θ and the score function $S(\theta) = dlogf(y;\theta)/d\theta$. In view of the identity in (11.42) we can write:

$$
\begin{aligned}
[Corr(g, S(\theta))]^2 &= \frac{[E(g, S(\theta))]^2}{E(g^2)E[(S(\theta))^2]} \\
&= \frac{[E(dg/d\theta)]^2}{E(g)^2} \frac{1}{E[(S(\theta))^2]} \\
&= \frac{1}{Var(g_s)} \frac{1}{Var(S(\theta))}.
\end{aligned}
\tag{11.48}
$$

Therefore, choosing g with the minimum variance of its standardized version is equivalent to maximizing the correlation of g with the score function. Second, consider the L_2 distance of g_s from the standardized score function $S_s(\theta)$. Upon noting that the variance of the standardized score is $1/Var(S(\theta))$ and using (11.42), we obtain

$$
E[(g_s - S_s(\theta))^2] = Var(g_s) - \frac{1}{Var(S(\theta))}.
\tag{11.49}
$$

Thus, minimization of the variance of g_s is equivalent to minimizing the Euclidean distance of g_s from the score function. The two results above certainly highlight the nature of the optimal EF as a best approximation to the score function, which, in general, is unknown.

Kale (1962) independently proved the result in (11.41), and called it an extension of the CRLB for the variance of an EF $g(y; \theta)$ instead of a statistic (which is a function of the sample alone). He also proved that if the variance of $g(y; \theta)$ attains the lower bound given by the extended inequality, then $g(y; \theta)$ is a sufficient EF in the sense of Kimball (1946) (as discussed in section 11.5). Kale (1962, p. 82) expressed his result as

$$
Var[g] \geq \frac{[d\psi/d\theta - E(dg/d\theta)]^2}{\mathcal{I}(\theta)},
\tag{11.50}
$$

where $E[g(y;\theta)] = \psi(\theta) = \psi$ and $\mathcal{I}(\theta)$ is the Fisher information in the whole sample, $y = (y_1, y_2, \ldots, y_n)$. He also noted that the score function $dlogf(y;\theta)/d\theta$ is a sufficient EF since it attains the extended CRLB. The extended inequality (11.50) reduces to the standard Cramér–Rao inequality by putting $g(y;\theta) = T(y) - \theta$ and writing

$$
Var[T(y)] \geq \frac{1}{\mathcal{I}(\theta)},
\tag{11.51}
$$

where $T(y)$ is an unbiased estimator for θ. We should, however, note that the CRLB is attained only exceptionally, whereas the optimality of ML equations among EEs holds merely under regularity conditions.

Bhapkar (1972) defined the information contained in an EF $g(y; \theta)$ about θ by the reciprocal of the variance of the standardized EF g_s, i.e.,

$$\mathcal{I}_g(\theta) = \frac{1}{Var[g_s]} = \frac{[E(dg/d\theta)]^2}{E(g^2)}, \tag{11.52}$$

and the ratio

$$RE(g) = \frac{\mathcal{I}_g(\theta)}{\mathcal{I}(\theta)}, \tag{11.53}$$

as the efficiency of the EF $g(y; \theta)$. Therefore, we can rewrite inequality (11.41) simply as

$$\mathcal{I}_g(\theta) \leq \mathcal{I}(\theta), \tag{11.54}$$

and hence,

$$RE(g) \leq 1, \tag{11.55}$$

for all $\theta \in \Theta$ and $g \in \mathcal{G}$. Therefore, $\mathcal{I}(\theta)$ is the maximum amount of information contained in a regular EF $g \in \mathcal{G}$. Let $T \equiv t(y)$ be sufficient for θ and define $\tilde{g} \equiv \tilde{g}(y; \theta) = E[g(y; \theta)|t]$, which is a Rao–Blackwellization of the original unbiased EF $g(y; \theta)$. Bhapkar (1972, p. 469) showed that

$$\mathcal{I}_g(\theta) \leq \mathcal{I}_{\tilde{g}}(\theta), \tag{11.56}$$

with equality iff $g(y; \theta) = \tilde{g}(t(y); \theta)$. In other words, if we start with a EF that is already a function of the sufficient statistic T, there is no room for improvement. Also combining (11.54) and (11.56), it is easy to see that

$$\mathcal{I}_g(\theta) \leq \mathcal{I}_{\tilde{g}}(\theta) \leq \mathcal{I}(\theta) = \mathcal{I}_{g^*}(\theta), \tag{11.57}$$

where $\mathcal{I}_{g^*}(\theta)$ denotes the information contained in the optimal EF $g^*(y; \theta)$.

Wedderburn (1974) observed that, from a computational point of view, the only assumptions on a generalized linear model necessary to estimate the model were a specification of the mean and the relationship between the mean and variance, without specifying the probability density function. Let us consider a very simple model where the random variable y has mean μ and variance $V(\mu)$ that may be dependent on the mean. Define the function

$$g(y; \mu) = \frac{\sum_{i=1}^{n}(y_i - \mu)}{V(\mu)}. \tag{11.58}$$

Wedderburn (1974) noticed that (11.58) is very close to the true score of all the distributions that belong to the exponential family. In addition, $g(y; \mu)$ has properties similar to those of a score function in the sense that

(i) $E[g(y; \mu)] = 0$,
(ii) $E[g^2(y; \mu)] = -E[dg(y; \mu)/d\mu]$.

Wedderburn termed $g(y; \mu)$ in (11.58) as the "quasi-score function," the integral of $g(y; \mu)$ the "quasi-likelihood," and the equation $g(y; \mu) = 0$, the "quasi-likelihood equation." Godambe and Heyde (1987) showed that Wedderburn's method can be regarded as a particular case of the optimal EF approach (see also Heyde, 1997, pp. 21–6; Desmond, 1997, pp. 78–80). The attractive feature of the EF approach is that we do not need to assume that the true underlying distribution belongs to the exponential family.

Since one good example is worth a thousand theories, we now discuss an example, often used in the context of EFs (for example, see Godambe and Kale, 1991; Desmond, 1997; and Bera and Bilias, 2002).

Example 2.1 Let $y_i, i = 1, \ldots, n$ be independent random variables with $E(y_i) = \mu_i(\theta)$ and $Var(y_i) = \sigma_i^2(\theta)$, where θ is a scalar parameter. The quasi-score approach of Wedderburn (1974) suggests that, in the class of linear EFs, we should solve

$$g^*(y; \mu) = \sum_{i=1}^{n} \frac{[y_i - \mu_i(\theta)]}{\sigma_i^2} \frac{d\mu_i(\theta)}{d\theta} = 0. \tag{11.59}$$

Under the assumption of normality of y_i, the ML equation

$$\frac{d\log f(y; \mu)}{d\theta} = g^*(y; \theta) + \frac{1}{2} \sum_{i=1}^{n} \frac{[y_i - \mu_i(\theta)]^2}{\sigma_i^4(\theta)} \frac{d\sigma_i^2(\theta)}{d\theta} - \frac{1}{2} \sum_{i=1}^{n} \frac{d\log \sigma_i^2(\theta)}{d\theta} = 0, \tag{11.60}$$

is globally optimal and estimation based on the quasi-score (11.59) is inferior. If one is unwilling to assume normality, one could claim that the weighted LS approach that minimizes $\sum_i [y_i - \mu_i(\theta)]^2/\sigma_i^2(\theta)$ and yields the EE

$$w(y; \mu) = g^*(y; \theta) + \frac{1}{2} \sum_{i=1}^{n} \frac{[y_i - \mu_i(\theta)]^2}{\sigma_i^4(\theta)} \frac{d\sigma_i^2(\theta)}{d\theta} = 0 \tag{11.61}$$

is preferable. However, because of the dependence of the variance on θ, (11.61) delivers an inconsistent root, in general; see Crowder (1986), McLeish (1984) and Sørensen (1999). The application of a law of large numbers shows that $g^*(y; \theta)$ is stochastically closer to the score (11.60) than is $w(y; \theta)$. In a way, the second term in (11.61) creates a bias in $w(y; \theta)$, and the third term in (11.60) "corrects" for this bias in the score equation.

Let us now consider the optimal EF for this model. We start with a linear EF of the form

$$g(y; \theta) = \sum_{i=1}^{n} [y_i - \mu_i(\theta)] b_i(\theta), \tag{11.62}$$

where the $b_i(\theta)$'s need to be determined. Its standardized version is

$$\begin{aligned}
g_s(y; \theta) &= \frac{g(y; \theta)}{E[dg(y; \theta)/d\theta]} \\
&= \frac{\sum_{i=1}^{n} [y_i - \mu_i(\theta)] b_i(\theta)}{E\left[-\sum_{i=1}^{n} (d\mu_i(\theta)/d\theta) b_i(\theta) + \sum_{i=1}^{n} [y_i - \mu_i(\theta)] db_i(\theta)/d\theta \right]} \\
&= -\frac{\sum_{i=1}^{n} [y_i - \mu_i(\theta)] b_i(\theta)}{\sum_{i=1}^{n} (d\mu_i(\theta)/d\theta) b_i(\theta)},
\end{aligned} \tag{11.63}$$

whose variance is equal to

$$Var[g_s(y; \theta)] = \frac{\sum_{i=1}^{n} \sigma_i^2(\theta) b_i^2(\theta)}{\left[\sum_{i=1}^{n} (d\mu_i(\theta)/d\theta) b_i(\theta) \right]^2}. \tag{11.64}$$

The variance in (11.64) is minimized at

$$b_i(\theta) \propto \frac{d\mu_i(\theta)}{d\theta} \sigma_i^{-2}(\theta). \tag{11.65}$$

Using this value of $b_i(\theta)$ in (11.65) leads to the optimal EF

$$\sum_{i=1}^{n} \frac{[y_i - \mu_i(\theta)]}{\sigma_i^2(\theta)} \frac{d\mu_i(\theta)}{d\theta}, \tag{11.66}$$

which is identical to that obtained from the Wedderburn quasi-likelihood approach as in equation (11.59). Now assume that $Var(y_i) = c\sigma_i^2(\theta)$, where c is an unknown positive constant not depending on θ: then under the ML approach, θ and c cannot be estimated separately. For a specified value $c = c_0$, the ML equation now changes from (11.60) to

$$\frac{dlogf(y; \mu)}{d\theta} = \frac{g^*(y; \theta)}{c_0} + \frac{1}{2c_0} \sum_{i=1}^{n} \frac{[y_i - \mu_i(\theta)]^2}{\sigma_i^4(\theta)} \frac{d\sigma_i^2(\theta)}{d\theta} - \frac{1}{2} \sum_{i=1}^{n} \frac{dlog\sigma_i^2(\theta)}{d\theta} = 0, \tag{11.67}$$

with

$$E\left[\frac{dlogf(y; \mu)}{d\theta} \right] = \frac{1}{2} \left(\frac{c}{c_0} - 1 \right) \sum_{i=1}^{n} \frac{dlog\sigma_i^2(\theta)}{d\theta}, \tag{11.68}$$

which is also zero only when $c = c_0$. Thus the ML equation is biased, as was the LS equation in (11.61). However, the optimal EF in (11.62) [and also the quasi-score in (11.59)] remains unaffected by the value of c. Therefore, here we have situations in which both the LS and ML methods could be inconsistent while the EF retains its optimality property.

11.2.2 Generalization to the multiparameter case

The extension of the EF approach from the single parameter case to the multi-parameter framework with $\theta = (\theta_1, \theta_2, \ldots, \theta_p)'$ is quite natural and straightforward. The basic technique is to replace the scalars by $(p \times 1)$ vectors and variances by $(p \times p)$ variance–covariance matrices. Therefore, instead of presenting all generalizations to the multiparameter case, we will only mention the key results. We start with a $(p \times 1)$ vector EF, $g(y; \theta) = (g_1(y; \theta), g_2(y; \theta), \ldots, g_p(y; \theta))'$, satisfying the regularity conditions stated in section 11.2.1 for the single parameter case. Let us denote the class of regular unbiased EFs by $\mathcal{G}$ and define

$$\Sigma_g = Var[g(y; \theta)] = E[g(y; \theta)g'(y; \theta)], \tag{11.69}$$

and

$$D_g = E\left[\frac{\partial g(y; \theta)}{\partial \theta}\right], \tag{11.70}$$

both being $(p \times p)$ nonsingular matrices. The standardized vector EF can be written as

$$g_s(y; \theta) = D_g^{-1} g(y; \theta), \tag{11.71}$$

and hence

$$Var[g(y; \theta)] = D_g^{-1} \Sigma_g D_g'^{-1} = \Sigma_{g_s}, \quad \text{say.} \tag{11.72}$$

Therefore, our objective could be stated as to minimize (maximize) a scalar measure corresponding to $D_g^{-1} \Sigma_g D_g'^{-1} (D_g \Sigma_g^{-1} D_g')$. Bhapkar (1972) defined an optimal EF g^* as follows:

Definition 2.2   *A $g^* \in \mathcal{G}$ is said to be optimal if*

$$Var[g_s^*] \leq Var[g_s] \tag{11.73}$$

or,

$$\Sigma_{g_s^*} \leq \Sigma_{g_s} \tag{11.74}$$

or,

$$D_{g^*}^{-1} \Sigma_{g^*} D_{g^*}'^{-1} \leq D_g^{-1} \Sigma_g D_g'^{-1} \tag{11.75}$$

i.e., the difference of the left-hand-side matrix from the right-hand-side matrix is non-negative definite (nnd) for all $g \in \mathcal{G}$.

This is the multiparameter counterpart of Definition 2.1, given in section 11.2.1. The above criterion is called the *matrix optimality* of g^*. Unlike in the scalar case, there could be many ways to compare the two matrices, say, in (11.74) and define optimality of g^*; for example, two other ways could be through

(i) trace optimality, i.e., $Tr(\Sigma_{g_s^*}) \leq Tr(\Sigma_{g_s})$,
(ii) determinant optimality, i.e., $|\Sigma_{g_s^*}| \leq |\Sigma_{g_s}|$.

Chandrasekhar and Kale (1984) proved that these three criteria are equivalent in the sense that if g^* is optimal with respect to one criterion then it is also optimal with respect to the remaining two (see also Heyde, 1997, pp. 19–21). Godambe–Durbin's optimality result can now be presented as: for all $g \in \mathcal{G}$ and $\theta \in \Theta$

$$D_g^{-1}\Sigma_g D_g^{-1} - \mathcal{I}^{-1} \geq 0, \tag{11.76}$$

where $\mathcal{I} \equiv \mathcal{I}(\theta) = E[\partial \log f(y; \theta)/\partial\theta\partial\theta']$ is the ($p \times p$) Fisher information matrix. The equality in (11.76) holds since the optimal EF $g^*(y; \theta) = \partial logf(y; \theta)/\partial\theta = S(\theta)$, the ($p \times 1$) score vector. From (11.76) it follows that

$$|\Sigma_g| \geq |D_g \mathcal{I}^{-1} D_g'| = \frac{|D_g|^2}{|\mathcal{I}|}. \tag{11.77}$$

Following the scalar case, Bhapkar (1972) defined the amount of information contained in the EF $g(y; \theta)$ about θ, by

$$\mathcal{I}_g(\theta) = \frac{|D_g|^2}{|\Sigma_g|}. \tag{11.78}$$

The equality

$$RE(g) = \frac{\mathcal{I}_g(\theta)}{|\mathcal{I}(\theta)|} \tag{11.79}$$

provides a measure of efficiency of g. Clearly $0 \leq RE(g) \leq 1$, and the upper bound is attained by the score function $S(\theta)$. In the multiparameter case, alternative measures of efficiency can also be defined, such as,

$$\frac{Tr\left(D_g \Sigma_g^{-1} D_g'\right)}{Tr(\mathcal{I})}. \tag{11.80}$$

Both the measures, (11.79) and (11.80), reduce to (11.53) in the scalar case.

11.2.3 Estimating function in the presence of nuisance parameters

In the 1930s, the controversy between Karl Pearson and Fisher spilled over to Jerzy Neyman. Neyman found it difficult to accept the ML method as a *general* method of estimation. As Barnard (1973, p. 133) stated, Neyman's objection to the ML method arose not because of its failure in unusual pathological cases, but because it seemed to give "wrong" answers for some simple cases. One of the simplest cases is estimation of θ_1 when $Y \sim N(\theta_2, \theta_1)$. The ML method gives a biased estimate for θ_1. A more serious objection to the ML approach was raised by Neyman and Scott (1948), who showed that when the number of nuisance parameters increases with the sample size, the MLE of a parameter of interest could be

inefficient or even *inconsistent*. Perhaps, for problems involving nuisance parameters, the EF approach has the most potential.

Let us partition the $p \times 1$ parameter vector θ by $\theta = (\theta_1', \theta_2')' \in \Theta$, where $\theta_1 \in \Theta_1$
is an $r \times 1 (r < p)$ vector of unknown parameters of interest, and $\theta_2 \in \Theta_2$ is a
$(p - r) \times 1$ vector of "nuisance" or "incidental" parameters. As noted, nuisance
parameters can have a major influence on the estimation of parameters of interest.

The problem of estimating a real parameter θ_1, in the presence of a nuisance
parameter θ_2, was first addressed by Godambe and Thompson (1974), yet another
"conceptually clean" and pathbreaking paper – just over three pages long. They
first defined a class $\mathcal{G}_1$ of regular unbiased EFs of the form $g(y; \theta_1)$. The generalization of the earlier optimality criteria [see equations (11.38) and (11.46)] now
defines an optimal EF $g^* \in \mathcal{G}_1$ for which

$$Var[g_s^*] \le Var[g_s], \tag{11.81}$$

for all $g \in \mathcal{G}_1$. Taking θ_1 and θ_2 as scalars, Godambe and Thompson (1974) showed
that, under the regularity conditions, the function $g^* \in \mathcal{G}_1$ satisfying (11.81) is
given by

$$g^* = c_1(\theta_1, \theta_2) \frac{\partial logf(y; \theta)}{\partial \theta_1}$$
$$+ c_2(\theta_1, \theta_2) \left\{ \left[\frac{\partial logf(y; \theta)}{\partial \theta_2} \right]^2 + \frac{\partial^2 logf(y; \theta)}{\partial \theta_2^2} \right\}, \tag{11.82}$$

where $c_1(\theta_1, \theta_2)$ and $c_2(\theta_1, \theta_2)$ are such that the resulting g^* is free of θ_2.

Example 2.2   Godambe and Thompson (1974) considered the $N(\theta_2, \theta_1)$ case. Here

$$f(y; \theta) = \frac{1}{(\sqrt{2\pi\theta_1})^n} e^{-\frac{1}{2\theta_1} \sum_{i=1}^{n} (y_i - \theta_2)^2}, \tag{11.83}$$

$$\frac{\partial logf(y; \theta)}{\partial \theta_1} = -\frac{n}{2\theta_1} + \frac{(n-1)\hat{\theta}_1 + n(\bar{y} - \theta_2)^2}{2\theta_1^2}, \tag{11.84}$$

$$\frac{\partial logf(y; \theta)}{\partial \theta_2} = \frac{n(\bar{y} - \theta_2)}{\theta_1}, \tag{11.85}$$

$$\frac{\partial^2 logf(y; \theta)}{\partial \theta_2^2} = -\frac{n}{\theta_1}, \tag{11.86}$$

where $\hat{\theta}_1 = \sum_{i=1}^{n}(y_i - \bar{y})^2/(n-1)$ with $\bar{y} = \sum_{i=1}^{n} y_i/n$. Using (11.84)–(11.86), it is
essay to see that by choosing $c_1(\theta_1, \theta_2) = 1$ and $c_1(\theta_1, \theta_2) = -1/2n$, we can get a g^*
which is free of θ_2, and it is given by

$$g^* = \frac{n-1}{2\theta_1^2}(\hat{\theta}_1 - \theta_1), \tag{11.87}$$

and $g^* = 0$ gives an unbiased estimator. In this connection we should mention that Fisher (1912), while proposing his ML method, also produced an unbiased estimator of θ_1 from the mode of the posterior distribution (inverse probability) with a non-informative prior for θ_2. At a later stage, Fisher (1922, p. 326) himself did not approve of basing his argument upon the principle of inverse probability.

Toward the end of their paper, without any fanfare, Godambe and Thompson (1974) suggested an EF $g_1(y; \theta_1)$ of the form

$$g_1(y;\theta_1) = \left[\frac{\partial logf(y;\theta)}{\partial\theta_1}\bigg|_{\theta_2 = \hat{\theta}_2}\right] - E\left[\frac{\partial logf(y;\theta)}{\partial\theta_1}\bigg|_{\theta_2 = \hat{\theta}_2}\right] \tag{11.88}$$

where $\hat{\theta}_2$ is the MLE of θ_2. They attributed their result to George Barnard (through oral communication) who was then visiting their Department of Statistics, University of Waterloo. Eight years later, as we discuss below, in a very influential paper, Lindsay (1982) considered precisely this form of EF and established its importance and usefulness.

Example 2.3 Let us consider $y_{ij} = \mu_i + \epsilon_{ij}, \epsilon_{ij} \sim IIDN(0, \theta_1)$, $i = 1, 2, \ldots, k, j = 1, 2$. Here $\theta_2 = (\mu_1, \mu_2, \ldots, \mu_k)'$ is the nuisance parameter vector. Neyman and Scott (1948) used this model for their famous illustration of the inconsistency of MLE of a parameter of interest when the number of nuisance parameter increases with the sample size. The loglikelihood and score functions, respectively, are given by

$$\log f(y;\theta) = -k\log(2\pi) - k\log\theta_1 - \frac{1}{2\theta_1}\sum_{i=1}^{k}\sum_{j=1}^{2}(y_{ij} - \mu_i)^2,$$

$$\frac{\partial \log f(y;\theta)}{\partial\theta_1} = -\frac{k}{\theta_1} + \frac{1}{2\theta_1^2}\sum_{i=1}^{k}\sum_{j=1}^{2}(y_{ij} - \mu_i)^2,$$

$$\frac{\partial \log f(y;\theta)}{\partial\mu_i} = \frac{1}{\theta_1}\sum_{j=1}^{2}(y_{ij} - \mu_i), \quad i = 1, 2, \ldots, k.$$

Therefore,

$$\hat{\theta}_1 = \frac{1}{2k}\sum_{i=1}^{k}\sum_{j=1}^{2}(y_{ij} - \bar{y}_i)^2, \tag{11.89}$$

where $\bar{y}_i = \sum_{j=1}^{2} y_{ij}/2$ is the MLE for θ_1. Since $\frac{1}{\theta_1}\sum_{j=1}^{2}(y_{ij} - \bar{y}_i)^2 \sim \chi_1^2$, if we define $z_i = \frac{1}{2}\sum_{j=1}^{2}(y_{ij} - \bar{y}_i)^2$, then $z_i \sim IID(\theta_1/2, \theta_1^2/2)$. By the weak law of large numbers, as $k \to \infty$, $\hat{\theta}_1 = \sum_{i=1}^{k} z_i/k$ converges to $E(z_i) = \theta_1/2$.

Godambe resolved this inconsistency of the MLE problem by showing that, under certain conditions, the optimal EF leads to a *conditional* ML approach and provides a consistent estimator for θ_1. The basic problem for the ML approach is that, although

$$E[\partial \log f(y;\theta_1, \theta_2)/\partial\theta_1] = 0, \tag{11.90}$$

$$E[\partial \log f(y; \theta_1, \hat{\theta}_{2.1})/\partial \theta_1] \neq 0, \tag{11.91}$$

where $\hat{\theta}_{2.1}$ is the MLE of θ_2 for fixed θ_1. Therefore, the use of (11.91) will lead to a biased EF for θ_1. Let $T \equiv t(y)$ be a complete sufficient statistic for the parameter θ_2, for every fixed θ_1, and also assume that T does not involve θ_1. Suppose we can decompose the likelihood function as

$$f(y; \theta) = f(y|t; \theta_1)h(t; \theta_1, \theta_2), \tag{11.92}$$

where $f(y|t; \theta_1)$ is the conditional pdf of y given t, and h is the pdf of T. Then Godambe (1976, Theorem 3.2) showed that the "conditional" score function $\partial \log f(y|t; \theta_1)/\partial \theta_1$ gives a *unique optimal* EF.

Example 2.3   *(Continued)* It can be shown that $T(y) = (\bar{y}_1, \bar{y}_2, \ldots, \bar{y}_k)'$ is complete sufficient for $\theta_1 = (\mu_1, \mu_2, \ldots, \mu_k)'$. Using (11.92), we can show that

$$g^* = \frac{\partial \log f_t(y|t; \theta_1)}{\partial \theta_1} = -\frac{k}{2\theta_1} + \frac{1}{2\theta_1^2} \sum_{i=1}^{k}\sum_{j=1}^{2}(y_{ij} - \bar{y}_i)^2 \tag{11.93}$$

is the optimal EF. The difference between the score $\partial \log f(y; \theta)/\partial \theta$, and the conditional score g^* is quite obvious. Solving $g^* = 0$, we have the solution

$$\tilde{\theta}_1 = \frac{1}{k}\sum_{i=1}^{k}\sum_{j=1}^{2}(y_{ij} - \bar{y}_i)^2 = \frac{1}{4k}\sum_{i=1}^{k}(y_{i1} - y_{i2})^2 = 2\hat{\theta}_1, \tag{11.94}$$

which converges to θ_1, and hence is consistent. This was Godambe's (1976) solution to the Neyman–Scott (1948) problem through the EF approach.

Godambe's method works well as long as the conditioning statistic $T(y)$ does not involve θ_1, which will be the case when $f(y; \theta)$ has the exponential family structure. However, that will exclude a large class of distributions. To accommodate a general situation, Lindsay (1982) extended Godambe's (1976) conditional score function $\partial \log f(y|t; \theta_1)/\partial \theta_1$ to

$$S_1^*(\theta) = \frac{\partial \log f(y; \theta)}{\partial \theta_1} - E\left[\frac{\partial \log f(y; \theta)}{\partial \theta_1} | t_{\theta_1}\right], \tag{11.95}$$

where t_{θ_1} is the minimal sufficient statistic for θ_2 and the notation signifies that t is functionally dependent on θ_1. When $t_{\theta_1} \equiv t$, $S_1^*(\theta)$ reduces to $\partial \log f(y|t; \theta)/\partial \theta_1$. The closeness of (11.88) and (11.95) is unmistakable. $S_1^*(\theta)$, which is sometimes also called the effective score, is orthogonal to the space spanned by the sufficient statistic t_{θ_1}. Though $S_1^*(\theta)$ will continue to depend on θ_2, the representation in (11.95) implies that the dependence on θ_2 is now reduced. For a rigorous discussion of these issues and further results see, for instance, Lindsay and Waterman (1992) and Liang and Zeger (1995).

We end our discussion on nuisance parameter issues by giving another, though asymptotic, justification for Lindsay's conditional (effective) score (11.95) by following Neyman's (1959) approach to testing in the presence of nuisance parameters (see Bera and Bilias, 2001a, 2001b). For simplicity, we assume that both θ_1 and θ_2 are scalars. The need to leave the asymptotic distribution of EF unchanged after the substitution of a $\sqrt{n}$-*consistent* estimate of θ_2 leads to the orthogonalization step: starting from an arbitrary EF g, we will regress g on the part of the score for the nuisance parameter $S_2 = \partial logf(y; \theta)/\partial\theta_2$ and keep the residual. The new EF will be

$$g - bS_2,$$

where b denotes the regression coefficient. Next, we want to choose $(g - bS_2)$, and therefore g, according to the Godambe–Durbin optimality criterion. This dictates that the optimal EF, in its standardized form, should have minimum variance. By differentiating the moment condition

$$E[g - bS_2] = 0 \tag{11.96}$$

with respect to θ_1, we have

$$E\left[\frac{\partial(g - bS_2)}{\partial\theta_1}\right] + Cov[(g - bS_2), S_1] = 0,$$

where S_1 is the score for the parameter of interest. Since $(g - bS_2)$ is *orthogonal* to S_2, $Cov[(g - bS_2), S_1] = Cov[(g - bS_2), (S_1 - bS_2)]$. Therefore,

$$E\left[\frac{\partial(g - bS_2)}{\partial\theta_1}\right] = -Cov[(g - bS_2), (S_1 - bS_2)], \tag{11.97}$$

which, using the Cauchy-Schwartz inequality, yields:

$$\left\{E\left[\frac{\partial(g - bS_2)}{\partial\theta_1}\right]\right\}^2 = \{Cov[(g - bS_2), (S_1 - bS_2)]\}^2$$
$$\leq Var(g - bS_2)Var(S_1 - bS_2). \tag{11.98}$$

The inequality (11.98) can be rearranged so that a lower bound for the variance of the standardized EF is formed as

$$\frac{Var[(g - bS_2)]}{\left\{E\left[\frac{\partial(g-bS_2)}{\partial\theta_1}\right]\right\}^2} \geq \frac{1}{Var(S_1 - bS_2)}. \tag{11.99}$$

The bound is reached when $g = S_1$. Thus the optimal EF in the presence of nuisance parameters is given by the effective score $(S_1 - bS_2)$, where $b = Cov(S_2, S_1)/Var(S_1)$. However, it should be remarked that, in contrast to Godambe's result (Theorem 2.1) that the score is the optimal EF, our argument in the presence of nuisance parameters holds only asymptotically.

11.2.4 The dependent case and optimal combination of (elementary) estimating functions

As noted in section 11.2.1, for some time it was believed that the MM estimators are inefficient compared to the ML estimators. Godambe's (1960) analysis highlights, for the IID case, the equivalence of MM and ML estimation when one replaces an arbitrary moment function with the score function. Much of his analysis also carries over to the dependent situation. For a general discrete time stochastic process, an optimality criterion for an EF was established in two important papers by Godambe (1985) and Godambe and Thompson (1989) using a "flexible" *conditioning* method. Their flexible set up can cope with the estimation of parameters in dependent data, such as those from time series processes on a real line or a spatial process on a lattice. In this section we present the theory developed for the optimum combination of (elementary) EFs for the estimation of parameters of stochastic processes. In section 11.3, we will provide applications to some widely used models in the applied econometrics and statistics literature.

Let us consider a discrete time stochastic process $\{y_t; t \geq 0\}$ taking values on the real line $\mathbf{R}$. Also let $\mathcal{F} = \{F\}$ be a class of probability distributions on $\mathbf{R}^n$ and $\theta = \theta(F) \in \Theta$, be a real parameter. The objective is to estimate θ by an estimator $\hat{\theta}_n$ which is a function of observations $\{y_t; 0 \leq t \leq n\}$. By definition, the EF $g(y_1, \ldots, y_n; \theta(F))$ is a real valued function of both the observation $\{y_t\}$ and the parameter θ, that satisfies certain regularity conditions (such as square-integrability and differentiability, given in section 11.2.1). It is called a regular unbiased EF if

$$E_F\{g(y_1, \ldots, y_n; \theta(F))\} = 0, \quad F \in \mathcal{F}.$$

Among all regular unbiased EFs $g(y_1, \ldots, y_n; \theta(F))$, $g^*(y_1, \ldots, y_n; \theta(F))$ is said to be optimum if

$$E_F[g(y_1, \ldots, y_n; \theta(F))^2] \Big/ \left[E_F \left(\frac{\partial g(y_1, \ldots, y_n; \theta)}{\partial \theta} \right)_{\theta = \theta(F)} \right]^2 \tag{11.100}$$

is minimized $\forall F \in \mathcal{F}$ at $g = g^*$. An estimator $\hat{\theta}_n$ is obtained by solving

$$g^*(y_1, \ldots, y_n; \theta(F)) = 0.$$

Suppose that we have the unbiased EFs $\psi_t, t = 1, \ldots, n$ involving θ. The question is what is the best way of combining these n EFs into one EF for estimation of θ. Godambe (1985) restricted his search to the class $\mathcal{L}$ of linear combinations of $\psi_t's$ namely,

$$\left\{ g : g(\theta) = \sum_{t=1}^n a_{t-1} \psi_t \right\}, \tag{11.101}$$

where the coefficient a_{t-1} is arbitrary function of $\{y_1, \ldots, y_{t-1}\}$ and θ. Also, the elementary EF ψ_t is such that $E_F[\psi_t | \mathcal{F}_{t-1}^y] = 0$, with $\mathcal{F}_{t-1}^y$ as the σ-field generated by $\{y_s; s \leq t - 1\}$. This further implies that $\forall F \in \mathcal{F}$,

$$E_F(\psi_t \psi_{t'}) = 0, \quad \text{for } t \neq t' \tag{11.102}$$

i.e., ψ_t and $\psi_{t'}$ are orthogonal. Under this set up a new definition follows. Among all unbiased EFs g, an optimal EF g^* is the one that provides the smallest value of

$$E[g(y_1, \ldots, y_n; \theta)^2 | \mathcal{F}_{t-1}^y] \Big/ \left[E\left\{ \left(\frac{\partial g(y_1, \ldots, y_n; \theta)}{\partial \theta} \right) \Big| \mathcal{F}_{t-1}^y \right\} \right]^2. \tag{11.103}$$

Note that $\mathcal{L}$ is a subset of the class of all unbiased EFs where ψ_t and a_{t-1} are assumed to be differentiable with respect to $\theta, \forall t = 1, \ldots, n$. Now we state and prove Godambe's (1985) result on the optimal EF for the dependent case.

Theorem 2.2 *Within a class of estimating functions $\mathcal{L}$ defined in (11.101), the optimal estimating function g^* that minimizes (11.103) is given by $g^*(\theta) = \sum_{t=1}^n \psi_t a_{t-1}^*$ where $a_{t-1}^* = [E(\partial \psi_t / \partial \theta | \mathcal{F}_{t-1}^y)] / [E(\psi_t^2 | \mathcal{F}_{t-1}^y)].$*

Proof. Using the equations (11.101) and (11.102), we have

$$E(g^2) = E\left\{ \sum_{t=1}^n a_{t-1}^2 E(\psi_t^2 | \mathcal{F}_{t-1}^y) \right\} \tag{11.104}$$

and

$$\left[E\left(\frac{\partial g}{\partial \theta} \right) \right]^2 = \left[E \sum_{t=1}^n \left\{ a_{t-1} E\left(\frac{\partial \psi_t}{\partial \theta} \Big| \mathcal{F}_{t-1}^y \right) + \left(\frac{\partial a_{t-1}}{\partial \theta} \right) E(\psi_t | \mathcal{F}_{t-1}^y) \right\} \right]^2$$

$$= \left\{ E \sum_{t=1}^n a_{t-1} E\left(\frac{\partial \psi_t}{\partial \theta} \Big| \mathcal{F}_{t-1}^y \right) \right\}^2, \tag{11.105}$$

as $E(\psi_t | \mathcal{F}_{t-1}^y) = 0.$ Letting $B = \sum_{t=1}^n a_{t-1} E(\partial \psi_t / \partial \theta | \mathcal{F}_{t-1}^y)$ and $A^2 = \sum_{t=1}^n a_{t-1}^2 E(\psi_t^2 | \mathcal{F}_{t-1}^y)$, we have

$$\frac{\left\{ E\left(\frac{\partial g}{\partial \theta} \right) \right\}^2}{E(g)^2} = \frac{\{E(B)\}^2}{E(A^2)} \leq E\left(\frac{B^2}{A^2} \right) \tag{11.106}$$

by the Cauchy–Schwartz inequality. The equality in (11.106) holds if $A^2 \propto B$, i.e., if $a_{t-1} = a_{t-1}^*$, and the Theorem follows.

Example 2.4 Estimating function (11.3) for the AR(1) model in (11.1) can be obtained through Godambe's (1985) approach and this sheds light on the distinctive nature of the theory of EF. Here $\psi_t = u_t = y_t - \theta y_{t-1}, t = 2, 3, \ldots, n$ are n elementary EFs, and the issue is how we should combine these $(n-1)$ functions into one to solve for the parameter θ. Let us consider the class of EFs

$$g = \sum_{t=2}^{n} a_{t-1} \psi_t,$$

where the weights a_{t-1} depend only on the conditioning event $(y_1, y_2, \ldots, y_{t-1})$. Theorem 2.2 yields the optimal weights as

$$a_{t-1}^* = \frac{E_{t-1}[\partial(y_t - \theta y_{t-1})/\partial \theta]}{E_{t-1}[(y_t - \theta y_{t-1})^2]} = \frac{-y_{t-1}}{\sigma^2},$$

where $\sigma^2 = \text{var}(u_t)$. Therefore, the optimal EF for θ is

$$g^* = \sum_{t=2}^{n} y_{t-1}(y_t - \theta y_{t-1}) = 0$$

which is the same as (11.3). Durbin (1960) arrived at the same EF by starting with an unbiased linear EF $g = T_1(y) + \theta T_2(y)$, where $T_1(y)$ and $T_2(y)$ are functions of data $(y_1, y_2, \ldots, y_n)$ only. Then he imposed a minimum variance requirement on g, reminiscent of Gauss–Markov theorem.

Godambe (1985, p. 424) also established that, in the class of all EFs of the form (11.101), the partial likelihood score is the optimum EF. For this consider the joint density function of $(y_1, \ldots, y_n)$, involving the parameter of interest θ and the nuisance parameter δ

$$f(y_1, \ldots, y_n; \theta, \delta) = \prod_{t=1}^{n} f_{t-1}(y_t; \theta, \delta),$$

where f_{t-1} denotes the conditional density of y_t given $y_1, \ldots, y_{t-1}(t = 1, \ldots, n)$. Let $T_t(t = 1, \ldots, n)$ be minimal sufficient for δ in the density $f_{t-1}(y_t; \theta, \delta)$, so that $f_{t-1}(y_t|T_t; \theta, \delta) = f_{t-1}(y_t|T_t; \theta)$ is independent of δ. Now, by considering the partial likelihood score for θ,

$$\sum_{t=1}^{n} \frac{\partial \log f_{t-1}(y_t|T_t; \theta)}{\partial \theta} = \sum_{t=1}^{n} \psi_t, \text{ say.} \tag{11.107}$$

It is easy to see that $E_{t-1}(\psi_t) = 0$ and $E(\psi_t \psi_{t'}) = 0$, $t \neq t' = 1, \ldots, n$. Therefore, from Theorem 2.2, it follows that the optimal EF within the class of linear combinations of ψ_t's is $\sum_{t=2}^{n} \psi_t a_{t-1}^*$, where

$$a_{t-1}^* = \frac{E_{t-1}[\partial^2 \log f_{t-1}(y_t|T_t; \theta)/\partial \theta^2]}{E_{t-1}[\partial \log f_{t-1}(y_t|T_t; \theta)/\partial \theta]^2} = -1.$$

This establishes the optimality of the partial likelihood score function in (11.107).

As we discussed in section 11.2.1, in a parametric model the score function provides the optimum EF; the result of Theorem 2.2 can be extended to a theory of the pseudo-score function and the associated Fisher information. Utilizing the pseudo-score function

$$\Psi = -\sum_{t=1}^{n} \psi_t a_{t-1}^*,$$

we derive

$$E\left[\frac{\partial(-\Psi)}{\partial \theta}\right] = E\left[\sum_{t=1}^{n} a_{t-1}^* E_{t-1}\left(\frac{\partial \psi_t}{\partial \theta}\right)\right] = E\left[\sum_{t=1}^{n} a_{t-1}^{*2} E_{t-1}(\psi_t^2)\right] = E(\Psi^2)$$

and obtain the EF

$$\left(\sum_{t=1}^{n} \psi_t a_{t-1}^*\right) \bigg/ \left[\sum_{t=1}^{n} (a_{t-1}^{*2}) E_{t-1}(\psi_t^2)\right]^{1/2}, \tag{11.108}$$

which is a standardized martingale. Asymptotically, the density of EF in (11.108) converges to $N(0, 1)$. This suggests the existence of an associated pseudo Fisher information, independent of the parameter θ, given by

$$\mathcal{I} = \sum_{t=1}^{n} a_{t-1}^{*2} E_{t-1}(\psi_t^2).$$

Interestingly, one can interpret $\mathcal{I}$ as an unbiased estimate of the variance of Ψ.

Another justification of the Godambe optimality criterion is the fact that, under standard regularity conditions, the EF estimator $\hat{\theta}_n^*$ that solves the optimal EE $g^*(y_1, \ldots, y_n; \theta(F)) = 0$, also minimizes, at least asymptotically, the mean squared error $E(\hat{\theta} - \theta)^2$, where $\hat{\theta}$ is the estimator from $g(y_1, \ldots, y_n; \theta(F)) = 0$. Also, one can utilize the choice of weights a_{t-1}^* to get the most benefit from any knowledge about the unknown distribution of $\{y_t; t \geq 0\}$, especially when specifications of third and fourth moments are unknown. The suboptimal weights can reduce the efficiency of the estimator significantly without affecting its consistency and asymptotic normality properties.

It is important to note that the optimal estimation procedure of Godambe (1985) is based on a martingale structure with the corresponding filtering method which, in some sense, restricts the nature of the stochastic process. However, Godambe and Thompson (1989) provided an extension of the concept of optimality of such an EF into a general setting using a more "flexible" *conditioning* method which is related to the concept of the quasi-likelihood approach. This broadens the applicability of their method to a wider class. Using the same set up with $\mathcal{Y}$ as an arbitrary sample space, they considered the class of EFs ψ_j, which is a real function defined on $\mathcal{Y} \times \Theta$ such that

$$E_F[\psi_j(y_1, \ldots, y_n; \theta(F)) | \mathcal{Y}_j] = 0, \quad F \in \mathcal{F}, \tag{11.109}$$

where $E_F[\cdot|\mathcal{Y}_j]$ is the expectation under F, conditional on $\mathcal{Y}_j$, $\mathcal{Y}_j(j = 1, \ldots, k)$ being a σ-field generated by a specified partition on the sample space $\mathcal{Y}$. To estimate θ on the basis of observations $\{y_t\}$ they considered the class of EFs $\mathcal{H} = \{h\}$, where

$$h = \sum_{j=1}^{k} a_j \psi_j$$

and a_j is a real function on $\mathcal{Y} \times \Theta$. The EFs $\psi_j, j = 1, \ldots, k,$ satisfying (11.109) are said to be mutually orthogonal if $E_F(\psi_i\psi_j|\mathcal{Y}_j) = 0$ and $E_F(\psi_j\psi_i|\mathcal{Y}_i) = 0$ for $F \in \mathcal{F}$ and $i \neq j, i, j = 1, \ldots, k$. An estimate of θ based on the EF h is obtained by solving the equation $h(y_1, \ldots, y_n; \theta(F)) = 0$. For the optimal EF they defined

$$h^* = \sum_{j=1}^{k} a_j^* \psi_j, \tag{11.110}$$

where

$$a_j^* = \frac{E_F\left\{\left(\partial\psi_j/\partial\theta\right)_{\theta=\theta(F)}\Big|\mathcal{Y}_j\right\}}{E_F\{[\psi_j(y_1, \ldots, y_n; \theta(F))]^2|\mathcal{Y}_j\}}.$$

The following result, a proof of which is given in Godambe and Thompson (1989, p. 140), demonstrates how to construct such an optimal EF.

Theorem 2.3   *The estimating function h^* of (11.110) is optimum in the class $\mathcal{H}$, if the elementary estimating functions ψ_j are mutually orthogonal.*

The above theorem provides an optimal EF in a wide class of functions $\mathcal{H}$ when the ψ_j's need not necessarily be linear functions of y_i's and can be formed using an optimal orthogonal combination involving the first few moments of y_i. In some cases, the function a_j can be the functions of all y_i's except the y_j itself. A similar criterion of optimality, but without the notion of orthogonality, was also used by Crowder (1986) based on optimum quadratic EFs. However, in Crowder (1986), the criterion of optimality is in terms of the asymptotic variance of the estimate, whereas for Godambe (1985) the finite sample optimality criterion for a general stochastic process is for the EF. Also the class of unbiased and orthogonal EFs in Godambe and Thompson (1989) is broader than the class of quadratic EFs. For more on the theory of optimum orthogonal EFs, see Godambe (1991b).

11.2.5   Estimating functions and generalized method of moments

The EF approach to estimation, while very popular among statisticians, has been largely ignored by econometricians, who were mainly absorbed by the use of generalized method of moments (GMM). Today it looks as if the two methods produce the same results from the point of view of the user. The EF methodology started by defining a concrete optimality criterion for the choice of *elementary* EFs. In many instances, these elementary EFs were essentially what was called in econometrics *conditional moments*; compare Godambe (1985) and Chamberlain (1987). Then, the EF approach went on with the issue of how best to combine these elementary EFs into a number of EEs that equals the number of the unknown parameters of the statistical model. In particular, as we discussed in section 11.2.4, Godambe (1985) worked out the problem for stochastic processes, where the conditioning information set is formed naturally from the past of the process. According to his solution, if we restrict ourselves to linear combinations of the various EFs, then an optimal combination is formed by utilizing weights given in Theorem 2.2. This result was generalized by Godambe and Heyde (1987), who termed the optimal EF as the quasi-score.

In the econometric practice of GMM, the emphasis seems to be on the formation of convenient unconditional moments from the conditional restrictions. Then, the question of optimality usually concerns the optimal choice of the weighting matrix in the objective function for a *given* set of *unconditional* moments. Consider the framework of the generalized linear regression with strictly exogenous regressors. The econometric practice will be to form the unconditional moments that eventually lead to the least squares estimator. The optimal EF approach will point to the first order conditions that correspond to generalized least squares. It is true that the first approach is adopted by applied researchers who want to avoid making specific assumptions about the variances and covariances of the responses. However, it is certainly useful to know what is the benchmark for optimality.

In the econometric literature, a result similar to the one given by Godambe (1985) is now well known and it seems that it was first given by Chamberlain (1987); see also Newey (2004) for more results and examples, and Davidson and MacKinnon (1993, section 17.4) for a textbook discussion.

It should be noted that the result in the econometric literature was produced from asymptotic considerations by studying the variance matrix of the estimator, while in the statistical literature the focus was on finite sample optimality of the EF.

11.3 Applications

In this section we apply the optimal EF approach of estimation discussed in previous sections to a number of widely used econometric models. First, we demonstrate its applicability to various nonlinear time series models and then utilize it for the spatial regression model. This is followed by applications to longitudinal data and the median regression model.

The general expression of a nonlinear univariate time series model is

$$X_t = \varphi(X_{t-1}, \ldots, X_{t-p}; \epsilon_{t-1}, \ldots, \epsilon_{t-q}; \theta) + \epsilon_t, t \in \mathbf{Z}, \tag{11.111}$$

where $\varphi(.)$ is some known nonlinear function with finite dimensional parameter vector θ, $\{\epsilon_t\}$ is strictly white noise, p, q are non-negative integers and $\mathbf{Z}$ denotes the set of all integers. For a description of the nonlinear time series models we use, see Teräsvirta (2006). In sections 11.3.1–11.3.4 we discuss the EF approach to

estimate θ for such nonlinear time series models that are frequently used, sometimes even as competing models. As long as we express the first two conditional
moments of the observed series, the EF theory is readily applicable. Our discussion
is valid for observed time series data as well as estimated residuals in a regression
set up.

11.3.1   Random coefficient autoregressive model

An important class of nonlinear time series model is the random coefficient
autoregressive (RCA) model, for which a fairly extensive theory of estimation
exists based on LS and ML procedures (see, for example, Nicholls and Quinn,
1982). One of the common features of the RCA model is the *varying conditional
variance* that is similar to autoregressive conditional heteroskedastic (ARCH)-type
models (Tsay, 1987; Bera and Lee, 1993; Granger and Teräsvirta, 1993, ch. 4). Also,
since many properties of ARCH models, both conditional and unconditional, can
be derived directly from the RCA model, the usefulness of the latter becomes more
appealing in both a theoretical and an applied context. Therefore, it makes sense
to apply an optimal EF approach to obtain a more *efficient* estimate without any
distributional assumptions, which has important finite sample properties. The
important references on this topic are Thavaneswaran and Abraham (1988), Heyde
(1997) and Chandra and Taniguchi (2001).

A stochastic process $\{X_t, t \in \mathbf{Z}\}$ is said to follow a RCA model of order p if it
satisfies

$$
\begin{aligned}
X_t &= \sum_{i=1}^{p} \theta_{it} X_{t-i} + \epsilon_t \\
&= \sum_{i=1}^{p} (\theta_i + \eta_{it}) X_{t-i} + \epsilon_t,
\end{aligned}
\tag{11.112}
$$

where $\theta = (\theta_1, \ldots, \theta_p)'$ is the parameter to be estimated, η_{it} are random components and ϵ_t is the innovation term. For model (11.112), it is customary to define
$\mathbf{X}_{t-1} = (X_{t-1}, \ldots, X_{t-p})'$ and to make the following assumptions: (i) For
$t = 1, \ldots, n, \{\eta_t = (\eta_{1t}, \ldots, \eta_{pt})'\}$ is a sequence of IID random vectors with zero
mean and variance $E(\eta_t \eta_t') = \Sigma$, a $p \times p$ matrix; (ii) $\{\epsilon_t\}$ is a sequence of IID random
variables with $E(\epsilon_t) = 0$ and $E(\epsilon_t^2) = \sigma_\epsilon^2 < \infty$; (iii) $\{\eta_t\}$ and $\{\epsilon_t\}$ are mutually
independent; (iv) $\{\eta_t\}$ and $\{\mathbf{X}_{t-1}\}$ are mutually independent.

For simplicity, let us consider the estimation of the parameter θ assuming that
the nuisance parameters $(\sigma_\epsilon^2, \Sigma)$ are known. Consider a linear class of EFs of the
form $g_i = \sum_{t=1}^{n} \psi_t a_{i,t-1}$, with

$$
\psi_t = X_t - E[X_t | \mathcal{F}_{t-1}^X] = X_t - \sum_{i=1}^{p} \theta_i X_{t-i} = X_t - \mathbf{X}_{t-1}' \theta.
$$

Note that the information set $\mathcal{F}_t^X$ is now based on $\{\eta_s; s \le t\}$ and $\{X_s; s \le t\}$; so
$\mathbf{X}_{t-1} \in \mathcal{F}_{t-1}^X$ and $E[(\partial \psi_t / \partial \theta) | \mathcal{F}_{t-1}^X] = -\mathbf{X}_{t-1}$. We derive the optimal EF using

Theorem 2.3 as

$$g_i^* = \sum_{t=1}^{n} \psi_t a_{i,t-1}^* \tag{11.113}$$

where $a_{i,t-1}^* = -X_{t-i}/Q_t$ with $Q_t = E[\psi_t^2 | \mathcal{F}_{t-1}^X] = \sigma_\epsilon^2 + X_{t-1}'\Sigma X_{t-1}$. Therefore, by solving the EF $g_i^* = 0$ we obtain the optimal estimate of θ as

$$\hat{\theta}_n^{EF} = \left[\sum_{t=p+1}^{n} \left(\frac{X_{t-1}X_{t-1}'}{Q_t} \right) \right]^{-1} \left[\sum_{t=p+1}^{n} \left(\frac{X_{t-1}X_t}{Q_t} \right) \right]. \tag{11.114}$$

The scaling factor Q_t is nothing but the conditional variance of the original random process X_t (Bera, Higgins and Lee, 1992), as can be seen from

$$
\begin{aligned}
Var(X_t | \mathcal{F}_{t-1}^X) &= E\left[\left(\sum_{i=1}^{p} X_{t-i}\eta_{it} + \epsilon_t \right)^2 \Bigg| \mathcal{F}_{t-1}^X \right] \\
&= E\left[\left\{ \left(\sum_{i=1}^{p} X_{t-i}\eta_{it} \right)^2 + 2\epsilon_t \left(\sum_{i=1}^{p} X_{t-i}\eta_{it} \right) + \epsilon_t^2 \right\} \Bigg| \mathcal{F}_{t-1}^X \right] \\
&= X_{t-1}'\Sigma X_{t-1} + \sigma_\epsilon^2 \\
&= Q_t.
\end{aligned} \tag{11.115}
$$

When $\Sigma = 0$, both LS and EF estimates of θ become the same, but when $\Sigma \neq 0$ Q_t has an ARCH type form that needs to be taken into consideration. Also, whether Σ is diagonal or a full matrix has important implications for the joint presence of autocorrelation and conditional heteroskedasticity. If Σ is diagonal then the scaling factor of the optimal EF will be same as in Engle (1982). However, if Σ has non-zero off-diagonal terms, the interpretation of the scaling factor becomes closer to the *asymmetric* ARCH, model proposed by Nelson (1991). For diagonal Σ, we can write $E(\eta_t \eta_t') = \sigma_\eta^2 . I_p$, where I_p is the identity matrix of dimension p. The optimal estimate for a first-order RCA model based on EF $g_i^* = \sum_{t=1}^{n} \psi_t a_{i,t-1}^*$ is given by $\hat{\theta}_n^{EF}$ in (11.114), with $Q_t = \sigma_\epsilon^2 + \sum_{i=1}^{p} X_{t-i}^2 \sigma_\eta^2$. This is similar to the traditional generalized LS estimator and is an improvement over the naive LS. This estimator was first proposed by Thavaneswaran and Abraham (1988). To implement (11.114), in the first step LS estimation can be used to obtain initial estimates of σ_ϵ^2 and σ_η^2. Then, in the second step, plugging in all the relevant information an efficient estimate can be obtained as $\hat{\theta}_n^{EF}$. For example, if $p=1$, the optimal EF turns out to be

$$g_i^* = \sum_{t=2}^{n} \left(\frac{X_{t-1}}{Q_t} \right) \psi_t, \tag{11.116}$$

where $\psi_t = (X_t - \theta X_{t-1})$ and $Q_t = E[\psi_t^2 | \mathcal{F}_{t-1}^X] = \sigma_\epsilon^2 + X_{t-1}^2 \sigma_\eta^2$. Therefore, the solution of (11.116) becomes

$$\hat{\theta}_n^{EF} = \frac{\sum_{t=2}^n a_{t-1}^* X_t}{\sum_{t=2}^n a_{t-1}^* X_{t-1}}, \tag{11.117}$$

with $a_{t-1}^* = -X_{t-1}/(\sigma_\epsilon^2 + X_{t-1}^2 \sigma_\eta^2)$. By letting $u_t = \psi_t^2 - \sigma_\epsilon^2 - X_{t-1}^2 \sigma_\eta^2$, the estimates of $\hat{\sigma}_\epsilon^2$ and $\hat{\sigma}_\eta^2$ can be obtained by minimizing $\sum_{t=2}^n u_t^2$ with respect to $\sigma_\epsilon^2, \sigma_\eta^2$ (Nicholls and Quinn, 1982, p. 43), i.e., by regressing ψ_t^2 on 1 and X_{t-1}^2. The LS estimate $\hat{\theta}_n^{LS} = (\sum_{t=2}^n X_t X_{t-1})/(\sum_{t=2}^n X_{t-1}^2)$ can be used to obtain $\hat{\psi}_t^2$.

11.3.2   Threshold autoregressive model

It is widely known that many nonlinear features such as limit cycles and asymmetry can be explained by threshold autoregressive (TAR) models (Tong, 1990, chapter 1), where we assume that the function $\varphi(\cdot)$ in (11.111) is piecewise linear and allow the parameters to be determined partly by past data. In the simplest form of TAR model, a time series $\{X_t, t \in \mathbf{Z}\}$ is given by

$$X_t = \theta_1 X_{t-1}^+ + \theta_2 X_{t-1}^- + \epsilon_t, \tag{11.118}$$

where $X_t^+ = \min(X_t, 0), X_t^- = \max(X_t, 0)$ and $\{\epsilon_t\} \sim \text{IID}(0, \sigma_\epsilon^2)$. The process is known as "double threshold" if both the conditional mean and variance change with thresholds (Granger, 1998).

For the general expression of model (11.118), we partition the range of X_t into k parts by the set of ordered values $r_1 < \cdots < r_{k-1}$. If the value X_t lies in the interval $D_j = (r_j, r_{j+1}]$, with r_j, r_{j+1} as threshold values, the jth set of parameters is used to generate $X_{t+d(d<k)}$, where d is the delay (lag) parameter. The zero mean threshold AR(p) (TAR(p)) process can be expressed as

$$X_t = \sum_{i=1}^p \theta_i^j X_{t-i} I(X_{t-d} \in D_j) + \epsilon_t,$$

where $I(.)$ is the indicator function, ϵ_t is a white noise and $j \in \{1, \ldots, k\}$ is determined by $X_{t-d} \in d_j$. By considering the elementary EF $\psi_t = X_t - \sum_{i=1}^p \sum_{j=1}^k \theta_i^j X_{t-i} I(X_{t-d} \in D_j)$ and noting that $E(\psi_t^2) = \sigma_\epsilon^2$, the optimal EF for the set of parameters (θ_i^j) becomes (see Ainkaran, 2004)

$$g_{\theta_i^j}^* = \sum_{t=k+1}^n \psi_t a_{t-1,\alpha_i}^*$$

$$= -\sum_{t=k+1}^n X_{t-i} I(X_{t-d} \in D_j) \left(X_t - \sum_{i=1}^p \sum_{j=1}^k \theta_i^j X_{t-i} I(X_{t-d} \in D_j) \right) \Big/ \sigma_\epsilon^2.$$

Solving the corresponding EEs, we obtain the optimal EF estimates for the *TAR* (p) parameters. For a generalized kernel smoothing estimate using an optimal EF approach for threshold models, see Thavaneswaran and Peiris (1996).

11.3.3 Bilinear model

In the bilinear class, we incorporate cross-product terms involving lagged values of the time series and of the disturbance process. This class of models, originally introduced by Granger and Anderson (1978), has many interesting statistical properties and act as competing models with ARCH for *nonlinear dependence* (e.g., see Weiss, 1986; Bera and Higgins, 1997). However, it is important to note that, even though both ARCH and bilinear processes have similar unconditional moments, conditionally their moment structure is different. The simplest form of bilinear time series $\{X_t, t \in \mathbf{Z}\}$ model is given by

$$X_t = \sum_{i=1}^{r} \sum_{j=1}^{s} \theta_{ij} X_{t-i} \epsilon_{t-j} + \epsilon_t \tag{11.119}$$

where $\{\epsilon_t\} \sim IID(0, \sigma_\epsilon^2)$ is the innovation that drives the bilinear process and $\{\theta_{ij}, i = 1, \ldots, r, j = 1, \ldots, s\}$ are parameters to be estimated. Here the conditional mean is a nonlinear function of past values of $\{X_t, \epsilon_t\}$ while the conditional variance is constant. This is in contrast to the ARCH process, for which, as we will see in section 11.3.4, the conditional mean is, in general, a constant, but the conditional variance is time varying.

The general expression for the bilinear model $(BL(p, q, r, s))$ can be obtained by adding a linear ARMA component to (11.120), such as

$$X_t = \sum_{i=1}^{p} \alpha_i X_{t-i} + \sum_{i=1}^{r} \sum_{j=1}^{s} \theta_{ij} X_{t-i} \epsilon_{t-j} + \epsilon_t + \sum_{j=1}^{q} \beta_j \epsilon_{t-j}. \tag{11.120}$$

Here, in addition to θ_{ij}, we need to estimate $p + q$ parameters α_i and β_j. As before, let us assume that the conditioning information set $\mathcal{F}_t^X$ is a σ-field, based on $\{X_r; r \leq t\}$ and $\{\epsilon_r; r \leq t\}$; so $X_{t-1} \in \mathcal{F}_{t-1}^X$ and $E[\epsilon_{t-i}|\mathcal{F}_{t-1}^X] = \epsilon_{t-i}, i \geq 1$. Also, as $\{\epsilon_t\} \sim IID(0, \sigma_\epsilon^2)$, an obvious choice for an elementary EF becomes $\psi_t = X_t - E[X_t|\mathcal{F}_{t-1}^X]$, where

$$E[X_t|\mathcal{F}_{t-1}^X] = \sum_{i=1}^{p} \alpha_i X_{t-i} + \sum_{i=1}^{r} \sum_{j=1}^{s} \theta_{ij} X_{t-i} \epsilon_{t-j} + \sum_{j=1}^{q} \beta_j \epsilon_{t-j}.$$

Therefore, following Theorem 2.3, the optimal EF is given by the following set of equations (see Ainkaran, 2004):

$$g_{\alpha_i}^* = \sum_{t=m+1}^{n} \psi_t a_{t-1,\alpha_i}^*,$$

$$g_{\beta_j}^* = \sum_{t=m+1}^{n} \psi_t a_{t-1,\beta_j}^*, \tag{11.121}$$

$$g_{\theta_{ij}}^* = \sum_{t=m+1}^{n} \psi_t a_{t-1,\theta_{ij}}^*,$$

where

$$a^*_{t-1,\alpha_i} = E\left(\frac{\partial\psi_t}{\partial\alpha_i}\Big|\mathcal{F}^X_{t-1}\right)\Big/Q_t = -X_{t-i}/Q_t,$$

$$a^*_{t-1,\beta_j} = E\left(\frac{\partial\psi_t}{\partial\beta_j}\Big|\mathcal{F}^X_{t-1}\right)\Big/Q_t = \left(-\epsilon_{t-j} - \beta_j\frac{\partial\epsilon_{t-j}}{\partial\beta_j} - \sum_{i=1}^r \theta_{ij}X_{t-i}\frac{\partial\epsilon_{t-j}}{\partial\beta_j}\right)\Big/Q_t,$$

$$a^*_{t-1,\theta_{ij}} = E\left(\frac{\partial\psi_t}{\partial\theta_{ij}}\Big|\mathcal{F}^X_{t-1}\right)\Big/Q_t = \left(-X_{t-i}\epsilon_{t-j} - \beta_j\frac{\partial\epsilon_{t-j}}{\partial\theta_{ij}} - \theta_{ij}X_{t-i}\frac{\partial\epsilon_{t-j}}{\partial\theta_{ij}}\right)\Big/Q_t,$$

$$Q_t = E[\psi_t^2|\mathcal{F}^X_{t-1}] = \sigma_\epsilon^2\left(1 + \sum_{j=1}^q \beta_j^2 + \sum_{i=1}^r\sum_{j=1}^s \theta_{ij}^2 X_{t-i}^2\right)$$

and $m = max(p, r)$. Solving the EEs corresponding to the EFs in (11.121), the estimates of the bilinear model's $p + q + rs$ parameters can be obtained.

11.3.4   ARCH and GARCH models

The ARCH model introduced by Engle (1982), and its various extensions, have become arguably the most popular and extensively used financial econometric models (for surveys on this topic, see Bera and Higgins, 1993; Bollerslev, Engle and Nelson, 1994; and Engle, 2002). The standard procedure is to estimate an ARCH or GARCH model using an ML approach assuming a normal or Student's t distribution. However, such assumptions are hard to justify in practice due to the presence of asymmetry and high excess kurtosis in real data. Li and Turtle (2000) and Chandra and Taniguchi (2001) proposed an EF method that is free of any distributional assumptions.

A general expression for an ARCH(p) model is given by

$$X_t = \epsilon_t\sqrt{h_t}, \quad h_t = \alpha_0 + \sum_{i=1}^p \alpha_i X_{t-i}^2, \tag{11.122}$$

where $\{\epsilon_t\} \sim IID(0, \sigma_\epsilon^2)$ with fourth-order cumulant κ_4 and $\alpha_0 > 0, \alpha_j \geq 0$, $\forall j = 1, \ldots, p$. A candidate class for an unbiased and mutually orthogonal EFs is $\psi_t = X_t^2 - h_t, \forall t = 1, \ldots, n$. The linear combination of which becomes $g_\alpha = \sum_{t=1}^n a_t\psi_t$, where the weights a_t are functions of the data and the unknown parameter $\alpha = (\alpha_0, \alpha_1, \ldots, \alpha_p)'$. Using Theorem 2.3, we can derive the optimal EF as $g_\alpha^* = \sum_{t=1}^n a_t^*\psi_t$, where

$$a_t^* = \frac{E(\partial\psi_t/\partial\alpha|\mathcal{F}^X_{t-1})}{E(\psi_t^2|\mathcal{F}^X_{t-1})}$$

$$= -\frac{\partial h_t}{\partial\alpha}\Big/\{E(X_t^4|\mathcal{F}^X_{t-1}) - h_t^2\}$$

$$= -\frac{\partial h_t}{\partial\alpha}\Big/\{(\kappa_4 + 2)h_t^2\},$$

and $\mathcal{F}^X_{t-1}$ is the σ-field generated by $\{X_s; s \leq t-1\}$. Therefore, the optimal EF estimate of the ARCH(p) parameters turns out to be the solution of

$$g^*_\alpha = -\sum_{t=1}^n \frac{(\partial h_t/\partial\alpha)(X_t^2 - h_t)}{\{(\kappa_4 + 2)h_t^2\}} = 0.$$

Next let us consider ARCH(p) errors in the context of a linear regression model:

$$y_t = z_t\beta + X_t, \quad X_t|\mathcal{F}^X_{t-1} \sim (0, h_t), \tag{11.123}$$

where z_t is a non-stochastic regressor and β represents the regression coefficient. The conditional mean from (11.123) becomes nonzero as $E(y_t|\mathcal{F}^X_{t-1}) = z_t\beta$ and $\mathcal{F}^X_{t-1}$ is now generated by $\{z_t, X_{t-1}, X_{t-2}, \ldots\}$. The objective is to estimate the set of parameters α and β. Let us denote the skewness and excess kurtosis coefficients as $\gamma_{1t} = E[(y_t - z_t\beta)^3|\mathcal{F}^X_{t-1}]/h_t^{3/2}$ and $\gamma_{2t} = E[(y_t - z_t\beta)^4|\mathcal{F}^X_{t-1}]/h_t^2 - 3$, respectively, and choose the following two orthogonal EFs $\psi_{1t} = (y_t - z_t\beta)$ and $\psi_{2t} = (y_t - z_t\beta)^2 - h_t - \gamma_{1t}h_t^{1/2}(y_t - z_t\beta)$. Then, following Theorem 2.3, the optimal EF becomes $g^*_{\alpha,\beta} = g^*_1 + g^*_2 = 0$, with

$$g^*_1 = \sum_{t=1}^n \frac{E(\partial\psi_{1t}/\partial\alpha|\mathcal{F}^X_{t-1})}{E(\psi_{1t}^2|\mathcal{F}^X_{t-1})}\psi_{1t} + \sum_{t=1}^n \frac{E(\partial\psi_{2t}/\partial\alpha|\mathcal{F}^X_{t-1})}{E(\psi_{2t}^2|\mathcal{F}^X_{t-1})}\psi_{2t}$$

$$= -\sum_{t=1}^n \frac{\partial h_t/\partial\alpha}{h_t^2(\gamma_{2t} + 2 - \gamma_{1t}^2)}\psi_{2t},$$

and

$$g^*_2 = \sum_{t=1}^n \frac{E(\partial\psi_{1t}/\partial\beta|\mathcal{F}^X_{t-1})}{E(\psi_{1t}^2|\mathcal{F}^X_{t-1})}\psi_{1t} + \sum_{t=1}^n \frac{E(\partial\psi_{2t}/\partial\beta|\mathcal{F}^X_{t-1})}{E(\psi_{2t}^2|\mathcal{F}^X_{t-1})}\psi_{2t}$$

$$= -\sum_{t=1}^n \frac{\partial z_t\beta/\partial\beta}{h_t}\psi_{1t} - \sum_{t=1}^n \frac{h_t^{1/2}\gamma_{1t}(\partial z_t\beta/\partial\beta) - (\partial h_t/\partial\beta)}{h_t^2(\gamma_{2t} + 2 - \gamma_{1t}^2)}\psi_{2t}.$$

The above discussion is also valid for the class of GARCH processes with

$$h_t = \text{Var}(X_t|\mathcal{F}^X_{t-1}) = \alpha_0 + \sum_{i=1}^p \alpha_i X_{t-i}^2 + \sum_{j=1}^q \delta_j h_{t-j}. \tag{11.124}$$

Here, in addition to α and β, we need to estimate q additional parameters $\delta = (\delta_1, \ldots, \delta_q)'$. It is easy to see that $E(X_t X_{t-k}) = E[E(X_t X_{t-k}|\mathcal{F}^X_{t-1})] = 0, \forall k \geq 1$, and hence GARCH errors are uncorrelated.

To illustrate the usefulness of the optimal EF approach, we concentrate on a simple GARCH(1, 1) process given by $h_t = \alpha_0 + \alpha_1 X_{t-1}^2 + \delta_1 h_{t-1}$. As in the ARCH model, let us choose the same two orthogonal EFs ψ_{1t} and ψ_{2t}. Then, by denoting $\theta = (\alpha_0, \alpha_1, \delta_1)'$, following Theorem 2.3, we obtain the optimal EF as $g_{\theta,\beta}^* = g_1^* + g_2^* = 0$, where

$$g_1^* = \sum_{t=1}^{n} \frac{E(\partial\psi_{1t}/\partial\theta | \mathcal{F}_{t-1}^X)}{E(\psi_{1t}^2 | \mathcal{F}_{t-1}^X)} \psi_{1t} + \sum_{t=1}^{n} \frac{E(\partial\psi_{2t}/\partial\theta | \mathcal{F}_{t-1}^X)}{E(\psi_{2t}^2 | \mathcal{F}_{t-1}^X)} \psi_{2t}$$

$$= -\sum_{t=1}^{n} \frac{\partial h_t/\partial\theta}{h_t^2(\gamma_{2t} + 2 - \gamma_{1t}^2)} \psi_{2t},$$

$$q_2^* = \sum_{t=1}^{n} \frac{E(\partial\psi_{1t}/\partial\beta | \mathcal{F}_{t-1}^X)}{E(\psi_{1t}^2 | \mathcal{F}_{t-1}^X)} \psi_{1t} + \sum_{t=1}^{n} \frac{E(\partial\psi_{2t}/\partial\beta | \mathcal{F}_{t-1}^X)}{E(\psi_{2t}^2 | \mathcal{F}_{t-1}^X)} \psi_{2t}$$

$$= -\sum_{t=1}^{n} \frac{\partial z_t \beta/\partial\beta}{h_t} \psi_{1t} + \sum_{t=1}^{n} \frac{h_t^{1/2} \gamma_{1t}(\partial z_t \beta/\partial\beta) - (\partial h_t/\partial\beta)}{h_t^2(\gamma_{2t} + 2 - \gamma_{1t}^2)} \psi_{2t}.$$

If we impose conditional normality, i.e., $\gamma_{1t} = 0$, $\gamma_{2t} = 0$, the optimal EFs become

$$g_1^* = -\sum_{t=1}^{n} \frac{1}{2h_t} \frac{\partial h_t}{\partial\theta} \left(\frac{X_t^2}{h_t} - 1\right) = 0,$$

$$g_2^* = -\sum_{t=1}^{n} \frac{z_t X_t}{h_t} - \sum_{t=1}^{n} \frac{1}{2h_t} \frac{\partial h_t}{\partial\beta} \left(\frac{X_t^2}{h_t} - 1\right) = 0$$

which are, as expected, similar to the first-order conditions for MLE under the normality assumption.

11.3.5   Spatial regression model

Recently there has been considerable interest among economists in the application of spatial econometric techniques to an increasing number of problems (see Anselin and Bera, 1998; Anselin, 2006). Due to its unique nature and defining characteristic, no existing method is dominant for modeling spatial data, and diffierent operational implementation is still a debatable issue. In this section, we discuss the implementation of the optimal EF technique of section 11.2.4 into a simple spatial regression set up following Naik-Nimbalkar (1996) (for additional references, see Lele, 1997; Yasui and Lele, 1997).

Consider the following simple simultaneous model, known as a spatial autoregressive model of first order: $y = \rho W y + \epsilon$, where $W = ((w_{ij}))$ is a $n \times n$ weights matrix. For the ith observation, the model can be written as

$$y_i = \rho \sum_{j \neq i}^{n} w_{ij} y_j + \epsilon_i, \quad i = 1, \ldots, n, \tag{11.125}$$

where we use the sum over "neighbors j" of the ith cross-sectional observation and assume $\epsilon_i \sim IID(0, \sigma_\epsilon^2)$. We are interested in estimating the spatial dependence parameter ρ and the distribution of the error term is not known. It is very difficult to derive the optimal EF for a general W matrix. However, assuming $w_{i,i+1} = w_{i,i-1} = 1$ for all $i = 1, \ldots, n$ with all other $w_{ij} = 0$, we can easily obtain an optimal EF. Define $\psi_i = \epsilon_i \epsilon_{i+1}$, where $\epsilon_i = y_i - \rho(y_{i-1} + y_{i+1})$ and $\epsilon_{i+1} = y_{i+1} - \rho(y_i + y_{i+2})$. The implication becomes clear as due to the independence of ϵ_i's, $\psi_i, i = 2, \ldots, n-2$, are mutually orthogonal for any trivial conditioning σ-field. The optimal EF in the class $\left\{ \sum_{i=2}^{n-2} \psi_i a_i \right\}$ with a_i as nonrandom functions of ρ, becomes

$$g^* = \sum_{i=2}^{n-2} \left\{ E\left[\frac{\partial \psi_i}{\partial \rho} \right] / \sigma_\epsilon^4 \right\} \psi_i. \tag{11.126}$$

Since stationary implies $E[\partial \psi_i / \partial \rho]$ is constant $\forall i$, the optimal EF becomes $\sum_{i=2}^{n-2} \psi_i = \sum_{i=2}^{n-2} \epsilon_i \epsilon_{i+1} = 0$, which is basically the weighted LS equation suggested by Ord (1975).

We can generalize the above discussion by using conditional moment functions and exploiting their optimal orthogonal combinations. For example, consider the σ-field $Q_i = \sigma\{J(i)|i \neq j; i, j = 1, \ldots, n\}$ defined over the information set $J(i)$, which includes all locations other than i. Then if we define the following conditional moments

$$E[y_i|Q_i] = m_{1i}(\theta; y_{i-1}, y_{i+1}) = m_{1i},$$
$$Var[y_i|Q_i] = m_{2i}(\theta; y_{i-1}, y_{i+1}) = m_{2i},$$

the possible elementary EFs turns out to be $\psi_i = y_i - m_{1i}(\theta; y_{i-1}, y_{i+1})$, with $E[\psi_i|Q_i] = 0, \forall i = 1, \ldots, n$. But since the $\{\psi_i\}$'s are not mutually orthogonal, using Besag's (1974) coding method we obtain a set of mutually orthogonal EFs as the subclass of functions $\{\psi_i \text{ for } i\text{-even}\}$ and $\{\psi_i \text{ for } i\text{-odd}\}$. Therefore, the optimal combination of EFs becomes

$$g_1^* = \sum_{i=odd} (y_i - m_{1i}) \frac{1}{m_{2i}} \left[\frac{\partial m_{1i}}{\partial \theta} \right] \tag{11.127}$$

and

$$g_2^* = \sum_{i=even} (y_i - m_{1i}) \frac{1}{m_{2i}} \left[\frac{\partial m_{1i}}{\partial \theta} \right]. \tag{11.128}$$

Then, under the assumption of strong stationarity of the underlying process, the optimal linear combination of g_1^* and g_2^* will be in the class $\mathcal{G} = \{ag_1^* + bg_2^*\}$, with a, b being real functions of θ. This class of optimum EFs is more meaningful if either a and b are known, or $a = b$, suggesting the optimal equation as $g_1^* + g_2^* = 0$; this is basically the same as the equation obtained from maximizing Besag's pseudo-likelihood (Besag 1974, 1977).

Therefore, we can see that the usefulness of EF optimality in both simultaneous and conditional spatial models can be interpreted as the existing methods of Ord (1975) and Besag (1974, 1977). Interestingly, the underlying notion of orthogonality is not unique and can be achieved by many alternative ways as discussed above, i.e., by constructing different sub-lattices such that one is independent of the others and then reversing the procedure and combining all separate estimates. For future research, Godambe's flexible approach can be generalized to accommodate higher dimensional spatial autoregressive processes with non-stochastic regressors and a general form of simultaneous or conditional specification.

11.3.6 Longitudinal data analysis

The Generalized EE (GEE) approach was devised by Liang and Zeger (1986) to deal with longitudinal data. In longitudinal data, we are presented with repeated measurements on different cross-sectional units over time. It is typically assumed that the cross-sectional units are independent, but the time series data on the same subject are positively correlated. The GEE methodology was formulated especially from the need to handle discrete-type data where no Gaussian likelihood seemed to be appropriate. At the end, the approach looks like an extension of Wedderburn's (1974) quasi-likelihood to a class of correlated data, which models only the mean and the variance of the responses instead the full joint distribution.

To establish notation, suppose the (balanced) panel data set consists of responses y_{it}, $i = 1, 2, \ldots, n$; $t = 1, 2, \ldots, T$, on n units over T periods. The $nT \times 1$ vector $\mathbf{y} = (y_{11}, \ldots, y_{1T}, \ldots, y_{n1}, \ldots, y_{nT})'$ has a corresponding mean model $\boldsymbol{\mu} = (\mu_{11}, \ldots, \mu_{1T}, \ldots, \mu_{n1}, \ldots, \mu_{nT})'$ and, by assumption, has a variance–covariance matrix $\mathbf{V}$ with block-diagonal structure

$$\mathbf{V} = diag(\mathbf{V}_1, \mathbf{V}_2, \ldots, \mathbf{V}_n).$$

Also, we will assume that $\mathbf{V}_i = \mathbf{V}_i(\mu_{i1}, \ldots, \mu_{iT}, \lambda_i)$ for $i = 1, 2, \ldots, n$, where λ_i is a parameter characterizing the variance and correlation components. In addition, each mean $\mu_{it} = \mu_{it}(\theta)$ depends on a $p \times 1$ coefficient vector θ.

From the family of EFs

$$\{A(\mathbf{y} - \boldsymbol{\mu})\} \tag{11.129}$$

where $A = nT \times nT$, the quasi-score EF, i.e., the optimal EF, is given by

$$\dot{\boldsymbol{\mu}}'\mathbf{V}^{-1}(\mathbf{y} - \boldsymbol{\mu})$$

or, by exploiting the block-diagonal structure of the covariance matrix $\mathbf{V}$,

$$U(\theta) = \sum_{i=1}^{n} \dot{\boldsymbol{\mu}}_{\mathbf{i}}'\mathbf{V}_{\mathbf{i}}^{-1}(\mathbf{y_i} - \boldsymbol{\mu_i}), \tag{11.130}$$

where $\mathbf{y_i} = (y_{i1}, \ldots, y_{iT})$, $\boldsymbol{\mu_i} = (\mu_{i1}, \ldots, \mu_{iT})$, and $\dot{\boldsymbol{\mu}}_i = \partial \boldsymbol{\mu}_i / \partial \theta$. The GEE is based on the EF $U(\theta)$ in (11.130), and the estimator is obtained by finding the root of (11.130).

One characteristic of the GEE methodology is the use of the so-called "working" covariance matrix in place of the generally unknown matrix $\mathbf{V}$. Even if the "working" covariance matrices are misspecified, Liang and Zeger (1986) show that the GEE estimator will be consistent, although generally inefficient. When a consistent estimator of the true V is utilized, then the estimator from (11.130) is efficient. The consistency of the estimator requires only correct specification of the mean functions μ_{it}.

As it has been presented in the literature, GEE corresponds to the random effects model, but it treats the variance components λ_i as nuisance parameters. The advantage of this approach is that it can handle in a unified way a variety of types of data, such as continuous data, discrete data, or count data. For a detailed review of the literature and related references, see Fitzmaurice, Laird and Rotnitzky (1993).

11.3.7 Median regression model

Consider the median regression model proposed by Koenker and Basset (1978):

$$y_i = \mu_i(\beta) + \epsilon_i, \quad i = 1, 2, \dots, n$$

where ϵ_i is a random variable with median zero and marginal pdf f_i. Let

$$f_i(0) = \frac{1}{\phi}\gamma(\mu_i),$$

be the pdf of y_i at μ_i, where $\phi > 0$ is a scale parameter, and γ is considered a known function. We will assume the regularity condition that $\gamma(\mu_i) > 0$, which is needed for the median to be unique. For later use we will denote the $n \times 1$ vector of medians of y_i's by $\mu = (\mu_1(\beta), \dots, \mu_n(\beta))'$. Jung (1996) analyzed the estimation of median regression models using the approach of Wedderburn (1974) and Godambe and Heyde (1987). In the following we use Jung's framework and notation; a similar analysis is given by Godambe (2001). For more on combining median and mean EFs; see Judge and Mittelhammer (2005).

For estimation of β, the $p \times 1$ parameter vector, we start from the n elementary EFs

$$\left\{ I(y_i - \mu_i(\beta) \geq 0) - \frac{1}{2} \right\}, \quad i = 1, 2, \dots, n; \tag{11.131}$$

which clearly have zero expectation. Let V denote the $n \times n$ variance–covariance matrix of the elementary EFs; the n diagonal elements of V equal 1/4.

The n elementary EFs can be combined linearly in an optimal way by using the theory developed by Godambe and Heyde (1987). Consider any $n \times p$ matrix H of rank p. The unbiasedness of the elementary EFs ensures that the $p \times 1$ EF

$$U_H(\beta) = \phi^{-1} H' \begin{pmatrix} I(y_1 - \mu_1(\beta) \geq 0) - \frac{1}{2} \\ \vdots \\ I(y_n - \mu_n(\beta) \geq 0) - \frac{1}{2} \end{pmatrix}$$

will deliver a consistent estimator of β.

The choice of weighting matrix $H' = D'\Gamma V^{-1}$, where $D = \partial\mu/\partial\beta$, and $\Gamma = diag\{\gamma(\mu_1), \ldots, \gamma(\mu_n)\}$, yields the optimal EF U_{opt} within the class of linear combinations of (11.131). By solving the system of p equations $U_{opt}(\beta) = 0$, we obtain the so-called quasi-likelihood estimator $\hat{\beta}$. If the true model is double exponential, $\hat{\beta}$ is the MLE. We note that the use of optimal EF theory makes clear from the outset the role of the density f_i of y_i's. Optimality dictates weighting the elementary EFs (11.131) in a way that is reminiscent of weighted LS. In case of identically and independently distributed random variables, the density is constant and it falls out of the picture. The optimum EF reduces to

$$U_{opt} = D' \begin{pmatrix} I(y_1 - \mu_1(\beta) \geq 0) - \frac{1}{2} \\ \vdots \\ I(y_n - \mu_n(\beta) \geq 0) - \frac{1}{2} \end{pmatrix}. \tag{11.132}$$

Furthermore, in case of the linear median regression model, $\mu_i(\beta) = x_i'\beta$, the resulting system of EEs (11.132) is the familiar sum of cross products of the x_i's with the elementary EF's (11.131).

The advantage of the optimal EF approach to estimation of the median regression model is that the form of the optimal EEs, $U_{opt}(\beta) = 0$, allows for a wide variety of data structures, such as dependent or heteroscedastic data, thus offering a unified treatment. In addition, due to the invariance of medians to monotone transformations, we can handle censored (Powell, 1984) or binary data (Manski, 1975) as well.

11.4   Epilogue

It was the 1930s: the conflict between the two statistical giants Karl Pearson and R.A. Fisher was at its height. One issue of their heated arguments was the relative merits of the MM and ML approaches. "I am even ready to adopt new methods," Karl Pearson wrote to Fisher on August 28, 1935, "if they are quicker and more exact than the old. Now I do not suppose you spend much, if any, time in fitting frequency curves; nevertheless I should like to have your method of fitting them to observations, which avoids the 'traditional but inefficient method of fitting them by moments.' (*Annals of Eugenics*, vol. VI, p. 252). It would aid me in many inquiries, if you would let me know the more efficient way." On August 30, 1935, Fisher sent a prompt reply, "The fullest examination of the method of moments in fitting the Pearsonian curves is in a paper 'On the mathematical foundations of theoretical statistics' (*Phil. Trans. A*, vol. 122, 309–68). High efficiencies are only obtained in the neighborhood of the normal curve. Efficient equations of estimation may always be obtained by the maximum likelihood." The acrimonious debate culminated in two final papers. Karl Pearson, in one of his very last papers that was published in the June 1936 issue of *Biometrika* after he passed away on April 26, 1936, began with the italized and striking line, "*Wasting your time fitting curves by moments, eh?*" Fisher, not to be outdone, sent an equally scathing reply. After his step-by-step rebuttal of

Pearson's (1936) arguments, Fisher (1937, p. 317), now feeling free after Pearson's death, bluntly stated: "So long as 'fitting curves by moments' stands in the way of students' obtaining proper experience of these other activities, all of which require time and practice, so long will it be judged with increasing confidence to be waste of time." MM was basically swept away by the ML revolution; Fisher and his method came out to be the winner from this battle. For several decades chapters were devoted to the ML method in statistics (and econometrics) text-books, while MM had only scant mentions. However, it now appears that, after all, MM did not lose the war, and econometricians can take credit in reviving the MM approach through GMM.

Looking back at the Fisher–Pearson conflict after nearly seven decades in the light of Godambe's EF approach, much of the sharpness of their debate is lost, as Desmond (1997, pp. 116–17) noted, "One of the advantages of the estimating function framework is that the apparent dichotomy between these two methods [MM and ML] is nullified and it is possible to see these methods as lying within a unifying framework of continuum, ranging from weak second-order assumption to fully specified parametric models." It is indeed ironic that the EF method, which is essentially a Pearsonian-type moment-based approach, provides, as we discussed in section 11.2, a *finite sample* justification of Fisher's *asymptotically* efficient ML method. Following Godambe and Kale (1991, p. 3), one may even say that the EF approach combines the strength of both MM and ML methods and eliminates the weaknesses of both! Apart from the potential practical applications, some of which are discussed in section 11.3, these unifying features of the EF method are very attractive along with its philosophical and foundational approach.

Of course, we could not do full justice to the proliferation of papers written on the theory and applications of EFs. For instance, we have not covered the topic of hypothesis testing based on EFs. McLeish and Small (1988, p. 10) argued that EFs can be regarded as vehicles for more general focus on inference than simple esti-mation, and they preferred to call these functions "inference functions." For dis-cussion on tests utilizing EFs, see Basawa (1985, 1991), Hall and Mathiason (1990), Thavaneswaran (1991), Bhat (1996) and Heyde (1997, ch. 9). A related area to the EF method of estimation is the empirical likelihood (EL) approach. The links between the EF and EL methods and how to combine different sources of infor-mation on parameters are discussed in Qin and Lawless (1994) and Owen (2001, pp. 39–42, 51–5). We have tried to project the EF method by emphasizing its finite sample justification. However, the consistency and asymptotic normality of the resulting estimator are also important issues and good references on these are Crowder (1986), Heyde (1997, ch. 12) and Sørensen (1999).

To conclude, in this chapter we have reviewed the important phases in the development of the EF method, which now appears to have at least a century-old history. We have stressed the historical continuity in our discussion. It appears that, regarding the choice of estimation techniques, we are now back to the Pearsonian MM paradigm which looks more useful than ever after a very long devotion to Fisher's ML approach. Given that economic theory provides char-acterizations of stochastic laws mostly in terms of moment restrictions and the

EF approach is a sufficiently flexible moment-based method, the usefulness of this estimation technique looks very promising in econometric applications.

Acknowledgments

We are most grateful to Kerry Patterson for his constant encouragement and very helpful comments on an earlier draft. Without his many kind and gentle proddings this chapter would not have been completed. We are also most thankful to Vidhyadhar Godambe, George Judge, James MacKinnon, Peter Phillips and Jun Yan for many pertinent comments and suggestions. However, we retain the responsibility for any remaining errors. A part of the work was done during a visit by the first author to the Department of Economics, University of Cyprus, whose financial support is gratefully acknowledged.

References

Ainkaran, P. (2004) Analysis of some linear and nonlinear time series models, unpublished thesis, School of Mathematics and Statistics, University of Sydney.

Anselin, L. (2006) Spatial econometrics. In *Palgrave Handbook of Econometrics*, vol. 1. Basingstoke: Palgrave Macmillan.

Anselin, L. and Bera, A.K. (1998) Spatial dependence in linear regression models with an introduction to spatial econometrics. In A. Ullah and D.E.A. Giles (eds), *Handbook of Applied Economic Statistics*, pp. 237–89.

Barnard, G.A. (1973) Maximum likelihood and nuisance parameters. *Sankhya. The Indian Journal of Statistics* A **35**, 133–8.

Basawa, I.V. (1985) Neyman–LeCam tests based on estimating functions. In *Proceedings of the Berkeley Conference in Honor of Jerzy Neyman and Jack Keifer*, vol. 2. Monterey: Wadsworth, pp. 811–26.

Basawa, I.V. (1991) Generalized score tests for composite hypothesis. In V.P. Godambe (ed.), *Estimating Functions*. Oxford: Oxford University Press, pp. 121–31.

Basawa, I.V., V.P. Godambe and R.L. Taylor (eds) (1997) *Selected Proceedings of the Symposium on Estimating Functions*, Institute of Mathematical Statistics, Lecture Notes – Monograph Series, vol. 32.

Bellhouse, D.R. (1992) The life and times of V.P. Godambe. In J. Chen (ed.), *Recent Concepts in Statistical Inference*, Proceedings of a Symposium in Honor of Prof. V.P. Godambe. Waterloo, ONT: University of Waterloo, pp. 1–5.

Bera, A.K. and Y. Bilias (2001a) On some optimality properties of Fisher–Rao score function in testing and estimation. *Communications in Statistics – Theory and Methods* **30**, 1533–1559.

Bera, A.K. and Y. Bilias (2001b) Rao's score, Neyman's $C(\alpha)$ and Silvey's LM tests: an essay on historical developments and some new results. *Journal of Statistical Planning and Inference* **97**, 9–44.

Bera, A.K. and Y. Bilias (2002) The MM, ME, ML, EL, EF and GMM approaches to estimation: a synthesis. *Journal of Econometrics* **107**, 51–86.

Bera, A.K. and M.L. Higgins (1993) ARCH models: properties, estimation and testing. *Journal of Economic Surveys* **7**, 305–66.

Bera, A.K. and M.L. Higgins (1997) ARCH and bilinearity as competing models for nonlinear dependence. *Journal of Business and Economic Statistics* **15**, 43–50.

Bera, A.K., M.L. Higgins and S. Lee (1992) Interaction between autocorrelation and conditional heteroscedasticity: a random coefficient approach. *Journal of Business and Economic Statistics* **10**, 133–42.

Bera, A.K. and S. Lee (1993) Information matrix test, parameter heterogeneity and ARCH: a synthesis. *Review of Economic Studies* **60**, 229–40.

Besag, J. (1974) Spatial interaction and the statistical analysis of lattice systems (with discussion). *Journal of Royal Statistical Society* 36, Series B, 192–236.
Besag, J. (1977) Efficiency of pseudo-likelihood estimators for simple Gaussian fields. *Biometrika* 64, 616–18.
Bhapkar, V.P. (1972) On a measure of efficiency of an estimating equation. *Sankhya: The Indian Journal of Statistics* A, 34, 467–72.
Bhapkar, V.P. (1991) Sufficiency, ancillarity and information in estimating functions. In V.P. Godambe (ed.), *Estimating Functions*. New York: Oxford University Press, pp. 241–54.
Bhat, B.R. (1990) Optimal statistical estimating functions. Paper presented at the Indian Science Congress, Cochin.
Bhat, B.R. (1996) Tests based on estimating functions. In: B.L.S. Prakasa Rao and B.R. Bhat (eds), *Stochastic Processes and Statistical Inference*. New Delhi: New Age International Publishers, pp. 20–38.
Bollerslev, T., R.F. Engle and D.B. Nelson (1994) ARCH models. In R.F. Engle and D. McFadden (eds), *Handbook of Econometrics*, vol. 4. Amsterdam: North-Holland, pp. 2959–3038.
Chamberlain, G. (1987) Asymptotic efficiency in estimation with conditional moment restrictions. *Journal of Econometrics* 34, 305–34.
Chandrasekhar, B. and B.K. Kale (1984) Unbiased statistical estimating functions in presence of nuisance parameters. *Journal of Statistical Planning and Inference* 9, 45–54.
Chandra, A.S. and M. Taniguchi (2001) Estimating functions for non-linear time series models. *Annals of the Institute of Statistical Mathematics* 53, 125–41.
Chen, J. (ed.) (1992) *Recent Concepts in Statistical Inference*. Proceedings of a Symposium in Honor of Prof. V. P. Godambe. Waterloo, Ontario: University of Waterloo.
Cramér, H. (1946) *Mathematical Methods of Statistics*. Princeton, NJ: Princeton University Press.
Crowder, M. (1986) On consistency and inconsistency of estimating equations. *Econometric Theory* 2, 305–30.
Davidson, R. and J.G. MacKinnon (1993) *Estimation and Inference in Econometrics*. New York: Oxford University Press.
Davidson, R. and J.G. MacKinnon (2004) *Econometric Theory and Methods*. New York: Oxford University Press.
Desmond, A.F. (1989) The theory of estimating equations. In S. Kotz, N.L. Johnson, and C.B. Read (eds), *Encyclopedia of Statistical Sciences*, Supplement Volume. New York: Wiley, pp. 56–9.
Desmond, A.F. (1997) Optimal estimating functions, quasi-likelihood and statistical modelling (with discussion). *Journal of Statistical Planning and Inference* 60, 116–21.
Durbin, J. (1960) Estimation of parameters in time-series regression models. *Journal of the Royal Statistical Society* 22, Series B, 139–53.
Durbin, J. (1997) Optimal estimating equations for state vectors in non-Gaussian and non-linear space time series models. In I.V. Basawa, V.P. Godambe and R.L. Taylor (eds), *Selected Proceedings of the Symposium on Estimating Functions*. IMS Lecture Note-Monograph Series, vol. 32, pp. 285–91.
Edgeworth, F.Y. (1908) On the probable errors of frequency-constants. *Journal of the Royal Statistical Society* 71, 381–97, 499–512, 651–78.
Edgeworth, F.Y. (1909) Addendum on "Probable errors of frequency-constants". *Journal of the Royal Statistical Society* 72, 81–90.
Engle, R.F. (1982) Autoregressive conditional heteroscedasticity with estimates of the variance of United Kingdom inflation. *Econometrica* 50, 987–1007.
Engle, R.F. (2002) New frontiers for ARCH models. *Journal of Applied Econometrics* 17, 425–46.
Fitzmaurice, G.M., N.M. Laird and A.G. Rotnitzky (1993) Regression models for discrete longitudinal responses (with discussion). *Statistical Science* 8, 284–309.
Fisher, R.A. (1912) On an absolute criterion for fitting frequency curves. *Messenger of Mathematics* 41, 155–60.

Fisher, R.A. (1922) On the mathematical foundations of theoretical statistics. *Philosophical Transactions of the Royal Society of London* **222**, Series A, 309–68.

Fisher, R.A. (1924) The conditions under which χ^2 measures the discrepancy between observation and hypothesis. *Journal of the Royal Statistical Society* **87**, 442–50.

Fisher, R.A. (1935a) The logic of inductive inference. *Journal of the Royal Statistical Society* **98**, 39–54.

Fisher, R.A. (1935b) The fiducial argument in statistical inference. *Annals of Eugenics* **6**, 391–6.

Fisher, R.A. (1937) Professor Karl Pearson and the method of moments. *Annals of Eugenics* **7**, 303–18.

Godambe, V.P. (1960) An optimum property of regular maximum likelihood estimation. *Annals of Mathematical Statistics* **31**, 1208–1212.

Godambe, V.P. (1976) Conditional likelihood and unconditional optimum estimating equations. *Biometrika* **63**, 277–84.

Godambe, V.P. (1984) On ancillary and Fisher information in the presence of nuisance parameter. *Biometrika* **71**, 626–9.

Godambe, V.P. (1985) The foundations of finite sample estimation in stochastic processes. *Biometrika* **72**, 419–28.

Godambe, V.P. (ed.) (1991a) *Estimating Functions*. New York: Oxford Science Publications.

Godambe, V.P. (1991b) Orthogonality of estimating functions and nuisance parameters. *Biometrika* **78**, 143–51.

Godambe, V.P. (2001) Estimation of median: quasi-likelihood and optimum estimating functions, Working Paper 2001–01, Department of Statistics and Actuarial Science, University of Waterloo, Canada.

Godambe, V.P. and C.C. Heyde (1987) Quasi-likelihood and optimal estimation. *International Statistical Review* **55**, 231–44.

Godambe, V.P. and B.K. Kale (1991) Estimating functions: an overview. In V.P. Godambe (ed.), *Estimating Functions*. Oxford: Oxford University Press, pp. 3–20.

Godambe, V.P. and M.E. Thompson (1974) Estimating equations in the presence of a nuisance parameter. *Annals of Statistics* **2**, 568–71.

Godambe, V.P. and M.E. Thompson (1978) Some aspects of the theory of estimating equations. *Journal of Statistical Planning and Inference* **2**, 95–104.

Godambe, V.P. and M.E. Thompson (1984) Robust estimation through estimating equations. *Biometrika* **71**, 115–25.

Godambe, V.P. and M.E. Thompson (1989) An extension of quasi-likelihood estimation. *Journal of Statistical Planning and Inference* **22**, 137–52.

Granger, C.W.J. (1998) Overview of nonlinear time series specification in economics. NSF Symposium on Nonlinear Time Series Models, University of California, Berkeley.

Granger, C.W.J. and A.P. Anderson (1978) *An Introduction to Bilinear Time Series Models*. Göttingen: Vandenhoeck and Ruprecht.

Granger, C.W.J. and T. Teräsvirta (1993) *Modelling Nonlinear Economic Relationships*. New York: Oxford University Press.

Hald, A. (1998) *A History of Mathematical Statistics: From 1750 to 1930*. New York: John Wiley and Sons.

Hall, W.J. and D.J. Mathiason (1990) On largesample estimation and testing in parametric models. *International Statistical Review* **58**, 77–97.

Heyde, C.C. (1989) Quasi-likelihood and optimality of estimating functions: some current unifying themes. *Bulletin International Statistical Institute*, Book 1, 19–29.

Heyde, C.C. (1997) *Quasi-likelihood and Its Applications: A General Approach to Optimal Parameter Estimation*. New York: Springer.

Judge, G.G. and R.C. Mittelhammer (2005) Estimation and inference in case of competing sets of estimating equations. *Journal of Econometrics*, forthcoming.

Jung, S.H. (1996) Quasi-likelihood for median regression models. *Journal of the American Statistical Association* **91**, 251–7.

Kale, B.K. (1962) An extension of the Cramér–Rao inequality for statistical estimation functions. *Skandinaviske Akturietidskrift* **45**, 80–9.

Kale, B.K. (2001–02) Estimating functions and equations. *Journal of the Indian Society for Probability and Statistics* **6**, 1–27.

Kendall, M.G. (1951) Regression, structure and functional relationship – I. *Biometrika* **38**, 11–25.

Kimball, B.F. (1946) Sufficient statistical estimation functions for the parameters of the distribution of maximum values. *Annals of Mathematical Statistics* **17**, 299–309.

Koenker, R. and G. Bassett (1978) Regression quantiles. *Econometrica* **46**, 33–50.

Lele, S. (1994) Estimating functions in chaotic systems. *Journal of the American Statistical Association* **89**, 512–16.

Lele, S. (1997) Estimating functions for semivariogram estimation. In I.V. Basawa, V.P. Godambe and R.L. Taylor (eds), *Selected Proceedings of the Symposium on Estimating Functions*. IMS Lecture Note-Monograph Series, vol. 32, 381–96.

Li, D.X. and H.J. Turtle (2000) Semiparametric ARCH models: an estimating function approach. *Journal of Business and Economic Statistics* **18**, 174–86.

Liang, K.Y. and S.L. Zeger (1986) Longitudinal data analysis using generalized linear models. *Biometrika* **73**, 13–22.

Liang, K.Y. and S.L. Zeger (1995) Inference based on estimating functions in the presence of nuisance parameter. *Statistical Science* **10**, 158–73.

Lindsay, B.G. (1982) Conditional score functions: some optimality results. *Biometrika* **69**, 503–12.

Lindsay, B.G. and R.P. Waterman (1992) Extending Godambe's method in nuisance parameter problems. In J. Chen (ed.), *Recent Concepts in Statistical Inference*, Proceedings of a Symposium in Honor of Prof. V.P. Godambe, University of Waterloo, Canada.

Manski, C.F. (1975) Maximum score estimation of the stochastic utility model of choice. *Journal of Econometrics* **3**, 205–28.

McLeish, D.L. (1984) Estimation for aggregate models: the aggregate Markov chain. *Canadian Journal of Statistics* **12**, 265–82.

McLeish, D.L. and C.G. Small (1988) *The Theory and Applications of Statistical Inference Functions*, Lecture Notes in Statistics, 44. New York: Springer-Verlag.

Mittelhammer, R.C., G.G. Judge and D.J. Miller (2000) *Econometric Foundations*. Cambridge: Cambridge University Press.

Mukhopadhyay, P. (2004) *An Introduction to Estimating Functions*. New Delhi: Narosa Publishing House.

Naik-Nimbalkar, U.V. (1996) Estimating functions for stochastic processes. In B.L.S. Prakasa Rao and B.R. Bhat (eds), *Stochastic Processes and Statistical Inference*. New Delhi: New Age International Publishers, pp. 52–72.

Nelson, D.B. (1991) Conditional heteroscedasticity in asset returns: a new approach. *Econometrica* **59**, 347–70.

Newey, W.K. (2004) Efficient semiparametric estimation via moment restrictions. *Econometrica* **72**, 1877–1897.

Neyman, J. (1959) Optimal asymptotic test of composite statistical hypothesis. In U. Grenander (eds), *Probability and Statistics: the Herald Cramér Volume*. Uppsala: Almqvist and Wiksell, pp. 213–34.

Neyman, J. and E. Pearson (1933) On the problem of the most efficient tests of statistical hypothesis. *Philosophical Transactions of the Royal Society* A, **231**, 289–337.

Neyman, J., and E.L. Scott (1948) Consistent estimates based on partially consistent observations. *Econometrica* **16**, 1–32.

Nicholls, D.F and B.G. Quinn (1982) *Random Coefficient Autoregressive Models: An Introduction*. New York: Springer-Verlag.

Okuma, A. (1976) On invariance of estimating equations. *Bulletin of Kyushu Institute of Technology* **23**, 11–16.

Ord, J.K. (1975) Estimation methods for models of spatial interaction. *Journal of the American Statistical Association* 70, 120–6.

Owen, A.B. (2001) *Empirical Likelihood*, Monographs on Statistics and Applied Probability Series. London: Chapman and Hall/CRC Press.

Pearson, K. (1894) Contribution to the mathematical theory of evolution. *Philosophical Transactions of the Royal Society of London* 185, Series A, 71–110.

Pearson, K. (1902) On the systematic fitting of curves to observations and measurements, Parts I and II. *Biometrika* 1, 265–303; 2, 1–23.

Pearson, K. (1936) Method of moments and method of maximum likelihood. *Biometrika* 28, 34–59.

Phillips, P.C.B. (1988) The ET interview: Professor James Durbin. *Econometric Theory* 4, 125–57.

Powell, J.L. (1984) Least absolute deviations estimation for the censored regression model. *Journal of Econometrics* 25, 303–25.

Qin, J. and J. Lawless (1994) Empirical likelihood and general estimating equations. *Annals of Statistics* 22, 300–25.

Rao, C.R. (1945) Information and accuracy attainable in the estimation of statistical parameters. *Bulletin of Calcutta Mathematical Society* 37, 81–91.

Sørensen, M. (1999) On asymptotics of estimating functions. *Brazilian Journal of Probability and Statistics* 13, 111–36.

Teräsvirta, T. (2006) Univariate nonlinear time series models. In *Palgrave Handbook of Econometrics*, vol. 1. Basingstoke: Palgrave Macmillan.

Thavaneswaran, A. (1991) Tests based on optimal estimate. In V.P. Godambe (ed.), *Estimating Functions*. New York: Oxford University Press, pp. 189–97.

Thavaneswaran, A. and B. Abraham (1988) Estimation for non-linear time series models using estimating equations. *Journal of Time Series Analysis* 9, 99–108.

Thavaneswaran, A. and S. Peiris (1996) Nonparametric estimation for some non-linear models. *Statistics and Probability Letters* 28, 227–33.

Thompson, M.E. (2002) A conversation with V.P. Godambe. *Statistical Science* 17, 458–66.

Tong, H. (1990) *Nonlinear Time Series: A Dynamical System Approach*. Oxford: Oxford University Press.

Tsay, R.S. (1987) Conditional heteroscedastic time series models. *Journal of the American Statistical Association* 82, 590–604.

Vinod, H.D. (1998) Foundations of statistical inference based on numerical roots of robust pivot functions. *Journal of Econometrics* 86, 387–96.

Wald, A. (1940) The fitting of straight lines if both variables are subject to error. *Annals of Mathematical Statistics* 11, 284–300.

Wald, A. (1942) Asymptotically shortest confidence intervals. *Annals of Mathematical Statistics* 13, 127–37.

Wedderburn, R.W.M. (1974) Quasi-likelihood functions, generalized linear models and the Gauss–Newton method. *Biometrika* 61, 439–47.

Weiss, A.A. (1986) ARCH and bilinear time series models: comparison and combinations. *Journal of Business and Economics Statistics* 4, 59–70.

Wilks, S.S. (1938) Shortage average confidence intervals from large samples. *Annals of Mathematical Statistics* 9, 166–75.

Wilks, S.S. (1962) *Mathematical Statistics*. New York: John Wiley and Sons.

Yanagimoto, T. and E. Yamamoto (1991) The role of unbiasedness in estimating equations. In V.P. Godambe (ed.), *Estimating Functions*. New York: Oxford University Press, pp. 89–101.

Yanagimoto, T. and E. Yamamoto (1993) A criterion of sensitivity of an estimating function. *Communications in Statistics – Theory and Methods* 22, 451–60.

Yasui, Y. and S. Lele (1997) A regression method for spatial disease rates: an estimating function approach. *Journal of the American Statistical Association* 92, 21–32.

Yule, G.U. (1902) Mendel's laws and their probable relations to intra-racial heredity. *New Phytologist* 1, 193–207.

12

Vector Autoregressive Models

Helmut Lütkepohl

Abstract

Vector autoregressive (VAR) models are important tools for economic analysis and forecasting multiple time series. The first step in a VAR analysis is to specify and estimate a model. Specification involves lag order determination and possibly imposing parameter restrictions. Estimation is usually done by least squares, generalized least squares or maximum likelihood methods. Once a VAR model is set up, a range of checks is performed to ensure that it represents the data generation process adequately. All these steps are reviewed in the present chapter. In addition, forecasting, causality analysis and impulse response analysis are considered as possible uses of VAR models. The problem of nonuniqueness of the impulse responses is discussed and a framework for imposing structural information is presented.

12.1	Introduction	478
	12.1.1 Characteristics of variables	479
	12.1.2 Organization of the chapter	480
	12.1.3 Notational conventions	481
12.2	VAR models	481
	12.2.1 The levels VAR representation	482
	12.2.2 The VECM representation	482
	12.2.3 Structural forms	484
12.3	Estimation of reduced form models	484
	12.3.1 Estimation of unrestricted VARs	484
	12.3.2 Estimation with linear restrictions	486
12.4	Model specification	488
	12.4.1 Lag order selection	488
	12.4.2 Subset modeling	490
12.5	Model checking	491
	12.5.1 Tests for residual autocorrelation	492
	12.5.2 Tests for nonnormality	494
	12.5.3 Stability analysis	495

12.6   Forecasting and Granger-causality   495
    12.6.1   Forecasting with VAR processes   495
    12.6.2   Granger-causality analysis   498
12.7   Structural VARs and impulse response analysis   501
    12.7.1   Basic ideas   501
    12.7.2   Estimating impulse responses   503
    12.7.3   Forecast error variance decompositions   504
12.8   Conclusions and extensions   505

12.1   Introduction

Since the 1950s econometric simultaneous equations models have become standard tools for economic analysis and forecasting. They have been constructed for more and more refined analyses and their sizes have also grown considerably since the required computer technology and statistical tools have become available. Clearly, it was hoped that bigger, more detailed models would result in better approximations to the underlying data generation mechanisms. However, the availability of longer and more frequently observed time series and the development of methods for analyzing univariate time series have cast doubt on the usefulness of some of the large simultaneous equations models. In fact, in some forecast comparisons, univariate time series models provided better forecasts than the competing large scale econometric models. The insufficient representation of the dynamic interactions in simultaneous equations models was seen as one possible problem.

Therefore it was only natural that macroeconometric modeling was reassessed and, in an influential article, Sims (1980) advocated using vector autoregressive (VAR) models as alternatives which allow for a rich dynamic structure. He also criticized the exogeneity assumptions for some of the variables in simultaneous equations models which are often not supported by fully developed theories but reflect the preferences and prejudices of the model builders. In contrast, in VAR models often all observed variables are treated as a priori endogenous. Restrictions are imposed to a large extent by statistical tools rather than by prior beliefs based on uncertain theoretical considerations.

Sims (1980) also proposed to analyze the dynamic interactions between the variables of a VAR model by impulse response analysis or forecast error variance decompositions. It quickly became apparent, however, that such analyses usually also require a priori assumptions which cannot be checked by statistical tools and *structural* VAR (SVAR) models were developed as a framework for incorporating such restrictions. In addition, it was discovered that the trending properties of the variables under consideration are of major importance in econometric modeling and the associated statistical analysis. The spurious regression problem pointed out by Granger and Newbold (1974) made it clear that ignoring stochastic trends can lead to seriously misleading conclusions when modeling relations between time series variables. Hence, the stochastic trends, unit roots or integratedness of the variables of interest became of major concern to time series econometricians. The subsequent development of cointegration by Granger (1981), Engle and Granger (1987), Johansen (1995) and many others has opened the stage for a different view of the relations between time series variables. In particular, the long-run relations are now often distinguished from the short-run dynamics. The latter determine the adjustment path if deviations from the long-run relations occur. The cointegrating or long-run relations are often associated with relations derived from economic theory and are consequently of particular interest. It is therefore useful to construct models which explicitly separate the long-run and short-run parts of a stochastic process. Vector error correction or equilibrium correction models (VECMs) offer a convenient framework for this purpose. Because the trending properties of the variables are of importance in this context, the related terminology will be introduced next.

12.1.1 Characteristics of variables

Integrated variables, unit roots and stochastic trends have already been discussed in Chapter 7. We will also use this terminology in the present chapter and call a variable *integrated of order* d $(I(d))$ if stochastic trends or unit roots can be removed by differencing the variable d times and a stochastic trend still remains after differencing only $d - 1$ times. In particular, a variable without a stochastic trend or unit root is sometimes called $I(0)$. To simplify matters, in this chapter all variables are assumed to be either $I(0)$ or $I(1)$ if not otherwise stated. Also seasonal unit roots are excluded if not explicitly mentioned otherwise. In other words, for any time series variable y_{kt}, the first differences, $\Delta y_{kt} \equiv y_{kt} - y_{k, t-1}$, are assumed to have no stochastic trend. The variables Δy_{kt} may still have deterministic components such as a polynomial trend, however. A set of $I(1)$ variables is called *cointegrated* if a linear combination exists which is $I(0)$. This concept will be used extensively in the present chapter and is also discussed further in Chapters 14 to 16. In the present chapter it is occasionally convenient to consider systems with both $I(1)$ and $I(0)$ variables. If $I(0)$ variables are present, any linear combination which is $I(0)$ is called a cointegration relation, although this terminology is not quite in the spirit of the original definition of cointegration. In this case it can happen that a linear combination of $I(0)$ variables is called a cointegration relation. In the present chapter this terminology is convenient, however, and the reader should be aware of it.

Regarding deterministic terms, it was already mentioned that there may be deterministic polynomial trends. To simplify the exposition it is assumed that they are at most linear trends, unless stated otherwise. In other words, deterministic terms will usually be of the form $\mu_t = \mu_0 + \mu_1 t$. Of course, μ_1 may be zero in which case there is just a constant or intercept term in the process. Moreover, $\mu_t = 0$ will sometimes be assumed. Extensions to other deterministic terms such as seasonal dummies are not difficult. They are not discussed explicitly to avoid more elaborate notation.

12.1.2   Organization of the chapter

In practice, the initial step of a VAR analysis is to specify and estimate a model for a given multiple time series. Then the model adequacy has to be checked. If model defects are detected at this stage, model revisions are necessary. Otherwise the model can be used for forecasting, causality and structural analysis. The main steps of a VAR analysis are outlined in the diagram in Figure 12.1. This chapter is organized accordingly. In particular, in the next section the basic VARs and VECMs will be introduced. Estimation and specification of such models will be considered in sections 12.3 and 12.4, respectively, and model checking is discussed in section 12.5. Generally, the focus will be on levels VAR models because VECMs are treated in detail in Chapter 14. Forecasting and Granger-causality analysis will be dealt with in section 12.6 and impulse response analysis and forecast error variance decomposition are discussed in section 12.7. The latter issues will also require the discussion of SVARs. Conclusions are drawn and some extensions are mentioned in section 12.8.

Nowadays a number of textbooks are available which treat VAR modeling and dynamic econometric analysis more generally. Examples are Lütkepohl (2005), Banerjee, Dolado, Galbraith and Hendry (1993), Hamilton (1994), Hendry (1995), Johansen (1995), Hatanaka (1996), Hayashi (2000) and Lütkepohl and Krätzig (2004). They provide more details on the theoretical and related applied issues covered in this chapter. In addition there are a number of recent survey articles with a similar coverage as the present chapter. Examples are Watson (1994) and

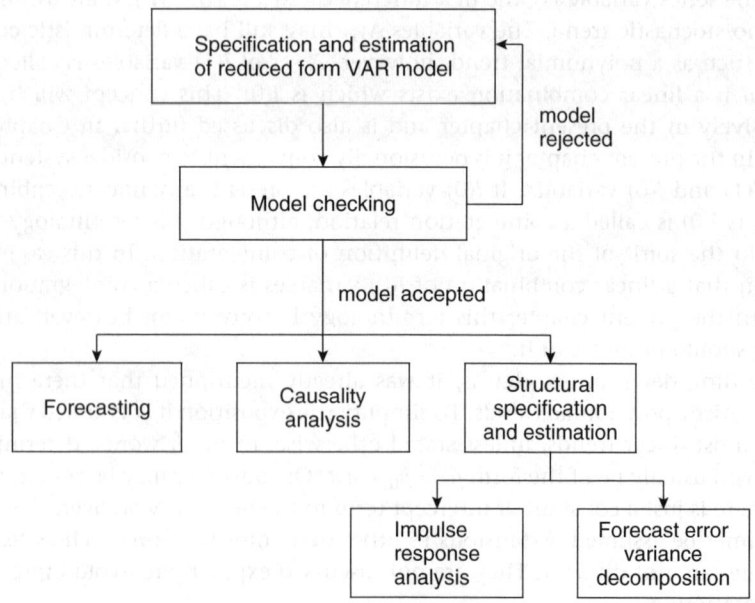

Figure 12.1   VAR analysis

Lütkepohl (2001). The present chapter draws partly on the latter article. More recent developments and references are taken into account, however.

12.1.3 Notational conventions

In this chapter the following notation and terminology will be used. The sets of all integers and positive integers are signified by $\mathbb{Z}$ and $\mathbb{N}$, respectively. The differencing and lag operators are denoted by Δ and L, respectively. The symbol "$\sim (\mu, \Sigma)$" is used for "has a distribution with mean (vector) μ and (co)variance (matrix) Σ" and $N(\mu, \Sigma)$ denotes a (multivariate) normal distribution with mean (vector) μ and (co)variance (matrix) Σ. Convergence in distribution and "is asymptotically distributed as" are signified by $\xrightarrow{d}$ and $\overset{a}{\sim}$, respectively. Independently, identically distributed is abbreviated as i.i.d.. A stochastic process u_t with $t \in \mathbb{Z}$ or $t \in \mathbb{N}$ is called *white noise* if the u_t are i.i.d. with mean zero, $E(u_t) = 0$, positive definite covariance matrix $\Sigma_u = E(u_t u_t')$ and finite fourth order moments. The i.i.d. assumption is stronger than actually necessary for many of the forthcoming results to hold. It is made here for convenience.

The transpose, inverse, trace, determinant and rank of the matrix A are denoted by A', A^{-1}, $\text{tr}(A)$, $\det(A)$ and $\text{rk}(A)$, respectively. The symbol vec is used for the column vectorization operator, $\otimes$ signifies the Kronecker product and I_n denotes an $(n \times n)$ identity matrix. The natural logarithm is denoted by log. The abbreviations ML, LS, GLS, EGLS, LM, LR and MSE are used for maximum likelihood, least squares, generalized least squares, estimated generalized least squares, Lagrange multiplier, likelihood ratio and mean squared error, respectively. Moreover, VAR, SVAR, VECM and MA abbreviate vector autoregression, structural vector autoregression, vector error correction model and moving average, respectively. A sum is defined to be zero if the lower bound of the summation index exceeds the upper bound.

12.2 VAR models

For a set of K observable time series variables $y_t = (y_{1t}, \ldots, y_{Kt})'$ the DGP is assumed to be of the following form:

$$y_t = \mu_t + x_t, \tag{12.2.1}$$

where μ_t is the deterministic part and x_t is a purely stochastic process with zero mean. Thus the deterministic part is simply added to the stochastic part. Although most procedures covered in the following can be generalized easily to other deterministic terms, it will be assumed that μ_t is a constant or linear trend, $\mu_t = \mu_0$ or $\mu_t = \mu_0 + \mu_1 t$, to simplify the exposition. Occasionally it will also be convenient to assume $\mu_t = 0$, in which case $y_t = x_t$. The stochastic part x_t includes all stochastic trends, of course, and, hence, the cointegration properties of the process are captured in x_t. Generally the unobserved purely stochastic part x_t is assumed to have a VAR or VECM representation which then implies a similar representation for the observed process y_t and the latter process also inherits the order of integration and the cointegration properties from x_t. The VAR and VECM forms for x_t and y_t will be introduced more formally in the next subsections.

12.2.1 The levels VAR representation

The basic VAR model of order p (VAR(p)) for x_t has the form

$$x_t = A_1 x_{t-1} + \cdots + A_p x_{t-p} + u_t. \qquad (12.2.2)$$

Here the A_i ($i = 1, \ldots, p$) are $(K \times K)$ coefficient matrices and the error process $u_t = (u_{1t}, \ldots, u_{Kt})'$ is assumed to be an unobservable white noise process with covariance matrix $E(u_t u_t') = \Sigma_u$, that is, $u_t \sim (0, \Sigma_u)$. The process x_t is *stable* if

$$\det(I_K - A_1 z - \cdots - A_p z^p) \neq 0 \quad \text{for } |z| \leq 1. \qquad (12.2.3)$$

If this condition is satisfied, it is convenient to assume that the DGP is defined for all integer values t, that is, $t \in \mathbb{Z}$ in (12.2.2). The process x_t is then stationary ($I(0)$), that is, it has time-invariant means, variances and covariance structure. Therefore, without prior notice, we assume $t \in \mathbb{Z}$ if x_t is stable and, hence, stationary. If the determinantal polynomial in (12.2.3) has a root for $z = 1$ (i.e., a unit root), then some or all of the variables are nonstationary and they may also be cointegrated. In that case, assuming $t \in \mathbb{N}$ is often convenient and the initial values $x_{-p+1}, \ldots, x_0$ are assumed to be constants or random vectors with some fixed probability distribution. If not otherwise mentioned, this assumption will be made if x_t is $I(1)$. Recall that we only consider $I(0)$ and $I(1)$ variables and no higher-order integration if not explicitly stated otherwise.

If x_t has the VAR(p) representation (12.2.2) and $\mu_t = \mu_0 + \mu_1 t$, then y_t has the VAR(p) representation

$$y_t = v_0 + v_1 t + A_1 y_{t-1} + \cdots + A_p y_{t-p} + u_t, \qquad (12.2.4)$$

where $v_0 = (I_K - \sum_{j=1}^{p} A_j)\mu_0 + (\sum_{j=1}^{p} jA_j)\mu_1$ and $v_1 = (I_K - \sum_{j=1}^{p} A_j)\mu_1$. Note, however, that if (12.2.4) is regarded as the basic model without restrictions for v_i, $i = 0, 1$, the model can in principle generate quadratic trends if $I(1)$ variables are involved, whereas in our model setup (12.2.1) with $\mu_t = \mu_0 + \mu_1 t$, a linear trend term is permitted only. Starting from the model (12.2.1) with additive deterministic and stochastic terms is sometimes helpful in theoretical derivations. It is also useful to think about the possible deterministic term at the beginning of the analysis and allow for the appropriate polynomial order. Moreover, in some situations it is useful to subtract the deterministic term first and then focus the analysis on the stochastic part. The latter part is often of primary interest in econometric analyses because it usually contains the behavioral relations.

12.2.2 The VECM representation

Although the levels VAR representation (12.2.2) is general enough to accommodate variables with stochastic trends, it is often not the most suitable representation. In particular, if the cointegration relations are of primary importance, it is a disadvantage that they do not appear explicitly in (12.2.2). They are more easily analyzed within the VECM representation

$$\Delta x_t = \Pi x_{t-1} + \Gamma_1 \Delta x_{t-1} + \cdots + \Gamma_{p-1} \Delta x_{t-p+1} + u_t, \qquad (12.2.5)$$

which may be obtained from (12.2.2) by subtracting x_{t-1} on both sides of the equation and rearranging terms. Thereby it is seen that $\Pi = -(I_K - A_1 - \cdots - A_p)$ and $\Gamma_j = -(A_{j+1} + \cdots + A_p)$ for $j = 1, \ldots, p-1$. Because Δx_t does not contain stochastic trends by the assumption that all variables can be at most $I(1)$, the term Πx_{t-1} is the only one which includes $I(1)$ variables. Hence, Πx_{t-1} must also be $I(0)$ and, consequently, it must contain the cointegrating relations. The Γ_j ($j = 1, \ldots, p-1$) are often referred to as the *short-term* or *short-run parameters* while Πx_{t-1} is called the *long-run* or *long-term part* or the *error correction* or *equilibrium correction term* of the model.

If the condition (12.2.3) does not hold and $\det(I_K - A_1 z - \cdots - A_p z^p) = 0$ for $z = 1$, the matrix Π is singular. Suppose $\text{rk}(\Pi) = r$ with $0 < r < K$. Then there exist $(K \times r)$ matrices α and β with $\text{rk}(\alpha) = \text{rk}(\beta) = r$ such that $\Pi = \alpha\beta'$. Premultiplying an $I(0)$ vector by some matrix results again in an $I(0)$ process. Hence, premultiplying $\Pi x_{t-1} = \alpha\beta' x_{t-1}$ by $(\alpha'\alpha)^{-1}\alpha'$ shows that $\beta' x_{t-1}$ is $I(0)$. Thus, there are r linearly independent cointegrating relations among the components of x_t and the rank r of the matrix Π is called the *cointegrating rank* of the process. Because the matrices α and β are not unique, the cointegrating relations are also not unique. Specifying cointegrating relations with economic content usually requires restrictions for the β matrix which may result in unique or identified relations.

Necessarily, $0 \le r \le K$. $I(0)$ processes for which $r = K$ are included as special cases. Moreover, systems with a stable VAR representation in first differences result for $r = 0$. In the latter case, the term Πx_{t-1} disappears in (12.2.5). Clearly, these boundary cases do not represent cointegrated systems in the usual sense. There are also other cases where no cointegration in a strict sense is present although the representation (12.2.5) has a cointegrating rank strictly between 0 and K. For example, if all variables but one are $I(0)$ then the cointegrating rank is $K - 1$ although the $I(1)$ variable is not cointegrated with the other variables. Such cases are not excluded when we consider systems with $I(1)$ variables in the following.

If x_t has the representation (12.2.5) and the deterministic term is a linear trend, it can be shown that y_t has the VECM representation

$$\Delta y_t = v_0 + v_1 t + \alpha\beta' y_{t-1} + \Gamma_1 \Delta y_{t-1} + \cdots + \Gamma_{p-1} \Delta y_{t-p+1} + u_t, \qquad (12.2.6)$$

where v_0 and v_1 are as in (12.2.4). In particular, $v_1 = -\Pi\mu_1 = -\alpha\beta'\mu_1$. Thus, the trend term can be absorbed into the cointegrating relations,

$$\Delta y_t = v + \alpha[\beta', \eta] \begin{bmatrix} y_{t-1} \\ t-1 \end{bmatrix} + \Gamma_1 \Delta y_{t-1} + \cdots + \Gamma_{p-1} \Delta y_{t-p+1} + u_t, \qquad (12.2.7)$$

with $\eta = -\beta'\mu_1$ being an $(r \times 1)$ vector and $v = v_0 + v_1$.

12.2.3 Structural forms

The models discussed so far are reduced forms because all right-hand side variables are predetermined. Later in this chapter structural forms, where contemporaneous relations between the variables are also modeled, will be of interest. As an example consider a structural form associated with the VAR representation (12.2.4),

$$Ay_t = v_0^* + v_1^* t + A_1^* y_{t-1} + \cdots + A_p^* y_{t-p} + v_t, \tag{12.2.8}$$

where $v_i^* = A v_i$ $(i = 0, 1)$, $A_j^* = A A_j$ $(j = 1, \ldots, p)$ and $v_t = A u_t$ is the structural form error term. It is again i.i.d. white noise with covariance matrix $\Sigma_v = A \Sigma_u A'$. The matrix A is a nonsingular $(K \times K)$ coefficient matrix which describes the instantaneous relations between the variables. The parameters of the structural form (12.2.8) are not identified without further restrictions. More discussion of structural models will be provided in section 12.7.1. Typically reduced form VAR models or VECMs are specified first and then structural restrictions are imposed. Therefore, in the following sections we will first deal with estimation and specification of reduced form models. The specification of a VAR model requires the choice of the VAR order p and possibly further parameter restrictions. Similarly, specifying a VECM requires in addition the choice of the cointegrating rank. Before specification issues are dealt with, it is useful to consider estimation problems for fully specified models because estimation of various models is usually necessary at the specification stage. Estimation of VARs is therefore discussed next.

12.3   Estimation of reduced form models

Because estimating unrestricted reduced form VAR models is particularly easy and still of considerable practical importance, this case will be treated first. A discussion of estimation under linear restrictions follows in subsection 12.3.2.

12.3.1   Estimation of unrestricted VARs

To simplify matters, a VAR(p) process without deterministic terms ($\mu_t = 0$) is considered first,

$$y_t = A_1 y_{t-1} + \cdots + A_p y_{t-p} + u_t. \tag{12.3.1}$$

It is assumed that a sample of size T, $y_1, \ldots, y_T$, and p presample values, $y_{-p+1}, \ldots, y_0$, are available. Defining

$$Y = [y_1, \ldots, y_T], \quad \mathbf{Y} = [Y_0, \ldots, Y_{T-1}], \quad \text{where } Y_{t-1} = \begin{pmatrix} y_{t-1} \\ \vdots \\ y_{t-p} \end{pmatrix}, \tag{12.3.2}$$

$$A = [A_1, \ldots, A_p] \quad \text{and} \quad U = [u_1, \ldots, u_T],$$

the model can be written compactly as

$$Y = A \mathbf{Y} + U. \tag{12.3.3}$$

As shown by Zellner (1962), for this model, estimating the K equations separately by LS is identical to GLS estimation, if there are no restrictions on the parameters A. In fact, if the white noise process u_t is Gaussian, $u_t \sim N(0, \Sigma_u)$, and, hence, y_t is also normally distributed, the LS estimator is identical to the ML estimator and, thus, there is no loss in asymptotic estimation efficiency.

The estimator can be written as

$$\hat{A} = [\hat{A}_1, \ldots, \hat{A}_p] = YY'(YY')^{-1}. \tag{12.3.4}$$

If the process is stable ($I(0)$), the LS estimator $\hat{A}$ is consistent and asymptotically normally distributed under our assumptions for u_t (see, e.g., Lütkepohl, 2005),

$$\sqrt{T}\text{vec}(\hat{A} - A) \xrightarrow{d} N(0, \Sigma_{\hat{A}}) \quad \text{or, more intuitively,} \quad \text{vec}(\hat{A}) \overset{a}{\sim} N(\text{vec}(A), \Sigma_{\hat{A}}/T). \tag{12.3.5}$$

The covariance matrix of the asymptotic distribution is $\Sigma_{\hat{A}} = \text{plim}(YY'/T)^{-1} \otimes \Sigma_u$, so that an even more intuitive, albeit imprecise, way of writing the result in (12.3.5) is

$$\text{vec}(\hat{A}) \approx N(\text{vec}(A), (YY')^{-1} \otimes \Sigma_u). \tag{12.3.6}$$

In fact, this way to write the result is useful in setting up the usual test statistics like t-, χ^2- and F-statistics. All these statistics can be set up pretending that the left-hand side vector in (12.3.6) has a normal distribution and treating the stochastic matrix $(YY')^{-1} \otimes \Sigma_u$ as the covariance matrix. Asymptotically the statistics will then have the usual distributions.

Similar results also hold if some or all of the variables are $I(1)$ and they are potentially cointegrated (see Park and Phillips, 1988, 1989; Sims, Stock and Watson, 1990; Lütkepohl, 2005, chapter 7). In that case, however, the covariance matrix $\Sigma_{\hat{A}}$ is singular, whereas it is nonsingular in the usual $I(0)$ case. In other words, in the $I(1)$ case, the asymptotic distribution of $\hat{A}$ is singular and some estimated coefficients or linear combinations of coefficients converge with a faster rate than $\sqrt{T}$. In general, the usual t-, χ^2- and F-tests for inference regarding the VAR parameters will therefore not be valid (Toda and Phillips, 1993). Clearly, this result is not surprising given that, for a univariate first-order autoregressive $I(1)$ process $y_t = \alpha y_{t-1} + u_t$ with $\alpha = 1$, the LS estimator $\hat{\alpha}$ converges with rate T (see Chapter 7). In other words, $\sqrt{T}(\hat{\alpha} - \alpha)$ converges to zero in probability and, thus, the limiting distribution has zero variance and is degenerate, whereas $T(\hat{\alpha} - \alpha)$ has a nondegenerate nonnormal limiting distribution.

In VAR models with $I(1)$ variables the situation is not quite so extreme and many of the standard statistics converge to their usual asymptotic distributions. Dolado and Lütkepohl (1996) and Toda and Yamamoto (1995) have shown that, if all variables are $I(1)$ or $I(0)$ and if a null hypothesis is considered which does not restrict elements of each of the A_i's ($i = 1, \ldots, p$), then the usual tests have their standard asymptotic properties. Thus, for example, if the VAR order is $p \geq 2$, then the t-ratios have their usual asymptotic standard normal distributions because they are test statistics for hypotheses regarding individual coefficients and, hence, the null hypothesis specifies a restriction for one of the coefficient matrices only. On the other hand, if a VAR(1) model is considered, even the t-ratios may have nonstandard asymptotic distributions.

In setting up test statistics it is usually necessary to have an estimator of the residual covariance matrix Σ_u as well. It can be estimated in the usual way as

$$\hat{\Sigma}_u = \frac{1}{T - Kp} \sum_{t=1}^{T} \hat{u}_t \hat{u}_t' \quad \text{or} \quad \tilde{\Sigma}_u = \frac{1}{T} \sum_{t=1}^{T} \hat{u}_t \hat{u}_t', \tag{12.3.7}$$

where $\hat{u}_t = y_t - \hat{A} Y_{t-1}$ are the LS residuals. Both estimators are consistent and asymptotically normally distributed independently of $\hat{A}$, that is, $\sqrt{T}(\hat{\Sigma}_u - \Sigma_u)$ and $\sqrt{T}(\tilde{\Sigma}_u - \Sigma_u)$ have asymptotic normal distributions independent of $\hat{A}$ if sufficient moment conditions are assumed for u_t (see Lütkepohl, 2005; and Lütkepohl and Saikkonen, 1997). These properties are convenient for inference purposes.

It is also easy to include deterministic terms in the model (12.3.1). For example, if a linear trend term $v_0 + v_1 t$ is included, the regressor vectors Y_{t-1} just have to be augmented by additional regressors 1 and t and the vectors v_0 and v_1 have to be included in the coefficient matrix. With these modifications the foregoing formulas apply. Some more care is necessary in this case in stating the asymptotic distributions of the estimators because the slope parameters converge at a faster rate than $\sqrt{T}$. Interestingly, the result (12.3.6) survives in the stationary case because the convergence rates do not appear explicitly in that formulation. In the $I(1)$ case, the situation is not quite so simple and further assumptions regarding the deterministic terms are necessary to state their precise distributions. Recall that under our assumptions the linear trend term can be absorbed in the cointegration relations and a similar possibility exists for the constant term in some situations. We will not give the precise conditions and results because these issues are discussed in Chapter 14. It may be of interest to note, however, that the asymptotic properties of the VAR coefficients remain essentially the same as in the case without deterministic terms (Sims *et al.*, 1990). Thus, the previous comments on inference for these coefficients apply.

12.3.2   Estimation with linear restrictions

To simplify the exposition of estimation under parameter restrictions, it is again assumed that (12.3.1) is the model of interest so that there are no deterministic terms. It is also assumed that the process is $I(0)$. In practice, the most common restrictions for A are zero restrictions. Therefore we will study such restrictions here. They can be written in the form

$$\alpha = R\gamma, \tag{12.3.8}$$

where $\alpha = \text{vec}(A)$ is a $(K^2p \times 1)$ vector, R is a known $(K^2p \times M)$ matrix of zeros and ones with rank M and γ is the $(M \times 1)$ vector of all unrestricted parameters. To impose the restrictions in the estimation procedure it is convenient to vectorize the model (12.3.3),

$$\text{vec}(Y) = (\mathbf{Y}' \otimes I_K)\text{vec}(A) + \text{vec}(U) = (\mathbf{Y}' \otimes I_K)R\gamma + \text{vec}(U). \qquad (12.3.9)$$

Because the covariance matrix of $\text{vec}(U)$ is $I_T \otimes \Sigma_u$, the GLS estimator for γ is

$$\hat{\gamma} = [R'(\mathbf{YY}' \otimes \Sigma_u^{-1})R]^{-1}R'(\mathbf{Y} \otimes \Sigma_u^{-1})\text{vec}(Y). \qquad (12.3.10)$$

The estimator has standard asymptotic properties, that is, it is consistent and asymptotically normally distributed,

$$\sqrt{T}(\hat{\gamma} - \gamma) \overset{d}{\to} N(0, (R'\Sigma_{\hat{A}}^{-1}R)^{-1}). \qquad (12.3.11)$$

Because the white noise covariance matrix is usually unknown, the GLS estimator is of limited value in practice. Using, for example, the estimator $\hat{\Sigma}_u$ from (12.3.7), gives an EGLS estimator

$$\hat{\hat{\gamma}} = [R'(\mathbf{YY}' \otimes \hat{\Sigma}_u^{-1})R]^{-1}R'(\mathbf{Y} \otimes \hat{\Sigma}_u^{-1})\text{vec}(Y), \qquad (12.3.12)$$

which has the same asymptotic properties as the GLS estimator $\hat{\gamma}$. The EGLS estimator can also be used to construct an estimator for $\alpha, \hat{\hat{\alpha}} = R\hat{\hat{\gamma}}$, which is also consistent and asymptotically normal,

$$\sqrt{T}(\hat{\hat{\alpha}} - \alpha) \overset{d}{\to} N(0, R(R'\Sigma_{\hat{A}}^{-1}R)^{-1}R'). \qquad (12.3.13)$$

The EGLS estimator may be iterated by reestimating the white noise covariance matrix from the EGLS residuals and computing a new estimator for γ with the new covariance estimator. This procedure may be continued until convergence. The asymptotic properties of the resulting estimators for γ and α are unaffected by such iterations. Also, if u_t is Gaussian white noise, Gaussian ML estimation can be used. In small samples the ML estimator for γ is generally different from the EGLS or iterated EGLS estimators. On the other hand, the asymptotic properties are the same. It is also easy to include deterministic terms in the model. Technically the required modifications are straightforward, as in the unrestricted case.

So far it has been assumed that the process is $I(0)$. If there are $I(1)$ components, restricted estimation of the levels VAR form can be done in principle in the same way. The asymptotic properties may be more complicated in that case. The reason is that in the levels VAR form there is no clear distinction between stationary and nonstationary components. Recall that some linear combinations of $I(1)$ variables may be cointegrated and, hence, stationary. Therefore it is preferable to impose restrictions on the VECM form. As mentioned earlier, estimation of VECMs is dealt with in detail in Chapter 14 and will therefore not be considered here.

12.4 Model specification

To specify a VAR model, the lag order has to be determined. In addition, it is often desirable to reduce the parameter space by imposing restrictions, because the number of parameters in an unrestricted VAR model increases with the square of the number of variables and therefore quickly becomes large. Estimating a large number of parameters from a limited data set may result in imprecise estimators which, in turn, may make the interpretation of the models and forecasting difficult. If zero restrictions are imposed, the resulting models are commonly referred to as *subset VAR models*. In this section lag order selection is discussed first. In practice it is often the first step in the specification procedure. Zero restrictions are then imposed on the parameter matrices in a second stage. Some statistical procedures for that purpose will be considered in section 12.4.2. Of course, sometimes it may also be possible to use economic subject matter theory to identify possible restrictions. Both lag order selection and imposing subset restrictions are also relevant for specifying VECMs. In these models the cointegrating rank has to be specified in addition. Relevant statistical procedures will again be discussed in Chapter 14 and are therefore not treated here.

12.4.1 Lag order selection

12.4.1.1 Sequential testing

If, for a given set of variables, a maximum order, say p_{max}, for a VAR model is available, a sequential testing procedure for the lag order can be set up. For example, a sequence of null hypotheses $H_0 : A_{p_{max}} = 0, H_0 : A_{p_{max}-1} = 0$, etc., may be tested until the null hypothesis is rejected for the first time. In this procedure standard tests for zero restrictions, such as Wald or LR tests, may be used because we have seen that these tests have standard asymptotic distributions. This result even holds if some of the variables are $I(1)$, as long as the null hypothesis $H_0 : A_1 = 0$ is not tested. Recall from the discussion in section 12.3.1 that if restrictions on a VAR(1) model are tested, the usual tests may not be valid. Also, there is some evidence that the tests are strongly distorted in small samples and have small sample distributions which are quite different from their asymptotic counterparts, especially if systems with more than a couple of variables are considered (e.g., Lütkepohl, 2005). Therefore small sample adjustments, possibly based on bootstrap methods, may be worth considering (e.g., Li and Maddala, 1996; Berkowitz and Kilian, 2000).

Clearly, the choice of p_{max} is important in this procedure. If this quantity is chosen very large, a long sequence of tests may be necessary before the null hypothesis is rejected for the first time. A long testing sequence, in turn, will have an impact on the overall Type I error of the testing procedure. If, on the other hand, p_{max} is chosen quite small, an appropriate model may not be in the set of possibilities and therefore cannot be found with a sequential procedure of the type described earlier. In choosing the maximum lag order, it should be kept in mind that making an error at this stage may result in model deficiencies which may be uncovered at the model checking stage (see section 12.5). Increasing the lag order is one possible course of action at that stage. Therefore starting with a moderately large $p_{\max}$ appears to be a useful strategy.

It is also possible that the actual DGP does not have a finite-order VAR representation. Ng and Perron (1995) have considered some consequences for choosing the lag order by sequential testing procedures in univariate models when the true lag length is infinite. Rather than using sequential tests, one may alternatively choose the lag order by model selection procedures which will be discussed next.

12.4.1.2 Model selection criteria

Various model selection criteria are available for choosing the VAR order. They are applied by fitting VAR(m) models with orders $m = 0, \ldots, p_{\max}$ and choosing an estimator of the order p which minimizes the prespecified criterion. Many of the criteria used in this context are of the general form

$$C(m) = \log \det(\tilde{\Sigma}_m) + c_T \varphi(m), \qquad (12.4.1)$$

where $\tilde{\Sigma}_m = T^{-1} \sum_{t=1}^{T} \hat{u}_t \hat{u}_t'$ is the residual covariance matrix estimator for a model of order m and c_T is a sequence which may depend on the sample size. The quantity $\varphi(m)$ is a function of m which penalizes large VAR orders. On the other hand, the term $\log \det(\tilde{\Sigma}_m)$ measures the fit of a model of order m. This quantity declines, or at least does not increase, with increasing order m because there is no correction for degrees of freedom in the covariance matrix estimator. In the selection procedure the sample size is assumed to be held constant and, hence, the number of presample values set aside for estimation is given by the maximum order $p_{\max}$. The estimator $\hat{p}$ of p is chosen to be the order which minimizes the criterion (12.4.1).

Examples of criteria in widespread use in applied work are Akaike's information criterion (Akaike, 1973, 1974),

$$\text{AIC}(m) = \log \det(\tilde{\Sigma}_m) + \frac{2}{T} mK^2,$$

where $\varphi(m) = mK^2$ and $c_T = 2/T$, the Hannan–Quinn criterion (Hannan and Quinn, 1979; Quinn, 1980),

$$\text{HQ}(m) = \log \det(\tilde{\Sigma}_m) + \frac{2 \log \log T}{T} mK^2,$$

where again $\varphi(m) = mK^2$ and $c_T = 2 \log \log T/T$, and the Schwarz (or Rissanen) criterion (Schwarz, 1978; Rissanen, 1978),

$$\text{SC}(m) = \log \det(\tilde{\Sigma}_m) + \frac{\log T}{T} mK^2,$$

where $\varphi(m) = mK^2$, as for the other two criteria, and $c_T = \log T/T$. The AIC criterion tends to overestimate the order asymptotically and the HQ and SC criteria are both consistent, that is, plim $\hat{p} = p$ or $\hat{p} \to p$ a.s., under quite general conditions, if the actual DGP has a finite VAR order and the maximum order, p_{max}, is larger than or at least equal to the true order. Paulsen (1984) has shown that these results not only hold for $I(0)$ processes but also for $I(1)$ processes with cointegrated variables. Generally, in small samples of fixed size $T \geq 16$,

$$\hat{p}(SC) \leq \hat{p}(HQ) \leq \hat{p}(AIC),$$

where $\hat{p}(AIC)$, $\hat{p}(HQ)$ and $\hat{p}(SC)$ denote the orders selected by AIC, HQ and SC, respectively (Lütkepohl, 2005, chapters 4 and 8). Thus, when the VAR order is estimated by these three criteria, SC always chooses the smallest order while AIC delivers the largest estimate. Of course, all three order estimates can be identical.

12.4.2   Subset modeling

As mentioned earlier, once a VAR(p) model has been specified, it is often a good idea to consider further restrictions on the parameters because the dimension of the parameter space increases quickly with the number of variables. Zero restrictions are the most common restrictions that are imposed on VAR coefficients. As discussed in section 12.3, the usual test statistics for testing hypotheses regarding individual parameters or groups of coefficients are asymptotically valid in stable models and in many situations also for models involving $I(1)$ variables. Still, it is preferable to set up a VECM in the latter case and impose restrictions on the VECM parameters. In any case, using statistical tests in deciding on the restrictions is justified on the basis of asymptotic theory. Small sample adjustments of the usual statistics, possibly based on bootstrap methods (e.g., Li and Maddala, 1996; Berkowitz and Kilian, 2000) or Bartlett corrections (Omtzigt, 2003, chapter 5), may be desirable in some situations, however. Alternatively, restrictions for individual parameters or groups of parameters in VARs or VECMs may be based on model selection criteria.

   If nothing is known about possible zero restrictions one could consider all possible combinations of coefficients and test whether they may be replaced by zero. Such a strategy would be extremely computer intensive and also its statistical properties are unclear. Therefore some computationally more efficient subset modeling procedures are often used in practice. For instance, individual parameters may be checked for their significance, one at a time, by statistical tests or model selection criteria and this is often not done on the full system at once but equation by equation. Consider, for instance, the kth equation of a VAR or VECM,

$$y_{kt} = z_{1t}\theta_1 + \cdots + z_{Nt}\theta_N + u_t, \quad t = 1, \ldots, T. \tag{12.4.2}$$

Here all right-hand side variables are denoted by z_{nt}, including deterministic terms, and if a VECM is considered, the cointegration relations may also be included. For example, $z_{nt} = \beta' y_{t-1}$ may be a regressor if the cointegrating rank $r = 1$ and β is a known vector. If β is unknown, it may be replaced by an estimator and the following procedures can still be justified under general conditions. For the regression (12.4.2) a model selection criterion corresponding to (12.4.1) has the form

$$C(i_1, \ldots, i_n) = \log T^{-1} SSE(i_1, \ldots, i_n) + c_T n/T, \qquad (12.4.3)$$

where $SSE(i_1, \ldots, i_n)$ is the sum of squared errors obtained by including $z_{i_1 t}, \ldots, z_{i_n t}$ in the regression model (12.4.2) and c_T is a sequence as in (12.4.1). A criterion of this form can in principle be used to compare all possible subsets of regressors and choose the one which minimizes the criterion. Clearly, such a procedure is computationally expensive for large N because the set $\{1, \ldots, N\}$ has 2^N subsets. Therefore 2^N models have to be compared.

In practice short-cuts may be considered such as a procedure which sequentially eliminates those regressors which lead to the largest reduction of the given selection criterion until no further reduction is possible (e.g., Brüggemann and Lütkepohl, 2001). In this procedure, one variable only is eliminated in each step. A decision on which variable to eliminate could also be based on the t-ratios of the parameter estimators. A possible strategy is to sequentially delete those regressors with the smallest absolute values of t-ratios until all t-ratios (in absolute value) are greater than some threshold value c. Brüggemann and Lütkepohl (2001) show that this strategy is equivalent to the sequential elimination based on model selection criteria if the threshold value c is chosen accordingly. Other possible subset specification strategies are discussed and investigated by Lütkepohl (2005, chapter 5) Penm, Brailsford and Terrell (2000), Brüggemann and Lütkepohl (2001) and Brüggemann (2004). Rather than considering individual equations one by one, it is of course also possible to focus on the full system at once. Moreover, it is also possible to combine testing procedures for individual coefficients with tests for groups of coefficients and also integrate model checking procedures in the model selection stage. Such a more elaborate approach is, in fact, available in the *PcGets* software package (Hendry and Krolzig, 2001).

12.5 Model checking

Once a model has been specified and estimated, one should check whether it represents the DGP adequately. A wide range of statistical procedures is available for this purpose. Many model-checking procedures are based on the residuals of the final model. Some of them are applied to the residuals of individual equations and others are based on the full residual vectors. They range from visual inspection of the plots of the residuals and their autocorrelations to formal tests for deviations from the underlying assumptions. For example, tests for residual autocorrelation are in common use to check that the model residuals conform to the white noise assumption. Two such tests will be considered in the following. Moreover, tests for nonnormality are routinely applied and they will be discussed in section 12.5.2. Although normality is not a necessary condition for the validity of many of the statistical procedures related to VAR models, deviations from the normality assumption may indicate that model improvements are possible. Stability tests are another important class of model checking tools because the validity of the model for the whole sample period is usually one of the crucial assumptions for valid inference. Brief remarks on possible tools are provided in section 12.5.3.

12.5.1   Tests for residual autocorrelation

12.5.1.1   *Portmanteau test*

A popular test for residual autocorrelation is the so-called portmanteau test. Its null hypothesis is that all residual autocovariances are zero, $H_0 : E(u_t u'_{t-i}) = 0$ $(i = 1, 2, \ldots)$, which is tested against the alternative that at least one auto-covariance and, hence, one autocorrelation is nonzero. The test statistic is

$$Q_h = T \sum_{j=1}^{h} \text{tr}(\tilde{C}'_j \tilde{C}_0^{-1} \tilde{C}_j \tilde{C}_0^{-1}),$$

where $\tilde{C}_j = T^{-1} \sum_{t=j+1}^{T} \hat{u}_t \hat{u}'_{t-j}$ and the $\hat{u}_t$'s are the estimated residuals from an unrestricted VAR(p) process. If the VAR process is stable, then, under the null hypothesis, Q_h has an approximate $\chi^2(K^2(h-p))$ distribution if T and h approach infinity such that $h/T \to 0$. More generally, the degrees of freedom of the approximate distribution are the difference between the number of autocorrelations included in the statistic (K^2h) and the number of estimated VAR coefficients. For subset models the latter number will be smaller than K^2p (Ahn, 1988; Hosking, 1980, 1981a, 1981b; Li and McLeod, 1981; or Lütkepohl, 2005). As pointed out by Brüggemann, Lütkepohl and Saikkonen (2001), the situation is a bit more complicated for VAR processes with integrated and cointegrated variables. In that case the approximate test distribution depends also on the cointegrating rank of the system. Therefore the portmanteau test should only be applied to VECMs for which the cointegrating rank has been specified properly. For a VECM of the form (12.2.7) with cointegrating rank r and no restrictions on α and $\Gamma_1, \ldots, \Gamma_{p-1}$, the proper approximate distribution is $\chi^2(K^2h - K^2(p-1) - Kr)$.

In small samples the approximate χ^2-distribution was found to be a poor approximation to the actual null distribution. An adjusted statistic with potentially superior small sample properties is therefore recommended (Hosking, 1980),

$$Q_h^* = T^2 \sum_{j=1}^{h} \frac{1}{T-j} \text{tr}(\tilde{C}'_j \tilde{C}_0^{-1} \tilde{C}_j \tilde{C}_0^{-1}).$$

In practice, a suitable choice of h is important for good small sample properties of the test. Clearly, h has to be bigger than p to get a useful approximate distribution with positive degrees of freedom. In fact, h should usually be considerably larger than p to get a good approximation to the null distribution. On the other hand, using an h which is very large may result in a loss of power for the portmanteau test. In practice, different values of h are therefore often checked. Generally, the portmanteau test should be applied primarily to test for autocorrelation of high order. Low order residual autocorrelation is better checked with the LM or Breusch–Godfrey test which is presented in the next subsection.

12.5.1.2 LM test

The LM or Breusch–Godfrey test for residual autocorrelation of order h can be regarded as a test for zero coefficient matrices in the model

$$u_t = B_1 u_{t-1} + \cdots + B_h u_{t-h} + e_t,$$

where e_t denotes a white noise error term. In other words, the pair of hypotheses is

$$H_0 : B_i = 0 \ (i = 1, \ldots, h) \quad \text{versus} \quad H_1 : B_i \neq 0 \text{ for at least one } i \in \{1, \ldots, h\}.$$

The test statistic can be computed easily by considering the auxiliary model

$$\hat{u}_t = A_1 y_{t-1} + \cdots + A_p y_{t-p} + B_1 \hat{u}_{t-1} + \cdots + B_h \hat{u}_{t-h} + e_t^* \tag{12.5.1}$$

or a similar version which also involves deterministic terms if they are included in the original model. Here the $\hat{u}_t$ are again the estimated residuals from the original model and e_t^* is an auxiliary error term. If the underlying model for which residual autocorrelation is to be checked is a VECM, the corresponding auxiliary model has the form

$$\hat{u}_t = \alpha \hat{\beta}' y_{t-1} + \Gamma_1 \Delta y_{t-1} + \cdots + \Gamma_{p-1} \Delta y_{t-p+1} + B_1 \hat{u}_{t-1} + \cdots + B_h \hat{u}_{t-h} + e_t^*, \tag{12.5.2}$$

where $\hat{\beta}$ is the ML estimator of the cointegration matrix. Again deterministic terms should be added if they are present in the original model. In both models, the $\hat{u}_t$ with $t \leq 0$ should be replaced by zero.

Denoting the estimated residuals from (12.5.1) and (12.5.2) by $\hat{e}_t^* (t = 1, \ldots, T)$ and the corresponding residual covariance matrix estimator by $\tilde{\Sigma}_e = \frac{1}{T} \sum_{t=1}^T \hat{e}_t^* \hat{e}_t^{*\prime}$, the relevant LM statistic can be written as

$$Q_{LM} = T \big(K - \text{tr}(\tilde{\Sigma}_u^{-1} \tilde{\Sigma}_e) \big).$$

Under the null hypothesis it has an asymptotic $\chi^2(hK^2)$-distribution for both $I(0)$ and $I(1)$ systems (Brüggemann *et al.*, 2005).

For medium-sized or large models the asymptotic distribution is again no good guide for the small sample distribution of the test statistic. Edgerton and Shukur (1999) have performed a large Monte Carlo study for stationary processes and found that the following related test statistic has a small sample distribution which can be well approximated by an F-distribution:

$$LMF_h = \left[\left(\frac{\det(\tilde{\Sigma}_u)}{\det(\tilde{\Sigma}_e)} \right)^{1/s} - 1 \right] \cdot \frac{Ns - q}{Km}$$

with

$$s = \left(\frac{K^2 m^2 - 4}{K^2 + m^2 - 5} \right)^{1/2}, \quad q = \frac{1}{2} Km - 1, \quad N = T - n - m - \frac{1}{2}(K - m + 1),$$

n is the number of regressors in each equation of the original system and $m = Kh$ is the number of additional regressors in the auxiliary system. The statistic should be used with critical values from an $F(hK^2, Ns - q)$-distribution.

12.5.2   Tests for nonnormality

Multivariate tests for nonnormality may be based on ideas used by Lomnicki (1961) and Jarque and Bera (1987) for univariate models. These authors propose to check whether the third and fourth moments of the residuals are conformable with those of a normal distribution. For the multivariate case, the idea is that the residual vector of a VAR or VECM is first transformed to make the individual components independent and then it is checked to determine whether they all have third and fourth moments corresponding to those of normal distributions. More precisely, for given residuals $\hat{u}_t(t = 1, \ldots, T)$ of an estimated VAR process or VECM, the residual covariance matrix $\tilde{\Sigma}_u$ is determined and the corresponding square root matrix $\tilde{\Sigma}_u^{1/2}$ is computed (see Lütkepohl, 1996). The tests for non-normality can then be based on the skewness and kurtosis of the standardized residuals $\hat{u}_t^s = (\hat{u}_{1t}^s, \ldots, \hat{u}_{Kt}^s)' = \tilde{\Sigma}_u^{-1/2}\hat{u}_t$:

$$\mathbf{b}_1 = (b_{11}, \ldots, b_{1K})' \quad \text{with} \quad b_{1k} = T^{-1}\sum_{t=1}^{T}(\hat{u}_{kt}^s)^3$$

and

$$\mathbf{b}_2 = (b_{21}, \ldots, b_{2K})' \quad \text{with} \quad b_{2k} = T^{-1}\sum_{t=1}^{T}(\hat{u}_{kt}^s)^4.$$

Notice that the standardized residuals should also be mean-adjusted if the $\hat{u}_t$'s do not have a sample mean of zero. Tests can be based on the third moments only, using the test statistic $s_3^2 = T\mathbf{b}_1'\mathbf{b}_1/6$, or on the fourth moments only, using $s_4^2 = T(\mathbf{b}_2 - \mathbf{3}_K)'(\mathbf{b}_2 - \mathbf{3}_K)/24$. Here $\mathbf{3}_K = (3, \ldots, 3)'$ is a $(K \times 1)$ vector. Both statistics have asymptotic $\chi^2(K)$-distributions if the underlying white noise process u_t is normally distributed. Moreover, they can be combined as $JB_K = s_3^2 + s_4^2$ to check the third and fourth moments jointly. The statistic JB_K has a $\chi^2(2K)$ limiting distribution under normality of the process.

The standardization of the residuals used here was proposed by Doornik and Hansen (1994). An alternative possibility for standardizing the residuals was discussed by Lütkepohl (2005, chapter 4). He used a Choleski decomposition of the residual covariance matrix to standardize the residuals. The literature on testing for nonnormality is extensive and many other tests are available. Still, the ones presented here are probably the most popular ones in applied time series econometrics.

If normality of the residuals is rejected this is not necessarily a problem for many of the inference procedures discussed so far. It is, however, often regarded as a signal that model improvements are possible. In particular, nonlinearities are not captured by linear VARs or VECMs and may show up as nonnormality of the residuals. Specific nonlinearity tests are available and can be used for more refined investigations of model defects (see, e.g., Granger and Teräsvirta, 1993). Non-normality is also a likely problem if the residuals are conditionally heteroskedastic and special tests for this feature exist. Conditional heteroskedasticity is discussed in Chapters 20 and 21. The issue is therefore not pursued here.

12.5.3 Stability analysis

There is also a wide range of procedures for checking the stability or time invariance of a given model (e.g., Doornik and Hendry, 1997; Lütkepohl, 2004). These procedures are used for detecting potential structural breaks during the sample period. For example, prediction tests as discussed in Lütkepohl (2005, chapter 4), recursive estimates and Chow tests (Doornik and Hendry, 1997) or CUSUM type tests (Krämer, Ploberger and Alt, 1988) may be performed. Furthermore, recursive tests for cointegration (Hansen and Johansen, 1999) may be considered for VECMs.

Generally, if model defects of some sort are detected at the checking stage, then this is usually regarded as an indication that the model is a poor representation of the DGP. In that case attempts should be made to find a better representation. Possible actions include adding other variables or further lags to the model, including nonlinear terms or changing the functional form. Also the sampling period may be modified or getting other data may be considered.

12.6 Forecasting and Granger-causality

VARs and VECMs are very well suited for forecasting and they can also be used for economic analysis. In this section, it is convenient to use the levels VAR representation in discussing forecasting and the concept of Granger-causality, which presents one possibility for economic analysis and which is closely related to forecasting. We will therefore primarily use the VAR representation.

12.6.1 Forecasting with VAR processes

We will first discuss the somewhat unrealistic situation that the DGP is fully known – that is, all parameters are given. This simplifying assumption makes the analysis easy and it is also easy to explain the modifications which are necessary if the true parameters are replaced by estimators.

12.6.1.1 Known processes

Because the future values of deterministic terms are known with certainty by their very nature, they will be neglected for the moment and the focus will be on the stochastic part first. Suppose x_t is generated by a VAR(p) process as in (12.2.2) and u_t is an i.i.d. white noise process. Then the optimal (minimum MSE) h-step ahead forecast in period T is the conditional expectation given $x_t, t \leq T$,

$$x_{T+h|T} \equiv E(x_{T+h}|x_T, x_{T-1}, \ldots) = A_1 x_{T+h-1|T} + \cdots + A_p x_{T+h-p|T}, \tag{12.6.1}$$

where $x_{T+j|T} = x_{T+j}$ for $j \leq 0$. These forecasts can easily be computed recursively for $h = 1, 2, \ldots$, starting with $x_{T+1|T} = A_1 x_T + \cdots + A_p x_{T+1-p}$. The forecast error of an h-step forecast is

$$x_{T+h} - x_{T+h|T} = u_{T+h} + \Phi_1 u_{T+h-1} + \cdots + \Phi_{h-1} u_{T+1}, \qquad (12.6.2)$$

where

$$\Phi_i = \sum_{j=1}^{i} \Phi_{i-j} A_j, \quad i = 1, 2, \ldots, \qquad (12.6.3)$$

with $\Phi_0 = I_K$ and $A_j = 0$ for $j > p$ (e.g., Lütkepohl, 2005). Hence, u_t represents the 1-step forecast error in period $t-1$, the forecasts are unbiased, that is, $E(y_{T+h} - y_{T+h|T}) = 0$ and the MSE matrix or forecast error covariance matrix is

$$\Sigma_x(h) \equiv E[(x_{T+h} - x_{T+h|T})(x_{T+h} - x_{T+h|T})'] = \sum_{j=0}^{h-1} \Phi_j \Sigma_u \Phi_j'. \qquad (12.6.4)$$

The minimum MSE property of the forecasts relies on the independence of the u_t's, i.e., u_t and u_s are independent for $s \neq t$. If u_t is uncorrelated white noise and not necessarily independent over time, the forecasts obtained recursively as in (12.6.1) are still best *linear* forecasts.

The forecast results discussed so far are valid for stable, stationary $I(0)$ processes and for integrated processes as well. For the latter processes, the forecast MSEs are generally unbounded as the horizon h goes to infinity. Hence, the forecast uncertainty increases without bound for forecasts of the distant future. In contrast, the forecast MSEs for $I(0)$ variables are bounded by the unconditional covariance $\Sigma_x \equiv E(x_t x_t')$ of x_t, that is, $\Sigma_x(h) \to \Sigma_x$ for $h \to \infty$. This result means, in particular, that forecasts of cointegration relations have bounded MSEs even for horizons approaching infinity.

If a nonzero deterministic term is present, $y_t = \mu_t + x_t$, the h-step forecast of y_t at origin T is $y_{T+h|T} = \mu_{T+h} + x_{T+h|T}$ and the forecast errors are identical to those of the x_t process,

$$y_{T+h} - y_{T+h|T} \sim (0, \Sigma_x(h)).$$

Hence, the forecasts for y_t have the same properties as those of x_t.

The previous results can also be used to set up forecast intervals. If the process y_t is Gaussian, that is, $u_t \sim$ i.i.d. $N(0, \Sigma_u)$, the forecast errors are also multivariate normal and, thus, forecast intervals of the form

$$[y_{k, T+h|T} - c_{1-\gamma/2} \sigma_k(h), \ y_{k, T+h|T} + c_{1-\gamma/2} \sigma_k(h)] \qquad (12.6.5)$$

can be set up. Here $c_{1-\gamma/2}$ is the $(1 - \frac{\gamma}{2})100$ percentage point of the standard normal distribution, $y_{k, T+h|T}$ denotes the kth component of $y_{T+h|T}$ and $\sigma_k(h)$ denotes the square root of the kth diagonal element of $\Sigma_x(h)$, that is, $\sigma_k(h)$ is the standard deviation of the h-step forecast error for the kth component of y_t. If $y_{k,t}$ is an $I(1)$ variable, $\sigma_k(h)$ is unbounded for $h \to \infty$ and, thus, the same is true for the length of the interval in (12.6.5). In contrast, forecast intervals associated with $I(0)$ variables have bounded length. Also, of course, forecast intervals of cointegration relations are therefore bounded in length.

The forecast interval in (12.6.5) is based on the assumption of a Gaussian process. In practice the distribution of y_t will often be nonnormal and in many cases it will be unknown. In that situation constructing forecast intervals is still possible. Findley (1986), Masarotto (1990), Grigoletto (1998), Kabaila (1993), Kim (1999) and Pascual, Romo and Ruiz (2004) consider bootstrap methods for forecasting nonnormal processes. In that case forecast intervals may not represent the best way to report the forecast uncertainty, however. A survey of related issues is given by Tay and Wallis (2002).

12.6.1.2 Estimated processes

In practice the parameters of a VAR process have to be replaced by estimators. Clearly, this has implications for forecast precision. To study the consequences of forecasting with estimated processes, the counterpart of $y_{T+h|T}$ based on estimated parameters will be signified by a hat, that is,

$$\hat{y}_{T+h|T} = \hat{\mu}_{T+h} + \hat{A}_1(\hat{y}_{T+h-1|T} - \hat{\mu}_{T+h-1}) + \cdots + \hat{A}_p(\hat{y}_{T+h-p|T} - \hat{\mu}_{T+h-p}), \qquad (12.6.6)$$

where $\hat{y}_{T+j|T} = y_{T+j}$ for $j \leq 0$, the $\hat{A}_i$'s $(i = 1, \ldots, p)$ are estimated parameters and the $\hat{\mu}_t$'s are also based on estimated parameters. The corresponding forecast error is

$$\begin{aligned} y_{T+h} - \hat{y}_{T+h|T} &= (y_{T+h} - y_{T+h|T}) + (y_{T+h|T} - \hat{y}_{T+h|T}) \\ &= \sum_{j=0}^{h-1} \Phi_j u_{T+h-j} + (y_{T+h|T} - \hat{y}_{T+h|T}). \end{aligned} \qquad (12.6.7)$$

At the forecast origin T, the first term on the right-hand side involves future residuals only, whereas the second term involves $y_T, y_{T-1}, \ldots$ only, provided only variables up to time T have been used for estimation. Consequently, if u_t is independent white noise, the two terms are independent. Moreover, under standard assumptions, the difference $y_{T+h|T} - \hat{y}_{T+h|T}$ is small in probability as the sample size used for estimation gets large. Hence, the forecast error covariance matrix in this case is

$$\Sigma_{\hat{y}}(h) \equiv E[(y_{T+h} - \hat{y}_{T+h|T})(y_{T+h} - \hat{y}_{T+h|T})'] = \Sigma_x(h) + o(1), \qquad (12.6.8)$$

where $o(1)$ denotes a term which approaches zero as the sample size tends to infinity. Thus, in large samples the forecast uncertainty attributable to estimation uncertainty may be ignored in evaluating forecast precision and the setting up of forecast intervals. A correction term may be advisable in finite sample situations, however. In this case the precision of the forecasts will depend on the precision of the estimators. Hence, precise estimators are a prerequisite for precise forecasts.

For the stationary case, possible correction factors are given, e.g., in Yamamoto (1980), Baillie (1981) and Lütkepohl (2005, chapter 3), whereas Hoque, Magnus and Pesaran (1988) presented an exact treatment of univariate first-order autoregressive models.

The previous results have been extended in various directions. For example, Lewis and Reinsel (1985) and Lütkepohl (1985) considered the forecast MSE for the case where the true process may be of infinite order and they considered approximating it by a finite order VAR, thereby extending earlier univariate results by Bhanasali (1978). Reinsel and Lewis (1987), Basu and Sen Roy (1987), Engle and Yoo (1987), Sampson (1991), Reinsel and Ahn (1992) and Clements and Hendry (1998, 2001) presented results for processes with unit roots. Stock (1996) and Kemp (1999) assumed that the forecast horizon h and the sample size T both go to infinity simultaneously. Clements and Hendry (1998, 2001) also considered various other sources of possible forecast errors. Taking into account the specification and estimation uncertainty in multi-step forecasts, one may also consider constructing separate models for different forecast horizons h. This approach was discussed in detail by Bhansali (2002).

12.6.2 Granger-causality analysis

12.6.2.1 *Intuition and Theory*

Granger (1969) presented a definition of causality which is intimately related to forecasting and has become quite popular in time series econometrics. He called a variable y_1 causal for another time series variable y_2 if the information in y_1 is helpful for predicting y_2. To present a formal definition, let $y_{2, t+h|\Omega_t}$ be the optimal h-step predictor of y_{2t} at origin t, based on the set of all the relevant, available information in the universe, denoted by Ω_t. Using this notation, y_{1t} is said to be *Granger-noncausal* for y_{2t} if and only if

$$y_{2, t+h|\Omega_t} = y_{2, t+h|\Omega_t \setminus \{y_{1, s}, |s \leq t\}}, \qquad h = 1, 2, \ldots . \tag{12.6.9}$$

In this relation $\Omega_t \setminus \mathbb{A}$ denotes the set containing all elements of Ω_t which are not in the set $\mathbb{A}$. In other words, y_{1t} is not causal for y_{2t} if and only if removing the past information in the process y_{1t} from the information set does not change the optimal forecast for y_{2t} at any forecast horizon h. Thus, y_{1t} is *Granger-causal* for y_{2t} if a better forecast of y_{2t} is obtained for some forecast horizon by including the past of y_{1t} in the information set.

To operationalize the definition, the information set is usually reduced to the information in the variables of interest in a particular analysis. For example, if a causal relation between two time series variables y_1 and y_2 is of interest, $\Omega_t = \{(y_{1,s}, y_{2,s})' | s \leq t\}$ is usually used. Assuming that $(y_{1t}, y_{2t})'$ is generated by a bivariate VAR(p) process,

$$\begin{pmatrix} y_{1t} \\ y_{2t} \end{pmatrix} = \sum_{i=1}^{p} \begin{bmatrix} \alpha_{11,i} & \alpha_{12,i} \\ \alpha_{21,i} & \alpha_{22,i} \end{bmatrix} \begin{pmatrix} y_{1,t-i} \\ y_{2,t-i} \end{pmatrix} + u_t, \tag{12.6.10}$$

then (12.6.9) is equivalent to

$$\alpha_{21,i} = 0, \quad i = 1, 2, \ldots, p \tag{12.6.11}$$

(Lütkepohl, 2005, section 2.3.1).

These results also hold for stationary and integrated systems because the forecast formulas for $I(1)$ systems are the same as for $I(0)$ systems. It can still be preferable to investigate Granger-causal relations within a VECM if $I(1)$ variables are involved. The VECM corresponding to the bivariate process (12.6.10) is

$$\begin{pmatrix} \Delta y_{1t} \\ \Delta y_{2t} \end{pmatrix} = \alpha \beta' \begin{pmatrix} y_{1,t-1} \\ y_{2,t-1} \end{pmatrix} + \sum_{i=1}^{p-1} \begin{bmatrix} \gamma_{11,i} & \gamma_{12,i} \\ \gamma_{21,i} & \gamma_{22,i} \end{bmatrix} \begin{pmatrix} \Delta y_{1,t-i} \\ \Delta y_{2,t-i} \end{pmatrix} + u_t.$$

In this representation the condition (12.6.11) is satisfied if and only if $\gamma_{21,i} = 0$ $(i = 1, \ldots, p-1)$ and the element in the lower left-hand corner of $\alpha \beta'$ is also zero. In a bivariate model, the cointegrating rank r can only be 0, 1 or 2, and $r = 1$ is the only case where a VECM is of interest because in the other cases a VAR in first differences or levels may be set up. If $r = 1$, α and β are (2×1) vectors and

$$\alpha \beta' = \begin{pmatrix} \alpha_1 \\ \alpha_2 \end{pmatrix} (\beta_1, \beta_2) = \begin{bmatrix} \alpha_1 \beta_1 & \alpha_1 \beta_2 \\ \alpha_2 \beta_1 & \alpha_2 \beta_2 \end{bmatrix}.$$

Thus, in this case, $\alpha_2 \beta_1 = 0$ needs to be checked in addition to $\gamma_{21,i} = 0$ $(i = 1, \ldots, p-1)$ (see also Mosconi and Giannini, 1992). Note also that if $r = 1$, there must be Granger-causality in at least one direction (from y_{1t} to y_{2t} or from y_{2t} to y_{1t} or both).

Many economic systems of interest consist of more than two relevant variables. Therefore extending the concept of Granger-causality to higher dimensional systems is desirable. Possible extensions have been considered, e.g., by Lütkepohl (1993) and Dufour and Renault (1998). One possibility is to partition the vector of all variables into two subvectors so that $y_t = (y'_{1t}, y'_{2t})'$ and to use the definition in (12.6.9) for the two subvectors y_{1t}, y_{2t} rather than individual variables. If $\Omega_t = \{y_s | s \leq t\}$ and y_t is a VAR process of the form (12.6.10), it still holds that y_{1t} is Granger-noncausal for y_{2t} if $\alpha_{21,i} = 0$ for $i = 1, \ldots, p$, where the $\alpha_{21,i}$'s are now matrices of appropriate dimensions (Lütkepohl, 2005, section 2.3.1).

If a causal relation between two variables within a higher dimensional system is of interest, then this generalization is not satisfactory. In that case one would like to consider causality of an individual variable y_{1t} to a single variable y_{2t} given that there are further variables in the system. Again the general definition in (12.6.9) can be used, but the causality restrictions become more complicated. To see this, consider the three-dimensional VAR process,

$$y_t = \begin{pmatrix} y_{1t} \\ y_{2t} \\ y_{3t} \end{pmatrix} = \sum_{i=1}^{p} \begin{bmatrix} \alpha_{11,i} & \alpha_{12,i} & \alpha_{13,i} \\ \alpha_{21,i} & \alpha_{22,i} & \alpha_{23,i} \\ \alpha_{31,i} & \alpha_{32,i} & \alpha_{33,i} \end{bmatrix} \begin{pmatrix} y_{1,t-i} \\ y_{2,t-i} \\ y_{3,t-i} \end{pmatrix} + u_t. \tag{12.6.12}$$

Within this system the restrictions

$$\alpha_{21,i} = 0, \quad i = 1,\ldots,p, \tag{12.6.13}$$

are equivalent to equality of the 1-step forecasts, $y_{2,t+1|\Omega_t} = y_{2,t+1|\Omega_t \setminus \{y_{1,s}|s\leq t\}}$ only. Even if (12.6.13) holds, the information in past y_{1t} may still be helpful for improving the forecasts of y_{2t} more than one period ahead because there may be indirect causal links, e.g., y_{1t} may have an impact on y_{3t} which in turn may affect y_{2t} (Lütkepohl, 1993). Thus, the definition of noncausality corresponding to the restrictions in (12.6.13) is not in line with an intuitive notion of the term. Using the more general definition (12.6.9) for higher dimensional processes, more complicated nonlinear restrictions for the VAR coefficients are obtained (Dufour and Renault, 1998).

There has been an extensive discussion of causality concepts in econometrics. For instance, it has been argued that predictability and causality are different concepts. Also, operationalizing causality in a more general probability context and not just within the linear VAR models considered here is of interest. Moreover, causality is not only discussed in time series econometrics but also in describing economic relations more generally (e.g., Granger, 1982; Angrist, Imbens and Rubin, 1996; Heckman, 2000; Pearl, 2000; Hoover, 2001).

12.6.2.2   Testing for Granger-causality

The restrictions characterizing Granger-noncausality in (12.6.11) are linear parameter restrictions and standard χ^2- or F-tests of the Wald type can be applied for stationary processes. Unfortunately, these tests may have nonstandard asymptotic properties if some of the variables are $I(1)$ (Toda and Phillips, 1993). Dolado and Lütkepohl (1996) have suggested a simple possibility to resolve the problems in the present context. As mentioned in section 12.3, whenever the elements in at least one of the complete coefficient matrices A_i are not restricted at all under the null hypothesis, the Wald statistic has its usual limiting χ^2-distribution. Thus, if elements from all matrices $A_1,\ldots,A_p$ are involved in the restrictions as, for instance, in the noncausality restrictions (12.6.11), adding an extra redundant lag in estimating the parameters of the process ensures standard asymptotics for the Wald tests. Notice that if the true DGP is a VAR(p) process, then a VAR($p+1$) with $A_{p+1} = 0$ is also an appropriate model. The test is then performed on the $A_1,\ldots,A_p$ only. This approach is feasible even if the cointegration properties of the system are unknown. Unfortunately, the procedure is not fully efficient due to the redundant parameters.

It may be worth noting that the procedure remains valid if deterministic terms are included in the VAR model, as a consequence of results due to Park and Phillips (1989) and Sims et al. (1990). A generalization of these ideas to Wald tests for nonlinear restrictions representing, for instance, other causality definitions, is discussed by Lütkepohl and Burda (1997). Furthermore, testing for Granger-causality in infinite order VAR processes is considered by Lütkepohl and Poskitt (1996b) and Saikkonen and Lütkepohl (1996).

12.7   Structural VARs and impulse response analysis

12.7.1   Basic ideas

Tracing out the effects of changes in or shocks to the variables of a given system is one popular way of investigating the relationships between the variables of a VAR model. If the process y_t is stable and stationary, it has a Wold MA representation of the form

$$y_t = \sum_{j=0}^{\infty} \Phi_j u_{t-j}, \tag{12.7.1}$$

where $\Phi_0 = I_K$ and deterministic terms are ignored to simplify the exposition. The Φ_j's $(j=1,2,\dots)$ are $(K \times K)$ coefficient matrices which can be computed as in (12.6.3). The (n, m)th elements of the matrices Φ_j, viewed as a function of j, trace out the marginal response of $y_{n,t+j}$ to a unit change in y_{mt}, holding constant all past values of y_t. Since the change in y_{it} given $\{y_{t-1}, y_{t-2}, \dots\}$ is measured by the innovation u_{it}, the elements of Φ_j represent the impulse responses of the components of y_t with respect to the u_t innovations. They are sometimes called *forecast error impulse responses* because the u_t's are the 1-step ahead forecast errors, as seen in section 12.6.1 (Lütkepohl, 2005, section 2.3.2). In the presently considered $I(0)$ case, $\Phi_j \to 0$ as $j \to \infty$. Hence, the effect of an impulse vanishes over time and is thus transitory.

It has been noted that forecast error impulse responses may not be interesting from the point of view of economic analysis because they may not properly reflect what is actually happening in the system of variables when a shock occurs. The reason is that forecast error shocks are not likely to occur in isolation if the components of u_t are correlated, that is, if Σ_u is not diagonal. Clearly, the MA representation (12.7.1) is not unique. Using any nonsingular matrix P and defining $\varepsilon_t = P^{-1} u_t$ and $\Psi_i = \Phi_i P$ $(i = 0, 1, 2, \dots)$, we get a new MA representation,

$$y_t = \sum_{j=1}^{\infty} \Phi_j P P^{-1} u_{t-j} = \sum_{j=1}^{\infty} \Psi_j \varepsilon_{t-j}. \tag{12.7.2}$$

Here the ε_t are the innovations and the elements of the Ψ_j's supposedly reflect the movement in the variables caused by ε shocks. If P is chosen such that $PP' = \Sigma_u$, we have $\varepsilon_t \sim (0, I_K)$ and, hence, the ε shocks are instantaneously uncorrelated. Thus, they may be better suited to learn about the effects of individual shocks to the system. The problem is, however, that many different P matrices with the property $PP' = \Sigma_u$ exist and for economic analysis the question arises as to which one of them reflects the actual ongoings in the economic system of interest. It is here where structural VAR analysis comes in. It offers a number of ways to identify the impulse responses of a VAR model. In other words, it imposes restrictions which make the innovations and, hence, the impulse responses unique.

Historically, a popular way to achieve uniqueness of P is to compute the matrix by a lower triangular Choleski decomposition. In that situation the matrix $\Psi_0 = P$ of instantaneous effects of the innovations is also lower triangular and a recursive structure is imposed on the system. Notice that in this case an innovation in the first equation can have instantaneous effects on all the variables, while a shock in the second equation can only have instantaneous impacts on the second to last variables and not on the first one. Finally, an innovation in the last equation affects only the last variable instantaneously and none of the other variables. The resulting impulse responses are often referred to as *orthogonal* or *orthogonalized impulse responses*. Using this approach to making the impulse responses unique requires a proper ordering of the variables because a different ordering will generally result in different impulse responses.

The recent SVAR literature has proposed a number of different possibilities for identifying the relevant innovations and impulse responses by considering the so-called AB-model of the form

$$A y_t = A_1^* y_{t-1} + \cdots + A_p^* y_{t-p} + B \varepsilon_t \tag{12.7.3}$$

with $\varepsilon_t \sim (0, I_K)$, as before. This model is a structural form model similar to (12.2.8) which allows us to model instantaneous relations between the components of y_t via A and, in addition, it permits us to impose restrictions on the relations between the residuals via B (Giannini, 1992; Amisano and Giannini, 1997; Breitung, Brüggemann and Lütkepohl, 2004). Relating this model form to the reduced form (12.3.1) shows that

$$u_t = A^{-1} B \varepsilon_t,$$

and, hence, $P = B^{-1} A$ in (12.7.2).

Different types of identifying restrictions for the matrices A and B have been considered (e.g., Sims, 1986; Bernanke, 1986; Blanchard and Quah, 1989; Galí, 1999; Pagan, 1995). Many of them can be written as linear restrictions of the form $\text{vec}(A) = R_A \gamma_A + r_A$ and $\text{vec}(B) = R_B \gamma_B + r_B$, where γ_A and γ_B contain all unrestricted elements of A and B, respectively, R_A and R_B are suitable matrices with 0–1 elements and r_A and r_B are known vectors.

For $I(1)$ systems, forecast error impulse response matrices can also be computed (Lütkepohl, 2005, chapter 6; Lütkepohl and Reimers, 1992). In this case, some forecast error shocks may have permanent effects, however. Apart from that, the AB-model may also be used for $I(1)$ systems to specify identifying restrictions for impulse responses. Because the distinction between shocks with permanent and transitory effects is usually of importance in such systems, a different setup is often preferred, however (King, Plosser, Stock and Watson, 1991; Gonzalo and Ng, 2001; Fisher and Huh, 1999; Breitung *et al.*, 2004). The interested reader is referred to these references.

It may also be worth noting that a unique specification of impulse responses within a given model is not the only problem related to their interpretation.

Also omitted variables, filtering and adjusting series prior to using them for a VAR analysis and using aggregated or transformed data can lead to major changes in the dynamic behavior of the model. For instance, if an important variable is omitted from a system of interest, adding it can change in principle all the impulse responses. Similarly, using seasonally adjusted and, hence, filtered data can change the dynamic structure of the variables and, thus, may lead to impulse responses which are quite different from those for unadjusted variables.

12.7.2 Estimating impulse responses

Estimation of forecast error impulse responses is straightforward because they depend solely upon the reduced form parameters of the levels VAR for which we have discussed estimation in section 12.3. For the structural impulse responses we also need the structural parameters. Thus, for example, for the AB-model we need estimates of A and B. For this purpose, an ML or quasi ML approach under normality assumptions is often used. If the reduced form is unrestricted, the A_i's $(i = 1, \ldots, p)$ can be concentrated out of the likelihood function by replacing them by their LS estimators which are identical to the ML estimators in this case. Thereby a concentrated log-likelihood function,

$$l(\mathsf{A}, \mathsf{B}) = \text{constant} + \frac{T}{2} \log \det(\mathsf{A})^2 - \frac{T}{2} \log \det(\mathsf{B})^2 - \frac{T}{2} \text{tr}(\mathsf{A}'\mathsf{B}'^{-1}\mathsf{B}^{-1}\mathsf{A}\tilde{\Sigma}_u), \quad (12.7.4)$$

is obtained with $\tilde{\Sigma}_u = T^{-1}(Y - \hat{A}Y)(Y - \hat{A}Y)'$, as usual (cf. Breitung *et al.*, 2004). This function can be optimized with respect to the free parameters in A and B by numerical algorithms. The resulting estimators have the usual asymptotic properties under standard assumptions, that is, they are consistent and asymptotically normally distributed.

Collecting all structural form coefficients in a vector $\boldsymbol{\alpha}$ and denoting its estimator by $\hat{\boldsymbol{\alpha}}$, any specific impulse response coefficient ψ will be a (nonlinear) function of $\boldsymbol{\alpha}$ and can be estimated as

$$\hat{\psi} = \psi(\hat{\boldsymbol{\alpha}}). \quad (12.7.5)$$

If $\hat{\boldsymbol{\alpha}}$ is asymptotically normal,

$$\sqrt{T}(\hat{\boldsymbol{\alpha}} - \boldsymbol{\alpha}) \xrightarrow{d} N(0, \Sigma_{\hat{\alpha}}), \quad (12.7.6)$$

then $\hat{\psi}$ is also asymptotically normally distributed,

$$\sqrt{T}(\hat{\psi} - \psi) \xrightarrow{d} N(0, \sigma_\psi^2), \quad (12.7.7)$$

where

$$\sigma_\psi^2 = \frac{\partial \psi}{\partial \boldsymbol{\alpha}'} \Sigma_{\hat{\alpha}} \frac{\partial \psi}{\partial \boldsymbol{\alpha}} \quad (12.7.8)$$

and $\partial\psi/\partial\boldsymbol{\alpha}$ denotes the vector of first-order partial derivatives of ψ with respect to the elements of $\boldsymbol{\alpha}$. The limiting result in (12.7.7) holds if σ_ψ^2 is nonzero, which in turn is guaranteed if $\Sigma_{\hat{\alpha}}$ is nonsingular and $\partial\psi/\partial\boldsymbol{\alpha} \neq 0$. The covariance matrix $\Sigma_{\hat{\alpha}}$ may be singular if there are constraints on the coefficients or, as mentioned earlier, if there are $I(1)$ variables. The partial derivatives will also usually be zero in parts of the parameter space because the impulse responses generally consist of sums of products of the VAR coefficients and, hence, the partial derivatives will also be sums of products of such coefficients which may be zero in some points of the parameter space. Thus, there may be points in the parameter space where $\sigma_\psi^2 = 0$ and $\hat{\psi}$ actually converges at a faster rate than $\sqrt{T}$ (cf. Benkwitz, Lütkepohl and Neumann, 2000).

Because asymptotic theory does not provide good approximations to the distributions of impulse responses in small samples, bootstrap methods are often used in applied work to construct confidence intervals for impulse responses (e.g., Kilian, 1998; Benkwitz, Lütkepohl and Wolters, 2001). Another advantage of using bootstrap methods in this context is that deriving the rather complicated analytical expressions of the asymptotic variances of the impulse response coefficients can be avoided by using bootstrap methods. It is important to note, however, that the bootstrap does not necessarily overcome the problems due to a singularity in the asymptotic distribution which results from a zero variance in (12.7.7). In these cases bootstrap confidence intervals may not have the desired coverage. For further discussion see Benkwitz *et al.* (2000).

Impulse response analysis and the related inference problems have been discussed extensively in the recent literature. Further methodological contributions are, for instance, due to Koop (1992) who considers confidence bands for impulse responses constructed with Bayesian methods and Sims and Zha (1999) who question the practice of reporting confidence intervals around individual impulse response coefficients and propose likelihood-characterizing error bands as alternatives. Moreover, Uhlig (2005) proposes inequality constraints for identifying impulse responses and Lee, Pesaran and Pierse (1992) and Pesaran and Shin (1996) consider persistence profiles which measure the persistence of certain shocks without imposing structural identification restrictions.

12.7.3   Forecast error variance decompositions

Forecast error variance decompositions are closely related to impulse responses. Expressing the h-step forecast error from (12.6.2) in terms of the structural innovations ε_t gives

$$y_{T+h} - y_{T+h|T} = \Psi_0\varepsilon_{T+h} + \Psi_1\varepsilon_{T+h-1} + \cdots + \Psi_{h-1}\varepsilon_{T+1}.$$

Denoting the (n, m)th element of Ψ_j by $\psi_{nm,j}$, the forecast error variance of the kth element of the forecast error vector is seen to be

$$\sigma_k^2(h) = \sum_{j=0}^{h-1}(\psi_{k1,j}^2 + \cdots + \psi_{kK,j}^2) = \sum_{j=1}^{K}(\psi_{kj,0}^2 + \cdots + \psi_{kj,h-1}^2).$$

The term $(\psi_{kj,0}^2 + \cdots + \psi_{kj,h-1}^2)$ may be interpreted as the contribution of the jth innovation to the h-step forecast error variance of variable k. Dividing the term by $\sigma_k^2(h)$ gives the percentage contribution of innovation j to the h-step forecast error variance of variable k. These quantities can be estimated easily when estimates of the structural impulse responses are available. They are often reported and interpreted for various forecast horizons. For such an interpretation to make sense it is, of course, important to have identified impulse responses which adequately reflect what is going on in the underlying economic system.

12.8 Conclusions and extensions

In this chapter the VAR methodology for time series econometrics is reviewed with special emphasis on issues related to integrated and cointegrated variables. The most popular models have been introduced and their estimation and specification has been discussed. Moreover, forecasting, Granger-causality and impulse response analysis, including structural modeling, have been considered. In this chapter the levels VAR model is the standard workhorse, although it has been pointed out that VECMs are often more useful if integrated variables are involved. Many procedures discussed in this chapter can be generalized for VECMs and in some cases the extensions have been mentioned. A more detailed discussion of VECMs will be given in Chapter 14.

To perform the computations related to a VAR analysis, specialized easy-to-use software packages are available. Examples are *PcGive* (Doornik and Hendry, 1997), *EViews* (EViews, 2000) or *JMulTi* (Krätzig, 2004).

There are many possible generalizations of the presently considered models which are of interest in applied and theoretical work. For a more parsimonious parameterization it may be useful to consider the class of vector autoregressive moving average processes, where the residuals of a VAR model may have a MA structure. For the stationary case these models have been considered, for instance, by Hannan and Deistler (1988), Lütkepohl (2005, Part IV) and Lütkepohl and Poskitt (1996a). Extensions to cointegrated systems have been discussed by Lütkepohl and Claessen (1997), Bartel and Lütkepohl (1998) and Poskitt (2003). Seasonal fluctuations in economic time series often require special models or model features which were not discussed in the present chapter. Seasonality is considered in Chapter 29. In the present chapter the order of integration has been assumed to be at most one. In economic analysis, allowing for higher order integration is sometimes useful. For further discussion see Chapter 14. In particular for modeling financial time series the conditional second moments are often of interest. Suitable multivariate models that can be used for this purpose are presented in Chapter 21.

Acknowledgment

The author thanks Søren Johansen for helpful comments on an earlier draft of this chapter.

References

Ahn, S.K. (1988) Distribution for residual autocovariances in multivariate autoregressive models with structured parameterization. *Biometrika* **75**, 590–3.

Akaike, H. (1973) Information theory and an extension of the maximum likelihood principle. In B. Petrov and F. Csáki (eds), *2nd International Symposium on Information Theory*. Budapest: Acadêmiai Kiadó, pp. 267–81.

Akaike, H. (1974) A new look at the statistical model identification. *IEEE Transactions on Automatic Control* **AC-19**, 716–23.

Amisano, G. and C. Giannini (1997) *Topics in Structural VAR Econometrics*, 2nd edn. Berlin: Springer.

Angrist, J.D., G.W. Imbens and D.B. Rubin (1996) Identification of causal effects using instrumental variables. *Journal of the American Statistical Association* **91**, 444–72.

Baillie, R.T. (1981) Prediction from the dynamic simultaneous equation model with vector autoregressive errors. *Econometrica* **49**, 1331–1337.

Banerjee, A., J.J. Dolado, J.W. Galbraith and D.F. Hendry (1993) *Co-integration, Error-Correction, and the Econometric Analysis of Non-stationary Data*. Oxford: Oxford University Press.

Bartel, H. and H. Lütkepohl (1998) Estimating the Kronecker indices of cointegrated echelon form VARMA models. *Econometrics Journal* **1**, C76–C99.

Basu, A.K. and S. Sen Roy (1987) On asymptotic prediction problems for multivariate autoregressive models in the unstable nonexplosive case. *Calcutta Statistical Association Bulletin* **36**, 29–37.

Benkwitz, A., H. Lütkepohl and M. Neumann (2000) Problems related to bootstrapping impulse responses of autoregressive processes. *Econometric Reviews* **19**, 69–103.

Benkwitz, A., H. Lütkepohl and J. Wolters (2001) Comparison of bootstrap confidence intervals for impulse responses of German monetary systems. *Macroeconomic Dynamics* **5**, 81–100.

Berkowitz, J. and L. Kilian (2000) Recent developments in bootstrapping time series. *Econometric Reviews* **19**, 1–48.

Bernanke, B. (1986) Alternative explanations of the money–income correlation. *Carnegie-Rochester Conference Series on Public Policy*. Amsterdam: North-Holland.

Bhansali, R.J. (1978) Linear prediction by autoregressive model fitting in the time domain. *Annals of Statistics* **6**, 224–31.

Bhansali, R.J. (2002) Multi-step forecasting. In M.P. Clements and D.F. Hendry (eds), *A Companion to Economic Forecasting*. Oxford: Blackwell, pp. 206–21.

Blanchard, O. and D. Quah (1989) The dynamic effects of aggregate demand and supply disturbances. *American Economic Review* **79**, 655–73.

Breitung, J., R. Brüggemann and H. Lütkepohl (2004) Structural vector autoregressive modeling and impulse responses. In H. Lütkepohl and M. Krätzig (eds), *Applied Time Series Econometrics*. Cambridge: Cambridge University Press, pp. 159–96.

Brüggemann R. (2004) *Model Reduction Methods for Vector Autoregressive Processes*. Berlin: Springer Verlag.

Brüggemann, R. and H. Lütkepohl (2001) Lag selection in subset VAR models with an application to a U.S. monetary system. In R. Friedmann, L. Knüppel and H. Lütkepohl (eds), *Econometric Studies: A Festschrift in Honour of Joachim Frohn*. Münster: LIT Verlag, pp. 107–28.

Brüggemann, R., H. Lütkepohl and P. Saikkonen (2005) Residual autocorrelation testing for vector error correction models. *Journal of Econometrics*, forthcoming.

Clements, M.P. and D.F. Hendry (1998) *Forecasting Economic Time Series*. Cambridge: Cambridge University Press.

Clements, M.P. and D.F. Hendry (1999) *Forecasting Non-stationary Economic Time Series*. Cambridge, MA: MIT Press.

Dolado, J.J. and H. Lütkepohl (1996) Making Wald tests work for cointegrated VAR systems. *Econometric Reviews* **15**, 369–86.

Doornik, J.A. and H. Hansen (1994) A practical test of multivariate normality. Unpublished paper, Nuffield College.

Doornik, J.A. and D.F. Hendry (1997) *Modelling Dynamic Systems Using PcFiml 9.0 for Windows*. London: International Thomson Business Press.

Dufour, J.-M. and E. Renault (1998) Short run and long run causality in time series: theory. *Econometrica* **66**, 1099–1125.

Edgerton, D. and G. Shukur (1999) Testing autocorrelation in a system perspective. *Econometric Reviews* **18**, 343–86.

Engle, R.F. and C.W.J. Granger (1987) Cointegration and error correction: representation, estimation and testing. *Econometrica* **55**, 251–76.

Engle, R.F. and B.S. Yoo (1987) Forecasting and testing in cointegrated systems. *Journal of Econometrics* **35**, 143–59.

EViews (2000) *EViews 4.0 User's Guide*. Irvine, CA: Quantitative Micro Software.

Findley, D.F. (1986) On bootstrap estimates of forecast mean square errors for autoregressive processes. In D.M. Allen (ed.), *Computer Science and Statistics: The Interface*. Amsterdam: North-Holland, pp. 11–17.

Fisher, L.A. and H. Huh (1999) Weak exogeneity and long-run and contemporaneous identifying restrictions in VEC models. *Economics Letters* **63**, 159–65.

Galí, J. (1999) Technology, employment, and the business cycle: do technology shocks explain aggregate fluctuations? *American Economic Review* **89**, 249–71.

Giannini, C. (1992) *Topics in Structural VAR Econometrics*. Heidelberg: Springer.

Gonzalo, J. and S. Ng (2001) A systematic framework for analyzing the dynamic effects of permanent and transitory shocks. *Journal of Economic Dynamics & Control* **25**, 1527–1546.

Granger, C.W.J. (1969) Investigating causal relations by econometric models and cross-spectral methods. *Econometrica* **37**, 424–38.

Granger, C.W.J. (1981) Some properties of time series data and their use in econometric model specification. *Journal of Econometrics* **16**, 121–30.

Granger, C.W.J. (1982) Generating mechanisms, models, and causality. In W. Hildenbrand (ed.), *Advances in Econometrics*. Cambridge: Cambridge University Press, pp. 237–53.

Granger, C.W.J. and P. Newbold (1974) Spurious regressions in eonometrics. *Journal of Econometrics* **2**, 111–20.

Granger, C.W.J. and T. Teräsvirta (1993) *Modelling Nonlinear Economic Relationships*. Oxford: Oxford University Press.

Grigoletto, M. (1998) Bootstrap prediction intervals for autoregressions: some alternatives. *International Journal of Forecasting* **14**, 447–56.

Hamilton, J.D. (1994) *Time Series Analysis*. Princeton, NJ: Princeton University Press.

Hannan, E.J. and M. Deistler (1988) *The Statistical Theory of Linear Systems*. New York: Wiley.

Hannan, E.J. and B.G. Quinn (1979) The determination of the order of an autoregression. *Journal of the Royal Statistical Society* **B41**, 190–95.

Hansen, H. and S. Johansen (1999) Some tests for parameter constancy in cointegrated VAR-models. *Econometrics Journal* **2**, 306–33.

Hatanaka, M. (1996) *Time-Series-Based Econometrics: Unit Roots and Co-Integration*. Oxford: Oxford University Press.

Hayashi, F. (2000) *Econometrics*. Princeton, NJ: Princeton University Press.

Heckman, J.J. (2000) Causal parameters and policy analysis in econometrics: a twentieth century retrospective. *Quarterly Journal of Economics* **105**, 45–97.

Hendry, D.F. (1995) *Dynamic Econometrics*. Oxford: Oxford University Press.

Hendry, D.F. and H.-M. Krolzig (2001) *Automatic Econometric Model Selection with PcGets*. London: Timberlake Consultants Press.

Hogue, A., J. Magnus and B. Pesaran (1988) The exact multi-period mean-square forecast error for the first-order autoregressive model. *Journal of Econometrics* **39**, 327–46.

Hoover, K.D. (2001) *Causality in Macroeconomics*. Cambridge, MA: Cambridge University Press.

Hosking, J.R.M. (1980) The multivariate portmanteau statistic. *Journal of the American Statistical Association* 75, 602–8.

Hosking, J.R.M. (1981a) Equivalent forms of the multivariate portmanteau statistic. *Journal of the Royal Statistical Society* B43, 261–2.

Hosking, J.R.M. (1981b). Lagrange-multiplier tests of multivariate time series models. *Journal of the Royal Statistical Society* B43, 219–30.

Jarque, C.M. and A.K. Bera (1987) A test for normality of observations and regression residuals. *International Statistical Review* 55, 163–72.

Johansen, S. (1995) *Likelihood-based Inference in Cointegrated Vector Autoregressive Models*. Oxford: Oxford University Press.

Kabaila, P. (1993) On bootstrap predictive inference for autoregressive processes. *Journal of Time Series Analysis* 14, 473–84.

Kemp, G.C.R. (1999) The behavior of forecast errors from a nearly integrated AR(1) model as both sample size and forecast horizon become large. *Econometric Theory* 15, 238–56.

Kilian, L. (1998) Small-sample confidence intervals for impulse response functions. *Review of Economics and Statistics* 80, 218–30.

Kim, J.H. (1999) Asymptotic and bootstrap prediction regions for vector autoregression. *International Journal of Forecasting* 15, 393–403.

King, R.G., C.I. Plosser, J.H. Stock, and M.W. Watson (1991) Stochastic trends and economic fluctuations. *American Economic Review* 81, 819–40.

Koop, G. (1992) Aggregate shocks and macroeconomic fluctuations: a Bayesian approach. *Journal of Applied Econometrics* 7, 395–411.

Krämer, W., W. Ploberger, and R. Alt (1988) Testing for structural change in dynamic models. *Econometrica* 56, 1355–69.

Krätzig, M. (2004) The software JMulTi. In H. Lütkepohl and M. Krätzig (eds), *Applied Time Series Econometrics*. Cambridge: Cambridge University Press, pp. 289–99.

Lee, K.C., M.H. Pesaran and R.G. Pierse (1992) Persistence of shocks and its sources in a multisectoral model of UK output growth. *Economic Journal* 102, 342–56.

Lewis, R. and G.C. Reinsel (1985) Prediction of multivariate time series by autoregressive model fitting. *Journal of Multivariate Analysis* 16, 393–411.

Li, H. and G.S. Maddala (1996) Bootstrapping time series models. *Econometric Reviews* 15, 115–58.

Li, W.K. and A.I. McLeod (1981) Distribution of the residual autocorrelations in multivariate ARMA time series models. *Journal of the Royal Statistical Society* B43, 231–9.

Lomnicki, Z.A. (1961) Tests for departure from normality in the case of linear stochastic processes. *Metrika* 4, 37–62.

Lütkepohl, H. (1985) The joint asymptotic distribution of multistep prediction errors of estimated vector autoregressions. *Economics Letters* 17, 103–6.

Lütkepohl, H. (1993) Testing for causation between two variables in higher dimensional VAR models. In H. Schneeweiss and K.F. Zimmermann (eds), *Studies in Applied Econometrics*. Heidelberg: Physica-Verlag, pp. 75–91.

Lütkepohl, H. (1996) *Handbook of Matrices*. Chichester: John Wiley & Sons.

Lütkepohl, H. (2001) Vector autoregressions. In B.H. Baltagi (ed.), *A Companion to Theoretical Econometrics*. Oxford: Blackwell, pp. 678–99.

Lütkepohl, H. (2004) Vector autoregressive and vector error correction models. In H. Lütkepohl and M. Krätzig (eds), *Applied Time Series Econometrics*. Cambridge: Cambridge University Press, pp. 86–158.

Lütkepohl, H. (2005) *New Introduction to Multiple Time Series Analysis*. Berlin: Springer Verlag.

Lütkepohl, H. and M.M. Burda (1997) Modified Wald tests under nonregular conditions. *Journal of Econometrics* 78, 315–32.

Lütkepohl, H. and H. Claessen (1997) Analysis of cointegrated VARMA processes. *Journal of Econometrics* **80**, 223–39.

Lütkepohl, H. and M. Krätzig (eds) (2004) *Applied Time Series Econometrics*. Cambridge: Cambridge University Press.

Lütkepohl, H. and D.S. Poskitt (1996a) Specification of echelon form VARMA models. *Journal of Business & Economic Statistics* **14**, 69–79.

Lütkepohl, H. and D.S. Poskitt (1996b) Testing for causation using infinite order vector autoregressive processes. *Econometric Theory* **12**, 61–87.

Lütkepohl, H. and H.-E. Reimers (1992) Impulse response analysis of cointegrated systems. *Journal of Economic Dynamics and Control* **16**, 53–78.

Lütkepohl, H. and P. Saikkonen (1997) Impulse response analysis in infinite order cointegrated vector autoregressive processes. *Journal of Econometrics* **81**, 127–57.

Masarotto, G. (1990) Bootstrap prediction intervals for autoregressions. *International Journal of Forecasting* **6**, 229–39.

Mosconi, R. and C. Giannini (1992) Non-causality in cointegrated systems: representation, estimation and testing. *Oxford Bulletin of Economics and Statistics* **54**, 399–417.

Ng, S. and P. Perron (1995) Unit root tests in ARMA models with data-dependent methods for the selection of the truncation lag. *Journal of the American Statistical Association* **90**, 268–81.

Omtzigt, P. (2003) *Essays on Cointegration Analysis*, PhD thesis, European University Institute, Florence.

Pagan, A. (1995) Three econometric methodologies: an update. In L. Oxley, D.A.R. George, C.J. Roberts and S. Sayer (eds), *Surveys in Econometrics*. Oxford: Basil Blackwell.

Park, J.Y. and P.C.B. Phillips (1988) Statistical inference in regressions with integrated processes: part 1. *Econometric Theory* **4**, 468–97.

Park, J.Y. and P.C.B. Phillips (1989) Statistical inference in regressions with integrated processes: part 2. *Econometric Theory* **5**, 95–131.

Pascual, L., J. Romo and E. Ruiz (2004) Bootstrap predictive inference for ARIMA processes. *Journal of Time Series Analysis* **25**, 449–65.

Paulsen, J. (1984) Order determination of multivariate autoregressive time series with unit roots. *Journal of Time Series Analysis* **5**, 115–27.

Pearl, J. (2000) *Causality: Models, Reasoning, and Inference*. Cambridge, MA: Cambridge University Press.

Penm, J.H.W., T.J. Brailsford and R.D. Terrell (2000) A robust algorithm in sequentially selecting subset time series systems using neural networks. *Journal of Time Series Analysis* **21**, 389–412.

Pesaran, M.H. and Y. Shin (1996) Cointegration and speed of convergence to equilibrium. *Journal of Econometrics* **71**, 117–43.

Poskitt, D.S. (2003) On the specification of cointegrated autoregressive moving-average forecasting systems. *International Journal of Forecasting* **19**, 503–19.

Quinn, B.G. (1980) Order determination for a multivariate autoregression. *Journal of the Royal Statistical Society* **B42**, 182–5.

Reinsel, G.C. and S.K. Ahn (1992) Vector autoregressive models with unit roots and reduced rank structure: estimation, likelihood ratio test, and forecasting. *Journal of Time Series Analysis* **13**, 353–75.

Reinsel, G.C. and A.L. Lewis (1987). Prediction mean square error for non-stationary multivariate time series using estimated parameters. *Economics Letters* **24**, 57–61.

Rissanen, J. (1978) Modeling by shortest data description. *Automatica* **14**, 465–71.

Saikkonen, P. and H. Lütkepohl (1996) Infinite order cointegrated vector autoregressive processes: estimation and inference. *Econometric Theory* **12**, 814–44.

Sampson, M. (1991) The effect of parameter uncertainty on forecast variances and confidence intervals for unit root and trend stationary time-series models. *Journal of Applied Econometrics* **6**, 67–76.

Schwarz, G. (1978) Estimating the dimension of a model. *Annals of Statistics* **6**, 461–4.

Sims, C.A. (1980) Macroeconomics and reality. *Econometrica* **48**, 1–48.

Sims, C.A. (1986) Are forecasting models usable for policy analysis? *Quarterly Review, Federal Reserve Bank of Minneapolis* **10**, 2–16.

Sims, C.A., J.H. Stock and M.W. Watson (1990) Inference in linear time series models with some unit roots. *Econometrica* **58**, 113–44.

Sims, C.A. and T. Zha (1999) Error bands for impulse responses. *Econometrica* **67**, 1113–1155.

Stock, J.H. (1996) VAR, error correction and pretest forecasts at long horizons. *Oxford Bulletin of Economics and Statistics* **58**, 685–701.

Tay, A.S. and K.F. Wallis (2002) Density forecasting: a survey. In M.P. Clements and D.F. Hendry (eds), *Companion to Economic Forecasting*. Oxford: Blackwell, pp. 45–68.

Toda, H.Y. and P.C.B. Phillips (1993) Vector autoregressions and causality. *Econometrica* **61**, 1367–1393.

Toda, H.Y. and T. Yamamoto (1995) Statistical inference in vector autoregressions with possibly integrated processes. *Journal of Econometrics* **66**, 225–50.

Uhlig, H. (2005) What are the effects of monetary policy on output? Results from an agnostic identification procedure. *Journal of Monetary Economics* **52**, 381–419.

Watson, M.W. (1994) Vector autoregressions and cointegration. In R.F. Engle and D.L. McFadden (eds), *Handbook of Econometrics*, vol. IV. New York: Elsevier.

Yamamoto, T. (1980) On the treatment of autocorrelated errors in the multiperiod prediction of dynamic simultaneous equation models. *International Economic Review* **21**, 735–48.

Zellner, A. (1962) An efficient method of estimating seemingly unrelated regressions and tests of aggregation bias. *Journal of the American Statistical Association* **57**, 348–68.

13
Nonstationary Panels

In Choi

Abstract

This chapter surveys major developments in the econometrics of nonstationary panels since the early 1990s. The survey starts from unit root and stationarity tests for independent panels. These include unit root tests by Levin, Lin and Chu (2002), Im, Pesaran and Shin (2003), Maddala and Wu (1999) and Choi (2001a). The stationarity tests included are Hadri's LM test and the combination tests due to Choi (2001a) and Yin and Wu (2000). Extensions of the unit root tests to cross-sectionally dependent panels are also discussed. These use either factor modeling as in Bai and Ng (2002), Philips and Sul (2003), Moon and Perron (2004a), or cross-sectional averages as additional regressors as in Pesaran (2003). In addition, properties of the OLS, modified OLS, IV and VAR regressions for independent and cross-sectionally dependent panels are summarized. Residual-based panel cointegration tests of Kao (1999) and Pedroni (1999) and panel VAR cointegration tests of Larsson, Lyhagen and Löthgren (2001), Larsson and Lyhagen (1999) and Groen and Kleibergen (2003) are also discussed.

13.1	Introduction	512
13.2	Tests for a unit root and stationarity	513
	13.2.1 Unit root tests for independent panels	513
	13.2.2 Asymptotic power analysis of panel unit root tests	519
	13.2.3 Stationarity tests for independent panels	520
	13.2.4 Unit root tests for cross-sectionally correlated panels	522
	13.2.5 Stationarity tests for cross-sectionally correlated panels	525
13.3	Panel regressions	526
	13.3.1 OLS and modified OLS estimation	526
	13.3.2 IV estimation	528
	13.3.3 Regressions for cross-sectionally correlated panels	529
	13.3.4 Panel VAR	529
13.4	Tests for panel cointegration	530
	13.4.1 Residual-based panel cointegration tests	530
	13.4.2 Panel VAR cointegration tests	531
13.5	Other topics and further comments	534

13.1   Introduction

Recent years have seen a growing interest in nonstationary panels. The initial motivation for using panel data was to increase the power of unit root tests. Levin and Lin's (1992)[1] tests and subsequent panel unit root tests demonstrated the power advantage of panel data by simulation. Levin and Lin's and other tests have been applied on a large scale for different purposes (see the list below) and numerous theories for nonstationary panels have also been developed. These developments resemble those for nonstationary time series in the 1980s and 1990s, when empirical applications and econometric theory grew side by side, satisfying each other's needs and posing new problems for each other. Indeed, anyone who has observed the evolution of the econometric theory of nonstationary time series since those days will realize that the research paradigm of nonstationary panels is similar to that of nonstationary time series during that time, although nonstationary panels raise some unique issues, such as cross-sectional correlation and ways to handle two indices going to infinity. As with nonstationary time series, interest in the panel unit root test has extended to the panel cointegration test, panel cointegrating regression, panel VAR, and optimal unit root testing, as will be discussed later.

The purpose of this chapter is to survey major developments in the econometrics of nonstationary panels since the early 1990s, complementing earlier surveys by Baltagi and Kao (2000), Banerjee (1999), and Phillips and Moon (2000). Topics that will be discussed include panel tests for a unit root and stationarity for both independent and dependent panels, panel regressions and tests for panel cointegration, among others.

Econometric methods for nonstationary panels have been applied extensively in the empirical literature.[2] A partial list of related articles studying the PPP (purchasing power parity) hypothesis includes Frankel and Rose (1996); Oh (1996); Lothian (1997); MacDonald (1996); Wu (1996); Coakley and Fuertes (1997); Papell (1997); O'Connell (1998); Bleaney and Leybourne (2003); Taylor and Sarno (1998); Herwartz and Reimers (2002); Smith, Leybourne, Kim and Newbold (2004); Wu and Wu (2001); Fleissig and Strauss (2000); and Luintel (2001). Other applications include Estrin and Urga (1997), Fleissig and Strauss (2001), and McCoskey (2002) on growth and convergence; Mark and Sul (2003) on money demand; Groen (2002), Mark and Sul (2001), and Oh (1999) on the monetary exchange rate model; Culver and Papell (1997), Holmes (2002), and Lee and Wu (2001) on inflation-rate convergence; Wu and Chen (1998), Wu and Chen (2001), Wu and Zhang (1996), and Wu and Zhang (1997) on interest rates; Gerdtham and Löthgren (2000), Gerdtham and Löthgren (2002), Hansen and King (1998), Jewell, Lee, Tieslau and Strazicich (2003), McCoskey and Selden (1998), McDonald and Hopkins (2002), and Okunade and Karakus (2001) on health care expenditures; Edmond (2001), Frantzen (1998), Funk (2001), Gutierrez and Gutierrez (2003), Kao, Chiang and Chen (1999), and Los and Verspagen (2000) on R&D spillovers; and Leon (2002), Smyth (2003), Song and Wu (1998) on hysteresis in unemployment. No doubt this list is incomplete and more applications can be found throughout the literature.

The remainder of this chapter is structured as follows. Section 13.2 introduces tests for a unit root and stationarity for both independent and dependent panels. Section 13.3 discusses panel regressions. Section 13.4 explains tests for panel cointegration. Section 13.5 summarizes some other developments in nonstationary panels.

13.2 Tests for a unit root and stationarity

13.2.1 Unit root tests for independent panels

This subsection reviews unit root tests for independent panels that have often been used in practice. These are the pooled *t*-test proposed by Levin, Lin and Chu (2002; LLC hereafter), the averaged *t*-test of Im, Pesaran and Shin (2003; IPS hereafter) and the combination tests of Maddala and Wu (1999) and Choi (2001a).[3] The LLC test is based on Levin and Lin (1992), but improves on it in the sense that heterogeneity of cross-sectional units is allowed.

In addition to these tests, there are several other panel unit root tests that are designed for a fixed number of time series, as in the conventional dynamic panel literature.[4] These include Breitung and Meyer (1994); Harris and Tzavalis (1999); and Binder, Hsiao and Pesaran (2002). For these tests, homogeneity of slope coefficients should be imposed, which may be too restrictive for applications.

In practice, panels from macroeconomics and international finance are seldom cross-sectionally independent. However, existing panel unit root tests that allow cross-sectional correlation are mostly extensions of the tests for independent panels, which warrants careful study of the unit root tests for independent panels.

The tests can coherently be introduced using the autoregressive models[5]

$$\Delta y_{it} = \rho_i y_{i,t-1} + \sum_{j=1}^{k_i} \varphi_{ij} \Delta y_{i,t-j} + \mu_i + u_{it}, \quad (i = 1, \dots, N; t = k_i + 2, \dots, n), \quad (13.1)$$

and

$$\Delta y_{it} = \rho_i y_{i,t-1} + \sum_{j=1}^{k_i} \varphi_{ij} \Delta y_{i,t-j} + \mu_i + \beta_i t + u_{it}, \quad (i = 1, \dots, N; t = k_i + 2, \dots, n), \quad (13.2)$$

where $u_{it} \sim iid(0, \sigma_i^2)$ for $t = k_i + 2, \dots, n$ and $\{y_{1t}\}_{t=k_1+2}^n, \dots, \{y_{Nt}\}_{t=k_N+2}^n$ are independent. We assume k_i are known, though in practice these can be estimated using information criteria and sequential testing. In addition, for all i, characteristic roots of models (13.1) and (13.2) are assumed to lie outside the unit circle with possibly one root taking the value one.

It will be convenient to write model (13.1) in matrix notation as

$$\Delta \mathbf{y}_{in} = \rho_i \mathbf{y}_{i,-1,n} + \mathbf{Q}_{in}\gamma_i + u_{in}, \quad (i = 1, \ldots, N),$$

where $\Delta \mathbf{y}_{in} = [\Delta y_{i,k_i+2}, \ldots, \Delta y_{i,n}]'$, $\mathbf{Q}_{in} = (\mathbf{1}, \Delta \mathbf{y}_{i,-1,n}, \Delta \mathbf{y}_{i,-2,n}, \ldots, \Delta \mathbf{y}_{i,-k_i,n})$ with $\mathbf{1} = [1, \ldots, 1]'$, $\mathbf{y}_{i,-1,n} = [y_{i,k_i+2-1}, \ldots, y_{i,n-1}]'$ and $\gamma_i = (\mu_i, \varphi_{i1}, \ldots, \varphi_{ik_i})$. In the same manner, we write model (13.2) as

$$\Delta \mathbf{y}_{in} = \rho_i \mathbf{y}_{i,-1,n} + \ddot{\mathbf{Q}}_{in}\delta_i + u_{in}, \quad (i = 1, \ldots, N),$$

where $\ddot{\mathbf{Q}}_{in} = (\mathbf{1}, \mathbf{t}, \Delta \mathbf{y}_{i,-1,n}, \Delta \mathbf{y}_{i,-2,n}, \ldots, \Delta \mathbf{y}_{i,-k_i,n})$ with $\mathbf{t} = [k_i + 2, \ldots, n]'$ and $\delta_i = (\mu_i, \beta_i, \varphi_{i1}, \ldots, \varphi_{ik_i})$.

The null hypothesis for the panel unit root tests is:

$$H_0 : \rho_i = 0 \quad \text{for all } i. \tag{13.3}$$

Our discussions in this section will mainly be based on the so-called sequential asymptotics, where $n \to \infty$ and then $N \to \infty$. This approach is intuitive and easy to understand. One may also be interested in joint asymptotics where n and N are sent to infinity simultaneously or diagonal asymptotics, where N is assumed to be a function of n. Though these approaches are theoretically interesting and sometimes provide useful implications, the limiting results are essentially the same as those of the sequential asymptotics but require more stringent conditions. From a practical viewpoint, therefore, sequential asymptotic results will suffice in most cases.

13.2.1.1 The LLC test

We introduce the LLC test for model (13.1) first. Once this is done, its extension to model (13.2) is straightforward. For the LLC test, we estimate σ_i^2 first by the time series regression on each individual. This gives a consistent estimator of σ_i^2

$$\hat{\sigma}_{in}^2 = \frac{1}{n - k_i - 1} \left(\mathbf{M}_{\mathbf{Q}_{in}} \Delta \mathbf{y}_{in} - \hat{\rho}_{in} \mathbf{M}_{\mathbf{Q}_{in}} \mathbf{y}_{i,-1,n} \right)' \left(\mathbf{M}_{\mathbf{Q}_{in}} \Delta \mathbf{y}_{in} - \hat{\rho}_{in} \mathbf{M}_{\mathbf{Q}_{in}} \mathbf{y}_{i,-1,n} \right), \tag{13.4}$$

where $\mathbf{M}_{\mathbf{Q}_{in}} = I - \mathbf{Q}_{in}(\mathbf{Q}_{in}'\mathbf{Q}_{in})^{-1}\mathbf{Q}_{in}'$ and $\hat{\rho}_{in} = \mathbf{y}_{i,-1,n}'\mathbf{M}_{\mathbf{Q}_{in}}\Delta \mathbf{y}_{in}/\mathbf{y}_{i,-1,n}'\mathbf{M}_{\mathbf{Q}_{in}}\mathbf{y}_{i,-1,n}$ is the OLS estimator of ρ_i. After normalizing each individual by $\hat{\sigma}_{in}$, LLC consider the following t-test using the normalized, pooled data

$$t_{Nn} = \frac{\hat{\rho}_{Nn}^p}{\sqrt{\hat{\sigma}_{Nn}^2 \left(\sum_{i=1}^N \mathbf{y}_{i,-1,n}'\mathbf{M}_{\mathbf{Q}_{in}}\mathbf{y}_{i,-1,n}/\hat{\sigma}_{in}^2 \right)^{-1}}} \tag{13.5}$$

for null hypothesis (13.3). In (13.5), $\hat{\rho}_{Nn}^p$ is a pooled OLS estimator of ρ_i defined by

$$\hat{\rho}_{Nn}^p = \frac{\sum_{i=1}^N \mathbf{y}_{i,-1,n}' \mathbf{M}_{Q_{in}} \Delta \mathbf{y}_{in} / \hat{\sigma}_{in}^2}{\sum_{i=1}^N \mathbf{y}_{i,-1,n}' \mathbf{M}_{Q_{in}} \mathbf{y}_{i,-1,n} / \hat{\sigma}_{in}^2}$$

and

$$\hat{\sigma}_{Nn}^2 = \frac{1}{N(n - \bar{k} - 1)} \sum_{i=1}^N \left(\mathbf{M}_{Q_{in}} \Delta \mathbf{y}_{in} - \hat{\rho}_{Nn}^p \mathbf{M}_{Q_{in}} \mathbf{y}_{i,-1,n} \right)'$$

$$\times \left(\mathbf{M}_{Q_{in}} \Delta \mathbf{y}_{in} - \hat{\rho}_{Nn}^p \mathbf{M}_{Q_{in}} \mathbf{y}_{i,-1,n} \right) / \hat{\sigma}_{in}^2,$$

with $\bar{k}$ denoting the mean of k_i. The t_{Nn} statistic is the usual t-test for the null hypothesis (13.3) when each set of time series data are normalized by $\hat{\sigma}_{in}$. It follows that $\hat{\rho}_{Nn}^p \xrightarrow{P} 0$ and $\hat{\sigma}_{Nn}^2 \xrightarrow{P} 1$ under the null hypothesis (13.3) as $n \to \infty$ and $N \to \infty$.
It is convenient for later analysis to rewrite (13.5) as

$$t_{Nn} = \frac{\sum_{i=1}^N \mathbf{y}_{i,-1,n}' \mathbf{M}_{Q_{in}} \Delta \mathbf{y}_{in} / \hat{\sigma}_{in}^2}{\sqrt{\hat{\sigma}_{Nn}^2 \sum_{i=1}^N \mathbf{y}_{i,-1,n}' \mathbf{M}_{Q_{in}} \mathbf{y}_{i,-1,n} / \hat{\sigma}_{in}^2}}$$

Using this formula, we obtain under the null hypothesis (13.3), as $n \to \infty$,

$$t_{Nn} \Rightarrow \frac{\sum_{i=1}^N s_i \int_0^1 \bar{W}_i(r) dW_i(r)}{\sqrt{\hat{\sigma}_N^2 \sum_{i=1}^N s_i^2 \int_0^1 \bar{W}_i^2(r) dr}} = \zeta_N, \text{ say,} \qquad (13.6)$$

where $\bar{W}_i(r) = W_i(r) - \int_0^1 W_i(s) ds$, $W_i(r)$ is standard Brownian motion, $\hat{\sigma}_N^2$ is the weak limit of $\hat{\sigma}_{Nn}^2$ as $n \to \infty$, and $s_i = \sigma_{li}/\sigma_i$ with σ_{li}^2 being the long-run variance of Δy_{it}. Since $E\left(\int_0^1 \bar{W}_i(r) dW_i(r) \right) = -\frac{1}{2}$,

$$\frac{1}{N} \sum_{i=1}^N s_i \int_0^1 \bar{W}_i(r) dW_i(r) \xrightarrow{P} \lim_{N \to \infty} \left(-\frac{1}{2N} \sum_{i=1}^N s_i \right) \text{ as } N \to \infty \qquad (13.7)$$

by the law of large numbers for a sequence of independent random variables. In addition, the law of large numbers applied to the denominator in relation (13.6) gives

$$\frac{1}{N} \sum_{i=1}^N s_i^2 \int_0^1 \bar{W}_i^2(r) dr \xrightarrow{P} \lim_{N \to \infty} \frac{1}{6N} \sum_{i=1}^N s_i^2, \qquad (13.8)$$

because $E\left(\int_0^1 \bar{W}_i^2(r)dr\right) = 1/6$. Assuming that the limits in relations (13.7) and (13.8) exist, we infer from (13.7) and (13.8) that the pooled t-test diverges in probability. This is the reason for the modification of the t-test.

In order to pursue the modification of the pooled t-test, apply the central limit theorem to the demeaned numerator in relation (13.6). This yields, as $N \to \infty$,

$$\frac{1}{\sqrt{N}}\sum_{i=1}^N s_i\left(\int_0^1 \bar{W}_i(r)dW_i(r) - E\left(\int_0^1 \bar{W}_i(r)dW_i(r)\right)\right)$$

$$= \frac{1}{\sqrt{N}}\sum_{i=1}^N s_i\left(\int_0^1 \bar{W}_i(r)dW_i(r) + \frac{1}{2}\right) \tag{13.9}$$

$$\Rightarrow N\left(0, \lim_{N\to\infty}\frac{1}{12N}\sum_{i=1}^N s_i^2\right),$$

where $\Rightarrow$ denotes weak convergence. Note that $Var\left(\int_0^1 \bar{W}_i(r)dW_i(r)\right) = \frac{1}{12}$. Relations (13.8) and (13.9) imply

$$\zeta_N \Rightarrow N\left(0, \frac{1}{2}\right). \tag{13.10}$$

Asymptotic results (13.8), (13.9) and (13.10) indicate that the pooled t-test should have mean and scale adjustments in order to have a standard normal distribution in the limit. If we assume $n = \infty$, the modification should be of the form[6]

$$\frac{\sum_{i=1}^N \left(\mathbf{y}_{i,-1}'{}_n \mathbf{M}_{Q_{in}}\Delta\mathbf{y}_{in}/\hat{\sigma}_{in}^2 + \frac{1}{2}n\hat{s}_i\right)}{\sqrt{\frac{1}{2}}\sqrt{\hat{\sigma}_{Nn}^2 \sum_{i=1}^N \mathbf{y}_{i,-1}'{}_n \mathbf{M}_{Q_{in}}\mathbf{y}_{i,-1,n}/\hat{\sigma}_{in}^2}}$$

$$= \frac{t_{Nn}}{\sqrt{\frac{1}{2}}} - \frac{\left(-\frac{1}{2}\right)n\sum_{i=1}^N \hat{s}_i}{\sqrt{\frac{1}{2}}\sqrt{\hat{\sigma}_{Nn}^2 \sum_{i=1}^N \mathbf{y}_{i,-1}'{}_n \mathbf{M}_{Q_{in}}\mathbf{y}_{i,-1,n}/\hat{\sigma}_{in}^2}}, \tag{13.11}$$

where $\hat{s}_i = \hat{\sigma}_{in}/\hat{\sigma}_{li}$, with $\hat{\sigma}_{li}^2$ being a consistent estimator of the long-run variance σ_{li}^2 that uses $\Delta y_{it} - \frac{1}{n-1}\sum_{i=2}^n \Delta y_{it}$. Using the same methods as above, we can show that the test statistic (13.11) has a standard normal distribution in the limit.

For the case of finite sample time series, LLC propose to use the mean and variance adjustment factors that were calculated by simulation. Using μ_n^* as a mean adjustment factor instead of $-\frac{1}{2}$ and σ_n^* as a variance adjustment factor instead of $\sqrt{1/2}$ in relation (13.11), the LLC test for model (13.1) using the finite sample mean and variance adjustments is defined by

$$LLC = \frac{t_{Nn}}{\sigma_n^*} - \frac{\mu_n^* n\sum_{i=1}^N \hat{s}_i}{\sigma_n^*\sqrt{\hat{\sigma}_{Nn}^2 \sum_{i=1}^N \mathbf{y}_{i,-1}'{}_n \mathbf{M}_{Q_{in}}\mathbf{y}_{i,-1,n}/\hat{\sigma}_{in}^2}}.$$

Values of μ_n^* and σ_n^* for various sample sizes are simulated using generated random normal numbers and reported in Table 2 of LLC (p. 14). In using the LLC test, we reject null hypothesis (13.3) when the LLC test is smaller than a critical value from the lower tail of a standard normal distribution.

The LLC test for model (13.2) is obtained in exactly the same manner by replacing $\mathbf{Q}_{in}$ with $\ddot{\mathbf{Q}}_{in}$, but the mean and variance adjustment factors should change because of the demeaned and detrended Brownian motion that emerges instead of the demeaned Brownian motion when n is sent to infinity. Values of the adjustment factors for finite n are also reported in Table 2 of LLC.

LLC also report the asymptotic distributions of the pooled t-test when N is a function of n. In this setup, N and n grow along the same path. The resulting distributions are no different from those of the sequential asymptotics but require more stringent conditions.

13.2.1.2 The IPS test

IPS propose to use the average of individual t-tests for the null hypothesis (13.3). To this end, they strengthen the assumption $u_{it} \sim iid(0, \sigma_i^2)$ to $u_{it} \sim iidN(0, \sigma_i^2)$. The individual t-test is defined by

$$t_{in} = \frac{\hat{\rho}_{in}}{\sqrt{\hat{\sigma}_{in}^2 \left(\mathbf{y}_{i,-1,n}' \mathbf{M}_{\mathbf{Q}_{in}} \mathbf{y}_{i,-1,n} \right)^{-1}}},$$

where $\hat{\rho}_{in} = \mathbf{y}_{i,-1,n}' \mathbf{M}_{\mathbf{Q}_{in}} \Delta \mathbf{y}_{in} / \mathbf{y}_{i,-1,n}' \mathbf{M}_{\mathbf{Q}_{in}} \mathbf{y}_{i,-1,n}$ is the OLS estimator of ρ_i and $\hat{\sigma}_{in}^2$ is a consistent estimator of $\hat{\sigma}_i^2$ defined by (13.4). The IPS t-bar statistic is the average of the individual augmented Dickey–Fuller tests defined by

$$\bar{t}_{Nn} = \frac{1}{N} \sum_{i=1}^{N} t_{in}.$$

For fixed N, as $n \to \infty$

$$\bar{t}_{Nn} \Rightarrow \frac{1}{N} \sum_{i=1}^{N} \frac{\int_0^1 \bar{W}_i(r) dW_i(r)}{\sqrt{\int_0^1 \bar{W}_i^2(r) dr}}$$

under null hypothesis (13.3). This can be shown to have a degenerate distribution when N goes to infinity using the same arguments as for the LLC test. For the case of large N and n, IPS propose a modified average t-test,

$$W_{tbar} = \frac{\sqrt{N} \left(\bar{t}_{Nn} - \frac{1}{N} \sum_{i=1}^{N} E(t_{in}(k_i, 0) | \rho_i = 0) \right)}{\sqrt{\frac{1}{N} \sum_{i=1}^{N} Var(t_{in}(k_i, 0) | \rho_i = 0)}},$$

where $t_{in}(k_i, 0)$ denotes the individual t-test using the AR order k_i and the restrictions $\varphi_{i1} = \ldots = \varphi_{ik_i} = 0$. In finite samples, the latter restrictions do not affect the W_{tbar}-test. The moments $E(t_{in}(k_i, 0)|\rho_i = 0)$ and $Var(t_{in}(k_i, 0)|\rho_i = 0)$ are obtained by simulation assuming $\rho_i = 0$ for all i and are reported in Table 3 of IPS (p. 66). IPS show that

$$W_{tbar} \Rightarrow \mathbf{N}(0, 1) \text{ as } n \to \infty \text{ and } N \to \infty.$$

In using the W_{tbar}-test, we reject the null hypothesis (13.3) when the W_{tbar}-test is smaller than a critical value from the lower tail of a standard normal distribution. For model (13.2), we follow the same procedure but use the moment estimates reported in Table 3 of IPS.

13.2.1.3   Combination tests

Combination tests have been proposed independently by Maddala and Wu (1999) and Choi (2001a). Suppose that we reject the null hypothesis $H_0 : \rho_i = 0$ when a realized value of the unit root test G_{in} is smaller than a constant. The asymptotic p-value for the G_{in} test is defined as

$$p_i = F(G_{in})$$

where $F(\cdot)$ denotes the distribution function of the G_{in} test when n is sent to infinity.

Maddala and Wu (1999) propose using the inverse chi-square test (Fisher's test), defined by

$$P = -2 \sum_{i=1}^{N} \ln(p_i). \tag{13.12}$$

Choi (2001a) considers various tests, including the inverse chi-square test, but the most promising is the inverse normal test defined by

$$Z = \frac{1}{\sqrt{N}} \sum_{i=1}^{N} \Phi^{-1}(p_i) \tag{13.13}$$

where $\Phi(\cdot)$ is the standard normal cumulative distribution function.

For fixed N, as $n \to \infty$,

$$P \Rightarrow \chi^2_{2N} \tag{13.14}$$

and

$$Z \Rightarrow \mathbf{N}(0, 1). \tag{13.15}$$

As $n \to \infty$ and $N \to \infty$, P diverges to infinity in probability, rendering it unusable for large N. But because relation (13.15) continues to hold, the Z test can be used for any N. Simulation results in Choi (2001a) indicate that the Z test performs better than other types of combination tests including the chi-square test.

In using the Z test, we reject null hypothesis (13.3) when the Z test is smaller than a critical value from the lower tail of a standard normal distribution. By contrast, critical values for the P test are taken from the upper tail of the chi-square distribution.

For the underlying test G_{in}, Maddala and Wu (1999) employ the augmented Dickey–Fuller test. According to unreported simulations by the author, however, using Elliott, Rothenberg and Stock's (1996) Dickey–Fuller–GLS test brings significant size and power advantages in finite samples. Simulation results in Choi (2001a) also indicate that the Z test is more powerful in finite samples than others when the Dickey–Fuller–GLS test is used as an underlying test.

13.21.4 Test consistency

In order for the unit root tests introduced so far to be consistent when $N \to \infty$, we need to assume that the number of individuals that are stationary when the null is not true, denoted as N_h, is large enough such that

$$N_h/N \to h \quad \text{(a fixed constant) as } N \to \infty. \tag{13.16}$$

This indicates that enough individuals must violate the null hypothesis of a unit root for the tests to be consistent. This is analyzed for the combination tests in Choi (2001a) and the same is true for those tests. This also implies that the null of a unit root may be true for some individuals even when the tests reject null hypothesis (13.3). In other words, rejection of the null hypothesis does not imply that every individual is stationary when N is large.

13.2.2 Asymptotic power analysis of panel unit root tests

Moon, Perron and Phillips (2003) consider the following model of independent panels

$$z_{it} = b_{0i} + b_{1i}t + y_{it};$$
$$y_{it} = \rho_i y_{i,t-1} + u_{it},$$

where $u_{it} \sim iid(0, \sigma^2)$, $\rho_i = 1 - \theta_i/N^{1/4}n$ and θ_i is a sequence of iid random variables. Using the Neyman–Pearson framework, they derive the asymptotic power envelope for the null hypothesis,

$$H_0 : \theta_i = 0 \quad \text{a.s. for all } i,$$

against the alternative

$$H_1 : \theta_i \neq 0 \quad \text{for some } i.$$

The power envelope is found to depend on $E(\theta_i^4)$. Comparing Ploberger and Phillips' (2002) and Moon and Phillips' (2004) tests,[7] they report that the power envelope is not achieved by both tests for the heterogeneous alternative H_1 and that Moon and Phillips' test is dominated by Ploberger and Phillips'. Unfortunately, the IPS and combination tests, particularly designed for heterogeneous panels, cannot be studied in their framework, and more work is needed to investigate whether or not there exist tests that achieve the asymptotic power envelope.

13.2.3 Stationarity tests for independent panels

This section reviews tests for the null of stationarity that are designed for independent panels. The tests we will consider are Hadri's (2000) Lagrange Multiplier test and Yin and Wu's (2000) and Choi's (2001) combination tests. The tests can be based on the models

$$y_{it} = \mu_i + u_{it}, \quad u_{it} = \rho_i u_{i,t-1} + v_{it}, \quad (i = 1, \ldots, N; t = 2, \ldots, n), \qquad (13.17)$$

and

$$y_{it} = \mu_i + \beta_i t + u_{it}, \quad u_{it} = \rho_i u_{i,t-1} + v_{it}, \quad (i = 1, \ldots, N; t = 2, \ldots, n). \qquad (13.18)$$

Assuming that the v_{it} are $I(0)$ for all i and that they are cross-sectionally independent, the null hypothesis of the tests is

$$H_0 : |\rho_i| < 1 \quad \text{for all } i. \qquad (13.19)$$

13.23.1 The Hadri test

Hadri's (2000) Lagrange Multiplier test for null hypothesis (13.19) is based on the "random walk plus noise" model, and can be defined by using the regression residuals of models (13.17) and (13.18). Letting $r_{it} = \sum_{k=1}^{t}(y_{ik} - \bar{y}_i)$ with $\bar{y}_i = \frac{1}{n}\sum_{t=1}^{n} y_{it}$, Hadri's test for model (13.17) is defined by (cf. Hadri's equations (27) and (28))

$$LM_{Nn} = \frac{1}{N}\sum_{i=1}^{N}\frac{1}{n^2\hat{\sigma}_i^2}\sum_{t=1}^{n} r_{it}^2,$$

where $\hat{\sigma}_i^2$ is an estimator of the long-run variance of y_{it} defined by $\hat{\sigma}_i^2 = \sum_{j=-l}^{l} C_i(j)k_l^j$, with $C_i(j) = \frac{1}{n}\sum_{t=1}^{n-j}(y_{it} - \bar{y}_i)(y_{i,t+j} - \bar{y}_i)$ and $k(\cdot)$ being a lag window. The lag length, l, is assumed to satisfy $l/n \to 0$ as $n \to \infty$. This test may be considered as the average of Kwiatkowski, Phillips, Schmidt and Shin's (1992) test of level-stationarity for each individual.

Since

$$LM_{Nn} \Rightarrow \frac{1}{N}\sum_{i=1}^{N}\int_0^1 (W_i(r) - rW_i(1))^2 dr \quad \text{as } n \to \infty$$

under some regularity conditions on $\{v_{it}\}$ and $E \iint (W_i(r) - rW_i(1))^2 dr = \frac{1}{6}$, Hadri proposes a modification of the Lagrange Multiplier test for large N along the lines of IPS. The modified test is defined by

$$W_{LMbar} = \frac{\sqrt{N}(LM_{Nn} - \frac{1}{6})}{\sqrt{\frac{1}{45}}} \tag{13.20}$$

and, as $n \to \infty$ and $N \to \infty$,

$$W_{LMbar} \Rightarrow N(0, 1).$$

For model (13.18), using the demeaned and detrended y_{it} for r_{it}, we proceed in the same way but replace $\frac{1}{6}$ and $\frac{1}{45}$ in formula (13.20) with $\frac{1}{15}$ and $\frac{11}{6300}$, respectively, in order to reflect the different weak limit of LM_{Nn} when $n \to \infty$. The limiting distribution of the test is the same as the test for model (13.17).

In order to analyze the behavior of the Hadri test under the violation of the null hypothesis, let the number of individuals having unit roots when null hypothesis (13.19) is not true be N_h and assume relation (13.16) holds true. Also, let $LM_{Nn} = \frac{1}{N} \sum_{i=1}^{N} \eta_{in}$ and assume $\rho_i = 1$ for $i = 1, \ldots, N_h$. Then,

$$W_{LMbar} = \frac{\sqrt{N}(\frac{1}{N}\sum_{i=1}^{N} \eta_{in} - \frac{1}{6})}{\sqrt{\frac{1}{45}}}$$

$$= \frac{\sqrt{N}(\frac{1}{N}(\sum_{i=1}^{N_h} \eta_{in} + \sum_{i=N_h+1}^{N} \eta_{in}) - \frac{1}{6})}{\sqrt{\frac{1}{45}}}$$

$$= \frac{\sqrt{(N_h/N)}(1/\sqrt{N_h}) \sum_{i=1}^{N_h} \eta_{in}}{\sqrt{\frac{1}{45}}} + \frac{\sqrt{N}(\frac{1}{N}\sum_{i=N_h+1}^{N} \eta_{in} - \frac{1}{6})}{\sqrt{\frac{1}{45}}}$$

$$= A_{Nn} + B_{Nn}, \text{ say}.$$

Because $\eta_{in} = O_p(n/\ell)$ for $i = 1, \ldots, N_h$ (cf. Kwiatkowski, Phillips, Schmidt and Shin, 1992, p. 169), $A_{Nn} = O_p(\frac{n\sqrt{N}}{\ell})$ and it diverges to plus infinity in probability. Moreover,

$$B_{Nn} = \frac{\sqrt{N}\left(((N - N_h)/N)(1/(N - N_h)) \sum_{i=N_h+1}^{N} \eta_{in} - \frac{1}{6}\right)}{\sqrt{\frac{1}{45}}}$$

$$= \frac{\sqrt{N}(((N - N_h)/N)\bar{\eta} - \frac{1}{6})}{\sqrt{\frac{1}{45}}}$$

$$= \sqrt{\frac{N}{N - N_h}} \frac{\sqrt{N - N_h}(\bar{\eta} - \frac{1}{6})}{\sqrt{\frac{1}{45}}} - \frac{N_h/\sqrt{N}}{6\sqrt{\frac{1}{45}}}$$

$$= O_p(1) + O_p(\sqrt{N})$$

because $\sqrt{N - N_h}(\bar{\eta} - \frac{1}{6}) = O_p(1)$. Thus, $W_{LMbar} \xrightarrow{P} -\infty$ as $n \to \infty$ and $N \to \infty$ when condition (13.16) is satisfied. But A_{Nn} dominates B_{Nn} because it diverges at a faster rate than B_{Nn}. Thus we have $W_{LMbar} \xrightarrow{P} \infty$, and this implies that we should use the right-hand tail of a standard normal distribution for critical values of Hadri's test.

13.2.3.2 Combination tests

Suppose that we reject the null hypothesis, $H_0 : |\rho_i| < 1$, when a realized value of the stationarity test G_{in} is greater than a constant. The asymptotic p-value for the G_{in} test is defined as

$$p_i = 1 - F(G_{in_i}),$$

where $F(\cdot)$ denotes the distribution function of the G_{in} test when n is sent to infinity. Yin and Wu (2000) employ Kwiatkowski, Phillips, Schmidt and Shin's (1992) and Leybourne and McCabe (1994) tests for G_{in} and combine the resulting p-values using Fisher's test defined in (13.12). The limiting distribution of the combination test for fixed N is given in (13.14). Instead of Fisher's test, we may also use the Z test defined by (13.13). Its distribution is a standard normal for both finite and infinite N.

Time series tests for the null of stationarity tend to have serious size distortions when the null is close to the alternative of a unit root. Panel tests for the null of stationarity are no different in this respect, and caution should be exercised when interpreting the results of panel stationarity tests.

13.2.4 Unit root tests for cross-sectionally correlated panels

This subsection reviews unit root tests for cross-sectionally correlated panels. O'Connell (1998) and Maddala and Wu (1999) report size distortions of some panel unit root tests when errors are cross-sectionally correlated. This prompted much interest in panel unit root tests for cross-sectionally correlated panels. This subsection reviews tests using common factors and some other approaches.

13.2.4.1 Tests using common factors

Bai and Ng (2002; BN hereafter), Moon and Perron (2004a; MP hereafter), Phillips and Sul (2003; PS hereafter), and Pesaran (2003) model cross-sectional correlation by common factors.[8] They all develop tests using large n and large N asymptotics. PS's and Pesaran's panel unit root tests use models (13.1) and (13.2),[9] but assume

$$u_{it} = \gamma_i f_t + \varepsilon_{it},$$

where f_t is an unobserved common factor, γ_i is a factor loading coefficient and the ε_{it} are idiosyncratic errors. When there are enough lagged variables in models (13.1) and (13.2), it is reasonable to assume that $\{f_t\}$ and $\{\varepsilon_{it}\}$ are white noise processes as in PS and Pesaran, though their theories are expected to work for stationary f_t as well. Since it is assumed that ε_{it} is independent of ε_{js} and f_s for all $i \neq j$ and for all s and t, cross-sectional correlation is embodied in the common factor f_t. If $\gamma_i = 0$ for all i, there will be no cross-sectional correlation. The main idea of PS's and Pesaran's tests is to eliminate the common factor f_t and apply the panel unit root tests developed for independent panels.

PS estimate $[\gamma_1, \ldots, \gamma_N]$ and $[\sigma_1^2, \ldots, \sigma_N^2]$ by the principal-component method and use the estimates to transform the observed time series $\{y_{it}\}$ for each i such that the common factor is eliminated from the series. They recommend using the inverse normal test (13.13) for the transformed time series. PS show by simulation that their method works reasonably well in finite samples.

Pesaran uses regressions augmented by the cross-sectional averages of lagged levels and first-differences, whose presence eliminates the cross-sectional correlation embodied in $\gamma_i f_t$. In order to understand this idea, consider the cross-sectional average of the homogenous AR model with one lagged difference,

$$
\begin{aligned}
\frac{1}{N}\sum_{i=1}^{N}\Delta y_{it} &= \frac{\rho}{N}\sum_{i=1}^{N}y_{i,\,t-1} + \varphi\frac{1}{N}\sum_{i=1}^{N}\Delta y_{i,\,t-1} + \frac{f_t}{N}\sum_{i=1}^{N}\gamma_i + \frac{1}{N}\sum_{i=1}^{N}\varepsilon_{it} \\
&\approx \frac{\rho}{N}\sum_{i=1}^{N}y_{i,\,t-1} + \frac{\varphi}{N}\sum_{i=1}^{N}\Delta y_{i,\,t-1} + \frac{f_t}{N}\sum_{i=1}^{N}\gamma_i,
\end{aligned}
$$

where the approximate relation holds for large N by the law of large numbers. This relation shows that f_t is expressible as a linear combination of cross-sectional averages of the lagged level $y_{i,\,t-1}$ and the differences Δy_{it} and $\Delta y_{i,\,t-1}$ as long as $\frac{1}{N}\sum_{i=1}^{N}\gamma_i \neq 0$. Thus, if we run the time series OLS regression for each i,

$$
\Delta y_{it} = \hat{\rho} y_{i,\,t-1} + \hat{\varphi}\Delta y_{i,\,t-1} + \hat{\alpha}_1 \bar{y}_{t-1} + \hat{\alpha}_2 \Delta \bar{y}_t + \hat{\alpha}_3 \Delta \bar{y}_{t-1} + \hat{u}_{it},
$$

where ‾ denotes the cross-sectional average, the residual $\hat{u}_{it}$ will be devoid of $\gamma_i f_t$ in the limit that brings cross-sectional correlation. Using this regression, *t*-tests are devised and combined as in IPS. The *t*-tests' limiting distributions are different from the Dickey–Fuller distribution due to the presence of the cross-sectional average of the lagged level. Pesaran uses a truncated version of the IPS test that avoids the problem of moment calculation. In addition, the *t*-tests are also used to formulate a combination test. His experimental results show that the IPS test using truncation and the combination test using the inverse normal principle perform well. A limitation of the model Pesaran uses is that the model imposes homogeneity across cross-sectional units. Certainly, this is a restriction empirical researchers do not wish to entertain, but it seems possible to relax the restriction. A major novelty of Pesaran's approach is that the cross-sectional correlation is eliminated by simple OLS without estimating factor-loading coefficients as others do.

BN use the models

$$
X_{it} = c_i + \lambda_i' f_t + y_{it} \tag{13.21}
$$

and

$$X_{it} = c_i + \beta_i t + \lambda_i' f_t + y_{it} \qquad (13.22)$$

where f_t is a vector of unobserved common factors, γ_i is a vector of factor loading coefficients and the y_{it} are idiosyncratic components that are independent across cross-sectional units. The number of factors is assumed to be unknown and f_t is allowed to be nonstationary. They estimate the number of factors, f_t and λ_i, that provides an estimate of y_{it}. The modified Fisher test (cf. Choi, 2001a,b) using the Dickey–Fuller test as an underlying test is then applied to the defactored and detrended time series to test for unit roots in y_{it}. Furthermore, they suggest methods that can test for the number of cointegrating vectors in f_t. Experimental results in BN confirm that their methods work reasonably well in finite samples.

MP's tests for panel unit roots are based on similar models, but the common factor appears as an error term for observed time series. Thus, the common factor should be stationary. Otherwise, it should be differenced. The models they use are

$$X_{it} = c_i + y_{it}$$

and

$$X_{it} = c_i + \beta_i t + y_{it},$$

with

$$y_{it} = \rho_i y_{i,t-1} + \lambda_i' f_t + \varepsilon_{it}.$$

After estimating the number of factors and λ_i, they defactor and detrend X_{it} and apply semiparametric, pooled panel t-tests for unit roots to $\{y_{it}\}$. The tests have a standard normal distribution in the limit, but they are subject to serious size distortions, particularly when the number of factors is estimated, as shown in their experimental results.

13.2.4.2 Other tests

When errors are cross-sectionally correlated, it is natural to consider SUR estimation for models (13.1) and (13.2). In fact, O'Connell (1998)[10] and Taylor and Sarno (1998) use it for examining the PPP hypothesis. But they do not provide a theoretical analysis of the SUR approach for panel unit root testing. In fact, it is straightforward to show that the limiting distributions of the SUR-based panel unit root tests depend on nuisance parameters in general, unless the AR order is one across all cross-sectional units (cf. Chang, 2004, and Breitung and Das, 2004, BD hereafter).[11] As a remedy for this, Chang (2004) uses bootstrapping. However, whether bootstrapped or not, the SUR method requires the condition $n \geq N$,[12] which may be too restrictive in applications. Even if the condition is satisfied, it is highly likely that the SUR method does not work properly unless n is substantially larger than N.[13]

Relative to the SUR-based tests, BD's robust t-test is more promising and does not require the condition $n \geq N$. Assuming the same number[14] of lagged differences, k, for all cross-sectional units and letting $E(u_t u_t') = \Omega$ for all t($u_t = [u_{1t}, \ldots, u_{Nt}]'$), it can be calculated using the following steps.

Step 1: Run the OLS regression[15]

$$\Delta y_{it} = \hat{\rho}_i y_{i,t-1} + \sum_{j=1}^{k} \hat{\phi}_{ij} \Delta y_{i,t-j} + \hat{u}_{it}.$$

Step 2: Calculate

$$y_{it}^* = y_{it} - \sum_{j=1}^{k} \hat{\phi}_{ij} y_{i,t-j}.$$

This behaves like a unit root process under the null.[16]

Step 3: The robust t-test for panel unit roots is defined by

$$t_{rob} = \frac{\sum_{t=2}^{n} y_{t-1}^{*\prime} \Delta y_t^*}{\sqrt{\sum_{t=2}^{n} y_{t-1}^{*\prime} \hat{\Omega} y_{t-1}^*}},$$

where $y_t^* = [y_{1t}^*, \ldots, y_{Nt}^*]'$ and $\hat{\Omega}$ is a consistent estimator of Ω using $\hat{u}_{it}$.

BD shows that t_{rob} has a standard normal distribution in the limit as $n \to \infty$ and $N \to \infty$ and that it has good finite sample properties.

Another method that can profitably be used for cross-sectionally correlated panels is subsampling. Let ξ_{Nn} be a panel unit root test that uses the whole sample. Its limiting distribution is likely to depend on nuisance parameters for cross-sectionally correlated panels. As a way to approximate the limiting distribution, letting ξ_{Nbs} be a panel unit root test that uses the subsample $\{y_{is}, \ldots, y_{i,s+b-1}\}_{i=1}^{N}$, consider the statistic

$$L_{Nnb}^{\xi}(x) = \frac{1}{n-b+1} \sum_{s=1}^{n-b+1} 1\{\xi_{Nbs} \leq x\}, \tag{13.23}$$

where if $1\{\xi_{Nbs} \leq x\} = 1$ if $\xi_{Nbs} \leq x$ and $1\{\xi_{Nbs} \leq x\} = 0$ if $\xi_{Nbs} > x$. If $b \to \infty$ and $b/n \to 0$ as $n \to \infty$, $L_{Nnb}^{\xi}(x)$ approximates the limiting cumulative distribution uniformly in x for fixed N and can thus be used for panel unit root testing. Details for this are reported in Choi and Chue (2004). Choi and Chue subsample the LLC, IPS and combination tests for panel unit roots and report that the subsample method works well in finite samples.

13.2.5 Stationarity tests for cross-sectionally correlated panels

In the light of the various methods introduced so far for cross-sectionally correlated panels, it would seem to be straightforward to devise tests for the null of stationarity. Bai and Ng (2004) extend their method for panel unit root testing to tests for the null of stationarity. Using models (13.21) and (13.22), they defactor and detrend the series and apply Kwiatkowski, Phillips, Schmidt and Shin's (1992) tests and the modified Fisher test to test the null of stationarity for idiosyncratic errors. They also apply Kwiatkowski, Phillips, Schmidt and Shin's tests to the estimated factors. Tests for the null of stationarity are subject to size distortions in general and Bai and Ng's tests are not exceptions.[17] When they are used in applications, researchers should bear in mind that they tend to overreject under the null of stationarity.

If the number of cross-sectional units is not large, Choi and Ahn's (1999) multivariate tests for stationarity can also be used for cross-sectionally correlated panels. Unlike Bai and Ng's (2004) tests, these tests are applied directly to observed time series. In addition, Choi and Chue's (2004) subsampling method can also be used. In relation (13.23), by replacing ξ_{Nbs} by a panel test for the null of stationarity – for example, Hadri's (2000) test – we can obtain the critical values of the test under cross-sectional correlation.

13.3 Panel regressions

13.3.1 OLS and modified OLS estimation

It is well known that the OLS estimator is consistent in cointegrating regressions even when the errors and regressors are correlated. But because the OLS estimator has second-order bias, various modifications of the OLS estimator have been proposed in the context of time series (see, e.g., Phillips and Hansen, 1990; Saikkonen, 1991) and these are known to be more efficient than the OLS estimator.

Cointegrating panel regressions are studied in Kao and Chiang (2000), Pedroni (2000), Phillips and Moon (1999) and Mark and Sul (2003). Kao and Chiang, Pedroni and Phillips and Moon consider the model

$$y_{it} = \beta_i + \alpha' x_{it} + u_{it}, \quad (t = 1, \ldots, n; i = 1, \ldots, N)$$
$$x_{it} = x_{i,t-1} + \varepsilon_{it},$$
(13.24)

for which the assumption of cross-sectional independence is maintained. Mark and Sul study a similar model with a common time-specific factor and an individual-specific linear trend. We will focus on model (13.24) for the sake of simplicity. First, we consider OLS estimation of this model under regressor-error dependence. The following OLS estimation result is reported in Kao and Chiang. Letting $w_{it} = (u_{it}, \varepsilon'_{it})'$, assume

$$\frac{1}{\sqrt{n}} \sum_{t=1}^{[nr]} w_{it} \Rightarrow B_i(r)$$

where $B_i(r)$ is a vector Brownian motion with the homogenous long-run covariance matrix

$$\Omega = \sum_{j=-\infty}^{\infty} E(w_{ij} w'_{i0}) = \Sigma + \Gamma + \Gamma' = \begin{bmatrix} \Omega_{uu} & \Omega_{u\varepsilon} \\ \Omega'_{u\varepsilon} & \Omega_{\varepsilon\varepsilon} \end{bmatrix},$$

with $\Gamma = \sum_{j=1}^{\infty} E(w_{ij}w_{i0}')$ and $\Sigma = E(w_{i0}w_{i0}')$. We also let $\Delta = \Sigma + \Gamma$. The matrices Σ, Γ and Δ are partitioned conformably as

$$\Sigma = \begin{bmatrix} \Sigma_{uu} & \Sigma_{u\varepsilon} \\ \Sigma_{u\varepsilon}' & \Sigma_{\varepsilon\varepsilon} \end{bmatrix}, \quad \Gamma = \begin{bmatrix} \Gamma_{uu} & \Gamma_{u\varepsilon} \\ \Gamma_{u\varepsilon}' & \Gamma_{\varepsilon\varepsilon} \end{bmatrix} \quad \text{and} \quad \Delta = \begin{bmatrix} \Delta_{uu} & \Delta_{u\varepsilon} \\ \Delta_{u\varepsilon}' & \Delta_{\varepsilon\varepsilon} \end{bmatrix}.$$

Kao and Chiang (2000) report that the OLS estimator of α, defined by

$$\hat{\alpha} = \left(\sum_{i=1}^{N} \sum_{t=1}^{n} (x_{it} - \bar{x}_i)(x_{it} - \bar{x}_i)' \right)^{-1} \left(\sum_{i=1}^{N} \sum_{t=1}^{n} (x_{it} - \bar{x}_i)(y_{it} - \bar{y}_i) \right),$$

has the limiting distribution

$$\sqrt{N}n(\hat{\alpha} - \alpha) - \sqrt{N}\delta_{Nn} \Rightarrow N(0, 6\Omega_{\varepsilon\varepsilon}^{-1}\Omega_{u\varepsilon}) \quad \text{as } n \to \infty \quad \text{and} \quad N \to \infty,$$

where

$$\delta_{Nn} = \left(\frac{1}{Nn^2} \sum_{i=1}^{N} \sum_{t=1}^{n} (x_{it} - \bar{x}_i)(x_{it} - \bar{x}_i)' \right)^{-1}$$

$$\times \left(\frac{1}{N} \sum_{i=1}^{N} \Omega_{\varepsilon\varepsilon}^{1/2} \left(\int_0^1 \bar{W}_i(r)dW_i'(r) \right) \Omega_{\varepsilon\varepsilon}^{-1/2}\Omega_{u\varepsilon}' + \Delta_{u\varepsilon}' \right)$$

and $\bar{W}_i(r) = W_i(r) - \int_0^1 W_i(s)ds$. This result shows that the pooled panel OLS estimator is inconsistent under regressor-error dependence, in contrast with the consistency property of time series OLS under the same circumstances.

To remedy the deficiencies of pooled panel OLS, Kao and Chiang (2000), Pedroni (2000), and Phillips and Moon (1999) consider the fully modified OLS (FM-OLS) estimator of α, defined by

$$\hat{\alpha}_{FM} = \left(\sum_{i=1}^{N} \sum_{t=1}^{n} (x_{it} - \bar{x}_i)(x_{it} - \bar{x}_i)' \right)^{-1} \left(\sum_{i=1}^{N} \left(\sum_{t=1}^{n} (x_{it} - \bar{x}_i)\hat{y}_{it}^+ - n\hat{\Delta}_{\varepsilon u}^+ \right) \right),$$

where $\hat{y}_{it}^+ = y_{it} - \hat{\Omega}_{u\varepsilon}\hat{\Omega}_{\varepsilon\varepsilon}^{-1}\Delta x_{it}$ and $\hat{\Delta}_{\varepsilon u}^+ = \hat{\Delta}_{\varepsilon u} - \hat{\Delta}_{\varepsilon\varepsilon}\hat{\Omega}_{\varepsilon\varepsilon}^{-1}\hat{\Omega}_{\varepsilon u}$. This estimator extends the FM-OLS estimator of Phillips and Hansen (1990) to panel regression. As $n \to \infty$ and $N \to \infty$,

$$\sqrt{N}n(\hat{\alpha}_{FM} - \alpha) \Rightarrow N(0, 6\Omega_{\varepsilon\varepsilon}^{-1}\Omega_{u.\varepsilon})$$

where $\Omega_{u.\varepsilon} = \Omega_{uu} - \Omega_{u\varepsilon}\Omega_{\varepsilon\varepsilon}^{-1}\Omega_{\varepsilon u}$. This result shows that the pooled FM-OLS estimator is consistent and normally distributed in the limit. Kao and Chiang also consider the pooled FM-OLS estimator for heterogeneous long-run variance matrices. Details can be found in their article.

Kao and Chiang (2000) also consider the leads-and-lags regression

$$y_{it} = \beta_i + \alpha' x_{it} + \sum_{j=-q}^{q} \zeta'_{ij} \Delta x_{it} + \dot{v}_{it}$$

(see Phillips and Loretan, 1991; Saikkonen, 1991; and Stock and Watson, 1993) and show that the pooled OLS estimator of the parameter vector α from this regression has the same distribution as the FM-OLS estimator.

13.3.2   IV estimation

The asymptotic normality of the pooled FM-OLS estimator depends on the assumption of exact unit roots for all the regressors. When regressors are endogenous and nearly nonstationary, in the sense that $x_{it} - \exp(C/n)x_{i,\,t-1}$ is $I(0)$ with C being a constant matrix, Kauppi (2000) shows that the FM-OLS estimator does not, in general, provide asymptotically normal distributions.

By contrast, Choi (2002) shows that IV estimation can be used for panel regression with endogenous, nearly nonstationary regressors. To understand this estimator, consider a simple model,

$$y_{it} = \beta + \alpha x_{it} + u_{it},$$

where x_{it} is nearly nonstationary and u_{it} is the $I(0)$ disturbance term. When $N=1$, the IV estimator, $\tilde{\alpha}$, using a nearly integrated process, z_{1t}, as an instrument, has the following limiting distribution under the proper moment conditions (cf. Phillips, 1988):

$$n(\tilde{\alpha} - \alpha) \Rightarrow \frac{\int_0^1 \bar{K}_{z_1}(r)dB_{u_1}(r)}{\int_0^1 \bar{K}_{x_1}(r)\bar{K}_{z_1}(r)dr}, \qquad \text{as } n \to \infty, \tag{13.25}$$

where $\bar{K}_{x1}(r)$ and $\bar{K}_{z1}(r)$ are Ornstein–Uhlenbeck processes and $B_{u_1}(r)$ is the weak limit of $\frac{1}{\sqrt{n}}\Sigma_{t=1}^{[nr]} u_{1t}$. If $E[\epsilon_{z_{1t}} u_{1s}] = 0$ for all t and s (i.e., z_{1t} are strictly exogenous), $\int_0^1 \bar{K}_{z_1}(r)dB_{u_1}(r)$ is a mixture normal random variable. But still, the weak limit in relation (13.25) is not a mixture normal random variable because $\bar{K}_{x_1}(r)$ is not independent of $B_{u_1}(r)$ due to the endogeneity of x_t. Thus, standard hypothesis testing cannot be performed based on the IV estimator $\tilde{\alpha}$. The situation does not change even when $C=0$. This indicates that IV estimation is not suitable for use in the time series context when regressors are endogenous and have either a near or exact unit root.

However, as $n \to \infty$, the panel IV estimator of parameter α, $\check{\alpha}$, has the weak limit

$$\sqrt{N}n(\check{\alpha} - \alpha) = \frac{\sum_{i=1}^{N} \sum_{t=1}^{n} (z_{it} - \bar{z}_i)u_{it}/(n\sqrt{N})}{\sum_{i=1}^{N} \sum_{t=1}^{n} (z_{it} - \bar{z}_i)(x_{it} - \bar{x}_i)/(n^2 N)}$$

$$\Rightarrow \frac{\sum_{i=1}^{N} \int_0^1 \bar{K}_{z_i}(r)dB_{u_i}(r)/\sqrt{N}}{\sum_{i=1}^{N} \int_0^1 \bar{K}_{z_i}(r)\bar{K}_{x_i}(r)dr/N}. \tag{13.26}$$

The numerator of the weak limit in relation (13.26) is a standardized sum of zero-mean random variables when $E(z_{it}u_{is}) = 0$, for all t and s, and the denominator is a standardized sum of random variables. Thus, when proper conditions are given and N is large, we may apply the central limit theorem and law of large numbers for the numerator and denominator, respectively, which leads to the asymptotic normality result for the panel estimator. This intuition forms the basis of the asymptotic normality results for more involved IV estimators such as the Within-IV-OLS, IV-GLS and Within-IV-GLS estimator in Choi (2002). Note that no modification of the IV estimator is required for the asymptotic normality results. The results in Choi (2002) show that the panel regression has an added advantage in the sense that the sharp assumption of unit roots for regressors can be relaxed for asymptotic normality of pooled estimators as long as the proper instruments are available.

13.3.3   Regressions for cross-sectionally correlated panels

Regressions for nonstationary, cross-sectionally correlated panels can be devised using experience from unit root testing. In regression model (13.24) with $I(1)$ regressors and dynamic factor structures for Δx_{it} and u_{it}, Pesaran's (2002) regression augmented by cross-section averages of the regressors and regressand can be used to deal with cross-sectionally correlated panels. Though Pesaran studies stationary regressions only, his method can readily be extended to nonstationary regressions.

Alternatively, one can use the SUR approach used in the panel unit root test for fixed N. Indeed, Mark, Ogaki and Sul (2000) and Moon and Perron (2004b) adopt this approach and show that the dynamic GLS estimator is most efficient. For fixed N, Choi and Chue's (2004) subsampling method can also be used for statistical inference on possibly nonstationary, cross-sectionally correlated panels. The method for this is similar to that for unit root testing.

13.3.4   Panel VAR

The panel VAR model with unit roots is studied in Binder, Hsiao and Pesaran (2003), extending the results of Hsiao, Pesaran and Tahmiscioglu (2002) to the case of VAR and unit roots. They consider the panel VAR model of order one,

$$\mathbf{w}_{it} = (I_m - \Phi)\mu_i + \Phi \mathbf{w}_{i, t-1} + \varepsilon_{it}, \quad (i = 1, \ldots, N; t = 1, \ldots, n), \tag{13.27}$$

where Φ denotes an $m \times m$ matrix of slope coefficients, μ_i is an $m \times 1$ vector of individual-specific effects, ε_{it} is an $m \times 1$ vector of disturbances and I_m denotes the identity matrix of dimension $m \times m$. This model is equivalent to the VAR(1) model for $\mathbf{w}_{it} - \mu_i$ with coefficient matrix Φ. For model (13.27), it is assumed that the eigenvalues of Φ are either equal to unity or fall inside the unit circle. For fixed n, Binder, Hsiao and Pesaran derive asymptotic $(N \to \infty)$ normality of the QMLEs (Quasi Maximum Likelihood Estimators) using specifications of both random and fixed effects. These distributions are robust to the presence of unit roots. They also study a consistent GMM estimator, but favor the fixed effects QMLE over it in terms of efficiency. In addition, using standard orthogonality conditions, Binder, Hsiao and Pesaran show how the presence of unit roots causes the GMM estimators to fail. However, because n is fixed in their work, homogeneity of the VAR coefficient should be imposed, which may be considered too restrictive in applications using VAR.

13.4 Tests for panel cointegration

As is the case with time series analysis, there are two types of cointegration tests for panel data in the literature: residual-based tests and tests based on vector autoregressive processes. This section introduces both types of tests.

13.4.1 Residual-based panel cointegration tests

Suppose that y_{it} and x_{it} are $I(1)$ and noncointegrated. Let $z_{i\cdot} = \frac{1}{n}\sum_{t=1}^{n} z_{it}$ be the time series average of $\{z_{it}\}$ for individual i. Then, in the panel least squares regression

$$y_{it} - y_{i\cdot} = \hat{\alpha}'(x_{it} - x_{i\cdot}) + \hat{u}_{it}, \tag{13.28}$$

$\hat{u}_{it}$ will behave like an integrated process for large n and N.[18] Thus, applying unit root tests to $\hat{u}_{it}$ provides tests for the null of noncointegration. This is the idea used in Kao (1999) and Pedroni (1999).

Kao (1999) considers his tests in a bivariate setting and assumes for i

$$\Sigma = E\begin{pmatrix} \Delta y_{it} \\ \Delta x_{it} \end{pmatrix}(\Delta y_{it} \quad \Delta x_{it})' = \begin{bmatrix} \Sigma_{yy} & \Sigma_{yx} \\ \Sigma_{xy} & \Sigma_{xx} \end{bmatrix}$$

and

$$\Omega = E\left[\sum_{t=1}^{n}\begin{pmatrix} \Delta y_{it} \\ \Delta x_{it} \end{pmatrix}\right]\left[\sum_{t=1}^{n}\begin{pmatrix} \Delta y_{it} \\ \Delta x_{it} \end{pmatrix}\right]' = \begin{bmatrix} \Omega_{yy} & \Omega_{yx} \\ \Omega_{xy} & \Omega_{xx} \end{bmatrix}.$$

Note that Σ and Ω can be estimated using $\{\Delta y_{it}, \Delta x_{it}\}$, the latter by the method of long-run variance estimation. For the case where Δy_{it} and Δx_{it} are correlated for all i, Kao considers the following modifications of the Dickey–Fuller coefficient and t-tests applied to $\hat{u}_{it}$

$$DF_{\rho}^{*} = \frac{\sqrt{N}n(\hat{\rho}-1) + 3\sqrt{N}\hat{\sigma}_{v}^{2}/\hat{\sigma}_{0v}^{2}}{\sqrt{3 + (36\hat{\sigma}_{v}^{4}/5\hat{\sigma}_{0v}^{4})}},$$

$$DF_{t}^{*} = t_{\rho} + \frac{\sqrt{6N}\hat{\sigma}_{v}/2\hat{\sigma}_{0v}}{\sqrt{(\hat{\sigma}_{0v}^{2}/2\hat{\sigma}_{v}^{2}) + (3\hat{\sigma}_{v}^{2}/10\hat{\sigma}_{0v}^{2})}},$$

where $\hat{\rho} = \sum_{i=1}^{N} \sum_{t=2}^{n} \hat{u}_{it}\hat{u}_{i,t-1} / \sum_{i=1}^{N} \sum_{t=2}^{n} \hat{u}_{i,t-1}^2, t_\rho = (\hat{\rho} - 1)/\sqrt{s_e^2 \left(\sum_{i=1}^{N} \sum_{t=2}^{n} \hat{u}_{it-1}^2 \right)^{-1}}$

with $s_e^2 = \frac{1}{Nn} \sum_{i=1}^{N} \sum_{t=2}^{n} (\hat{u}_{it} - \hat{\rho}\hat{u}_{it-1})^2, \hat{\sigma}_v^2 = \hat{\Sigma}_{yy} - \hat{\Sigma}_{yx}\hat{\Sigma}_{xx}^{-1}$ and $\hat{\sigma}_{0v}^2 = \hat{\Omega}_{yy} - \hat{\Omega}_{yx}\hat{\Omega}_{xx}^{-1}$. Note that $\hat{\rho}$ is the pooled AR(1) coefficient estimator using $\{\hat{u}_{it}\}$ and t_ρ is the associated, conventional t-test for a unit root. The modifications are needed to make the tests have the following limiting distributions:

$$DF_\rho^*, DF_t^* \Rightarrow N(0, 1) \quad \text{as } n \to \infty \quad \text{and} \quad N \to \infty.$$

Extending Kao's tests to the case of multiple regressors is straightforward. No changes in the tests are required except that $\hat{\sigma}_v^2$ and $\hat{\sigma}_{0v}^2$ now require estimating vectors and matrices. In addition, Kao also considers a modification of the augmented Dickey–Fuller test using $\{\hat{u}_{it}\}$.

Pedroni (1999) bases his test on the regression residuals of regression (13.28). He introduces seven tests, but simulation results in Gutierrez (2003) indicate that the group ρ-test is most promising. Similar to the IPS test, the test is a normalized sum of Phillips and Ouliaris' (1990) coefficient test for cointegration using the residuals from the i-th individual. The normalization requires the mean and variance of Phillips and Ouliaris' (1990) test, which are reported in Pedroni. In addition, the test allows the long-run variance of $\{\Delta y_{it}, \Delta x_{it}\}$ to be heterogeneous.

McCoskey and Kao (1998) consider the null of cointegration. For the test, we run Phillips and Hansen's (1990) FM-OLS or the dynamic least squares of Saikkonen (1991), Stock and Watson (1993), and Phillips and Loretan (1991) on each individual. The residuals from the regressions are used to formulate a test similar to (13.20). McCoskey and Kao use simulation to provide the moments required to formulate the test. In the limit, the test follows a standard normal distribution.

All the tests discussed so far assume cross-sectional independence. Residual-based tests for cointegration that incorporate cross-sectional correlation are not yet available. But, for fixed N, the critical values of the tests under cross-sectional correlation can be estimated by subsampling. Details can be found in Choi and Chue (2004).

13.4.2 Panel VAR cointegration tests

Larsson, Lyhagen and Löthgren (2001) consider the heterogeneous vector error-correction model of order k_i,

$$\Delta Y_{it} = \Pi_i Y_{i,t-1} + \sum_{j=1}^{k_i} \Gamma_{ij} \Delta Y_{i,t-j} + \varepsilon_{it}, \tag{13.29}$$

where the p-dimensional vector $\varepsilon_{it} \overset{iid}{\sim} N_p(0, \Omega_i)$. Conditions for Johansen's (1988) likelihood ratio test are assumed to be satisfied. Larsson, Lyhagen and Löthgren test the null hypothesis

$$H_0 : \text{rank}(\Pi_i) = r_i \le r \quad \text{for all } i = 1, \ldots, N \tag{13.30}$$

against the alternative

$$H_1 : \text{rank}(\Pi_i) = p \quad \text{for all } i = 1, \ldots, N.$$

Denote Johansen's likelihood ratio test for this hypothesis for individual i by $LR_{in}\{H(r)|H(p)\},$[19] and the cross-section average of $LR_{in}\{H(r)|H(p)\}$ by $LRB_{N_n}\{H(r)|H(p)\}$. Then, Larsson, Lyhagen and Löthgren's test is defined by

$$\Upsilon\{H(r)|H(p)\} = \frac{\sqrt{N}(LRB_{Nn} - E(Z_{p-r}))}{\sqrt{Var(Z_{p-r})}}$$

and its limiting distribution is $N(0,1)$ as N and n go to infinity such that $\sqrt{N}/n \to 0$. Essentially, this test uses the same idea as in IPS. Using combination tests for the null hypothesis (13.30) would also be possible, though it has not been pursued in the literature. One shortcoming of this test is that cross-sectional units are assumed to be independent.

Extending Larsson, Lyhagen and Löthgren (2001), Larsson and Lyhagen (1999) consider the stacked vector error-correction model

$$
\begin{bmatrix} \Delta Y_{1t} \\ \vdots \\ \Delta Y_{Nt} \end{bmatrix} = \begin{bmatrix} \Pi_{11} & \Pi_{12} & \cdots & \Pi_{1N} \\ \Pi_{21} & \Pi_{22} & & \\ \vdots & & \ddots & \\ \Pi_{N1} & \Pi_{N2} & & \Pi_{NN} \end{bmatrix} \begin{bmatrix} Y_{1,t-1} \\ \vdots \\ Y_{N,t-1} \end{bmatrix}
$$
$$
+ \cdots + \sum_{j=1}^{k} \begin{bmatrix} \Gamma_{11,j} & \cdots & \Gamma_{1N,j} \\ \vdots & & \vdots \\ \Gamma_{N1,j} & \cdots & \Gamma_{NN,j} \end{bmatrix} \begin{bmatrix} \Delta Y_{1,t-j} \\ \vdots \\ \Delta Y_{N,t-j} \end{bmatrix} + \begin{bmatrix} \varepsilon_{1t} \\ \vdots \\ \varepsilon_{Nt} \end{bmatrix},
$$

and assume $\begin{bmatrix} \varepsilon_{1t} \\ \vdots \\ \varepsilon_{Nt} \end{bmatrix} \sim N(0, \Omega)$ without any restrictions on the matrix Ω except that it should be positive definite. They assume

$$\text{rank}(\Pi) = \sum_{i=1}^{N} r_i, \quad 0 \le r_i < p,$$

with $\Pi = (\Pi_{ij})_{i,j=1,\ldots,N}$ and that the matrix Π is written as

$$\Pi = AB',$$

where the matrix B is restricted to be

$$
B = \begin{bmatrix} \beta_{11} & & \underset{\sim}{0} \\ & \ddots & \\ \underset{\sim}{0} & & \beta_{NN} \end{bmatrix}.
$$

These restrictions, $\beta_{ij} = 0 \, (i \neq j)$, imply that cointegrating relationships are allowed only within each of the N individuals in the panel. There are no restrictions on the short-run dynamics in this model because matrix A is not restricted. They consider the same null and alternative hypothesis as in Larsson, Lyhagen and Löthgren (2001) and devise the likelihood ratio test for finite N.

Groen and Kleibergen (2003) consider stacking model (13.29) (with $k_i = 0$) and base their tests for cointegration on the model

$$
\Delta Y_t - \begin{pmatrix} \Pi_1 & & \underset{\sim}{0} \\ & \ddots & \\ \underset{\sim}{0} & & \Pi_N \end{pmatrix} Y_{t-1} + \varepsilon_t \tag{13.31}
$$

$$
= \Pi_A Y_{t-1} + \varepsilon_t,
$$

where

$$
Y_t = \begin{pmatrix} Y_{1t} \\ \vdots \\ Y_{Nt} \end{pmatrix}, \varepsilon_t \sim N(0, \Omega) \quad \text{and} \quad \Omega = \begin{pmatrix} \Omega_{11} & \cdots & \Omega_{1N} \\ \vdots & & \vdots \\ \Omega_{N1} & \cdots & \Omega_{NN} \end{pmatrix}.
$$

There are no restrictions on the variance–covariance matrix Ω for model (13.31) so that cross-sectional correlation is allowed. But the coefficient matrix Π_A is restricted to being off-diagonal. If the number of cointegrating vectors is r for all individuals, model (13.31) is written as

$$
\Delta Y_t = \begin{pmatrix} \alpha_1 \beta_1' & & \underset{\sim}{0} \\ & \ddots & \\ \underset{\sim}{0} & & \alpha_N \beta_N' \end{pmatrix} Y_{t-1} + \varepsilon_t
$$

$$
= \Pi_B Y_{t-1} + \varepsilon_t,
$$

where $\beta_i = \begin{bmatrix} I_r \\ -\beta_{2i} \end{bmatrix}$. A more restrictive model they consider is

$$
\Delta Y_t = \begin{pmatrix} \alpha_1 \beta' & & \underset{\sim}{0} \\ & \ddots & \\ \underset{\sim}{0} & & \alpha_N \beta' \end{pmatrix} Y_{t-1} + \varepsilon_t
$$

$$
= \Pi_C Y_{t-1} + \varepsilon_t,
$$

which assumes the common cointegrating vector β for all individuals. Groen and Kleibergen consider testing

$$H_0 \, : \, \Pi_B \quad \text{vs} \quad H_1 \, : \, \Pi_A$$

and

$$H_0 \, : \, \Pi_C \quad \text{vs} \quad H_1 \, : \, \Pi_A$$

by using likelihood ratio tests for both fixed and infinite N. The test for infinite N again uses essentially the same idea as in IPS. They also consider extending these tests to a model of higher-order dynamics and a model with deterministic components.

Both Larsson and Lyhagen (1999) and Groen and Kleibergen (2003) improve on Larsson, Lyhagen and Löthgren (2001) by allowing cross-sectional correlation, but their tests also depend on the restrictive assumption that cointegration is allowed only within each individual.

13.5   Other topics and further comments

Moon and Phillips (2004) study a generalized method of moments approach to the estimation of common autoregressive roots near unity. Assuming that the localizing parameter takes a nonpositive value, they establish the consistency of the GMM estimator and derive its limiting distribution.

Nonlinear, nonstationary panel regressions are still at the infant stage and have not yet been studied much. One notable exception is Jin (2004), who studies discrete choice nonstationary panels with large n and N. She derives consistency and asymptotic normality of the MLE. An application to exchange rate regime choice is also reported.

Econometric methods for nonstationary panels have developed at a rapid pace for the last few years. Nowadays, more focus is on cross-sectionally correlated panels because these are more realistic in applications. Attention is still being given to the question of how best we can model cross-sectional correlation and accommodate it in econometric theory for nonstationary panels. For nonlinear models, this will be a more challenging problem. Empirical researchers should also re-examine what has been done based on the assumption of independent panels using more recent methods for dependent panels. Many surprises may be hidden there. Using nonlinear panel data models is also deemed to be a promising path for empirical research. Unlike in time series analysis, more data can be used for parameter estimation in nonlinear panel data analysis which may bring more reliable estimation results. These await more endeavors and challenges from researchers.

Acknowledgments

The author thanks Kerry Patterson, Donggyu Sul, Roger Moon and Benoit Perron for helpful comments. The author acknowledges financial support for this paper from the RGC Competitive Earmarked Research Grant 2003–2004 under Project No. HKUST6223/03H.

Notes

1. Subsequently, Levin, Lin and Chu (2002).
2. An EconLit search of May, 2004, provided more than 150 papers that use econometric methods for nonstationary panels.
3. Quah (1994) also studies panel unit root tests for large numbers of time series observations and cross-sectional units. But the model he considers seems to be too specialized for practical use.
4. See Baltagi (2001) and Hsiao (2003) for the literature of dynamic panels.
5. LLC uses the $AR(1)$ model with ARMA residuals. From a practical viewpoint, this model and the autoregressive model do not have any differences for unit root testing because LLC also use the autoregressive model as an approximation to their $AR(1)$ model.
6. LLC use $n - \bar{k} - 1$ instead of n. Using n simplifies the discussions without bringing any changes in the limiting distribution.
7. These are Sargan–Bhargava-type tests (cf. Sargan and Bhargava, 1983), using different detrending methods.
8. A related paper is Choi (2001b), which uses the model with $u_{it} = \gamma_i + f_t + \varepsilon_{it}$. Cross-sectional demeaning can eliminate the cross-sectional correlation embodied by f_t in this model.
9. Pesaran (2003) assumes homogenous AR processes.
10. O'Connell considers only the $AR(1)$ model.
11. However, Breitung and Das' GLS-based test has a standard normal limiting distribution. Their test is calculated using methods different from those of Taylor and Sarno (1998).
12. Otherwise, the estimator of the variance–covariance matrix becomes singular.
13. See the simulation results in BD.
14. If this condition is not satisfied, the maximum AR order may be used as the common AR order.
15. For the AR model with an intercept, BD suggests using $y_{it} - y_{i0}$ instead of y_{it}.
16. Suppose for simplicity that $\Delta y_{it} = \rho_i y_{i,t-1} + \varphi_{i1} \Delta y_{i,t-1} + \mu_i + u_{it}$. Then, $y_{it} - \varphi_{i1} y_{i,t-1} = y_{i,t-1} - \varphi_{i1} y_{i,t-2} + \mu_i + u_{it}$ which shows that $y_{it} - \varphi_{i1} y_{i,t-1}$ is a unit root process. BD shows that $y_{it} - \hat{\varphi}_{i1} y_{i,t-1}$ resembles a unit root process in the limit.
17. Using Lanne and Saikkonen's (2003) new procedure may improve the situation.
18. Since $\hat{\alpha}$ converges to a constant vector in probability in this regression (cf. Phillips and Moon, 1999), $\hat{u}_{it}$ is a linear combination of y_{it} and x_{it} in the limit.
19. The weak limit Z_{p-r} is derived in Johansen (1988). Its simulated moments required for Larsson, Lyhagen and Löthgren's test are reported in Table 1 of their paper.

References

Bai, J. and S. Ng (2002) A panic attack on unit roots and cointegration. Mimeo, Boston College.

Bai, J. and S. Ng (2004) A new look at panel testing of stationarity and the PPP hypothesis. Mimeo, NYU.

Baltagi, B. (2001) *Econometric Analysis of Panel Data*, 2nd edition. New York: Wiley.

Baltagi, B. and C. Kao (2000) Nonstationary panels, cointegration in panels and dynamic panels: A survey. In B. Baltagi (ed.), *Advances in Econometrics 15*. New York: JAI, pp. 7–51.

Banerjee, A. (1999) Panel data unit roots and cointegration: An overview. *Oxford Bulletin of Economics and Statistics* 61, 607–29.

Binder, M., C. Hsiao and M.H. Pesaran (2002) Estimation and inference in short panel vector autoregressions with unit roots and cointegration. Mimeo, Trinity College, Cambridge.

Bleaney, M. and S.J. Leybourne (2003) Real exchange rate dynamics under the current float: A re-examination. *Manchester School* 71, 156–71.

Breitung, J. and S. Das (2004) Panel unit root tests under cross sectional dependence. Mimeo, University of Bonn.

Breitung, J. and W. Meyer (1994) Testing for unit roots in panel data: Are wages on different bargaining levels cointegrated? *Applied Economics* **26**, 353–61.

Chang, Y. (2004) Bootstrap unit root tests in panels with cross-sectional dependency. *Journal of Econometrics* **120**, 263–93.

Choi, I. (2001a) Unit root tests for panel data. *Journal of International Money and Finance* **20**, 249–72.

Choi, I. (2001b) Unit root tests for cross-sectionally correlated panels. In D. Corbae, S. Durlauf and B. Hansen (eds), *Econometric Theory and Practice: Frontiers of Analysis and Applied Research. Essays in Honor of Peter C.B. Phillips*. New York: Cambridge University Press.

Choi, I. (2002) Instrumental variables estimation of a nearly nonstationary, heterogeneous error component model. *Journal of Econometrics* **109**, 1–32.

Choi, I. and B.C. Ahn (1999) Testing the null of stationarity for multiple time series. *Journal of Econometrics* **88**, 41–77.

Choi, I. and T.K. Chue (2004) Subsampling hypothesis tests for nonstationary panels with applications to the PPP hypothesis. Mimeo, HKUST.

Coakley, J. and A.M. Fuertes (1997) New panel unit root tests of PPP. *Economics Letters* **57**, 17–22.

Culver, S.E. and D.H. Papell (1997) Is there a unit root in the inflation rate? Evidence from sequential break and panel data models. *Journal of Applied Econometrics* **12**, 435–44.

Edmond, C. (2001) Some panel cointegration models of international R&D spillovers. *Journal of Macroeconomics* **23**, 241–60.

Elliott, G., T.J. Rothenberg and J.H. Stock (1996). Efficient tests for an autoregressive unit root. *Econometrica* **64**, 813–36.

Estrin, S. and G. Urga (1997) *Convergence in output in transition economies: Central and Eastern Europe, 1970–1995*. Centre for Economic Policy Research Discussion Paper, 23.

Fleissig, A.R. and J. Strauss (2000) Panel unit root tests of purchasing power parity for price indices. *Journal of International Money and Finance* **19**, 489–506.

Fleissig, A. and J. Strauss (2001) Panel unit root tests of OECD stochastic convergence. *Review of International Economics* **9**, 153–62.

Frankel, J.A. and A.K. Rose (1996) A panel project on purchasing power parity: Mean reversion within and between countries. *Journal of International Economics* **40**, 209–24.

Frantzen, D. (1998) R&D, international technical diffusion and total factor productivity. *Kyklos* **51**, 489–508.

Funk, M. (2001) Trade and international R&D spillovers among OECD countries. *Southern Economic Journal* **67**, 725–36.

Gerdtham, U.G. and M. Löthgren (2000) On stationarity and cointegration of international health expenditure and GDP. *Journal of Health Economics* **19**, 461–75.

Gerdtham, U.G. and M. Löthgren (2002) New panel results on cointegration of international health expenditures and GDP. *Applied Economics* **34**, 1679–1686.

Groen, J.J.J. (2002) Cointegration and the monetary exchange rate model revisited. *Oxford Bulletin of Economics and Statistics* **64**, 361–80.

Groen, J.J.J. and F.R. Kleibergen (2003) Likelihood-based cointegration analysis in panels of vector error correction models. *Journal of Business and Economic Statistics* **21**, 295–318.

Gutierrez, L. (2003) On the power of panel cointegration tests: A Monte Carlo comparison. *Economics Letters* **80**, 105–11.

Gutierrez, L. and M.M. Gutierrez (2003) International R&D spillovers and productivity growth in the agricultural sector: A panel cointegration approach. *European Review of Agricultural Economics* **30**, 281–303.

Hadri, K. (2000) Testing for stationarity in heterogeneous panel data. *Econometrics Journal* **3**, 148–61.

Hansen, P. and A. King (1998) Health care expenditure and GDP: Panel data unit root test results—Comment. *Journal of Health Economics* **17**, 377–81.

Harris, R.D.F. and E. Tzavalis (1999) Inference for unit roots in dynamic panels where the time dimension is fixed. *Journal of Econometrics* **91**, 201–26.

Herwartz, H. and H.E. Reimers (2002) Testing the purchasing power parity in pooled systems of error correction models. *Japan and the World Economy* **14**, 45–62.

Holmes, M.J. (2002) Convergence in international output: Evidence from panel data unit root tests. *Journal of Economic Integration* **17**, 826–38.

Hsiao, C. (2003) *Analysis of Panel Data*, 2nd edn. New York: Cambridge University Press.

Hsiao, C., M.H. Pesaran and A.K. Tahmiscioglu (2002) Maximum likelihood estimation of fixed effects dynamic panel data models covering short time periods. *Journal of Econometrics* **109**, 107–50.

Im, K.S., M.H. Pesaran and S. Shin (2003) Testing for unit roots in heterogeneous panels. *Journal of Econometrics* **115**, 53–74.

Jewell, T., J. Lee, M. Tieslau and M.C. Strazicich (2003) Stationarity of health expenditures and GDP: Evidence from panel unit root tests with heterogeneous structural breaks. *Journal of Health Economics* **22**, 313–23.

Jin, S. (2004) Discrete choice modeling with nonstationary panels applied to exchange rate regime choice. Mimeo, Department of Economics, Yale University.

Johansen, S. (1988) Statistical analysis of cointegrating vectors. *Journal of Economic Dynamics and Control* **12**, 231–54.

Kao, C. (1999) Spurious regression and residual-based tests for cointegration in panel data. *Journal of Econometrics* **90**, 1–44.

Kao, C. and M.-H. Chiang (2000) On the estimation and inference of a cointegrated regression in panel data. In B. Baltagi (ed.), *Advances in Econometrics* **15**. New York: JAI, pp. 179–222.

Kao, C., M.-H. Chiang and B. Chen (1999) International R&D spillovers: an application of estimation and inference in panel cointegration. *Oxford Bulletin of Economics and Statistics* **61**, 691–709.

Kauppi, H. (2000) Panel data limit theory and asymptotic analysis of a panel regression with near integrated regressors. In B. Baltagi (ed.), *Advances in Econometrics* **15**. New York: JAI, pp. 239–74.

Kwiatkowski, D., P.C.B. Phillips, P. Schmidt and Y. Shin (1992) Testing the null hypothesis of stationarity against the alternative of a unit root: How sure are we that economic time series have a unit root? *Journal of Econometrics* **54**, 159–78.

Lanne, M. and P. Saikkonnen (2003) Reducing size distortions of parametric stationarity tests. *Journal of Time Series Analysis* **24**, 423–39.

Larsson, R. and J. Lyhagen (1999) Likelihood-based inference in multivariate panel cointegration model. Mimeo, Stockholm School of Economics.

Larsson, R., J. Lyhagen and M. Löthgren (2001) Likelihood-based cointegration tests in heterogeneous panels. *Econometrics Journal* **4**, 109–47.

Lee, H.Y. and J.L. Wu (2001) Mean reversion of inflation rates: evidence from 13 OECD countries. *Journal of Macroeconomics* **23**, 477–87.

Leon, L.M.A. (2002) Unemployment hysteresis in the US states and the EU: a panel approach. *Bulletin of Economic Research* **54**, 95–103.

Levin, A. and C.-F. Lin (1992) Unit root tests in panel data: Asymptotic and finite-sample properties. U.C. San Diego Discussion Paper 92–23.

Levin, A., C.-F. Lin and C.-S.J. Chu (2002) Unit root tests in panel data: Asymptotic and finite-sample properties. *Journal of Econometrics* **108**, 1–25.

Leybourne, S.J. and B.P.M. McCabe (1994) A consistent test for a unit root. *Journal of Business and Economic Statistics* **12**, 157–66.

Los, B. and B. Verspagen (2000) R&D spillovers and productivity: Evidence from US manufacturing microdata. *Empirical Economics* **25**, 127–48.

Lothian, J.R. (1997) Multi-country evidence on the behavior of purchasing power parity under the current float. *Journal of International Money and Finance* 16, 19–35.

Luintel, K.B. (2001) Heterogeneous panel unit root tests and purchasing power parity. *Manchester School Supplement* 69, 42–56.

MacDonald, R. (1996) Panel unit root tests and real exchange rates. *Economics Letters* 50, 7–11.

Maddala, G.S. and S. Wu (1999) A comparative study of unit root tests with panel data and a new simple test. *Oxford Bulletin of Economics and Statistics* 61, 631–52.

Mark, N., M. Ogaki and D. Sul (2000) Dynamic seemingly unrelated cointegrating regression. Mimeo, University of Auckland.

Mark, N.C. and D. Sul (2001) Nominal exchange rates and monetary fundamentals: Evidence from a small post-Bretton Woods panel. *Journal of International Economics* 53, 29–52.

Mark, N.C. and D. Sul (2003) Cointegration vector estimation by panel DOLS and long-run money demand. *Oxford Bulletin of Economics and Statistics* 65, 655–80.

McCoskey, S.K. (2002) Convergence in sub-Saharan Africa: A nonstationary panel data approach. *Applied Economics* 34, 819–29.

McCoskey, S. and C. Kao (1998) A residual-based test of the null of cointegration in panel data. *Econometric Review* 17, 57–84.

McCoskey, S.K. and T.M. Selden (1998) Health care expenditures and GDP: Panel data unit root test results. *Journal of Health Economics* 17, 369–76.

McDonald, G. and S. Hopkins (2002) Unit root properties of OECD health care expenditure and GDP data. *Health Economics* 11, 371–6.

Moon, H.R. and B. Perron (2004a) Testing for a unit root in panels with dynamic factors. *Journal of Econometrics* 122, 81–126.

Moon, H.R. and B. Perron (2004b) Efficient estimation of the SUR cointegration regression model and testing for purchasing power parity. Forthcoming in *Econometric Reviews*.

Moon, H.R., B. Perron and P.C.B. Phillips (2003) Incidental trends and the power of panel unit root tests. Mimeo, Cowles Foundation, Yale University.

Moon, H.R. and P.C.B. Phillips (2004) GMM estimation of autoregressive roots near unity with panel data. *Econometrica* 72, 467–522.

O'Connell, P.G.J. (1998) The overvaluation of purchasing power parity. *Journal of International Economics* 44, 1–19.

Oh, K.-Y. (1996) Purchasing power parity and unit root tests using panel data. *Journal of International Money and Finance* 15, 405–18.

Oh, K.-Y. (1999) Are exchange rates cointegrated with monetary model in panel data? *International Journal of Finance and Economics* 4, 147–54.

Okunade, A.A. and M.C. Karakus (2001) Unit root and cointegration tests: time-series versus panel estimates for international health expenditure models. *Applied Economics* 33, 1131–1137.

Papell, D.H. (1997) Searching for stationarity: purchasing power parity under the current float. *Journal of International Economics* 43, 313–32.

Pedroni, P. (1999) Critical values for cointegration tests in heterogeneous panels with multiple regressors. *Oxford Bulletin of Economics and Statistics* 61, 653–70.

Pedroni, P. (2000) Fully modified OLS for heterogeneous cointegrated panels and the case of purchasing power parity. In B. Baltagi (ed.), *Advances in Econometrics* 15. New York: JAI Press, pp. 93–130.

Pesaran, M.H. (2002) Estimation and inference in large heterogenous panels with cross-section dependence. Mimeo, Trinity College, Cambridge.

Pesaran, M.H. (2003) A simple panel unit root test in the presence of cross-section dependence. Mimeo, Trinity College, Cambridge.

Phillips, P.C.B. (1988) Multiple regression with integrated processes. In N.U. Prabhu (ed.), *Contemporary Mathematics 80*. Providence, RI: American Mathematical Society, pp. 79–105.

Phillips, P.C.B. and B. Hansen (1990) Statistical inference in instrumental variables regression with I(1) processes. *Review of Economic Studies* 57, 99–125.

Phillips, P.C.B. and M. Loretan (1991) Estimating long run economic equilibria. *Review of Economic Studies* 58, 407–36.

Phillips, P.C.B. and H. Moon (1999) Linear regression limit theory for nonstationary panel data. *Econometrica* 67, 1057–1112.

Phillips, P.C.B. and H. Moon (2000) Nonstationary panel data analysis: An overview of some recent developments. *Econometric Review* 19, 263–86.

Phillips, P.C.B. and S. Ouliaris (1990) Asymptotic properties of residual based tests for cointegration. *Econometrica* 58, 165–93.

Phillips, P.C.B. and D. Sul (2003) Dynamic panel estimation and homogeneity testing under cross section dependence. *Econometrics Journal* 6, 217–59.

Ploberger, W. and P.C.B. Phillips (2002) Optimal testing for unit roots in panel data. Mimeo, Cowles Foundation, Yale University.

Quah, D. (1994) Exploiting cross-section variations for unit root inference in dynamic panels. *Economics Letters* 44, 9–19.

Saikkonen, P. (1991) Asymptotically efficient estimation of cointegration regressions. *Econometric Theory* 7, 1–21.

Sargan, J.D. and A. Bhargava (1983) Maximum likelihood estimation of regression models with first order moving average errors when the root lies on the unit circle. *Econometrica* 51, 799–820.

Smith, L.V., S. Leybourne, T.-H. Kim and P. Newbold (2004) More powerful panel data unit root tests with an application to mean reversion in real exchange rates. *Journal of Applied Econometrics* 19, 147–70.

Smyth, R. (2003) Unemployment hysteresis in Australian states and territories: Evidence from panel data unit root tests. *Australian Economic Review* 36, 181–92.

Song, F.M. and Y. Wu (1998) Hysteresis in unemployment: Evidence from OECD countries. *Quarterly Review of Economics and Finance* 38, 181–92.

Stock, J.H. and M.W. Watson (1993) A simple estimator of cointegrating vectors in higher order integrated systems. *Econometrica* 61, 783–820.

Taylor, M.P. and L. Sarno (1998) The behavior of real exchange rates during the post-Bretton Woods period. *Journal of International Economics* 46, 281–312.

Wu, J.L. and S.L. Chen (1998) Foreign exchange market efficiency revisited. *Journal of International Money and Finance* 17, 831–8.

Wu, J.L. and S.L. Chen (2001) Mean reversion of interest rates in the Eurocurrency market. *Oxford Bulletin of Economics and Statistics* 63, 459–73.

Wu, J.L. and S.W. Wu (2001) Is purchasing power parity overvalued? *Journal of Money, Credit, and Banking* 33, 804–12.

Wu, Y. (1996) Are real exchange rates nonstationary? Evidence from a panel-data test. *Journal of Money, Credit, and Banking* 28, 54–63.

Wu, Y. and H. Zhang (1996) Mean reversion in interest rates: New evidence from a panel of OECD countries. *Journal of Money, Credit, and Banking* 28, 604–21.

Wu, Y. and H. Zhang (1997) Do interest rates follow unit root processes? Evidence from cross-maturity Treasury bill yields. *Review of Quantitative Finance and Accounting* 8, 69–81.

Yin, Y. and S. Wu (2000) Stationarity tests in heterogeneous panels. In B. Baltagi (ed.), *Advances in Econometrics* 15. New York: JAI, pp. 275–96.

14
Cointegration: An Overview

Søren Johansen

Abstract

An overview is given of cointegration analysis in the framework of the vector autoregressive model for processes integrated of order one. We find the representation of the solution and discuss briefly the role of the deterministic terms. We discuss the interpretation of cointegrating vectors and adjustment coefficients and show how many hypotheses can be formulated in terms of cointegrating vectors. The reduced rank approach to inference is discussed and we show that many hypotheses on cointegrating vectors and adjustment vectors can be estimated and tested using Gaussian likelihood methods. The asymptotic analysis is outlined and a small sample correction is discussed. The mixed Gaussian distribution is used for inference on the cointegrating vectors. Finally we treat briefly some further topics like rational expectations, analysis of explosive and seasonal roots and outline some results for the I(2) model. We conclude with a few results related to nonlinear cointegration and panel data cointegration.

14.1	Introduction and methodology	541
	14.1.1 The regression formulation	541
	14.1.2 The autoregressive formulation	542
	14.1.3 The unobserved component formulation	542
	14.1.4 The statistical methodology for the analysis of cointegration	542
14.2	The vector autoregressive process and Granger's Representation Theorem	544
	14.2.1 The stationary vector autoregressive process and the definition of integration and cointegration	544
	14.2.2 The Granger Representation Theorem	546
	14.2.3 The role of the deterministic terms	549
	14.2.4 Interpretation of cointegrating coefficients	550
14.3	Interpretation of the $I(1)$ model for cointegration	552
	14.3.1 Normalization of the parameters of the $I(1)$ model	552
	14.3.2 Hypotheses on the long-run coefficients β	553
	14.3.3 Hypotheses on the adjustment coefficients α and $\alpha_\perp$	554
	14.3.4 The structural error correction model	555
	14.3.5 Shocks, changes and impulse responses	556

14.4   Likelihood analysis of the $I(1)$ model   557
    14.4.1   Checking the specifications of the model   557
    14.4.2   Reduced rank regression   558
    14.4.3   Reduced rank regression in the $I(1)$ model and derivation
          of the rank test   559
    14.4.4   Hypothesis testing for the long-run coefficients β 560
    14.4.5   Tests on adjustment coefficients   561
    14.4.6   Partial systems   561
14.5   Asymptotic analysis   562
    14.5.1   The asymptotic distribution of the rank test   562
    14.5.2   Determination of cointegrating rank   563
    14.5.3   A small sample correction of the rank test   564
    14.5.4   The asymptotic distribution of β 565
14.6   Further topics in cointegration   567
    14.6.1   Rational expectations   568
    14.6.2   Seasonal cointegration   568
    14.6.3   Models for explosive roots   569
    14.6.4   The $I(2)$ model   570
    14.6.5   Nonlinear cointegration   571
    14.6.6   Panel data cointegration   573
14.7   Conclusion   573

14.1   Introduction and methodology

The phenomenon that nonstationary processes can have linear combinations that are stationary was termed cointegration by Granger (1983), who used it for modeling long-run economic relations. The paper by Engle and Granger (1987), which showed the equivalence of the error correction formulation and the phenomenon of cointegration, started a rapid development of the statistical and probabilistic analysis of the idea.

There are now three different ways of modeling cointegration in a statistical framework. To illustrate the ideas we formulate these in the simplest possible case, leaving out deterministic terms.

14.1.1   The regression formulation

The multivariate process $x_t = (x'_{1t}, x'_{2t})'$ of dimension $p = p_1 + p_2$ is given by the regression equations

$$x_{1t} = \beta' x_{2t} + u_{1t},$$
$$\Delta x_{2t} = u_{2t},$$

where we assume that u_t is a linear invertible process defined by i.i.d. errors ε_t with mean zero and finite variance. The assumptions behind the model imply that x_{2t} is nonstationary and not cointegrating, and hence that the cointegrating rank, p_1, is known so that the models for different ranks are not nested. The first estimation method used in this model is least squares regression, see Engle and Granger

(1987), which gives superconsistent estimators, as shown by Stock (1987), and which gives rise to residual-based tests for cointegration. It was shown by Phillips and Hansen (1990) and Park (1992) that a modification of the regression, involving a correction using the long-run variance of the process u_t, would give useful inference for the coefficients of the cointegrating relations, see also Phillips (1991).

14.1.2   The autoregressive formulation

In this case the process x_t is given by the equations

$$\Delta x_t = \alpha \beta' x_{t-1} + \varepsilon_t,$$

where ε_t are i.i.d. errors with mean zero and finite variance, and α and β are $p \times r$ matrices. The formulation allows modeling of both the long-run relations and the adjustment, or feedback, towards the attractor set $\{\beta' x = 0\}$ defined by the long-run relations, and this is the model we shall focus upon in this chapter. The models for different cointegrating ranks are nested and the rank can be analysed by like-lihood ratio tests. The methods usually applied for the analysis are derived from the Gaussian likelihood function (Johansen, 1996), which we shall discuss here: see also Ahn and Reinsel (1990) and Reinsel and Ahn (1992).

14.1.3   The unobserved component formulation

Let x_t be given by

$$x_t = \xi \eta' \sum_{i=1}^{t} \varepsilon_i + u_t$$

where u_t is a linear process, typically independent of the process ε_t, which is i.i.d. with mean zero and finite variance.

In this formulation too, the hypotheses of different ranks are nested. The parameters are linked to the autoregressive formulation by $\xi = \beta_\perp$ and $\eta = \alpha_\perp$, where for any $p \times r$ matrix a of rank $r \leq p$, we define $a_\perp$ as a $p \times (p - r)$ matrix of rank $p - r$, for which $a' a_\perp = 0$. Thus both adjustment and cointegration can be discussed in this formulation. Rather than testing for unit roots, one tests for stationarity, which is sometimes a more natural formulation. The estimation is usually per-formed by the Kalman filter, and the asymptotic theory of the rank tests has been worked out by Harvey and Nyblom (2000).

14.1.4   The statistical methodology for the analysis of cointegration

In this chapter we analyse cointegration as modeled by the vector autoregressive model

$$\Delta x_t = \alpha \beta' x_{t-1} + \sum_{i=1}^{k-1} \Gamma_i \Delta x_{t-i} + \Phi d_t + \varepsilon_t, \tag{14.1}$$

where ε_t are i.i.d. with mean zero and variance Ω, and d_t are deterministic terms, like constant, trend, seasonals or intervention dummies. Under suitable conditions, see section 14.2, the process $(\beta'x_t, \Delta x_t)$ is stationary around its mean, and subtracting the mean from (14.1) we find

$$\Delta x_t - E(\Delta x_t) = \alpha(\beta'x_{t-1} - E\beta'x_{t-1}) + \sum_{i=1}^{k-1} \Gamma_i(\Delta x_{t-i} - E(\Delta x_{t-i})) + \varepsilon_t.$$

This shows how the changes of the process react to feedback from the disequilibrium errors $\beta'x_{t-1} - E(\beta'x_{t-1})$ and $\Delta x_{t-i} - E(\Delta x_{t-i})$, $i = 1, \ldots, k-1$, via the short-run adjustment coefficients α and Γ_i, $i = 1, \ldots, k-1$. The equation $\beta'x_t - E(\beta'x_t) = 0$ defines the long-run relations between the variables.

By working throughout with a statistical model we ensure that we get a coherent framework for formulating and testing economic hypotheses. Thus our understanding of the dynamic behavior of the economic processes is expressed by the model.

The application of the likelihood approach gives a set of methods for conducting inference without having to derive properties of estimators and tests since they have been derived once and for all. Thus, one can focus on applying the methods, using the now standard software available, provided the questions of interest can be formulated in the framework of the model.

The price paid for all this is that one has to be reasonably sure that the framework one is working in, the vector error correction model, is in fact a good description of the data. This implies that one should always ask the fundamental question:

WHICH STATISTICAL MODEL DESCRIBES THE DATA?

That means that one should carefully check that the basic assumptions are satisfied and, if they are not, one should be prepared to change the model or find out what are the implications of deviations in the underlying assumptions for the properties of the procedures employed.

The statistical methodology employed is to analyze the Gaussian likelihood function with the purpose of deriving estimators and test statistics. Once derived under the ideal Gaussian assumptions, one then derives the properties of the estimators and test statistics under more general assumptions.

The rest of this chapter deals with the following topics. In section 14.2 we give the definitions of integration and cointegration and the basic properties of the vector autoregressive $I(1)$ process as formulated in the Granger Representation Theorem, which is then used to discuss the role of the deterministic terms and the interpretation of cointegrating coefficients. In section 14.3 we show how various hypotheses can be formulated in the cointegrated model and discuss briefly the impulse response function. In section 14.4 we give the likelihood theory and discuss the calculation of maximum likelihood estimators under various restrictions on the parameters. Section 14.5 has a brief discussion of the asymptotics, including the different Dickey–Fuller distributions for the determination of rank and the mixed Gaussian distribution for the asymptotic distribution of $\hat{\beta}$, which leads to asymptotic χ^2 inference. We briefly mention the small sample improvements.

In section 14.6, we discuss some further topics that involve cointegration, like the implication of rational expectations for the cointegration model and models for seasonal cointegration, explosive roots, the model for $I(2)$ variables, nonlinear cointegration, and a few comments on models for panel data cointegration. These topics are still to be developed in detail and thus offer scope for a lot more research.

There are many surveys of the theory of cointegration (see, for example, Watson (1994)), and the topic has become part of most text books in econometrics; see, among others, Lütkepohl (2005), Banerjee, Dolado, Galbraith and Hendry (1993), Hamilton (1994), and Hendry (1995). It is not possible to mention all the papers that have contributed to the theory and we shall use as a general reference the monograph by Johansen (1996), where many earlier references can be found. The purpose of this survey is to explain some basic ideas, and show how they have been extended since 1996 for the analysis of new problems in the autoregressive model, and for the analysis of some new models. The theory of cointegration is an interesting econometric technique, but the main interest and usefulness of the methods lies in their application to macroeconomic problems. We do not deal with the many applications of cointegration techniques, but refer to the monograph by Juselius (2006) for a detailed treatment of the macroeconomic applications.

14.2 The vector autoregressive process and Granger's Representation Theorem

In this section we first formulate the well-known conditions for stationarity of an autoregressive process and then show how these results generalize to integrated variables of order 1. The solution of the equations, the Granger Representation Theorem, is applied to discuss the role of deterministic terms, the interpretation of the cointegrating coefficients and, in section 14.5, the asymptotic properties of the process.

14.2.1 The stationary vector autoregressive process and the definition of integration and cointegration

The vector autoregressive model for the p-dimensional process x_t

$$\Delta x_t = \Pi x_{t-1} + \sum_{i=1}^{k-1} \Gamma_i \Delta x_{t-i} + \Phi d_t + \varepsilon_t \tag{14.2}$$

is a dynamic stochastic model for all the variables x_t. The model is discussed in detail in Chapter 5. We assume that ε_t is i.i.d. with mean zero and variance Ω. By recursive substitution, the equations define x_t as a function of initial values,

$x_0, \ldots, x_{-k+1}$, errors $\varepsilon_1, \ldots, \varepsilon_t$, deterministic terms $d_1, \ldots, d_t$, and the parameters $(\Pi, \Gamma_1, \ldots, \Gamma_{k-1}, \Phi, \Omega)$. The deterministic terms are constants, linear terms, seasonals, or intervention dummies. The properties of x_t are studied through the characteristic polynomial

$$\Pi(z) = (1 - z)I_p - \Pi z - (1 - z) \sum_{i=1}^{k-1} \Gamma_i z^i$$

with determinant $\det(\Pi(z)) = |\Pi(z)|$ of degree at most kp. Let ρ_i^{-1} be the roots of $|\Pi(z)| = 0$. Then $\det(\Pi(z)) = \prod_{i=1}^{kp}(1 - z\rho_i)$ and the inverse matrix is given by

$$C(z) = \Pi^{-1}(z) = \frac{\text{adj}(\Pi(z))}{\det(\Pi(z))}, \quad z \neq \rho_i^{-1}$$

We mention the well-known result, see Chapter 5,

Theorem 1 *If $|\rho_i| < 1$, the coefficients of $\Pi^{-1}(z) = C(1) = \sum_{i=0}^{\infty} C_i z^i$ are exponentially decreasing. Let $\mu_t = \sum_{i=0}^{\infty} C_i \Phi d_{t-i}$. Then the initial values of x_t can be given a distribution so that $x_t - \mu_t$ is stationary. The moving average representation of x_t is*

$$x_t = \sum_{i=0}^{\infty} C_i(\varepsilon_{t-i} + \Phi d_{t-i}). \tag{14.3}$$

Thus the exponentially decreasing coefficients are found by simply inverting the characteristic polynomial if the roots are outside the unit disk. If this condition fails, the equations will generate nonstationary processes of various types and the coefficients will not be exponentially decreasing. The process (14.3) is called a linear process and will form the basis for the definitions of integration and cointegration.

Definition 2 *We say that the process x_t is integrated of order 1, I(1), if Δx_t is a linear process, with $C(1) = \sum_{i=0}^{\infty} C_i \neq 0$. If there is a vector $\beta \neq 0$ so that $\beta' x_t$ is stationary, then x_t is cointegrated with cointegrating vector β. The number of linearly independent cointegrating vectors is the cointegrating rank.*

Example 3 *A bivariate cointegrated process given by the moving average representation*

$$x_{1t} = a \sum_{i=1}^{t} \varepsilon_{1i} + \varepsilon_{2t}$$

$$x_{2t} = b \sum_{i=1}^{t} \varepsilon_{1i} + \varepsilon_{3t}$$

is a cointegrated I(1) process with $\beta = (b, -a)'$ because $\Delta x_{1t} = a\varepsilon_{1t} + \Delta\varepsilon_{2t}, \Delta x_{2t} = b\varepsilon_{1t} + \Delta\varepsilon_{3t}$ and $bx_{1t} - ax_{2t} = b\varepsilon_{2t} - a\varepsilon_{3t}$ are stationary.

Example 4   *A bivariate process given by the vector autoregressive model allowing for adjustment is*

$$\Delta x_{1t} = \alpha_1 (x_{1t-1} - x_{2t-1}) + \varepsilon_{1t},$$
$$\Delta x_{2t} = \alpha_2 (x_{1t-1} - x_{2t-1}) + \varepsilon_{2t}.$$

Subtracting the equations we find that the process $y_t = x_{1t} - x_{2t}$ is autoregressive and stationary if $|1 + \alpha_1 - \alpha_2| < 1$. Similarly we find that $S_t = \alpha_2 x_{1t} - \alpha_1 x_{2t}$ is a random walk, so that

$$x_{1t} = (S_t - \alpha_1 y_t)/(\alpha_2 - \alpha_1),$$
$$x_{2t} = (S_t - \alpha_2 y_t)/(\alpha_2 - \alpha_1).$$

This shows that if $|1 + \alpha_1 - \alpha_2| < 1$, x_t is I(1), $x_{1t} - x_{2t}$ is stationary, and $\alpha_2 x_{1t} - \alpha_1 x_{2t}$ is a random walk, so that x_t is a cointegrated I(1) process with cointegrating vector $\beta' = (1, -1)$. We call S_t a common stochastic trend and α the adjustment coefficients. Note that the properties of the processes are derived from the equations and depend on the parameters of the model.

Example 2 presents a special case of the Granger Representation Theorem, which we give next.

14.2.2   The Granger Representation Theorem

If the characteristic polynomial $\Pi(z)$ has a unit root, then $\Pi(1) = -\Pi$ is singular, of rank r, say, and the process is not stationary. We let the $r \times p$ matrix β' denote the r linearly independent rows of Π, and let the $p \times r$ matrix α contain the coefficients that express each row of $-\Pi$ as a combination of the vectors β', so that $\Pi = \alpha\beta'$. Equation (14.2) becomes

$$\Delta x_t = \alpha\beta' x_{t-1} + \sum_{i=1}^{k-1} \Gamma_i \Delta x_{t-i} + \Phi d_t + \varepsilon_t. \tag{14.4}$$

This is called the error or equilibrium correction model. We next formulate a condition, the I(1) condition, which guarantees that the solution of (14.4) is a cointegrated I(1) process. We define $\Gamma = I_p - \sum_{i=1}^{k-1} \Gamma_i$.

Condition 5   *(The I(1) condition). We assume that $\det(\Pi(z)) = 0$ implies that $|z| > 1$ or $z = 1$ and assume that*

$$\det(\alpha'_\perp \Gamma \beta_\perp) \neq 0. \tag{14.5}$$

This condition is needed to avoid solutions which have seasonal roots or explosive roots, and solutions which are integrated of order 2 or higher (see section 14.6). The condition is equivalent to the condition that the number of roots of $\det \Pi(z) = 0$ is $p - r$.

Theorem 6 (*The Granger Representation Theorem*) *If* $\Pi(z)$ *has unit roots and the* $I(1)$ *condition (14.5) is satisfied, then*

$$(1-z)\Pi^{-1}(z) = C(z) = \sum_{i=0}^{\infty} C_i z^i = C(1) + (1-z)C^*(z) \qquad (14.6)$$

is convergent for $|z| \le 1 + \delta$ *for some* $\delta > 0$ *and*

$$C = C(1) = \beta_\perp (\alpha'_\perp \Gamma \beta_\perp)^{-1} \alpha'_\perp. \qquad (14.7)$$

The process x_t *has the moving average representation*

$$x_t = C\sum_{i=1}^{t}(\varepsilon_i + \Phi d_i) + \sum_{i=0}^{\infty} C_i^*(\varepsilon_{t-i} + \Phi d_{t-i}) + A, \qquad (14.8)$$

where A depends on initial values, so that $\beta'A = 0$. *It follows that* x_t *is a cointegrated* $I(1)$ *process with* r *cointegrating vectors* β *and* $p - r$ *common stochastic trends* $\alpha'_\perp \sum_{i=1}^{t} \varepsilon_i$.

The result (14.6) rests on the observation that the singularity of $\Pi(z)$ for $z = 1$ implies that $\Pi(z)^{-1}$ has a pole at $z = 1$. Condition (14.5) is a condition for this pole to be of order one. We shall not prove this here, but will show how this result can be applied to prove the representation result (14.8). We multiply $\Pi(L)x_t = \Phi d_t + \varepsilon_t$ by

$$(1-L)\Pi^{-1}(L) = C(L) = C(1) + (1-L)C^*(L)$$

and find

$$\Delta x_t = (1-L)\Pi^{-1}(L)\Pi(L)x_t = C(1)(\varepsilon_t + \Phi d_t) + \Delta C^*(L)(\varepsilon_t + \Phi d_t).$$

Now define the stationary process $z_t = C^*(L)\varepsilon_t$ and the deterministic function $\mu_t = C^*(L)\Phi d_t$. Then

$$\Delta x_t = C(\varepsilon_t + \Phi d_t) + \Delta(z_t + \mu_t),$$

which cumulates to

$$x_t = C\sum_{i=1}^{t}(\varepsilon_i + \Phi d_i) + z_t + \mu_t + A,$$

where $A = x_0 - z_0 - \mu_0$. We choose the distribution of x_0 so that $\beta'x_0 = \beta'(z_0 + \mu_0)$, and hence $\beta'A = 0$. It is seen that x_t is $I(1)$, that $\beta'x_t = \beta'z_t + \beta'\mu_t$, so that $\beta'x_t$ is stationary around its mean $E(\beta'x_t) = \beta'\mu_t$, and that Δx_t is stationary around its mean $E(\Delta x_t) = C\Phi d_t + \Delta\mu_t$ (see Figure 14.1).

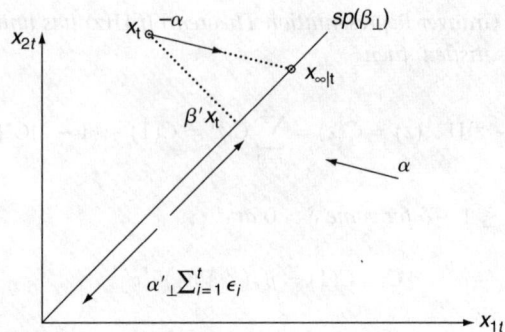

Figure 14.1   In the model $\Delta x_t = \alpha \beta' x_{t-1} + \varepsilon_t$, the point $x_t = (x_{1t}, x_{2t})$ is moved towards the long-run value $x_{\infty|t}$ on the attractor set $\{x | \beta' x = 0\} = sp(\beta_\perp)$ by the force $-\alpha$ or $+\alpha$, and pushed along the attractor set by the common trends $\alpha'_\perp \sum_{i=1}^t \varepsilon_i$.

It is easy to see that, for a process with one lag, we have $\Gamma = I_p$ and

$$\beta' x_t = (I_r + \beta'\alpha)\beta' x_{t-1} + \beta'\varepsilon_t,$$

so that the $I(1)$ condition is that the eigenvalues of $I_r + \beta'\alpha$ are bounded by one.

Engle and Granger (1987) show this result in the form that, if $\Delta x_t = C(L)\varepsilon_t$ with $|C(1)| = 0$, then x_t satisfies an (infinite order) autoregressive model. We have chosen to start with the autoregressive formulation, which is the one estimated and which has the coefficients that have immediate interpretations, and derive the (infinite order) moving average representation. Both formulations require the $I(1)$ condition (5). We next give three examples to illustrate the use of the Granger Representation Theorem.

Example 7   *First consider*

$$\Delta x_{1t} = -\frac{1}{4}(x_{1t-1} - x_{2t-1}) + \varepsilon_{1t},$$

$$\Delta x_{2t} = \frac{1}{4}(x_{1t-1} - x_{2t-1}) + \varepsilon_{2t},$$

which gives an $I(1)$ process, with $\alpha' = \frac{1}{4}(-1, 1)$, $\beta' = (1, -1)$, and $|1 + \alpha'\beta| = \frac{1}{2} < 1$.

Example 8   *Next consider*

$$\Delta x_{1t} = \frac{1}{4}(x_{1t-1} - x_{2t-1}) + \varepsilon_{1t},$$

$$\Delta x_{2t} = -\frac{1}{4}(x_{1t-1} - x_{2t-1}) + \varepsilon_{2t},$$

for which $\alpha' = \frac{1}{4}(1, -1)$, $\beta' = (1, -1)$, and $|1 + \alpha'\beta| = \frac{3}{2} > 1$. This describes an explosive process, and the $I(1)$ condition is not satisfied because there are roots inside the unit disk.

Example 9 *Finally consider a strange example:*

$$\Delta x_{1t} = \frac{1}{4}(x_{1t-1} - x_{2t-1}) + \frac{9}{4}\Delta x_{2t-1} + \varepsilon_{1t},$$

$$\Delta x_{2t} = -\frac{1}{4}(x_{1t-1} - x_{2t-1}) + \varepsilon_{2t}.$$

This process is a cointegrated I(1) process with cointegrating relation $\beta' = (1, -1)$, because the I(1) condition is satisfied despite the fact that the adjustment coefficients point in the wrong direction. The adjustment of the process towards equilibrium comes through the term Δx_{2t-1}.

14.2.3 The role of the deterministic terms

We apply the result (14.8) to discuss the role of a deterministic term in the equations, which could be called an "innovation" term. It follows from (14.8) that d_t is cumulated into the trend $C\Phi \sum_{i=1}^{t} d_i$. We consider some special cases first. Let $\Phi d_t = \mu_0 + \mu_1 t$, so that

$$x_t = C\sum_{i=1}^{t}(\varepsilon_i + \mu_0 + \mu_1 i) + \sum_{i=0}^{\infty} C_i^*(\varepsilon_{t-i} + \mu_0 + \mu_1(t - i)) + A,$$

which shows that, in general, a linear term in the equation becomes a quadratic trend with coefficient $\frac{1}{2}C\mu_1 t^2$ in the process. We decompose $\mu_i = \alpha \rho_i' + \alpha_\perp \gamma_i'$, where $\bar{\alpha}' \mu_i = \rho_i'$, and $\bar{\alpha}_\perp' \mu_i = \gamma_i'$. It is then seen that if $\gamma_1 = 0$, so that $\mu_1 = \alpha \rho_1'$, or $\alpha_\perp' \mu_1 = 0$, then the quadratic term has coefficient zero, $C\mu_1 = C\alpha\gamma_1' = 0$, so that only a linear trend is present. We therefore distinguish five cases, as shown in Table 14.1.

We also consider a "linear additive term" defined by

$$x_t = \tau_0 + \tau_1 t + z_t,$$

$$\Delta z_t = \alpha \beta' z_{t-1} + \sum_{i=1}^{k-1} \Gamma_i \Delta z_{t-i} + \varepsilon_t,$$

Table 14.1 The five models defined by restrictions on the deterministic terms in the equations. We decompose $\mu_i = \alpha \rho_i' + \alpha_\perp \gamma_i'$ ($\bar{\alpha}' \mu_i = \rho_i'$, $\bar{\alpha}_\perp' \mu_i = \gamma_i'$) and express the models by restrictions on ρ_i and γ_i

Model	Linear term	Restriction	Trend in x_t	$E(\Delta x_t)$	$E(\beta' x_t)$
1	$\mu_0 + \mu_1 t$	none	quadratic	linear	linear
2	$\mu_0 + \alpha \rho_1' t$	$\gamma_1 = 0$	linear	constant	linear
3	μ_0	$\mu_1 = 0$	linear	constant	constant
4	$\alpha \rho_0'$	$\mu_1 = 0, \gamma_0 = 0$	constant	zero	constant
5	0	$\mu_1 = \mu_2 = 0$	zero	zero	zero

so that the deterministic part and the stochastic part are modeled independently. We eliminate z_t and find an error correction model (14.4) with

$$\mu_0 = -\alpha\beta'\tau_0 + \alpha\beta'\tau_1 + \Gamma\tau_1, \quad \mu_1 = -\alpha\beta'\tau_1,$$

thus corresponding to case 2 in Table 14.1. Similarly, if we take $\tau_1 = 0$, we get case 4, where the constant is restricted through $\alpha'_\perp \mu_0 = 0$.

Finally we consider the case of an "innovation dummy." We define

$$d_t = 1_{\{t=t_0\}} = \begin{cases} 1, t = t_0 \\ 0, t \neq t_0 \end{cases}.$$

In this case the deterministic part of x_t is

$$C\Phi 1_{\{t \geq t_0\}} + \sum_{i=0}^{\infty} C_i^* \Phi d_{t-i} = (C\Phi + C_{t-t_0}^* \Phi) 1_{\{t \geq t_0\}}.$$

Because $C_{t-t_0}^* \to 0$, for $t \to \infty$, it is seen that the effect of an innovation dummy is that x_t changes from having "level" zero up to time $t_0 - 1$ to having "level" $C\Phi$ for large t.

On the other hand, if we model an "additive dummy"

$$x_t = \Phi d_t + z_t,$$

$$\Delta z_t = \alpha\beta' z_{t-1} + \sum_{i=1}^{k-1} \Gamma_i \Delta z_{t-i} + \varepsilon_t,$$

we get the equation for x_t as

$$\Delta x_t = \alpha\beta' x_{t-1} + \sum_{i=1}^{k-1} \Gamma_i \Delta z_{t-i} + \Phi\Delta d_t - \alpha\beta'\Phi d_{t-1} - \sum_{i=1}^{k-1} \Phi\Gamma_i \Delta d_{t-i} + \varepsilon_t,$$

which shows that, in the autoregressive formulation, we need the deterministic terms $\Delta d_t, d_{t-1}, \Delta d_{t-1}, \ldots, d_{t-k+1}$, with coefficients depending on $\Phi, \alpha, \beta, \Gamma_i$. The inclusion of deterministic terms in the equations thus requires careful consideration of which trending behavior or deterministic term is relevant for the data.

14.2.4 Interpretation of cointegrating coefficients

Usually regression coefficients in a regression like

$$x_{1t} = \gamma_2 x_{2t} + \gamma_3 x_{3t} + \varepsilon_t \tag{14.9}$$

are interpreted via a counterfactual experiment of the form: The coefficient γ_2 is the effect on x_{1t} of a change in x_{2t}, keeping x_{3t} constant. It is not relevant if, in fact, x_{3t} can in reality be kept constant when x_{2t} is changed: the experiment is purely a counterfactual or thought experiment.

The cointegrating relations are long-run relations. This is not taken to mean that these relations will eventually materialize if we wait long enough, but rather that these are relations which have been there all the time and which influence the movement of the process x_t via the adjustments α, in the sense that the more the process $\beta' x_t$ deviates from $E\beta' x_t$, the more the adjustment coefficients pull the process back towards its mean.

It is therefore natural that the interpretation of cointegrating coefficients involves the notion of a long-run value. From the Granger Representation Theorem (14.8) applied to the model with no deterministic terms, one can find an expression for $E(x_{t+s}|x_t)$, which shows that

$$x_{\infty|t} = \lim_{h \to \infty} E(x_{t+h}|x_t, \ldots, x_{t-k+1}) = C\left(x_t - \sum_{i=1}^{k-1} \Gamma_i x_{t-i}\right) = C\sum_{i=1}^{t} \varepsilon_i + x_{\infty|0}.$$

This limiting conditional expectation is the so-called long-run value of the process, which is a point in the attractor set, see Figure 14.1, because $\beta' x_{\infty|t} = 0$. The cointegrating relation can be formulated as a relation between long-run values: $\beta' x_{\infty|t} = 0$.

We see that if the current value is shifted from x_t to $x_t + h$, then the long-run value is shifted from $x_{\infty|t}$ to $x_{\infty|t} + Ch$, which is still a point in the attractor set because $\beta' x_{\infty|t} + \beta' Ch = 0$. If we want to achieve a given long-run change $k = C\xi$, say, we must add Γk to the current value, as the long-run value becomes

$$x_{\infty|t} + C\Gamma k = x_{\infty|t} + C\Gamma C\xi = x_{\infty|t} + C\xi = x_{\infty|t} + k,$$

because $C\Gamma C = C$, see (14.7). This idea is now used to give an interpretation of a cointegrating coefficient in the simple case of $r = 1$, and where the relation is normalized on x_1

$$x_1 = \gamma_2 x_2 + \gamma_3 x_3, \tag{14.10}$$

so that $\beta' = (1, -\gamma_2, -\gamma_3)$. In order to give the usual interpretation as a regression coefficient (or elasticity if the variables are in logs), we would like to implement a long-run change so that x_2 changes by one, x_1 changes by γ_2, and x_3 is kept fixed. Thus the long-run change should be the vector $k = (\gamma_2, 1, 0)$, but this satisfies $\beta' k = 0$, and hence $k = C\xi$ for some ξ, so we can achieve the long-run change k by moving the current value to $x_t + C\Gamma k$.

In this sense, a coefficient in an identified cointegrating relation can be interpreted as the effect of a long-run change to one variable on another, keeping all others fixed. The difference with the usual interpretation of a regression coefficient is that, because the relation is a long-run relation, that is, a relation between long-run values, the counterfactual experiment should involve a long-run change in the variables. More details can be found in Johansen (2005a), see also Proietti (1997).

14.3   Interpretation of the $I(1)$ model for cointegration

We discuss here the model $H(r)$ defined by (14.1). The parameters are

$$(\alpha, \beta, \Gamma_1, \ldots, \Gamma_{k-1}, \Phi, \Omega).$$

All parameters vary freely, and α and β are $p \times r$ matrices. The models $H(r)$ form a nested sequence of hypotheses

$$H(0) \subset \cdots \subset H(r) \subset \cdots \subset H(p),$$

where $H(p)$ is the unrestricted vector autoregressive model, or the $I(0)$ model, and $H(0)$ corresponds to the restriction $\Pi = 0$, which is the vector autoregressive model for the process in differences. The models in between, $H(1), \ldots, H(p-1)$, ensure cointegration and are the models of primary interest to us here. Note that in order to have nested models we allow in $H(r)$ all processes with rank less than or equal to r.

The formulation allows us to derive likelihood ratio tests for the hypothesis $H(r)$ in the unrestricted model $H(p)$. These tests can then be applied to check if one's prior knowledge of the number of cointegrating relations is consistent with the data, or alternatively to construct an estimator of the cointegrating rank.

Note that when the cointegrating rank is r, the number of common trends is $p - r$. Thus, if one can explain the presence of r cointegrating relations, one should also explain the presence of $p - r$ independent stochastic trends in the data.

14.3.1   Normalization of the parameters of the $I(1)$ model

The parameters α and β in (14.1) are not uniquely identified in the sense that, given any choice of α and β and any non-singular matrix $\xi(r \times r)$, the choice $\alpha\xi^{-1}$ and $\beta\xi'$ will give the same matrix $\Pi = \alpha\beta' = \alpha\xi^{-1}(\beta\xi')'$ and hence determine the same probability distribution for the variables.

If $x_t = (x_{1t}', x_{2t}')'$ and $\beta = (\beta_1', \beta_2')'$, with $|\beta_1| \neq 0$, we can solve the cointegrating relations as

$$x_{1t} = \theta' x_{2t} + u_t$$

where u_t is stationary and $\theta' = -(\beta_1')^{-1}\beta_2'$. This represents cointegration as a regression equation.

A normalization of this type is sometimes convenient for estimation and calculation of "standard errors" of the estimate (see section 14.5), but many hypotheses are invariant to a normalization of β and, thus, in a discussion of a test of such a hypothesis, β does not require normalization. On the other hand, as seen in the next subsection, many economic hypotheses are expressed in terms of different restrictions, for which the regression formulation is not convenient.

Similarly, $\alpha_\perp$ and $\beta_\perp$ are not uniquely defined, so that the common trends are not unique. From the Granger Representation Theorem we see that common trends contribute with the nonstationary random walk term $C\sum_{i=1}^{t} \varepsilon_i$. For any full rank $(p-r) \times (p-r)$ matrix η, we have that $\eta\alpha'_\perp \sum_{i=1}^{t} \varepsilon_i$ could also be used because

$$C\sum_{i=1}^{t} \varepsilon_i = \beta_\perp(\alpha'_\perp\Gamma\beta_\perp)^{-1}\left(\alpha'_\perp\sum_{i=1}^{t}\varepsilon_i\right) = \beta_\perp(\eta\alpha'_\perp\Gamma\beta_\perp)^{-1}\left(\eta\alpha'_\perp\sum_{i=1}^{t}\varepsilon_i\right).$$

This shows that we could have defined the common trends as $\eta\alpha'_\perp \sum_{i=1}^{t} \varepsilon_i$, so that identifying restrictions are needed in order to make sense of them.

14.3.2 Hypotheses on the long-run coefficients β

The main use of the concept of cointegration is as a precise definition of the economic concept of a long-run relation or equilibrium relation. In order to illustrate these ideas, consider the variables: m_t, log real money, y_t, log real income, $\pi_t = \Delta\log(p_t)$, the inflation rate, and two interest rates: a deposit rate i_t^d and a bond rate i_t^b. For simplicity, we first assume that we have only one cointegrating relation between the variables and formulate some natural hypotheses below.

The inverse money velocity is defined as $m_t - y_t$. We do not find that $m_t - y_t = c$ holds in the data, but instead interpret the statement that money velocity is constant as the statement that the process $m_t - y_t$ is stationary, or, in terms of cointegration, that $\beta = (1, -1, 0, 0, 0)'$ is a cointegrating relation. Another hypothesis of interest is that velocity is a function of the interest rates only, which we formulate as $\beta = (1, -1, 0, \psi, \eta)'$, for some parameters ψ, η. We can formulate the question of whether the interest rate spread is stationary as the hypothesis that $\beta = (0, 0, 0, 1, -1)'$ and, finally, we can investigate the question of the stationarity of the inflation rate as the hypothesis $\beta = (0, 0, 1, 0, 0)'$.

Notice that stationarity of a variable is formulated as a question about the parameters of the model, that is, the model allows for both $I(0)$ variables and $I(1)$ variables.

If the cointegrating rank is two, we have more freedom in formulating hypotheses. In this situation we could ask if, in both relations, the coefficients to m and y add to zero, and that the coefficient to the inflation rate is zero. This hypothesis is expressed as a restriction on the cointegrating relations

$$\beta = H\phi, \quad \text{or} \quad R'\beta = 0,$$

where

$$R' = \begin{pmatrix} 1 & 1 & 0 & 0 & 0 \\ 0 & 0 & 1 & 0 & 0 \end{pmatrix}, H = R_\perp.$$

The stationarity of velocity is formulated as the existence of a cointegrating relation of the form $b' = (1, -1, 0, 0, 0)$, that is, $\beta = (b, \phi)$, where b is known and the vector ϕ is the remaining unrestricted cointegrating vector.

A general formulation of linear restrictions on individual cointegrating relations is

$$\beta = (H_1 \varphi_1, \ldots, H_r \varphi_r), \quad \text{or } R_i' \beta_i = 0, \quad i = 1, \ldots, r, \tag{14.11}$$

where $H_i = R_{i\perp}$ is $p \times s_i$ and φ_i is $s_i \times 1$. In this way we impose $p - s_i$ restrictions on β_i. In order to identify the vector ϕ_i, we also have to normalize on one of its coefficients. An example of (14.11) for the case $r = 2$ is given by the hypotheses that m_t and y_t cointegrate and that i_t^d cointegrates with π_t. This hypothesis can be formulated as the existence of two cointegrating vectors of the form $(\varphi_{11}, \varphi_{12}, 0, 0, 0)$ and $(0, 0, \varphi_{21}, \varphi_{22}, 0)$ for some $\varphi_1 = (\phi_{11}, \phi_{12})'$, and $\varphi_2 = (\phi_{21}, \phi_{22})$. For this case we would take

$$H_1' = \begin{pmatrix} 1 & 0 & 0 & 0 & 0 \\ 0 & 1 & 0 & 0 & 0 \end{pmatrix}, \quad H_2' = \begin{pmatrix} 0 & 0 & 1 & 0 & 0 \\ 0 & 0 & 0 & 1 & 0 \end{pmatrix}.$$

The formulation (14.11) is the general formulation of linear restrictions on individual equations and identification is therefore possible, provided the identification condition is satisfied. In this particular case this means that, for instance, the first equation is identified by $R_1' \beta_1 = 0$, provided the rank condition is satisfied at the true value, that is, rank $(R_1'(\beta_2, \ldots, \beta_r)) \geq r - 1$.

Another set of conditions, which do not involve the true value, is given by

$$\text{rank}(R_1'(H_{i_1}, \ldots, H_{i_k})) \geq k,$$

for all $2 \leq i_1 \leq \cdots \leq i_k \leq r, k = 1, \ldots, r - 1$. These ensure that, for almost all values of the true parameter β, the rank condition is satisfied.

Finally one can, of course, impose general (cross-equation) restrictions of the form $R' \text{vec}(\beta) = r_0$.

14.3.3 Hypotheses on the adjustment coefficients α and $\alpha_\perp$

There are two type of hypotheses on α that are of primary interest. The first is the hypothesis of weak exogeneity, see Engle, Hendry and Richard (1983), of some of the variables x_{2t}, say. We decompose x_t as $(x_{1t}', x_{2t}')'$ and the matrices similarly. The model equations without deterministics are then

$$\Delta x_{1t} = \alpha_1 \beta' x_{t-1} + \sum_{i=1}^{k-1} \Gamma_{1i} \Delta x_{t-i} + \varepsilon_{1t},$$

$$\Delta x_{2t} = \alpha_2 \beta' x_{t-1} + \sum_{i=1}^{k-1} \Gamma_{2i} \Delta x_{t-i} + \varepsilon_{2t}.$$

The conditional model for Δx_{1t} given Δx_{2t} and the past variables is

$$\Delta x_{1t} = \omega \Delta x_{2t} + (\alpha_1 - \omega \alpha_2) \beta' x_{t-1} + \sum_{i=1}^{k-1} (\Gamma_{1i} - \omega \Gamma_{2i}) \Delta x_{t-i} + \varepsilon_{1t} - \omega \varepsilon_{2t}, \tag{14.12}$$

where $\omega = \Omega_{12} \Omega_{22}^{-1}$, if the errors are Gaussian. It is seen that, if $\alpha_2 = 0, x_{2t}$ is weakly exogenous for α_1 and β, if there are no further restrictions on the parameters. This implies that efficient inference can be conducted on α_1 and β in the conditional model.

Another interpretation of the hypothesis of weak exogeneity is the following: if $\alpha_2 = 0$ then $\alpha_\perp = (0, I_{p-r})'$, so that the common trends are $\alpha'_\perp \sum_{i=1}^{t} \varepsilon_i = \sum_{i=1}^{t} \varepsilon_{2i}$. Thus the errors in the equations for x_{2t} cumulate in the system and give rise to the nonstationarity. This does not mean that the process x_{2t} cannot cointegrate: in fact it can be stationary for specific parameter values, as the next example shows.

Example 10 *Consider the model*

$$\Delta x_t = \begin{pmatrix} \alpha_1 \\ 0 \end{pmatrix} \beta' x_{t-1} + \Gamma_1 \Delta x_{t-1} + \varepsilon_{1t},$$

where evidently x_{2t} is weakly exogenous for the parameters α_1 and β, if all parameters are varying freely. The data-generating process given by the equations

$$\Delta x_{1t} = x_{2t-1} + \varepsilon_{1t},$$

$$\Delta x_{2t} = -\frac{1}{4} \Delta x_{1t-1} + \varepsilon_{2t},$$

is a special case with parameter values

$$\alpha' = (1, 0), \quad \beta' = (0, 1), \quad \Gamma_1 = -\frac{1}{4} \begin{pmatrix} 0 & 0 \\ 1 & 0 \end{pmatrix},$$

which satisfy the I(1) condition (14.5), and for which the weakly exogenous variable x_{2t} is stationary.

A general formulation of this type of hypothesis is

$$\alpha = A\psi,$$

which has the interpretation that $A'_\perp x_t$ is weakly exogenous for $A'\alpha_1$ and β.

Another hypothesis of interest is that there are some cointegrating relations that only appear in one equation. In this case one of the adjustment vectors is a unit vector, a say, or equivalently $\alpha_\perp$ has a zero row. The interpretation of this is that the shocks to the corresponding equation are not contributing to the common trends. This hypothesis can be formulated as $\alpha = (a, \phi)$, or equivalently that $\alpha_\perp = a_\perp \psi$. This is an example where a hypothesis on $\alpha_\perp$ is formulated as a hypothesis on α. Another example is the hypothesis $\alpha_\perp = (a, \psi)$, which is equivalent to $\alpha = a_\perp \phi$.

14.3.4   The structural error correction model

Multiplying equation (14.1) by a nonsingular matrix A_0 gives the structural error (or equilibrium) correction model

$$A_0 \Delta x_t = \alpha^* \beta' x_{t-1} + \sum_{i=1}^{k-1} \Gamma_i^* \Delta x_{t-i} + \Phi^* d_t + \varepsilon_t^*, \tag{14.13}$$

where the * indicates that the matrices have been multiplied by A_0. Note that the parameter β is the same as in (14.1), but that all the other coefficients have changed. In particular, A_0 is often chosen so that Ω^* is diagonal. Usually β is identified first, by suitable restrictions, and then the remaining parameters are identified by imposing restrictions on

$$\vartheta = (\alpha^*, \Gamma_0^*, \ldots, \Gamma_{k-1}^*, \Phi^*, \Omega^*). \tag{14.14}$$

Such restrictions are, of course, well known from econometric textbooks (see Fisher, 1966), and the usual rank condition applies, as well as the formulations in connection with the identification of β.

The conclusion of this is that the presence of nonstationary variables allows two distinct identification problems to be formulated. First, the long-run relations must be identified uniquely in order that one can estimate and interpret them, and then the short-run parameters ϑ must be identified uniquely in the usual way.

The cointegration analysis allows us to formulate long-run *relations between variables*, but the structural error correction model formulates *equations for the variables* in the system. Thus if $r = 1$ in the example with money, income, the inflation rate and interest rates, we can think of the cointegrating relation as a *money relation* if we solve it for money, but the equation for Δm_t in the structural model is a *money equation* and models the dynamic adjustment of money to the past and the other simultaneous variables in the system. The structural VAR is treated in Chapter 5, section 7.

14.3.5 Shocks, changes and impulse responses

Model (14.1) shows that a change in $\varepsilon_t (\varepsilon_t \mapsto \varepsilon_t + c)$ is equivalent to a change in $x_t (x_t \mapsto x_t + c)$. We shall call ε_t a shock and c a change. The Granger Representation Theorem shows that the effect at time $t + h$ of a change c to ε_t (or x_t) is

$$\frac{\partial x_{t+h}}{\partial \varepsilon_t}(c) = (C + C_h)c \to Cc, h \to \infty,$$

so that the impulse response function converges to Cc, which we shall call the long-run (or permanent) impact of the change c.

Sometimes one can give an economic meaning to a linear combinations of shocks $e_i = v_i' \varepsilon_t$ and therefore one may want to induce changes to one of these and keep the remaining ones fixed. We introduce the notation

$$B^{-1} = (w_1, \ldots, w_p), B' = (v_1, \ldots, v_p),$$

and call $e_i = v_i' \varepsilon_t$ the structural shock and w_i its loading. We find

$$(C + C_h)\varepsilon_t = \sum_{i=1}^p (C + C_h)w_i v_i' \varepsilon_t = \sum_{i=1}^p (C + C_h)w_i e_i.$$

Now a change of one unit, say, to the structural shock e_i, keeping the others fixed, gives the impulse response function

$$h \mapsto (C + C_h)w_i.$$

One such possibility is to choose the Cholesky decomposition, so that B is triangular and $B\Omega B' = I_p$.

Because the shocks $\alpha'_\perp \varepsilon_t$ cumulate to the common trends, we define them as *permanent* shocks. It is natural to define *transitory* shocks as independent of the permanent ones, that is as $\alpha'\Omega^{-1}\varepsilon_t$. The decomposition

$$\varepsilon_t = \underbrace{\alpha(\alpha'\Omega^{-1}\alpha)^{-1}}_{loading} \underbrace{\alpha'\Omega^{-1}\varepsilon_t}_{trans.\,shock} + \underbrace{\Omega\alpha_\perp(\alpha'_\perp\Omega\alpha_\perp)^{-1}}_{loading} \underbrace{\alpha'_\perp\varepsilon_t}_{perm.\,shock}$$

is a decomposition of the shocks ε_t into the transitory shocks and the permanent shocks. Note that the transitory shock has a loading proportional to α, so that the long-run effect of a transitory shock is zero. Note also that the loadings of the permanent shocks are suitable combinations of columns of Ω. Such loadings are used in the so-called generalized impulse response analysis (see Koop, Pesaran and Potter, 1996).

14.4 Likelihood analysis of the *I*(1) model

This section contains first some comments on what aspects are important for checking for model misspecification, and then introduces a notation for the calculations of reduced rank regression, introduced by Anderson (1951). We then discuss how reduced rank regression and modifications thereof are used to estimate the parameters of the *I*(1) model (1) and various submodels.

14.4.1 Checking the specifications of the model

In order to apply the Gaussian maximum likelihood methods one has to check the assumptions behind the model carefully, so that one is convinced that the statistical model chosen contains the density that describes the data. If this is not the case, the asymptotic results available from the Gaussian analysis need not hold. The methods for checking the VAR model are outlined in chapter 5, including the choice of lag length, a test for normality and tests for autocorrelation and heteroskedasticity in the errors. The asymptotic results for estimators and tests derived from the Gaussian likelihood turn out to be robust to some types of deviations from the above assumptions. Thus the limit results hold for i.i.d. errors with finite variance, and not just for Gaussian errors. It turns out that heteroscedasticity does not influence the limit distributions (see Rahbek, Hansen, and Dennis, 2002), whereas autocorrelated error terms will influence limit results, so this has to be checked carefully. Finally, and perhaps most importantly, the assumption of constant parameters is crucial.

In practice it is important to model outliers by suitable dummy variables, but it is also important to model breaks in the dynamics, breaks in the cointegrating properties, breaks in the stationarity properties, etc. The papers by Seo (1998) and Hansen and Johansen (1999) contain a theory for recursive estimation in the cointegrating model.

14.4.2   Reduced rank regression

Let U_t, W_t, and Z_t be three multivariate time series of dimensions p_u, p_w, p_z respectively. We define a notation, which can be used to describe the calculations performed in regression and reduced rank regression: see Anderson (1951). We consider a regression model

$$U_t = \Pi W_t + \Gamma Z_t + \varepsilon_t, \tag{14.15}$$

where ε_t are the errors with variance Ω. The product moments are

$$S_{uw} = T^{-1} \sum_{t=1}^{T} U_t W_t',$$

and the residuals we get by regressing U_t on W_t are

$$(U|W)_t = U_t - S_{uw} S_{ww}^{-1} W_t,$$

so that the conditional product moments are

$$S_{uw.z} = S_{uw} - S_{uz} S_{zz}^{-1} S_{zw} = T^{-1} \sum_{t=1}^{T} (U|Z)_t (W|Z)_t'$$

$$S_{uu.w,z} = T^{-1} \sum_{t=1}^{T} (U|W,Z)_t (U|W,Z)_t' = S_{uu.w} - S_{uz.w} S_{zz.w}^{-1} S_{zu.w}.$$

The unrestricted regression estimates are $\hat{\Pi} = S_{uw.z} S_{ww.z}^{-1}, \hat{\Gamma} = S_{uz.w} S_{zz.w}^{-1}$ and $\hat{\Omega} = S_{uu.w,z}$. Reduced rank regression of U_t on W_t corrected for Z_t gives estimates of α, β and Ω in (14.15), when we assume that $\Pi = \alpha\beta'$ and α is $p_u \times r$ and β is $p_w \times r$. We first solve the eigenvalue problem

$$|\lambda S_{ww.z} - S_{wu.z} S_{uu.z}^{-1} S_{uw.z}| = 0. \tag{14.16}$$

The eigenvalues are ordered $\hat{\lambda}_1 \geq \ldots \geq \hat{\lambda}_{pw}$, and the corresponding eigenvectors are $\hat{v}_1, \ldots, \hat{v}_{pw}$. The interpretation of $\hat{\lambda}_1$, say, is as the maximal squared canonical correlation between U and W corrected for Z, that is,

$$\hat{\lambda}_1 = \max_{\xi, \eta} \frac{(\xi' S_{uw.z} \eta)^2}{\xi' S_{uu.z} \xi \eta' S_{ww.z} \eta}.$$

The reduced rank estimates of β, α, Γ and Ω are given by

$$\hat{\beta} = (\hat{v}_1, \ldots, \hat{v}_r),$$
$$\hat{\alpha} = S_{uw.z}\hat{\beta}(\hat{\beta}' S_{ww.z}\hat{\beta})^{-1},$$
$$\hat{\Gamma} = S_{uz.\hat{\beta}'w} S_{zz.\hat{\beta}'w}^{-1},$$
$$\hat{\Omega} = S_{uu.z} - S_{uw.z}\hat{\beta}(\hat{\beta}' S_{ww.z}\hat{\beta})^{-1}\hat{\beta}' S_{wu.z},$$

and we find $|\hat{\Omega}| = |S_{uu.z}| \prod_{i=1}^{r}(1 - \hat{\lambda}_i)$. Often the eigenvectors are normalized on $\hat{v}_i' S_{ww.z}\hat{v}_j = 0$, if $i \neq j$, and 1 if $i = j$. The calculations described here are called a reduced rank regression and will be denoted by $RRR(U, W|Z)$.

14.4.3 Reduced rank regression in the $I(1)$ model and derivation of the rank test

We saw in section (14.2.3) that the role of a deterministic term changes when its coefficient is proportional to α. We therefore consider a model where some deterministic terms have this property, that is, the model

$$\Delta x_t = \alpha(\beta' x_{t-1} + \Upsilon D_t) + \sum_{i=1}^{k-1} \Gamma_i \Delta x_{t-i} + \Phi d_t + \varepsilon_t, \tag{14.17}$$

where D_t and d_t are deterministic terms. Note that the coefficient on D_t, $\alpha\Upsilon$, has been restricted to be proportional to α. We assume for the derivations of maximum likelihood estimators and likelihood ratio tests that ε_t is i.i.d. $N_p(0, \Omega)$. The Gaussian likelihood function shows that maximum likelihood estimation can be solved by the reduced rank regression

$$RRR(\Delta x_t, (x_{t-1}', D_t')' | \Delta x_{t-1}, \ldots, \Delta x_{t-k+1}, d_t).$$

With the notation

$$R_{0t} = (\Delta x_t | \Delta x_{t-1}, \ldots, \Delta x_{t-k+1}, d_t),$$
$$R_{1t} = ((x_{t-1}', D_t')' | \Delta x_{t-1}, \ldots, \Delta x_{t-k+1}, d_t),$$
$$S_{ij} = T^{-1} \sum_{t=1}^{T} R_{it} R_{jt}',$$

we find that $(\hat{\beta}', \hat{\Upsilon})'$ solves the eigenvalue problem

$$|\lambda S_{11} - S_{10} S_{00}^{-1} S_{01}| = 0,$$

and that the maximized likelihood is, apart from a constant, given by

$$L_{\max}^{-2/T} = |\hat{\Omega}| = |S_{00}| \prod_{i=1}^{r}(1 - \hat{\lambda}_i). \tag{14.18}$$

Note that we have solved all the models $H(r)$, $r = 0, \ldots, p$, by the same eigenvalue calculation. The maximized likelihood is given for each r by (14.18) and by dividing the maximized likelihood function for r with the corresponding expression for $r = p$ we get the likelihood ratio test for cointegrating rank, the so-called rank test or trace test:

$$-2 \log LR(H(r)|H(p)) = -T \sum_{i=r+1}^{p} \log(1 - \hat{\lambda}_i). \tag{14.19}$$

The asymptotic distribution of this test statistic and the estimators will be discussed in section 14.5. Next we discuss how a number of hypotheses or submodels can be analysed by reduced rank regression.

14.4.4   Hypothesis testing for the long-run coefficients β

We first consider the hypothesis $H_0 : \beta = H\phi$. Under H_0, the equation becomes

$$\Delta x_t = \alpha \begin{pmatrix} \phi \\ \Upsilon' \end{pmatrix}' \begin{pmatrix} H'x_{t-1} \\ D_t \end{pmatrix} + \sum_{i=1}^{k-1} \Gamma_i \Delta x_{t-i} + \Phi d_t + \varepsilon_t,$$

which is solved by

$$RRR(\Delta x_t, (x'_{t-1}H, D'_t)' | \Delta x_{t-1}, \ldots, \Delta x_{t-k+1}, d_t).$$

If $\hat{\lambda}_i^*$ denote the eigenvalues derived under H_0, we find

$$-2 \log LR(H_0|H(r)) = T \sum_{i=1}^{r} \log\{(1 - \hat{\lambda}_i^*)/(1 - \hat{\lambda}_i)\}. \tag{14.20}$$

Similarly, the hypotheses $\beta = b$ and $\beta = (b, H\phi)$ can be solved by reduced rank regression, but the more general hypothesis

$$\beta = (H_1 \varphi_1, \ldots, H_r \varphi_r),$$

cannot be solved by reduced rank regression. With $\alpha = (\alpha_1, \ldots, \alpha_r)$ and $\Upsilon = (\Upsilon'_1, \ldots \Upsilon'_r)'$, the equation becomes

$$\Delta x_t = \sum_{j=1}^{r} \alpha_j (\varphi'_j H'_j x_{t-1} + \Upsilon_j D_t) + \sum_{i=1}^{k-1} \Gamma_i \Delta x_{t-i} + \Phi d_t + \varepsilon_t.$$

This is evidently a reduced rank problem, but with r reduced rank matrices of rank one. The solution is not given by an eigenvalue problem, but there is a simple modification of the reduced rank algorithm, which is easy to implement and is found to converge quite often. The algorithm has the property that the likelihood function is maximized in each step. The algorithm switches between the reduced rank regressions

$$RRR(\Delta x_t, (x'_{t-1}H_i, D'_t)' | (x'_{t-1}H_j\phi_j, D'_t\Upsilon_j)'_{j\neq i}, \Delta x_{t-1}, \ldots, \Delta x_{t-k+1}, d_t).$$

This result can immediately be applied to calculate likelihood ratio tests for many different restrictions on the coefficients of the cointegrating relations. Thus, in particular, this can give a test of over-identifying restrictions.

Another useful algorithm (see Boswijk, 1992) consists of noticing that, for fixed $\{\phi_j, \Upsilon_j\}^r_{j=1}$, the likelihood is easily maximized by regression of Δx_t on $\{\phi'_jH'_jx_{t-1} + \Upsilon_jD_t\}^r_{j=1}$, the lagged differences and d_t. This gives estimates of $\{\alpha_j\}^r_{j=1}, \{\Gamma_i\}^{k-1}_{i=1}, \Phi$, and Ω. For fixed values of these, however, the equations are linear in $\{\phi_j, \Upsilon_j\}^r_{j=1}$, which can therefore be estimated by generalized least squares. By switching between these steps until convergence one can calculate the maximum likelihood estimators. This algorithm has the further advantage that one can impose restrictions of the form $R'vec(\beta) = r_0$, and the second step is still feasible.

14.4.5 Tests on adjustment coefficients

Under the hypothesis $H_0 : \alpha = A\psi$, in particular the hypothesis of weak exogeneity, we have the model

$$\Delta x_t = A\psi \left(\begin{matrix} \beta \\ \Upsilon' \end{matrix} \right)' \left(\begin{matrix} x_{t-1} \\ D_t \end{matrix} \right) + \sum_{i=1}^{k-1} \Gamma_i\Delta x_{t-i} + \Phi d_t + \varepsilon_t.$$

Multiplying by $\bar{A}' = (A'A)^{-1}A'$ and $A'_\perp$ and conditioning on $A'_\perp\Delta x_t$, we get the marginal and conditional models

$$\bar{A}'\Delta x_t = \omega A'_\perp \Delta x_t + \psi \left(\begin{matrix} \beta \\ \Upsilon' \end{matrix} \right)' \left(\begin{matrix} x_{t-1} \\ D_t \end{matrix} \right) + \sum_{i=1}^{k-1} \Gamma_{Ai}\Delta x_{t-i} + \Phi_A d_t + \varepsilon_{At} \qquad (14.21)$$

$$A'_\perp \Delta x_t = \sum_{i=1}^{k-1} \Gamma_{A_\perp i}\Delta x_{t-i} + \Phi_{A_\perp} d_t + \varepsilon_{A_\perp t}. \qquad (14.22)$$

where $\omega = \bar{A}'\Omega A_\perp (A'_\perp \Omega A_\perp)^{-1}$. The parameters in the marginal and the conditional model are variation independent, and β is estimated from the first equation by

$$RRR(\bar{A}'\Delta x_t, (x'_{t-1}, D'_t)' | A'_\perp \Delta x_t, \Delta x_{t-1}, \ldots, \Delta x_{t-k+1}, d_t).$$

14.4.6 Partial systems

The usual economic distinction between endogenous and exogenous variables is not present in the VAR formulation. If we decompose $x_t = (x'_{1t}, x'_{2t})'$ of dimension

p_1 and p_2 and the matrices similarly, we get weak exogeneity when $\alpha_2 = 0$. Inference on β is efficiently conducted in the conditional model (14.21) with $A = (I_{p_1}, 0)$. Thus we can model the changes of the variables x_{1t} conditional on current changes of x_{2t} and lagged values of both variables, under the assumption of weak exogeneity. It is therefore tempting to use this conditional or partial model to make inferences on both the cointegrating rank and the cointegrating relations.

The partial model is estimated by reduced rank regression

$$RRR(\Delta x_{1t}, (x'_{t-1}, D'_t)' | \Delta x_{2t}, \Delta x_{t-1}, \ldots, \Delta x_{t-k+1}, d_t).$$

and tests of rank and hypotheses on β and α_1 can be calculated as for the full model. However, the assumption of weak exogeneity, without which the analysis would not be efficient, has to be checked in the full model. If the full system is too large to analyse by cointegration, one can determine β from the conditional model and then test for the absence of $\hat{\beta}' x_{t-1}$ in a regression model for Δx_{2t}, see (14.22).

14.5 Asymptotic analysis

This section contains a brief discussion of the most important aspects of the asymptotic analysis of the cointegrating model without proofs and details. We give the result that the rank test requires a family of Dickey–Fuller type distributions, depending on the specification of the deterministic terms of the model. The tests for hypotheses on β are asymptotically distributed as χ^2, and the asymptotic distribution of $\hat{\beta}$ is mixed Gaussian. The asymptotic results are supplemented by a discussion of small sample corrections of the tests.

14.5.1 The asymptotic distribution of the rank test

We give the asymptotic distribution of the rank test when the deterministic term is a polynomial of order d.

Theorem 11 *In model (14.17) with $D_t = t^d$ and $d_t = (1, t, \ldots, t^{d-1})$, the likelihood ratio test statistic $LR(H(r)|H(p))$ is given in (14.19). Under the assumption that the cointegrating rank is r, and ε_t i.i.d. $(0, \Omega)$, the asymptotic distribution is*

$$\mathrm{tr}\left\{ \int_0^1 (dB)F' \left(\int_0^1 FF'du \right)^{-1} \int_0^1 F(dB)' \right\}, \qquad (14.23)$$

where F is defined by

$$F(u) = \begin{pmatrix} B(u) \\ u^d \end{pmatrix} \begin{vmatrix} \\ 1, \ldots, u^{d-1} \end{vmatrix},$$

and where B(u) is the p − r dimensional Brownian motion. This distribution is tabulated by simulating the distribution of the test of no cointegration in the model for a p − r dimensional process with one lag and the same deterministic terms.

Note that the limit distribution does not depend on the parameters $\Gamma_1, \ldots, \Gamma_{k-1}$, Υ, Φ, Ω, but only on the dimension $p - r$, the number of common trends, and the order of the trend d. If $p = 1$ the limit distribution is the squared Dickey–Fuller distribution (see Dickey and Fuller, 1981), and we therefore call the distribution (14.23) the Dickey–Fuller distribution with $p - r$ degrees of freedom, $DF_{p-r}(d)$.

If the deterministic terms are more complicated, they sometimes change the asymptotic distribution. It follows from the Granger Representation Theorem that the deterministic term d_t is cumulated to $C\Phi \sum_{i=1}^{t} d_i$. In deriving the asymptotics, we normalize x_t by $T^{-1/2}$. If $\sum_{i=1}^{t} d_i$ is bounded, this normalization implies that the limit distribution does not depend on the precise form of $\sum_{i=1}^{t} d_i$. Thus, if we let d_t be a centered seasonal dummy, or a "innovation dummy" $d_t = 1_{\{t \geq t_0\}}$, they do not change the asymptotic distribution. If, on the other hand, we include the "step dummy" $d_t = 1_{\{t \geq t_0\}}$, then the cumulation of this is a broken linear trend, and that will influence the limit distribution and requires special tables (see Johansen, Mosconi and Nielsen, 2000).

For the partial models we also need special tables (see Harbo, Johansen, Nielsen and Rahbek, 1998; or Pesaran, Shin and Smith, 2000). The problem is that because $\alpha_2 = 0$, the cointegrating rank has to be less than the dimension, p_1, of the modeled variables, as all the $\varepsilon's$ from the p_2 conditioning variables generate common trends. Thus the tables depends on the indices p_2 and $p_1 - r$. The general problem of including stationary regressors in the VAR has been treated by Mosconi and Rahbek (1999).

One can also test for rank when some of the cointegrating relations are known: see Horvath and Watson (1995) and Paruolo (2001). In that case we get new limit distributions which are convolutions of the Dickey–Fuller distributions for rank determination and the χ^2 distributions used for inference for β.

14.5.2 Determination of cointegrating rank

Consider again model (14.17), with $D_t = t^d$ and $d_t = (1, \ldots, t^{d-1})$, where the limit distribution is given by (14.23). The tables are used as follows. If r represents prior knowledge that we want to test, we simply calculate the test statistic $Q_r = -2 \log LR(H(r)|H(p))$ and compare it with the relevant quantile. Note that the tables give the asymptotic distribution only, and that the actual distribution depends not only on the finite value of T but also on the parameters $(\alpha, \beta, \Gamma_1, \ldots, \Gamma_{k-1})$, although not on Φ, Υ, and Ω.

A common situation is that one has no, or very little, prior knowledge about r, and in this case it seems more reasonable to estimate r from the data. This is done as follows. First compare Q_0 with its quantile c_0, say. If $Q_0 < c_0$, we let $\hat{r} = 0$, if $Q_0 \geq c_0$ we calculate Q_1 and compare it with c_1. If now $Q_1 < c_1$ we define $\hat{r} = 1$, and if not we compare Q_2 with its quantile c_2, etc. This defines an estimator $\hat{r}$:

$$\{\hat{r} = r\} = \{Q_r < c_r, Q_{r-1} \geq c_{r-1}, \ldots, Q_0 \geq c_0\},$$

which takes on the values $0, 1, \ldots, p$, and which converges in probability to the true value in the sense that, if 95 per cent quantiles are used for the estimation, then

$$P_r(\hat{r} = r) \to 95\% \quad \text{and} \quad P_r(\hat{r} < r) \to 0.$$

14.5.3 A small sample correction of the rank test

In Johansen (2002a, 2004) a small sample correction for the rank test is developed under the assumption of Gaussian errors, which improves the useful-ness of the asymptotic tables for the rank test. For finite samples, the distribution of the likelihood ratio test statistic depends on the unknown parameters under the null hypothesis. For $T \to \infty$ the dependence on the parameters disappears, but not uniformly in the parameter. Usually the distribution is shifted to higher values for finite T, and the more so, the closer we are to the $I(2)$ boundary of the para-meter space.

As an illustration of the results, consider the test for $\pi = \mu_1 = 0$ in the model for the univariate process x_t, with $k = 2s + 1$

$$\Delta x_t = \pi x_{t-1} + \sum_{i=1}^{2s} \gamma_i \Delta x_{t-i} + \mu_0 + \mu_1 t + \varepsilon_t.$$

Under the assumption that the process is $I(1)$, the limit distribution of the like-lihood ratio test is the (squared) Dickey–Fuller test. We can then prove that if, instead of using $-2 \log LR(\pi = \mu_1 = 0)$, we divide by the quantity

$$(1 + 0.12T^{-1} + 4.05T^{-2})\left(1 + \frac{1.72}{T}\left[s + \frac{\sum_{i=1}^{2s} i\hat{\gamma}_i}{1 - \sum_{i=1}^{2s} \hat{\gamma}_i}\right]\right),$$

then the approximation to the limit distribution is improved. Note how the cor-rection depends on the estimated parameters, in particular on values of $\sum_{i=1}^{k} \gamma_i$ close to one, where the correction tends to infinity. This corresponds to the process being almost $I(2)$. The numerical coefficients are determined by simulation of the various moments of a random walk for various values of T, and depend on the type of deterministics in the model.

Another example is given by the model with one lag and p dimensions

$$\Delta x_t = \Pi x_{t-1} + \mu_1 t + \mu_0 + \varepsilon_t,$$

where we test $\Pi = \alpha\beta'$ and $\mu_1 = \alpha\beta'_1$, where α and β are $p \times 1$. Under the null we have

$$H_0 : \Delta x_t = \alpha(\beta' x_{t-1} + \beta'_1 t) + \mu_0 + \varepsilon_t.$$

In this case the correction factor takes the form

$$(1 + T^{-1}a_1(p) + T^{-2}a_2(p))\left(1 + \frac{1}{T}\frac{k(\alpha,\beta,\Omega)}{\beta'\alpha}\right)$$

where

$$k = -(2 + \beta'\alpha)m(p)\kappa + \{2(1 + \beta'\alpha)(p - 1) - 2\kappa(4 + 3\beta'\alpha)\}g(p)/(p - 1)^2$$

and where $\kappa = 1 - (\beta'\alpha)^2/\alpha'\Omega^{-1}\alpha\beta'\Omega\beta$, and the coefficients $a_1(p), a_2(p), m(p)$, and $g(p)$ are found by simulation. Notice that again the correction, and the test, give problems when $\alpha'\beta = 0$, which happens close to the $I(2)$ boundary.

14.5.4   The asymptotic distribution of β

The main result here is that the estimator of β, suitably normalized, converges to a mixed Gaussian distribution, even when estimated under continuously differentiable restrictions. The result is taken from Johansen (1996), but see also Anderson (2002). This result implies that likelihood ratio tests on β are asymptotically χ^2 distributed. We normalize $\hat{\beta}$ on $\bar{\beta}$, so that $\bar{\beta}'\hat{\beta} = I_r$, and find

Theorem 12   *In model (14.1) the asymptotic distribution of $\hat{\beta}$ is given by*

$$T\bar{\beta}'_\perp(\hat{\beta} - \beta) \xrightarrow{w} \left(\int_0^1 HH'du\right)^{-1}\int_0^1 H(dV)', \tag{14.24}$$

where

$$H = \beta'_\perp CW, \quad \text{and} \quad V = (\alpha'\Omega^{-1}\alpha)^{-1}\alpha'\Omega^{-1}W$$

are independent Brownian motions. An estimator of $\int_0^1 HH'du$ is $T^{-1}\hat{\beta}'_\perp S_{11}\hat{\beta}_\perp$.

Because H and V are independent, it follows that the limiting random variable Z, say, has a distribution given H that is Gaussian

$$Z|H \sim N_{(p-r)\times r}\left(0, (\alpha'\Omega^{-1}\alpha)^{-1} \otimes \left(\int_0^1 HH'du\right)^{-1}\right), \tag{14.25}$$

or, equivalently,

$$\left(\int_0^1 HH'du\right)^{1/2} Z(\alpha'\Omega^{-1}\alpha)^{1/2}|H \sim N_{(p-r)\times r}(0, I_r \otimes I_{p-r}), \tag{14.26}$$

so that

$$\left(\hat{\beta}'_\perp \sum_{t=1}^T R_{1t}R'_{1t}\hat{\beta}_\perp\right)^{1/2} \bar{\beta}'_\perp(\hat{\beta} - \beta)(\hat{\alpha}'\hat{\Omega}^{-1}\hat{\alpha})^{1/2} \xrightarrow{w} N_{(p-r)\times r}(0, I_r \otimes I_{p-r}).$$

This implies that Wald and likelihood ratio tests on β can be conducted using the asymptotic χ^2 distribution. Note that the asymptotic distribution is not Gaussian and that the scaling factor $\left(\int_0^1 HH'du\right)^{1/2}$ is not an inverse standard deviation, as we usually employ in inference for stationary processes. It is correct that the deviation $(\hat{\beta} - \beta)$ can be scaled to converge to the Gaussian distribution, but it is not correct that this scaling is done by an estimator of the asymptotic standard deviation.

One could say that the proper scaling is an estimator of the asymptotic conditional variance, given the function H, see Johansen (1995). The available information in the data is measured by the matrix $\hat{\alpha}'\hat{\Omega}^{-1}\hat{\alpha} \otimes \hat{\beta}'_\perp \sum_{t=1}^{T} R_{1t}R'_{1t}\hat{\beta}_\perp$, and if this is very large, $\hat{\beta}$ has a small "standard error," but occasionally the information is small, and then large deviations of $\hat{\beta} - \beta$ can occur. We end by giving, without proof, a result on the test for identifying restrictions on β. We denote by $\{A_{ij}\}$ the matrix with blocks A_{ij}.

Theorem 13 *Let β be identified by the restrictions $\beta = \{h_i + H_i\varphi_i\}_{i=1}^{r}$, where H_i is $p \times (s_i - 1)$ and φ_i is $(s_i - 1) \times 1$. Then the asymptotic distribution of $T(\hat{\beta} - \beta)$ is mixed Gaussian with an estimate of the asymptotic conditional variance given by*

$$T diag(\{H_i\}_{i=1}^{r})\{\hat{\rho}_{ij}H'_iS_{11}H_j\}^{-1}diag(\{H'_i\}_{i=1}^{r}),$$

with $\rho_{ij} = \alpha'_i\Omega^{-1}\alpha_j$. The asymptotic distribution of the likelihood ratio test statistic for these restrictions is χ^2 with degrees of freedom given by $\sum_{i=1}^{r}(p - r - s_i + 1)$.

A small sample correction for the test on β has been developed by Johansen (2000, 2002b); see also Omtzigt and Fachin (2006) for a discussion of this result and a comparison with the bootstrap.

To illustrate how to conduct inference on a cointegrating coefficient, and why it becomes asymptotic χ^2 despite the asymptotic mixed Gaussian limit of $\hat{\beta}$, we may consider a very simple case. Let x_t be a bivariate process with one lag for which $\alpha' = (-1, 0)$ and $\beta = (1, \theta)'$. The equations become

$$x_{1t} = \theta x_{2t-1} + \varepsilon_{1t},$$
$$\Delta x_{2t} = \varepsilon_{2t}. \tag{14.27}$$

If we add the assumption that ε_t is Gaussian with mean zero and variance $\Omega = diag(\sigma_1^2, \sigma_2^2)$, the maximum likelihood estimator satisfies

$$\hat{\theta} = \frac{\sum_{t=1}^{T} x_{1t}x_{2t-1}}{\sum_{t=1}^{T} x_{2t-1}^2} = \theta + \frac{\sum_{t=1}^{T} \varepsilon_{1t}x_{2t-1}}{\sum_{t=1}^{T} x_{2t-1}^2}.$$

Let us first analyse the distribution of $\hat{\theta}$ conditional on the process $\{x_{2t}\}$. We find that

$$\hat{\theta}|\{x_{2t}\} \text{ is distributed as } N\left(\theta, \sigma_1^2/\sum_{t=1}^{T} x_{2t-1}^2\right).$$

It follows that $\hat{\theta}$ is mixed Gaussian with mixing parameter $1/\sum_{t=1}^{T} x_{2t-1}^2$, and hence has mean θ and variance $\sigma_1^2 E(1/\sum_{t=1}^{T} x_{2t-1}^2)$. When constructing a test for $\theta = \theta_0$

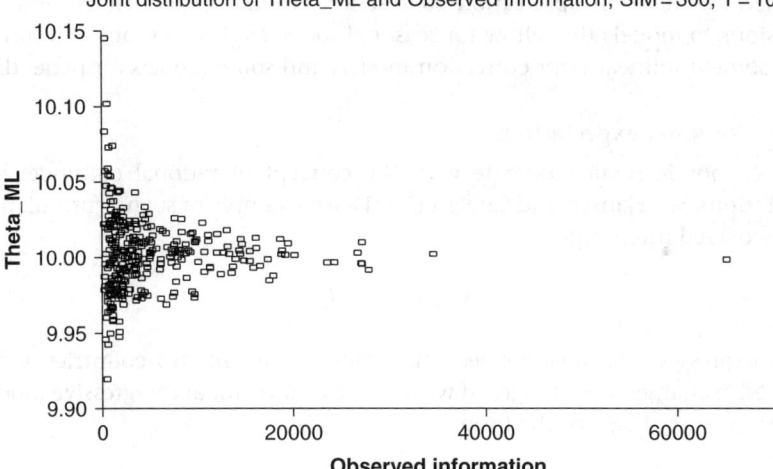

Figure 14.2 The joint distribution of $\hat{\theta}$ and the observed information ($\sum_{i=1}^{T} x_{2t-1}^2/\hat{\sigma}^2$) in the model (14.27). Note that the larger the information, the smaller is the uncertainty in the estimate $\hat{\theta}$

we do not base our inference on the Wald test

$$\frac{\hat{\theta} - \theta}{\sqrt{Var(\hat{\theta})}} = \frac{\hat{\theta} - \theta}{\sqrt{E(1/\sum_{t=1}^{T} x_{2t-1}^2)}},$$

but rather on the Wald test which comes from an expansion of the likelihood function and is based on the observed information:

$$\left(\sum_{t=1}^{T} x_{2t-1}^2\right)^{1/2} (\hat{\theta} - \theta), \tag{14.28}$$

which is distributed as $N(0, \sigma_1^2)$. Thus we normalize by the observed information, not the expected information often used when analysing stationary processes. In order to conduct inference we should therefore not consider the marginal distribution of the estimator, but the joint distribution of the estimator, $\hat{\theta}$, and the information in the data, $\sum_{t=1}^{T} x_{2t-1}^2/\sigma_1^2$, see Figure 14.2. The information should be exploited by conditioning, in order to achieve Gaussian inference (see Johansen, 1995), and because the information and the t-ratio (28) are asymptotically independent, we can perform the conditioning (asymptotically) by simply considering the marginal distribution of the t-ratio instead.

14.6   Further topics in cointegration

The basic model for $I(1)$ variables can be applied to test economic hypotheses of different types and extended to allow for other types of nonstationarity.

We mention here an application to test for rational expectations, and some extensions to models that allow for seasonal roots, explosive roots, and $I(2)$ variables, some nonlinear error correction models and some models for panel data.

14.6.1　Rational expectations

Many economic models operate with the concept of rational or model based expectations, see Hansen and Sargent (1991). An example of such a formulation is the uncovered interest parity,

$$\Delta^e e_{t+1} = i_t^1 - i_t^2, \tag{14.29}$$

which expresses a balance between the interest rates in two countries and the expected exchange rate changes. If we have fitted a vector autoregressive model to the data $x_t = (e_t, i_t^1, i_t^2)'$ of the form

$$\Delta x_t = \alpha \beta' x_{t-1} + \Gamma_1 \Delta x_{t-1} + \varepsilon_t, \tag{14.30}$$

the assumption of model-based expectations (Muth, 1961) means that $\Delta^e e_{t+1}$ can be replaced by $E_t \Delta e_{t+1}$ based upon the model (14.30). That is

$$\Delta^e e_{t+1} = E_t \Delta e_{t+1} = \alpha_1 \beta' x_t + \Gamma_{11} \Delta x_{t-1}.$$

The assumption (14.29) implies the identity

$$i_t^1 - i_t^2 = \alpha_1 \beta' x_t + \Gamma_{11} \Delta x_{t-1}.$$

Hence the cointegrating relation has to have the form

$$\beta' x_{t-1} = i_t^1 - i_t^2,$$

the adjustment is $\alpha_1 = 1$ and, finally, the first row of Γ_1 is zero: $\Gamma_{11} = 0$. Thus, the hypothesis (14.29) implies a number of testable restrictions on the vector autoregressive model. The implications of model-based expectations and the cointegrated vector autoregressive model is explored in Johansen and Swensen (1999, 2004), where it is shown that, as in the example above, the rational expectation restrictions have information on the cointegrating relations and the short run adjustments. It is demonstrated how estimation under the rational expectation restrictions can be performed by regression and reduced rank regression in certain cases. See also Campbell and Shiller (1987) for an analysis of the expectation hypothesis in the cointegration model.

14.6.2　Seasonal cointegration

The cointegration theory so far described works under the assumption that the only unstable root of the process is $z = 1$. If roots are allowed at $z = -1, i, -i$ we get models that exhibit quarterly seasonal non-stationary variation.

This model has been analysed from the point of view of maximum likelihood by Lee (1992), Ahn and Reinsel (1994), and Johansen and Schaumburg (1998). In order to illustrate the concepts in a simple setting, we consider the model with roots only at $z = 1$ and $z = -1$, where we need $(1 - L)(1 + L)x_t = (1 - L^2)x_t$ to achieve stationarity under a condition corresponding to (14.5).

The error correction model (see Hylleberg, Engle, Granger, and Yoo, 1990), in this case is found by expanding the autoregressive polynomial around $z = 1$ and $z = -1$ and a simplified version, without deterministics and lags, is

$$(1 - L)(1 + L)x_t = (1 + L)\alpha_1\beta_1'x_{t-1} + (1 - L)\alpha_{-1}\beta_{-1}'x_{t-1} + \varepsilon_t. \tag{14.31}$$

The Granger Representation Theorem can be generalized to this case and gives the solution of the equations, or the moving average representation, under an $I(1)$ condition of the form (14.5)

$$x_t = C_1 \sum_{i=1}^{t} \varepsilon_i + C_{-1}(-1)^t \sum_{i=1}^{t}(-1)^i\varepsilon_i + A_1 + (-1)^tA_{-1} \mid y_t,$$

where y_t is stationary and A_1 and A_{-1} depend on initial values and satisfy $\beta_1'A_1 = 0$ and $\beta_{-1}'A_{-1} = 0$, and C_1 and C_{-1} have expressions like (14.7). This implies that the processes

$$(1 - L)(1 + L)x_t = C_1(1 + L)\varepsilon_t + C_{-1}(1 - L)\varepsilon_t + (1 + L)(1 - L)y_t,$$
$$(1 + L)\beta_1'x_t = \beta_1'C_{-1}\varepsilon_t + (1 + L)\beta_1'y_t,$$
$$(1 - L)\beta_{-1}'x_t = \beta_{-1}'C_1\varepsilon_t + (1 - L)\beta_{-1}'y_t,$$

are stationary. The nonstationarity of x_t is due to the processes $S_t^{(1)} = \sum_{i=1}^{t} \varepsilon_i$ and $S_t^{(-1)} = (-1)^t \sum_{i=1}^{t}(-1)^i\varepsilon_i$, for which $(1 - L)S_t^{(1)} = \varepsilon_t$, and $(1 + L)S_t^{(-1)} = \varepsilon_t$. Maximum likelihood estimation of (14.31) involves two reduced rank regressions and can be performed by a switching algorithm: see also Cubadda (2001) for complex reduced rank regression in this model. Asymptotic inference can be conducted much along the same lines as for the usual $I(1)$ model, and we get the same basic results: inference on the rank requires new Dickey–Fuller distributions which can be expressed as stochastic integrals of complex Brownian motions, and inference on the remaining parameters is asymptotic χ^2.

14.6.3 Models for explosive roots

If the characteristic polynomial has one real explosive root $z = \lambda < 1$ and roots at $z = 1$, we get explosive processes for which $(1 - L)(1 - \lambda^{-1}L)x_t$ is stationary under an $I(1)$ condition corresponding to (14.5). We find, by expanding around $z = \lambda^{-1}$ and $z = 1$, the error correction model

$$(1 - L)(1 - \lambda^{-1}L)x_t = \alpha_1\beta_1'(1 - \lambda^{-1}L)x_{t-1} + \alpha_\lambda\beta_\lambda'(1 - L)x_{t-1} + \varepsilon_t.$$

The solution under the $I(1)$ condition is

$$x_t = C_1 \sum_{i=1}^{t} \varepsilon_i + C_\lambda \lambda^{-t} \sum_{i=1}^{t} \lambda^i \varepsilon_i + \lambda^{-t} A_\lambda + A_1 + y_t,$$

where A_1 and A_λ depend on initial values and satisfy $\beta_1' A_1 = 0$ and $\beta_\lambda' A_\lambda = 0$, and y_t is stationary. The matrices C_1 and C_λ have expressions as given in (14.7). The nonstationarity is due to $S_t^{(1)} = \sum_{i=1}^{t} \varepsilon_i$, and $S_t^{(\lambda)} = \lambda^{-t} \sum_{i=1}^{t} \lambda^i \varepsilon_i$, which satisfy $(1 - L)S_t^{(1)} = \varepsilon_t$ and $(1 - \lambda^{-1}L)S_t^{(\lambda)} = \varepsilon_t$. Cointegration can remove one root, and the other is removed by either $(1 - L)$ or $(1 - \lambda^{-1}L)$, so that the processes

$$(1 - L)(1 - \lambda^{-1}L)x_t = C_1(1 - \lambda^{-1}L)\varepsilon_t + C_\lambda(1 - L)\varepsilon_t + (1 - L)(1 - \lambda^{-1}L)y_t,$$
$$(1 - \lambda^{-1}L)\beta_1' x_t = \beta_1' C_1 \varepsilon_t + (1 - \lambda^{-1}L)\beta_1' y_t,$$
$$(1 - L)\beta_\lambda' x_t = \beta_\lambda' C_1 \varepsilon_t + (1 - L)\beta_\lambda' y_t,$$

are stationary. The sum $\sum_{i=0}^{t} \lambda^i \varepsilon_i$ converges for $t \to \infty$, and the explosiveness is due to the factor $\lambda^{-t} \to \infty$. This implies that the asymptotic theory is much more complicated as no central limit theorem can be invoked, but the limit distributions involve the random variable $\sum_{i=0}^{\infty} \lambda^i \varepsilon_i$, see Anderson (1959). The asymptotic theory is developed by Nielsen (2001, 2002, 2005). Maximum likelihood estimation of the model involves two reduced rank regressions and an estimation of λ. This can be performed by a suitable switching algorithm.

14.6.4   The $I(2)$ model

If $z = 1$ is the only unstable root and $\alpha_\perp' \Gamma \beta_\perp$ has reduced rank, see (14.5), then we get integration of orders more than one. Under suitable conditions, similar to (14.5), we find that we need two differences to make the process stationary. We find an error correction model which can be parameterized as

$$\Delta^2 x_t = \alpha(\beta' x_{t-1} + \psi' \Delta x_{t-1}) + \Omega \alpha_\perp (\alpha_\perp' \Omega \alpha_\perp)^{-1} \kappa' \tau' \Delta x_{t-1} + \varepsilon_t, \quad \beta = \tau \rho, \qquad (14.32)$$

where α and β are $p \times r$ and τ is $p \times (r + s)$ (see Johansen, 1997), or

$$\Delta^2 x_t = \alpha \begin{pmatrix} \beta \\ \delta' \end{pmatrix}' \begin{pmatrix} x_{t-1} \\ \tau_\perp' \Delta x_{t-1} \end{pmatrix} + \zeta \tau' \Delta x_{t-1} + \varepsilon_t, \qquad (14.33)$$

see Paruolo and Rahbek (1999). Here $\delta = \psi \tau_\perp$ is of dimension $r \times (p - r - s)$. Under suitable conditions on the parameters, the equation has a solution of the form

$$x_t = C_2 \sum_{i=1}^{t} \sum_{j=1}^{i} \varepsilon_j + C_1 \sum_{i=1}^{t} \varepsilon_i + A_1 + tA_2 + y_t.$$

The coefficient matrices satisfy

$$\tau' C_2 = 0, \quad \beta' C_1 + \psi' C_2 = 0, \quad \tau'(A_1, A_2) = 0, \quad \beta' A_1 + \psi' A_2 = 0,$$

so that the processes

$$\Delta^2 x_t = C_2 \varepsilon_t + C_1 \Delta \varepsilon_t + \Delta^2 y_t,$$
$$\beta' x_t + \psi' \Delta x_t = \beta' y_t + \psi' C_1 \varepsilon_t + \psi' \Delta y_t$$
$$\tau' \Delta x_t = \tau' C_1 \varepsilon_t + \tau' \Delta y_t,$$

are stationary. Thus the solution is an $I(2)$ process, and the cointegrating relations are given by $\tau' x_t$ (and hence $\beta' x_t = \rho' \tau' x_t$ is $I(1)$), but the model also allows for multicointegration (see Engle and Yoo, 1991), that is, cointegration between the levels and the differences: $\beta' x_t + \psi' \Delta x_t$ is stationary. Equivalently one can say, since $\tau' \Delta x_t$ is stationary, that $\beta' x_t + \delta \tau'_\perp \Delta x_t$ is stationary, where δ is the so-called multicointegration parameter. Maximum likelihood estimation can be performed by a switching algorithm using the two parametrizations given in (14.32) and (14.33). The same techniques can be used for a number of hypotheses on the cointegrating parameters β and τ.

The asymptotic theory of likelihood ratio tests and maximum likelihood estimators is developed by Johansen (1997), Rahbek, Kongsted, and Jørgensen (1999), and Paruolo (1996, 2000). It is shown that the likelihood ratio test for rank involves not only Brownian motion, but also integrated Brownian motion and hence some new Dickey–Fuller-type distributions that have to be simulated. The asymptotic distribution of the maximum likelihood estimator is quite involved as it is not mixed Gaussian. Many different hypotheses on the parameters can be tested using asymptotic χ^2 tests: see Boswijk (2000) and Johansen (2006).

14.6.5 Nonlinear cointegration

There are obviously many different ways in which a linear model can be generalized to a nonlinear model. We focus here on the nonlinear error correction model, without deterministic terms, formulated as

$$\Delta x_t = f(\beta' x_{t-1}) + \sum_{i=1}^{k-1} \Gamma_i \Delta x_{t-i} + \varepsilon_t, \qquad (14.34)$$

see Bec and Rahbek (2004) for a survey and recent results. For linear $f(\beta' x_{t-1}) = \alpha \beta' x_{t-1}$ we get model (14.1), and for the choice

$$f(\beta' x_{t-1}) = \begin{cases} \alpha_1 \beta' x_{t-1}, & \text{if } |\beta' x_{t-1}| > \lambda, \\ \alpha_2 \beta' x_{t-1}, & \text{if } |\beta' x_{t-1}| \leq \lambda \end{cases}$$

we get the Threshold Autoregressive (TAR) model, where the adjustment coefficients switch between α_1 and α_2, depending on the regime defined by the size of the disequilibrium error $|\beta' x_{t-1}|$. This kind of model has been used for testing for no cointegration (see Enders and Siklos, 2001), and for testing, for linear cointegration (see Balke and Fomby, 1997; Hansen and Seo, 2002). No general results exist for inference on β, which is difficult to even calculate because of the discontinuous function f.

If we take

$$f(\beta' x_{t-1}) = \alpha_1 \exp(-|\beta' x_{t-1}|) + \alpha_2(1 - \exp(-|\beta' x_{t-1}|))$$

we get a smooth transition model, see Granger and Teräsvirta (1993).

In both cases one should think of the function f as modeling that the reaction to a disequilibrium error is different depending on the regime, but the switching is endogenous and does not depend on any outside influence.

Another type of model is where f is allowed to depend on an outside shock. Consider, as an example, a zero-one variable s_t, and a model of the form

$$\Delta x_t = f(\beta' x_{t-1}, s_t) + \sum_{i=1}^{k-1} \Gamma_i \Delta x_{t-i} + \varepsilon_t, \qquad (14.35)$$

with f given by

$$f(\beta' x_{t-1}, s_t) = (s_t \alpha_1 + (1 - s_t)\alpha_2)\beta' x_{t-1}.$$

The distribution of s_t given the past and ε_t may be defined as, for example,

$$P\{s_t = 1 | x_{t-1}, \ldots, x_{t-k+1}, \varepsilon_t\} = (1 - \exp(-|\beta' x_{t-1}|))/(1 + \exp(-|\beta' x_{t-1}|)).$$

In this case the adjustment coefficient switches between two states, where the probability of the two states is a smooth function of the process. Such a process is considered by Rahbek and Shephard (2002). The Markov switching models, where s_t is an independent Markov chain, were introduced into econometrics for stationary autoregressive processes by Hamilton (1989), and have gained widespread use. Only recently (see Douc, Moulines, and Rydén, 2003) have the properties of maximum likelihood estimators been established, but extensions of the results to the cointegrated model are still to be developed.

In general, this kind of model is difficult to analyse because of the nonlinear reaction function. Instead of finding a linear representation of the process in terms of the errors, one has instead to prove the properties of the process directly. One can replace the usual notion of $I(0)$ by the notion of "geometric ergodicity" (Bec and Rahbek 2004) or "near epoch dependence" (Escribano and Mira, 2002), and attempt to define $I(1)$ by the requirement that x_t converges weakly to a Brownian motion, but the final concepts have not been developed yet. What replaces the Granger Representation Theorem are results about $\beta' x_t$ and Δx_t being $I(0)$, whereas, under regularity conditions, x_t is not, so that the process is cointegrated. Furthermore, one can discuss the existence of moments of the process x_t, which is useful for developing an asymptotic theory for the process and eventually for the estimators. Estimation of this model is relatively straightforward if β is known, but, as mentioned, the theory has yet to be developed for β unknown.

14.6.6 Panel data cointegration

If we follow a panel of N units (countries), each with p variables, the data comes in the form $x_{it}, i = 1, \ldots, N, \ t = 1, \ldots, T$. We stack the vectors into the Np dimensional vector x_t and want to build a statistical model for x_t that reflects the panel structure. For illustration we assume that x_t satisfies the simple $I(1)$ model

$$\Delta x_t = \alpha \beta' x_{t-1} + \varepsilon_t.$$

The panel structure could then be formulated by the conditions that α, β and Ω are block diagonal corresponding to no feedback from one unit to another, no cointegration between units, and independent units. This model has been investigated by Larsson, Lyhagen and Løthgren (2001) and Groen and Kleibergen (2003) for general Ω.

For macro data, this is not a useful set of assumptions, and the problem is to model a large dimensional vector so that there is the possibility of: (1) cointegration within a unit; (2) some cointegration between units; (3) the possibility of feedback from disequilibrium in other units; and, finally, (4) some possibility of correlation between the shocks to different units.

An interesting solution has been proposed by Pesaran, Schuermann and Weiner (2004), who suggest constructing for each unit a "rest of the world" index $x_{it}^* = \sum_{j \neq i} w_{ij} x_{jt}$, and modeling the ith unit as

$$\Delta x_{it} = \alpha_i (\beta_i' x_{it-1} + \beta_i^{*'} x_{it-1}^*) + \varepsilon_{it}.$$

By stacking the observations into x_t and solving the models for x_t they obtain a model that takes into account all the four requirements above.

All the models are, of course, submodels of the basic $I(1)$ model but the asymptotic theory is different, because we can let $N \to \infty$ or $T \to \infty$ or both, see Phillips and Moon (1999).

14.7 Conclusion

Granger (1983) coined the term cointegration, and it was his investigations of the relation between cointegration and error correction in Engle and Granger (1987) that brought the modeling of vector autoregressions with unit roots to the center of attention in macroeconometrics.

During the last 20 years, many have contributed to the development of the theory and applications of cointegration. The account given here focuses on theory, more precisely on likelihood-based theory for the vector autoregressive model and its extensions. The reason for focusing on model-based inference is that, although we hope to derive methods with wide applicability, all methods have a limited applicability. By building a statistical model as a framework for hypothesis testing, one has to make explicit assumptions about the model used.

Therefore it becomes a natural part of the methodology to check assumptions, because if the assumptions are not satisfied, the same may hold for the results derived. Applying a rank test to some given data, without checking that the underlying vector autoregressive model has errors with no residual autocorrelation, and that the parameters of the model are constant, is as wrong as applying the continuous mapping theorem in asymptotic analysis, without checking that the function in question is in fact continuous.

What has been developed for the cointegrated vector autoregressive model is a set of useful tools for the analysis of macroeconomic and financial time series. The theory is part of many textbooks, and the $I(1)$ procedures have been implemented in many different software packages, CATS in RATS, Givewin, Eviews, Microfit, Shazam, etc. The $I(2)$ model is less developed but a version will appear in CATS.

Many theoretical problems remain unsolved, however. Time series rely heavily on asymptotic methods and it is often a problem to obtain long series in economics which actually measure the same variables for the whole period. Therefore periods which can be modeled by constant parameters are often rather short, and it is therefore extremely important to develop methods for small sample correction of the asymptotic results. When these become part of the software packages, they will be routinely applied and ensure more reliable inference.

A very interesting and promising development lies with nonlinear time series analysis, where the statistical theory is still in its beginning. There are many different types of nonlinearities possible, and the theory has to be developed in close contact with the applications in order to ensure that useful models and concepts are developed.

Apart from this there is going to be a development and extension of cointegration in the area of panel data cointegration, seasonal cointegration, and the models for explosive roots. This development should also include software for the various models, in order that the theory can be easily applied and extended in interaction with applications.

Most importantly, however, a totally different development is needed, and that is a development of economic theory, which takes into account the findings of the empirical analysis of nonstationary economic data.

For a long time, regression analysis and correlations have been standard ways of analysing relations between variables and cause and effect in economics. Economic theory has incorporated regression analysis as a useful tool for checking or falsifying economic predictions.

Similarly, empirical cointegration analysis of economic data reveals new ways of understanding economic data, and there is a need for building an economic theory that supports and explains these understanding.

References

Ahn, S.K. and G.C. Reinsel (1990) Estimation for partially non-stationary multivariate autoregressive models. *Journal of the American Statistical Association* **85**, 813–23.

Ahn, S.K. and G.C. Reinsel (1994) Estimation of partially non-stationary vector autoregressive models with seasonal behavior. *Journal of Econometrics* **62**, 317–50.

Anderson, T.W. (1951) Estimating linear restrictions on regression coefficients for multivariate normal distributions. *Annals of Mathematical Statistics* **22**, 327–51.

Anderson, T.W. (1959) On asymptotic distributions of estimates of parameters of stochastic difference equations. *Annals of Mathematical Statistics* **30**, 676–87.

Anderson, T.W. (2002) Reduced rank regression in cointegrated models. *Journal of Econometrics* **106**, 203–16.

Balke, N.S. and T.B. Fomby (1997) Threshold cointegration. *International Economic Review* **38**, 627–45.

Banerjee, A., J.J. Dolado, J.W. Galbraith and D.F. Hendry (1993) *Co-integration Error-Correction and the Econometric Analysis of Non-Stationary Data.* Oxford: Oxford University Press.

Bec, F. and A.C. Rahbek (2004) Vector equilibrium correction models with non-linear discontinuous adjustments. *Econometrics Journal* **72**, 641–6.

Boswijk, P. (1992) *Cointegration, Identification and Exogeneity: Inference in Structural Error Correction Models.* Amsterdam: Thesis Publisher, Tinbergen Institute.

Boswijk, P. (2000) Mixed normality and ancillarity in $I(2)$ systems. *Econometric Theory* **16**, 878–904.

Campbell, J. and R.J. Shiller (1987) Cointegration and tests of present value models. *Journal of Political Economy* **95**, 1062–1088.

Cubadda, G. (2001) Complex reduced rank models for seasonally cointegrated time series. *Oxford Bulletin of Economics and Statistics* **63**, 497–511.

Dickey, D.A. and W.A. Fuller (1981) Likelihood ratio statistics for autoregressive time series with a unit root. *Econometrica* **49**, 1057–1072.

Douc, R., É. Moulines and T. Rydén (2004) Asymptotic properties of the maximum likelihood estimator in autoregressive models with Markov regime. *Annals of Statistics* **32**, 2254–2304.

Enders, W. and P.L. Siklos (2001) Cointegration and threshold adjustment. *Journal of Business and Economic Statistics* **19**, 166–76.

Engle, R.F. and C.W.J. Granger (1987) Co-integration and error correction: representation, estimation and testing. *Econometrica* **55**, 251–76.

Engle, R.F. and B.S. Yoo (1991) Cointegrated economic time series: A survey with new results. In C.W.J. Granger and R.F. Engle (eds), *Long-run Economic Relations: Readings in Cointegration.* Oxford: Oxford University Press.

Engle, R.F., D.F. Hendry and J.-F. Richard (1983) Exogeneity. *Econometrica* **51**, 277–304.

Escribano, A. and S. Mira (2002) Nonlinear error correction models. *Journal of Time Series Analysis* **23**, 509–22.

Granger, C.W.J. (1983) Cointegrated variables and error correction models. UCSD Discussion paper 83–13a.

Granger C.W.J. and T. Teräsvirta (1993) *Modelling Non-linear Economic Relationships.* Oxford: Oxford University Press.

Groen, J. and F.R. Kleibergen (2003) Likelihood based cointegration analysis in panels of vector error correction models. *Journal of Business and Economic Statistics* **21**, 295–318.

Hamilton, D.J. (1989) A new approach to economic analysis on non stationary time series and the business cycle. *Econometrica* **57**, 357–84.

Hamilton, D.J. (1994) *Time Series Analysis.* Princeton: Princeton University Press.

Hansen, H. and S. Johansen (1999) Some tests for parameter constancy in the cointegrated VAR. *Econometrics Journal* **2**, 306–33.

Hansen, L.P. and T.J. Sargent (1991) Exact linear rational expectations models: Specification and estimation. In L.P. Hansen and T.J. Sargent (eds), *Rational Expectations Econometrics.* Boulder, CO: Westview Press.

Hansen, B.E. and B. Seo (2002) Testing for two-regime threshold cointegration in vector error-correction models. *Journal of Econometrics* **110**, 293–318.

Harbo, I., S. Johansen, B.G. Nielsen and A.C. Rahbek (1998) Asymptotic inference on cointegrating rank in partial systems. *Journal of Business Economics and Statistics* **16**, 388–99.

Harvey, A. and J. Nyblom (2000) Tests of common stochastic trends. *Econometric Theory* **16**, 151–75.

Hendry, D.F. (1995) *Dynamic Econometrics*. Oxford: Oxford University Press.

Horvath, M.T.K. and M. Watson (1995) Testing for cointegration when some of the cointegrating vectors are prespecified. *Econometric Theory* 11, 952–84.

Hylleberg, S., R.F. Engle, C.W.J. Granger and S.B. Yoo (1990) Seasonal integration and cointegration. *Journal of Econometrics* 44, 215–38.

Johansen, S. (1995) The role of ancillarity in inference for non-stationary variables. *Economic Journal* 13, 302–20.

Johansen, S. (1996) *Likelihood-Based Inference in Cointegrated Vector Autoregressive Models*. Oxford: Oxford University Press.

Johansen, S. (1997) Likelihood analysis of the $I(2)$ model. *Scandinavian Journal of Statistics* 24, 433–62.

Johansen, S. (2000) A Bartlett correction factor for tests on the cointegrating relations. *Econometric Theory* 16, 740–78.

Johansen, S. (2002a) A small sample correction of the test for cointegrating rank in the vector autoregressive model. *Econometrica* 70, 1929–1961.

Johansen, S. (2002b) A small sample correction for tests of hypotheses on the cointegrating vectors. *Journal of Econometrics* 111, 195–221.

Johansen, S. (2004) A small sample correction for the Dickey–Fuller test. In A. Welfe (ed.), *New Directions in Macromodelling*. Amsterdam: Elsevier.

Johansen, S. (2005) The interpretation of cointegrating coefficients in the cointegrated vector autoregressive model. *Oxford Bulletin of Economics and Statistics* 67, 93–104.

Johansen, S. (2006) The statistical analysis of hypotheses on the cointegrating relations in the $I(2)$ model. *Journal of Econometrics*.

Johansen, S. and E. Schaumburg (1998) Likelihood analysis of seasonal cointegration. *Journal of Econometrics* 88, 301–39.

Johansen, S. and A.R. Swensen (1999) Testing rational expectations in vector autoregressive models. *Journal of Econometrics* 93, 73–91.

Johansen, S. and A.R. Swensen (2004) More on testing exact rational expectations in cointegrated vector autoregressive models: restricted drift terms. *Econometric Journal* 7, 389–397.

Johansen, S., R. Mosconi and B. Nielsen (2000) Cointegration analysis in the presence of structural breaks in the determinstic trend. *Econometric Journal* 3, 1–34.

Juselius, K. (2006) *The Cointegrated VAR Model: Econometric Methodology and Macroeconomic Applications*. Oxford: Oxford University Press.

Koop, G., H.M. Pesaran and S.M. Potter (1996) Impulse response analysis in nonlinear multivariate models. *Journal of Econometrics* 74, 119–47.

Larsson, R.L., J. Lyhagen and M. Löthgren (2001) Likelihood based cointegration tests in heterogenous panels. *Econometric Journal* 4, 109–42.

Lee, H.S. (1992) Maximum likelihood inference on cointegration and seasonal cointegration. *Journal of Econometrics* 54, 1–47.

Lütkepohl, H. (2005) *New Introduction to Multiple Times Series*. Berlin: Springer-Verlag.

Mosconi, R. and A.C. Rahbek (1999) Cointegration rank inference with stationary regressors in VAR models. *Econometrics Journal* 2, 76–91.

Muth, J.F. (1961) Rational expectations and the theory of price movements. *Econometrica* 29, 315–35.

Nielsen, B. (2001) The asymptotic distribution of likelihood ratio test statistics for cointegration in unstable vector autoregressive processes. Discussion paper, Nuffield College, Oxford.

Nielsen, B. (2002) Cointegration analysis of explosive processes. Discussion paper, Nuffield College, Oxford.

Nielsen, B. (2005) Strong consistency results for least squares estimators in general vector autoregressions with deterministic terms. *Econometric Theory* 21, 534–61.

Omtzigt, P. and S. Fachin (2006) The size and power of bootstrap and Bartlett-corrected tests of hypotheses on the cointegrating vectors. *Econometric Reviews*.

Park, J.Y. (1992) Canonical cointegrating regressions. *Econometrica* 60, 119–43.

Paruolo, P. (1996) On the determination of integration indices in $I(2)$ systems. *Journal of Econometrics* 72, 313–56.

Paruolo, P. (2000) Asymptotic efficiency of the two stage estimator in $I(2)$ systems. *Econometric Theory* 16, 524–50.

Paruolo, P. (2001) LR tests for cointegration when some cointegrating relations are known. Statistical methods and applications. *Journal of the Italian Statistical Society* 10, 123–37.

Paruolo, P. and A.C. Rahbek (1999) Weak exogeneity in $I(2)$ VAR systems. *Journal of Econometrics* 93, 281–308.

Pesaran, M.H., T. Schuermann and S. Weiner (2004) Modelling regional interdependencies using a global error-correction macroeconometric model. *Journal of Business Economics and Statistics* 22, 129–62.

Pesaran, M.H., Y. Shin and R.J. Smith (2000) Structural analysis of vector error correction models with exogenous $I(1)$ variables. *Journal of Econometrics* 97, 293–343.

Phillips, P.C.B. (1991) Optimal inference in cointegrated systems. *Econometrica* 59, 283–306.

Phillips, P.C.B. and B.E. Hansen (1990) Statistical inference on instrumental variables regression with $I(1)$ processes. *Review of Economic Studies* 57, 99–124.

Phillips, P.C.B. and H.R. Moon (1999) Linear regression limit theory for nonstationary panel data. *Econometrica* 67, 1057–1111.

Proietti, T. (1997) Short-run dynamics in cointegrated systems. *Oxford Bulletin of Economics and Statistics* 59, 405–22.

Rahbek, A.C., H.C. Kongsted and C. Jørgensen (1999) Trend-stationarity in the $I(2)$ cointegration model. *Journal of Econometrics* 90, 265–89.

Rahbek, A.C., E. Hansen and J.G. Dennis (2002) ARCH innovations and their impact on cointegration rank testing. Preprint 12, 1998, University of Copenhagen.

Rahbek, A.C. and N. Shephard (2002) Autoregressive conditional root model: inference and geometric ergodicity. Working paper, Nuffield College, Oxford.

Reinsel, G.C. and S.K. Ahn (1992) Vector autoregressive models with unit roots and reduced rank structure, estimation, likelihood ratio test, and forecasting. *Journal of Time Series Analysis* 13, 353–75.

Stock, J.H. (1987) Asymptotic properties of least squares estimates of cointegration vectors. *Econometrica* 55, 1035–1056.

Seo, B. (1998) Tests for structural change in cointegrated systems. *Econometric Theory* 14, 222–59.

Watson, M. (1994) Vector autoregressions and cointegration. In R.F. Engle and D. McFadden (eds), *Handbook of Econometrics*, vol. 4. Amsterdam: North-Holland.

15
Threshold Effects in Multivariate Error Correction Models

Jesús Gonzalo and Jean-Yves Pitarakis

Abstract

We propose a testing procedure for assessing the presence of threshold effects in nonstationary vector autoregressive models with or without cointegration. Our approach involves first testing whether the long-run impact matrix characterizing the VECM type representation of the VAR switches according to the magnitude of some threshold variable and is valid regardless of whether the system is purely I(1), I(1) with cointegration or stationary. Once the potential presence of threshold effects is established we subsequently evaluate the cointegrating properties of the system in each regime through a model selection based approach whose asymptotic and finite sample properties are also established. This subsequently allows us to introduce a novel non-linear permanent and transitory decomposition of the vector process of interest.

15.1	Introduction	578
15.2	Testing threshold effects in a multivariate framework	582
	15.2.1 The model and test statistic	582
	15.2.2 Assumptions and limiting distributions	585
	15.2.3 Simulation-based evidence	587
15.3	Estimation of the threshold parameter	589
15.4	Stochastic properties of the system and rank configuration of the VECM with threshold effects	591
	15.4.1 Stability properties of the system	591
	15.4.2 I(1)ness and cointegration within a nonlinear VECM	592
	15.4.3 Rank configuration under alternative stochastic properties of Y_t	595
	15.4.4 Estimation of r_1 and r_2	596
15.5	A nonlinear permanent and transitory decomposition	600
15.6	Conclusions	601

15.1 Introduction

A growing body of research in the recent time series literature has concentrated on incorporating nonlinear behavior into conventional linear reduced form specifications such as autoregressive and moving average models. The motivation for moving away from the traditional linear model with constant parameters has typically come from the observation that many economic and financial time series are often characterized by regime-specific behavior and asymmetric responses to shocks. For such series the linearity and parameter constancy restrictions are typically inappropriate and may lead to misleading inferences about their dynamics.

Within this context, and a univariate setting, a general class of models that has been particularly popular from both a theoretical and applied perspective is the family of threshold models, which are characterized by piecewise linear processes separated according to the magnitude of a threshold variable which triggers the changes in regime. When each linear regime follows an autoregressive process, we have the well-known threshold autoregressive class of models, the statistical properties of which have been investigated in the early work of Tong and Lim (1980), Tong (1983, 1990), Tsay (1989) and Chan (1990, 1993), and more recently reconsidered and extended in Hansen (1996, 1997, 1999a, 1999b, 2000), Caner and Hansen (2001), Gonzalez and Gonzalo (1997), Gonzalo and Montesinos (2000) and Gonzalo and Pitarakis (2002), among others. The two key aspects on which this theoretical research has focused is the development of a distributional theory for tests designed to detect the presence of threshold effects and the statistical properties of the resulting parameter estimators characterising such models.

Given their ability to capture a very rich set of dynamic behavior, including persistence and asymmetries, the use of this class of models has been advocated in numerous applications aiming to capture economically meaningful non-linearities. Examples include the analysis of asymmetries in persistence in US output growth (Beaudry and Koop, 1993; Potter, 1995), asymmetries in the response of output prices to input price increases versus decreases (Borenstein, Cameron and Gilbert, 1997; Peltzman, 2000), nonlinearities in unemployment rates (Hansen, 1997; Koop and Potter, 1999), and threshold effects in cross-country growth regressions (Durlauf and Johnson, 1995) and in international relative prices (Michael, Nobay and Peel, 1997; Obstfeld and Taylor, 1997; O'Connell and Wei, 1997; Lo and Zivot, 2001), among numerous others.

Although the vast majority of the theoretical developments in the area of testing and estimation of univariate threshold models have been obtained under the assumption of stationarity and ergodicity, another important motivation for their popularity came from the observation that a better description of the dynamics of numerous economic variables can be achieved by interacting the pervasive nature of unit roots with that of threshold effects within the same specification. This was also motivated by the observation that there might be much weaker support for the unit root hypothesis when the alternative hypothesis under consideration allows for the presence of threshold type effects in the time series of interest. In Pippenger and Goering (1993), for example, the authors documented a substantial fall in the power of the Dickey–Fuller test when the stationary alternative was allowed to include threshold effects. This also motivated the work of Enders and Granger (1998), who proposed a simple test of the null hypothesis of a unit root against asymmetric adjustment instead of a linear stationary alternative.

One important property of threshold models that contributed to this line of research is their ability to capture persistent behavior while remaining globally stationary. This can be achieved, for example, by allowing a time series to follow a unit-root-type process such as a random walk within one regime while being stationary in another. Numerous economic and financial variables, such as unemployment rates or interest rates, must be stationary by the mere fact that they are bounded. However, at the same time, conventional unit roots tests are typically unable to reject the null hypothesis of a unit root in their auto-regressive representation. This observation has prompted numerous researchers to explore the possibility that the dynamics of these series may be better described by threshold models that allow the nonstationary component to occur within a corridor regime. A well-known example highlighting this point is the behavior of real exchange rate series, which are typically found to be unit root processes, implying a lack of international arbitrage and violation of the PPP hypothesis. Once allowance is made for the presence of threshold effects, capturing aspects such as transaction costs, it has typically been found that this nonstationarity only occurs locally (e.g., between transaction cost bounds) and that the process is, in fact, globally stationary (see Bec, Ben-Salem and Carrasco, 2001, and references therein). Within a related context, Gonzalez and Gonzalo (1998) introduced a globally stationary process, referred to as a threshold unit root model, that combines the presence of a unit root with threshold effects, and found strong support in favor of such a specification when modeling interest rate series.

Although all of this research lay within a univariate setup, the recent time series literature has also witnessed a growing interest in the inclusion of threshold effects in multivariate settings such as vector error correction models. A key factor that triggered this research was the observation that threshold effects may also have an intuitive appeal when it comes to modeling the adjustment process toward a long-run equilibrium characterizing two or more variables.

From the early work of Engle and Granger (1987), for instance, it is well known that two or more variables that behave like unit root processes individually may, in fact, be linked via a long-run equilibrium relationship that makes particular linear combinations of these variables stationary or, as it is commonly known, coin-tegrated. When this happens, the variables in question admit an error correction model representation that allows for the joint modeling of both their long-run and short-run dynamics. In its linear form, such an error correction specification restricts the adjustment process to remain the same across time, thereby ruling out the possibility of lumpy and discontinuous adjustment. An important paper, which relaxed this linearity assumption by introducing the possibility of threshold effects in the adjustment process toward the long-run equilibrium, thereby cap-turing phenomena such as changing speeds of adjustment, was Balke and Fomby

(1997), where the authors introduced the concept of threshold cointegration (see also Tsay, 1998).

The inclusion of such nonlinearities in error correction models has been found to have a very strong intuitive and economic appeal, allowing, for example, for the possibility that the adjustment process toward the long-run equilibrium behaves differently depending on how far off the system is from the long-run equilibrium itself (i.e., depending on the magnitude of the equilibrium error). This also allows for the possibility that the adjustment process shuts down over certain periods. Consider, for instance, the prices of the same asset in two different geographical regions. Although both prices will be equal in the long-run equilibrium, due to the presence of transaction costs, arbitrage only kicks in when the difference in price (i.e., the equilibrium error) is sufficiently large.

The concept of threshold cointegration, as introduced in Balke and Fomby (1997), has attracted considerable attention from practitioners interested in uncovering nonlinear adjustment patterns in relative prices and other variables (see Wohar and Balke, 1998; Baum, Barkoulas and Caglayan, 2001; Enders and Falk, 1998; Lo and Zivot, 2001; O'Connell and Wei, 1997). From a methodological point of view, Balke and Fomby (1997) proposed to assess such occurences within a simple setup which consisted of adapting the approach developed in Hansen (1996) to an Engle–Granger type test performed on the cointegrating residuals. Their setup also implicitly assumed the existence of a known and single cointegrating vector linking the variables of interest. In a related study, Enders and Siklos (2001) extended Balke and Fomby's methodology by adapting the work of Enders and Granger (1998) to a cointegrating framework.

Despite the substantial interest generated by the introduction of the concept of threshold cointegration in Balke and Fomby (1997), a full statistical treatment within a formal multivariate error correction type of specification has only been available since the recent work of Hansen and Seo (2002) (see also Tsay (1998), who introduced an arranged regression approach for testing for the presence of threshold effects in VARs). Although also dealing with a multivariable cointegration setup, the methodology proposed in Balke and Fomby (1998) or Enders and Siklos (2001) focused on the direct treatment of the cointegrating residuals akin to the familiar Engle–Granger test for cointegration. In Hansen and Seo (2002), however, the authors developed a maximum likelihood based estimation and testing theory, starting directly from a vector error correction model representation of a cointegrated system with potential threshold effects in its adjustment process. More specifically, Hansen and Seo (2002) considered a VECM, assumed to contain a single cointegrating vector, in which the threshold effects are driven by the error correction term. Their analysis also implicitly assumes that the researcher knows in advance the cointegration properties of the system (i.e., the system is known to be cointegrated with a single cointegrating vector) and interest solely lies in detecting the presence of threshold effects in the adjustment process toward the equilibrium. This simplifying assumption avoids the need to test for cointegration in the presence of a potentially nonlinear adjustment process. In more recent research, Seo (2004) concentrated on this latter issue by developing a new distributional theory for directly testing the null of no cointegration against the alternative of threshold cointegration. In Seo's (2004) framework it is again the case that cointegration, if present, is solely characterized by a single cointegrating vector and, as in Hansen and Seo (2002), the threshold variable of interest is taken to be the error correction term itself.

In the present chapter our goal is to contribute further to the analysis of threshold effects in possibly cointegrated multivariate systems of the vector error correction type. Our initial goal is to evaluate the properties of a Wald-type test for testing the null of linearity against threshold nonlinearity in the long-run impact matrix of a VECM. Our analysis does not presume any specific coin-tegration properties of the system and is valid regardless of whether the system is cointegrated or not. One additional difference from previous work is our view about the threshold variable that induces the presence of threshold effects. Instead of taking the error correction term to be the variable whose magnitude triggers threshold effects, we consider a general external threshold variable, which could be any economic or financial variable that is stationary and ergo-dic, such as the growth rate in the economy. Having established the existence of threshold effects in the VECM representation of our system, we subsequently evaluate the properties of least squares based estimators of the threshold para-meter, focusing on both its large and small sample properties, followed by an analysis of the formal cointegration properties of the system when applicable. This then allows us to formally obtain a nonlinear permanent and transitory decomposition of the vector process of interest following the same methodology as in Gonzalo and Granger (1995).

The rest of this chapter is as follows. Section 15.2 develops the theory for testing for the presence of threshold effects in a Vector Error Correction type of model. Section 15.3 focuses on the theoretical properties of estimators of the threshold parameters. Section 15.4 proposes a methodology for assessing the cointegration properties of the system, Section 15.5 introduces a nonlinear permanent and transitory decomposition based on a VECM with threshold effects and Section 15.6 concludes. All proofs are relegated to the appendix.

15.2 Testing for threshold effects in a multivariate framework

15.2.1 The model and test statistic

We let the p-dimensional time series $\{Y_t\}$ be generated by the following vector error correction type specification, which allows for the presence of threshold effects in its long run impact matrix:

$$\Delta Y_t = \mu + \mathbf{\Pi}_1 Y_{t-1} I(q_{t-d} \leq \gamma) + \mathbf{\Pi}_2 Y_{t-1} I(q_{t-d} > \gamma) + \sum_{j=1}^{k} \Gamma_j \Delta Y_{t-j} + u_t \qquad (15.1)$$

where Π_1, Π_2 and Γ_j are $p \times p$ constant parameter matrices, q_{t-d} is a scalar threshold variable, $I(.)$ is the indicator function, γ the threshold parameter, k and d the known lag length and delay parameters and u_t is the p-dimensional random disturbance vector.

The model in (15.1) is a multivariate generalization of an autoregressive model with threshold effects whose dynamics are characterized by a piecewise linear vector autoregression. The regime switches are governed by the magnitude of the threshold variable q_t crossing an unknown threshold value γ. The specification in (15.1) is similar to that considered in Seo (2004), except that no assumptions are made about the rank structure of either Π_1 or Π_2, and the threshold variable is not necessarily given by an error correction term such as $q_t = \beta' Y_t$, with β denoting the single cointegrating vector.

The initial question of interest in the context of the specification in (15.1) is whether the long-run impact matrix is truly characterized by threshold effects driven by the threshold variable q_t. In the absence of such effects we have a standard linear VECM with $\Pi_1 = \Pi_2$, and this restriction can be tested via a conventional Wald-type test statistic against the alternative $H_1 : \Pi_1 \neq \Pi_2$.

At this stage it is important to note that the sole purpose of testing the above null hypothesis is to uncover the presence or absence of threshold effects in the long run impact matrix. More importantly, we wish to conduct this set of inferences regardless of the stationarity properties of Y_t, in the sense that our null hypothesis may hold under a purely stationary set up or a unit root set up with or without cointegration. If the null hypothesis is not rejected we can then carry on with the process of exploring the stochastic properties of the data following, for example, Johansen's methodology (see Johansen, 1998 and references therein). Before proceeding further, and to motivate our working model, we consider two simple examples illustrating particular cases of our specification in (15.1).

EXAMPLE 1: Here we present a bivariate system of cointegrated I(1) variables with threshold effects in their adjustment process. Specifically, with $Y_t = (y_{1t}, y_{2t})'$ we write $y_{1t} = \beta y_{2t} + z_t$, where $\Delta y_{2t} = \epsilon_{2t}$ and $\Delta z_t = \rho_1 z_{t-1} I(q_{t-1} \leq \gamma) + \rho_2 z_{t-1} I(q_{t-1} > \gamma) + \epsilon_{1t}$ with $\rho_i < 0$ for $i = 1, 2$, and for simplicity we take q_t to be an iid random variable. In this example both y_{1t} and y_{2t} are I(1) and cointegrated with cointegrating vector $(1, -\beta)$, since z_t is a covariance stationary process following a threshold autoregressive scheme. It is now straightforward to reformulate the above model as in (15.1) by writing

$$
\begin{pmatrix} \Delta y_{1t} \\ \Delta y_{2t} \end{pmatrix} = \begin{pmatrix} \rho_1 \\ 0 \end{pmatrix} (1 - \beta) \begin{pmatrix} y_{1t-1} \\ y_{2t-1} \end{pmatrix} I(q_{t-1} \leq \gamma)
$$

$$
+ \begin{pmatrix} \rho_2 \\ 0 \end{pmatrix} (1 - \beta) \begin{pmatrix} y_{1t-1} \\ y_{2t-1} \end{pmatrix} I(q_{t-1} \geq \gamma) + \begin{pmatrix} u_{1t} \\ u_{2t} \end{pmatrix}
$$

(15.2)

with $u_{1t} = \epsilon_{1t} + \beta \epsilon_{2t}$ and $u_{2t} = \epsilon_{2t}$.

EXAMPLE 2: Here we consider a purely stationary bivariate system with both variables following a threshold autoregressive process. Consider $\Delta y_{1t} = \rho_{11} y_{1t-1} I(q_{t-1} \leq \gamma) + \rho_{21} y_{1t-1} I(q_{t-1} > \gamma) + u_{1t}$ and $\Delta y_{2t} = \rho_{12} y_{2t-1} I(q_{t-1} \leq \gamma) + \rho_{22} y_{2t-1} I(q_{t-1} > \gamma) + u_{2t}$ with $\rho_{i1} < 0$ and $\rho_{i2} < 0$ for $i = 1, 2$. We can again reformulate this system as in (15.1) by writing

$$
\begin{pmatrix} \Delta y_{1t} \\ \Delta y_{2t} \end{pmatrix} = \begin{pmatrix} \rho_{11} & 0 \\ 0 & \rho_{12} \end{pmatrix} \begin{pmatrix} y_{1t-1} \\ y_{2t-1} \end{pmatrix} I(q_{t-1} \leq \gamma) +
$$
$$
\begin{pmatrix} \rho_{21} & 0 \\ 0 & \rho_{22} \end{pmatrix} \begin{pmatrix} y_{1t-1} \\ y_{2t-1} \end{pmatrix} I(q_{t-1} > \gamma) + \begin{pmatrix} u_{1t} \\ u_{2t} \end{pmatrix}.
\tag{15.3}
$$

In order to explore the properties of the Wald-type test for the above null hypothesis, it will be convenient to reformulate (15.1) in matrix form. In what follows, for clarity and simplicity of exposition we focus on a restricted version of (1) which sets the constant term as well as the coefficients on the lagged dependent variables equal to zero. Since our framework does not consider threshold effects in those parameters, it would be straightforward to concentrate (15.1) with respect to Π_1 and Π_2 using an appropriate projection matrix. This leads to no loss of generality since our distributional results presented in Propositions 1 and 2 below would remain unaffected. We now write

$$
\Delta Y = \Pi_1 Z_1 + \Pi_2 Z_2 + U
\tag{15.4}
$$

where $\Delta Y, Z_1$ and Z_2 are all $p \times T$ matrices stacking the vectors $\Delta Y_t, Y_{t-1} I(q_{t-d} \leq \gamma)$ and $Y_{t-1} I(q_{t-d} > \gamma)$, respectively. Within the formulation (15.4) we have $\Delta Y = (\Delta y_1, \Delta y_2, \ldots, \Delta y_T), Z_1 = (y_0 I(q_{0-d} \leq \gamma), \ldots, y_{T-1} I(q_{T-d} \leq \gamma))$ and $Z_2 = (y_0 I(q_{0-d} > \gamma), \ldots_{T-1} I(q_{T-d} > \gamma))$. Similarly U is a $p \times T$ matrix of random disturbances given by $U = (u_1, \ldots, u_T)$. We note that within our parameterization the regressor matrices Z_1 and Z_2 are orthogonal due to the presence of the two indicator functions. Their dependence on γ is omitted for notational parsimony. For later use we also introduce the $p \times T$ matrix $Z = (y_0, \ldots, y_{T-1})$, which is such that $Z = Z_1 + Z_2$.

The unknown parameters of the model (15.4) can be estimated via concentrated least squares, proceeding conditionally on a known γ. Indeed, since given γ the model is linear in its parameters, the least squares estimators of Π_1 and Π_2 are $\hat{\Pi}_1(\gamma) = \Delta Y Z_1'(Z_1 Z_1')^{-1}$ and $\hat{\Pi}_2(\gamma) = \Delta Y Z_2'(Z_2 Z_2')^{-1}$. For later use we also introduce the vectorised versions of the parameter matrices, writing $\hat{\pi}_1 \equiv vec\ \hat{\Pi}_1$ and $\hat{\pi}_2 \equiv vec\ \hat{\Pi}_2$, and the null hypothesis of interest can be equivalently expressed as $H_0 : \pi_1 = \pi_2$ or $H_0 : R\pi = 0$ with $R = [I_{p^2}, -I_{p^2}]$ and $\pi = (\pi_1', \pi_2')'$.

The Wald statistic for testing the above null hypothesis takes the following form

$$
W_T(\gamma) = (R\hat{\pi})' \left[R((DD')^{-1} \otimes \hat{\Omega}_u) R' \right]^{-1} (R\hat{\pi})
\tag{15.5}
$$

where $\otimes$ is the Kronecker product operator, $\hat{\pi}_1 = [(Z_1Z_1')^{-1}Z_1 \otimes I_p]\ vec\ \Delta Y$, $\hat{\pi}_2 = [(Z_2Z_2')^{-1}Z_2 \otimes I_p]\ vec\ \Delta Y$ and $D = [Z_1\ Z_2]$. The $p \times p$ matrix $\hat{\Omega}_u$ refers to the least squares estimator of the covariance matrix defined as $\hat{\Omega}_u = \hat{U}\hat{U}'/T$, with $\hat{U} = \Delta Y - \hat{\Pi}_1(\gamma)Z_1 - \hat{\Pi}_2(\gamma)Z_2$. Since Z_1 and Z_2 are orthogonal, it also immediately follows that $DD' = diag(Z_1Z_1', Z_2Z_2')$ and $(DD')^{-1} \otimes \hat{\Omega}_u = diag[(Z_1Z_1')^{-1} \otimes \hat{\Omega}_u, (Z_2Z_2')^{-1} \otimes \hat{\Omega}_u]$. We can thus also reformulate the Wald statistic in (15.5) as

$$W_T(\gamma) = (\hat{\pi}_1 - \hat{\pi}_2)'\left[(Z_2Z_2')(ZZ')^{-1}(Z_1Z_1') \otimes \hat{\Omega}_u^{-1}\right](\hat{\pi}_1 - \hat{\pi}_2) \tag{15.6}$$

where $ZZ' = Z_1Z_1' + Z_2Z_2'$.

At this stage it is also important to reiterate the fact that, when implementing our test of the null hypothesis of linearity with, say, $\Pi_1 = \Pi_2 = \Pi$, the corresponding characteristic polynomial $\Phi(z) = (1 - z)I_p - \Pi z$ will be assumed to have all its roots either outside or on the unit circle and the number of unit roots present in the system will be given by $p - r$ with $0 \leq r \leq p$. Our analysis rules out instances of explosive behavior or processes that may be integrated of order two. This also allows us to have a direct correspondence between the stochastic properties of Y_t under the null hypothesis and the rank structure of the long-run impact matrix Π. In the particular case where all the roots of the characteristic polynomial are outside the unit circle, the series will be referred to as $I(0)$.

15.2.2 Assumptions and limiting distributions

Throughout this section we will be operating under the following set of assumptions

(A1) $u_t = (u_{1t}, \ldots, u_{pt})'$ is a zero mean iid sequence of p-dimensional random vectors with a bounded density function, covariance matrix $E[u_tu_t'] = \Omega_u > 0$ and with $E|u_{it}|^{2\delta} < \infty$ for some $\delta > 2$ and $i = 1, \ldots, p$;

(A2) q_t is a strictly stationary and ergodic sequence that is independent of $u_{is}\forall t, s, i = 1, \ldots, p$ and has distribution function F that is continuous everywhere;

(A3) the threshold parameter γ is such that $\gamma \in \Gamma = [\gamma_L, \gamma_U]$, a closed and bounded subset of the sample space of the threshold variable.

Assumption (A1) above is required for our subsequent limiting distribution theory. It will ensure, for instance, that the functional central limit theorem can be applied to the sample moments used in the construction of Wald and related tests. Assumption (A2) restricts the behavior of the scalar random variable that induces threshold effects in the model (15.1). Although it allows q_t to follow a very rich class of processes, it requires it to be external, in the sense of being independent of the u_t sequence, and also rules out the possibility of q_t being I(1) itself. Finally, assumption (A3) is standard in this literature. The threshold variable sample space Γ is typically taken to be $[\gamma_L, \gamma_U]$, with γ_L and γ_U chosen such that $P(q_{t-d} \leq \gamma_L) = \theta_1 > 0$ and $P(q_{t-d} \leq \gamma_U) = 1 - \theta_1$. The choice of θ_1 is commonly taken to be 10 or 15 percent. Restricting the parameter space of the threshold in this fashion ensures that there are enough observations in each regime and also guarantees the existence of nondegenerate limits for the test statistics of interest.

In what follows, we will be interested in obtaining the limiting behavior of $W_T(\gamma)$ defined in (15.6). In this context it will be important to explore the distinctive features of the limiting null distribution of the test statistic when the maintained model is either a pure multivariate unit root process with no cointegration (i.e., $\Delta Y_t = u_t$) or a VECM in the form $\Delta Y_t = \Pi Y_{t-1} + u_t$ with $Rank(\Pi) = r$ such that $0 < r \le p$. The case where $r = p$ would correspond to a purely stationary specification. We note that under all these cases the null hypothesis of linearity holds. Before proceeding further it is also important to emphasize the fact that we are facing a nonstandard inference problem, since under the null hypothesis the threshold parameter γ is not unidentified. This is now a well-known and documented problem in the literature on testing for the presence of various forms of nonlinearities in regression models and is commonly referred to as the Davies problem. Under a stationary setting, where $Rank(\Pi) = p$ and taking γ as fixed and given, we would expect $W_T(\gamma)$ to behave like a χ^2 random variable in large samples. Since we will not be assuming that γ is known, however, we will follow Davies (1977, 1987) and test the null hypothesis of linearity using $SupW = \sup_{\gamma \in \Gamma} W_T(\gamma)$. In what follows we also make use of the equality $I(q_{t-d} \le \gamma) = I(F(q_{t-d}) \le F(\gamma))$, which allows us to use uniform random variables (see Caner and Hansen, 2001, p. 1586). In this context we let $\lambda \equiv F(\gamma) \in \Lambda$ with $\Lambda = [\theta_1, 1 - \theta_1]$, and throughout this chapter we will be using λ and $F(\gamma)$ interchangeably.

In the following proposition we summarize the limiting behavior of the Wald statistic for testing the null hypothesis of linearity when it is assumed that the system is purely stationary.

Proposition 1   *Under assumptions A1–A3, $H_0 : \Pi_1 = \Pi_2$ and Y_t a p-dimensional I(0) vector we have*

$$SupW \Rightarrow Sup_{\lambda \in \Lambda} G(\lambda)' V(\lambda)^{-1} G(\lambda) \tag{15.7}$$

where $G(\lambda)$ is a zero mean p^2-dimensional Gaussian random vector with covariance $E[G(\lambda_1)G(\lambda_2)] = V(\lambda_1 \wedge \lambda_2)$ and $V(\lambda) = \lambda(1 - \lambda)(Q \otimes \Omega_u)$ with $Q = E[ZZ']$.

REMARK 1: It is interesting to note that the above limiting distribution is equivalent to a normalized squared Brownian Bridge process identical to the one arising when testing for the presence of structural breaks as in Andrews (1993, Theorem 3, p. 838). The same distribution also arises in particular parameterizations of self-exciting threshold autoregressive models when only the constant terms are allowed to be different in each regime (see Chan, 1990). We also note that, for known and given γ, the quantity $G(\lambda)' V(\lambda)^{-1} G(\lambda)$ reduces to a χ^2 random variable with p^2 degrees of freedom. Since $G(\lambda)$ is $(Q \otimes \Omega_u)^{\frac{1}{2}} N(0, \lambda(1 - \lambda)I_{p^2}) \equiv (Q \otimes \Omega_u)^{\frac{1}{2}}[W(\lambda) - \lambda W(1)]$, with $W(.)$ denoting a p^2-dimensional standard Brownian Motion, the result follows from the above definition of $V(\lambda)$. We also note that the limiting process is free of nuisance parameters, solely depending on the number of parameters being tested under the null hypothesis and is tabulated in Andrews (1993, table 1, p. 840). For a more extensive set of p-values of the corresponding limiting distributions, see also Hansen (1997).

In the next proposition we summarize the limiting behavior of the same Wald test statistic when the system is assumed to be a p-dimensional pure I(1) process as $\Delta Y_t = u_t$ or, alternatively, I(1) but cointegrated as in $\Delta Y_t = \alpha \beta' Y_{t-1} + u_t$, with α and β having reduced ranks. In what follows, a standard Brownian Sheet $W(s, t)$ is defined as a zero mean two-parameter Gaussian process indexed by $[0, 1]^2$ and having a covariance function given by $Cov[W(s_1, t_1), W(s_2, t_2)] = (s_1 \wedge t_1)(s_2 \wedge t_2)$, while a Kiefer process K on $[0, 1]^2$ is given by $K(s, t) = W(s, t) - tW(s, 1)$. The Kiefer process is also a two-parameter Gaussian process with zero mean and covariance function $Cov[K(s_1, t_1), K(s_2, t_2)] = (s_1 \wedge s_2)(t_1 \wedge t_2 - t_1 t_2)$.

Proposition 2   *Under assumptions A1–A3, $H_0 : \Pi_1 = \Pi_2$ and Y_t a p-dimensional I(1) vector cointegrated or not:*

$$SupW \Rightarrow Sup_{\lambda \in \Lambda} \frac{1}{\lambda(1-\lambda)} tr\left(\int_0^1 W(r)dK(r, \lambda)'\right)' \left(\int_0^1 W(r)W(r)'\right)^{-1}$$
$$\times \left(\int_0^1 W(r)dK(r, \lambda)'\right)$$

(15.8)

where $K(r, \lambda)$ is a Kiefer process given by $K(r, \lambda) = W(r, \lambda) - \lambda W(r, 1)$, with $W(.)$ denoting a p-dimensional standard Brownian Motion and $W(r, \lambda)$ a p-dimensional standard Brownian Sheet.

Looking at the expression of the limiting distribution in Proposition 2, we again observe that for given and known λ, the limiting random variable is $\chi^2(p^2)$, exactly as occurred under the purely stationary setup of proposition 1. This follows from the observation that $W(r)$ and $K(r, \lambda)$ are independent. Note that we have $E[W(r)K(r, \lambda)] = E[W(r)W(r, \lambda)] - \lambda E[W(r)^2]$ and since $E[W(r)W(r, \lambda)] = r\lambda$ and $E[W(r)^2] = r$ the result follows. It also follows that the limiting random variables in (15.7) and (15.8) are equivalent in distribution.

15.2.3   Simulation-based evidence

Having established the limiting behavior of the Wald statistic for testing the null of no threshold effects within the VECM type representation, we next explore the adequacy of the asymptotic approximations presented in Propositions 1–2 when dealing with finite samples. This will also allow us to explore the documented robustness of the above limiting distributions to the absence or presence of unit roots and cointegration, and to the stochastic properties of the threshold variable q_t when faced with limited sample sizes.

We initially consider a purely stationary bivariate DGP as the model under the null hypothesis, parameterised as $Y_t = \Phi Y_{t-1} + u_t$ with $\Phi = diag(0.5, 0.8)$ and

$u_t = NID(0, I_2)$. As a candidate threshold variable required in the construction of the Wald statistic, we consider two options; one in which q_t is taken to be a normal iid random variable (independent of $u_{it}, i = 1, 2$) and one where q_t follows a stationary AR(1) process given by $q_t = \theta q_{t-1} + \epsilon_t$, with $\theta = 0.5$ and $\epsilon_t = NID(0, 1)$ with $Cov(\epsilon_t, u_{is}) = 0 \ \forall t, s$ and $i = 1, 2$. Regarding the magnitude of the delay parameter, we set $d = 1$ throughout all our experiments, all conducted using samples of size $T = 200, 400, 2000$ across $N = 5000$ replications and with a 10 percent trimming of the sample space of the threshold variable. Another important purpose of our experiments is to construct a range of critical values for the distributions presented in (15.7)–(15.8) and to compare them with the corresponding tabulations in Andrews (1993, Table 1, p. 840). Results for the purely stationary system are presented in Table 15.1.

The critical values tabulated in Table 15.1 suggest that the finite sample distributions of the Wald statistic track their asymptotic counterpart (as judged by a sample of size $T = 2,000$) very accurately. As discussed in Remark 1 above, we can also observe that the critical values obtained in Andrews (1993) are virtually identical to the ones obtained using our DGPs and multivariate framework with thresholds (note that within our bivariate VAR we are testing for the presence of threshold effects across p^2 parameters).

In Tables 15.2 and 15.3 we concentrate on the limiting and finite sample behavior of the Wald statistic for testing the absence of threshold effects when the true DGP is a system of I(1) variables. Table 15.2 focuses on the case of a purely I(1) system with no cointegration, given by $\Delta Y_t = u_t$, while Table 15.3 focuses on a cointegrated system given by $\Delta y_{1t} = u_{1t}$ and $y_{2t} = 0.8y_{2t-1} + u_{2t}$. In this latter case the bivariate system is characterized by the presence of one stationary relationship and the corresponding rank of the long-run impact matrix is one. The dynamics of q_t were maintained as above in both sets of experiments.

The empirical results presented in Tables 15.2–15.3 clearly illustrate the robustness of the limiting distributions to various parameterizations of the threshold variable. Our tabulations also corroborate our earlier observation that the limiting distributions are unaffected by the presence or absence of I(1) components.

Table 15.1   Critical values under an I(0) system and $p^2 = 4$

	T	90%	95%	99%
		$q_t : NID(0, 1)$		
SupW	200	14.946	16.909	21.246
SupW	400	14.606	16.686	21.239
SupW	2,000	14.762	16.596	20.741
		$q_t : AR(1)$		
SupW	200	15.135	17.252	21.331
SupW	400	14.836	17.024	21.323
SupW	2,000	14.829	16.737	20.854
Andrews	∞	14.940	16.980	21.040

Table 15.2 Critical values under a pure I(1) system and $p^2 = 4$

	T	90%	95%	99%
		$q_t : NID(0, 1)$		
SupW	200	14.970	17.023	22.098
SupW	400	14.858	18.578	21.205
SupW	2,000	15.012	16.947	20.967
		$q_t : AR(1)$		
SupW	200	15.369	17.197	22.164
SupW	400	14.948	18.527	21.358
SupW	2,000	14.904	16.840	21.212
Andrews	∞	14.940	16.980	21.040

Table 15.3 Critical values under a cointegrated system and $p^2 = 4$

	T	90%	95%	99%
		$q_t : NID(0, 1)$		
SupW	200	15.030	17.236	21.431
SupW	400	14.685	16.879	20.926
SupW	2,000	14.723	16.739	20.911
		$q_t : AR(1)$		
SupW	200	15.068	16.903	21.074
SupW	400	15.150	17.040	21.153
SupW	2,000	14.961	16.758	21.013
Andrews	∞	14.940	16.980	21.040

15.3 Estimation of the threshold parameter

Once inferences based on the Wald test reject the null hypothesis of a linear VECM, our next objective is to obtain a consistent estimator of the threshold parameter. The model under which we operate is now given by $\Delta Y = \Pi_1 Z_1 + \Pi_2 Z_2 + U$. We propose to obtain an estimator of γ based on the least squares principle. Letting $\hat{U}(\gamma) = \Delta Y - \hat{\Pi}_1(\gamma)Z_1(\gamma) - \hat{\Pi}_2(\gamma)Z_2(\gamma)$, we consider

$$\hat{\gamma} = \arg \min_{\gamma \in \Gamma} |\hat{U}(\gamma)\hat{U}(\gamma)'|. \tag{15.9}$$

Before establishing the large sample behavior of $\hat{\gamma}$ introduced in (15.9), it is important to highlight the fact that a VECM type of representation with threshold effects as in (15.4) is compatible with either a purely stationary Y_t or a system of I(1) variables that is cointegrated in a conventional sense and with threshold effects present in its adjustment process. Examples of such processes are provided in (15.2) and (15.3) above, while a formal discussion of the stationarity properties of Y_t generated from (15.4) is provided below.

The following proposition summarizes the limiting behavior of the threshold parameter estimator defined above, with γ_0 referring to its true magnitude.

Proposition 3   *Under assumptions (A1)–(A3) with Y_t I(0) or I(1) but cointegrated and generated as in (15.4) we have $\hat{\gamma} \xrightarrow{p} \gamma_0$ as $T \to \infty$.*

From the above proposition it is clear that the consistency property of the threshold parameter estimator remains unaffected by the presence of I(1) components. In order to empirically illustrate the above proposition, and to explore the behavior of $\hat{\gamma}$ in smaller samples, we conducted a Monte-Carlo experiment covering a range of parameterizations, including purely stationary and cointegrated systems. Our objective was to assess the finite sample performance of the least squares based estimator of γ_0 in moderate to large samples in terms of bias and variability.

For the purely stationary case we consider the specification introduced in (15.3), setting $(\rho_{11}, \rho_{21}) = (-0.8, -0.4)$ and $(\rho_{12}, \rho_{22}) = (-0.2, -0.6)$. Regarding the choice of threshold variable, we consider the case of a purely Gaussian iid process as well as an AR(1) specification given by $q_t = 0.5q_{t-1} + u_t$ with $u_t = NID(0, 1)$. The true threshold parameter is set to $\gamma_0 = 0.25$ under the AR(1) dynamics and to $\gamma_0 = 0$ when q_t is iid. The delay parameter is fixed at $d = 1$. For the cointegrated case we consider a system given by $y_{1t} = 2y_{2t} + z_t$ with $\Delta y_{2t} = \epsilon_{2t}$ and $z_t = 0.2z_{t-1}I(q_{t-1} \leq \gamma_0) + 0.8z_{t-1}I(q_{t-1} > \gamma_0) + v_t$, while retaining the same dynamics for q_t and the same threshold parameter configurations as above. Both ϵ_{2t} and v_t are chosen as NID(0,1) random variables.

Results for these two classes of DGPs are presented in Table 15.4, which displays the empirical mean and standard deviation of $\hat{\gamma}$ estimated as in (15.9) using samples of size $T = 200$ and $T = 400$ across $N = 5,000$ replications.

From both of the above experiments we note that $\hat{\gamma}$ as defined in (15.9) displays a reasonably small and negative finite sample bias of approximately 0.5 percent under both configurations of the dynamics of the threshold variable and system properties. At the same time, however, we note that $\hat{\gamma}$ is characterized by a substantial variability across all model configurations. Its empirical standard deviation is virtually twice the magnitude of γ_0 under $T = 200$ and, although clearly

Table 15.4   Empirical mean and standard deviation of $\hat{\gamma}$

	q_t AR(1), $\gamma_0 = 0.15$		q_t iid, $\gamma_0 = 0$	
	$E(\hat{\gamma})$	$Std(\hat{\gamma})$	$E(\hat{\gamma})$	$Std(\hat{\gamma})$
	Stationary system			
$T = 200$	0.142	0.278	−0.014	0.247
$T = 400$	0.145	0.108	−0.004	0.100
	Cointegrated system			
$T = 200$	0.140	0.266	−0.006	0.229
$T = 400$	0.144	0.101	−0.003	0.091

declining with sample size, remains substantial even under $T = 400$. Similar features of threshold parameter estimators have also been documented in Gonzalo and Pitarakis (2002).

Taking the presence of threshold effects as given, together with the availability of a consistent estimator of the unknown threshold parameter, our next concern is to explore further the stochastic properties of the p-dimensional vector Y_t.

15.4 Stochastic properties of the system and rank configuration of the VECM with threshold effects

So far the test developed in the previous sections allows us to decide whether the inclusion of threshold effects into a VECM-type specification is supported by the data. Given the simplicity of its implementation, and the fact that the limiting distribution of the test statistic is unaffected by the stationarity properties of the variables being modeled, the proposed Wald-based inferences can be viewed as a useful pre-test before implementing a formal analysis of the integration and cointegration properties of the system. If the null hypothesis is not rejected, we can proceed with the specification of a linear VECM using the methodology developed in Johansen (1995 and references therein).

Our next concern is to explore the implications of the rejection of the null hypothesis of linearity for the stability and, when applicable, cointegration properties of Y_t, whose dynamics are now known to be described by the specification (15.4). Although rejecting the hypothesis that $\Pi_1 = \Pi_2$ rules out the scenario of a purely I(1) system with no cointegration as traditionally defined, since having $\Pi_1 \neq \Pi_2$ is trivially incompatible with the specification $\Delta Y = U$, as shown below, it remains possible that the system is either purely covariance stationary or I(1) with cointegration in a sense to be made clear (see, for example, the formulation in (15.2) under Example 1).

15.4.1 Stability properties of the system

In the context of our specification in (15.4), and maintaining the notation $\Phi_1 = I_p + \Pi_1$ and $\Phi_2 = I_p + \Pi_2$, so that the system can be formulated as $Y_t = \Phi_t Y_{t-1} + u_t$ with $\Phi_t = \Phi_1 I(q_{t-d} \leq \gamma) + \Phi_2 I(q_{t-d} > \gamma)$, the stability properties of the system are summarized in the following proposition, where for a square matrix $\mathbf{M}$ the notation $\rho(\mathbf{M})$ refers to its spectral radius.

Proposition 4 *Under assumptions (A1)–(A3), Y_t generated from (15.4) is covariance stationary iff $\rho(F(\gamma)(\Phi_1 \otimes \Phi_1) + (1 - F(\gamma))(\Phi_2 \otimes \Phi_2)) < 1$.*

From the above proposition it is interesting to note that, even if one of the two regimes has a root on the unit circle, the model could still be covariance stationary. In fact, the system could even be characterized by an explosive behavior in one of its regimes while still being covariance stationary, if, for example, the magnitudes of the transition probabilities are such that switching occurs very often. Note also that the condition ensuring the covariance stationarity of Y_t is also equivalent to requiring the eigenvalues of $E[\Phi_t \otimes \Phi_t]$ to have moduli less than one.

EXAMPLE 3: We can here consider the example of a bivariate process given by $Y_t = I_2 Y_{t-1} I(q_{t-d} \leq \gamma) + \Phi_2 Y_{t-1} I(q_{t-d} > \gamma) + u_t$ and let $\Phi_2 = \phi I_2$ with $|\phi| < 1$, where I_2 denotes a two-dimensional identity matrix. This system can be seen to be characterized by a random walk type of behavior in one regime and covariance stationarity in the second regime. In matrix form we have

$$
\begin{pmatrix} \Delta y_{1t} \\ \Delta y_{2t} \end{pmatrix} = \begin{pmatrix} 0 & 0 \\ 0 & 0 \end{pmatrix} \begin{pmatrix} y_{1t-1} \\ y_{2t-1} \end{pmatrix} I(q_{t-1} \leq \gamma)
$$
$$
+ \begin{pmatrix} \phi - 1 & 0 \\ 0 & \phi - 1 \end{pmatrix} \begin{pmatrix} y_{1t-1} \\ y_{2t-1} \end{pmatrix} I(q_{t-1} > \gamma) + \begin{pmatrix} \epsilon_{1t} \\ \epsilon_{2t} \end{pmatrix}. \tag{15.10}
$$

Letting $M = F(\gamma)(\Phi_1 \otimes \Phi_1) + (1 - F(\gamma))(\Phi_2 \otimes \Phi_2))$, it is straightforward to establish that, in the case of (15.10), we have $\rho(M) = F(\gamma) + \phi^2(1 - F(\gamma)) < 1$, since $\phi^2 < 1$, thus implying that $Y_t = (y_{1t}, y_{2t})'$ is covariance stationary.

EXAMPLE 4: Another example of a covariance stationary system is given by

$$
\begin{pmatrix} \Delta y_{1t} \\ \Delta y_{2t} \end{pmatrix} = \begin{pmatrix} 0 & 0 \\ 0 & \phi - 1 \end{pmatrix} \begin{pmatrix} y_{1t-1} \\ y_{2t-1} \end{pmatrix} I(q_{t-1} \leq \gamma)
$$
$$
+ \begin{pmatrix} \phi - 1 & 0 \\ 0 & 0 \end{pmatrix} \begin{pmatrix} y_{1t-1} \\ y_{2t-1} \end{pmatrix} I(q_{t-1} > \gamma) + \begin{pmatrix} \epsilon_{1t} \\ \epsilon_{2t} \end{pmatrix} \tag{15.11}
$$

for which we have $\rho(M) = (1 - F(\gamma))(1 - \phi)^2 < 1$ if $F(\gamma) < 0.5$, and $\rho(M) = F(\gamma)(1 - \phi)^2 < 1$ if $F(\gamma) > 0.5$. On the other hand, if we concentrate on the specification given in (15.2), it is straightforward to establish that $\rho(M) = 1$, thus violating the requirement for Y_t to be covariance stationary.

For later use it is also important at this stage to observe the correspondence between the ranks of the long-run impact matrices presented in the above example and the covariance stationarity of each system. In example 3, for examples, we note that $r_1 \equiv Rank(\Pi_1) = 0$ and $r_2 \equiv Rank(\Pi_2) = 2$, while in model (15.11) we have $(r_1, r_2) = (1, 1)$. This highlights the fact that within a nonlinear specification, as in (15.4), the correspondence between the rank structure of the long-run impact matrices and the stability/cointegration properties of the system will be less clearcut than within a simple linear VECM. Before exploring further this issue, it will be important to clarify the type of threshold nonlinearities that are compatible with an I(1) system and its VECM representation in (15.4).

15.4.2 I(1)ness and cointegration within a nonlinear VECM

The recent literature on the inclusion of nonlinear features in models with I(1) variables and cointegration can typically be categorized into two strands. Single equation approaches aim to detect the presence of nonlinearities in regressions with I(1) processes known to be cointegrated (see Saikkonen and Choi, 2004;

Hong, 2003; Arai, 2004). In Saikkonen and Choi (2004), the authors included a smooth transition type of function $g(.)$ within a postulated cointegrating regression model of the form $y_{1t} = \beta y_{2t} + \theta y_{2t} g(y_{2t}; \gamma) + u_t$ and proposed a methodology for testing the null hypothesis of no such effects, given here by $H_0 : \theta = 0$. The presence of such nonlinearities within a cointegrating relationship implies some form of switching equilibria, in the sense that the cointegrating vector is allowed to be different depending on the magnitude of y_{2t}. In both Hong (2003) and Arai (2004), the authors focused on a similar setup without an explicit choice of functional form. This was achieved through the inclusion of additional polynomial terms in the y_2 variable on the right-hand side of a cointegrating regression.

Another strand of the same literature focused on the treatment of nonlinearities within a multivariate error correction framework. The motivation underlying this research was again to detect the presence of nonlinear cointegration, but here defined as a nonlinear adjustment towards the long-run equilibrium while maintaining the assumption that the cointegration relationship is itself linear. Another important maintained assumption in this line of research is the existence of a single cointegrating vector (see Balke and Fomby, 1997; Seo and Hansen, 2002; Seo, 2004). Regarding the theoretical properties of multivariate models with nonlinearities, Bec and Rahbek (2004) have explored the strict stationarity and ergodicity properties of multivariate error correction models with general cointegrating rank and nonlinearities in their adjustment process.

One aspect that seems not to have been emphasized in the literature is the fact that, when operating within a VECM-type framework, an important aspect of restricting the presence of nonlinearity to occur solely in the adjustment process stems from representation concerns. More specifically, it can be shown that two I(1) variables that are linearly cointegrated but with a nonlinear adjustment process continue to admit a "nonlinear" VECM representation similar to (15.4) above. If we also wish to explore the possibility of nonlinearities in the cointegrating relationship itself, however, it becomes difficult to justify the existence of a VECM representation à la Granger.

To highlight this point, let us consider the following simple *nonlinear* cointegrating relationship, which is characterized by the presence of a threshold type of nonlinearity

$$y_{1t} = \beta y_{2t} + \theta y_{2t} I(q_{t-1} > \gamma) + z_t$$
$$\Delta y_{2t} = \epsilon_{2t} \tag{15.12}$$
$$\Delta z_t = \rho z_{t-1} + u_t$$

with $\rho < 0$ and z_t representing the stationary equilibrium error.

If we were in a linear setup with $\theta = 0$, it would be straightforward to reformulate the above specification as $\Delta y_{1t} = \rho z_{t-1} + v_t$, with $v_t = u_t + \beta \epsilon_{2t}$, and we would have a traditional VECM representation with ρ playing the role of the adjustment coefficient to equilibrium and $z_{t-1} = (y_{1t-1} - \beta y_{2t-1})$ denoting the previous period's equilibrium error. At this stage it is important to note that a key aspect of the linear setup that allows us to move toward an ECM type representation is the fact that taking y_{2t} to be an I(1) variable, as in (15.12), directly implies that y_{1t} is also difference stationary, since taking the first difference of both sides of the first equation gives $\Delta y_{1t} = \beta \Delta y_{2t} + \Delta z_t$ and both the left- and right-hand sides are characterized by the same integration properties.

When we introduce nonlinearities in the relationship linking y_{1t} and y_{2t}, however, the stochastic properties of the system become less obvious. Specifically, taking y_{2t} to be I(1), or equivalently difference stationary, no longer implies that y_{1t} is also difference stationary. Indeed, it becomes straightforward to show that, although the I(1)ness of y_{2t} makes y_{1t} nonstationary, this nonstationarity of y_{1t} can no longer be removed by first differencing. Put differently, although the variance of y_{1t} behaves in a manner similar to the variance of a random walk, first differencing y_{1t} will no longer make it stationary. More formally, if we take the first difference of the first equation in (15.12) and use the notation $I_t \equiv I(q_t > \gamma)$, we have

$$\Delta y_{1t} = \beta \Delta y_{2t} + \theta \Delta(y_{2t} I_{t-1}) + \Delta z_t$$
$$= \rho z_{t-1} + \theta y_{2t-1} \Delta I_{t-1} + v_t \tag{15.13}$$

where $v_t = \theta \epsilon_{2t} I_{t-1} + \beta \epsilon_{2t} + u_t$. Clearly, the presence of the term $y_{2t-1} \Delta I_t$ in the right-hand side of (15.13) precludes the possibility of a traditional ECM-type representation à la Granger. If we take q_t to be an iid process, then it is straightforward to establish that $V(y_{2t-1} \Delta I_t) = 2F(\gamma)(1 - F(\gamma))(t - 1)$. Similarly, y_{1t} cannot really be viewed as a difference stationary process, as would have been the case within a linear framework. As dicussed in Granger, Inoue and Morin (1997), where the authors introduced a specification similar to (15.13), the correct but not directly operational form of the error correction model could be formulated as

$$\Delta y_{1t} - \theta y_{2t-1} \Delta I_{t-1} = \rho z_{t-1} + v_t$$

where now both the left- and right-hand side components are stationary. Practical tools and their theoretical properties for handling models such as the above are developed in Gonzalo and Pitarakis (2005a).

Our specification in (15.13) has highlighted the difficulties of handling switching phenomena within the cointegrating relationship itself if we want to operate within the traditional VECM framework. It is also worth emphasizing that similar conceptual difficulties will arise in non-VECM-based approaches to the treatment of nonlinearities in cointegrating relationships. Writing $y_{1t} = \beta_t y_{2t} + u_t$, with y_{2t} an I(1) variable and u_t an I(0) error term, defines a stationary relationship between y_{1t} and y_{2t} which is not invalid per se. However, it would be inaccurate to refer to it as a cointegrating relationship linking two I(1) variables since y_{1t} cannot be difference stationary due to the time varying nature of β_t.

In summary, a system such as (15.12), which has a switching cointegrating vector, cannot admit a VECM representation as in (15.4) in which both the left- and right-hand sides are balanced in the sense of both being stationary. Equivalently, for an I(1) vector to admit a formal VECM representation as in (15.4), it must be the case that the threshold effects are only present in the adjustment process.

15.4.3 Rank configuration under alternative stochastic properties of Y_t

Our objective here is to explore further the correspondence between the rank characteristics of Π_1 and Π_2 and the stability properties of Y_t, akin to the well-known relationship between the rank of the long-run impact matrix of a linear VECM specification and its cointegration properties. We are interested in the rank configurations of Π_1 and Π_2 that are consistent with covariance stationarity of Y_t. Similarly, we also wish to explore the correspondence between the presence of threshold effects in the adjustment process of a cointegrated I(1) system and the rank configurations of the two long-run impact matrices that are compatible with such a system.

Within a linear VECM specification, whose corresponding lag polynomial has roots either on or outside the unit circle, it is well known that having a matrix Π that has full rank also implies that the underlying process is I(0). Although from our result in proposition 4 it is straightforward to see that, if both *or either* of Π_1 and Π_2 have full rank, then Y_t generated from (15.4) is going to be covariance stationary as well, it is also true that the full rank condition is not necessary for covariance stationarity. Our examples in (15.2) and (15.11), for instance, have illustrated the fact that two identical rank configurations, say $(r_1, r_2) = (1, 1)$ may be compatible with either a purely I(1) system as in (15.2) or a covariance stationary system as in (15.11). Similarly, Example 3 with $(r_1, r_2) = (0, 2)$ illustrated the possibility of having a covariance stationary DGP in which either Π_1 or Π_2 have zero rank. These observations highlight the difficulties that may arise when attempting to clearly define the meaning of "nonlinear cointegration" when operating within an Error Correction type of model.

Drawing from our analysis in section 15.4.2, if we take the a priori view that Y_t is I(1) and (15.4) is the correct specification, then it must be the case that the rejection of the null hypothesis of linearity $H_0 : \Pi_1 = \Pi_2$ *directly* implies that we have threshold cointegration, here understood to mean that the adjustment process has a threshold type nonlinearity driven by the external variable q_t while the cointegrating relationship itself is stable over time. Differently put, we can formulate Π_1 and Π_2 as $\Pi_1 = \alpha_1 \beta'$ and $\Pi_2 = \alpha_2 \beta'$.

At this stage it is also important to note that, even under the maintained assumption that the cointegrating relationship itself is linear and is not characterized by threshold effects, this does not necessarily imply that Π_1 and Π_2 must have identical ranks. This feature of the system can be illustrated by considering our earlier example in (15.2), in which we set $\rho_1 = 0$ and $\rho_2 < 0$. This specific parameterization implies, for instance, that $r_1 \equiv Rank(\Pi_1) = 0$ and $r_2 \equiv Rank(\Pi_2) = 1$. Alternatively, we could also have set $\rho_2 = 0$ and $\rho_1 < 0$, implying the rank configuration $(r_1, r_2) = (1, 0)$ within the same example. Obviously our system could also be characterized by a parameterization such as

$\rho_1 < 0$ and $\rho_2 < 0$ with a corresponding rank configuration given by $(r_1, r_2) = (1, 1)$ as in example 1.

Using our result in Proposition 4 and our discussion above, it is straightforward to observe that within a system whose characteristic roots may lie either on or outside the complex unit circle (excluding roots that induce explosive behavior), I(1)ness with cointegration characterized by threshold adjustment may only occur if the rank configuration of $\mathbf{\Pi}_1$ and $\mathbf{\Pi}_2$ is such that $(r_1, r_2) \in \{(0, 1), (1, 0), (1, 1)\}$. Note, however, that the scenario whereby $(r_1, r_2) = (1, 1)$ may also be compatible with a purely stationary Y_t, as in example 2 above with $\rho_{11} = 0$ and $\rho_{12} = 0$, among other possible configurations. At this stage it is also important to recall that, within our operating framework, cases involving processes that are integrated of order greater than one are ruled out. The above observations are summarized more formally in the following proposition.

Proposition 5 *Letting $r_j \equiv Rank(\mathbf{\Pi}_j)$ for $j = 1, 2$ and assuming that $p = 2$, we have that (i) Y_t is covariance stationary if either r_1 or r_2 is equal to 2, (ii) Y_t is I(1) with threshold cointegration if $(r_1, r_2) = (0, 1)$ or $(r_1, r_2) = (1, 0)$, (iii) Y_t is either covariance stationary or I(1) with threshold cointegration if $r_1 = r_2 = 1$.*

According to the above proposition, even if at most one of the two long-run impact matrices characterizing the model in (15.4) is found to have full rank, it must be that Y_t itself is covariance stationary. On the other hand, if we have a rank configuration such as $(r_1, r_2) = (0, 1)$ or $(r_1, r_2) = (1, 0)$ then this would imply that Y_t described by (4) is I(1) and the model is characterized by threshold effects in its adjustment process towards its long-run equilibrium. Intuitively, such a rank configuration captures the idea of an adjustment process that shuts off when the threshold variable q_t crosses above or below a certain magnitude given by γ. Finally, the case whereby $(r_1, r_2) = (1, 1)$ is compatible with either a purely covariance stationary system or an I(1) system with an underlying adjustment process characterized by different speeds of adjustment depending on the magnitude of q_t.

15.4.4   Estimation of r_1 and r_2

Having established the correspondence between alternative rank configurations and the stochastic properties of Y_t, our next objective is to estimate each individual rank r_1 and r_2. In what follows we will take the view that Y_t is known to be I(1), so that the rejection of the null hypothesis of linearity directly implies threshold effects in the adjustment process towards equilibrium. Furthermore, for the simplicity of the exposition, we will assume that the system under consideration is bivariate, setting $p = 2$ in (15.4). Thus we wish to decide whether $(r_1, r_2) = (0, 1)$, $(r_1, r_2) = (1, 0)$ or $(r_1, r_2) = (1, 1)$ in the true specification. Note that any other configuration of (r_1, r_2) would imply that Y_t is covariance stationary and is therefore ruled out by our operating framework.

Before introducing our proposed methodology for estimating r_1 and r_2, we define the following sample quantities. We let $\widehat{\Delta Y_1} = \Delta Y * I(q \leq \hat{\gamma})$, $\widehat{\Delta Y_2} = \Delta Y * I(q > \hat{\gamma})$ and $\hat{Z}_1$ and $\hat{Z}_2$ are as in (15.4) with γ replaced with its estimated counterpart $\hat{\gamma}$. The residual vector is obtained as $\hat{U} = \Delta Y - \hat{\Pi}_1 \hat{Z}_1 - \hat{\Pi}_2 \hat{Z}_2$ and we also define $\hat{U}_1 = \widehat{\Delta Y_1} - \hat{\Pi}_1 \hat{Z}_1$ and $\hat{U}_2 = \widehat{\Delta Y_2} - \hat{\Pi}_2 \hat{Z}_2$, from which we note the equality $\hat{\Omega} = \hat{\Omega}_1 + \hat{\Omega}_2$, where $\hat{\Omega}_1 = \hat{U}_1 \hat{U}_1' / T, \hat{\Omega}_2 = \hat{U}_2 \hat{U}_2' / T$ and $\hat{\Omega} = \hat{U}\hat{U}'/T$. For later use we also introduce the following moment matrices corresponding to each regime j

$$
\begin{aligned}
S_{11}^j &= \frac{\hat{Z}_j \hat{Z}_j'}{T}, \\
S_{00}^j &= \frac{\widehat{\Delta Y_j} \widehat{\Delta Y_j}'}{T}, \\
S_{01}^j &= \frac{\widehat{\Delta Y_j} \hat{Z}_j'}{T}, \\
S_{10}^j &= (S_{01}^j)'
\end{aligned} \tag{15.14}
$$

with $j = 1, 2$. Using (15.14) we can now reformulate the estimated covariance matrices as $\hat{\Omega}_j = S_{00}^j - S_{01}^j (S_{11}^j)^{-1} S_{10}^j, j = 1, 2$, and for later use it will also be useful to note that the eigenvalues of $(S_{00}^j)^{-1} S_{01}^j (S_{11}^j)^{-1} S_{10}^j$ are the same as those of $I - (S_{00}^j)^{-1} \hat{\Omega}_j$ for $j = 1, 2$.

We now propose to estimate the unknown ranks of Π_1 and Π_2 using a model selection approach as introduced and investigated in Gonzalo and Pitarakis (1998, 1999, 2002). We view the problem of the estimation of r_1 and r_2 from a model selection perspective in which our main task is to select the optimal model among a portfolio of nested specifications. The selection is made via the optimization of a penalized objective function. The latter has one component which decreases as the number of estimated parameters increases (e.g., as r_j increases) and another component that increases to penalize overfitting. The use of a model selection based approach for inferences similar to the above has been advocated in numerous related areas of the econometric literature. In Gonzalo and Pitarakis (2002), for example, the authors explore the properties of a model selection based approach for estimating the number of regimes of a stationary time series characterized by threshold effects. In Cragg and Donald (1997), the authors used AIC and BIC type criteria for estimating the rank of a normally distributed matrix. Similarly, in Phillips and Chao (1999) the authors developed a new information theoretic criterion used to determine the rank and short-run dynamics of error correction models.

Formally, letting $\hat{\Omega}_j(r_j)$ denote the sample covariance matrices obtained from each regime characterizing (15.4) under the restriction that $rank(\Pi_j) = r_j$, our estimator of r_j is defined as

$$
\hat{r}_j = \arg \min_{r_j} IC_j(r_j) \tag{15.15}
$$

where

$$
IC(r_j) = \ln |\hat{\Omega}_j(r_j)| + \frac{c_T}{T} m(r_j) \tag{15.16}
$$

with $m(r_j)$ denoting the number of estimated parameters (here $m(r_j) = 2pr_j - r_j^2$) and c_T a deterministic penalty term. Next, using the fact that

$$\ln |\hat{\Omega}_j(r_j)| = \ln |S_{00}^j| + \sum_{i=1}^{r_j}(1 - \hat{\lambda}_i^j) \qquad (15.17)$$

and noting that S_{00}^j is independent of the magnitude of r_j, we can instead focus on the optimization of the following modified criterion

$$\overline{IC}(r_j) = \sum_{i=1}^{r_j} \ln(1 - \hat{\lambda}_i^j) + \frac{c_T}{T}(2pr_j - r_j^2). \qquad (15.18)$$

A clear advantage of using (15.18) stems from the simplicity of its empirical implementation, requiring solely the availability of the eigenvalues of $I - (S_{00}^j)^{-1}\hat{\Omega}_j$ for $j = 1, 2$. It is also interesting to observe the close similarity between conducting inferences using (15.18) and, for example, a formal likelihood ratio-based testing procedure. Focusing on the estimation of r_1, our model selection-based approach involves selecting $\hat{r}_1 = 0$ as the optimal choice if $\overline{IC}(r_1 = 0) < \overline{IC}(r_1 = 1)$ and $\hat{r}_1 = 1$ if $\overline{IC}(r_1 = 1) < \overline{IC}(r_1 = 0)$. Equivalently, the model selection-based approach points to $\hat{r}_1 = 1$ if $-T \ln(1 - \hat{\lambda}_1^1) > 3c_T$ and to $\hat{r}_1 = 0$ otherwise under a bivariate setting. This is equivalent to the formulation of a likelihood ratio statistic for testing the null $H_0 : r_1 = 0$ against $H_1 : r_1 = 1$, except that here the decision rule is dictated by the magnitude of the penalty term and the number of estimated parameters. A formal distribution theory for an LR test-based approach for the determination of r_1 and r_2 à la Johansen can be found in Gonzalo and Pitarakis (2005a). We next summarize the asymptotic properties of the model selection approach in the following proposition.

Proposition 6   *Letting r_j^0 denote the true rank of Π_j for $j = 1, 2$, $\hat{r}_j$ defined as in (15.15), with c_T such that (i) $c_T \to \infty$ and (ii) $c_T/T \to 0$ as $T \to \infty$, we have $\hat{r}_j \xrightarrow{p} r_j^0$.*

The above proposition establishes the weak consistency of the rank estimators obtained through the model selection-based approach. A possible candidate for the choice of the penalty term satisfying both (i) and (ii) is $c_t = \ln T$, corresponding to the well-known BIC-type criterion. It is clear, however, that other functionals of the sample size may be equally valid (e.g. $c_T = 2 \ln \ln T$), making it difficult to argue in favor of a universally optimal criterion.

Having established the limiting properties of our rank estimators, we next concentrate on their finite and large sample performance across a wide range of possible model configurations. Following Gonzalo and Pitarakis (2002), we implement our experiments using $c_T = \ln T$ as the penalty term in (15.18).

We initially consider the DGP given in (15.2) under example 1. We have a bivariate system that is I(1) with a single cointegrating vector $(1, -\beta)$. We set $\beta = 2$ and consider $(\rho_1, \rho_2) = (0, -0.4)$, so that the system is characterized by a true rank configuration given by $(r_1, r_2) = (0, 1)$. In a second set of experiments we set

$(\rho_1, \rho_2) = (-0.2, -0.6)$, so that this second system has $(r_1, r_2) = (1, 1)$. Our results are summarized in Table 15.5, which presents the decision frequencies for each possible magnitude of r_j. Throughout all our experiments q_t is assumed to follow the AR(1) process given by $q_t = 0.5q_{t-1} + \epsilon_t$ with $\epsilon_t = iid(0, 1)$ and the true threshold parameter is set at $\gamma_0 = 0$. As in our earlier experiments the delay parameter is set at $d = 1$ throughout.

From the decision frequencies presented in Table 15.5 it is clear that the proposed model selection procedure performs remarkably well across the three alternative specifications. As expected from our result in Proposition 6, it is selecting the true magnitude of each rank 100% of the times under $T = 1000$, while maintaining very high correct decision frequencies even under $T = 200$. Under the specification in (2), for instance, with $(r_1^0, r_2^0) = (0, 1)$, the procedure picked $r_1 = 0$ about 85% of the times and $r_2 = 1$ 100% of the times under $T = 200$, with the correct decision frequency increasing to about (93%, 100%) under $T = 400$.

To provide further empirical support for our proposed approach, we next consider a set of threshold DGPs that restrict Y_t to being covariance stationary. For this purpose we have focused on the specification given in (15.3) under Example 2 and considered two alternative rank configurations. First, imposing $(\rho_{11}, \rho_{12}) = (0, 0)$ and $(\rho_{21}, \rho_{22}) = (-0.2, -0.4)$, we have a covariance stationary system with $(r_1, r_2) = (0, 2)$. Second, setting $(\rho_{11}, \rho_{12}, \rho_{21}, \rho_{22}) = (-0.4, 0.0, 0.0, -0.2)$, we have another covariance stationary system, this time with $(r_1, r_2) = (1, 1)$. All simulation results are presented in Table 15.6.

From the empirical decision frequencies presented in Table 15.6 it is again the case that the various estimators of r_1 and r_2 point to their true counterparts as T is allowed to increase. Although the accuracy of the estimators is somehow determined by the DGP specific parameters, it is also clear that, under both experiments, the frequency of selecting the true rank is high, reaching levels of between 90 and 100% accuracy.

Table 15.5 Decision frequencies in an I(1) system

	$\hat{r}_1 = 0$	$\hat{r}_1 = 1$	$\hat{r}_1 = 2$	$\hat{r}_2 = 0$	$\hat{r}_2 = 1$	$\hat{r}_2 = 2$
		\multicolumn — $(r_1^0 = 0, r_2^0 = 1), \beta = 2, (\rho_1, \rho_2) = (0.0, -0.4)$				
$T = 200$	85.26	14.74	0.00	0.00	100.00	0.00
$T = 400$	93.42	6.58	0.00	0.00	100.00	0.00
$T = 1{,}000$	100.00	0.00	0.00	0.00	100.00	0.00
		$(r_1^0 = 1, r_2^0 = 1), \beta = 2, (\rho_1, \rho_2) = (-0.2, -0.6)$				
$T = 200$	34.76	65.24	0.00	0.02	99.98	0.00
$T = 400$	10.16	89.84	0.00	0.00	100.00	0.00
$T = 1{,}000$	0.00	100.00	0.00	0.00	100.00	0.00
		$(r_1^0 = 1, r_2^0 = 0), \beta = 2, (\rho_1, \rho_2) = (-0.4, 0.0)$				
$T = 200$	0.02	99.98	0.00	84.76	15.24	0.00
$T = 400$	0.00	100.00	0.00	93.50	0.00	0.00
$T = 1{,}000$	0.00	100.00	0.00	100.00	0.00	0.00

Table 15.6 Decision frequencies in a stationary system

	$\hat{r}_1 = 0$	$\hat{r}_1 = 1$	$\hat{r}_1 = 2$	$\hat{r}_2 = 0$	$\hat{r}_2 = 1$	$\hat{r}_2 = 2$
		$(r_1^0 = 0, r_2^0 = 2), (\rho_{11}, \rho_{12}, \rho_{21}, \rho_{22}) = (0.0, 0.0, -0.2, -0.4)$				
$T = 200$	88.36	10.24	1.40	0.00	0.00	100.00
$T = 400$	94.16	5.32	0.52	0.00	0.00	100.00
$T = 1,000$	100.00	0.00	0.00	0.00	0.00	100.00
		$(r_1^0 = 1, r_2^0 = 1), (\rho_{11}, \rho_{12}, \rho_{21}, \rho_{22}) = (-0.4, 0.0, 0.0, -0.2)$				
$T = 200$	0.00	86.90	13.10	0.56	86.94	12.50
$T = 400$	0.00	90.38	0.00	0.00	91.00	9.00
$T = 1,000$	0.00	92.64	7.36	0.00	92.96	7.04

15.5   A nonlinear permanent and transitory decomposition

Having established the threshold cointegration properties of Y_t, we next investigate how this vector process of interest can be decomposed into a permanent and transitory component following the methodology developed in Gonzalo and Granger (1995).

Recall that in the linear case with Y_t following a VECM of the form $\Delta Y_t = \alpha \beta' Y_{t-1} + u_t$, we are interested in decomposing the p-dimensional vector Y_t into two sets of components as

$$Y_t = A_1 f_t + \tilde{Y}_t \tag{15.19}$$

where A_1 is the $p \times (p - r)$ loading matrix, f_t the $(p - r) \times 1$ common I(1) factors and $\tilde{Y}_t$ is the I(0) component. The above decomposition of Y_t is such that the factors f_t are linear combinations of Y_t and $A_1 f_t$ and $\tilde{Y}_t$ form a Permanent-Transitory decomposition (see Gonzalo and Granger, 1995 for the detailed definitions of each component).

As shown in Gonzalo and Granger (1995), the above two conditions are sufficient to identify the permanent and transitory components. Formally we can write

$$Y_t = A_1 f_t + A_2 z_t \tag{15.20}$$

with $f_t = \alpha_\perp Y_t$, $z_t = \beta' Y_t$ and $A_1 = \beta_\perp (\alpha'_\perp \beta_\perp)^{-1}$, $A_2 = \alpha(\beta'\alpha)^{-1}$.   Note that $\alpha'_\perp \alpha = \beta'_\perp \beta = 0$.

Now, let us consider the following VECM with threshold effects

$$\Delta Y_t = \alpha_1 \beta' Y_{t-1} I(q_{t-d} \le \gamma) + \alpha_2 \beta' Y_{t-1} I(q_{t-d} > \gamma) + u_t.$$

Following the same reasoning as in Gonzalo and Granger (1995), it is now straightforward to establish the following Threshold Permanent-Transitory decomposition for Y_t

$$Y_t = A_1 f_{1t} I(q_{t-d} \leq \gamma) + A_2 f_{2t} I(q_{t-d} > \gamma) + A_3 I(q_{t-d} \leq \gamma) + A_4 I(q_{t-d} > \gamma) z_t \quad (15.21)$$

where $f_{1t} = \alpha'_{1\perp} Y_t, f_{2t} = \alpha'_{2\perp} Y_t$ and $z_t = \beta' Y_t$. The corresponding loading matrices are then given by $A_1 = \beta_\perp (\alpha'_{1\perp} \beta_\perp)^{-1}, A_2 = \beta_\perp (\alpha'_{2\perp} \beta_\perp)^{-1}$ and, similarly, $A_3 = \alpha_1 (\beta' \alpha_1)^{-1}$ and $A_4 = \alpha_2 (\beta' \alpha_2)^{-1}$. Given our estimator of the threshold parameter γ defined in (15.9), together with the corresponding sample moment matrices introduced in (15.14), the practical implementation of the above Threshold Permanent and Transitory decomposition becomes straightforward (see Gonzalo and Pitarakis, 2005b) and is obtained following the same approach as in Gonzalo and Granger (1995).

Despite the representational complications that would arise if we were to also allow the cointegrating vector β to be characterized by the presence of threshold effects, as say $\beta_t = \beta_1 I(q_{t-d} \leq \gamma) + \beta_2 I(q_{t-d} > \gamma)$ (see our discussion in section 15.4.2), the above threshold-based decomposition would translate naturally to such a framework by reformulating it as $Y_t = A_1 f_{1t} I(q_{t-d} \leq \gamma) + A_2 f_{2t} I(q_{t-d} > \gamma) + A_3 z_{1t} I(q_{t-d} \leq \gamma) + A_4 z_{2t} I(q_{t-d} > \gamma)$, with $z_{1t} = \beta'_1 Y_t, z_{2t} = \beta'_2 Y_t$. The corresponding loading matrices would then be given by $A_1 = \beta_{1\perp} (\alpha'_{1\perp} \beta_{1\perp})^{-1}, A_2 = \beta_{2\perp} (\alpha'_{2\perp} \beta_{2\perp})^{-1}, A_3 = \alpha_1 (\beta'_1 \alpha_1)^{-1}$ and $A_4 = \alpha_2 (\beta'_2 \alpha_2)^{-1}$.

15.6 Conclusions

This chapter has focused on the issue of introducing and testing for threshold-type nonlinear behavior into the conventional multivariate error correction model. The threshold nonlinearities we considered were driven by a stationary and external random variable triggering the regime switches. Within this context we obtained the limiting properties of a Wald-type test statistic for testing for the presence of such threshold effects characterizing the long-run impact matrix of the VECM. An interesting property of the proposed test is its robustness to the presence or absence of unit roots in the system, displaying the same limiting null distribution under a wide range of stochastic properties of the system.

We subsequently proceeded with the interpretation and further analysis of the system following a rejection of the null hypothesis of linearity. We showed that cointegration as traditionally defined was compatible with such an error correction type specification only if the nonlinearities are present in the adjustment process rather than the long-run equilibrium itself. We then introduced a model selection-based approach designed to gain further insight into the stochastic properties of the system through the determination of the rank structure of the long-run impact matrices characterizing each regime. This then allowed us to extend the permanent and transitory decomposition of Gonzalo and Granger (1995) into a nonlinear permanent and transitory decomposition.

Much remains to be done in the area of nonlinear multivariate specifications such as the VAR/VECMs considered here. In this chapter we restricted our analysis to models with no deterministic trends. Similarly, our results also ignored the possibility of having such components together with the lagged dependent variables and cointegrating vectors displaying threshold switching behavior.

Extensions along these lines, together with a formal representation theory for such models, are topics currently being investigated by the authors.

Appendix

Lemma A1   *Under assumptions A1–A3 and Y_t a p-dimensional vector of I(0) variables we have as $T \to \infty$*

(a) $\frac{ZZ'}{T} \overset{P}{\to} Q \equiv E[ZZ']$,

(b) $\frac{Z_1 Z_1'}{T} \overset{P}{\to} F(\gamma)Q$, $\frac{Z_2 Z_2'}{T} \overset{P}{\to} (1 - F(\gamma))Q$,

(c) $\frac{UZ'}{T} \overset{P}{\to} 0$, $\frac{UZ_j'}{T} \overset{P}{\to} 0$ for $j = 1, 2$,

(d) $\hat{\Omega}_u \overset{P}{\to} \Omega_u$.

where Q denotes a positive definite $p \times p$ matrix.

Proof.   Under the stated assumptions parts (a) and (d) follow directly from the ergodic theorem. Parts (b) and (d) follow from Lemma 1 in Hansen (1996) and part (e) is obvious.

Lemma A2   *Letting $H_T(\gamma) \equiv \frac{1}{\sqrt{T}}(Z_1 \otimes I)\text{vec } U$, under assumptions A1–A3 and Y_t a p-dimensional vector of I(0) variables we have $H_T(\gamma) \Rightarrow H(\gamma)$ as $T \to \infty$, where $H(\gamma)$ is a zero mean Gaussian process with covariance kernel $F(\gamma_1 \wedge \gamma_2)(Q \otimes \Omega_u)$.*

Proof.   The use of the central limit therem for martingale differences applied to the sequence $\{Y_{t-1} u_t I(q_{t-d} \leq \gamma)\}$ leads to the required Gaussianity for each $\gamma \in \Gamma$. This, combined with the componentwise tightness of $H_T(\gamma)$, which follows from Hansen (1996, Theorem 1), leads to the desired result.

Proof of Proposition 1   From Lemma A1 it directly follows that

$$(Z_2 Z_2'/T)(ZZ'/T)^{-1}(Z_1 Z_1'/T) \otimes \hat{\Omega}_u^{-1} \overset{P}{\to} F(\gamma)(1 - F(\gamma))Q \otimes \Omega_u^{-1} \qquad (15.22)$$

and the Wald statistic in (15.6) can be formulated as

$$W_T(\gamma) = F(\gamma)(1 - F(\gamma))\sqrt{T}(\hat{\pi}_1 - \hat{\pi}_2)'(Q \otimes \Omega_u^{-1})\sqrt{T}(\hat{\pi}_1 - \hat{\pi}_2) + o_p(1). \qquad (15.23)$$

Standard least squares algebra together with Lemma A1 also imply

$$
\begin{aligned}
\sqrt{T}(\hat{\pi}_1 - \pi) &= \sqrt{T}[(Z_1 Z_1')^{-1} Z_1 \otimes I_p]\text{vec } U \\
&= \left[\left(\frac{Z_1 Z_1'}{T} \right)^{-1} \otimes I_p \right] \frac{1}{\sqrt{T}}(Z_1 \otimes I_p)\text{vec } U \\
&= \frac{1}{F(\gamma)}(Q^{-1} \otimes I_p) \frac{1}{\sqrt{T}}(Z_1 \otimes I_p)\text{vec } U + o_p(1)
\end{aligned}
\qquad (15.24)
$$

and

$$\sqrt{T}(\hat{\pi}_2 - \pi) = \left[\left(\frac{Z_2 Z_2'}{T}\right)^{-1} \otimes I_p\right] \frac{1}{\sqrt{T}}(Z_2 \otimes I_p) vec\, U$$

$$= \frac{1}{(1 - F(\gamma))}(Q^{-1} \otimes I_p) \frac{1}{\sqrt{T}}(Z_2 \otimes I_p) vec\, U + o_p(1). \tag{15.25}$$

Combining (15.24) and (15.25) above and using the fact that $Z_2 = Z - Z_1$, we have

$$\sqrt{T}(\hat{\pi}_1 - \hat{\pi}_2) = \frac{(Q^{-1} \otimes I)}{F(\gamma)(1 - F(\gamma))}\left[\frac{1}{\sqrt{T}}(Z_1 \otimes I) vec\, U - F(\gamma)\frac{1}{\sqrt{T}}(Z \otimes I) vec\, U\right] + o_p(1). \tag{15.26}$$

We can now write the Wald statistic as

$$W_T(\gamma) = \left[\frac{1}{\sqrt{T}}(Z_1 \otimes I) vec\, U - F(\gamma)\frac{1}{\sqrt{T}}(Z \otimes I) vec\, U\right]' V(\gamma)^{-1}$$

$$\times \left[\frac{1}{\sqrt{T}}(Z_1 \otimes I) vec\, U - F(\gamma)\frac{1}{\sqrt{T}}(Z \otimes I) vec\, U\right] + o_p(1) \tag{15.27}$$

where $V(\gamma) = F(\gamma)(1 - F(\gamma))(Q \otimes \Omega_u)$. Next letting $G_T(\gamma) \equiv [(Z_1 \otimes I) vec\, U - F(\gamma)(Z \otimes I) vec\, U]/\sqrt{T}$, Lemmas A1–A2, together with the fact that $\frac{1}{\sqrt{T}}(Z \otimes I) vec\, U \xrightarrow{d} N(0, Q \otimes \Omega_u)$, which follows directly from the CLT, imply $G_T(\gamma) \Rightarrow G(\gamma)$, where $G(\gamma)$ is a zero mean Gaussian random vector with covariance $E[G(\gamma_1)G(\gamma_2)] = V(\gamma_1 \wedge \gamma_2) \equiv F(\gamma_1 \wedge \gamma_2)(1 - F(\gamma_1 \wedge \gamma_2))(Q \otimes \Omega_u)$. It now follows that the limiting distribution of the Wald statistic $W_T(\gamma)$ is given by $W_T(\gamma) \Rightarrow G(\gamma)'V(\gamma)^{-1}G(\gamma)$ and the final result follows from the continuous mapping theorem.

Lemma A3 *Under assumptions A1–A3 and Y_t a p-dimensional vector of I(1) variables with $\Delta Y = U$ we have as $T \to \infty$*

(a) $\frac{ZZ'}{T^2} \Rightarrow \int_0^1 W(r)W(r)'dr$,

(b) $\frac{Z_1 Z_1'}{T^2} \Rightarrow F(\gamma) \int_0^1 W(r)W(r)'dr$,

(c) $\frac{Z_2 Z_2'}{T^2} \Rightarrow (1 - F(\gamma)) \int_0^1 W(r)W(r)'dr$

where $W(r)' = (W_1(r), \ldots, W_p(r))$ is a p-dimensional standard Brownian motion.

Proof. Part (a) follows directly from Phillips and Durlauf (1986). For part (b) we first write

$$\frac{Z_1 Z_1'}{T^2} = F(\gamma)\frac{ZZ'}{T^2} + \frac{W_1 W_1'}{T^2} \tag{15.28}$$

where $W_1 W_1'$ stacks the elements of the form $Y_{t-1} Y_{t-1}' (I(q_{t-d} \leq \gamma) - F(\gamma))$. It now suffices to show that $\frac{W_1 W_1'}{T^2} = o_p(1)$. We let $S_t = \sum_{i=1}^t (I(q_{t-1} \leq \gamma) - F(\gamma))$ and with no loss of generality set $d = 1$ and take zero initial conditions. Using summation by parts we can write $\sum_{t=1}^T (I(q_{t-1} \leq \gamma) - F(\gamma)) Y_{t-1} Y_{t-1}' = S_{T-1} Y_T Y_T' - \sum_{t=1}^{T-1} S_t (Y_{t+1} Y_{t+1}' - Y_t Y_t')$. Next, using the fact that $Y_{t+1} Y_{t+1}' = Y_t Y_t' + Y_t u_{t+1}' + u_{t+1} Y_t' + u_{t+1} u_{t+1}'$, we also have

$$\frac{1}{T^2} W_1 W_1' = \frac{S_{T-1}}{T} \frac{Y_T Y_T'}{T} - \frac{1}{T^2} \sum_{t=1}^{T-1} Y_t u_{t+1}' S_t - \frac{1}{T^2} \sum_{t=1}^{T-1} u_{t+1} Y_t' S_t$$
$$- \frac{1}{T^2} \sum_{t=1}^{T-1} (u_{t+1} u_{t+1}' - \Omega_u) S_t - \frac{1}{T^2} \Omega_u \sum_{t=1}^{T-1} S_t. \tag{15.29}$$

Under the maintained assumptions the ergodic theorem ensures that $S_{T-1}/T \xrightarrow{p} 0$. Since $Y_T Y_T'/T$ is stochastically bounded, it thus follows that the first term in the right-hand side of (15.29) is $o_p(1)$. Next, we consider the components $y_{it} u_{jt+1} S_t$. We have $E[y_{it} u_{jt+1} S_t] = 0$ and it is also straightforward to establish that

$$\lim_{T \to \infty} E\left[\frac{1}{T^2} \sum_{t=1}^{T-1} y_{it-1} u_{jt} S_t S_t \right]^2 = 0$$

and both the second and third terms in the right-hand side of (15.29) are also $o_p(1)$. Proceeding similarly, the third and fourth components can also be seen to be $o_p(1)$ and the final result follows from (a). Part (c) can be shown to hold in exactly the same manner as part (b).

Lemma A4   *Under assumptions A1–A3 and Y_t a p-dimensional vector of I(1) variables with $\Delta Y = U$ we have as $T \to \infty$*

(a) $\frac{1}{T}(Z \otimes I_p) vec\, U \Rightarrow vec\left[\int_0^1 dW(r) W(r)' \right]$,

(b) $\frac{1}{T}(Z_1 \otimes I_p) vec\, U \Rightarrow vec\left[\int_0^1 dW(r, F(\gamma)) W(r)' \right]$

Proof.   Part (a) follows directly from Phillips and Durlauf (1986). For part (b), the result follows from $L_T(\gamma) \equiv \frac{1}{\sqrt{T}} \sum_{t=1}^{[Tr]} u_t I(q_{t-1} \leq \gamma) \Rightarrow W(r, F(\gamma))$, where $W(r, F(\gamma))$ denotes a standard Brownian Sheet (see Theorem 1 in Diebolt, Laib and Wandji, 1997; and Theorem 2 in Caner and Hansen, 2001).

Proof of Proposition 2   We assume that the underlying null model is a pure unit root process as $\Delta Y = U$. Within the present I(1) framework we consider the following normalization of the Wald statistic

$$T(\hat{\pi}_1 - \hat{\pi}_2)' \left[\left(\frac{Z_2 Z_2'}{T^2} \right) \left(\frac{Z Z'}{T^2} \right)^{-1} \left(\frac{Z_1 Z_1'}{T^2} \right) \otimes \hat{\Omega}_u^{-1} \right] T(\hat{\pi}_1 - \hat{\pi}_2).$$

and with no loss of generality in what follows we will impose $\Omega_u = I_p$. Next, from Lemma A3 it follows that

$$\left[\left(\frac{Z_2 Z_2'}{T^2}\right)\left(\frac{ZZ'}{T^2}\right)^{-1}\left(\frac{Z_1 Z_1'}{T^2}\right) \otimes \hat{\Omega}_u^{-1}\right] \Rightarrow F(\gamma)(1 - F(\gamma)) \int_0^1 W(r)W(r)' dr \otimes I_p \quad (15.30)$$

and we formulate the test statistic of interest as

$$W_T(\gamma) = F(\gamma)(1 - F(\gamma))T(\hat{\pi}_1 - \hat{\pi}_2)'\left[\int_0^1 W(r)W(r)' dr \otimes I_p\right]T(\hat{\pi}_1 - \hat{\pi}_2) + o_p(1).$$

We next focus on the large sample behavior of $T(\hat{\pi}_1 - \hat{\pi}_2)$ when the true DGP is given by $\Delta Y = U$. We have

$$\begin{aligned} T\hat{\pi}_1 &= \left[\left(\frac{Z_1 Z_1'}{T^2}\right)^{-1} \otimes I_p\right]\frac{1}{T}(Z_1 \otimes I_p)vec\ U \\ &= \frac{1}{F(\gamma)}\left[\left(\int_0^1 W(r)W(r)' dr\right)^{-1} \otimes I_p\right]\frac{1}{T}(Z_1 \otimes I_p)vec\ U + o_p(1). \end{aligned} \quad (15.31)$$

Proceeding similarly for $\hat{\pi}_2$ and rearranging as above we have

$$T(\hat{\pi}_1 - \hat{\pi}_2) = \frac{1}{F(\gamma)(1 - F(\gamma))}\left[\left(\int_0^1 WW'\right)^{-1} \otimes I_p\right]\left[\frac{1}{T}(Z_1 \otimes I_p)vec\ U - F(\gamma)\frac{1}{T}(Z \otimes I_p)vec\ U\right]$$

Next, using Lemma A4 it follows that

$$\begin{aligned} \frac{1}{T}(Z_1 \otimes I)vec\ U - F(\gamma)\frac{1}{T}(Z \otimes I)vec\ U &\Rightarrow vec\left[\int_0^1 dW(r, F(\gamma))W(r)'\right] \\ &\quad - F(\gamma)vec\left[\int_0^1 dW(r, 1)W(r)'\right] \\ &= vec\left[\int_0^1 [dW(r, F(\gamma)) - F(\gamma)dW(r, 1)]W(r)'\right] \\ &= vec\left[\int_0^1 dK(r, F(\gamma))W(r)'\right] \end{aligned} \quad (15.32)$$

where we let $K(r, F(\gamma)) = W(r, F(\gamma)) - F(\gamma)W(r, 1)$. Using the above in the expression of the Wald test statistic and rearranging we obtain the required result. The case for a cointegrated system follows along the same lines.

Proof of Proposition 3 From $\hat{U}(\gamma) = \Delta Y - \hat{\Pi}_1 Z_1 - \hat{\Pi}_2 Z_2 + U$ we can write

$$\begin{aligned} \hat{U}(\gamma)\hat{U}(\gamma)' &= (\Delta Y - \hat{\Pi}_1 Z_1 - \hat{\Pi}_2 Z_2)(\Delta Y' - Z_1'\hat{\Pi}_1' - Z_2'\hat{\Pi}_2') \\ &= \Delta Y \Delta Y' - \Delta Y Z_1'(Z_1 Z_1')^{-1}Z_1 \Delta Y' - \Delta Y Z_2'(Z_2 Z_2')^{-1}Z_2 \Delta Y' \end{aligned} \quad (15.33)$$

where we made use of the fact that $Z_i Z_j' = 0 \; \forall i \neq j$ and $i, j = 1, 2$. Next, letting γ_0 denote the true threshold parameter, we write the model evaluated at γ_0 as $\Delta Y = \mathbf{\Pi}_1 Z_1^0 + \mathbf{\Pi}_2 Z_2^0 + U$, where $Z_1^0 = (y_0 I(q_{0-d} \leq \gamma_0), \ldots, y_{T-1} I(q_{T-d} \leq \gamma_0))$ and $Z_2^0 = Z - Z_1^0$ with $Z_1^0 Z_2^{0} = 0$. Inserting into (15.33) and rearranging gives

$$
\begin{aligned}
\hat{U}(\gamma)\hat{U}(\gamma)' ={} & \mathbf{\Pi}_1 Z_1^0 Z_1^{0} \mathbf{\Pi}_1' + \mathbf{\Pi}_2 Z_2^0 Z_2^{0} \mathbf{\Pi}_2' + 2\mathbf{\Pi}_1 Z_1^0 U' + 2\mathbf{\Pi}_2 Z_2^0 U' + UU' - \mathbf{\Pi}_1 Z_1^0 M_1 Z_1^{0} \mathbf{\Pi}_1' \\
& - \mathbf{\Pi}_2 Z_2^0 M_1 Z_2^{0} \mathbf{\Pi}_1' - 2\mathbf{\Pi}_1 Z_1^0 M_1 Z_2^{0} \mathbf{\Pi}_2' - 2\mathbf{\Pi}_1 Z_1^0 M_1 U' - 2\mathbf{\Pi}_2 Z_2^0 M_1 U' - U M_1 U' \\
& - \mathbf{\Pi}_1 Z_1^0 M_2 Z_1^{0} \mathbf{\Pi}_1' - \mathbf{\Pi}_2 Z_2^0 M_2 Z_2^{0} \mathbf{\Pi}_2' - 2\mathbf{\Pi}_1 Z_1^0 M_2 Z_2^{0} \mathbf{\Pi}_2' - 2\mathbf{\Pi}_1 Z_1^0 M_2 U' \\
& - 2\mathbf{\Pi}_2 Z_2^0 M_2 U' - U M_2 U'
\end{aligned}
$$

where $M_1 = Z_1'(Z_1 Z_1')^{-1} Z_1$ and $M_2 = Z_2'(Z_2 Z_2')^{-1} Z_2$. We next evaluate the limiting behavior of the above quantity for $\gamma < \gamma_0, \gamma = \gamma_0$ and $\gamma > \gamma_0$. Applying appropriate normalizations, we obtain the following uniform convergence in probability result over $\gamma \in \Gamma$ for the case $\gamma < \gamma_0$

$$
\begin{aligned}
\frac{\hat{U}(\gamma)\hat{U}(\gamma)'}{T} \overset{p}{\to} {}& (\mathbf{\Pi}_1 - \mathbf{\Pi}_2)[(G(\gamma_0) - G(\gamma))(G - G(\gamma))^{-1}(G - G(\gamma_0))](\mathbf{\Pi}_1 - \mathbf{\Pi}_2)' + \Omega_u \\
\equiv {}& \frac{(F(\gamma_0) - F(\gamma))(1 - F(\gamma_0))}{1 - F(\gamma)} (\mathbf{\Pi}_1 - \mathbf{\Pi}_2) Q (\mathbf{\Pi}_1 - \mathbf{\Pi}_2)' + \Omega_u.
\end{aligned}
$$

$$(15.34)$$

Proceeding similarly for the case $\gamma > \gamma_0$ we have

$$
\begin{aligned}
\frac{\hat{U}(\gamma)\hat{U}(\gamma)'}{T} \overset{p}{\to} {}& (\mathbf{\Pi}_1 - \mathbf{\Pi}_2)[G(\gamma_0)G(\gamma)^{-1}(G(\gamma) - G(\gamma_0))](\mathbf{\Pi}_1 - \mathbf{\Pi}_2)' + \Omega_u \\
\equiv {}& \frac{F(\gamma_0)(F(\gamma) - F(\gamma_0))}{F(\gamma)} (\mathbf{\Pi}_1 - \mathbf{\Pi}_2) Q (\mathbf{\Pi}_1 - \mathbf{\Pi}_2)' + \Omega_u.
\end{aligned}
$$

Finally with

$$
\frac{\hat{U}(\gamma_0)\hat{U}(\gamma_0)'}{T} \overset{p}{\to} \Omega_u
$$

we have that the objective function converges uniformly in probability to a nonstochastic limit that is uniquely minimized at $\gamma = \gamma_0$ and the required result follows from Theorem 2.1 in Newey and McFadden (1994).

Proof of Proposition 4 We are interested in the covariance stationarity of the stochastic recurrence given by $Y_t = \mathbf{\Phi}_1 Y_{t-1} I_{1t-d} + \mathbf{\Phi}_2 Y_{t-1} I_{2t-d} + u_t$, where we use the notation $I_{1t-d} \equiv I(q_{t-d} \leq \gamma)$ and $I_{2t-d} \equiv I(q_{t-d} > \gamma)$. Note first that, given Assumption A2, we have $E[Y_{t-1} I_{1t-d}] = E[I_{1t-d}] E[Y_{t-1}] = F(\gamma) E[Y_{t-1}]$ and $E[Y_{t-1} I_{2t-1}] = (1 - F(\gamma)) E[Y_{t-1}]$. With Y_t denoting a solution to the stochastic recurrence, we have $\forall t \; E[Y_t] = 0$ and

$$
\begin{aligned}
E[Y_t Y_t'] ={} & E[\mathbf{\Phi}_1 Y_{t-1} Y_{t-1}' \mathbf{\Phi}_1 I_{1t-1}] + E[\mathbf{\Phi}_2 Y_{t-1} Y_{t-1}' \mathbf{\Phi}_2 I_{2t-1}] + E[u_t u_t'] \\
={} & F(\gamma) \mathbf{\Phi}_1 E[Y_{t-1} Y_{t-1}'] \mathbf{\Phi}_1 + (1 - F(\gamma)) \mathbf{\Phi}_2 E[Y_{t-1} Y_{t-1}'] \mathbf{\Phi}_2 + \Omega_u.
\end{aligned}
$$

Letting $V_t = E[Y_t Y_t']$, the above stochastic difference equation can be written more compactly as $V_t = F(\gamma)\Phi_1 V_{t-1}\Phi_1' + (1 - F(\gamma))\Phi_2 V_{t-1}\Phi_2' + \Omega_u$. Next, vectorizing both sides and letting $v_t \equiv vec(V_t)$ and $\omega \equiv vec(\Omega_u)$, we have $v_t = [F(\gamma)(\Phi_1 \otimes \Phi_1) + (1 - F(\gamma))(\Phi_2 \otimes \Phi_2)]v_{t-1} + \omega$. For Y_t to be covariance stationary, it is thus necessary that V_t converges and this is ensured by the requirement that $\rho(F(\gamma)(\Phi_1 \otimes \Phi_1) + (1 - F(\gamma))(\Phi_2 \otimes \Phi_2)) < 1$. Following the same line of proof as in Brandt (1986) and Karlsen (1990), it is also straightforward to establish that, if $\rho(F(\gamma)(\Phi_1 \otimes \Phi_1) + (1 - F(\gamma))(\Phi_2 \otimes \Phi_2)) < 1$, then the above stochastic recurrence admits a unique covariance stationary solution. We can thus conclude that the above threshold VAR admits a unique covariance stationary solution *if and only if* $\rho(F(\gamma)(\Phi_1 \otimes \Phi_1) + (1 - F(\gamma))(\Phi_2 \otimes \Phi_2)) < 1$.

Proof of Proposition 6   We first consider the case $r_j > r^0$ and establish that under the stated conditions, $P[\overline{IC}(r_j) < \overline{IC}(r^0)] \to 0$ as $T \to \infty$. From the definition of $\overline{IC}(.)$ in (15.18) we have $P[\overline{IC}(r_j) < \overline{IC}(r^0)] = P[-T \sum_{i=r^0+1}^{r_j} \ln(1 - \hat{\lambda}_i^j) > c_T(2pr_j - 2pr^0 - r_j^2 + (r^0)^2)]$. Since $-T \sum_{i=r^0+1}^{r_j} \ln(1 - \hat{\lambda}_i^j)$ is $O_p(1)$ and the right-hand side diverges towards infinity we have that $\lim_{T\to\infty} P[\overline{IC}(r_j) < \overline{IC}(r^0)] = 0$ and thus the procedure does not overrank asymptotically. For the case $r_j < r^0$ we have $P[\overline{IC}(r_j) < \overline{IC}(r^0)] = P[\sum_{i=r_j+1}^{r^0} \ln(1 - \hat{\lambda}_i^j) < \frac{c_T}{T}(2pr^0 - (r^0)^2 + r_j^2 - 2pr_j)]$. Since $-\sum_{i=r_j+1}^{r^0} \ln(1 - \hat{\lambda}_i^j) \xrightarrow{p} \theta > 0$ and $\frac{c_T}{T} \to 0$, it follows that, for $r_j < r^0$, $\lim_{T\to\infty} P[\overline{IC}(r_j) < \overline{IC}(r^0)] = 0$ as required.

Acknowledgments

We wish to thank the Spanish Ministry of Education for supporting this research under grants No. SEC01-0890 and SEJ2004-0401ECON.

References

Andrews, D.W.K. (1993) Tests for parameter stability and structural change with unknown change point. *Econometrica* **61**, 821–56.

Arai, Y. (2004) Testing for linearity in regressions with I(1) processes. CIRJE Discussion Paper No. F-303, University of Tokyo.

Balke, N. and T. Fomby (1997) Threshold Cointegration. *International Economic Review* **38**, 627–45.

Baum, C.F., J.T Barkoulas and M. Caglayan (2001) Nonlinear adjustment to purchasing power parity in the post-Bretton Woods era. *Journal of International Money and Finance* **20**, 379–99.

Beaudry, P. and G. Koop (1993) Do recessions permanently change output? *Journal of Monetary Economics* **31**, 149–64.

Bec, F., M. Ben-Salem and M. Carrasco (2001) Tests for unit-root versus threshold specification with an application to the PPP. *Journal of Business and Economic Statistics*, forthcoming.

Bec, F. and A. Rahbek (2004) Vector equilibrium correction models with nonlinear discontinuous adjustments. *Econometrics Journal* **7**, 1–24.

Borenstein, S.A., A.C. Cameron and R. Gilbert (1997) Do gasoline prices respond asymmetrically to crude oil prices? *Quarterly Journal of Economics* **112**, 305–39.

Brandt, A. (1986) The stochastic equation $Y_{n+1} = A_n Y_n + B_n$ with stationary coefficients. *Advances in Applied Probability* **18**, 211–20.

Caner, M. and B.E. Hansen (2001) Threshold autoregression with a unit root. *Econometrica* **69**, 1555–1596.

Chan, K.S. (1990) Testing for threshold autoregression. *Annals of Statistics* **18**, 1886–1894.

Chan, K.S. (1993) Consistency and limiting distribution of the least squares estimator of a threshold autoregressive model. *Annals of Statistics* **21**, 520–33.

Cragg, J.G. and S.G. Donald (1997) Inferring the rank of a matrix. *Journal of Econometrics* **76**, 223–50.

Diebolt, J., N. Laib and J. Ngatchou-Wandji (1997) Limiting distributions of weighted processes of residuals. Application to parametric nonlinear autoregressive models. *Comptes Rendus de l'Académie des Sciences de Paris, Series 1*, **325**, 535–40.

Durlauf, S.N. and P.A. Johnson (1995) Multiple regimes and cross-country growth behaviour. *Journal of Applied Econometrics* **10**, 365–84.

Enders, W. and B. Falk (1998) Threshold-autoregressive, median-unbiased, and cointegration tests of purchasing power parity. *International Journal of Forecasting* **14**, 171–86.

Enders, W. and C.W.J. Granger (1998) Unit-root tests and asymmetric adjustment with an example using the term structure of interest rates. *Journal of Business and Economic Statistics* **16**, 304–11.

Enders, W. and P.L. Siklos (2001) Cointegration and threshold adjustment. *Journal of Business and Economic Statistics* **19**, 166–76.

Engle, R.F. and C.W.J. Granger (1987) Cointegration and error correction: representation, estimation and testing. *Econometrica* **55**, 251–76.

Gonzalez, M. and J. Gonzalo (1997) Threshold unit root processes. Unpublished manuscript, Department of Statistics and Econometrics, Universidad Carlos III de Madrid.

Gonzalo, J. and C.W.J. Granger (1995) Estimation of common long-memory components in cointegrated systems. *Journal of Business and Economic Statistics* **13**, 27–35.

Gonzalo, J. and R. Montesinos (2000) Threshold stochastic unit root models. Unpublished manuscript, Department of Statistics and Econometrics, Universidad Carlos III de Madrid.

Gonzalo, J. and J.-Y. Pitarakis (1998) Specification via model selection in vector error correction models. *Economics Letters* **60**, 321–8.

Gonzalo, J. and J.-Y. Pitarakis (1999) Dimensionality effect in cointegration analysis. In R.F. Engle and H. White (eds). *Cointegration, Causality and Forecasting: a Festschrift in Honour of C.W.J. Granger*. Oxford: Oxford University Press, pp. 212–29.

Gonzalo, J. and J.-Y. Pitarakis (2002) Estimation and model selection based inference in single and multiple threshold models. *Journal of Econometrics* **110**, 319–52.

Gonzalo, J. and J.-Y. Pitarakis (2005a) Threshold nonlinearities in cointegrated systems. Unpublished manuscript.

Gonzalo, J. and J.-Y. Pitarakis (2005b) Estimation of common long-memory components in threshold cointegrated systems. Unpublished manuscript.

Granger, C.W.J., T. Inoue and N. Morin (1997) Nonlinear stochastic trends. *Journal of Econometrics* **81**, 65–92.

Hansen, B.E. (1996) Inference when a nuisance parameter is not identified under the null hypothesis. *Econometrica* **64**, 413–30.

Hansen, B.E. (1997) Approximate asymptotic p-values for structural change tests. *Journal of Business and Economic Statistics* **15**, 60–7.

Hansen, B.E. (1999a) Testing for linearity. *Journal of Economic Surveys* **13**, 551–76.

Hansen, B.E. (1999b) Threshold effect in nondynamic panels: estimation, testing and inference. *Journal of Econometrics* **93**, 345–68.

Hansen, B.E. and B. Seo (2002) Testing for two-regime threshold cointegration in vector error correction models. *Journal of Econometrics* **110**, 293–318.

Hong, S. (2003) Testing linearity in cointegrating relations: application to PPP. Mimeo, Yale University. Unpublished manuscript.

Johansen, S. (1988) Statistical analysis of cointegrating vectors. *Journal of Economic Dynamics and Control* **12**, 231–54.

Johansen, S. (1991) Estimation and hypothesis testing of cointegrating vectors in Gaussian vector autoregressive models. *Econometrica* **59**, 1551–1580.

Johansen, S. (1995) *Likelihood Based Inference in Cointegrated Vector Autoregressive Models.* Oxford: Oxford University Press.

Karlsen, H.A. (1990) Existence of moments in a stationary stochastic difference equation. *Advances in Applied Probability* **22**, 129–46.

Koop, G. and S.M. Potter (1999) Dynamic asymmetries in US unemployment. *Journal of Business and Economic Statistics* **17**, 298–312.

Lo, M.C. and E. Zivot (2001) Threshold cointegration and nonlinear adjustment to the law of one price. *Macroeconomic Dynamics* **5**, 533–76.

Michael, P., A.R. Nobay and D.A. Peel (1997) Transaction costs and nonlinear adjustment in real exchange rates: an empirical investigation. *Journal of Political Economy* **105**, 862–79.

Newey, W.K. and D.L. McFadden (1994) Large sample estimation and hypothesis testing. In R.F. Engle and D.L. McFadden (eds), *Handbook of Econometrics*, vol. 4. New York: Elsevier, pp. 2113–2245.

Obstfeld, M. and A.M. Taylor (1997) Nonlinear aspects of goods-market arbitrage and adjustment: Heckscher's commodity points revisited. *Journal of the Japanese and International Economies* **11**, 441–79.

O'Connell, P.G.J. and S. Wei (1997) The bigger they are the harder they fall: how price differences across US cities are arbitraged. *Journal of International Economics* **56**, 21–53.

Peltzman, S. (2000) Prices rise faster than they fall. *Journal of Political Economy* **108**, 466–502.

Phillips, P.C.B. and J.C. Chao (1999) Model selection in partially nonstationary vector autoregressive processes with reduced rank structure. *Journal of Econometrics* **91**(2), 227–71.

Phillips, P.C.B. and S. Durlauf (1986) Multiple time series regression with integrated processes. *Review of Economic Studies* **53**, 473–95.

Pippenger, M.K. and G.E. Goering (1993) A note on the empirical power of unit root tests under threshold processes. *Oxford Bulletin of Economics and Statistics* **55**, 473–81.

Potter, S.M. (1995) A nonlinear approach to US GNP. *Journal of Applied Econometrics* **2**, 109–25.

Saikkonen, P. and I. Choi (2004) Cointegrating smooth transition regressions, *Econometric Theory* **20**, 301–40.

Seo, M. (2004) Bootstrap testing for the presence of threshold cointegration in a threshold vector error correction model. Unpublished manuscript, Department of Economics, University of Wisconsin-Madison.

Tong, H. and K.S. Lim (1980) Threshold autoregression, limit cycles and cyclical data. *Journal of the Royal Statistical Society* **4**, Series B, 245–92.

Tong, H. (1983) Threshold models in non-linear time series analysis. *Lecture Notes in Statistics*, vol. 21. Berlin: Springer-Verlag.

Tong, H. (1990) *Non-Linear Time Series: A Dynamical System Approach*. Oxford: Oxford University Press.

Tsay, R.S. (1989) Testing and modeling threshold autoregressive processes. *Journal of the American Statistical Association* **84**, 231–40.

Tsay, R.S. (1998) Testing and modeling multivariate threshold models. *Journal of the American Statistical Association* **93**, 1188–1202.

Wohar, M.E. and N.S. Balke (1998) Nonlinear dynamics and covered interest rate parity. *Empirical Economics* **23**, 535–59.

16
Common Cycles

Farshid Vahid

Abstract

This chapter provides an overview of several existing methods for studying and estimating common cycles in multiple time series. These methods differ in their definition of "the cycle," the extent of assumptions that they impose on the dynamic structure of the underlying data-generating process, and the applications for which they are most appropriate. I study Beveridge–Nelson and unobserved component methods that are appropriate for decomposing a small number of series into trends and cycles. I also study common-idiosyncratic decomposition of cycles, which relies on the use of a large number of time series. Finally, I review a nonparametric method that uncovers the common cycle by identifying clusters of turning points in levels of time series. This last method is close in spirit to economists' dating of turning points of the "business cycle."

16.1	Introduction		610
16.2	Common trends and common cycles as common features		613
	16.2.1	Common Beveridge–Nelson cycles	615
	16.2.2	Implications and extensions	617
16.3	Common unobserved factors		619
	16.3.1	Common unobserved trends and cycles	619
	16.3.2	Common and idiosyncratic cycles	622
16.4	Common classical cycles		626
16.5	Conclusion		627

16.1 Introduction

It is commonly agreed that most macroeconomic variables are best modeled as difference stationary, i.e., I(1), processes, and a difference stationary variable has a stochastic, as well as, or instead of, a deterministic trend. It is often of some importance to decompose a time series into its trend and transitory deviations from the trend, and as long as these deviations are serially correlated, they are called the "cycle."[1] For example, in the case of economic output, the trend innovations, i.e., innovations that have permanent effects, are often associated with supply-side innovations, while the innovations that only have transitory effects are associated with demand-side shocks. Since the innovations with permanent effects are the innovations of the stochastic trend, the decomposition of output into its trend and cycle becomes an essential requirement for measuring the relative importance of supply and demand innovations in total output.

The sole distinction that trend is I(1) and cycle is I(0) is not sufficient for the identification of the trend and cycle. With the additional assumption that the trend is a random walk (with drift when appropriate), we can turn an estimated ARIMA model of a time series into a random walk trend and stationary deviations from that trend. This is the univariate Beveridge–Nelson (BN) decomposition (Beveridge and Nelson, 1981). The attractiveness of BN trends and cycles are that they are implied by the reduced form dynamic equation chosen by the data. The disadvantage is that they are both driven by the innovation (the unpredictable part given the past) in the series, and therefore they cannot be split into two components, one driven by supply shocks and the other by demand shocks. If BN trends and cycles are inappropriately given a structural interpretation, one comes to the extreme conclusion that all cyclical variation in output is driven by supply shocks only. Given that a single series has only a single innovation, splitting this innovation into more than one unobserved component requires extraneous restrictions. These restrictions can be in the form of a restriction on the covariance between the trend and cycle, as in Harvey (1985) and Watson (1986), or a restriction on the dynamic structure of the cycle, as in Morley *et al.* (2003). However, since more than one unobserved component structure may lead to the same or similar reduced form, and these structures can have vastly different implications, which structure to choose is a matter of judgement (see Watson, 1986; Proietti, 2002).

The estimation of the permanent component can be sharpened in multivariate models with cointegration. Cointegration implies that the stochastic trends in n cointegrated variables are linear combinations of a smaller number of common trends. As shown in Chapter 14, the reduced form for a cointegrated set of n time series with r ($< n$) cointegrating vectors is a vector error correction (VECM) model. This model can be inverted into the sum of $n - r$ common random walk trends and n cycles. Here, only $n - r$ linear combinations of n innovations drive the common trends (i.e., have permanent effects), which implies that we can find r combinations of innovations that have only transitory effects. While this is less restrictive than the univariate case, it is still a reduced form analysis. In particular, the n cycles are, by construction, driven both by the innovations with permanent effects and those with transitory effects. This must not be interpreted structurally, as there can be many underlying structural forms that lead to the same reduced form. Cointegration only determines the number of random walk trends in the structural form.

It is natural to think of possible restrictions on the cycles to narrow down the space of structural forms that are compatible with a reduced form. Section 16.2 of this essay refers to this as a "common feature" (Engle and Kozicki, 1993) question and discusses the test for common cycles suggested by Vahid and Engle (1993). It also discusses some recent extensions and applications of this idea.

Time series analysts usually think of a time series as the sum of independent unobserved components. For non-seasonal data, these components are an unobserved trend, an unobserved cycle and perhaps a measurement error. A top-down approach to modeling time series, advocated by Harvey (1989), is to write down plausible models for the dynamics of each component, and then estimate the parameters of the model using the data. Until a few years ago, activity in this line of research was almost entirely focused on univariate time series. Recently, however, there has been an upsurge of activity in multivariate generalizations of this approach and, in particular, in the analysis of common trends and common cycles within this approach. I provide an overview of these advances in the first part of section 16.3.

The general-to-specific methodology of identifying trends and cycles that starts with a general reduced form dynamic model, finds restrictions on the trends and cycles that are supported by the data, and thereby narrows down the set of structural forms that are compatible with the reduced form, is quite appealing. However, this strategy is impractical when working with a large number of variables. A VARMA model with just 10 variables is quite difficult to identify and estimate. The determination of cointegration rank in large systems is also problematic (see Gonzalo and Pitarakis, 1999). Even the determination of lag length, which has serious implications for all subsequent analysis, can be tricky (see Vahid and Issler, 2002). Therefore, in situations with a large number of variables, one has no choice but to start from a simple identifiable structure, and if that structure produces features that are not supported by the data in directions that are of importance, one then makes it slightly more general. This approach is particularly apt when we model many similar variables, for example, a model of GDP of all European countries, or a model of the top 200 stock prices. In the second part of section 16.3, I review the recent advances in this direction, in particular the dynamic factor models proposed by Forni *et al.* (2000). In this line of research, attention has shifted from cycles defined as deviations from random walk trends to cycles in the first difference of I(1) variables.

Business cycle analysis is an important driving factor in the study of common trends and common cycles. The methods discussed above define cycles either as deviations from random walk trends, or as dynamic factors in the growth rates. In each case, one can go somewhat further and use frequency domain theory to design filters that extract periodic components with "business cycle frequencies," as in Baxter and King (1999) and Christiano and Fitzgerald (2003). Groups of respected economists often monitor and determine the turning points of the phenomenon known as "the business cycle", and we need to ask whether any of the above parametric models capture this phenomenon. Perhaps none do since, after all, models of cycles are, by definition, models, i.e., simple constructs that are supposed to (but might not) provide a satisfactory representation of particular features of the data. Instead of using a parametric model, Harding and Pagan (2004) propose an algorithm for dating the turning points of a "common cycle" in a set of variables. Section 16.4 provides a summary of their procedure.

Finally, a word on what this chapter does not include. It is not intended to provide a comprehensive survey of the literature on common cycles and related topics. The literature on common cycles is growing at an increasing rate, largely because of interest in the question of a European cycle and the proliferation of factor models in finance. There are annual conferences around the world on regional and international business cycles, common features and dynamic factor analysis, and the subject has now become very broad. Only a few representative definitions of common cycles are considered in this chapter, and only a few papers for each of these definitions are cited in order to keep the number of references manageable. This chapter does not include a discussion of similarity of cycles in structural vector autoregressive (SVAR) models. In SVAR models, restrictions from economic theory are used to identify trends. After identifying and estimating the trend, one can then look at the similarity of deviations from trend in different variables (as in, for example, Lippi and Reichlin, 1994). Although this is a sound approach to applied economic modeling, there is little more to say about it. Since structural identifying restrictions are problem specific, it is not possible to come up with a general theory of how to test for common deviations from trend, or how to use the similarity of these deviations to improve the quality of inference in SVAR models. Finally, there are also important issues, such as nonlinear dynamics, coupling of nonlinear dynamic systems, measures of coherence and other measures of similarity of dynamics, that are obviously relevant to the topic of common cycles, and have been, or can be, fruitfully used in this line of research. However, the discussion of these topics is beyond the scope of this chapter.

16.2 Common trends and common cycles as common features

The decomposition of time series into trends, cycles and seasonals has been an important objective of time series analysts. For a time series analyst, it is natural to seasonally adjust time series and detrend them (often by differencing), and then to model the seasonally adjusted and detrended series jointly. Although econometricians tend to also use seasonally adjusted data, they pay more careful attention to trends. We know that economic variables, at least at the aggregate level, obey some rules in the long run that makes them interdependent. For example, we know that not everybody in an economy can be a net borrower at all times. For the same reason, no nation can run a current account deficit indefinitely. Similarly, prices of the same good in different locations cannot differ systematically by more than the cost of transporting the good from one location to another. Hence, it is natural to suspect that some economic variables have common trends. This, and the rather small sample size of aggregate economic time series, have led econometricians to consider how to improve the estimation of the trend in one variable by using data on that variable and all other variables that are likely to have the same trend.

Economists have also observed that cyclical variations in economic aggregates seem to be related. It is often said that monetary aggregates are "pro-cyclical," or that business profits are "pro-cyclical," meaning that they go up, reach their peak, come down and reach their trough at the same time as aggregate output. Hence, it is also natural to think about how common cycles might improve the precision of trend cycle decompositions. However, it is appropriate to test whether the assumption of commonality is supported or rejected by the data before one attempts to use this assumption to estimate trends and cycles.

Engle and Kozicki (1993) provided a general framework for testing common statistical features such as trends and cycles. They define a statistical property to be a "feature" if it satisfies a set of axioms. The following definitions are from Engle and Kozicki (1993).

Definition 1   *A "feature" is a property that satisfies the following three axioms:*

1. *If y has (does not have) the feature, then λy will have (not have) the feature for any $\lambda \neq 0$.*
2. *If y does not have the feature and x does not have the feature, then $z = x + y$ will not have the feature.*
3. *If y does not have the feature but x does have the feature, then $z = x + y$ will have the feature.*

Definition 2   *A feature that is present in each of a group of series is said to be common to those series if there exists a non-zero linear combination of the series that does not have the feature. Such a linear combination is called a* cofeature combination *and the vector that represents it is called a* cofeature *vector. There can exist $s(< n)$ linearly independent cofeature vectors. The set of all linearly independent cofeature vectors span the* cofeature space.

The significance of these definitions is twofold. Firstly, they imply that if a set of variables has common features, they are consistent with a common factor structure in which the common factors have the feature and the remaining factors do not. Secondly, they suggest simple directions to design tests for common features. These implications are made explicit in Anderson and Vahid (1998), who outline the following theorem:

Theorem 3   *A common feature implies and is implied by a common factor representation in which common factors have the feature and other factors do not have the feature.*

Proof. Let $x \in F$ stand for "x has the feature F" and $x \in NF$ stand for "x does not have the feature." Suppose that the n-vector $y_t \in F$ and that there are s linearly independent linear combinations of y_t that belong to NF, i.e.

$$\underset{s \times n}{\beta'} \quad \underset{n \times 1}{y_t} \quad = \quad \underset{s \times 1}{c_t}$$

where $c_t \in NF$. Without loss of generality, take $\beta' = (I_s | \beta^*_{s \times (n-s)})$ and partition y_t accordingly as $\begin{pmatrix} ly_{1t} \\ y_{2t} \end{pmatrix}$. y_{2t} can be arbitrarily decomposed to:

$$
\begin{array}{ccccc}
y_{2t} & = & f_t & + & c^*_t \\
(n-s) \times 1 & & (n-s) \times 1 & & (n-s) \times 1
\end{array}
$$

where $f_t \in F$ and $c^*_t \in NF$. This implies:

$$
\begin{pmatrix} y_{1t} \\ y_{2t} \end{pmatrix} = \begin{pmatrix} -\beta^*_{s \times (n-s)} \\ I_{(n-s)} \end{pmatrix} f_t + \begin{pmatrix} c^{**}_t \\ c^*_t \end{pmatrix}
$$

where $c^{**}_t = -\beta^*_{s \times (n-s)} c^*_t + c_t \in NF \Rightarrow$ the n-vector y_t can be represented by n-s common factors. Obviously this decomposition is not unique. The only if proof is obvious.

Whenever a feature can be detected in each of a group of series by means of a conditional moment test based on the same conditioning information, GMM tests for common features and for the determination of the dimension of the cofeature space can readily be designed. This has been proven in the context of the special case of common nonlinearity in Anderson and Vahid (1998), and the proof for a general case is along similar lines and will not be repeated here.

16.2.1   Common Beveridge–Nelson cycles

Let us consider the special case of common trends and common cycles. A trend, when its order of magnitude is defined, e.g., a deterministic trend or an I(1) trend, is a feature. Tests for common trends or cointegration are discussed elsewhere in this handbook. A cycle, defined as cyclical deviations from the trend, is not determined unless we completely specify what the trend is. If the trend is specified as a random walk (with drift where appropriate), then a cycle is a feature, and it can be detected by the presence of serial correlation in the first difference of the time series. A test for a common serial correlation feature in the first differences of a group of I(1) series is therefore a test for a common cycle in those series. The implications of this for the reduced form dynamic equations are explained in terms of familiar notation below.

Starting from the Wold representation of an n-vector of I(1) variables (ignoring deterministic terms for simplicity), we have

$$
\Delta y_t = C(L)\epsilon_t, \tag{16.1}
$$

where $C(L)$ is a matrix polynomial in the lag operator L, with $C(0) = I_n$, and $\sum_{j=1}^{\infty} ||C_j|| < \infty$, where $||X||$ denotes a norm for the matrix X such as $||X||^2 = tr(X'X)$. The vector ϵ_t is a $n \times 1$ vector of stationary one-step-ahead linear forecast errors in y_t, given information on the lagged values of y_t. We can rewrite equation (16.1) as:

$$
\Delta y_t = C(1)\epsilon_t + \Delta C^*(L)\epsilon_t \tag{16.2}
$$

where $C^*_i = \sum_{j>i} -C_j$ for all i. In particular $C^*_0 = I_n - C(1)$.

If we integrate both sides of equation (2) we get:

$$y_t = C(1) \sum_{s=0}^{\infty} \epsilon_{t-s} + C^*(L)\epsilon_t \tag{16.3}$$

$$= \tau_t + c_t$$

Equation (16.3) is the multivariate version of the Beveridge–Nelson trend-cycle representation (Beveridge and Nelson, 1981). The series y_t are represented as the sum of an n-vector of random walks τ_t which is called the trend, and an n-vector of I(0) components c_t, which is called the cycle. The variables in y_t have common trends (or cointegrate) if there are r linearly independent vectors, $r < n$, stacked in an $r \times n$ matrix α', with the property that

$$\underset{r \times n}{\alpha'} \, C(1) = 0.$$

The variables in y_t have common cycles if there are s linearly independent vectors, $s \le n - r$, stacked in an $s \times n$ matrix $\tilde{\alpha}'$, with the property that

$$\underset{s \times n}{\tilde{\alpha}'} \, C^*(L) = 0.$$

The reason that s has to be less than $n - r$ is that columns of $\tilde{\alpha}$ must be linearly independent of columns of α, otherwise it would imply that elements of y_t are exactly linearly dependent. Hence, s can at most be $n - r$. Given the definition of $C^*(L)$, common cycles imply

$$\tilde{\alpha}'C_j = 0 \qquad \text{for } j = 1, 2, \dots$$
$$\Longleftrightarrow \tilde{\alpha}' \Delta y_t \text{ is unpredictable from the past.}$$

By the Granger representation theorem (Engle and Granger, 1987), inverting equation (16.1) under the restrictions implied by cointegration, leads to a vector error correction model (VECM). Making the additional customary assumption that a VECM with a finite number of autoregressive lags and no moving average terms can adequately capture the dynamics of y_t, this leads to

$$\Delta y_t = \Gamma_1 \Delta y_{t-1} + \cdots + \Gamma_p \Delta y_{t-p} + \gamma \alpha' y_{t-1} + \epsilon_t \tag{16.4}$$

where γ and α are $n \times r$ matrices of rank r, the rank of the cointegrating space. The common cycles requirement that $\tilde{\alpha}' \Delta y_t$ must be unpredictable from the past leads to the following conditional moment restriction:

$$E(\tilde{\alpha}' \Delta y_t | \Delta y_{t-1}, \dots, \Delta y_{t-p}, \alpha' y_{t-1}) = 0. \tag{16.5}$$

This is a test of reduced rank in $B = (\Gamma_1, \dots, \Gamma_p, \gamma)$, i.e., testing the null hypothesis that there are s unpredictable combinations of Δy_t versus the alternative that are no such combinations is the same as testing the null hypothesis that B has rank $n - s$ versus the alternative that B is of full rank. Obviously, $\tilde{\alpha}$ is only identified up to a normalization. Anderson and Vahid (1998) show that, under a convenient normalization, the GMM estimator of the columns of $\tilde{\alpha}$ are the canonical coefficient vectors of Δy_t corresponding to $\{\lambda_i^2, i = 1, \ldots, s\}$, the s smallest estimated squared canonical correlations between Δy_t and $(\Delta y_{t-1}, \ldots, \Delta y_{t-p}, \alpha' y_{t-1})$. Moreover, the test statistic for the null hypothesis that there are s unpredictable combinations of Δy_t which is also the test for over-identifying restrictions in this system, is $T \sum_{i=1}^{s} \lambda_i^2$. This statistic has the same asymptotic distribution as the statistic $-T \sum_{i=1}^{s} \ln(1 - \lambda_i^2)$. This latter statistic is the standard likelihood ratio test of the null that the s smallest canonical correlations are zero under the assumption of normality (Anderson, 1984). The test statistic has an asymptotic χ^2 distribution with $s(np + r - n + s)$ degrees of freedom under the null. The factor T in this statistic can be replaced by a function of T, n and p to improve the performance of the test in finite samples (see Kshirsagar, 1972, chapters 7 and 8). Alternatively, the rank of B and the lag length can be simultaneously determined using a model selection criterion (see Vahid and Issler, 2002).

In closing, I mention two points. First, cointegration is not a prerequisite for common cycles. We can, and should, test for common cycles regardless of whether there are any common trends. When there are no common trends, there will not be any cointegrating vectors in the conditioning set of (16.5). Second, when the cointegrating vectors α are not known, they can be replaced by consistent estimates without affecting the asymptotic distribution of the common cycle test, because of the super consistency for the estimators of cointegrating vectors. However, as shown by Hecq *et al.* (2004), the uncertainty in the rank of the cointegration space can have a considerable effect on the small sample performance of the common cycle test. I discuss this further below.

16.2.2 Implications and extensions

The tests described above determine the number of common cycles, i.e., the rank of the matrix of coefficients $B = (\Gamma_1, \ldots, \Gamma_p, \gamma)$ of the VECM. After determining this, the reduced rank VECM can be estimated using a reduced rank regression estimation method. The estimated reduced rank VECM will have the properties that (i) its long-run forecasts will obey the cointegration restrictions, and (ii) its short-run forecasts will be collinear. When this reduced rank VECM is inverted to decompose the series into BN-trends and BN-cycles, these components will satisfy the cointegration and the common cycle cofeature restrictions. For example, in a bivariate case with a common cycle, the BN cycles will be completely in sync, i.e., they will have coherency of one at all frequencies. It is important to note that this will only be true for the BN-cycles delivered by the rank restricted VECM, a multivariate one-sided filter that has data-supported common trend and cycle restrictions built into its construction. If another detrending filter, such as the first difference filter, the Hodrick–Prescott filter or a univariate band pass filter, is used, the resulting detrended series need not be perfectly coherent at any frequency. This point is elaborated in Cubadda (1999).

Data-supported common cycle restrictions reduce the number of parameters in the VECM, and sharpen the inference about the relative importance of innovations with permanent and transitory effects, as shown by Issler and Vahid (2001). In contrast with the univariate BN trend and cycle decomposition, in the multivariate case with $n - r$ common trends and $n - s$ common cycles, it is no longer necessary that the innovations to BN trends are spanned by the innovations driving BN cycles. There can be s out of $n - r$ innovations to BN trends that are uncorrelated with the $n - s$ innovations that drive the BN cycles (recall that $s \leq n - r$). In the extreme case that $s = n - r$, there will be no perfect linear relationship between the innovations of BN trends and cycles. In the special case in which $s = n - r$, it is possible to obtain the BN trend-cycle decomposition using the estimated cointegration and cofeature vectors only, without estimating the reduced rank VECM. This has been shown in Vahid and Engle (1993), and it is just a minor point pertaining to an extreme special case. Unfortunately, some researchers have incorrectly assumed that this is the only case where common cycle restrictions should be taken into account to improve multivariate BN decompositions.

An advantage of common cycle restrictions is their sharpness. That is, if they are supported in a multivariate data set, they deliver sharp implications about comovement in the BN-cycles and they imply many restrictions on the VECM, far more than those implied by cointegration. This eases the problem of excess uncertainty caused by redundant parameters in vector autoregressive models, and therefore leads to real advantages for forecasting (Vahid and Issler, 2002). At the same time, this sharpness is also a disadvantage, in the sense that BN-cycles that are not perfectly coherent are all considered to be equally dissimilar. If the data does not support exact coherency in BN-cycles, does it mean that these cycles are not similar at all?

While the two extremes of perfectly coherent cycles and independent cycles are easy to define, the concept of similarity in cycles is much more difficult. Rather than concentrating on providing a measure of similarity, the literature on reduced rank VECMs has moved in the direction of providing answers for three "What if?" questions, namely: (i) What if the variables are observed with measurement error?; (ii) What if the only difference in cycles are very local blips, as in moving averages with very short memory?; and (iii) What if the cycle in one variable is just the lagged version of the cycle in another? In all three situations, the common cycle hypothesis is rejected, but with any sensible definition, these cycles must be recognized as similar. In the first two cases, there are no white noise linear combinations of Δy_t, but there is a linear combination that is a low order MA, a lower MA order than any of the elements of Δy_t. This is what Gourieroux and Peaucelle (1992) call "codependence." Vahid and Engle (1997) suggest a test for codependent cycles to test for this type of similar, but not perfectly coherent BN-cycles. In the third case, a linear combination of elements of Δy_t at different lags will be unpredictable from the past. Cubadda and Hecq (2001) use this to develop a test for common, but out of phase, cycles. Another suggestion for relaxing the strict restrictions of common cycles has been put forward by Breitung and Candelon (2000), who propose a test for common periodic components of specific frequencies, instead of testing for comovement at all frequencies.

There have also been some recent developments in the study of reduced rank VECMs. Hecq *et al.* (2004) have studied the implication of rank restrictions on just $(\Gamma_1, \ldots, \Gamma_p)$ in the VECM in equation (16.4). Their study shows that these restriction can be detected more reliably than common BN cycles restrictions when the cointegration rank is misspecified. Work on whether this result can be exploited to develop better forecasting models, or to improve inference about cointegration in large systems, is currently in progress. The analysis of common trends and common cycles becomes more involved in I(2) systems. Paruolo (2004) examines the question of common trends and common cycles in I(2) systems.

16.3 Common unobserved factors

The discussion in the previous section implies a general to specific modeling strategy for multiple I(1) series comprising of the following steps: (i) Start from an unrestricted VAR model; (ii) Test for cointegration and if it is found move to a VECM, otherwise move to a VAR in differences; (iii) Test for common cycles and if they are found estimate a reduced rank VECM; (iv) Derive the implied BN trends and cycles. As an alternative, some find it more intuitive to think about the components of a time series as independent unobserved factors. If there is a possibility of common unobserved components in several time series, then there will be significant gains in modeling these series together. I consider two applications of common unobserved factor models that have been put forward for the study of common cycles. The first has been developed to estimate trends and cycles of a finite number of time series, and can be considered an alternative to the BN methodology. The second has been developed to estimate common cycles in a large panel of time series, each of which has its own idiosyncratic cycle as well as being influenced by common cycles.

16.3.1 Common unobserved trends and cycles

These models are discussed in Harvey and Koopman (1997) and are multivariate extensions of the unobserved components (UC) models[2] of Harvey (1989). They start by assuming a dynamic structure for the trend and cycle in each series, and then multivariate time series are modeled as a system of seemingly unrelated univariate time series. For example, trends are usually assumed to be random walks with drift, and sometimes growth rates are also assumed to change smoothly, implying that the time series is I(2). Cycles are assumed to be at least AR(2) processes with complex roots. Harvey (1989) prefers to parameterize the cycle in terms of the damping factor and frequency of oscillations of the auto-covariance function. Assuming that the trend is a random walk with drift and that there are no measurement errors, this leads to the structure for each time series being given by

$$y_t = \tau_t + \varphi_t$$
$$\tau_t = \beta + \tau_{t-1} + \eta_t$$
$$\begin{pmatrix} \varphi_t \\ \varphi_t^* \end{pmatrix} = \begin{pmatrix} \rho \cos \lambda_c & \rho \sin \lambda_c \\ -\rho \sin \lambda_c & \rho \cos \lambda_c \end{pmatrix} \begin{pmatrix} \varphi_{t-1} \\ \varphi_{t-1}^* \end{pmatrix} + \begin{pmatrix} \kappa_t \\ \kappa_t^* \end{pmatrix}$$

(16.6)

where η_t, κ_t and κ_t^* are independent of each other. The reduced form for the cycle φ_t is an ARMA(2,1) with autoregressive polynomial $(1 - 2\rho \cos \lambda_c L + \rho^2 L^2)$. Having two errors κ_t and κ_t^* influencing the cycle is not essential, and one can assume that $\kappa_t^* = 0$ to simplify the model. In the multivariate case, all of the above will have an additional index i. Trend innovations can be contemporaneously correlated across time series and cycle innovations can be correlated across series, but trend and cycle innovations are assumed to be independent of each other. These models are effortlessly expressed in state space form, and the Kalman filter is used to compute the likelihood function, which is maximized to yield estimates of the parameters of the model. With the assumption of normality, the Kalman filter delivers the conditional expectation of trends and cycles at time $t + 1$ given the information at time t, and the Kalman smoother delivers the conditional expectation of trends and cycles at every t given the entire sample information.

Common trends will require all β_i to be equal and the covariance matrix Σ_η of $(\eta_{1t}, \eta_{2t}, \dots, \eta_{nt})'$ to be singular. As structural time series models are considered in greater detail in the chapter of this handbook contributed by Harvey and de Rossi, I, therefore, concentrate here on just the characterization of cycles and common cycles. Common cycles will require all ρ_i to be equal, all λ_{ci} to be equal, and Σ_κ, the covariance matrix of $(\kappa_{1t}, \kappa_{2t}, \dots, \kappa_{nt})'$, to be singular. Testing the hypothesis of common cycles in this framework is difficult because the singularity of Σ_κ means that, under the null hypothesis, these parameters will be on the boundary of the parameter space. However, a necessary condition for common cycles in this framework is that the moment condition expressed in equation (16.5) is satisfied. To see this, consider the case of two variables ($n = 2$). The singularity of Σ_κ implies that the innovations that generate cycles in the two variables are perfectly correlated. Let the ratio of the variance of these innovations be q^2. This implies that

$$y_{1t} = \tau_{1t} + \varphi_{1t},$$
$$y_{2t} = \tau_{2t} + q\varphi_{1t}$$

Here we have not made any assumptions about common trends. This implies that $qy_{1t} - y_{2t} = q\tau_{1t} - \tau_{2t}$, which leads to

$$q\triangle y_{1t} - \triangle y_{2t} = q\beta_1 - \beta_2 + q\eta_{1t} - \eta_{2t}.$$

That is, there is a linear combination of mean subtracted $\triangle y_{1t}$ and $\triangle y_{2t}$ that is not predictable from the past. The necessary and sufficient condition for common cycles is therefore

$$E(q(\triangle y_{1t} - \beta_1) - (\triangle y_{2t} - \beta_2)|\eta_{1t-1}, \eta_{2t-1}, \varphi_{1t-1}, \eta_{1t-2}, \eta_{2t-2}, \varphi_{1t-2} \dots) = 0. \quad (16.7)$$

While the observed histories of $\triangle y_1$ and $\triangle y_2$ are included in the conditioning set, they do not exhaust it. Therefore, the above moment condition implies

$$E(q(\triangle y_{1t} - \beta_1) - (\triangle y_{2t} - \beta_2)|\triangle y_{1t-1}, \triangle y_{2t-1}, \triangle y_{1t-2}, \triangle y_{2t-2}, \ldots) = 0 \qquad (16.8)$$

but (16.8) does not imply (16.7). Because this moment condition is easy to check, it will be wise to check it before assuming that an unobserved component model has a common cycle.

There is one special case where the moment condition (16.8) is both necessary and sufficient, and this is when the number of common trends and common cycles adds up to n. For example, if we also have cointegration in the above two variable example, then

$$y_{1t} = \tau_{1t} + \varphi_{1t}$$
$$y_{2t} = \alpha\tau_{1t} + q\varphi_{1t},$$

and the space spanned by $(\eta_{1t-1}, \varphi_{1t-1}, \eta_{1t\ 2}, \varphi_{1t-2}, \ldots)$ will be the same as the space spanned by $(\alpha y_{1t-1} - y_{2t-1}, \triangle y_{1t-1}, \triangle y_{2t-1}, \triangle y_{1t-2}, \triangle y_{2t-2}, \ldots)$. In this special case, the moment condition (16.5) is both necessary and sufficient for a common cycle. The considerations for the situation where the cointegrating relationship is estimated, and the required modifications when allowing for observation errors, are similar to the discussions for common BN cycles. This demonstrates that developments in testing for common BN cycles are useful for unobserved component modeling.

The criticisms listed for the BN common cycles also apply to UC common cycles. In particular, cycles are assumed to be perfectly synchronized. However, in this framework, since cycles are assumed to have a simple structure with parameters that directly measure the frequency and the amplitude of the auto-covariance function of the cyclical component, it is easier (in theory) to study cycles that are common but not in phase. Rünstler (2004) shows that, in the context of the UC model specified in (16.6), stochastic cycles with phase shifts can be characterized by

$$\cos(\theta)\varphi_t + \sin(\theta)\varphi_t^*.$$

This implies an ARMA(2,1) cycle with the same autoregressive polynomial as φ_t, generated by the same underlying white noise process[3] κ_t, but the MA polynomial is $(\cos(\theta) - \rho\cos(\lambda_c - \theta)L)$. Hence, y_{1t} and y_{2t} have common non-synchronous cycles when

$$y_{1t} = \tau_{1t} + \varphi_t$$
$$y_{2t} = \tau_{2t} + q(\cos(\theta)\varphi_t + \sin(\theta)\varphi_t^*).$$

While imposing this structure and estimating its parameters is straightforward, testing if variables have common shifted cycles is not. Rünstler (2004, p. 238) suggests that this may be done by inspecting the eigenvalues of the estimated covariance matrix of cycle innovations in a model that is estimated without restricting cycles to be common. Whether it is possible to design a test to provide some information about such cycles prior to estimation is an interesting topic for future research.

16.3.2 Common and idiosyncratic cycles

In section 16.2, I explained how tests for common trends and common cycles can be designed on the basis of a test for a common feature. Common feature tests exploit the fact that the common factor has a different statistical property than other constituent factors. However, there are situations where the objective is to decompose series into components with similar statistical properties. For instance, the dynamics of returns or volatilities of different stocks can be modeled as the sum of a market factor, which reacts to overall market news and is common to all stocks, and an idiosyncratic factor that reacts to firm specific news. Both common and idiosyncratic factors are I(0) dynamic factors, which we call cycles. With a small number of time series, one can impose the number of common factors, impose specific dynamic structures for the common and idiosyncratic factors, assume that all factors are independent of each other, and then estimate the resulting unobserved component model. The goodness of the assumptions underlying such a model can be evaluated, for example, by an encompassing test against a fitted VARMA model. However, when the number of variables n is large, such a strategy is infeasible.

Recently, researchers have exploited the large cross-section dimension to develop consistent estimators for the common dynamic factors as both n and T go to infinity. The idea of exploiting the cross-sectional dimension goes back at least to Chamberlain and Rothschild (1983). In the model

$$\underset{(n\times 1)}{Y_t} = \underset{(n\times r)}{A} \underset{(r\times 1)}{F_t} + \underset{(n\times 1)}{u_t} \qquad (16.9)$$

in which the Y_t are assumed to have mean zero for simplicity, the F_t are r common factors, and the u_t are n idiosyncratic factors that are independent of F_t and independent of each other,[4] Chamberlain and Rothschild (1983) show that the r largest eigenvalues of $\frac{1}{T}\sum_{t=1}^{T} Y_t Y_t'$ will go to infinity as n goes to infinity, while the $(r+1)^{\text{th}}$ eigenvalue remains bounded. This property is exploited by Forni *et al.* (2000) to suggest an ocular test for determining the number of common factors by examining how the few largest eigenvalues increase as n increases. For example, Figure 16.1, taken from Anderson and Vahid (2004), shows the evolution of the largest five eigenvalues of the variance-covariance matrix of the logarithms of volatility of the weekly returns of n Australian stocks as n increases from 5 to 21. This graph shows that the largest eigenvalue increases at a much faster rate than other eigenvalues, and this suggests one common factor for the 21 series. For more information about this graph refer to Anderson and Vahid (2004).

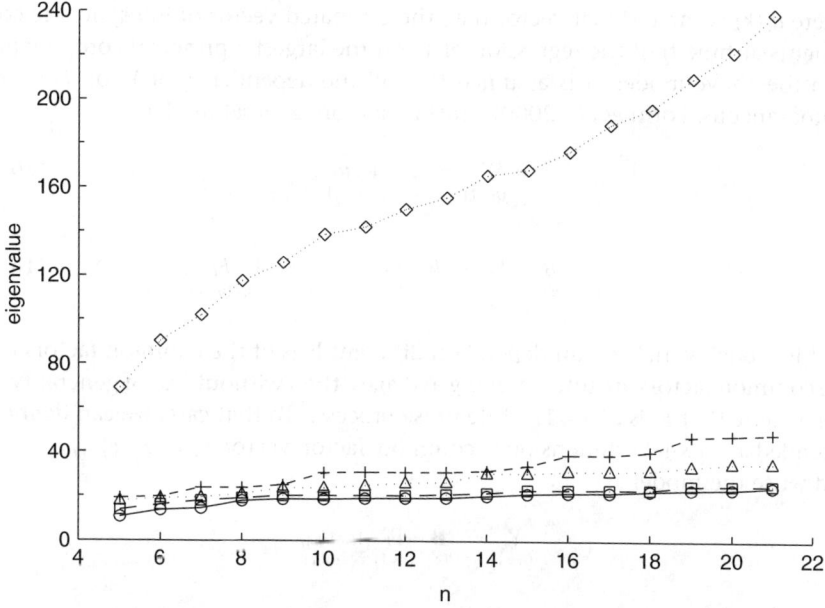

Figure 16.1 The largest five eigenvalues of log-volatility of Australian stock returns

The setup in (16.9) is similar to traditional factor models, and naturally the first r principal components of Y_t, i.e., the r weighted averages of elements of Y_t which explain the largest part of cross-section variation in Y_t relative to any other possible weighted average, are candidate estimators for the common factors. The intuitive idea is that, in this framework, the influence of any of the idiosyncratic factors in the cross section averages of Y_{it} goes to zero, and asymptotically such averages are driven purely by the common factors. Indeed, principal components are not only consistent, but also asymptotically efficient if the model is correct. After common factors are estimated, a simple OLS regression of Y_t on estimated factors delivers estimates of factor loadings and idiosyncratic components.

Bai and Ng (2002) suggest model selection criteria that determine the number of common factors consistently (as n and T go to infinity). Their simulation showed that the following model selection criteria worked well in finite samples when finding the number of common factors based on the principal component estimator of common factors:

$$IC_1(k) = \ln\left(\frac{1}{nT}\sum_{t=1}^{T}\hat{u}_t'(k)\hat{u}_t(k)\right) + k\left(\frac{n+T}{nT}\right)\ln\frac{nT}{n+T}$$

$$IC_2(k) = \ln\left(\frac{1}{nT}\sum_{t=1}^{T}\hat{u}_t'(k)\hat{u}_t(k)\right) + k\left(\frac{n+T}{nT}\right)\ln(\min\{n,T\}),$$

where $\hat{u}_t(k)$ is the residual vector (i.e., the estimated vector of idiosyncratic components at time t) of the regression of Y_t on the largest k principal components.

In the above model, it is assumed that all the dependence of Y_t on F_t is contemporaneous. Forni *et al.* (2000) consider a more general model,

$$\underset{(n\times1)}{Y_t} = \underset{(n\times1)}{\chi_t} + \underset{(n\times1)}{u_t} \tag{16.10}$$

$$\underset{(n\times1)}{\chi_t} = \underset{(n\times q)}{B_0}\ \underset{(q\times1)}{F_t} + \underset{(n\times q)}{B_1}\ \underset{(q\times1)}{F_{t-1}} + \cdots + \underset{(n\times q)}{B_s}\ \underset{(q\times1)}{F_{t-s}}. \tag{16.11}$$

In this model, variables can depend on different lags of the common factors F_t. If the common factors are finite moving averages, then without loss of generality, we can assume that F_t is a $(q \times 1)$ white noise process.[5] In that case, we can define an extended $r = q(s + 1)$ dimensional common factor vector $\mathbf{F}_t = (F'_t, F'_{t-1}, \ldots, F'_{t-s})'$ and write the model as

$$\underset{(n\times1)}{Y_t} = \underset{(n\times r)}{\mathbf{B}}\ \underset{(r\times1)}{\mathbf{F}_t} + \underset{(n\times1)}{u_t}\ ,$$

and then use the principal component estimator (see, e.g., Stock and Watson, 2002). This estimator is often called the *static* principal component estimator. Note that it will suffer from an extra approximation error when the common factors have autoregressive dynamics, in which case the model selection criteria above will not be applicable.

Forni *et al.* (2000) suggest an estimator of the common component based on *dynamic* principal components. The latter are based on the eigenvalues and eigenvectors of the spectral density matrices of Y_t at different frequencies. A description of their idea is as follows. The spectral representation theorem tells us that each of the n stationary time series can be regarded as random coefficient sums of the harmonics of all frequencies between $(-\pi, \pi)$. For each variable, the random coefficients of the components of each frequency ω are the sum of (i) how important that frequency is in explaining the variation of the common factors; and (ii) how important that frequency is in explaining the idiosyncratic variation in that variable. Each additional variable contains some additional information about (i), but only local information about (ii). Therefore, it is intuitive that, for every frequency ω, q eigenvalues of $\Sigma(\omega)$, the $n \times n$ covariance matrix of coefficients of harmonics of frequency ω, will diverge as n goes to infinity, while all other eigenvalues remain bounded. The $(n \times 1)$ eigenvectors corresponding to the q largest eigenvalues of $\Sigma(\omega)$ show the contribution of the frequency ω component of the common factors to each of the n variables. Therefore, the q combinations of the frequency ω spectral coordinates of n variables will determine the importance of harmonics of frequency ω in the q common factors as n goes to infinity. To translate this information into the time domain, an inverse transform delivers the weights of filters that extract the common component from n time series. The ideal filter will be two-sided and infinite, and in practice it is truncated. The practical recipe of this approach, taken from Forni *et al.* (2000), is provided below.

1. Compute a consistent estimate of the spectral density matrix of Y at frequency ω using

$$\underset{n \times n}{\hat{\Sigma}(\omega_h)} = \frac{1}{2\pi} \sum_{j=-M}^{+M} W(j, M) \hat{\Gamma}_j e^{-ij\omega_h}$$

where

$$\omega_h = \frac{2\pi h}{2M+1} \quad \text{with } h = 0, 1, \ldots, 2M, \quad \hat{\Gamma}_j = \frac{1}{T} \sum_{t=1}^{T} Y_t Y_{t-j}',$$

and $W(.,.)$ is a weight function, such as the Bartlett or Parzen window functions. Based on simulation results, Forni *et al.* (2000) recommend that the truncation lag M be chosen to be the closest integer to $\frac{2}{3} T^{\frac{1}{3}}$.

2. Compute $\mathbf{p}_1(\omega_h), \ldots, \mathbf{p}_q(\omega_h)$, the row eigenvectors corresponding to the q largest (in absolute value) eigenvalues of $\hat{\Sigma}(\omega_h)$ for $h = 0, 1, \ldots, 2M$, and use them to compute $1 \times n$ vectors

$$\mathbf{K}_i(\omega_h) = p_{1,i}^*(\omega_h) \mathbf{p}_1(\omega_h) + \cdots + p_{q,i}^*(\omega_h) \mathbf{p}_q(\omega_h),$$

where $p_{.,i}^*(\omega_h)$ denotes the complex conjugate of the ith element of $\mathbf{p}(\omega_h)$. These vectors show how the frequency ω_h components of each variable should be combined to generate the contribution of the common factors to the variation at frequency ω_h of variable i.

3. Use the inverse Fourier transform of $\mathbf{K}_i(\omega_h), h = 1, \ldots, 2M$, to deliver the filter weights that extract χ_{it}:

$$\underline{\mathbf{K}}_{i,k} = \frac{1}{2M+1} \sum_{h=0}^{2M} \mathbf{K}_i(\omega_h) e^{ik\omega_h} \quad \text{for } k = -M, \ldots, M,$$

$$\hat{\chi}_{it} = \sum_{k=-M}^{M} \underline{\mathbf{K}}_{i,k} L^k Y_t.$$

The truncated filter is a two-sided filter and, although it will be useful for in-sample common and idiosyncratic decomposition, it is not useful for forecasting. Forni *et al.* (2003) propose an alternative estimator of the common factor that is a linear combination of contemporaneous Y_t only. Another estimator for the common factor in large n and T models has been proposed by Kapetianos and Marcellino (2003).

In closing, I emphasize that the theory of dynamic factors makes constructive use of the large cross-section dimension n, and it depends on $\min\{n, T\} \to \infty$. In practice, one should be careful when $\min\{n, T\}$ is not large. For example, an n of 20, which is too large to be handled by the VARMA or UC models described in the previous sections, may not be large enough to give a reliable estimator of the common factor in this framework, especially if the common factor is not strong relative to the idiosyncratic factors. As Boivin and Ng (2004) show, enlarging the cross-section dimension with variables that only weakly depend on the common factor will not help with estimating the common factor. Also, in an application to modeling volatility of stock returns, Anderson and Vahid (2004) have found that, if these volatilities are not pre-purged of their idiosyncratic jumps, the largest of these jumps can be picked up by the static principal component method as the estimate of the common factor. Of course, this is a reflection of the finiteness of n, because asymptotically the influence of idiosyncratic jumps will go to zero. However, it highlights the fact that there are many issues that need to be addressed to make sure that these methods produce a reasonable estimator of the common factor in finite samples.

16.4   Common classical cycles

A major impetus for the study of common cycles is to study the business cycle, to find an index that is coincident with the business cycle, and to find an index that leads the business cycle. All of the above methods have been used to study common cycles in the GDP of different groups of countries or in different regions of the same country (Engle and Issler, 1995; Carvalho and Harvey, 2002; Forni and Reichlin, 1998, to cite just one example of each approach). All have been used to design coincident indicators of economic activity by extracting the common cycle of a group of coincident variables (Issler and Vahid, 2004; Stock and Watson, 1998; Forni *et al.*, 2000, to give just one example of each approach). However, all of these focus on the cycles as detrended GDP or cycles in the growth rate of GDP.

Harding and Pagan (2002) point out the gap between academic interest in modeling the movements of detrended variables and policy makers' focus on turning points in the *level* of variables. They contend that the classical cycle is the movement from a turning point to the next turning point in the *level* of economic activity. They use a version of the Bry–Boschan (1971) algorithm to identify the turning points as local minima and maxima subject to some minimum requirements related to the length of each phase of a cycle as well as the length of a complete cycle.

After constructing binary indicators representing recessions and expansions in a series of variables, Harding and Pagan (2004) provide tests of perfect synchronization, and a non-parametric method for extracting turning points of a "reference cycle" from these binary indicators. Their test for perfect synchronization is basically a test for correlation of one between a pair of binary indicators. Since each indicator is strongly dependent over time, this dependence must be accounted for in the derivation of the standard error of the sample correlation coefficient. Also, since the null-value of the correlation parameter is on the boundary of the parameter space, the asymptotic distribution of the test statistic is non-standard. See Harding and Pagan (2004) for more details.

The Harding and Pagan (2004) procedure for extracting the turning points of the common cycle is based on identifying clusters of turning points. A summary of their algorithm is as follows. Suppose that there are T observations on n variables. The Bry–Boschan algorithm dates peaks and troughs in each variable. For each variable, we construct a distance-to-nearest-peak vector of size T whose t-th element shows the distance between t and the time of the nearest peak. Then, we compute a $T \times 1$ vector M^P whose t-th element is the median of the t-th elements of the n distance-to-nearest-peak vectors. Looking at M^P as a time series, the dates of the local minima in this series are the candidate dates for the peak of the common cycle. For each candidate peak date τ^P, we find the date of the nearest peak in each of the n variables. If all of these peaks are less than a threshold distance away from τ^P (for example, less than 24 months for monthly series), and they are closer to τ^P than to any other candidate peak date, then this cloud of peaks is recognized as a cluster of turning points, and τ^P, the centre of this cluster, is chosen as a turning point of the common or the "reference" cycle. A similar procedure identifies clusters of troughs and dates of the troughs of the common cycle. Finally, the requirement that peaks and troughs must alternate and the Bry–Boschan requirements on the minimum duration of each phase of the business cycle and the minimum length of a complete cycle eliminate some of the turning points identified in the previous stage. The remaining peaks and troughs are taken as the turning points of the common cycle.

   This method is useful for identifying turning points in the common classical cycle of a group of time series, and it can be used for dating the peaks and troughs of historical business cycles. Obviously, it cannot produce probabilities of turning points in the future. However, it can be used as a good specification test for parametric models that claim to be a model of the business cycle; for example, statistical models that produce an index that is supposed to be coincident with the business cycle. Based on the peaks and troughs of the reference cycle identified by this procedure, one can come up with average peak to trough and trough to peak duration of the business cycle. Any parametric model of the business cycle must be able to produce cycles of the same duration. Harding and Pagan (2002) suggest simulation based tests for the hypothesis that a statistical model can produce cycles with the same characteristics as those of the observed cycles.

16.5 Conclusion

This chapter gives a summary of several approaches to tackle the question "Are cycles in a group of variables common?," and, when common cycles are found, how to estimate them. The approaches differ in their applicability and in their definition of a "cycle." One approach starts from a fitted unrestricted VARMA model or a VECM and asks if the Beveridge–Nelson cycles implied by this model are common. Another starts from assuming dynamic equations for trend and cycle of each variable, and then asks if the number of cycles can be reduced to a smaller number of common cycles. Both of these methods are designed for studying trends and cycles in a small number of variables. A third approach ignores the trends, and decomposes the cycles into common and idiosyncratic components. This is appropriate for studying a large number of variables, and uses the large dimension to produce estimates of common factors. Finally, the chapter reviews a nonparametric method for studying common classical cycles, i.e., cycles extracted from actual series via a dating algorithm.

One objective of this chapter is to give an overview of these recent advances in the study of common cycles. It is unfortunate that publications in academic journals have to be narrowly focused. It is quite possible that four papers, one on each of the approaches discussed here, are all presented in a single session titled "Common Cycles" in a conference, but overlap only in that they cite a few classic papers. My focus has been to put these approaches under a unifying umbrella, and to discuss the similarity and the difference in the questions that they are addressing, and the situations where each is most appropriate.

Another objective of this chapter has been to point out the possibilities for cross-fertilization among these approaches. For example, I show that unobserved component common cycles are a common feature that implies a necessary, but not sufficient, moment condition. Such conditions can be checked before assuming a common cycle structure. Also, the new directions for defining shifted cycles in unobserved component methodology may point to a new way to study common but not synchronized cycles within the BN framework. There is also scope for combining some of these methods in applications. For example, after estimating the common market factor in the volatilities of returns of a large number of stocks using principal components, the common sectoral factor in the idiosyncratic components of volatilities of stock returns in different sectors can be estimated using one of the other approaches. Finally, if any of the multivariate models discussed here are put forward as a model of the business cycle, they must be confronted with the Harding and Pagan test to see if they are capable of reproducing the features of classical cycles.

I have focused on theory and methods rather than on applications. All of the above methods were developed to answer applied questions in empirical macroeconomics and finance. These include empirical business cycle analysis, the construction of coincident and leading indicators, and estimating regional and sectoral cycles. It also includes estimating common factors in empirical finance, forecasting growth and inflation, and many other applications. Good sources of recent articles on the application of these methods are the web pages of annual conferences on common features,[6] and the dynamic factors web page.[7]

Acknowledgments

I thank the editors, an associate editor, Heather Anderson and Alain Hecq for their helpful comments and suggestions.

Notes

1. The term "cycle" in different parts of this chapter will refer to different things. This is deliberate and intended to reflect the fact that, in different parts of the literature, the word "cycle" has been used to mean different things. Each subsection of the chapter defines "the cycle" in that subsection.
2. Harvey (1989) and Harvey and Koopman (1997) call their models "structural time series models." However, to avoid possible confusion with structural models in econometrics, in particular structural VAR models, I refer to them as unobserved components models.

3. Recall that we set κ^* to zero for simplicity. None of the arguments in this section are affected by this simplifying assumption.
4. Some controlled local dependence among idiosyncratic factors is allowed. Also, there can be some weak local dependence between the common factors and some of the idiosyncratic factors. We do not get into such technicalities here. Interested readers can refer to Bai and Ng (2002) or Forni *et al.* (2000).
5. This is because a k_1 moving average of an MA (k_2) is an MA $(k_1 + k_2)$. Therefore, s in equation (16.11) can be taken to be $k_1 + k_2$.
6. http://www.cass.city.ac.uk/conferences/cfl, http://www.fdewb.unimaas.nl/cfmaas, http://epge.fgv.br/cfrio.
7. http://www.dynfactors.org.

References

Anderson, H.M. and F. Vahid (1998) Testing multiple equation systems for common non-linear components. *Journal of Econometrics* **84**, 1–37.
Anderson, H.M. and F. Vahid (2004) Forecasting the volatility of Australian stock returns: do common factors help? Working paper, Australian National University.
Anderson, T.W. (1984) *An Introduction to Multivariate Statistical Analysis*, 2nd edn. New York: Wiley.
Bai, J. and S. Ng (2002) Determining the number of factors in approximate factor models. *Econometrica* **70**, 191–222.
Baxter, M. and R.G. King (1999) Measuring business cycles: approximate band-pass filters for economic time series. *Review of Economics and Statistics* **81**, 575–93.
Beveridge, S. and C.R. Nelson (1981) A new approach to the decomposition of economic time series into permanent and transitory components with particular attention to measurement of the "business cycle." *Journal of Monetary Economics* **7**, 151–74.
Boivin J. and S. Ng (2004) Are more data always better for factor analysis? *Journal of Econometrics*, forthcoming.
Breitung, J. and B. Candelon (2000) Common cycles: a frequency domain approach. Humboldt Universitaet Berlin working paper 2000–99.
Bry, G. and C. Boschan (1971) *Cyclical Analysis of Time Series: Selected Procedures and Computer Programs*. New York: National Bureau of Economic Research.
Burns, A.F. and W.C. Mitchell (1946) *Measuring Business Cycles*. New York: National Bureau of Economic Research.
Carvalho, V.M. and A.C. Harvey (2002) Growth, cycles and convergence in US regional time series. University of Cambridge, Department of Applied Economics working paper 0221.
Chamberlain, G. and M. Rothschild (1983) Arbitrage, factor structure and mean-variance analysis in large asset markets. *Econometrica* **51**, 1305–1324.
Christiano, L.J. and T.J. Fitzgerald (2003) The band pass filter. *International Economic Review* **44**, 435–65.
Cubadda, G. (1999) Common serial correlation and common business cycles: a cautious note. *Empirical Economics* **24**, 529–35.
Cubadda, G. and A. Hecq (2001) On non-contemporaneous short-run comovements. *Economics Letters* **73**, 389–97.
Engle, R.F. and C.W.J. Granger (1987) Cointegration and error correction: representation, estimation and testing. *Econometrica* **55**, 251–76.
Engle, R.F. and J.V. Issler (1995) Estimating common sectoral cycles. *Journal of Monetary Economics* **35**, 83–113.
Engle, R.F. and S. Kozicki (1993) Testing for common features. *Journal of Business and Economic Statistics* **11**, 369–80.
Forni, M., M. Hallin, M. Lippi and L. Reichlin (2000) The generalized factor model: identification and estimation. *The Review of Economics and Statistics* **82**, 540–54.

Forni, M., M. Hallin, M. Lippi and L. Reichlin (2003) The generalized factor model: one-sided estimation and forecasting. LEM working paper series 2003/13.

Forni, M. and L. Reichlin (1998) Let's get real: a factor analytical approach to disaggregated business cycle dynamics. *Review of Economic Studies* **65**, 453–73.

Gonzalo, J. and J.Y. Pitarakis (1999) Dimensionality effect in cointegration analysis. In R.F. Engle and H. White (eds), *Cointegration, Causality and Forecasting: A Festschrift in Honour of Clive W. J. Granger*. New York: Oxford University Press.

Gourieroux, C. and I. Peaucelle (1992) Series codependantes: application a l'hypothese de parite du pouvoir d'achat. *Revue d'Analyse Economique* **68**, 283–304.

Harding, D. and A.R. Pagan (2002) Dissecting the cycle: a methodological investigation. *Journal of Monetary Economics* **49**, 365–81.

Harding, D. and A.R. Pagan (2004) Synchronisation of cycles. *Journal of Econometrics*, forthcoming.

Harvey, A.C. (1985) Trends and cycles in macroeconomic time series. *Journal of Business and Economic Statistics* **3**, 216–27.

Harvey, A.C. (1989) *Forecasting, Structural Time Series Models and the Kalman Filter*. Cambridge: Cambridge University Press.

Harvey, A.C. and S.J. Koopman (1997) Multivariate structural time series models. In C. Heij, H. Schumacher, B. Hanzon and C. Praagman (eds), *Systematic Dynamics in Economic and Financial Models*. Chichester: Wiley.

Hecq, A., F.C. Palm and J.P. Urbain (2004) Testing for common cyclical features in VAR models with cointegration. *Journal of Econometrics*, forthcoming.

Issler, J.V. and F. Vahid (2001) Common cycles and the importance of transitory shocks to macroeconomic aggregates. *Journal of Monetary Economics* **47**, 449–75.

Issler, J.V. and F. Vahid (2004) The missing link: using the NBER recession indicator to construct coincident and leading indices of economic activity. *Journal of Econometrics*, forthcoming.

Kapetianos, G. and M. Marcellino (2003) A comparison of estimation methods for dynamic factor models of large dimensions. Queen Mary University of London working paper 489.

Kshirsagar, A.M. (1972) *Multivariate Analysis*. New York: Marcel Dekker.

Lippi, M. and L. Reichlin (1994) Common and uncommon trends and cycles. *European Economic Review* **38**, 624–35.

Morley, J.C., C.R. Nelson and E. Zivot (2003) Why are Beveridge–Nelson and unobserved-component decompositions of GDP so different?, *Review of Economic and Statistics* **85**, 235–43.

Paruolo, P. (2004) Common trends and cycles in I(2) VAR systems. *Journal of Econometrics*, forthcoming.

Proietti, T. (2002) Some reflections on trend-cycle decompositions with correlated components. Economics working paper 2002/23, European University Institute.

Rünstler, G. (2004) Modelling phase shifts among stochastic cycles. *Econometrics Journal* **7**, 232–48.

Stock, J.H. and M.W. Watson (2002) Macroeconomic forecasting using diffusion indexes. *Journal of Business and Economic Statistics* **20**, 147–62.

Vahid, F. and R.F. Engle (1993) Common trends and common cycles. *Journal of Applied Econometrics* **8**, 341–60.

Vahid, F. and R.F. Engle (1997) Codependent cycles. *Journal of Econometrics* **80**, 199–221.

Vahid, F. and J.V. Issler (2002) The importance of common cyclical features in VAR analysis: a Monte-Carlo study. *Journal of Econometrics* **109**, 341–63.

Watson, M.W. (1986) Univariate detrending methods with stochastic trends. *Journal of Monetary Economics* **18**, 49–75.

Part VI

Cross-Section and Panel Data Models

17
Panel Data Models

Badi H. Baltagi

Abstract

Panel data is used to describe the pooling of time series observations across a variety of cross-sectional units, typically households. Some of the benefits of using panel data sets include a much larger data set with more variability and less collinearity among the variables. Limitations of panel data sets include problems of nonresponse and measurement errors. This chapter introduces the one-way error component model and discusses the fixed and random effects models as well as the Hausman (1978) specification test. Then it surveys the estimation of these models under endogeneity of the regressors of the simultaneous equation type, as well as the Hausman and Taylor (1981) type. Finally, it introduces some of the standard GMM methods for the estimation of dynamic panel data models and concludes with an update on the current status of this literature.

17.1	Introduction	633
17.2	The one-way error component regression model	634
	17.2.1 The fixed effects model	635
	17.2.2 The random effects model	637
	17.2.3 Hausman's specification test	639
17.3	Simultaneous equations with error components	641
17.4	Fixed vs random: the Hausman and Taylor estimator	645
17.5	Dynamic panel data models	649
17.6	Conclusion	658

17.1 Introduction

Panel data is used to describe the pooling of time series observations across a variety of cross-sectional units, including countries, regions, states, firms or households. Some of the benefits and limitations of using panel data sets are given in Baltagi (2005) and Hsiao (2003). Obvious benefits include a much larger data set with more variability and less collinearity among the variables than is typical of cross-sectional or time series data. With more informative data, one can get more reliable estimates and test more sophisticated behavioral models with less restrictive assumptions. Another advantage of panel data sets is their ability to control for individual heterogeneity. Not controling for these unobserved individual specific effects leads to bias in the resulting estimates. Panel data sets are also better able to identify and estimate effects that are simply not detectable in pure cross-sections or pure time series data. In particular, panel data sets are better able to study complex issues of dynamic behavior. Limitations of panel data sets include problems of nonresponse and measurement errors. Panel data sets may also exhibit bias due to sample selection problems. For the initial wave of the panel, respondents may refuse to participate or the interviewer may not find anybody at home. This may cause some bias in the inference drawn from this sample. While such nonresponse can also occur in cross-sectional data sets, it is more serious with panels because subsequent waves of the panel are still subject to nonresponse. Respondents may die, or move, or find that the cost of responding is high. Macro and financial panel data with long time series have standard distributions for panel unit roots tests, unlike their counterparts in time series analysis where unit root tests have non-standard asymptotic distributions; see chapter 13 by Choi on nonstationary panels.

Two well-known examples of US panel data are the Panel Study of Income Dynamics (PSID) and the National Longitudinal Surveys of Labor Market Experience (NLS). An inventory of national studies using panel data is given at (http://www.isr.umich.edu/src/psid/panelStudies.html). These include the German Socio-Economic panel, the British Household Panel Survey and, more recently, the European Community Household Panel. Virtually every graduate text in econometrics contains a chapter on the econometrics of panel data. There are two chapters in the *Handbook of Econometrics*, one by Chamberlain (1984) and another by Arellano and Honoré (2001). There is also a handbook on the econometrics of panel data edited by Mátyás and Sevestre (1996). Classic papers on this subject have been collected in two volumes by Maddala (1993) and updated with two additional volumes by Baltagi (2002).

This chapter reviews some of the basic material on panel data econometrics. Section 17.2 introduces the one-way error component model and discusses the fixed and random effects models as well as the Hausman (1978) specification test. Section 17.3 surveys the estimation of these models under endogeneity of the regressors, while section 17.4 considers the Hausman and Taylor (1981) type model. Section 17.5 surveys dynamic panel data models, while section 17.6 concludes.

17.2 The one-way error component regression model

Consider the panel data regression

$$y_{it} = \alpha + X'_{it}\beta + u_{it} \quad i = 1, \dots, N; \quad t = 1, \dots, T \tag{17.2.1}$$

with i denoting households, individuals, firms, countries, etc., and t denoting time. The i subscript, therefore, denotes the cross-section dimension whereas t denotes the time series dimension. The panel data is *balanced* in that none of the observations are missing, whether randomly or nonrandomly due to attrition or sample selection. α is a scalar, β is $K \times 1$ and X_{it} is the itth observation on K explanatory variables. Most of the panel data applications utilize a one-way error component model for the disturbances, with

$$u_{it} = \mu_i + v_{it} \tag{17.2.2}$$

where μ_i denotes the *unobservable* individual specific effect and v_{it} denotes the remainder disturbance. For example, in an earnings equation in labor economics, y_{it} will measure earnings of the head of the household, whereas X_{it} may contain a set of variables like experience, education, union membership, sex, race, etc. Note that μ_i is time-invariant and accounts for any individual specific effect that is not included in the regression. In this case we could think of it as the individual's unobserved ability. The remainder disturbance v_{it} varies with individuals and time and can be thought of as the usual disturbance in the regression. In vector form, (17.2.1) can be written as

$$y = \alpha \iota_{NT} + X\beta + u = Z\delta + u \tag{17.2.3}$$

where y is $NT \times 1$, X is $NT \times K$, $Z = [\iota_{NT}, X]$, $\delta' = (\alpha', \beta')$ and ι_{NT} is a vector of ones of dimension NT. Also, (17.2.2) can be written as

$$u = Z_\mu \mu + v \tag{17.2.4}$$

where $u' = (u_{11}, \ldots, u_{1T}, u_{21}, \ldots, u_{2T}, \ldots, u_{N1}, \ldots, u_{NT})$, with the observations stacked such that the slower index is over individuals and the faster index is over time. $Z_\mu = I_N \otimes \iota_T$, where I_N is an identity matrix of dimension N, ι_T is a vector of ones of dimension T and $\otimes$ denotes the Kronecker product. Z_μ is a selector matrix of ones and zeroes, or simply the matrix of individual dummies that one may include in the regression to estimate the μ_i if they are assumed to be fixed parameters. $\mu' = (\mu_1, \ldots, \mu_N)$ and $v' = (v_{11}, \ldots, v_{1T}, \ldots, v_{N1}, \ldots, v_{NT})$. Note that $Z_\mu Z'_\mu = I_N \otimes J_T$, where J_T is a matrix of ones of dimension T, and that $P = Z_\mu (Z'_\mu Z_\mu)^{-1} Z'_\mu$, the projection matrix on Z_μ, reduces to $I_N \otimes \bar{J}_T$, where $\bar{J}_T = J_T/T$. P is a matrix which averages the observations across time for each individual, and $Q = I_{NT} - P$ is a matrix which obtains the deviations from individual means. For example, Py has typical element $\bar{y}_{i.} = \sum_{t=1}^{T} y_{it}/T$, repeated T times for each individual, and Qy has typical element $(y_{it} - \bar{y}_{i.})$. P and Q are (*i*) symmetric idempotent matrices, i.e., $P' = P$ and $P^2 = P$. This means that $\text{rank}(P) = tr(P) = N$ and $\text{rank}(Q) = tr(Q) = N(T-1)$. This uses the result that the rank of an idempotent matrix is equal to its trace. Also, (*ii*) P and Q are orthogonal, i.e., $PQ = 0$, and (*iii*) they sum to the identity matrix, $P + Q = I_{NT}$.

17.2.1 The fixed effects model

In this case, the μ_i are assumed to be fixed parameters to be estimated and the remainder disturbances are assumed to be stochastic with v_{it} independent and identically distributed, IID $(0, \sigma_v^2)$. The X_{it} are assumed independent of the v_{it} for all i and t. The fixed effects model is an appropriate specification if we are focusing on a specific set of N firms, say, IBM, GE, Westinghouse, etc., and our inference is restricted to the behavior of these sets of firms. Alternatively, it could be a set of N OECD countries, or N American states. Inference in this case is conditional on the particular N firms, countries or states that are observed. One can substitute the disturbances given by (17.2.4) into (17.2.3) to get

$$y = \alpha \iota_{NT} + X\beta + Z_\mu \mu + v = Z\delta + Z_\mu \mu + v \qquad (17.2.5)$$

and then perform ordinary least squares (OLS) on (17.2.5) to get estimates of α, β and μ. Note that Z is $NT \times (K+1)$ and Z_μ, the matrix of individual dummies, is $NT \times N$. If N is large, (17.2.5) will include too many individual dummies, and the matrix to be inverted by OLS is large and of dimension $(N+K)$. In fact, since α and β are the parameters of interest, one can obtain the LSDV (least squares dummy variables) estimator from (17.2.5) by premultiplying the model by Q and performing OLS on the resulting transformed model:

$$Qy = QX\beta + Qv \qquad (17.2.6)$$

This uses the fact that $QZ_\mu = Q\iota_{NT} = 0$, since $PZ_\mu = Z_\mu$. In other words, the Q matrix wipes out the individual effects. This is a regression of $\tilde{y} = Qy$, with typical element $(y_{it} - \bar{y}_{i.})$, on $\tilde{X} = QX$, with typical element $(X_{it,k} - \bar{X}_{i.,k})$ for the kth regressor, $k = 1, 2, \ldots, K$. This involves the inversion of a $(K \times K)$ matrix rather than an $(N+K) \times (N+K)$ matrix as in (17.2.5). The resulting OLS estimator is

$$\tilde{\beta} = (X'QX)^{-1}X'Qy \qquad (17.2.7)$$

with var $(\tilde{\beta}) = \sigma_v^2(X'QX)^{-1} = \sigma_v^2(\tilde{X}'\tilde{X})^{-1}$. For large labor or consumer panels, where N is very large, regressions like (17.2.5) may not be feasible, since one is including $(N-1)$ dummies in the regression. This fixed effects (FE) least squares, also known as least squares dummy variables (LSDV), suffers from a large loss of degrees of freedom. We are estimating $(N-1)$ extra parameters, and too many dummies may aggravate the problem of multicollinearity among the regressors. In addition, this FE estimator cannot estimate the effect of any time-invariant variable like sex, race, religion, schooling or union participation. These time-invariant variables are wiped out by the Q transformation, the deviations from means transformation. This can be done with Stata using the (xtreg, fe) command. If (17.2.5) is the true model, LSDV is the best linear unbiased estimator (BLUE) as long as v_{it} is the standard classical disturbance with mean 0 and variance-covariance matrix $\sigma_v^2 I_{NT}$. Note that, if T is fixed and $N \to \infty$, as is typical in short labor panels, then only the FE estimator of β is consistent; the FE estimators of the individual effects $(\alpha + \mu_i)$ are not consistent since the number of these parameters increases as N increases. This is the incidental parameter problem discussed recently by Lancaster (2000). Note that when the true model is fixed effects as in (17.2.5), OLS on (17.2.1) yields biased and inconsistent estimates of the regression parameters. This is an omitted variables bias due to the fact that OLS deletes the individual dummies when, in fact, they are relevant.

One could test the joint significance of these dummies, i.e., $H_0 : \mu_1 = \mu_2 = \cdots = \mu_{N-1} = 0$, by performing an F-test. This is a simple Chow test with the restricted residual sum of squares (RRSS) being that from OLS on the pooled model and the unrestricted residual sum of squares (URSS) being that from the LSDV regression. If N is large, one can perform the Within (Q) transformation and use that residual sum of squares as the URSS. In this case

$$F_0 = \frac{(RRSS - URSS)/(N - 1)}{URSS/(NT - N - K)} \overset{H_0}{\sim} F_{N-1,N(T-1)-K} \tag{17.2.8}$$

For the Within estimator, Arellano (1987) suggests a simple method for obtaining robust estimates of the standard errors that allow for a general variance–covariance matrix on the v_{it}.

17.2.2 The random effects model

There are too many parameters in the fixed effects model and the loss of degrees of freedom can be avoided if the μ_i can be assumed random. In this case $\mu_i \sim \text{IID}(0, \sigma_\mu^2)$, $v_{it} \sim \text{IID}(0, \sigma_v^2)$ and the μ_i are independent of the v_{it}. In addition, the X_{it} are independent of the μ_i and v_{it}, for all i and t. The random effects model is an appropriate specification if we are drawing N individuals randomly from a large population. This is usually the case for household panel studies. Care is taken in the design of the panel to make it "representative" of the population we are trying to make inferences about. In this case, N is usually large and a fixed effects model would lead to an enormous loss of degrees of freedom. The individual effect is characterized as random and inference pertains to the population from which this sample was randomly drawn. From (17.2.4), one can compute the variance–covariance matrix

$$\Omega = E(uu') = Z_\mu E(\mu\mu')Z_\mu' + E(vv')$$
$$= \sigma_\mu^2(I_N \otimes J_T) + \sigma_v^2(I_N \otimes I_T) \tag{17.2.9}$$

This implies a homoskedastic variance var $(u_{it}) = \sigma_\mu^2 + \sigma_v^2$ for all i and t, and an equicorrelated block-diagonal covariance matrix which exhibits serial correlation over time only between the disturbances of the same individual. For extensions of this model to allow for heteroskedasticity and serial correlation, see Baltagi (2005, chapter 5).

In order to obtain the GLS estimator of the regression coefficients, we need Ω^{-1}. This is a huge matrix for typical panels and is of dimension $(NT \times NT)$. No brute force inversion should be attempted even if the researcher's application has a small N and T. We will follow a simple trick devised by Wansbeek and Kapteyn (1982) that allows the derivation of Ω^{-1} and $\Omega^{-1/2}$. Essentially, one replaces J_T by $T\bar{J}_T$, and I_T by $(E_T + \bar{J}_T)$, where E_T is by definition $(I_T - \bar{J}_T)$. In this case

$$\Omega = T\sigma_\mu^2(I_N \otimes \bar{J}_T) + \sigma_v^2(I_N \otimes E_T) + \sigma_v^2(I_N \otimes \bar{J}_T)$$

Collecting terms with the same matrices, we get

$$\Omega = (T\sigma_\mu^2 + \sigma_v^2)(I_N \otimes \bar{J}_T) + \sigma_v^2(I_N \otimes E_T) = \sigma_1^2 P + \sigma_v^2 Q \tag{17.2.10}$$

where $\sigma_1^2 = T\sigma_\mu^2 + \sigma_v^2$. Equation (17.2.10) is the spectral decomposition representation of Ω, with σ_1^2 being the first unique characteristic root of Ω of multiplicity N and σ_v^2 being the second unique characteristic root of Ω of multiplicity $N(T-1)$. It is easy to verify, using the properties of P and Q, that

$$\Omega^r = (\sigma_1^2)^r P + (\sigma_v^2)^r Q \tag{17.2.11}$$

where r is an arbitrary scalar including -1 and $-1/2$. Now we can obtain the GLS estimator from a weighted least squares regression. Fuller and Battese (1973) suggested premultiplying the regression equation given in (17.2.3) by $\sigma_v\Omega^{-1/2} = Q + (\sigma_v/\sigma_1)P$ and performing OLS on the resulting transformed regression. In this case, $y^* = \sigma_v\Omega^{-1/2}y$ has typical element $y_{it} - \theta\bar{y}_{i.}$, where $\theta = 1 - (\sigma_v/\sigma_1)$. This transformed regression inverts a matrix of dimension $(K+1)$ and can be easily implemented using any regression package. The random effects estimator can be implemented with Stata using the (xtreg, re) command.

The best quadratic unbiased (BQU) estimators of the variance components arise naturally from the spectral decomposition of Ω. In fact, $Pu \sim (0, \sigma_1^2 P)$ and $Qu \sim (0, \sigma_v^2 Q)$ and

$$\hat{\sigma}_1^2 = \frac{u'Pu}{tr(P)} = T\sum_{i=1}^{N} \bar{u}_{i.}^2/N \tag{17.2.12}$$

and

$$\hat{\sigma}_v^2 = \frac{u'Qu}{tr(Q)} = \frac{\sum_{i=1}^{N}\sum_{t=1}^{T}(u_{it} - \bar{u}_{i.})^2}{N(T-1)} \tag{17.2.13}$$

provide the BQU estimators of σ_1^2 and σ_v^2, respectively.

Swamy and Arora (1972) suggest running two regressions to get estimates of the variance components from the corresponding mean square errors of these regressions. The first regression is the Within regression, given in (17.2.6), which yields the following s^2:

$$\tilde{\sigma}_v^2 = [y'Qy - y'QX(X'QX)^{-1}X'Qy]/[N(T-1)-K] \tag{17.2.14}$$

The second regression is the Between regression, which runs the regression of averages across time, i.e.

$$\bar{y}_{i.} = \alpha + \bar{X}'_{i.}\beta + \bar{u}_{i.} \qquad i = 1, \ldots, N \tag{17.2.15}$$

This is equivalent to premultiplying the model in (17.2.5) by P and running OLS. The only caution is that the latter regression has NT observations because it repeats the averages T times for each individual, while the cross-section regression in (17.2.15) is based on N observations. To remedy this, one can run the cross-section regression

$$\sqrt{T}\bar{y}_{i.} = \alpha\sqrt{T} + \sqrt{T}\bar{X}'_{i.}\beta + \sqrt{T}\bar{u}_{i.} \qquad (17.2.16)$$

where one can easily verify that $\text{var}(\sqrt{T}\bar{u}_{i.}) = \sigma_1^2$. This regression will yield an s^2 given by

$$\tilde{\sigma}_1^2 = (y'Py - y'PZ(Z'PZ)^{-1}Z'Py)/(N - K - 1) \qquad (17.2.17)$$

Taylor (1980) derived exact finite sample results for the one-way error component model. He compared the Within estimator with the Swamy–Arora feasible GLS estimator. He found the following important results:

(1) Feasible GLS is more efficient than LSDV for all but the fewest degrees of freedom.
(2) The variance of feasible GLS is never more than 17 percent above the Cramer–Rao lower bound.
(3) More efficient estimators of the variance components do not necessarily yield more efficient feasible GLS estimators.

These finite sample results are confirmed by the Monte Carlo experiments carried out by Maddala and Mount (1973) and Baltagi (1981a).

For the random two-way error component model, Breusch and Pagan (1980) derived a Lagrange-multiplier (LM) test of $H_0 : \sigma_\mu^2 = 0$. The log-likelihood function under normality of the disturbances is given by

$$L(\delta, \theta) = \text{constant} - \frac{1}{2}\log |\Omega| - \frac{1}{2}u'\Omega^{-1}u \qquad (17.2.18)$$

where $\theta' = (\sigma_\mu^2, \sigma_\nu^2)$ and Ω is given by (17.2.9). The information matrix is block-diagonal between θ and δ. Since H_0 involves only θ, the part of the information matrix due to δ is ignored. The resulting LM statistic is given by

$$LM = \frac{NT}{2(T-1)} \left[1 - \frac{\tilde{u}'(I_N \otimes J_T)\tilde{u}}{\tilde{u}'\tilde{u}} \right]^2 \qquad (17.2.19)$$

Under H_0, LM is asymptotically distributed as χ_1^2. This LM test requires only OLS residuals and is easy to compute. For more diagnostics and test of hypotheses, see Baltagi (2005, chapter 4). For a survey of specification tests in panel data models using artificial regressions, see Baltagi (1999).

17.2.3 Hausman's specification test

A critical assumption in the error component regression model is that $E(u_{it}/X_{it}) = 0$. This is important given that the disturbances contain individual invariant effects (the μ_i) which are unobserved and may be correlated with the X_{it}. For example, in an earnings equation the μ_i may denote the unobservable ability of the individual and may be correlated with the schooling variable included on the right-hand side of the equation. In this case, $E(u_{it}/X_{it}) \neq 0$ and the GLS estimator $\hat{\beta}_{GLS}$ becomes biased and inconsistent for β. However, the Within transformation wipes out these μ_i and leaves the Within estimator $\tilde{\beta}_{Within}$ unbiased and consistent for β. Hausman (1978) suggests comparing $\hat{\beta}_{GLS}$ and $\tilde{\beta}_{Within}$, both of which are consistent under the null hypothesis $H_0 : E(u_{it}/X_{it}) = 0$, but which will have different probability limits if H_0 is not true. In fact, $\tilde{\beta}_{Within}$ is consistent whether H_0 is true or not, while $\hat{\beta}_{GLS}$ is BLUE, consistent and asymptotically efficient under H_0, but is inconsistent when H_0 is false. A natural test statistic would be based on $\hat{q}_1 = \hat{\beta}_{GLS} - \tilde{\beta}_{Within}$. Under H_0, plim $\hat{q}_1 = 0$, and cov $(\hat{q}_1, \hat{\beta}_{GLS}) = 0$.

Using the fact that $\hat{\beta}_{GLS} - \beta = (X'\Omega^{-1}X)^{-1}X'\Omega^{-1}u$ and $\tilde{\beta}_{Within} - \beta = (X'QX)^{-1}X'Qu$, one gets $E(\hat{q}_1) = 0$ and

$$
\begin{aligned}
\text{cov}(\hat{\beta}_{GLS}, \hat{q}_1) &= \text{var}(\hat{\beta}_{GLS}) - \text{cov}(\hat{\beta}_{GLS}, \tilde{\beta}_{Within}) \\
&= (X'\Omega^{-1}X)^{-1} - (X'\Omega^{-1}X)^{-1}X\Omega^{-1}E(uu')QX(X'QX)^{-1} \\
&= (X'\Omega^{-1}X)^{-1} - (X'\Omega^{-1}X)^{-1} = 0
\end{aligned}
$$

Using the fact that $\tilde{\beta}_{Within} = \hat{\beta}_{GLS} - \hat{q}_1$, one gets

$$
\text{var}(\tilde{\beta}_{Within}) = \text{var}(\hat{\beta}_{GLS}) + \text{var}(\hat{q}_1)
$$

since cov $(\hat{\beta}_{GLS}, \hat{q}_1) = 0$. Therefore

$$
\text{var}(\hat{q}_1) = \text{var}(\tilde{\beta}_{Within}) - \text{var}(\hat{\beta}_{GLS}) = \sigma_v^2 (X'QX)^{-1} - (X'\Omega^{-1}X)^{-1} \tag{17.2.20}
$$

Hence, the Hausman test statistic is given by

$$
m_1 = \hat{q}_1' [\text{var}(\hat{q}_1)]^{-1} \hat{q}_1 \tag{17.2.21}
$$

and under H_0 is asymptotically distributed as χ_K^2, where K denotes the dimension of the slope vector β. In order to make this test operational, Ω is replaced by a consistent estimator $\hat{\Omega}$, and GLS by its corresponding feasible GLS. This can be implemented in Stata using the Hausman command.

An alternative asymptotically equivalent test can be obtained from the augmented regression

$$
y^* = X^*\beta + \tilde{X}\gamma + w \tag{17.2.22}
$$

where $y^* = \sigma_v \Omega^{-1/2} y, X^* = \sigma_v \Omega^{-1/2} X$ and $\tilde{X} = QX$. Hausman's test is now equivalent to testing whether $\gamma = 0$. This is a standard Wald test for the omission of the variables $\tilde{X}$ from (17.2.22). In fact, Hausman and Taylor (1981) showed that H_0 can be tested using any of the following three paired differences: $\hat{q}_1 = \hat{\beta}_{GLS} - \tilde{\beta}_{Within}$; $\hat{q}_2 = \hat{\beta}_{GLS} - \hat{\beta}_{Between}$; or $\hat{q}_3 = \tilde{\beta}_{Within} - \hat{\beta}_{Between}$. The corresponding test statistics can be computed as $m_i = \hat{q}'_i V_i^{-1} \hat{q}_i$, where $V_i = \text{var}(\hat{q}_i)$. These are asymptotically distributed as χ^2_K for $i = 1, 2, 3$ under H_0. More recently, Arellano (1993) provided an alternative variable addition test to the Hausman test which is robust to autocorrelation and heteroskedasticity of arbitrary form.

Chamberlain (1982) showed that the fixed effects specification imposes testable restrictions on the coefficients from regressions of all leads and lags of dependent variables on all leads and lags of independent variables. Chamberlain specified the relationship between the unobserved individual effects and X_{it} as follows:

$$\mu_i = X'_{i1} \lambda_1 + \cdots + X'_{iT} \lambda_T + \varepsilon_i \qquad (17.2.23)$$

where each λ_t is of dimension $K \times 1$ for $t = 1, 2, \ldots, T$. Let $y'_i = (y_{i1}, \ldots, y_{iT})$ and $X'_i = (X'_{i1}, \ldots, X'_{iT})$ and denote the "reduced form" regression of y'_i on X'_i by

$$y'_i = X'_i \pi + \eta_i \qquad (17.2.24)$$

The restrictions between the reduced form and the structural parameters are given by

$$\pi = (I_T \otimes \beta) + \lambda \iota'_T \qquad (17.2.25)$$

with $\lambda' = (\lambda'_1, \ldots, \lambda'_T)$. Chamberlain (1982) suggested that estimation and testing be carried out using the minimum chi-square method, where the minimand is a χ^2 goodness of fit statistic for the restrictions on the reduced form. However, Angrist and Newey (1991) showed that this minimand can be obtained as the sum of T terms. Each term of this sum is simply the degrees of freedom times the R^2 from a regression of the within residuals for a particular period on all leads and lags of the independent variables. Angrist and Newey (1991) illustrate this test using two examples. The first example estimates and tests a number of models for the union-wage effect using five years of data from the National Longitudinal Survey of Youth (NLSY). They find that the assumption of fixed effects in an equation for union-wage effects is not at odds with the data. The second example considers a conventional human capital earnings function. They find that the fixed effects estimates of the return to schooling in the NLSY are roughly twice those of ordinary least squares. However, the over-identification test suggests that the fixed effects assumption may be inappropriate for this model.

17.3 Simultaneous equations with error components

Endogeneity of the right-hand regressors is a serious problem in econometrics. By endogeneity we mean the correlation of the right-hand side regressors with the disturbances. This may be due to the omission of relevant variables, measurement error, sample selectivity, self-selection or other reasons. Endogeneity causes inconsistency of the usual OLS estimates and requires instrumental variable (IV) methods, like two-stage least squares (2SLS), to obtain consistent parameter estimates. The applied literature is full of examples of endogeneity: demand and supply equations for labor, money, goods and commodities, to mention a few.

Consider the following first structural equation of a simultaneous equation model

$$y_1 = Z_1 \delta_1 + u_1 \tag{17.3.1}$$

where $Z_1 = [Y_1, X_1]$ and $\delta_1' = (\gamma_1', \beta_1')$. As in the standard simultaneous equation literature, Y_1 is the set of g_1 right-hand side endogenous variables, and X_1 is the set of k_1 included exogenous variables. Let $X = [X_1, X_2]$ be the set of all exogenous variables in the system. This equation is identified with k_2, the number of excluded exogenous variables from the first equation (X_2), being larger than or equal to g_1. Using the one-way error component model defined in (17.2.4), we get

$$u_1 = Z_\mu \mu_1 + v_1 \tag{17.3.2}$$

where $Z_\mu = (I_N \otimes \iota_T)$ and $\mu_1' = (\mu_{11}, \ldots, \mu_{N1})$ and $v_1' = (v_{111}, \ldots, v_{NT1})$ are random vectors with zero means and covariance matrix

$$E\begin{pmatrix} \mu_1 \\ v_1 \end{pmatrix}(\mu_1', v_1') = \begin{bmatrix} \sigma_{\mu_{11}}^2 I_N & 0 \\ 0 & \sigma_{v_{11}}^2 I_{NT} \end{bmatrix} \tag{17.3.3}$$

In this case,

$$E(u_1 u_1') = \Omega_{11} = \sigma_{v_{11}}^2 I_{NT} + \sigma_{\mu_{11}}^2 (I_N \otimes J_T) \tag{17.3.4}$$

In other words, the first structural equation has the typical variance–covariance matrix of a one-way error component model described in (17.2.9). The only difference is that now a double subscript $(1,1)$ is attached to the variance components to specify that this is the first equation. One can transform (17.3.1) by $Q = I_{NT} - P$, with $P = I_N \otimes \bar{J}_T$, to get

$$Qy_1 = QZ_1 \delta_1 + Qu_1 \tag{17.3.5}$$

Let $\tilde{y}_1 = Qy_1$ and $\tilde{Z}_1 = QZ_1$. Performing 2SLS on (17.3.5), with $\tilde{X} = QX$ as the set of instruments, one gets Within 2SLS (or Fixed Effects 2SLS)

$$\hat{\delta}_{1,W2SLS} = (\tilde{Z}_1' P_{\tilde{X}} \tilde{Z}_1)^{-1} \tilde{Z}_1' P_{\tilde{X}} \tilde{y}_1 \tag{17.3.6}$$

with var $(\hat{\delta}_{1,W2SLS}) = \sigma_{v_{11}}^2 (\tilde{Z}_1' P_{\tilde{X}} \tilde{Z}_1)^{-1}$. This can be obtained using the Stata command (xtivreg, fe), specifying the endogenous variables Y_1 and the set of instruments X. Within 2SLS can also be obtained as GLS on

$$\tilde{X}' \tilde{y}_1 = \tilde{X}' \tilde{Z}_1 \delta_1 + \tilde{X}' \tilde{u}_1 \tag{17.3.7}$$

Similarly, if we let $\bar{y}_1 = P y_1$ and $\bar{Z}_1 = P Z_1$, we can transform (17.3.1) by P and perform 2SLS with $\bar{X} = P X$ as the set of instruments. In this case, we get the Between 2SLS estimator

$$\hat{\delta}_{1,B2SLS} = (\bar{Z}_1' P_{\bar{X}} \bar{Z}_1)^{-1} \bar{Z}_1' P_{\bar{X}} \bar{y}_1 \tag{17.3.8}$$

with var $(\hat{\delta}_{1,B2SLS}) = \sigma_{1_{11}}^2 (\bar{Z}_1' P_{\bar{X}} \bar{Z}_1)^{-1}$, where $\sigma_{1_{11}}^2 = T \sigma_{\mu_{11}}^2 + \sigma_{\nu_{11}}^2$. This can also be obtained using the Stata command (xtivreg, be), specifying the endogenous variables Y_1 and the set of instruments X. Between 2SLS can also be obtained as GLS on

$$\bar{X}' \bar{y}_1 = \bar{X}' \bar{Z}_1 \delta_1 + \bar{X}' \bar{u}_1 \tag{17.3.9}$$

Stacking the two transformed equations in (17.3.7) and (17.3.9) as a system, and noting that δ_1 is the same for these two transformed equations, one gets

$$\begin{pmatrix} \tilde{X}' \tilde{y}_1 \\ \bar{X}' \bar{y}_1 \end{pmatrix} = \begin{pmatrix} \tilde{X}' \tilde{Z}_1 \\ \bar{X}' \bar{Z}_1 \end{pmatrix} \delta_1 + \begin{pmatrix} \tilde{X}' \tilde{u}_1 \\ \bar{X}' \bar{u}_1 \end{pmatrix} \tag{17.3.10}$$

where

$$E \begin{pmatrix} \tilde{X}' \tilde{u}_1 \\ \bar{X}' \bar{u}_1 \end{pmatrix} = 0 \quad \text{and} \quad \text{var} \begin{pmatrix} \tilde{X}' \tilde{u}_1 \\ \bar{X}' \bar{u}_1 \end{pmatrix} = \begin{bmatrix} \sigma_{\nu_{11}}^2 \tilde{X}' \tilde{X} & 0 \\ 0 & \sigma_{1_{11}}^2 \bar{X}' \bar{X} \end{bmatrix}$$

Performing GLS on (3.10) yields the error component two-stage least squares (EC2SLS) estimator of δ_1 derived by Baltagi (1981b):

$$\hat{\delta}_{1,EC2SLS} = \left[\frac{\tilde{Z}_1' P_{\tilde{X}} \tilde{Z}_1}{\sigma_{\nu_{11}}^2} + \frac{\bar{Z}_1' P_{\bar{X}} \bar{Z}_1}{\sigma_{1_{11}}^2} \right]^{-1} \left[\frac{\tilde{Z}_1' P_{\tilde{X}} \tilde{y}_1}{\sigma_{\nu_{11}}^2} + \frac{\bar{Z}_1' P_{\bar{X}} \bar{y}_1}{\sigma_{1_{11}}^2} \right] \tag{17.3.11}$$

with var $(\hat{\delta}_{1,EC2SLS})$ given by the inverted term in (17.3.11). Note that $\hat{\delta}_{1,EC2SLS}$ can also be written as a matrix-weighted average of $\hat{\delta}_{1,W2SLS}$ and $\hat{\delta}_{1,B2SLS}$, with the weights depending on their respective variance–covariance matrices. Consistent estimates of $\sigma_{\nu_{11}}^2$ and $\sigma_{1_{11}}^2$ can be obtained from W2SLS and B2SLS residuals, respectively. In fact

$$\hat{\sigma}_{\nu_{11}}^2 = (y_1 - Z_1 \hat{\delta}_{1,W2SLS})' Q (y_1 - Z_1 \hat{\delta}_{1,W2SLS}) / N(T - 1) \tag{17.3.12}$$

$$\hat{\sigma}_{1_{11}}^2 = (y_1 - Z_1 \hat{\delta}_{1,B2SLS})' P (y_1 - Z_1 \hat{\delta}_{1,B2SLS}) / N \tag{17.3.13}$$

Substituting these variance components estimates into (17.3.11) one gets a feasible estimate of EC2SLS. Note that, unlike the usual 2SLS procedure, EC2SLS requires estimates of the variance components. One can correct for degrees of freedom in (17.3.12) and (17.3.13), especially for small samples, but the panel is assumed to have large N. Also, one should check that $\hat{\sigma}_{\mu_{11}}^2 = (\hat{\sigma}_{1_{11}}^2 - \hat{\sigma}_{\nu_{11}}^2)/T$ is positive.

Alternatively, one can premultiply (17.3.1) by $\Omega_{11}^{-1/2}$, where Ω_{11} is given in (17.3.4), to get

$$y_1^* = Z_1^* \delta_1 + u_1^* \tag{17.3.14}$$

with $y_1^* = \Omega_{11}^{-1/2} y_1, Z_1^* = \Omega_{11}^{-1/2} Z_1$ and $u_1^* = \Omega_{11}^{-1/2} u_1$. In this case, $\Omega_{11}^{-1/2}$ is given by (17.2.11) with the additional subscripts (1,1) for the variance components, i.e.

$$\Omega_{11}^{-1/2} = (P/\sigma_{1_{11}}) + (Q/\sigma_{v_{11}}) \tag{17.3.15}$$

Therefore, the typical element of y_1^* is $y_{1_{it}}^* = (y_{1_{it}} - \theta_1 \bar{y}_{1_{i.}})/\sigma_{v_{11}}$, where $\theta_1 = 1 - (\sigma_{v_{11}}/\sigma_{1_{11}})$ and $\bar{y}_{1_{i.}} = \sum_{t=1}^{T} y_{1_{it}}/T$.

Given a set of instruments A, then 2SLS on (17.3.15) using A gives:

$$\hat{\delta}_{1,2SLS} = (Z_1^{*'} P_A Z_1^*)^{-1} Z_1^{*'} P_A y_1^* \tag{17.3.16}$$

where $P_A = A(A'A)^{-1}A'$. Using the results in White (1986), the optimal set of instrumental variables in (17.3.14) is

$$X^* = \Omega_{11}^{-1/2} X = \frac{QX}{\sigma_{v_{11}}} + \frac{PX}{\sigma_{1_{11}}} = \frac{\tilde{X}}{\sigma_{v_{11}}} + \frac{\bar{X}}{\sigma_{1_{11}}}$$

Using $A = X^*$, one gets the Balestra and Varadharajan-Krishnakumar (1987) generalized two-stage least squares estimator (G2SLS):

$$\hat{\delta}_{1,G2SLS} = (Z_1^{*'} P_{X^*} Z_1^*)^{-1} Z_1^{*'} P_{X^*} y_1^* \tag{17.3.17}$$

Cornwell, Schmidt and Wyhowski (1992) showed that Baltagi's (1981b) EC2SLS can be obtained from (17.3.16), i.e., using a 2SLS package on the transformed equation (17.3.14) with the set of instruments $A = [QX, PX] = [\tilde{X}, \bar{X}]$. In fact, QX is orthogonal to PX and $P_A = P_{\tilde{X}} + P_{\bar{X}}$. This also means that $\hat{\delta}_{1,EC2SLS}$ given by (17.3.11) is the same as (17.3.16) with $A = [\tilde{X}, \bar{X}]$.

Note that the set of instruments $A = [\tilde{X}, \bar{X}]$ spans the set of instruments $X^* = [\tilde{X}/\sigma_{v_{11}} + \bar{X}/\sigma_{1_{11}}]$. In fact, one can show that $A = [\tilde{X}, \bar{X}], B = [X^*, \tilde{X}]$ and $C = [X^*, \bar{X}]$ yield the same projection, and therefore the same 2SLS estimator given by EC2SLS; see Baltagi (2005). In fact, $\hat{\delta}_{1,G2SLS}$ and $\hat{\delta}_{1,EC2SLS}$ yield the same asymptotic variance–covariance matrix. Therefore, using White's (1986) terminology, $\tilde{X}$ in B and $\bar{X}$ in C are *redundant* with respect to X^*. Redundant instruments can be interpreted loosely as additional sets of instruments that do not yield extra gains in asymptotic efficiency.

For applications, it is easy to obtain EC2SLS using a standard 2SLS package:

Step 1: Run W2SLS and B2SLS using a standard 2SLS package on (17.3.5) and (17.3.9), i.e., run 2SLS of $\tilde{y}$ on $\tilde{Z}$ using $\tilde{X}$ as instruments, and run 2SLS of $\bar{y}$ on $\bar{Z}$ using $\bar{X}$ as instruments. This yields (17.3.6) and (17.3.8), respectively. Alternatively, this can be computed using the (xtivreg,fe) and (xtivreg,be) commands in Stata, specifying the endogenous variables and the set of instruments.

Step 2: Compute $\hat{\sigma}^2_{v_{11}}$ and $\hat{\sigma}^2_{1_{11}}$ from (17.3.12) and (17.3.13) and obtain y^*_1, Z^*_1 and X^* as described below (17.3.16). This transforms (17.3.1) by $\hat{\Omega}^{-1/2}_{11}$ as in (17.3.14).

Step 3: Run 2SLS on the transformed equation (17.3.14) using the instrument set $A = X^*$ or $A = [QX, PX]$ as suggested above, i.e., run 2SLS of y^*_1 on Z^*_1 using X^*_1 as instruments to get G2SLS, or $[\tilde{X}, \bar{X}]$ as instruments to get EC2SLS. This yields (17.3.17) and (17.3.11), respectively. These computations are easy. They involve simple transformations on the data and the application of 2SLS three times. Alternatively, this can be done with Stata using the (xtivreg, re) command to get G2SLS, and (xtivreg, re ec2sls) to get EC2SLS.

17.4 Fixed vs random: the Hausman and Taylor estimator

Let us reconsider the single equation estimation case, but now focus on endogeneity occurring through the unobserved individual effects. Examples where μ_i and the explanatory variables may be correlated include an earnings equation, where unobserved individual ability may be correlated with schooling and experience, and a production function, where managerial ability may be correlated with the inputs. Mundlak (1978) considered the one-way error component regression model in (17.2.5) but with the additional auxiliary regression:

$$\mu_i = \bar{X}'_{i.}\pi + \epsilon_i \qquad (17.4.1)$$

where $\epsilon_i \sim \text{IIN}(0, \sigma^2_\epsilon)$ and $\bar{X}'_{i.}$ is $1 \times K$ vector of observations on the explanatory variables averaged over time. In other words, Mundlak assumed that the individual effects are a linear function of the averages of *all* the explanatory variables across time. These effects are uncorrelated with the explanatory variables if and only if $\pi = 0$. Mundlak (1978) assumed, without loss of generality, that the X are deviations from their sample mean. In vector form, one can write (17.4.1) as

$$\mu = Z'_\mu X\pi/T + \epsilon \qquad (17.4.2)$$

where $\mu' = (\mu_1, \ldots, \mu_N)$, $Z_\mu = I_N \otimes \iota_T$ and $\epsilon' = (\epsilon_1, \ldots, \epsilon_N)$. Substituting (17.4.2) into (17.2.5), with no constant, one gets

$$y = X\beta + PX\pi + (Z_\mu\epsilon + v) \qquad (17.4.3)$$

where $P = I_N \otimes \bar{J}_T$. Using the fact that ε and v are uncorrelated, the new error in (17.4.3) has zero mean and variance–covariance matrix

$$V = E(Z_\mu\epsilon + v)(Z_\mu\epsilon + v)' = \sigma^2_\epsilon(I_N \otimes J_T) + \sigma^2_v I_{NT} \qquad (17.4.4)$$

Using the partitioned inverse, one can verify that GLS on (17.4.3) yields

$$\hat{\beta}_{GLS} = \tilde{\beta}_{Within} = (X'QX)^{-1}X'Qy \qquad (17.4.5)$$

and

$$\hat{\pi}_{GLS} = \hat{\beta}_{Between} - \hat{\beta}_{Within} = (X'PX)^{-1}X'Py - (X'QX)^{-1}X'Qy \qquad (17.4.6)$$

with

$$\text{var}(\hat{\pi}_{GLS}) = \text{var}(\hat{\beta}_{Between}) + \text{var}(\hat{\beta}_{Within})$$
$$= (T\sigma_{\epsilon}^2 + \sigma_v^2)(X'PX)^{-1} + \sigma_v^2(X'QX)^{-1} \qquad (17.4.7)$$

Therefore, Mundlak (1978) showed that the best linear unbiased estimator of (17.2.5) becomes the fixed effects (Within) estimator once these individual effects are modeled as a linear function of *all* the X_{it} as in (17.4.1). The random effects estimator, on the other hand, is biased because it ignores (17.4.1). Note that Hausman's test based on the Between minus Within estimators is basically a test for $H_0:\pi = 0$ and this turns out to be another natural derivation for the Hausman test, namely,

$$\hat{\pi}'_{GLS}(\text{var}(\hat{\pi}'_{GLS}))^{-1}\hat{\pi}_{GLS} \overset{H_0}{\to} \chi_K^2$$

Mundlak's (1978) formulation in (17.4.3) assumes that *all* the explanatory variables are related to the individual effects. The random effects model, on the other hand, assumes *no* correlation between the explanatory variables and the individual effects. The random effects model generates the GLS estimator, whereas Mundlak's formulation produces the Within estimator. Instead of this "all or nothing" correlation among the X and the μ_i, Hausman and Taylor (1981) consider a model where some of the explanatory variables are related to the μ_i. In particular, they consider the following model:

$$y_{it} = X_{it}\beta + Z_i\gamma + \mu_i + v_{it} \qquad (17.4.8)$$

where the Z_i are cross-sectional time-invariant variables. Hausman and Taylor (1981), hereafter HT, split X and Z into two sets of variables: $X = [X_1; X_2]$ and $Z = [Z_1; Z_2]$, where X_1 is $n \times k_1$, X_2 is $n \times k_2$, Z_1 is $n \times g_1$, Z_2 is $n \times g_2$ and $n = NT$. X_1 and Z_1 are assumed exogenous in that they are not correlated with μ_i and v_{it}, while X_2 and Z_2 are endogenous because they are correlated with the μ_i, but not the v_{it}. The Within transformation would sweep the μ_i and remove the bias, but in the process it would also remove the Z_i and hence the Within estimator will not give an estimate of γ. To get around that, HT suggest premultiplying the model by $\Omega^{-1/2}$ and using the following set of instruments; $A_0 = [Q, X_1, Z_1]$, where $Q = I_{NT} - P$ and $P = (I_N \otimes \bar{J}_T)$. Breusch, Mizon and Schmidt (1989), hereafter BMS, show that this set of instruments yields the same projection and is therefore equivalent to another set, namely $A_{HT} = [QX_1, QX_2, PX_1, Z_1]$. The latter set of instruments A_{HT} is feasible, whereas A_0 is not. The order condition for identification gives the result that k_1, the number of variables in X_1, must be at least as large as g_2, the number of variables in Z_2. Note that $\tilde{X}_1 = QX_1, \tilde{X}_2 = QX_2, \bar{X}_1 = PX_1$

and Z_1 are used as instruments. Therefore X_1 is used twice, first as averages and then as deviations from these averages. This is an advantage of panel data allowing instruments from *within* the model. Note that the Within transformation wipes out the Z_i and does not allow the estimation of γ. In order to get consistent estimates of γ, HT propose obtaining the Within residuals and averaging them over time

$$\hat{d}_i = \bar{y}_{i.} - \bar{X}'_{i.}\tilde{\beta}_W \tag{17.4.9}$$

Then, (17.4.8) averaged over time can be estimated by running 2SLS of $\hat{d}_i$ on Z_i with the set of instruments $A = [X_1, Z_1]$. This yields

$$\hat{\gamma}_{2SLS} = (Z'P_A Z)^{-1} Z'P_A \hat{d} \tag{17.4.10}$$

where $P_A = A(A'A)^{-1}A'$. It is clear that the order condition has to hold $(k_1 \geq g_2)$ for $(Z'P_A Z)$ to be nonsingular. Next, the variance–components estimates are obtained as follows:

$$\hat{\sigma}_v^2 = \tilde{y}'\bar{P}_{\tilde{X}}\tilde{y}/N(T-1) \tag{17.4.11}$$

where $\tilde{y} = Qy, \tilde{X} = QX, \bar{P}_A = I - P_A$ and

$$\hat{\sigma}_1^2 = \frac{(y_{it} - X_{it}\tilde{\beta}_W - Z_i\hat{\gamma}_{2SLS})'P(y_{it} - X_{it}\tilde{\beta}_W - Z_i\hat{\gamma}_{2SLS})}{N} \tag{17.4.12}$$

This last estimate is based upon an NT vector of residuals. Once the variance–components estimates are obtained, the model in (17.4.8) is transformed using $\hat{\Omega}^{-1/2}$ as follows:

$$\hat{\Omega}^{-1/2} y_{it} = \hat{\Omega}^{-1/2} X_{it}\beta + \hat{\Omega}^{-1/2} Z_i\gamma + \hat{\Omega}^{-1/2} u_{it} \tag{17.4.13}$$

The HT estimator is basically 2SLS on (17.4.13) using $A_{HT} = [\tilde{X}, \bar{X}_1, Z_1]$ as a set of instruments.

(1) If $k_1 < g_2$, then the equation is under-identified. In this case $\hat{\beta}_{HT} = \tilde{\beta}_W$ and $\hat{\gamma}_{HT}$ does not exist.
(2) If $k_1 = g_2$, then the equation is just-identified. In this case, $\hat{\beta}_{HT} = \tilde{\beta}_W$ and $\hat{\gamma}_{HT} = \hat{\gamma}_{2SLS}$ given by (17.4.10).
(3) If $k_1 > g_2$, then the equation is over-identified and the HT estimator obtained from (17.4.13) is more efficient than the Within estimator.

A test for over-identification is obtained by computing

$$\hat{m} = \hat{q}'[\text{var}(\tilde{\beta}_W) - \text{var}(\hat{\beta}_{HT})]^{-}\hat{q} \tag{17.4.14}$$

with $\hat{q} = \hat{\beta}_{HT} - \tilde{\beta}_W$ and $\hat{\sigma}_v^2\hat{m} \overset{H_0}{\to} \chi_l^2$, where $l = \min[k_1 - g_2, NT - K]$.

Note that $y^* = \hat{\sigma}_v \hat{\Omega}^{-1/2} y$ has typical element $y_{it}^* = y_{it} - \hat{\theta} \bar{y}_{i.}$, where $\hat{\theta} = 1 - \hat{\sigma}_v / \hat{\sigma}_1$ and similar terms exist for X_{it}^* and Z_i^*. In this case 2SLS on (17.4.13) yields

$$\begin{pmatrix} \hat{\beta} \\ \hat{\gamma} \end{pmatrix} = \left[\begin{pmatrix} X^{*\prime} \\ Z^{*\prime} \end{pmatrix} P_A(X^*, Z^*) \right]^{-1} \begin{pmatrix} X^{*\prime} \\ Z^{*\prime} \end{pmatrix} P_A y^* \tag{17.4.15}$$

where P_A is the projection matrix on $A_{HT} = [\tilde{X}, \bar{X}_1, Z_1]$. This can be implemented in Stata using the xthtaylor command.

Amemiya and MaCurdy (1986), hereafter AM, suggest a more efficient set of instruments $A_{AM} = [QX_1, QX_2, X_1^*, Z_1]$, where $X_1^* = X_1^0 \otimes \iota_T$ and

$$X_1^0 = \begin{bmatrix} X_{11} & X_{12} & \cdots & X_{1T} \\ \vdots & \vdots & \cdots & \vdots \\ X_{N1} & X_{N2} & \cdots & X_{NT} \end{bmatrix} \tag{17.4.16}$$

is an $N \times k_1 T$ matrix. So X_1 is used $(T+1)$ times, once as $\tilde{X}_1$ and T times as X_1^*. The order condition for identification is now more likely to be satisfied $(Tk_1 > g_2)$. However, this set of instruments requires a stronger exogeneity assumption than that of Hausman and Taylor (1981). The latter requires only uncorrelatedness of the mean of X_1 from the μ_i, i.e.

$$\text{plim}\left(\frac{1}{N} \sum_{i=1}^{N} \bar{X}_{1i.} \mu_i \right) = 0$$

while AM require

$$\text{plim}\left(\frac{1}{N} \sum_{i=1}^{N} X_{1it} \mu_i \right) = 0 \quad \text{for } t = 1, \ldots, T$$

i.e., uncorrelatedness at each point in time. This can be implemented in Stata using the xthtaylor command with amacurdy option. Breusch, Mizon and Schmidt (1989) suggest a yet more efficient set of instruments

$$A_{BMS} = [QX_1, QX_2, PX_1, (QX_1)^*, (QX_2)^*, Z_1]$$

so that X_1 is used $(T+1)$ times and X_2 is used T times. This requires even more exogeneity assumptions, i.e., $\tilde{X}_2 = QX_2$ should be uncorrelated with the μ_i effects. The BMS order condition becomes $Tk_1 + (T-1)k_2 \geq g_2$.

For the Hausman and Taylor (1981) model given in (17.4.8), Metcalf (1996) shows that using less instruments may lead to a more powerful Hausman specification test. Asymptotically, more instruments lead to more efficient estimators. However, the asymptotic bias of the less efficient estimator will also be greater as the null hypothesis of no correlation is violated. Metcalf argues that, if the bias increases at the same rate as the variance (as the null is violated) for the less efficient estimator, then the power of the Hausman test will increase. This is due to the fact that the test statistic is linear in variance but quadratic in bias. The number of instruments used by the AM and BMS procedures can increase rapidly as T and the number of variables in the equation get large.

17.5 Dynamic panel data models

Many economic relationships are dynamic in nature and one of the advantages of panel data is that they allow the researcher to better understand the dynamics of adjustment. See, for example, Arellano and Bond (1991) on a dynamic model of employment. These dynamic relationships are characterized by the presence of a lagged dependent variable among the regressors, i.e.

$$y_{it} = \delta y_{i,t-1} + x'_{it}\beta + u_{it} \quad i = 1, \ldots, N \quad t = 1, \ldots, T \quad (17.5.1)$$

where δ is a scalar, x'_{it} is $1 \times K$ and β is $K \times 1$. We will assume that the u_{it} follow a one-way error component model as in (17.2.2)

$$u_{it} = \mu_i + v_{it} \quad (17.5.2)$$

where $\mu_i \sim \text{IID}(0, \sigma_\mu^2)$ and $v_{it} \sim \text{IID}(0, \sigma_v^2)$ are independent of each other and among themselves. The dynamic panel data regression described in (17.5.1) and (17.5.2) are characterized by two sources of persistence over time: autocorrelation due to the presence of a lagged dependent variable among the regressors and individual effects characterizing the heterogeneity among the individuals.

Let us start with some of the basic problems introduced by the inclusion of a lagged dependent variable. Since y_{it} is a function of μ_i, it immediately follows that $y_{i,t-1}$ is also a function of μ_i. Therefore, $y_{i,t-1}$, a right-hand regressor in (17.5.1), is correlated with the error term. This renders the OLS estimator biased and inconsistent even if the v_{it} are not serially correlated. For the fixed effects (FE) estimator, the Within transformation wipes out the μ_i, but $(y_{i,t-1} - \bar{y}_{i,-1})$, where $\bar{y}_{i,-1} = \sum_{t=2}^{T} y_{i,t-1}/(T-1)$, will still be correlated with $(v_{it} - \bar{v}_{i.})$ even if the v_{it} are not serially correlated. This is because $y_{i,t-1}$ is correlated with $\bar{v}_{i.}$ by construction. The latter average contains $v_{i,t-1}$, which is obviously correlated with $y_{i,t-1}$. In fact, the Within estimator will be biased of $O(1/T)$ and its consistency will depend upon T being large; see Nickell (1981). More recently, Kiviet (1995) derives an approximation for the bias of the Within estimator in a dynamic panel data model with serially uncorrelated disturbances and strongly exogenous regressors. Kiviet (1995) proposed a corrected Within estimator that subtracts a consistent estimator of this bias from the original Within estimator. For the typical labor panel where N is large and T is fixed, the Within estimator is biased and inconsistent. It is worth emphasizing that only if $T \to \infty$ will the Within estimator of δ and β be consistent for the dynamic error component model. For macro-panels, studying, for example, long-run growth, the data covers a large number of countries N over a moderate size T. In this case, T is not very small relative to N. Hence, some researchers may still favor the Within estimator, arguing that its bias may not be large. Judson and

Owen (1999) performed some Monte Carlo experiments for $N = 20$ or 100 and $T = 5, 10, 20$ and 30 and found that the bias in the Within estimator can be sizeable, even when $T = 30$. This bias increases with δ and decreases with T. But even for $T = 30$, this bias could be as much as 20 percent of the true value of the coefficient of interest.

The random effects GLS estimator is also biased in a dynamic panel data model. In order to apply GLS, quasi-demeaning is performed and $(y_{i,t-1} - \theta \bar{y}_{i,-1})$ will be correlated with $(u_{i,t} - \theta \bar{u}_{i,-1})$. An alternative transformation that wipes out the individual effects is the first difference (FD) transformation. In this case, correlation between the predetermined explanatory variables and the remainder error is easier to handle. In fact, Anderson and Hsiao (1981) suggested first differencing the model to get rid of the μ_i and then using $\Delta y_{i,t-2} = (y_{i,t-2} - y_{i,t-3})$, or simply $y_{i,t-2}$, as an instrument for $\Delta y_{i,t-1} = (y_{i,t-1} - y_{i,t-2})$. These instruments will not be correlated with $\Delta v_{i,t} = v_{i,t} - v_{i,t-1}$, as long as the v_{it} themselves are not serially correlated. This instrumental variable (IV) estimation method leads to consistent, but not necessarily efficient, estimates of the parameters in the model because it does not make use of all the available moment conditions (see Ahn and Schmidt, 1995), and it does not take into account the differenced structure on the residual disturbances (Δv_{it}).

Arellano (1989) finds that, for simple dynamic error components models, the estimator that uses the differences $\Delta y_{i,t-2}$, rather than the levels $y_{i,t-2}$, for instruments has a singularity point and very large variances over a significant range of parameter values. In contrast, the estimator that uses instruments in levels, i.e., $y_{i,t-2}$, has no singularities and much smaller variances and is therefore recommended. Arellano and Bond (1991) proposed a Generalized Method of Moments (GMM) procedure that is more efficient than the Anderson and Hsiao (1981) estimator. Arellano and Bond (1991) argue that additional instruments can be obtained in a dynamic panel data model if one utilizes the orthogonality conditions that exist between lagged values of y_{it} and the disturbances v_{it}. Let us illustrate this with the simple autoregressive model with no regressors:

$$y_{it} = \delta y_{i,t-1} + u_{it} \quad i = 1, \ldots, N \quad t = 1, \ldots, T \qquad (17.5.3)$$

where $u_{it} = \mu_i + v_{it}$ with $\mu_i \sim \text{IID}(0, \sigma_\mu^2)$ and $v_{it} \sim \text{IID}(0, \sigma_v^2)$, independent of each other and among themselves. In order to get a consistent estimate of δ as $N \to \infty$ with T fixed, we first difference (17.5.3) to eliminate the individual effects

$$y_{it} - y_{i,t-1} = \delta(y_{i,t-1} - y_{i,t-2}) + (v_{it} - v_{i,t-1}) \qquad (17.5.4)$$

and note that $(v_{it} - v_{i,t-1})$ is MA(1) with a unit root. For $t = 3$, the first period we observe this relationship, we have

$$y_{i3} - y_{i2} = \delta(y_{i2} - y_{i1}) + (v_{i3} - v_{i2})$$

In this case, y_{i1} is a valid instrument, since it is highly correlated with $(y_{i2} - y_{i1})$ and not correlated with $(v_{i3} - v_{i2})$ as long as the v_{it} are not serially correlated. But note what happens for $t = 4$, the second period we observe (17.5.4):

$$y_{i4} - y_{i3} = \delta(y_{i3} - y_{i2}) + (v_{i4} - v_{i3})$$

In this case, y_{i2} as well as y_{i1} are valid instruments for $(y_{i3} - y_{i2})$, since both y_{i2} and y_{i1} are not correlated with $(v_{i4} - v_{i3})$. One can continue in this fashion, adding an extra valid instrument with each forward period, so that for period T, the set of valid instruments becomes $(y_{i1}, y_{i2}, \ldots, y_{i,T-2})$.

This instrumental variable procedure still does not account for the differenced error term in (17.5.4). In fact,

$$E(\Delta v_i \Delta v_i') = \sigma_v^2 (I_N \otimes G) \tag{17.5.5}$$

where $\Delta v_i' = (v_{i3} - v_{i2}, \ldots, v_{iT} - v_{i,T-1})$ and

$$G = \begin{pmatrix} 2 & -1 & 0 & \cdots & 0 & 0 & 0 \\ -1 & 2 & -1 & \cdots & 0 & 0 & 0 \\ \vdots & \vdots & \vdots & \ddots & \vdots & \vdots & \vdots \\ 0 & 0 & 0 & \cdots & -1 & 2 & -1 \\ 0 & 0 & 0 & \cdots & 0 & -1 & 2 \end{pmatrix}$$

is $(T-2) \times (T-2)$, since Δv_i is MA(1) with a unit root. Define

$$W_i = \begin{bmatrix} [y_{i1}] & & & 0 \\ & [y_{i1}, y_{i2}] & & \\ & & \ddots & \\ 0 & & & [y_{i1}, \ldots, y_{i,T-2}] \end{bmatrix} \tag{17.5.6}$$

Then, the matrix of instruments is $W = [W_1', \ldots, W_N']'$ and the moment equations described above are given by $E(W_i' \Delta v_i) = 0$. Premultiplying the differenced equation (17.5.4) in vector form by W', one gets

$$W'\Delta y = W'(\Delta y_{-1})\delta + W'\Delta v \tag{17.5.7}$$

Performing GLS on (17.5.7) one gets the Arellano and Bond (1991) preliminary one-step consistent estimator

$$\hat{\delta}_1 = [(\Delta y_{-1})'W(W'(I_N \otimes G)W)^{-1}W'(\Delta y_{-1})]^{-1} \\ \times [(\Delta y_{-1})'W(W'(I_N \otimes G)W)^{-1}W'(\Delta y)] \tag{17.5.8}$$

The optimal GMM estimator of δ_1 for $N \to \infty$ and T fixed, using only the above moment restrictions, yields the same expression as in (17.5.8) except that

$$W'(I_N \otimes G)W = \sum_{i=1}^{N} W_i'GW_i$$

is replaced by

$$V_N = \sum_{i=1}^{N} W_i'(\Delta v_i)(\Delta v_i)' W_i$$

This GMM estimator requires no knowledge concerning the initial conditions or the distributions of v_i and μ_i. To operationalize this estimator, Δv is replaced by the differenced residuals obtained from the preliminary consistent estimator $\hat{\delta}_1$. The resulting estimator is the two-step Arellano and Bond (1991) GMM estimator:

$$\hat{\delta}_2 = [(\Delta y_{-1})' W \hat{V}_N^{-1} W'(\Delta y_{-1})]^{-1} [(\Delta y_{-1})' W \hat{V}_N^{-1} W'(\Delta y)] \tag{17.5.9}$$

A consistent estimate of the asymptotic var $(\hat{\delta}_2)$ is given by the first term in (17.5.9),

$$\text{var}(\hat{\delta}_2) = [(\Delta y_{-1})' W \hat{V}_N^{-1} W'(\Delta y_{-1})]^{-1} \tag{17.5.10}$$

Note that $\hat{\delta}_1$ and $\hat{\delta}_2$ are asymptotically equivalent if the v_{it} are IID $(0, \sigma_v^2)$.

Arellano and Bond (1991) propose a test for the hypothesis that there is no second-order serial correlation for the disturbances of the first-differenced equation. This test is important because the consistency of the GMM estimator relies upon the fact that $E[\Delta v_{it} \Delta v_{i,t-2}] = 0$. The test statistic is given in equation (8) of Arellano and Bond (1991, p. 282) and will not be reproduced here. This hypothesis is true if the v_{it} are not serially correlated or follow a random walk. Under the latter situation, both OLS and GMM of the first-differenced version of (17.5.1) are consistent and Arellano and Bond (1991) suggest a Hausman-type test based on the difference between the two estimators. Additionally, Arellano and Bond (1991) suggest Sargan's test of over-identifying restrictions given by

$$m = \Delta \hat{v}' W \left[\sum_{i=1}^{N} W_i'(\Delta \hat{v}_i)(\Delta \hat{v}_i)' W_i \right]^{-1} W'(\Delta \hat{v}) \sim \chi_{p-K-1}^2 \tag{17.5.11}$$

where p refers to the number of columns of W and $\Delta \hat{v}$ denote the residuals from a two-step estimation given in (17.5.9). This can be implemented in Stata using the xtabond command.

Using Monte Carlo experiments, Bowsher (2002) finds that the use of too many moment conditions causes the Sargan test for overidentifying restrictions to be undersized and have extremely low power. Fixing N at 100, and letting T increase over the range (5, 7, 9, 11, 13, 15), the performance of the Sargan test using the full set of Arellano–Bond moment conditions is examined for $\delta = 0.4$. For $T = 5$, the Monte Carlo mean of the Sargan χ_5^2 statistic is 5.12 when it should be 5, and its Monte Carlo variance is 9.84 when it should be 10. The size of the test is 0.052 at the 5% level and the power under the alternative is 0.742. For $T = 15$, the Sargan χ_{90}^2 statistic has a Monte Carlo mean of 91.3 when its theoretical mean is 90. However, its Monte Carlo variance is 13.7 when it should be 180.

This underestimation of the theoretical variance results in zero rejection rates under the null and alternative. In general, the Monte Carlo mean is a good estimator of the mean of the asymptotic χ^2 statistic. However, the Monte Carlo variance is much smaller than its asymptotic counterpart when T is large. The Sargan test never rejects when T is too large for a given N. Zero rejection rates under the null and alternative were also observed for the following (N, T) pairs (125, 16), (85, 13), (70, 112), and (40, 10). This is attributed to poor estimates of the weighting matrix in GMM rather than to weak instruments.

Ziliak (1997) asks the question of whether the bias/efficiency trade-off for the GMM estimator for the time series case is still binding in panel data, where the sample size is normally larger than 500. This problem becomes more pronounced with panel data since the number of moment conditions increase dramatically as the number of strictly exogenous variables and the number of time series observations increase. Even though it is desirable from an asymptotic efficiency point of view to include as many moment conditions as possible, it may be infeasible or impractical to do so in many cases. For example, for $T = 10$ and five strictly exogenous regressors, this generates 500 moment conditions for GMM. Ziliak (1997) performs an extensive set of Monte Carlo experiments for a dynamic panel data model and finds that the same trade-off between bias and efficiency exists for GMM as the number of moment conditions increase, and that one is better off with sub-optimal instruments. In fact, Ziliak finds that GMM performs well with suboptimal instruments, but is not recommended for panel data applications when all the moments are exploited for estimation. Ziliak attributes the bias in GMM to the correlation between the sample moments used in estimation and the estimated weight matrix. Interestingly, Ziliak finds that the forward filter 2SLS estimator proposed by Keane and Runkle (1992) performs best in terms of the bias/efficiency trade-off and is recommended. For more on the Keane and Runkle, as well as other dynamic panel data estimators, see Baltagi (2005, chapter 8).

Ahn and Schmidt (1995) derived additional nonlinear moment conditions not exploited by Arellano and Bond (1991). In fact Arellano and Bover (1995), Ahn and Schmidt (1995) and Blundell and Bond (1998) generalize and extend the Arellano and Bond estimator. The latter paper revisits the importance of exploiting the initial condition in generating efficient estimators of the dynamic panel data model when T is small. It considers a simple autoregressive panel data model with no exogenous regressors

$$y_{it} = \delta y_{i,t-1} + \mu_i + v_{it} \tag{17.5.12}$$

with $E(\mu_i) = 0; E(v_{it}) = 0;$ and $E(\mu_i v_{it}) = 0$ for $i = 1, 2, \ldots, N; t = 1, 2, \ldots, T$. Blundell and Bond (1998) focus on the case where $T = 3$ and therefore there is only one orthogonality condition, given by $E(y_{i1} \Delta v_{i3}) = 0$, so that δ is just-identified. In this case, the first-stage IV regression is obtained by regressing Δy_{i2} on y_{i1}. Note that this regression can be obtained from (17.5.12) evaluated at $t = 2$ by subtracting y_{i1} from both sides of this equation, i.e.,

$$\Delta y_{i2} = (\delta - 1)y_{i,1} + \mu_i + v_{i2} \tag{17.5.13}$$

Since we expect $E(y_{i1}\mu_i) > 0$, $(\delta - 1)$ will be biased upwards with

$$\text{plim}(\hat{\delta} - 1) = (\delta - 1)\frac{c}{c + (\sigma_\mu^2/\sigma_u^2)} \qquad (17.5.14)$$

where $c = (1 - \delta)/(1 + \delta)$. The bias term effectively scales the estimated coefficient on the instrumental variable y_{i1} towards zero. They also find that the F-statistic of the first stage IV regression converges to χ_1^2 with noncentrality parameter

$$\tau = \frac{(\sigma_u^2 c)^2}{\sigma_\mu^2 + \sigma_u^2 c} \to 0 \text{ as } \delta \to 1 \qquad (17.5.15)$$

As $\tau \to 0$, the instrumental variable estimator performs poorly. Hence, Blundell and Bond attribute the bias and the poor precision of the first difference GMM estimator to the problem of weak instruments and characterize this by its concentration parameter τ.

Next, Blundell and Bond (1998) show that an additional mild stationarity restriction on the initial conditions of the process allows the use of an extended system GMM estimator that uses lagged differences of y_{it} as instruments for equations in levels, in addition to lagged levels of y_{it} as instruments for equations in first differences, see Arellano and Bover (1995). The system GMM estimator is shown to have dramatic efficiency gains over the basic first difference GMM as $\delta \to 1$ and $(\sigma_\mu^2/\sigma_u^2)$ increases. In fact, for $T = 4$ and $(\sigma_\mu^2/\sigma_u^2) = 1$, the asymptotic variance ratio of the first difference GMM estimator to this system GMM estimator is 1.75 for $\delta = 0$ and increases to 3.26 for $\delta = 0.5$ and 55.4 for $\delta = 0.9$. This clearly demonstrates that the levels restrictions suggested by Arellano and Bover (1995) remain informative in cases where first differenced instruments become weak. Things improve for first difference GMM as T increases. However, with short T and persistent series, the Blundell and Bond findings support the use of the extra moment conditions.

Hahn (1999) examined the role of the initial condition imposed by the Blundell and Bond (1998) estimator. This was done by numerically comparing the semi-parametric information bounds for the case that incorporates the stationarity of the initial condition and the case that does not. Hahn (1999) finds that the efficiency gain can be substantial. The Alonso-Borrego and Arellano (1999) paper is also motivated by the finite sample bias in panel data instrumental variable estimators when the instruments are weak. The dynamic panel model generates many overidentifying restrictions even for moderate values of T. Also, the number of instruments increases with T, but the quality of these instruments is often poor because they tend to be only weakly correlated with the first-differenced endogenous variables that appear in the equation. Limited information maximum likelihood (LIML) is strongly preferred to 2SLS if the number of instruments gets large as the sample size tends to infinity. The alternative normalization rules adopted by LIML and 2SLS are at the root of their different sampling behavior. Alonso-Borrego and Arellano (1999) derive a symmetrically normalized GMM (SNM) estimator and compare it with ordinary GMM and LIML analogues by means of simulations. Monte Carlo and empirical results show that GMM can exhibit large biases when the instruments are poor, while LIML and SNM remain essentially unbiased. However, LIML and SNM always had a larger interquartile range than GMM. For $T=4$, $N=100$, $\sigma_\mu^2 = 0.2$ and $\sigma_v^2 = 1$, the bias for $\delta = 0.5$ was 6.9 percent for GMM, 1.7 percent for SNM and 1.7 percent for LIML. This bias increases to 17.8 percent for GMM, 3.7 percent for SNM and 4.1 percent for LIML for $\delta = 0.8$.

Alvarez and Arellano (2003) studied the asymptotic properties of FE, one-step GMM and non-robust LIML for a first-order autoregressive model when both N and T tend to infinity with $(N/T) \rightarrow c$ for $0 \leq c < 2$. For this autoregressive model, the FE estimator is inconsistent for T fixed and N large, but becomes consistent as T gets large. GMM is consistent for fixed T, but the number of orthogonality conditions increases with T. The common conclusion among the studies cited above is that GMM estimators that use the full set of available moments can be severely biased, especially when the instruments are weak and the number of moment conditions is large relative to N. Alvarez and Arellano show that, for $T<N$, GMM bias is always smaller than FE bias and LIML bias is smaller than the other two. In a fixed T framework, GMM and LIML are asymptotically equivalent, but as T increases, LIML has a smaller asymptotic bias than GMM. These results provide some theoretical support for LIML over GMM. Alvarez and Arellano (2003) derive the asymptotic properties of the FE, GMM and LIML estimators of a dynamic model with random effects. When both T and $N \rightarrow \infty$, GMM and LIML are *consistent* and asymptotically equivalent to the FE estimator. When $(T/N \rightarrow 0)$, the fixed T results for GMM and LIML remain valid, but FE, although consistent, still exhibits an asymptotic bias term in its asymptotic distribution. When $T/N \rightarrow c$, where $0 < c \leq 2$, all three estimators are consistent. The basic intuition behind this result is that, contrary to the structural equation setting, where too many instruments produce over-fitting and undesirable closeness to OLS, here a larger number of instruments is associated with larger values of T, and closeness to FE is desirable since the endogeneity bias $\rightarrow 0$ as $T \rightarrow \infty$. Nevertheless, FE, GMM and LIML exhibit a bias term in their asymptotic distributions; the biases are of order $1/T$, $1/N$ and $1/(2N-T)$, respectively. Provided $T<N$, the asymptotic bias of GMM is always smaller than the FE bias, and the LIML bias is smaller than the other two. When $T=N$, the asymptotic bias is the same for all three estimators.

Alvarez and Arellano (2003) also consider a random effects MLE that leaves the mean and variance of the initial conditions unrestricted but enforces time series homoskedasticity. This estimator has no asymptotic bias because it does not entail incidental parameters in the N and T dimensions, and it becomes robust to heteroskedasticity as $T \rightarrow \infty$. For the simple autoregressive model in (17.5.12) with $|\delta| < 1$ and v_{it} being *iid* across time and individuals and independent of μ_i and y_{i0}, Alvarez and Arellano (2003) find that, as $T \rightarrow \infty$, regardless of whether N is fixed or tends to ∞, and provided $N/T^3 \rightarrow 0$,

$$\sqrt{NT}\left[\tilde{\delta}_{FE} - (\delta - \frac{1}{T}(1+\delta))\right] \rightarrow N(0, 1-\delta^2) \qquad (17.5.16)$$

Also, as N, $T \to \infty$ such that $(\log T^2)/N \to 0, \hat{\delta}_{GMM} \to \delta$. Moreover, provided $T/N \to c, 0 < c < \infty$,

$$\sqrt{NT}\left[\hat{\delta}_{GMM} - (\delta - \frac{1}{N}(1+\delta))\right] \to N(0, 1-\delta^2) \qquad (17.5.17)$$

When $T \to \infty$, the number of GMM orthogonality conditions $T(T-1)/2 \to \infty$. In spite of this fact, $\hat{\delta}_{GMM} \to \delta$. Also, as $N, T \to \infty$ provided $T/N \to c, 0 \le c \le 2$, $\hat{\delta}_{LIML} \to \delta$. Moreover,

$$\sqrt{NT}\left[\hat{\delta}_{LIML} - (\delta - \frac{1}{2N-T}(1+\delta))\right] \to N(0, 1-\delta^2) \qquad (17.5.18)$$

LIML, like GMM, is consistent for δ despite $T \to \infty$ and $T/N \to c$. Provided $T < N$, the bias of LIML < bias of GMM < bias of FE. In fact, for $\delta = 0.2$, $T = 11$, $N = 100$, the median of $\hat{\delta}$ for 1,000 Monte Carlo replications yields 0.063 for FE, 0.188 for GMM and 0.196 for LIML. For $\delta = 0.8$, $T = 11$, $N = 100$, the median of $\hat{\delta}$ for 1,000 Monte Carlo replications yields 0.554 for FE, 0.763 for GMM and 0.792 for LIML. When we increase T to 51, $N = 100$ and $\delta = 0.8$, the median of 1,000 Monte Carlo replications for $\hat{\delta}$ yields 0.760 for FE, 0.779 for GMM and 0.789 for LIML.

Wansbeek and Knaap (1999) consider a simple dynamic panel data model with heterogeneous coefficients on the lagged dependent variable and the time trend, i.e.,

$$y_{it} = \delta_i y_{i,t-1} + \xi_i t + \mu_i + u_{it} \qquad (17.5.19)$$

They show that double differencing gets rid of the individual country effects (μ_i) on the first round of differencing and the heterogeneous coefficient on the time trend (ξ_i) on the second round of differencing. Modified OLS, IV and GMM methods are adapted to this model and LIML is suggested as a viable alternative to GMM to guard against the small sample bias of GMM. Simulations show that LIML is the superior estimator for $T \ge 10$ and $N \ge 50$. Macroeconomic data are subject to measurement error and Wansbeek and Knaap (1999) show how these estimators can be modified to account for measurement error that is white noise. For example, GMM is modified so that it discards the orthogonality conditions that rely on the absence of measurement error.

Andrews and Lu (2001) develop consistent model and moment selection criteria and downward testing procedures for GMM estimation that are able to select the correct model and moments with probability that goes to one as the sample size goes to infinity. This is applied to dynamic panel data models with unobserved individual effects. The selection criteria can be used to select the lag length for the lagged dependent variables, to determine the exogeneity of the regressors, and/or to determine the existence of correlation between some regressors and the individual effects. Monte Carlo experiments are performed to study the small sample performance of the selection criteria and the testing procedures and their impact on parameter estimation.

Hahn and Kuersteiner (2002) consider the simple autoregressive model given in (17.5.12) with $v_{it} \sim N(0, \Omega)$ *iid* across $i, 0 < \lim(N/T) = c < \infty, |\delta| < 1$ and $\sum_{i=1}^{N} y_{i0}^2/N = O(1)$ and $\sum_{i=1}^{N} \mu_i^2/N = O(1)$. The MLE of δ is the FE estimator, which is inconsistent for fixed T and $N \to \infty$. For large T, large N, as in cross-country studies, such that $\lim(N/T) = c$ is finite, Hahn and Kuersteiner derive a bias-corrected estimator which reduces to

$$\hat{\delta}_c = \left(\frac{T+1}{T}\right)\tilde{\delta}_{FE} + \frac{1}{T}$$

with $\sqrt{NT}(\hat{\delta}_c - \delta) \to N(0, 1 - \delta^2)$. Under the assumption of normality of the disturbances, $\hat{\delta}_c$ is asymptotically efficient as $N, T \to \infty$ at the same rate. Monte Carlo results for $T = 5$, 10, 20 and $N = 100$, 200 show that this bias-corrected MLE has comparable bias properties to the Arellano and Bover (1995) GMM estimator and often dominates in terms of RMSE for $T = 10$, 20 and $N = 100$, 200. Kiviet (1995) showed that a bias-corrected MLE (knowing δ) has much more desirable finite sample properties than various instrumental variable estimators. However, in order to make this estimator feasible, an initial instrumental variable for δ is used and its asymptotic properties are not derived. In contrast, the Hahn and Kuersteiner (2002) correction does not require a preliminary estimate of δ and its asymptotic properties are well derived. They also showed that this bias-corrected MLE is not expected to be asymptotically unbiased under a unit root ($\delta = 1$).

Hahn, Hausman and Kuersteiner (2003) consider the simple autoregressive panel data model in (17.5.12) with the following strong assumptions: (i) $v_{it} \sim IIN(0, \sigma_v^2)$ over i and t, (ii) stationarity conditions $(y_{i0}/\mu_i) \sim N((\mu_i/(1-\delta)), (\sigma_v^2/(1-\delta^2)))$ and $\mu_i \sim N(0, \sigma_\mu^2)$. They show that the Arellano and Bover (1995) GMM estimator, based on the forward demeaning transformation, can be represented as a linear combination of 2SLS estimators and therefore may be subject to a substantial finite sample bias. Based on 5,000 Monte Carlo replications, they show that this is indeed the case for $T = 5,10$; $N = 100$, 500 and $\delta = 0.1, 0.3, 0.5, 0.8$ and 0.9. For example, for $T = 5$, $N = 100$ and $\delta = 0.1$, the %bias of the GMM estimator is -16%, for $\delta = 0.8$, this %bias is -28% and for $\delta = 0.9$, this %bias is -51%. Hahn, Hausman and Kuersteiner attempt to eliminate this bias using two different approaches. The first is a second-order Taylor series type approximation and the second is a long-difference estimator. The Monte Carlo results show that the second-order Taylor series type approximation does a reasonably good job except when δ is close to 1 and N is small. Based on this, the bias corrected (second order theory) estimator should be relatively free of bias. Monte Carlo results show that this is the case unless δ is close to 1. For $T = 5$, $N = 100$ and $\delta = 0.1, 0.8, 0.9$, the %bias for this bias corrected estimator is 0.25%, -11% and -42%, respectively.

The second-order asymptotics fail to be a good approximation around $\delta = 1$. This is due to the *weak instrument* problem, see Blundell and Bond (1998). In fact, this paper argued that the weak IV problem can be alleviated by assuming stationarity of the initial observation y_{i0}. The stationarity condition turns out to be a predominant source of information around $\delta = 1$, as noted by Hahn (1999). The stationarity condition may or may not be appropriate for particular applications, and substantial finite sample biases due to inconsistency will result under violations of stationarity. Hahn, Hausman and Kuersteiner turn to the long-difference estimator to deal with weak IV around the unit circle, so avoiding the stationarity assumption:

$$y_{it} - y_{i1} = \delta(y_{it} - y_{i0}) + v_{it} - v_{i1} \qquad (17.5.20)$$

Here y_{i0} is a valid instrument. The residuals $(y_{i,T-1} - \delta y_{i,T-2}), \ldots, (y_{i,2} - \delta y_{i,1})$ are also valid instruments. To make it operational, they suggest using the Arellano and Bover estimator for the first step and iterating using the long difference estimator. The bias of the 2SLS (GMM) estimator depends on four factors: the sample size, the number of instruments, the covariance between the stochastic disturbance of the structural equation and the reduced form equation, and the explained variance of the first stage reduced form. The long difference estimator increases the R^2, but decreases the covariance between the stochastic disturbance of the structural equation and the reduced form equation. This alleviates the weak instruments problem. Further, the number of instruments is smaller for the long difference specification than for the first difference GMM and therefore one should expect smaller bias. The actual properties of the long-difference estimator turn out to be much better than those predicted by higher order theory, especially around the unit circle. Monte Carlo results show that the long-difference estimator does better than the other estimators for large δ and not significantly different for moderate δ.

Hahn, Hausman and Kuersteiner analyze the class of GMM estimators that exploit the Ahn and Schmidt complete set of moment conditions and show that a strict subset of the full set of moment restrictions should be used in estimation in order to minimize bias. They show that the long difference estimator is a good approximation to the bias minimal procedure. They report the numerical values of the biases of the Arellano and Bond, Arellano and Bover and Ahn and Schmidt estimators under near unit root asymptotics and compare them with biases for the long difference estimator as well as the bias minimal estimator. Despite the fact that the long difference estimator does not achieve as small a bias reduction as the fully optimal estimator, it has significantly less bias than the more commonly used implementations of the GMM estimator.

17.6   Conclusion

The panel data econometrics literature has exhibited rapid growth in recent years and one cannot do justice to the many theoretical contributions to date. Space limitations prevented the inclusion of many worthy topics, such as attrition, sample selection, non-linear panel models, semiparametric, nonparametric and Bayesian methods using panel data, unbalanced panels, problems associated with heteroskedasticity, serial as well as spatial correlation in panels, measurement error, limited dependent variables, duration and count panel data models, to mention a few. More extensive treatments of these and other topics are given in textbooks on the subject by Baltagi (2005), Wooldridge (2002), Hsiao (2003) and Arellano (2003).

References

Ahn, S.C. and P. Schmidt (1995) Efficient estimation of models for dynamic panel data. *Journal of Econometrics* **68**, 5–27.

Alonso-Borrego, C. and M. Arellano (1999) Symmetrically normalized instrumental variable estimation using panel data. *Journal of Business and Economic Statistics* **17**, 36–49.

Alvarez, J. and M. Arellano (2003) The time series and cross-section asymptotics of dynamic panel data estimators. *Econometrica* **71**, 1121–1159.

Amemiya, T. and T.W. MaCurdy (1986) Instrumental-variable estimation of an error components model. *Econometrica* **54**, 869–81.

Anderson, T.W. and C. Hsiao (1981) Estimation of dynamic models with error components. *Journal of the American Statistical Association* **76**, 598–606.

Andrews, D.W.K. and B. Lu (2001) Consistent model and moment selection procedures for GMM estimation with application to dynamic panel data models. *Journal of Econometrics* **101**, 123–64.

Angrist, J.D. and W.K. Newey (1991) Over-identification tests in earnings functions with fixed effects. *Journal of Business and Economic Statistics* **9**, 317–23.

Arellano, M. (1987) Computing robust standard errors for within-groups estimators. *Oxford Bulletin of Economics and Statistics* **49**, 431–4.

Arellano, M. (1989) A note on the Anderson–Hsiao estimator for panel data. *Economics Letters* **31**, 337–41.

Arellano, M. (1993) On the testing of correlated effects with panel data. *Journal of Econometrics* **59**, 87–97.

Arellano, M. (2003) *Panel Data Econometrics*. Oxford: Oxford University Press.

Arellano, M. and S. Bond (1991) Some tests of specification for panel data: Monte Carlo evidence and an application to employment equations. *Review of Economic Studies* **58**, 277–97.

Arellano, M. and O. Bover (1995) Another look at the instrumental variables estimation of error-component models. *Journal of Econometrics* **68**, 29–51.

Arellano, M. and B. Honoré (2001) Panel data models: some recent developments. In J. Heckman and E. Leamer (eds), *Handbook of Econometrics*. Amsterdam: North-Holland, pp. 3229–96.

Balestra, P. and J. Varadharajan-Krishnakumar (1987) Full information estimations of a system of simultaneous equations with error components structure. *Econometric Theory* **3**, 223–46.

Baltagi, B.H. (1981a) Pooling: An experimental study of alternative testing and estimation procedures in a two-way error components model. *Journal of Econometrics* **17**, 21–49.

Baltagi, B.H. (1981b) Simultaneous equations with error components. *Journal of Econometrics* **17**, 189–200.

Baltagi, B.H. (1999) Specification tests in panel data models using artificial regressions. *Annales D'Économie et de Statistique* **55–6**, 277–97.

Baltagi, B.H. (2005) *The Econometrics of Panel Data*. Chichester: Wiley.

Baltagi, B.H. (ed.) (2002) *Recent Developments in the Econometrics of Panel Data*, vols I and II. Cheltenham: Edward Elgar Publishing.

Blundell, R. and S. Bond (1998) Initial conditions and moment restrictions in dynamic panel data models. *Journal of Econometrics* **87**, 115–43.

Bowsher, C.G. (2002) On testing overidentifying restrictions in dynamic panel data models. *Economics Letters* **77**, 211–20.

Breusch, T.S., G.E. Mizon and P. Schmidt (1989) Efficient estimation using panel data. *Econometrica* **57**, 695–700.

Breusch, T.S. and A.R. Pagan (1980) The Lagrange Multiplier test and its applications to model specification in econometrics. *Review of Economic Studies* **47**, 239–53.

Chamberlain, G. (1982) Multivariate regression models for panel data. *Journal of Econometrics* **18**, 5–46.

Chamberlain, G. (1984) Panel data. In Z. Griliches and M. Intrilligator (eds), *Handbook of Econometrics*. Amsterdam: North-Holland, pp. 1247–1318.

Cornwell, C., P. Schmidt and D. Wyhowski (1992) Simultaneous equations and panel data. *Journal of Econometrics* **51**, 151–81.

Fuller, W.A. and G.E. Battese (1973) Transformations for estimation of linear models with nested error structure. *Journal of the American Statistical Association* **68**, 626–32.

Hahn, J. (1999) How informative is the initial condition in the dynamic panel model with fixed effects? *Journal of Econometrics* **93**, 309–26.

Hahn, J., J. Hausman and G. Kuersteiner (2003) Bias corrected instrumental variables estimation for dynamic panel models with fixed effects. Working paper, MIT, Massachusetts.

Hahn, J. and G. Kuersteiner (2002) Asymptotically unbiased inference for a dynamic model with fixed effects when both n and T are large. *Econometrica* **70**, 1639–1657.

Hausman, J.A. (1978) Specification tests in econometrics. *Econometrica* **46**, 1251–1271.

Hausman, J.A. and W.E. Taylor (1981) Panel data and unobservable individual effects. *Econometrica* **49**, 1377–1398.

Hsiao, C. (2003) *Analysis of Panel Data*, Cambridge: Cambridge University Press.

Judson, R.A. and A.L. Owen (1999) Estimating dynamic panel data models: a guide for macroeconomists. *Economics Letters* **65**, 9–15.

Keane, M.P. and D.E. Runkle (1992) On the estimation of panel-data models with serial correlation when instruments are not strictly exogenous. *Journal of Business and Economic Statistics* **10**, 1–9.

Kiviet, J.F. (1995) On bias, inconsistency and efficiency of various estimators in dynamic panel data models. *Journal of Econometrics* **68**, 53–78.

Lancaster, T. (2000) The incidental parameter problem since 1948. *Journal of Econometrics* **95**, 391–413.

Maddala, G.S. (ed.) (1993) *The Econometrics of Panel Data*, vols I and II. Cheltenham: Edward Elgar Publishing.

Maddala, G.S. and T.D. Mount (1973) A comparative study of alternative estimators for variance components models used in econometric applications. *Journal of the American Statistical Association* **68**, 324–8.

Mátyás, L. and P. Sevestre (eds) (1996) *The Econometrics of Panel Data: A Handbook of the Theory With Applications*. Dordrecht: Kluwer Academic Publishers.

Metcalf, G.E. (1996) Specification testing in panel data with instrumental variables. *Journal of Econometrics* **71**, 291–307.

Mundlak, Y. (1978) On the pooling of time series and cross-section data. *Econometrica* **46**, 69–85.

Nickell, S. (1981) Biases in dynamic models with fixed effects. *Econometrica* **49**, 1417–1426.

Swamy, P.A.V.B. and S.S. Arora (1972) The exact finite sample properties of the estimators of coefficients in the error components regression models. *Econometrica* **40**, 261–75.

Taylor, W.E. (1980) Small sample considerations in estimation from panel data. *Journal of Econometrics* **13**, 203–23.

Wansbeek, T.J. and A. Kapteyn (1982) A simple way to obtain the spectral decomposition of variance components models for balanced data. *Communications in Statistics A11*, 2105–2112.

Wansbeek, T.J. and T. Knapp (1999) Estimating a dynamic panel data model with heterogeneous trends. *Annales D'Économie et de Statistique* **55–6**, 331–49.

White, H. (1986) Instrumental variables analogs of generalized least squares estimators. In R.S. Mariano (ed.), *Advances in Statistical Analysis and Statistical Computing*, vol. 1. New York: JAI Press, pp. 173–277.

Wooldridge, J.M. (2002) *Econometric Analysis of Cross Section and Panel Data*. Cambridge: MIT Press.

Ziliak, J.P. (1997) Efficient estimation with panel data when instruments are predetermined: An empirical comparison of moment-condition estimators. *Journal of Business and Economic Statistics* 15, 419–31.

18
Nonstandard Dependent Variables Models: Some Common Structures of Simulated Specification Tests

Lung-fei Lee

Abstract

Specification tests in nonstandard dependent variables models, which include multinormal discrete variables models, limited dependent variables models, and disequilibrium market models, via simulation estimation methods are considered. We investigate the formulation of simulated scores for a model on which the likelihood function under the null hypothesis has been estimated by some practical simulated methods. Specification tests for omitted dynamics, higher order serial correlations, normal distribution or heteroskedastic disturbances, etc., in discrete choice, dynamic Tobit and dynamic disequilibrium market models all have some common and intuitive appealing structures. Monte Carlo results on the test of normality in a dynamic model provide practical guidance on its implementation.

18.1	Introduction	663
18.2	Specification tests in latent variables models and the simulated EM algorithm	664
18.3	Importance sampler and specification tests	670
18.4	The multinormal discrete choice model	673
	18.4.1 The omitted variables test	675
	18.4.2 A normality test	675
18.5	Dynamic discrete choice panel data models	676
	18.5.1 Omitted variables, higher-order serial correlation or state dependence tests	677
	18.5.2 A normality test	678
18.6	Dynamic Tobit models	679
	18.6.1 Omitted variables or state dependence tests	680
	18.6.2 A test for heteroskedasticity in the Tobit GARCH model	680
	18.6.3 A normality test	681

18.7	Dynamic disequilibrium models	681
	18.7.1 Omitted variables, higher-order serial correlation or state dependence tests	683
	18.7.2 A normality test	683
18.8	Monte Carlo results on the testing of normality in a dynamic discrete choice panel model	684
18.9	Conclusions	689
Appendix:	Dynamic Latent Models and the Exponential Family of Conditional Densities	689

18.1 Introduction

Because of nonlinear probability structures in nonstandard dependent variables models, such as the discrete choice and limited dependent variables models, it is known that misspecification errors such as omitted variables, nonnormal distributions or heteroskedastic variances may lead to inconsistent estimators under a conventional parametric specification. There exists a literature, developed in the 1980s, on specification error tests for cross-section or panel data models where likelihood functions are analytically tractable and can be evaluated without simulation. Surveys on that literature can be found in Pagan and Vella (1989) and Maddala (1995). For those models, various test statistics have some common features in that they are testing some orthogonal conditions based on conditional moments or generalized residuals (see, for example, Lee and Maddala, 1985; Gourieroux, Monfort, Renault and Trognon, 1987a).

Recent developments in computationally intensive methods have proposed various simulation methods and probability simulators for the estimation of complicated structural models, such as the multinormal discrete choice model (e.g., McFadden, 1989; Geweke, 1992; Borsch-Supan and Hajivassiliou, 1993; Geweke, Keane and Runkle, 1994; Hajivassiliou, and McFadden and Ruud, 1996), the mixed multinomial logit model (McFadden and Train 2000), and latent dynamic models (Hendry and Richard, 1992; Laroque and Salanie, 1993; Shephard, 1993; Danielsson and Richard, 1993; Keane, 1994), etc. Surveys on simulation estimation methods can be found in Gourieroux and Monfort (1993), Hajivassiliou (1993), Keane (1993), Hajivassiliou and Ruud (1994), McFadden and Ruud (1994), Chib (2001), Geweke and Keane (2001), and Train (2003). The recent book by Train (2003) focuses on discrete choice models and their simulation based estimation. The literature so far has focused on computationally tractable and adequate simulators. Simulation methods are designed for the estimation of parametric models. As multivariate and dynamic discrete choice and limited dependent variable models may be sensitive to misspecification errors, specification tests will be valuable for diagnostic purposes.

The literature on hypothesis testing within simulation estimation methods is limited in scope. There are only a few papers on this topic. For example, Lee (1999a) discusses the classical likelihood ratio, Wald and efficient score tests in the framework of simulated maximum likelihood estimation; McFadden and Train (2002) consider the test of mixing in the multinomial and mixed multinomial logit models; and Ghysels and Guay (2003) have suggested tests for structural change in the framework of simulation method of moments. There is a literature on the use of simulation to construct confidence intervals of test statistics when the statistics are pivotal, for example, Dufour and Khalaf (2002) and Dufour *et al.* (2004). More generally, the bootstrapping is a simulation-based method of constructing confidence intervals. But those are not necessarily related to the estimation of models via simulation methods. In this chapter, we provide some possible formulations of specification tests for complicated structural models with nonstandard dependent variables. As an extension of tests in the cross-section and panel data models, we emphasize common structures of efficient score (or Lagrange multiplier) tests formulated with simulation. This extends the literature of the 1980s with the use of generalized and simulated residuals for specification tests.

The efficient score test approach is attractive for diagnostic purposes because its formulation requires only the estimation of a restricted but computationally simpler model. For simulated statistics, computational simplicity can be preserved if an accurate and tractable sampler can be designed. As the sampler for the simulation estimation of the restricted model should be tractable and has provided an adequate likelihood simulator, we investigate the possible use of such a sampler for the construction of simulated diagnostic test statistics and the structures of such statistics. We illustrate such specification test statistics, in particular, for omitted dynamics, serial correlation structures and the normality assumptions for multivariate discrete choice, limited dependent variables, and disequilibrium models, in which estimation can only be done via simulation methods. Heteroskedasticity tests in ARCH and GARCH Tobit models will also be of interest.

This chapter is organized as follows. In section 18.2, we pinpoint an important feature of the score and its relation to the conditional score of a latent variable model, which provides a possible common structure for the Lagrangian multiplier test statistic. We consider the simulated EM (expectation and maximization algorithm) approach and its relevance in the formulation of simulated specification tests for latent dynamic models. Within the simulated EM framework, specification test statistics have some common elegant structures. In section 18.3, common features on simulated specification tests via importance samplers are highlighted. Specification tests for omitted variables and normality assumptions are developed in section 18.4 for the multinormal discrete choice model. Section 18.5 considers specification tests for dynamic discrete choice models. Sections 18.6 and 18.7 consider dynamic Tobit and disequilibrium markets models. Monte Carlo results on the implementation of a normality test in a dynamic discrete choice model and its finite sample properties are reported in section 18.8. Conclusions are drawn in section 18.9.

18.2 Specification tests in latent variables models and the simulated EM algorithm

In an econometric model with latent variables, suppose that $g(y^*, y|\theta)$ is the joint density of the vector of latent variables y^* and the vector of observed sample variables y, where θ is the vector of unknown parameters in the model. Let $f(y|\theta)$ be the density of y, and $g(y^*|y, \theta)$ be the conditional density of y^* given y. Since $g(y^*, y|\theta) = g(y^*|y, \theta)f(y|\theta)$,

$$\ln f(y|\theta) = \ln g(y^*, y|\theta) - \ln g(y^*|y, \theta), \tag{18.2.1}$$

and

$$\frac{\partial \ln f(y|\theta)}{\partial \theta} = \frac{\partial \ln g(y^*, y|\theta)}{\partial \theta} - \frac{\partial \ln g(y^*|y, \theta)}{\partial \theta}. \tag{18.2.2}$$

Integrating the right-hand side expressions of (18.2.1) and (18.2.2) with respect to $g(y^*|y, \theta^+)$, where θ^+ is an arbitrary value of θ, it follows that

$$\ln f(y|\theta) = \int_{-\infty}^{\infty} [\ln g(y^*, y|\theta)]g(y^*|y, \theta^+)dy^*$$
$$- \int_{-\infty}^{\infty} [\ln g(y^*|y, \theta)]g(y^*|y, \theta^+)dy^*, \tag{18.2.3}$$

and

$$\frac{\partial \ln f(y|\theta)}{\partial \theta} = \int_{-\infty}^{\infty} \frac{\partial \ln g(y^*, y|\theta)}{\partial \theta} g(y^*|y, \theta^+)dy^*$$
$$- \int_{-\infty}^{\infty} \frac{\partial \ln g(y^*|y, \theta)}{\partial \theta} g(y^*|y, \theta^+)dy^*. \tag{18.2.4}$$

At $\theta^+ = \theta$, the first order derivative of the log likelihood (18.2.4) becomes

$$\frac{\partial \ln f(y|\theta)}{\partial \theta} = \int_{-\infty}^{\infty} \frac{\partial \ln g(y^*, y|\theta)}{\partial \theta} g(y^*|y, \theta)dy^* - \int_{-\infty}^{\infty} \frac{\partial \ln g(y^*|y, \theta)}{\partial \theta} g(y^*|y, \theta)dy^*$$
$$= \int_{-\infty}^{\infty} \frac{\partial \ln g(y^*, y|\theta)}{\partial \theta} g(y^*|y, \theta)dy^*$$
$$= E_\theta \left(\frac{\partial \ln g(y^*, y|\theta)}{\partial \theta} \bigg| y \right), \tag{18.2.5}$$

because $E_\theta((\partial \ln g(y^*|y, \theta)/\partial \theta)|y) = 0$. From (18.2.5) and (18.2.2), the second-order derivative matrix of the log likelihood is

$$\frac{\partial^2 \ln f(y|\theta)}{\partial \theta \partial \theta'}$$
$$= \int_{-\infty}^{\infty} \left[\frac{\partial^2 \ln g(y^*, y|\theta)}{\partial \theta \partial \theta'} + \frac{\partial \ln g(y^*, y|\theta)}{\partial \theta} \left(\frac{\partial \ln g(y^*, y|\theta)}{\partial \theta'} - \frac{\partial \ln f(y|\theta)}{\partial \theta} \right) \right] g(y^*|y, \theta)dy^*$$
$$= E_\theta \left(\frac{\partial^2 \ln g(y^*, y|\theta)}{\partial \theta \partial \theta'} \bigg| y \right) + V_\theta \left(\frac{\partial \ln g(y^*, y|\theta)}{\partial \theta} \bigg| y \right), \tag{18.2.6}$$

where V_θ is the variance function. The formulations in (18.2.5) and (18.2.6) are revealing in that the first- and second-order derivatives of the log likelihood depend only on the conditional density $g(y^*|y, \theta)$ and the first- and second-order derivatives of the joint density $g(y^*, y|\theta)$. In a specification test, the Lagrangian multiplier (efficient score) test statistic will be based on the score $(\partial \ln f(y|\theta))/\partial \theta$ evaluated at the relevant restricted likelihood estimate. The relation (18.2.5) links the relevant score vector to the conditional score vector of the latent variables model. It reveals a common structure and the intuition underlying a specification test statistic in terms of conditional moments for testing a relevant hypothesis.

In the nonstandard dependent variables models that require simulation estimation, an evaluation of the likelihood $f(y|\theta)$ is not analytically tractable but $g(y^*, y|\theta)$ is. The tractability of $g(y^*, y|\theta)$ and the feasibility of drawing the random variable y^* from the conditional density $g(y^*|y, \theta)$ provide the simulated EM (SEM) approach. Define

$$Q(y, \theta, \theta^+) = \int_{-\infty}^{\infty} [\ln g(y^*, y|\theta)] g(y^*|y, \theta^+) dy^*. \tag{18.2.7}$$

The EM algorithm approach is to maximize $Q(y, \theta, \theta^+)$ with respect to θ starting from an initial estimate $\theta^{(1)}$ for θ^+, and update the maximization with a new estimate replacing the old one. The EM algorithm for latent models has the advantage of avoiding a direct but difficult maximization of $\ln f(y|\theta)$ by using $Q(y, \theta, \theta^+)$ instead as the objective function for maximization (Dempster *et al.*, 1977). The reasoning of the EM algorithm depends crucially on the information inequality that $\int_{-\infty}^{\infty} [\ln g(y^*|y, \theta^{(2)})] g(y^*|y, \theta^{(1)}) dy^* \leq \int_{-\infty}^{\infty} [\ln g(y^*|y, \theta^{(1)})] g(y^*|y, \theta^{(1)}) dy^*$, for any two values $\theta^{(1)}$ and $\theta^{(2)}$. Given an initial estimate $\theta^{(1)}$ and that $\theta^{(2)}$ maximizes $Q(y, \theta, \theta^{(1)})$ with respect to θ, the information inequality guarantees that $\ln f(y|\theta^{(2)}) \geq \ln f(y|\theta^{(1)})$ from (18.2.3). At convergence, the estimate converges to a local maximum of the log likelihood function (Wu, 1983). This is so, since, from (18.2.7), $(\partial Q(y, \theta, \theta^+))/\partial \theta = \int_{-\infty}^{\infty} (\partial \ln g(y^*, y|\theta))/\partial \theta g(y^*|y, \theta^+) dy^*$, and hence

$$\frac{\partial Q(y, \theta, \theta^+)}{\partial \theta} \bigg|_{\theta^+ = \theta} = \frac{\partial \ln f(y|\theta)}{\partial \theta}, \tag{18.2.8}$$

from (18.2.5). At convergence, the EM estimate $\hat{\theta}$ satisfies the condition $(\partial Q(y, \hat{\theta}, \hat{\theta}))/\partial \theta = 0$. Therefore, $(\partial \ln f(y|\hat{\theta}))/\partial \theta = 0$ and $\hat{\theta}$ is a local maximum of $\ln f(y|\theta)$. The E step in an EM algorithm is to evaluate the expectation in (18.2.7). The expectation can be difficult when the integral is of a high dimension. An SEM evaluates $Q(y, \theta, \theta^+)$ by a Monte Carlo simulation and uses the simulated function for maximization (Tanner, 1987; Ruud, 1991; Shephard, 1993). Let $y^{*(r)}(\theta), r = 1, \ldots, m$, be m independent draws from $g(y^*|y, \theta)$. Q can be simulated by

$$Q_m(y, \theta, \theta^+) = \frac{1}{m} \sum_{r=1}^{m} \ln g(y^{*(r)}(\theta^+), y|\theta). \tag{18.2.9}$$

This $Q_m(y, \theta, \theta^+)$ can be used in the search of a simulated maximum likelihood estimator (SMLE) of the model. The computational tractability of the SEM approach will depend on the computational tractability of $g(y^*, y|\theta)$ and feasible samplers of drawing random variables from $g(y^*|y, \theta)$. The $g(y^*|y, \theta)$ is a conditional density of latent variables y^* conditional on sample y, with which, for certain models, the Gibbs sampler can be feasible. However, for some models, sophisticated Markov chain samplers need to be designed (Shephard, 1993). The Gibbs sampler is a member of the broad class of Markov chain samplers. The Markov Chain Monte Carlo approach is important for Bayesian, non-Bayesian and classical estimation approaches. Recent surveys on those can be found in Chib (2001) and Geweke and Keane (2001). Chernozhukov and Hong (2003) discuss the usefulness of the Markov Chain Monte Carlo method as a computationally tractable approach for a quasi-Bayesian estimation approach.

The relation in (18.2.8) indicates that an efficient score test can be implemented with the derivative of $Q(y, \theta, \theta^+)$. A simulated specification test can be based on the corresponding simulated score (SSC):

$$\left.\frac{\partial Q_m(y, \theta, \theta^+)}{\partial \theta}\right|_{\theta^+=\theta} = \frac{1}{m}\sum_{r=1}^{m}\left.\frac{\partial \ln g(y^{*(r)}(\theta^+), y|\theta)}{\partial \theta}\right|_{\theta^+=\theta}, \tag{18.2.10}$$

evaluated at the SMLE of the restricted model. Consider the situation when $\theta = (\theta_1, \theta_2)$ and a restricted model corresponds to $\theta_2 = 0$. The SSC for testing $H_0 : \theta_2 = 0$ will be

$$\left.\frac{\partial Q_m(y, (\hat{\theta}_1, 0), \theta^+)}{\partial \theta}\right|_{\theta^+=(\hat{\theta}_1, 0)} = \frac{1}{m}\sum_{r=1}^{m}\frac{\partial \ln g(y^{*(r)}(\hat{\theta}_1, 0), y|(\hat{\theta}_1, 0))}{\partial \theta}, \tag{18.2.11}$$

where $\hat{\theta}_1$ is the SMLE of the restricted model. Similarly, the second-order derivatives (Hessian matrix) of the log likelihood (18.2.6) can be simulated by

$$S_m(\theta) = \left(\frac{1}{m}\sum_{r=1}^{m}\frac{\partial^2 \ln g(y^{*(r)}(\theta^+), y|\theta)}{\partial\theta\partial\theta'} + \frac{1}{m}\sum_{r=1}^{m}\frac{\partial \ln g(y^{*(r)}(\theta^+), y|\theta)}{\partial \theta}\frac{\partial \ln g(y^{*(r)}(\theta^+), y|\theta)}{\partial \theta'}\right.$$

$$\left.\left.-\frac{\partial Q_m(y, \theta, \theta^+)}{\partial \theta}\frac{\partial Q_m(y, \theta, \theta^+)}{\partial \theta'}\right)\right|_{\theta^+=\theta}. \tag{18.2.12}$$

An SSC test statistic can be formed as[1]

$$\left.\frac{\partial Q_m(y, (\hat{\theta}_1, 0), \theta^+)}{\partial \theta'}\right|_{\theta^+=(\hat{\theta}_1, 0)}[-S_m(\hat{\theta}_1, 0)]^{-1}\left.\frac{\partial Q_m(y, (\hat{\theta}_1, 0), \theta^+)}{\partial \theta}\right|_{\theta^+=(\hat{\theta}_1, 0)}. \tag{18.2.13}$$

In the formulation of the SSC statistics (18.2.13), the simulated random variables are $y^{*(r)}(\hat{\theta}_1, 0)$, which correspond to draws from the density $g(y^*|y, (\hat{\theta}_1, 0))$.

This sampler is essentially the one used for the SEM estimation of the restricted model. This is so, because, for the estimation of the restricted model, all the densities and likelihood functions in (18.2.1) will be restricted to the parameter subspace Θ_1 of θ_1. The maximization step will be applied to the objective function (18.2.9) defined on $\Theta_1 \times \Theta_1$. Furthermore, from the construction of the SSC in (18.2.10), the derivatives with respect to θ in (18.2.11) and (18.2.12) do not involve any derivatives of the simpler $y^{*(r)}(\theta)$. Thus, the formulation of a diagnostic efficient score test (18.2.13) in an SEM approach does not require any more general sampler than the one already used for the restricted model. This is an interesting feature of the SSC test within the SEM framework. The classical efficient score test is known to be computationally simpler than the likelihood ratio or Wald tests for certain models as it requires only the computation of the MLE of the restricted model. The SEM approach reveals that simulation may not create additional complexity in the formulation of an SSC statistic. The SSC in (18.2.10) is an estimate of the exact score. As the score (18.2.5) is simply the conditional expectation of the score of the latent model conditional on sample observations, intuitive interpretations of tests for certain hypotheses in terms ofconditional moments are possible. This provides a common structure for score test statistics of various hypotheses, as in Maddala and Lee (1985) and Gourieroux, Monfort, Renault and Trognon (1987a). Such a common structure may therefore be carried over to the SSC test statistic.

The specification tests for limited dependent variables in the 1980s concern null hypotheses where restricted models do not involve high dimensional integrals in their likelihood functions and the resultant test statistics do not involve any complicated integrals at all. These hypotheses are quite strong and special. For the testing of serial correlation in Tobit or disequilibrium market models in Lee (1984a), Lee and Maddala (1985), Robinson, Bera and Jarque (1985) and Bera and Robinson (1989), the null hypothesis is no serial correlation and the alternative hypothesis is an autoregressive moving average process of certain finite orders. The statistics considered in this chapter are more general in that null hypotheses can be less restrictive. For example, one may consider the null hypothesis being an AR(1) process and the alternative a high order autoregressive moving average process. However, under the strong hypothesis of no serial correlation being considered, the SSC in (18.2.10) does not necessarily reduce to an existing test. The difference is that the SSC in (18.2.10) will involve simulation even under the strong hypothesis.[2] It is possible to construct an SSC which can be reduced to existing ones without simulation under those strong hypotheses. To do that, one has to consider a different way of simulating the $Q(y, \theta, \theta^+)$ in (18.2.7). The issue under consideration concerns dynamic models. Consider a dynamic model with a latent dependent variable y_t^* at t. Let y_t be the corresponding sample observation. With a time series of length T, the time series of latent variables is $\bar{y}_T^* = (y_1^*, \ldots, y_T^*)$ and the vector of sample observations is $\bar{y}_T$. Furthermore, for any t, define $\bar{y}_t^* = (y_1^*, \ldots, y_t^*)$ and $\bar{y}_t = (y_1, \ldots, y_t)$. Also, denote $\bar{y}_{T,-t}^* = (y_1^*, \ldots, y_{t-1}^*, y_t^*, \ldots, y_T^*)$, the vector $\bar{y}_T^*$ with its component y_t^* deleted. The corresponding objective function for maximization of (18.2.7) is

$$Q(\bar{y}_T, \theta, \theta^+) = \int_{-\infty}^{\infty} [\ln g(\bar{y}_T^*, \bar{y}_T|\theta)] g(\bar{y}_T^*|\bar{y}_T, \theta^+) d\bar{y}_T^*. \tag{18.2.14}$$

In a time series context, the joint density can be factorized in a natural way as

$$g(\bar{y}_T^*, \bar{y}_T|\theta) = \prod_{t=1}^{T} g(y_t^*, y_t|\bar{y}_{t-1}^*, \bar{y}_{t-1}, \theta). \tag{18.2.15}$$

It follows that

$$\begin{aligned} Q(\bar{y}_T, \theta, \theta^+) = \sum_{t=1}^{T} \int_{-\infty}^{\infty} \int_{-\infty}^{\infty} & [\ln g(y_t^*, y_t|\bar{y}_{t-1}^*, \bar{y}_{t-1}, \theta)] \\ & \times g(y_t^*|\bar{y}_{T,-t}^*, \bar{y}_T, \theta^+) g(\bar{y}_{T,-t}^*|\bar{y}_T, \theta^+) dy_t^* d\bar{y}_{T,-t}^*. \end{aligned}$$

Let

$$R(\bar{y}_{T,-t}^*, \bar{y}_T, \theta, \theta^+) = \int_{-\infty}^{\infty} [\ln g(y_t^*, y_t|\bar{y}_{t-1}^*, \bar{y}_{t-1}, \theta)] g(y_t^*|\bar{y}_{T,-t}^*, \bar{y}_T, \theta^+) dy_t^*. \tag{18.2.16}$$

Then

$$\begin{aligned} Q(\bar{y}_T, \theta, \theta^+) &= \sum_{t=1}^{T} \int_{-\infty}^{\infty} R(\bar{y}_{T,-t}^*, \bar{y}_T, \theta, \theta^+) g(\bar{y}_{T,-t}^*|\bar{y}_T, \theta^+) d\bar{y}_{T,-t}^* \\ &= \sum_{t=1}^{T} \int_{-\infty}^{\infty} R(\bar{y}_{T,-t}^*, \bar{y}_T, \theta, \theta^+) g(\bar{y}_T^*|\bar{y}_T, \theta^+) d\bar{y}_T^* \tag{18.2.17} \\ &= \int_{-\infty}^{\infty} \left[\sum_{t=1}^{T} R(\bar{y}_{T,-t}^*, \bar{y}_T, \theta, \theta^+) \right] g(\bar{y}_T^*|\bar{y}_T, \theta^+) d\bar{y}_T^*. \end{aligned}$$

Instead of (18.2.9), the Q can be simulated by

$$\tilde{Q}_m(\bar{y}_T, \theta, \theta^+) = \frac{1}{m} \sum_{r=1}^{m} \left[\sum_{t=1}^{T} R(\bar{y}_{T,-t}^{*(r)}, \bar{y}_T, \theta, \theta^+) \right]. \tag{18.2.18}$$

The corresponding SSC is

$$\frac{\partial \tilde{Q}_m(\bar{y}_T, \theta, \theta^+)}{\partial \theta} = \frac{1}{m} \sum_{r=1}^{m} \left[\sum_{t=1}^{T} \frac{\partial R(\bar{y}_{T,-t}^{*(r)}, \bar{y}_T, \theta, \theta^+)}{\partial \theta} \right]. \tag{18.2.19}$$

The SSC for testing $H_0: \theta_2 = 0$ will be

$$\frac{\partial \tilde{Q}_m(\bar{y}_T, (\hat{\theta}_1, 0), \theta^+)}{\partial \theta} \bigg|_{\theta^+ = (\hat{\theta}_1, 0)} = \frac{1}{m} \sum_{r=1}^{m} \left[\sum_{t=1}^{T} \frac{\partial R(\bar{y}_{T,-t}^{*(r)}, \bar{y}_T, (\hat{\theta}_1, 0), \theta^+)}{\partial \theta} \right] \bigg|_{\theta^+ = (\hat{\theta}_1, 0)}. \tag{18.2.20}$$

This SSC will reduce to an exact score without simulation under the hypothesis of no latent dynamics because, under such a situation, $g(y_t^*, y_t | \bar{y}_{t-1}^*, \bar{y}_{t-1}, (\theta_1, 0)) = g(y_t^*, y_t | \bar{y}_{t-1}, (\theta_1, 0))$ and $g(y_t^* | \bar{y}_{T,-t}^*, \bar{y}_t, (\theta_1, 0)) = g(y_t^* | \bar{y}_t, (\theta_1, 0))$, hence the SSC in (18.2.20) does not depend on $\bar{y}_T^*$. The SSC (18.2.19) may have smaller simulation error than the one in (18.2.10) because it involves a smaller order of integrals. Its tractability, however, depends on the feasibility of an analytical evaluation of the integral in (18.2.16).[3] Models with the exponential family of distributions discussed in the Appendix provide some interesting examples.

18.3   Importance sampler and specification tests

The SEM is one of many possible approaches to the simulation estimation of an econometric model. For certain models, various computationally simple and adequate simulators unrelated to the SEM have been proposed. For the simulation estimation of multinormal choice probability models, the GHK simulator due to Geweke (1992), Borsch-Supan and Hajivassiliou (1993) and Keane (1994) is known to be accurate. The GHK simulator has been generalized to the simulation estimation of dynamic switching and disequilibrium market models and dynamic Tobit models in Lee (1997, 1999b). In this section, we consider the formulation of SSC test statistics which can accommodate such samplers and have similar conditional moment interpretations.

In an econometric model with latent dependent variables, the density or probability function of the general model is

$$f(y|\theta) = \int_{-\infty}^{\infty} g(y^*, y|\theta) dy^*. \tag{18.3.1}$$

The density (probability) function for the restricted model with $\theta_2 = 0$ is $f_c(y|\theta_1) = \int_{-\infty}^{\infty} g(y^*, y|(\theta_1, 0)) dy^*$. For the restricted model, suppose $g(y^*, y|(\theta_1, 0))$ can be decomposed as

$$g(y^*, y|(\theta_1, 0)) = h(y^*, y, \theta_1)\psi(y^*; y, \theta_1) \tag{18.3.2}$$

where $\psi(y^*; y, \theta_1)$ is a nonnegative function such that $\int_{-\infty}^{\infty} \psi(y^*; y, \theta_1) dy^* = 1$. Thus, $\psi(y^*; y, \theta_1)$ is a certain parametric density function even though it may not be equal to the conditional density $g(y^*|y, (\theta_1, 0))$ of y^* given y of the model. With such a decomposition, ψ can be used as a sampler and random variables $y^{*(r)}$ can be drawn with it. For simulation estimation, common random draws which do not change during parameter estimation guarantee equicontinuity of simulated estimating functions (McFadden, 1989; Pakes and Pollard, 1989). Without loss of generality, assume that y^* is a univariate latent random variable. The common random draws requirement can usually be achieved by drawing a set of uniform random variables $\xi^{(r)}, r = 1, \ldots, m$, which are fixed once they are drawn. For example, let $\Psi(y^*; y, \theta_1)$ be the corresponding distribution function of $\psi(y^*; y, \theta_1)$.

Then $y^{*(r)} = \Psi^{-1}(\xi^{(r)}; y, \theta_1)$ will be the desired random draws with the density $\psi(y^*; y, \theta_1)$. Since

$$f_c(y|\theta_1) = \int_{-\infty}^{\infty} h(y^*, y, \theta_1)\psi(y^*; y, \theta_1)dy^* \qquad (18.3.3)$$

from (18.3.1) and (18.3.2), the logarithmic restricted likelihood function can be simulated as

$$\ln L_{c,m}(\theta_1) = \ln\left\{\frac{1}{m}\sum_{r=1}^{m}h(\Psi^{-1}(\xi^{(r)}; y, \theta_1), y, \theta_1)\right\}. \qquad (18.3.4)$$

The corresponding simulated score vector for the restricted model is

$$\frac{\partial \ln L_{c,m}(\theta_1)}{\partial \theta_1} = \sum_{r=1}^{m}\left[\frac{\partial h(y^{*(r)}, y, \theta_1)}{\partial y^*}\frac{\partial \Psi^{-1}(\xi^{(r)}; y, \theta_1)}{\partial \theta_1} + \frac{\partial h(y^{*(r)}, y, \theta_1)}{\partial \theta_1}\right]\bigg/\sum_{s=1}^{m}h(y^{*(s)}, y, \theta_1).$$

$$(18.3.5)$$

For the testing of $\theta_2 = 0$, the general likelihood function is needed and shall be simulated. A feasible approach is to generalize the simulation in (18.3.4). The general likelihood in (18.3.1) can be rewritten as $f(y|\theta) = \int_{-\infty}^{\infty}[(g(y^*, y|\theta))/\psi((y^*; y, \theta_1))]\psi(y^*; y, \theta_1)dy^*$, under the assumption that the support of $\psi(y^*; y, \theta_1)$ in y^* is not a proper subset of that of $g(y^*, y|\theta)$. This suggests that the log likelihood function of the general model can be simulated as

$$\ln L_m(\theta) = \ln\left\{\frac{1}{m}\sum_{r=1}^{m}\frac{g(\Psi^{-1}(\xi^{(r)}; y, \theta_1), y|\theta)}{\psi(\Psi^{-1}(\xi^{(r)}; y, \theta_1); y, \theta_1)}\right\}. \qquad (18.3.6)$$

It follows from (18.3.6) that $(\partial \ln L_m(\theta))/\partial \theta_2 = \sum_{r=1}^{m}((\partial \ln g(y^{*(r)}, y|\theta))/\partial \theta_2((g(y^{*(r)}, y|\theta))/(\psi(y^{*(r)}; y, \theta_1))))/\sum_{s=1}^{m}(g(y^{*(s)}, y|\theta))/(\psi(y^{*(s)}; y, \theta_1))$. At $\theta_2 = 0$, it follows from (18.3.2) that

$$\frac{\partial \ln L_m(\theta_1, 0)}{\partial \theta_2} = \sum_{r=1}^{m}\frac{\partial \ln g(y^{*(r)}, y|(\theta_1, 0))}{\partial \theta_2}h(y^{*(r)}, y, \theta_1)\bigg/\sum_{s=1}^{m}h(y^{*(s)}, y, \theta_1)$$

$$= \sum_{r=1}^{m}\frac{\partial \ln g(y^{*(r)}, y|(\theta_1, 0))}{\partial \theta_2}\omega_r(\theta_1), \qquad (18.3.7)$$

where $\omega_r(\theta_1) = h(y^{*(r)}, y, \theta_1)/\sum_{s=1}^{m}h(y^{*(s)}, y, \theta_1)$ can be regarded as weights. Similarly,

$$\frac{\partial \ln L_m(\theta)}{\partial \theta_1} = \sum_{r=1}^{m}\left[\frac{\partial \ln g(y^{*(r)}, y|\theta)}{\partial y^*}\frac{\partial \Psi^{-1}(\xi^{(r)}; y, \theta_1)}{\partial \theta_1} + \frac{\partial \ln g(y^{*(r)}, y|\theta)}{\partial \theta_1}\right.$$

$$\left. -\frac{\partial \ln \psi(y^{*(r)}; y, \theta_1)}{\partial y^*}\frac{\partial \Psi^{-1}(\xi^{(r)}; y, \theta_1)}{\partial \theta_1} - \frac{\partial \ln \psi(y^{*(r)}; y, \theta_1)}{\partial \theta_1}\right]$$

$$\times \frac{g(y^{*(r)}, y|\theta)/\psi(y^{*(r)}; y, \theta)}{\sum_{s=1}^{m}g(y^{*(s)}|y, \theta)/\psi(y^{*(s)}; y, \theta_1)}.$$

At $\theta_2 = 0$, because

$$\frac{\partial \ln g(y^{*(r)}, y|(\theta_1, 0))}{\partial y^*} = \frac{\partial \ln h(y^{*(r)}, y, \theta_1)}{\partial y^*} + \frac{\partial \ln \psi(y^{*(r)}; y, \theta_1)}{\partial y^*}$$

and

$$\frac{\partial \ln g(y^{*(r)}, y|(\theta_1, 0))}{\partial \theta_1} = \frac{\partial \ln h(y^{*(r)}, y, \theta_1)}{\partial \theta_1} + \frac{\partial \ln \psi(y^{*(r)}; y, \theta_1)}{\partial \theta_1}$$

from (18.3.2),

$$\frac{\partial \ln L_m(\theta_1, 0)}{\partial \theta_1} = \sum_{r=1}^{m} \left[\frac{\partial \ln h(y^{*(r)}, y, \theta_1)}{\partial y^*} \frac{\partial \Psi^{-1}(\xi^{(r)}; y, \theta_1)}{\partial \theta_1} + \frac{\partial \ln h(y^{*(r)}, y, \theta_1)}{\partial \theta_1} \right] \omega_r(\theta_1),$$

$$(18.3.5)'$$

which is equal to $(\partial \ln L_{c,m}(\theta_1))/\partial \theta_1$ in (18.3.5) as expected. With the second-order derivatives derived from (18.3.6), the SSC statistic is

$$\frac{\partial \ln L_m(\theta_1, 0)}{\partial \theta'} \left[-\frac{\partial^2 \ln L_m(\theta_1, 0)}{\partial \theta \partial \theta'} \right]^{-1} \frac{\partial \ln L_m(\theta_1, 0)}{\partial \theta} \bigg|_{\theta_1 = \hat{\theta}_1}. \qquad (18.3.8)$$

This formulation of the simulated score statistic in (18.3.8) involves only the same sampler for the simulation estimation of the restricted model.[4] Simulation does not create additional complexity in this formulation of the SSC. The SSC in (18.3.7) has a similar interpretation as the one in (18.2.10) for the simulated EM approach. The only differences are the samplers and the weights $w_j(\theta_1)$ used in (18.3.7) instead of identical weights in (18.2.11).

A version of the SSC corresponding to (18.2.20) for a dynamic model can also be derived. In a time series context, $f(\bar{y}_T|\theta) = \int_{-\infty}^{\infty} g(\bar{y}_T^*, \bar{y}_T|\theta) d\bar{y}_T^*$. With the density factorization in (18.2.15),

$$\frac{\partial f(\bar{y}_T|\theta)}{\partial \theta} = \int_{-\infty}^{\infty} \left(\sum_{t=1}^{T} \frac{\partial \ln g(y_t^*, y_t|\bar{y}_{t-1}^*, \bar{y}_{t-1}, \theta)}{\partial \theta} \right) g(\bar{y}_T^*, \bar{y}_T|\theta) d\bar{y}_T^*$$

$$= \sum_{t=1}^{T} \int_{-\infty}^{\infty} \int_{-\infty}^{\infty} \frac{\partial \ln g(y_t^*, y_t|\bar{y}_{t-1}^*, \bar{y}_{t-1}, \theta)}{\partial \theta}$$

$$\times g(\bar{y}_t^*|\bar{y}_{T,-t}^*, \bar{y}_T, \theta) g(\bar{y}_{T,-t}^*, \bar{y}_T|\theta) dy_t^* d\bar{y}_{T,-t}^*.$$

Denote $R_\theta(\bar{y}_{T,-t}^*, \bar{y}_T, \theta) = \int_{-\infty}^{\infty} (\partial \ln g(y_t^*, y_t|\bar{y}_{t-1}^*, \bar{y}_{t-1}, \theta))/\partial \theta \, g(\bar{y}_t^*|\bar{y}_{T,-t}^*, \bar{y}_T, \theta) dy_t^*$. It follows that

$$\frac{\partial f(\bar{y}_T|\theta)}{\partial \theta} = \sum_{t=1}^{T} \int_{-\infty}^{\infty} R_\theta(\bar{y}_{T,-t}^*, \bar{y}_T, \theta) g(\bar{y}_{T,-t}^*, \bar{y}_T|\theta) d\bar{y}_{T,-t}^*$$

$$= \int_{-\infty}^{\infty} \left[\sum_{t=1}^{T} R_\theta(\bar{y}_{T,-t}^*, \bar{y}_T, \theta) \right] g(\bar{y}_T^*, \bar{y}_T|\theta) d\bar{y}_T^*.$$

Suppose that the corresponding decomposition of (18.3.2) is $g(\bar{y}_T^*, \bar{y}_T|(\theta_1, 0)) = h(\bar{y}_T^*, \bar{y}_T, \theta_1)\psi(\bar{y}_T^*; \bar{y}_T, \theta_1)$, then

$$\frac{\partial f(\bar{y}_T|(\theta_1, 0))}{\partial \theta} = \int_{-\infty}^{\infty} \left[\sum_{t=1}^{T} R_\theta(\bar{y}_{T, -t}^*, \bar{y}_T, (\theta_1, 0))\right] h(\bar{y}_T^*, \bar{y}_T, \theta_1)\psi(\bar{y}_T^*; \bar{y}_T, \theta_1)d\bar{y}_T^*. \quad (18.3.9)$$

This score can be simulated as

$$S_m(\theta_1) = \sum_{r=1}^{m}\left[\sum_{t=1}^{T} R_\theta\left(\bar{y}_{T, -t}^{*(r)}, \bar{y}_T, (\theta_1, 0)\right)\right]\omega_r(\theta_1), \quad (18.3.10)$$

where

$$\omega_r(\theta_1) = h\left(\bar{y}_T^{*(r)}, \bar{y}_T, \theta_1\right) \bigg/ \sum_{s-1}^{m} h\left(\bar{y}_T^{*(s)}, \bar{y}_T, \theta_1\right) \quad (18.3.11)$$

with $\bar{y}_T^*(r)$ being a random draw with the density $\psi(\bar{y}_T^*; \bar{y}_T, \theta_1)$. This SSC generalizes the one in (18.2.20) to the case with an importance sampler.

18.4 The multinormal discrete choice model

A general polychotomous choice model with $J + 1$ choice alternatives under utility maximization is

$$y_j^* = x_j\beta + \sigma_j u_j, \quad j = 1, \ldots, J+1, \quad (18.4.1)$$

where y_j^* is the utility of the choice alternative j. The observed dependent variable y is the index of the chosen alternative. The alternative j is chosen, i.e., $y = j$, if $y_j^* \geq y_l^*$ for all $l \neq j$; $l = 1, \ldots, J+1$. For normalization, $y_{J+1}^* = 0$ and $\sigma_1 = 1$. Let $u = (u_1, \ldots, u_J)'$ and $\bar{y}_J^* = (y_1^*, \ldots, y_J^*)'$. The joint density of $(\bar{y}_J^*, y)$ conditional on all exogenous variables x (with x and θ suppressed) is

$$g(\bar{y}_J^*, y) = S(\bar{y}_J^*|y)g(\bar{y}_J^*), \quad (18.4.2)$$

where $S(\bar{y}_J^*|y) = I_{\{\bar{y}_J^*: y_y^* = \max_{l=1, \ldots, J+1} y_l^*\}}(\bar{y}_J^*)$ is the indicator of a choice y and $I_A(\bar{y}_J^*)$ is the indicator of a set A. The choice probability is

$$P(y) = \int_{-\infty}^{\infty} \cdots \int_{-\infty}^{\infty} S(\bar{y}_J^*|y)g(\bar{y}_J^*)dy_1^* \cdots dy_J^*. \quad (18.4.3)$$

For the multinormal probit model, numerical evidence shows that its choice probabilities can be accurately approximated by the GHK simulator

(Geweke, 1992; Borsch-Supan and Hajivassiliou, 1993; Keane, 1994). The formulation of the GHK simulator can be generalized to models beyond the multinormal probit. For notational simplicity, let $\bar{y}_j^* = (y_1^*, \ldots, y_j^*)'$ be a vector consisting of elements from y_1^* to y_j^*. Let I_j be a dichotomous indicator such that $I_j = 1$ if $y = j$; 0 otherwise. Consider $g(\bar{y}_J^*, I_1 = 1)$. This mixed joint density can be decomposed into a product of conditional densities and probabilities:

$$
g(\bar{y}_J^*, I_1 = 1) = \prod_{j=2}^{J} g(y_j^* | \bar{y}_{j-1}^*, y_1^* > y_j^*) P(y_1^* > y_j^* | \bar{y}_{j-1}^*) \cdot g(y_1^* | y_1^* > 0) P(y_1^* > 0)
$$

$$
= \left[\prod_{j=2}^{J} P(y_1^* > y_j^* | \bar{y}_{j-1}^*) \cdot P(y_1^* > 0) \right] \left[\prod_{j=2}^{J} g(y_j^* | \bar{y}_{j-1}^*, y_1^* > y_j^*) g(y_1^* | y_1^* > 0) \right].
$$

Since $P(y_1 = 1) = \int_{-\infty}^{\infty} g(\bar{y}_J^*, y_1 = 1) d\bar{y}_J^*$, the sampler is to draw random variables with the density $\prod_{j=2}^{J} g(y_j^* | \bar{y}_{j-1}^*, y_1^* > y_j^*) \cdot g(y_1^* | y_1^* > 0)$ and estimate the probability by the simulator $\frac{1}{m} \sum_{r=1}^{m} \prod_{j=2}^{J} P(y_1^* > y_j^{*(r)} | \bar{y}_{j-1}^{*(r)}) \cdot P(y_1^* > 0)$. Probabilities for other choice alternatives can similarly be simulated. The likelihood function for a sample observation can be simulated with the GHK sampler as

$$
L_m = \prod_{j=1}^{J} \left\{ \frac{1}{m} \sum_{r=1}^{m} \prod_{l=1, l \neq j}^{J} P\left(y_l^{*(r)} > y_l^* | \bar{y}_{(l-1,+j)}^{*(r)}\right) \cdot P\left(y_j^* > 0\right) \right\}^{I_j} \left\{ \frac{1}{m} \sum_{r=1}^{m} \prod_{l=1}^{J} P\left(0 > y_l^* | \bar{y}_{l-1}^{*(r)}\right) \right\}^{I_{J+1}}
$$

$$
= \frac{1}{m} \sum_{r=1}^{m} \left\{ \sum_{j=1}^{J} I_j \left[\prod_{l=1, l \neq j}^{J} P\left(y_j^{*(r)} > y_l^* | \bar{y}_{(l-1,+j)}^{*(r)}\right) \cdot P\left(y_j^* > 0\right) \right] + I_{J+1} \left[\prod_{l=1}^{J} P\left(0 > y_l^* | \bar{y}_{l-1}^{*(r)}\right) \right] \right\},
$$

$$(18.4.4)$$

where $\bar{y}_{(k,+j)}^* = (y_j^*, y_1^*, \ldots, y_{k-1}^*, y_k^*)$ when $j > k$, and $\bar{y}_{(k,+j)}^* = (y_j^*, y_1^*, \ldots, y_{j-1}^*, y_{j+1}^*, \ldots, y_k^*)$ when $j \leq k$; and as a convention, $\bar{y}_{(0,+j)}^* = y_j^*$. With the GHK sampler, the weight for the rth simulation run is

$$
\omega_r = \frac{\sum_{j=1}^{J} I_j \left[\prod_{l=1, l \neq j}^{J} P\left(y_l^{*(r)} > y_l^* | \bar{y}_{(l-1,+j)}^{*(r)}\right) \cdot P(y_j^* > 0) \right] + I_{J+1} \left[\prod_{l=1}^{J} P\left(0 > y_l^* | \bar{y}_{l-1}^{*(r)}\right) \right]}{\sum_{s=1}^{m} \left\{ \sum_{j=1}^{J} I_j \left[\prod_{l=1, l \neq j}^{J} P\left(y_j^{*(s)} > y_l^* | \bar{y}_{(l-1,+j)}^{*(s)}\right) \cdot P(y_j^* > 0) \right] + I_{J+1} \left[\prod_{l=1}^{J} P\left(0 > y_l^* | \bar{y}_{l-1}^{*(s)}\right) \right] \right\}}.
$$

$$(18.4.5)$$

A multinormal choice model assumes that the distribution of u is $N(0, R)$ where R is a correlation matrix. Let $\bar{x} = (x_1', \ldots, x_J')'$. The $\bar{y}_J^*$ is normally distributed with the density

$$
g(\bar{y}_J^*; \Omega) = \frac{1}{(2\pi)^{J/2} |\Omega|^{1/2}} \exp\left\{ -\frac{1}{2} (\bar{y}_J^* - \bar{x}\beta)' \Omega^{-1} (\bar{y}_J^* - \bar{x}\beta) \right\}, \qquad (18.4.6)
$$

where $\Omega = \Lambda R \Lambda$ and Λ is a diagonal matrix with diagonal elements $\sigma_1, \ldots, \sigma_J$. In this case, the density functions $g(y_j^*|\bar{y}_{j-1}^*, y_1^* > y_j^*)$ in the sampler are univariate truncated normal densities, and $P(y_1^* > y_j^*|\bar{y}_{j-1})$ are truncated univariate normal probabilities.

18.4.1 The omitted variables test

A test of omitted variables in a multinormal choice model is simple. For example, testing that a subset of variables $\bar{x}_2$ in $\bar{x} = (\bar{x}_1, \bar{x}_2)$ does not enter the utilities is a test of the corresponding coefficient vector β_2 in $\beta = (\beta_1', \beta_2')$ being zero. Since $(\partial \ln g(\bar{y}_j^*))/\partial \beta = \bar{x}'\Omega^{-1}(\bar{y}_j^* - \bar{x}\beta)$, $(\partial \ln P(y))/\partial \beta = \bar{x}'\Omega^{-1}E(\bar{y}_j^* - \bar{x}\beta|y)$ from (18.2.5). With the GHK sampler, the SSC of (18.3.7) for a sample of size n is

$$\frac{\partial \ln L_{n,m}}{\partial \beta} = \sum_{i=1}^{n} \bar{x}_i'\Omega^{-1}\left(\sum_{r=1}^{m} \left(\bar{y}_{ji}^{*(r)} - \bar{x}_i\beta\right)\omega_{is}\right), \tag{18.4.7}$$

where the subscript i refers to the ith sample observation. This specification test is a test of whether the variables in $\bar{x}_2$ are correlated with the generalized residual $E(\bar{y}_j^* - \bar{x}_1\beta_1|y)$, after proper weighting with Ω^{-1}. The GHK sampler provides a simulator $\sum_{r=1}^{m}(\bar{y}_{ji}^{*(r)} - \bar{x}_{i1}\beta_1)\omega_{is}$ for $E(\bar{y}_j^* - \bar{x}_1\beta_1|y)$.

18.4.2 A normality test

Suppose that the density of u admits a J-variate Gram–Charlier expansion as $f(u) = K(u)\phi(u; 0, R)$, where $K(u) = \left[1 + \sum_{j_1 + \cdots + j_J \geq 3} c_{j_1 \ldots j_J} H(u; j_1, \ldots, j_J, R)\right]$ and $\phi(u; 0, R)$ is a standardized J-variate normal density with the correlation matrix R, and Hs are Hermite polynomials (see Kendall and Stuart, 1977; Johnson and Kotz, 1976). A test of normality will test the parameters $c_{j_1 \ldots j_J}$ being zero for all $j_1 + \cdots + j_J \geq 3$. The nesting of the normality distribution within a Gram–Charlier expansion in limited dependent variable models can be found in Lee (1984b) and Smith (1987), among others.[5] The density of $\bar{y}_j^*$ under this representation is

$$g(\bar{y}_j^*) = K(\Lambda^{-1}(\bar{y}_j^* - \bar{x}\beta))g(\bar{y}_j^*; \Omega). \tag{18.4.8}$$

The log density of $(\bar{y}_j^*, y)$ is

$$\ln g(\bar{y}_j^*, y) = S(\bar{y}_j^*|y)\{\ln K(\Lambda^{-1}(\bar{y}_j^* - \bar{x}\beta)) + \ln g(\bar{y}_j^*; \Omega)\}, \tag{18.4.9}$$

from (18.4.1), (18.4.6) and (18.4.8). It follows that $(\partial \ln g(\bar{y}_j^*, y))/\partial c_{j_1 \ldots j_J} = S(\bar{y}_j^*|y)$ $(H(\Lambda^{-1}(\bar{y}_j^* - \bar{x}\beta); j_1, \ldots, j_J, R))/(K(\Lambda^{-1}(\bar{y}_j^* - \bar{x}\beta)))$. Hence, a normality test will be based on $(\partial \ln P(y))/(\partial c_{j_1 \ldots j_J})|_{c=0} = E_{c=0}[H(\Lambda^{-1}(\bar{y}_j^* - \bar{x}\beta); j_1, \ldots, j_J, R)|y]$. With the GHK sampler, the SSC of (18.3.7) is

$$\frac{\partial \ln L_{n,m}}{\partial c_{j_1 \ldots j_J}}\bigg|_{c=0} = \sum_{i=1}^{n}\sum_{r=1}^{m} H\left(\Lambda^{-1}\left(\bar{y}_{ji}^{*(r)} - \bar{x}_i\beta\right); j_1, \ldots, j_J, R\right)\omega_{ir}. \tag{18.4.10}$$

This specification test is a test of normality based on simulated conditional higher order moment properties of the multivariate normal distribution.

18.5   Dynamic discrete choice panel data models

Consider the general dynamic discrete choice panel data model of Heckman (1981):

$$y_{it}^* = x_{it}\beta + \sum_{l=1}^{L_1} \gamma_l y_{i,t-l} + \sum_{k=1}^{L_2} \lambda_k \prod_{l=1}^{k} y_{i,t-l} + \sum_{l=1}^{L_3} \delta_l y_{i,t-l}^* + v_{it}, \tag{18.5.1}$$

where the observed dependent variable is

$$y_{it} = \begin{cases} 1 & \text{if } y_{it}^* > 0, \\ 0 & \text{if } y_{it}^* \le 0. \end{cases}$$

The disturbance process is $v_{it} = \sigma\xi_i + \varepsilon_{it}$, where ε_{it} is an ARMA(p,q) process: $\varepsilon_{it} = \sum_{l=1}^{p} \rho_l \varepsilon_{i,t-l} + w_{it} + \sum_{j=1}^{q} \psi_j w_{i,t-j}$. For normalization, w_{it} has a unit variance. The ξ_i and w_{it} are independently $N(0,1)$ distributed for all i and t and are independent of all x's. The ξ_i is a random component.

Consider the likelihood function of an individual time series (with the subscript i suppressed for simplicity). Let $\bar{y}_t = (y_1, \dots, y_t)$ denote the observed ys preceding and up to the time period t. The observed sample for an individual is $\bar{y}_T$. Similarly, denote $\bar{y}_t^*$ for the y^*s. The joint probability of a $\bar{y}_T$ conditional on all exogenous variables x and ξ (with x and the parameter vector θ suppressed) is $P(\bar{y}_T|\xi) = \int_{-\infty}^{\infty} \cdots \int_{-\infty}^{\infty} g(\bar{y}_T^*, \bar{y}_T|\xi)d\bar{y}_T^*$ and the unconditional probability is

$$P(\bar{y}_T) = \int_{-\infty}^{\infty} \cdots \int_{-\infty}^{\infty} g(\bar{y}_T, \bar{y}_T^*|\xi)\phi(\xi)d\bar{y}_T^*d\xi, \tag{18.5.2}$$

where ϕ is the standard normal density function.[6] The mixed joint density of $(\bar{y}_T, \bar{y}_T^*)$ can be factorized in various ways. One of the decompositions is $g(\bar{y}_T^*, \bar{y}_T|\xi) = \prod_{t=1}^{T} S(y_t^*|y_t)g(y_t^*|\bar{y}_{t-1}^*, \bar{y}_{t-1}, \xi)$, where $S(y_t^*|y_t) = y_t I_{(0,\infty)}(y_t^*) + (1-y_t)I_{(-\infty,0)}(y_t^*)$. Hence

$$g(\bar{y}_T^*, \bar{y}_T, \xi) = \prod_{t=1}^{T} S(y_t^*|y_t)g(y_t^*|\bar{y}_{t-1}^*, \bar{y}_{t-1}, \xi) \cdot \phi(\xi). \tag{18.5.3}$$

The GHK simulation of these probabilities and the likelihood function is as follows. Let $a_t = x_t\beta + \sum_{l=1}^{L_1} \gamma_l y_{t-l} + \sum_{k=1}^{L_2} \lambda_k \prod_{l=1}^{k} y_{t-l} + \sum_{l=1}^{L_3} \delta_l y_{t-l}^* + \sigma\xi$. The joint probability of $\bar{y}_T$ conditional on ξ is

$$P(\bar{y}_T|\xi) = \int_{L_1}^{U_1} \cdots \int_{L_T}^{U_T} g(\varepsilon_T|\varepsilon_{T-1}, \dots, \varepsilon_1)g(\varepsilon_{T-1}|\varepsilon_{T-2}, \dots, \varepsilon_1), \dots, g(\varepsilon_1)d\varepsilon_T, \dots, d\varepsilon_1,$$

where the integral limits are

$$L_t = \begin{cases} -a_t & \text{if } y_t = 1, \\ -\infty & \text{if } y_t = 0, \end{cases} \qquad U_t = \begin{cases} \infty & \text{if } y_t = 1, \\ -a_t & \text{if } y_t = 0. \end{cases}$$

Denote $b_t = a_t + \sum_{l=1}^{p} \rho_l \varepsilon_{t-l} + \sum_{j=1}^{q} \psi_j w_{t-j}$ and

$$
\bar{L}_t = \begin{cases} -b_t & \text{if } y_t = 1, \\ -\infty & \text{if } y_t = 0, \end{cases} \qquad \bar{U}_t = \begin{cases} \infty & \text{if } y_t = 1, \\ -b_t & \text{if } y_t = 0. \end{cases}
$$

By a transformation of variables, $P(\bar{y}_T | \xi) = \int_{\bar{L}_1}^{\bar{U}_1} \cdots \left(\int_{\bar{L}_{T-1}}^{\bar{U}_{T-1}} \left[\int_{\bar{L}_T}^{\bar{U}_T} \phi(w_T) dw_T \right] \phi(w_{T-1}) dw_{T-1} \right), \ldots, \phi(w_1) dw_1$. The joint probability can then be written as

$$
\begin{aligned}
P(\bar{y}_T) &= \int_{-\infty}^{\infty} \cdots \int_{-\infty}^{\infty} [\Phi(\bar{U}_T) - \Phi(\bar{L}_T)] \prod_{t=1}^{T-1} [\Phi(\bar{U}_t) - \Phi(\bar{L}_t)] \phi_{[\bar{L}_t, \bar{U}_t]}(w_t) dw_t \cdot \phi(\xi) d\xi \\
&= \int_{-\infty}^{\infty} \cdots \int_{-\infty}^{\infty} \Phi(D_T b_T) \prod_{t=1}^{T-1} \Phi(D_t b_t) \phi_{[\bar{L}_t, \bar{U}_t]}(w_t) dw_t \cdot \phi(\xi) d\xi,
\end{aligned} \tag{18.5.4}
$$

where $\phi_{[\bar{L}_t, \bar{U}_t]}(w_t)$ is a truncated standard normal density function with support $[\bar{L}_t, \bar{U}_t]$, Φ is the standard normal distribution function, and D_t is an indicator such that $D_t = 1$ if $y_t = 1$ and $D_t = -1$ if $y_t = 0$. The GHK simulator is constructed with random draws from the density $\prod_{t=1}^{T} \phi_{[\bar{L}_t, \bar{U}_t]}(w_t) \cdot \phi(\xi)$. With m simulation runs, the log likelihood for a panel with n cross-section units can be simulated as

$$
\ln L_{n, m} = \sum_{i=1}^{n} \ln \left\{ \frac{1}{m} \sum_{r=1}^{m} \left[\prod_{t=1}^{T} \Phi \left(D_{it} b_{it}^{(r)} \right) \right] \right\}, \tag{18.5.5}
$$

where $b_{it}^{(r)} = x_{it} \beta + \sum_{l=1}^{L_1} \gamma_l y_{i, t-l} + \sum_{k=1}^{L_2} \lambda_k \prod_{l=1}^{k} y_{i, t-l} + \sum_{l=1}^{L_3} \delta_l y_{i, t-l}^{*(r)} + \sigma \xi_i^{(r)} + \sum_{l=1}^{p} \rho_l$ $\varepsilon_{i, t-l}^{*(r)} + \sum_{l=1}^{q} \psi_l w_{i, t-l}^{(r)}$. Equivalently, this simulator is based on the decomposition $g(\bar{y}_T^*, \bar{y}_T, \xi) = \prod_{t=1}^{T} \Phi(D_t b_t) \phi_{[\bar{L}_t, \bar{U}_t]}(w_t) \cdot \phi(\xi)$. Therefore, with the GHK sampler, the weights are

$$
\omega_{ir} = \prod_{t=1}^{T} \Phi \left(D_{it} b_{it}^{(r)} \right) \bigg/ \sum_{s=1}^{m} \prod_{t=1}^{T} \Phi \left(D_{it} b_{it}^{(s)} \right). \tag{18.5.6}
$$

Monte Carlo results on the performance of the GHK simulator for the estimation of the general dynamic model (18.5.1) can be found in Lee (1998). Unless the time dimension of the panel data is quite lengthy, the GHK simulator provides accurate parameter estimates of the model. With lengthy panels, an accelerated importance sampler can provide a better simulator, as demonstrated in Zhang and Lee (2004).[7]

18.5.1 Omitted variables, higher-order serial correlation or state dependence tests

As (18.5.1) can be rewritten as $y_t^* = b_t + w_t$, $g(y_t^* | \bar{y}_{t-1}^*, \bar{y}_{t-1}, \xi) = \phi(y_t^* - b_t)$. From (18.5.3),

$$
\ln g(\bar{y}_T^*, \bar{y}_T, \xi) = \sum_{t=1}^{T} S(y_t^* | y_t) \ln \phi(y_t^* - b_t) + \ln \phi(\xi). \tag{18.5.7}
$$

Under the normality assumption, as $(\partial \ln \phi(y_t^* - b_t))/\partial \theta = (y_t^* - b_t)(\partial b_t/\partial \theta)$ and $\phi(\xi)$ does not depend on θ, it follows from (18.5.7) that $(\partial \ln g(\bar{y}_T^*, \bar{y}_T, \xi))/\partial \theta = \sum_{t=1}^{T} S(y_t^*|y_t)(y_t^* - b_t)(\partial b_t/\partial \theta)$. Therefore, from (18.5.2),

$$
\begin{aligned}
\frac{\partial \ln P(\bar{y}_T)}{\partial \theta} &= \int_{-\infty}^{\infty} \cdots \int_{-\infty}^{\infty} \left(\frac{\partial \ln g(\bar{y}_T^*, \bar{y}_T, \xi)}{\partial \theta} \right) \frac{g(\bar{y}_T^*, \bar{y}_T, \xi)}{P(\bar{y}_T)} d\bar{y}_T^* d\xi \\
&= \sum_{t=1}^{T} E_\theta \left[(y_t^* - b_t) \frac{\partial b_t}{\partial \theta} \bigg| \bar{y}_T \right].
\end{aligned}
$$

The tests of omitted variables in x or higher order serial correlation or state dependence are different only in the expressions for $\partial b_t/\partial \theta$. All these tests can be broadly treated as a test of omitted variables, where the omitted variables can be variables in x, lagged dependent variables of y or y^*, or lagged disturbances of ε^* or $w_{i,t-1}$. This specification is to test the conditional correlation of the omitted variables with the residual $(y_t^* - b_t)$ under the null hypothesis.

With the GHK sampler, the SSC corresponding to (18.3.7) of the model (18.5.1) is

$$
\frac{\partial \ln L_{n,m}(\theta)}{\partial \theta} = \sum_{i=1}^{n} \left\{ \frac{1}{m} \sum_{r=1}^{m} \left[\sum_{t=1}^{T} \left(y_{it}^{*(r)} - b_{it}^{(r)} \right) \frac{\partial b_{it}^{(r)}}{\partial \theta} \right] \omega_{ir} \right\}. \tag{18.5.8}
$$

18.5.2 A normality test

Suppose that the density $g(w)$ of w can be represented by a Gram–Charlier Series $g(w) = [1 + \sum_{j \geq 3} c_j H_j(w)]\phi(w)$ and the density $g(\xi)$ of ξ by $g(\xi) = [1 + \sum_{j \geq 3} d_j H_j(\xi)]\phi(\xi)$. These expansions imply that $g(\bar{y}_T^*, \bar{y}_T, \xi) = \left\{ \prod_{t=1}^{T} S(y_t^*|y_t) \left[1 + \sum_{j \geq 3} c_j H_j(y_t^* - b_t)]\phi(y_t^* - b_t) \right\} \left[1 + \sum_{j \geq 3} d_j H_j(\xi) \right] \phi(\xi)$. It contains (18.5.7) as a special case with $c = d = 0$. It follows that $(\partial \ln g(\bar{y}_T^*, \bar{y}_T, \xi))/\partial c_j = \sum_{t=1}^{T} S(y_t^*|y_t)(H_j(y_t^* - b_t))/(1 + \sum_{j \geq 3} c_j H_j(y_t^* - b_t))$, and $(\partial \ln g(\bar{y}_T^*, \bar{y}_T, \xi))/\partial d_j = H_j(\xi)/(1 + \sum_{j \geq 3} d_j H_j(\xi))$ for $j \geq 3$. Hence $((\partial \ln P(\bar{y}_T))/\partial c_j)|_{c=0} = \sum_{t=1}^{T} E_{H_o}[H_j(y_t^* - b_t)|\bar{y}_T]$, and $((\partial \ln P(\bar{y}_T))/\partial d_j)|_{d=0} = \sum_{t=1}^{T} E_{H_o}[H_j(\xi)|\bar{y}_T]$. The test for normality can be based on these functions of conditional high-order moments.

For the GHK simulation approach, as

$$
\begin{aligned}
P(\bar{y}_T) = \int_{-\infty}^{\infty} \cdots \int_{-\infty}^{\infty} \prod_{t=1}^{T} \left(1 + \sum_{j \geq 3} c_j H_j(w_t) \right) \Phi(D_t b_t) \phi_{[\bar{L}_t, \bar{U}_t]}(w_t) dw_t \\
\times \left(1 + \sum_{j \geq 3} d_j H_j(\xi) \right) \phi(\xi) d\xi,
\end{aligned}
$$

the simulated log likelihood function for the general model is

$$
\ln L_{n,m} = \sum_{i=1}^{n} \ln \left\{ \frac{1}{m} \sum_{r=1}^{m} \left[\prod_{t=1}^{T} \left(1 + \sum_{j \geq 3} c_j H_j\left(w_{it}^{(r)} \right) \right) \Phi\left(D_{it} b_{it}^{(r)} \right) \right] \left(1 + \sum_{j \geq 3} d_j H_j\left(\xi_i^{(r)} \right) \right) \right\}.
$$

$$\tag{18.5.9}$$

Under the null hypothesis $H_0 : c = 0, d = 0$, $(\partial \ln L_{n,m}(\theta_1, 0))/\partial \theta_1 = \sum_{i=1}^{n} \sum_{r=1}^{m}$ $\left(\sum_{t=1}^{T}(\partial \ln \Phi(D_{it} b_{it}^{(r)}))/\partial \theta_1\right) \omega_{ir}$, where θ_1 is the vector of parameters of the model (18.5.1) under the normality hypothesis.

The SSC of (18.3.7) for the normality test are

$$\frac{\partial \ln L_{n,m}(\theta_1, 0)}{\partial c_l} = \sum_{i=1}^{n} \sum_{r=1}^{m} \left(\sum_{t=1}^{T} H_l\left(y_{it}^{*(r)} - b_{it}^{(r)}\right)\right) \omega_{ir}, \tag{18.5.10}$$

as $w_{it}^{(r)} = y_{it}^{*(r)} - b_{it}^{(r)}$, and

$$\frac{\partial L_{n,m}(\theta_1, 0)}{\partial d_l} = \sum_{i=1}^{n} \sum_{r=1}^{m} H_l(\varsigma_i^{(r)}) \omega_{ir}. \tag{18.5.11}$$

18.6   Dynamic Tobit models

Consider the following general dynamic Tobit model:

$$y_t^* = x_t \beta + \sum_{j=1}^{J} y_{t-j} \gamma_j + \sum_{l=1}^{L} y_{t-l}^* \delta_l + \sigma_t u_t,$$

where u_t are i.i.d. $N(0,1)$. The observed sample is $y_t = \max\{y_t^*, c_t\}$, where c_t are known constants. In a dynamic model with homoskedastic disturbances, $\sigma_t = \sigma$, a constant, for all t. If $\sigma_t^2 = \alpha_{1,1} + \sum_{j=1}^{p} \alpha_{2,j} \varepsilon_{t-j}^2$, where $\varepsilon_t = \sigma_t u_t$, it is a Tobit ARCH model with an ARCH(p) process. If $\sigma_t^2 = \alpha_{1,1} + \sum_{j=1}^{p} \alpha_{2,j} \varepsilon_{t-j}^2 + \sum_{k=1}^{q} \alpha_{3,k} \sigma_{t-k}^2$, it is a Tobit GARCH model with a GARCH(p,q) process. For a given time series of length T, suppose that censoring occurs at $t_1, \ldots, t_m$, with $t_1 < \cdots < t_m$. Define dichotomous censoring indicators I_t such that $I_t = 0$ if $y_t^* \le c_t$; 1 otherwise. Let $\bar{I}_t = (I_1, \ldots, I_t)$. The mixed joint density of latent and observed dependent variables (with x and parameters suppressed) is

$$g(\bar{y}_T^*, \bar{y}_T, \bar{I}_T) = S(\bar{y}_T^* | \bar{y}_T, \bar{I}_T) \prod_{s \notin \{t_1, \ldots, t_m\}} g(y_s | \bar{y}_{s-1}^*, \bar{y}_{s-1}) \cdot \prod_{s \in \{t_1, \ldots, t_m\}} g(y_s^* | \bar{y}_{s-1}^*, \bar{y}_{s-1}),$$

$$\tag{18.6.1}$$

where $S(\bar{y}_T^* | \bar{y}_T, \bar{I}_T) = \prod_{s \in \{t_1, \ldots, t_m\}} I_{(-\infty, c_s)}(y_s^*)$ is the indicator of censoring occurs at $t_1, \ldots, t_m$ for the sample path $\bar{I}_T$. The likelihood function is

$$f(\bar{y}_T, \bar{I}_T) = \int_{-\infty}^{\infty} \cdots \int_{-\infty}^{\infty} S(\bar{y}_T^* | \bar{y}_T, \bar{I}_T) \left[\prod_{s \notin \{t_1, \ldots, t_m\}} g(y_s | \bar{y}_{s-1}^*, \bar{y}_{s-1}) \right.$$

$$\tag{18.6.2}$$

$$\left. \times \prod_{s \in \{t_1, \ldots, t_m\}} g(y_s^* | \bar{y}_{s-1}^*, \bar{y}_{s-1}) \right] dy_{t_1}^*, \ldots, dy_{t_m}^*.$$

Define $\tilde{y}_t = I_t y_t + (1 - I_t) y_t^*$, which is, in fact, y_t^* but emphasizes that $y_t^* = y_t$ when y_t^* is not censored. Similarly, $\tilde{\sigma}_t$ is σ_t with lagged y^*s replaced by $\tilde{y}$s. Under the normality assumption,

$$\ln g(\bar{y}_T^*, \bar{y}_T, \bar{I}_T) = S(\bar{y}_T^*|\bar{y}_T, \bar{I}_T)\left\{-\frac{T}{2}\ln(2\pi) - \frac{1}{2}\sum_{t=1}^{T}\left[\ln \tilde{\sigma}_t^2 + \frac{\tilde{\varepsilon}_t^2}{\tilde{\sigma}_t^2}\right]\right\}, \tag{18.6.3}$$

where $\tilde{\varepsilon}_t = \tilde{y}_t - x_t\beta - \sum_{j=1}^{J} y_{t-j}\gamma_j - \sum_{l=1}^{L} \tilde{y}_{t-l}\delta_l$.

The GHK sampler for the discrete choice model can be generalized to the dynamic Tobit model. The mixed joint density of latent and observed dependent variables can be factorized into

$$g(\bar{y}_T^*, \bar{y}_T, \bar{I}_T) = \prod_{t=1}^{T}[g(y_t|\bar{y}_{t-1}^*, \bar{y}_{t-1})]^{I_t}[P(I_t = 0|\bar{y}_{t-1}^*, \bar{y}_{t-1})]^{1-I_t}$$
$$\times \prod_{s\in\{t_1, \ldots, t_m\}} g(y_s^*|I_s = 0, \bar{y}_{s-1}^*, \bar{y}_{s-1}). \tag{18.6.4}$$

With this decomposition, $y_{t_1}^*, \ldots, y_{t_m}^*$ can be recursively drawn from univariate truncated densities $g(y_s^*|I_s = 0, \bar{y}_{s-1}^*, \bar{y}_{s-1})$. With m simulation runs, the likelihood function can be simulated as

$$L_{T,m} = \frac{1}{m}\sum_{r=1}^{m}\prod_{t=1}^{T}\left[g\left(y_t|\bar{y}_{t-1}^{*(r)}, \bar{y}_{t-1}\right)\right]^{I_t}\left[P\left(I_t = 0|\bar{y}_{t-1}^{*(r)}, \bar{y}_{t-1}\right)\right]^{1-I_t}. \tag{18.6.5}$$

With this sampler, the implied weights are

$$\omega_r = \frac{\prod_{t=1}^{T}[g(y_t|\bar{y}_{t-1}^{*(r)}, \bar{y}_{t-1})]^{I_t}[P(I_t = 0|\bar{y}_{t-1}^{*(r)}, \bar{y}_{t-1})]^{1-I_t}}{\sum_{s=1}^{m}\prod_{t=1}^{T}[g(y_t|\bar{y}_{t-1}^{*(s)}, \bar{y}_{t-1})]^{I_t}[P(I_t = 0|\bar{y}_{t-1}^{*(s)}, \bar{y}_{t-1})]^{1-I_t}}, \tag{18.6.6}$$

for $r = 1, \ldots, m$. The performance of this sampler for the estimation of dynamic Tobit models can be found in Lee (1999b).[8]

18.6.1   Omitted variables or state dependence tests

Let $b_t = (x_t\beta + \sum_{j=1}^{J} y_{t-j}\gamma_j + \sum_{l=1}^{L} \tilde{y}_{t-l}\delta_l)$. As θ_2 is in b's, it follows from (18.6.3) that $(\partial \ln g(\bar{y}_T^*, \bar{y}_T, \bar{I}_T))/\partial\theta_2 = S(\bar{y}_T^*|\bar{y}_T, \bar{I}_T)\sum_{t=1}^{T}((\tilde{y}_t - b_t)/\tilde{\sigma}_t^2)\partial b_t/\partial\theta_2$. The test of omitted variables or higher-order dynamics will be based on $(\partial \ln f(\bar{y}_T, \bar{I}_T))/\partial\theta_2 = \sum_{t=1}^{T} E((((\tilde{y}_t - b_t)/\tilde{\sigma}_t^2)\partial b_t/\partial\theta_2)|\bar{y}_T, \bar{I}_T)$.

For example, the test of state dependence on the jth lag of y_t, which is a test of $\gamma_j = 0$, will be based on $(\partial \ln f(\bar{y}_T, \bar{I}_T))/\partial\gamma_j = \sum_{t=1}^{T} E(((\tilde{y}_t - b_t)/\tilde{\sigma}_t^2 \tilde{y}_{t-j})|\bar{y}_T, \bar{I}_T)$. With the GHK sampler, the SSC is $(\partial \ln L_{T,m})/\partial\gamma_j = \sum_{r=1}^{m}\left(\sum_{t=1}^{T}((\tilde{y}_t^{(r)} - b_t^{(r)})/\tilde{\sigma}_t^{2(r)})\tilde{y}_{t-j}^{(r)}\right)\omega_r$.

18.6.2   A test for heteroskedasticity in the Tobit GARCH model

Consider a GARCH(p,q) process, $\sigma_t^2 = \alpha_{1,1} + \sum_{j=1}^{p} \alpha_{2,j}\varepsilon_{t-j}^2 + \sum_{k=1}^{q} \alpha_{3,k}\sigma_{t-k}^2$. For such a model,

$$\frac{\partial \ln g(\bar{y}_T^*, \bar{y}_T, \bar{I}_T)}{\partial\alpha} = S(\bar{y}_T^*|\bar{y}_T, \bar{I}_T) \cdot \frac{1}{2}\sum_{t=1}^{T}\frac{1}{\sigma_t^4}[(\tilde{y}_t - b_t)^2 - \sigma_t^2]\frac{\partial\sigma_t^2}{\partial\alpha}.$$

A test of heteroskedasticity can be based on $(\partial \ln f(\bar{y}_T, \bar{I}_T))/\partial \alpha = (1/2)\sum_{t=1}^{T}$
$E(((1/\sigma_t^2)(u_t^2 - 1)(\partial\sigma_t^2/\partial\alpha))|\bar{y}_T, \bar{I}_T)$. For example, a test of an ARCH against a GARCH
model is to test $\alpha_{3,1} = \cdots = \alpha_{3,q} = 0$, which can be based on $(\partial \ln f(\bar{y}_T, \bar{I}_T))/$
$\partial\alpha_{3,k}|_{\alpha_3=0} = \frac{1}{2}\sum_{t=1}^{T} E_{\alpha_3=0}((1/\sigma_t^2(u_t^2 - 1)\sigma_{t-k}^2)|\bar{y}_T, \bar{I}_T)$. With the GHK sampler, the SSC
of (18.3.7) is $((\partial \ln L_{T,m})/\partial\alpha_{3,k})|_{\alpha_3=0} = \frac{1}{2}\sum_{r=1}^{m}\sum_{t=1}^{T} \frac{1}{\sigma_t^{4(r)}}[(\tilde{y}_t - b_t)^{2(r)} - \tilde{\sigma}_t^{2(r)}]\sigma_{t-k}^{2(r)}\omega_r.$

18.6.3   A normality test

Suppose that the density of u is $g(u) = [1 + \sum_{j\geq 3} c_j H_j(u)]\phi(u)$. It follows that the
density of ε_t is $g(\varepsilon_t) = [1 + \sum_{j\geq 3} c_j H_j(\varepsilon_t/\sigma_t)]\cdot\frac{1}{\sigma_t}\phi(\varepsilon_t/\sigma_t)$. Hence

$$\ln g(\bar{y}_T^*, \bar{y}_T, \bar{I}_T) = S(\bar{y}_T^*|\bar{y}_T, \bar{I}_T)\sum_{t=1}^{T}\left\{\ln\left[1 + \sum_{j\geq 3} c_j H_j(\tilde{u}_t)\right] + \ln\left[\frac{1}{\tilde{\sigma}_t}\phi(\tilde{u}_t)\right]\right\},$$

where $\tilde{u}_t = (\tilde{\varepsilon}_t/\sigma_t)$, which generalizes (18.6.3). It follows that

$$\frac{\partial \ln g(\bar{y}_T^*, \bar{y}_T, \bar{I}_T)}{\partial c_l} = S(\bar{y}_T^*|\bar{y}_T, \bar{I}_T)\sum_{t=1}^{T} H_l(\tilde{u}_t)/[1 + \sum_{j\geq 3} c_j H_j(\tilde{u}_t)].$$

A normality test is a test of $c=0$ and it can be based on $((\partial \ln f(\bar{y}_T, \bar{I}_T))/\partial c_l)|_{c=0} =$
$\sum_{t=1}^{T} E_{c=0}(H_l(u_t)|\bar{y}_T, \bar{I}_T)$. With the GHK sampler, the SSC of (18.3.7) is
$((\partial \ln L_{T,m})/\partial c_l)|_{c=0} = \sum_{r=1}^{m}\left(\sum_{t=1}^{T} H_l\left(\tilde{u}_t^{(r)}\right)\right)\omega_r.$

18.7   Dynamic disequilibrium models

Consider a disequilibrium market model under voluntary participation. The
traded quantity at each time period will be the minimum of notional demand and
supply quantities at that time period. Let y_{1t}^* and y_{2t}^* denote notional supply and
demand quantities at t. The observed traded quantity is $y_t = \min\{y_{1t}^*, y_{2t}^*\}$.
A general system of dynamic notional demand and supply equations can be
specified as

$$y_{1t}^* = x_{1t}\beta_1 + \sum_{j=1}^{J_1} y_{t-j}\gamma_{1j} + \sum_{l=1}^{L_1} y_{1,t-1}^*\delta_{1l} + \varepsilon_{1t},$$

$$\tag{18.7.1}$$

$$y_{2t}^* = x_{2t}\beta_2 + \sum_{j=1}^{J_2} y_{t-j}\gamma_{1j} + \sum_{l=1}^{L_2} y_{2,t-1}^*\delta_{2l} + \varepsilon_{2t},$$

where $(\varepsilon_{1t}, \varepsilon_{2t}), t = 1, \ldots, T$, are i.i.d. $N(0, \Omega)$.

Consider the general case where there is no sample separation information,
that is, it is unknown whether y_t lies on the notional demand equation or the
notional supply equation. In that case, it is convenient to introduce a latent
regime indicator I_t^* at each t, such that $I_t^* = 1$ if $y_{1t}^* \leq y_{2t}^*; I_t^* = 0$ if $y_{1t}^* > y_{2t}^*$.

Denote $z_t^* = \max\{y_{1t}^*, y_{2t}^*\}$. The latent variable vector at t is $y_t^* = (z_t^*, I_t^*)$ for this model. The joint density of all latent variables and sample observations can be factorized into a product of conditional densities, $g(\bar{y}_T^*, \bar{y}_T) = g(\bar{z}_T^*, \bar{I}_T^*, \bar{y}_T) = \prod_{t=1}^{T} g(z_t^*, I_t^*, y_t | \bar{z}_{t-1}^*, \bar{I}_{t-1}^*, \bar{y}_{t-1})$. Let $g(y_{1t}^*, y_{2t}^* | \bar{z}_{t-1}^*, \bar{I}_{t-1}^*, \bar{y}_{t-1})$ be the conditional density of (y_{1t}^*, y_{2t}^*) given $\bar{z}_{t-1}^*, \bar{I}_{t-1}^*$ and $\bar{y}_{t-1}$. One has

$$g(z_t^*, I_t^*, y_t | \bar{z}_{t-1}^*, \bar{I}_{t-1}^*, \bar{y}_{t-1}) = I_t^* g(y_t, y_{2t}^* | \bar{z}_{t-1}^*, \bar{I}_{t-1}^*, \bar{y}_{t-1})$$
$$+ (1 - I_t^*) g(y_{1t}^*, y_t | \bar{z}_{t-1}^*, \bar{I}_{t-1}^*, \bar{y}_{t-1}).$$

Hence

$$\ln g(\bar{y}_T^*, \bar{y}_T) = \sum_{t=1}^{T} \{I_t^* \ln g(y_t, y_{2t}^* | \bar{z}_{t-1}^*, \bar{I}_{t-1}^*, \bar{y}_{t-1}) + (1 - I_t^*) \ln g(y_{1t}^*, y_t | \bar{z}_{t-1}^*, \bar{I}_{t-1}^*, \bar{y}_{t-1})\}.$$

$$(18.7.2)$$

These conditional densities can be expressed as follows. From the definitions of y_t and z_t^*, it is apparent that $y_{1t}^* = I_t^* y_t + (1 - I_t^*) z_t^*$ and $y_{2t}^* = I_t^* z_t^* + (1 - I_t^*) y_t$. Denote

$$b_{1t} = x_{1t}\beta_1 + \sum_{j=1}^{J_1} y_{t-j}\gamma_{1j} + \sum_{l=1}^{L_1} (I_{t-l}^* y_{t-l} + (1 - I_{t-l}^*) z_{t-l}^*) \delta_{1l},$$

$$b_{2t} = x_{2t}\beta_2 + \sum_{j=1}^{J_2} y_{t-j}\gamma_{2j} + \sum_{l=1}^{L_2} (I_{t-l}^* z_{t-l}^* + (1 - I_{t-l}^*) y_{t-l}) \delta_{2l}.$$

The system of equations can then be rewritten as $y_{1t}^* = b_{1t} + \varepsilon_{1t}$ and $y_{2t}^* = b_{2t} + \varepsilon_{2t}$. Under the normality assumption,

$$g(y_{1t}^*, y_{2t}^* | \bar{z}_{t-1}^*, \bar{I}_{t-1}^*, \bar{y}_{t-1}) = \frac{1}{2\pi |\Omega|^{1/2}} \exp\left\{ -\frac{1}{2} (y_{1t}^* - b_{1t}, y_{2t}^* - b_{2t}) \Omega^{-1} \begin{pmatrix} y_{1t}^* - b_{1t} \\ y_{2t}^* - b_{2t} \end{pmatrix} \right\}.$$

$$(18.7.3)$$

A general simulation method for the estimation of this model has been suggested in Lee (1997). In that simulation method, the following density factorization is used:

$$g(\bar{z}_T^*, \bar{I}_T^*, \bar{y}_T) = \prod_{t=1}^{T} g(z_t^* | \bar{I}_t^*, \bar{z}_{t-1}^*, \bar{y}_t) f(y_t | \bar{I}_t^*, \bar{z}_{t-1}^*, \bar{y}_{t-1}) P(I_t^* | \bar{z}_{t-1}^*, \bar{y}_{t-1}).$$

With this factorization, the likelihood function of the model can be written as

$$f(\bar{y}_T) = \sum_{I_1=1}^{2} \cdots \sum_{I_T=1}^{2} \int_{-\infty}^{\infty} \cdots \int_{-\infty}^{\infty} \prod_{t=1}^{T} g(z_t^* | \bar{I}_t^*, \bar{z}_{t-1}^*, \bar{y}_t) f(y_t | \bar{I}_t^*, \bar{z}_{t-1}^*, \bar{y}_{t-1}) P(I_t^* | \bar{I}_{t-1}^*, \bar{z}_{t-1}^*, \bar{y}_{t-1}) dz_t^*.$$

$$(18.7.4)$$

The latent variables $\bar{I}_T^*$ and $\bar{z}_T^*$ can be drawn recursively. Given simulated $\bar{I}_{t-1}^*$ and $\bar{z}_{t-1}^*$, the I_t^* can be simulated as a binomial variable with the probability $P(I_t^* = 1|\bar{I}_{t-1}^*, \bar{z}_{t-1}^*, \bar{y}_{t-1})$ and z_t^* is simulated with the density $g(z_t^*|\bar{I}_t^*, \bar{z}_{t-1}^*, \bar{y}_t)$. With m simulation runs, the likelihood can be simulated by

$$L_{T,m} = \frac{1}{m}\sum_{r=1}^{m}\prod_{t=1}^{T}f\left(y_t|\bar{I}_t^{*(r)}, \bar{z}_{t-1}^{*(r)}, \bar{y}_{t-1}\right). \tag{18.7.5}$$

The weights implied by this simulator are

$$\omega_r = \frac{\prod_{t=1}^{T}f\left(y_t|\bar{I}_t^{*(r)}, \bar{z}_{t-1}^{*(r)}, \bar{y}_{t-1}\right)}{\sum_{s=1}^{m}\prod_{t=1}^{T}f\left(y_t|\bar{I}_t^{*(s)}, \bar{z}_{t-1}^{*(s)}, \bar{y}_{t-1}\right)}. \tag{18.7.6}$$

18.7.1 Omitted variables, higher-order serial correlation or state dependence tests

Let θ_2 be parameters in $b_t = (b_{1t}, b_{2t})$. Let $w_t = I_t^*\left(\begin{smallmatrix} y_t \\ z_t^* \end{smallmatrix}\right) + (1 - I_t^*)\left(\begin{smallmatrix} z_t^* \\ y_t \end{smallmatrix}\right)$. It follows from (18.7.2) and (18.7.3) that $(\partial \ln g(\bar{y}_T^*, \bar{y}_T))/\partial\theta_2 = \sum_{t=1}^{T}(\partial b_t'/\partial\theta_2)\Omega^{-1}(w_t - b_t)$. A test of omitted variables can be based on $(\partial \ln f(\bar{y}_T))/\partial\theta_2 = \sum_{t=1}^{T}E((\partial b_t'/\partial\theta_2)\Omega^{-1}(w_t - b_t)|\bar{y}_T)$. With the likelihood simulation in (18.7.5), the SSC of (18.3.7) is

$$\frac{\partial L_{T,m}}{\partial\theta_2} = \sum_{r=1}^{m}\left[\sum_{t=1}^{T}\left(\frac{\partial b_t'^{(r)}}{\partial\theta_2}\Omega^{-1}\left(w_t^{(r)} - b_t^{(r)}\right)\right)\right]\omega_r.$$

18.7.2 A normality test

Let $\varepsilon_{jt} = \sigma_j u_{jt}$ for $j = 1, 2$. Let $f(u) = \left[1 + \sum_{j_1+j_2\geq 3}c_{j_1j_2}H(u; j_1, j_2, \rho)\right]\phi(u; 0, \rho)$ be a bivariate Gram–Charlier expansion of the density of $u = (u_1, u_2)$, where ρ is the correlation coefficient of u_1 and u_2 and $\phi(u; 0, \rho)$ is the bivariate standard normal density function. It follows that $g(y_{1t}^*, y_{2t}^*|\bar{z}_{t-1}^*, \bar{I}_{t-1}^*, \bar{y}_{t-1}) = K(y_{1t}^*, y_{2t}^*)g_\Omega(y_{1t}^*, y_{2t}^*|\bar{z}_{t-1}^*, \bar{I}_{t-1}^*, \bar{y}_{t-1})$, where $K(y_{1t}^*, y_{2t}^*) = \left[1 + \sum_{j_1+j_2\geq 3}c_{j_1j_2}H((y_{1t}^* - b_{1t})/\sigma_1, (y_{2t}^* - b_{2t})/\sigma_2; j_1, j_2, \rho)\right]$ and $g_\Omega(y_{1t}^*, y_{2t}^*|\bar{z}_{t-1}^*, \bar{I}_{t-1}^*, \bar{y}_{t-1})$ is the conditional bivariate normal density derived from (18.7.1) for the restricted normal model, with $\varepsilon_t = (\varepsilon_{t1}, \varepsilon_{t2})$ being $N(0, \Omega)$ with $\Omega = \left(\begin{smallmatrix} \sigma_1^2 & \sigma_1\sigma_2\rho \\ \sigma_1\sigma_2\rho & \sigma_2^2 \end{smallmatrix}\right)$. Hence,

$$\ln g(\bar{y}_T^*, \bar{y}_T) = \sum_{t=1}^{T}\left\{I_t^*\ln K(y_t, y_{2t}^*) + (1 - I_t^*)\ln K(y_{1t}^*, y_t)\right.$$
$$\left. + I_t^*\ln g_\Omega(y_t, y_{2t}^*|\bar{z}_{t-1}^*, \bar{I}_{t-1}^*, \bar{y}_{t-1}) + (1 - I_t^*)\ln g_\Omega(y_{1t}^*, y_t|\bar{z}_{t-1}^*, \bar{I}_{t-1}^*, \bar{y}_{t-1})\right\}.$$

It follows that

$$\frac{\partial \ln g(\bar{y}_T^*, \bar{y}_T)}{\partial c_{j_1j_2}} = \sum_{t=1}^{T}\left\{I_t^*\frac{H((y_t - b_{1t})/\sigma_1, (y_{2t}^* - b_{2t})/\sigma_2; j_1, j_2, \rho)}{K(y_t, y_{2t}^*)}\right.$$
$$\left. + (1 - I_t^*)\frac{H((y_{1t}^* - b_{1t})/\sigma_1, (y_t - b_{2t})/\sigma_2; j_1, j_2, \rho)}{K(y_{1t}^*, y_t)}\right\}.$$

A normality test can be based on

$$\left.\frac{\partial \ln f(\bar{y}_T)}{\partial c_{j_1 j_2}}\right|_{c=0} = \sum_{t=1}^{T} E_{c=0}\left\{I_t^* H\left(\frac{y_t - b_{1t}}{\sigma_1}, \frac{y_{2t}^* - b_{2t}}{\sigma_2}; j_1, j_2, \rho\right)\right.$$

$$\left. + (1 - I_t^*)H\left(\frac{y_{1t}^* - b_{1t}}{\sigma_1}, \frac{y_t - b_{2t}}{\sigma_2}; j_1, j_2, \rho\right)\middle|\bar{y}_T\right\}.$$

With the likelihood sampler in (18.7.5), the SSC of (18.3.7) is

$$\left.\frac{\partial \ln L_{T,m}}{\partial c_{j_1 j_2}}\right|_{c=0} = \sum_{r=1}^{m} \sum_{t=1}^{T}\left\{I_t^{*(r)} H\left(\frac{y_t - b_{1t}^{(r)}}{\sigma_1}, \frac{y_{2t}^{*(r)} - b_{2t}^{(r)}}{\sigma_2}; j_1, j_2, \rho\right)\right.$$

$$\left. + (1 - I_t^{*(r)})H\left(\frac{y_{1t}^{*(r)} - b_{1t}^{(r)}}{\sigma_1}, \frac{y_t - b_{2t}^{(r)}}{\sigma_2}; j_1, j_2, \rho\right)\right\}\omega_r.$$

18.8   Monte Carlo results on the testing of normality in a dynamic discrete choice panel model

The model for the Monte Carlo experiment is a habit persistence probit model with a random component and an $AR(1)$ disturbance:

$$y_{it}^* = x_{it}\beta + \lambda y_{i,t-1}^* + \sigma\xi_i + \varepsilon_{it}, \tag{18.8.1}$$

where $\varepsilon_{it} = \rho\varepsilon_{i,t-1} + w_{it}$ and ξ_i and w_{it} are $N(0,1)$. The x_{it} are generated as $x_{it} = (1/\sqrt{2})r_{it} + \sqrt{6}s_i$, where r_{it} are i.i.d. truncated normal $N(0,1)$ variables with support on $[-2, 2]$ and s_i are independent uniform variables with support on $[-1/2, 1/2]$. The variance of x is about 1 and its correlation coefficient over time is over 0.5. The process starts at $y_{i0}^* = 0$ and $\varepsilon_{i0} = 0$. The true parameters which generate the sample are $\beta = 1$, $\lambda = 0.2$, $\sigma^2 = 0.5$, and $\rho = 0.4$.

We investigate the general formulation of the SSC in (18.5.10) for the normality test of the ε_{it} in this model. The restricted model is the multinormal dynamic model where both ξ_i and ε_{it} are normally distributed. The alternative hypothesis is that ε_{it} is nonnormal. The multinormal likelihood function can be simulated with the GHK simulator as in (18.5.5). We investigate the finite-sample properties of the SSC normality test statistic in terms of levels of significance and power against some nonnormal alternatives. We have experimented with panel data models with 200 cross-section units and time lengths T of 8 and 15. For each reported case, the summary statistics are constructed with 300 replications. To investigate the power of the simulated normality test, three alternative nonnormal distributions for w_{it} are used. The first alternative is a Student's $t(5)$ distribution with five degrees of freedom. The Student t distribution is symmetric and its kurtosis is 9. The second alternative is an extreme value (Gumbel) distribution. The Gumbel distribution has a skewed density. Its skewness is about 1.14 and kurtosis is 5.4. The third alternative is a 50–50 mixture of $N(-3, 1)$ and $N(3, 1)$ variables. This normal mixture has a bimodal distribution. All these variables are normalized to have zero means and unit variances and are used to generate the disturbance w_{it}.

As this model is a panel data model, several consistent estimates of the information matrix can be constructed. One of the estimates can be the inverse of the negative Hessian matrix of the simulated log likelihood function. The second one can be constructed from the outer product of the gradient vector of the simulated log likelihood across cross-section units. A third alternative has been considered in Lee (1999a), which is based on a robust formulation of the quasi-ML approach. To be specific, the simulated log likelihood function for the model in (18.8.1) is $\ln L_{n,m}(\theta) = \sum_{i=1}^{n} \ln l_{i,m}(\theta)$, where $l_{i,m}(\theta)$ is the simulated log likelihood for the ith observation:

$$l_{i,m}(\theta) = \frac{1}{m} \sum_{j=1}^{m} \prod_{t=1}^{T} [1 + c_3 H_3(w_{it}^{(j)})$$
$$+ c_4 H_4(w_{it}^{(j)})] \Phi(D_{it}(x_{it}\beta + \lambda y_{i,t-1}^{*(j)} + \sigma \xi_i^{(j)} + \rho \varepsilon_{i,t-1}^{(j)})), \qquad (18.8.2)$$

where $D_{it} = (2y_{it} - 1)$ and $w_{it}^{(j)} = -D_{it}\Phi^{-1}[u_{it}^{(j)}\Phi(D_{it}(x_{it}\beta + \lambda y_{i,t-1}^{*(j)} + \sigma \xi_i^{(j)} + \rho \varepsilon_{i,t-1}^{(j)}))]$ are simulated truncated normal variables. The test of normality in this setting is to test that $\iota' = (c_3, c_4) = 0$.[9] The negative Hessian matrix of the simulated log likelihood is $V_{h,m} = -\sum_{i=1}^{n}(\partial^2 \ln l_{i,m}(\hat\theta))/\partial\theta\partial\theta$ evaluated at the SMLE $\hat\theta$ of the normal model. The outer product matrix of the simulated gradient vector is $V_{p,m} = \sum_{i=1}^{n}((\partial \ln l_{i,m}(\hat\theta))/\partial\theta)((\partial \ln l_{i,m}(\hat\theta))/\partial\theta')$. Let J be the selection matrix such that $J\theta = c$. The SSC statistic with $V_{h,m}$ is $S_h = (\partial \ln L_{n,m}(\hat\theta))/\partial\theta' J' [JV_{h,m}^{-1}J'] J(\partial \ln L_{n,m}(\hat\theta))/\partial\theta$, and the SSC statistic with $V_{h,m}$ is $S_p = (\partial \ln L_{n,m}(\hat\theta))/\partial\theta' J' [JV_{p,m}^{-1}J'] J(\partial \ln L_{n,m}(\hat\theta))/\partial\theta$. The third SSC statistic is $S_r = ((\partial \ln L_{n,m}(\hat\theta))/\partial\theta') V_{h,m}^{-1}J' [JV_{r,m}J']^{-1}JV_{h,m}^{-1}(\partial \ln L_{n,m}(\hat\theta))/\partial\theta$, where $V_{r,m} = V_{h,m}^{-1}V_{p,m}V_{h,m}^{-1}$ is a robust estimate of the variance of a quasi-likelihood estimate.[10] These test statistics are asymptotically chi-square distributed with two degrees of freedom under the normal hypothesis.[11]

Table 18.1 reports the empirical levels of significance and the powers of these SSC tests at the nominal 5 and 10 percent levels of significance. We have varied the number of simulation runs m from 50 to 200. There are some variations of the empirical levels of significance with m, but there is no general pattern with it. Overall, the empirical levels of significance seem reasonably adequate for the S_p and S_r statistics. The empirical levels of S_h tend to be slightly higher than the nominal levels of significance. These test statistics do not seem to have good power against the $t(5)$ distribution. The normalized $t(5)$ distribution has thicker tails and larger kurtosis than the $N(0,1)$ but is symmetric. The weak power might be due to the similar shapes of these distributions and the simulated likelihood depends only on choice probabilities but not on a density function. The SMLEs from the simulated normal likelihood function with data generated by various distributions are reported in Table 18.2. Those SMLEs are revealing. The estimates do not seem to be sensitive to the number of simulation runs. The SMLEs based on the misspecified (normal) likelihood of the $t(5)$ distribution model are robust. Except that the estimate of σ is slightly biased upward for $T = 15$, the estimates of β, λ and ρ are as good as those of the correct normal case. The robustness of the SMLEs might explain the weak power of the tests against t alternatives. The statistics have more

Table 18.1 Significant levels and power of simulated efficient score tests for normality Common random draws for estimation and SSC

Data	T	m	S_p	S_h	S_r	S_p	S_h	S_r
				10% level of significance			*5% level of significance*	
				Empirical level of significance				
Normal	8	50	0.1067	0.1200	0.0900	0.0567	0.0900	0.0467
	8	100	0.1067	0.1633	0.0833	0.0567	0.1100	0.0367
	8	200	0.0967	0.1100	0.0733	0.0467	0.0767	0.0367
	15	50	0.1067	0.1100	0.0900	0.0367	0.0733	0.0333
	15	100	0.0700	0.1000	0.0633	0.0500	0.0633	0.0533
	15	200	0.0967	0.1367	0.0933	0.0567	0.0933	0.0467
				Power of test				
Student-t(5)	8	50	0.0867	0.1233	0.0700	0.0367	0.0900	0.0333
	8	100	0.1300	0.1600	0.1200	0.0867	0.1067	0.0633
	8	200	0.1167	0.1367	0.1067	0.0633	0.1000	0.0567
	15	50	0.1167	0.1367	0.0967	0.0533	0.0700	0.0500
	15	100	0.1433	0.1433	0.1267	0.0667	0.0733	0.0500
	15	200	0.1400	0.1400	0.1267	0.0567	0.0900	0.0467
Gumbel	8	50	0.1000	0.1733	0.0833	0.0600	0.1167	0.0467
	8	100	0.1433	0.2167	0.1233	0.0933	0.1367	0.0767
	8	200	0.1933	0.2467	0.1467	0.1167	0.1767	0.0767
	15	50	0.2100	0.2167	0.1833	0.1233	0.1400	0.1067
	15	100	0.3567	0.3733	0.3233	0.2333	0.2567	0.2067
	15	200	0.4633	0.4600	0.4333	0.3533	0.3367	0.3167
Mixed normal	8	50	0.2033	0.2533	0.1767	0.1100	0.1767	0.1033
	8	100	0.2633	0.2800	0.2433	0.1733	0.1967	0.1533
	8	200	0.3500	0.2733	0.3133	0.2333	0.2033	0.2133
	15	50	0.2233	0.2367	0.2333	0.1367	0.1833	0.1300
	15	100	0.3333	0.3300	0.3267	0.2267	0.2433	0.2367
	15	200	0.5167	0.4633	0.4933	0.4033	0.3467	0.3900

power against the Gumbel and mixed normal alternatives for panels with longer time length $T = 15$ and with larger simulation runs. Table 18.2 shows that the Gumbel and normal mixture distributions have larger misspecification effects on the SMLEs. For the Gumbel case, the estimates of β and λ are still quite accurate but the estimates of σ are more biased upward. For the normal mixture case, there are severe downward biases in all the estimates of β, σ and ρ.[12]

The SSC statistics of the normality test under the Gumbel and normal mixture distributions seem to have some power but the power is moderate. As the power for these cases tends to increase with a larger number of simulation runs, it will be of interest to increase the number of simulation runs m beyond those used for the simulation estimation and reported in Table 18.1. To do that, we consider the approach of directly simulating the score instead of constructing the score as derivatives from a simulated likelihood function. Table 18.3 reports the corresponding SSC statistics with large simulation runs m, while the SMLEs for the

Table 18.2 SMLEs of heterogeneous habit persistence models
True parameters: $\beta = 1$, $\lambda = 0.2$, $\sigma = \sqrt{0.5}(= 0.7071)$, and $\rho = 0.4$; sample size $n = 200$
Simulated likelihood based on the normal distribution specification

T	m	β	λ	σ	ρ
			Standard Normal w-disturbance		
8	50	0.9872 (.0711)	.1992 (.0651)	.6893 (.1104)	.3842 (.1086)
8	100	0.9938 (.0709)	.2030 (.0630)	.6966 (.1048)	.3829 (.1044)
8	200	0.9983 (.0721)	.2047 (.0624)	.7021 (.1011)	.3825 (.0994)
15	50	0.9771 (.0497)	.1977 (.0500)	.7013 (.0809)	.3716 (.0740)
15	100	0.9868 (.0490)	.2013 (.0484)	.7055 (.0806)	.3789 (.0695)
15	200	0.9937 (.0489)	.2035 (.0475)	.7057 (.0792)	.3845 (.0681)
			Standarized t(5) w-disturbance		
8	50	1.0651 (.0767)	.1968 (.0599)	.7230 (.1246)	.4278 (.1096)
8	100	1.0734 (.0774)	.2004 (.0589)	.7340 (.1165)	.4249 (.1040)
8	200	1.0775 (.0762)	.2024 (.0577)	.7360 (.1164)	.4283 (.1009)
15	50	1.0507 (.0570)	.1941 (.0457)	.7501 (.0854)	.3961 (.0633)
15	100	1.0619 (.0577)	.1987 (.0431)	.7548 (.0821)	.4040 (.0578)
15	200	1.0690 (.0590)	.2019 (.0427)	.7532 (.0812)	.4106 (.0567)
			Standarized Gumbel w-disturbance		
8	50	1.0978 (.0909)	.1951 (.0677)	1.0077 (.1497)	.4618 (.1495)
8	100	1.1098 (.0900)	.2011 (.0677)	1.0187 (.1362)	.4609 (.1390)
8	200	1.1154 (.0919)	.2045 (.0649)	1.0225 (.1309)	.4598 (.1339)
15	50	1.0946 (.0616)	.2034 (.0504)	1.0977 (.1038)	.3837 (.0786)
15	100	1.1084 (.0623)	.2074 (.0491)	1.1006 (.1007)	.3963 (.0729)
15	200	1.1183 (.0634)	.2111 (.0477)	1.0966 (.0982)	.4048 (.0714)
			Standarized 50–50 mixture of N(−3,1) and N(3,1) disturbance		
8	50	0.9120 (.0628)	.1949 (.0712)	.6267 (.1044)	.3394 (.1224)
8	100	0.9183 (.0626)	.1977 (.0687)	.6378 (.0943)	.3384 (.1145)
8	200	0.9212 (.0632)	.1997 (.0688)	.6432 (.0943)	.3347 (.1125)
15	50	0.9136 (.0508)	.1934 (.0476)	.6589 (.0665)	.3275 (.0716)
15	100	0.9204 (.0524)	.1953 (.0457)	.6601 (.0664)	.3357 (.0686)
15	200	0.9241 (.0526)	.1970 (.0444)	.6618 (.0659)	.3392 (.0658)

Note: The reported values are empirical means based on 300 sample replications, and the values in brackets are empirical standard deviations.

restricted model are those in Table 18.2 with 100 simulation runs. The empirical levels of significance are not very sensitive to larger simulation runs. The empirical levels of S_p and S_r seem reasonably accurate. The empirical levels of S_h tend to be larger than the actual levels of significance. The power against the $t(5)$ alternative is only slightly improved even for $m = 800$. All tests do not have good power against the t alternatives. For the Gumbel and normal mixtures, for $T = 15$ and with large $m = 800$ or 1500, the powers are greatly improved. The statistics can have good power against those skew and bimodal distributions. Relatively, S_p and S_r are better than the S_h statistics.

Table 18.3 Significant levels and power of simulated efficient score tests for normality Independent random draws for estimation and SSC

Data	T	m	S_p	S_h	S_r	S_p	S_h	S_r
				10% level of significance			*5% level of significance*	
			Empirical level of significance					
Normal	8	100	0.0900	0.1567	0.0733	0.0467	0.1033	0.0433
	8	200	0.1233	0.1867	0.1033	0.0500	0.1267	0.0333
	8	400	0.1367	0.1333	0.1267	0.0700	0.0933	0.0633
	8	800	0.1233	0.1667	0.1067	0.0667	0.1100	0.0533
	15	100	0.0900	0.1667	0.0833	0.0567	0.1267	0.0400
	15	200	0.0933	0.1267	0.0867	0.0533	0.0933	0.0433
	15	400	0.0967	0.1233	0.0833	0.0467	0.0833	0.0500
	15	800	0.0900	0.1500	0.1000	0.0467	0.0867	0.0433
			Power of test					
Student-t(5)	8	100	0.0933	0.1467	0.0800	0.0467	0.1067	0.0367
	8	200	0.1200	0.1933	0.1033	0.0633	0.1333	0.0533
	8	400	0.1200	0.1667	0.1133	0.0633	0.1067	0.0433
	8	800	0.1667	0.2267	0.1267	0.0867	0.1500	0.0633
	15	100	0.1233	0.1633	0.1100	0.0467	0.1100	0.0367
	15	200	0.1533	0.1767	0.1400	0.0967	0.1167	0.0933
	15	400	0.1567	0.1500	0.1600	0.0867	0.0667	0.0733
	15	800	0.2233	0.2500	0.2000	0.1367	0.1533	0.1133
Gumbel	8	100	0.1400	0.2733	0.1133	0.0733	0.2000	0.0567
	8	200	0.1900	0.2100	0.1633	0.1233	0.1700	0.0833
	8	400	0.2233	0.2733	0.1800	0.1533	0.1967	0.0900
	8	800	0.2100	0.2867	0.1833	0.1200	0.2167	0.0833
	15	100	0.3867	0.4200	0.3700	0.2767	0.3233	0.2467
	15	200	0.4700	0.4900	0.4533	0.3367	0.3833	0.3133
	15	400	0.5600	0.5467	0.5333	0.4700	0.4600	0.4500
	15	800	0.6833	0.6533	0.6433	0.5567	0.5300	0.5500
	15	1500	0.7167	0.6900	0.7233	0.6400	0.6233	0.5967
Mixed normal	8	100	0.2533	0.3133	0.2267	0.1633	0.2533	0.1400
	8	200	0.3200	0.3267	0.3133	0.2367	0.2500	0.2033
	8	400	0.4833	0.3767	0.4933	0.4000	0.2667	0.3933
	8	800	0.6300	0.4533	0.6067	0.5233	0.4033	0.5200
	8	1500	0.7800	0.3967	0.7767	0.6633	0.3600	0.6767
	15	100	0.3267	0.4067	0.3167	0.2333	0.3167	0.2300
	15	200	0.4567	0.4833	0.4867	0.3367	0.3800	0.3767
	15	400	0.6900	0.5767	0.7400	0.5667	0.4767	0.6333
	15	800	0.7800	0.5933	0.8500	0.7000	0.5133	0.7600
	15	1500	0.9233	0.6733	0.9567	0.8767	0.6300	0.9000

So for empirical applications of such simulated specification tests, we suggest the use of a large number of random simulation in the construction of simulated score test statistics. This is computationally tractable as the construction of simulated test statistics does not require iterations, once simulated estimates of the parameters for the restricted model are available.

18.9 Conclusions

This chapter has considered diagnostic tests for complicated nonstandard dependent variables models, which include multinormal and dynamic models with discrete choices and/or limited dependent variables. Diagnostic tests that are of particular interest can be the test for the normality assumption in the multinormal probit model, and the tests of normality, omitted high-order dynamics, or serial correlations in dynamic models, and heteroskedasticity in GARCH models. As the estimation of those models is feasible only via simulation estimation, tractable diagnostic test statistics are also simulated.

We have considered the formulation of simulated efficient score test statistics which do not require additional simulation design beyond the sampler for the simulation estimation of the restricted model. These simulated efficient score statistics have some common features in terms of simulated conditional moments. For the simulated EM approach, all these are immediate consequences of the approach. Other simulated likelihood approaches can have these features when the sampler under the null hypothesis is used for the construction of the simulated scores. These simulated efficient score test statistics extend the familiar diagnostic tests in cross-section probit and Tobit models in the 1980s to the multivariate and dynamic models, which can only be estimated by simulation methods.

A Monte Carlo experiment is performed to investigate a general simulated normality score test statistic for a dynamic discrete choice model. The finite sample performance of the test in terms of accuracy at the conventional levels of significance and power is investigated. The empirical levels of significance seem to be adequate for a moderate amount of simulation. The simulated MLE of the restricted normal model does not seem sensitive to the amount of simulation. This is also the case for the empirical level of significance. However, for the power, it is important to simulate the score directly with a larger number of simulation runs. This design is computationally tractable as the simulation of the score does not require iteration once the restricted SMLE is available. Because the importance sampler designed for the simulation estimation of the restricted model might not be adequate enough for the specification test statistics, a large number of simulations will remedy this possible deficiency by reducing the simulation error.

Appendix: Dynamic Latent Models and the Exponential Family of Conditional Densities

Gourieroux, Monfort, Renault and Trognon (1987a) have considered the formulation of generalized residuals for latent variables models within the exponential family of densities. The models analyzed are mainly cross-sectional or panel data models. The exponential densities are either univariate or multivariate densities with a finite dimension. In this Appendix, we point out the possible generalization of these results on score vectors (Theorems 1 and 2) to latent dynamic models.

In a dynamic model with a time series of length T, because of the presence of observed lagged dependent variables or nonlinear structures, the joint density of the underlying latent dependent variables will not, in general, be in a T-dimensional exponential family of densities, even though the disturbances of the latent equations are jointly normal. However, the conditional density of the latent dependent variable at each time period, conditional on all the past lagged latent and observable dependent variables, can be exponential. The score vector results of Gourieroux *et al.* (1987a) can be generalized.

Suppose that the conditional density of y_t^* conditional on $\bar{y}_{t-1}^*$ and $\bar{y}_{t-1}$ (as well as strictly exogenous variables) belongs to the exponential family:

$$g(y_t^*|\bar{y}_{t-1}^*, \bar{y}_{t-1}, \theta) = \exp[A(\bar{y}_{t-1}^*, \bar{y}_{t-1}, \theta)T(y_t^*) + B(\bar{y}_{t-1}^*, \bar{y}_{t-1}, \theta) + C(\bar{y}_t^*, \bar{y}_{t-1})]. \quad (A.1)$$

The log-likelihood of the latent dependent variables is

$$\ln L(\bar{y}_T^*|\theta) = \sum_{t=1}^{T}\{A(\bar{y}_{t-1}^*, \bar{y}_{t-1}, \theta)T(y_t^*) + B(\bar{y}_{t-1}^*, \bar{y}_{t-1}, \theta) + C(\bar{y}_T^*, \bar{y}_{t-1})\}. \quad (A.2)$$

As has been pointed out in Gourieroux *et al.* (1987a), an exponential latent model can be associated with a second-order model. This is so for the conditional exponential density model (A.1) with the following second-order conditional model:

$$T(y_t^*) = m(\bar{y}_{t-1}^*, \bar{y}_{t-1}, \theta) + u_t(\theta), \quad (A.3)$$

where $E_\theta(u(\theta)|\bar{y}_{t-1}^*, \bar{y}_{t-1}) = 0$ and $V_\theta(u(\theta)|\bar{y}_{t-1}^*, \bar{y}_{t-1}) = \Omega(\bar{y}_{t-1}^*, \bar{y}_{t-1}, \theta)$, where $m(\bar{y}_{t-1}^*, \bar{y}_{t-1}, \theta)$ is the conditional mean of the canonical statistic $T(y_t^*)$.

The following theorem generalizes Theorem 1 in Gourieroux *et al.* (1987a) to dynamic latent models. Its proof follows the same arguments as Gourieroux *et al.*

Theorem 1:   The score vector in the dynamic latent model is equal to

$$\frac{\partial \ln L(\bar{y}_T^*|\theta)}{\partial\theta} = \sum_{t=1}^{T}\frac{\partial A(\bar{y}_{t-1}^*, \bar{y}_{t-1}, \theta)}{\partial\theta}u_t(\theta),$$

or equivalently,

$$\frac{\partial \ln L(\bar{y}_T^*|\theta)}{\partial\theta} = \sum_{t=1}^{T}\frac{\partial m'(\bar{y}_{t-1}^*, \bar{y}_{t-1}, \theta)}{\partial\theta}\Omega^{-1}(\bar{y}_{t-1}^*, \bar{y}_{t-1}, \theta)u_t(\theta).$$

The score vector of the observed data can be expressed in the following theorem. It is an immediate result of Theorem 1 by using the relation (18.2.5).

Theorem 2:   The score vector in the observed model is equal to

$$\frac{\partial \ln L(\bar{y}_T|\theta)}{\partial\theta} = \sum_{t=1}^{T}E_\theta\left[\frac{\partial A(\bar{y}_{t-1}^*, \bar{y}_{t-1}, \theta)}{\partial\theta}u_t(\theta)\Big|\bar{y}_T\right],$$

or equivalently,

$$\frac{\partial \ln L(\bar{y}_T|\theta)}{\partial\theta} = \sum_{t=1}^{T}E_\theta\left[\frac{\partial m'(\bar{y}_{t-1}^*, \bar{y}_{t-1}, \theta)}{\partial\theta}\Omega^{-1}(\bar{y}_{t-1}^*, \bar{y}_{t-1}, \theta)u_t(\theta)\Big|\bar{y}_T\right].$$

Define the full conditional mean of $T(y_t^*)$ as

$$M(\bar{y}_{T,-t}^*, \bar{y}_T, \theta) = \int T(y_t^*) g(y_t^* | \bar{y}_{T,-t}^*, \bar{y}_T) dy_t^*.$$

The other useful expression of the score vector is

Theorem 3: The score vector in the observed model is equal to

$$\frac{\partial \ln L(\bar{y}_T | \theta)}{\partial \theta} = \sum_{t=1}^{T} E_\theta \left[\frac{\partial A(\bar{y}_{t-1}^*, \bar{y}_{t-1}, \theta)}{\partial \theta} \left(M(\bar{y}_{T,-t}^*, \bar{y}_T, \theta) - m(\bar{y}_{t-1}^*, \bar{y}_{t-1}, \theta) \right) \Big| \bar{y}_T \right],$$

or equivalently,

$$\frac{\partial \ln L(\bar{y}_T | \theta)}{\partial \theta}$$
$$= \sum_{t=1}^{T} E_\theta \left[\frac{\partial m'(\bar{y}_{t-1}^*, \bar{y}_{t-1}, \theta)}{\partial \theta} \Omega^{-1}(\bar{y}_{t-1}^*, \bar{y}_{t-1}, \theta) \left(M(\bar{y}_{T,-t}^*, \bar{y}_T, \theta) - m(\bar{y}_{t-1}^*, \bar{y}_{t-1}, \theta) \right) \Big| \bar{y}_T \right].$$

Proof: It is sufficient to prove the first expression. The second can be derived in a similar way. The result follows from Theorem 2 because

$$E_\theta \left[\frac{\partial A(\bar{y}_{t-1}^*, \bar{y}_{t-1}, \theta)}{\partial \theta} u_t(\theta) \Big| \bar{y}_T \right]$$
$$= \int \frac{\partial A(\bar{y}_{t-1}^*, \bar{y}_{t-1}, \theta)}{\partial \theta} u_t(\theta) g(\bar{y}_T^* | \bar{y}_T, \theta) d\bar{y}_T^*$$
$$= \int \frac{\partial A(\bar{y}_{t-1}^*, \bar{y}_{t-1}, \theta)}{\partial \theta} \left(\int u_t(\theta) g(y_t^* | \bar{y}_{T,-t}^*, \bar{y}_T, \theta) dy_t^* \right) g(\bar{y}_{T,-t}^* | \bar{y}_T, \theta) d\bar{y}_{T,-t}^*$$
$$= \int \frac{\partial A(\bar{y}_{t-1}^*, \bar{y}_{t-1}, \theta)}{\partial \theta} \left(M(\bar{y}_{T,-t}^*, \bar{y}_T, \theta) - m(\bar{y}_{t-1}^*, \bar{y}_{t-1}, \theta) \right) g(\bar{y}_{T,-t}^* | \bar{y}_T, \theta) d\bar{y}_{T,-t}^*$$
$$= E_\theta \left[\frac{\partial A(\bar{y}_{t-1}^*, \bar{y}_{t-1}, \theta)}{\partial \theta} \left(M(\bar{y}_{T,-t}^*, \bar{y}_T, \theta) - m(\bar{y}_{t-1}^*, \bar{y}_{t-1}, \theta) \right) \Big| \bar{y}_T \right].$$

Q.E.D.

Acknowledgments

I appreciate having received valuable comments and suggestions from a referee and the volume editors, Kerry Patterson and Terence Mills.

Notes

1. For a valid justification of its limiting distribution being an asymptotic chi-square, it is necessary that the number of simulation runs m goes to infinity at a rate such that $\sqrt{m}/n$, where n is the sample size, goes to zero as n goes to infinity (see, e.g., Lee, 1995). Alternative formulas may use different consistent estimates of the information matrix instead of the negative Hessian matrix.

2. The difference is similar in a way to the difference between generalized residuals and simulated residuals defined in Gourieroux, Monfort, Renault and Trognon (1987a,b).
3. The $g(y_t^*|\bar{y}_{T,-t}^*, \bar{y}_T, \theta)$ in (18.2.16) is a full conditional density. Its tractability is related to the feasibility of the Gibbs sampler for the model.
4. In some situations, simulated scores of both general and restricted models can be constructed (Hajivassiliou and McFadden 1998). Such a sampler has been considered in Lee (1999a) for simulated efficient score tests. For the latter simulated statistics, for some cases, its algebraic structure may not provide simple interpretations. This can be seen from (18.3.5)′ (with the derivatives replaced by the derivatives with respect to θ_2).
5. In Bera, Jarque and Lee (1984), the normality assumption is tested against alternatives in the Pearson family of distributions. The derived score at the null hypothesis is identical to that derived with the truncated Gram–Charlier or Edgeworth expansions.
6. In this formulation and those for subsequent dynamic models, we have implicitly assumed that x's are strictly exogenous. However, the general features of the simulated score testing statistics described below are valid when x's are weakly exogenous (Hendry and Richard, 1983). This is so because, under weak exogeneity, the parameter of interest does not appear in the feed back equations of y to x, i.e., the conditional density of x_t conditional on $\bar{y}_{t-1}$ and the past $(x_{t-1}, \ldots, x_1)$ does not involve the parameter of interest.
7. This paper also contains a recent empirical application of the discrete dynamic panel data model. In the application, the observed lagged y is an explanatory variable. There is no latent lagged y^* included as explanatory variables but there are unobservable heteroskedasticity ξ_i and the disturbances ε_{it}s are serially correlated. Thus, a simulated method is needed for the estimation of such a model.
8. The sampler (18.6.6) can be improved for models with simpler dynamics such as a model with an AR(1) process. The details can be found in Lee (1999b). For the latter case, the improved sampler can be used instead of (18.6.6). For long time series, a direct evaluation of (18.6.6) may be subject to numerical underflow. Lee (1999b) has suggested an iterative weighting algorithm which can overcome the possible numerical difficulty.
9. This is a truncated version of the Gram–Charlier expansion for practical use. It can also be regarded as a likelihood function for a parametric distribution model. See Lee (1984b).
10. The simulated likelihood function is a quasi-likelihood function. Justifications for this formulation are given in Lee (1999a).
11. In Lee (1995, 1999a), we have also considered issues of asymptotic bias in SMLE and SSC statistics. Some bias-adjusted estimates and statistics are derived. With the amount of simulation runs of 100 or more used in this experiment, the bias is not an issue and will not be considered here.
12. The normal mixture has been investigated in Manski and Thompson (1986) and Horowitz (1992) for the effect of misspecification in the binary logit model. Downward biases in regression coefficients are also found in the binary logit MLE.

References

Bera, A.K., C.M. Jarque and L.F. Lee (1984) Testing the normality assumption in limited dependent variable models. *International Economic Review* 25, 563–78.

Bera, A.K. and P.M. Robinson (1989) Tests for serial dependence and other specification analysis in models of markets in disequilibrium. *Journal of Business and Economic Statistics* 7, 343–52.

Borsch-Supan, A. and V.A. Hajivassiliou (1993) Smooth unbiased multivariate probability simulators for maximum likelihood estimation of limited dependent variable models. *Journal of Econometrics* 58, 347–68.

Chernozhukov, V. and H. Hong (2003) An MCMC approach to classical estimation. *Journal of Econometrics* 115, 293–346.

Chib, S. (2001) Markov chain Monte Carlo methods: computation and inference. In J.J. Heckman and E. Leamer (eds), *Handbook of Econometrics*, vol. 5. Amsterdam: Elsevier Science, pp. 3569–3649.

Danielsson, J. and J.F. Richard (1993) Accelerated Gaussian importance sampler with application to dynamic latent variable models. *Journal of Applied Econometrics* **8**, S153–S173.

Dempster, A.P., N.M. Laird and D.B. Rubin (1977) Maximum likelihood from incomplete data via the EM algorithm. *Journal of the Royal Statistical Society* B **39**, 1–22.

Dufour, J.-M. and L. Khalaf (2002) Simulation based finite and large sample tests in multivariate regressions. *Journal of Econometrics* **111**, 303–22.

Dufour, J.-M., L. Khalaf, J.-T. Bernard and I. Genest (2004) Simulation-based finite-sample tests for heteroskedasticity and ARCH effects. *Journal of Econometrics* **122**, 317–47.

Engle, R.F., D.F. Henry, and J.-F. Richard (1983) Exogeneity. *Econometrica* **55**, 277–304.

Geweke, J. (1992) Efficient simulation from the multivariate normal and student-t distributions subject to linear constraints. In *Computer Science and Statistics: Proceedings of the Twenty-Third Symposium on the Interface*. Alexandria, VA: American Statistical Association, pp. 571–8.

Geweke, J. and M. Keane (2001) Computationally intensive methods for integration in econometrics. In J.J. Heckman and E. Leamer (eds), *Handbook of Econometrics*, vol. 5. Amsterdam: Elsevier Science, pp. 3465–3568.

Geweke, J., M. Keane and D. Runkle (1994) Alternative computational approaches to inference in the multinomial probit model. *The Review of Economics and Statistics* **76**, 609–32.

Ghysels, E. and A. Guay (2003) Structural change tests for simulated method of moments. *Journal of Econometrics* **115**, 91–123.

Gourieroux, C. and A. Monfort (1993) Simulation-based inference: a survey with special reference to panel data models. *Journal of Econometrics* **59**, 5–33.

Gourieroux, C., A. Monfort, E. Renault and A. Trognon (1987a) Generalised residuals. *Journal of Econometrics* **34**, 5–32.

Gourieroux, C., A. Monfort, E. Renault and A. Trognon (1987b) Simulated residuals. *Journal of Econometrics* **34**, 201–52.

Hajivassiliou, V. (1993) Simulation estimation methods for limited dependent variable models. In G.S. Maddala, C.R. Rao and H.D. Vinod (eds), *Handbook of Statistics (Econometrics)*, vol. 11. Amsterdam: North-Holland, pp. 519–43.

Hajivassiliou, V. and D. McFadden (1998) The method of simulated scores for the estimation of LDV models. *Econometrica* **66**, 863–96.

Hajivassiliou, V. and P. Ruud (1994) Classical estimation methods for LDV models using simulation. In R.F. Engle and D.L. McFadden (eds), *Handbook of Econometrics*, vol. IV. Amsterdam: Elsevier Science, pp. 2384–2441.

Hajivassiliou, V., D. McFadden and P. Ruud (1996) Simulation of multivariate normal rectangle probabilities and their derivatives: theoretical and computational results. *Journal of Econometrics* **72**, 85–134.

Heckman, J.J. (1981) Statistical models for discrete panel data. In C.F. Manski and D. McFadden (eds), *Structural Analysis of Discrete data with Econometric Applications*. Cambridge, MA: MIT Press, pp. 114–78.

Hendry, D.F. and J.F. Richard (1983) The econometric analysis of economic time series. *International Statistical Review* **51**, 111–63.

Hendry, D.F. and J.F. Richard (1992) Likelihood evaluation for dynamic latent variables models. In H.M. Amman, D.A. Belsley and L.F. Pau (eds), *Computational Economics and Econometrics*. Amsterdam: Kluwer.

Horowitz, J.L. (1992) A smoothed maximum score estimator for the binary response model. *Econometrica* **60**, 505–31.

Johnson, N.L. and S. Kotz (1976) *Distributions in Statistics: Continuous Multivariate Distributions*. New York: John Wiley and Sons.

Keane, M.P. (1993) Simulation methods for panel data limited dependent variable models. In G.S. Maddala, C.R. Rao and H.D. Vinod (eds), *Handbook of Statistics (Econometrics)*, vol. 11. Amsterdam: North-Holland, pp. 545–71.

Keane, M.P. (1994) A computationally practical simulation estimator for panel data. *Econometrica* **62**, 95–116.

Kendall, M. and A. Stuart (1977) *The Advanced Theory of Statistics*, vol. 1, 4th edn. London: Charles Griffin.

Laroque, G. and B. Salanie (1993) Simulation-based estimation of models with lagged latent variables. *Journal of Applied Econometrics* **8**, S119–S133.

Lee, L.F. (1984a) The likelihood function and a test for serial correlation in a disequilibrium market model. *Economics Letters* **14**, 195–200.

Lee, L.F. (1984b) Tests for the bivariate normal distribution in the econometric models with selectivity. *Econometrica* **52**, 843–63.

Lee, L.F. (1995) Asymptotic bias in simulated maximum likelihood estimation of discrete choice models. *Econometric Theory* **11**, 437–83.

Lee, L.F. (1997) Simulation estimation of dynamic switching regression and dynamic disequilibrium models. *Journal of Econometrics* **78**, 179–204.

Lee, L.F. (1998) Simulated maximum likelihood estimation of dynamic discrete choice statistical models – some Monte Carlo results. *Journal of Econometrics* **82**, 1–35.

Lee, L.F. (1999a) Statistical inference with simulated likelihood functions. *Econometric Theory* **15**, 337–60.

Lee, L.F. (1999b) Estimation of dynamic and ARCH Tobit models. *Journal of Econometrics* **92**, 355–90.

Lee, L.F. and G.S. Maddala (1985) The common structure of tests for selectivity bias, serial correlation, heteroskedasticity and non-normality in the Tobit model. *International Economic Review* **26**, 1–20.

Maddala, G.S. (1995) Specification tests in limited dependent variable models. In G.S. Maddala, P.C.B. Phillips and T.N. Srinivasan (eds), *Advances in Econometrics and Quantitative Economics*. Oxford: Blackwell, pp. 1–49.

Manski, C.F. and T.S. Thompson (1986) Operational characteristics of maximum score estimation. *Journal of Econometrics* **32**, 65–108.

McFadden, D. (1989) A method of simulated moments for estimation of discrete response models without numerical integration. *Econometrica* **57**, 995–1026.

McFadden, D. and P.A. Ruud (1994) Estimation by simulation. *The Review of Economics and Statistics* **76**, 591–608.

McFadden, D. and K. Train (2002) Mixed MNL models of discrete response. *Journal of Applied Econometrics* **15**, 447–70.

Pagan, A.R. and F. Vella (1989) Diagnostic tests for models based on unit record data: a survey. *Journal of Applied Econometrics* **4**, S29–S59.

Pakes, A. and D. Pollard (1989) Simulation and the asymptotics of optimization estimators. *Econometrica* **54**, 755–85.

Robinson, P.M., A.K. Bera and C.M. Jarque (1985) Tests for serial dependence in limited dependent variable models. *International Economic Review* **26**, 629–38.

Ruud, P. (1991) Extensions of estimation methods using the EM algorithm. *Journal of Econometrics* **49**, 305–41.

Shephard, N. (1993) Fitting nonlinear time-series models with applications to stochastic variance models. *Journal of Applied Econometrics* **8**, S135–S152.

Smith, R. (1987) Testing the normality assumption in multivariate simultaneous limited dependent variable models. *Journal of Econometrics* **34**, 105–23.

Tanner, M.A. (1987) *Tools for Statistical Inference*. New York: Springer-Verlag.

Train, K.E (2003) *Discrete Choice Methods with Simulation*. Cambridge: Cambridge University Press.

Wu, C.F.J. (1983) On the convergence properties of the EM-algorithm. *Annals of Statistics* **11**, 95–103.

Zhang, W. and L.F. Lee (2004) Simulation estimation of dynamic discrete choice panel models with accelerated importance samplers. *The Econometrics Journal* **7**, 120–42.

19
Censored Data and Truncated Distributions

William Greene

Abstract

We detail the basic theory for regression models in which dependent variables are censored or underlying distributions are truncated. The model is extended to models for counts, sample selection models, and hazard models for duration data. Entry-level theory is presented for the practitioner. We then describe a few of the recent, frontier developments in theory and practice.

19.1	Introduction	695
19.2	Truncation	697
19.3	Censored data and the censored regression model	701
	19.3.1 Estimation and inference	704
	19.3.2 Specification analysis	705
	19.3.3 Heteroskedasticity	706
	19.3.4 Unobserved heterogeneity	707
	19.3.5 Distribution	707
	19.3.6 Other models with censoring	708
19.4	Incidental truncation and sample selection	712
19.5	Panel data	715
	19.5.1 Estimating fixed effects models	716
	19.5.2 Estimating random effects models	719
	19.5.3 An application of fixed and random effects estimators	719
	19.5.4 Sample selection models for panel data	721
19.6	Recent developments	724
19.7	Summary and conclusions	728

19.1 Introduction

The analysis of censoring and truncation arises not from a free-standing body of theory and economic/econometric modeling, but from a subsidiary set of results that treat a practical problem of how data are gathered and analyzed. Thus, we have chosen the title "Censored Data and Truncated Distributions" for this chapter, rather than the more often used rubric "Limited Dependent Variables" (see, e.g., Maddala, 1983) specifically to underscore the relationship between the results and this practical issue. The results that we examine here arise because otherwise ordinary data are censored between generation and observation. Likewise, truncation arises because of something the analyst or the sample-generating mechanism specifically does to the data-generating process that produces the data in hand. Formally, censored data arise through a transformation of a variable of interest, say y^*, through the many to one transformation $y = T(y^*)$. (It is the data on y^* that are censored.) Perhaps the most familiar example is the latent regression interpretation of binary choice; e.g., where y^* designates a one-dimensional representation of a voter's preferences and y denotes which of two parties the voter chooses in an election, so that $T(y^*) = 1(y^* > \alpha)$; an analogous representation might describe labor force participation y as a reflection of y^*, the difference between an underlying (and unobserved) reservation wage and an offered wage. Truncation likewise is a feature of the data-gathering (as opposed to -generating) mechanism. When data are drawn from a clearly defined subset of a larger population, the probability distribution that applies to the observed data will arise as a conditional distribution within that of the larger population – hence the "truncation" will usefully be analyzed in the framework of conditional probabilities. Consider, for example, modeling the probabilities of visits to recreation sites based only on individuals who visited those sites at least once. Likewise, we consider modeling family size by analyzing only families with at least one child. In this instance, while we might have interest in the characteristics of the population at large, $f(y^*)$, what we have direct access to via familiar tools to $f(y^* | T(y^*))$, the relationship between this and $f(y^*)$ remains to be established.

This chapter will survey the basic theory and a few recent developments in models based on censoring and truncation. It has numerous precedents, notably Maddala (1983) and Dhrymes (1986), as well as numerous more recent treatments such as Long (1997) and DeMaris (2004). Terra firma in this literature is the classical linear regression with normally distributed disturbances; indeed, most of the early development focused on this exclusively. Standard analyses examined the (undesirable) properties of least squares and the (more desirable) behavior of the maximum likelihood estimator. More recent treatments have examined less fragile specifications based, for example, on semiparametric specifications. We are also interested in models that extend beyond the linear regression platform, such as models for counts, ordered choice, and so on. We begin on terra firma, with a review of the firmly established results in the standard models. As noted, we are interested in more robust model specifications and estimators. We will also examine the special features of applications to panel data. This being an applied literature at its core, we will also be interested in the situations and modeling frameworks that give rise to problems of censoring and truncation.

We need to draw two distinctions to define the analytical arena of interest in this survey:

(a) The estimation and inference problem. Interest will be on a specific class of models, defined by the conditional density of a response variable y, conditioned on a set of variables **x** and unobservable characteristics, ε. The problems analyzed here arise from censoring, truncation, or selection with respect to y, not **x**, that is, ultimately, on the unobservables, ε. Since the model is defined with respect to the conditional distribution, problems, though they may apply to observed data on **x**, will not affect our estimation problem, since the conditional model will apply to the observations that remain. Problems such as they are will apply to analysis of the marginal distribution of x, but that will generally not be of concern here.

(b) It is important to make the distinction between censoring and truncation. Censoring is a feature of the data-gathering mechanism. Truncation, whether direct or indirect, is a characteristic of the population under study, and its relation to the population that has generated the data in hand. The distinction is occasionally loose. Indeed, the second condition can be created from the first. The most pedestrian example, long a staple of the pedagogical literature, is that in which the analyst holding a data set in which some observations are censored, discards the censored observations. The distribution of the uncensored data which remain in hand is truncated with respect to the population of interest. It is useful, as well, to draw a second distinction with respect to certain types of censoring – we will treat both types in this study. In certain cases, the data gathering process produces censoring. Greene (2003) suggests the example of ticket sales to sporting events, in which the actual latent demand is censored in translation to ticket sales because some events will sell out, that is, fill the facility to capacity. In other cases, the censoring is actually a natural part of the data generating mechanism. Duration data behave this way – when one observes spells of unemployment, for example, the survey period may end while some individuals under study remain unemployed. There is a possibly unwarranted assumption that were the survey period long enough, the spell would in fact, eventually end. But this need not be the case. We will consider the implied "split population" models below.

This survey proceeds as follows: section 19.2 will present results for truncated distributions. In terms of the received literature, this part of the theory is less often used. However, the central distributional results here are extended to produce the more common censored data models. These will be developed in section 19.3. Section 19.4 will present the central features of models of sample selection. Since Heckman's (1979) seminal work, a vast literature on this subject has appeared, and continues to draw a large amount of attention. We will present little more than a simple gateway to that literature. Section 19.5 presents some of the model extensions that are made possible by panel data. Some conclusions are drawn in section 19.6.

19.2 Truncation

In their pioneering study of income and education, Hausman and Wise (1977) make the strong distinction (as we do) between censored data which are "piled up" at a censoring point and truncation, which occurs when a relevant subset of the population which generates the data is *unobserved*. The foundation of this class of models, and our departure point, is a classical linear regression model with uncorrelated normally distributed disturbances,

$$y_i^* = \mathbf{x}_i'\boldsymbol{\beta} + \varepsilon_i, \varepsilon_i \sim N[0, \sigma^2], \quad i = 1, \ldots, N. \tag{19.2.1}$$

It follows, then, that the regression of y_i on $\mathbf{x}_i$ is $E[y_i^* | \mathbf{x}_i] = \mathbf{x}_i'\boldsymbol{\beta}$. The log likelihood for this model is

$$\ln L = \sum_{i=1}^{N} \left[-\frac{1}{2}\ln 2\pi - \ln \sigma - \frac{1}{2}((y_i^* - \mathbf{x}_i'\boldsymbol{\beta})/\sigma)^2 \right]. \tag{19.2.2}$$

In this basic foundation, all the familiar properties (finite sample and asymptotic) apply to the usual least squares estimators, $\mathbf{b}$ and s^2. (All the results that will interest us here will be asymptotic, so we will ignore degrees of freedom corrections in what follows.)

Consider, then, analysis of the subset of the population defined by

$$
\begin{aligned}
y_i &= y_i^* \quad \text{if } y_i^* \geq 0 \\
y_i &\text{ is unobserved if } y_i^* < 0.
\end{aligned}
\tag{19.2.3}
$$

(The choice of zero as the truncation point is innocent if $\mathbf{x}_i$ contains a constant term, which we assume here. The choice of lower truncation is a minor complication which we will deal with in passing below.) The truncation mechanism implies that for the observed data,

$$\varepsilon_i \geq -\mathbf{x}_i'\boldsymbol{\beta} \tag{19.2.4}$$

so the normal distribution assumed above is inappropriate. The regression is also inappropriate since, using known results for truncation in the normal distribution (Greene, 2003, ch. 22),

$$
\begin{aligned}
E[y_i|\mathbf{x}_i] &= E[y_i^*|\mathbf{x}_i, y_i^* \geq 0] = \mathbf{x}_i'\boldsymbol{\beta} + E[\varepsilon_i|\varepsilon_i \geq -\mathbf{x}_i'\boldsymbol{\beta}] \\
&= \mathbf{x}_i'\boldsymbol{\beta} + \sigma \frac{\phi(-\mathbf{x}_i'\boldsymbol{\beta}/\sigma)}{1 - \Phi(-\mathbf{x}_i'\boldsymbol{\beta}/\sigma)}.
\end{aligned}
\tag{19.2.5}
$$

where $\phi(.)$ and $\Phi(.)$ are the standard normal density and cdf, respectively. If we write this as $E[y_i | \mathbf{x}_i] = \mathbf{x}_i'\boldsymbol{\beta} + \sigma\lambda_i$ where

$$\lambda_i = \frac{\phi(-\mathbf{x}_i'\boldsymbol{\beta}/\sigma)}{1 - \Phi(-\mathbf{x}_i'\boldsymbol{\beta}/\sigma)} = \frac{\phi(\mathbf{x}_i'\boldsymbol{\beta}/\sigma)}{\Phi(\mathbf{x}_i'\boldsymbol{\beta}/\sigma)}, \tag{19.2.6}$$

we can see immediately that linear regression of y_i on $\mathbf{x}_i$ will omit a variable that is surely correlated with $\mathbf{x}_i$ (see Heckman, 1979). (The variable λ_i is called the inverse Mills ratio.) The implication is that linear least squares regression of y_i on $\mathbf{x}_i$ will produce a biased and inconsistent estimator of $\boldsymbol{\beta}$. (An early thread of the literature on this model considered the possibility of *nonlinear* regression of y_i on $\mathbf{x}_i$ which would produce consistent estimators of $\boldsymbol{\beta}$ and σ. The NLS estimator here would be demonstrably inefficient (compared to MLE), very inconvenient, and not robust to any violations of the model assumptions. So, we will not consider it any further.) The magnitude and direction of the bias in the least squares estimator will be data dependent, so little can be said analytically. For reasons that will be suggested shortly, the often observed empirical regularity is that the least squares estimator in this setting is *attenuated* (biased toward zero), approximately by the relationship

$$\text{plim } \mathbf{b} \approx \boldsymbol{\beta}[1 - a\lambda(a) - \lambda(a)^2] \qquad (19.2.7)$$

where a would be approximated by $-\bar{\mathbf{x}}'\boldsymbol{\beta}/\sigma$ (see Greene, 1983). The bracketed term is strictly bounded by zero and one, so we expect $\mathbf{b}$ to be attenuated as an estimator of $\boldsymbol{\beta}$. (An exact result due to Cheung and Goldberger (1984), which parallels this, states that if $E[\mathbf{x}_i | y_i]$ is linear in y_i, then plim $\mathbf{b} = \boldsymbol{\beta}\tau$ for some proportionality constant τ. The condition is unlikely to hold in practice – most models contain dummy variables, for example – but it does provide a commonly observed approximation.)

Estimation of the parameters can be accomplished by maximum likelihood. We write the log likelihood function for the untruncated case as

$$\ln L = \sum_{i=1}^{N} \ln\left[\frac{1}{\sigma}\phi\left(\frac{y_i^* - \mathbf{x}_i'\boldsymbol{\beta}}{\sigma}\right)\right]. \qquad (19.2.8)$$

The density for the truncated random variable must be scaled to integrate to one over the range $\varepsilon_i > -\mathbf{x}_i'\boldsymbol{\beta}$, so for the truncated case,

$$\ln L = \sum_{i=1}^{N} \ln\left[\frac{(1/\sigma)\phi((y_i - \mathbf{x}_i'\boldsymbol{\beta})/\sigma)}{\Phi(\mathbf{x}_i'\boldsymbol{\beta}/\sigma)}\right]. \qquad (19.2.9)$$

Maximization of this log likelihood is fairly straightforward – it is preprogrammed into several widely used commercial software packages. The analytical first and second derivatives are very cumbersome (e.g., Wooldridge (2002, p. 526)) but are made vastly simpler by Olsen's (1978) transformation, which is a useful device for many models of this sort. Let $\theta = 1/\sigma$ and $\boldsymbol{\gamma} = (1/\sigma)\boldsymbol{\beta}$. Then, the log likelihood function and its derivatives become

$$\ln L = \sum_{i=1}^{N} -\frac{1}{2}\ln 2\pi + \ln \theta - \frac{1}{2}(\theta y_i - \mathbf{x}_i'\boldsymbol{\gamma})^2 - \ln \Phi(\mathbf{x}_i'\boldsymbol{\gamma}),$$

$$\frac{\partial \ln L}{\partial \boldsymbol{\gamma}} = \sum_{i=1}^{N} (\theta y_i - \mathbf{x}_i'\boldsymbol{\gamma})\mathbf{x}_i - \lambda_i \mathbf{x}_i,$$

$$\frac{\partial \ln L}{\partial \theta} = \sum_{i=1}^{N} [-(\theta y_i - \mathbf{x}_i'\boldsymbol{\gamma})y_i + (1/\theta)],$$

$$\frac{\partial^2 \ln L}{\partial \boldsymbol{\gamma}\partial \boldsymbol{\gamma}'} = \sum_{i=1}^{N} -\delta_i \mathbf{x}_i \mathbf{x}_i', \quad 0 < \delta_i = 1 - (\mathbf{x}_i'\boldsymbol{\gamma})\lambda_i - \lambda_i^2 < 1, \qquad (19.2.10)$$

$$\frac{\partial^2 \ln L}{\partial \boldsymbol{\gamma}\partial \theta} = \sum_{i=1}^{N} \mathbf{x}_i y_i,$$

$$\frac{\partial^2 \ln L}{\partial \theta^2} = \sum_{i=1}^{N} [-y_i^2 - (1/\theta)^2].$$

After estimation of γ and θ, the original parameters are recovered from $\sigma = 1/\theta$ and $\beta = (1/\theta)\gamma$. The asymptotic covariance matrix for the estimators of (β, σ) is derived from that for γ and θ via the delta method

$$Asy.Var[(\hat{\beta}', \hat{\sigma})'] = G \times Asy.Var[(\hat{\gamma}', \hat{\theta})'] \times G', G = \begin{bmatrix} \frac{1}{\theta}I & \frac{-1}{\theta^2}\gamma \\ 0' & \frac{-1}{\theta^2} \end{bmatrix}. \tag{19.2.11}$$

For later reference, we note in $\partial^2 \ln L / \partial\gamma\partial\gamma'$ the appearance of $\delta_i = 1 - a_i\lambda_i - \lambda_i^2$. This quantity appears at various points in the analysis of models with censoring and truncation, and derives from

$$Var[\varepsilon_i | x_i, \varepsilon_i \geq -x_i'\beta] = \sigma^2 \delta_i. \tag{19.2.12}$$

As (it has been shown elsewhere, for example, as in Maddala (1983)) we have that $0 < \delta_i < 1$, it follows that the truncation has the effect of reducing the variation in the truncated population.

Since this "truncated regression model" is also a nonlinear regression, the slopes (derivatives of the conditional mean function) are not equal to the parameters. Returning to the conditional mean function, we find that $E[y_i | x_i] = x_i'\beta + \sigma\lambda_i$. Differentiating with respect to β and using the results we have above, we find (not surprisingly) that

$$\frac{\partial E[y_i | x_i]}{\partial x_i} = \beta \delta_i \tag{19.2.13}$$

Note that the approximate result for the least squares estimator mimics this result for the true marginal effects.

This set of results has been widely applied to models with continuous dependent variables, such as hours equations and earnings models in finance. Another common application of truncation modeling occurs in analysis of data on counts. A particular application is counts of site visits, taken on site; see Shaw (1988). Consider recreation site "q," and we are interested in the number of visits that individual i makes to that site in a given period (year, for example). Survey data taken on site that ask the respondent for numbers of visits are truncated by construction – since they are there to answer, the response must be at least one. The Poisson regression model is commonly used for this application. Under the assumptions just made, the appropriate model for on site responses would be

$$\begin{aligned} Prob[y_i = j] &= \frac{\exp(-\mu_i)\mu_i^j}{j!Prob[y_i \geq 1]}, \quad \mu_i = \exp(x_i'\beta) \\ &= \frac{\exp(-\mu_i)\mu_i^j}{j!\{1 - Prob[y_i = 0]\}} \\ &= \frac{\exp(-\mu_i)\mu_i^j}{j!\{1 - \exp(-\mu_i)\}}. \end{aligned} \tag{19.2.14}$$

As before, estimation is not complicated. But we do note that the force of the truncation is likely to substantially change the estimated coefficients. The marginal effects are obtained from

$$E[y_i|\mathbf{x}_i] = \mu_i/[1 - \exp(-\mu_i)]. \tag{19.2.15}$$

After some tedious algebra, we find

$$\frac{\partial E[y_i|\mathbf{x}_i]}{\partial x_i} = E[y_i \,|\, \mathbf{x}_i]\{1 + \mathrm{Prob}[y_i = 0 \,|\, \mathbf{x}_i]E[y_i \,|\, \mathbf{x}_i]\}\boldsymbol{\beta} = \kappa_i\boldsymbol{\beta}. \tag{19.2.16}$$

It is unclear how this compares to the derivative of the original conditional mean, $\mu_i\boldsymbol{\beta}$.

Truncation of this form is straightforward to build into the model – assuming that the larger population can be characterized. We label this form of truncation "direct." It takes the form of a reduction in the range of variation of the observed variable of interest. As we've seen in the two examples described, building it into the regression model of interest, and into the likelihood for estimation purposes, is accomplished by using the laws of probability; if y_i^* is the "untruncated" random variable and y_i is observed counterpart,

$$E[y_i|\mathbf{x}_i] = E[y_i^*|\mathbf{x}_i, y_i^* \text{ is in the observed range}] \tag{19.2.17}$$

and

$$\ln f(y_i|\mathbf{x}_i) = \ln f(y_i^*|\mathbf{x}_i) - \ln[\mathrm{Prob}(y_i^* \text{ is in the observed range}|\mathbf{x}_i)] \tag{19.2.18}$$

When these have known forms, modification of regression functions and the log likelihood function is straightforward. Note, however, that in terms of these marginal effects of interest, the attenuation result of the linear model is not general – even in the simple Poisson model, the magnitude of the marginal effects can change substantially.

19.3 Censored data and the censored regression model

In terms of received applications, censoring is much more common than truncation; applications can be found throughout and beyond all the social sciences. (There are numerous surveys, beginning with Maddala (1983) and more recently, Long (1997) and DeMaris (2004).) Here, we will establish a few of the essential elements of a model with censoring, then point toward some more elaborate specifications and methods of analysis.

As before, we depart from the classical normal, linear regression model,

$$y_i^* = \mathbf{x}_i'\boldsymbol{\beta} + \varepsilon_i, \varepsilon_i \sim N[0, \sigma^2], \quad i = 1, \ldots, N. \tag{19.3.1}$$

In this setting, the observed data, y_i are obtained by a many to one transformation of y_i^*,

$$y_i = \Sigma_{j=1}^{J} d_j T_j(y_i^*) \tag{19.3.2}$$

where $T_j(y_i^*)$ partitions the range of y_i^* into J ranges and maps the values of y_i^* in the specific range into a specific value and d_j equals one if y_i^* falls in range j and zero otherwise; $d_j = 1[y_i^*$ is in range $j]$. The most familiar case [the tobit model, from Tobin (1958)[1]] has $J = 2$, where the first range is $-\infty$ to 0, which is mapped to 0 and the second range is 0 to ∞ where y_i^* is mapped to itself. (Thus, we formalize the simple case of censoring values below zero to zero.) Another familiar case with $J = 2$ is the same as the first, save that the second range is mapped to one – the probit model for binary choice. The case of sellouts at sporting events represents a case in which actual ticket sales are a censored version of true demand. Another form of the data generating mechanism which is not censoring but which produces pre-cisely the same specification is the *corner solution model* (Wooldridge, 2002), in which, for example, zero emerges as the choice outcome in one circumstance while a continuous y_i emerges in another. The choice of insurance coverage that one chooses might be such a case – zero amounts to a specific choice, not a cen-sored value of some latent negative value. In the model as stated, censoring may be incomplete, when one or more of the ranges is uncensored $(T_j(y_i^*) = y_i^*)$, or it may be complete, as in the binary choice model just mentioned.

For simplicity, we consider the simplest case first; censoring at zero a range of values. In order to form the quantities of interest in this model, we apply the laws of probability to the underlying regression model. Thus, the model that applies to the observed data in this case is

$$y_i = \max(0, y_i^*) \tag{19.3.3}$$

(that is, $d_1 = 1(y_i^* < 0), d_2 = 1(y_i^* > 0), T_1(y_i^*) = 0, T_2(y_i^*) = y_i^*$). The conditional mean function in this model is

$$E[y_i|\mathbf{x}_i] = \text{Prob}[y_i^* < 0|\mathbf{x}_i] \times 0 + \text{Prob}[y_i^* \geq 0|\mathbf{x}_i]E[y_i^*|\mathbf{x}_i, y_i^* \geq 0]. \tag{19.3.4}$$

We obtained the necessary parts in our discussion of truncation. Using the probability and conditional mean function obtained there, we have

$$E[y_i|\mathbf{x}_i] = \Phi(\mathbf{x}_i'\boldsymbol{\beta}/\sigma) \times (\mathbf{x}_i'\boldsymbol{\beta} + \sigma\lambda_i). \tag{19.3.5}$$

(Note that in this partially censored data case, $\Phi(\mathbf{x}_i'\boldsymbol{\beta}/\sigma)$ is the probability attached to the uncensored region.) The conditional mean function for this model is noteworthy. Figure 19.1 shows the function for the standard case. Referring back to the linear specification for y_i^*, we see that y_i^* and $E[y_i^*|\mathbf{x}_i]$ can take either sign. However, $\mathbf{x}_i'\boldsymbol{\beta}$ cannot serve as the regression model for the observed y_i, which is either zero or positive. The function $E[y_i|\mathbf{x}_i]$ given above is always positive, even

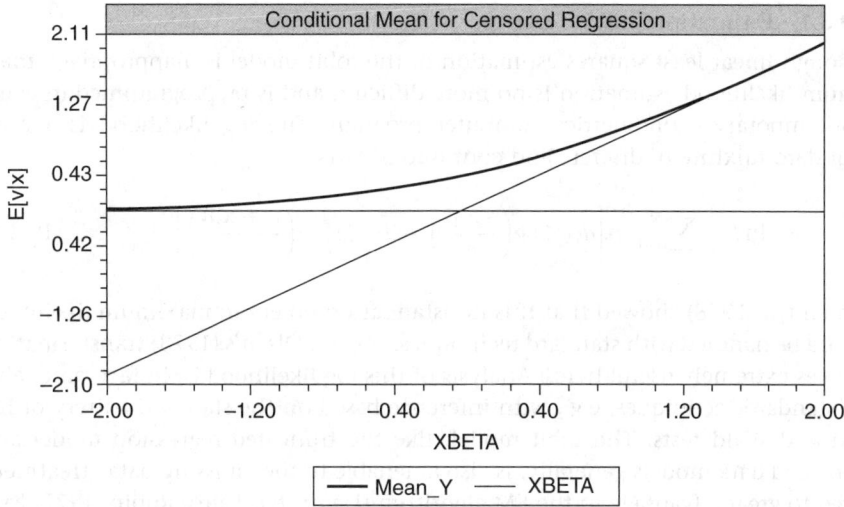

Figure 19.1 Conditional mean function for the censored regression model

when $x_i'\beta$ is negative. As in the truncation model examined earlier, the non-linearity of the conditional mean function suggests that linear regression of y_i on x_i is unlikely to produce an estimate that resembles β. Indeed, a surprising result emerges. Marginal effects are obtained by using our earlier results and, to some advantage, the Olsen transformation of the parameters;

$$\frac{\partial E[y_i|x_i]}{\partial x_i} = \Phi\left(\frac{x_i'\beta}{\sigma}\right)\beta. \tag{19.3.6}$$

That is, the partial effect in this model is equal to the coefficient times the probability attached to the noncensored region. Greene (1999, 2003) shows that this result extends to the "two-tailed" censoring model – that is below zero and above some positive value – and is not specific to the normal distribution but occurs regardless of the distribution of ε_i as long as it is continuous. On reflection, it should make sense. In the uncensored region, $E[y_i|x_i]$ responds to changes in x_i directly in measure β, but in the censored region, we have a range of values for which changes in the value of x_i do not induce changes in y_i.

Faced with substantial censoring in the data, the researcher might be tempted simply to discard the "limit" observations and apply conventional techniques, for example, least squares, to the observations that remain. But, assembling the parts above, we see that the nonlimit observations are governed by the truncated regression model of the preceding section. This does not solve the problem; it merely moves it to a different modeling platform. Dionne *et al.* (1998) apply this principle to an "incomplete" panel of cost data on Canadian trucking firms. In their application, the specification is further complicated because the incompleteness of the data set results from "attrition," a form of sample selection that we consider in section 19.5.

19.3.1   Estimation and inference

Though linear least squares estimation of the tobit model is inappropriate, maximum likelihood estimation is no more difficult, and is preprogrammed in every contemporary econometrics computer program. The log likelihood is a non-standard mixture of discrete and continuous parts;

$$\ln L = \sum_{i=1}^{N} \ln\left[d_1(y_i^*)\Phi\left(\frac{-\mathbf{x}_i'\boldsymbol{\beta}}{\sigma}\right) + d_2(y_i^*)\frac{1}{\sigma}\phi\left(\frac{y_i - \mathbf{x}_i'\boldsymbol{\beta}}{\sigma}\right) \right]. \tag{19.3.7}$$

Amemiya (1978) showed that this nonstandard problem in maximum likelihood could be handled with standard techniques. (Again, Olsen's (1978) transformation proves extremely useful here.) Analysis of this log likelihood is, in fact, amenable to standard techniques, e.g., with inference based on the standard battery of LR, LM and Wald tests. The tobit model, like the truncated regression model and censored data models generally, is also amenable to the "missing data" treatment used to great advantage in the EM algorithm (Dempster, Laird, Rubin, 1977; Fair, 1977). Here, we note, if the censored observations were not censored, the appropriate estimator for $\boldsymbol{\beta}$ would be least squares. Given the actual data, we can compute the expectations of the missing data, as

$$E[y_i^*|\mathbf{x}_i, y_i = 0] = \mathbf{x}_i'\boldsymbol{\beta} + \sigma[-\phi(-\mathbf{x}_i'\boldsymbol{\beta}/\sigma)/\Phi(-\mathbf{x}_i'\boldsymbol{\beta}/\sigma)]. \tag{19.3.8}$$

The EM algorithm proceeds, with minor modification, by using this expression to compute the estimates for the missing observations, then using least squares based on the partially reconstructed sample. (This is the algorithm proposed in Fair (1978), though he did not treat it as an EM method.) Not surprisingly, the Bayesian MCMC estimator of the tobit model with data augmentation (see Chib, 1992) is, with trivial modification, the same computation.[2]

Construction of fit measures and predictions in this model are less straightforward than in the linear regression case. There is no counterpart to R^2 since one is not using OLS (with a constant term). Simply computing a prediction using $\mathbf{x}_i'\hat{\boldsymbol{\beta}}$ is unsatisfactory since, for some of the sample, the linear predictor is being used to predict observations known to be zero, and none can legitimately be predicted to be less than zero. Likewise, the correlation between y_i and this prediction will give a misleading indication of how well the model fits the data. For prediction, the estimated conditional mean, $\hat{E}[y_i|\mathbf{x}_i] = \Phi(\mathbf{x}_i'\hat{\boldsymbol{\beta}})[\mathbf{x}_i'\hat{\boldsymbol{\beta}} + \hat{\sigma}\hat{\lambda}_i]$ makes more sense. Even with this predictor, however, summarizing the fit of the model to the data in an R^2-like measure is problematic because of the ambiguity of the limit observations. There is no consensus on how fit should be measured in this setting. Many contemporary researchers report the "pseudo-R^2,"

$$pseudo\text{-}R^2 = 1 - \ln L / \ln L_0 \tag{19.3.9}$$

where $\ln L$ is evaluated at the unrestricted maximum likelihood estimates and $\ln L_0$ is computed for a model which contains only a constant term. Whether this is truly useful as a fit measure is debatable as the log likelihood is not maximized to optimize "fit." It does have the virtues of lying between zero and one, and it does increase as variables are added to the model.[3]

19.3.2 Specification analysis

The corner solution interpretation of the model raises a question about the model. Under the assumptions already made, the probability that a corner solution emerges, i.e., $\text{Prob}[y_i^* < 0]$, has the same underlying specification as the regression model applied in the nonlimit case; in both cases, the index function in the density is $x_i'\boldsymbol{\beta}$. One might be interested in whether the impact on the limit probability is different from that on the regression model given that it is not a limit case. To analyze this possibility, we write the log likelihood (using Olsen's transformation) for the corner solution model in the form

$$\ln L = \sum_{y_i=0} \ln \Phi(-x_i'\boldsymbol{\gamma}) + \sum_{y_i>0} \ln\{\theta\phi[(\theta y_i - x_i'\boldsymbol{\gamma})]\}$$

$$= \sum_{y_i=0} \ln \Phi(-x_i'\boldsymbol{\gamma}) + \sum_{y_i>0} \ln \Phi(x_i'\boldsymbol{\gamma}) \qquad (19.3.10)$$

$$+ \sum_{y_i>0} \ln\{\theta\phi[(\theta y_i - x_i'\boldsymbol{\gamma})]\} - \sum_{y_i>0} \ln \Phi(x_i'\boldsymbol{\gamma})$$

Note that the second form is obtained simply by adding and subtracting the nonlimit probability. The first line is the log likelihood for a binary probit model for the probability of the corner solution. The second line is the log density for the observation conditioned on their having a nonlimit solution. It is also precisely the log density for the truncated regression model discussed in the preceding section. A natural specification test for whether the impact of the regressors is the same in the probability equation and in the conditional regression equation is a test of whether the coefficients in an independently estimated probit equation are the same as those in the truncated regression model for the nonlimit observations. Fin and Schmidt (1984) proposed a Lagrange multiplier test for this specification based on the results of the tobit model. A simpler computation which requires only that it be possible to compute the MLEs for all three models is the *LR* statistic

$$LR = 2 \left[\ln L_{probit} + \ln L_{truncated\ regression} - \ln L_{tobit}\right]. \qquad (19.3.11)$$

The test statistic will have a limiting chi-squared distribution with degrees of freedom equal to the number of variables in x_i.

The preceding might be extended a step further to allow for different specifications in the probability equation in the regression. This produces a simple version of the *hurdle model* (Cragg, 1971). Estimation of this form of the model is quite simple, though again it requires estimation of the truncated regression model. Indeed, computation of the likelihood ratio statistic defined above actually requires fitting this hurdle model with the additional restriction that the regressor vectors are the same in the two equations. This is not required, of course. Two extensions of the hurdle model are also useful. Having bifurcated the model into the "participation" equation (the probability model) and the regression model, we are no longer required to specify a linear regression model for the "regression" equation. Jones (1994) analyzes a model of this sort in which the participation equation is a conventional probit model while the regression equation is a count (Poisson) model for smoking behavior. A second extension involves the underlying unobservables in the structural equations. A model which produces the hurdle log likelihood function

$$z_i^* = \mathbf{w}_i'\boldsymbol{\alpha} + u_i, \quad u_i \sim N[0, 1]$$
$$z_i = d_1(z_i^*) = 1(z_i^* > 0) \quad \text{(a probit model)} \tag{19.3.12}$$
$$y_i^* = \mathbf{x}_i'\boldsymbol{\beta} + \varepsilon_i|\varepsilon_i \sim N[0, \sigma^2], \quad z_i = 1.$$

The model considered so far includes the assumption that u_i and ε_i are uncorrelated (independent). If they are allowed to be correlated (bivariate normally distributed), then this form of the hurdle model produces the sample selection model that is discussed in section 19.4, below.

19.3.3 Heteroskedasticity

Since these models are typically employed with microeconomic data, two other specifications, heteroskedasticity (heterogeneity in scaling) and omitted heterogeneity (unobserved heterogeneity in the levels). In the linear regression model, conventional estimation and inference techniques are (more or less) robust to these failures of the model assumptions. Here, the estimators are not robust to any of these failures. (Nor, by large, are they to any other failures of the model assumptions, which calls into question "robust" estimators. We turn to this issue below.)

Consider, first, a tobit model with heteroskedasticity. The modification of the model is straightforward. We define the model in terms of the log likelihood;

$$\ln L = \sum_{i=1}^{N} \ln \left[d_1(y_i^*)\Phi\left(\frac{-\mathbf{x}_i'\boldsymbol{\beta}}{\sigma_i}\right) + d_2(y_i^*)\frac{1}{\sigma_i}\phi\left(\frac{y_i - \mathbf{x}_i'\boldsymbol{\beta}}{\sigma_i}\right) \right]. \tag{19.3.13}$$

Conventional ML (or Bayesian MCMC) estimation of the model parameters that ignores the heteroskedasticity is not robust to this failure of the model assumptions. Assuming that σ_i is a function of $\mathbf{x}_i$ (or variables that are correlated with $\mathbf{x}_i$), conventional estimators are not consistent, and nothing can be said about the magnitude or direction of the bias. There is no counterpart to White's robust, heteroskedasticity corrected estimator for the linear model either; the often cited Huber–White "sandwich" estimator, $\mathbf{H}^{-1}(\mathbf{G}'\mathbf{G})\mathbf{H}^{-1}$ where $\mathbf{H}$ is the negative of the inverse of the Hessian and $\mathbf{G}$ is the matrix (row by row) of first derivatives of $\ln L$, does not solve the problem; it is merely a "robust" covariance matrix for an inconsistent estimator. (Robustness is a moot point.) Extension of the tobit model to allow for heteroskedasticity is straightforward, though it does require the analyst to specify the heteroskedasticity. For a model such as

$$\sigma_i = \sigma \times \exp(\mathbf{x}_i'\boldsymbol{\delta}) \tag{19.3.14}$$

the log likelihood or posterior can simply be augmented to include the additional parameters. (We have written the scedastic function in terms of the same x_i that appears in the regression purely for convenience as will be clear below. Appropriately placed zeros in β and/or δ can produced the desired different specifications.) With a formal specification in place, a test for heteroskedasticity in the tobit model can be based on the Wald or LR statistics by fitting the model with heteroskedasticity or by using an Lagrange multiplier statistic as shown in Greene (2003, p. 769). (Note that the ML statistic does not free the analyst from the necessity of specifying precisely what variables must appear in the scedastic function.) Partial effects in the model with heteroskedasticity are (after some tedious algebra)

$$\frac{\partial E[y_i|x_i]}{\partial x_i} = \Phi(a_i)\beta + \sigma_i\phi(a_i)\delta, \quad a_i = x_i'\beta/\sigma. \tag{19.3.15}$$

For variables which appear in both the mean and variance components of the model, we see that both sign and magnitude of the partial effect can differ from those of the coefficients in β. This suggests some care is called for in the interpretation of the estimated model components.

19.3.4 Unobserved heterogeneity

Unobserved heterogeneity in the tobit model that is uncorrelated with x_i is, surprisingly, benign. There is no need to prove the result analytically. If the model changes from

$$y_i^* = x_i'\beta + \varepsilon_i, \varepsilon_i \sim N[0, \sigma^2], \quad i = 1, \ldots, N. \tag{19.3.16}$$

to

$$y_i^* = x_i'\beta + c_i + \varepsilon_i, \varepsilon_i \sim N[0, \sigma^2], c_i \sim N[0, \tau^2], \quad i = 1, \ldots, N, \tag{19.3.17}$$

then the heterogeneity simply becomes part of the disturbance, which now has variance $\sigma^2 + \tau^2$. This simple result doesn't arise, for example, in the probit model because here, unlike the probit model, the sample data contain information on the scale of the latent y_i^* whereas in the binary choice model, they do not.

19.3.5 Distribution

The specification of the tobit model, thus far, hangs crucially on the assumption of normality. How fragile the model is because of this is unknown; the only received results are (and will almost surely be) based on Monte Carlo studies of very limited generality. For better or worse, the normal distribution has provided the platform for nearly all the research on this model. One can, of course, specify an alternative distribution – we will explore how below. Of course, the resulting model is no less fragile than the censored normal model. A preferable alternative would be a less heavily parameterized, more robust estimator, such as Powell's (1981, 1984) least absolute deviations estimator. (See Melenberg and van Soest, 1996 for an application and Duncan, 1983, 1986; Newey, Powell and Walker, 1990; Lee, 1996; and Lee, 2002 for further theoretical development.)

Though estimation with an alternative model is computationally complicated, testing for the normality assumption remains worthwhile.[4] Several approaches have been devised, including a Hausman test that compares the robust LAD estimator to the tobit/normal estimator (Melenberg and van Soest, 1996), LM tests (Bera and Jarque, 1981, 1982) and conditional moment tests (Nelson, 1981; Chesher and Irish, 1987; and Pagan and Vella, 1989). The LM and conditional moment and LM tests require a set of residuals that contain information about the distribution – and nonnormality in particular. As noted above, the conventional residual, y_i – anything, has a built in problem whenever y_i equals zero. Chesher and Irish (1987) proposed the *generalized residual* for models such as this one. For the tobit (and many other models), the generalized residual can be computed as the derivative of the log-density with respect to the constant term, computed at the maximum likelihood estimators. Using the Olsen form of the log likelihood, we have

$$e_i = d_1 \frac{-\phi(-\mathbf{x}_i'\boldsymbol{\gamma})}{\Phi(-\mathbf{x}_i'\boldsymbol{\gamma})} + d_2(\theta y_i - \mathbf{x}_i'\boldsymbol{\gamma}) \tag{19.3.18}$$

This residual has expectation and sample mean zero and accounts for the censoring.[5] A chi-squared test of the normality assumption (actually a test of whether the residual moments conform to what would be expected from a normal distribution) is computed using

$$LM = \mathbf{i}'\mathbf{M}(\mathbf{M}'\mathbf{M})^{-1}\mathbf{M}'\mathbf{i} \tag{19.3.19}$$

where $\mathbf{i}$ is a column of ones and $\mathbf{M}$ is $N \times K + 3$, where each row contains

$$\mathbf{m}_i' = [e_i\mathbf{x}_i', b_i, e_i^3, e_i^4 - 3] \tag{19.3.20}$$

$$b_i = \frac{1}{2}\{d_1[(\theta y_i - \mathbf{x}_i'\boldsymbol{\gamma})^2 - 1] + d_2[\mathbf{x}_i'\boldsymbol{\gamma}\phi(-\mathbf{x}_i'\boldsymbol{\gamma})/\Phi(-\mathbf{x}_i'\boldsymbol{\gamma})]\} \tag{19.3.21}$$

(Pagan and Vella (1989) propose a variety of similar conditional moment tests for the tobit model.) Skeels and Vella (1999) have examined the behavior of this test in an extensive Monte Carlo study. The same style of specification test is extended to tests for the sample selection model examined in section 19.4 below by Vella (1992).

19.3.6   Other models with censoring

Censoring is found in many different types of applications. To suggest the range of possibilities, we note a few of them here. As in the tobit model above, the general approach to estimation and inference is generally to formulate the model in terms of the "latent" data, then deal with the censoring in the likelihood function or posterior density in the case of a Bayesian approach by using the basic laws of probability to modify the model.

The logical limit of the censoring model set out at the outset occurs when data are completely censored – none of the transformation functions $T(y_i^*)$ is one to one as it is in the uncensored region of the tobit model. Perhaps the most familiar case is the binary choice model noted at the outset,

$$y_i^* = \mathbf{x}_i\boldsymbol{\beta} + \varepsilon_i, \varepsilon_i \sim N[0, \sigma^2], \quad i = 1, \dots, N$$

$$y_i = \sum_{j=1}^{2} d_j T_j(y_i^*), d_1 = 1(y_i^* < 0), T_1(y_i^*) = 0, d_2 = 1 - d_1, T_2(y_i^*) = 1. \tag{19.3.22}$$

A less extreme case is the *ordered probit model*, which maps ranges with unknown boundary points to the integers $0, 1, \dots, J$. The second equation in the structure above is

$$\text{Prob}[\mu_{j-1} < y_i^* \leq \mu_j] = \Phi[\mu_j - \mathbf{x}_i'\boldsymbol{\beta}] - \Phi[\mu_{j-1} - \mathbf{x}_i'\boldsymbol{\beta}], \quad \mu_j > \mu_{j-1}, \quad j = 0, \dots, J, \tag{19.3.23}$$

with normalizations $\mu_{-1} = -\infty, \mu_0 = 0, \mu_J = +\infty$. Familiar applications include opinion measures, where the strength of opinions or preferences are expressed on a scale (usually zero to four). Another natural application (which remains to be explored at length) is self reported health status, such as the variable contained in Winkelmann (2004). In the ordered probit model, information about the scale of the dependent variable is lost – in the case of latent preference, it would have no meaning in any event. When data are censored to mask within range variation, the observed response may be *interval censored*. In Bhat (1994) a latent income variable is reported only in ranges. The structural model is identical to that of the ordered probit, except that the threshold parameters are known. This obviates the normalizations, and reveals the scaling information, so that an estimate of σ can be computed with the estimate of $\boldsymbol{\beta}$. As a consequence, the density for y_i is redefined to be

$$\text{Prob}[y_i = j] = \Phi\left(\frac{a_j - \mathbf{x}_i'\boldsymbol{\beta}}{\sigma}\right) - \Phi\left(\frac{a_{j-1} - \mathbf{x}_i'\boldsymbol{\beta}}{\sigma}\right). \tag{19.3.24}$$

Each of these represents a method of modeling censoring in the context of the classical normal linear regression model. Two other leading cases of censored data are in models of counts and in duration data. In the count data model, we have the generic structure

$$\text{Prob}[y_i = j | \mathbf{x}_i] = f(j; \boldsymbol{\beta})$$

(The parameter vector may include other ancilliary parameters, such as the over-dispersion parameter in the negative binomial model.) The most familiar case is the Poisson (loglinear) regression model,

$$\text{Prob}[y_i = j | \mathbf{x}_i] = \frac{\exp(-\mu_i)\mu_i^j}{j!}, \quad \mu_i = \exp(\mathbf{x}_i'\boldsymbol{\beta}), \quad j = 0, 1, \dots \tag{19.3.25}$$

Data may be censored at either end, though the leading case is *top coding*, in which the censoring takes the form of piling all values above a limit value into that value (see Terza, 1985). An example is Fair's (1978) study of extramarital affairs in which the reported count was censored at 12.[6] The censored Poisson model follows naturally from the definitions. For example, for censoring at upper limit C, we would have the model

$$\text{Prob}[y_i = j|\mathbf{x}_i] = \frac{\exp(-\mu_i)\mu_i^j}{j!}, \mu_i = \exp(\mathbf{x}_i'\boldsymbol{\beta}), j = 0, 1, \ldots, C-1,$$

$$\text{Prob}[y_i = C|\mathbf{x}_i] = 1 - \sum_{j=0}^{C-1} \frac{\exp(-\mu_i)\mu_i^j}{j!}.$$

(19.3.26)

The conditional mean is altered in an expected fashion (see Greene, 2000);

$$E[y_i|\mathbf{x}_i] = \mu_j - \sum_{j=C}^{\infty}(j-C)\text{Prob}[y_i = j|\mathbf{x}_i]$$

$$= C - \sum_{j=0}^{C-1}(C-j)\text{Prob}[y_i = j|\mathbf{x}_i].$$

(19.3.27)

The marginal effects also change;

$$\frac{E[y_i|\mathbf{x}_i]}{\partial x_i} = \left[\sum_{j=0}^{C-1}(j-C)(j-\mu_i)\text{Prob}[y_i = j|\mathbf{x}_i]\right]\boldsymbol{\beta}.$$

(19.3.28)

These can be substantially smaller than their uncensored counterparts, $\mu_i\boldsymbol{\beta}$.

The foregoing illustrate the effect of censoring on regression models, that is in models in which the conditional mean function and its derivatives is the central focus. A vast variety of other models, in which some variation of the regressand is masked by censoring, are all handled similarly and similar results emerge. Censoring, which masks variation brings predictable changes in the location of the mean, generally reduces marginal effects because in the censored region changes in the stimuli (independent variables) are not associated with changes in the response.

Another leading class of models in which censoring is an important feature is models of duration. In this setting, we model the length of time, t, from a "baseline" until a "transition" takes place (see Kiefer, 1985 for a survey). Familiar applications include the time until business failure, length of a spell of unemployment or the lengths of the intervals between children at the household level, or between wars at a global level. In all cases, what is typically of interest is not the length of time, but the *hazard rate*, which is roughly the probability that the transition takes place in interval t to $t+\Delta t$ given that it has not taken place up to time t. We consider a few of the formalities of hazard models to illustrate an extension of our class of censored data models.

For the random variable t, the time until an event occurs, $t \geq 0$, the density, cdf and *survival function* are denoted $f(t)$, $F(t)$ and $S(t) = 1 - F(t)$. The probability of an event occurring at or before time t is $F(t)$. The conditional probability that an event occurs in the interval t to $t+\Delta$ given that it has not occurred by time t is

$$h(t) = \text{Prob}(\text{event occurs in time } t \text{ to } t+\Delta| \text{ event occurs after time } t)$$

$$= \frac{F(t+\Delta) - F(t)}{1 - F(t)}.$$

(19.3.29)

As $\Delta \to 0$, the function $[F(t + \Delta) - F(t)]/[\Delta(1 - F(t))]$ converges to $f(t)/S(t)$, which is called the *hazard function*, often denoted $\lambda(t)$. (This is not to be confused with λ_i as used in the preceding discussions, though there is clearly a relationship for the normal distribution.) Note that $\Delta\lambda(t)$ equals the probability sought, Prob $[t \leq T \leq t + \Delta|T \geq t]$. The hazard function is a descriptor of the probability distribution, as are the pdf and cdf. Indeed, we see the simple relationship $\lambda(t)S(t) = f(t)$. There are many different specifications that can be used to model the hazard for the duration variable T. The simplest is a function with "no memory;" that is, one with a constant hazard rate. For this model, we would have $\lambda(t) = \lambda$, a constant. It follows from the definition that the hazard follows the simple differential equation $\lambda(t) = -d \ln S(t)/dt$. The solution to $-d \ln S(t)/dt = \lambda$ is $S(t) = K \exp(-\lambda t)$, where K is the constant of integration. The boundary condition $S(0) = 1$ implies $K = 1$, which leaves $S(t) = \exp(-\lambda t)$. This is the exponential density,

$$f(t) = \lambda \exp(-\lambda t), \quad \lambda > 0, \quad t \geq 0. \tag{19.3.30}$$

This is the most basic hazard function model. Some other candidates are

Weibull: $\quad \lambda(t) = \lambda p(\lambda t)^{p-1}, p = 1$ implies exponential,

log logistic: $\quad \lambda(t) = \lambda p(\lambda t)^{p-1}/[1 + (\lambda t)^p], \tag{19.3.31}$

log normal: $\quad \lambda(t) = \phi[-p \ln(\lambda t)]/\Phi[-p \ln(\lambda t)]$

Figure 19.2 shows the behavior of these hazard functions for a standard data set on strike duration (see Kennan, 1985).

Note that the hazard for the Weibull model declines monotonically – this is known as *negative duration dependence*. Over some ranges, the lognormal and log logistic have *positive duration dependence*, while the exponential model has no duration dependence.

The counterpart to the familiar regression models in this context would be the *accelerated failure time models*, in which the hazard function is modeled as a function of covariates. A familiar example is the loglinear model. For the Weibull model, this would be

$$\lambda(t|\mathbf{x}) = \exp(\mathbf{x}'\boldsymbol{\beta})p[\exp(\mathbf{x}'\boldsymbol{\beta})t]^{p-1} \tag{19.3.32}$$

Most data sets have incomplete observations. The observation consists of the time of the measurement and the indication that the transition (business failure, death, warranty exercise, next insurrection, next child) has not yet occurred. Such observations are censored at time t, the same as the censoring phenomenon observed earlier.

We now construct the log likelihood for a sample of duration data. For an uncensored observation, the contribution to the likelihood is the density. For a censored observation, it is the survival function. (Note that this is precisely the

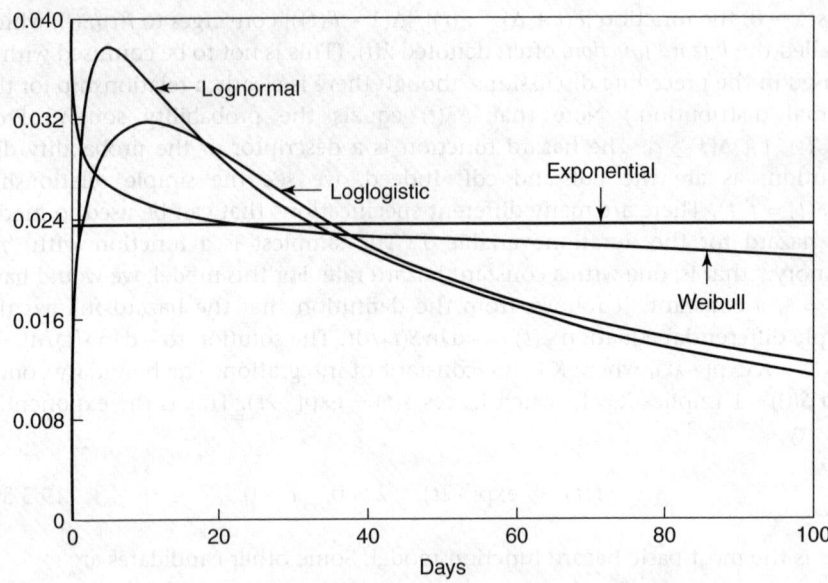

Figure 19.2 Hazard functions

format the likelihood takes for the regression model with right tail censoring that was discussed above.) Let d be a noncensoring indicator; $d=0$ for a censored observation and $d=1$ for an uncensored observation. We will also use the result noted earlier, $f(t|\mathbf{x}) = \lambda(t|\mathbf{x})S(t|\mathbf{x})$. Then, the log likelihood for a sample that contains both censored and uncensored observations is

$$\ln L = \sum_{i=1}^{N} d_i \ln[\lambda(t_i|\mathbf{x}_i)] + \ln S(t_i|\mathbf{x}_i) \qquad (19.3.33)$$

For the parametric models shown earlier, this is now a standard problem for maximum likelihood estimation and inference. To close the loop here, so to speak, we note that the preceding shows how different distribution could be used for a censored regression model. We used the normal distribution in our earlier discussion. This derivation shows how the exponential, Weibull and other models could be used. Moreover, to use this template to accommodate our standard model with left censoring at zero, we can simply use $-\ln t$ as the dependent variable (see Greene, 2000 for discussion).

19.4 Incidental truncation and sample selection

The results of the preceding sections have been extended to a "two-part" model that extends the hurdle model. Consider an observation mechanism that departs from the familiar regression model,

$$y_i^* = \mathbf{x}_i'\boldsymbol{\beta} + \varepsilon_i, \varepsilon_i \sim N[0, \sigma^2], \quad i = 1, \ldots, N, \tag{19.4.1}$$

and adds a "sample selection mechanism" to a binary probit model;

$$
\begin{aligned}
d_i^* &= \mathbf{z}_i'\boldsymbol{\alpha} + u_i \\
T(d_i^*) &= 1(d_i^* > 0) \\
T(y_i^*|d_i^*) &= y_i^* \quad \text{if } d_i^* > 0, y_i^* \text{ is unobserved otherwise.}
\end{aligned}
\tag{19.4.2}
$$

This is a modification of the truncated regression model discussed in section 19.2, where $d_i^* = y_i^*$. Here, d_i^* is another variable in this two equation model. If u_i and ε_i are correlated, then the observed values of y_i^* are unusual compared to the full population. Hence we use the term "incidental truncation" for this specification. Applications of this sort of model abound in the literature, beginning with Heckman's pioneering work (e.g., 1979) on labor supply.[7] Some examples, in addition to this one, include analysis of returns in long time series of financial data ("survivorship" effects), analysis of program participation where observation at the end of the program is affected by attrition of the participants, count models of recreation site use, health care usage, and a vast catalog of other settings.

In all cases, it is the relationship between the unobservables in the models that exerts the impact on the estimation and inference procedures. Consider, in the model above, the standard case in which (ε_i, u_i) are bivariate normally distributed with correlation ρ. In the observed data, we will have

$$
\begin{aligned}
\mathbb{E}[y_i|\mathbf{x}_i, y_i \text{ is observed}] &= \mathbb{E}[y_i^*|\mathbf{x}_i, d_i^* > 0] = \mathbb{E}[y_i^*|\mathbf{x}_i, d_i = 1] \\
&= \mathbf{x}_i'\boldsymbol{\beta} + \mathbb{E}[\varepsilon_i|d_i = 1] \\
&= \mathbf{x}_i'\boldsymbol{\beta} + \mathbb{E}[\varepsilon_i|u_i > -\mathbf{z}_i'\boldsymbol{\alpha}].
\end{aligned}
\tag{19.4.3}
$$

From results for the bivariate normal distribution, this is

$$
\begin{aligned}
\mathbb{E}[y_i|\mathbf{x}_i, y_i \text{ is observed}] &= \mathbf{x}_i'\boldsymbol{\beta} + \rho\sigma_\varepsilon\phi(-\mathbf{z}_i'\boldsymbol{\alpha})/[1 - \Phi(-\mathbf{z}_i'\boldsymbol{\alpha})] \\
&= \mathbf{x}_i'\boldsymbol{\beta} + \kappa\lambda_i
\end{aligned}
\tag{19.4.4}
$$

where $\lambda_i = \phi(\mathbf{z}_i'\boldsymbol{\alpha})/\Phi(\mathbf{z}_i'\boldsymbol{\alpha})$ is the inverse Mills ratio discussed earlier. Two conclusions follow from this derivation, before we consider estimation. First, by dint of the excluded variable, λ_i, it is clear that linear regression of y_i on $\mathbf{x}_i$ in the observed data will produce an inconsistent estimator of $\boldsymbol{\beta}$ if κ is not equal to zero (which we assumed) and if λ_i is correlated with $\mathbf{x}_i$, which is almost surely going to be the case, particularly if $\mathbf{z}_i$ and $\mathbf{x}_i$ have variables in common. To underscore the point, consider a modification of the model, known as the *treatment effects* model, where

$$y_i^* = \mathbf{x}_i'\boldsymbol{\beta} + \delta d_i + \varepsilon_i, \varepsilon_i \sim N[0, \sigma^2], \quad i = 1, \ldots, N,$$
$$d_i^* = \mathbf{z}_i'\boldsymbol{\alpha} + u_i, d_i = 1[d_i^* > 0] \tag{19.4.5}$$

and $(y_i^*, \mathbf{x}_i)$ is observed for all cases. In an intriguing recent example [Dale and Krueger (1999)], consider the case in which y_i^* is an income variable and d_i is an indicator of whether the individual attended an elite college. Clearly in this model, the "regressor" d_i is correlated with the disturbance ε_i, producing "simultaneous equations bias." With a bit of manipulation, we can recast this model as another example of our selection model – at least it shares the fundamental features. Returning to the original model, a second question arises; it is unclear whether $\boldsymbol{\beta}$ is even the quantity of interest. Using the device we used before, assume that $\mathbf{z}_i = \mathbf{x}_i$ (with appropriate zeros in $\boldsymbol{\beta}$ or $\boldsymbol{\alpha}$ as needed). Then, again using our earlier results, we find in this basic model,

$$\frac{\partial E[y_i|\mathbf{x}_i]}{\partial \mathbf{x}_i} = \boldsymbol{\beta} - (a_i\lambda_i + \lambda_i^2)\boldsymbol{\alpha}. \tag{19.4.6}$$

We conclude that, even after dealing appropriately with the estimation issues, some care is needed in interpreting the results.

There are two methods of estimating this model, *two-step* (not two-stage) least squares and maximum likelihood. The two-step method was proposed by Heckman (1979) (see also Greene, 1981, 2003). The logic of Heckman's method is strikingly simple. If λ_i were observed, ordinary least squares would provide a consistent (though not necessarily efficient) estimator of $(\boldsymbol{\beta}, \kappa)$. Since the parameters in λ_i can be consistently estimated by applying a binary probit model to the model for d_i, and $\mathbf{z}_i$ is observed, a "pointwise" consistent estimator of λ_i is obtained by using $\hat{\boldsymbol{\alpha}}$ from the probit model. This is the first step of the two-step estimator. The second step is least squares regression of y_i on $\mathbf{x}_i$ and $\hat{\lambda}_i$. The conventionally estimated asymptotic covariance matrix for this least squares estimator is inappropriate for two reasons; first, the implied disturbance in the regression is heteroskedastic and, second, it does not account for the variation in the estimated parameter vector used to compute $\hat{\lambda}_i$ (see Murphy and Topel, 1985). Expressions for computing the appropriate covariance matrix appear in Heckman (1979) and Greene (1980, 2003). The treatment effects model is handled similarly. In this case, the counterpart to "λ_i" is the generalized residual from the probit model,

$$\hat{\lambda}_i = d_i \frac{\phi(\mathbf{z}_i'\boldsymbol{\alpha})}{\Phi(\mathbf{z}_i'\boldsymbol{\alpha})} + (1 - d_i)\frac{-\phi(-\mathbf{z}_i'\boldsymbol{\alpha})}{\Phi(-\mathbf{z}_i'\boldsymbol{\alpha})} \tag{19.4.7}$$

After estimation, a "test" for "selectivity" is based on the estimate of κ; a simple "t-test" of the significance of the coefficient on $\hat{\lambda}_i$ is equivalent to a test that ρ equals zero.

The second estimator is maximum likelihood. The log likelihood function for this model is constructed from the joint density for d_i and y_i for those observations for which y_i is observed. As usual, the Olsen transformation simplifies the notation;

$$\ln L = \sum_{d_i=1} \ln[\theta\phi(\theta y_i - \mathbf{x}_i'\boldsymbol{\gamma})] + \ln \Phi\left[\frac{\rho(\theta y_i - \mathbf{x}_i'\boldsymbol{\gamma}) + \mathbf{z}_i'\boldsymbol{\alpha}}{\sqrt{1 - \rho^2}}\right]$$
$$+ \sum_{d_i=0} \ln \Phi[-\mathbf{z}_i'\boldsymbol{\alpha}].$$
(19.4.8)

(There is yet another simplification possible by transforming ρ.) This is a compli-cated (because of ρ) but otherwise standard problem in maximum likelihood estimation. In addition to its theoretically greater efficiency, the MLE has another advantage over the Heckman two step estimator. The variable λ_i is a nonlinear function of z_i that is essentially linear in $\mathbf{z}_i'\boldsymbol{\alpha}$ over much of its range. This implies that if there is not much difference between x_i and z_i – in many applications they are the same – then there is the potential for serious multicollinearity in the augmented regression. Most researchers seek to accommodate this problem of "weak" identification by ensuring that there is at least one variable in z_i that is not in x_i and that has substantial variation.

We note an aspect of estimation here for the interested practitioner. The appearance of Heckman's "lambda" in the estimated selection equation has produced a temptation to augment other kinds of selection models likewise and thereby "take care of the selection problem." This form of the model is specific to the linear regression case. Notice, for example, that there is no inverse Mills ratio in the log likelihood for the model. Thus, for example, it is not appropriate to correct a Poisson regression model for selectivity by just adding an inverse Mills ratio to the index function in the model. See Terza (1998) and Greene (1995, 1997, 2000) for applications of sample selection corrections to the Poisson regression model. In these and other models, it is necessary to reconstruct the log likelihood function, somewhat similar to the form as it appears above.

The literature on selection models and treatment effects is vast and varied. This is an active and ongoing area of research in econometrics (see, for example, Angrist, 2001). The above discussion suggests only the most basic form of the model.

19.5   Panel data

Microeconomic data increasingly come in the form of extensive panel data sets, such as the National Longitudinal Surveys of Labor Market Experience (NLS), the German SocioEconomics Panel or the British Household Panel Survey (BHPS) which, among many others, contain rich multiple wave surveys of individual health and labor market behavior. Interesting response variables in these data sets, such as income, fertility and labor market experience, often come in the form of discrete, truncated, limited and otherwise range restricted variables to which the methods described here apply. We consider a few of the basic issues in analysis of panel data in the censoring and truncation models considered here. The issues are relatively common across modeling platforms, so to present the essential results, we will focus on the tobit model, and add some details about panel data and sample selection at the end of the section.

Thinking about incorporating individual heterogeneity in models such as the tobit model usually focuses on the two standard approaches, fixed and random effects. We modify the basic model to include the heterogeneity as

$$y_{it}^* = \alpha_i + \mathbf{x}_{it}'\boldsymbol{\beta} + \varepsilon_{it}, \varepsilon_i \sim N[0, \sigma^2], \quad i = 1, \ldots, N,$$
$$y_{it} = \max(0, y_{it}^*).$$
(19.5.1)

Conventional wisdom about the model is guided by the linear model with individual heterogeneity. As we will see, some of that wisdom is useful, while some is not.

19.5.1 Estimating fixed effects models

The fixed effects model in the preceding specification allows correlation between α_i and $\mathbf{x}_{it}$. It is useful to digress briefly to explore the practical implication of the assumption, $\text{Cov}[\mathbf{x}_{it}, \alpha_i] \neq 0$. Suppose individual i is observed T_i times (where T_i may vary across individuals). Let $\mathbf{X}_i$ denote the $T_i \times K$ matrix of observations on the regressors and let $\mathbf{j}\alpha_i$ denote the $T_i \times 1$ column of observations (repeated) on the individual heterogeneity, α_i; $\mathbf{j}$ is a column of ones. Consider, then, the "estimator" of the covariance,

$$\text{Est.Cov}[\alpha_i, \mathbf{x}_{it}] = \frac{\sum_{i=1}^N \sum_{t=1}^{T_i} \mathbf{x}_{it}\alpha_i}{\sum_{i=1}^N T_i} = \frac{\sum_{i=1}^N \alpha_i T_i (1/T_i) \sum_{t=1}^{T_i} \mathbf{x}_{it}}{\sum_{i=1}^N T_i}$$
$$= \frac{\sum_{i=1}^N T_i \alpha_i \bar{\mathbf{X}}_i}{\sum_{i=1}^N T_i} = \sum_{i=1}^N w_i \alpha_i \bar{\mathbf{X}}_i$$
(19.5.2)
$$\rightarrow \text{Cov}[\alpha_i, \bar{\mathbf{X}}_i].$$

(The weights in the sum, w_i, $0 < w_i < 1$, $\sum_{i=1}^N w_i = 1$, accommodate an unbalanced panel. If T_i is the same for all i, then $w_i = 1/N$.) This suggests that the relationship between the invariant "effect" and the exogenous variables will be reflected in covariation between the effect and the group means. (We will employ this idea below with the "Mundlak (1978) correction" for the random effects model.) For reasons that will soon become clear, typically no distribution is assumed in the fixed effects model. The random effects model, in contrast, begins with an assumption that the effect, α_i and the data, $\mathbf{x}_{it}$ are uncorrelated. Also, it is typical to assume that the random effect is normally distributed with zero mean and constant variance. We will explore this issue in more detail below.

The fixed effects model is estimated by including in the model a set of N group dummy variables, $\mathbf{d}_i = $ the dummy variable indicating membership in group i. With this specification, the model becomes

$$y_{it}^* = \sum_{i=1}^N d_{it}\alpha_i + \mathbf{x}_{it}'\boldsymbol{\beta} + \varepsilon_{it}, \varepsilon_i \sim N[0, \sigma^2], \quad i = 1, \ldots, N,$$
$$y_{it} = \max(0, y_{it}^*).$$
(19.5.3)

The log likelihood function for the tobit model with fixed effects is

$$\ln L = \sum_{i=1}^{N} \sum_{t=1}^{T_i} (1 - c_{it}) \ln \Phi(-\eta_i - \mathbf{x}'_{it}\boldsymbol{\gamma}) + c_{it} \ln[\phi(\theta y_{it} - \eta_i - \mathbf{x}'_{it}\boldsymbol{\gamma})] \qquad (19.5.4)$$

where $c_{it} = 1$ if $y_{it} > 0$ and 0 otherwise and, as usual, we employ the Olsen transformation so that $\eta_i = \alpha_i/\sigma$. In practical terms, there are two problems with application of the fixed effects model in limited dependent variable models such as the tobit or truncated regression model. First, the number of individuals, N, is typically large, which implies that it is necessary to estimate a potentially very large number of parameters. In the linear model, this difficulty is handled by transforming observations to deviations from group means or by using first differences. In the Poisson model, there is a transformed likelihood that can be constructed that is free of the dummy variable coefficients. None of these approaches work here; since y_{it} is observed only after transformation, deviations of y_{it} from group means produces deviations in the transformations, not deviations in y_{it}^*. There is no transformation of the log likelihood that removes the dummy variable coefficients. In order to fit this model by maximum likelihood, it is necessary to estimate all $N + K + 1$ parameters simultaneously.[8] This can, in fact be done – our example below includes estimates of 7,293 dummy variable coefficients – using the method described, e.g., in Greene (2005). Before turning to the theoretical shortcoming of the fixed effects estimator, we note one additional complication. It is easy to show that for any individual for which all observations are censored, the parameter η_i is inestimable. (For such an individual, the derivative of the log likelihood with respect to η_i is $\Sigma_t - \phi(-\eta_i - \mathbf{x}'_{it}\boldsymbol{\gamma})/\Phi(-\eta_i - \mathbf{x}'_{it}\boldsymbol{\gamma})$, which is always negative and hence cannot be equated to zero.) Note, finally, another shortcoming of the fixed effects model is that like the linear regression model, it is not estimable if $\mathbf{x}_{it}$ contains any time invariant regressors.

The practical issue has discouraged use of the fixed effects estimator.[9] However, the more vexing problem is the *incidental parameters problem* of the maximum likelihood estimator in the presence of fixed effects (Neyman and Scott, 1948). Note that in the log likelihood function above, the number of parameters increases with N – each individual specific constant term is estimated with T_i observations. Since T_i is fixed, one can expect a problem with consistency of the estimator. This is generally expected to introduce a "small sample bias" into the parameter estimator. The thinking on this issue has long been guided by some well established results on binary choice models. It has been shown analytically (Andersen, 1970; Abrevaya, 1997) that in the binary logit model, the MLE of $\boldsymbol{\beta}$ in the presence of fixed effects, is biased by a factor of two (plim $\hat{\beta}_{MLE} = 2\boldsymbol{\beta}$) when T_i equals 2.

A long history of Monte Carlo work (for example, Greene, 2004) has suggested that the essentially the same result applies to the binary probit model – it has not been shown analytically. Analytic results for T greater than 2 have not been shown for any model, but, again, the Monte Carlo studies suggest, as intuition might also, that the bias in binary choice estimators diminishes as T increases, but relatively slowly – it remains substantial for T as large as 10. Until recently, analysis of this sort was limited to binary choice models, but it was, by and large, taken as a given (see, for example, Wooldridge, 2000) that similar results apply to other models. In fact, this appears not to be the case. Table 19.1 shows the results of an analysis of the tobit model under the specification,

$$y_{it}^* = \alpha_i + x_{it}\beta + z_{it}\delta + \varepsilon_{it}$$
$$y_{it} = \max(0, y_{it}^*)$$
(19.5.5)

The two regressors are a continuous variable x_{it} and a dummy variable z_{it}. The R^2 in the latent regression is about .77 and about 40 percent of the observations are censored. The values in the table are the percentage biases against the known true values of the items shown; the true values of β, δ and σ were all one. The results are strongly at odds with the conventional wisdom. First, there is essentially no bias in the estimated slope parameters (far less then one percent), but there is some bias in the estimated marginal effects (at the data means), but not very much in view of what is known about the binary choice models. The results do suggest that estimated standard errors are biased downward somewhat. As noted, these results are not consistent with those for the binary choice models. They are consistent with the original Neyman and Scott results, who found that the bias in the MLE of σ^2 in the linear model was downward, by a factor of $(T-1)/T$.[10] Surprisingly, and in conflict with our intuition, the results above seem not to extend to the truncated regression. The same study produces the results in Table 19.2. Note, in this case, everything is biased toward zero, rather than away.

The end result would seem to be that estimation of fixed effects models with censoring and truncation presents no practical obstacle. The incidental parameters problem is to be reckoned with, but if the Monte Carlo results given here have any

Table 19.1 Tobit model: effect of group size on estimates

Estimate	$T=2$	$T=3$	$T=5$	$T=8$	$T=12$	$T=15$	$T=20$
β	0.67	0.53	0.50	0.29	0.098	0.082	0.047
δ	0.33	0.90	0.57	0.54	0.32	0.16	0.14
σ	-36.14	-23.54	-13.78	-8.40	-5.54	-4.43	-3.30
ME_x	15.83	8.85	3.65	1.30	0.44	0.22	0.081
ME_z	19.67	11.85	5.08	2.16	0.89	0.46	0.27
S.E.(β)	-32.92	-19.00	-11.30	-8.36	-6.21	-4.98	0.63
S.E.(δ)	-32.87	-22.75	-12.66	-7.39	-5.56	-6.19	0.25

Table 19.2 Truncated regression model: behavior of the MLE/FE

Estimate	$T=2$	$T=3$	$T=5$	$T=8$	$T=12$	$T=15$	$T=20$
β	-17.13	-11.97	-7.64	-4.92	-3.41	-2.79	-2.11
δ	-22.81	-17.08	-11.21	-7.51	-5.16	-4.14	-3.27
σ	-35.36	-23.42	-14.28	-9.12	-6.21	-4.94	-3.75
ME_x	-7.52	-4.85	-2.87	-1.72	-1.14	-0.94	-0.67
ME_z	-11.64	-8.65	-5.49	-3.64	-2.41	-1.90	-1.53

generality, then the IP problem in this setting is far less severe than in the binary choice case.

19.5.2 Estimating random effects models

In the random effects model, the heterogeneity is assumed to be uncorrelated with the regressors. This suggests an altogether different approach to estimation and inference. The conditional log likelihood in the presence of the random effect is

$$\ln L^C = \sum_{i=1}^{N} \ln \prod_{t=1}^{T_i} [\Phi(-\tau w_i - \mathbf{x}'_{it}\boldsymbol{\gamma})]^{1-c_{it}} [\theta \phi(\theta y_{it} - \tau w_i - \mathbf{x}'_{it}\boldsymbol{\gamma})]^{c_{it}} \qquad (19.5.6)$$

where $\tau = \sigma_\alpha/\sigma$ and $w_i \sim N[0,1]$. Estimation of the model entails estimation of the unknown parameters γ, θ and τ. Since the conditional log likelihood function includes the unobserved random effect, it cannot serve as the basis for estimation. The unconditional log likelihood function is

$$\ln L = \sum_{i=1}^{N} \ln \int_{-\infty}^{\infty} \prod_{t=1}^{T_i} [\Phi(-\tau w_i - \mathbf{x}'_{it}\boldsymbol{\gamma})]^{1-c_{it}} [\theta \phi(\theta y_{it} - \tau w_i - \mathbf{x}'_{it}\boldsymbol{\gamma})]^{c_{it}} \phi(w_i) dw_i$$

$$(19.5.7)$$

Estimation of the random effects model can be done by Gauss–Hermite quadrature as designed by Butler and Moffitt (1982) or by Monte Carlo integration (Greene, 2000).

The random effects form of the model is much more manageable than the fixed effects form. Here, however, one trades the difficulty of the incidental parameters problem and the practical complication of time invariant regressors in the fixed effects case for the possibly unpalatable assumption that the effects are uncorrelated with the regressors in the random effects model. A path between the horns of this dilemma (see Wooldridge, 2005, for example) is suggested by the Mundlak idea outlined at the beginning of this section. Suppose in either the fixed or random effects specification, we project the unknown effect on the means of the time varying variables; then,

$$y_{it}^* = \alpha_i + \mathbf{x}'_{it}\boldsymbol{\beta} + \varepsilon_{it}, \varepsilon_{it} \sim N[0, \sigma^2],$$
$$\alpha_i = \bar{\mathbf{x}}'_i \boldsymbol{\pi} + \tau w_i, w_i \sim N[0, 1], \qquad (19.5.8)$$
$$y_{it} = \max(0, y_{it}^*).$$

This produces a random effects model which can be estimated by either method mentioned above and in which, one hopes, the effect of correlation between the unobserved effects and the regressors, is picked up by the group means.

19.5.3 An application of fixed and random effects estimators

To illustrate a few of the models discussed above, we will fit and analyze the data used in Winkelmann (2004). This is an unbalanced panel survey of health care utilization of 27,326 German individuals. The sample contains 7,293 individuals observed from one to seven times in the panel. Counts for the group sizes are 1,525, 1,079, 825, 926, 1,051, 1,000 and 887 for $T_i = 1, \ldots, 7$, respectively. We have fit a model for household income as a function of age, education, marital status and whether there are children in the household. Descriptive statistics for the data are given in Table 19.3. The raw income data in the survey range from zero (a handful of observations) to about 2. We have "top coded" ("for privacy") the income variable at 0.35, thus censoring 12,369 observations, or 45.4 percent of the sample. Assuming that a linear regression model applies to the raw data, the tobit and truncated regression models should likewise be appropriate for the censored data.

Table 19.4 presents least squares and maximum likelihood estimates for several approaches.[11] The OLS estimates, compared to their ML counterparts, clearly

Table 19.3 Panel data on income and sociodemographic variables. $N = 27,326$

Variable	Mean	Standard deviation	Minimum	Maximum
Income	.288208986	.0754686019	0	0.35
Age	43.5256898	11.3302475	25	64
Education	11.3206310	2.32488546	7	18
Married	.758618166	.427929136	0	1
Children in household	.402730001	.490456267	0	1

Table 19.4 Estimates of model parameters

Estimator	Constant	Age	Education	Married	Children	σ
OLS Nonlimit Data	0.1772	−0.0006	0.004497	0.05341	−0.0018	0.0633
Logl = 20012.91	(0.0044)	(0.00005)	(0.00029)	(0.00126)	(0.0012)	
MLE Truncation	0.1699	−0.0008	0.00641	0.07070	−0.0011	0.0756
Logl = 21110.15	(0.0064)	(0.00007)	(0.0004)	(0.00177)	(0.0018)	
OLS All Data	0.1931	−0.0007	0.0073	0.0602	−0.01025	0.0698
Logl = 33965.22	(0.0031)	(0.00004)	(0.0002)	(0.0011)	(0.0010)	
MLE Tobit	0.1169	−0.00071	0.01599	0.09105	−0.0176	0.1117
Logl = 2745.94	(0.0058)	(0.00007)	(0.00037)	(0.0019)	(0.0018)	
Tobit Fixed Effects		0.02406	0.03043	0.1553	−0.0657	0.0832
Logl = 17957.33		(0.00027)	(0.00230)	(0.00365)	(0.0027)	
Tobit RE (B&M)	0.03662	0.00098	0.0180	0.07426	−0.0207	
Logl = 7133.42	(0.00697)	(0.00008)	(0.00047)	(0.00164)	(0.0015)	0.0706
σ_u0.09117						
Tobit RE (MSL)	0.03073	0.00119	0.01798	0.07345	−0.02103	
Logl = 7167.50	(0.00285)	(0.000034)	(0.00018)	(0.0008)	(0.0009)	0.0693
$\sigma_u = 0.09708$						
Tobit RE-Mundlak	0.1668	0.00905	0.01641	0.07107	−0.02223	
Logl = 8325.72	(0.0008)	(0.00015)	(0.00121)	(0.0020)	(0.0017)	0.0662
$\sigma_u = 0.08609$		−0.01041	−0.00220	0.01643	0.0119	
		(0.00018)	(0.0032)	(0.00319)	(0.0031)	

illustrate the attenuation effect noted earlier. The remaining results are for the tobit model. Comparing either the random effects or the fixed effects results to the restricted MLE, the difference in the log likelihoods strongly suggests that some model with unobserved heterogeneity is appropriate. As for choosing between the fixed and random effects models, there is no simple test with known properties. A Hausman test of the random effects alternative against the fixed effects null hypothesis would appear to be inappropriate. Whether the MLE slope estimator with fixed effects is consistent or not remains to be established – based on the Monte Carlo study, it appears to be consistent – but there is little doubt that the variance estimator for the MLE of β in the fixed effects model is inconsistent when T is small. Note, as well, that the sample standard deviation of the 7,293 estimated fixed effects (dummy variable coefficients) is 0.58 compared to a random effects estimate of the standard deviation of the effects of about 0.086 in the final set of results. There is far more variation in the fixed effects estimates, doubtless due to the small samples (one to seven observations) used to estimate them. The random effects estimator is consistent and efficient under the alternative hypothesis. The final set of results in the table use the Mundlak correction to accommodate correlation between the unobserved effects and the regressors. In the limited range of this study, these would probably be the preferred estimates.

19.5.4 Sample selection models for panel data

The development of methods for extending sample selection models to panel data settings parallels the literature on cross-section methods. It begins with Hausman and Wise (1979) who devised a maximum likelihood estimator for a two-period model with attrition – the "selection equation" was a formal model for attrition from the sample. The subsequent literature on attrition has formally drawn the analogy between attrition and sample selection in a variety of applications, such as Keane *et al.* (1988) and Nijman and Verbeek (1992). A formal "effects" treatment for sample selection was first suggested in complete form by Verbeek (1990), who formulated a random effects model for the probit equation and a fixed effects approach for the main regression. Zabel (1992) criticized the specification for its asymmetry in the treatment of the effects in the two equations, and for the likelihood that neglected correlation between the effects and regressors in the probit model would render the FIML estimator inconsistent. His proposal involved fixed effects in both equations. Recognizing the difficulty of fitting such a model (as noted above), he then proposed using the Mundlak correction. It is useful to lay out the model in full: (The original notation has been changed slightly to conform with the preceding.)

$$y_{it}^* = \eta_i + x_{it}'\beta + \varepsilon_{it}, \quad \eta_i = \bar{x}_i'\pi + \tau w_i, w_i \sim N[0, 1]$$

$$d_{it}^* = \theta_i + z_{it}'\alpha + u_{it}, \quad \theta_i = \bar{z}_i'\delta + \omega v_i, v_i \sim N[0, 1] \tag{19.5.9}$$

$$(\varepsilon_{it}, u_{it}) \sim N_2[(0, 0), (\sigma^2, 1, \rho\sigma)].$$

The "selectivity" in the model is carried through the correlation between ε_{it} and u_{it}. The resulting log likelihood is built up from the contribution of individual i,

$$L_i = \int_{-\infty}^{\infty} \prod_{d_{it}=0} \Phi[-z'_{it}\alpha - \bar{z}'_i\delta - \omega v_i]\phi(v_i)dv_i$$

$$\times \int_{-\infty}^{\infty}\int_{-\infty}^{\infty} \prod_{d_{it}=1} \Phi\left[\frac{z'_{it}\alpha + \bar{z}'_i\delta + \omega v_i + (\rho/\sigma)\varepsilon_{it}}{\sqrt{1-\rho^2}}\right]\frac{1}{\sigma}\phi\left(\frac{\varepsilon_{it}}{\sigma}\right)\phi_2(v_i, w_i)dv_idw_i$$

$$\varepsilon_{it} = y_{it} - x'_{it}\beta - \bar{x}'_i\pi - \tau w_i$$

The log likelihood is then $\ln L = \Sigma_i \ln L_i$. The log likelihood is formidable, and does require integration in two dimensions for any selected observations. We do note, however, that the bivariate normal integration is actually the product of two univariate normals, because in the specification above, v_i and w_i are assumed to be uncorrelated. Vella (1998) notes, "given the computational demands of estimating by maximum likelihood induced by the requirement to evaluate multiple integrals, we consider the applicability of available simple, or two step procedures." Before we examine a few of those, we note that with simulation methods developed since this survey, the likelihood function above can be readily evaluated using relatively straightforward (and available) techniques. (Vella and Verbeek (1999) do suggest this in a footnote, but do not pursue it.) To show this, we note that the first line in the log likelihood is of the form $E_v[\prod_{d=0}\Phi(\dots)]$ and the second line is of the form $E_w[E_v[\Phi(\dots)\phi(\dots)/\sigma]]$. Either of these expectations can be satisfactorily approximated with the average of a sufficient number of draws from the standard normal populations that generate w_i and v_i. The term in the simulated likelihood that follows this prescription is

$$L_i^S = \frac{1}{R}\sum_{r=1}^{R} \prod_{d_{it}=0} \Phi[-z'_{it}\alpha - \bar{z}'_i\delta - \omega v_{i,r}]$$

$$\times \frac{1}{R}\sum_{r=1}^{R} \prod_{d_{it}=1} \Phi\left[\frac{z'_{it}\alpha + \bar{z}'_i\delta + \omega v_{i,r} + (\rho/\sigma)\varepsilon_{it,r}}{\sqrt{1-\rho^2}}\right]\frac{1}{\sigma}\phi\left(\frac{\varepsilon_{it,r}}{\sigma}\right)$$

$$\varepsilon_{it,r} = y_{it} - x'_{it}\beta - \bar{x}'_i\pi - \tau w_{i,r}$$

Maximization of this log likelihood with respect to (β, σ, ρ, α, δ, π, τ, ω) by conventional gradient methods is quite feasible. Indeed, this formulation provides a means by which the likely correlation between v_i and w_i can be accommodated in the model. Suppose that w_i and v_i are bivariate standard normal with correlation ρ_{vw}. We can project w_i on v_i and write

$$w_i = \rho_{vw}v_i + (1 - \rho_{vw}^2)^{1/2}h_i \tag{19.5.12}$$

where h_i has a standard normal distribution. To allow the correlation, we now simply substitute this expression for w_i in the simulated (or original) log likelihood, and add ρ_{vw} to the list of parameters to be estimated. The simulation is then over the still independent normal variates, v_i and h_i.[12]

Notwithstanding the derivation above, much of the recent attention has focused on simpler two-step estimators. Building on Ridder (1990) and Verbeek and Nijman (1992) (see Vella, 1998, for numerous additional references), Vella and Verbeek (1999) propose a two-step methodology that involves a random effects framework similar to the one above. As they note, there is some loss in efficiency by not using the FIML estimator. But, with the sample sizes typical in contemporary panel data sets, that efficiency loss may not be large. As they note, their two-step template encompasses a variety of models including the tobit model examined in the preceding sections and the mover stayer model noted above.

The Vella and Verbeek procedures require some fairly intricate maximum likelihood procedures. Wooldridge (1995) proposes an estimator that, with a few probably but not necessarily innocent assumptions, can be based on straightforward applications of conventional, everyday methods. We depart from a fixed effects specification,

$$y_{it}^* = \eta_i + \mathbf{x}_{it}'\boldsymbol{\beta} + \varepsilon_{it},$$
$$d_{it}^* = \theta_i + \mathbf{z}_{it}'\boldsymbol{\alpha} + u_{it}, \tag{19.5.13}$$
$$(\varepsilon_{it}, u_{it}) \sim N_2[(0, 0), (\sigma^2, 1, \rho\sigma)].$$

Under the mean independence assumption $E[\varepsilon_{it}|\eta_i, \theta_i, \mathbf{z}_{i1}, \ldots, \mathbf{z}_{iT}, v_{i1}, \ldots, v_{iT}, d_{i1}, \ldots, d_{iT}] = \rho u_{it}$, it will follow that

$$E[y_{it}|\mathbf{x}_{i1}, \ldots, \mathbf{x}_{iT}, \eta_i, \theta_i, \mathbf{z}_{i1}, \ldots, \mathbf{z}_{iT}, v_{i1}, \ldots, v_{iT}, d_{i1}, \ldots, d_{iT}]$$
$$= \eta_i + \mathbf{x}_{it}'\boldsymbol{\beta} + \rho u_{it}. \tag{19.5.14}$$

This suggests an approach to estimating the model parameters, however it requires computation of u_{it}. That would require estimation of θ_i which cannot be done, at least not consistently – and that precludes simple estimation of u_{it}. To escape the dilemma, Wooldridge suggests Chamberlain's approach to the fixed effects model,

$$\theta_i = f_0 + \mathbf{z}_{i1}'\mathbf{f}_1 + \mathbf{z}_{i2}'\mathbf{f}_2 + \cdots + \mathbf{z}_{iT}'\mathbf{f}_T + h_i. \tag{19.5.15}$$

With this substitution,

$$d_{it}^* = \mathbf{z}_{it}'\boldsymbol{\alpha} + f_0 + \mathbf{z}_{i1}'\mathbf{f}_1 + \mathbf{z}_{i2}'\mathbf{f}_2 + \cdots + \mathbf{z}_{iT}'\mathbf{f}_T + h_i + u_{it}$$
$$= \mathbf{z}_{it}'\boldsymbol{\alpha} + f_0 + \mathbf{z}_{i1}'\mathbf{f}_1 + \mathbf{z}_{i2}'\mathbf{f}_2 + \cdots + \mathbf{z}_{iT}'\mathbf{f}_T + w_{it} \tag{19.5.16}$$

where w_{it} is independent of $\mathbf{z}_{it}, t = 1, \ldots, T$. This now implies that

$$E[y_{it}|\mathbf{x}_{i1}, \ldots, \mathbf{x}_{iT}, \eta_i, \theta_i, \mathbf{z}_{i1}, \ldots, \mathbf{z}_{iT}, v_{i1}, \ldots, v_{iT}, d_{i1}, \ldots, d_{iT}] = \eta_i + \mathbf{x}_{it}'\boldsymbol{\beta} + \rho(w_{it} - h_i)$$
$$= (\eta_i - \rho h_i) + \mathbf{x}_{it}'\boldsymbol{\beta} + \rho w_{it}. \tag{19.5.17}$$

To complete the estimation procedure, we now compute T cross-sectional probit models (reestimating $f_0, f_1, \ldots$ each time), and compute $\hat{\lambda}_{it}$ from each one.

The resulting equation,

$$y_{it} = a_i + \mathbf{x}'_{it}\boldsymbol{\beta} + \rho\hat{\lambda}_{it} + v_{it} \tag{19.5.18}$$

now forms the basis for estimation of $\boldsymbol{\beta}$ and ρ by using a conventional fixed effects linear regression with the observed data.

19.6 Recent developments

As with all areas in econometrics – one of the most active and heavily populated fields in economics – many researchers are extending the models we have discussed here in many directions. Space hardly allows even a cursory review of the literature. What follows is a small sampler chosen more or less haphazardly from the vast recent literature.

We note, first, consistent with other areas, recently developed simulation methods, the Gibbs sampler and Markov Chain Monte Carlo methods, have enabled researchers to extend classical methods into Bayesian frameworks. For example, Bayesian techniques have been developed for the sample selection model, including those by Li, Poirier and Tobias (2004) and Li (1998). The first of these examines a type of sample selection model sometimes called the *mover-stayer model*,

$$
\begin{aligned}
d_i^* &= \mathbf{z}'_i\boldsymbol{\alpha} + u_i, d_i = 1[d_i^* > 0]\\
y_i|(d_i = 1) &= \mathbf{x}'_i\boldsymbol{\beta}_1 + \varepsilon_{i1}\\
y_i|(d_i = 0) &= \mathbf{x}'_i\boldsymbol{\beta}_0 + \varepsilon_{i0}\\
\varepsilon_{i1}, \varepsilon_{i0} &\sim N_2[(0.0), (\sigma_1^2, \sigma_0^2, \rho\sigma_1\sigma_0)], i = 1, \ldots, N
\end{aligned}
\tag{19.6.1}
$$

The name of the model derives from studies of migration, in which income is analyzed after migration or nonmigration. There are two intriguing aspects of the model that Poirier and Tobias examine. First, a crucial parameter, ρ, is not identified in the observed data. Second, the model specification suggests an interesting problem of predicting the outcome variable on the road not taken. (This theme figures prominently in the treatment effects literature, where the question of how the treatment would affect those not treated if they had taken it for example, job training, assistance, drug). The authors use the model to study incomes of high school students, some of whom drop out before their third year. Li (1998) examined a treatment effects model

$$
\begin{aligned}
y_i^* &= \mathbf{x}'_i\boldsymbol{\beta} + \delta d_i + \varepsilon_i, \varepsilon_i \sim N[0, \sigma^2], i = 1, \ldots, N\\
y_i &= \max(0, \mathbf{x}'_i\boldsymbol{\beta} + \delta d_i + \varepsilon_i)\\
d_i^* &= \mathbf{z}'_1\boldsymbol{\alpha} + u_i, d_i = 1[d_i^* > 0]
\end{aligned}
\tag{19.6.2}
$$

with the added complication that the outcome variable is censored. This precludes two-step least squares based estimation strategies, and mandates a likelihood based procedure instead. Li uses a Bayesian, MCMC procedure to estimate the parameters of the model. The technique is applied to a sample of times in default for firms who declare bankruptcy.

The strict normality assumptions that underlie the familiar tobit, probit, truncated regression and Heckman's sample selection model have perhaps attracted the most attention of contemporary researchers. Moon (1989) reconsidered the nonlinear least squares estimators mentioned earlier. The conditional mean function defined for the tobit model,

$$E[y|\mathbf{x}] = \Phi(\mathbf{x}_i'\boldsymbol{\gamma})\sigma[\mathbf{x}_i'\boldsymbol{\gamma} + \lambda(\mathbf{x}_i'\boldsymbol{\gamma})] \tag{19.6.3}$$

is amenable to nonlinear least squares. However, it is no less reliant on the normality assumption than is the likelihood function, so it has no advantage over the MLE and one shortcoming – it is less efficient. Moon (1989) examines ways to relax the assumptions to produce a more robust estimator that can be estimated by nonlinear least squares.

Many recent studies, both theoretical and applied, have proposed semiparametric estimators that rely on fewer or less stringent distributional assumptions. Powell (1984, 1986) is an early contribution. The censored least absolute deviations estimator (CLAD),

$$\hat{\boldsymbol{\beta}} = \arg\ \min_{\boldsymbol{\beta}} \sum_{i=1}^{N} |y_i - \max(0, \mathbf{x}_i'\boldsymbol{\beta})| \tag{19.6.4}$$

is consistent even in the absence of normality – it requires only that the conditional median of y_i^* be zero. There are several practical problems in implementing the CLAD estimator, including the possibility of multiple optima. Bilias *et al.* (2000) proposed a bootstrapping method that they argue is better behaved. The programming problem is asymptotically equivalent to

$$\hat{\boldsymbol{\beta}}* = \arg\ \min_{\boldsymbol{\beta}} \sum_{i=1}^{N} |y_i - \mathbf{x}_i'\boldsymbol{\beta}| \times 1(\mathbf{x}_i'\boldsymbol{\beta}_0 > 0) \tag{19.6.5}$$

where $\boldsymbol{\beta}_0$ is the true value of $\boldsymbol{\beta}$, that is, the parameter we are trying to estimate. We do note that, if we had the true $\boldsymbol{\beta}$ that we were trying to estimate, this minimization would be unnecessary. The authors suggest substituting Powell's consistent estimator for $\boldsymbol{\beta}_0$, then using a bootstrapping procedure to sharpen the estimator of $\boldsymbol{\beta}$. Chen and Khan (2000) further extend Powell's approach to allow for unspecified heteroskedasticity. Moon's (1989) proposed estimator is not unrelated to this, and he, as these authors do, takes the CLAD estimator as a benchmark for comparison. Honore (1992) suggests how the CLAD estimator can be extended to accommodate panel data models with fixed effects. (It is worth noting that these estimators focus on estimation of a constant multiple of $\boldsymbol{\beta}$. Without information about scaling, further computation of partial effects and/or predictions is not possible. Since the models are "robust" to heteroskedasticity, no such information will be forthcoming.) An empirical exploration of the semiparametric estimators is given in Chay and Honore (1998).

One extension of the semiparametric methods is to the panel data models of sample selection. Several studies have pursued this, including Kyriazidou (1997), Honore and Kyriazidou (2000) and Lee (2001). (See Vella (1998) for a lengthy survey of these and other semiparametric and nonparametric approaches to modeling selection.) In general, the recent applications have considered the assumptions under which first differences of y_{it} and x_{it} can be used for adjacent pairs of "selected observations". Kyriazidou's (1997) estimator builds on a fixed effects model,

$$y_{it}^* = \mathbf{x}_{it}'\boldsymbol{\beta} + \eta_i + \varepsilon_{it}, \varepsilon_{it} \sim N[0, \sigma^2], i = 1, \ldots, N, \text{ observed when } d_{it} = 1$$
$$d_{it}^* = \mathbf{z}_{it}'\boldsymbol{\alpha} + \theta_i + u_{it} \ d_{it} = 1(d_{it}^* > 0).$$

(19.6.6)

Minimal assumptions are made about the conditional distributions – that is, the point of the semiparametric approach. The estimator proceeds in two steps. At the first, a robust (semiparametric) estimator of $\boldsymbol{\alpha}$ in the binary choice model is obtained (Manski's (1985, 1986, 1987) maximum score estimator or Klein and Spady's (1993) semiparametric estimator). At the second step, the estimator is weighted least squares using adjacent (both selected) observations,

$$\hat{\beta} = \left[\sum_{i=1}^{N} D_i \hat{\psi}_i (\Delta \mathbf{x}_i)(\Delta \mathbf{x}_i)'\right]^{-1} \left[\sum_{i=1}^{N} D_i \hat{\psi}_i (\Delta \mathbf{x}_i)(\Delta y_i)'\right]$$

(19.6.7)

where Δ creates the first differences of the observations, D_i equals 1 if $d_{it} = d_{i,t-1}$ (that is, if the two adjacent observations are both selected) and zero otherwise, and $\hat{\psi}_i$ is a weight that declines to zero as the magnitude of $|z_{i,t}\hat{\alpha} - z_{i,t-1}'\hat{\alpha}|$ increases; the author suggests a *kernel function* for the weight. Honore and Kyriazidou (2000) and Lee (2001) explore various aspects of this estimator. Note that the use of differences eliminates the- time-invariant effect from the equations, so it has the virtue of obviating any strong assumptions (such as random effects). On the other hand, using first differences removes any interesting time invariant independent variables, as well. Another interesting aspect of this class of estimators is that it allows the use of pairs of observations that are not adjacent in time. This *exchangeability* aspect is pursued at length in the papers mentioned. Rochina-Barrachina (1999) and Dustman and Rochina-Barrachina (2000) proposes a similar estimator based on differences of the selected observations.

The semiparametric approach has been applied to a variety of settings. Gurmu (1997) has used a hurdle/Poisson model with a semiparametric framework for unobserved heterogeneity in a model for the number of doctor visits in a sample of Medicaid patients. Lee (2004) also examined a count response variable; like Gurmu, he examined the number of doctor visits in a sample on health and retirement (see Lee (2004, p. 332) for discussion). In his study, the Poisson model is extended to accommodate an endogenous treatment effect, the amount of exercise. The treatment here is an ordinal variable – high, medium, low – so this model is a bit different (and somewhat more complicated) than the usual case in which the treatment is simply on or off, a binary variable. The hurdle model for counts in a study of health care outcomes is a frequent subject of analysis. Winkelmann (2004) (the source for the data in our application above) is another application.

The programming estimators considered here are "direct" estimators based on minimizing a particular criterion function, either the sum of absolute values or, in Moon's (1989) case, the sum of squares. A number of authors have approached the problem from the direction of moment based (GMM) estimation. Lee (2002) suggests an approach to estimation of the basic censored regression model, while Honore (2002) and Kyriazidou (1997, 2001) extend the model to the sample selection specification. In these cases, the estimators are highly robust, but at the high cost of limiting attention to the $T = 2$ case. Research on this type of estimation methodology is ongoing.

The models discussed above are all static – there are no considerations of dynamic behavior thus far. That is a moot point in the cross-section variants of the models considered, but a crucial assumption of the panel data approaches described in section 19.5.[13] The issue of dynamics in panel data models is a vast literature in itself – at this late juncture, we eschew even a hint at a survey style list. The form in which dynamics should be introduced into the model (any model) is, itself, not a simple issue. Wooldridge (2005) proposes the following general specification for the tobit model (among several he considers) with unobserved time invariant effects.

$$
y_{it} = \max(0, \mathbf{x}'_{it}\boldsymbol{\beta} + g(y_{i,t-1})\rho + \alpha_i + \varepsilon_{it})
$$
$$
\varepsilon_{it} | \mathbf{x}_{it}, \alpha_i, y_{i,0}, y_{i,1}, \ldots, y_{i,t-1} \sim N[0, \sigma^2].
$$
(19.6.8)

where $g(\cdot)$ is some transformation of the lagged observed value – it will usually be $y_{i,t-1}$ itself – and $y_{i,0}$ is the observed initial condition. (We have changed the notation slightly to conform to ours, and limited attention to a single lagged value (as he actually does as well).) Wooldridge explores the conditions under which we may write the density for the observed variable (using the Olsen transformation as usual), as

$$
\ln f(y_{i,t} | x_{i,t}, \alpha_i, y_{i,t-1}) = 1[y_{i,t} = 0] \ln \Phi\left[\mathbf{x}'_{i,t}\boldsymbol{\gamma} + y_{i,t-1}\mu + \sigma_\alpha a_i\right]
$$
$$
+ 1[y_{i,t} > 0] \ln \theta\phi\left[(\theta y_{i,t} - \mathbf{x}'_{i,t}\boldsymbol{\gamma} - y_{i,t-1}\mu - \sigma_\alpha a_i)\right].
$$
(19.6.9)

We have isolated the standard deviation of α_i, and consistent with the normalization of the model by $1/\sigma$, what we have labeled σ_α above is actually $\mathrm{Var}[\alpha_i]^{1/2}/\sigma$. The crucial step in Wooldridge's analysis is the assumptions that allow projection of a_i on known information; he writes

$$
a_i = \alpha_0 + \alpha_1 y_{i,0} + \mathbf{x}'_i\boldsymbol{\alpha}_2 + w_i
$$
(19.6.10)

where $\mathbf{x}_i$ is (a bit ambiguously) defined to include some or all observations on $\mathbf{x}_{it}$, and w_i is normally distributed with zero mean and constant variance. (Asymptotics and other technical details may be found in Wooldridge's study.) Inserting the equation for a_i into the density for $y_{i,t}$, and summing the logs produces, as he notes, a "simple solution" to the initial conditions problem in a dynamic tobit model. The end result is a tobit random effects model, precisely the one we examined in section 19.5.[14]

19.7   Summary and conclusions

The preceding sections has outlined the basic modeling frameworks that are used in analyzing microeconomic data when the response variable is truncated, censored, or otherwise affected by transformation before being observed. The essential models for truncation, censoring and sample selection have provided the starting points for a vast array of applications and theoretical developments. The full set of results for the fully parametric models based on the normal distribution are well established. Ongoing contemporary research is largely focused on less parametric approaches, on panel data, and on different kinds of data generating mechanisms, such as models for counts and for discrete choices.

Appendix: LIMDEP Commands for Model Estimation

```
? Generic - File will be loaded from the File menu on the desktop
? Load ; File = Health.lpj $
Namelist ; xt = age, educ, married, hhkids$
? Censor the income data
Create ; income = hhninc; if (income > .35) income = .35$
Dstat ; rhs = income, xt$
Reject ; income >= .35$
? Pooled OLS nonlimit data
Regress ; lhs = income; rhs = one, xt$
? Pooled truncation using nonlimit data
Truncation ; lhs = income; rhs = one, xt; limit = .35; upper$
? Restore full sample
Sample ; All $
? Pooled OLS using full sample
Regress ; lhs = income; rhs = one, xt$
? Pooled tobit using full sample
Tobit; lhs = income; rhs = one, xt; limit = .35; upper$
? Tobit with fixed effects. Retain dummy variable coefficients
Tobit ; lhs = income; rhs = one, xt
        ; limit = .35 ; upper; pds = numobs; fem; parameters$
Sample ; 1-7293$
Create ; ai = alphafe$
Calc ; list ; sdv(ai) $$
Sample ; all$
? Tobit with random effects using quadrature
Tobit ; lhs = income ; rhs = one, xt ; limit = .35 ; upper; pds = numobs$
? For MSL program convert to a zero censored variable
Create ; income35 = .35 - income$
? Tobit with random effects using Monte Carlo integration.
? Need to reverse signs of coefficients and adjust constant
? Appropriate constant is .35-b0. Reported in Table 4.
```

```
Tobit ; lhs = income35; rhs = one, xt; pds = numobs
        ; rpm; fcn = one (n) ; Halton draws ; pts = 50 $
? Get group means for Mundlak correction
Matrix ; meanx = gxbr (xt, id) $
Create ; xbage = meanx (id, 1) $
Create ; xbeduc = meanx (id, 2) $
Create ; xbmarr = meanx (id, 3) $
Create ; xbkids = meanx (id, 4) $
? Random effects model with group means added to the model
Tobit ; lhs = income; rhs = one, xt, xbage, xbeduc, xbmarr, xbkids
        ; limit = .35; upper; pds = numobs$
```

Notes

1. The origin of the model's name, "tobit", is the subject of some speculation. Popular lore has it as a play on "Tobin's probit", in reference to Tobin (1958) and his model's connection to the probit (binary choice) model. However, a deeper look into the archives uncovers the same James Tobin's appearance as Tobit, the midshipman "with a mind like a sponge..." in Tobin's Columbia friend, Herman Wouk's (1951) classic work, *The Caine Mutiny* (http://www.economyprofessor.com/theorists/jamestobin.php).

2. The differences between these estimators is illusory. In all cases, they are equivalent to gradient methods each using its own weighting matrix. Some, e.g., Newton's method, are more efficient (computationally) than others (e.g., the EM method).

3. Surprisingly, this fit measure has become a required standard in some fields in some journals. This fit measure bears only a slight connection to the fit of the model to the data, even in the linear regression model. For the linear model, a little algebra shows it to equal $\ln(s^2/s_0^2)/[\ln(s^2/s_0^2) + 1 + \ln 2\pi + \ln s_0^2)]$, which can be distressingly low even in models that have "excellent fit." Note that it is a function of the scale of the data. In a simple experiment, we used a random number generator to generate 1000 standard normal observations on x_i and ε_i, then, $y_i = x_i + \varepsilon_i$. Linear regression of y_i on x_i and a constant produces an R^2 of .5193 and a pseudo-R^2 of .20602. Multiplying y_i by 10 and repeating the exercise leaves R^2 unchanged (of course), but reduces the pseudo-R^2 to .09. To cite another example, in the author's experience, values of .02 appear to be routine in ordered probit models for which conventional prediction procedures based on the estimated model give the correct value for the dependent variable 90% of the time.

4. We note that, among the other shortcomings of most semiparametric estimators of the censored regression model, they are estimated "up to (an unknown) scale." Some are even robust to heteroskedasticity. This is not a virtue – it precludes prediction and estimation of partial effects.

5. The counterpart for the truncated regression model is $e_i = (\theta y_i - \mathbf{x}'_i\boldsymbol{\gamma}) - \lambda_i$.

6. The dependent variable analyzed in Fair (1978) was a reported count that was censored in several ranges. The reported count variable was transformed to 0,1,2,3,(4–10) = 7, (anything else) = 12. Fair analyzed this count variable with the tobit model discussed above as if it were continuous, and treated the censoring as having occurred at the zero point. These data obviously fall more naturally into the corner solution interpretation (see Wooldridge, 2002). See Greene (2003, chapter 22) for a reanalysis of these data using the censored count data model suggested here.

7. Vella (1998) is a thorough, excellent survey of this topic recounted clearly from a practitioner's viewpoint.

8. Heckman and MaCurdy (1981) suggested an iterative procedure whereby, given initial estimates of the parameters, the dummy variable coefficients be estimated conditionally, one at a time each based on T_i observations, then with estimates of α_i in hand, the slopes be estimated, then back and forth until convergence. Because the Hessian is not block

diagonal – the parameter space cannot be partitioned – this procedure does not maximize the full log likelihood function. It can only be done directly, by "brute force."

9. The computational method for fittting the model with large numbers of dummy variables appears not to be widely known.

10. The exact expected value of the variance estimator in the linear model with fixed effects is easy to find with elementary matrix algebra – see any graduate-level textbook in econometrics, for example.

11. All computations reported were done using LIMDEP Version 8.0. Readers who wish to replicate (or extend) the results will find the data on the Journal of Applied Econometrics data archive website for 2004. They are also stored in the forms of an Excel™ spreadsheet and a LIMDEP project file on the author's website at http://www.stern.nyu.edu/~wgreene/Econometrics/healthcare.lpj (and .xls). The commands for LIMDEP are given in the appendix.

12. The estimator is contained in the current version of LIMDEP (Econometric Software, 2006).

13. There are very few strict time series applications of the models discussed in this chapter. Censoring and truncation are generally viewed as signature features of microeconomic (cross section and panel) data. However, Lee (1999, 2004) does consider a time series specification of the tobit model, extending it to a GARCH framework. This extension is, as one might expect, extremely complicated. Relevant applications remain forthcoming. Lee (1999) cites a number of natural candidates involving, for example, intervention in foreign exchange markets intended to limit movement of exchange rates.

14. In an application with more than a trivial number of periods and a substantial number of regressors, the expression for a_i is likely to have an excessive number of terms. As a useful approximation, one might want just to use the Mundlak approach, and replace the full set of vectors x_{it} with the group means of the time-varying variables.

References

Abrevaya, J. (1997) The equivalence of two estimators of the fixed effects logit model. *Economics Letters* 55(1), 41–4.

Amemiya, T. (1978) The estimation of a simultaneous equation generalized probit model. *Econometrica* 46(5), 1193–1205.

Andersen, E. (1970) Asymptotic properties of conditional maximum likelihood estimators. *Journal of the Royal Statistical Society, Series B* 32, 283–301.

Angrist, J. (2001) Estimation of limited dependent variable models with binary endogenous regressors: simple strategies for empirical practice. *Journal of Business and Economic Statistics* 19(1), 1–14.

Bera, A. and C. Jarque (1982) Model specification tests: a simultaneous approach. *Journal of Econometrics* 20, 59–82.

Bera, A., C. Jarque and L. Lee (1981) Testing for the normality assumption in limited dependent variable models. Manuscript, Department of Economics, University of Minnesota.

Bhat, C. (1994) Imputing a continuous income variable from grouped and missing income observations. *Economics Letters* 46(4), 311–20.

Bilias, Y., S. Chen and Z. Ying (2000) Simple resampling methods for censored regression quantiles. *Journal of Econometrics* 99(2), 373–86.

Butler, J. and R. Moffitt (1982) A computationally efficient quadrature procedure for the one factor multinomial probit model. *Econometrica* 50, 761–4.

Chay, K. and B. Honore (1998) Estimation of semiparametric censored regression models: an application to changes in black–white earnings inequality during the 1960s. *Journal of Human Resources* 33(1), 4–38.

Chen, S. and S. Khan (2000) Estimating censored regression models in the presence of nonparametrtic multiplicative heteroskedasticity. *Journal of Econometrics* 98(2), 283–316.

Chesher, A. and M. Irish (1987) Residual analysis in the grouped data and censored normal linear model. *Journal of Econometrics* 34, 33–62.

Cheung, C. and A. Goldberger (1984) Proportional projections in limited dependent variable models. *Econometrica* 52, 531–4.

Chib, S. (1992) Bayes regression for the Tobit censored regression model. *Journal of Econometrics* 51, 79–99.

Cragg, J. (1971) Some statistical models for limited dependent variables with application to the demand for durable goods. *Econometrica* 39, 829–44.

Dale, S. and A. Krueger (1999) Estimating the payoff to attending a more selective college: an application of selection on observables and unobservables. Princeton University Industrial Relations Section Working Paper Number 409.

DeMaris, A. (2004) *Regression with Social Data: Modeling Continuous and Limited Response Variables.* New York: John Wiley and Sons.

Dempster, A., N. Laird and D. Rubin (1977) Maximum likelihood estimation from incomplete data via the EM algorithm. *Journal of the Royal Statistical Society, Series B* 39, 1–38.

Dhrymes, P. (1986) Limited dependent variables. In Z. Griliches and M. Intriligator (eds), *Handbook of Econometrics*, vol. 2. Amsterdam: North-Holland.

Dionne, G., R. Gagne and C. Vanesse (1998) Inferring technological parameters from incomplete panel data. *Journal of Econometrics* 87(2), 303–29.

Duncan, G. (1983) Sample selectivity as a proxy variable problem: on the use and misuse of Gaussian selectivity corrections. *Research in Labor Economics*, Supplement 2, 333–45.

Duncan, G. (1986) A Semiparametric censored regression estimator. *Journal of Econometrics* 31, 5–34.

Dustman, C. and M. Rochina-Barrachina (2000) Selection correction in panel data models: an application to labour supply and wages. Discussion Paper No. 162, IZA, Bonn, Germany.

Econometric Software, Inc. (2006) *LIMDEP*, Version 9.0. Plainview, NY: Econometric Software, Inc.

Fair, R. (1977) A note on computation of the Tobit estimator. *Econometrica* 45, 1723–1727.

Fair, R. (1978) A theory of extramarital affairs. *Journal of Political Economy* 86, 45–61.

Fin, T. and P. Schmidt (1984) A test of the Tobit specification against an alternative suggested by Cragg. *Review of Economics and Statistics* 66, 174–7.

Greene, W. (1981) Sample selection bias as a specification error: comment. *Econometrica* 49, 795–8.

Greene, W. (1983) Estimation of limited dependent variable models by ordinary least squares and the method of moments. *Journal of Econometrics* 21, 195–212.

Greene, W. (1995) Sample selection in the Poisson regression model. Working Paper No. EC-95-6, Department of Economics, Stern School of Business, New York University.

Greene, W. (1997) FIML estimation of sample selection models for count data. Stern School, Department of Economics, Working Paper 97–02.

Greene, W. (1999) Marginal effects in the censored regression model. *Economics Letters* 64(1), 43–50.

Greene, W. (2000) *LIMDEP, User's Manual.* Plainview, NY: Econometric Software.

Greene, W. (2003) *Econometric Analysis*, 5th edn. Upper Saddle River: Prentice Hall.

Greene, W. (2004) Fixed effects and the incidental parameters problem in the tobit model. *Econometric Reviews* 23(2), 125–48.

Gurmu, S. (1997) Semi-parametric estimation of hurdle regression models with an application to medicaid utilization. *Journal of Applied Econometrics* 12(3), 225–42.

Hausman, J. and D. Wise (1977) Social experimentation, truncated distributions, and efficient estimation. *Econometrica* 45, 919–38.

Hausman, J. and D. Wise (1979) Attrition bias in experimental and panel data: the Gary income maintenance experiment. *Econometrica* **47**(2), 1979, 455–573.

Heckman, J. (1979) Sample selection bias as a specification error. *Econometrica* **47**, 153–61.

Heckman, J. and T. MaCurdy (1981) A life cycle model of female labor supply. *Review of Economic Studies* **47**, 247–83.

Honore, B. (1992) Trimmed LAD and least squares estimation of truncated and censored regression models with fixed effects. *Econometrica* **60**, 533–65.

Honore, B. (2002) Non-linear models with panel data. Insititute For Fiscal Studies, CEMMAP, Working Paper CWP13/02.

Honore, B. and E. Kyriazidou (2000) Panel data discrete choice models with lagged dependent variables. *Econometrica* **68**(4), 839–74.

Honore, B. and E. Kyriazidou (2000) Estimation of tobit-type models with individual specific effects. *Econometric Reviews* **19**(3), 341–66.

Jensen, P., M. Rosholm and M. Verner (2001) A comparison of different estimators for panel data sample selection models. Manuscript, Department of Economics, CIM, CLS, Aarhus School of Business.

Jones, A. (1994) Health, addiction, social interaction and the decision to quit smoking. *Journal of Health Economics* **13**, 93–110.

Keane, M., R. Moffitt and D. Runkle (1988) Real wages over the business cycle: estimating the impact of heterogeneity with micro-data. *Journal of Political Economy* **96**(6), 1232–1265.

Kiefer, N. (ed.) (1993) Econometric analysis of duration data. *Journal of Econometrics* **28**(1), 1–169.

Klein, R. and R. Spady (1993) An efficient semiparametric estimator for discrete choice. *Econometrica* **61**, 387–421.

Kyriazidou, E. (1997) Estimation of a panel data sample selection model. *Econometrica* **65**(6), 1335–1364.

Kyriazidou, E. (2001) Estimation of dynamic panel data sample selection models. *Review of Economic Studies* **68**, 543–72.

Lee, L. (1999) Estimation of dynamic and ARCH tobit models. *Journal of Econometrics* **92**, 355–90.

Lee, L. (2004) Nonstandard dependent variables: some common structures of simulated specifications tests. Manuscript, Department of Economics, The Ohio State University.

Lee, M. (1996) *Method of Moments and Semiparametric Econometrics for Limited Dependent Variables*. New York: Springer-Verlag.

Lee, M. (2001) First difference estimators for panel censored selection models. *Economics Letters* **70**(1), 43–50.

Lee, M. (2002) *Panel Data Econometrics: Methods of Moments and Limited Dependent Variables*. New York: John Wiley.

Lee, M. (2004) Selection correction and sensitivity analysis for ordered treatment effect on count response. *Journal of Applied Econometrics* **19**(3), 323–37.

Li, K. (1998) Bayesian inference in a simultaneous equation model with limited dependent variables. *Journal of Econometrics* **85**(2), 387–400.

Li, M., D. Poirier and J. Tobias (2004) Do dropouts suffer from dropping out? Estimation and prediction of outcome gains in generalized selection models. *Journal of Applied Econometrics* **19**(2), 203–26.

Long, S. (1997) *Regression Models for Categorical and Limited Dependent Variables*. Thousand Oaks, CA: Sage Publications.

Maddala, G. (1983) *Limited Dependent and Qualitative Variables in Econometrics*. New York: Cambridge University Press.

Manski, C. (1985) Semiparametric analysis of discrete response: asymptotic properties of the maximum score estimator. *Journal of Econometrics* **27**, 313–33.

Manski, C. (1986) Operational characteristics of the maximum score estimator. *Journal of Econometrics* **32**, 85–100.

Manski, C. (1987) Semiparametric analysis of the random effects linear model from binary response data. *Econometrica* **55**, 357–62.

Melenberg, B. and A. van Soest (1996) Parametric and semi-parametric modelling of vacation expenditures. *Journal of Applied Econometrics* **11**(1), 59–76.

Moon, C. (1989) A Monte Carlo comparison of semiparametric Tobit estimators. *Journal of Applied Econometrics* **4**(4), 361–82.

Mundlak, Y. (1978) On the pooling of time series and cross sectional data. *Econometrica* **56**, 69–86.

Murphy, K. and R. Topel (1985) Estimation and inference in two step econometric models. *Journal of Business and Economic Statistics* **3**, 370–9.

Nelson, F. (1981) A test for misspecification in the censored normal model. *Econometrica* **49**, 1317–1329.

Newey, W., J. Powell and J. Walker (1990) Semiparametric estimation of selection models. *American Economic Review* **80**, 324–8.

Neyman, J. and E. Scott (1948) Consistent estimates based on partially consistent observations. *Econometrica* **16**, 1–32.

Nijman, T. and M. Verbeek (1992) Nonresponse in panel data: the impact on estimates of the life cycle consumption function. *Journal of Applied Econometrics* **7**(3), 243–57.

Olsen, R. (1978) A note on the uniqueness of the maximum likelihood estimator in the Tobit model. *Econometrica* **46**, 1211–1215.

Pagan, A. and F. Vella (1989) Diagnostic tests for models based on individual data: a survey. *Journal of Applied Econometrics* **4**, Supplement, S29–S59.

Powell, J. (1984) Least absolute deviations estimation for the censored regression model. *Journal of Econometrics* **25**, 303–25.

Powell, J. (1986) Censored regression quantiles. *Journal of Econometrics* **32**, 143–55.

Ridder, G. (1990) Attrition in multiwave panel data. In J. Hartog, E. Ridder and J. Theeuwes (eds), *Panel Data and Labor Market Studies*. Amsterdam: Elsevier.

Rochina-Barrachina, M. (1999) A new estimator for panel data sample selection models. *Annales d'Economie et de Statistique* **55/56**, 153–81.

Schafgans, M. (1998) Ethnic wage differences in Malaysia: parametric and semiparametric estimation of the Chinese–Malay wage gap. *Journal of Applied Econometrics* **13**(5), 481–504.

Shaw, D. (1988) " 'On-Site Samples' Regression Problems of Nonnegative Integers, Truncation, and Endogenous Stratification." *Journal of Econometrics* **37**, 211–23.

Skeels, C. and F. Vella (1999) A Monte Carlo investigation of the sampling behavior of conditional moment tests in Tobit and probit models. *Journal of Econometrics* **92**(2), 275–94.

Terza, J. (1985) A Tobit type estimator for the censored poisson regression model. *Economics Letters* **18**, 361–5.

Terza, J. (1998) Estimating count data models with endogenous switching: sample selection and endogenous treatment effects. *Journal of Econometrics* **84**(1), 129–54.

Tobin, J. (1958) Estimation of relationships for limited dependent variables. *Econometrica* **26**, 24–36.

Vella, F. (1992) Simple tests for sample selection bias in censored and discrete choice models. *Journal of Applied Econometrics* **7**(4), 413–22.

Vella, F. (1998) Estimating models with sample selection bias: a survey. *Journal of Human Resources* **33**(1), 127–69.

Vella, F. and M. Verbeek (1999) Two-step estimation of panel data models with censored endogenous variables and selection bias. *Journal of Econometrics* **90**, 239–63.

Verbeek, M. (1990) On the estimation of a fixed effects model selectivity bias. *Economics Letters* **34**, 267–70.

Verbeek, M. and T. Nijman (1992) Testing for selectivity bias in panel data models. *International Economic Review* **33**(3), 681–703.

Winkelmann, R. (2004) Health care reform and the number of doctor visits – an econometric analysis. *Journal of Applied Econometrics* **19**(4), 455–72.

Wooldridge, J. (1995) Selection corrections for panel data models under conditional mean independence assumptions. *Journal of Econometrics* **68**(1), 115–32.

Wooldridge, J. (2002) *Econometric Analysis of Cross Section and Panel Data*. Cambridge, MA: MIT Press.

Wooldridge, J. (2005) Simple solutions to the initial conditions problem in dynamic, non-linear panel data models with unobserved heterogeneity. *Journal of Applied Econometrics* **20**(1), 39–54.

Wouk, H. (1951) *The Caine Mutiny*. New York: Alden Press.

Zabel, J. (1992) Estimating fixed and random effects models with selectivity. *Economics Letters* **40**, 269–72.

Part VII

Stochastic Volatility

20
Modeling Volatility
Richard T. Baillie

Abstract

This chapter reviews some of the major econometric models, approaches and issues in the area of volatility. Particular emphasis is placed on the basic properties of the models and associated inferential procedures. Given the vast literature on this still rapidly expanding subject, the survey is inevitably very selective. Most attention in the chapter is concentrated on the family of univariate ARCH and GARCH processes, since these appear to be the most widely used techniques. The application of these methods to problems in financial economics and asset pricing and related areas are discussed throughout the chapter. There is also a short discussion on stochastic volatility models, volatility in high frequency financial market returns and the relatively new area of realized volatility.

20.1	Introduction	737
20.2	Informal measures of volatility	739
20.3	*ARCH* models	741
	20.3.1 Conditional moments	741
	20.3.2 Linear *ARCH* and *GARCH* models	742
	20.3.3 Regression with *ARCH* effects	747
	20.3.4 Moment structure of *GARCH* models	749
	20.3.5 Prediction from *GARCH* models	751
	20.3.6 Variants of *GARCH* models	752
	20.3.7 Estimation and inference in *ARCH* models	755
20.4	Stochastic volatility	757
20.5	High frequency returns and realized volatility	759
20.6	Conclusion	761

20.1 Introduction

There are many possible definitions of *volatility* and there seems to be no exact definition to meet all circumstances. However, the term volatility generally means a period in the history of a time series realization that is associated with high variability, or increasing variance. The phenomenon is very relevant in the analysis of many economic, and particularly financial, time series. These series often appear to be characterized by alternating periods of relative tranquility and relative high variability, or volatility.

Many theories of asset pricing in finance emphasize the role of variances and covariances to explain the behavior of asset prices; for example, the capital asset pricing model (CAPM). From an empirical perspective, financial market returns typically have relatively little serial correlation but, conversely, periods of extreme tranquility and volatility. This type of behavior intuitively implies that, while returns may be uncorrelated, they are certainly not independent, and often have rich dynamics in their higher moments and interesting non-Gaussian distributional properties. Hence both the theoretical models and empirical stylized facts require the appropriate econometric procedures to focus on higher moment characteristics, especially volatility, rather than modeling the conditional mean as in many other areas of econometrics.

It should be noted that many of the remarks and techniques discussed in this chapter are relevant for all forms of time series analysis, including those from the physical sciences. However, our emphasis is on methods that have been directly relevant to economic and financial theories and applications. Also, this chapter is mainly concerned with modeling volatility in univariate time series and only passing reference is made to generalizations involving multivariate time series, which are covered in detail in chapter 21.

The second section of this chapter discusses some of the historical, and to some extent rather more informal, measures of volatility. Section 20.3 then describes the foundations and properties of the basic *ARCH* and *GARCH* models, including some of the more widely used parametric variants of these models. The same section also discusses estimation and some of the inferential issues that arise in the area of *ARCH* modeling. This section is by far the most comprehensive of the chapter due to the fact that the area of *ARCH* modeling has been the most widely applied and has attracted so much attention, both in terms of theory and applications. Section 20.4 then describes some of the main properties of stochastic volatility models, while section 20.5 is concerned with modeling volatility from high frequency financial market data and the relatively new, but very important subject of realized volatility. The application of volatility models to problems in asset pricing and financial economics are briefly discussed throughout the text, although it is not possible, due to space constraints, to really do justice to much of the very interesting applied work that has taken place in this area. The same comment also applies to stochastic volatility and realized volatility, which are also becoming huge bodies of literature in their own right. The chapter finishes with a brief conclusion.

It is convenient to begin by establishing some basic notation to be used throughout the chapter. The univariate time series of interest is y_t, which is observed for $t = 1, 2, \ldots, T$. In many situations y_t will be assumed to be covariance stationary with Wold decomposition

$$y_t = \sum_{j=0}^{\infty} \psi_j \varepsilon_{t-j},$$

$$(20.1.1)$$

where $E(\varepsilon_t) = 0, E(\varepsilon_t^2) = \sigma^2$ and $E(\varepsilon_t \varepsilon_s) = 0$, for $s \neq t$. Additionally, the square summability condition that $\sum_{j=0}^{\infty} \psi_j^2 < \infty$ is imposed. Hence the unconditional variance of the process y_t is given by $Var(y_t) = \sigma^2 \sum_{j=0}^{\infty} \psi_j^2$ and is finite and constant over time. It should be noted that the assumptions on the disturbance of constant variance and lack of serial correlation allow for the possibility that its higher moments are correlated. This idea will be explored further in the detailed description of volatility models.

20.2 Informal measures of volatility

For simplicity, this chapter mainly focuses on situations where the dependent variable measures *returns* and is assumed to be serially uncorrelated in its conditional mean, but to nevertheless exhibit volatility. The motivation for this comes from the fact that many of the techniques and applications for models of volatility have been derived from financial econometrics. Formally, let P_t be the nominal price of an asset at time t, and let $y_t = \Delta \ln(P_t)$. Then y_t can easily be shown to be the continuously compounded rate of return. If returns are unpredictable in their conditional mean, then they are consistent with a martingale model, which was originally suggested by Bachelier (1900). The model only implies that returns are uncorrelated. A considerable amount of interest in modeling volatility has arisen from theories such as the CAPM, since the characteristics of asset pricing data are typically rather uninteresting in the conditional mean, because the first differences of the logged price series are usually close to being uncorrelated. Hence the continuously compounded rate of returns are uncorrelated or unpredictable, so that the asset prices are approximately martingale difference sequences. This property was first recognized by Bachelier (1900) and, subsequently, Mandelbrot (1963) noted the further stylized fact that changes in asset prices have pronounced volatile and tranquil periods, so that their volatility was time dependent. A third stylized fact was that the returns series exhibited extreme nonnormality and excess kurtosis. Some of these stylized features of returns can be captured by models to describe volatility, such as *ARCH*.

Many of the original methods for measuring changing variances, or volatility, were relatively informal in nature. While actual returns y_t are generally close to being serially uncorrelated, their squares y_t^2, absolute values $|y_t|$ and powers of absolute returns $|y_t|^\delta$, for some $\delta > 0$ are generally very highly serially correlated. The sample autocorrelation functions of these transformations of returns can all be indicative of volatility in financial markets. An algorithmic approach, which is not obviously based on an underlying model, was devised by Mandelbrot (1963), who calculated recursive estimates of the variance over time. Similarly, Klein (1977) constructed rolling moving averages around sample means. Hence a simple measure of volatility is

$$\bar{\sigma}_t^2 = \left(\frac{1}{m+1}\right) \sum_{j=0}^{m} y_{t-j}^2 \qquad (20.2.1)$$

which moves throughout the sample and gives equal weight to the last m observations. The analyst or trader has to choose m. Another measure used by market practitioners is a simple *Exponential smoothing* approach of the form

$$\sigma_t^2 = \alpha\sigma_{t-1}^2 + (1 - \alpha)y_{t-1}^2, \tag{20.2.2}$$

where $0 < \alpha < 1$ and usually the smoothing parameter α is chosen to be about 0.8, so that the estimated variance changes quite slowly. The model implies exponentially declining weight on past squared returns, so that

$$\sigma_t^2 = (1 - \alpha)\sum_{j=0}^{\infty} \alpha^{j-1}y_{t-j}^2, \tag{20.2.3}$$

and there is an infinite horizon for the memory of volatility. As is well known, the exponential smoothing method provides the minimum mean squared forecast error when the true data generating process for volatility is the ARIMA(0,1,1) model,

$$\Delta\sigma_t^2 = v_t - (1 - \alpha)v_{t-1}, \tag{20.2.4}$$

where v_t is a white noise process.

Much of the historical motivation to modeling volatility comes from very practical problems in financial economics. In particular, in a series of articles Schwert (1989, 1990a, 1990b) considered various formal and informal models of stock market volatility when considering the relationship between the US stock market and the macroeconomy over long historical periods of data stretching back to the early 1800s. Schwert used several estimators of the variance of monthly returns. One method was to take the sum of squared daily returns, after subtracting out the average daily return within the month. The estimate of volatility in month t is $\hat{\sigma}_t^2$ and is derived from the demeaned returns for day i and month t, denoted by y_{it}, as

$$\hat{\sigma}_t^2 = \sum_{i=1}^{N_t} y_{it}^2 \tag{20.2.5}$$

where N_t is the number of trading days within the month i, so that usually $N_t = 22$. The method uses non-overlapping samples of daily data to estimate the monthly variance. Hence the errors from estimating volatility should be close to being uncorrelated over time. On denoting Y_t as the monthly returns, Schwert used an $AR(12)$ model for the returns, including 12 dummy variables D_{jt} to allow for different monthly mean returns,

$$Y_t = \sum_{j=1}^{12} \alpha_j D_{jt} + \sum_{j=1}^{12} \beta_j Y_{t-j} + \varepsilon_t. \tag{20.2.6}$$

The estimated model is

$$Y_t = \sum_{j=1}^{12} \hat{\alpha}_j D_{jt} + \sum_{j=1}^{12} \hat{\beta}_j Y_{t-j} + \hat{\varepsilon}_t \tag{20.2.7}$$

This procedure is intended to remove autocorrelation in $\hat{\varepsilon}_t$, although it is expected that $E(\hat{\varepsilon}_t^2 \hat{\varepsilon}_{t-k}^2) \neq 0$ and $E|\hat{\varepsilon}_t^2||\hat{\varepsilon}_{t-k}^2| \neq 0$ for $k \neq 0$, since the mean adjusted returns are not independent. The approach is to then estimate another AR(12) for the absolute values of the errors from the above regression, to allow for different monthly standard deviations,

$$|\hat{\varepsilon}_t| = \sum_{j=1}^{12} \gamma_j D_{jt} + \sum_{j=1}^{12} \rho_j |\hat{\varepsilon}_{t-j}| + u_t \tag{20.2.8}$$

The predicted value of the dependent variable $|\hat{\varepsilon}_t|$ is then an estimate of the standard deviation of the stock market return for month t and hence is a measure of one definition of volatility. It is also likely that a satisfactory ARMA or ARFIMA model could be found to describe the $|\hat{\varepsilon}_t|$ series. French, Schwert and Stambaugh (1987) calculated the monthly variances of the S&P returns using

$$s_t^2 = \sum_{i=1}^{N_t} y_{i,t}^2 + 2 \sum_{i=1}^{N_t-1} y_{i,t} y_{i+1,t}, \tag{20.2.9}$$

where there are N_t trading days in month t. The second term aims to remove the effects of first-order autocorrelation due to non-synchronous trading. These authors typically find that estimates of the standard deviation of monthly stock returns varies between 2 and 20 percent between 1857 and 1985, with stock market volatility being particularly high between 1929 through 1939. Historically high levels of volatility also occurred in macro aggregates such as inflation, the index of industrial production and money growth. There is a view, or concern, in some of this literature that the 1929 to 1939 period can bias measures of stock market volatility which use long historical data series. Some authors, notably Shiller (1979), have focused on *excess volatility*, which implies that the level of stock market volatility is too high relative to ex-post variability of dividends. Leverage has also been claimed to be one of the strongest forces in raising stock market volatility. Having briefly discussed some of the reasons for the interest in volatility in finance, this chapter now turns to some of the econometric procedures for measuring volatility.

20.3 ARCH models

20.3.1 Conditional moments

In order to motivate the underlying ideas of autoregressive conditional hetero-skedastic (*ARCH*) processes, it is first worthwhile considering the problem of predicting the future level of the mean of a random variable, which is recorded from time series data. The relative success of forecasting from any dynamic econometric model essentially comes from the use of the *conditional mean* rather than the *unconditional* mean. As an illustration, consider the simple scalar first-order autoregression, i.e., the $AR(1)$ model $y_t = \phi y_{t-1} + \varepsilon_t$, where $E(\varepsilon_t) = 0, E(\varepsilon_t^2) = \sigma^2$ and $E(\varepsilon_t \varepsilon_s) = 0$ for $s \neq t$. Since

$$y_t = \sum_{j=0}^{t-1} \phi^j \varepsilon_{t-j} + \phi^t y_0,$$

and assuming that the initial value is $y_0 = 0$, then $E(y_t) = 0$ and hence $Var(y_t^2) = \sigma^2(1 - \phi^2)^{-1}$. Rather than use the unconditional mean of zero, an efficient forecasting procedure implements the use of the conditional mean,

$$E_t y_{t+1} = E(y_{t+1}|\Omega_t), \qquad (20.3.1)$$

where Ω_t is a sigma field of all relevant, worthwhile information available at time t. In the case of the $AR(1)$ process, $E_t y_{t+1} = E(y_{t+1}|\Omega_t) = \phi y_t$. Clearly this forecast will be time dependent as the current information set, reflected in y_t, changes over time. The conditional variance of the y_t process will be

$$Var_t y_{t+1} = E_t(y_{t+1} - E_t y_{t+1})^2 = E_t[\phi y_t + (\varepsilon_{t+1} - \phi y_t)]^2 = E_t(\varepsilon_{t+1})^2 = \sigma_{t+1}^2, \quad (20.3.2)$$

where σ_{t+1}^2, the conditional variance, is generally assumed to be constant over time. One of the insights in the pioneering work of Engle (1982) is to analyze conditional, rather than unconditional, second moments and to allow the conditional variance, σ_{t+1}^2, to be time dependent.

20.3.2   Linear *ARCH* and *GARCH* models

The simplest model involving *ARCH* is the Martingale Difference Sequence with *ARCH(q)* innovations, which can be expressed as,

$$y_t = \varepsilon_t = z_t \sigma_t \qquad (20.3.3)$$

$$z_t \sim IID(0, 1) \qquad (20.3.4)$$

$$\sigma_t^2 = \omega + \sum_{j=1}^{q} \alpha_j y_{t-j}^2, \qquad (20.3.5)$$

$$\omega > 0 \quad \text{and} \quad \alpha_j \geq 0, \quad \text{for } j = 1, 2, \ldots, q, \qquad (20.3.6)$$

where the parameter restrictions (20.3.6) are required to avoid negativity of the conditional variance. The variable σ_t^2 is a time-varying positive, and measurable function of the time $t-1$ information set, Ω_{t-1}. While the y_t process is serially uncorrelated, the σ_t^2 process is changing over time. Hence,

$$E[y_t|\Omega_{t-1}] = \sigma_t E[z_t|\Omega_{t-1}] = 0$$

and

$$Var[y_t|\Omega_{t-1}] = \sigma_t^2 Var[z_t|\Omega_{t-1}] = \sigma_t^2,$$

so that the *ARCH* process in y_t arises as a rescaled normal innovation sequence. From Engle (1982), the volatility process at time t is a deterministic function of the last q squared shocks of the uncorrelated process y_t The model implies an absence of dynamics in the conditional mean, while the *ARCH* model allows for serial correlation in the volatility process and specifies the conditional variance, or volatility, to be a linear function of the last q squared returns. Hence, a series of large positive, or large negative, values of the dependent variable y_t are associated with increasing future volatility.

The *ARCH* model specifies the form of the *conditional* variance of a process, and from this representation it is generally possible to derive the corresponding *unconditional* variance. From the Law of Iterated Expectations, if Ω_1 and Ω_2 are two information sets of random variables and Ω_1 is a subset of Ω_2, then for any random variable y, it follows that $E(y|\Omega_1) = E[E(y|\Omega_2)|\Omega_1]$. For example, if $\Omega_2 = (y_t, y_{t-1}, \ldots\ldots)$ and $\Omega_1 = (y_{t-k}, y_{t-k-1}, \ldots)$, then $E(y) = E[E(y|\Omega_2)]$. To derive the mean and variance of the unconditional distribution of the *ARCH(q)* process in equations (20.3.3) through (20.3.6), we note that

$$E(y_t) = E[E(y_t|\Omega_{t-1})] = 0,$$

and

$$E(y_t^2) = E[E(y_t^2|\Omega_{t-1})] = \sigma_t^2, \tag{20.3.7}$$

so that

$$E(y_t^2) = \omega + E\left[\sum_{j=1}^{q} \alpha_j y_{t-j}^2|\Omega_{t-1}\right] = \omega + \sum_{j=1}^{q} \alpha_j E(y_{t-j}^2)|\Omega_{t-1})$$

A necessary requirement for the stationarity of the process is for its unconditional variance to be finite and constant. Then $E(y_{t-j}^2) = \sigma^2$, for $j = 0,1,2,\ldots$, where σ^2 is a finite and positive constant such that

$$\sigma^2 = \omega \left(1 - \sum_{j=1}^{q} \alpha_j\right)^{-1} \tag{20.3.8}$$

and a necessary condition for the stationarity and existence of a finite unconditional variance of the *ARCH(q)* process is thus

$$\sum_{j=1}^{q} \alpha_j < 1.$$

The *ARCH* modeling approach indicates that potentially very volatile economic and financial time series can arise from processes with changing conditional variances, which at the same time have constant unconditional variances.

The original application of *ARCH* models in Engle (1982, 1983) concerned monthly UK inflation series, with applications in finance appearing some time later. Initial difficulties in the practical application of *ARCH* models centered on the implementation of the parameter restrictions (20.3.6) during estimation and the excessively large numbers of parameters required to successfully represent the level of persistence in volatility generally found in data. One method for reducing the parameter space was used by Engle (1983) and consisted of imposing the condition that the *ARCH* parameters linearly decayed with lag, so that

$$\alpha_j = \left(\frac{\alpha}{q}\right)\left[\frac{(q+1-j)}{(q+1)}\right] \text{ for } j = 0, 1, 2, \ldots, q-1 \quad \text{and} \quad \alpha_j = 0 \text{ for } j = q, q+1, \ldots.$$

An alternative parameterization, due to Geweke (1986), was to consider a Bayesian approach which introduced a prior distribution that guaranteed the parameter estimates to lie in a feasible region.

The Generalized *ARCH* or *GARCH* (p, q), process introduced by Bollerslev (1986) is

$$\sigma_t^2 = \omega + \sum_{j=1}^{q} \alpha_j y_{t-j}^2 + \sum_{j=1}^{p} \beta_j \sigma_{t-j}^2, \tag{20.3.9}$$

so that the *ARCH(q)* model is appended with p lagged conditional variance terms. The above *GARCH(p, q)* process can be expressed in lag operator form as

$$\sigma_t^2 = \omega + \alpha(L)y_t^2 + \beta(L)\sigma_t^2 \tag{20.3.10}$$

where $\alpha(L) = \sum_{j=1}^{q} \alpha_j L^j, \beta(L) = \sum_{j=1}^{p} \beta_j L^j$; and $\omega > 0, \alpha_j \geq 0$, for $j = 1, 2, \ldots, q$, and $\beta_j \geq 0$ for $j = 1, 2, \ldots, p$. On taking iterated expectations throughout (20.3.10),

$$E(\sigma_t^2) = \omega + \sum_{j=1}^{q} \alpha_j E(y_{t-j}^2) + \sum_{j=1}^{p} \beta_j E(\sigma_{t-j}^2)$$

Since $E(\sigma_{t+j}^2) = E(y_{t+j}^2) = \sigma^2$, it follows that the unconditional variance is

$$\sigma^2 = \omega \left(1 - \sum_{j=1}^{q} \alpha_j - \sum_{j=1}^{p} \beta_j\right)^{-1} = \omega[1 - \alpha(1) - \beta(1)]^{-1}. \tag{20.3.11}$$

One main attraction of *GARCH* models compared to *ARCH* models is the reduction in the parameter space. A necessary condition for the *GARCH(p, q)* process to be covariance stationary is then seen to be

$$0 < \left(\sum_{j=1}^{q} \alpha_j + \sum_{j=1}^{p} \beta_j\right) < 1. \tag{20.3.12}$$

The *GARCH* (p, q) process in (20.3.9) and (20.3.10) can be written as

$$[1 - \beta(L)]\sigma_t^2 = \omega + \alpha(L)y_t^2,$$

If all the roots of $[1 - \beta(L)]$ lie outside the unit circle, then the *GARCH* (p, q) process can be excpressed as an infinite-order *ARCH* process,

$$\sigma_t^2 = [1 - \beta(1)]^{-1}\omega + \delta(L)y_t^2 = \gamma + \sum_{j=1}^{\infty} \delta_j y_{t-j}^2, \tag{20.3.13}$$

where $\delta(L) = [1 - \beta(L)]^{-1}\alpha(L)$ is an infinite-order power series in the lag operator. A valid representation for the infinite distributed lag on past squared returns requires nonnegative coefficients. For the *GARCH*(1,1) process this trivially amounts to the model's parameters being nonnegative. Nelson and Cao (1992) have derived the corresponding restrictions in higher-order *GARCH*(p,q) processes.

The linear *GARCH*(p, q) process can also be easily reparameterized to obtain an interesting representation as an *ARMA*(m, p) process for y_1^2, where $m = \max(p, q)$. Since

$$y_{t+1}^2 = \omega + \alpha(L)y_{t+1}^2 + \beta(L)\sigma_{t+1}^2,$$

then

$$[1 - \alpha(L) - \beta(L)]y_{t+1}^2 = \omega + (y_{t+1}^2 - \sigma_{t+1}^2) - \beta(L)(y_{t+1}^2 - \sigma_{t+1}^2)$$

and

$$[1 - \alpha(L) - \beta(L)]y_{t+1}^2 = \omega + (1 - \beta(L))v_{t+1}, \tag{20.3.14}$$

where

$$v_{t+1} = (y_{t+1}^2 - \sigma_{t+1}^2) = (z_{t+1}^2 - 1)\sigma_{t+1}^2, \tag{20.3.15}$$

and v_{t+1} is a white noise process and has the interpretation of being the innovation in the conditional variance process. First, note that since $E[v_{t+1}|\Omega_t] = E[(y_{t+1}^2 - \sigma_{t+1}^2)|\Omega_t] = 0$, it follows that v_{t+1} is a martingale. Also, v_{t+1} is serially uncorrelated since $E[v_{t+i}v_{t+j}|\Omega_t] = 0$, for any $i, j > 0$. However,

$$Var[v_{t+1}|\Omega_t] = E[v_{t+1}^2|\Omega_t] = E[(y_{t+1}^4 - 2\sigma_{t+1}^2 y_{t+1}^2 + \sigma_{t+1}^4)|\Omega_t]$$

and, since σ_{t+1}^2 is known at time $t + 1$ and is included in the information set Ω_t, then

$$Var_t v_{t+1} = E_t y_{t+1}^4 - 2\sigma_{t+1}^2 E_t y_{t+1}^2 + \sigma_{t+1}^4 \tag{20.3.16}$$

Under conditional normality, so that (20.3.4) is replaced with $Z_t \sim NID(0, 1)$, then $E_t y_{t+1}^4 = 3\sigma_{t+1}^4$ and (20.3.16) reduces to $Var_t v_{t+1} = 2\sigma_{t+1}^4$. Hence, v_{t+1} possesses a form of time-dependent heteroskedasticity and is bounded in the range $(-\sigma_{t+1}^2, \infty)$.

The value $-\sigma_{t+1}^2$ is known as the "support" of the distribution. Thus v_{t+1} satisfies all the conditions to be a white noise process and hence y_{t+1}^2 is *ARMA(m, p)*, where $m = \max(p, q)$.

The most widely used model is the *GARCH*(1,1) process, given by

$$y_t = \varepsilon_t = \sigma_t z_t, \tag{20.3.3}$$

$$z_t \sim IID(0, 1) \tag{20.3.4}$$

$$\sigma_{t+1}^2 = \omega + \alpha y_t^2 + \beta \sigma_t^2, \tag{20.3.17}$$

$$\omega > 0, \alpha \geq 0 \text{ and } \beta \geq 0 \tag{20.3.18}$$

where (20.3.18) ensures nonnegative conditional variances, while the condition $0 < (\alpha + \beta) < 1$ ensures stationarity and a finite variance of the unconditional returns. The unconditional variance of returns is then $E(y_t^2) = \sigma^2 = \omega(1 - \alpha - \beta)^{-1}$. The *ARCH*($\infty$) representation is obtained in the same manner as for (20.3.13) as

$$(1 - \beta L)\sigma_t^2 = \omega + (\alpha L)y_t^2,$$
$$\sigma_t^2 = \omega(1 - \beta)^{-1} + (1 - \beta L)^{-1}(\alpha L)y_t^2,$$
$$\sigma_t^2 = \omega(1 - \beta)^{-1} + \alpha \sum_{j=0}^{\infty} \beta^j y_{t-1-j}^2, \tag{20.3.19}$$

so that the weights on past squared innovations (returns) are exponentially decaying. From (20.3.14) it can be seen that the *GARCH*(1,1) process in (20.3.17) can be expressed as the *ARMA*(1,1) process in squared returns. For expositional purposes, it is worth noting that, from first principles (20.3.17) can be rewritten by introducing y_{t+1}^2 on both sides of the equation:

$$y_{t+1}^2 = \omega + y_{t+1}^2 - \sigma_{t+1}^2 + \alpha y_t^2 + \beta \sigma_t^2,$$

and hence

$$y_{t+1}^2 = \omega + (\alpha + \beta)y_t^2 + v_{t+1} - \beta v_t, \tag{20.3.20}$$

where v_t is defined in equation (20.3.15). Since

$$[1 - (\alpha + \beta)L]y_{t+1}^2 = \omega + (1 - \beta L)v_{t+1},$$

the Wold decomposition for the squared returns process is

$$y_{t+1}^2 = \frac{\omega}{1 - (\alpha + \beta)} + \sum_{j=0}^{\infty} (\alpha + \beta)^j \beta v_{t+1-j}, \tag{20.3.21}$$

which also shows that the unconditional variance of returns is $E(y_{t+1}^2) = \omega[1 - (\alpha + \beta)]^{-1}$. This representation also neatly illustrates how the parameter

$(\alpha + \beta)$ represents the degree of persistence of the volatility process, which is also the autoregressive component of the *ARMA* representation for squared returns. Clearly, if $0 < (\alpha + \beta) < 1$, the squared returns will be generated by a stationary *ARMA*(1,1) model and the variance of the unconditional returns will be finite. If $(\alpha + \beta) = 1$, there will be a unit root in the autoregressive representation for squared returns, which will then be generated by a nonstationary *ARIMA*(0,1,1) model, and the unconditional returns will have an infinite variance.

20.3.3 Regression with *ARCH* effects

For pedagogic reasons, the discussion so far has been restricted to a martingale process with no dynamics in the conditional mean, but with *ARCH* effects. In many practical situations *ARCH*-type models are used in more general regression settings. Indeed, this was the original formulation by Engle (1982). For example, the regression model with *ARMA(P,Q)* disturbances and innovations that are *GARCH (p, q)* process is

$$y_t = x_t'b + u_t, \tag{20.3.22}$$

$$\phi(L)u_t = \theta(L)\varepsilon_t, \quad \varepsilon_t = \sigma_t z_t, \tag{20.3.23}$$

$$z_t \sim IID(0,1) \tag{20.3.24}$$

$$\sigma_t^2 = \omega + \sum_{j=1}^{q} \alpha_j \varepsilon_{t-j}^2 + \sum_{j=1}^{p} \beta_j \sigma_{t-j}^2 \tag{20.3.9}$$

where $\phi(L)$ and $\theta(L)$ are respectively P and Q ordered polynomials in the lag operator, (20.3.22) represents a regression with a k-dimensional vector of explanatory variables x_t', with corresponding vector of parameters b. Variants of this model are widely used in applications, with possible cointegration being exhibited in the structural variables y_t and x_t'.

Many applications of *GARCH* models have included specifications containing explanatory variables in the conditional variance equation. For example, Lamoureux and Lastrapes (1990a, 1990b) have investigated the effects of volume of trading on volatility in currency options markets. From French and Roll (1986), the volatility of a market is hypothesized to be proportional to the length of the market closure before trading commences. Hence studies of this type generally include day of the week dummy variables D_{it}, a dummy variable for market holidays and reopens and x_{it}, to measure volume of trading. Recent work has also emphasized order flow dynamics. Models of the form,

$$y_t = \varepsilon_t = \sigma_t z_t, \quad z_t \sim IID(0,1)$$

$$\sigma_{t+1}^2 = \omega + \alpha y_t^2 + \beta \sigma_t^2 + \sum_{i=1}^{4} \lambda_i D_{it} + \sum_{i=1}^{k} \gamma_i x_{it},$$

do not pose any particular problems except that the conditions that guarantee the nonnegativity of the conditional variance depend on the range of the explanatory variables as well as the parameter values. These are often neglected in practice. The interim dynamics of the explanatory variables on the conditional variance can then be obtained from

$$y_{t+1}^2 = [1 - (\alpha + \beta)L]^{-1}\left[\omega + \sum_{i=1}^{4}\lambda_i D_{it} + \sum_{i=1}^{k}\gamma_i x_{it}\right] + \sum_{i=0}^{\infty}\delta_i v_{t+1-i}$$

where

$$\delta(L) = [1 - (\alpha + \beta)L]^{-1}(1 - \beta L) = \sum_{i=0}^{\infty}\beta(\alpha + \beta)^i L^i.$$

A further issue in this area concerns the probable joint endogeneity of volume and volatility. One possible method suggested by Lamoureux and Lastrapes (1990a) is to use an instrument in the conditional variance equation for volume. Another approach, which is unfortunately beyond the scope of this chapter, would be to estimate a simultaneous equation *GARCH* model for volatility and volume separately, with interaction terms being included.

A special and very interesting type of regression with *GARCH* is the *ARCH in Mean Model*, or *ARCH – M* model, which was originally suggested by Engle, Lilien and Robins (1987). In this model a function of lagged volatility is allowed to effect the current level of the process. Hence,

$$y_t = x_t'\beta + \gamma f(\sigma_t^2) + u_t, \tag{20.3.25}$$

with equations (20.3.22), (20.3.24) and (20.3.9) also included. The parameter γ is known as the *ARCH* in mean parameter. The choice of functional form is fairly flexible; usually the conditional standard deviation, σ_t, is used since this preserves the same scaling as the mean of the process y_t. Sometimes the conditional variance σ_t^2 itself, or $\ln(\sigma_t^2)$, is the chosen function. This model can be used to represent the "market model" in finance, where the return's own volatility is allowed to effect mean returns. The original application of Engle, Lilien and Robins (1987) was the term structure of interest rates and γ has the interpretation of being a liquidity premium. In their formulation, y_t is the excess holding yield on long term bonds relative to a one-period Treasury Bill, σ_t is interpreted as the risk premium and ε_t is the ex-ante rate of return and would be expected to be uncorrelated in an efficient market.

There are many other examples from finance where the *ARCH – M* model is very relevant. In particular, Campbell and Hentschel (1992) use a volatility feedback hypothesis, where a positive shock to volatility drives down returns. If expected returns increase when volatility increases and if expected dividends are unchanged, then stock prices should fall when volatility increases. Other researchers have considered the conditional covariance of the returns for two stocks, i.e., $Cov_{t-1}(R_{it}, R_{jt})$ to be related to the conditional standard deviation of the market index in the form of

$$Cov_{t-1}(R_{it}, R_{jt}) = \alpha_{0ij} + \alpha_{1ij}\sqrt{Var_{t-1}(R_{et})},$$

which is clearly a far more complex form of the *ARCH – M* model and involves some multivariate formulations, which is beyond the scope of this chapter. There are also some examples in macroeconomics; Baillie, Chung and Tieslau (1996) show that long memory processes in the conditional mean with *GARCH* innovations describe quite well the monthly inflation series for post-WWII G7 countries. They then test the Friedman hypothesis concerning the relationship between the mean level and variability of inflation; and find evidence for some countries that high volatility of inflation may Granger cause higher levels of inflation.

20.3.4 Moment structure of *GARCH* models

There are some interesting relationships between the conditional returns density with a *GARCH* process and the implied density for the unconditional returns. As noted by Hsieh (1989), Jensen's inequality implies that the excess kurtosis in the unconditional returns y_t, defined in (20.3.2), must be at least as great as the excess kurtosis in the conditional returns density $z_t = y_t \sigma_t^{-1}$. Hence the focus on modeling volatility (the second stylized fact in asset prices) naturally has implications for the non-Gaussianity in unconditional returns (the third stylized fact of asset prices). For the *ARCH*(1) process with $\omega > 0$ and $\alpha_1 > 0$, Engle (1982) showed that the $2m^{\text{th}}$ unconditional moment exists if and only if

$$\alpha_1^m \prod_{j=1}^{m} (2j - 1) < 1. \tag{20.3.26}$$

Hence, for $E(y_t^2)$ and $E(y_t^4)$ to exist, necessary conditions are that $\alpha_1 < 1$ and $3\alpha_1^2 < 1$, respectively. Engle (1982) showed that

$$E(y_t^4) = 3 \left(\frac{\omega}{1 - \alpha} \right)^2 \frac{(1 - \alpha^2)}{(1 - 3\alpha^2)} \tag{20.3.27}$$

so that κ the coefficient of excess kurtosis, is

$$\kappa = \frac{\left\{ E(y_t^4) - 3[E(y_t^2)]^2 \right\}}{[E(y_t^2)]^2} = \left(\frac{6\alpha^2}{1 - 3\alpha^2} \right) \tag{20.3.28}$$

and, since $E(y_t^2) = \omega(1 - \alpha)^{-1} = \sigma^2$, it follows that $E(y_t^4) > 3Var(y_t)$, so that the *ARCH*(1) model generates excess kurtosis. Hence a martingale process with *ARCH*(1) innovations is consistent with uncorrelated returns with time-dependent volatility and excess kurtosis in the density of unconditional returns. These three aspects of the model are entirely consistent with the major stylized facts of asset prices.

Bollerslev (1986) has also derived necessary and sufficient conditions for the existence of the $2m^{\text{th}}$ moment of the *GARCH*(1,1) process, under Gaussianity of the conditional density so that $z_t \sim NID(0, 1)$. Define

$$\mu(\alpha, \beta, m) = \sum_{j=0}^{m} C_j^m a_j \alpha_j \beta_{m-j} < 1, \tag{20.3.29}$$

where

$$C_j^m = \left[\frac{m!}{j!(m-j)!}\right], a_0 = 1 \quad \text{and} \quad a_j = \prod_{i=1}^{j}(2i-1) \quad \text{for } j = 1, 2, \ldots.$$

The $2m^{\text{th}}$ moment of the unconditional distribution of ε_t is expressed by the recursive formula

$$E(y_t^{2m}) = a_m\left[\sum_{n=0}^{m-1}\alpha_n^{-1}E(y_t^{2n})\omega^{m-n}C_{m-n}^m\mu(\alpha, \beta, n)\right][1 - \mu(\alpha, \beta, m)]^{-1} \qquad (20.3.30)$$

In particular, if $3\alpha^2 + 2\alpha\beta + \beta^2 < 1$, then the fourth-order moment exists and the moments of the unconditional density are given by

$$E(y_t^2) = \sigma^2 = \omega(1 - \alpha - \beta)^{-1} \qquad (20.3.31)$$

and

$$E(y_t^4) = 3\omega^2(1 + \alpha + \beta)[(1 - \alpha - \beta)(1 - \beta^2 - 2\alpha\beta - 3\alpha^2)]^{-1}. \qquad (20.3.32)$$

For the normal density $\kappa = 0$ and for the $GARCH(1,1)$ process,

$$\kappa = 6\alpha^2(1 - \beta^2 - 2\alpha\beta - 3\alpha^2)^{-1}. \qquad (20.3.33)$$

Given the existence of the fourth moment, it can be seen that $\kappa > 0$, which implies that the $GARCH(1,1)$ process gives rise to excess kurtosis, i.e., it is leptokurtic. He and Terasvirta (1999a) have extended the results to non-Gaussian situations for a family of $GARCH(1,1)$ models. Some results also exist for the autocorrelations of the squared process y_t^2. In particular, Bollerslev (1988) found the autocorrelation function for squared returns from the martingale–$GARCH(1,1)$ model in (20.3.14) with conditionally Gaussian errors; i.e., $y_t = \varepsilon_t = \sigma_t z_t$, $z_t \sim NID(0,1)$, and $\sigma_{t+1}^2 = \omega + \alpha y_t^2 + \beta\sigma_t^2$, with $\omega > 0$, $\alpha \geq 0$ and $\beta \geq 0$. Then the autocorrelation function at lag k for the squared returns is

$$\rho_k = (\alpha + \beta)^{k-1}\rho_1, \qquad (20.3.34)$$

and

$$\rho_1 = \alpha(1 - \alpha\beta - \beta^2)(1 - 2\alpha\beta - \beta^2)^{-1}. \qquad (20.3.35)$$

Bollerslev (1988) also shows that analysis based on Yule–Walker-type equations indicates the shape and patterns of the autocorrelation functions and partial autocorrelation functions for higher order $GARCH(p, q)$ processes. Milhoj (1985) has some results for the $ARCH(q)$ model. As noted by Bollerslev (1988), the information on the sample autocorrelation and sample partial autocorrelation functions can potentially be used in model selection. However, the sampling distribution of autocorrelations from y_t^2 is more complicated due to the dependence structure, so that the conventional Bartlett standard errors will be inappropriate. He and Terasvirta (1999b) have derived the autocorrelation function for $GARCH(1,1)$ models with conditional nonnormality. Some extremely complicated theoretical results on the fourth moments of $GARCH(p, q)$ models with nonnormal conditional densities are also given by He and Terasvirta (1999c) and analogous results for Gaussian conditional densities by Karanasos (1999).

There has also been extensive recent work on other theoretical issues relating to the probabilistic structure of $GARCH$ models. Although there is insufficient space to do justice to all this work, it should be noted that Carrasco and Chen (2002) derive mixing conditions for the existence of higher moments of various nonlinear $GARCH$ models. Also, Berkes, Horvath and Kokoszka (2003) provide a potentially useful and unique representation for the conditional variance of the $GARCH(p, q)$ process.

20.3.5 Prediction from *GARCH* models

In many practical situations it is of interest to make predictions in models with time-dependent heteroskedasticity. The presence of *ARCH* effects will have implications for forming confidence intervals of predictions of the conditional mean and also for predicting future volatility. On considering the regression with *ARMA(P, Q)* disturbances with $GARCH(p, q)$ innovations, as in (20.3.22) through (20.3.24) and (20.3.9), and with known parameters, the functional form of the minimum MSE predictor will be unaffected by the presence of the time-dependent heteroskedasticity. The only exception to this would be in the case of an $ARCH-M$ model with volatility feedback into the conditional mean equation. Otherwise, for a dependent variable which is covariance stationary and has a Wold decomposition given by (20.1.1), the variance of the minimum MSE s-step ahead predictor, $y_{t,s}$, is

$$Var_t(y_{t,s}) = \sum_{i=1}^{s} \psi_{s-i}^2 E_t \sigma_{t+i}^2, \tag{20.3.36}$$

so that predictions of future volatility have to be made in order to calculate confidence intervals for predictions of the *conditional mean*. Clearly, in the case of conditional homoskedasticity, the prediction MSE reduces to the usual formula of $MSE(y_{t,s}) = \sigma^2 \sum_{i=1}^{s} \psi_{i-1}^2$. In order to implement equation (20.3.36) it is necessary to forecast future volatility. Baillie and Bollerslev (1992) have derived the form of the minimum MSE predictor for a $GARCH(p, q)$ process. For example, for the $GARCH(1,1)$ model in equation (20.3.17), the predictor of future volatility s periods ahead is,

$$E_t \sigma_{t+s}^2 = \sigma^2 + (\alpha + \beta)^{s-1} (\sigma_{t+1}^2 - \sigma^2), \tag{20.3.37}$$

which implies that the optimal prediction is based on the average, or unconditional volatility, plus an adjustment term of geometrically declining weight on the last "surprise" in the variance. The surprise in this context is the distance of the last observed conditional variance from its average value of σ^2. Baillie and Bollerslev (1992) derive the moments of the s-step ahead conditional prediction density from a $GARCH(1,1)$ process and use a Cornish Fisher expansion to approximate the percentiles of the prediction density.

Further issues arise in option pricing settings, when forecasts of future volatility are required and it may also be desirable to know about the distribution of these volatility predictions. Often σ_t^2 can be regarded as a regular covariance stationary stochastic process with a Wold decomposition in terms of the lagged innovations in the conditional variance, namely v_t. In this case $\sigma_t^2 = \sum_{j=1}^{\infty} \xi_j v_{t-j}$, which can be used to determine the properties of the s-step ahead prediction error for the conditional variance.

20.3.6   Variants of *GARCH* models

It has been said that there are as many *ARCH* models as the investigator's imagination. To an extent this is a similar attribute to the use of nonlinear models in general and new parameterizations of *GARCH* models have frequently been developed to meet new financial and economic situations. This section briefly reviews some of the more widely used varieties.

Integrated GARCH

In many empirical studies it is often found that the sum of the parameters in a $GARCH(1,1)$ model is close to unity. Hence Engle and Bollerslev (1986) suggested the model

$$\sigma_{t+1}^2 = \omega + \alpha y_t^2 + (1 - \alpha)\sigma_t^2,$$

where $0 < \alpha < 1$ and, from equation (20.3.11), it is seen that the unconditional variance of the *IGARCH* model is undefined, while the s-step ahead predictor is

$$E_t \sigma_{t+s}^2 = (s - 1)\omega + \sigma_{t+1}^2, \tag{20.3.38}$$

so there is a direct analogy with the Random Walk with drift in the conditional mean model. The optimal prediction is the current value of the process plus a linearly increasing term. This is one reason why this *GARCH* model is said to be "integrated." The $GARCH(1,1)$ model is an $ARIMA(0,1,1)$ model in squared returns, so that

$$(1 - L)y_{t+1}^2 = \omega + (1 - \beta L)v_{t+1} \tag{20.3.39}$$

In many applications, the estimate of β is found to be close to 0.8, which is the typical choice of the smoothing constant in the informal exponential smoothing method discussed earlier in section 20.1. In general, the $GARCH(p, q)$

process reduces to an *IGARCH(p,q)* process when the factorization of the polynomial gives

$$[1 - \alpha(L) - \beta(L)] \equiv (1 - L)\Phi(L), \tag{20.3.40}$$

where $\Phi(L)$ is a polynomial of degree $m - 1$ in the lag operator and has all its roots outside the unit circle. Then, the *IGARCH(p, q)* process is,

$$(1 - L)\Phi(L)y_t^2 = \omega + [1 - \beta(L)]v_t. \tag{20.3.41}$$

Nelson (1990a) has shown that the *IGARCH* process is strongly stationary, but not weakly stationary. On starting with a continuous time diffusion process, which is often specified in finance theory, taking discrete observations at finer and finer sampling intervals leads to a discrete time volatility process which tends to *IGARCH* with a zero intercept. This is an interesting relationship between two previously different specifications.

Exponential GARCH

Nelson (1990c) introduced the *EGARCH* process to allow for asymmetric effects between volatility and shocks, which can account for leverage. Black and Scholes (1972) noted that when the total value of a levered firm falls, the value of the equity becomes a smaller share of the total. Since equity bears the full risk of the firm the percentage volatility of equity should rise. Subsequent empirical work by Christie (1982) tended to confirm this theory. Nelson's *EGARCH(1,1)* model is used to represent these market features and is given by

$$\ln(\sigma_{t+1}^2) = \omega + \alpha z_t + \gamma[|z_t| - E|z_t|] + \beta \ln(\sigma_t^2), \tag{20.3.42}$$

and does not require any nonnegativity restrictions on the parameters. The variable $g(z_t) = \alpha z_t + \gamma[|z_t| - E|z_t|]$ has a mean of zero and is serially uncorrelated. This function is piecewise linear in z_t since it can be written as

$$g(z_t) = (\alpha + \gamma)z_t I(z_t > 0) + (\alpha - \gamma)z_t I(z_t < 0) - \gamma E|z_t| \tag{20.3.43}$$

where $I(z_t > 0)$ is the standard indicator function and is one for all positive z_t and zero otherwise. The *EGARCH(1,1)* model implies that a negative return has an effect $(\alpha - \gamma)$ on the log of the conditional variance, while a positive return has an effect of $(\alpha + \gamma)$ on the log of the conditional variance. Extensions to higher-order parametric *EGARCH* models are not difficult conceptually, but are rarely used in practice.

GJR asymmetric GARCH

This model provides another formulation for introducing asymmetry into the volatility process and is an alternative to Nelson's *EGARCH* model. Glosten, Jagannathan and Runkle (1993) modified the standard *GARCH(1,1)* model to allow for the parameter of lagged squared returns to depend on the sign of the shock, so that

$$\sigma_{t+1}^2 = \omega + \alpha y_t^2(1 - I[y_t > 0]) + \gamma y_t^2(1 - I[y_t < 0]) + \beta\sigma_t^2 \tag{20.3.44}$$

The model requires the restrictions $\omega > 0$, $[(\alpha + \gamma)/2] \geq 0$ and $\beta > 0$ to ensure nonnegative conditional variances. The further restriction that $(\alpha + \gamma)(1/2) + \beta < 1$ ensures stationarity and a finite variance of unconditional returns.

Long memory ARCH

Taylor (1986) and Ding, Granger and Engle (1993) made the important empirical observations that squared returns, and particularly absolute returns, from many speculative auction financial markets tend to have very slowly decaying auto-correlation functions that are consistent with the long memory property, or Hurst effect. There are several possible ways of incorporating these features into *ARCH* models. First, Baillie, Bollerslev and Mikkelsen (1996) introduced the Fractionally Integrated *GARCH* model, known as *FIGARCH* On modifying the *IGARCH(p, q)* model in equation (20.3.41), the *FIGARCH(p, d, q)* model can be expressed as

$$\phi(L)(1 - L)^d y_{t+1}^2 = \omega + [1 - \beta(L)]v_{t+1}, \tag{20.3.45}$$

In most applications low-order models are found to be expedient and, in parti-cular, the *FIGARCH(0, d, 1)* model can be expressed as,

$$(1 - L)^d y_{t+1}^2 = \omega + (1 - \beta L)v_{t+1}, \tag{20.3.46}$$

where $0 < d < 1$ is the long memory volatility parameter and v_{t+1} is defined as in equation (20.3.15). The model can also be written as

$$\sigma_{t+1}^2 = \left(\frac{\omega}{1 - \beta}\right) + \lambda(L)y_t^2 \tag{20.3.47}$$

where

$$\lambda(L) = \left\{1 - (1 - \beta L)^{-1}(1 - L)^d\right\} = \sum_{k=0}^{\infty} \lambda_k L^k.$$

From Sterling's approximation it can be shown that, for high lags,

$$\lambda_k \approx ck^{d-1} \tag{20.3.48}$$

where $c = (1 - \beta)/\Gamma(d)$ is a constant and $\Gamma(\cdot)$ is the gamma function. Equation (20.3.48) then displays the *long memory property*, or "Hurst effect," where the distributed lag coefficients decay at the very slow hyperbolic rate, as opposed to the regular exponential rate associated with the conventional stable *GARCH* family. The attraction of the *FIGARCH* process is that, for $0 < d < 1$, it is sufficiently flexible to allow for intermediate ranges of persistence. It should also be noted that squared returns from the martingale-*FIGARCH*(0,*d*,1) process are the *ARFIMA*(0,*d*,1) process given in (20.3.46), which helps to motivate the parameterization. The generalization to higher-order processes is straightforward. For example the *FIGARCH*(1,*d*,1) model,

$$(1 - \phi L)(1 - L)^d y_{t+1}^2 = \omega + v_{t+1} - \beta v_t \tag{20.3.49}$$

can be expressed as

$$\sigma_{t+1}^2 = \omega + [1 - \beta L - (1 - \phi L)(1 - L)^d]y_t^2 + \beta \sigma_t^2, \tag{20.3.50}$$

and will also have the same hyperbolic rate of decay at high lags, i.e., $\lambda_k \approx k^{d-1}$. The theoretical properties of the low-order *FIGARCH* processes are discussed in more detail by Baillie, Bollerslev and Mikkelsen (1996). They conjecture that the process is strictly stationary and ergodic for $0 \leq d < 1$, and shocks to the conditional variance will ultimately die out in a forecasting sense.

Bollerslev and Mikkelsen (1996) have considered the application of long memory *FIGARCH* models to the problem of forecasting volatility in options pricing frameworks and for stock returns as opposed to currencies. They consider the modified *FIEGARCH* model

$$\ln(\sigma_{t+1}^2) = \omega + \phi(L)^{-1}(1 - L)^{-d}[1 + \pi(L)]g(z_t), \tag{20.3.51}$$

which nests the conventional *EGARCH* model for $d = 0$. Davidson (2004) discusses other parametric structures for hyperbolically decaying *ARCH* models and their related moment properties.

20.3.7 Estimation and inference in *ARCH* models

To maintain sufficient generality, consider the model given by equations (20.3.9) and (20.3.23) with $y_t = h(x_t; b) + \varepsilon_t$, and define Θ to represent a vector of unknown parameters in both the conditional mean and the conditional variance. For estimation it is necessary to specify the density $f(z_t)$ of the process $\varepsilon_t = z_t \sigma_t$, where $z_t \sim IID(0, 1)$. The log likelihood of the sample is then

$$L(\Theta) = \sum_{t=1}^{T} \left[\ln \left[f(\varepsilon_t \sigma_t^{-1}) \right] - \ln(\sigma_t) \right] \tag{20.3.52}$$

where the second term represents the Jacobian of transforming from z_t to ε_t Under conditional normality, so that $z_t \sim NID(0, 1)$, then

$$\ln(L) = -\left(\frac{T}{2}\right) \ln(2\pi) - (1/2) \sum_{t=1}^{T} \left[\left(\frac{\varepsilon_t^2}{\sigma_t^2}\right) + \ln(\sigma_t^2) \right] \tag{20.3.53}$$

Standard numerical optimization methods can be used to find the maximum MLE. The estimate of Θ at the ith iteration is given by $\hat{\Theta}^i$ and, in general,

$$\hat{\Theta}^i = \hat{\Theta}^{i-1} - H(\Theta)^{-1}s(\Theta) \tag{20.3.54}$$

where $H(\Theta)$ is the hessian and $s(\Theta)$ is the score vector. A major area of interest concerns *ARCH* models with non-Gaussian conditional densities. Although the combination of an *ARCH*-type process with a conditional normal density generates an unconditional returns density with implied excess kurtosis, the degree of excess kurtosis is frequently insufficient to represent the behavior of daily or higher frequency returns data. For this reason, there has been some experimentation on using conditional densities which have greater kurtosis than the normal distribution, since they can generate still greater excess kurtosis in the unconditional returns distribution. In particular, Bollerslev (1987) used the Student-*t* density, so that $z_t \sim t(0, \sigma_t^2, v)$, where v is the degrees of freedom, and the log likelihood is, therefore,

$$\ln(L) = \sum \left[\ln\left(\Gamma\left(\frac{v+1}{2}\right)\right) - \ln\left(\Gamma\left(\frac{v}{2}\right)\right) - (1/2)\ln(v-2)\sigma_t^2 \right. $$
$$\left. - \left(\frac{v+1}{2}\right)\ln\left(1 + \left(\frac{y_t^2}{\sigma_t^2}\right)\right) \right]$$

The kurtosis of the Student-*t* density is $3(v-2)/(v-4)$, so that it is necessary for $v > 4$, for the conditional density to have a finite kurtosis. In order to represent non-Gaussian data with excess kurtosis, conditional densities of Student-*t* or power exponential are sometimes used. However, high frequency financial market returns data is generally difficult to model in terms of an appropriate conditional density. Also, it is desirable to have an inferential procedure which is robust to misspecification of the conditional density. Such a technique is the Quasi MLE method, or QMLE, which has been implemented by Bollerslev and Wooldridge (1992) for the case of parameter estimation in *ARCH* models when the conditional density may have been misspecified. The technique maximizes the Gaussian density as usual and shows that, under standard regularity conditions,

$$T^{1/2}(\hat{\Theta} - \Theta_0) \rightarrow N\left[0, A(\Theta_0)^{-1}(\Theta_0)A(\Theta_0)^{-1}\right], \tag{20.3.55}$$

where $A(.)$ and $B(.)$ are the Hessian and outer product gradient respectively, when evaluated at the true parameter values Θ_0.

The formal statistical properties of MLE for *ARCH* models have only been derived for some special cases. Berkes, Horvath and Kokoszka (2003) have proved the consistency and asymptotic normality of the parameters of a *GARCH(p, q)* process under extremely mild conditions. Lumsdaine (1996) showed similar results for the stable *GARCH(1,1)* process; but required much stronger conditions involving the existence of moments up to order thirty two and the assumption that y_0 has a symmetric unimodal distribution which is bounded in a neighborhood of zero.

Results for integrated *GARCH* processes have been previously obtained by Lee and Hansen (1994) and Lumsdaine (1996). Their proofs require z_t to be stationary and ergodic, together with three other relatively mild conditions on the z_t process, in order for a central limit theorem to be applicable to derive the limiting distribution of the QMLE. For many of the variants of *GARCH* considered in section 20.3.6 there is an absence of theory to justify the asymptotic properties of the MLE. However, in many cases detailed simulation evidence has led researchers to believe that the QMLE often possesses asymptotic normality and $T^{1/2}$ consistency; e.g., the *FIGARCH* model in Baillie, Bollerslev and Mikkelesen (1996).

Some alternative methods to MLE have also been considered for *GARCH*-type models. In particular, Glosten, Jagannathan and Runkle (1993) have used Generalized Method of Moments (GMM) and Rich, Raymond and Butler (1991) have used instrumental variable methods. Baillie and Chung (2001) use a minimum distance estimator to estimate the parameters of the *GARCH*(1,1) model from the autocorrelations of the squared returns process in equation (20.3.15). They find that, for some very non-Gaussian conditional densities, their procedure compares very favorably to that of QMLE for some regions of the parameter space.

A considerable amount of literature has also considered issues of testing for *ARCH* effects in the residuals of models. Engle (1982) demonstrated that a Lagrange Multiplier (LM) test for *ARCH*(q) innovations could be computed by taking $T \cdot R^2$ of the regression of ε_t^2 on $\varepsilon_{t-1}^2, \ldots, \varepsilon_{t-q}^2$; where T is the sample size. An asymptotically equivalent alternative test is to replace the squared innovations with squared residuals from the model in equations (20.3.23). The resulting test statistic has the usual asymptotic χ_q^2 distribution: see Weiss (1986) for further discussion of these tests.

20.4 Stochastic volatility

One interesting characteristic of the *GARCH* modeling paradigm is that the conditional variance is a deterministic function of the set of information in the previous time period. An alternative approach is to introduce a stochastic disturbance term into the volatility equation. This results in a family of stochastic volatility (*SV*) models that have also been quite popular in representing volatility dynamics. The *SV* models are best illustrated with a simple example, where the driving part of the *SV* model is an *AR*(1) process,

$$y_t = \sigma_t z_t, \tag{20.4.1}$$

$$\ln\left(\sigma_{t+1}^2\right) = \omega + \beta \ln\left(\sigma_t^2\right) + \gamma \eta_t, \tag{20.4.2}$$

where $z_t \sim NID(0,1)$ and $\eta_t \sim NID(0,1)$ and the two innovations are mutually uncorrelated at all lags. The *SV* model implies that η_t represents shocks to the intensity of flow of new information, while z_t represents the content of the news.

If $\beta < 0$ in equation (20.4.2), then the logged volatility, $\ln(\sigma_{t+1}^2)$ will follow an $AR(1)$ process in equation (20.4.2). Then

$$\ln(\sigma_{t+1}^2) \sim N(\mu, \sigma^2) \qquad (20.4.3)$$

$$\mu = E[\ln(\sigma_{t+1}^2)] = \left(\frac{\omega}{1-\beta}\right) \qquad (20.4.4)$$

$$\sigma^2 = Var[\ln(\sigma_{t+1}^2)] = \left(\frac{\gamma^2}{1-\beta^2}\right) \qquad (20.4.5)$$

and the SV process $\ln(\sigma_{t+1}^2)$ will have a lognormal distribution. For the returns series this implies that $E(y_t^r) = 0$ for r odd, while the unconditional variance and fourth moment of returns are given by

$$E(y_t^2) = E(z_t^2 \sigma_t^2) = E(z_t^2)E(\sigma_t^2) = \exp(\mu + \sigma^2) \qquad (20.4.6)$$

and

$$E(y_t^4) = E(z_t^4 \sigma_t^4) = E(z_t^4)E(\sigma_t^4) = 3\exp(2\mu + 2\sigma^2) \qquad (20.4.7)$$

The autocovariance function of the squared returns process can be derived as

$$E(y_t^2 y_{t-k}^2) = E(z_t^2 \sigma_t^2 z_{t-k}^2 \sigma_{t-k}^2) = E(\sigma_t^2 \sigma_{t-k}^2) = \frac{\exp(\sigma^2 \gamma_1^k) - 1}{3\exp(\sigma^2) - 1} \approx \left[\frac{\exp(\sigma^2) - 1}{3\exp(\sigma^2) - 1}\right] \gamma_1^k,$$

and hence

$$E(y_t^2 y_{t-k}^2) \approx \left[\frac{\exp(\sigma^2) - 1}{3\exp(\sigma^2) - 1}\right] \gamma_1^k, \qquad (20.4.8)$$

which implies an exponential rate of decay in the autocorrelation function of the squared returns. Clearly this property is very similar to the behavior of squared returns from the $GARCH(1,1)$ model. It can also be shown from the above that the simple SV–$AR(1)$ model implies excess kurtosis in the unconditional returns distribution.

The SV models have some extra flexibility for modeling kurtosis compared to the $GARCH$ family, but at the cost of introducing an additional stochastic term. Also, the expressions for the moments and autocorrelations are generally more complicated for SV compared with $GARCH$ models. However, the real disadvantage in using SV models arises from the additional complexity of estimation. The mathematical structure of $GARCH$ models has σ_t^2 as a deterministic function of a measurable set of information in Ω_{t-1} which, given the conditional density of z_t allows the construction of the form of the likelihood function. Since σ_t^2 cannot be directly observed in SV models due to its stochastic nature, the conditional density of returns does not have an explicit form, which prevents the standard MLE approach from being directly applicable. Therefore, many less efficient methods and many extremely computationally complex methods have been utilized to estimate the parameters of the *SV* model. For example, Gallant, Hsieh and Tauchen (1997) use an Efficient Method of Moments estimator; Kim, Shephard and Chib (1998) use a Markov chain Monte Carlo sampling method to find an MLE; Duffie and Singleton (1993) use a GMM approach; while Jacquier, Polson and Rossi (1994) use a Bayesian method. At the current time a wide range of competing methods exist for conducting inference in *SV* models.

20.5 High frequency returns and realized volatility

In the last ten years a considerable amount of high frequency data on equity and currency markets has become available. In this context, *high frequency* generally refers to data sampled more often than once an hour and usually every ten or twenty minutes, depending on the level of signal to noise in the data. Goodhart and O'Hara (1997) survey some of the market microstructure theories and econometric issues in the analysis of high frequency data. The use of high frequency financial market returns data seems to be potentially very important for issues such as the pricing of risk, exploring possible arbitrage opportunities, implementing value at risk calculations, exploring the role of "fundamentals" in changing asset prices at high frequencies, and also in terms of price discovery between upstairs and downstairs markets.

Andersen and Bollerslev (1997, 1998) have developed methods for analyzing high frequency returns, which have particularly addressed the extreme intra-day periodicity that is pervasive in the high frequency volatility process. The intra-day periodicity turns out to be extremely stable and predictable across days, weeks and years in equity and currency markets and is largely due to institutional features of very regular market behavior related to the opening and closing of markets. The volatility in currency markets depends on the trading patterns of the European, Asian and North American markets. This gives rise to recurrent U-shape patterns in the correlograms of the squared and absolute returns data in currency markets and was first noticed by Dacorogna *et al.* (1993) when dealing with DM/$ returns measured very 20 minutes for three years. Domestic equity markets tend to have one U-shaped pattern of trading volume and volatility within the day. Superimposed on this very regular periodicity are jumps and discontinuities associated with the announcement of economic news. Hence the intra-day periodicity is both intriguing and an obstacle to more fundamental analysis. Andersen and Bollerslev (1997, 1998) have advocated eliminating the intra-day periodicity by means of a deterministic Flexible Fourier Form (FFF) filter originally suggested by Gallant (1981). The method is based on the equation,

$$R_{t,n} = E\left(R_{t,n}\right) + \frac{\sigma_t S_{t,n} Z_{t,n}}{N^{1/2}}, \tag{20.5.1}$$

where $R_{t,n}$ is the return for intra-day period n for day t, while $E(R_{t,n})$ is the unconditional mean of returns, and σ_t^2 is the conditional variance of daily returns, obtained from a *GARCH* model estimated from the daily returns series. Andersen and Bollerslev (1997, 1998) denote $S_{t,n}$ as a deterministic function to represent intra-day periodicity and, as usual, $z_t \sim NID(0, 1)$ and is independent of the daily volatility process σ_t^2. The variable $x_{t,n}$ is defined as

$$x_{t,n} = 2 \ln |R_{t,n} - E(R_{t,n})| - \ln \sigma_t^2 + \ln N = \ln s_{t,n}^2 + \ln z_{t,n}^2 \qquad (20.5.2)$$

which is fully observable except for the last term, $\ln z_{t,n}^2$, which is regarded as a disturbance. The modeling approach is then based on a nonlinear regression in the intra-day time interval, n, and the daily volatility factor, σ_t; i.e., $x_{t,n} = f(\theta; t, n) + u_{t,n}$, where the random variable $u_{t,n} = \ln z_{t,n}^2 - E(\ln z_{t,n}^2)$ is an *IID(0,1)* process. Thus

$$f(\theta; t, n) = \mu_0 + \mu_1 n/N_1 + \mu_2 n^2/N_2 + \lambda_k I_k(t, n) + \sum_{k=1}^{3} \theta_k D_k(t, n - k)$$

$$+ \sum_{p=1}^{k} [\delta_{c,p}. \cos(p2\pi n/N) + \delta_{s,p}. \sin(p2\pi n/N)], \qquad (20.5.3)$$

so the extremely regular intra day periodicity is modeled as a collection of harmonic terms with indicator variables to remove the effects of announcements. The practical estimation is to replace $E(R_{t,n})$ with the sample mean of returns $\bar{R}_{t,n}$ and σ_t with the estimates from a daily volatility model. The variable $\hat{x}_{t,n}$ is treated as the dependent variable in the regression and the parameters are estimated by OLS to obtain $\tilde{R}_{t,n} = (R_{t,n}/\hat{s}_{t,n})$, where $\tilde{R}_{t,n}$ is the "filtered" intra-day return with the intra-day periodicity removed. It has become standard in the analysis of high frequency returns data to use the above filtering method. Andersen and Bollerslev (1997) then report estimated *GARCH* models for different levels of temporal aggregation of high frequency returns and discuss the differences between the volatility process in equity and currency markets.

The relatively new topic of realized volatility (*RV*) from high frequency financial market data has the potential attraction of being a pure, observed measure of volatility, which does not depend on the specification of an underlying *GARCH* or stochastic volatility model and is computationally and conceptually quite simple. The initial justification for the approach has been based on quadrature approximations to continuous time diffusion processes, which are assumed to be a realistic model for the returns generating process. At the simplest approximation, *RV* is simply obtained by summing the high frequency squared returns throughout the day to obtain a measure of *RV* at the end of the day, so that

$$\sum_{n=1}^{N} y_{n,t}^2 = RV_t \qquad (20.5.4)$$

Anderson, Bollerslev, Diebold and Labys (2001) have introduced the measure and applied it to long series of high frequency returns on the Yen/$ and DM/$ currencies; while Anderson, Bollerslev, Diebold and Embens (2001) have applied similar techniques to stock indices. They find that there is a strong long memory feature in the RV series, so that an appropriate model for RV is a fractional white noise, or $ARFIMA(0, d, 0)$ model of the form $(1 - L)^d(y_t - \mu) = \varepsilon_t$, where ε_t is a white noise process. Anderson, Bollerslev, Diebold and Labys (2003) have estimated a multivariate system for three currencies and find extremely similar estimates of the fractional integration parameter for all three currencies. The method of using RV also promises interesting possibilities on unraveling the effects of announcements and news on fundamentals on the volatility in financial markets.

20.6 Conclusion

This chapter has surveyed some of the econometric methods currently used for modeling volatility in economics and finance. Where appropriate, some detail has been given on the underlying theoretical properties of the models and processes. It has concentrated heavily on *ARCH*-type models; and one justification for this is that they are the most widely used models in applied work. After reviewing the various *GARCH*-type models, this chapter has discussed the currently known properties of MLE and QMLE and inferential procedures. Both the theoretical models and inferential techniques form an attractive and coherent body of statistical literature.

Later sections have discussed some of the main theoretical aspects of stochastic volatility models and the modeling of volatility from high frequency financial market data, and the concept of realized volatility. Due to space constraints, it has not been possible to fully do justice to these fascinating and important topics. Nor has it been possible to address the large subject of multivariate volatility processes. It is likely that much of the current research being undertaken in the area of high frequency financial returns data, and the associated realized volatility, will have a very significant impact on future developments of modeling volatility in financial markets.

Where appropriate reference has been made to some of the many applications of volatility models to problems in asset pricing and financial economics. Again, a separate survey could be written on this area alone. It is hoped that this chapter will stimulate further interest and work in the area of modeling volatility.

References

Andersen, T.G. and T. Bollerslev (1997) Intraday periodicity and volatility persistence in financial markets. *Journal of Empirical Finance* **4**, 115–58.

Andersen, T.G. and T. Bollerslev (1998) Deutsche mark–dollar volatility: intraday activity, patterns, macroeconomic announcements and longer run dependence. *Journal of Finance* **53**, 219–65.

Andersen, T.G., T. Bollerslev, F.X. Diebold and P. Labys (2001) The distribution of realized exchange rate volatility. *Journal of the American Statistical Association* **96**, 42–55.

Andersen, T.G., T. Bollerslev, F.X. Diebold and H. Ebens (2001) The distribution of realized stock return volatility. *Journal of Financial Economics* **61**, 43–76.

Andersen, T.G., T. Bollerslev, F.X. Diebold and P. Labys (2003) Modeling and forecasting realized volatility. *Econometrica* **71**, 579–626.

Bachelier, L.J.B.A. (1900) *Theorie de la speculation*. Paris: Gauthier-Villars.

Baillie, R.T. and T. Bollerslev (1992) Prediction in dynamic models with time dependent conditional variances. *Journal of Econometrics* **52**, 91–113.

Baillie, R.T., T. Bollerslev and H.-O. Mikkelsen (1996) Fractionally integrated generalized autoregressive conditional heteroskedasticity. *Journal of Econometrics* **74**, 3–30.

Baillie, R.T. and H. Chung (2001) Estimation of GARCH models from the autocorrelations of the squares of a process. *Journal of Time Series Analysis* **22**, 631–50.

Baillie, R.T., C.-F. Chung and M.A. Tieslau (1996) Analysing inflation by the fractionally integrated ARFIMA-GARCH model. *Journal of Applied Econometrics* **11**, 23–40.

Berkes, I., L. Horvath and P. Kokoszka (2003) GARCH processes: structure and estimation. *Bernoulli* **9**, 201–27.

Black, F. and M. Scholes (1972) The valuation of option contracts and a test of market efficiency. *Journal of Finance* **37**, 399–417.

Bollerslev, T. (1986) Generalized autoregressive conditional heteroskedasticity. *Journal of Econometrics* **31**, 307–27.

Bollerslev, T. (1987) A conditional heteroskedastic time series model for speculative prices and rates of return. *Review of Economics and Statistics* **69**, 542–7.

Bollerslev, T. (1988) On the correlation structure for the generalized autoregressive conditional heteroskedastic process. *Journal of Time Series Analysis* **9**, 121–31.

Bollerslev, T and H.-O. Mikkelsen (1996) Modeling and pricing long-memory in stock market volatility. *Journal of Econometrics* **73**, 151–85.

Bollerslev, T. and J.M. Wooldridge (1992) Quasi-maximum likelihood estimation of dynamic models with time varying covariances. *Econometric Reviews* **11**, 143–72.

Bollerslev, T., R.Y. Chou and K.F. Kroner (1992) ARCH models in finance: a review of the theory and empirical evidence. *Journal of Econometrics* **52**, 5–59.

Bollerslev, T., R.F. Engle and D.B. Nelson (1994) ARCH models. In *Handbook of Econometrics* vol. 4. Amsterdam: Elsevier, pp. 2959–3038.

Bougerol, P. and N. Picard (1992) Stationarity of GARCH processes and of some nonnegative time series. *Journal of Econometrics* **52**, 115–27.

Campbell, J.Y. and L. Hentschel (1992) No news is good news: an asymmetric model of changing volatility in stock returns. *Journal of Financial Economics* **31**(3), 281–318.

Carrasco, M. and X. Chen (2002) Mixing and moment properties of various GARCH and stochastic volatility models. *Econometric Theory* **18**, 17–39.

Chou, R.Y. (1988) Volatility persistence and stock valuations: some empirical evidence using GARCH. *Journal of Applied Econometrics* **3**, 279–94.

Christie, A.A. (1982) The stochastic behavior of common stock variances: value, leverage and interest rate effects. *Journal of Financial Economics* **10**, 407–32.

Dacorogna, M.M., U.A. Muller, R.J. Nagler, R.B. Olsen and O.V. Pictet (1993) A geographical model for daily and weekly seasonal volatility in the foreign exchange markets. *Journal of International Money and Finance* **12**, 413–38.

Davidson, J.E.H. (2004) Moment and memory properties of linear conditional heteroscedasticity models, and a new model. *Journal of Business and Economic Statistics* **22**, 16–29.

Ding, Z. and C.W.J. Granger (1996) Modeling volatility persistence of speculatrive returns: a new approach. *Journal of Econometrics* **73**, 185–215.

Ding, Z., C.W.J. Granger and R.F. Engle (1993) A long memory property of stock market returns and a new model. *Journal of Empirical Finance* **1**, 83–106.

Drost, F.C. and T. Nijman (1993) Temporal aggregation of GARCH processes. *Econometrica* **61**(4), 909–27.

Duffie, D. and K.J. Singleton (1993) Simulated moments estimation of Markov models of asset prices. *Econometrica* **61**, 929–52.

Engle, R.F. (1982) Autoregressive conditional heteroskedasticity with estimates of the variance of UK inflation. *Econometrica* **50**, 987–1008.

Engle, R.F. (1983) Estimates of the variance of UK inflation based on the ARCH model. *Journal of Money, Credit and Banking* 15, 286–301.

Engle, R.F. and T. Bollerslev (1986) Modelling the persistence of conditional variances. *Econometric Reviews* 5, 1–50.

Engle, R.F., D.M. Lilien and R.P. Robins (1987) Estimating time varying risk in the term structure: the ARCH–M model. *Econometrica* 55, 391–407.

Engle, R.F. and C. Mustafa (1992) Implied ARCH models from options prices. *Journal of Econometrics* 52, 289–311.

Engle, R.F. and V. Ng (1993) Measuring and testing the impact of news on volatility. *Journal of Finance* 48, 1749–1778.

French, K.R. and R. Roll (1986) Stock return variances: the arrival of information and the reaction of traders. *Journal of Financial Economics* 17, 5–26.

French, K.R., G.W. Schwert and R.F. Stambaugh (1987) Expected stock returns and volatility. *Journal of Financial Economics* 19, 3–30.

Gallant, A.R. (1981) On the bias in flexible function forms and an essentially unbiased form: the Fourier flexible form. *Journal of Econometrics* 15, 211–45.

Gallant, A.R., D.A. Hsieh and G. Tauchen (1997) Estimation of stochastic volatility models with diagnostics. *Journal of Econometrics* 81, 159–92.

Geweke, J. (1986) Modelling the persistence of conditional variances: a comment. *Econometric Reviews* 5, 57–61.

Giraitis, L., P. Kokoszka and R. Leipus (2000) Stationary ARCH models: dependence structure and central limit theorem. *Econometric Theory* 16, 3–22.

Giraitis, L., R. Leipus and D. Surgailis (2003) Recent advances in ARCH modeling. Preprint.

Glosten, L.R., R. Jagannathan and D.E. Runkle (1993) On the relation between the expected value and the volatility of the nominal excess return on stocks. *Journal of Finance* 48, 1779–1801.

Goodhart, C.A.E. and M. O'Hara (1997) High frequency data in financial markets: issues and applications. *Journal of Empirical Finance* 4, 73–114.

Granger, C.W.J. and T. Teräsvirta (1993) *Modeling Nonlinear Economic Relationships*. Oxford: Oxford University Press.

He, C. and T. Teräsvirta (1999a) Properties of moments of a family of GARCH processes. *Journal of Econometrics* 92, 173–92.

He, C. and T. Teräsvirta (1999b) Properties of the autocorrelation function of squared observations for second order GARCH processes under two sets of parameter constraints. *Journal of Time Series Analysis* 20, 23–30.

He, C. and T. Teräsvirta (1999c) Fourth moment structure of the GARCH(p, q) process. *Econometric Theory* 15, 824–46.

Hsieh, D.A. (1989) Modeling heteroskedasticity in daily foreign exchange rates. *Journal of Business and Economic Statistics* 7, 307–17.

Jacquier, E., N.G. Polson and P.G. Rossi (1994) Bayesian analysis of stochastic volatility models. *Journal of Business and Economic Statistics* 12, 371–417.

Karanasos, M. (1999) The second moment and the autocovariance function of the squared errors of the GARCH model. *Journal of Econometrics* 90, 63–76.

Kazakevicius, V. and R. Leipus (2002) On stationarity in the ARCH model. *Econometric Theory* 18, 1–16.

Kim, S., N. Shephard and S. Chib (1998) Stochastic volatility: likelihood inference and comparison with ARCH models. *Review of Economic Studies* 65(3), 361–93.

Klein, B. (1977) The demand for quantity adjusted cash balances: price uncertainty in the US demand for money function, 85, 692–715.

Lamoureux, C.G. and W.D. Lastrapes (1990a) Persistence in variance, structural change and the GARCH model. *Journal of Business and Economic Statistics* 8, 225–34.

Lamoureux, C.G. and W.D. Lastrapes (1990b) Heteroskedasticity in stock return data: volume versus GARCH effects. *Journal of Finance* 45, 221–9.

Lee, S.-W.W. and B. Hansen (1994) Asymptotic theory for the IGARCH(1,1) quasi maximum likelihood estimator. *Econometric Theory* 10, 29–52.

Lumsdaine, R.L. (1996) Consistency and asymptotic normality for the quasi maximum likelihood estimator IGARCH(1,1) and covariance stationary GARCH(1,1) models. *Econometrica* 64, 573–96.

Mandelbrot, B. (1963) The variation of certain speculative prices. *Journal of Business* 36, 394–419.

Milhoj, A. (1985) The moment structure of ARCH processes. *Scandinavian Journal of Statistics* 12, 281–92.

Nelson, D.B. (1990a) Stationarity and persistence in the GARCH(1,1) model. *Econometric Theory* 6, 318–34.

Nelson, D.B. (1990b) ARCH models as diffusion approximations. *Journal of Econometrics* 45, 7–38.

Nelson, D.B. (1990c) Conditional heteroskedasticity in asset returns: a new approach. *Econometrica* 59, 347–70.

Nelson, D.B. and C.Q. Cao (1992) Inequality constraints in the univariate GARCH model. *Journal of Business and Economic Statistics* 10, 229–35.

Newey, W.K. and K.D. West (1987) A simple, positive, semi-definite, heteroskedasticity and autocorrelation consistent covariance matrix. *Econometrica* 55, 703–8.

Rich, R., J. Raymond and J.S. Butler (1991) Generalized instrumental variables estimation of autoregressive conditional heteroskedastic models. *Economics Letters* 2, 179–85.

Schwert, G.W. (1989) Why does stock market volatility change over time? *Journal of Finance* 44, 1115–1153.

Schwert, G.W. (1990a) Stock volatility and the crash of 87. *Review of Financial Studies* 3, 77–102.

Schwert, G.W. (1990b) Indexes of United States stock prices from 1802 to 1987. *Journal of Business* 63, 399–431.

Shiller, R.J. (1979) The volatility of long term interest rates and expectations models of the term structure. *Journal of Political Economy* 87, 1190–1219.

Taylor, S. (1986) *Modeling Financial Time Series*. New York: Wiley.

Weiss, A.A. (1984) ARMA models with ARCH errors. *Journal of Time Series Analysis* 5, 129–43.

Weiss, A.A. (1986) Asymptotic theory for ARCH models: estimation and testing. *Econometric Theory* 2, 107–31.

21

Multivariate Volatility Models*

Chris Brooks

Abstract

This chapter examines both multivariate stohastic volatility and the more common multivariate GARCH models that are now widely used in finance and other fields for modeling conditional variances and covariances. After presenting the basic multivariate stochastic volatility model, the review continues by examining the various estimation options available, including Bayesian Markov Chain Monte Carlo and the efficient method of moments. There then follows a discussion of some possible extensions of the model, such as asymmetric and factor approaches. In the context of multivariate GARCH models, estimation involving maximum likelihood is first examined, as are the numerous extensions to the basic framework that are now available, including an asymmetric formulation and a factor specification. The latter is related to the orthogonal GARCH, or principal components GARCH model, as it is sometimes known, which sets up a multivariate GARCH model as a linear combination of univariate GARCH building blocks, Distributional alternatives to the normal, in particular the student's t, are discussed. The chapter continues by considering a number of residual-based specification tests for multivariate GARCH models. Finally, some of the alternative multivariate approaches to modeling volatilities and correlations that have been recently proposed are examined, including the dynamic conditional correlatilon model.

21.1 Introduction   765
21.2 Multivariate stochastic volatility models   767
    21.2.1   Model description   767
    21.2.2   Estimating the multivariate stochastic volatility model   769
    21.2.3   Extensions to the multivariate stochastic volatility model   770
21.3 Multivariate GARCH models   771
    21.3.1   The basic multivariate GARCH framework   771
    21.3.2   Estimation of multivariate GARCH models   772
    21.3.3   Extensions to the basic multivariate GARCH model   773
    21.3.4   Misspecification tests for multivariate GARCH models   776
21.4 Alternative models for volatility   778
21.5 Concluding remarks   779

21.1 Introduction

Inevitably, when modeling volatility in either a univariate or a multivariate context, one is faced with the choice between two broad classes of specifications: stochastic volatility or autoregressive conditionally heteroskedastic models. Both classes of models are designed to capture the stylized characteristic of time series, and those of financial asset returns in particular, that they exhibit volatility clustering. Large innovations, of either sign, tend to occur in bunches so that volatility may be viewed as being positively serially correlated. One plausible explanation for this phenomenon, which seems to be an almost universal feature of asset return series in finance, is that the information arrivals that drive changes in prices themselves occur in bunches rather than being evenly spaced through time. A further common feature of both approaches to modeling volatility is that the conditional mean is usually entirely ignored. Sometimes the series under investigation is demeaned, but it is almost invariably assumed to be entirely free of other influences.

Stochastic volatility models are closely related to the financial theories used in the options pricing literature. Early work by Black and Scholes (1973) had assumed that volatility is constant through time. Such an assumption was made largely for simplicity, although it could hardly be considered realistic. One unappealing side effect of employing a model with the embedded assumption that volatility is fixed is that options deep in-the-money and far out-of-the-money are underpriced relative to actual traded prices. This empirical observation provided part of the genesis for stochastic volatility models, where the logarithm of an unobserved variance process is modeled by a linear stochastic specification, such as an autoregressive model. The primary advantage of stochastic volatility models is that they can be viewed as discrete time approximations to the continuous time models employed in options pricing frameworks (see, for example, Hull and White, 1987). However, such models are hard to estimate. For reviews of univariate stochastic volatility models, see Taylor (1994), Ghysels *et al.* (1995) or Shephard (1996) and the references therein.

Autoregressive conditionally heteroskedastic (ARCH) models, introduced by Engle (1982) and generalized (GARCH) by Bollerslev (1986), represent an alternative approach to capturing the autocorrelation in volatility. These models posit the current estimate of the conditional variance to be a function of its lagged values, and of lagged squared innovations. While GARCH-type models are further from their continuous time theoretical underpinnings than stochastic volatility, they are much simpler to estimate using maximum likelihood (ML). ML estimation of GARCH models is now routinely discussed even in introductory level econometrics textbooks (for example, Brooks, 2002). Consequently, the GARCH route has been favored in the vast majority of applications, and a large number of variants on and extensions to the basic model have been proposed. See Bollerslev *et al.* (1992) or Bollerslev *et al.* (1994) for a survey of theory and applications in the context of the univariate GARCH model.

Both the stochastic volatility and GARCH classes of models are available in multivariate forms, and these form the substance of the present chapter. Bauwens,

Laurent and Rombouts (2003) have thoroughly reviewed model developments and their application in the context of multivariate GARCH (MGARCH) models; inevitably there will be some overlap between their paper and the latter part of this chapter. At the time of writing, no survey articles have yet been drafted that focus on multivariate stochastic volatility (MSV) models. It is worth noting at this stage that, while the term "stochastic volatility" is commonly used to describe models from the GARCH family, strictly they do not fit well under this umbrella because the conditional variance (and covariance) equations are deterministic, given the information set up to the previous period. That is, there is no additional source of noise in the conditional variance (or covariance) equation of a GARCH model.

While multivariate models for volatilities are by their very nature inherently more complex and more difficult to estimate than their univariate counterparts, they are significantly more useful. In finance alone, many applications in asset pricing, risk measurement and option pricing require an examination of the extent to which asset returns move together over time. Multivariate models have been the subject of numerous empirical studies, including the estimation of conditional capital asset pricing model (CCAPM) betas (e.g. Brooks and Henry, 2002), and the determination of optimal hedge ratios (e.g. Brooks, Henry and Persand, 2002).

The remainder of this chapter is organized as follows. Section 21.2 will discuss MSV models, beginning with a description of the fundamentals of the model before moving on to estimation issues and possible extensions. Section 21.3 will similarly describe MGARCH models. The very limited number of alternatives to the two approaches are then discussed in section 21.4 before section 21.5 offers some concluding remarks.

21.2 Multivariate stochastic volatility models

21.2.1 Model description

The number of different notations and possible estimation approaches for multivariate stochastic volatility models is almost as large as the number of theoretical papers in this area, indicating that this literature is still very much in its infancy. The MSV model was initially proposed by Harvey, Ruiz and Shephard (1994) and the notation here will closely follow theirs. Let y_{it} be the elements of an $N \times 1$ vector of observations at time t on a series i, with time-varying variance σ_i^2, defined as

$$y_{it} = \varepsilon_{it}(\exp\{h_{it}\})^{1/2} \quad i = 1, \ldots, N; \ t = 1, \ldots, T \tag{21.1}$$

where $\varepsilon_t = (\varepsilon_{lt}, \ldots, \varepsilon_{Nt})'$ is a vector of disturbances with zero mean and covariance matrix Σ, and where

$$h_{it} = \log(\sigma_{it}^2) \tag{21.2}$$

This covariance matrix, Σ, is defined to have unity on the leading diagonal (and Σ is therefore also a correlation matrix), while its off-diagonal elements are termed ρ_{ij}.

Under the stochastic volatility model, the h_{it} would be specified to evolve as an autoregressive (AR) process of order P:

$$h_{it} = \gamma_i + \sum_{p=1}^{P} \varphi_{ip} h_{ip,\,t-1} + \eta_{it} \quad i = 1, \ldots, N \tag{21.3}$$

$\eta_t = (\eta_{1t}, \ldots, \eta_{Nt})'$ is a vector of disturbances to the conditional variance having zero mean and covariance matrix Σ_η. It is usually further assumed that ε_{it} and η_{it} are mutually independent and that each are multivariate normally distributed. Usually, $P = 1$ is deemed sufficient so that the variance dynamics for each series in the system are AR(1). Moving average terms or even exogenous variables could be added to the variance specification but rarely are in practice.

Taking logarithms of each side of equation (21.1), multiplying through by 2 and rearranging gives

$$\log(y_{it}^2) = h_{it} + \log(\varepsilon_{it}^2) \tag{21.4}$$

The mean of $\log(\varepsilon_{it}^2)$ is -1.27, and its variance is $\pi^2/2$, so (21.4) may be written

$$\log(y_{it}^2) = -1.27 + h_{it} + \xi_{it} \tag{21.5}$$

where $\xi_{it} = \log(\varepsilon_{it}^2) + 1.27$. Now $\xi_{it} \sim \mathrm{NID}(0, \Sigma_\xi)$, where Σ_ξ has $\pi^2/2$ on the leading diagonal and zeros elsewhere. Equations (21.3) and (21.5) describe the basic MSV model. Finally, writing the stacked forms of the vectors $\log(y_{it}^2)$, h_{it}, and ξ_{it} as w_t, h_t, and ξ_t, the model is

$$w_t = -1.27\iota + h_t + \xi_t \tag{21.6a}$$

$$h_t = \phi_1 h_{t-1} + \eta_t \tag{21.6b}$$

where ι is a vector of ones and ϕ_1 is a vector of AR(1) parameters. Harvey *et al.* (1994) set all elements of this vector to unity, although this seems excessively restrictive.

It is worth noting that in this model, the correlations, ρ_{ij}, between the mean equation disturbances are required to be fixed over time. Thus the covariances across the N series evolve as functions of the variances rather than independently of them. This formulation parallels the constant conditional correlation MGARCH model of Bollerslev (1990) discussed below, and represents an important limitation of the model. It does, however, imply that MSV models are highly parsimonious, and the number of parameters scales directly with the number of variables in the system. For example, in the context of a bivariate MSV model, there are eight parameters to estimate.[1]

21.2.2 Estimating the multivariate stochastic volatility model

Harvey *et al.* (1994) propose estimating the model in state space form (equations (21.6a) and (21.6b) with ϕ_1 set to a vector of ones) using quasi-maximum likelihood (QML) via the Kalman filter. However, Danielsson (1998) argues that their QML approach results in inefficient estimation.

An alternative approach to estimating MSV models is to make use of Bayesian Markov Chain Monte Carlo (MCMC) methods, as proposed by Jacquier, Polson and Rossi (1995).[2] This involves sampling via a simulation, with the draws from the simulation being employed to determine the characteristics of the posterior distribution. Following closely the notation of Nadari and Scruggs (2003, pp. 8–9), let $\psi = (\gamma, \phi_1, \Sigma_\varepsilon, \Sigma_\eta)$ denote the complete parameter vector ($\gamma = (\gamma_1, \ldots, \gamma_N)$, with all other notation as above). Then the joint posterior density of the parameters will be proportional to the product of the likelihood function and the prior density

$$\pi(\psi|y) \propto p(y|\psi)\phi(\psi) \tag{21.7}$$

where $p(y|\psi)$ is the likelihood of the data given all of the parameters. If the history of $\{y_t\}$ to time $t-1$ is given by $\mathcal{J}_{t-1}$, and the density of the latent log variances (h_t), conditioned upon $(\mathcal{J}_{t-1}, \psi)$, is given by $p(h_t|\mathcal{J}_{t-1}, \psi)$, then the likelihood function for the model described by equations (21.6) is given by

$$p(y|\psi) = \prod_{t=1}^{T} \int p(y_t|h_t)p(h_t|\mathcal{J}_{t-1}, \psi)dh_t \tag{21.8}$$

A further approach to estimating MSV models was proposed by Danielsson (1998), involving the use of simulated maximum likelihood (SML). Here, the latent volatilities are simulated conditional upon $\mathcal{J}_{t-1}$ and these simulated values are employed to reconstruct the marginal densities of the observed variables.

A fourth possibility is a method of moments-based technique, such as the Efficient Method of Moments (EMM) suggested by Gallant and Tauchen (1996) and Gallant, Hsieh and Tauchen (1997) in the context of univariate stochastic volatility models. The EMM approach follows the same intuition as the generalized method of moments (GMM) but, by matching the score vector of an auxiliary probability model that closely fits the actual data, a procedure that is as efficient as maximum likelihood can be obtained.

A final approach to be found in the extant literature involves maximum likelihood based on efficient importance sampling (EIS) – see Liesenfeld and Richard (2003). EIS is a Monte Carlo method used to numerically solve the high dimensional integral arising from the nonlinear way in which the latent volatility process enters the model. To this author's knowledge, no comparative studies have yet been undertaken to determine the optimality of each of the available estimation methods, and neither have a sufficient number of applications of MSV models been implemented for one approach to have emerged as dominant.

21.2.3 Extensions to the multivariate stochastic volatility model

Again, in part due to the relative infancy of the MSV model, the number of extensions to the basic framework that have been proposed is rather limited. The most obvious and simple enhancement is to place additional variables in the conditional mean equation. Following on from earlier work by Pitt and Shephard (1999), Nardari and Scruggs (2003), for example, combine MSV with an arbitrage pricing theory (APT)-style factor model. In this model, excess stock and bond returns depend on a set of latent systematic factor shocks, each with an associated risk premium. The factor shocks and idiosyncratic shocks follow a MSV specification. The factor SV model of Pitt and Shephard (1999) will be discussed in subsection 21.2.3.1 below. Chib, Nardari and Shephard (2001) further extend the framework to allow for both latent factors and series-specific independent Bernoulli jumps in the mean equation.

A second relatively trivial extension would be to modify the conditional variance equations to allow for asymmetries in the response of volatility to good and bad news. This could be achieved by adding a Glosten, Jaganathan and Runkle (1993)-style indicator function that picks out negative innovations. Alternatively, Jiang and van der Sluis (2000) allow for asymmetries by adopting a mixture of normals in the conditional variance equation. Their approach does not, however, allow for conditional asymmetries in volatility related to the sign of previous returns (i.e., the "leverage effect").

Harvey *et al.* (1994) argue that, in common with GARCH, stochastic volatility models generate unconditional distributions for the fitted y_t series that are fat tailed, but not sufficiently so to capture the extent of leptokurtosis found in most actual financial time series. A natural way to achieve the required tail fatness is by assuming that the disturbances are conditionally Student's t rather than Gaussian. Liesenfeld and Richard (2003) examine such a model, but only in the context of a univariate stochastic volatility model. Chib *et al.* (2001) propose a MSV model that allows for Student's t disturbances with unknown degrees of freedom, but the model is examined only via simulation and is not estimated using real data.

21.2.3.1 *Factor stochastic volatility*

Kim, Shephard and Chib (1998) propose a factor stochastic volatility model where the factors and the disturbances follow their own stochastic volatility processes. Pitt and Shephard (1999) enhance the estimation approach, again based on Bayesian MCMC, and they also examine the performance of the model using daily exchange rate data. Their model has a direct analogy with similar specifications developed with ARCH models in place of stochastic volatility by Diebold and Nerlove (1989) and by King, Sentana and Wadhwani (1994).

The factor SV model may be written

$$y_t = \beta f_t + \omega_t, \quad t = 1, \ldots, T$$
$$\omega_{j,t} \sim ISV(\phi^{w_j}; \sigma_\eta^{\omega_j}; \mu^{\omega_j}), \quad j = 1, \ldots, N \qquad (21.9)$$
$$f_k \sim ISV(\phi^{f_k}; \sigma_\eta^{f_k}; 0), \quad k = 1, \ldots, K$$

where *ISV* denote independent, mean-adjusted stochastic volatility models. Thus the K zero mean latent factors, $f_k(k = 1, \ldots, K)$, follow a stochastic volatility process, as do the idiosyncratic shocks, $\omega_{j,t}(j = 1, \ldots, N; t = 1, \ldots, T)$, and β is a $K \times N$ matrix of factor loadings.

In order for the model to be identified, the factor loading matrix must be restricted, and Pitt and Shephard (1999) choose the extreme simplification $\beta_{ij} = 0$ and $\beta_{ij} = 1$ and, in their application, they also set $K = 1$. This leads to a highly parsimonious model where the number of parameters to be estimated varies linearly with the number of series (financial assets in their case) in the system. Therefore, in this setup, the covariances between the series in y_t arise from the factors, and the disturbances in the mean equation follow stochastic volatility processes that are independent of one another, unlike the Harvey *et al.* (1994) approach described above.

21.3 Multivariate GARCH models

Bollerslev, Engle and Wooldridge (1988) first proposed a very general form of multivariate generalized conditionally heteroskedastic model. The number of related studies developed rapidly thereafter, to the extent that there are now hundreds of published papers in this area in addition to the thousands that employ or propose new variants upon their univariate counterparts. Consequently, this review will devote proportionally more space to MGARCH than to MSV models.

21.3.1 The basic multivariate GARCH framework

As with MSV, the conditional mean equation may be parameterized in any way desired, although it is worth noting that, since the conditional variances are measured about the mean, misspecification of the latter is likely to imply misspecification of the former. To introduce some notation, suppose, as above, that y_t is an $N \times 1$ vector of time series observations, each with zero mean, and

$$y_t = \varepsilon_t \quad \text{with} \quad \varepsilon_t \sim \text{NID}(0, H_t) \tag{21.10}$$

Under the unrestricted form of the model, which has been termed the "VECH," the conditional variance–covariance equations could be written in matrix form as

$$\text{VECH}(H_t) = C + A\text{VECH}(\varepsilon_{t-1}\varepsilon'_{t-1}) + B\text{VECH}(H_{t-1}) \tag{21.11}$$

where $\text{VECH}(\bullet)$ denotes the vector half-stacking operator that stacks the upper triangular portion of the symmetric matrix $(\bullet)$ into a column vector. C is an $N(N + 1)/2$ column vector of conditional variance and covariance intercepts, and A and B are square parameter matrices of order $N(N + 1)/2$. As Bauwens *et al.* (2003) note, the unconditional variance matrix for the VECH will be given by $C[I - A - B]^{-1}$, where I is an identity matrix of order $N(N + 1)/2$. Stationarity of the VECH model requires that the eigenvalues of $[A + B]$ are all less than one in absolute value.

This unrestricted model is highly parameterized, and is almost infeasible to estimate for $N > 2$.[3] This issue led Bollerslev *et al.* (1988) to propose the diagonal VECH model, where the matrices A and B are forced to be diagonal. This restriction implies that there are no direct volatility spillovers from one series to another, and this significantly reduces the number of parameters.[4] Even with fewer parameters, the matrix H_t must still be everywhere positive definite and imposing this condition is still difficult. This led Engle and Kroner (1995) to suggest the BEKK[5] model, where a quadratic form for the conditional variance–covariance equations ensures positive definiteness:

$$H_t = C^{*\prime}C^* + A^{*\prime}\varepsilon_{t-1}\varepsilon_{t-1}^{\prime}A^* + B^{*\prime}H_{t-1}B^* \tag{21.12}$$

where C^* is an upper triangular parameter matrix, and A^* and B^* are $N \times N$ parameter matrices. A drawback of the BEKK formulation is that the elements of A^* and B^* no longer provide a direct interpretation of the impact of a particular lagged variance on an element of H_t.

An alternative method for reducing the number of parameters in the MGARCH framework is to require the correlations between the disturbances, ε_t, (or equivalently between the observed variables, y_t) to be fixed through time. Thus, although the conditional covariances are not fixed, they are tied to the variances[6] as proposed in the constant conditional correlation model due to Bollerslev (1990). The conditional variances in the fixed correlation model are identical to those of a set of univariate GARCH specifications (although they are estimated jointly)

$$h_{ii,t} = c_i + a_i\varepsilon_{i,t-1}^2 + b_ih_{ii,t-1} \quad i = 1, \ldots, N \tag{21.13}$$

The off-diagonal elements of H_t, $h_{ij,t}(i \neq j)$, are defined indirectly via the correlations, denoted ρ_{ij}

$$h_{ij,t} = \rho_{ij}h_{ii,t}^{1/2}h_{jj,t}^{1/2} \quad i,j = 1, \ldots, N, i < j \tag{21.14}$$

Is it empirically plausible to assume that the correlations are constant through time? Several tests have been developed, including a test based on the information matrix due to Bera and Kim (2002) and a Lagrange Multiplier test due to Tse (2000). The conclusions reached appear dependent on which test is used, but there seems to be non-negligible evidence against the constant correlations assumption, particularly in the context of stock returns.

To summarize, the four models described above – the unrestricted VECH, the diagonal VECH, the BEKK and the constant conditional correlations specification – comprise the main building blocks of multivariate GARCH analysis. They can be augmented or enhanced in a number of ways, and this issue shall be returned to after the following section considers estimation issues.

21.3.2 Estimation of multivariate GARCH models

Parameter estimation of all of the above models can be achieved most simply using maximum likelihood. The process is intellectually fairly simple, although one frequently runs into estimation problems (e.g., negative estimated parameter values, non-convergence or convergence to local maxima) as a result of the large number of parameters and the interconnectedness of the equations. Given the assumption that ε_t are multivariate normally distributed, the sample log likelihood function for any of the above models may be written

$$l(\theta) = \frac{-TN}{2}\log(2\pi) - \frac{1}{2}\sum_{t=1}^{T}\log|H_t| - \frac{1}{2}\sum_{t=1}^{T}\varepsilon_t'H_t^{-1}\varepsilon_t \qquad (21.15)$$

where θ denotes all of the parameters to be estimated. Even if the true ε_t are not conditionally Gaussian, consistent parameter estimates may be obtained by maximizing this log-likelihood function, in which case it is termed quasi-maximum likelihood (QML) – see Bollerslev and Wooldridge (1992).

Multivariate GARCH models are now available as pre-programmed sets of instructions in several packages[7] – see Brooks, Burke and Persand (2003), although not all of the MGARCH variants are available with all packages, and the results from each package may represent very different characterizations of the same set of data.

21.3.3 Extensions to the basic multivariate GARCH model

Numerous extensions to the univariate specification have been proposed, and many of these carry over to the multivariate case. For example, conditional variance or covariance terms can be included in the conditional mean equation (see Bollerslev *et al.*, 1988, for instance). In the context of financial applications, where the y_t are returns, the parameters on these variables can be loosely interpreted as risk premia.

21.3.3.1 *Asymmetric multivariate GARCH*

Asymmetric models have become very popular in empirical applications, where the conditional variances and/or covariances are permitted to react differently to positive and negative innovations of the same magnitude. In the multivariate context, this is usually achieved in the Glosten *et al.* (1993) framework, rather than the EGARCH specification of Nelson (1991). Kroner and Ng (1998), for example, suggest the following extension to the BEKK formulation (with obvious related modifications for the VECH or diagonal VECH models)

$$Ht = C^{*\prime}C^* + A^{*\prime}\varepsilon_{t-1}\varepsilon_{t-1}'A^* + B^{*\prime}H_{t-1}B^* + D^{*\prime}z_{t-1}z_{t-1}'D^* \qquad (21.16)$$

where z_{t-1} is an N-dimensional column vector with elements taking the value $-\varepsilon_{t-1}$ if the corresponding element of ε_{t-1} is negative and zero otherwise. The asymmetric properties of time-varying covariance matrix models are analysed by Kroner and Ng (1998), who identify three possible forms of asymmetric behavior. Firstly, the covariance matrix displays own variance asymmetry if the conditional variance of one series is affected by the sign of the innovation in that series. Secondly, the covariance matrix displays cross variance asymmetry if the conditional variance of one series is affected by the sign of the innovation of another series. Finally, if the conditional covariance is sensitive to the sign of the innovation in the return for either series, then the model is said to display covariance asymmetry.

21.3.3.2 Alternative distributional assumptions

As was the case for multivariate stochastic volatility and univariate GARCH models, an assumption of (multivariate) conditional normality cannot generate sufficiently fat tails to accurately model the distributional properties of financial data. A better approximation to the actual distributions of (especially financial) time series can be obtained using a Student's t distribution. Ignoring the constant for simplicity, the loglikelihood function (21.15) for each observation t would be

$$l_t = \log(\Gamma[(v+N)/2]) - \log(\Gamma[v/2]) - \frac{1}{2}\log|H_t| - \frac{1}{2}\log(v-2)$$
$$- \frac{v+N}{2} \log\left(1 + \frac{\varepsilon_t' H_t^{-1}\varepsilon_t}{(v-2)}\right)$$

(21.17)

where Γ is the gamma function.

Note that this formulation assumes a single degree of freedom parameter, v, which applies to all of the series in the system. An additional potential drawback of this approach is that the tail fatness embodied in the degrees of freedom parameter is fixed over time. Brooks, Burke and Persand (2002) propose a model where both of these limitations are removed. However, some identifying restrictions are still required. A further issue is the extent to which the unconditional distribution of the shocks is skewed. If this is the case, then a model based on the Student's t will be inadequate, and an alternative such as the multivariate skew Student's t of Bauwens and Laurent (2002) must be used.

Although many other extensions of the basic models may be conceived of, such as periodic or seasonal MGARCH, the range of specifications employed in the existing literature is narrower than for the corresponding univariate models. A major drawback for even the more parsimonious of the models above is that they are too highly parameterized, and yet many potential applications in economics and finance are in the context of high dimensional systems (such as asset alloca-tion among a number of stocks). Thus, an important innovation was the devel-opment of orthogonal and factor models. Both have the same fundamental idea that by forcing some structure on the variance–covariance matrix, a simplification can be achieved.

21.3.3.3 Factor GARCH models

Engle, Ng and Rothschild (1990) derive a factor GARCH model in a conditional capital asset pricing model framework for asset returns. Defining the conditional mean vector of the observed series y_t as μ_t, its conditional covariance matrix, H_t, is specified as

$$H_t = \sum_{k=1}^{K} \beta_k \beta_k' \lambda_{k,t} + \Omega$$

(21.18)

where Ω is an $N \times N$ positive semi-definite matrix, β_k are uncorrelated $N \times 1$ vectors and λ_{kt} are positive random variables. The conditional mean equation for their model may be written

$$y_t = \mu_t + \sum_{k=1}^{K} g_{kt} f_{kt} + e_t \qquad (21.19)$$

where the f_{kt} are a set of $K(K < N)$ factors affecting y_t, g_{kt} are the factor loadings and e_t is a vector of disturbances that are mutually and temporally uncorrelated and are independent of the factors. The conditional expectation at $t - 1$ of $(e_t e_t')$ is Ω. In Engle *et al.* (1990), the variance–covariance matrix, H_t, of y_t is related to the factors in two different ways. First, $g_{kt} = \beta_k \lambda_{kt}^{1/2}$ and the conditional variance of the factors is everywhere unity, or second, $g_{kt} = \beta_k$ and the conditional factor variance is λ_{kt}. The conditional variance-covariance matrix of y_t may then be expressed as a GARCH-type model in the factors

$$H_t = C^* + \sum_{k=1}^{K} \left\{ \gamma_k \beta_k \beta_k' (\alpha_k' \varepsilon_{t-1})^2 + \delta_k \beta_k \beta_k' (\alpha_k' H_{t-1} \alpha_k) \right\} \qquad (21.20)$$

where the α_k are orthogonal to the $\beta_j (k \neq j)$ and are chosen such that $\alpha_k' \beta_k = 1$, and γ_k, δ_k are parameters. The factor GARCH model was further refined by Bollerslev and Engle (1993).

21.3.3.4 Orthogonal GARCH models

The orthogonal GARCH (OGARCH) or principal components GARCH model, as it is sometimes known, sets up a multivariate GARCH model as a linear combination of univariate GARCH building blocks. Bauwens *et al.* (2003) argue that OGARCH can be viewed as a factor model, where the factors are $m < N$ univariate GARCH processes. Introduced by Ding (1994) and by Alexander and Chibumba (1996), the OGARCH model has more recently been generalized by van der Weide (2002). His model is set up such that the observed series, y_t, are related to a series of unobserved uncorrelated components x_t via a linear map Z

$$y_t = Zx_t, \quad x_t \sim N(0, H_t) \qquad (21.21)$$

Thus, the unobserved components follow separate GARCH processes and H_t is therefore defined to be a diagonal matrix. The conditional covariances of the observed series y_t are given by

$$V_t = ZH_t Z' \qquad (21.22)$$

The unobserved components are assumed to have unit variance. The implied correlation matrix of the y_t can be written as

$$R_t = D_t^{-1} V_t D_t^{-1} \qquad (21.23)$$

where $D_t = (V_t \circ I)^{1/2}$ and $\circ$ denotes the Hadamard product.

Letting P and Λ denote matrices containing a set of orthonormal eigenvectors and eigenvalues, respectively, of the unconditional covariance matrix ZZ', an orthogonal matrix U_0 is constructed via a singular value decomposition

$$P\Lambda^{1/2}U_0 = Z \qquad (21.24)$$

This orthogonal matrix can be parameterised using a set of rotation matrices, with the angles being estimated by maximum likelihood.

21.3.4 Misspecification tests for multivariate GARCH models

A number of different approaches to diagnostic testing were developed for determining the adequacy of particular univariate GARCH specifications, and most of these carry over to the multivariate context. There are also tests specifically designed for multivariate models that are applied to the vectors of residuals together. Popular univariate procedures that are also relevant for multivariate models include asymmetry tests and residual-based conditional moment tests. These approaches will be discussed only briefly since they are now routinely applied in the extant univariate literature, and then two multivariate diagnostics will be presented.

21.3.4.1 Asymmetry tests

Engle and Ng (1993) have proposed a set of tests for asymmetry in volatility, known as sign and size bias tests. The Engle and Ng tests should thus be used to determine whether an asymmetric model is required for a given series, or whether a symmetric GARCH model can be deemed adequate. Although they can be applied to raw data, in practice, the Engle–Ng tests are usually applied to the residuals of a univariate GARCH fit to individual series. Denote an individual series of disturbances as u_t, and define S_{t-1}^- as an indicator dummy that takes the value 1 if $\hat{u}_{t-1} < 0$ and zero otherwise. Then the test for sign bias is based on the significance or otherwise of ϕ_1 in the regression

$$\hat{u}_t^2 = \phi_0 + \phi_1 S_{t-1}^- + v_t \qquad (21.25)$$

where v_t is an IID error term. If positive and negative shocks to $\hat{u}_{t-1}$ impact differently upon the conditional variance, then ϕ_1 will be statistically significant.

It could also be the case that the magnitude or size of the shock will affect whether the response of volatility to shocks is symmetric or not. In this case, a negative sign bias test would be conducted, based on a regression in which S_{t-1}^- is now used as a slope dummy variable. Negative sign bias is argued to be present if ϕ_1 is statistically significant in the regression

$$\hat{u}_t^2 = \phi_0 + \phi_1 S_{t-1}^- u_{t-1} + v_t \qquad (21.26)$$

Finally, defining $S_{t-1}^+ = 1 - S_{t-1}^-$, so that S_{t-1}^+ picks out the observations with positive innovations, Engle and Ng propose a joint test for sign and size bias based on the regression

$$\hat{u}_t^2 = \phi_0 + \phi_1 S_{t-1}^- + \phi_2 S_{t-1}^- u_{t-1} + \phi_3 S_{t-1}^+ u_{t-1} + v_t \tag{21.27}$$

Significance of ϕ_1 indicates the presence of sign bias, where positive and negative shocks have differing impacts upon future volatility, compared with the symmetric response required by the standard GARCH formulation. On the other hand, the significance of ϕ_2 or ϕ_3 would suggest the presence of size bias, where not only the sign, but also the magnitude, of the shock is important. A joint test statistic is formulated in the standard fashion by calculating TR^2 from regression (21.27), which will asymptotically follow a χ^2 distribution with 3 degrees of freedom under the null hypothesis of no asymmetric effects.

21.3.4.2   Residual-based conditional moment tests

If the model is correctly specified, and represents an adequate characterization of the data, certain moment relationships should hold on an appropriately standardized measure of the residuals. Let θ denote a $k \times 1$ parameter vector (containing all model parameters) and $r(\theta)$ denote the restrictions function required for the test. The null hypothesis is:

$$H_0 : r(\theta) = 0. \tag{21.28}$$

Let

$$\Omega = \mathrm{var}(r(\hat{\theta})). \tag{21.29}$$

Then the Wald test statistic is given by

$$W = r(\hat{\theta})^T \hat{\Omega}^{-1} r(\hat{\theta}). \tag{21.30}$$

Under the null, $W^a \sim \chi_J^2$, and so the null hypothesis is rejected if $W > \chi_{J,a}^2$, where α is the size of the test and J is the number of restrictions. The variance–covariance in (21.29), $\hat{\Omega}$, may be calculated from the residual sum of squares of the regression of $\hat{m}$ (the values of elements of the moment restriction function by observation) on $\hat{d}_1, \hat{d}_2, \ldots, \hat{d}_k$, the values of each of the derivatives of the log-likelihood, observation by observation. The residual sum of squares of this regression is given by

$$R = \hat{m}^T \hat{m} - \hat{m}^T D(D^T D)^{-1} D^T \hat{m}. \tag{21.31}$$

The required variance is then

$$\hat{\Omega} = \frac{R}{T^2}. \tag{21.32}$$

See Newey (1985) for further details.

21.3.4.3   *Multivariate model diagnostics*

Among the specific multivariate model diagnostics, Bauwens *et al.* (2003) propose the use of a multivariate version of the Ljung–Box test due to Hosking (1980). Letting $\hat{s}_t = \hat{H}_t^{-1/2}\hat{\varepsilon}_t$ denote the N-vector of standardized residuals, the test statistic is given by

$$HM(M) = T^2 \sum_{t=1}^{M}(T-j)^{-1}tr\left\{C_{S_t}^{-1}(0)C_{S_t}(j)C_{S_t}^{-1}(0)C_{S_t}'(j)\right\} \qquad 21.33$$

where $S_t = \text{VECH}(s_t s_t')$ and $C_{S_t}(j)$ is the sample autocovariance matrix of order j. Under the null hypothesis of no dependence in the standardized residuals, the test statistic is asymptotically distributed as a $\chi^2(N^2 M)$.

Ling and Li (1997) develop another diagnostic test for unparameterized heteroskedasticity in the standardized residuals.[8] Their formulation resembles a multivariate version of the Durbin–Watson test applied to the squares of the standardized residuals

$$LL(M) = T \sum_{h=1}^{M}\tilde{R}^2(h) \qquad (21.34)$$

which asymptotically follows a $\chi^2(M)$ under the null, and where

$$\tilde{R} = \frac{\displaystyle\sum_{t=h+1}^{T}(\hat{\varepsilon}_t'\hat{H}_t^{-1}\hat{\varepsilon}_t - N)(\hat{\varepsilon}_{t-h}'\hat{H}_{t-h}^{-1}\hat{\varepsilon}_{t-h} - N)}{\displaystyle\sum_{t=h+1}^{T}(\hat{\varepsilon}_t'\hat{H}_t^{-1}\hat{\varepsilon}_t - N)^2}$$

21.4   Alternative models for volatility

Multivariate stochastic volatility and multivariate GARCH models have dominated empirical work, and there are only a very small number of alternatives available. A very simple approach that seems to work reasonably well is the exponentially weighted moving average (EWMA) model used, for example, in the RiskMetrics system for calculating value at risk. Here, the conditional variances and conditional covariances are modeled as

$$h_{ij,t} = \lambda h_{ij,t-1} + (1-\lambda)r_{i,t-1}r_{j,t-1} \qquad (21.35)$$

where $i=j$ for the variance specifications. λ is a decay factor that could be estimated (for example, by maximum likelihood), but is often set arbitrarily (e.g., to 0.94). While this is probably the simplest way to allow for time-varying variances and covariances, the model is a restricted version of an integrated GARCH (IGARCH) specification, and it does not guarantee the fitted variance–covariance matrix to be positive definite. As a result of the parallel with IGARCH, EWMA models also cannot allow for the observed mean reversion in volatilities of asset returns that is particularly prevalent at lower frequencies of observation.

Another possible setup that appears to have been largely overlooked in the existing literature is to model an *ex post* measure of volatility or covariances or correlations directly. Such an approach would contrast with both MSV models, where the volatilities are latent, and MGARCH models, where they are modeled indirectly as the variances of the observed data. A VAR or VARMA model, for example, could then be used to capture the temporal dependencies within or between these volatilities.

A final and very promising alternative model is the dynamic conditional correlation (DCC) specification due to Engle (2002). The model is related to Bollerslev's (1990) constant conditional correlation formulation described above, but where the correlations are allowed to vary over time. Defining the variance–covariance matrix, H_t, as

$$H_t = D_t R_t D_t \tag{21.36}$$

D_t is a diagonal matrix containing the conditional standard deviations on the leading diagonal, and R_t is the conditional correlation matrix. Forcing R_t to be time-invariant would lead to the constant conditional correlation model of Bollerslev (1990). Note that, unlike the orthogonal model described above, there are no unobserved components in this setup.

Numerous explicit parameterizations of R_t are possible, including an exponential smoothing approach discussed in Engle (2002). More generally, a model of the MGARCH form could be specified as

$$Q_t = S \circ (\iota \iota' - A - B) + A \circ u_{t-1} u'_{t-1} + B \circ Q_{t-1} \tag{21.37}$$

where S is the unconditional correlation matrix of the vector of standardized disturbances, $u_t = D_t^{-1} \varepsilon_t$ and $R_t = diag\{Q_t\}^{-1} Q_t diag\{Q_t\}^{-1}$. This specification for the intercept term simplifies estimation and reduces the number of parameters to be estimated, but is not necessary. Engle (2002) also proposes a GARCH-esque formulation for dynamically modeling D_t^2.

The model may be estimated in a single stage using maximum likelihood, although this will still be a difficult exercise in the context of large systems. Consequently, Engle advocates a two-stage estimation procedure where each variable in the system is first modeled separately as a univariate GARCH process and then, in a second stage, the conditional likelihood is maximized with respect to any unknown parameters in the correlation matrix. Under some regularity conditions, estimation using this two-step procedure will be consistent but inefficient.

21.5 Concluding remarks

Univariate GARCH and stochastic volatility models revolutionized the way that researchers thought about and modeled variances. Their multivariate extensions are, potentially, even more useful because they permit the explicit parameterization of conditional covariances as well as variances. Again, the vast majority of applied researchers seem more comfortable with the GARCH than the stochastic volatility framework. Early multivariate GARCH models suffered from severe overparameterization, making a system involving more than two time series virtually infeasible. Recently proposed factor and orthogonal specifications have proved extremely useful in this regard, but at the expense of simplicity and interpretability. Numerous extensions and enhancements to the basic MGARCH model have been proposed, and a battery of diagnostic tests is now available. Thus, in the relatively short time since these models were first proposed, a great deal of progress has been made.

Bauwens *et al.* (2003) suggest ten "open issues" in multivariate GARCH modeling, with the improvement of software for inference appearing at the top of their agenda. The review by Brooks *et al.* (2003) concurs that there is much to be done here, with the development of a benchmark for the determination of estimation accuracy a priority. They demonstrate that researchers who assume their software will give accurate and reliable results are at best naïve, since different packages and different optimization routines can give radically different parameter and standard error estimates.

Secondly, there has been very little comparative work on the relative merits of the many available alternative specifications, especially across the MGARCH and MSV paradigms (with the exception of Danielsson, 1998). Which model produces the most accurate volatility or correlation forecasts? Which provides the most accurate option prices? Which supplies optimal hedge ratios and optimal asset allocations? None of these questions have yet to be addressed satisfactorily. The further development of misspecification tests, particularly for MSV models, would also be a worthwhile activity for further research.

Both multivariate GARCH and MSV models have their limitations. A simple model that can be estimated by maximum likelihood, that is sufficiently flexible to capture the salient features of the data, that can be intuitively interpreted and that can be used on relatively large systems without being excessively parameterized, has yet to be found. Such a model, if it existed, would be very widely used by practitioners, and the pace at which this literature is developing suggests that it may not be too far away.

Acknowledgments

The author thanks Terry Mills for useful comments on a previous version of the paper. The usual disclaimer applies.

Notes

1. This compares with 9 for a diagonal VECH MGARCH model and 21 for the unrestricted MGARCH: see section 21.3.1.
2. See Chib and Greenberg (1996) for an extensive discussion of the intricacies of the MCMC technique.

3. For $N = 2$ there are 21 parameters, while for $N = 3$ there are 78, and $N = 4$ implies 210 parameters.
4. Now 7 and 12 parameters are required in the case where $N = 2$ and $N = 3$ respectively.
5. The BEKK acronym arises from the fact that early versions of the paper also listed Baba and Krafts as co-authors.
6. The bivariate and trivariate systems now entail estimation of only 7 and 12 parameters respectively.
7. At the time of writing, these are available in EVIEWS, GAUSS with the FANPAC add-in, RATS, SAS and S-PLUS. It is anticipated that they will become more widely available in the near future.
8. Their test can also be applied directly to raw data.

References

Alexander, C. and A. Chibumba (1996) Multivariate orthogonal factor GARCH. Mimeo, University of Sussex.

Bauwens, L. and S. Laurent (2002) A new class of multivariate skew densities with application to GARCH models. CORE discussion paper 2002/20.

Bauwens, L., S. Laurent and J.V.K. Rombouts (2003) Multivariate GARCH models: a survey. CORE discussion paper 2003/31.

Bera, A. and S. Kim (2002) Testing constancy of correlation and other specifications of the BGARCH model with an application to international equity returns. *Journal of Empirical Finance* 9, 171–95.

Black, F. and M. Scholes (1973) The pricing of options and corporate liabilities. *Journal of Political Economy* 81, 637–54.

Bollerslev, T. (1986) Generalised autoregressive conditional heteroscedasticity. *Journal of Econometrics* 31, 307–27.

Bollerslev, T. (1990) Modelling the coherence in short-run nominal exchange rates: a multivariate generalised ARCH model. *Review of Economics and Statistics* 72, 498–505.

Bollerslev, T. and R.F. Engle (1993) Common persistence in conditional variances. *Econometrica* 61, 167–86.

Bollerslev, T., R. Chou and K. Kroner (1992) ARCH modelling in finance: a review of the theory and empirical evidence. *Journal of Econometrics* 52, 5–59.

Bollerslev, T., R.F. Engle and D. Nelson (1994). ARCH models in R. Engle and D. McFadden (eds) *Handbook of Econometrics*. Amsterdam: North-Holland, pp. 2959–3038.

Bollerslev, T., R.F. Engle and J. Wooldridge (1988) A capital asset pricing model with time-varying covariances. *Journal of Political Economy* 96, 116–31.

Bollerslev, T. and J. Wooldridge (1992) Quasi-maximum likelihood estimation and inference in dynamic models with time-varying covariances. *Econometric Reviews* 11, 143–72.

Brooks, C. (2002) *Introductory Econometrics for Finance*. Cambridge: Cambridge University Press.

Brooks, C., S.P. Burke and G. Persand (2002) Autoregressive conditional kurtosis. ISMA Centre discussion papers in finance 2002–05, University of Reading, UK.

Brooks, C., S.P. Burke and G. Persand (2003) Multivariate GARCH models: software choice and estimation issues. *Journal of Applied Econometrics* 18, 725–34.

Brooks, C. and O.T. Henry (2002) The impact of news on measures of undiversifiable risk: evidence from the UK stock market. *Oxford Bulletin of Economics and Statistics* 64(5), 487–508.

Brooks, C., O.T. Henry and Persand G. (2002) The effect of asymmetries on optimal hedge ratios. *Journal of Business* 75(2), 333–52.

Chib, S. and E. Greenberg (1996) Markov chain Monte Carlo simulation methods in econometrics. *Econometric Theory* 12, 409–31.

Chib, S., F. Nardari and N. Shephard (2001) Analysis of high dimensional multivariate stochastic volatility models. Mimeo, Washington University, St Louis.

Danielsson, J. (1998) Multivariate stochastic volatility models: estimation and comparison with VGARCH models. *Journal of Empirical Finance* 5, 155–73.

Diebold, F.X. and M. Nerlove (1989) The dynamics of exchange rate volatility: a multivariate latent factor ARCH model. *Journal of Applied Econometrics* 4, 1–21.

Ding, Z. (1994) Time series analysis of speculative returns. PhD thesis, University of California, San Diego.

Engle, R.F. (1982) Autoregressive conditional heteroscedasticity with estimates of the variance of United Kingdom inflation. *Econometrica* 50, 987–1007.

Engle, R.F. (2002) Dynamic conditional correlation – a simple class of multivariate GARCH models. *Journal of Business and Economic Statistics* 20, 339–50.

Engle, R.F. and K. Kroner (1995) Multivariate simultaneous generalised ARCH. *Econometric Theory* 11, 122–50.

Engle, R.F. and V. Ng (1993) Measuring and testing the impact of news on volatility. *Journal of Finance* 48, 1749–1778.

Engle, R,F., V.K. Ng and M. Rothschild (1990) Asset pricing with a factor-ARCH covariance structure: empirical estimates for Treasury bills. *Journal of Econometrics* 45, 213–38.

Gallant, A.R., D.A. Hsieh and G.E. Tauchen (1997) Estimation of stochastic volatility models with diagnostics. *Journal of Econometrics* 81, 159–92.

Gallant, A.R. and G.E. Tauchen (1996) Which moments to match? *Econometric Theory* 12, 657–81.

Ghysels, E., A.C. Harvey and E. Renault (1995) Stochastic volatility. In G.S. Maddala and C.R. Rao (eds), *Handbook of Statistics*, vol. 14. Amsterdam: Elsevier, pp. 119–91.

Glosten, L., R. Jaganathan and D. Runkle (1993) On the relation between expected value and the volatility of the nominal excess return on stocks. *Journal of Finance* 48, 1779–1801.

Harvey, A., E. Ruiz and N. Shephard (1994) Multivariate stochastic variance models. *Review of Economic Studies* 61, 247–64.

Hosking, J. (1980) The multivariate portmanteau statistic. *Journal of the American Statistical Association* 75, 602–8.

Hull, J. and A. White (1987) The pricing of options on assets with stochastic volatilities. *Journal of Finance* 42, 281–300.

Jacquier, E., N.G. Polson and P. Rossi (1995). Stochastic volatility: univariate and multivariate extensions. Mimeo, Cornell University.

Jiang, G.J. and P.J. van der Sluis (2000) Index option pricing models with stochastic volatility and stochastic interest rates. Centre for Economic Research Discussion Paper 2000–36.

Kim, S., N. Shephard and S. Chib (1998) Stochastic volatility: likelihood inference and comparison with ARCH models. *Review of Economic Studies* 65, 361–93.

King, M., E. Sentana and S. Washwani (1994) Volatility and links between national stock markets. *Econometrica* 62, 901–33.

Kroner, K. and V.K. Ng (1998) Modelling asymmetric comovements of asset returns. *Review of Financial Studies* 11(4), 817–44.

Liesenfeld, R. and J.-F. Richard (2003) Univariate and multivariate stochastic volatility models: estimation and diagnostics. *Journal of Empirical Finance* 10(4), 505–31.

Ling, S. and W. Li (1997) Diagnostic checking of nonlinear multivariate time series with multivariate ARCH errors. *Journal of Time Series Analysis* 18, 447–64.

Nardari, F. and J.T. Scruggs (2003) Analysis of linear factor models with multivariate stochastic volatility for stock and bond returns. Mimeo, University of Georgia.

Nelson, D. (1991) Conditional heteroscedasticity in asset returns: a new approach. *Econometrica* 59, 349–70.

Newey, W. (1985) Generalised method of moments specification testing. *Journal of Econometrics* 29, 229–56.

Pitt, M.K. and N. Shephard (1999) Time varying covariances: a factor stochastic volatility approach. In J.M. Bernardo, J.O. Berger, A.P. Dawid and A.F.M. Smith (eds), *Bayesian Statistics 6, Proceedings of the Sixth Valencia International Meeting.* Oxford: Oxford University Press, pp. 547–70.

Shephard, N. (1996) Statistical aspects of ARCH and stochastic volatility. In D.R. Cox, D.V. Hinkley and O.E. Barndorff-Nielsen (eds), *Time series Models: in Econometrics, Finance, and Other Fields.* London: Chapman and Hall, pp. 1–67.

Taylor, S.J. (1994) Modelling stochastic volatility: a review and comparative study. *Mathematical Finance* **4**, 183–204.

Tse, Y.K. (2000) A test for constant correlations in a multivariate GARCH model. *Journal of Econometrics* **98**, 107–27.

Van der Weide, R. (2002) GO-GARCH: a multivariate generalised orthogonal GARCH model. *Journal of Applied Econometrics* **17**, 549–64.

Part VIII

Computation and Econometrics

22

The Role of Simulation in Econometrics

Jurgen A. Doornik

Abstract

Simulation methods pervade all aspects of econometrics. Major factors in this are the analytical intractability of many modern econometric techniques (in particular at small samples) and the availability of low cost computing. Recent developments in random number generation, which are at the core of econometric simulations, are reviewed. Notably, these are very high-period generators that are also computationally efficient, together with their extension to the generation of standard normal random numbers. Next, an introduction is provided, discussing techniques that reduce the efficiency of experiments, and those that enhance their generality.

22.1	Introduction		787
22.2	Random number generation		790
	22.2.1	Uniform random numbers	790
	22.2.2	Non-uniform random numbers	796
	22.2.3	Some further issues	801
22.3	Monte Carlo methods in econometrics		803
	22.3.1	Introduction	803
	22.3.2	Simple Monte Carlo	804
	22.3.3	Enhancing the efficiency of Monte Carlo experiments	804
	22.3.4	Enhancing the generality of Monte Carlo experiments	807
22.4	Conclusion		808

22.1 Introduction

The enormous increase of computational power at falling prices, in particular the exponential growth of personal computing from 1980 onward, has made it possible to estimate ever more complex econometric models. Often, these models are not amenable to a fully theoretical analysis, which is why simulation methods are used to understand their properties. In a Monte Carlo study, a deterministic problem is replaced by an analogous stochastic process which can be analyzed in a computer experiment. For example, consider calculating:

$$\int_a^b x e^{-\frac{1}{2}x^2} \, dx.$$

When an integral such as this has no straightforward analytical solution, numerical integration could be used to obtain an answer. Alternatively, the integral corresponds to the mean value over the interval $[a, b]$ of a random variable X distributed as $(2\pi)^{1/2}$ times the standard normal density. If random numbers from the standard normal can be created on a computer, then the mean over $[a, b]$ of a large sample also provides a numerical estimate (on scaling by $(2\pi)^{1/2}$).

Famous early applications of simulation are by W.S. Gosset, who used it to check a theoretical result (the Student-t distribution, Student, 1908a) and, in a second paper, to guess a parameter in a formula (the distribution of the correlation coefficient, Student, 1908b). In the former case, subsequent tightening of the proof makes the simulation redundant, as would finding the proof in the latter case. Such uses of simulation are less common, but can still be useful. Normally distributed random numbers for these experiments were provided by a previously published table of correlations of finger measurements of 3,000 criminals. The classic paper of Yule (1926) illustrates the problem of nonsense correlation by plotting the correlation between (a) two independent random series, (b) two independent series with random first differences, and (c) two independent series with random second differences. In modern terminology these would be described as I(0), I(1), and I(2) series (see Chapter 17). Despite being independent, the plot for the I(1) series looks nearly uniform, while the I(2) case is U shaped. The uniform random series underlying these experiments were obtained by drawing cards, which Yule described as a very time-consuming process. The work of Student and Yule are examples of distribution sampling: the experimental representation of the properties of a distribution function. Teichrow (1965) reviews the literature from the early twentieth century onward, while Stigler (1991) reproduces three interesting examples that precede this.

The Monte Carlo method originated toward the end of World War II at Los Alamos as a tool to aid the development of the atomic bomb. Von Neumann and Ulam are generally credited with the invention of the procedure and the "Monte Carlo" label. It was seen as quite different from distribution sampling, which solves a problem that is already probabilistic. The Monte Carlo method, by contrast, solves an analytical problem through a simulation experiment. An early example of this was the Monte Carlo computation of eigenvalues of the Schrödinger equation. Solving an analogous stochastic problem, together with the clever use of variance-reduction techniques, were considered to be the distinguishing features of the Monte Carlo method. Subsequently, the development of digital electronic computing, combined with a realization of the wide applicability of Monte Carlo methods, led to its increasing popularity.

In econometrics, Monte Carlo is primarily used as a device to investigate the behavior in finite samples of various statistics of interest (estimators, standard errors, tests, etc.). A Monte Carlo experiment, therefore, typically involves directly mimicking on a computer the desired data generation process

(DGP) for the type of system and data to which the statistical methods are to be applied. The artificial DGP is fully specified by the researcher, and should reflect all relevant aspects of the economy, in order to produce data that are applicable to the real world econometric problem under study. The generated data provides the input for the econometric model, of which some aspect of interest is studied. For example, the researcher can decide whether the model is correctly specified for the DGP or not. Hendry (1984) discusses those aspects of Monte Carlo that are relevant for econometric applications, with an in-depth treatment of variance reduction techniques (also see section 22.3.3) and response surfaces (section 22.3.4). Davidson and MacKinnon (1993, chapter 21) provide a useful introduction to this material.

There have been several important developments since the publication of the authoritative survey by Hendry (1984):

- Twenty years later, computers are about 10,000 times faster. A simulation experiment that takes one minute today would have taken 7 days in 1984. A quick scan of the recent literature shows that simulation methods permeate all aspects of econometrics.
- A switch to higher-level programming tools, in particular matrix-programming languages, has reduced the programming effort that is required to implement an experiment. The introduction of object-oriented programming into econometrics (Doornik, 2002) has provided additional labour savings.
- Introduction of interactive software for Monte Carlo experiments in econometrics (Hendry, 1990; Hendry, Neale and Ericsson, 1991; Doornik and Hendry, 2001). This enables the teaching of Monte Carlo principles without the need for students to learn a programming language.
- Development of high-period random number generators, and a move away from old-fashioned linear congruential generators, see section 22.2.
- Development of bootstrap methods and bootstrap testing, see Chapter 25.
- Development of simulation estimation methods for Bayesian models, see Chapter 26, with wide applicability to models that involve high-dimensional integrals and otherwise intractable likelihoods.

Despite these major developments, much of Hendry (1984) remains pertinent. However, the availability of faster computers has reduced the emphasis on variance reduction techniques (suprisingly, Marshall, 1954, had already noted this effect). As a consequence, the delineation between the Monte Carlo method, distribution sampling, and simulation in general is of much less relevance today.

The main focus of this chapter is on recent developments in random number generation (section 22.2). While a fundamental starting point, this aspect is often neglected in the econometric literature. This is followed in section 22.3 by a discussion of Monte Carlo methods that introduces the main concepts.

22.2   Random number generation

The basic building block of a simulation experiment is the random number generator (RNG). This produces a stream of random numbers, and the experiment is nothing more than an average of some complicated function of these random numbers.

It may seem surprising that a computer, which is a purely deterministic device, can produce a stream of random numbers. Perhaps it is helpful to use the mathematical constant π as an example. Assume that an infinite stream of digits is available from an algorithm to compute π to arbitrary precision. Then each group of 15 digits could form the decimal part of a uniform random number, thus providing a sequence of U(0,1)-distributed numbers.[1] This requires that the digits are random, which is as yet unresolved (see Bailey and Crandall, 2001, for a recent contribution). Assuming that this is the case, the purely deterministic and known sequence of digits has been transformed into a series that is sufficiently random to be used for simulation experiments. The quality of the random numbers can be tested on a computer, for example by comparison of higher sample moments with their theoretical values, absence of autocorrelation, etc. Because the random numbers are generated from a deterministic formula, they are called *pseudo random numbers*, and the corresponding method a pseudo random number generator. Because only pseudo random number generators are considered in this chapter (quasi-random numbers are not discussed), I shall omit the "pseudo" adjective.

Physical devices have been used to generate random numbers in the past (Tocher, 1963), and are still used when they have more popular appeal, such as in the lotto, where numbered rubber balls are mechanically picked out of a rotating container. It is very difficult to design physical systems that are flawless and not influenced by their environment. In contrast, the pseudo-random number generators are open to rigorous mathematical analysis and are easy to implement on a computer. More importantly, replicability of experiments is lost when using a physical device.

It is convenient to start from a uniform random number generator. Other distributions can then be derived from the uniform RNG, see section 22.2.2.

22.2.1   Uniform random numbers

22.2.1.1   The linear congruential generator

Until recently, one of the most popular methods used to generate uniform random numbers $u_i \sim U(0, 1)$ was the linear congruential generator (LCG):

$$z_{i+1} = (bz_i + c)\mathrm{mod}\ m \quad \text{for } i = 0, 1, \ldots, P. \tag{22.1}$$

The modulo operator takes the remainder after division by m; for example, 34 mod 16 gives 2. When $c=0$, the generator is called multiplicative congruential. In (22.1), b, c, and z_i are integers between 0 and $m-1$.

Clearly, this procedure cannot yield more than m random integers, and may produce fewer. Therefore P is called the period: after reaching P, the generator starts repeating itself, so that $z_P = z_0$. A careful choice of b and m ensures that the maximum period is reached ($P=m$). Zero is usually excluded, so that division by m gives $m-1$ uniformly distributed random numbers with the floating-point representation:

$$u_i = z_i/m \in (0,1).$$

On current computer architecture it is convenient to take $m = 2^{31} - 1$, because this is a prime number (of the form $2^n - 1$, a so-called Mersenne prime), and corresponds to the largest signed integer when using 4-byte values.

The initial value z_0 is called the seed of the random number generator. When $P=m$, the seed just picks an entry point in the sequence of m numbers, and it is irrelevant where we start. In the multiplicative case, the seed cannot be zero. Some matrix programming languages start from a random seed (based on the computer time, for example). This comes at a cost: when the experiment is rerun the next day, different outcomes will entail. But when simulation is used as a scientific tool, it is useful to be able to exactly replicate the results, for example to ensure that no mistakes were introduced by recent changes to the code. Cryptographic applications have quite the opposite need.

The $\{u_i\}$ are really only pseudo-random, in that from knowing the algorithm and the seed z_0, they can be exactly reproduced. This means that there is never a need to store the actual random numbers on disk for later use. Instead, the data can be "compressed" to a single number z_0.

The choices of b and m (and, to a lesser extent, c) influence the quality of the RNG. It is important that they are such that the stream is not detectably non-random on statistical tests and has the maximum feasible period $P=m$. LCGs can have a lattice structure (see, e.g., Ripley, 1987, sections 2.2, 2.4), i.e., the output falls on a small number of (hyper)planes, which effectively corresponds to some form of autocorrelation, thus making them useless. Park and Miller (1988) pointed out that many readily available random number generators (including many implementations in popular programming languages) are actually quite bad. In addition, many "casual" improvements, such as swapping bytes, may actually destroy the randomness of the LCG. They propose a multiplicative generator with $b=48{,}271$, $c=0$ and $m=2^{31}-1$ as a minimal standard (Park, Miller and Stockmeyer, 1993). This is a simple and efficient LCG which passes many statistical tests; Knuth (1998, section 3.3.4, Table 1, Line 20) gives its properties on the spectral test, which looks at the randomness of short sequences.

For a more detailed analysis of congruential generators, see Knuth (1998, section 3.1), Press, Flannery, Teukolsky and Vetterling (1993, section 7.1), L'Ecuyer (1997), and Ripley (1987, section 2.2), among many others.

22.2.1.2 High-period generators

A period of nearly $2^{31} \approx 2.15 \times 10^9$ may seem high, but it takes less than a minute to generate all uniform random numbers and compute their average. Therefore, recent research has focussed on high-period generators that can also be computed efficiently. One could argue that the quality of the randomness is more important than the period. After all, it will be very unlikely that the numbers start to repeat in such a way that matters for the econometric experiment. On the other hand, there are situations where it may matter. For example, when selecting from a very large choice set, it may be desirable that every choice is possible. This would require a period larger than the number of possible choices (see Marsaglia, 2003b, for some examples). High-period generators also tend to have better high-dimensional structure – so even if only a relatively small subset is used, their properties tend to be better. Finally, one may as well take a high-period generator if it comes at low additional cost. In most econometric experiments, model estimation is much more time consuming than the generation of the underlying random numbers.

One method of achieving a high period is to combine different RNGs. Marsaglia (1997) suggests a combination of two multiply-with-carry (MWC) generators. The MWC generator is a simple extension of (22.1):

$$z_{i+1} = (bz_i + c_i) \bmod m \quad \text{for } i = 0, 1, \dots, P, \quad \text{and} \quad P = bm - 1 \text{ is prime,}$$
$$c_{i+1} = (bz_i + c_i) \operatorname{div} m, \tag{22.2}$$

where the div operator returns the integer part of the division. When m is a power of two, the div and mod operations can be implemented efficiently. The proposed combination of two MWC generators with $m = 2^{16}$ yields a generator with period close to 2^{60}. This combination requires two seeds.

L'Ecuyer (1996) proposes a combination of linear feedback shift register (LFSR) generators. This is essentially a binary autoregression with lag length k:

$$x_{i+1} = (\beta_1 x_i + \dots + \beta_k x_{i-k+1}) \bmod 2, \quad x_i, \beta_i \in \{0, 1\}. \tag{22.3}$$

The computational appeal is that the evaluation can be implemented efficiently using bitwise operators. Because

$$[(0, 0, 1, 1) + (0, 1, 0, 1)] \bmod 2 = [(0, 1, 1, 2)] \bmod 2 = (0, 1, 1, 0),$$

addition mod 2 is equivalent to the exclusive-or operator and can be done on a vector of bits (i.e., an integer) at once.

The properties of (22.3) depend on the characteristic polynomial. In particular, when the polynomial cannot be factorized, it will have maximum period $2^k - 1$ (and is called primitive). A 32-bit binary integer can then be formed by 'glueing' the random bits together at step size s:

$$z_{i+1} = (x_h x_{h+1} \dots x_{h+31}),$$

where $h = (i + 1)s$. When the largest common divisor of s and $2^k - 1$ is one (i.e., they are coprime), then the period of z_n is also $2^k - 1$. A combination of LFSR generators is necessary to improve statistical properties and increase the period. L'Ecuyer (1999) gives tables of specifications for s and k that produce maximally-equidistributed sequences (roughly: the hypercube generated by a vector of successive random numbers is subdivided into equal-sized cells, and each cell contains the same number of points). For example, LFSR113 is a combination of 4 LFSR generators resulting in a period of 2^{113}.

22.2.1.3 Very high-period generators

In general, very high-period generators use a seed that consists of an array of integers. For example, one could imagine that a 1024 integer seed may have a period of $2^{32 \times 1024}$. Efficient implementation is achieved by either updating the seed once every k steps (with intermediate steps just requiring a look-up), or by touching only a few elements at a time. The Mersenne twister of Matsumoto and Nishimura (1998) falls into the former category. It uses an array of 624 integers that is updated once every 624 steps. The version for which they provide computer code is called MT19937, with period $2^{19937} - 1$ (a Mersenne prime). The basic building block for the Mersenne twister is the binary autoregression (22.3).

The Mersenne twister provided impetus for further research into very high-period generators. In particular, the WELL generators (Panneton, L'Ecuyer and Matsumoto, 2005), again based on binary autoregressions, generalize the Mersenne twister by providing generators that are maximally equidistributed (or nearly so). They also argue that, for better randomness, about half of the autoregressive coefficients in (22.3) should be non-zero. WELL performs better on this metric than the Mersenne twister.

Simple very-high period RNGs, based on the multiply-with-carry generators (22.2), have been proposed by Marsaglia (2003b, 2003a). There are, of course, many other generators, including those that are more relevant for cryptographical applications. At some point, there is a limit to the usefulness of an extremely high period: if generating 2^{32} numbers takes a second, drawing "only" 2^{64} would take 136 years.

22.2.1.4 Testing random numbers

The quality of the random number generator is of paramount importance. The advances in computing have also made testing much easier, and most recently published algorithms have been tested extensively. Certain theoretical properties are desirable, such as being maximally equidistant, as discussed above. Statistical tests, on the other hand, are empirical inspections of the $U(0, 1)$ properties of the generated series. There is a wide range of tests that are used in practice: see, e.g., Knuth (1998, section 3.3) and Fishman Moore (1982). A standard for testing was established by Marsaglia (1995) in the form of the DIEHARD battery of tests: also see Gentle (1998, section 6.2.1) for a description of the DIEHARD tests. This uses quite a small amount of random numbers (relative to modern computational power), and some of the tests are not suitable for periodicity less than 2^{32} (such as the Park and Miller minimum standard of section 22.1.1).

L'Ecuyer and Simard (2005) provide a useful library for statistical testing of random numbers, including, among others, the tests proposed by Knuth (1998) and DIEHARD. They provide test suites which are named "small crush," "crush," and "big crush," using increasing amounts of random numbers. The crush suite has 94 tests in total, using about 2^{35} random numbers, while the big crush involves 60 tests, requiring close to 2^{38} random numbers; these are much more stringent than the diehard tests. The objective of this section is to apply the crush and big crush test suites to a selection of uniform random number generators. Table 22.1 lists six RNGs that are representative for the algorithms discussed above, with their approximate period.

Table 22.2 reports the number of failures in the crush and big crush test suites (L'Ecuyer and Simard, 2005) at p-values of 10^{-300}, 10^{-15}, and 10^{-5} respectively. Both LCG31 and MWC60 fail a large number of tests, and seem unsatisfactory as a uniform RNG. LFSR113 and WELL1024 fail the tests that look for linear dependence in long sequences of bits. Panneton, L'Ecuyer and Matsumoto (2005) note that all generators of the form (22.3), including the Mersenne Twister, will fail such tests. It is likely that the tempering used in MT19937, together with the very long period, requires a longer sequence to get failure. MWC8222 also performs very well, while being simple to implement.

I also timed the generators on a range of hardware platforms. On Intel and AMD 32-bit platforms, LCG31 is the fastest of the RNGs under consideration. All others are roughly equally fast, but take about 1.5 times longer than LCG31. The relative performance on a 64-bit AMD platform, using 64-bit code, is different, with MWC60 and MWC8222 about 1.5 times faster than the others.

Table 22.1 Random number generators used in this chapter

RNG	Reference	Approximate period
LCG31	(Park and Miller, 1988)	2^{31}
MWC60	(Marsaglia, 1997)	2^{60}
LFSR113	(L'Ecuyer, 1999)	2^{113}
WELL1024	(Panneton, L'Ecuyer and Matsumoto, 2005)	2^{1024}
MWC8222	(Marsaglia, 2003a)	2^{8222}
MT19937	(Matsumoto and Nishimura, 1998)	2^{19937}

Table 22.2 Number of failures in the crush battery of tests (94 tests in total), and the big-crush battery (60 in total) at three significance levels

	Crush			Big crush		
	10^{-300}	10^{-15}	10^{-5}	10^{-300}	10^{-15}	10^{-5}
LCG31	11	11	3	20	9	5
MWC60	13	7	7	26	8	9
LFSR113	4	2	0	2	1	0
WELL1024	2	2	0	1	1	0
MWC8222	0	0	0	0	0	0
MT19937	0	0	1	0	0	0

22.2.1.5 *Parallel random number generation*

Doornik, Hendry and Shephard (2002) consider the use of small clusters of personal computers for econometric applications. In particular, Monte Carlo experiments, bootstrapping and simulation estimation are prime candidates for a distributed framework. However, in parallel applications it is essential that each process has its own random numbers: otherwise, each would do exactly the same experiment, thus wasting the parallel resources. Above it was advocated that, in the interest of scientific replicability, computational outcomes should be deterministic. However, starting from the same seed is clearly not an option in parallel computation.

An early solution, suggested by Smith, Reddaway and Scott(1985), was to split a linear congruential generator (1) into Q sequences which are spaced by Q (so each process gets a different slice; on processor i: $U_i, U_{i+Q}, U_{i+2Q}, \ldots$). As argued by Coddington (1996), this leapfrog method can be problematic: LCG numbers tend to have a lattice structure, which can cause correlation between streams even when Q is large. In particular, the method is likely to be flawed when the number of processors is a power of two, which happens quite commonly. Another method is to split the generation into L sequences, with processor i using $U_{iL}, U_{iL+1}, U_{iL+2}, \ldots$. This ensures that there is no overlap, but the fixed spacing could still result in correlation between sequences. Both methods produce different results when the number of processors changes.

Recently, methods of parameterization have become popular. The aim is to use a parameter of the underlying recursion that can be varied, resulting in independent streams of random numbers. An example is provided by the SPRNG library (Mascagni and Srinivasan, 2000), see SCAN (1999) for an introduction. The SPRNG library has the ability to achieve the same results independently of the number of processors, by assigning a separate parameter to each replication.

An alternative method for the WELL algorithms is to use the fact that it is a linear recurrence to jump ahead in the stream efficiently.

The approach of Doornik, Hendry and Shephard (2002) sits half-way between sequence splitting and the method of parameterization. They assign a seed to each replication (i.e., each iteration of the loop), instead of each process, as follows. The master process runs LCG31, assigning a seed to each replication block. The slaves are told to execute B replications. At the start of the block, they use the received seed to set LCG31 to the correct state. Then, for each replication, LCG31 is used to create four random numbers as a seed for LFSR113. All subsequent random numbers for that replication are then generated with LFSR113. On the master, LCG31 must be advanced by $4B$ after each send, because LFSR113 uses 4 seeds. This can simply be done by drawing $B \times 4$ random numbers.

Although the replications may arrive at the master in a different order if the number of processes changes, this is still the same set of replications, so the results are independent of the number of processes. Randomizing the seed avoids the problem that is associated with a fixed sequence split. There is a probability of overlap but, because the period of the generator is so high, this is very small.

With M replications, an RNG period of P, and L random numbers consumed in each replication, the effective period becomes $P^* = P/L$. For large M and P^* considerably larger than M, Doornik, Hendry and Shephard (2002) show that the probability of overlap is approximately equal to $1 - \exp[-0.5M^2L/P]$. The bigger P^*, the closer to one this probability is.

This procedure can be emulated on a single processor by setting the seed of the second RNG according to the first RNG after each Lth call. Table 22.3 reports the number of failures when the crush test suite is applied for different values of L. In the first case, LCG31 is used to seed LFSR113. Crush uses about 2^{35} random numbers, so using $ML = 2^{35}$, the probability of overlap is roughly $1 - \exp(-2^{-44}L^{-1})$. This is 5.7×10^{-13} for $L = 10$. The last three columns of Table 22.3 consider the case where MWC8222, which requires 256 seeds, is seeded by LFSR113. This has a probability of overlap of $1 - \exp(-2^{-8153}L^{-1})$, which is exceedingly small. Table 22.3 shows that the properties of the combined parallel generators are essentially the same as for their scalar versions: the number of serious failures remains four for LFSR113 and none for MWC8222.

22.2.2   Non-uniform random numbers

22.2.2.1   Principles

The uniform distribution is rarely used directly in any econometric model. Other distributions, in particular the normal or Gaussian distribution, are much more prevalent. Various methods exist to transform a uniform RNG into a non-uniform counterpart.

When it is feasible, the most convenient method to derive random number generators for a non-uniform distribution is the inversion principle. This derives from the property:

$$\Pr(U_i \leq u) = P(u) = u \quad \text{for } U_i \sim U(0, 1) \quad \text{and} \quad u \in [0, 1].$$

Consequently, $P(u)$ and u can be interchanged in any derivation. Let $F(\cdot)$ denote the cumulative distribution function of a random variable $\{e_i\}$; if $F(\cdot)$ can be analytically inverted, then $e_i = F^{-1}(u_i)$ implies that $u_i = F(e_i)$ and hence:

$$\Pr(e_i \leq u) = \Pr(F(e_i) \leq F(u)) = \Pr(U_i \leq F(u)) = P(F(u)) = F(u).$$

as required.

Table 22.3 Number of failures in the crush test-suite of two combined parallel generators

L	LCG31–LFSR113			LFSR113–MWC8222		
	10^{-300}	10^{-5}	10^{-15}	10^{-300}	10^{-15}	10^{-15}
10	2	0	0	0	0	0
100	4	0	0	0	0	0
1,000	4	2	0	0	0	0
100,000	4	2	0	0	0	0
∞	4	2	0	0	0	0

Using the exponential distribution as an example: $X \sim \exp(\lambda)$, with CDF $F(x) = 1 - \exp(-\lambda x)$ where $\lambda > 0$, the draws can be obtained from uniform random numbers u_i as:

$$x_i = -\lambda^{-1} \log(1 - u_i).$$

Excluding zero and one from the uniform random numbers ensures that $-\infty$ and zero are avoided for the exponential distribution.

If a cumulative distribution function and density are available, but no analytical formula for the inverse, it is simple to implement the quantile function (i.e., the inverse function) using the Newton–Raphson method. This could then provide a generator for random numbers. However, while this can be a convenient approach, it is usually very much slower than direct methods. The rejection method, which can be traced back to Von Neumann, often provides an efficient alternative when inversion is slow. Suppose we wish to sample from a density $f(\cdot)$, and that f is bounded by another density g: $f(\cdot) \le cg(\cdot)$. Sampling from $f(\cdot)$ can then be implemented as:

> repeat
> > generate a random observation v_i from $g(\cdot)$, $\hspace{2em}$ (22.4)
> until $u_i cg(v_i) \le f(v_i)$,

where u_i is independently $\mathsf{U}(0, 1)$ distributed. The potential benefit comes when it is difficult to sample from f, but easy for g. The closer cg is to f, the better the bound, and the more efficient the rejection method. An example for the normal distribution is given below.

The most important non-uniform distribution is the standard normal, which, unfortunately, does not have an analytical inverse. Accurate, non-iterative, approximations to the normal quantiles exist, but would lead to a relatively slow procedure.

A rough method for generating $e_i \sim \mathsf{IN}[0, 1]$ is based on the approximate central limit result:

$$\left(\sum_{j=1}^{12} u_j - 6 \right) = e_i. \hspace{2em} (22.5)$$

While this is simple, it is 12 times slower than the uniform RNG, and of limited accuracy.

The method of Box and Muller (1958) transforms two uniform random numbers into two independent standard normals:

$$(e_i, e_{i+1}) = h_i(\cos 2\pi u_{i+1}, \sin 2\pi u_{i+1}) \quad \text{where} \quad h_i = (-2 \log u_i)^{\frac{1}{2}}. \hspace{2em} (22.6)$$

A well-tested and empirically satisfactory generator must be used for input to the Box–Muller method when (u_i, u_{i+1}) are successively generated. In particular, an LCG with poor lattice structure could be problematic. The most popular method is the polar–Marsaglia method (Marsaglia and Bray, 1964), which is based on Box–Muller as follows:

$$
\begin{aligned}
&\text{repeat}\\
&\quad v_1 = 2u_1 - 1, \quad v_2 = 2u_2 - 1\\
&\quad d = v_1^2 + v_2^2 \qquad\qquad\qquad\qquad\qquad\qquad (22.7)\\
&\text{until } d < 1\\
&\quad e_1 = [-2\log(d)/d]^{1/2}v_1, \quad e_2 = [-2\log(d)/d]^{1/2}v_2.
\end{aligned}
$$

This requires, on average, 1.27 as many uniforms as (22.6) but avoids the trigonometric function.

As an example of the rejection method, consider the logistic distribution as a bound for the standard normal. From discrete choice methods, it is known that binary probit and binary logit are very similar (Chambers and Cox, 1967), so the logistic may be a good candidate that can be inverted analytically. The logistic distribution with scale zero and variance $\beta^2 \pi^2/3$ has cdf:

$$
G(x) = [1 + \exp(-x/\beta)]^{-1}.
$$

The corresponding density is $g(x) = \beta^{-1}G(x)[1 - G(x)]$ and the quantiles are $G^{-1}(u) = -\beta \log[(1 - u)/u]$. Implementation requires a choice for the scaling parameter c in (22.4) and the variance of the logistic distribution through β, such that the rejection probability is (approximately) minimized. Devroye (1986, ch. 2) illustrates the principle of how these parameters can be computed. Following this, we maximize $f(x)/g_\beta(x)$ or, more conveniently, $d(x) = \log f(x) - \log g_\beta(x)$ to find one solution at zero for $\beta \geq 0.71$. For smaller β's, zero is a local minimum. Solving numerically, it is found that $\min_\beta \max_x d(x)$ is at $x_m = 0.98226$ when $\beta_m = 0.65$. The value of c is then $f(x_m)/g_{\beta_m}(x_m) = 1.081$. This specifies a rejection algorithm:

$$
\begin{aligned}
&\text{repeat}\\
&\quad w_1 = \log(u_1), \quad w_2 = \log(1 - u_1)\\
&\quad v = 0.65 * (w_1 - w_2);\qquad\qquad\qquad\qquad\qquad (22.8)\\
&\text{until } \log(u_2) + w_1 + w_2 + \log(1.081/0.65) < -v^2/2 - \log(2\pi)/2\\
&\text{return } v.
\end{aligned}
$$

It will be slower than (22.7), because it requires at least two uniforms and three logarithms per standard normal.

There is a large literature on the generation of non-uniform random numbers. Good starting points are Ripley (1987, chapter 3), Knuth (1998, section 3.4), and the monograph by Devroye (1986). The volumes by Johnson, Kotz and Balakrishnan (1994) also include discussions of random number generation.

22.2.2.2 Efficient methods for the standard normal distribution

The aforementioned polar method is simple to implement, but not particularly fast. Because of the importance of the normal distribution, many more efficient methods have been proposed. The method of Wallace (1996) is interesting, because it generates normal random numbers directly, in addition to being very efficient. However, because of this it is also somewhat harder to understand the properties of this method.

Probably the fastest available rejection method at the moment is the so-called "ziggurat method," introduced by Marsaglia and Tsang (1984) and subsequently refined (Marsaglia and Tsang, 2000). This method has some deficiencies, which were corrected by Doornik (2005b) at the expense of some of its speed.

The ziggurat partitions the standard normal density into horizontal blocks of equal area. The standardization can be omitted, using $f(x) = \exp(-x^2/2)$ instead. All blocks are rectangular boxes, except the bottom one, which consists of a box joined with the remainder of the density. This is illustrated in Figure 22.1, using four boxes, labeled from bottom to top as B_0, B_1, B_2, B_3. Equal areas of size V implies:

$$x_3[f(x_4) - f(x_3)] = x_2[f(x_3) - f(x_2)] = x_1[f(x_2) - f(x_1)] = x_1 f(x_1) + \int_{x_1}^{\infty} f(x)dx = V.$$

Note that, working backward along the X-axis, previous values of x can easily be derived. For example, if x_1 is known:

$$x_2 = f^{-1}(f(x_1) + V/x_1).$$

In general, when dividing in to C blocks, the partitioning can be found by solving the non-linear equation:

$$x_{C-1}(r)[f(0) - f(x_{C-1}(r))] - V(r) = 0, \tag{22.9}$$

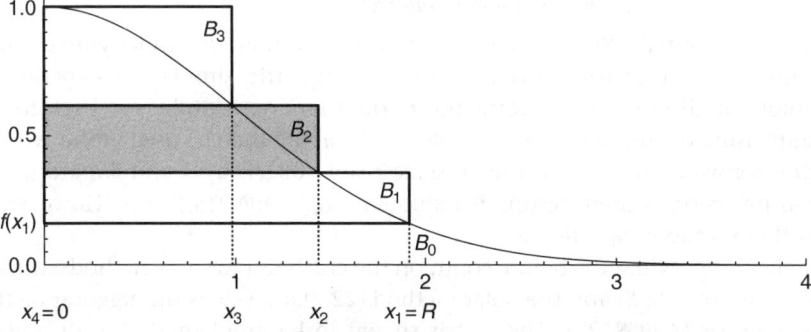

Figure 22.1 Example of a four-way ziggurat partitioning of the standard normal density

where r denotes the right-most x_1, $x_C = 0$, and:

$$V(r) = rf(r) + \int_r^\infty f(x)dx.$$

The value of $x_{C-1}(r)$ can be found by substitution from:

$$x_i = f^{-1}(f(x_{i-1}) + V(r)/x_{i-1}), \quad i = 2, \ldots, C - 1, \quad x_1 = r.$$

Denote the solution of (22.9) by R, then the complete partitioning has been found. The rejection method for the ziggurat is quite straightforward:

(1) Draw a box at random with probability $1/C$, say B_i.
(2) Draw a random number in the box as $z = (2u_0 - 1)x_i$ for $i > 0$ and $z = (2u_0 - 1)V/f(x_1)$ for $i = 0$.
(3) If $|z| < x_{i+1}$ accept z.
(4.1) If $i = 0$, draw v from the tail using Marsaglia (1964), accept sign (z) v.
(4.2) Else if $i > 0$ and $u_1f(x_i) - f(x_{i+1})] < f(z) - f(x_{i+1})$ accept z.
(5) Return to step 1.

u_0 and u_1 denote $U(0, 1)$ random numbers. The efficiency of this rejection algorithm is $0.5 * (2\pi)^{1/2}/(VC)$. Using $C = 4$, as in Figure 22.1, this is only about 83 percent. The benefit comes for higher values of C: for $C = 128$ it climbs to 98.78 percent with an average acceptance rate of 98.05 percent at step 3. The efficiency comes from the fact that the test at step 3 can be rewritten as $|(2u_0 - 1)| < x_{i+1}/x_i$, of which the right-hand side can be precomputed and stored (similarly for $i = 0$). The most efficient implementation uses integers instead of floating point numbers for the test. The standard ziggurat method is at least twice as fast as the polar method, with the most efficient implementation about three to four times faster. Details can be found in Doornik (2005b).

22.2.2.3   Testing non-uniform random numbers

Testing the normal RNG is perhaps more important than the underlying uniform, because it provides the basis for most econometric simulation experiments. A simple method is to transform the normal random numbers e_i back to uniformity using the normal cdf $\Phi : \tilde{u}_i = \Phi(e_i)$. The $\tilde{u}_i$ can then be used in the available testing software, in our case the crush test suite of L'Ecuyer and Simard (2005). When inversion is used, testing is redundant: $\tilde{u}_i = \Phi(\Phi^{-1}(u_i)) = u_i$. However, for the other methods: $\tilde{u}_i \neq u_i$.

Table 22.4 provides the failure count on the crush test for two methods: the sum of 12 uniforms (22.5) and the polar method (22.7), as well as the ziggurat method (but only for MWC8222). The first is shown to be problematic for all uniform RNGs. The results for the polar method are interesting, because it shows that the

Table 22.4 Number of failures in the crush battery of tests (94 tests in total) for some standard normal random number generators

	Sum of 12 uniforms			Polar method			Ziggurat method		
	10^{-300}	10^{-15}	10^{-5}	10^{-300}	10^{-15}	10^{-5}	10^{-300}	10^{-15}	10^{-5}
LCG31	13	7	4	1	5	0			
MWC60	10	3	2	3	3	0			
LFSR113	10	3	2	0	0	0			
WELL1024	10	4	0	0	0	0			
MWC8222	10	4	1	0	0	0	0	0	0
MT19937	10	4	0	0	0	0			

Table 22.5 Number of failures in the crush battery of tests (94 tests in total) for Student-*t* random number generators

	Student-t(6)			Student-t(12)		
	10^{-300}	10^{-15}	10^{-5}	10^{-300}	10^{-15}	10^{-5}
LCG31	4	0	1	3	0	1
MWC60	1	0	1	1	0	1
LFSR113	0	0	0	0	0	0
WELL1024	0	0	0	0	0	0
MWC8222	0	0	0	0	0	0
MT19937	0	0	0	0	0	0

new uniform random numbers $\tilde{u}_i$ are considerably more uniform than the underlying u_i for LCG31 and MWC60, but also somewhat for LFSR113 and WELL1024. This is largely the effect of using the rejection method, while there is no added problem from using consecutive numbers. So, while LCG31 and MWC60 were rejected as uniform RNGs, they are more acceptable for standard normal RNGs based on the polar method.

Finally, consider the Student-$t(n)$ distribution. This can be generated as

$$\phi\left(\frac{n}{x}\right)^{1/2}, \quad \phi \sim N[0,1], x \sim \chi^2(n).$$

The χ^2 distribution in turn can be generated from a gamma distribution, for which algorithms 3.19 and 3.20 from Ripley (1987) can be used. Table 22.5 provides the failure count on the crush test for $n=6$ and $n=12$ after mapping the Student-t numbers back to uniformity. Again, LCG31 and MWC60 do not behave as well as the others, but not disastrously so.

22.2.3 Some further issues

22.2.3.1 Smoothness

There are several levels at which smoothness can be discussed. First, most efficient algorithms to sample from statistical distributions use the rejection method.

The consequence is that there is no one-to-one mapping from an underlying uniform random number to the derived distribution. The exception is when inversion is used, in which case one can go back and forth between the uniform and non-uniform random number. This lack of one-to-one mapping usually does not matter.

The second level is smoothness with respect to the parameters of the distribution. This is generally the case for location and scale parameters. For example, $x_i = z_i \sigma + \mu$ is a drawing from $N[\mu, \sigma^2]$ when $z_i \sim N[0, 1]$. So given a μ and σ, one can go back and forth between z_i and x_i. With respect to other parameters this is not always the case. For the gamma distribution, $\Gamma(a, r)$:

$$\frac{a^r}{\Gamma(r)} x^{r-1} e^{-ax}$$

a is a scale parameter, so can be set to one in the underlying RNG. But rejection methods often use a different method for $r < 1, r = 1$ (exponential distribution) and $r > 1$. This will cause a lack of smoothness around $r = 1$: starting from a specific seed, a stream with r just below one may look quite different from a stream with r just larger than one. On rare occasions this may matter, in which case the solution is to use inversion instead, at the expense of computational efficiency.

Related to this is the smoothness of an econometric estimator that requires simulations, for example, a Markov Chain Monte Carlo estimator. Denote the log-likelihood as $\ell(\theta|u_1, \ldots, u_m)$. If derivatives are required, these are usually computed numerically. However, subsequent evaluation at θ_1 and $\theta_1 + \varepsilon$, where ε is an appropriate small number, computes:

$$\ell_1 = \ell(\theta_1|u_1, \ldots, u_m),$$
$$\ell_2 = \ell(\theta_1 + \varepsilon|u_{m+1}, \ldots, u_{2m}),$$

Because different random numbers were used, the function subtly changes and numerical differentiation breaks down. The solution is to reset the seed for every function evaluation, making the log-likelihood a function of the chosen seed. Choosing a different seed will give a different model.

22.2.3.2   Are 0 and 1 included?

Many rejection methods, as well as statistical applications, take logarithms of random numbers. If the uniforms are $U[0, 1]$ instead of $U(0, 1)$ these would break down, as in (22.8).

The value one is excluded by virtue of the conversion to floating point. When using a 32-bit unsigned integer, the largest value possible is $(2^{32} - 1)/2^{32}$, which is less than unity.

The case of zero is less obvious. LCG31 never returns zero, so will return $U(0, 1)$. The same holds for MWC60: setting the two seeds to zero will result in a stream of zeros. For the other generators it is difficult to see if zero is possible, but there seems to be no inherent reason why not. In that case, doing the conversion differently and adding a tiny offset, as suggested in Doornik (2005a), provides a solution (with the added benefit of being faster too).

22.2.3.3 Precision of uniform random numbers

Most simulations are implemented in double precision, but run with much more limited precision: the 64-bit floating point value provides for a mantissa of 53 bits, but the conversion discussed in section 22.2.3.2 uses only 32. In decimal terms, this corresponds roughly to using only about 9–10 digits of the available 15–16. One can envisage situations, such as randomized searches or maximization, where this matters.

One solution would be to use an RNG that uses double precision throughout (Marsaglia and Tsang, 2004), avoiding the use of integers. Another solution is to use two 32-bit integers: 32 bits from the first, and 20 from the second to allow 52 bits of significance. Efficient implementation of this for MWC8222 is roughly as fast as the standard (but inefficient) implementation of dividing a single unsigned integer by 2^{32} (Doornik, 2005a).

In other words, the uniform random numbers that are generated on the computer are not really continuous, but are drawn on the grid $[\varepsilon, 2\varepsilon, \ldots, 1 - \varepsilon]$, where $\varepsilon = 2^{-32} = 2.32830643653870 \times 10^{-10}$. The proposal of Doornik (2005a) refines the grid to $\varepsilon = 2^{-52} = 2.22044604925031 \times 10^{-16}$. These limits are reflected in the non-uniform RNGs, depending on the transformation method that is used. For example, the approximate limits for the standard normal RNG are:

Method	Precision	Minimum	Maximum
inversion	32 bits	− 6.23	6.23
inversion	52 bits	− 8.12	8.12
ziggurat	32 bits	− 9.89	9.89
ziggurat	52 bits	− 11.9	11.9

The ziggurat implementation used here is based on a partition into 128 blocks, with the tail block starting at 3.44. Therefore, 7 additional random bits are needed to decide on the particular box, while the 32 (or 52) bits can be used entirely in the tail, resulting in higher limits than straightforward inversion.

22.3 Monte Carlo methods in econometrics

22.3.1 Introduction

For a given and fixed numerical choice of the parameters determining the data generation process, a random sample of size T on the variables in the model is then drawn from that DGP, and the modeling methods and/or statistics of interest are calculated from the resulting sample of artificial data. A Monte Carlo experiment involves repeating this process many times (M say) in order to create a large Monte Carlo sample on the behavior of the relevant statistics, where M is called the number of replications or the Monte Carlo sample size. The empirical distributions of the statistics based on the artificial data then simulate the actual, but unknown, theoretical distributions which we seek.

Following Hendry (1984), we use the AR(1) process as an example:

- The **data generation process** is:

$$y_t = \alpha y_{t-1} + \varepsilon_t \quad \text{with } \varepsilon_t \sim \text{IN} \, [0, \sigma_\varepsilon^2], \tag{22.10}$$

  where $|\alpha| < 1$, and $t = 0, \dots, T$.
- The **econometric relationship of interest** is:

$$y_t = \alpha y_{t-1} + u_t \quad \text{with } u_t \sim \text{IN} \, [0, \sigma^2], \tag{22.11}$$

  which is the same as the DGP, except for the absence of the restriction on α when using OLS.

The objective of the experiment could be to understand the finite sample properties of the OLS estimator $\hat{\alpha}$ of α. The Monte Carlo **design variables** are then $\psi = (\alpha, \sigma_\varepsilon^2)'$ and the econometric sample size is T.

Notice that σ is an invariant here as the intercept is zero. It is usually the case in stationary DGPs that the outcomes do not fundamentally depend on the scale. Such invariance arguments provide a valuable simplification of the Monte Carlo experiment by reducing the parameter space over which we may wish to simulate.

22.3.2   Simple Monte Carlo

A simple Monte Carlo, in which we directly compute the statistic of interest, and average it over M replications, is convenient, but naïve. At best it has an accuracy which improves at a rate of $M^{-1/2}$ for a given sample size T. This generates rapid improvements for little cost initially (e.g., consider an increase in M from 25 to 100 replications: accuracy doubles on average). However, high accuracy is hard to achieve, especially for (say) test powers where the probability of a rejection is p, and the usual average of the binary estimator (unity if reject, zero otherwise) has a standard error of $s = [p(1-p)/M]^{1/2}$. For example, if $p = 0.05$, then the asymptotic standard error is 0.0022 for $M = 10,000$, so that a 95 percent confidence interval around the estimated p is about 17 percent of p. Whether there is an interest in deriving more efficient methods, such as those introduced below, depends on the relative costs of computer time versus labour as well as the objective of the study.

22.3.3   Enhancing the efficiency of Monte Carlo experiments

Variance reduction techniques are used to get more precise Monte Carlo estimates for a certain amount of computational power. The cost is the additional effort required in designing and implementing the more sophisticated experiment.

22.3.3.1   Antithetic variates

Antithetic variates involve a second estimator, whose variability offsets that of the first. Consider, for example, the simple case where the DGP and econometric model are a normal regression with just an intercept, in the former fixed at μ, in the latter estimated. The simple estimate from T observations using normal random numbers ε_i is $\hat{\mu}_1 = \mu + T^{-1}\sum_{i=1}^{T}\varepsilon_i$. Because ε_i is just as likely to happen as $-\varepsilon_i$, a second estimator $\hat{\mu}_2$ can be based on that. The average of this is μ with variance zero, and only two replications were needed to show this.

Antithetic variates can be used to establish the unbiasedness of some estimators which are too complex to analyze algebraically, and are members of a class of sophisticated Monte Carlo methods called variance reduction techniques (see, for example, Hammersley and Handscomb, 1964; Hendry and Trivedi, 1972; and Hendry, 1984). Unfortunately, antithetic variates obtained by changing the sign of the random numbers do not always work well, even for symmetric distributions. For example, the estimate of the autoregressive coefficient α in an AR(1) model is unchanged by such a sign change, making this form of antithetic variate useless.

22.3.3.2 Control variables

An alternative approach to variance reduction is provided by the method of control variables. The reason for using Monte Carlo to study the distribution of (say) the OLS estimator in (22.10) and (22.11) is the mathematical intractability of deriving exact sampling results, due to the dependence between the numerator and denominator of the OLS estimate. That does not entail that all aspects of the problem are intractable.

Continuing with the AR(1) example, the distribution of the OLS estimator of α in the econometric model is:

$$\hat{\alpha} = \sum_{t=1}^{T} y_t y_{t-1} \Big/ \sum_{t=1}^{T} y_{t-1}^2 = \alpha + \sum_{t=1}^{T} y_{t-1}\varepsilon_t \Big/ \sum_{t=1}^{T} y_{t-1}^2, \tag{22.12}$$

with asymptotic distribution:

$$\sqrt{T}(\hat{\alpha} - \alpha) \xrightarrow{D} N\,[0, (1 - \alpha^2)]. \tag{22.13}$$

Now define the control variable $\tilde{\alpha}$, defined by:

$$\tilde{\alpha} = \alpha + T^{-1}\sum_{t=1}^{T} y_{t-1}\varepsilon_t / [\sigma^2/(1 - \alpha^2)]. \tag{22.14}$$

We can calculate $\tilde{\alpha}$ in a Monte Carlo, since we know, or can generate, all of its components, even though we could not calculate it in any practical econometric analysis where (α,σ) and $\{\varepsilon_t\}$ are unknown. The construction of $\tilde{\alpha}$ is based on $\hat{\alpha}$, but replaces the denominator of the latter by its population value, scaled to the relevant sample size T.

Three important consequences follow. First, it follows from (22.14) that, in the Monte Carlo, $\tilde{\alpha}$ is an unbiased estimator of α. With some algebra, it can be shown that:

$$V[\tilde{\alpha}] = (1 - \alpha^2)/T.$$

Hence, from Cramér's theorem, $\sqrt{T}(\tilde{\alpha} - \alpha)$ has the same limiting distribution as $\sqrt{T}(\hat{\alpha} - \alpha)$. Consequently:

$$\sqrt{T}(\hat{\alpha} - \tilde{\alpha}) \xrightarrow{P} 0.$$

In fact, for the present problem (and usually true for stationary processes), $(\hat{\alpha} - \tilde{\alpha})$ is $O_p(T^{-1})$, so that is the approximate rate at which their difference vanishes. This contrasts with the original formulation in terms of $(\hat{\alpha} - \alpha)$, which is $O_p(T^{-1/2})$. Finally, in the identity:

$$\hat{\alpha} \equiv \tilde{\alpha} + (\hat{\alpha} - \tilde{\alpha}), \tag{22.15}$$

the first term on the right has a known expectation, and the second is $O_p(1/T)$. Thus, a more precise outcome can be obtained by calculating $\hat{\alpha}$ and $\tilde{\alpha}$ in every replication, recording their difference and at the completion of the replications adding back the known value of $\mathcal{E}[\tilde{\alpha}]$ (the expectation in the Monte Carlo), which corresponds to using the Monte Carlo estimator $\hat{\alpha}_c$:

$$\hat{\alpha}_c = \hat{\alpha} - \tilde{\alpha} + \alpha. \tag{22.16}$$

An alternative interpretation of the role of control variables is to note that (22.14) defines a function of the $\{\varepsilon_t\}$ which can help control for variation in the Monte Carlo due to the particular random numbers generated. That notion is similar to the role of antithetic variates above and, continuing that reasoning, we see that (writing $\mathcal{V}, \mathcal{C}$ for the variance and covariance in the Monte Carlo experiment):

$$\mathcal{V}[\hat{\alpha}_c] = \mathcal{V}[\hat{\alpha} - \tilde{\alpha}] = \mathcal{V}[\hat{\alpha}] + \mathcal{V}[\tilde{\alpha}] - 2\mathcal{C}[\hat{\alpha}, \tilde{\alpha}] \leq \mathcal{V}[\hat{\alpha}], \tag{22.17}$$

if:

$$\mathcal{V}[\tilde{\alpha}] \leq 2\mathcal{C}[\hat{\alpha}, \tilde{\alpha}].$$

The variance of the controlled experiment will be less than that of the uncontrolled if the correlation between $\hat{\alpha}$ and $\tilde{\alpha}$ is sufficiently high, which it must be for large enough T from Cramér's theorem (see, e.g., Sargan, 1988).

There is a close link between control variates and asymptotic distribution theory in the above approach. In effect, the control variable simulates the limiting distribution directly in finite samples. Other functions of the $\{\varepsilon_t\}$ than those based on Cramér's theorem could be used to control the experimental variation, but may not yield large improvements in precision. Ripley (1987) and Davidson and MacKinnon (1992) consider the use of control variables whose effects can be estimated by inter-replication regression, rather than having a known coefficient of unity as in (22.15) above.

22.3.3.3 Common random numbers

An example of the use of common random numbers is where we study two different estimators and apply them to the identical artificial data set. Using common random numbers was already standard practice in early studies (such as Summers, 1965). The difference between two unbiased estimators remains an unbiased estimator of the difference, even if the estimators are dependent, but the variance of the estimated difference will be smaller if there is positive dependence. If sampling variation leads to over (under)-estimation in the first estimate, the dependence leads to a similar over (under)-estimation in the second estimate, so this contamination is reduced by examining their difference. Thus, positive dependence can be beneficial.

A second example is when we estimate at sample sizes $T = 50$ and 100 (say), using M replications. Then, common random numbers are used if, at each replication, the sample of size 50 corresponds to the first 50 observations of the sample for $T = 100$. This can be implemented without saving the random numbers, even when the experiments are run separately. In simple cases it is sufficient to always generate a data set for the maximum required sample size, and then only use a subset for the required T. An example is given in section 22.3.4.2.

22.3.4 Enhancing the generality of Monte Carlo experiments

The presenter of Monte Carlo results faces two challenges. The first is how to make the experiment less specific: the usual objective is not simply to calculate the properties of a distribution at a few points in the parameter space, but to come closer to the corresponding mathematical analysis by providing results that are applicable to the complete parameter space.

The second challenge is how to present the output. Tabulation is possible, but is both hard to remember and not conducive to general findings – graphical presentation of the results is usually much more incisive. The need to summarize, and the aim of simulation itself, both motivate a more general technique known as response surfaces.

22.3.4.1 *Response surfaces*

The DGP is the joint density of the observables given the parameters, and for different parameter values, different samples of observables result. In turn, the distributions of statistics of interest depend on the parameters of the DGP. A response surface provides a parametric approximation to the variability over the Monte Carlo parameter space (which normally includes the sample size).

For example, the expected value of the OLS estimator from (22.12) depends on α and T, and can be written as the conditional expectation:

$$E\left[\hat{\alpha} \mid \alpha, T\right] = G(\alpha, T). \tag{22.18}$$

In principle, σ might also matter, but it does not do so here. Thus, the objective of Monte Carlo studies of finite-sample behavior of statistics is to numerically establish functions like $G(\alpha, T)$.

We know the large-sample behavior of the OLS estimator of α from (22.13), so the limiting form of the function $G(\cdot)$ can be deduced, and this can aid formulating the response surface approximating $G(\alpha, T)$. Specifically, since $\hat{\alpha}$; is consistent for α and has a symmetric asymptotic distribution, a first approximation to the unknown function $G(\alpha, T)$ in (22.18) might take the form $H(\alpha, T)$, where:

$$H(\alpha, T) = \alpha + \gamma_1 \frac{\alpha}{T} + \gamma_2 \frac{\alpha}{T^2} + \cdots$$
$$\approx G(\alpha, T).$$

(22.19)

The form of $H(\alpha, T)$ ensures consistency because $H(\alpha, T) \to \alpha$ as $T \to \infty$, and asymptotic unbiasedness because $T^{1/2}[H(\alpha, T) - \alpha] \to 0$ as $T \to \infty$. Given simulation results from a set of experiments across a range of values of α and T, the unknown γ_i could be estimated by regression of the (observed) Monte Carlo estimates of $E[\hat{\alpha}]$ on $\alpha, \alpha/T, \alpha/T^2$, etc. For example, Hendry (1984) reports a response surface for $H(\alpha, T)$ as $[\alpha - 1.8\alpha/(T+2)]$.

Response surfaces for higher-order moments, test powers, etc., can be developed in a similar fashion: see, e.g. Hendry (1984) and Doornik and Hendry (2001, chapter 15).

Other approaches to response surfaces are possible. For example, Doornik (1998) uses the Gamma distribution to approximate the asymptotic distribution of I(1) and I(2) cointegration tests. Values for the two parameters (the mean and variance) are determined by response surfaces. This approach is convenient, because p values and quantiles can be computed easily. Boswijk and Doornik (2005) extend this to the case with stationary regressors using theoretical results for the mean and variance of correlated Brownian motions. This replaces more than twenty pages of tables with a small set of approximations that are much more general and accurate.

22.3.4.2 Recursive Monte Carlo

The second important specificity of the experiments is analyzing only one sample size T. This limitation can be overcome by a different approach, known as recursive Monte Carlo (see Hendry and Neale, 1987). Instead of simply calculating the Monte Carlo at the largest sample size T, it is possible to compute all the relevant statistics recursively as the sample is generated, from T_0 (the smallest feasible sample size of interest) up to T. This approach facilitates the use of recursive updating techniques for estimators to reduce the amount of computation. However, the extra effort required for that is rarely justified nowadays, and it is therefore more efficient to select a set of sample sizes instead (for example, growing 25 observations at a time for small samples, and then taking larger steps).

By using common random numbers, we obtain a proper recursive Monte Carlo: the first 25 observations for $T_i = 50$ (say), are precisely the observations used for $T_i = 25$. As a consequence, successive results are not independent and so are not equivalent to conducting separate experiments. However, they will act as a variance reduction technique. By using the same stream of random numbers as T_i varies, the estimate of the outcome difference between T_j and ($j > i$) will have lower variance than if separate independent streams of random numbers were used.

22.4 Conclusion

While the principles of Monte Carlo have changed little, the practice has changed enormously under the influence of technological change. This chapter has focussed on recent advances in random number generation. Very-high period generators based on binary autoregressions or of the multiply-with-carry type are ready to supersede the traditional linear congruential generators. They have much higher period, appear to be more random, and are not much slower.

From the teaching perspective, with graphical computer facilities, recursive Monte Carlo procedures offer excellent classroom demonstrations of absolute and comparative properties of estimators and tests, under correct and incorrect specifications, as the sample size varies from very small to fairly large.

Acknowledgments

This research was supported by ESRC grant RES-000-23-0539. Helpful comments and suggestions from David Hendry are gratefully acknowledged.

Note

1. A floating point number on the computer takes 8 bytes, which is 64 bits. All modern hardware follows the IEEE standard, with a 53-bit mantissa (normalized, so stored in 52 bits), 10 bit exponent plus one bit for the sign. This corresponds to 15 to 16 significant digits when using decimal representation.

References

Bailey, D.H. and R.E. Crandall (2001) On the random character of fundamental constant expansions. *Experimental Mathematics* **10**, 175–90.

Boswijk, H.P. and J.A. Doornik (2005) Distribution approximations for cointegration tests with stationary exogenous regressors. *Journal of Applied Econometrics* **20**, 797–810.

Box, G.E.P. and M.E. Muller (1958) A note on the generation of random normal deviates. *Annals of Mathematical Statistics* **29**, 610–11.

Chambers, E.A. and D.R. Cox, (1967) Discrimination between alternative binary response models. *Biometrika* **54**, 573–8.

Coddington, P.D. (1996) Random number generators for parallel computers. *The NHSE Review* 2. Version 1.1, April 1997, www.crpc.rice.edu/NHSEreview/RNG/.

Davidson, R. and J.G. MacKinnon (1992) Regression-based methods for using control variates in Monte Carlo experiments. *Journal of Econometrics* **54**, 203–22.

Davidson, R. and J.G. MacKinnon (1993) *Estimation and Inference in Econometrics*. New York: Oxford University Press.

Devroye, L. (1986) *Non-Uniform Random Variate Generation*. New York: Springer-Verlag.

Doornik, J.A. (1998) Approximations to the asymptotic distribution of cointegration tests. *Journal of Economic Surveys* **12**, 573–93. Reprinted in M. McAleer and L. Oxley (eds) (1999) *Practical Issues in Cointegration Analysis*. Oxford: Blackwell Publishers.

Doornik, J.A. (2002) Object-oriented programming in econometrics and statistics using Ox: a comparison with C++, Java and C#. In S.S. Nielsen (ed.), *Programming Languages and Systems in Computational Economics and Finance*. Dordrecht: Kluwer Academic Publishers, pp. 115–47.

Doornik, J.A. (2005a) Conversion of high-period random numbers to floating point. Mimeo, Nuffield College.

Doornik, J.A. (2005b) An improved ziggurat method to generate normal random samples. Mimeo, Nuffield College.

Doornik, J.A. and D.F. Hendry (2001) *Interactive Monte Carlo Experimentation in Econometrics Using PcNaive*. London: Timberlake Consultants Press.

Doornik, J.A., D.F. Hendry and N. Shephard (2002) Computationally-intensive econometrics using a distributed matrix-programming language. *Philosophical Transactions of the Royal Society of London, Series A* **360**, 1245–1266.

Fishman, G.S. and L.R. Moore (1982) A statistical evaluation of multiplicative congruential random number generators with modules $2^{31} - 1$. *Journal of the American Statistical Association* **77**, 129–36.

Gentle, J.E. (1998) *Random Number Generation and Monte Carlo Methods*. New York: Springer-Verlag.

Hammersley, J.M. and D.C. Handscomb (1964) *Monte Carlo Methods*. London: Chapman and Hall.

Hendry, D.F. (1984) Monte Carlo experimentation in econometrics. In Z. Griliches and M.D. Intriligator (eds), *Handbook of Econometrics*, vol. 2–3. Amsterdam: North-Holland, pp. 937–76.

Hendry, D.F. (1990) Using PC-NAIVE in teaching econometrics. *Oxford Bulletin of Economics and Statistics* **53**, 199–223.

Hendry, D.F. and A.J. Neale (1987) Monte Carlo experimentation using PC-NAIVE. In T. Fomby and G.F. Rhodes (eds), *Advances in Econometrics*, vol. 6. Greenwich, CT: JAI Press Inc, pp. 91–125.

Hendry, D.F., A.J. Neale and N.R. Ericsson (1991) *PC-NAIVE: An Interactive Program for Monte Carlo Experimentation in Econometrics. Version 6.0.* Oxford: Institute of Economics and Statistics, University of Oxford.

Hendry, D.F. and P.K. Trivedi (1972) Maximum likelihood estimation of difference equations with moving-average errors: A simulation study. *Review of Economic Studies* **32**, 117–45.

Johnson, N.L., S. Kotz and N. Balakrishnan (1994) *Continuous Univariate Distributions – 1*, 2nd edn. New York: John Wiley.

Knuth, D.E. (1998) *The Art of Computer Programming. Volume 2: Seminumerical Algorithms*, 3rd edn. Reading, MA: Addison Wesley.

L'Ecuyer, P. (1996) Maximally equidistributed combined tausworthe generators. *Mathematics of Computation* **65**, 203–13.

L'Ecuyer, P. (1997) Uniform random number generators: A review. In *Proceedings of the 1997 Winter Simulation Conference*. IEEE Press, pp. 127–34. www.informs-cs.org/wsc97papers.

L'Ecuyer, P. (1999) Tables of maximally-equidistributed combined LFSR generators. *Mathematics of Computation* **68**, 261–9.

L'Ecuyer, P. and R. Simard (2005) Testu01. A software library in ANSI C for empirical testing of random number generators. Mimeo, University of Montreal, Canada.

Marsaglia, G. (1964) Generating a variable from the tail of the normal distribution. *Technometrics* **6**, 101–2.

Marsaglia, G. (1995) The Marsaglia random number cdrom including the diehard battery of tests of randomness. Mimeo, University of Florida, stat.fsu.edu/pub/diehard/.

Marsaglia, G. (1997) A random number generator for C. Posting, Usenet newsgroup sci.stat.math. 29-Sep-1997.

Marsaglia, G. (2003a) Re: good C random number generator. Posting, Usenet newsgroup sci.lang.c. 13-May-2003.

Marsaglia, G. (2003b) Seeds for random number generators. *Communications of the ACM* **46**, 90–3.

Marsaglia, G. and T.A. Bray (1964) A convenient method for generating random normal variables. *SIAM Review* **6**, 260–4.

Marsaglia, G. and W.W. Tsang (1984) A fast, easily implemented method for sampling from decreasing or symmetric unimodal density functions. *SIAM Journal on Scientific and Statistical Computing* **5**, 349–59.

Marsaglia, G. and W.W. Tsang (2000) The ziggurat method for generating random variables. *Journal of Statistical Software* **5**, 1–7. www.jstatsoft.org.

Marsaglia, G. and W.W. Tsang (2004) The 64-bit universal RNG. *Statistics & Probability Letters* 66, 183–7.

Marshall, A.W. (1954) An introductory note. In H.A. Meyer (ed), *Symposium on Monte Carlo Methods*. New York: John Wiley & Sons, pp. 1–14.

Mascagni, M. and A. Srinivasan (2000) Algorithm 806: SPRNG: A scalable library for pseudorandom number generation. *ACM Transactions on Mathematical Software* 26, 436–61.

Matsumoto, M. and T. Nishimura (1998) Mersenne Twister: A 623-dimensionally equidistributed uniform pseudorandom number generator. *ACM Transactions on Modeling and Computer Simulation* 8, 3–30.

Panneton, F., P. L'Ecuyer and M. Matsumoto (2005) Improved long-period generators based on linear recurrences modulo 2. *ACM Transactions on Mathematical Software*, forthcoming.

Park, S.K. and K.W. Miller (1988) Random number generators: good ones are hard to find. *Communications of the ACM* 31, 1192–1201.

Park, S.K., K.W. Miller and P.K. Stockmeyer (1993) Response. *Communications of the ACM* 36, 108–10.

Press, W.H., B.P. Flannery, S.A. Teukolsky and W.T. Vetterling (1993) *Numerical Recipes in C*, 2nd edn. New York: Cambridge University Press.

Ripley, B.D. (1987) *Stochastic Simulation*. New York: John Wiley & Sons.

Sargan, J.D. (1988) *Lectures on Advanced Econometric Theory*. Oxford: Basil Blackwell.

SCAN (1999) Parallel random number generators. *Scientific Computing at NPACI*, vol. 3, March 31, www.npaci.edu/online/v3.7/SCAN1.html.

Smith, K.A., S.F. Reddaway and D.M. Scott (1985) Very high performance pseudo-random number generation on DAP. *Computer Physics Communications* 37, 239–44.

Stigler, S.M. (1991) Stochastic simulation in the nineteenth century. *Statistical Science* 6, 89–97. Reprinted in S.M. Stigler (1999), *Statistics on the Table*. Cambridge, MA: Harvard University Press.

Student (1908a) On the probable error of the mean. *Biometrika* 6, 1–25.

Student (1908b) Probable error of a correlation coefficient. *Biometrika* 6, 302–10.

Summers, R. (1965) A capital intensive approach to the small sample properties of various simultaneous equation estimators. *Econometrica* 33, 1–41.

Teichrow, D. (1965) A history of distribution sampling prior to the era of the computer and its relevance to simulation. *Journal of the American Statistical Association* 60, 27–49.

Tocher, K.D. (1963) *The Art of Simulation*. London: English Universities Press.

Wallace, C.S. (1996) Fast pseudorandom generators for normal and exponential variates. *ACM Transactions on Mathematical Software* 22, 119–27.

Yule, G.U. (1926) Why do we sometimes get nonsense-correlations between time-series? A study in sampling and the nature of time series (with discussion). *Journal of the Royal Statistical Society* 89, 1–64.

23
Bootstrap Methods in Econometrics

Russell Davidson and James G. MacKinnon

Abstract

Although it is common to refer to "the bootstrap," there are actually a great many different bootstrap methods that can be used in econometrics. We emphasize the use of bootstrap methods for inference, particularly hypothesis testing, and we also discuss bootstrap confidence intervals. There are important cases in which bootstrap inference tends to be more accurate than asymptotic inference. However, it is not always easy to generate bootstrap samples in a way that makes bootstrap inference even asymptotically valid.

23.1	Introduction	812
23.2	Monte Carlo tests	814
23.3	The parametric bootstrap	817
23.4	Bootstrap DGPs based on resampling	820
23.5	Heteroskedasticity	821
23.6	Covariance matrices and bias correction	825
23.7	More than one dependent variable	826
23.8	Bootstrap DGPs for dependent data	828
23.9	Confidence intervals	831
23.10	The performance of bootstrap methods	834

23.1 Introduction

When we perform a hypothesis test in econometrics, we reject the null hypothesis if the test statistic is unlikely to have occurred by chance for the distribution that it should follow under the null. Traditionally, this distribution is obtained by theoretical methods. In many cases, we use asymptotic distributions that are strictly valid only if the sample size is infinitely large. In others, such as the classical normal linear regression model with its associated t and F statistics, we use finite-sample distributions that depend on very strong distributional assumptions.

Bootstrap methods, which have become increasingly popular in econometrics during the last decade as the cost of computation has fallen dramatically, provide an alternative way of obtaining the distributions to which test statistics are to be compared. The idea is to generate a large number of simulated *bootstrap samples*, use each of them to calculate a *bootstrap test statistic*, and then compare the actual test statistic with the empirical distribution of the bootstrap statistics. When the latter provides a good approximation to the unknown true distribution of the test statistic under the null hypothesis, bootstrap tests should lead to accurate inferences. In some cases, they lead to very much more accurate inferences than using asymptotic distributions in the traditional way.

Because of the close connection between hypothesis tests and confidence intervals, we can also obtain *bootstrap confidence intervals*. The ends of a confidence interval generally depend on the quantiles of the distribution that some test statistic is supposed to follow. We "invert" the test to find the interval that contains all the parameter values that would not be rejected by the test. One way to construct a bootstrap confidence interval is to use the quantiles of the empirical distribution of a set of bootstrap test statistics instead of the quantiles of a theoretical distribution.

In the next section, we discuss the basic ideas of bootstrap testing for the special case in which the bootstrap statistics follow exactly the same distribution as the actual test statistic under the null hypothesis. We show that, in this special case, it is possible to perform a *Monte Carlo test* that is exact, in the sense that the actual probability of Type I error is equal to the nominal significance level of the test. This is an important result, in part because there are valuable applications of Monte Carlo tests in econometrics, and in part because this case serves as a benchmark for bootstrap tests more generally.

In most cases, it is impossible to find a *bootstrap data-generating process*, or *bootstrap DGP*, such that the bootstrap statistics follow exactly the same distribution as the actual test statistic under the null hypothesis. In section 23.3, we discuss the *parametric bootstrap*, for which the bootstrap DGP is completely characterized by a set of parameters that can be consistently estimated. We show that, under mild regularity conditions likely to be satisfied in many cases of interest in econometrics, the error in rejection probability (ERP) of a parametric bootstrap test, that is, the difference between the true probability of rejecting a true null hypothesis and the nominal level, tends to zero as the sample size tends to infinity faster than does the ERP of conventional asymptotic tests.

In sections 23.4–23.8, we discuss various methods for the construction of bootstrap DGPs that are applicable to a variety of problems in econometrics. In our view, this is where the principal impediments to the widespread adoption of bootstrap methods lie. Methods that work well for some problems may be invalid or may perform poorly for others. Econometricians face a great many challenges in devising bootstrap DGPs that will lead to accurate inferences for many of the models that we commonly estimate.

In section 23.9, we extend the methods of bootstrap testing discussed earlier in the chapter to the construction of confidence intervals. Finally, section 23.10 contains a general discussion of the accuracy of bootstrap methods and some concluding remarks.

23.2   Monte Carlo tests

The simplest type of bootstrap test, and the only type that can be exact in finite samples, is called a *Monte Carlo test*. This type of test was first proposed by Dwass (1957). Monte Carlo tests are available whenever a test statistic is *pivotal*. Let τ denote a statistic intended to test a given null hypothesis. By *hypothesis* we mean a set of DGPs that satisfy some condition or conditions that we wish to test. Then the statistic τ is pivotal for this null hypothesis if and only if, for each possible fixed sample size, the distribution of τ is the same for all of the DGPs that satisfy the hypothesis. Such a test statistic is said to be a *pivot*.

Suppose we compute a realization $\hat{\tau}$ of a pivotal test statistic using real data, and then compute B independent bootstrap test statistics $\tau_j^*, j = 1, \ldots, B$, using data simulated using any DGP that satisfies the null hypothesis. Since τ is a pivot, it follows that the τ_j^* and $\hat{\tau}$ are independent drawings from one and the same distribution, *provided* that the true DGP, the one that generated $\hat{\tau}$, also satisfies the null hypothesis.

Imagine that we wish to perform a test at significance level α, where α might, for example, be .05 or .01, and reject the null hypothesis when the value of $\hat{\tau}$ is unusually large. Given the actual and simulated test statistics, we can compute a *bootstrap P value* as

$$\hat{p}^*(\hat{\tau}) = \frac{1}{B} \sum_{j=1}^{B} \mathrm{I}(\tau_j^* > \hat{\tau}), \tag{23.1}$$

where $\mathrm{I}(\cdot)$ is the *indicator function*, with value 1 when its argument is true and 0 otherwise. Evidently, $\hat{p}^*(\hat{\tau})$ is just the fraction of the bootstrap samples for which τ_j^* is larger than $\hat{\tau}$. If this fraction is smaller than α, we reject the null hypothesis. This makes sense, since $\hat{\tau}$ is extreme relative to the empirical distribution of the τ_j^* when $\hat{p}^*(\hat{\tau})$ is small.

Now suppose that we sort the original test statistic $\hat{\tau}$ and the B bootstrap statistics τ_j^* in decreasing order. Define the rank r of $\hat{\tau}$ in the sorted set in such a way that there are exactly r simulations for which $\tau_j^* > \hat{\tau}$. Then r can have $B + 1$ possible values, $r = 0, 1, \ldots, B$, all of them equally likely under the null. The estimated P value $\hat{p}^*(\hat{\tau})$ is then just r/B.

The Monte Carlo test rejects if $r/B < \alpha$, that is, if $r < \alpha B$. Under the null, the probability that this inequality is satisfied is the proportion of the $B + 1$ possible values of r that satisfy it. If we denote by $[\alpha B]$ the largest integer that is smaller than αB, there are exactly $[\alpha B] + 1$ such values of r, namely, $0, 1, \ldots, [\alpha B]$. Thus the probability of rejection is $([\alpha B] + 1)/(B + 1)$. We want this probability to be exactly equal to α. For that to be true, we require that

$$\alpha(B + 1) = [\alpha B] + 1.$$

Since the right-hand side above is the sum of two integers, this equality can hold only if $\alpha(B + 1)$ is also an integer. In fact, it is easy to see that the equation holds whenever $\alpha(B + 1)$ is an integer. In that case, therefore, the rejection probability under the null, that is, the Type I error of the test, is precisely α, the desired significance level.

Of course, using simulation injects randomness into this test procedure, and the cost of this randomness is a loss of power. A test based on $B = 99$ simulations will be less powerful than a test based on $B = 199$, which in turn will be less powerful than one based on $B = 299$, and so on; see Jöckel (1986) and Davidson and MacKinnon (2000). Notice that all of these values of B have the property that $\alpha(B + 1)$ is an integer whenever α is an integer percentage like .01, .05, or .10.

For an example of a Monte Carlo test, consider the classical normal linear regression model

$$y_t = X_t\beta + u_t, \quad u_t \sim \text{NID}(0, \sigma^2), \tag{23.2}$$

where there are n observations, β is a k-vector, and the $1 \times k$ vector of regressors X_t, which is the tth row of the $n \times k$ matrix X, is treated as fixed. Every DGP belonging to this model is completely characterized by the values of the parameter vector β and the variance σ^2. Thus any test statistic the distribution of which does not depend on these values is a pivot for the hypothesis that (23.2) is correctly specified. In particular, a statistic that depends on y only through the OLS residuals and is invariant to the scale of y is pivotal. To see this, note that the vector of OLS residuals is $\hat{u} = M_X y = M_X u$, where M_X is the orthogonal projection matrix $I - X(X^\top X)^{-1}X^\top$. Thus $\hat{u}$ is unchanged if the value of β changes, and a change in the variance σ^2 changes $\hat{u}$ only by a scale factor of σ.

One such pivotal test statistic is the estimated autoregressive parameter $\hat{\rho}$ that is obtained by regressing the tth residual $\hat{u}_t$ on its predecessor $\hat{u}_{t-1}$. The estimate $\hat{\rho}$ can be used as a test for serial correlation of the error terms in (23.2). Evidently,

$$\hat{\rho} = \frac{\sum_{t=2}^{n} \hat{u}_{t-1}\hat{u}_t}{\sum_{t=2}^{n} \hat{u}_{t-1}^2}. \tag{23.3}$$

Since $\hat{u}_t$ is proportional to σ, there are implicitly two factors of σ in the numerator and two in the denominator of (23.3). Thus $\hat{\rho}$ is independent of the scale factor σ.

Of course, the distribution of $\hat{\rho}$ *does* depend on the regressor matrix X. But recall that we assumed that X is fixed in the definition of the model (23.2). This means that it is the same for every DGP in the model. With this definition, then, $\hat{\rho}$ is indeed pivotal. If we are unwilling to assume that X is a fixed matrix, then we can interpret (23.2) as a model defined conditional on X, in which case $\hat{\rho}$ is pivotal conditional on X.

The fact that $\hat{\rho}$ is a pivot means that we can perform an exact Monte Carlo test of the hypothesis that $\rho = 0$ without knowing the distribution of $\hat{\rho}$. The bootstrap DGP used to generate simulated samples can be any DGP in the model (23.2), and so we may choose the simplest such model, which has $\beta = 0$ and $\sigma^2 = 1$. This bootstrap DGP can be written as

$$y_t^* = \varepsilon_t^*, \quad \varepsilon_t^* \sim \text{NID}(0, 1).$$

For each of B bootstrap samples, we then proceed as follows:

1. Generate the vector y^* as an n-vector of IID standard normal variables.
2. Regress y^* on X and save the vector of residuals $\hat{u}^*$.
3. Compute ρ^* by regressing $\hat{u}_t^*$ on $\hat{u}_{t-1}^*$ for observations 2 through n.

Denote by $\rho_j^*, j = 1, \ldots, B$, the bootstrap statistics obtained by performing the above three steps B times. We now have to choose the alternative to our null hypothesis of no serial correlation. If the alternative is positive serial correlation, then, analogously to (23.1), we perform a one-tailed test by computing the bootstrap P value as

$$\hat{p}^*(\hat{\rho}) = \frac{1}{B} \sum_{j=1}^{B} I(\rho_j^* > \hat{\rho}).$$

This P value is small when $\hat{\rho}$ is positive and sufficiently large, thereby indicating positive serial correlation. However, we may wish to test against both positive and negative serial correlation. In that case, there are two possible ways to compute a P value corresponding to a two-tailed test. The first is to assume that the distribution of $\hat{\rho}$ is symmetric, in which case we can use the bootstrap P value

$$\hat{p}^*(\hat{\rho}) = \frac{1}{B} \sum_{j=1}^{B} I(|\rho_j^*| > |\hat{\rho}|). \tag{23.4}$$

This is implicitly a symmetric two-tailed test, since we reject when the fraction of the ρ_j^* that exceed $\hat{\rho}$ in absolute value is small. Alternatively, if we do not assume symmetry, we can use

$$\hat{p}^*(\hat{\rho}) = 2 \min \left(\frac{1}{B} \sum_{j=1}^{B} I(\rho_j^* \leq \hat{\rho}), \frac{1}{B} \sum_{j=1}^{B} I(\rho_j^* > \hat{\rho}) \right). \tag{23.5}$$

In this case, for level α, we reject whenever $\hat{\rho}$ is either below the $\alpha/2$ quantile or above the $1 - \alpha/2$ quantile of the empirical distribution of the ρ_j^*. Although tests based on these two P values are both exact, they may yield conflicting results, and their power against various alternatives will differ.

Many common test statistics for serial correlation, heteroskedasticity, skewness, and excess kurtosis in the classical normal linear regression model (23.2) are pivotal, since they depend on the regressand only through the least squares residuals $\hat{u}$ in a way that is invariant to the scale factor σ. The Durbin–Watson d statistic is a particularly well-known example. We can perform a Monte Carlo test based on d just as easily as a Monte Carlo test based on $\hat{\rho}$, and the two tests should give very similar results. Since we condition on X, the infamous upper and lower bounds from the classic tables of the d statistic are quite unnecessary.

With modern computers and appropriate software, it is extremely easy to perform a variety of exact tests in the context of the classical normal linear regression model. These procedures also work when the error terms follow a nonnormal distribution that is known up to a scale factor; we just have to use the appropriate distribution in step 1 above. For further references and a detailed treatment of Monte Carlo tests for heteroskedasticity, see Dufour, Khalaf, Bernard, and Genest (2004).

23.3 The parametric bootstrap

When a hypothesis is tested using a statistic that is not pivotal for that hypothesis, the bootstrap procedure described in the previous section does not lead to an exact Monte Carlo test. However, with a suitable choice of bootstrap DGP, inference that is often more accurate than that provided by conventional asymptotic tests can be performed by use of bootstrap P values. In this section, we focus on the *parametric bootstrap*, in which the bootstrap DGP is completely specified by one or more parameters, some of which have to be estimated.

Examples of the parametric bootstrap are encountered frequently when models are estimated by maximum likelihood. For fixed parameter values, a likelihood function is a probability density which fully characterizes a DGP. The aim of all bootstrap tests is to estimate the distribution of a test statistic under the DGP that generated it, provided that the DGP satisfies the null hypothesis. When a statistic is not pivotal, it is no longer a matter of indifference what DGP is used to generate simulated statistics. Instead, it is desirable to get as good an estimate as possible of the true DGP for the bootstrap DGP. In the context of the parametric bootstrap, this means that we want to estimate the unknown parameters of the true DGP as accurately as possible, since those estimates are used to define the bootstrap DGP.

Consider as an example the probit model, a binary choice model for which each observation y_t on the dependent variable is either 0 or 1. For this model,

$$\Pr(y_t = 1) = \Phi(X_t \boldsymbol{\beta}), \quad t = 1, \ldots, n, \tag{23.6}$$

where $\Phi(\cdot)$ is the cumulative distribution function (CDF) of the standard normal distribution, and X_t is a $1 \times k$ vector of explanatory variables, again treated as fixed. The parameter vector $\boldsymbol{\beta}$ is usually estimated by maximum likelihood (ML).

Suppose that $\boldsymbol{\beta}$ is partitioned into two subvectors, $\boldsymbol{\beta}_1$ and $\boldsymbol{\beta}_2$, and that we wish to test the hypothesis that $\boldsymbol{\beta}_2 = 0$. The first step in computing a parametric bootstrap P value is to estimate a restricted probit model in which $\boldsymbol{\beta}_2 = 0$, again by ML, so as to obtain restricted estimates $\tilde{\boldsymbol{\beta}}_1$. Next, we compute a suitable test statistic, which would usually be a Lagrange multiplier statistic, a likelihood ratio statistic, or a Wald statistic, although there are other possible choices.

The bootstrap DGP is defined by (23.6) with $\boldsymbol{\beta}_1 = \tilde{\boldsymbol{\beta}}_1$ and $\boldsymbol{\beta}_2 = 0$. Bootstrap samples can be generated easily as follows:

1. Compute the vector of values $X_{t1}\tilde{\boldsymbol{\beta}}_1$, where X_{t1} is the subvector of X_t that corresponds to the nonzero parameters $\boldsymbol{\beta}_1$.

2. For each bootstrap sample, generate a vector of random numbers $u_t^*, t = 1, \ldots, n$, drawn from the standard normal distribution.
3. Set the simulated y_t^* equal to 1 if $X_{t1}\hat{\boldsymbol{\beta}}_1 + u_t^* > 0$, and to 0 otherwise. By construction (23.6) is satisfied for the y_t^*.

For each bootstrap sample, a bootstrap statistic is then computed using exactly the same procedure as the one used to compute the test statistic with the real data. The bootstrap P value is the proportion of bootstrap statistics that are more extreme than the one from the real data. If $\boldsymbol{\beta}_2$ has only one component, the test could be performed using an asymptotic t statistic, and then it would be possible, as we saw in the previous section, to perform one-tailed tests.

Bootstrap DGPs similar to the one described above can be constructed whenever a set of parameter estimates is sufficient to characterize a DGP completely. This is the case for a wide variety of limited dependent variable models, including more complicated discrete choice models, count data models, and models with censoring, truncation, or sample selection. Hypotheses that can be tested are not restricted to hypotheses about the model parameters. Various specification tests, such as tests for heteroskedasticity or information matrix tests, can be carried out in just the same way.

Why should we expect that a parametric bootstrap test will lead to inference that is more reliable than conventional asymptotic inference? In fact, it does so only if the test statistic τ on which the test is based is *asymptotically pivotal*, which means that its asymptotic distribution, as the sample size $n \to \infty$, is the same for all DGPs that satisfy the null hypothesis. This is not a very strong condition. All statistics that are asymptotically standard normal, or asymptotically chi-squared with known degrees of freedom, or even distributed asymptotically as a Dickey–Fuller distribution, are asymptotically pivotal, since these asymptotic distributions depend on nothing that is specific to a particular DGP in the null hypothesis.

Let us define what in Davidson and MacKinnon (1999a) is called the *rejection probability function*, or *RPF*. The value of this function is the probability that a true null hypothesis is rejected by a test based on the asymptotic distribution of the statistic τ, as a function of the nominal level α and the parameter vector $\boldsymbol{\theta}$ that characterizes the true DGP. Thus the RPF $R(\alpha, \boldsymbol{\theta})$ satisfies the relation

$$R(\alpha, \boldsymbol{\theta}) = \Pr_{\boldsymbol{\theta}}(\tau \in \text{Rej}(\alpha)), \tag{23.7}$$

where $\text{Rej}(\alpha)$ is the rejection region for an asymptotic test at level α. We use this notation so as to be able to handle one-tailed and two-tailed tests simultaneously. The notation "$\Pr_{\boldsymbol{\theta}}$" indicates that we are evaluating the probability under the DGP characterized by $\boldsymbol{\theta}$. If τ were pivotal, R would not depend on $\boldsymbol{\theta}$.

Suppose now that we carry out a parametric bootstrap test using a realized test statistic $\hat{\tau}$ and a bootstrap DGP characterized by a parameter vector $\boldsymbol{\theta}^*$ that satisfies the null hypothesis. Let $\hat{p}$ be the *asymptotic P* value associated with $\hat{\tau}$; $\hat{p}$ is defined so that $\hat{\tau}$ is on the boundary of the rejection region $\text{Rej}(\hat{p})$. If we let the number B of bootstrap samples tend to infinity, then the bootstrap P value is $R(\hat{p}, \boldsymbol{\theta}^*)$. To see this, observe that this quantity is the probability, according to the bootstrap DGP associated with $\boldsymbol{\theta}^*$, that $\tau \in \text{Rej}(\hat{p})$. For large B, the proportion of bootstrap statistics more extreme than $\hat{\tau}$ tends to this probability.

By a first-order Taylor series approximation around the true parameter vector θ_0,

$$R(\hat{p}, \boldsymbol{\theta}^*) - R(\hat{p}, \boldsymbol{\theta}_0) \cong \boldsymbol{R}^\top(\hat{p}, \boldsymbol{\theta}_0)(\boldsymbol{\theta}^* - \boldsymbol{\theta}_0), \tag{23.8}$$

where $\boldsymbol{R}(\hat{p}, \boldsymbol{\theta})$ denotes a vector of derivatives of $R(\hat{p}, \boldsymbol{\theta})$ with respect to the elements of $\boldsymbol{\theta}$. The quantity $R(\hat{p}, \boldsymbol{\theta}_0)$ can be interpreted as the ideal P value that we would like to compute if it were possible to do so. Under the DGP associated with $\boldsymbol{\theta}_0$, the probability that $R(\hat{p}, \boldsymbol{\theta}_0)$ is less than α is exactly α. To see this, notice from (23.7) that

$$R(\alpha, \boldsymbol{\theta}) = \text{Pr}_\theta(\tau \in \text{Rej}(\alpha)) = \text{Pr}_\theta(p < \alpha),$$

where p is the asymptotic P value associated with τ. Thus, under the DGP characterized by θ_0, $R(\alpha, \boldsymbol{\theta}_0)$ is the CDF of p evaluated at α. The random variable $R(p, \boldsymbol{\theta}_0)$, of which $R(\hat{p}, \boldsymbol{\theta}_0)$ is a realization, is therefore distributed as $U(0,1)$.

Equation (23.8) tells us that the difference between the parametric bootstrap P value and the ideal P value is given approximately by the expression $\boldsymbol{R}^\top(\hat{p}, \boldsymbol{\theta}_0)(\boldsymbol{\theta}^* - \boldsymbol{\theta}_0)$. Since τ is asymptotically pivotal, the limit of the function $R(\alpha, \boldsymbol{\theta})$ as $n \to \infty$ does not depend on $\boldsymbol{\theta}$. Thus the derivatives in the vector $R(\alpha, \boldsymbol{\theta})$ tend to zero as $n \to \infty$, in regular cases with the same rate of convergence as that of $R(\alpha, \boldsymbol{\theta})$ to its limiting value. This latter rate of convergence is easily seen to be the rate at which the ERP of the asymptotic test tends to zero. The parameter estimates in the vector $\boldsymbol{\theta}^*$ are root-n consistent whenever they are obtained by ML or by any ordinary estimation method. Thus $\boldsymbol{R}^\top(\hat{p}, \boldsymbol{\theta}_0)(\boldsymbol{\theta}^* - \boldsymbol{\theta}_0)$, the expectation of which is approximately the ERP of the bootstrap test, tends to zero faster than the ERP of the asymptotic test by a factor of $n^{-1/2}$.

This heuristic argument provides some intuition as to why the parametric bootstrap, when used in conjunction with an asymptotically pivotal statistic, generally yields more reliable inferences than an asymptotic test based on the same statistic. See Beran (1988) for a more rigorous treatment. Whenever the ERP of a bootstrap test declines more rapidly as n increases than that of the asymptotic test on which it is based, the bootstrap test is said to offer *higher-order accuracy* than the asymptotic one, or to benefit from *asymptotic refinements*.

It is important to note that the left-hand side of (23.8), which is a random variable through the asymptotic P value $\hat{p}$, is not the ERP of the bootstrap test. The bootstrap ERP is rather the expectation of that random variable, which can be seen to depend on the joint distribution of the statistic τ and the estimates $\boldsymbol{\theta}^*$. In some cases, this expectation converges to zero as $n \to \infty$ at a rate even faster than the left-hand side of (23.8); see Davidson and MacKinnon (1999a) and Davidson and MacKinnon (2006) for more details.

Although the result just given is a very powerful one, it does not imply that a parametric bootstrap test will always be more accurate than the asymptotic test on which it is based. In some cases, an asymptotic test may just happen to perform extremely well even when n is quite small, and the corresponding bootstrap test may perform a little less well. In other cases, neither test may perform at all well in small samples, and the sample size may have to be quite large before the bootstrap test establishes its superiority.

23.4   Bootstrap DGPs based on resampling

The bootstrap, when it was first proposed by Efron (1979, 1982), was an entirely nonparametric procedure. The idea was to draw bootstrap samples from the empirical distribution function (EDF) of the data, a procedure that Efron called *resampling*. Since the EDF assigns probability $1/n$ to each point in the sample, this procedure amounts to drawing each observation of a bootstrap sample randomly, with replacement, from the original sample. Each bootstrap sample thus contains some of the original data points once, some of them more than once, and some of them not at all. Resampling evidently requires the assumption that the data are IID.

In regression models, it is unusual to suppose that the observations are IID. On the other hand, we often suppose that the error terms of a regression model are IID. We do not observe error terms, and so cannot resample them, but we can resample residuals, which are then interpreted as estimates of the error terms. As an example of a bootstrap DGP based on resampling, consider the dynamic linear regression model

$$y_t = X_t\boldsymbol{\beta} + \gamma y_{t-1} + u_t, \quad u_t \sim \text{IID}(0, \sigma^2), \tag{23.9}$$

in which we suppose that y_0 is observed, so that the regression can be run for observations 1 through n. Statistics used to test hypotheses about the parameters $\boldsymbol{\beta}$ and γ are not pivotal for this model. If we assume that the errors are normal, we can use a parametric bootstrap, as described below, but for the moment we are not willing to make that assumption.

We begin by estimating (23.9), subject to the restrictions we wish to test, by ordinary or nonlinear least squares, according to the nature of the restrictions. This gives us restricted estimates $\tilde{\boldsymbol{\beta}}$ and $\tilde{\gamma}$ and a vector of residuals, say $\tilde{\boldsymbol{u}}$. If there is a constant or its equivalent in the regression, then the mean of the elements of $\tilde{u}$ is zero. If not, then it is necessary to center these elements by subtracting their mean, since one of the key assumptions of any regression model is that the errors have an expectation of 0. If we were to resample a set of uncentered residuals, the bootstrap DGP would not belong to the null hypothesis and would give erroneous results.

After recentering, if needed, we can set up a bootstrap DGP as follows. Bootstrap samples are generated recursively from the equation

$$y_t^* = X_t\tilde{\boldsymbol{\beta}} + \tilde{\gamma}y_{t-1}^* + u_t^*, \tag{23.10}$$

where $y_0^* = y_0$, and the u_t^* are resampled from the vector $\tilde{\boldsymbol{u}}$ centered. This is an example of a *semiparametric bootstrap DGP*. The error terms are obtained by resampling, but equation (23.10) also depends on the parameter estimates $\tilde{\boldsymbol{\beta}}$ and $\tilde{\gamma}$.

A parametric bootstrap DGP would look just like (23.10) as regards its recursive nature, but the u_t^* would be generated from the $N(0,s^2)$ distribution, where s^2 is the least squares variance estimate from the restricted version of (23.9), that is, $1/(n-k)$ times the sum of squared residuals, where k is the number of regression parameters to be estimated under the null hypothesis.

The variance of the resampled bootstrap error terms is the sum of the squared (centered) residuals divided by the sample size n. But this is *not* the least squares estimate s^2, for which one divides by $n - k$. Unless the statistic being bootstrapped is scale invariant, we can get a bootstrap DGP that is a better estimate of the true DGP by rescaling the residuals so as to make their variance equal to s^2. The simplest rescaled residuals are the elements of the vector

$$\ddot{u} \equiv \left(\frac{n}{n-k} \right)^{1/2} \tilde{u}, \tag{23.11}$$

which do indeed have variance s^2. A more sophisticated rescaling method, which takes into account the leverage of each observation, uses the vector with typical element

$$\ddot{u}_t = \lambda \left(\frac{\tilde{u}_t}{(1-h_t)^{1/2}} - \frac{1}{n} \sum_{s=1}^{n} \frac{\tilde{u}_s}{(1-h_s)^{1/2}} \right), \tag{23.12}$$

where h_t denotes the tth diagonal element of the matrix $P_X \equiv X(X^\top X)^{-1} X^\top$. This is the matrix that projects orthogonally on to the subspace spanned by the regressors of the model used to obtain the residual vector $\tilde{u}$. The second term inside the large parentheses in (23.12) ensures that the rescaled residuals have mean zero, and the factor λ is chosen so that the sample variance of the $\ddot{u}_t$ is equal to s^2. In our experience, methods based on (23.11) and (23.12) generally yield very similar results. However, it may be worth using (23.12) when a few observations have very high leverage.

The recursive relation (23.10) that defines the bootstrap DGP must be initialized, and above we chose to do so with the observed value of y_0. This is usually a good choice, and in some cases it is the only reasonable choice. In other cases, the process y_t defined by (23.10) may have a stationary distribution, and we may be prepared to assume that the observed series y_t is drawn from that stationary distribution. If so, it may be preferable to take for y_0^* a drawing from an estimate of that stationary distribution.

23.5 Heteroskedasticity

Resampling residuals is reasonable if the error terms are homoskedastic or nearly so. If instead they are heteroskedastic, bootstrap DGPs based on resampled residuals are generally not valid. In this section, we discuss three other methods of constructing bootstrap DGPs, all based on some sort of resampling, which can be used when the error terms of a regression model are heteroskedastic.

To begin with, consider the static linear regression model

$$y = X\beta + u, \quad E(u) = 0, \quad E(uu^\top) = \Omega, \tag{23.13}$$

where Ω is an unknown, diagonal $n \times n$ covariance matrix. For any model with heteroskedasticity of unknown form, the test statistics which are bootstrapped should always be computed using a heteroskedasticity-consistent covariance matrix estimate, or HCCME. The best-known of these is the one proposed by White (1980) for the model (23.13), namely,

$$\widehat{\mathrm{Var}}(\hat{\beta}) = (X^\top X)^{-1} X^\top \hat{\Omega} X (X^\top X)^{-1}, \tag{23.14}$$

where $\hat{\Omega}$ is an $n \times n$ diagonal matrix with squared residuals, possibly rescaled, on the principal diagonal.

The first type of bootstrap DGP that we will discuss is the so-called *pairs bootstrap*, which was originally proposed by Freedman (1981). This is a fully nonparametric procedure that is applicable to a wide variety of models. Unlike resampling residuals, the pairs bootstrap is not limited to regression models. The idea is to resample entire observations from the original data in the form of $[y_t, X_t]$ pairs. Each bootstrap sample consists of some of the original pairs once, some of them more than once, and some of them not at all. This procedure does not condition on X and does not assume that the error terms are IID. Instead, it assumes that all the data are IID drawings from a multivariate distribution, which may permit heteroskedasticity of the y_t conditional on X_t.

Although it does not appear to be directly applicable to a dynamic model like (23.9), the pairs bootstrap can be used with dynamic models that have serially independent error terms. The idea is simply to treat lagged values of the dependent variable in the same way as other regressors when X_t includes lagged values of y_t. See Gonçalves and Kilian (2004) and the discussion of the block-of-blocks bootstrap in section 23.8.

When we use a semiparametric bootstrap DGP like (23.10), it is generally easy to ensure that the parameter estimates used to define that DGP satisfy the requirements of the null hypothesis. However, when we use the pairs bootstrap, we cannot impose any restrictions on β. Therefore, we may have to modify the null hypothesis when we calculate the bootstrap test statistics. If the actual null hypothesis is that $\beta_2 = 0$, where β_2 is a subvector of the regression parameters, we must instead calculate bootstrap test statistics for the null hypothesis that $\beta_2 = \hat{\beta}_2$, where $\hat{\beta}_2$ is the unrestricted estimate. For some specification tests, such as tests for serial correlation, the null imposes no restrictions on β, and, in such cases, this device is unnecessary.

The trick of changing the null hypothesis so that the bootstrap data automatically satisfy it can be used whenever it is not possible to impose the null hypothesis on the bootstrap DGP. It is also widely used in constructing bootstrap confidence intervals, as we will see in section 23.9. However, we recommend imposing the null hypothesis whenever possible, because it generally results in better finite-sample performance. The improvement occurs because restricted estimates are more efficient than unrestricted ones. This improvement is often modest, but it can be substantial in some cases; see Davidson and MacKinnon (1999a).

Flachaire (1999) proposed an alternative version of the pairs bootstrap which makes it possible to impose parametric restrictions. First, the regression model is estimated under the restrictions imposed by the null hypothesis. This yields restricted estimates $\tilde{\beta}$. Estimating the unrestricted model provides residuals $\hat{u}_t$, which are then transformed using (23.12) to yield rescaled residuals $\ddot{u}_t$. The bootstrap DGP then resamples the pairs $[\ddot{u}_t, X_t]$ and reconstructs the bootstrap dependent variable y_t^* by the formula

$$y_t^* = X_t^* \tilde{\beta} + u_t^*,$$

where each pair $[u_t^*, X_t^*]$ is randomly resampled from the set of pairs $[\ddot{u}_t, X_t]$. This bootstrap DGP accounts for heteroskedasticity conditional on the regressors and imposes the parametric restrictions of the null hypothesis. Flachaire gives some limited simulation results in which tests based on his modified pairs bootstrap have a smaller ERP than ones based on the conventional pairs bootstrap.

The pairs bootstrap is not the only type of bootstrap DGP that allows for heteroskedasticity of unknown form in a regression model. A very different technique called the *wild bootstrap* is also available. It very often seems to work better than the pairs bootstrap when it is applicable; see MacKinnon (2002) and Flachaire (2005) for some simulation evidence. The wild bootstrap is a semiparametric procedure, in some ways quite similar to the one discussed in section 23.4, but the IID assumption is not imposed by the method used to simulate the bootstrap errors. Key early references are Wu (1986), Liu (1988), and Mammen (1993).

For testing restrictions on the model (23.13), the wild bootstrap DGP would be

$$y_t^* = X_t \tilde{\beta} + f(\tilde{u}_t) v_t^*, \tag{23.15}$$

where $\tilde{\beta}$ denotes the least-squares estimates subject to the restrictions being tested, $f(\tilde{u}_t)$ is a transformation of the tth restricted residual $\tilde{u}_t$, and v_t^* is a random variable with mean 0 and variance 1. The simplest choice for $f(\cdot)$ is just $f(\tilde{u}_t) = \tilde{u}_t$, but another natural choice is

$$f(\tilde{u}_t) = \frac{\tilde{u}_t}{(1 - h_t)^{1/2}},$$

which ensures that the $f(\tilde{u}_t)$ would have constant variance if the error terms were homoskedastic.

There are, in principle, many ways to specify v_t^*. The most popular approach is to use the two-point distribution

$$F_1 : v_t^* = \begin{cases} -(\sqrt{5} - 1)/2 & \text{with prob. } (\sqrt{5} + 1)/(2\sqrt{5}), \\ (\sqrt{5} + 1)/2 & \text{with prob. } (\sqrt{5} - 1)/(2\sqrt{5}), \end{cases}$$

which was suggested by Mammen (1993). However, a much simpler two-point distribution is the *Rademacher distribution*

$$F_2 : v_t^* = \begin{cases} -1 & \text{with probability } \frac{1}{2}, \\ 1 & \text{with probability } \frac{1}{2}. \end{cases}$$

Davidson and Flachaire (2001) have shown, on the basis of both theoretical analysis and simulation experiments, that wild bootstrap tests based on F_2 usually perform better than ones based on F_1, especially when the conditional distribution of the error terms is approximately symmetric.

The error terms for the wild bootstrap DGP (23.15) do not look very much like those for the true DGP (23.13). When a two-point distribution is used, the bootstrap error term can take on only two possible values for each observation. With F_2, these are just plus and minus $f(\tilde{u}_t)$. Nevertheless, the wild bootstrap apparently mimics the essential features of many actual DGPs well enough for it to be useful in many cases.

It is possible to use the wild bootstrap with dynamic models. What Gonçalves and Kilian (2004) call the *recursive-design wild bootstrap* is simply a bootstrap DGP that combines recursive calculation of the regression function, as in (23.10), with wild bootstrap error terms, as in (23.15). They provide theoretical results to justify the use of the F_1 form of the recursive-design wild bootstrap for pure autoregressive models with ARCH errors, and they provide simulation evidence that symmetric confidence intervals work well for AR(1) models with ARCH errors.

In a related paper, Godfrey and Tremayne (2005) have provided evidence that heteroskedasticity-robust tests for serial correlation in dynamic linear regression models like (23.9) perform markedly better when they are bootstrapped using either the F_1 or F_2 form of the recursive-design wild bootstrap than when asymptotic critical values are used.

Although the wild bootstrap often works well, it is possible to find combinations of X matrix and pattern of heteroskedasticity for which tests and/or confidence intervals based on it are not particularly reliable in finite samples; see, for example, MacKinnon (2002). Problems are most likely to arise when there is severe heteroskedasticity and a few observations have exceptionally high leverage.

The pairs bootstrap and the wild bootstrap are primarily used when it is thought that the heteroskedasticity is conditional on the regressors. For conditional heteroskedasticity of the ARCH/GARCH variety, a parametric or semiparametric bootstrap DGP can be used instead. The GARCH (p,q) process is defined by $p+q+1$ parameters, of which one is a scale factor. All these parameters can be estimated consistently. As an example, consider the GARCH(1,1) process, defined by the recurrence

$$u_t = \sigma_t \varepsilon_t, \quad \varepsilon_t \sim \text{IID}(0,1), \quad \sigma_t^2 = \alpha + \gamma u_{t-1}^2 + \delta \sigma_{t-1}^2. \tag{23.16}$$

For a bootstrap DGP, we may use estimates of the GARCH parameters α, γ, and δ, and, for the ε_t^*, we may use either independent standard normal random numbers, if we prefer a parametric bootstrap, or resampled residuals, recentered if necessary, and rescaled so as to have variance 1.

As with all recursive relationships, (23.16) must be initialized. In fact, we need values for both u_1^2 and σ_1^2 in order to use it to generate a GARCH(1,1) process. If u_1 is observed, or if a residual $\hat{u}_1$ can be computed, then it makes sense to use it to initialize (23.16). For σ_1^2, a good choice in most circumstances is to use an estimate of the stationary variance of the process, here $\alpha/(1 - \gamma - \delta)$.

23.6   Covariance matrices and bias correction

If we generate a number of bootstrap samples and use each of them to estimate a parameter vector, it seems natural to use the sample covariance matrix of the bootstrap parameter estimates as an estimator of the covariance matrix of the original parameter estimates. In fact, early work such as Efron (1982) emphasized the use of the bootstrap primarily for this purpose.

Although there are cases in which *bootstrap covariance matrices*, or *bootstrap standard errors*, are useful, that is not true for regression models. Consider the semiparametric bootstrap DGP (23.10) that we discussed in section 23.4, in which the bootstrap error terms are obtained by resampling rescaled residuals. Suppose we use this bootstrap DGP with the static linear regression model (23.13). If $\bar{\beta}^*$ denotes the sample mean of the bootstrap parameter estimates $\hat{\beta}_j^*$, then the sample covariance matrix of the $\hat{\beta}_j^*$ is

$$\widehat{\text{Var}}(\hat{\beta}_j^*) = \frac{1}{B} \sum_{j=1}^{B} (\hat{\beta}_j^* - \bar{\beta}^*)(\hat{\beta}_j^* - \bar{\beta}^*)^\top. \tag{23.17}$$

The probability limit of this *bootstrap covariance matrix*, as $B \to \infty$, is

$$\plim_{B \to \infty} \left(\frac{1}{B} \sum_{j=1}^{B} (X^\top X)^{-1} X^\top u_j^* u_j^{*\top} X (X^\top X)^{-1} \right) = \sigma_*^2 (X^\top X)^{-1}, \tag{23.18}$$

where σ_*^2 is the variance of the bootstrap errors, which should be equal to s^2 if the error terms have been rescaled properly before resampling.

This example makes two things clear. First, it is just as necessary to make an appropriate choice of bootstrap DGP for covariance matrix estimation as for hypothesis testing. In the presence of heteroskedasticity, the semiparametric bootstrap DGP (23.10) is not appropriate, because (23.18) is not a valid estimator of the covariance matrix of $\hat{\beta}$. Second, when the errors are homoskedastic, so that (23.18) is valid, it is neither necessary nor desirable to use the bootstrap to calculate a covariance matrix. Every OLS regression package can calculate the matrix $s^2(X^\top X)^{-1}$. The semiparametric bootstrap simply replaces s^2 by an estimate that converges to it as $B \to \infty$.

The pairs bootstrap does lead to a valid covariance matrix estimator for the model (23.13). In fact, it can readily be shown that, as $B \to \infty$, the bootstrap estimate (23.17) tends to the White estimator (23.14); see Flachaire (2002) for details. It therefore makes little sense to use the pairs bootstrap when it is so easy to calculate the HCCME (23.14) without doing any simulation at all. In general, it makes sense to calculate covariance matrices via the bootstrap only when it is very difficult to calculate reliable ones in any other way. The linear regression model is not such a case.

This raises an important theoretical point. Even when it does make sense to compute a bootstrap standard error, a test based on it does not benefit from the asymptotic refinements that accrue to a bootstrap test based on an asymptotically pivotal test statistic. Consider a test statistic of the form

$$\frac{\hat{\theta} - \theta_0}{s_{\theta}^*},\tag{23.19}$$

where $\hat{\theta}$ is a parameter estimate, θ_0 is the true value, and s_{θ}^* is a bootstrap standard error. When $n^{1/2}(\hat{\theta} - \theta_0)$ is asymptotically normal, and the bootstrap DGP yields a valid standard error estimate, the statistic (23.19) is asymptotically distributed as N(0,1). However, there is, in general, no reason to suppose that it yields more accurate inferences in finite samples than a similar statistic that uses some other standard error estimate.

It might seem natural to modify (23.19) by using a bias-corrected estimate of θ instead of $\hat{\theta}$. Suppose that $\bar{\theta}^*$ is the mean of a set of bootstrap estimates θ_j^* obtained by using a parametric or semiparametric bootstrap DGP characterized by the parameter $\hat{\theta}$. Then a natural estimate of bias is just $\bar{\theta}^* - \hat{\theta}$. This implies that a *bias-corrected* estimate is

$$\hat{\theta}^* \equiv \hat{\theta} - (\bar{\theta}^* - \hat{\theta}) = 2\hat{\theta} - \bar{\theta}^*.\tag{23.20}$$

In most cases, $\hat{\theta}^*$ is less biased than $\hat{\theta}$. However, the variance of $\hat{\theta}^*$ is

$$\text{Var}(\hat{\theta}^*) = 4\text{Var}(\hat{\theta}) + \text{Var}(\bar{\theta}^*) - 4\text{Cov}(\hat{\theta}, \hat{\theta}^*),$$

which is greater than $\text{Var}(\hat{\theta})$ except in the extreme case in which

$$\text{Var}(\hat{\theta}) = \text{Var}(\hat{\theta}^*) = \text{Cov}(\hat{\theta}, \hat{\theta}^*).$$

In general, using the bootstrap to correct bias results in increased variance. MacKinnon and Smith (1998) propose some alternative methods of simulation-based bias correction, which sometimes work better than (23.20). Davison and Hinkley (1997) discuss a number of other bias-correction methods.

23.7 More than one dependent variable

Although there is little difficulty in adapting the methods described so far to systems of equations that define more than one dependent variable, it is not so simple to set up adequate bootstrap DGPs when we are interested in only one equation of such a system. Econometricians very frequently estimate a regression model using instrumental variables in order to take account of possible endogeneity of the explanatory variables. If some or all of the explanatory variables are indeed endogenous, then they, as well as the dependent variable of the regression being estimated, must be explicitly generated by a bootstrap DGP. The question that arises is just how this should be done.

Consider the linear regression model

$$y_t = X_t\boldsymbol{\beta} + u_t \equiv Z_t\boldsymbol{\delta} + Y_t\boldsymbol{\gamma} + u_t, \tag{23.21}$$

where the variables in Z_t are treated as exogenous and those in Y_t as endogenous, that is, correlated with the error term u_t. If we form a set of instrumental variables W_t where W_t contains Z_t as a subvector and has at least as many additional exogenous elements as there are endogenous variables in Y_t, then the IV estimator

$$\hat{\boldsymbol{\beta}}_{\mathrm{IV}} \equiv (X^{\top}P_WX)^{-1}X^{\top}P_Wy \tag{23.22}$$

is root-n consistent under standard regularity conditions, with asymptotic covariance matrix

$$\lim_{n\to\infty} \mathrm{Var}\left(n^{1/2}(\hat{\boldsymbol{\beta}}_{\mathrm{IV}} - \boldsymbol{\beta}_0)\right) = \sigma_0^2 \operatorname*{plim}_{n\to\infty}(n^{-1}X^{\top}P_WX)^{-1},$$

where $\boldsymbol{\beta}_0$ is the true parameter vector and σ_0^2 the true error variance. The estimator (23.22) is asymptotically efficient in the class of IV estimators if the endogenous variables Y_t are related to the instruments by the set of linear relations

$$Y_t = W_t\boldsymbol{\Pi} + V_t, \tag{23.23}$$

where the error terms V_t have mean zero and are, in general, correlated with u_t.

If we are willing to assume that both (23.21) and (23.23) are correctly specified, then we can treat them jointly as a system of equations simultaneously determining y_t and Y_t. The parameters of the system can all be estimated, $\boldsymbol{\beta}$ by either (23.22) or a restricted version of it if we wish to test a set of restrictions, and $\boldsymbol{\Pi}$ least squares applied to the reduced-form equations (23.23). The covariance matrix of u_t and V_t, under the assumption that the pairs $[u_t, V_t]$ are IID, can be estimated using the squares and cross-products of the residuals given by estimating (23.21) and (23.23).

If we let the estimated covariance matrix be $\hat{\boldsymbol{\Sigma}}$, then a possible parametric bootstrap DGP is

$$y_t^* = Z_t\hat{\boldsymbol{\delta}} + Y_t^*\hat{\boldsymbol{\gamma}} + u_t^*, \quad Y_t^* = W_t\hat{\boldsymbol{\Pi}} + V_t^*, \quad \begin{bmatrix} u_t^* \\ V_t^* \end{bmatrix} \sim \mathrm{NID}(0, \hat{\boldsymbol{\Sigma}}). \tag{23.24}$$

Similarly, a possible semiparametric bootstrap DGP looks just like (23.24) except that the bootstrap errors $[u_t^*, V_t^*]$ are obtained by resampling from the pairs $[\hat{u}_t, \hat{V}_t]$

of residuals from the estimation of (23.21) and (23.23). If there is no constant in the set of instruments, then it is necessary to recenter these residuals before resampling. Some sort of rescaling procedure could also be used, but it is not at all clear whether doing so would have any beneficial effect.

Another nonparametric approach to bootstrapping a model like (23.21) is to extend the idea of the pairs bootstrap and construct bootstrap samples by resampling from the tuples $[y_t, X_t, W_t]$. This method makes very weak assumptions about the joint distribution of these variables, but it does assume that they are IID across observations. As we saw in section 23.5, the IID assumption allows for heteroskedasticity conditional on the exogenous variables W_t.

The parametric and semiparametric bootstrap procedures described above for the model specified by equations (23.21) and (23.23) can easily be extended to deal with any fully specified set of seemingly unrelated equations or simultaneous equation system. As long as the model provides a mechanism for generating *all* of its endogenous variables, and the parameters can be consistently estimated, a bootstrap DGP for such a model is conceptually no harder to set up than for a single-equation model. However, not much is yet known about the finite-sample properties of bootstrap procedures in multivariate models. See Rilstone and Veall (1996), Inoue and Kilian (2002), and MacKinnon (2002) for limited evidence about a few particular cases.

23.8   Bootstrap DGPs for dependent data

The bootstrap DGPs that we have discussed so far are not valid when applied to models with dependent errors having an unknown pattern of dependence. For such models, we wish to specify a bootstrap DGP which generates correlated error terms that exhibit approximately the same pattern of dependence as the real errors, even though we do not know the process that actually generated the errors. There are two main approaches, neither of which is entirely satisfactory in all cases.

The first approach is a semiparametric one called the *sieve bootstrap*. It is based on the fact that any linear, invertible time-series process can be approximated by an $AR(\infty)$ process. The idea is to estimate a stationary $AR(p)$ process and use this estimated process, perhaps together with resampled residuals from the estimation of the $AR(p)$ process, to generate bootstrap samples. For example, suppose we are concerned with the static linear regression model (23.13), but the covariance matrix Ω is no longer assumed to be diagonal. Instead, it is assumed that Ω can be well approximated by the covariance matrix of a stationary $AR(p)$ process, which implies that the diagonal elements are all the same.

In this case, the first step is to estimate the regression model, possibly after imposing restrictions on it, so as to generate a parameter vector $\hat{\beta}$ and a vector of residuals $\hat{u}$ with typical element $\hat{u}_t$. The next step is to estimate the $AR(p)$ model

$$\hat{u}_t = \sum_{i=1}^{p} \rho_i \hat{u}_{t-i} + \varepsilon_t \tag{23.25}$$

for $t = p+1, \ldots, n$. In theory, the order p of this model should increase at a certain rate as the sample size increases. In practice, p is most likely to be determined either by using an information criterion like the AIC or by sequential testing. Care should be taken to ensure that the estimated model is stationary. This may require the use of full maximum likelihood to estimate (23.25), rather than least squares.

Estimation of (23.25) yields residuals and an estimate $\hat{\sigma}_\varepsilon^2$ of the variance of the ε_t, as well as the estimates $\hat{\rho}_i$. We may use these to set up a variety of possible bootstrap DGPs, all of which take the form

$$y_t^* = X_t \hat{\beta} + u_t^*.$$

There are two choices to be made, namely, the choice of parameter estimates $\hat{\beta}$ and the generating process for the bootstrap errors u_t^*. One choice for $\hat{\beta}$ is just the OLS estimates from running (23.13). But these estimates, although consistent, are not efficient if Ω is not a scalar matrix. We might therefore prefer to use feasible GLS estimates. An estimate $\hat{\Omega}$ of the covariance matrix can be obtained by solving the Yule–Walker equations, using the $\hat{\rho}_i$ in order to obtain estimates of the auto-covariances of the AR(p) process. Then a Cholesky decomposition of $\hat{\Omega}^{-1}$ provides the feasible GLS transformation to be applied to the dependent variable y and the explanatory variables X in order to compute feasible GLS estimates of β, restricted as required by the null hypothesis under test.

For observations after the first p, the bootstrap errors are generated as follows:

$$u_t^* = \sum_{i=1}^{p} \hat{\rho}_i u_{t-i}^* + \varepsilon_t^*, \quad t = p+1, \ldots, n, \tag{23.26}$$

where the ε_t^* can either be drawn from the $N(0, \hat{\sigma}_\varepsilon^2)$ distribution for a parametric bootstrap or resampled from the residuals $\hat{\varepsilon}_t$ from the estimation of (23.25), preferably rescaled by the factor $\sqrt{n/(n-p)}$. Before we can use (23.26), of course, we must generate the first p bootstrap errors, the u_t^*, for $t = 1, \ldots, p$.

One way to do so is just to set $u_t^* = \hat{u}_t$ for the first p observations of each bootstrap sample. This is analogous to what we proposed for the bootstrap DGP (23.10) used in conjunction with the dynamic model (23.9): We initialize (23.26) with fixed starting values given by the real data. Unless we are sure that the AR(p) process is really stationary, rather than just being characterized by values of the ρ_i that correspond to a stationary covariance matrix, this is the only appropriate procedure.

If we are happy to impose full stationarity on the bootstrap DGP, then we may draw the first p values of the u_t^* from the p-variate stationary distribution. This is easy to do if we have solved the Yule–Walker equations for the first p auto-covariances, provided that we assume normality. If normality is an uncomfortably strong assumption, then we can initialize (23.26) in any way we please and then generate a reasonably large number (say 200) of bootstrap errors recursively, using resampled rescaled values of the $\hat{\varepsilon}_t$ for the ε_t^*. We then throw away all but the last p of these errors and use those to initialize (23.26). In this way, we approximate a stationary process with the correct estimated stationary covariance matrix, but with no assumption of normality.

The sieve bootstrap method has been used to improve the finite-sample properties of unit root tests by Park (2003) and Chang and Park (2003), but it has not yet been widely used in econometrics. The fact that it does not allow for heteroskedasticity is a limitation. Moreover, AR(p) processes do not provide good approximations to every time-series process that might arise in practice. An example for which the approximation is exceedingly poor is an MA(1) process with a parameter close to -1. The sieve bootstrap cannot be expected to work well in such cases. For more detailed treatments, see Bühlmann (1997, 2002), Choi and Hall (2000), and Park (2002).

The second principal method of dealing with dependent data is the *block bootstrap*, which was originally proposed by Künsch (1989). This method is much more widely used than the sieve bootstrap. The idea is to divide the quantities that are being resampled, which might be either rescaled residuals or $[y, X]$ pairs, into blocks of b consecutive observations, and then resample the blocks. The blocks may be either overlapping or nonoverlapping. In either case, the choice of block length, b, is evidently very important. If b is small, the bootstrap samples cannot possibly mimic the patterns of dependence in the original data, because these patterns are broken whenever one block ends and the next begins. However, if b is large, the bootstrap samples will tend to be excessively influenced by the random characteristics of the actual sample.

For the block bootstrap to work asymptotically, the block length must increase as the sample size n increases, but at a slower rate, which varies depending on what the bootstrap samples are to be used for. In some common cases, b should be proportional to $n^{1/3}$, but with a factor of proportionality that is, in practice, unknown. Unless the sample size is very large, it is generally impossible to find a value of b for which the bootstrap DGP provides a really good approximation to the unknown true DGP.

A variation of the block bootstrap is the *stationary bootstrap* proposed by Politis and Romano (1994), in which the block length is random rather than fixed. This procedure is commonly used in practice. However, Lahiri (1999) provides both theoretical arguments and limited simulation evidence which suggest that fixed block lengths are better than variable ones and that overlapping blocks are better than nonoverlapping ones. Thus, at the present time, the procedure of choice appears to be the *moving-block bootstrap*, in which there are $n - b + 1$ blocks, the first containing observations 1 through b, the second containing observations 2 through $b + 1$, and the last containing observations $n - b + 1$ through n.

It is possible to use block bootstrap methods with dynamic models. For example, consider the dynamic linear regression model (23.9). Let

$$Z_t \equiv [y_t, y_{t-1}, X_t].$$

For this model, we could construct $n - b + 1$ overlapping blocks

$$Z_1 \ldots Z_b, \; Z_2 \ldots Z_{b+1}, \; \ldots \ldots, Z_{n-b+1} \ldots Z_n$$

and resample from them. This is the moving-block analog of the pairs bootstrap. When there are no exogenous variables and several lagged values of the dependent variable, the Z_t are themselves blocks of observations. Therefore, this method is sometimes referred to as the *block-of-blocks bootstrap*. Notice that, when the block size is 1, the block-of-blocks bootstrap is simply the pairs bootstrap adapted to dynamic models, as in Gonçalves and Kilian (2004).

Block bootstrap methods are conceptually simple. However, there are many different versions, most of which we have not discussed, and theoretical analysis of their properties tends to require advanced techniques. The biggest problem with block bootstrap methods is that they often do not work very well. We have already provided an intuitive explanation of why this is the case. From a theoretical perspective, the problem is that, even when the block bootstrap offers higher-order accuracy than asymptotic methods, it often does so to only a modest extent. The improvement is always of higher order in the independent case, where blocks should be of length 1, than in the dependent case, where the block size must be greater than 1 and must increase at an optimal rate with the sample size. See Hall, Horowitz, and Jing (1995) and Andrews (2002, 2004), among others.

There are several valuable, recent surveys of bootstrap methods for time-series data. These include Bühlmann (2002), Politis (2003), and Härdle, Horowitz, and Kreiss (2003). Surveys that are older or deal with methods for time-series data in less depth include Li and Maddala (1996), Davison and Hinkley (1997, chapter 8), Berkowitz and Kilian (2000), and Horowitz (2001, 2003).

23.9 Confidence intervals

A confidence interval at level $1 - \alpha$ for some parameter θ can be constructed as the set of values of θ_0 such that the hypothesis $\theta = \theta_0$ is not rejected by a test at level α. This suggests that confidence intervals can be constructed using bootstrap methods, and that is indeed the case. Suppose that $\hat{\theta}$ is an estimate of θ, and $\hat{s}_\theta$ is its estimated standard error. Then, in many cases, the asymptotic t statistic

$$\tau = \frac{\hat{\theta} - \theta_0}{\hat{s}_\theta} \tag{23.27}$$

is pivotal or asymptotically pivotal when θ_0 is the true value of θ. As an example, θ might be one of the regression parameters of a classical normal linear regression model like (23.2). In this case, if $\hat{\theta}$ is the OLS estimator of θ, and $\hat{s}_\theta$ is the usual OLS standard error, we know that τ follows the Student's t distribution with a degrees-of-freedom parameter that depends only on the sample size.

When the distribution of τ is known, we can find the $\alpha/2$ and $1 - \alpha/2$ quantiles of that distribution, say $t_{\alpha/2}$ and $t_{1-\alpha/2}$, and use them to construct the confidence interval

$$[\hat{\theta} - \hat{s}_\theta t_{1-\alpha/2}, \ \hat{\theta} - \hat{s}_\theta t_{\alpha/2}]. \tag{23.28}$$

This interval contains all the values of θ_0 that satisfy the inequalities

$$t_{\alpha/2} \leq \frac{\hat{\theta} - \theta_0}{\hat{s}_\theta} \leq t_{1-\alpha/2}. \tag{23.29}$$

If θ_0 is the true parameter value, then the probability that $\hat{\theta}$ satisfies (23.29) is exactly $1 - \alpha$, by construction, and so the coverage probability of the interval (23.28) is also $1 - \alpha$. At first glance, the confidence interval (23.28) may seem odd, because the lower limit depends on an upper-tail quantile and the upper limit depends on a lower-tail quantile. This seeming inversion is not necessary when τ has a symmetric distribution, and is sometimes hidden when (23.28) is written in other ways which may be more familiar, but it is essential with an asymmetric distribution.

Whether or not the distribution of τ is known, we can replace $t_{\alpha/2}$ and $t_{1-\alpha/2}$ by the corresponding quantiles of the empirical distribution of B bootstrap statistics t_j^*. It is important to note that the bootstrap statistics must test a hypothesis that is true of the bootstrap DGP. This point was discussed in connection with the conventional (Freedman, 1981) version of the pairs bootstrap, in which the hypothesis tested is that $\theta = \hat{\theta}$, not $\theta = \theta_0$.

If $(1/2)\alpha(B+1)$ is an integer, and if τ is an exact pivot, using the quantiles of a bootstrap distribution leads to a confidence interval with coverage probability of exactly $1 - \alpha$, just as a P value based on an exact pivot gives a rejection probability equal to a desired significance level α if $\alpha(B+1)$ is an integer. In all cases, the bootstrap quantiles are calculated as the order statistics of rank $(\alpha/2)(B+1)$ and $(1 - \alpha/2)(B+1)$ in the set of the t_j^* sorted from smallest to largest. If $B = 199$ and $\alpha = .05$, for example, the empirical quantiles are t_5^* and t_{195}^*. Thus a confidence interval comparable to (23.28) has the form

$$\left[\hat{\theta} - \hat{s}_\theta t_{(1-\alpha/2)(B+1)}^*, \; \hat{\theta} - \hat{s}_\theta t_{(\alpha/2)(B+1)}^* \right]. \tag{23.30}$$

Such an interval is called a *Monte Carlo confidence interval* if τ is an exact pivot, and a *bootstrap confidence interval* otherwise. The cost of using quantiles estimated with a finite number of bootstrap statistics rather than the true quantiles of the distribution of τ is that, on average, confidence intervals constructed using the former are longer than ones constructed using the latter.

If the distribution of τ is believed to be symmetric around the origin, we can use the bootstrap confidence interval

$$\left[\hat{\theta} - \hat{s}_\theta |t^*|_{(1-\alpha)(B+1)}, \; \hat{\theta} + \hat{s}_\theta |t^*|_{(1-\alpha)(B+1)} \right]. \tag{23.31}$$

instead of (23.30). Here $|t^*|_{(1-\alpha)(B+1)}$ denotes number $(1 - \alpha)(B + 1)$ in the sorted list of the absolute values of the t_j^*. This *symmetric confidence interval* is related to a test based on the bootstrap P value (23.4) in the same way that the *equal-tailed confidence interval* (23.30) is related to a test based on (23.5).

The method of constructing bootstrap confidence intervals described above is often called the *bootstrap t method* or *percentile t method*, because it involves percentiles (that is, quantiles) of the distribution of bootstrap t statistics. If τ is merely asymptotically pivotal, bootstrap t confidence intervals are subject to coverage error. But just as bootstrap P values based on an asymptotic pivot have an ERP that benefits from asymptotic refinements, so do the coverage errors of bootstrap t confidence intervals decline more rapidly as the sample size increases than those of confidence intervals based on the nominal asymptotic distribution of τ; see Hall (1992).

The confidence interval (23.28) is obtained by "inverting" the test for which the t statistic (23.27) is the test statistic, in the sense that the interval contains exactly those values of θ_0 for which a two-tailed test of the hypothesis $\theta = \theta_0$ based on (23.27) is not rejected at level α. If instead we chose to invert a one-tailed test, we would obtain a confidence interval open to infinity in one direction. In this case, we would base the interval on the α or $1 - \alpha$ quantile of the bootstrap distribution.

The inversion of the test based on (23.27) is particularly easy to carry out because (23.27) depends linearly on θ_0. This is generally true if one uses an asymptotic t statistic. But such statistics are associated with Wald tests, and they may therefore suffer from the well-known disadvantages of Wald tests. It is not necessary to limit oneself to Wald tests when constructing confidence intervals. Davison, Hinkley, and Young (2003), for example, discuss the construction of confidence intervals based on inverting the signed square root of a likelihood ratio statistic. In general, let $\tau(y, \theta_0)$ denote a test statistic that depends on data y and tests the hypothesis that $\theta = \theta_0$. For any given distribution of $\tau(y, \theta_0)$ under the null hypothesis, exact, asymptotic, or bootstrap, the (two-tailed) confidence interval obtained by inverting the test based on $\tau(y, \theta_0)$ is the set of values of θ_0 that satisfy the inequalities

$$t_{\alpha/2} \leq \tau(y, \theta_0) \leq t_{1-\alpha/2},$$

where, as before, $t_{\alpha/2}$ and $t_{1-\alpha/2}$ are quantiles of the given distribution. It is clear that, when $\tau(y, \theta)$ is a nonlinear function of θ, solving the equations

$$\tau(y, \theta_+) = t_{\alpha/2} \quad \text{and} \quad \tau(y, \theta_-) = t_{1-\alpha/2}$$

that implicitly define the upper and lower limits $\theta_\pm$ of the confidence interval may be more computationally demanding than solving the equations that result from (23.29) in order to obtain the interval (23.28).

A great many other procedures have been proposed for constructing bootstrap confidence intervals. These include two very different procedures that are both confusingly called the *percentile method* by different authors. Neither of these is to be recommended in most cases, because they both involve inverting quantities that are not even asymptotically pivotal; see Hall (1992). They also include a number of more complicated techniques, such as the *grid bootstrap* of Hansen (1999). References that discuss a variety of methods for constructing confidence intervals include DiCiccio and Efron (1996) and Davison and Hinkley (1997). For reasons of space, however, we will not discuss any of them.

A bootstrap t confidence interval may be unreliable if τ is too far from being pivotal in finite samples. If so, a natural way to obtain a more reliable interval is to invert a test statistic that is closer to being pivotal. An approach that avoids the computational cost of inverting something other than a Wald test is to apply a nonlinear transformation to the parameter of interest, form a confidence interval for the transformed parameter, and then map from that interval to one for the original parameter. This can work well if the t statistic for the transformed parameter is closer to being pivotal than the one for the original parameter.

23.10   The performance of bootstrap methods

The bootstrap, whether used for hypothesis testing or the construction of confidence intervals, relies on the choice of a suitable bootstrap DGP for generating simulated data. We want the simulated data to have statistical properties as close as possible to those of the actual data, under the assumption that the latter were generated by a DGP that satisfies the requirements of the hypothesis under test or of the model for the parameters of which confidence intervals are sought. Consequently, we have tried to emphasize the importance of choosing a bootstrap DGP adapted to the problem at hand. Problems can and do arise if it is difficult or impossible to find a suitable bootstrap DGP. However, for many commonly used econometric models, it is not hard to do so if one takes a modest amount of care.

In this chapter, we have largely confined our discussion to linear models. This has been purely in the interests of clarity. Nonlinear regression models, with or without heteroskedasticity or serial correlation, can be handled using the sorts of bootstrap DGPs we have described. The same is true of multivariate nonlinear systems. The only disadvantage is that computing times are longer when nonlinear estimation is involved, and even this disadvantage can be minimized by use of techniques that we describe in Davidson and MacKinnon (1999b).

For a Monte Carlo test based on an exactly pivotal quantity, any DGP belonging to the model for which that quantity is pivotal can serve as the bootstrap DGP. We have seen that Monte Carlo tests are exact, and that Monte Carlo confidence intervals have exact coverage, if B is chosen properly. Intuitively, then, we expect bootstrapping to perform better the closer it is to a Monte Carlo procedure. This means that the quantity that is bootstrapped should be as close as possible to being pivotal, and that the bootstrap DGP should be as good an estimate as possible of the true DGP. As we saw in section 23.3, asymptotic refinements are available for the bootstrap when both these requirements are met. This is the case for the parametric bootstrap, which can be used with almost any fully parametric model. It is a natural choice if estimation is by maximum likelihood, but it makes sense only if one is confident of the specification of the model.

Once we get over the hurdle of finding a suitable bootstrap DGP, the delicate part of bootstrapping is over, since we can use the general techniques laid out in this chapter for using bootstrap samples to generate P values or confidence intervals.

In section 23.2, we saw that exact Monte Carlo procedures are available for univariate linear regression models with fixed regressors and IID normal errors, but that bootstrap methods which allow for lagged dependent variables and/or non-normal errors are no longer exact. If we can use a parametric bootstrap, using reasonably precise estimates of the nuisance parameters on which the distribution of the test statistic depends, bootstrap tests and confidence intervals can be remarkably accurate. In fact, numerous simulation experiments suggest that, for univariate regression models with IID errors, bootstrap methods generally work extremely well. In particular, this seems to be true for serial correlation tests (MacKinnon, 2002), tests of common factor restrictions (Davidson and MacKinnon, 1999b), and nonnested hypothesis tests (Godfrey, 1998; Davidson and MacKinnon, 2002). It would be surprising if it were not true for any sort of test on the parameters of a linear or nonlinear regression function, except perhaps in extreme cases like some of the ones considered by Davidson and MacKinnon (2002).

Once we move out of the realm of IID errors, the performance of bootstrap methods becomes harder to predict. The pairs bootstrap is very generally applicable when the data are independent, but its finite-sample performance can leave a lot to be desired; see, for example, MacKinnon (2002). The wild bootstrap is less widely applicable than the pairs bootstrap, but it generally outperforms the latter, especially when the F_2 variant is used. However, it is generally not as reliable as resampling rescaled residuals in the IID case.

With dependent data, bootstrap methods often do not perform well at all. Neither the sieve bootstrap nor the best available block bootstrap methods can be relied upon to yield accurate inferences in samples of moderate size. Even for quite large samples, they may perform little better than asymptotic tests, although there are cases in which they do perform well. At this stage, all we can recommend is that practitioners should, if possible, conduct their own simulation experiments, for the specific model and test(s) they are interested in, to see directly whether the available bootstrap procedures seem to yield reliable inferences.

Much modern bootstrap research deals with *bootstrap failure*, by which we mean that a bootstrap DGP gives such a poor approximation to the true DGP that bootstrap inference is severely misleading. It should be noted that a failure of one type of bootstrap DGP does not imply that all bootstrap methods are bound to fail; in many cases, a bootstrap failure has led to the development of more powerful methods. One case in which bootstrap failure can be a serious problem in applied work is when the true DGP generates random variables with fat tails. For instance, as long ago as the late 1980s, Athreya (1987) showed that resampling from data generated by a distribution with an infinite variance does not allow asymptotically valid inference about the mean of that distribution. Although better methods have been developed since then, fat tails still constitute a serious challenge for conventional bootstrap techniques.

There is an enormous variety of methods for constructing bootstrap DGPs that we have not been able to discuss here. Some interesting ones that potentially have econometric applications are discussed in Davison, Hinkley, and Young (2003),

Hu and Kalbfleisch (2000), Lahiri (2003), Lele (2003), and Shao (2003). Nevertheless, for some models, few or even none of the currently available methods may lead to asymptotically valid inferences. Fewer still may lead to reasonably accurate inferences in finite samples. Consequently, the bootstrap is an active research topic, and the class of models for which the bootstrap can be effectively used is continually growing.

References

Andrews, D.W.K. (2002) Higher-order improvements of a computationally attractive k-step bootstrap for extremum estimators. *Econometrica* **70**, 119–62.

Andrews, D.W.K. (2004) The block-block bootstrap: Improved asymptotic refinements. *Econometrica* **72**, 673–700.

Athreya, K.B. (1987) Bootstrap of the mean in the infinite variance case. *Annals of Statistics* **15**, 724–31.

Beran, R. (1988) Prepivoting test statistics: a bootstrap view of asymptotic refinements. *Journal of the American Statistical Association* **83**, 687–97.

Berkowitz, J. and L. Kilian (2000) Recent developments in bootstrapping time series. *Econometric Reviews* **19**, 1–48.

Bühlmann, P. (1997) Sieve bootstrap for time series. *Bernoulli* **3**, 123–48.

Bühlmann, P. (2002) Bootstraps for time series. *Statistical Science* **17**, 52–72.

Chang, Y. and J.Y. Park (2003) A sieve bootstrap for the test of a unit root. *Journal of Time Series Analysis* **24**, 379–400.

Choi, E. and P. Hall (2000) Bootstrap confidence regions computed from autoregressions of arbitrary order. *Journal of the Royal Statistical Society Series B*, **62**, 461–77.

Davidson, R. and E. Flachaire (2001) The wild bootstrap, tamed at last. GREQAM Document de Travail 99A32, revised.

Davidson, R. and J.G. MacKinnon (1999a) The size distortion of bootstrap tests. *Econometric Theory* **15**, 361–76.

Davidson, R. and J.G. MacKinnon (1999b) Bootstrap testing in nonlinear models. *International Economic Review* **40**, 487–508.

Davidson, R. and J.G. MacKinnon (2000) Bootstrap tests: how many bootstraps? *Econometric Reviews* **19**, 55–68.

Davidson, R. and J.G. MacKinnon (2002) Bootstrap J tests of nonnested linear regression models. *Journal of Econometrics* **109**, 167–93.

Davidson, R. and J.G. MacKinnon (2006) The power of bootstrap and asymptotic tests. *Journal of Econometrics*, forthcoming.

Davison, A.C. and D.V. Hinkley (1997) *Bootstrap Methods and Their Application*. Cambridge: Cambridge University Press.

Davison, A.C., D.V. Hinkley and G.A. Young (2003) Recent developments in bootstrap methodology. *Statistical Science* **18**, 141–57.

DiCiccio, T.J. and B. Efron (1996) Bootstrap confidence intervals (with discussion). *Statistical Science* **11**, 189–228.

Dufour, J.-M., L. Khalaf, J.-T. Bernard and I. Genest (2004) Simulation-based finite-sample tests for heteroskedasticity and ARCH effects. *Journal of Econometrics* **122**, 317–47.

Dwass, M. (1957) Modified randomization tests for nonparametric hypotheses. *Annals of Mathematical Statistics* **28**, 181–7.

Efron, B. (1979) Bootstrap methods: another look at the jackknife. *Annals of Statistics* **7**, 1–26.

Efron, B. (1982) *The Jackknife, the Bootstrap and Other Resampling Plans*. Philadelphia: Society for Industrial and Applied Mathematics.

Flachaire, E. (1999) A better way to bootstrap pairs. *Economics Letters* **64**, 257–62.

Flachaire, E. (2002) Bootstrapping heteroskedasticity consistent covariance matrix estimator. *Computational Statistics* **17**, 501–6.

Flachaire, E. (2005) Bootstrapping heteroskedastic regression models: wild bootstrap vs pairs bootstrap. *Computational Statistics and Data Analysis* **49**, 361–76.

Freedman, D.A. (1981) Bootstrapping regression models. *Annals of Statistics* **9**, 1218–1228.

Godfrey, L.G. (1998) Tests of non-nested regression models: some results on small sample behaviour and the bootstrap. *Journal of Econometrics* **84**, 59–74.

Godfrey, L.G. and A.R. Tremayne (2005) Using the wild bootstrap to implement heteroskedasticity-robust tests for serial correlation in dynamic regression models. *Computational Statistics and Data Analysis* **49**, 377–95.

Gonçalves, S. and L. Kilian (2004) Bootstrapping autoregressions with conditional heteroskedasticity of unknown form. *Journal of Econometrics* **123**, 89–120.

Hall, P. (1992) *The Bootstrap and Edgeworth Expansion.* New York: Springer-Verlag.

Hall, P., J.L. Horowitz and B.-Y. Jing (1995) On blocking rules for the bootstrap with dependent data. *Biometrika* **82**, 561–74.

Hansen, B.E. (1999) The grid bootstrap and the autoregressive model. *Review of Economics and Statistics* **81**, 594–607.

Härdle, W., J.L. Horowitz and J.-P. Kreiss (2003) Bootstrap methods for time series. *International Statistical Review* **71**, 435–59.

Horowitz, J.L. (2001) The bootstrap. In J.J. Heckman and E.E. Leamer (eds), *Handbook of Econometrics*, vol. 5. Amsterdam: North-Holland, pp. 3159–228.

Horowitz, J.L. (2003) The bootstrap in econometrics. *Statistical Science* **18**, 211–18.

Hu, F. and J.D. Kalbfleisch (2000) The estimating function bootstrap. *Canadian Journal of Statistics* **28**, 449–81.

Inoue, A. and L. Kilian (2002) Bootstrapping smooth functions of slope parameters and innovation variances in VAR(∞) models. *International Economic Review* **43**, 309–31.

Jöckel, K.-H. (1986) Finite sample properties and asymptotic efficiency of Monte Carlo tests. *Annals of Statistics* **14**, 336–47.

Künsch, H.R. (1989) The jackknife and the bootstrap for general stationary observations. *Annals of Statistics* **17**, 1217–41.

Lahiri, P. (2003) On the impact of the bootstrap in survey sampling and small-area estimation. *Statistical Science* **18**, 199–210.

Lahiri, S.N. (1999) Theoretical comparisons of block bootstrap methods. *Annals of Statistics* **27**, 386–404.

Lele, S.R. (2003) Impact of the bootstrap on the estimating functions. *Statistical Science* **18**, 185–90.

Li, H. and G.S. Maddala (1996) Bootstrapping time series models (with discussion). *Econometric Reviews* **15**, 115–95.

Liu, R.Y. (1988) Bootstrap procedures under some non-I.I.D. models. *Annals of Statistics* **16**, 1696–708.

MacKinnon, J.G. (2002) Bootstrap inference in econometrics. *Canadian Journal of Economics* **35**, 615–45.

MacKinnon, J.G. and A.A. Smith, Jr. (1998) Approximate bias correction in econometrics. *Journal of Econometrics* **85**, 205–30.

Mammen, E. (1993) Bootstrap and wild bootstrap for high dimensional linear models. *Annals of Statistics* **21**, 255–85.

Park, J.Y. (2002) An invariance principle for sieve bootstrap in time series. *Econometric Theory* **18**, 469–90.

Park, J.Y. (2003) Bootstrap unit root tests. *Econometrica* **71**, 1845–95.

Politis, D.N. (2003) The impact of bootstrap methods on time series analysis. *Statistical Science* **18**, 219–30.

Politis, D.N. and J.P. Romano (1994) The stationary bootstrap. *Journal of the American Statistical Association* **89**, 1303–13.

Rilstone, P. and M.R. Veall (1996) Using bootstrapped confidence intervals for improved inferences with seemingly unrelated regression equations. *Econometric Theory* **12**, 569–80.

Shao, J. (2003) Impact of the bootstrap on sample surveys. *Statistical Science* **18**, 191–8.

White, H. (1980) A heteroskedasticity-consistent covariance matrix estimator and a direct test for heteroskedasticity. *Econometrica* **48**, 817–38.

Wu, C.F.J. (1986) Jackknife, bootstrap and other resampling methods in regression analysis. *Annals of Statistics* **14**, 1261–95.

Part IX

Bayesian Analysis of Econometric Models

24
Bayesian Econometrics

Dale J. Poirier and Justin L. Tobias

Abstract

Basic principles of Bayesian statistics and econometrics are reviewed. The topics covered include point and interval estimation, hypothesis testing, prediction, model building and choice of prior. We also review in very general terms recent advances in computational methods and illustrate the use of these techniques with an application.

24.1	Introduction	841
24.2	Point estimation	843
24.3	Interval estimation	845
24.4	Hypothesis testing	845
24.5	Prediction	847
24.6	Choice of prior	848
24.7	Model building	851
24.8	Computation	852
	24.8.1 Non-iterative methods	853
	24.8.2 Iterative methods	854
24.9	Empirical example	856
	24.9.1 The model	857
	24.9.2 Fitting the model	858
	24.9.3 Diagnostics and estimation results	860
	24.9.4 Testing	861
	24.9.5 Prediction	862
24.10	Discussion and recommendations for further reading	864

24.1 Introduction

Statistics is the study of uncertainty. The Bayesian paradigm interprets "probability" similarly to ordinary everyday language, i.e., as a measure of "uncertainty" or "degree of belief" associated with the occurrence of a particular uncertain event, given the available information and any accepted assumptions. Degrees of belief can be operationalized into probabilities in terms of reference lotteries.[1] Bayesian statistics prescribes how an individual should act in the face of such uncertainty in order to avoid undesirable inconsistencies.[2] Expected utility maximization (or loss minimization) provides a basis for rational decision making, and Bayes Theorem describes how beliefs evolve as data are obtained.[3] While the descriptive accuracy of the Bayesian approach in capturing the actual behaviors of individuals is questioned by many opponents, Bayesians only claim that the Bayesian view provides *normative* guidelines for revising probabilities. Bayesian econometrics consists of the tools of Bayesian statistics applicable to economic phenomena.

The *subjective* interpretation of probability is based on an individual's personal assessment of a situation. Accordingly, probability is a property of an individual's perception of reality, whereas according to *objective* interpretations, probability is a property of reality itself. For subjectivists there are no "true unknown probabilities" in the world to be discovered. Instead, "probability" is in the eye of the beholder.[4] In de Finetti's words: "Probability does not exist."

Bruno de Finetti assigned a fundamental role in Bayesian analysis to the concept of *exchangeability*. A finite sequence of events (or random variables) is *exchangeable* iff the joint probability of the sequence, or any subsequence, is invariant under permutations of the subscripts. An infinite sequence is exchangeable iff any finite subsequence is exchangeable. Exchangeability involves recognizing symmetry in beliefs concerning *observables*, and presumably this is something about which a researcher may have intuition.[5] The links between exchangeable beliefs over uncertain observables and the parameters in statistical models are provided by various generalizations of de Finetti's celebrated *Representation Theorem* for infinite sequences of exchangeable Bernoulli random variables [Bernardo and Smith (1994, chapter 4)].[6] These theorems provide conditions under which exchangeability, and other symmetries, give rise to an isomorphic world consisting of i.i.d. observations conditional on a mathematical construct (a parameter), and guarantees the existence of a prior distribution.[7] De Finetti put parameters in their proper perspective: (i) they are mathematical constructs that provide a convenient index for a family of probability distributions, and (ii) they induce conditional independence in sequences of observables.

Bayesian inference involves updating prior beliefs into posterior beliefs conditional on observed data. Appealingly, Bayesian analysis requires only a few general principles that are applied over and over again in different settings. Bayesians begin by specifying a joint distribution of all quantities under consideration. The Bayesian paradigm reduces statistical inference to applied probability. Quantities that become known under sampling (data) are denoted by the T-dimensional vector $y \in Y$ and the remaining unknown (and unobserved) quantities (parameters) by the K-dimensional vector $\theta \in \Theta \subseteq \Re^K$. Unless noted otherwise, we treat y and θ as continuous random variables. Working in terms of densities, consider

$$f(y, \theta) = f(\theta)f(y \mid \theta) = f(\theta \mid y)f(y), \quad y, \theta \in Y \times \Theta, \tag{24.1}$$

where $Y \times \Theta$ is the product space containing the pair of variables y and θ, $f(\theta)$ is the *prior density*, the sampling density $f(y \mid \theta)$, viewed as a function of θ for known y, is the *likelihood function* [denoted $L(\theta; y)$], $f(\theta \mid y)$ is the *posterior density* and

$$f(y) = \int_\Theta f(\theta) L(\theta; y) \, d\theta, \quad y \in Y \tag{24.2}$$

is the *marginal likelihood* of the observed data y. From (24.1) *Bayes Theorem for densities* follows:

$$f(\theta \mid y) = \frac{f(\theta) L(\theta; y)}{f(y)} \propto f(\theta) L(\theta; y), \quad \theta \in \Theta, \tag{24.3}$$

with "$\propto$" denoting "is proportional to." We adopt (24.3) as the way we update our beliefs when $y = y$ is observed.[8] The choice of prior and likelihood are discussed in sections 24.6 and 24.7. Fortunately, sometimes the integration in (24.2) can be performed analytically and so the updating of prior beliefs in light of the data to obtain the posterior beliefs is straightforward. These situations correspond mostly to cases where $L(\theta; y)$ belongs to the *exponential family* of densities. In these cases the prior density can be chosen so that the posterior density falls within the same elementary family of distributions as the prior. These prior families are called *conjugate families*. Conjugate priors are more flexible than they may appear at first since mixtures of conjugate priors are themselves conjugate, although they may be daunting to elicit.

The denominator in (24.3) serves as an integrating constant. Hence, when considering experiments which yield proportional likelihoods for the observed data, and employing the same prior, identical posteriors will emerge, consistent with the *likelihood principle* (Berger and Wolpert, 1988).[9] Unlike the inherent *ex ante* perspective of frequentist statistics, which seeks properties of *procedures* in repeated sampling, posterior density (24.3) is *ex post*: it conditions on the observed data $y = y$, and dispenses with the part of the sample space Y that could have been observed but was not.

In most practical situations not all elements of θ are of interest. Let $\theta = [\beta' \ \gamma']' \in B \times \Gamma$ be partitioned into *parameters of interest* β and *nuisance parameters* γ not of direct interest. Nuisance parameters are well-named for frequentists, because dealing with them in a general setting is one of the major problems classical researchers face. In contrast, Bayesians have a universal approach to eliminating nuisance parameters from the problem: they are integrated-out of the posterior density, yielding the *marginal* posterior density for the parameters of interest, i.e.,

$$f(\beta \mid y) = \int_\Gamma f(\beta, \gamma \mid y) \, d\gamma, \quad \beta \in B. \tag{24.4}$$

24.2   Point estimation

Consider a *loss (cost) function* $C(\hat{\beta}, \beta)$ for the parameters of interest β, i.e., a non-negative function satisfying $C(\beta, \beta) = 0$, and which measures the consequences of using $\hat{\beta}$ when the parameter of interest is equal to β. Both frequentists and Bayesians seek to "minimize" (in some sense) $C(\hat{\beta}, \beta)$, but first its randomness must be eliminated. From the frequentist point of view, β is a degenerate random variable, but $C(\hat{\beta}, \beta)$ is stochastic because $\hat{\beta}$ is viewed *ex ante* as the estimator $\hat{\beta} = \hat{\beta}(y)$ depending on the data y which are random viewed *ex ante*. An obvious way to circumscribe the randomness of $C(\hat{\beta}, \beta)$ is to focus on its expected value, assuming it exists. Frequentists consider the *risk function* (assumed to exist):

$$R(\hat{\beta} \mid \beta, \gamma) = E_{y \mid \beta, \gamma}[C(\hat{\beta}(y), \beta)], \tag{24.5}$$

where the expectation is taken with respect to the sampling density $f(y \mid \beta, \gamma)$.

In contrast, the Bayesian perspective is entirely *ex post*, and it seeks a function of the observed data $y = \mathbf{y}$ to serve as a point estimate of the parameter of interest β. Unlike the frequentist approach, no role is provided for data that could have been observed, but were not. Since β is unknown, the Bayesian perspective suggests the formulation of subjective beliefs about it, given all the information at hand. Such information is fully contained in the marginal posterior density (24.4). In contrast to (24.5), Bayesians focus on *expected posterior loss*:

$$c(\hat{\beta} \mid y) = E_{\beta \mid y = \mathbf{y}}[C(\hat{\beta}, \beta)] = \int_B C(\hat{\beta}, \beta) f(\beta \mid y) d\beta. \tag{24.6}$$

The second Bayesian commandment (after Bayes Theorem), which guides most Bayesian statistical activities, is "act so as to minimize expected posterior loss," i.e., to find β^* where

$$\beta^* = \underset{\hat{\beta}}{\text{argmin}} \left[E_{\beta \mid y}[C(\hat{\beta}, \beta)] \right] = \underset{\hat{\beta}}{\text{argmin}} \left[c(\hat{\beta} \mid y) \right].$$

The posterior expectation (24.6) removes β from $[C(\hat{\beta}, \beta)]$, yielding a criterion function $c(\hat{\beta} \mid y)$ in (24.6), unlike the risk function (24.5), which involves only known quantities.[10]

For concreteness, focus on the case of univariate β and consider the following three loss functions in which c, c_1, c_2 and d are known constants: the *quadratic loss function* $C(\hat{\beta}, \beta) = (\hat{\beta} - \beta)^2$, the *asymmetric linear loss function*:

$$C(\hat{\beta}, \beta) = \begin{cases} c_1 |\hat{\beta} - \beta| & \text{if } \hat{\beta} \leq \beta \\ c_2 |\hat{\beta} - \beta| & \text{if } \hat{\beta} > \beta \end{cases}, \tag{24.7}$$

and the *all-or-nothing loss function* over $|\hat{\beta} - \beta| \leq d$:

$$C(\hat{\beta}, \beta) = \begin{cases} c & \text{if } |\hat{\beta} - \beta| > d \\ 0 & \text{if } |\hat{\beta} - \beta| \leq d \end{cases}. \tag{24.8}$$

It is then easy to show that the resulting Bayesian point estimates are the posterior mean, the qth posterior quantile, where $q = c_1/(c_1 + c_2)$, and the center of an interval of width $2d$ having maximum posterior probability (yielding the posterior mode as $d \to 0$), respectively.[11]

Minimum risk estimators do not exist in general because the risk function (24.5) depends on β and γ, and so an estimator that minimizes (24.5) will also depend on β and γ. Often extraneous side conditions are imposed (e.g., unbiasedness) to sidestep the problem. By construction, Bayesian point estimates are optimal from the *ex post* standpoint. In general they also have good *ex ante* risk properties. In other words, consider the solution to (24.6) viewed from the *ex ante* standpoint before the data are realized, i.e., consider the *Bayesian point estimator* $\hat{\beta} = \hat{\beta}(y)$. Provided the prior is *proper* (it integrates to unity), then $\hat{\beta}(y)$ satisfies the minimal frequentist requirement of *admissibility* (its risk cannot be dominated by another estimator everywhere in the parameter space). Furthermore, in most interesting settings, Wald (1950) showed that all admissible estimators are either Bayes or limits thereof, known as *generalized Bayes estimators*, based on an *improper prior* whose integral is unbounded (see section 24.6). In short, Bayes estimators based on proper priors have desirable properties in terms of final precision by construction, and also have many desirable initial precision properties.

24.3 Interval estimation

Bayesian interval estimation follows directly from the posterior density $f(\beta \mid y)$. Because opinions about the unknown parameter are treated in a probabilistic manner, there is no need to introduce the additional concept of "confidence." For example, given a region $B^{\dagger} \subset B$, it is meaningful to ask: given the data, what is the *probability* that β lies in $B^{\dagger}$? The answer is direct:

$$\Pr(\beta \in B^{\dagger} \mid y) = \int_{B^{\dagger}} f(\beta \mid y) d\beta. \tag{24.9}$$

We call $B^{\dagger}$ a $100(1 - \alpha)\%$ *credible set* if $\Pr(\beta \in B^{\dagger} \mid y) = 1 - \alpha$. Alternatively, given a desired probability of content $1 - \alpha$, it is possible to reverse this procedure and find a corresponding region $B^{\dagger}$. Since many sets $B^{\dagger}$ can be constructed which satisfy $\Pr(\beta \in B^{\dagger} \mid y) = 1 - \alpha$, one can find the "smallest" such region, say B^{*}, known as the *highest posterior density (HPD) region of content* $1 - \alpha$ for β. This HPD region satisfies the additional condition that $f(\beta \mid \beta \in B^{*}, y) \geq f(\beta \mid \beta \notin B^{*}, y)$.

Unlike point estimation, Bayesian interval estimation is rarely cast in a decision-theoretic form. Winkler (1972) is a rare exception. For a discussion of the confidence level (i.e., coverage probability) of HPD intervals, and the usefulness of frequentist matching in prior selection, see Ghosh and Mukerjee (1998).

24.4 Hypothesis testing

Consider a partition of the parameter space B for the parameter of interest β according to $B = B_1 \cup B_2$ where $B_1 \cap B_2$ is null. Suppose we are interested in testing $H_1 : \beta \in B_1$ versus $H_2 : \beta \in B_2$ based on a sample y yielding the likelihood $L(\beta, \gamma; y)$.

The relevant *decision space* is $D = \{d_1, d_2\}$, where d_j denotes the choice of hypothesis $H_j, j = 1, 2$. Extensions to cases involving more than two hypotheses are straightforward. Let $C(d; \beta) \geq 0$ denote the relevant *loss function*. Without loss of generality, assume that correct decisions yield zero loss.

From the Bayesian perspective a hypothesis is of interest only if the prior distribution assigns it positive probability. Therefore, assume $\underline{\pi}_j = \Pr(H_j) = \Pr(\beta \in B_j) > 0$, $j = 1, 2$ with $\underline{\pi}_1 + \underline{\pi}_2 = 1$. The prior probability function (density/mass function) can be decomposed as

$$f(\beta, \gamma) = \begin{cases} \underline{\pi}_1 f(\beta, \gamma \mid H_1) & \text{if } \beta \in B_1, \gamma \in \Gamma \\ \underline{\pi}_2 f(\beta, \gamma \mid H_2) & \text{if } \beta \in B_2, \gamma \in \Gamma \end{cases} \tag{24.10}$$

where $f(\beta, \gamma \mid H_j)$ is the prior under $H_j, j = 1, 2$. Under H_j the marginal likelihood is

$$f(y \mid H_j) = \int_\Gamma \int_{B_j} L(\beta, \gamma; y) \, dF(\beta, \gamma \mid H_j) = E_{\beta, \gamma \mid H_j}[L(\beta, \gamma; y)], j = 1, 2. \tag{24.11}$$

From Bayes Theorem it follows immediately that the posterior probability of H_j is

$$\bar{\pi}_j = \Pr(H_j \mid y) = \frac{\underline{\pi}_j f(y \mid H_j)}{f(y)} \quad j = 1, 2, \tag{24.12}$$

where the unconditional marginal density of the data is $f(y) = \underline{\pi}_1 f(y \mid H_1) + \underline{\pi}_2 f(y \mid H_2)$. Clearly $\bar{\pi}_1 + \bar{\pi}_2 = 1$. Under H_j, the posterior density of β and γ is (according to Bayes Theorem):

$$f(\beta, \gamma \mid y, H_j) = \frac{f(\beta, \gamma \mid H_j) L(\beta, \gamma; y)}{f(y \mid H_j)}, \quad \beta \in B_j, \quad \gamma \in \Gamma, \quad j = 1, 2. \tag{24.13}$$

Using posterior probabilities (24.12), the marginal posterior of θ (where $\theta = [\beta' \ \gamma']'$) is

$$f(\theta \mid y) = \begin{cases} \bar{\pi}_1 f(\theta \mid y, H_1) & \text{if } \theta \in \Theta_1 \\ \bar{\pi}_2 f(\theta \mid y, H_2) & \text{if } \theta \in \Theta_2 \end{cases} \tag{24.14}$$

where $\Theta_1 \equiv B_1 \times \Gamma$ and $\Theta_2 \equiv B_2 \times \Gamma$. As in the case of estimation, the Bayesian decision d^* in the hypothesis testing context minimizes expected posterior loss $c(d \mid y)$, i.e., $d^* = \underset{d}{\text{argmin}} \ c(d \mid y)$. Using (24.14), the *expected posterior loss* of decision d is

$$c(d \mid y) = \bar{\pi}_1 c(d \mid y, H_1) + \bar{\pi}_2 c(d \mid y, H_2), \tag{24.15}$$

where $c(d \mid y, H_j) = E_{\theta \mid y, H_j}[C(d; \theta)], j = 1, 2$. Specifically, $c(d_1 \mid y) = \bar{\pi}_2 c(d_1 \mid y, H_2)$ and $c(d_2 \mid y) = \bar{\pi}_1 c(d_2 \mid y, H_1)$. Therefore, it is optimal to choose H_2 (i.e., $c(d_2 \mid y) < c(d_1 \mid y)$), and therefore $d^* = d_2$, iff

$$\frac{\bar{\pi}_2}{\bar{\pi}_1} > \frac{c(d_2 \mid y, H_1)}{c(d_1 \mid y, H_2)}. \tag{24.16}$$

The quantities π_2/π_1 and $\bar{\pi}_2/\bar{\pi}_1$ are the *prior odds* and *posterior odds*, respectively, of H_2 versus H_1. From (24.12) it follows immediately that these two odds are related by $\bar{\pi}_2/\bar{\pi}_1 = B_{21}(\pi_2/\pi_1)$, where $B_{21} = f(y \mid H_2)/f(y \mid H_1)$ is the *Bayes factor for* H_2 *versus* H_1. A Bayes factor is a ratio of marginalized or expected likelihoods.[12] In terms of the Bayes factor B_{21}, (24.16) can be written

$$d^* = d_2 \text{ iff } B_{21} > \left[\frac{c(d_2 \mid y, H_1)}{c(d_1 \mid y, H_2)}\right]\left[\frac{\pi_1}{\pi_2}\right]. \tag{24.17}$$

In general, the expected posterior loss $c(d \mid y, H_j)$ depends on the data y and, hence, the Bayes factor B_{21} does *not* serve as a complete data summary because the right-hand side of the inequality in (24.17) also depends on the data. One exception is when both hypotheses are simple. Another is when an all-or-nothing loss is used such that the loss $C(d_j, \beta) = \bar{C}_i$ resulting from decision d_j when $\beta \in B_i$, $i \neq j$, is constant for all $\beta \in B_i$. In this case, for $i \neq j$, $c(d_i \mid y, H_j) = \bar{C}_j$ and the decision rule (24.17) reduces to

$$d^* = d_2 \text{ iff } B_{21} > \frac{\pi_1 \bar{C}_1}{\pi_2 \bar{C}_2}. \tag{24.18}$$

The right-hand side of the inequality in (24.18) is a known constant *Bayesian critical value*.

24.5   Prediction

The sampling distribution of an out-of-sample $y^* \in Y^*$ (possibly a vector) given $y = y$ and $\theta = [\beta' \ \gamma']'$ would be an acceptable predictive distribution if θ was known. However, without knowledge of θ this cannot be used. In its place is the *Bayesian predictive density*[13]

$$f(y^* \mid y) = \int_\Theta \frac{f(y^*, y, \theta)}{f(y)} d\theta = \int_\Theta f(y^* \mid y, \theta) f(\theta \mid y) \, d\theta$$
$$= E_{\theta \mid y}[f(y^* \mid y, \theta)], \quad y^* \in Y^*. \tag{24.19}$$

Given the predictive density (24.19), point and interval prediction proceeds analogous to sections 24.2 and 24.3. For example, letting $C(\hat{y}^*, y^*)$ denote a *predictive cost (loss) function* measuring the performance of a predictor $\hat{y}^*$ of y^*, the optimal point predictor $\tilde{y}^*$ is defined to be $\tilde{y}^* = \underset{\hat{y}^*}{\operatorname{argmin}} \ (E_{y^* \mid y}[C(\hat{y}^*, y^*)].)$ For example, if y^* is a scalar and predictive loss is quadratic, $C(\hat{y}^*, y^*) = (\hat{y}^* - y^*)^2$, then the optimal point estimate is the predictive mean $\tilde{y}^* = \int_{Y^*} y^* f(y^* \mid y) \, dy^*$.

The predictive density (24.19) treats all parameters as nuisance parameters and integrates them out of the predictive problem. A similar strategy is used when adding parametric hypotheses to the analysis as in section 24.4. Consider the hypotheses $H_j, j = 1, 2$, about $\theta = [\beta' \ \gamma']'$ and associated priors $f(\beta, \gamma \mid H_j), j = 1, 2$.

Given data y leading to the posterior $f(\beta, \gamma \mid y, H_j)$ the jth conditional predictive density of y^* is

$$f(y^* \mid y, H_j) = \int_\Theta f(y^* \mid \theta, y, H_j) f(\theta \mid y, H_j) \, d\theta. \tag{24.20}$$

Using the posterior probabilities (24.12), the marginal predictive density of y^* is the mixture density

$$f(y^* \mid y) = \bar{\pi}_1 f(y^* \mid y, H_1) + \bar{\pi}_2 f(y^* \mid y, H_2) \quad y^* \in Y^*, \tag{24.21}$$

and it serves as the new basis for interval and point prediction. For example, under quadratic loss the optimal Bayesian point estimate is the predictive mean

$$E(y^* \mid y) = \bar{\pi}_1 E(y^* \mid y, H_1) + \bar{\pi}_2 E(y^* \mid y, H_2), \tag{24.22}$$

which is a weighted average of the optimal point forecasts $E(y^* \mid y, H_j)$ under each hypothesis. The weights $\bar{\pi}_j$ in (24.22) have an intuitive appeal: the forecasts of more probable hypotheses *a posteriori* receive more weight. Combining quantities across hypotheses as in (24.21) and (24.22) is an example of *Bayesian model averaging* (for example, Hoeting *et al.*, 1999).

24.6   Choice of prior

Critics of Bayesianism find the choice of prior to be the major stumbling block in adopting the Bayesian approach. In contrast, proponents see the required effort to be manageable and well worth it. Usually the likelihood is parameterized to facilitate thinking in terms of θ, and so subject matter considerations should suggest plausible values of θ. Kadane and Wolfson (1998, p. 4) claim that economists are particularly open to thinking like this. But even when such direct thinking about θ is possible, we recommend also thinking *predictively* about the observable y and using (24.4) to back out a parametric prior $f(\theta \mid \lambda)$ for a specific value of the *hyperparameter* $\lambda \in \Lambda$ for some space Λ (for example, see Kadane and Wolfson, 1998).[14] This ideal, however, is difficult to achieve.

However, even if the prior elicitation of an expert's opinion is readily available, public research involving only a single prior is likely to draw few readers. Entertaining various professional positions in terms of θ can lead to different choices of λ. In other words, rather than thinking of eliciting *the* prior, it is more useful to think in terms of a set $\mathcal{F} = \{f(\theta \mid \lambda), \lambda \in \Lambda\}$ of priors. If a prior $f(\lambda)$ is available for λ, then we are back in the single prior case with *the* prior $f(\theta) = \int_\Lambda f(\theta \mid \lambda) f(\lambda) \, d\lambda$. In most practical problems, however, there will be no agreed-upon $f(\lambda)$.

Repeating the analysis of sections 24.2–24.5 for different λ, the sensitivity of the posterior to prior choice can be examined in whatever metric of interest. This is easier said than done, but in principle it can be done. The *extreme bounds analysis* developed in Leamer (1982, 1983) is a leading example. There is a certain element of art involved in communicating a sensitivity analysis to readers. For large dimensional θ, a compelling sensitivity analysis is likely to be difficult. Particularly in high-dimensional problems, the effects of the prior can be subtle: it may have little posterior influence on some functions of the data and have an overwhelming influence on other functions.

Numerous pseudo–Bayesian approaches exist which update the "prior" using Bayes Rule, argue on *a posteriori grounds*, but which employ a "prior" that is chosen in a decidedly nonsubjective Bayesian way. For example, *empirical Bayes analysis* uses the data to choose a value of λ (for example, see Maritz, 1970; Morris, 1983; or Deely and Lindley, 1981). Kass and Wasserman (1996) survey numerous formal rules that have been suggested for choosing a prior. Many of these rules reflect the desire to let the "data speak for themselves." This has led to variety of priors, with names like *conventional, default, diffuse, flat, formal, generic, indifference, neutral, non-informative, objective, reference,* and *vague* priors. We adopt the encompassing term: *non-subjective priors.* These priors are intended to lead to proper posteriors dominated by the data. They also serve as benchmarks for posteriors derived from ideal subjective considerations. At first many of these priors were also motivated on simplicity grounds. But as problems were discovered, and other issues were seen to be relevant, derivation of such priors became more complicated, possibly even more so than a legitimate attempt to elicit an actual subjective prior.

One interpretation of letting the data speak for themselves is to use classical techniques. Maximum likelihood estimates are rationalizable in a Bayesian framework by appropriate choice of prior distribution and loss function, specifically a uniform prior and an all-or-nothing loss function. But in what parameterization should one be uniform?

In order to overcome the reparameterization problem, Jeffreys sought a general rule for choosing a prior so that the same posterior inferences were obtained regardless of the parameterization chosen. Jeffreys (1961) makes a general (but not dogmatic) argument in favor of choosing a "non-informative" prior proportional to the square root of the determinant of the information matrix, i.e., $f(\theta) \propto |J(\theta)|^{1/2}$, where

$$J(\theta) = E_{y|\theta}\left[-\frac{\partial^2 \log L(\theta)}{\partial\theta\partial\theta'}\right]$$

is the *information matrix of the sample.* This prior has the desirable feature that if the model is reparameterized by a one-to-one transformation, say $\alpha = h(\theta)$, then choosing the non-informative prior

$$f(\alpha) \propto \left|E_{y|\alpha}\left[-\frac{\partial^2 \log L(\alpha)}{\partial\alpha\partial\alpha'}\right]\right|^{1/2}$$

will lead to identical posterior inferences as using $f(\theta)$. Such priors are said to follow *Jeffreys' Rule.*[15] There is a fair amount of agreement that such priors may be reasonable in one-parameter problems, but substantially less agreement (including Jeffreys) in multiple parameter problems (see, for example, Berger and Bernardo, 1989).

Usually, Jeffreys' Rule, and other formal rules surveyed by Kass and Wasserman (1996), lead to *improper priors*, i.e., priors which integrate to infinity rather than unity (as a *proper prior* would). When blindly plugged into Bayes Theorem as a prior they can lead to proper posterior densities, but not always. Furthermore, improper priors, in contrast to proper priors, are not guaranteed to lead to *admissible* Bayesian point estimators, and *marginalization paradoxes* can occur.[16]

Bernardo (1979) suggested a method for constructing *reference priors*, offering two innovations. First, he defined a notion of missing information in terms of the *Kullbach–Leibler distance* between the posterior and the prior density. Second, he developed a stepwise procedure for handling *nuisance parameters*. If there are no nuisance parameters, then his method usually leads to Jeffreys Rule. Subsequently, numerous refinements have been made in joint work with Berger (for example, Berger and Bernardo, 1989, 1992a, 1992b). A cottage industry has sprung up for generating reference priors leading to reference posteriors in a variety of situations. An excellent recent survey of reference analysis is Bernardo (2004).

There are many candidates for non-subjective priors. One problem is that there are too many candidates! Even in the simple Bernoulli case there are four legitimate candidates (see Geisser, 1984). Another problem is that they often have properties that seem rather non-Bayesian. Most non-subjective priors depend on some or all of the following: (a) the form of the likelihood, (b) the sample size, (c) an expectation with respect to the sampling distribution, (d) the parameters of interest, and (e) whether the researcher is engaged in estimating, testing or predicting. The dependency in (c) of Jeffreys prior on a sampling theory expectation makes it sensitive to a host of problems related to the Likelihood Principle. In light of (d), a *non-subjective* prior can depend on *subjective* choices, such as which are the parameters of interest and which are nuisance parameters. Different quantities of interest require different non-subjective priors which cannot be combined in a coherent manner.

Improper priors cause more problems in hypothesis testing and model selection than in estimation or in prediction. The reason is that improper priors involve arbitrary constants which are not restricted by the necessity of the prior to integrate to unity. Although these constants cancel when computing the posterior density, Bayes factors involve a ratio of arbitrary constants. This gives rise to questions such as: What does it mean to be equally non-informative in spaces of different dimension? Side-stepping such annoying questions, researchers have explored other non-subjective approaches to hypothesis testing. One idea (Berger and Pericchi, 1996) is to use enough data to update an improper prior into a proper posterior, and then use the latter to compute a Bayes factor using the remaining data. Of course, there are many such potential training samples. So, why not try all possible ways and then somehow combine (arithmetic or geometric average?) the different Bayes factors. Amazingly, sometimes this results in a legitimate Bayes factor corresponding to a proper prior called the *intrinsic prior*.

Our advice is *use a noninformative prior only with great care, and never alone*. We include non-subjective priors in the class of priors over which we perform a *sensitivity analysis*.[17]

24.7 Model building

A "true model" is an oxymoron. An *economic model* is an abstract representation of reality that highlights what a researcher deems relevant to a particular economic issue. By definition an economic model is literally false, and so questions regarding its literal truth are trivial. Whether the model is useful is another matter. A subjectivist's *econometric model* expresses probabilistically the researcher's beliefs concerning future observables of interest to economists. It has two components: (i) a *window* (likelihood) for viewing observables in the world, and (ii) a prior reflecting a professional position of interest.[18] Both components are subjective, and both involve mathematical constructs called *parameters*. Parameters simply index distributions; any correspondence to physical reality is a rare side bonus.

In choosing the window $L(\theta; y)$ the researcher is torn in two directions: choosing the dimensionality of θ to be large increases the chances of getting a bevy of researchers *to agree to disagree* in terms of the appropriate priors for θ, but a large dimensional θ necessitates increasingly more informative priors if anything useful is to be learned from a finite sample.[19] We seek a window that is *sophisticatedly simple*, to borrow a phrase from Arnold Zellner.[20]

Diagnostic checking of the maintained initial window can help achieve agreement on the initial window. If the diagnostic checks indicate window expansion, then rethinking is required, a new window must be introduced, and the diagnostic checking process repeated. The extent of diagnostic testing depends in part on the size of the initial window. Everything else being equal, small windows require more checking to convince others of their value than large windows. Reporting that the initial window passes diagnostic checks is intended to soothe the concerns of members of the research community. Due to space limitations we leave detailed discussion of diagnostic checking to others (e.g., Gelman *et al.*, 2004, chapter 6; Lancaster, 2004, chapter 2).

Conscientious empirical researchers provide their readers with a variety of ways of looking at the data. This amounts to checking how the observed data fit the marginal density (24.4), how out-of-sample observables fit the predictive density (24.19), and how the posterior density (24.14) is summarized and interpreted. This task is complicated when the dimension K of θ is large or when many hypotheses are entertained. Furthermore, the question arises: How should we bring together the results? Is one hypothesis to be chosen after an enlightened search of the data? If so, then the question is how to properly express uncertainty that reflects both sampling uncertainty from estimating the unknown parameters under a hypothesis and uncertainty over the hypothesis itself. The common practice of choosing a single hypothesis, and then proceeding conditionally on it, is difficult to rationalize because the researchers uncertainty is understated unless that hypothesis has a posterior probability near unity. Readers are interested in a clear articulation of the researcher's uncertainty because it can serve as a useful gauge or reference point for their own uncertainty.

When considering two hypotheses, H_1 and H_2, it is possible to assign only $\pi_1 + \pi_2 = 1 - \varepsilon$ prior probability to them, and to reserve ε, where $0 < \varepsilon < 1$, probability for an unspecified H_3 representing "something else." Then interpreting π_j relatively as $\Pr(H_j \mid H_1 \text{ or } H_2)$, posterior probabilities (26.12) can be computed and also interpreted relatively as $\Pr(H_j \mid H_1 \text{ or } H_2)$ *without specifying ε.* If in the process the researcher's creative mind has a new insight leading to specification of "something else," then some fraction π_3 of $1 - \varepsilon$ can be allocated to H_3 and the process repeated with the remaining portion allocated to another unspecified H_4. The catch here is that H_3 is data-instigated (i.e., created after looking at the data), and requires the appropriate choice of a "post-data prior," possibly involving π_3 and any parameters unrestricted under H_3. However, the need for sensitivity analysis in public research implies the researcher is left with the usual task of presenting a variety of mappings from "interesting" priors to posteriors. It is left to the reader to decide whether the priors are sufficiently plausible to warrant serious consideration of the data instigated hypothesis. Priors that have been contaminated by data can be presented as such – as always it remains for the reader to assess their plausibility.

24.8   Computation

Since the early 1990s, the statistics profession (and to a lesser extent the econometrics profession) has seen an explosion in applied Bayesian research. This explosion has had little to do with a warming of the statistics and econometrics communities to the theoretical foundation of Bayesianism, or to a sudden awakening to the merits of the Bayesian approach over frequentist methods, but instead can be primarily explained on pragmatic grounds. The development of powerful computational tools (and the realization that existing statistical tools could prove quite useful for fitting Bayesian models)[21] has drawn a number of researchers to use the Bayesian approach in practice. Indeed, the use of such tools often enables researchers to estimate complicated statistical models that would be quite difficult, if not virtually impossible, using standard frequentist techniques. The purpose of this section of the paper is to sketch, in very broad terms, basic elements of Bayesian computation. The reader is invited to see Casella and George (1992), Tierney (1994), Gilks *et al.* (1996), Chib and Greenberg (1995, 1996), Geweke (1999), Chen, Shao and Ibrahim (2000), Carlin and Louis (2000), Geweke and Keane (2001), Chib (2001), Koop (2003), Lancaster (2004) and Gelman *et al.* (2004) (among others) for more detailed and comprehensive descriptions of existing methods.

   To fix ideas, consider the problem faced by the applied Bayesian of evaluating the posterior mean of some function of interest, g:

$$E[g(\theta) \mid y] = \frac{\int_{\Theta} g(\theta) f(\theta) L(\theta; y) d\theta}{\int_{\Theta} f(\theta) L(\theta; y) d\theta}. \tag{24.23}$$

The denominator of the above expression represents the normalizing constant of the joint posterior, since it is only known up to proportionality by Bayes theorem. In virtually all problems of reasonable complexity, the above integration cannot be performed analytically, and we take it as given in the remainder of this discussion that no analytical solution for (24.23) exists.

24.8.1 Non-iterative methods

The first, and perhaps most obvious, way around direct calculation of the integral in (24.23) is to suppose that we can draw directly from the joint posterior $f(\theta \mid y)$. Denote a collection of N such draws (simulations) as $\{\theta_i\}_{i=1}^N$, where $\theta_i \overset{iid}{\sim} f(\theta \mid y)$. Provided the moment of interest exists, the Strong Law of Large Numbers guarantees that

$$\hat{E}[g(\theta) \mid y] = \frac{1}{N} \sum_{i=1}^N g(\theta_i) \qquad (24.24)$$

is a consistent estimator of $E[g(\theta) \mid y]$. It is useful to note that posterior means, posterior standard deviations, etc., of θ can be obtained in this way given suitable choices for g, and that the accuracy of the estimate improves with N. This simulation size N is under the control of the researcher and is in no way limited by the size of the data at hand. One can estimate the desired (finite sample) posterior moment with arbitrary accuracy by simply increasing the number of draws taken from the posterior.

The above approach, often referred to as *direct Monte Carlo integration*, has a very demanding and limiting prerequisite – in order to implement the method, we must be able to obtain i.i.d samples from the posterior distribution $f(\theta \mid y)$. Just as (24.23) can be evaluated analytically in only very few cases, i.i.d samples from $f(\theta \mid y)$ can seldom be obtained in problems of reasonable complexity.

To this end, a more applicable method is *importance sampling*, whose use was championed for Bayesian applications by Kloek and van Dijk (1978) and Geweke (1989). To provide an intuitive explanation behind the importance sampling estimator, note that the integral equations in (24.23) can be rewritten in the following way:

$$E[g(\theta) \mid y] = \frac{\int_\Theta g(\theta) f(\theta) L(\theta; y) d\theta}{\int_\Theta f(\theta) L(\theta; y) d\theta} \qquad (24.25)$$

$$= \frac{\int_\Theta [(g(\theta) f(\theta) L(\theta; y)) / I(\theta)] I(\theta) d\theta}{\int_\Theta [(f(\theta) L(\theta; y)) / I(\theta)] I(\theta) d\theta} \qquad (24.26)$$

for some *importance function* $I(\theta)$ whose support includes Θ. Written this way, one can see that the original integrals have been equivalently transformed into new problems of moment calculation, where the averaging is now performed with respect to $I(\theta)$ instead of $f(\theta \mid y)$. Provided one can draw from the importance function $I(\theta)$, direct Monte Carlo integration can be performed on the numerator and denominator individually to produce the *importance sampling estimator*:

$$\hat{E}[g(\theta) \mid y] = \frac{(1/N) \sum_{i=1}^{N} [g(\theta_i) f(\theta_i) L(\theta_i; y)] / I(\theta_i)}{(1/N) \sum_{i=1}^{N} f(\theta_i) L(\theta_i; y) / I(\theta_i)} = \frac{(1/N) \sum_{i=1}^{N} g(\theta_i) w(\theta_i)}{(1/N) \sum_{i=1}^{N} w(\theta_i)}$$
$$\equiv \sum_{i=1}^{N} g(\theta_i) \tilde{w}(\theta_i),$$
(24.27)

a weighted average of the $g(\theta_i)$, with $\tilde{w}(\theta_i) = w(\theta_i) / \sum_i w(\theta_i)$ denoting the (normalized) weight and $w(\theta_i) \equiv f(\theta_i) L(\theta_i; y) / I(\theta_i)$. Importantly, note that for the case of importance sampling, $\theta_i \overset{iid}{\sim} I(\theta)$, and are not draws from $f(\theta \mid y)$, as was the case in direct Monte Carlo integration. Since the importance function $I(\theta)$ is under the control of the researcher, it can (and should) be a density from which samples can easily be obtained.

Though the estimator in (24.27) may seem like a convenient way to solve all problems of posterior moment calculation, note that if $I(\theta)$ is a poor approximation to $f(\theta \mid y)$, then the "weights" $\tilde{w}(\theta)$ will typically be small for most values of θ_i, and thus the sum in (24.27) will be dominated by a few terms receiving large weight, resulting in a very inaccurate and unstable estimate. Common sense, of course, suggests that the accuracy of an importance sampling estimate will improve as $I(\theta)$ more closely approximates the target distribution $f(\theta \mid y)$. Indeed, if $I(\theta)$ and $f(\theta \mid y)$ coincide, then the "weights" $\tilde{w}(\theta) = 1/N$, and the estimator in (24.27) reduces to the ideal case, the direct Monte Carlo estimator. However, this is an ideal that we cannot achieve, as direct sampling from $f(\theta \mid y)$ is typically not possible.

To evaluate the performance of a particular importance sampling estimator, Geweke (1989) suggests a number of diagnostics, including monitoring the weights $\tilde{w}_i$ and calculating *relative numerical efficiency* (RNE), which quantifies how much is lost (owing to a choice of $I(\theta)$ that is far from the target $f(\theta \mid y)$) by using importance sampling relative to the numerical precision that would have obtained using direct Monte Carlo integration. Finally, Geweke also introduces conditions required for a central limit theorem to hold (and thus establish $\sqrt{N}$ convergence of the importance sampling estimator). In practice, satisfying these conditions may involve a reparameterization of the problem to compactify the parameter space or, more commonly, choosing the importance function to have heavier tails than the target density $f(\theta \mid y)$. Letting $\hat{\theta}$ denote an estimate of the posterior mode, $\hat{\Sigma}$ an estimate of the posterior covariance matrix and $t_\nu(x; \mu, \Omega)$ denote that x has a Student-t density with mean μ, scale matrix[22] Ω and ν degrees of freedom, a possible (and reasonably popular) choice is to select something like $t_4(\theta; \hat{\theta}, \hat{\Sigma})$ as an importance function. This choice may offer a reasonable starting point in practice, though application-specific refinements will almost surely offer an improvement in performance.[23]

24.8.2 Iterative methods

As discussed at the outset of this section, iterative simulation methods, particularly the *Gibbs sampler* and the *Metropolis–Hastings Algorithm*, are powerful statistical tools that facilitate computation in a variety of complex models. Though these two algorithms are commonly presented as useful yet distinct instruments for simulating joint posteriors, this distinction is rather artificial – indeed, one can regard the Gibbs sampler as a special case of the Metropolis–Hastings algorithm where jumps along the complete conditional distributions are accepted with probability one. In *conditionally conjugate* models, the Gibbs sampler is typically the algorithm of choice (since the complete posterior conditionals are easily sampled), giving the Gibbs sampler particular prominence in a wide array of models, and perhaps creating an artificial distinction between the algorithms. In our discussion below we follow this convention and thus discuss these two algorithms separately.

The general strategy with iterative methods is to follow the steps of the algorithm to generate a series of draws (sometimes called a *parameter chain*), say $\theta_0, \theta_1, \theta_2, \cdots$ that converge in distribution to some *target density* – in our case, the posterior $f(\theta \mid y)$. The algorithms are constructed so that the posterior $f(\theta \mid y)$ is the unique stationary distribution of the parameter chain. Once convergence to the target density is "achieved," we can use these draws in the same way as with direct Monte Carlo integration to calculate posterior means, posterior standard deviations, etc. In practice, we take care to diagnose that the parameter chain has approached convergence to the target density,[24] to discard the initial set of the pre-convergence draws (often called a *burn-in period*), and then to use the post-convergence sample to calculate the desired quantities. Unlike the non-iterative methods discussed previously, the post-convergence draws we obtain using these iterative methods will prove to be correlated, as the distribution of, say, θ_t depends on the last parameter sampled in the chain, θ_{t-1}.[25] If the correlation among the draws is severe, it may prove to be difficult to traverse the entire parameter space, and the numerical standard errors associated with the point estimates can be quite large. When the simulations are highly correlated, and our chain makes only small local movements from iteration to iteration, we refer to this as *slow mixing* of the parameter chain.

The Gibbs sampler

Let θ be a $K \times 1$ parameter vector with associated posterior distribution $f(\theta \mid y)$ and write $\theta = [\theta^1 \theta^2 \cdots \theta^K]$.[26] The *Gibbs sampling algorithm* proceeds as follows:

(i) Select an initial parameter vector $\theta_0 = [\theta_0^1 \theta_0^2 \cdots \theta_0^K]$. This initial condition could be arbitrarily chosen, sampled from the prior, or perhaps could be obtained from a crude estimation method such as least-squares.

    (1) Sample θ_1^1 from the *complete posterior conditional* density: $f(\theta^1 \mid \theta^2 = \theta_0^2, \theta^3 = \theta_0^3, \ldots, \theta^K = \theta_0^K, y)$.

    (2) Sample θ_1^2 from $f(\theta^2 \mid \theta^1 = \theta_1^1, \theta^3 = \theta_0^3, \ldots, \theta^K = \theta_0^K, y)$

              $\vdots$

  (K) Sample θ_1^K from $f(\theta^K \mid \theta^1 = \theta_1^1, \theta^2 = \theta_1^2, \ldots, \theta^{K-1} = \theta_1^{K-1}, y)$

(ii) Repeatedly cycle through (1) $\rightarrow$ (K) to obtain $\theta_2 = [\theta_2^1 \theta_2^2 \cdots \theta_2^K]$, θ_3, etc., always conditioning on the most recent values of the parameters drawn [e.g., to obtain θ_2^1, draw from $f(\theta^1 \mid \theta^2 = \theta_1^2, \theta^3 = \theta_1^3, \ldots, \theta^K = \theta_1^K, y)$, etc.].

To implement the Gibbs sampler we require the ability to draw from the posterior conditionals of the model. Although the joint posterior density $f(\theta \mid y)$ may often be intractable, the complete conditionals $\{f(\theta^j \mid \theta^{-j}, y)\}_{j=1}^{K}$, (with θ^{-j} denoting all parameters other than θ^j) prove to be of standard forms in many cases, particularly in hierarchical models and latent variable models using *data augmentation*[27] (see, for example, Tanner and Wong, 1987; or Albert and Chib, 1993). For this reason, the Gibbs sampler is now routinely used to fit a variety of popular econometric models, a point first demonstrated by Gelfand *et al.* (1990).

The Metropolis–Hastings algorithm

The Metropolis–Hastings (M–H) algorithm is an accept–reject type algorithm in which a candidate value, say θ_c, is proposed, and then one decides whether to set θ_{t+1} (the next value of the chain) equal to θ_c or to remain at the current value of the chain, θ_t. Formally, let $P(\theta \mid \theta_t)$ be an approximating *proposal density* (where the potential dependence on the current value of the chain is made explicit),[28] and consider generating samples from $P(\theta \mid \theta_t)$ instead of the target distribution $f(\theta \mid y)$. Supposing that θ_c is sampled from $P(\cdot \mid \theta_t)$, we will then set $\theta_{t+1} = \theta_c$ with (M–H) probability[29]

$$\min\left\{1, \frac{f(\theta_c \mid y)}{P(\theta_c \mid \theta_t)} \frac{P(\theta_t \mid \theta_c)}{f(\theta_t \mid y)}\right\} \tag{24.28}$$

and otherwise set $\theta_{t+1} = \theta_t$. In the case of a *symmetric* proposal density (the original Metropolis algorithm), the above probability of acceptance reduces to $f(\theta_c \mid y)/f(\theta_t \mid y)$, whence candidate draws from regions of higher density are always accepted in the algorithm, and draws from regions of lower density are occasionally accepted.

Often the Gibbs sampler and the Metropolis–Hastings algorithms are used in combination in a given application. For example, it might be the case that the complete conditionals for $K - 1$ of the elements of θ have convenient functional forms, whence the Gibbs sampler can be used to sample from these $K - 1$ posterior conditionals. The complete conditional for the remaining parameter, however, may not take a standard form, and for this parameter, one could use the Metropolis–Hastings algorithm to generate samples. This type of sampling is often referred to as a "Metropolis-within-Gibbs" step, and in (partially) non-conjugate situations, the use of both algorithms in combination often proves to be computationally attractive. We provide an example of such sampling in the following section.

24.9   Empirical example

In this section we provide a straightforward empirical example to illustrate the mechanics of posterior simulation. We choose an application which illustrates how the Gibbs sampler and Metropolis–Hastings algorithms are used to fit an econometric model and involves diagnosing convergence and possibly accelerating convergence through reparameterization. Finally, prediction and model selection (testing) using marginal likelihoods are also discussed in the context of our example.

Our particular application uses a portion of the data set provided by Butler *et al.* (1998) to investigate how mathematics SAT scores influence the number of semesters of calculus courses taken in college. The data were gathered from students at Vanderbilt University and, ultimately, the authors were interested in determining the "causal" effect of mathematics preparation on grades in intermediate-level theory courses in economics. In this illustrative application, however, we use this data simply to explore the relationship between SAT performance and semesters of college-level calculus taken prior to intermediate-level courses in economic theory.

24.9.1 The model

Our analysis divides the types of calculus courses students could possibly take into four categories: the least rigorous option: a one-semester calculus "survey" course, one semester of calculus,[30] two semesters of calculus, and more than two semesters of calculus. The choices are obviously ordered, leading us to consider adopting an ordered probit specification for our analysis:

$$z_i = x_i\beta + \varepsilon_i, \quad \varepsilon_i \overset{iid}{\sim} N(0,1), \tag{24.29}$$

and

$$y_i = \begin{cases} 1 & \text{if } \alpha_0 < z_i \leq \alpha_1 \\ 2 & \text{if } \alpha_1 < z_i \leq \alpha_2 \\ 3 & \text{if } \alpha_2 < z_i \leq \alpha_3 \\ 4 & \text{if } \alpha_3 < z_i \leq \alpha_4 \end{cases} \tag{24.30}$$

where (y_i, x_i) denotes the observed data and z_i represents an unobservable latent variable. The variable y_i denotes the amount of calculus taken, with $y_i = 1$ denoting the least rigorous survey option, and $y_i = 4$ denoting that more than 2 semesters were taken. The variables in x include an intercept, mathematics SAT score (the primary covariate of interest) and a dummy for having met a foreign language requirement.[31] For identification purposes in the ordered probit model, we set $\alpha_0 = -\infty$, $\alpha_1 = 0$ and $\alpha_4 = \infty$, and, of course, normalize the variance in the latent variable equation to unity.

For the parameters of the model, β and $\alpha = [\alpha_2 \ \alpha_3]$, we employ independent priors of the form

$$p(\beta, \alpha) = p(\alpha)p(\beta) \propto \phi[\beta; 0, \underline{V}_\beta], \tag{24.31}$$

with $\underline{V}_\beta$ denoting the prior covariance matrix and $\phi(x; \mu, \Sigma)$ denoting a Normal density for x with mean μ and covariance matrix Σ. In practice, we make the relatively vague choice of $\underline{V}_\beta = 100 I_K$, with I_K denoting the $K \times K$ identity matrix, so that the prior information will be quite small relative to information contained in the data.

24.9.2 Fitting the model

To facilitate computation, we choose to work with the *augmented* posterior distribution,[32] where the latent data $\{z_i\}_{i=1}^n$ are included as elements in the joint posterior density. Letting $z = [z_1 z_2 \dots z_n]'$ we note

$$
\begin{aligned}
p(\alpha, \beta, z \mid y) &\propto p(y, z, \beta, \alpha) \\
&= p(y, z \mid \beta, \alpha) p(\beta, \alpha) \\
&= p(y \mid z, \beta, \alpha) p(z \mid \beta, \alpha) p(\beta, \alpha) \\
&\propto \left[\prod_{i=1}^{N} \exp\left(-\frac{1}{2}(z_i - x_i \beta)^2 \right) I(\alpha_{y_{i-1}} \le z_i < \alpha_{y_i}) \right] \phi(\beta; 0, \underline{V}_\beta),
\end{aligned}
$$

where $I(\cdot)$ denotes the standard indicator function. The last line follows from the assumed conditional independence across observations, and notes that the distribution of y_i is degenerate given the latent data z and cutpoints α.

The standard Gibbs sampler would proceed by deriving and iteratively sampling from the three posterior conditionals: $f(z \mid \alpha, \beta, y), f(\alpha \mid z, \beta, y)$ and $f(\beta \mid \alpha, z, y)$. However, it has been noted that this standard Gibbs sampler in the ordered probit suffers from slow mixing, primarily due to high degrees of correlation between the simulated latent data z and cutpoints α.[33] To this end, we introduce a reparameterization[34] and blocking step which helps to mitigate this high degree of correlation. Specifically, we let

$$
\delta = (1/\alpha_3), \quad \alpha_2^* = \delta\alpha_2, \quad \beta^* = \delta\beta, \quad z^* = \delta z \tag{24.32}
$$

and seek to work with the posterior distribution $p(\alpha_2^*, \beta^*, \delta^2, z^* \mid y)$. In the case of a three-choice ordered probit model, this parameterization eliminates all the unknown cutpoints of the model, and δ^2 resembles a variance parameter from a linear regression model. In general, this reparameterization reduces the correlation between z and α and improves the performance of our sampler. Noting that the Jacobian of this transformation is $[\delta^2]^{-(N+K+4)/2}$, we obtain

$$
f(\alpha_2^*, \beta^*, \delta^2, z^* \mid y) \propto (\delta^2)^{-2} \left[\prod_{i=1}^{N} \phi(z_i^*; x_i \beta^*, \delta^2) I\left[\alpha_{y_{i-1}}^* < z_i^* \le \alpha_{y_i}^* \right] \right] \phi_k(\beta^*, 0, \delta^2 \underline{V}_\beta).
$$

$$\tag{24.33}$$

To fit this model we will employ the iterative simulation methods of the previous section and, specifically, we will successively sample from the following posterior conditionals: $f(\beta^* \mid \delta^2, \alpha_2^*, z^*, y), f(\delta^2 \mid \beta^*, \alpha_2^*, z^*, y)$ and $f(z^*, \alpha_2^* \mid \beta^*, \delta^2, y)$. In this sampling scheme, a *blocking step* is introduced where α_2^* and z^* are drawn together in a single block, resulting in improved mixing of our chains. The first two of the three conditionals above can be shown to have standard forms[35]

$$
\beta^* \mid \delta^2, \alpha_2^*, z^*, y \sim N(D_\beta d_\beta, D_\beta) \tag{24.34}
$$

where

$$D_\beta = \delta^2 \left(X'X + \underline{V}_\beta^{-1} \right)^{-1}, \quad d_\beta = X'z^*/\delta^2 \qquad (24.35)$$

and

$$\delta^2 \mid \beta^*, \alpha_2^*, z^*, y \sim IG \left(\frac{N+K+2}{2}, \left[\frac{1}{2} (z^* - X\beta^*)'(z^* - X\beta^*) + \frac{1}{2} \beta^{*'} \underline{V}_\beta^{-1} \beta^* \right]^{-1} \right),$$

$$(24.36)$$

where IG denotes the inverted Gamma distribution [see, for example, Poirier, (1995, p. 111)].

Though it is straightforward to generate draws from both distributions in (24.34) and (24.36), the remaining joint distribution $f(z^*, \alpha_2^* \mid \beta, \delta^2, y)$ is not as easily sampled. To generate draws from this distribution, we use the *method of composition* (e.g., Chib, 2001, section 2.3). First, a sample from the conditional for α_2^* marginalized over z^*, (i.e., $f(\alpha_2^* \mid \beta^*, \delta^2, y)$), is obtained. The realized draw from this density is then substituted into the full conditional $f(z^* \mid \alpha_2^*, \beta^*, \delta^2, y)$ and a draw from this density is obtained. Together, the generated α_2^* and z^* variates provide a draw from the desired joint distribution.

One can show that $f(\alpha_2^* \mid \beta^*, \delta^2, y)$ takes the form

$$f(\alpha_2^* \mid \beta^*, \delta^2, y) \propto \prod_{i:y_i=2} \left[\Phi\left(\frac{\alpha_2^* - x_i\beta^*}{\delta} \right) - \Phi\left(\frac{-x_i\beta^*}{\delta} \right) \right] \prod_{i:y_i=3} \left[\Phi\left(\frac{1 - x_i\beta^*}{\delta} \right) - \Phi\left(\frac{\alpha_2^* - x_i\beta^*}{\delta} \right) \right],$$

$$(24.37)$$

which is not a standard density function. However, one can use the Metropolis–Hastings algorithm to generate samples from this distribution once a reasonable proposal density has been selected. To embed key features of this conditional into our proposal density, we first calculate the mean $\mu = \mu(\beta^*, \delta^2)$ and variance $\sigma^2 = \sigma^2(\beta^*, \delta^2)$ numerically from (24.37), and then use a normal density with mean μ and standard deviation 3σ *truncated to the interval* $(0, 1)$ as our proposal density.[36] Candidate values are drawn from this truncated normal proposal density[37] and are accepted with probability given in (24.28), where ordinates of $f(\alpha_2^* \mid \beta^*, \delta^2, y)$ replace $f(\theta \mid y)$ in (24.28) and the truncated normal ordinates are calculated and inserted for $P(\theta)$ in (24.28). Once a sample from this distribution has been obtained, we draw independently from the complete conditionals for the transformed latent data:

$$z_i^* \mid \beta^*, \delta^2, \alpha_2^*, y \overset{ind}{\sim} TN_{(\alpha_{y_i-1}^*, \alpha_{y_i}^*)}(x_i\beta^*, \delta^2) \quad i = 1, 2, \ldots, n, \qquad (24.38)$$

where $TN_{(a,b)}(\mu, \sigma^2)$ denotes a normal density with mean μ and variance σ^2 truncated to the interval (a, b).

The posterior simulator is implemented by sampling from (24.34), (24.36), (24.37), and (24.38), conditioning at each step on the most recent set of parameters drawn. To recover the original coefficient vector β and cutpoints α_2 and α_3, we simply use the inverse transformations $\beta = (1/\delta)\beta^*, \alpha_3 = (1/\delta)$ and $\alpha_2 = \alpha_2^*/\delta$ at each iteration of the sampler.

24.9.3 Diagnostics and estimation results

We fit the model by drawing from the conditionals above for 5,000 iterations, discarding the first 500 draws as the burn-in period. Standard diagnostics (e.g., running multiple chains from overdispersed starting values) suggested that the parameter chains mixed well and converged reasonably quickly. As suggestive evidence of this, in Figure 24.1 we present a plot of lagged autocorrelations for the parameter that seemed to exhibit the highest degree of autocorrelation, α_3. As evident from this figure, even this parameter mixes quite well: taking every fifth or sixth draw from the parameter chain, for example, would result in a nearly independent sample of draws from the posterior.

In Table 24.1 we present posterior means, standard deviations and probabilities of being positive[38] for the parameters and cutpoints (α_2 and α_3) in our model. As one can see from the table, we find strong evidence that mathematics SAT scores play an important role in the level of calculus attained, and there is little evidence that satisfying the foreign language requirement at Vanderbilt reduces the number of calculus courses taken. In fact, there is modest evidence in this model that those satisfying the foreign language requirement actually take more calculus courses.

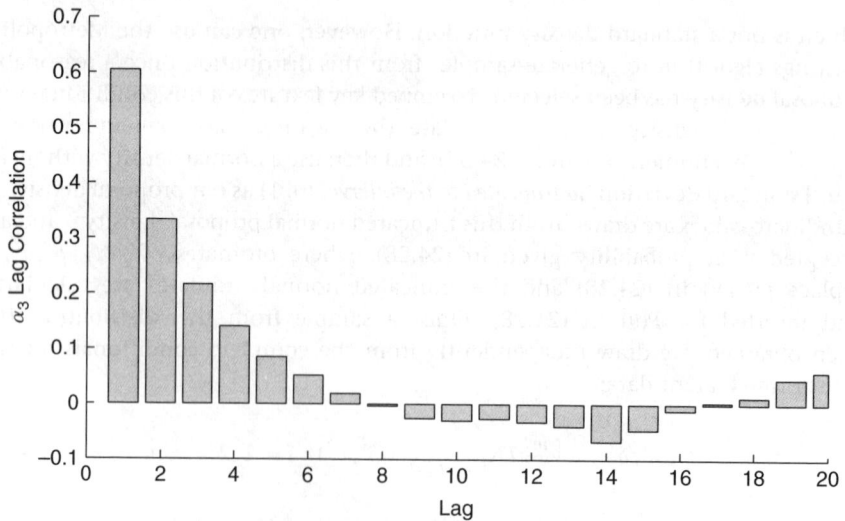

Figure 24.1 Lagged autocorrelation plot for α_3

Table 24.1 Parameter posterior means, standard deviations and probabilities of being positive: ordered probit model

Variable/Parameter	Post. Mean	Post. Std.	Pr(· 0|y)
Constant	−2.92	.509	0.00
Math SAT	.006	.001	1.00
Foreign Lang. Requirement	.116	.141	.784
α_2	.296	.034	1.00
α_3	1.58	.072	1.00

24.9.4 Testing

As discussed in section 24.4, Bayes factors, defined as the ratio of marginal likelihoods between two competing models, can be used to test both nested and nonnested hypotheses. Specifically, under equal prior odds between two models M_1 and M_2, the Bayes factor B_{12} gives the posterior odds in favor of model 1 relative to model 2.

In the context of our application, let us entertain the hypothesis that the coefficient on mathematics SAT scores, say β_{SAT}, equals 0 so that mathematics SAT scores play no role in predicting the number of calculus courses taken in college. As suggested by Table 24.1, this assertion seems greatly at odds with our data, yet we still wish to conduct a test to investigate this claim. To formally carry out such a test, let M_2 be the unrestricted version of our model, as estimated in the previous section, and let M_1 be the model imposing the restriction $\beta_{SAT} = 0$. As shown in Verdinelli and Wasserman (1995), in this case of a nested model comparision[39] the Bayes factor B_{12} reduces to:

$$B_{12} = \frac{f(\beta_{SAT} = 0 \mid y, M_2)}{f(\beta_{SAT} = 0 \mid M_2)},$$

the ratio of the ordinates of the marginal posterior for β_{SAT} at 0 to the prior for β_{SAT} at 0 under the unrestricted Model 2.

In practice, the above expression is typically easy to compute. The denominator can usually be calculated trivially, as one only has to evaluate the (marginal) prior at a particular point. The numerator can be calculated in several different ways using simulated output from the posterior. First, and most efficiently, one can use "Rao-Blackwellization" (for example, Gelfand and Smith, 1990) to calculate the desired ordinate. Formally, let γ denote all of the other parameters of our model. Then,

$$\frac{1}{N}\sum_{i=1}^{N} f(\beta_{SAT} = 0 \mid \gamma^i, y, M_2) \to f(\beta_{SAT} = 0 \mid y, M_2),$$

where γ^i represents the ith draw from the posterior of the remaining model parameters. The conditional distribution $f(\beta \mid \gamma, y, M_2)$ is known when using the Gibbs sampler, and thus ordinates of this conditional at 0 can often be easily obtained.

Secondly (and more generally in low dimension problems), one could use kernel density estimation[40] to estimate the desired ordinate at 0:

$$f(\beta_{SAT} = 0 \mid y, M_2) \approx \frac{1}{nh} \sum_{i=1}^{N} K\left(\frac{\beta_{SAT}^i}{h}\right),$$

with β_{SAT}^i representing the ith draw from the marginal posterior distribution of β_{SAT}, K is a kernel function (typically, a mean-zero, symmetric density function) and h is a bandwidth or smoothing parameter.

When implementing the above test we calculate B_{12} as approximately 2.0×10^{-83}, so that the unrestricted Model 2 is favored over the restricted Model 1 by the enormous factor of 5.0×10^{82}! This overwhelming preference makes sense given the concentration of β_{SAT} on positive regions away from zero (as suggested in Table 24.1) and provides convincing evidence that mathematics SAT scores are important predictors of the number of calculus courses taken in college.

24.9.5 Prediction

To get a better sense of how SAT scores affect the number of calculus courses taken, we will make predictions about the probabilities associated with each level of calculus, given SAT scores and other covariates in the model. To be a bit more formal, let y_f denote the as-yet unobserved quantity of calculus taken for some future, out-of-sample individual and note from our maintained model:

$$\Pr(y_f = j \mid \alpha, \beta, x_f, y) \equiv g_j(\alpha, \beta \mid x_f, y) = \Phi(\alpha_j - \beta_0 - \beta_1 SAT - \beta_2 FL)$$
$$- \Phi(\alpha_{j-1} - \beta_0 - \beta_1 SAT - \beta_2 FL), \tag{24.39}$$

with SAT denoting the mathematics SAT score, FL denoting the foreign language dummy and x_f generically capturing all future covariates. We have used the notation $g_j(\alpha, \beta \mid x_f, y)$ as we regard the conditional probability in (24.39) as a function of the model parameters α and β for given values of the covariates x_f. The added conditioning on y reflects that we will make *posterior* probability statements about this function of the parameters.

In Figure 24.2, we plot a point estimate of $\Pr(y_f = j \mid x_f, y) = E_{\alpha, \beta \mid y}[g_j(\alpha, \beta \mid x_f, y)] \approx N^{-1}\Sigma_i g_j(\alpha^i, \beta^i \mid x_f, y)$, with $(\alpha^i, \beta^i) \sim f(\alpha, \beta \mid y)$ for $j = 1, 2, 3, 4$. For each of the four states, we repeat this exercise over a grid of SAT values and then piece the estimated probabilities together. In a similar manner, we calculate the posterior standard deviations of $g_j(\alpha, \beta \mid x_f, y)$ and in Figure 24.2 report shaded regions, defined as two standard deviations above and below the posterior mean, together with the posterior mean.

From Figure 24.2 we see a wealth of information which generally agrees with our prior expectations. Students with low math SAT scores are likely to take the least rigorous calculus survey course, and are very unlikely to take more than two semesters of calculus prior to taking intermediate microeconomic theory. Conversely, those with very high math SATs are likely to take more than two semesters

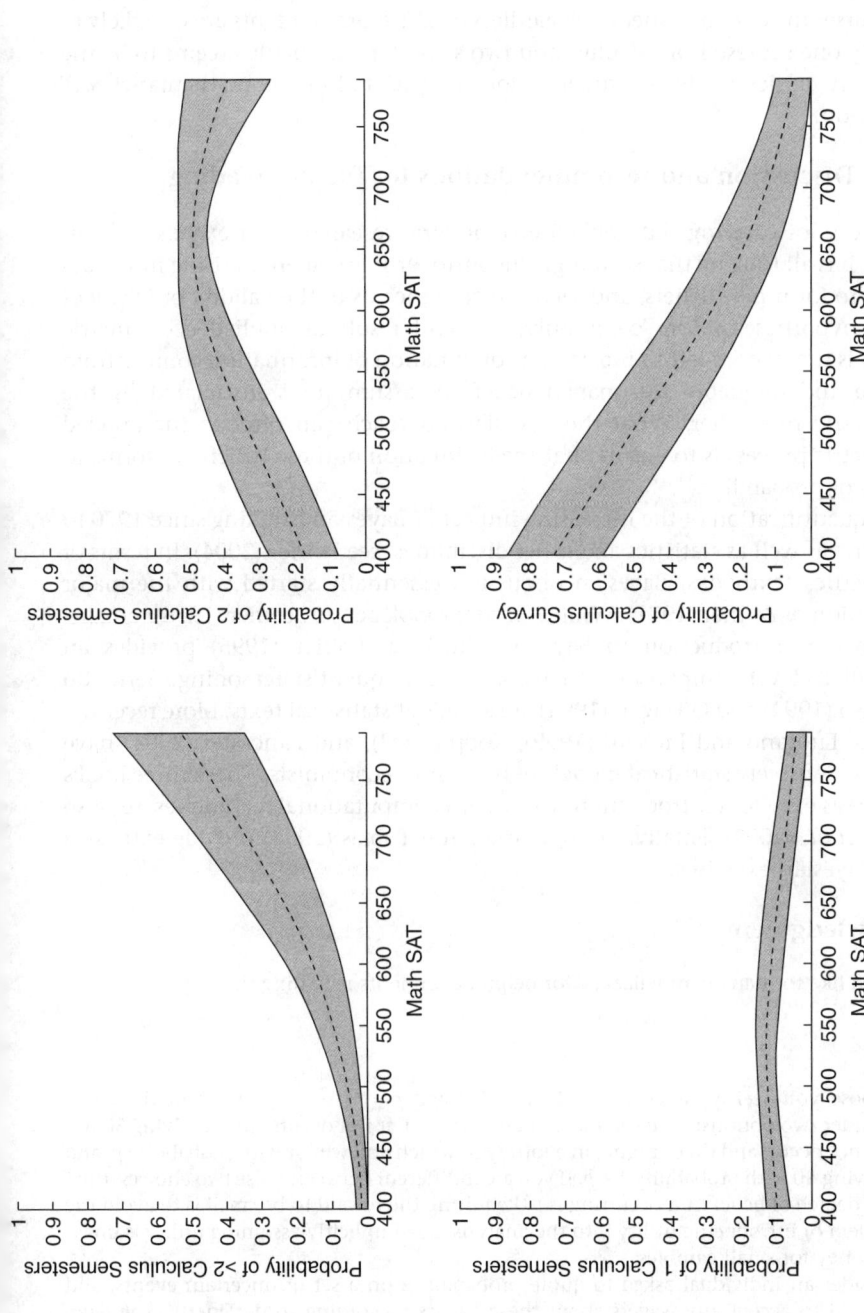

Figure 24.2 Predicted levels of calculus taken across math SAT scores. Dotted line is posterior mean, shaded region gives two standard deviations above and below mean

of calculus and are unlikely to take only the calculus survey prior to intermediate-level courses in economic theory. Regardless of SAT score, students are not likely to take only one semester of calculus, and two semesters of calculus seems to be the most likely choice for those students not in either tail of the mathematics SAT distribution.

24.10 Discussion and recommendations for further reading

The process of carrying out applied econometric research is an exercise in persuasion. It is all too rare that seemingly incontrovertible evidence arising from data leads us to form new beliefs, and serves to convince us of the validity or falsity of various hypotheses. More commonly, the end result of applied econometric research is that we are left to interpret a combination of information coming from the data and (arguably reasonable) beliefs or assumptions insinuated by the econometric researcher. What the Bayesian approach can offer to the applied econometric process is to ensure that the insinuation of these beliefs conforms to the laws of probability.[41]

For a quantification of the increasing impact of Bayesian thinking since 1970 in economics as well as statistics and other disciplines, see Poirier (2004). In terms of econometrics textbooks, Bayesian discussion essentially started with the major contribution of Zellner (1971). While not a textbook per se, Leamer (1978) remains a transparent introduction to Bayesian thinking. Poirier (1995) provides an intermediate level comparison of Bayesian and frequentist reasoning. Bernardo and Smith (1994) and O'Hagan (1994) are excellent statistical texts. More recently, Bauwens, Lubrano and Richard (1999), Koop (2003), and Lancaster (2004) have covered extensively statistical models of interest to economists. These three books also serve as excellent introductions to modern computational techniques: see also Gelman *et al.* (2004). Finally, Koop, Poirier, and Tobias (2004) provide extensive solved Bayesian exercises.

Acknowledgment

We would like to thank Ivan Jeliazkov for helpful comments regarding this paper.

Notes

1. Suppose you seek your degree of belief, denoted $p = Pr(A)$, that an event A occurs. Consider two options: (a) receiving a small reward of $r if A occurs, and receiving $0 if A does not occur, and (b) engaging in a lottery in which you win $r with probability p, and receiving $0 with probability $1 - p$. If you are indifferent between these two choices, then your degree of belief in A occurring is p. Requiring the reward to be small is to avoid the problem of introducing utility into the analysis, i.e., implicitly assuming utility is linear in money for small gambles.
2. Consider an individual asked to quote probabilities on a set of uncertain events, and required to accept any wagers about these events. According to de Finetti's *coherency principle*, such an individual should never assign probabilities so that someone else can select stakes that guarantee a sure loss (*Dutch book*) for the individual whatever the eventual outcome. This simple principle implies the usual axioms of probability except

that the additivity of probability for unions of disjoint events is required to hold only for *finite* unions.

3. There are numerous axiomatic formulations leading to the central unifying Bayesian prescription of maximizing expected subjective utility as the guiding principle of Bayesian statistical analysis. Bernardo and Smith (1994, chapter 2) is a valuable intro- duction to this vast literature.

4. For evidence of the use of subjectivity by history's most illustrious scientists, see Press and Tanur (2001).

5. Exchangeability provides an operational meaning to the weakest possible notion of a sequence of "similar" random quantities. It is operational because it only requires probability assignments of observable quantities, although admittedly this becomes problematic in the case of infinite exchangeability.

6. As in i.i.d. sequences, the individual elements in an exchangeable sequence are identi- cally distributed, but they are not necessarily independent, which has important pre- dictive implications for learning from experience.

7. Bernardo (2003) notes: "To ignore this mathematical fact, and to proceed as if a prior distribution did not exist, just because it is not easy to specify, is mathematically similar to working on a differential equation system as if no solution existed, *once it has been proven that a solution exists*, just because an explicit solution is not easily found."

8. Conditional probability $\Pr(B|A)$ is subjunctive – it refers to *ex ante* beliefs on events not yet decided. We adopt such conditioning as a basic principle. This rules out the possi- bility that the *ex post* experience of an event (e.g., a stock market crash) can bring with it more information than originally anticipated in the event.

9. Briefly, according to the likelihood principle, the evidence in the data of two propor- tional likelihoods, each involving the same unknown parameter, is the same. Replacing $f(\theta)$ by $cf(\theta)$, for some positive constant c in (24.2) and (24.3), it is seen that the same posterior emerges.

10. In other words, the frequentist approach emphasizes the sampling distribution $y \mid \beta, \gamma$, and the Bayesian approach emphasizes the posterior distribution $\beta \mid y = y$. Much of the debate is about the desired conditioning – as are most debates in statistics.

11. When there are more than one parameter of interest, the most popular loss function is the *weighted squared error* generalization of quadratic loss, $C(\hat{\beta}, \beta) = (\hat{\beta} - \beta)'Q(\hat{\beta} - \beta)$, where Q is a positive definite matrix, or the all-or-nothing loss function in (24.8). In these cases, the Bayesian point estimates are again the posterior mean and mode (as $d \to 0$), respectively.

12. See Kass and Raftery (1995) for an excellent review.

13. If the past and future are independent conditional on θ (as in random sampling) then $f(y^* \mid y, \theta) = f(y^* \mid \theta)$.

14. Usually such analyses restrict attention to conjugate priors. Why should prior beliefs conform to the conjugate prior form? One reason is that natural conjugate priors have an interpretation in terms of a prior fictitious sample from the same process that gives rise to the likelihood function. This corresponds to organizing prior beliefs by viewing the observable world through the same parametric window used for viewing the data.

15. Not all of Jeffreys recommendations followed Jeffreys' Rule. When Θ is finite, Jeffreys assigned equal probabilities to each of the values. When Θ is a bounded interval, Jeffreys assumed a constant proper prior. When $\Theta = \Re$, Jeffreys assumed a constant improper prior. When $\Theta = [0, \infty)$, Jeffreys chose $f(\theta) = 1/\theta$ because it is invariant under power transformations. When $\theta = [\theta_1, \theta_2]$, where θ_1 is a location parameter and θ_2 is a non- location parameter, Jeffreys chose $f(\theta) \propto |J(\theta)|^{1/2}$, where $J(\theta)$ is calculated holding θ_1 fixed. In the case of mixture models, Jeffreys argued that the mixing parameters should be treated independently from the other parameters.

16. As Bernardo (1997) notes, marginalization paradoxes imply that the concept of a unique non-subjective prior is untenable: we may only hope to agree on a unique non-subjective

prior for each quantity of interest. For example, consider the standardized mean $\beta = \mu/\sigma$ of a $N(\mu, \sigma^2)$ distribution. Stone and Dawid (1972) showed that the posterior distribution of β only depends on the data through some statistics b, whose sampling distributions only depend on β. It seems reasonable to expect that inferences derived from the model $f(b \mid \beta)$ would match those obtained from the full model $N(\mu, \sigma^2)$. However, this is not possible if the standard non-subjective prior $f(\mu, \sigma^{-2}) \propto \sigma^2$ is used. Marginalization paradoxes are ubiquitous in multiparameter problems. Note, however, that such problems disappear if a proper prior is used.

17. One reaction to the choice of prior is not to make one, and proceed with an asymptotic analysis. The same way sampling distributions of MLE's in regular situations are asymptotically normal, the posterior density (24.5) can be approximated as the sample size T approaches infinity by $\phi_K(\theta \mid \hat{\theta}_{ML}, [J_T(\cdot)]^{-1})$, where $\hat{\theta}_{ML}$ is the ML estimate and $J_T(\cdot)$ is the information matrix. This approximation also does not depend on the prior. As an approximation to the posterior density of θ, the approximation usually improves by replacing the information matrix by the observed Hessian of the log-likelihood evaluated at $\hat{\theta}_{ML}$. In addition, the quality of our approximation can usually be improved by incorporating some information on the prior. For example, by using $\phi_K(\theta \mid \hat{\theta}, [\bar{H}_T(\cdot)]^{-1})$, where $\hat{\theta}$ is the posterior mode and $\bar{H}_T(\hat{\theta})$ is the Hessian of the log posterior evaluated at $\hat{\theta}$. The BIC (Bayesian Information Criterion) approximation of $f(y \mid H)$ is $\ln L(\hat{\theta}_{ML}; y) - k_H \ln(T)$, with k_H denoting the number of parameters in the model. This approximation does not depend on the prior but has a multiplicative approximation error of order $O(1)$, dropping to $O(T^{-1/2})$ if the prior is a "unit information prior" of Kass and Wasserman (1996).

18. Poirier (1988) introduced the metaphor *window* for a likelihood function because it captures its essential role: a parametric medium for viewing the observable world.

19. In one sense this dichotomy between prior and likelihood is tautological: if there is no agreement, then the likelihood can always be expanded until agreement is obtained. The resulting window, however, may be hopelessly complex. The "bite" in the statement comes from the assertion that a researcher believes agreement is compelling in the case of a particular window.

20. Despite the many arguments in the literature over the wisdom of "general to specific" as opposed to "specific to general" modeling, observed behavior suggests researchers start with a finite parameterization of the problem that can be both simplified and expanded. The arguments are really over a matter of emphasis rather than kind.

21. See, for example, Gelfand *et al.* (1990).

22. With four degrees of freedom, this implies that the covariance matrix of x is 2Ω.

23. Geweke (1989) suggests other possibilities for importance functions, including the split Normal and split Student-t densities.

24. There is a large literature devoted to this topic and numerous diagnostics to use. Perhaps the most popular is to run multiple chains from "overdispersed" starting values, watch the progress of the chains for a representative set of parameters, and determine at what point the chains appear to "settle down" to explore the same region of the parameter space. Other possibilities include calculation of the *scale reduction factor* of Gelman and Rubin (1992), which again analyzes behavior across and within chains, and monitoring the *lag autocorrelations* and associated *numerical standard errors*. There are a variety of other diagnostics as well: see (among others) Cowles and Carlin (1996) and Brooks and Gelman (1998) for a review and Geweke (2004) for tests of posterior simulators. If the mixing is slow due to high autocorrelation in the parameter chains, reparameterizations may help to mitigate the problem, or parameters can be *blocked* together in one simulation step, when possible.

25. Because of this dependence, these algorithms are often referred to as *Markov Chain Monte Carlo* or *MCMC* methods.

26. We use superscripts to denote elements of the parameter vector and subscripts to denote iterations in the algorithm.
27. In data augmentation, one samples from the *complete* or *augmented* posterior density which includes both the parameters and the augmented data. Although this would seem to complicate the estimation exercise, the added conditioning on latent data often makes sampling from the conditional distribution of the model parameters straightforward.
28. If, for example, $\theta \mid \theta_t \sim N(\theta_t, \Sigma)$ for given Σ, the chain is termed a *random walk* chain. The last value of the chain θ_t does not, however, have to affect the sampling from the proposal density. If this dependence is suppressed, $P(\theta \mid \theta_t) = P(\theta)$ and the resulting chain is termed an *independence chain*. Such a chain would arise if one were to choose a *tailored proposal density* that calculated, say, the posterior mode and posterior covariance matrix and then used these to center and scale the proposal density.
29. Note that the acceptance probability depends on ratios of posterior ordinates. Thus, the unknown normalizing constant of the posterior conveniently cancels, leaving only the kernel of the posterior behind, which is known by Bayes theorem.
30. The authors actually differentiate even further, and separate semesters into what might be called "standard" calculus courses and more rigorous calculus for math majors courses. We do not make such a distinction here and group these into one category.
31. A satisfactory score on the College Board Foreign Language Achievement Test implied that the student did not have to meet a foreign language requirement at Vanderbilt. Since Vanderbilt's foreign language requirement could be met by taking higher level math courses, presumably those meeting the foreign language requirement would take less math courses, on average.
32. Albert and Chib (1993) discuss the uses of data augmentation in a variety of latent variable econometric models.
33. See Cowles (1996) and Nandram and Chen (1996).
34. This was suggested by Nandram and Chen (1996). Koop and Tobias (2004) use this transformation to fit a smooth coefficient ordered probit model with three choices.
35. Note the simplification induced by working with the *augmented posterior*. In this case, β is easily sampled given that the latent data z^* appears in the conditioning set.
36. Of course, the value of the transformed cutpoint α_2^* must lie between 0 and 1 in our model, making the truncation of the normal density a natural choice.
37. Draws from a truncated normal can be obtained rather easily using standard inversion methods.
38. We feel this is a very useful (and simple to calculate) quantity related to our intuitive notion of "significance."
39. This result holds if the prior for the remaining parameters in Model 1 is the same as the prior for those parameters in Model 2 given that $\beta_{SAT} = 0$. Typically, it is sensible to use the same priors for parameters that are common to both models. For more general methods for calculating Bayes factors using simulated output from a posterior sampler, see, for example, Gelfand and Dey (1994), Chib (1995) and Chib and Jeliazkov (2001), among others. In general, the problem of marginal likelihood calculation can be quite challenging, and in many cases, researchers make use of marginal likelihood approximations, such as the Bayesian Information Criterion [BIC (Schwarz, 1978)] to decide among competing specifications. Other "fit" measures, such as posterior-predictive p-values (for example, Gelman, Carlin, Stern and Rubin, 2004, pp. 162–3), can also be used to gauge the performance of a particular model.
40. See, for example, Silverman (1986) for more on nonparametric density estimation.
41. Much of this discussion, including our use of the phrase "exercise in persuasion" borrows from Lancaster (2004, pages 8359–64).

References

Albert, J. and S. Chib (1993) Bayesian analysis of binary and polychotomous response data. *Journal of the American Statistical Association* **88**, 669–79.

Bauwens, L., M. Lubrano and J.-F. Richard (1999) *Bayesian Inference in Dynamic Econometric Models*. Oxford: Oxford University Press.

Berger, J.O. and J.M. Bernardo (1989) Estimating a product of means: Bayesian analysis with Reference Priors. *Journal of the American Statistical Association* **95**, 200–7.

Berger, J.O. and J.M. Bernardo (1992a) Ordered group reference priors with applications to a multinomial problem. *Biometrika* **79**, 25–37.

Berger, J.O. and J.M. Bernardo (1992b) On the development of reference priors (with discussion). In J.M. Bernardo, J.O. Berger, A.P. Dawid and A.F.M. Smith (eds), *Bayesian Statistics*, vol. 4. Oxford: Oxford University Press, pp. 35–60.

Berger, J.O. and L.R. Pericchi (1996) The intrinsic Bayes factor for model selection and prediction. *Journal of the American Statistical Association* **91**, 109–22.

Berger, J.O. and R.L. Wolpert (1988) *The Likelihood Principle*, 2nd edn. Institute of Mathematical Statistics.

Bernardo, J.M. (1979) Reference posterior distributions for Bayesian inference (with discussion). *Journal of the Royal Statistical Society Series B*, **41**, 113–47.

Bernardo, J.M. (2003) Bayesian Statistics in Probability and Statistics. In R. Viertl (ed.), Encyclopedia of Life Support Systems (EOLSS) (UNESCO).

Bernardo, J.M. (2004) *Reference Analysis*. In D. Dey (ed.), *Handbook of Statistics*, vol. 25. Amsterdam: North-Holland.

Bernardo, J and A.F.M. Smith (1994) *Bayesian Theory*. New York: Wiley.

Brooks, S.P. and A. Gelman (1998) General methods for monitoring convergence of iterative simulations. *Journal of Computational and Graphical Statistics* **7**, 434–55.

Butler, J.S., T. Aldrich Finegan and J.J. Siegfried (1998) Does more calculus improve student learning in intermediate micro and macroeconomic theory? *Journal of Applied Econometrics* **13**, 185–202.

Carlin, B.P. and T.A. Louis (2000) *Bayes and Empirical Bayes Methods for Data Analysis*, 2nd edn. London: Chapman & Hall/CRC.

Casella, G. and E.I. George (1992) Explaining the Gibbs sampler. *The American Statistician* **46**, 167–74.

Chen, M.-H., Q.-M. Shao and J.G. Ibrahim (2000) *Monte Carlo Methods in Bayesian Computation*. New York: Springer-Verlag.

Chib, S. (1995) Marginal likelihood from the Gibbs output. *Journal of the American Statistical Association* **90**, 1313–1321.

Chib, S. (2001) Markov chain Monte Carlo methods: computation and inference. In J.J. Heckman and E. Leamer (eds), *Handbook of Econometrics*, vol. 5. Amsterdam: North-Holland and Elsevier Science, pp. 3569–3649.

Chib, S. and E. Greenberg (1995) Understanding the Metropolis–Hastings algorithm. *The American Statistician* **49**, 327–35.

Chib, S. and E. Greenberg (1996) Markov chain Monte Carlo simulation methods in econometrics. *Econometric Theory* **12**, 409–31.

Chib, S. and I. Jeliazkov (2001) Marginal likelihood from the Metropolis–Hastings output. *Journal of the American Statistical Association* **96**, 270–81.

Cowles, M. (1996) Accelerating Monte Carlo Markov chain convergence for cumulative-link generalized linear models. *Statistics and Computing* **6**, 101–11.

Cowles, M.C. and B.P. Carlin (1996) Markov chain Monte Carlo convergence diagnostics: a comparative review. *Journal of the American Statistical Association* **91**, 883–904.

Deely, J.J. and D.V. Lindley (1981) Bayes empirical Bayes. *Journal of the American Statistical Association* **76**, 833–41.

Geisser, S. (1984) On prior distributions for binary trials (with discussion). *The American Statistician* **38**, 244–51.

Gelfand, A.E. and D. Dey (1994) Bayesian model choice: asymptotics and exact calculations. *Journal of the Royal Statistical Society, Series B*, **56**, 501–14.

Gelfand, A.E., S.E. Hills, A. Racine-Poon and A.F.M. Smith (1990) Illustration of Bayesian inference in normal data models using Gibbs sampling. *Journal of the American Statistical Association* **85**, 972–85.

Gelfand, A.E. and A.F.M. Smith (1990) Sampling-based approaches to calculating marginal densities. *Journal of the American Statistical Association* **85**(410), 398–409.

Gelman, A., J.B. Carlin, H.S. Stern and D.B. Rubin (2004) *Bayesian Data Analysis*, 2nd edn. London: Chapman & Hall/CRC.

Gelman, A. and D.B. Rubin (1992) Inference from iterative simulation using multiple sequences (with discussion). *Statistical Science* **7**, 457–511.

Geweke, J. (1989) Bayesian inference in econometric models using Monte Carlo integration. *Econometrica* **57**, 1317–1339.

Geweke, J. (1999) Using simulation methods for Bayesian econometric models: inference, development and communication (with discussion and reply). *Econometric Reviews* **18**, 1–127.

Geweke, J. (2004) Getting it right: joint distribution tests of posterior simulators. *Journal of the American Statistical Association* **99**, 799–804.

Geweke, J. and M. Keane (2001) Computationally intensive methods for integration in econometrics. In J.J. Heckman and E. Leamer (eds), *Handbook of Econometrics*, vol. 5. Amstesdam: North-Holland and Elsevier Science, pp. 3463–3568.

Ghosh, M. and R. Mukerjee (1998) Recent developments on probability matching priors. In S.E. Ahmed, M. Ashanullah and B.K. Sinha (eds), *Applied Statistical Science*, III. New York: Science Publishers, pp. 227–52.

Gilks, W.R., S. Richardson and D.J. Spiegelhalter (eds) (1996) *Markov Chain Monte Carlo in Practice*. London: Chapman & Hall/CRC.

Hoeting, J.A., D. Madigan, A.E. Raftery and C.T. Volinsky (1999) Bayesian model averaging: a tutorial (with discussion). *Statistical Science* **19**, 382–417. (A version where the number of misprints has been significantly reduced is available at http://www.stat.washington.edu/raftery/.)

Jeffreys, H. (1961) *Theory of Probability*, 3rd edn. Oxford: Clarendon Press.

Kadane, J.B. and L.J. Wolfson (1988) Experiences in elicitation. *Statistician* **47**, 3–19.

Kass, R.E. and A.E. Raftery (1995) Bayes factors. *Journal of the American Statistical Association* **90**, 773–95.

Kass, R.E. and L. Wasserman (1995) A reference Bayesian test for nested hypotheses and its relationship to the Schwarz Criterion. *Journal of the American Statistical Association* **90**, 928–34.

Kass, R.E. and L. Wasserman (1996) The selection of prior distributions by formal rules. *Journal of the American Statistical Association* **91**, 1343–1370.

Kloek, T. and H.K. van Dijk (1978) Bayesian estimates of equation system parameters: an application of integration by Monte Carlo. *Econometrica* **46**, 1–19.

Koop, G. (2003) *Bayesian Econometrics*. New York: Wiley.

Koop, G., D.J. Poirier and J.L. Tobias (2004) *Bayesian Econometrics*, volume 12 of Econometric Exercises series, in preparation.

Koop, G. and J.L. Tobias (2004) Semiparametric Bayesian inference in smooth coefficient models. *Journal of Econometrics*, forthcoming.

Lancaster, T. (2004) *An Introduction to Modern Bayesian Econometrics*. Oxford: Blackwell.

Leamer, E.E. (1978) *Specification Searches: Ad Hoc Inference with Nonexperimental Data*. New York: Wiley.

Leamer, E.E. (1982) Sets of posterior means with bounded variance priors. *Econometrica* **50**, 725–36.

Leamer, E.E. (1983) Let's take the con out of econometrics. *American Economic Review* **73**, 31–43.

Maritz, J.S. (1970) *Empirical Bayes Methods*. London: Methuen.

Morris, C. (1983) Parametric empirical Bayes inference: theory and application (with discussion). *Journal of the American Statistical Association* **78**, 47–65.

Nandram, B. and M.-H. Chen (1996) Reparameterizing the generalized linear model to accelerate Gibbs sampler convergence. *Journal of Statistical Computation and Simulation* **54**, 129–44.

Poirier, D.J. (1988) Frequentist and subjectivist perspectives on the problems of model building in economics (with discussion). *Journal of Economic Perspectives* **2**, 121–70.

Poirier, D.J. (1995) *Intermediate Statistics and Econometrics*. Cambridge, MA: The MIT Press.

Poirier, D.J. (2004) What is in a word or two? Unpublished manuscript, University of California, Irvine.

Press, S.J. and J.M. Tanur (2001) *The Subjectivity of Scientists and the Bayesian Approach*. New York: Wiley.

Schwarz, G. (1978) Estimating the dimension of a model. *Annals of Statistics* **6**, 461–44.

Silverman, B.W. (1986) *Density Estimation for Statistics and Data Analysis*. London: Chapman & Hall.

Stone, M. and A.P. Dawid (1972) Un-Bayesian implications of improper Bayes inference in routine statistical problems. *Biometrika* **59**, 369–75.

Tanner, M.A. and W.H. Wong (1987) The calculation of posterior distributions by data augmentation. *Journal of the American Statistical Association* **82**, 528–49.

Tierney, L. (1994) Markov chains for exploring posterior distributions (with discussion). *Annals of Statistics* **22**, 1701–1762.

Verdinelli, I. and L. Wasserman (1995) Computing Bayes factors using a generalization of the Savage–Dickey density ratio. *Journal of the American Statistical Association* **90**, 614–18.

Wald, A. (1950) *Statistical Decision Functions*. New York: Wiley.

Winkler, R.L. (1972) A decision-theoretic approach to interval estimation. *Journal of the American Statistical Association* **67**, 187–91.

Zellner, A. (1971) *An Introduction to Bayesian Inference in Econometrics*. New York: Wiley.

25

Bayesian Approaches to Cointegration*

*Gary Koop, Rodney Strachan, Herman van Dijk
and Mattias Villani*

Abstract

In this chapter, we survey the Bayesian literature on cointegration. We begin with a discussion of early approaches based on vector autoregressions (VARs) before proceeding to more recent work using vector error correction models (VECMs). The reduced rank structure of the matrix of long-run multipliers in the VECM implies both a global and a local non-identification problem which complicates Bayesian analysis. We describe two approaches, the first based on the Jeffreys' prior and the second based on the concept of an embedding model, that have been suggested in the literature for surmounting the local non-identification problem. The global identification problem can be overcome by normalizing elements of the cointegrating vectors. However, some very recent Bayesian papers have argued that imposing standard normalizations can lead to misleading results. These papers recommend working directly with the space spanned by the cointegrating vectors (as opposed to the vectors themselves). We describe how priors (including a non-informative one) can be elicited on the cointegration space and posterior simulation can be carried out. If the feature of interest is the cointegrating space, then presenting posterior means and variances of particular identified cointegrating vectors can be misleading. Accordingly, we discuss the Bayesian literature on posterior inference about spaces. For all the different specifications we describe how Bayesian inference can be carried out in practice using posterior simulation. An empirical example illustrates how Bayesian methods work in practice, with a particular focus on Bayesian model averaging over the cointegrating rank and posterior analysis of the cointegrating space.

25.1	Introduction	872
25.2	Early work: unrestricted VARs and inference conditional upon the cointegration rank	873
25.3	Problems with the early work: identification and normalization issues	876
25.4	Prior distributions for the cointegratd ECM	877
	25.4.1 The Jeffreys' prior approach	878
	25.4.2 The embedding approach	878
	25.4.3 The cointegration space approach	880

25.5 Posterior distributions: $p(r \mid y)$ and $p(\beta \mid r, y)$ 885
    25.5.1   Analytical results   885
    25.5.2   Posterior simulation in the cointegrated ECM   886
    25.5.3   Posterior distribution of the cointegration rank   887
    25.5.4   Point estimation of the cointegrating space   889
25.6 Bayesian model averaging in cointegration models   890
25.7 Application   891
25.8 Conclusion   893

25.1   Introduction

Ever since the seminal work of Nelson and Plosser (1982), common wisdom has held that many macroeconomic and financial time series contain stochastic trends (such as a random walk process) or unit roots. When the stochastic trends in various time series are independent of one another, then no stable relationship exists among the different series. However, in practice one often observes that there exist linear combinations of different unit root time series that behave like stationary series. Examples in macroeconomics and finance abound, including consumption and permanent income, prices and dividends on the stock market and short- and long-term interest rate series. If linear combinations of unit root variables are stationary, then cointegration is said to occur. Since the fundamental work developing the concept of cointegration (Engle and Granger, 1987), an enormous literature has developed on estimation, testing and prediction in potentially cointegrated models. Most of the work has adopted a classical econometric perspective (see, for example, Johansen (1995) for an introduction to this literature). However, there has been a substantive amount of Bayesian work on cointegration. The purpose of this chapter is to survey and critically assess the Bayesian cointegration literature.

The chapter is aimed at Bayesians and non-Bayesians. For Bayesians, we offer discussion of the key issues which must be considered when specifying prior distributions and the likelihood and a description of the posterior simulation methods necessary to implement Bayesian methods empirically. As we shall see, the issues the Bayesian must address in cointegration analysis are somewhat different from those addressed by the classical econometrician. Hence, we feel that non-Bayesians should be interested in Bayesian cointegration methods as the different perspective they adopt sheds a new light on many key properties of cointegrated models.

To establish notation and illustrate the basic ideas underlying Bayesian cointegration analysis, let $\{x_t\}_{t=1}^{T}$ be a realization of the p-dimensional vector autoregressive (VAR) process of lag length k:

$$x_t = \sum_{i=1}^{k} \Gamma_i x_{t-i} + \Phi d_t + \varepsilon_t, \tag{25.1}$$

where $\varepsilon_t \overset{iid}{\sim} N_p(0, \Sigma)$.[1] d_t contains deterministic terms (i.e., an intercept, deterministic trends, dummy variables, etc.). This model can be written in error correction model (ECM) form as:

$$\Delta x_t = \Pi x_{t-1} + \sum_{i=1}^{k-1} \Psi_i \Delta x_{t-i} + \Phi d_t + \varepsilon_t, \tag{25.2}$$

where the matrix of long-run multipliers, Π, can be written as $\Pi = \alpha\beta'$, where α and β are both full rank $p \times r$ matrices and where $0 \leq r \leq p$ is the number of coin-tegrating relationships. Note that, if $r = p$ then all the elements of x_t are trend-stationary, while if $r = 0$ then the series all contain a unit root, but cointegration does not occur.

In one sense, Bayesian analysis of cointegration is straightforward. Equations (25.1) or (25.2) and the accompanying assumptions define the likelihood function. The researcher can combine the likelihood function with a prior and do Bayesian inference with the resulting posterior. However, interesting and empirically important issues of identification (and, as a result, prior elicitation) arise from the fact that Π is potentially of reduced rank. A global identification issue can be seen by noting that $\Pi = \alpha\beta'$ and $\Pi = \alpha A A^{-1}\beta'$ are identical for any nonsingular A. This indeterminacy is commonly surmounted by imposing the so-called *linear normalization*, where $\beta = [I_r, B']'$. However, as we shall see, there are some drawbacks to this linear normalization. Even if global identification is imposed, a local identification issue occurs at the point $\alpha = 0$ (i.e., at this point β does not enter the model). As we shall see, this local identification problem can cause serious problems for Bayesian inference. For instance, a common non-informative prior can lead to a posterior distribution which is improper (i.e., not a valid p.d.f. since it does not integrate to one), thus precluding valid statistical inference. This issue was advanced by Kleibergen and van Dijk (1994, 1998). The development of the Bayesian cointegration literature reflects an increasing awareness of these issues and this chapter is organized to reflect this development. In particular, we begin by discussing early work, based on VAR or Vector Moving Average (VMA) representations, which ignored these issues. We then proceed to a discussion of research based on the ECM representation, beginning with a simple specification using the linear normalization and Normal priors, before moving on to the recent literature which develops methods for sensible treatment of the identification issues.

25.2 Early work: unrestricted VARs and inference conditional upon the cointegration rank

Much of the earliest Bayesian work on cointegration (e.g., DeJong, 1992; Dorfman, 1994; Koop, 1991, 1994) did not work with the cointegrated ECM. This simplified Bayesian computation, but meant that the priors used by the authors did not reflect or consider the reduced rank restrictions implied by cointegration. As a representative example of this work, consider DeJong (1992), who worked with a VAR using a noninformative prior for the model parameters. Bayesian VAR methods are simple and well-established and, hence, DeJong (1992) remained within a familiar framework (see, e.g., Zellner, 1971). He used Monte Carlo integration to take random draws from the posterior of $(\Gamma_1, .., \Gamma_k)$, which are then transformed to build up posteriors of the roots of the VAR representation. Cointegration is related to the number of nonstationary roots in the VAR, the probability of which is calculated using output from the Monte Carlo integration procedure. Given future developments, it is interesting to note that DeJong (1992) discusses the properties of his prior and points out that, despite being Uniform and "noninformative" over the VAR coefficients, it is far from Uniform over the VAR roots which are the basis for cointegration inference.

The issue that a flat prior in one representation of a model may be very informative in an undesired way in another representation will return in the next section. It is, however, important to note that, in the case where data information on the number of stationary relations in a VAR is so strong that this information follows unambiguously from the posterior of the roots of the VAR, it follows that the choice of a Uniform prior, restricted by some inequality conditions to the regions where the data are informative, is a sensible choice. In many empirically relevant economic models, like the term structure of interest rates and present value models for stock and bond prices, the data information is usually not that informative and more informative priors than the Uniform (over the VAR coefficients) are necessary. Thus, an important research area became the search for a weakly informative prior where the information in the likelihood dominates strongly but where the posterior density of parameters of interest and posterior probabilities of model characteristics are well defined.

Influential early work using the ECM includes Bauwens and Lubrano (1996), Geweke (1996) and Kleibergen and van Dijk (1994). Since this work forms the basis of much of the future Bayesian cointegration work, it is instructive to consider these papers in some detail. The key innovation of these papers was to condition on a given number of cointegrating vectors, r, and directly work with α and β. In other words, unlike previous approaches, the reduced rank nature of Π is directly imposed in a posterior simulation algorithm. This allows for Bayesian estimation and inference on α and β (and all other model parameters) for a given r. By carrying out posterior inference for every possible r, the researcher can then use standard Bayesian model comparison methods (e.g., posterior or predictive odds ratios) to select r.

Relative to the VAR, Bayesian inference in the ECM is complicated by the fact that $\Pi = \alpha\beta'$ involves a product of parameters. This precludes direct use of analytical or Monte Carlo integration results for the VAR. However, Bauwens and Lubrano (1996), Geweke (1996) and Kleibergen and van Dijk (1994) note that once we condition on the cointegrating vectors, β, the otherwise nonlinear ECM becomes a linear one. This means that, under suitable informative priors (e.g., Normal priors of the form presented in Geweke, 1996), standard Bayesian analysis of the VAR model applies (conditional on β). Furthermore, for particular specifications, the posterior distribution of β conditional on α, Ψ, Φ and Σ has a standard distribution (where $\Psi = (\Psi_1, \ldots, \Psi_{k-1})$). This suggests that a posterior simulation method known as Gibbs sampling may be set up.

Gibbs sampling starts out from an initial value for all model parameters and then produces a sequence of random draws by cycling through the *full conditional posterior distributions*, always conditioning on the most recent draws of the conditioning parameters. Under weak conditions (verified by Geweke (1996) for the prior he considers), it can be shown that this sequence of draws from the full conditionals converges to a sequence of draws from the joint posterior density. Thus, Gibbs sampler output can be treated in the same fashion as output from a Monte Carlo integration procedure (e.g., averages of draws converge to posterior means).

A Gibbs sampling algorithm for the cointegrated ECM consists of the following steps:

1. Initialize all parameter matrices: $\alpha^{(0)}, \beta^{(0)}, \Psi^{(0)}, \Phi^{(0)}$ and $\Sigma^{(0)}$ with, for example, the maximum likelihood estimates in Johansen (1995).
2. Generate a draw $\Sigma^{(1)}$ from the posterior distribution of Σ conditional on $\alpha^{(0)}, \beta^{(0)}, \Psi^{(0)}, \Phi^{(0)}$.
3. Generate a draw $(\Psi^{(1)}, \Phi^{(1)})$ from the joint posterior distribution of Ψ and Φ conditional on $\alpha^{(0)}, \beta^{(0)}$ and $\Sigma^{(1)}$.
4. Generate a draw $\alpha^{(1)}$ from the joint posterior distribution of α conditional on $\beta^{(0)}, \Psi^{(1)}, \Phi^{(1)}$ and $\Sigma^{(1)}$.
5. Generate a draw $\beta^{(1)}$ from the joint posterior distribution of β conditional on $\alpha^{(1)}, \Psi^{(1)}, \Phi^{(1)}$ and $\Sigma^{(1)}$.
6. Repeat steps 2–5 until the sequence of draws $\{\alpha^{(i)}, \beta^{(i)}, \Psi^{(i)}, \Phi^{(i)}, \Sigma^{(i)}\}_{i=1}^N$ is large enough to provide an accurate approximation of the properties of $p(\alpha, \beta, \Psi, \Phi, \Sigma | Data)$.[2]

Geweke (1996) also discusses methods of evaluating the accuracy of estimates of posterior properties of functions of the parameters (e.g., posterior means) produced using the Gibbs sampler. The posterior density itself may be estimated from $\{\alpha^{(i)}, \beta^{(i)}, \Psi^{(i)}, \Phi^{(i)}, \Sigma^{(i)}\}_{i=1}^N$ using simple histograms or more sophisticated density estimates. Posterior moments are, in most cases, easily computed by arithmetic averages.

Geweke (1996) addressed the global identification issue described in section 25.1 through linear normalizations such as $\beta = [I_r \; B']'$. He showed that, if standard informative priors are used, the Gibbs sampling algorithm is of a particularly simple form, involving only draws from the multivariate Normal distribution (in Steps 3, 4 and 5) and the inverted Wishart (in Step 2). The standard prior considered by Geweke (1996) involved Normal forms for α, B, Ψ and Φ and an inverted Wishart form for Σ.

Even if the linear normalization is retained, the sampling scheme outlined above is not generally applicable for all of the priors for B that one may wish to choose. However, given the standard form of the posterior for $(\alpha, \Psi, \Phi, \Sigma | B)$, once a draw of B is obtained, the drawing of the remaining parameters is straightforward regardless of the form of the prior for B. This suggests, then, that a method of sampling B from its marginal posterior distribution is required. To this end, Bauwens and Lubrano (1996) present an approach to obtaining draws of B using importance sampling, while Bauwens and Giot (1998) demonstrate that a particular sort of Gibbs sampler known as griddy-Gibbs works well.

Bauwens and Lubrano (1996) and Geweke (1996), who developed computational methods which allowed for simple and efficient Bayesian inference in the cointegrated ECM under a range of commonly-used priors (including an apparently "noninformative" one), seemed to complete the research project establishing the basic tools for Bayesian analysis of cointegrated models. However, it soon became clear that there were problems with these early approaches (some of which were noted already by Kleibergen and van Dijk, 1994), which stimulated a flurry of additional approaches. Before describing these approaches, we first explain what these problems are.

25.3 Problems with the early work: identification and normalization issues

As we have seen in section 25.2, several standard prior distributions have emerged in the early Bayesian cointegration literature. Most of them are either non-informative or *conjugate*, i.e., priors with the attractive property of leading to posterior distributions in the same parametric family as the prior. Even when non-conjugate informative priors are used, it is common to stay within familiar frameworks which make computation easy. Typically, in Normal likelihood models, the use of Normal priors over regression coefficients and inverted-Wishart priors over error covariance matrices is particularly convenient. These prior choices are made, for example, in Geweke (1996). When designing priors for a new model class, it is common practice to use such standardized priors, at least as a first attempt, and the cointegrated VAR is no exception.

There are two main features of the cointegrated ECM which make the standard priors unsuitable for cointegration analysis, however. First, the reduced rank restriction of the cointegrated ECM introduces a rather complex nonlinearity into the otherwise linear VAR. Most standard priors have been developed and evaluated on linear models and there is no guarantee that their properties will carry over to nonlinear models. Second, the cointegrated ECM is inherently nonidentified in the sense that the cointegration vectors are only uniquely determined up to arbitrary linear combinations (see section 25.1), i.e., data only carries information about the cointegration space. This means that the cointegration vectors must be restricted for identification and that the set of unrestricted elements of β that remain to be estimated depends on the chosen identification scheme. As mentioned, a common choice of identifying restrictions is the set of linear restrictions. To implement these restrictions, we assume we know which r rows of β will be linearly independent, partition $\beta = (\beta_1', \beta_2')'$, where β_1 is $r \times r$, and specify a selection matrix c such that $c\beta$ is invertible ($|c\beta| \neq 0$). Next, we normalize upon these rows by $\beta(c\beta)^{-1}$. For example, assume we select the first r rows ($c = [I_r \, 0]$), then the resulting specification for β will be the linear normalization $\beta = [I_r \, B']'$, where $B = \beta_2\beta_1^{-1}$. This, however, will have implications for the specification of α as these two parameters always occur in the model as the product $\alpha\beta'$. The choice of prior is thus intertwined with the choice of identification, which makes the prior speci- fication a rather delicate problem.

An example of how a straightforward adoption of traditional priors to the cointegrated ECM brings unwanted distortion of prior beliefs is given by Strachan and van Dijk (2004). They show that a flat and apparently "noninformative" prior on B in the linear normalization $\beta = [I_r \, B']'$ favors the cointegration spaces near the region where the linear normalization is invalid ($|c\beta| = 0$). Hence, the linear nor- malization is used under the assumption that it is valid, while at the same time the prior says that the normalization is very likely to be invalid.

Assuming we use the linear identifying restrictions, another important issue identified by Kleibergen and van Dijk (1994) is that of local nonidentification. The issue here is that when α has reduced rank (e.g., $\alpha = 0$) the conditional posterior distribution for $B \,|\, \alpha$ is equal to its prior (i.e., since B does not enter the likelihood function at the point $\alpha = 0$ there is no data-based learning about B and, thus, its posterior equals its prior at this point). If the prior for $B \,|\, \alpha = 0$ is improper (as it is in the common "noninformative" case), then the posterior will also be improper. Formally, Kleibergen and van Dijk (1994) associate the local non-identification problem with nonexistence of posterior moments and non-integrability of the posterior (under a common noninformative prior). Kleibergen and van Dijk (1998) additionally point out that local non-identification implies an absorbing state in a Gibbs sampler, thereby violating the convergence conditions for the sampler.

Another issue with the identifying restrictions is the validity of the chosen normalization. Put differently, when we select c (and so the rows of β upon which to normalize), we may make an invalid selection such that $c\beta$ is singular. There has been much work in the classical framework addressing this issue (see, for example, Boswijk, 1996 and Luukkonen, Ripatti and Saikkonen, 1999), and a Bayesian investigation is provided in Strachan (2003). Finally, even if the chosen normal- ization is valid, the class of models that may be considered is restricted to exclude some that have proven very important in cointegration analysis generally. For example, Strachan and van Dijk (2004) show that imposing weak exogeneity results in an improper posterior not only when a noninformative prior is used, but also when particular informative priors are used.

25.4   Prior distributions for the cointegrated ECM

As discussed in the previous section, priors placed upon the elements of the cointegrating vectors B, even ones which appeared to be "noninformative," have many important (and often undesirable) impacts upon empirical analysis. In this section, we describe three key recent approaches for surmounting many of the problems outlined in the previous section. The first, which we only briefly discuss, is the Jeffreys' prior approach (e.g., Kleibergen and van Dijk (1994)). The second is the embedding approach due to Kleibergen (1997), Kleibergen and van Dijk (1998), Kleibergen and Paap (2002) and Kleibergen (2004), and extended in Strachan (2003). These approaches deal variously with issues of local non-identification and the possibility of using invalid identifying restrictions. The third line of research, see Villani (2000) and the further developments in Villani (2005a), Strachan (2003), Strachan and Inder (2004) and Strachan and van Dijk (2004), shifts the focus from the cointegrating vectors to treating the cointegrating space $\text{sp}(\beta)$ as the object of interest.

25.4.1 The Jeffreys' prior approach

In proposing the use of the Jeffreys' prior, Kleibergen and van Dijk (1994) were motivated by the result that at points of local nonidentification (such as where α has reduced rank) the Jeffreys' prior is zero. Thus these problematic points are excluded from the support of (α, B) in the posterior distribution. This approach has been extended by Martin (2001) to a fractional cointegration model. The Jeffreys' prior has the additional advantage that it is invariant with respect to certain specifications of the model and thus is more attractive than a Uniform prior. The posterior of several parameters of interest (such as r and k in (25.2)) becomes improper, however, due to the Jeffreys' prior being improper (see subsection 25.5.3 for further discussion on this issue, commonly termed Bartlett's paradox). In light of this, posterior probabilities on sharp nulls are not well defined (e.g., selecting a value for r cannot be done using posterior odds ratios). This point, which lessens the usefulness of the Jeffreys' prior for cointegration analysis, will be elaborated on in section 25.5. Another problem when using the Jeffreys' prior is the treatment of initial conditions. This matter is discussed in Kleibergen and van Dijk (1994), where a number of possible solutions are outlined.

25.4.2 The embedding approach

The embedding approach is a way of addressing the problems arising from the local identification problem discussed in section 25.3. This approach is based upon the insight that, while Π is globally identified, the problems arising from local non-identification exist because Π has reduced rank if cointegration occurs. However, a so-called *embedding model* can be constructed which nests the ECMs for various values of r and, crucially, contains a matrix of parameters, λ, which reflects the degree of rank reduction. In this approach, prior elicitation is carried out by first eliciting a prior for the unrestricted embedding model, i.e., $p(\Pi)$. Then a transformation from Π to α, β and λ is carried out to obtain the prior $p(\alpha, \beta, \lambda)$. Priors for the reduced rank ECMs are then obtained as this prior conditional on $\lambda = 0$, $p(\alpha, \beta | \lambda = 0)$. As we shall see in this subsection, such an approach has many desirable properties.

Kleibergen and van Dijk (1994) investigate the implications of employing a simple variable addition specification for the restriction of the $p \times p$ long-run multiplier matrix Π to reduced rank. They consider the decomposition

$$\Pi = \begin{bmatrix} \Pi_{11} & \Pi_{12} \\ \Pi_{21} & \Pi_{22} \end{bmatrix} = \begin{bmatrix} \alpha_1 \\ \alpha_2 \end{bmatrix} [I_r \quad B'] + \begin{bmatrix} 0 & 0 \\ 0 & \lambda \end{bmatrix}$$

where Π_{11} and α_1 are $r \times r$ matrices, Π_{12}, Π'_{21} and α_2 are $r \times (p - r)$ matrices and Π_{22} and λ are $(p - r) \times (p - r)$ matrices. The embedding model is (25.2) with this specification for Π. Note that, if $\lambda = 0$, then this model is the cointegrated ECM with r cointegrating vectors. The embedding approach involves putting a prior over the parameters in the embedding model, and the prior for the ECM with r cointegrating vectors is derived from this prior conditional on $\lambda = 0$.

The validity of this approach relies upon the following argument. If the matrix Π has reduced rank $r < p$, then it has r linearly independent rows and columns. If we know which rows and columns these are, we may rearrange the matrix such that these are the first r rows and columns and Π_{11} is of full rank r and we have the definitions $\alpha_1 = \Pi_{11}, \alpha_2 = \Pi_{21}, B' = \Pi_{11}^{-1}\Pi_{12}$ and $\lambda = \Pi_{22} - \Pi_{21}\Pi_{11}^{-1}\Pi_{12}$. In this case, if Π has reduced rank r (and, thus, $\lambda = 0$) then this implies $\Pi_{22} = \Pi_{21}\Pi_{11}^{-1}\Pi_{12}$.[3]

A local identification problem occurs where $\alpha_1 = \Pi_{11} = 0$ and, as we have seen in section 25.3, this causes problems for Bayesian analysis. If we knew which rows and columns of Π are linearly independent we could simply exclude from the support of Π_{11} the point where $|\Pi_{11}| = 0$. Problems arise, however, when we do not know which rows and columns of Π are linearly independent – which occurs in most practical situations. Kleibergen and Paap (2002) also link this approach to the problem of non-uniqueness of the posterior distribution of α and B conditional upon rank reduction, a manifestation of the Borel–Kolmogorov paradox.

For this reason, a direct application of the embedding approach along the lines outlined above is problematic. However, Kleibergen and van Dijk (1998), and subsequently Kleibergen and Paap (2002), address this issue by proposing a singular value decomposition (see, e.g., Golub and van Loan, 1989, p. 70). To see how this avoids the problem of not knowing which rows and columns of Π are linearly independent, consider the singular value decomposition of Π as

$$\Pi = USV' = U_1 S_1 V'_1 + U_2 S_2 V'_2$$

where

$$V = \begin{bmatrix} V_{11} & V_{12} \\ V_{21} & V_{22} \end{bmatrix}, U = \begin{bmatrix} U_{11} & U_{12} \\ U_{21} & U_{22} \end{bmatrix}, S = \begin{bmatrix} S_1 & 0 \\ 0 & S_2 \end{bmatrix}$$

S is a diagonal matrix with the (positive) singular values of Π in descending order down the diagonal and both U and V are orthonormal matrices such that $U'U = V'V = I_p$. Further, U_{11}, S_1 and V_{11} are $r \times r$ matrices such that, given Π is a $p \times p$ matrix, the dimensions of the remaining matrices are subsequently defined.

From the singular value decomposition above, the elements of the cointegrating model are defined by Kleibergen and Paap (2002) as $\alpha' = V_{11}S_1(U'_{11} \ U'_{21})$, $B = V_{11}^{-1}V_{12}$ and $\lambda = (V'_{22}V_{22})^{-1/2}V_{22}S_2U'_{22}(U_{22}U'_{22})^{-1/2}$. The decomposition of Π then becomes

$$\Pi = \alpha\beta' + \alpha_\perp\lambda\beta'_\perp$$

such that a rank of r implies $S_2 = 0$ and so $\lambda = 0$ and $\Pi = \alpha\beta'$. The implementation of this approach requires specification of the posterior for the full rank Π, $p_\pi(\Pi|y)$, and then the transformation to (α, B, λ) to obtain the posterior

$$p_\theta(\alpha, B, \lambda|y) = p_\pi(\alpha\beta' + \alpha_\perp\lambda\beta'_\perp|y)|J(\Pi : \alpha, B, \lambda)|,$$

where $|J(\Pi : \alpha, B, \lambda)|$ is the Jacobian for the transformation from Π to (α, B, λ). The reduced rank model obtains by considering this distribution at the point $\lambda = 0$. In the previous equation we have used y as generic notation for data and θ as generic notation for all parameters in the model.

It is interesting to note the relationship between the Jeffreys' prior and embedding approaches. As we have seen, an attractive property of the Jeffreys' prior is that it is zero at points of local nonidentification (such as where α has reduced rank) and, thus, these points are excluded from the support of (α, B) in the posterior distribution. The singular value approach uses a similar (related) behavior of the Jacobian for the transformation from Π to exclude points of local nonidentification from the support of the posterior. That is, when α has reduced rank, $|J(\Pi : \alpha, B, \lambda)| = 0$. Kleibergen and Zivot (2003) show that the Jeffreys' prior results from the embedding approach when the embedding specification is imposed upon $\Pi^* = (\Sigma x_{t-1}x'_{t-1})^{\frac{1}{2}}\Pi\Sigma^{-\frac{1}{2}}$ and a flat prior is specified on Π^*.

The embedding approach was a significant advance in Bayesian cointegration analysis in overcoming the problems associated with local nonidentification and results in a prior that is invariant to the chosen normalization (from the set of linear normalizations). However, the linear normalization was used in its development and, thus, does not address the problem of global nonidentification. This point is made in detail in Strachan (2003), who links the use of linear identifying restrictions to a range of problems (some discussed in section 25.3) and, in particular, to the issue that using linear identifying restrictions places a restriction on the estimable region of the cointegrating space (see subsection 25.5.3 for further discussion). Strachan and Inder (2004) provide an extensive discussion of further problems associated with the use of linear identifying restrictions. Strachan (2003) therefore proposes a specification of the identifying restrictions in an embedding approach that does not restrict the estimable cointegration space. The work discussed in the following section takes this concept further.

25.4.3 The cointegration space approach

The global identification problem (i.e., that there are an infinite number of ways of carrying out the decomposition $\Pi = \alpha\beta'$) mentioned in the introduction implies that the cointegration vectors are only identified up to arbitrary linear combinations. Thus, only the space spanned by the cointegrating vectors, $\mathfrak{p} = sp(\beta)$, can be estimated from data. Taking the cointegration space as the fundamental entity in cointegration models leads naturally to the view, expounded in Villani (2000), that a prior on the cointegration vectors should be evaluated by how it distributes probability mass across the support of p. For example, it is natural to use a Uniform distribution over the support of p to express ignorance. However, as demonstrated in Strachan and Inder (2004), a Uniform prior on B implies a very different informative, and undesirable, prior distribution on p. Developing a prior for p requires, therefore, a way of visualizing the parameter p, its support, and ways of placing priors upon this support.

Formally and generally, the cointegrating space p is an r-dimensional hyper-plane in a p-dimensional space and its relation to the cointegrating vectors β is that these vectors lie in and thereby identify that plane. To assist in visualizing the parameter p, we give two simple examples. Consider first the case where $p=2$ and $r=1$ such that β is a 2×1 vector. This vector is shown in Figure 25.1 as the black line with the open arrow head. The space spanned by this vector $p = sp(\beta)$ is the dashed line in which the vector lies. The support of p is, in this case, the collection of all possible lines passing through the origin. To generalize this slightly, consider the case $p=3$ and $r=2$ such that β is a 3×2 matrix and each of the 3×1 vectors are plotted in Figure 25.2. In this case p is the two-dimensional cross-hatched plane in which the vectors lie and the support of p is all of the two-dimensional planes passing through the origin such that all directions for the planes are covered.

The support for p (which we will formally define in a moment) in general, then, is a rather abstract space. Three questions come to mind: (i) is there a non-controversial definition of a Uniform distribution over the set of cointegra-tion spaces?; (ii) does such a distribution exist?; and (iii) is it unique? All three

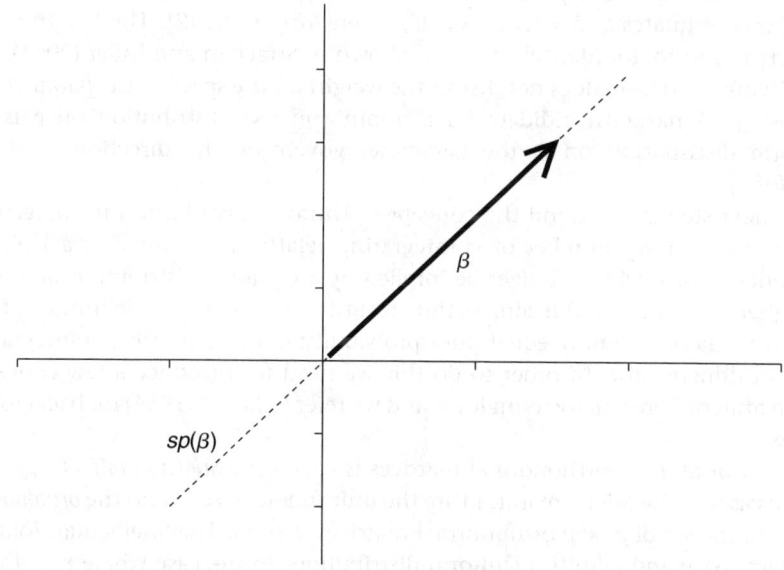

Figure 25.1   The cointegrating space is the one-dimensional plane, or line, represented by the dashed line. The vector lying in the cointegrating space is a cointegrating vector

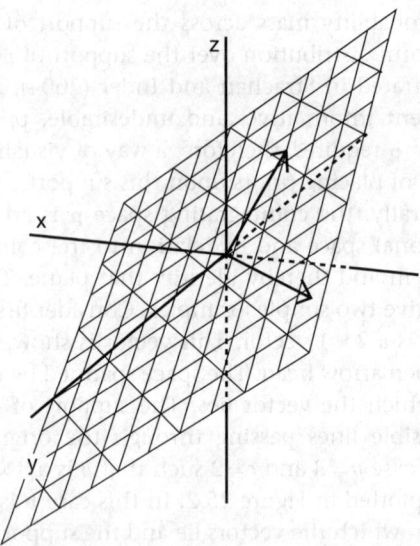

Figure 25.2 Two-dimensional cointegrating space represented by the cross-hatched plane. The two vectors lying in the plane are therefore cointegrating vectors

of these questions can be answered in the affirmative and the appropriate mathematical apparatus has been around for nearly a century.

In order to describe this line of research, we revert to the simplest case in Figure 25.1 of a bivariate process with a single cointegration vector parameterized in polar coordinates as $\beta = (\cos\theta \ \sin\theta)'$, where $\theta \in (-\pi/2, \pi/2)$. The length of β is restricted to unity for identification. As shown in Strachan and Inder (2004), this identifying restriction does not distort the weight on the space of the parameter of interest, p. A natural candidate for a noninformative distribution on p is the Uniform distribution on θ, the parameter governing the direction of β and therefore p.

The next step is to extend the concept of Uniform distribution to the general case of an arbitrary number of cointegrating relations. In this case a Uniform distribution for p will no longer be implied by a Uniform distribution on angles in higher dimensions. Our aim is thus to arrive at a rigorous definition of the intuitive idea of assigning equal prior probability to every possible cointegration space of dimension r. In order to do this we need to introduce a few concepts. Our treatment here will focus on ideas and we refer to James (1954) for background details.

The set of all $p \times r$ orthonormal matrices is called the *Stiefel manifold* $\mathbb{V}_{p,r}$. Two special cases of the Stiefel manifold are the unit sphere ($r = 1$) and the *orthonormal group* $\mathbb{O}_p$, the set of $p \times p$ orthonormal matrices ($r = p$). The Stiefel manifold is a compact space and admits a Uniform distribution. In the case where $r = 1$, one might conceptualize the collection of directions of all p-dimensional unit vectors, $\beta \in \mathbb{V}_{p,1}$, as describing a p-dimensional unit sphere centered at the origin. Thus, we may visualize a Uniform distribution on the p-dimensional unit sphere as characterizing a Uniform distribution on $\mathbb{V}_{p,1}$. For $r > 1$, we can think of each vector in β as describing a unit sphere with the additional restriction that the vectors are all orthogonal to each other.

The *Grassman manifold* $\mathbb{G}_{p,r}$ is the abstract space of all possible r-dimensional planes of $\mathbb{R}^p$. An example of an element of $\mathbb{G}_{3,2}$ is given as the two-dimensional cross-hatched plane in Figure 25.2. This defines the cointegrating space (the parameter of interest) as an element of the Grassman manifold (the support of the parameter), that is $\mathfrak{p} \in \mathbb{G}_{p,r}$. As stated earlier, in the ECM only the space spanned by the columns of β is identified, such that we only have information on $\mathfrak{p} = sp(\beta) \in \mathbb{G}_{p,r}$. A Uniform prior for the cointegration space is therefore given by the Uniform distribution on $\mathbb{G}_{p,r}$.

The next step is to make the notion of a Uniform prior distribution on $\mathbb{G}_{p,r}$ operational for a Bayesian analysis. Villani (2000, 2005a) develops the Uniform prior on the cointegrating space in the linear normalization of β. He shows that a matrix Cauchy prior on β, coupled with a specific normal prior on α, implies a uniformly distributed cointegration space.

The linear normalization may be regarded as convenient in many respects, but, as discussed in Strachan and Inder (2004) and Strachan and van Dijk (2004), it has a number of drawbacks (some discussed in section 25.3, but also some others which we will not elaborate on here). These papers develop an alternative approach which avoids the use of linear identifying restrictions through a more direct method of eliciting a prior on $\mathbb{G}_{p,r}$. This approach uses the natural relationship between the Grassman manifold and the Stiefel manifold and the development of measures on these spaces presented in James (1954). In particular, they use the result that the Uniform distribution on $\mathbb{V}_{p,r}$ induces a Uniform distribution on $\mathbb{G}_{p,r}$ (James, 1954; Strachan and Inder, 2004). Thus, it is possible to work with semiorthogonal matrices, i.e., $\beta \in \mathbb{V}_{p,r}$, and adjust all integrals by dividing with the volume of $\mathbb{O}_r$ (James, 1954; Strachan and van Dijk, 2004) to account for the fact that $\mathbb{V}_{p,r}$ is a larger space than $\mathbb{G}_{p,r}$. A convenient feature of this approach is that no normalization is imposed, but if a normalization is desired, this may be imposed after estimation of β.

So far, all our discussion in this subsection focusses on the prior for the cointegration space and ignores the other parameters in the model. For completeness, we should mention that the prior distribution on Σ, Γ and Φ may be chosen in many ways. For instance, ideas from the traditional VAR literature may be used (e.g., the well-known Minnesota prior in Litterman (1986) can be used). A common reference prior for the adjustment coefficients is $\alpha_i | \Sigma \overset{iid}{\sim} N(0, \sigma_\alpha^2 \Sigma)$, where α_i contains the adjustment coefficients for the ith cointegrating relation in the semiorthogonal normalization of β (see Strachan and Inder, 2004; and Villani, 2005a). The hyperparameter σ_α controls the shrinkage toward the zero matrix.

25.4.3.1 *Informative priors on the cointegrating space*

Although the Uniform prior is often used in theoretical work, it is common for practitioners to employ informative priors for parameters. Strachan and Inder

(2004) therefore present a method of eliciting an informative prior for p. The objectives of the method they propose are to place the mass of the prior distribution upon some preferred location, and to specify some level of dispersion for this distribution. The discussion here is cursory for brevity and we refer the reader to Strachan and Inder (2004) for details.

If a researcher believes a parameter is likely to have a particular value, to incorporate this prior belief she places more prior mass around this likely point. Here the "parameter" is the cointegrating space, p, and it will often be the case that a researcher has prior beliefs about plausible regions of this space. As a simple example, consider a vector of four interest rates $x_t = (x_{1,t}\ x_{2,t}\ x_{3,t}\ x_{4,t})$. Various expectations theories of the term structure of interest rates imply that, if each of the $x_{i,t}$ has a unit root, the spreads, $x_{i,t} - x_{j,t}$, will be stationary. This would suggest that such prior beliefs can be expressed through a matrix H (see Johansen, 1995 for examples and Strachan and van Dijk, 2003 for an application), such as

$$H = \begin{bmatrix} 1 & 0 & 0 \\ -1 & 1 & 0 \\ 0 & -1 & 1 \\ 0 & 0 & -1 \end{bmatrix}.$$

Since $sp(H) = sp(H\kappa)$ for any full rank square κ, after constructing H, we may innocuously map H to $V_{r,n}$ by the transformation $H \to H(H'H)^{-1/2}$. For the parameter p then, denote the likely or location value as $p^h = sp(H)$.

A dogmatic prior for p could be obtained by letting $\beta = H$ and this prior assigns probability one to the point $p = p^h$. However, it is common that the researcher will want to employ a less dogmatic prior. In our example, we may wish the random space p to have a mean under the prior of p^h, but be allowed to vary over the entire Grassman manifold. This is achieved by introducing a random scalar τ which performs a number of roles. First, it acts as a weight such that mass of the prior distribution is distributed over the Grassman manifold between the space of H and the space of $H_\perp$ which lies in the orthogonal complement of p^h. Second, the variance of τ controls the dispersion of the distribution of p around the location p^h. Finally, as the sign of τ may be positive or negative with equal probability, probability mass is allocated to all regions of the Grassman manifold, including between the spaces of H and $-H_\perp$.

One method of developing an informative prior is as follows. Let the random scalar τ have $E(\tau) = 0$ and $E(\tau^2) = \sigma_\tau^2$. For example, we may choose $\tau \sim N(0, \sigma_\tau^2)$. The value of σ_τ will control the tightness of the prior around p^h. Next construct $P_\tau = HH' + H_\perp H'_\perp \tau$ and let the $n \times r$ matrix Z be distributed as $vec(Z) \sim N(0, I_{nr})$. The matrix $X = P_\tau Z$ can be decomposed as $X = \beta \kappa$, where $\beta \in V_{r,n}$ and κ is an $r \times r$ lower triangular matrix. The resulting distribution for $p = sp(\beta)$ will then be centred upon p^h with its dispersion around this point determined by the value chosen for σ_τ. The reader interested in more detail is referred to Strachan and Inder (2004).

This completes our discussion of prior elicitation. Of course, a researcher may choose any prior she wishes to reflect her prior beliefs. In this section, we have described several common choices, ending with a discussion of prior elicitation (both informative and noninformative) directly over the cointegration space. We argue that this last approach, which surmounts the problems caused by global and local nonidentification in a sensible manner, will be the preferable one to use in most applications. Now that we have interesting classes of priors and a likelihood (given by equation 25.2 and the assumption of Normal errors), we can proceed to posterior analysis.

25.5 Posterior distributions: $p(r|y)$ and $p(\beta|r, y)$

In Bayesian cointegration analysis there are usually two primary aims. The first is to determine the dimension of the cointegrating space, r, and the second is to obtain an estimate of that space. From the decomposition $p(\beta, r|Data) = p(\beta|Data, r)p(r|Data)$, we can frame our discussion in terms of $p(\beta|Data, r)$ and $p(r|Data)$. In this section, we discuss both analytical expressions (where they exist) and posterior simulation algorithms. The final part of this section discusses point estimation of the cointegrating space. This is a non-trivial issue in cointegration analysis due to the non-identifiability of the cointegration vectors and, as we shall see, methods that might suggest themselves intuitively are, in fact, inappropriate.

25.5.1 Analytical results

As we have seen in section 25.2, most Bayesian treatments of the ECM use posterior simulation methods such as Gibbs sampling or importance sampling. However, a few analytical results have been derived and it is constructive to examine them to help understand the properties of the posterior in cointegrated models.

Bauwens and Lubrano (1996) show that the marginal posterior of β under a common noninformative prior $p(\alpha, \beta, \Gamma, \Phi, \Sigma) \propto |\Sigma|^{-(p+1)/2}$ is of the form

$$p(\beta|Data, r) \propto \frac{|\beta' C_1 \beta|^{l_1}}{|\beta' C_2 \beta|^{l_2}}, \tag{25.3}$$

where C_1 and C_2 are $p \times p$ data matrices and l_1 and l_2 are scalars (see Bauwens and Lubrano (1996) for precise definitions). In terms of B in the linear normalization $\beta = (I_r, B')'$, this density can be written as a ratio of two matrix t density kernels. This type of density has been termed a 1-1 poly matrix t density by Drèze (1978). Villani (2005a) shows that, for the specification used in that paper, the marginal posterior of B, with a Uniform prior on the Grassman manifold (see section 25.4.2) and a proper prior on α, is of the same form with different parameters C_1, C_2, l_1 and l_2.

The posterior distribution of B in (25.3) is integrable, but lacks moments of any order (see Kleibergen and van Dijk, 1994; or Bauwens and Lubrano, 1996). Villani (2005a) points out that this is a natural feature of the prior in the linear normalization. To see this, let $\beta \in \mathbb{V}_{p,r}$ such that a Uniform distribution on $\mathbb{V}_{p,r}$ implies a Uniform distribution on $\mathbb{G}_{p,r}$. Then B equals the matrix quotient $\beta_2 \beta_1^{-1}$, where β_1 and β_2 are the upper $r \times r$ and lower $(p - r) \times r$ submatrices of β, respectively, with a

Cauchy form for the Jacobian for this transformation $\beta \rightarrow B$, and B will therefore have very fat (Cauchy-like) tails in the posterior. In explaining why the maximum likelihood estimator occasionally produces very unreliable estimates of B, Phillips (1994) makes the same point in proving that this estimator has Cauchy tails. By contrast, Strachan and van Dijk (2004) prove that all posterior moments of β are finite in their approach, with β specified as a semiorthogonal matrix, $\beta \in \mathbb{V}_{p,r}$.

The analytical posterior results for B are useful for establishing some vital properties of the posterior, such as integrability, but are of limited value to practitioners as the class of poly matrix t distributions is, to a large extent, unexplored beyond the dimension $r = 1$. For example, marginal distributions and moments of poly matrix t variates (the case where $r > 1$) are not known. With the semi-orthogonal specification for β of Strachan and Inder (2004), many more analytical results can be obtained. However, analytical results for $p(\beta \,|\, Data, r)$ are not enough to deliver posterior distributions of various features of interest, such as forecasts and impulse response functions, which are important components in applied work. For these reasons, most Bayesian researchers use posterior simulation.

25.5.2   Posterior simulation in the cointegrated ECM

The Gibbs and importance samplers discussed previously (e.g., those in Geweke (1996) and Bauwens and Lubrano (1996) described at the end of section 25.2) were designed for models with computationally convenient priors. However, with the more sophisticated (and reasonable) priors of section 25.4, they cannot be directly applied. Kleibergen and van Dijk (1998) point out the complication that, due to the presence of local nonidentification, an inappropriately designed Gibbs sampler will have an absorbing state and so produce a reducible Markov chain, thus violating the conditions necessary for convergence of the chain to the posterior. Accordingly, it is useful to offer a more general discussion of posterior simulation methods. As discussed in section 25.2, the key challenges for posterior computation arise due to α and β entering the ECM in a nonlinear fashion. Hence, much of this discussion is focussed on these parameters. To simplify notation, we will collect the parameters other than α, β and r into the vector θ.

Posterior simulation with respect to θ and α is generally straightforward and integration with respect to (θ, α) can often be achieved analytically as the posterior distributions for elements of $(\theta\ \alpha)$ (conditional upon β and r) belong to well-understood standard classes of distributions, such as the multivariate Normal, inverted Wishart or Generalized Student-t distributions (see for example Zellner (1971) or Bauwens and van Dijk (1990)). For these parameters, methods such as those outlined in section 25.2 can be used. Notable exceptions to this case are the embedding specifications which incorporate a complicated Jacobian term, such as Kleibergen and van Dijk (1998), Kleibergen and Paap (2002), and Strachan (2003) (see subsection 25.4.2), and the Jeffreys' prior approach of Kleibergen and van Dijk (1994).

In contrast to $p(\theta, \alpha \,|\, Data, \beta, r)$, posterior simulation of β is not straightforward. There are three general approaches that have been taken. The first is to draw from $p(\beta \,|\, Data, \theta, \alpha, r)$ in the context of a Markov Chain Monte Carlo (MCMC) algorithm. Examples of this approach are Geweke (1996), Kleibergen and van Dijk (1998), Kleibergen and Paap (2002) and Strachan (2003). With the computationally convenient prior of Geweke (1996), $p\ (\beta\,|\,Data,\ \theta,\ \alpha,\ r)$ is Normal and Gibbs sampling is straightforward. However, for the other three studies, $p\ (\beta\,|\,Data,\ \theta,\ \alpha,\ r)$ is not of a simple form form and a standard Gibbs sampler cannot be employed. Thus, in these articles, a Metropolis–Hastings algorithm (see Chib and Greenberg (1995)) is developed in which the candidate density is derived from the full rank VAR.

A second approach uses the standard form for $p\ (\theta,\ \alpha\,|\,Data,\ \beta,\ r)$ to analytically integrate with respect to $(\theta,\ \alpha)$. Then draws from $p\ (\beta\,|\,Data,\ r)$ are taken. If $r = 1$ such that B has a 1-1 poly-t density, moments may be approximated using the approach detailed in Richard and Tompa (1980). For $r \geq 1$, Bauwens and Lubrano (1996) used an importance sampling scheme (see Kloek and van Dijk, 1978; or Geweke, 1989) to obtain draws from the posterior distribution of B. Alternatively, by showing that the conditional densities for $(\beta_1|\beta_2,\ldots,\beta_r), (\beta_2|\beta_1,\beta_3,\ldots,\beta_r),\ldots$ and so on, are 1-1 poly-t, they suggest a Gibbs sampling approach could be used and such an algorithm is presented in Bauwens and Richard (1985). This approach is useful only for a Uniform prior on B, and so Bauwens and Giot (1998) present a griddy-Gibbs sampler for obtaining draws on B for more general priors. Strachan and van Dijk (2004), who use both Uniform and informative priors over the cointegration space, also work with $p\ (\beta\,|\,Data,\ r)$ but use a Metropolis–Hastings algorithm.

A third approach is presented by Villani (2005a), in which θ is analytically integrated out and an MCMC scheme developed to draw from $p\ (\beta\,|\,Data,\ r,\ \alpha)$ and $p\ (\alpha\,|\,Data,\ r,\ \beta)$. This approach, which uses the linear normalization $\beta = [I_r\ B']'$, takes advantage of the result that the conditional densities for $\alpha\,|\,B$ and $B\,|\,\alpha$ are Generalized Student t such that a Gibbs sampler may be used.

An important advantage of a simulation-based evaluation of the posterior distribution is that the posterior distribution of any quantity which is a function of the parameters and the data can easily be computed from the generated posterior sample. So, for instance, posterior properties of impulse response functions and forecasts are immediately available.

25.5.3 Posterior distribution of the cointegration rank

It is common to select a value for r (e.g., the posterior mode) and then base empirical results (e.g., about the cointegration space) conditionally on this choice. However, one of the advantages of the Bayesian approach is that uncertainty about this parameter may be incorporated into the analysis by using $p\ (r\,|\,Data)$ to average across the various models. These two approaches relate, respectively, to model selection and Bayesian model averaging, the latter being a topic we will discuss in more detail below. Regardless of whether the researcher adopts a model selection or model averaging approach, it is necessary to know $p\ (r\,|\,Data)$.

In this subsection we will discuss several ways of learning about this density. Before we do this, the issue of Bartlett's paradox should be mentioned in passing. This issue arises when two models of different dimensions are being compared and is relevant here because deriving p $(r \,|\, Data)$ can be interpreted as comparing models of different dimension (e.g., $r=1$ and $r=2$ describe ECMs of different dimension). Bartlett's paradox is often informally expressed as saying improper priors[4] should be avoided when calculating Bayes factors (except over parameters common to both models), since then the Bayes factor can depend on arbitrary integrating constants. So, for instance, Bartlett's paradox implies that, with the Jeffreys' prior approach, $p(r \,|\, Data)$ cannot be obtained. Some of the technical issues in the recent literature relate to this point, although we will not elaborate on it in any detail in this survey.

Nesting the reduced rank cointegrated ECM within the embedding model (i.e., the unrestricted VAR), Kleibergen and Paap (2002) use MCMC output from a Metropolis–Hastings sampler and the Savage–Dickey density ratio (see Verdinelli and Wasserman (1995)) to estimate the Bayes factors for the model with rank $r<p$ to the model with full rank $r=p$. Using the embedding prior of subsection 25.4.2 makes estimation from the reduced rank model and its marginal likelihood computationally easy. However, the computation of the Bayes factors does require estimation of a correction factor (which is not defined for the improper prior due to Bartlett's paradox) for the ECM with $r<p$. Examples of the application of this approach are given in Paap and van Dijk (2003) and Strachan (2003). Interestingly, Kleibergen (2004) shows by use of Hausdorff measures and integrals that the posterior odds ratio developed in this way is well defined even with improper priors on the parameters of the full rank model (thus avoiding Bartlett's paradox) and negates the need to estimate the correction factor for the improper prior. The understanding of this argument requires that the researcher is comfortable with non-subjectively determined prior odds ratios and using the Hausdorff measure rather than the more commonly employed Lebesgue measure.

Villani (2005a) develops an efficient procedure for obtaining the posterior distribution of r using the (proper) Uniform prior on the cointegration space in the linear normalization. He derives closed form solutions for the posterior probabilities of $r=0$ and $r=p$. The posterior probabilities of $r=1, \ldots, p-1$ are computed from the posterior sample of α and B under each cointegration rank utilizing the method developed by Chib (1995).

Asymptotic approximations to the integral with respect to (θ, α) have also been used to obtain $p(r \,|\, Data)$. Corander and Villani (2004) use the fractional Bayes approach of O'Hagan (1995) to derive an approximation of the posterior distribution of the cointegration rank jointly with the lag length of the VAR and the deterministic trend model. The fractional Bayes approach has an intuitive appeal and has been supported by asymptotic arguments, but has also been criticized by a number of authors (see, e.g., the discussion of O'Hagan (1995) and Fernández, Ley and Steel (2001)) on the ground that it lacks a proper Bayesian interpretation.

After integrating out (θ, α) to provide an analytical form for p $(\beta, r \,|\, Data)$, Strachan and Inder (2004) use a Laplace approximation of the integral with respect to β to obtain an expression for $p(r \,|\, Data)$. This approach takes advantage of the Poincaré separation theorem from which we can obtain useful analytical results on the posterior, and utilizes techniques developed in James (1954, 1969). Chao and

Phillips (1999) use the posterior information criteria (PIC) developed in Phillips (1996) and Phillips and Ploberger (1996) to select the modal value for *r*. Related approaches are the common Schwarz Bayes information criteria (Schwarz, 1978) as a first order approximation to the marginal likelihood, while the PIC and Laplace methods use second-order approximations. A limitation of these approaches is that there is less control over the accuracy of the approximation than when using MCMC methods.

25.5.4   Point estimation of the cointegrating space

In standard inference problems one usually summarizes the posterior distribution with a measure of location, e.g., the posterior mean, median or mode, and a measure of posterior spread, e.g., the posterior standard deviation or interquartile range. The exact choice of location and spread is motivated by decision theory. The optimal posterior summary is the estimate minimizing the posterior expected loss

$$\hat{\theta} = \underset{\tilde{\theta}\in\Theta}{\operatorname{argmin}} E[l(\theta, \tilde{\theta})],$$

where $l(\theta, \tilde{\theta})$ is a loss function penalizing the discrepancy between the true parameter value and its estimate. For example, the mean, median and mode are the optimal estimates given a quadratic, absolute value or a 0-1 loss on the discrepancy $\theta - \tilde{\theta}$, respectively (see, e.g., Berger, 1985).

It may be tempting to use the standard point estimates on the unrestricted elements of β, e.g., the posterior mode or median of B in the linear normalization (as noted above, the posterior mean does not exist with some priors), and plugging these estimates into β to obtain an estimate of the cointegration vectors. Villani (2005b) criticizes this practice on two grounds. First, the loss functions underlying the standard estimates are not suitable for point estimation of the cointegrating vectors. Since only the cointegration space is identified, a loss function for estimating β should measure the discrepancy between *linear subspaces* rather than between real matrices. It is not true that if two matrices β_1 and β_2 are far apart then sp β_1 is distant from sp β_2. Optimal estimates of the cointegration vectors should thus be based on distance measures developed for the Grassman manifold. Second, by focusing on estimating unrestricted parameters under a given normalization rule, we may end up with estimates that are not invariant to the chosen normalization. For example, the estimators based on plugging in standard estimates of B into β in the linear normalization are dependent on the order of the variables in the system, even if the posterior distribution is invariant.

Strachan and Inder (2003) present a method for approximating the mode of the posterior for the cointegrating space using the Poincaré separation theorem. However, for various reasons, many Bayesians are more comfortable with or require mean estimates. Therefore, Villani (2005b) derives a more appropriate measure of location using the square of the projective Frobenius linear subspace distance

$$l(\beta, \tilde{\beta}) = \left\| \beta\beta' - \tilde{\beta}\tilde{\beta}' \right\|^2,$$

as loss function, where $\|A\| = tr(A'A)^{1/2}$ is the Frobenius norm for matrices and we have, without loss of generality, assumed that β is orthonormal. The optimal estimate, given the projective Frobenius loss, is the matrix of eigenvectors of $E(\beta\beta')$ corresponding to the r largest eigenvalues. Note that $\beta\beta'$ is the projection matrix of the linear subspace spanned by the columns of β. This estimate is thus based on a quadratic loss on the space of projection matrices and may therefore be interpreted as the mean cointegration space, rather than the mean of the unrestricted elements of β.

Villani (2005b) proposes a scalar measure of overall uncertainty in the posterior distribution of β based on the projective Frobenius linear subspace distance. He shows that this measure is independent of both the number of variables in the system and the number of cointegrating relations. It may therefore be used to compare the uncertainty regarding the estimated cointegration space in different studies. The measure is bounded between zero and one, where the upper bound is obtained if the posterior distribution is the Uniform distribution on $\mathbb{G}_{p,r}$.

25.6   Bayesian model averaging in cointegration models

As researchers usually have a range of models to use for their analysis and there is usually uncertainty as to which model generated the data, a growing area of interest in econometrics is the treatment of model uncertainty. Traditionally, choice of model form has been based on some criteria such as goodness-of-fit or on a series of nested or non-nested hypothesis tests designed to discriminate between alternative models. Inference is then based upon this chosen best model. One problem with this practice is that, once a particular model has been chosen, the fact that a number of other models have been discarded is usually ignored in measures of uncertainty for the object of interest. No allowance is made for the possibility of sample statistics yielding an incorrect choice and assessment of the precision of estimation via standard errors makes no provision for the preliminary-test implications for inference. Accounting for, and incorporating, model uncertainty can be achieved quite naturally in the Bayesian approach by using Bayesian model averaging (BMA).

The basic ideas underlying BMA can be demonstrated if we let M_i, for $i = 1, \ldots, M$, denote the ith model with parameters λ_i. Suppose we wish to learn about a function of interest common to all models (e.g., an impulse response) $\omega = g(\lambda_i)$. If we treat the M_i as random variables, then the rules of probability imply that:

$$p(\omega|Data) = \sum_{i=1}^{M} p(M_i|Data)\, p(\omega|Data, M_i).$$

In words, inferences about ω should be based on a weighted average of the posteriors in each model, where the weights are given by the posterior model probabilities $p(M_i|Data)$.[5]

Within the framework of cointegrated ECMs, a number of models can be defined based on the number of cointegrating vectors, lag lengths, or deterministic terms.

We may also have different specifications of cointegrating spaces which we may consider important. For instance, in an application involving foreign and domestic prices and an exchange rate, the theory of purchasing power parity suggests that a particular cointegrating vector should be present. Such a model implies a restricted version of $\mathfrak{p}$ such as $\mathfrak{p} = sp(H_1)$. Alternatively, one may not wish to impose the theory of purchasing power parity and express ignorance about $\mathfrak{p}$ through the Uniform priors discussed in subsection 25.4.2. Other restricted versions of the cointegrated ECM arise if exogeneity is present (Engle, Hendry and Richard (1983), Johansen (1992) and Urbain (1992)). Although exogeneity has statistical implications, it has also been given economic implications (e.g., Garratt *et al.*, 2003).

Given a set of models, the implementation of BMA in cointegrated ECMs is straightforward, requiring only a posterior simulator for every model (see the discussion in section 25.5) and a method for calculating $p(M_i | Data)$ (see the discussion in subsection 25.5.3). The use of BMA in forecasting with cointegrated ECMs is explored in Villani (2001). In a comprehensive study in which a range of methods were used, Strachan and van Dijk (2004) present posterior probabilities for very large classes of models covering all the issues we have mentioned so far: cointegrating rank; lag length; deterministic processes; overidentifying restrictions; and weak exogeneity. The empirical results suggest that BMA is an important issue in that results are substantially different from those obtained from a single model. This is undoubtedly an issue of empirical importance that will provoke a great deal of future research.

25.7 Application

In this section we provide a simple application to demonstrate some of the uniquely Bayesian aspects of the methods we have discussed, such as BMA and posterior analysis of the cointegrating space. King, Plosser, Stock and Watson (1991) investigate evidence in support of model features implied by the Balanced Growth Hypothesis within a Real Business Cycle model (RBC). The theory developed in the paper implies that there is a single common stochastic trend in log real US consumption (c_t), investment (i_t) and income (inc_t), and the log differences $c_t - inc_t$ and $i_t - inc_t$ form the cointegrating relations (if $r=2$). Collecting the variables into the vector $y_t = (c_t, i_t, inc_t)$, these restrictions imply the cointegrating vectors are overidentified as $\beta = H$, where $H = (h_1, h_2)$ and $h_1 = (1, 0, -1)'$ and $h_1 = (0, 1, -1)'$.

Using quarterly data covering the period from the first quarter 1951 to the final quarter of 1999 from the study by Paap and van Dijk (2003), Strachan and van Dijk (2004) investigate whether the restrictions of theory ($r = 2, \beta = H$) are supported. They consider a set of models involving this restriction, different numbers of cointegrating vectors, lag lengths and forms for the deterministic trends (see Strachan and van Dijk, 2004 for exact definitions). They find a high degree of posterior uncertainty about whether the implications of theory hold, but evidence against the features ($r = 2, \beta = H$) is not as strong as a sequential testing procedure might suggest. The reason why a sequential approach comes out so strongly against these features can be seen if we consider first testing $r = 2$ and then investigating whether $\beta = H$ is plausible. Without imposing the cointegrating space restrictions, we find $P(r = 2|y, \beta \neq H) \approx 0.004$. However $P(r = 2, \beta = H|y) = 0.414$ and this is the modal model (i.e., it has the highest posterior model probability). The marginal probability $P(r = 2|y)$ – averaged across models with and without the cointegrating space restrictions (and averaged across lag length and different forms for the deterministic terms) – is 0.430.

As a complementary view on the credibility of the restrictions, we may look at some measure of distance, $d = d(\beta,H)$, between the space of β, $\mathbf{p}^\beta$, and the space of H, $\mathbf{p}^H$. The fact that β is unknown causes no problems in a Bayesian analysis, as the whole posterior distribution of the distance $d(\beta,H)$ may be presented. This distribution, which is easily obtained from the simulated posterior draws of the cointegration vectors, is a clear presentation of how near the posterior distribution of β is to the subspace in β-space determined by H. As we have discussed in this chapter, the distance $d(\beta,H)$ should not be based on the usual Euclidean metric, but rather on a metric which measures the distance between two subspaces. We will use the distance measure in Larsson and Villani (2001), which in our case is conveniently bounded between zero and one. A value of $d = 1$ indicates that $\mathbf{p}^\beta$ lies in the orthogonal complement of $\mathbf{p}^H$–which is as far from $\mathbf{p}^H$ as $\mathbf{p}^\beta$ can get – and $d = 0$ indicates $\mathbf{p}^\beta = \mathbf{p}^H$.

The dashed line in Figure 25.3 is the posterior density of the distance $d = d(\beta,H)$ for the single best model chosen from the set of all possible models (assuming two cointegrating relations). This density is constructed by generating a sample $\beta^{(1)}, \ldots, \beta^{(M)}$ from the posterior $p(\beta|r = 2,y)$ and computing the distance to H for each draw. It is clear from Figure 25.3 that the main part of

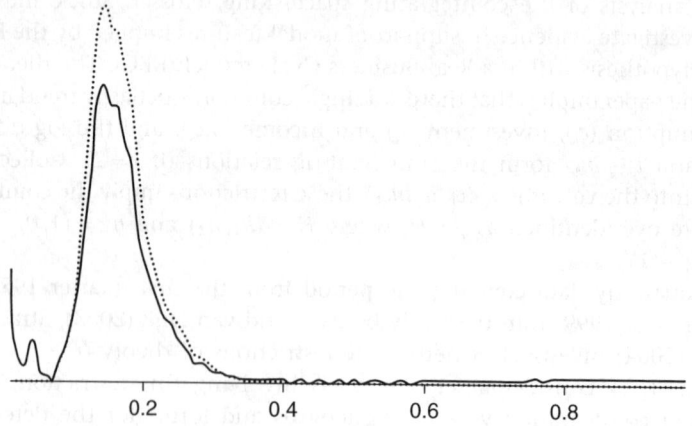

Figure 25.3　The solid line is the estimated unconditional posterior density of the distance, *d*, between the space of *β* and the space of *H*. The dashed line is the density of *d* conditional upon the best model

the posterior mass is not far from zero (the mean, median and mode are: 0.16, 0.15 and 0.14, respectively), suggesting support for $\beta = H$. The solid line in Figure 25.3 is the unconditional posterior density of the distance, where we average across lag length and deterministic processes to reduce the dependence of our results upon these features. The density is still conditional on $r = 2$. While the large bulk of the unconditional density still centers on a value slightly below 0.2, the averaging across models produces non-negligible probability mass near the point zero, thereby placing additional support on the restrictions given by H.

25.8 Conclusion

In this survey, we have discussed Bayesian inference in the cointegrated error correction model with a particular focus on r (the number of cointegrating vectors) and the cointegration space. A strong message of this survey is that, in light of global and local non-identification problems, prior elicitation is an important issue and that it is better to think in terms of the cointegration space than in terms of cointegrating vectors. In particular, apparently "noninformative" priors on cointegrating vectors can imply very (unreasonably) informative priors for the cointegration space and can even result in improper posteriors. In light of this, we have discussed in detail two main approaches to prior elicitation which surmount some or all of the problems caused by the identification problems. These approaches, which have been found to yield sensible inferences, we have called the Embedding Approach and the Cointegration Space Approach.

Fortunately, even using the Embedding and Cointegration Space approaches, posterior computation is relatively straightforward and simple MCMC algorithms can be derived. Accordingly, this chapter has only briefly discussed posterior computation.

As the majority of studies in the literature have used the traditional linear cointegrated error correction model, this has been our focus in this survey. A notable exception is G. Martin and V. Martin (2000), who present a method of obtaining inference on the triangular cointegration model of Phillips (1991) using the Jeffreys' prior. However, the models and methods we have described should also be useful when it comes to considering a myriad of possible extensions to the ECM (e.g., threshold/Markov switching cointegration models, ECMs with structural breaks or time varying parameters, different error structures, etc.).

Bayesian prior elicitation and posterior computation methods typically can be interpreted in terms of blocks of parameters. Many extensions can be interpreted as adding a new block of parameters to our current set. All the issues of prior elicitation and posterior computation described in this survey are relevant for the appropriate block of the extended model. As an example, collect all of the parameters r, α, β, Ψ, Φ and Σ into θ and consider our ECM, which is parameterized in terms of θ. We have discussed methods for eliciting the prior $p(\theta)$ and simulating from the posterior $p(\theta \mid Data)$. Now suppose we wish to extend this model to allow for a single structural break at unknown time, T^*, with θ_j for $j = 1,2$ denoting the ECM parameters before and after the break. Bayesian prior elicitation would typically involve specifying $p(\theta_j)$ and $p(T^*)$. But the issues and approaches described in this survey are relevant for $p(\theta_j)$ and, thus, the researcher need only worry about $p(T^*)$. Posterior simulation would typically involve drawing from $p(\theta_j|Data, T^*)$ (or $p(r_j, \beta_j|Data, T^*)$) and $p(T^*|Data)$ (or some posterior conditional such as $p(T^*|Data, \theta_1, \theta_2)$). But the discussion in this survey is relevant for $p(\theta_j|Data, T^*)$ and the researcher need only worry about developing a method for simulating from $p(T^*|Data)$.

Bayesian work on extensions of the cointegrated ECMs is still in its infancy and is a promising area for future research. One extension worth noting is by Paap and van Dijk (2003), who consider a Markov switching extension of a cointegrated ECM. Another is by Martin (2001), who considers a fractionally cointegrated model. Martin (2000) carries out a Bayesian analysis of a cointegration model with structural breaks. Finally, a recent PhD thesis (Sugita, 2004) considers both a Markov switching and a structural break extension of the cointegrated ECM.

Another interesting extension involves the issue of reduced rank in other classes of models, including instrumental variable regression models with weak instruments, simultaneous equations models with weak identification and factor models with common factors. Given that the same fundamental identification issues arise in cointegration, simultaneous equations and instrumental variable regression models (see Hoogerheide and van Dijk, 2001), it follows that the approaches discussed in this chapter are also applicable in those models. For instance, our terminology "Cointegration Space Approach" should not lead the reader into thinking that the approach applies only to cointegrated models.

Finally, we should also mention that there exists an extensive general discussion on the issues of identification and normalization in a Bayesian context. We refer the reader to Drèze (1974), Kadane (1974, 1978a, 1978b), Fisher (1976, 1977) and Poirier (1998) for a detailed and interesting exchange of viewpoints on these topics.

Acknowledgments

The authors would like to thank Luc Bauwens, Frank Kleibergen, Michel Lubrano, Gael Martin and Richard Paap for useful comments that have improved this chapter.

Notes

1. In this chapter, we will assume errors are Normally distributed. Extensions to more flexible distributions (for example, the Student-t) can easily be obtained by using mixtures of Normal distributions in the standard Bayesian manner. See, for instance, Geweke (1993) or Escobar and West (1995) for examples of such an approach.
2. N can be chosen using any of the standard convergence diagnostics. See, for instance, Gilks *et al.* (1996) or Geweke (1999).

3. This result must hold as, at rank r with Π_{11} full rank, each ij^{th} element of $\Pi_{22} = [\pi_{22,ij}]$ is determined by the determinant $\begin{vmatrix} \Pi_{11} & \pi_{12,j} \\ \pi_{21,i} & \pi_{22,ij} \end{vmatrix} = 0$, where $\pi_{12,j}$ is the jth column of Π_{12} and $\pi_{21,i}$ is the ith row of Π_{21}.

4. Improper priors are those which do not integrate to one. Thus, the integrating constant is not finite and must be selected/justified in some manner. Typically, for estimation of parameters, the integrating constant does not matter and use of improper priors is common. However, when doing model comparison (for example, using Bayes factors or posterior odds), the integrating constant cannot be ignored and, thus, problems such as Bartlett's paradox can arise with improper priors.

5. The posterior model probability is the prior model probability times the marginal likelihood. For cointegrated ECMs there are many ways to obtain the marginal likelihood. The discussion of subsection 25.5.3 implicitly describes some of these.

References

Bauwens, L. and A. Giot (1998) A Gibbs sampling approach to cointegration. *Computational Statistics* **13**, 339–68.

Bauwens, L. and M. Lubrano (1996) Identification restrictions and posterior densities in cointegrated Gaussian VAR systems. In *Advances in Econometrics, vol. 11, Part B*, Greenwich, CT: JAI Press, pp. 3–28.

Bauwens, L., M. Lubrano and J.-F. Richard (1999) *Bayesian Inference in Dynamic Econometric Models*. Oxford: Oxford University Press.

Bauwens, L. and J.-F. Richard (1985) A 1-1 poly-*t* random variable generator with application to Monte Carlo integration. *Journal of Econometrics* **29**, 19–46.

Bauwens, L. and H.K. van Dijk (1990) Bayesian limited information analysis revisited. In J. Gabszewicz, J.F. Richard and L. Wolsey (eds), *Economic Decision-Making: Games, Econometrics, and Decision-Making. Contributions in Honour of Jacques Drèze*. Amsterdam: North-Holland, pp. 385–424.

Berger, J.O. (1985) *Statistical Decision Theory and Bayesian Analysis*, 2nd edn. New York: Springer Verlag.

Boswijk, H.P. (1996) Testing identifiability of cointegrating vectors. *Journal of Business and Economic Statistics* **14**, 153–60.

Chao, J. and P.C.B. Phillips (1999) Model selection in partially nonstationary vector autoregressive processes with reduced rank structure. *Journal of Econometrics* **91**, 227–71.

Chib, S. (1995) Marginal likelihood from the Gibbs Sampler. *Journal of the American Statistical Association* **90**, 1313–1321.

Chib, S. and E. Greenberg (1995) Understanding the Metropolis–Hastings algorithm. *The American Statistician* **49**, 327–35.

Corander, J. and M. Villani (2004) Bayesian assessment of dimensionality in reduced rank regression. *Statistica Neerlandica* **58**, 255–70.

DeJong, D. (1992) Co-integration and trend-stationarity in macroeconomic time series. *Journal of Econometrics* **52**, 347–70.

Dorfman, J. (1994) A numerical Bayesian test for cointegration of AR processes. *Journal of Econometrics* **66**, 289–324.

Drèze, J. (1974) Bayesian theory of identification in simultaneous equations models. In S.E. Fienberg and A. Zellner (eds), *Studies in Bayesian Econometrics and Statistics*. Amsterdam: North-Holland, pp. 159–74.

Drèze, J.H. (1978) Bayesian regression analysis using poly-*t* densities. *Journal of Econometrics* **6**, 329–54.

Engle, R.F. and C.W.J. Granger (1987) Co-integration and error correction: representation, estimation and testing. *Econometrica* **55**, 251–76.

Engle, R.F., D.F. Hendry and J.-F. Richard (1983) Exogeneity. *Econometrica* **51**, 277–304.

Escobar, M. and M. West (1995) Bayesian density estimation using mixtures. *Journal of the American Statistical Association* **90**, 577–88.

Fernández, C., E. Ley and M.F.J. Steel (2001) Benchmark priors for Bayesian model averaging. *Journal of Econometrics* **100**, 381–427.

Fisher, W.D. (1976) Normalization in point estimation. *Journal of Econometrics* **4**, 243–52.

Fisher, W.D. (1978) Reply. *Journal of Econometrics* **7**, 127.

Garratt, A., K. Lee, M.H. Pesaran and Y. Shin (2003) A long run structural macroeconomic model of the UK. *Economic Journal* **113**, 412–55.

Geweke, J. (1993) Bayesian treatment of the independent Student-*t* linear model. *Journal of Applied Econometrics* **8**, S19–S40.

Geweke, J. (1996) Bayesian reduced rank regression in econometrics. *Journal of Econometrics* **75**, 121–46.

Geweke, J. (1999) Using simulation methods for Bayesian econometric models: Inference, development, and communication (with discussion and rejoinder). *Econometric Reviews* **18**, 1–126.

Gilks, W., S. Richardson and D. Speigelhalter (1996) *Markov Chain Monte Carlo in Practice*. New York: Chapman and Hall.

Golub, G. and C. van Loan (1989) *Matrix Computations*. Baltimore: Johns Hopkins University Press.

Hoogerheide, L.F. and H.K. van Dijk (2001) Comparison of the Anderson–Rubin test for overidentification and the Johansen test for cointegration. Report 2001–04 of the Econometric Institute, Erasmus University Rotterdam available at http://www.few.eur.nl/few/research/pubs/ei/2001/reports.htm.

James, A.T. (1954) Normal multivariate analysis and the orthogonal group. *Annals of Mathematical Statistic* **25**, 40–75.

James, A.T. (1969) Test of equality of the latent roots of the covariance matrix. In P.R. Krishnaiah (ed.), *Multivariate Analysis*. vol. II. New York: Academic Press, pp. 205–18.

Johansen, S. (1992) Cointegration in partial systems and the efficiency of single-equation analysis. *Journal of Econometrics* **52**, 389–402.

Johansen, S. (1995) *Likelihood-Based Inference in Cointegrated Vector Autoregressive Models*. Oxford: Oxford University Press.

Kadane, J.B. (1974) The role of identification in Bayesian theory. In S.E. Fienberg and A. Zellner (eds), *Studies in Bayesian Econometrics and Statistics*. Amsterdam: North-Holland, pp. 175–91.

Kadane, J.B. (1978a) A comment on "Normalization in point estimation." *Journal of Econometrics* **7**, 123–5.

Kadane, J.B. (1978b), Rejoinder. *Journal of Econometrics* **7**, 129.

Khatri, C.G. and K.V. Mardia (1977) The von Mises–Fisher distribution in orientation statistics. *Journal of Royal Statistical Society B* **39**, 95–106.

King, R.G., C. Plosser, J. Stock and M.W. Watson (1991) Stochastic trends and economic fluctuations. *American Economic Review* **81**, 819–40.

Kleibergen, F. (1997) Bayesian simultaneous equations analysis using equality restricted random variables. *1997 Proceedings of the Section on Bayesian Statistical Science*. American Statistical Association, pp. 141–7.

Kleibergen, F. (2004) How to overcome the Jeffreys'–Lindley paradox. Forthcoming in *Journal of Econometrics*.

Kleibergen, F. and R. Paap (2002) Prior, posteriors and Bayes factors for a Bayesian analysis of cointegration. *Journal of Econometrics* **111**, 223–49.

Kleibergen, F. and H.K. van Dijk (1994) On the shape of the likelihood/posterior in cointegration models. *Econometric Theory* **10**, 514–51.

Kleibergen, F. and H.K. van Dijk (1998) Bayesian simultaneous equations analysis using reduced rank structures. *Econometric Theory* **14**, 701–43.

Kleibergen, F. and E. Zivot (2003) Bayesian and classical approaches to instrumental variable regression. *Journal of Econometrics* **114**, 29–72.

Kloek, T. and H.K. van Dijk (1978) Bayesian estimates of equation system parameters: an application of integration by Monte Carlo. *Econometrica* **46**, 1–19.

Koop, G. (1991) Cointegration tests in present value relationships: a Bayesian look at the bivariate properties of stock prices and dividends. *Journal of Econometrics* **49**, 105–40.

Koop, G. (1994) An objective Bayesian analysis of common stochastic trends in international stock prices and exchange rates. *Journal of Empirical Finance* **1**, 343–64.

Larsson, R. and M. Villani (2001) A distance measure between cointegration spaces. *Economics Letters* **70**, 21–7.

Litterman, R. (1986) Forecasting with Bayesian vector autoregressions: five years of experience. *Journal of Business and Economic Statistics* **4**, 25–38.

Luukkonen, R., A. Ripatti and P. Saikkonen (1999) Testing for a valid normalisation of cointegrating vectors in vector autoregressive processes. *Journal of Business and Economic Statistics* **17**, 195–204.

Martin, G. (2000) US deficit sustainability: a new approach based on multiple endogenous breaks. *Journal of Applied Econometrics* **15**, 83–105.

Martin, G. (2001) Bayesian analysis of a fractional cointegration model. *Econometric Reviews* **20**, 217–34.

Martin, G. and V. Martin (2000) Bayesian inference in the triangular cointegration model using a Jeffreys prior. *Communications in Statistics, Theory and Methods* **29**, 1759–1785.

Nelson, C. and C. Plosser (1982) Trends and random walks in macroeconomic time series: some evidence and implications. *Journal of Monetary Economics* **10**, 139–62.

O'Hagan, A. (1995) Fractional Bayes factors for model comparison. *Journal of the Royal Statistical Society B* **57**, 99–138.

Paap, R. and H.K. van Dijk (2003) Bayes estimates of Markov trends in possibly cointegrated series: an application to US consumption and income. *Journal of Business and Economic Statistics* **21**, 547–63.

Phillips, P.C.B. (1991) Optimal inference in cointegrated systems. *Econometrica* **59**, 283–306.

Phillips, P.C.B. (1994) Some exact distribution theory for maximum likelihood estimators of cointegrating coefficients in error correction models. *Econometrica* **62**, 73–93.

Phillips, P.C.B. (1996) Econometric model determination. *Econometrica* **64**, 763–812.

Phillips, P.C.B. and W. Ploberger (1996) An asymptotic theory of Bayesian inference for time series. *Econometrica* **64**, 381–412.

Poirier, D. (1998) Revising beliefs in non-identified models. *Econometric Theory* **14**, 483–509.

Richard, J.-F. and H. Tompa (1980) On the evaluation of poly-*t* density functions. *Journal of Econometrics* **12**, 335–51.

Schwarz, G. (1978) Estimating the dimension of a model. *Annals of Statistics* **6**, 461–4.

Strachan, R. (2003) Valid Bayesian estimation of the cointegrating error correction model. *Journal of Business and Economic Statistics* **21**, 185–95.

Strachan, R. and B. Inder (2004) Bayesian analysis of the error correction model. *Journal of Econometrics* **123**, 307–25.

Strachan, R. and H.K. van Dijk (2004) Valuing structure, model uncertainty and model averaging in vector autoregressive processes. Econometric Institute Report EI 2004–23, Erasmus University, Rotterdam.

Strachan, R and H.K. van Dijk (2003) Bayesian model selection for a sharp null and a diffuse alternative with econometric applications. *Oxford Bulletin of Economics and Statistics* **65**, 681–8.

Sugita, K. (2004) Bayesian analysis of cointegrated vector autoregressive models. PhD thesis, Warwick University.

Urbain, J.P. (1992) On weak exogeneity in error correction models. *Oxford Bulletin of Economics and Statistics* **52**, 187–202.

Verdinelli, I. and L. Wasserman (1995) Computing Bayes factors using a generalization of the Savage–Dickey density ratio. *Journal of the American Statistical Association* **90**, 614–18.

Villani, M. (2000) Aspects of Bayesian cointegration. PhD thesis, Stockholm University.

Villani, M. (2001) Bayesian prediction with cointegrated vector autoregressions. *International Journal of Forecasting* **17**, 585–605.

Villani, M. (2005a) Bayesian reference analysis of cointegration. *Econometric Theory* **21**, 326–57.

Villani, M. (2005b) Bayesian point estimation of the cointegration space. Forthcoming in *Journal of Econometrics*.

Zellner, A. (1971) *An Introduction to Bayesian Inference in Econometrics*. New York: John Wiley and Sons Inc.

Part X

Special Topics

26
Spatial Econometrics
Luc Anselin

Abstract

Spatial econometrics is a collection of methods to deal with spatial effects in regression models. Spatial effects consist of spatial autocorrelation (cross-sectional dependence) and spatial heterogeneity (cross-sectional structural instability). This chapter reviews aspects of spatial econometrics pertaining to model specification, estimation and diagnostic checking, primarily in the context of the linear regression model. Some background is provided on theoretical motivations for incorporating spatial dependence in econometric models. This is followed by a review of a wide range of specifications used to model spatial covariance, including spatial stochastic processes, direct representation and non-parametric distance models. Estimation is considered by means of the maximum likelihood approach as well as by more recently developed method of moments and instrumental variables estimators. Specification tests include tests for spatial autocorrelation and diagnostics based on the maximum likelihood principle. Special attention is given to techniques to handle spatial panel data and models for limited dependent variables.

26.1	Introduction	902
26.2	Theoretical motivations	904
	26.2.1 Social and spatial interaction	905
	26.2.2 Measurement error and common shocks	907
	26.2.3 Identification issues	907
26.3	Specification of spatial error dependence	908
	26.3.1 Spatial stochastic processes	909
	26.3.2 Direct representation	913
	26.3.3 Nonparametric distance models	914
	26.3.4 Error component models	915
26.4	Specification of spatial lag dependence	916
	26.4.1 Mixed regressive spatial autoregressive model	916
	26.4.2 Higher-order models	918
26.5	Estimation	920
	26.5.1 Asymptotics in space	921
	26.5.2 Maximum likelihood estimation	922
	26.5.3 Method of moments/instrumental variables	927
26.6	Specification testing	931
	26.6.1 Tests against spatial autocorrelation	932
	26.6.2 Tests based on maximum likelihood	935

	26.6.3	Tests against multiple sources of misspecification	940
	26.6.4	Specification search	941
26.7	Spatial effects in panel data		941
	26.7.1	Spatial effects in pooled cross-section and time series models	942
	26.7.2	Spatial effects in error component models	945
	26.7.3	Spatial seemingly unrelated regression models (SUR)	949
26.8	Spatial effects in models with limited dependent variables		951
	26.8.1	Spatial probit	951
	26.8.2	Estimation of the spatial probit	953
	26.8.3	Specification tests in spatial probit	956
26.9	Future directions		958

26.1   Introduction

Spatial econometrics consists of a subset of econometric methods that is concerned with spatial aspects present in cross-sectional and space-time observations. Variables related to location, distance and arrangement (topology) are treated explicitly in model specification, estimation, diagnostic checking and prediction. More specifically, spatial econometrics deals with two basic forms of spatial effects in regression models, categorized as *spatial dependence* and *spatial heterogeneity* (Anselin, 1988b).

Spatial dependence is a special case of cross-sectional dependence, in the sense that the *structure* of the correlation or covariance between observations at different locations is derived from a specific ordering, determined by the relative position (distance, spatial arrangement) of the observations in geographic space (or, in general, in network space). While similar to correlation in the time domain, the distinct nature of spatial dependence requires a specialized set of techniques that are *not* a straightforward extension of time series methods to two dimensions (Anselin, 1988b).

Spatial heterogeneity is a special case of observed or unobserved heterogeneity, a familiar problem in standard econometrics. In contrast to spatial dependence, tackling this issue does not require a separate set of methods. The only spatial aspect of the heterogeneity is the additional information that may be provided by spatial structure. For example, this may inform models for heteroskedasticity, spatially varying coefficients, random coefficients and spatial structural change (spatial regimes). This will not be considered further here.[1]

The designation of a separate field of "spatial econometrics" was originally suggested by the Belgian economist Jean Paelinck in the early 1970s, to refer to methodological aspects associated with incorporating dependence in cross-sectional multiregional econometric models. An early overview is contained in the 1979 *Spatial Econometrics* book by Paelinck and Klaassen (Paelinck and Klaassen, 1979).[2] In it, they outlined five important characteristics of the field: (i) the role of spatial interdependence; (ii) the asymmetry in spatial relations; (iii) the importance of explanatory factors located in other spaces; (iv) differentiation between ex post and ex ante interaction; and (v) explicit modeling of space. In Anselin

(1988b), these ideas were elaborated upon and situated more formally within econometric estimation and specification testing.

Initially, the development and application of spatial econometric methods was largely confined to the applied fields of economics (for example, urban and regional economics, environmental economics, real estate economics), regional science and quantitative economic geography. Early reviews of the state of the art can be found in, among others, Cliff and Ord (1973, 1981), Hordijk (1974), Anselin (1980, 1988b, 1992), Upton and Fingleton (1985), Haining (1990), and Anselin and Florax (1995a). This early work was heavily influenced by the statistical literature, where the interest in spatial aspects dates back to the early twentieth century, dealing with concerns about the presence of spatial auto-correlation in the design of agricultural experiments (see Cressie 1993, p. 7). In spatial statistics, fundamental results regarding the estimation of spatial models were obtained by Whittle (1954), Besag (1974), Ord (1975), and Ripley (1981), among others (for more in-depth overviews, see Cressie, 1993 and Waller and Gotway, 2004).

Arguably, the distinction between spatial statistics and spatial econometrics is subtle. As suggested in Anselin (1988b), the main difference lies in the emphasis on the economic models (and the theory behind them) as the basis for econometric specification in spatial econometrics, whereas the data tend to be more central in spatial statistics. A great degree of cross fertilization has occurred, although distinct emphases remain, especially in terms of a greater prominence of a Bayesian (hierarchical) perspective in modern spatial statistics (see, for example, Waller *et al.*, 1997a,b; Wikle *et al.*, 1998; Royle and Berliner, 1999; Banerjee *et al.*, 2004, and the references cited therein).

The initially somewhat marginal status of spatial econometrics relative to other subfields of econometrics has changed dramatically. Spurred both by advances in theory (social and spatial interaction) and in technology (geographic information systems), interest in spatial modeling has grown considerably in economics, as evidenced by the large number of both applied and theoretical papers that have appeared in recent years (for extensive literature reviews, see Florax and van der Vlist, 2003; Anselin *et al.* 2004b). Several special journal issues have been devoted to the topic, including Nelson (2002), Anselin (2003a), Florax and van der Vlist (2003), and LeSage *et al.* (2004), as well as a number of edited volumes: Anselin *et al.* (2004a), Getis *et al.* (2004), and LeSage and Pace (2004).

This chapter reviews the basic methodology as well as recent advances in the specification, estimation and testing of spatial econometric models. It borrows from, builds upon and extends earlier reviews presented in Anselin and Bera (1998) and Anselin (2001a,b, 2002). In the next three sections, the basic specification problem of spatial econometrics is outlined, first motivated in terms of theory, then with regard to models of spatial error dependence and spatial lag dependence. This is followed by an overview of estimation and specification testing, presented in the context of the linear regression model. Two specialized sections deal with spatial effects in, respectively, panel data settings and models with limited dependent variables. The chapter closes with some comments on promising future directions.

26.2 Theoretical motivations

In general, spatial regression specifications fall into two broad categories, referred to in the literature as *spatial lag* and *spatial error* models (Anselin, 1988b). Before considering estimation and specification testing, in this section a few comments are formulated on the theoretical foundations for such specifications.

To focus the discussion, consider the regression model:

$$y_i = g(y_J, \theta) + x_i'\beta + \varepsilon_i, \tag{26.1}$$

where y_i is an observation on the dependent variable at location $i, i = 1, \dots, n$, $g(y_J, \theta)$ is a function of the values of the dependent variable observed at *neighboring* locations $j \in J$, with $j \neq i$ and with the set J of neighbors to be specified, x_i is a $k \times 1$ vector of observations on explanatory (exogenous) variables, ε_i is an error term, and θ and β are vectors of parameters. The function g of observations on the dependent variable at locations other than i is referred to as a *spatially lagged dependent variable*, or spatial lag term. It is typically formulated as a weighted average of neighboring values, where the neighbors are specified through the use of a so-called spatial weights matrix.[3] Specifically, a mixed regressive, spatial autoregressive model (Anselin, 1988b) takes the form (in matrix notation):

$$y = \rho W y + X\beta + \varepsilon, \tag{26.2}$$

where y is an $n \times 1$ vector of observations on the dependent variable, W is an $n \times n$ spatial weights matrix, which specifies the neighbors used in the averaging (resulting in the spatial lag term, Wy), ρ is a spatial autoregressive parameter, X an $n \times k$ matrix of observations on the explanatory variables, β a matching vector of parameters, and ε an $n \times 1$ vector of error terms.

The inclusion of the terms $g(y_J, \theta)$ or Wy on the right-hand side of the equation is motivated by theory as the equilibrium outcome of processes of social and spatial interaction, considered in section 26.2.1.

The case of spatial error autocorrelation is a special form of a non-spherical error variance–covariance matrix. Specifically,

$$E[\varepsilon_i \varepsilon_j] = \sigma_{ij} \neq 0, \tag{26.3}$$

for $j \neq i$, yielding a general variance–covariance matrix $E[\varepsilon\varepsilon'] = \Sigma$. The non-zero off-diagonal elements correspond to a notion of *spatial* covariance when they follow a given spatial structure or "spatial ordering" (Kelejian and Robinson, 1992). The spatial ordering specifies for which pairs of locations i, j (with $i \neq j$) the covariance will be non-zero. The ordering is based on concepts such as contiguity (neighbors in space) or on the use of a distance metric. The consideration of spatially correlated disturbance terms is motivated by measurement error or by the presence of common shocks, reviewed briefly in section 26.2.2.

A short overview of identification issues is presented in section 26.2.3.

26.2.1 Social and spatial interaction

Theoretical economic models of *interacting agents* and *social interaction* move away from the traditional notion of atomistic agents and instead formalize how interaction among the agents can lead to collective behavior and aggregate patterns. These models have recently received considerable attention, as evidenced in the development of theoretical frameworks to explain social phenomena such as peer effects, neighborhood effects, spatial spillovers, network effects, and the like (for examples and reviews, see, among others, Glaeser *et al.*, 1992, 1996; Akerlof, 1997; Durlauf, 1997, 2004; Brock and Durlauf, 2001a,b; Manski, 2000; Conley and Topa 2002). In his recent review, Manski (2000) suggests three specific channels of interaction from an economic perspective: constraint interactions, expectations interactions and preference interactions. This leads to specifications where the actions of other agents are included in the right hand side of a model for individual behavior. In the review of Brock and Durlauf (2001a), a further distinction is made between global interaction, specified as the average behavior of the population, and local interaction, specified as the average behavior of a reference group ("neighborhood"). The implications of these specifications for model identification and estimation are complex, and treated at length in Manski (1993, 1995) and Brock and Durlauf (2001a,b), among others.

In the spatial econometric literature, the spatial lag model is commonly conceptualized as representing the empirical counterpart to the equilibrium solution of strategic interaction, i.e., as a *spatial reaction function* (Brueckner, 1998, 2003). The reaction function of Brueckner (2003) takes the form:

$$y_i = R(y_{-i}, x_i), \tag{26.4}$$

where y_i stands for the level of decision variable y for decision maker i, y_{-i} reflects a function of the decision variables chosen by the other decision makers, and x_i is a vector of exogenous characteristics of i.[4] A linear functional form for R readily yields a specification such as equation (26.1) or (26.2).

Brueckner (2003) demonstrates how the reaction function (26.4) can be obtained through two different behavioral mechanisms for strategic interaction. In one, termed *spillover*, the level of the decision variable chosen by the other agents (y_{-i}) enters directly into the utility (objective function) of each individual agent. This yields a utility function such as:

$$U(y_i, y_{-i}; x_i).\tag{26.5}$$

This model can be extended to apply to a representative agent for an aggregate spatial unit, such as a state, for example, in the widely cited study of spillovers among state expenditures in Case *et al.* (1993). Other examples in the literature apply this framework as the motivation for the use of a spatial lag specification in studies of the demand for public goods, pollution abatement and other forms of yardstick competition (for example, Besley and Case, 1995; Murdoch *et al.*, 1993, 1997; Bivand and Szymanski 1997).

A second behavioral mechanism is termed *resource flow* by Brueckner (2003). In this approach, the agent's decision variable is indirectly affected by the decisions of other agents through their impact on an available resource. The utility function thus becomes:

$$U(y_i, s_i, x_i),\tag{26.6}$$

where s_i is the contribution of the resource used by the agent to the agent's utility. Interaction is induced through the effect of the actions of other agents on the resource use. Specifically, each agent's resource use is constrained by the actions taken by other agents, as in

$$s_i = H(y_i, y_{-i}, x_i).\tag{26.7}$$

After substituting this into the utility function, the same reaction function as in (26.4) obtains, again suggesting a spatial lag specification. Several tax competition and related strategic interaction models can be categorized as resource flow interactions (for further examples, see Brueckner, 1998, 2003; Saavedra, 2000; Brueckner and Saavedra, 2001).

In these frameworks, the use of the spatial lag specification follows from formal economic reasoning. However, the model itself cannot distinguish between which mechanism led to the equilibrium under consideration. The two processes are observationally equivalent and cannot be identified empirically. This is one example of many identification problems associated with spatial econometric model specifications (see section 26.2.3). In the statistical literature, it is referred to as the *inverse problem*, pervasive in the analysis of cross-sectional spatial data. It is also known as the problem of distinguishing *true* from *apparent* contagion, the latter being a case of spatial heterogeneity. Clusters in space may occur as the result of various mechanisms, including some that are not based on interaction or contagion. The information contained in the cross-sectional sample as such is insufficient to allow for the identification of the underlying mechanism.[5] This is a basic limitation of the cross-sectional setup, which is somewhat (but not completely) eliminated in spatial panel data settings.

26.2.2 Measurement error and common shocks

Unlike spatial lag models, spatial error specifications are typically not motivated by a theoretical economic model, but instead are formulated to deal with data problems. In other words, it is the cross-sectional nature of the data that causes correlation problems, not necessarily the "spatial" nature of the model. Therefore, error autocorrelation is more relevant in practice than lag correlation, since it pertains to both spatial and non-spatial models.

In many instances in applied econometrics using cross-sectional data, there is a mismatch between the spatial scale of the process under study (for example, a housing market or labor market) and the spatial unit of observation (for example, a census tract or county). As a result, measurement errors are likely to systematically vary across space (Anselin, 1988b, p. 12). In addition, the data integration (combination of observations from different spatial scales) and spatial interpolation that is facilitated by modern geographic information systems will tend to result in patterns of spatial correlation (Anselin, 2001c). The statistical issues related to the joint consideration of observations at different spatial scales is referred to as the "change of support problem" (COSP). The incorporation of these complexities into spatial econometric methodology is still limited to date (for an overview of the statistical issues, see Gotway and Young, 2002).

A theoretical framework for spatially correlated errors is provided by the general approach based on "common shocks" outlined by Andrews (2005). This focuses on the properties of estimators in a regression of a dependent variable $Y(\gamma)$ on explanatory variables $X(\gamma)$, where γ is a spatial sample from an arbitrary topological space Γ. Y and X are part of a random vector $W(\gamma) = (Y(\gamma), X(\gamma), S(\gamma))$ that contains observed and unobserved terms $S(\gamma)$ that are common to some units in the population. Common shocks are defined as random variables $C(\gamma)$ measurable on a σ-field such that, conditional on this field, a spatial sample $W_i : i = 1, \ldots$ is i.i.d. This general framework includes a wide range of forms of spatial correlation, as well as group effects and factor structures.[6] Factor structures are increasingly used in recently formulated models to deal with general forms of cross-sectional correlation in panel data settings (see section 26.3.4).

26.2.3 Identification issues

The degree of simultaneity and endogeneity inherent in spatial correlation creates a number of difficult identification problems. The best known of these is arguably the "reflection problem" outlined in Manski (1993), where it is shown that the parameters in models of social/spatial interaction are only identified under strict conditions. In Manski's model, three types of social interaction are considered, referred to as endogenous effects (interaction effects among individual agents), contextual effects (exogenous group characteristics) and correlated effects (observed or unobserved characteristics that agents have in common).

A general linear model for social interaction is then (using Manski's notation):

$$y = \alpha + \beta \, E(y|x) + E(z|x)'\gamma + z'\eta + u, \tag{26.8}$$

where y is the dependent variable (for example, participation in gangs), x are exogenous group characteristics (for example, census tract median income), and z and u are observed and unobserved variables that directly affect y (for example, age of the individual as observed, and "culture" as unobserved). The endogenous effect is specified in terms of the group mean, $E(y|x)$. The unobserved characteristics are further assumed to be correlated across individuals in the group, with $E(u|x, z) = x'\delta$. The resulting conditional expectation, or regression, is then:

$$E(y|x, z) = \alpha + \beta\,E(y|x) + E(z|x)'\gamma + x'\delta + z'\eta. \qquad (26.9)$$

Endogenous effects are present when $\beta \neq 0$, contextual effects when $\gamma \neq 0$, and correlated effects when $\delta \neq 0$. The reduced form of this regression yields:

$$E(y|x) = \alpha/(1 - \beta) + E(z|x)'(\gamma + \eta)/(1 - \beta) + x'\delta/(1 - \beta), \qquad (26.10)$$

which demonstrates how, without further restrictions, the different social effects cannot be separately identified. Manski (1993) outlines the types of constraints and instruments needed to obtain identification.[7]

In the spatial lag model, the reflection problem is avoided with a judicious specification of the spatial weights matrix. An important distinction between the endogenous effect $\beta\,E(y|x)$ in Manski's model and the spatially lagged effect ρWy is that the latter only pertains to a subset of the sample, not to the population conditional expectation (see also Irwin, 2004, for further discussion). Complications remain when both endogenous and correlated effects are present. An alternative approach to separately identify endogenous effects in the presence of correlated effects consists of a natural experiment design (Irwin, 2004).

While much of the discussion of social interaction is couched in terms of models for individual agents, in practice estimation is often carried out for aggregate spatial units of observation (for example, using the device of a representative agent). This can lead to an ecological fallacy or cross-level bias problem, where aggregate results are interpreted as if they pertained to individual behavior (for reviews of this issue, see, for example, Stoker, 1993; King, 1997; Greenland, 2002). When both individual characteristics as well as group effects are contained in a regression specification, estimation at the group level does not allow for the separate identification of individual and contextual effects (Greenland, 2002). Moreover, the coefficients in a spatial lag specification at the individual level are not estimated consistently by the coefficients in a spatially aggregate counterpart, as shown in Anselin (2002). Consequently, considerable care is needed in the specification as well as the interpretation of models for spatial and social interaction.

26.3   Specification of spatial error dependence

In the presence of spatial correlation, the error variance–covariance matrix $E[\varepsilon\varepsilon'] = \Sigma$ contains n variance terms and $n \times (n - 1)/2$ off-diagonal parameters. These cannot be separately estimated in a single cross-section with n observations.

A fundamental specification problem in spatial econometrics is the need to impose constraints or structure on the elements of Σ such that estimation becomes possible. Several approaches have been suggested. They can be categorized as spatial stochastic process models, direct representation, nonparametric distance models, and error component models. They are considered in turn.

26.3.1 Spatial stochastic processes

A spatial stochastic process, or spatial random field, is a collection of random variables, indexed by location. Using regression error terms (ε_i) as an example, this can be formally expressed as

$$\{\varepsilon_i \in D\}, \tag{26.11}$$

where D is a spatial index set, either a continuous surface or a finite set of discrete locations. The specification of the spatial process for the regression error terms gives rise to a particular covariance structure or pattern of spatial autocorrelation. A crucial element in the specification is the determination of the neighbor structure or, formally, which locations will be represented in the spatial lag term on the right-hand side of the equation. The connectedness structure is expressed by means of a spatial weights matrix, which is considered first. This is followed by a brief review of commonly used process specifications.

26.3.1.1 Spatial weights

The spatial weights matrix is an $n \times n$ positive matrix, W, through which the "neighborhood set" is specified for each observation. A location (observation) appears both as row and column, with non-zero matrix elements w_{ij} indicating a neighbor relation between observation (row) i and (column) j. By convention, self-neighbors are excluded, such that the diagonal elements $w_{ii} = 0$. Also, the weights matrix is often used in row-standardized form, with weights $w_{ij}^s = w_{ij}/\Sigma_j w_{ij}$.[8] The row-standardization facilitates the interpretation of the weights as constructing an average of the neighboring values in the so-called *spatial lag operator*, $\Sigma_j w_{ij} z_j$ (Anselin, 1988b, pp. 22–4). Since the traditional notion of a spatial shift is non-operational in irregular spatial layouts, this averaging is used instead (see Anselin and Bera, 1998, pp. 245–6, for a more in-depth discussion and further references). In matrix notation, the spatial lag of a random vector z is then Wz. In spatial econometric regression models, a range of specifications can be obtained by applying the spatial lag operator to the dependent variable, Wy, the explanatory variables, WX, or the error term, $W\varepsilon$.

There is very little formal guidance in the choice of the "correct" spatial weights for a given model specification. Typically, the definition of neighbor is based on geographic criteria, such as polygons having a common boundary (contiguity) or points being within a critical distance band. Other geographic criteria include combinations of contiguity and border length, or k-nearest neighbors. The literature on the specification of spatial weights is extensive, with early discussions in Cliff and Ord (1973, 1981), Upton and Fingleton (1985), and Anselin (1988b, chapter 3), and recent technical reviews in Dietz (2002), Leenders (2002) and Anselin (2002, pp. 256–60).

Spatial weights need not be limited to geographic considerations, and extensions to abstract spaces have been suggested, such as those arising from social networks or economic distance (for example, Case et al., 1993; Conley and Ligon, 2002; Conley and Topa, 2002). For example, the choice of a suitable metric can yield general measures of distance (d_{ij}), which are then converted into inverse distance spatial weights as $w_{ij} = 1/d_{ij}$. More complex functional forms have been suggested as well, including negative exponential and gravity-like measures that combine a "mass" measure at origin and destination with a distance decay effect (for example, Anselin, 1988b; Ferrándiz et al., 1995, 1999).

An interesting form of "economic" weights follows when a hierarchical or group structure is suggested by the data, as in Case (1991, 1992). All observations belonging to the same group (for example, a region) are considered to be neighbors, but the neighbor relation does not extend across groups. This results in a block-diagonal weights matrix, with each block consisting of weights $1/(n_g - 1)$ (with n_g as the number of observations belonging to the group). This structure has different properties from the distance or contiguity based weights, with important implications for estimation (see Lee, 2002; Kelejian and Prucha, 2002).

In order to obtain suitable asymptotic properties for estimators and specification tests, the weights matrix is subject to regularity conditions. These regularity conditions boil down to bounds on the weights and sums of the weights. Specifically, as pointed out in the work of Kelejian and Prucha (for example, Kelejian and Prucha, 1999, Assumption 3, p. 515), the sums $\Sigma_{i=1}^{n}|w_{ij}|$ and $\Sigma_{j=1}^{n}|w_{ij}|$ must be bounded by $c_w < \infty$. The bounds are related to summability conditions typically required to ensure that the error variance–covariance matrix is proper (see also Mandy and Martins-Filho, 1994). Spatial weights based on notions of contiguity easily satisfy these regularity conditions. For more complex weights, such as those derived from distance bands in economic space, careful consideration of the regularity conditions is required, especially when the weights also contain parameters.

26.3.1.2   Spatial autoregressive process – SAR

One of the earliest and simplest specifications considered for a spatial process is the simultaneous spatial autoregressive model (SAR), suggested by Whittle (1954). This specification applies to the special case where the data are located on a regular rectangular lattice. The right-hand side of the equation is simply a weighted sum of the North, South, East and West neighbors in the lattice, each assigned a separate parameter.

Using ε for the regression error term, and with the locations on the rectangular lattice labeled by row (r) and column (c), this model is:

$$\varepsilon_{r,c} = \xi_1 \varepsilon_{r-1,c} + \xi_2 \varepsilon_{r+1,c} + \xi_3 \varepsilon_{r,c-1} + \xi_4 \varepsilon_{r,c+1} + u_{r,c}, \qquad (26.12)$$

with $\xi_k, k = 1, \ldots, 4$, as the spatial autoregressive parameters and u as an idiosyncratic error term.[9] In irregular lattice layouts (such as a cross-section of counties or city neighborhoods), this simple specification is not applicable, since the number of neighbors typically varies by observation and the concept of a spatial shift has no meaning. Instead, a spatial weights matrix is used, as in:

$$\varepsilon_i = \lambda \sum_j w_{ij}\varepsilon_j + u_i, \qquad (26.13)$$

with λ as the autoregressive coefficient. Alternatively, in matrix notation, for the $n \times 1$ vector of error terms, ε:

$$\varepsilon = \lambda W \varepsilon + u. \qquad (26.14)$$

Since

$$\varepsilon = (I - \lambda W)^{-1} u, \qquad (26.15)$$

the error variance–covariance matrix follows as

$$E[\varepsilon\varepsilon'] = (I - \lambda W)^{-1} E[uu'](I - \lambda W')^{-1}. \qquad (26.16)$$

Under the standard assumption of i.i.d. errors u, with $E[uu'] = \sigma^2 I$, this expression simplifies to (after rearranging terms):

$$E[\varepsilon\varepsilon'] = \sigma^2[(I - \lambda W)'(I - \lambda W)]^{-1}. \qquad (26.17)$$

In the more general case where $E[uu'] = \sigma^2\Omega$, for example, to allow heteroskedastic errors, the full expression is:

$$E[\varepsilon\varepsilon'] = \sigma^2(I - \lambda W)^{-1}\Omega(I - \lambda W')^{-1}. \qquad (26.18)$$

Note that, in practice, the weights matrix W is typically not symmetric (for example, after row-standardization, or using k-nearest neighbors), so that $(I - \lambda W)^{-1} \neq (I - \lambda W')^{-1}$. In order to get a better insight into the structure of the covariance matrix induced by this process, consider the case where W corresponds to row-standardized first order contiguity. With $|\lambda| < 1$, the following expansion holds (also known as the Leontief expansion):

$$(I - \lambda W)^{-1} = I + \lambda W + \lambda^2 W^2 + \lambda^3 W^3 + \dots, \qquad (26.19)$$

and a similar expression with W'. The product of the two inverse terms then yields a sum of cross-products of the form

$$I + \lambda(W + W') + \lambda^2(WW + WW' + W'W')$$
$$+ \lambda^3(WWW + WWW' + WW'W') + \dots \qquad (26.20)$$

The resulting covariance is quite different from the familiar band structure for first order autoregressive processes in time. It is qualitatively similar, in that the strength of the covariance decreases (higher powers of λ) for higher orders of contiguity (powers of W), but the pattern is considerably more complex (due to the products of W and W'). Also, it is important to note that even though the W in the SAR process may only pertain to the first order neighbors, the resulting spatial covariance reaches far beyond those first order neighbors, in fact inducing *global* spatial autocorrelation.

Most importantly, when the number of neighbors (the nonzero elements in W) across locations is not constant (the typical case in practice), the diagonal elements in (26.20) are no longer constant, inducing heteroskedasticity. This heteroskedasticity is present even when u is i.i.d., greatly complicating estimation and specification testing.[10]

26.3.1.3 *Conditional autoregressive process – CAR*

The probabilistic model behind the SAR specification is based on the joint distribution of a random vector, such as ε. An alternative approach focuses on the conditional distribution. While originally outlined in Besag (1974), and very little used in the spatial econometric literature, this perspective is prevalent in the recent literature on Bayesian hierarchical spatial modeling (for example, Banerjee *et al.* 2004, pp. 76–84). It is used both as a model for spatial correlation itself, and as a spatial prior for parameters in a hierarchical setup.

In essence, the conditional approach consists of establishing conditions under which a density for the random variable at a given location, conditional on its neighbors, yields a proper joint density (Kaiser and Cressie, 2000). The formal result is contained in the Hammersley-Clifford theorem (Cressie, 1993, pp. 410–419).

Assuming normality, and ignoring complications from heteroskedasticity, the conditional expectation at location i, conditional upon all the other locations in the system ($j \neq i$), is expressed in the CAR model as a linear function of the neighbors:

$$E[\varepsilon_i|\varepsilon_j, j \neq i] = \lambda \sum_j w_{ij}\varepsilon_j. \tag{26.21}$$

Under the proper constraints on the elements of W (for example, Cliff and Ord, 1981, pp. 148, 179–83), this yields a joint multivariate normal distribution with variance

$$E[\varepsilon\varepsilon'] = \sigma^2(I - \lambda W)^{-1}. \tag{26.22}$$

Extensions to other distributions have been suggested as well, such as autologistic and auto-Poisson, but these only obtain under very restrictive conditions (Banerjee *et al.*, 2004, pp. 83–4).

Two important characteristics of the variance structure in (26.22) should be noted. First, it is required that the spatial weights matrix W be symmetric, which excludes the use of row-standardized weights (or k-nearest neighbor weights) and affects the parameter space for the autoregressive coefficient λ (typically making

λ much smaller than for corresponding row-standardized weights). Second, the range and strength of spatial covariance induced by this model is much smaller than for a corresponding SAR model. This can be seen by comparing the expansion in (26.19), which corresponds to the CAR model, to that in (26.20) for the SAR model (see also Wall, 2004).

26.3.1.4 *Spatial moving average process – SMA*

A third type of spatial stochastic process used to model the structure of spatial correlation is based on a moving average specification (see Haining, 1988, 1990, pp. 83–4).

For the individual error terms, this model is:

$$\varepsilon_i = \gamma \sum_j w_{ij} u_j + u_i, \tag{26.23}$$

where γ is the moving average parameter. In matrix notation, for the random vector ε, the corresponding expression is:

$$\varepsilon = \gamma W u + u. \tag{26.24}$$

Assuming i.i.d. errors u, the resulting error covariance matrix takes on the form:

$$E[\varepsilon\varepsilon'] = \sigma^2[I + \gamma(W + W') + \gamma^2 WW']. \tag{26.25}$$

In contrast to the SAR and CAR specifications, this represents a *local* pattern of autocorrelation. Inspection of (26.25) reveals that the only non-zero off-diagonal elements correspond to the nonzero elements of W (W') and WW'. In the case of first order contiguity for W, the matrix product WW' contains nonzero entries for the first and second order neighbors only. As a result, there is no spatial covariance beyond the second neighbor, hence the local characteristic (Anselin, 2003a, pp. 156–7).

As in the SAR model, a non-constant number of neighbors across observations will induce heteroskedasticity, even when u is i.i.d.

26.3.2 Direct representation

In a direct representation, the covariance between each pair or error terms is specified as an inverse function of the distance between them. Formally,

$$E[\varepsilon_i \varepsilon_j] = \sigma^2 f(d_{ij}, \phi), \tag{26.26}$$

with $\varepsilon_{i,j}$ as the regression error terms, σ^2 the error variance, d_{ij} the distance separating i and j, and f a distance function. The function f should be a distance *decay* function and ensure a positive definite covariance matrix. This requires $\partial f / \partial d < 0$ and $|f(d_{ij}, \phi)| \leq 1$, with $\phi \in \Phi$ as a $p \times 1$ vector of parameters on an open subset Φ of $\mathbb{R}^p$. This approach is closely related to variogram models used in geostatistics, and requires assumptions of stationarity and isotropy (see Cressie, 1993, for an extensive review). The complete variance–covariance is then:

$$E[\varepsilon\varepsilon'] = \sigma^2 \Omega(d_{ij}, \phi). \tag{26.27}$$

Note that, in contrast to the SAR and SMA specifications, the spatial autocorrelation in this model does *not* induce heteroskedasticity, since the diagonal terms of Ω are constant.

The direct representation specification of spatial autocovariance dates back to early papers by Cook and Pocock (1983), Mardia and Marshall (1984), Warnes and Ripley (1987), and Mardia and Watkins (1989), among others. Its application in spatial econometrics has been primarily in studies of real estate markets, such as Dubin (1988, 1992) and Basu and Thibodeau (1998) (see also the review in Dubin *et al.*, 1999).

The choice of the distance decay function is not arbitrary and the requirement of ensuring a positive definite covariance matrix imposes constraints on the functional form and the parameter space, as well as on the metric and scale used for the distance measure (for technical details, see, for example, Mardia and Marshall, 1984, pp. 138–9). The extent to which global, rather than local, autocorrelation is modeled depends on the slope of the distance decay function.

A commonly used specification is based on a negative exponential distance decay:

$$E[\varepsilon\varepsilon'] = \sigma^2[I + \gamma\Psi],   \tag{26.28}$$

where the off-diagonal elements of Ψ are given by $\Psi_{ij} = e^{-\phi d_{ij}}$, and where γ is a nonnegative scaling parameter. In order to facilitate interpretation and specification testing, the diagonal elements of Ψ are often set to zero (the variance is captured by the term $\sigma^2 I$). The distance metric and parameter space must be such that elements of $e^{-\phi d_{ij}}$ yield a valid spatial correlation matrix.[11]

26.3.3 Nonparametric distance models

An alternative to the parametric specification of spatial covariance as a function of a distance metric is a nonparametric approach. This is an extension to the spatial domain of the principle behind heteroskedastic and serially autocorrelation consistent covariance matrix estimation of Newey and West (1987) and Andrews (1991), among others.

As in the direct representation approach, the spatial covariance is a function of the distance separating two observations, but the functional form is left unspecified. For example, for the regression error terms:[12]

$$E[\varepsilon_i\varepsilon_j] = f(d_{ij}),   \tag{26.29}$$

where d_{ij} is a "proper" positive and symmetric distance metric (for regularity conditions on the distance metric, see Conley, 1999; Kelejian and Prucha, 2003).

This approach was first used in Conley (1999), and further elaborated upon in Conley and Ligon (2002) and Conley and Topa (2002). In its simplest form, the estimator for the familiar term $V = n^{-1}X'\Sigma X$ is:

$$\hat{V} = n^{-1}\sum_{d_{ij}<\delta} x_i x_j' \hat{\varepsilon}_i \hat{\varepsilon}_j,   \tag{26.30}$$

where δ is a distance cutoff, x_i is a column vector of observations at i, and $\hat{\varepsilon}_i$ is a residual at i. This estimator follows essentially the same principle as in the time series domain by adding up sample spatial autocovariances. In order to ensure positive definiteness of the estimator, a kernel is applied to the cross-products. For example, in the recent paper by Kelejian and Prucha (2003), a general covariance matrix estimator takes on the form:[13]

$$\hat{V} = n^{-1} \sum_i \sum_j x_i x_j' \hat{\varepsilon}_i \hat{\varepsilon}_j K(d_{ij}/d), \tag{26.31}$$

where $K()$ is a kernel function and d a suitable cut-off distance. Formal properties of the kernel estimator for a spatial autocovariance were also established in Hall and Patil (1994) (see also, Conley and Ligon, 2002; Conley and Topa, 2002, for further elaboration and examples).

Note that this structure results in zero spatial autocovariance beyond the distance cut-off. The latter is bounded but allowed to grow with the sample size, potentially yielding more global patterns of spatial correlation in larger samples.[14]

26.3.4 Error component models

In panel data models, it is customary to assume the existence of an unobserved error component, shared by all cross-sectional units in a given time period. This gives rise to a particular form of spatial autocorrelation, where all error terms are equicorrelated (see section 26.7.2). In a pure cross-section, such an approach is not feasible, but alternative concepts of error components are applicable.

In Kelejian and Robinson (1995), an error decomposition was proposed that combines a location-specific, or local component, with a regional or spillover component. Formally, the error term in this spatial error component process is:

$$\varepsilon = W\psi + \xi, \tag{26.32}$$

with ψ as an $n \times 1$ vector of errors that incorporate the spillover across neighbors, defined through a spatial weights matrix W, and ξ as a matching vector of location-specific disturbances. Each error component is i.i.d. with:

$$E[\psi] = E[\xi] = 0, \tag{26.33}$$

$$E[\psi\psi'] = \sigma_\psi^2 I, E[\xi\xi'] = \sigma_\xi^2 I, \tag{26.34}$$

$$E[\psi_i \xi_j] = 0, \forall i, j. \tag{26.35}$$

The error variance–covariance matrix then becomes:

$$E[\varepsilon\varepsilon'] = \sigma_\psi^2 WW' + \sigma_\xi^2 I, \tag{26.36}$$

with σ_ψ^2 as the spatial variance component, and σ_ξ^2 the remainder variance term. Since the matrix product WW' is positive definite, the error components variance–covariance matrix is positive definite with $\sigma_\psi^2 \geq 0$ and $\sigma_\xi^2 > 0$.

This particular specification is a model for *local* spatial correlation, as can be seen by comparing (26.36) to the terms in the SMA variance (26.25). The two models share the term in I and WW', but the spatial error components model does not have a term in W or W'. Using a first-order contiguity W as an example, this implies that the spatial error covariance only contains first-order neighbors that are also contained in the non-zero terms in WW'. More importantly, there is no spatial correlation beyond the second order neighbors.

The general framework outlined in Andrews (2005) provides a way to conceive of a mechanism for a broad range of common shocks. This includes the familiar error components from the panel data literature, where the error term is decomposed into a term associated with the location/individual (i), a term associated with the time period (t) and an idiosyncratic error term. Recent extensions to this model have been offered in the literature on heterogeneous panels. The time component can be generalized and expressed in the form of an unobserved common effect or *factor* f_t to which all cross-sectional units are exposed. However, unlike the standard error component model, each cross-sectional unit has a distinct factor *loading* on this factor. The simplest form is the so-called one factor structure, where the error term at location i and time t is specified as:

$$\varepsilon_{it} = \delta_i f_t + u_{it}, \tag{26.37}$$

with δ_i as the cross-sectional-specific loading on factor f_t, and u_{it} as an *i.i.d* zero mean error term. Consequently, cross-sectional (spatial) covariance between the errors at i and j follows from the the inclusion of the common factor f_t in both error terms:

$$E[\varepsilon_{it}\varepsilon_{jt}] = \delta_i \delta_j \sigma_f^2. \tag{26.38}$$

The common factor model has been extended to include multiple factors. In these specifications, a wide range of covariance structures can be expressed by including sufficient factors and through cross-sectional differences among the factor loadings (for further details, see Driscoll and Kraay, 1998; Coakley *et al.*, 2002; Pesaran, 2002; Hsiao and Pesaran, 2004).

26.4 Specification of spatial lag dependence

Spatial lag models include terms Wy and/or WX on the right-hand side of the equation. This leads to spatial multiplier effects, similar in nature to the social multiplier of Glaeser *et al.* (1996, 2002). In this section these specifications are further explored, with particular attention given to identification issues in higher order spatial models.

26.4.1 Mixed regressive spatial autoregressive model

The basic spatial lag specification is the mixed regressive, spatial autoregressive model, introduced in section 26.2, equation (26.2):

$$y = \rho Wy + X\beta + \varepsilon, \tag{26.39}$$

with the i.i.d. error vector ε. After some matrix algebra, the reduced form is obtained as:

$$y = (I - \rho W)^{-1} X\beta + (I - \rho W)^{-1}\varepsilon. \qquad (26.40)$$

This is a nonlinear model in ρ and β, with an error term that follows a SAR process. Consequently, the error variance will be as in (26.17).

The reduced form also illustrates how the spatially lagged dependent variable in (26.39), Wy, is *endogenous*, violating the assumptions of the standard regression model:

$$Wy = W(I - \rho W)^{-1} X\beta + W(I - \rho W)^{-1}\varepsilon, \qquad (26.41)$$

such that $E[(Wy)'\varepsilon] \neq 0$ (see also Anselin, 1988b, pp. 58–9).

It is worthwhile to consider further the similarity between the spatial lag model and the linear regression with a SAR error. Inserting the error equation (26.15) into the usual linear regression specification $y = X\beta + \varepsilon$ yields:

$$y = X\beta + (I - \lambda W)^{-1}u, \qquad (26.42)$$

or, alternatively,

$$y = \lambda Wy + X\beta - \lambda WX\beta + u. \qquad (26.43)$$

This latter specification is referred to as a *spatial Durbin* model or spatial common factor model, by analogy to the time series case (Anselin, 1980, 1988b; Burridge, 1981).

Comparison of (26.39) and (26.43) demonstrates how the spatial error model is a special case of a spatial lag model, but with additional nonlinear constraints on the parameters (the common factor constraints). Alternatively, comparison of (26.40) and (26.42) shows how the spatial lag model is a special case of a spatial error model that is nonlinear in the parameters. Also note how the two specifications are not nested. Setting either ρ or λ to zero in the respective models yields an ordinary linear regression equation, not one of the spatial models. The nonnested nature of the two specifications, together with their similarity, creates considerable problems in identification, estimation and diagnostic testing (for example, Anselin, 1988b; Kelejian and Prucha, 1997).

26.4.1.1 Spatial multipliers

An important aspect of the spatial lag model is the spatial multiplier, which can be illustrated by means of the reduced form (26.40). Consider the conditional expectation $E[y|X]$. Since $E[(I - \rho W)^{-1}\varepsilon|X] = 0$, it follows that

$$E[y|X] = (I - \rho W)^{-1} X\beta. \qquad (26.44)$$

Using the expansion of the inverse term, as in (26.19), yields:

$$E[y|X] = X\beta + \rho WX\beta + \rho^2 W^2 X\beta + \ldots, \tag{26.45}$$

which demonstrates how the value of y at i depends not only on x_i, but also on the x values at other locations, with locations further removed (higher powers of W) discounted by powers of the autoregressive parameter. This illustrates the *global* nature of the spatial multiplier effect in the spatial lag model. Specifically, if a unit change were introduced in a given explanatory variable X_k, the effect on y would amount to $[1/(1 - \rho)]\beta_k$ (Kim *et al.*, 2003, p. 35). More generally, for any vector of non-uniform changes in a given explanatory variable, ΔX_k, the resulting spatial pattern of changes in the dependent variable is:

$$\Delta y = (I - \rho W)^{-1} \Delta X_k \beta_k. \tag{26.46}$$

The global nature of the spatial multiplier in the spatial lag model contrasts with the local multiplier in a model with spatially lagged explanatory variables. Specifically, in a spatial cross-regressive model (Florax and Folmer, 1992),

$$y = X\beta + WX\gamma + \varepsilon, \tag{26.47}$$

WX is the set of spatially lagged explanatory variables (excluding the constant term) and γ is a matching vector of parameters. The impact on y of any change in a given explanatory variable, ΔX_k, is limited to the immediate effect $\Delta X_k \beta_k$ and the matching spatial lag effect (including only those neighbors as specified in W), $W\Delta X_k \gamma_k$ (for a review of a wide range of models incorporating spatial multipliers, see Anselin, 2003b).

26.4.2   Higher-order models

By analogy to higher-order autoregressive models in the time series domain, multiple spatial lagged dependent variables may be included in a spatial lag model. For example, Brandsma and Ketellapper (1979) suggested a biparametric spatial autoregressive model:

$$y = \rho_1 W_1 y + \rho_2 W_2 y + X\beta + \varepsilon, \tag{26.48}$$

where W_1 and W_2 are different spatial weights. Higher order SAR models were considered in Blommestein (1983, 1985):

$$y = \rho_1 W_1 y + \rho_2 W_2 y + \cdots + \rho_p W_p y + X\beta + \varepsilon, \tag{26.49}$$

with $W_i, i = 1, \ldots, p$, as the associated spatial weights. The weights are typically (but not necessarily) associated with increasing orders of contiguity.

In contrast to time series models, care must be taken to avoid redundancies and circularities in the higher order spatial weights. As shown in Blommestein (1985), simple powers of the first order contiguity weights W_1, for example, $W_p = (W_1)^p$, result in weights matrices that include lower order neighbors as well. These redundancies affect the properties of estimators and should be avoided (Blommestein, 1985; Blommestein and Koper, 1998). In order to ensure that the parameters in a higher-order model are properly identified and to avoid biased estimates, it is typically assumed that the spatial weights do not overlap. More formally, with w_{i*} as the i-th row of the weights matrix, and for any two orders of contiguity h, l:

$$(w_{i*}^h)(w_{i*}^l)' = 0. \tag{26.50}$$

In time series analysis, the problem of redundancy and circularity of higher order lags does not occur, due to the lack of two-way feedback in such models. In spatial analysis, consider the simple biparametric specification in (26.48), with $W_1 = W_{11} + W_0$ and $W_2 = W_{22} + W_0$, where W_0 is a weights matrix containing the common elements of W_1 and W_2. Taking into account this overlap yields:

$$y = \rho_1 W_{11} y + \rho_2 W_{22} y + (\rho_1 + \rho_2) W_0 y + X\beta + \varepsilon, \tag{26.51}$$

which illustrates the potential problems of identification and interpretation when the induced parameter constraints are not satisfied (for an extensive technical discussion, see, Anselin and Smirnov, 1996).

A more encompassing specification that includes both higher-order spatially lagged dependent variables, as well as spatial moving average error terms, was suggested by Huang (1984). The so-called SARMA(p, q) model takes the same form as equation (26.49) for the spatial autoregressive part, with the error term following:

$$\varepsilon = \lambda_1 W_1 u + \lambda_2 W_2 u + \cdots + \lambda_q W_q u + u, \tag{26.52}$$

a spatial moving average process of order q. The full order p, q has seen no application in practice. However, a SARMA(1,1) model is commonly considered as an alternative in specification testing (see, for example, Anselin, 2001a).

A different higher order specification that has received significant attention consists of a spatial lag model with a spatially autoregressive error term (Anselin, 1988b, p. 61):

$$y = \rho W_1 y + X\beta + \varepsilon \tag{26.53}$$

$$\varepsilon = \lambda W_2 \varepsilon + u, \tag{26.54}$$

with $E[uu'] = \sigma^2 \Omega$ to allow for heteroskedasticity. While similar to a first-order autoregressive model with serially correlated errors in time series, the spatial model is much more complex and requires great care to ensure identification of parameters.

After substituting (26.15) for the error term in the spatial lag specification and some further algebra, the following result is obtained:

$$y = \rho W_1 y + \lambda W_2 y - \rho \lambda W_2 W_1 y + X\beta - \lambda W_2 X\beta + u, \tag{26.55}$$

which simplifies when $W_2W_1 = 0$ (non-overlapping weights):

$$y = \rho W_1 y + \lambda W_2 y + X\beta - \lambda W_2 X\beta + u. \tag{26.56}$$

However, in practice, the same weights are often used for both the lag and the error part, $W_1 = W_2$, which yields:

$$y = (\rho + \lambda)Wy - \rho\lambda W^2 y + X\beta - \lambda WX\beta + u. \tag{26.57}$$

When all $\beta = 0$, this model will not be identified (for a technical discussion, see Kelejian and Prucha, 1998; Kelejian *et al.*, 2004; Das *et al.*, 2003; Lee, 2003). But even with some $\beta \neq 0$, there will be difficulty in disentangling the role of ρ and λ. For example, consider the covariance that is induced by this model for the dependent variable y. From the reduced form, ignoring heteroskedasticity ($\Omega = I$), and setting $W_1 = W_2$, some algebra yields the variance–covariance matrix for y as:

$$\text{Var}[y] = \sigma^2(I - \rho W)^{-1}(I - \lambda W)^{-1}(I - \lambda W')^{-1}(I - \rho W')^{-1}. \tag{26.58}$$

Using the familiar expansion (for example, equation 19) for the first two matrix inverses in this expression gives the following leading terms:

$$I + (\lambda + \rho)W + (\rho^2 + \lambda\rho + \lambda^2)W^2 + \ldots, \tag{26.59}$$

and a similar expression in the transpose W'. It is clear that λ and ρ are completely interchangeable, suggesting that the same spatial covariance structure for y can be obtained by a range of combinations of lag and error dependence.

In practice, higher-order models are typically used as alternatives in diagnostic tests. Rejection of the null may not necessarily imply that the higher order model is the proper alternative. Since the specification of the weights matrix is an additional source of uncertainty, it is possible (likely) that a different specification of the weights will eliminate the need for the higher order model (see Florax and Rey, 1995, for a discussion of the effects of misspecified weights).

26.5   Estimation

The estimation problems associated with spatial regression models are distinct for the spatial lag and spatial error case. Spatial error models are special instances of specifications with a non-spherical error. On the other hand, the inclusion of a spatially lagged dependent variable results in a form of endogeneity. Each of these complications can be tackled with the customary econometric methods. However, the two-directional (feedback) nature of spatial dependence and the reliance on a distance metric or spatial weights require specialized techniques to handle the associated probabilistic and computational aspects.

In this section, the two main approaches to estimation of spatial models are considered in turn. They are based on the maximum likelihood principle and the generalized method of moments. Other methods, such as the coding approach

(Besag, 1974, Haining, 1990), and Markov Chain Monte Carlo estimation in a Bayesian framework (LeSage, 1997, 1999), have been suggested as well, but they are not in common use and will not be considered further here (for an application of MCMC to the spatial probit model, see section 26.8.2). The review of estimation methods is prefaced by a brief discussion of the complexities of asymptotic reasoning in the spatial domain.

26.5.1 Asymptotics in space

The properties of estimators (and test statistics) in spatial econometrics are based on asymptotic considerations that use laws of large numbers (LLN) and central limit theorems (CLT) to establish consistency and asymptotic normality. These are not simple generalizations to two dimensions of results for the time domain, as there are differences in three important respects.

First, many spatial processes (for example, SAR and SMA) also induce heteroskedasticity, requiring a joint treatment of dependence and heterogeneity. Specifically, this non-stationarity precludes reliance on central limit theorems for stationary mixing spatial random fields (for example, Bolthausen, 1982), which have been used to obtain the properties of estimators in models where the dependence is based on a distance metric (Conley, 1999). The treatment of heterogeneous spatially dependent processes that include spatial weights is further complicated by the necessity to consider CLT and LLN for triangular arrays. This is caused by the fact that the weights depend on the sample size, and precludes "standard" results (for example, for maximum likelihood estimation) from being directly applicable. The importance of triangular arrays in the asymptotics of spatial econometrics is highlighted in the work of Kelejian and Prucha (1998, 1999).

A second important distinguishing characteristic is the way in which spatial sampling is conceptualized and the type of population it pertains to. Spatial data can be viewed as either constituting a continuous surface, or as a collection of discrete objects. The former view is prevalent in the physical sciences and geostatistical approaches (for example, Cressie, 1993; Stein, 1999). The latter is common in spatial econometrics. When considering a population of spatial objects, the mechanism through which observations or locations are selected is not arbitrary, and can be deterministic (fixed grid cells or points) or stochastic. In the stochastic case, an important concept is that of a *directing process*, which is the set of random indices (i.e., locations) used to draw samples from the population. As a consequence, the random spatial process itself becomes *subordinated* to the directing process, a complication which is typically not encountered in the time domain (see Conley, 1999; Andrews, 2005, for a technical discussion).

A third distinction pertains to the way in which the sample increases to reach the asymptotic limit, $n \to \infty$. A pure increasing domain structure is obtained when the minimum distance between neighboring locations remains bounded away from zero as the sample size grows (Cressie, 1993). One can conceive of this situation as a sampling structure where new data points are added at the edge such that the observation "region" becomes unbounded. In contrast, infill asymptotics are obtained when the sample region is bounded, but the number of data points increases. This yields a denser and denser sampling surface, with the minimum distance between sample locations approaching zero as $n \to \infty$. Asymptotic results that hold in the increasing domain case are often not transferable to the infill case, as shown in Lahiri (1996). Mixed situations can be considered as well, where an increasing domain "grid" is combined with infill in subregions (see, for example, Fazekas and Kukush, 2000; Lahiri and Mukherjee, 2004).

All asymptotic properties are based on regularity conditions that restrict the range and strength of spatial dependence and heterogeneity. In models using spatial weights, these conditions translate into constraints on the structure of the weights (see section 26.3.1.1). In practice, these are readily satisfied by contiguity-based weights, but not necessarily by more complex specifications. Similar regularity conditions on direct representation models are formulated in Mardia and Marshall (1984).

26.5.2 Maximum likelihood estimation

26.5.2.1 Spatial lag model

The point of departure for maximum likelihood (ML) estimation in spatial regression models is an assumption of normality for the error term. In general, allowing for heteroskedasticity and/or error correlation, the $n \times 1$ error vector has a multivariate normal distribution, $\varepsilon \sim N(0, \Sigma_\theta)$, with the subscript θ denoting that Σ may be a function of a $p \times 1$ vector θ of parameters. In the commonly considered i.i.d. case, this simplifies to $\varepsilon \sim N(0, \sigma^2 I)$, with $\theta = \sigma^2$.

To move from the likelihood for the error vector to a likelihood for the observed dependent variable, a *Jacobian* of the transformation needs to be inserted. In the spatial lag model (26.39), this corresponds to:

$$|\partial\varepsilon/\partial y| = |\partial(y - \rho W y - X\beta)/\partial y| = |I - \rho W|, \qquad (26.60)$$

the determinant of an $n \times n$ matrix. Note that this same Jacobian reduces to a scalar 1 in the standard regression model, since $|\partial(y - X\beta)/\partial y| = |I| = 1$. The presence of the Jacobian term constitutes a major computational complication (see section 26.5.2.3).

Using the standard result for a multivariate normal distribution, and taking into account the Jacobian term, the log-likelihood for the spatial lag model follows as:

$$L = - (n/2)(\ln 2\pi) - (1/2)\ln|\Sigma_\theta| + \ln|I - \rho W|$$
$$- (1/2)(y - \rho W y - X\beta)'\Sigma_\theta^{-1}(y - \rho W y - X\beta). \qquad (26.61)$$

Maximizing the log-likelihood is *not* equivalent to minimizing weighted least squares (the last term in L), as in the standard linear regression model. The main difference is in the presence of the log-Jacobian term $\ln|I - \rho W|$. This illustrates informally how weighted least squares will not yield a consistent estimator in the spatial lag model, due to the endogeneity in the Wy term (see section 26.4.1).[15] The log-Jacobian also implies constraints on the parameter space for ρ, which must be such that $|I - \rho W| > 0$.

ML estimates for β, ρ and θ are obtained as solutions to the usual first-order conditions (for technical details, see Ord, 1975; Cliff and Ord, 1981; Anselin, 1980, 1988b; Anselin and Bera, 1998, among others):

$$\partial L / \partial \beta = e' \Sigma_\theta^{-1} X = 0, \tag{26.62}$$

$$\partial L / \partial \rho = -tr[W(I - \rho W)^{-1}] + e' \Sigma_\theta^{-1} Wy = 0, \tag{26.63}$$

$$\partial L / \partial \theta_i = - (1/2)tr[\Sigma_\theta^{-1}(\partial \Sigma_\theta / \partial \theta_i)]$$
$$+ (1/2)e'\Sigma_\theta^{-1}(\partial \Sigma_\theta / \partial \theta_i)\Sigma_\theta^{-1}e = 0, \quad \text{for } i = 1, \ldots, p, \tag{26.64}$$

with $e = y - \rho Wy - X\beta$ and tr as the matrix trace operator. Solutions to these conditions need to be obtained through numerical optimization.

Inference is based on an asymptotic variance matrix, the inverse of the information matrix. In the general case considered here, the information matrix for $[\rho, \beta, \theta]$ is:

$$\begin{bmatrix} tr[W_\rho]^2 + tr[\Sigma_\theta W_\rho' \Sigma_\theta^{-1} W_\rho] + (\widehat{Wy})'\Sigma_\theta^{-1}(\widehat{Wy}) & (X'\Sigma_\theta^{-1}\widehat{Wy})' & \psi' \\ X'\Sigma_\theta^{-1}\widehat{Wy} & X'\Sigma_\theta^{-1}X & 0 \\ \psi & 0 & (1/2)\Psi \end{bmatrix} \tag{26.65}$$

with $W_\rho = W(I - \rho W)^{-1}$, $\widehat{Wy} = W(I - \rho W)^{-1}X\beta$, and ψ as a $p \times 1$ vector of matrix traces of the form:

$$\psi_i = tr[\Sigma_\theta^{-1}(\partial \Sigma_\theta / \partial \theta_i)W_\rho], \tag{26.66}$$

one for each parameter in θ. Similarly, Ψ is a $p \times p$ matrix containing matrix traces of the form:

$$\Psi_{i,j} = tr[\Sigma_\theta^{-1}(\partial \Sigma_\theta / \partial \theta_i)\Sigma_\theta^{-1}(\partial \Sigma_\theta / \partial \theta_j)]. \tag{26.67}$$

Note how the presence of the vectors ψ implies that the information matrix is not block-diagonal between the model parameters $[\rho, \beta]$ and the error parameters θ. This is an important distinguishing characteristic of the spatial lag model, and leads to some interesting results on the structure of specification tests (Anselin and Bera, 1998).

Consider the special case of groupwise heteroskedasticity, which has considerable appeal in practice.[16] The error variance–covariance matrix Σ is diagonal, with $q = 1, \ldots, p$ subdiagonals, each corresponding to a group (sorting the observations by group, without loss of generality):

$$\Sigma = \begin{bmatrix} \sigma_1^2 I_1 & 0 & \cdots & 0 \\ 0 & \sigma_2^2 I_2 & \cdots & 0 \\ \vdots & \vdots & \ddots & 0 \\ 0 & 0 & \cdots & \sigma_p^2 I_p \end{bmatrix} \tag{26.68}$$

with $I_g, g = 1, \ldots, p$ as an identity matrix, with n_g elements matching the number of observations in each group and $\Sigma_g n_g = n$.

Plugging these expressions into the first order conditions (26.62)–(26.64) yields analytical solutions for β_{ML} and $\sigma_{g,ML}$, conditional upon the value of ρ, as:

$$\beta_{ML} = (X'\Sigma^{-1}X)^{-1}X'\Sigma^{-1}(y - \rho Wy) \tag{26.69}$$

$$\sigma^2_{g,ML} = (y - \rho Wy - X\beta)'H_g(y - \rho Wy - X\beta)/n_g, \quad g = 1, \ldots, p \tag{26.70}$$

where H_g is an identity matrix with all diagonal elements except those corresponding to group g set to zero, making (26.70) the average sum of squared residuals for the respective group. The estimate of β_{ML} is a weighted sum of a FGLS estimation of X on y and X on Wy, with $-\rho$ as the weight. However, unlike the i.i.d. situation (Anselin, 1980, chapter 4), this does not lead to a simple concentrated likelihood, since the FGLS depends on the σ^2_g, which in turn depend on the unknown ρ. Estimates can be obtained in an iterative fashion by substituting values for β and Σ from a previous iteration into (26.63), solving this condition for ρ, which in turn yields new values for β and Σ from (26.69)–(26.70). Note that Σ^{-1} is a diagonal matrix with elements $1/\sigma^2_g$ corresponding to each group. Asymptotic inference can be based on the information matrix (26.65), with the simpler Σ^{-1} substituted for the general form, and with $\partial\Sigma/\partial\sigma^2_g = H_g$.

26.5.2.2 *Spatial error models*

Maximum likelihood estimation of the parameters in models with spatially dependent error terms follows as a special case of the results in Magnus (1978). For a general non-spherical error term Σ_θ, with θ as the parameters, the ML estimator for β is the familiar generalized least squares expression:

$$\hat{\beta}_{ML} = (X'\Sigma_\theta^{-1}X)^{-1}X'\Sigma_\theta^{-1}y. \tag{26.71}$$

This follows as the solution of the first order conditions, applied to the log-likelihood:

$$L = -(n/2)\ln(2\pi) - (1/2)\ln|\Sigma_\theta| - (y - X\beta)'\Sigma_\theta^{-1}(y - X\beta). \tag{26.72}$$

The estimators for the θ_i are obtained from the following first order conditions (Magnus, 1978, p. 283):

$$tr[(\partial\Sigma_\theta^{-1}/\partial\theta_i)\Sigma_\theta] = e'(\partial\Sigma_\theta^{-1}/\partial\theta_i)e, \tag{26.73}$$

with $e = y - X\hat{\beta}_{ML}$ as the residuals. With a consistent estimate for the parameters θ_i, consistent estimates for β are obtained through FGLS (26.71).

Asymptotic inference is based on the inverse of the information matrix, which is block-diagonal between the β and the parameters of the error variance–covariance matrix (Breusch, 1980). The asymptotic variance for $\hat{\beta}_{ML}$ takes on the familiar GLS form:

$$Asy\ Var[\hat{\beta}_{ML}] = (X'\Sigma_\theta^{-1}X)^{-1}, \tag{26.74}$$

while the block corresponding to the error variance–covariance matrix parameters is of the form $2\Psi^{-1}$, with the elements of Ψ as in (26.67).

The range of spatial error processes considered in section 26.3 will result in specialized forms for Σ_θ, some of which may simplify the expressions in (26.71)–(26.73). For example, consider the SAR error process outlined in section 26.3.1.2, without heteroskedasticity. The corresponding parameter vector is $\theta = [\sigma^2, \lambda]$, and the error variance–covariance matrix is as in (26.18).

As a result, the FGLS estimator in this model simplifies to:

$$\hat{\beta}_{ML} = [X'(I - \hat{\lambda}W)'(I - \hat{\lambda}W)X]^{-1}X'(I - \hat{\lambda}W)'(I - \hat{\lambda}W)y, \tag{26.75}$$

a regression of spatially filtered $X_L = X - \hat{\lambda}WX$ on spatially filtered $y_L = y - \hat{\lambda}Wy$, sometimes referred to as spatially weighted least squares. The partial derivative for use in condition (26.73) is:

$$\partial\Sigma^{-1}/\partial\lambda = -W - W' + \lambda W'W. \tag{26.76}$$

Unlike the time series counterpart, a consistent estimate for λ cannot be obtained from a simple auxiliary regression, but the first order condition (26.73) must be solved by numerical means. As for the spatial lag model, asymptotic inference is based on the inverse of the information matrix (for technical details, see Anselin, 1988b, chapter 6).

Other spatial error processes do not yield a simple expression for $\hat{\beta}_{ML}$ as in the spatially weighted regression (26.75). For example, in the SMA process (section 26.3.1.4), the error variance–covariance matrix is as in (26.25), and:

$$\Sigma^{-1} = (1/\sigma^2)[I + \gamma(W + W') + \gamma^2 WW']^{-1}, \tag{26.77}$$

requiring the inverse of an $n \times n$ matrix to carry out FGLS. Similarly, the partial derivatives required for condition (26.73) involve inverses of this order. Models for direct representation or error components suffer from the same problem. In addition, the functional forms and distance metric used in the direct representation approach may cause problems with multiple optima in the log-likelihood function (see, among others, Mardia and Marshall, 1984; Warnes and Ripley, 1987; Mardia and Watkins, 1989).

26.5.2.3 Computational issues

Maximum likelihood estimation in spatial regression models involves the application of nonlinear optimization techniques to the log-likelihood function. A main computational obstacle follows from the presence of the log-Jacobian term

$\ln|I - \rho W|$ in the log-likelihood. In addition, the first order conditions and information matrix involve the traces of matrix products such as $W(I - \rho W)^{-1}$. For even medium-sized data sets, the computation of these terms by "brute force" is impractical.

An early solution was suggested by Ord (1975), who exploited the decomposition of the Jacobian in terms of the eigenvalues of the spatial weights matrix:

$$|I - \rho W| = \prod_{i=1}^{n}(1 - \rho\omega_i), \tag{26.78}$$

where the ω_i, $i = 1, \ldots, n$, are the eigenvalues of W. The log-Jacobian then follows as:

$$\ln|I - \rho W| = \sum_{i=1}^{n}\ln(1 - \rho\omega_i). \tag{26.79}$$

This facilitates computation greatly, since the eigenvalues only need to be calculated once, and iterating over values of ρ in (26.79) is straightforward. The trace terms used in the information matrix can be expressed in terms of the eigenvalues as well (Anselin, 1980).

The eigenvalue decomposition also suggests a simple set of constraints for the parameter space. For (26.79) to be valid, the condition $(1 - \rho\omega_i) > 0$ must hold $\forall\, i$. This results in a parameter space of $(1/\omega_{min}, 1/\omega_{max})$, where ω_{min} and ω_{max} are, respectively, the smallest (most negative) and largest eigenvalues of W (Anselin, 1980). For row-standardized spatial weights, $\omega_{max} = 1$, but ω_{min} depends on the structure of the weights matrix and is typically < -1. While it is often suggested in the literature to constrain the parameter space to the interval $(-1, +1)$, this may be overly restrictive.[17]

The computation of eigenvalues becomes impractical and computationally unstable for medium and large-sized data sets ($n > 1000$). This precludes the application of the Ord approach. Several alternatives have been suggested that either approximate or bound the Jacobian or log-Jacobian term (for example, Martin, 1993; Griffith and Sone, 1995; Barry and Pace, 1999; Pace and LeSage, 2002, 2004), or exploit the sparse nature of spatial weights.[18] The latter include factorization methods for sparse matrices, such as Cholesky decomposition (Pace and Barry, 1997a,b), and a characteristic polynomial approach (Smirnov and Anselin, 2001). The characteristic polynomial approach, in particular, allows very large spatial regression models ($n > 1$ million) to be estimated in a realistic time.

A second important computational problem pertains to the presence of terms like $tr[W(I - \rho W)^{-1}]^2$ in the information matrix, such as in (26.65). The calculation of these inverse matrices is impractical in large data settings. As a result, most large data ML methods developed so far have not based inference on the asymptotic variance matrix, but instead use a sequence of Likelihood Ratio tests. Recently, Smirnov (2005) developed a solution to this problem, based on the use of a conjugate gradient approach.

While much progress has been made, several issues remain to be resolved to allow the full range of spatial models (for example, not just SAR models) to be estimated by maximum likelihood methods in large samples.

26.5.3 Method of moments/instrumental variables

26.5.3.1 Spatial two-stage least squares

An alternative to maximum likelihood estimation is to use the method of moments (including instrumental variables, generalized method of moments, and generalized moments). This approach does not require an assumption of normality and it avoids some of the computational problems associated with ML for very large data sets.

Consider the spatial lag model (26.2), rewritten as:

$$y = Z\gamma + \varepsilon, \tag{26.80}$$

with $Z = [Wy, X]$ and $\gamma = [\rho, \beta]$. This is a general specification of a linear model that contains endogenous variables (Wy) as well as exogenous variables (X).

A classic solution to the endogeneity problem is to use instrumental variables. In a two-stage least squares approach, the predicted value of Z in a regression on the instruments is obtained in a first stage, as:

$$\hat{Z} = Q(Q'Q)^{-1}Q'Z, \tag{26.81}$$

with Q as an $n \times q$ matrix of instruments (including the exogenous variables X), with $q \geq k+1$. Note how this has no impact on the exogenous variables X, but it yields:

$$\widehat{Wy} = Q(Q'Q)^{-1}Q'Wy. \tag{26.82}$$

The instrument $\hat{Z}$ replaces Z in the second stage, resulting in the spatial two-stage least squares estimator:

$$\hat{\gamma}_{2SLS} = [\hat{Z}'\hat{Z}]^{-1}\hat{Z}'y, \tag{26.83}$$

or, in full:

$$\hat{\gamma}_{2SLS} = [Z'Q(Q'Q)^{-1}Q'Z]^{-1}Z'Q(Q'Q)^{-1}Q'y. \tag{26.84}$$

Inference on γ is based on the asymptotic variance matrix:

$$AsyVar[\hat{\gamma}_{2SLS}] = \hat{\sigma}^2[Z'Q(Q'Q)^{-1}Q'Z]^{-1}, \tag{26.85}$$

with $\hat{\sigma}^2 = (y - Z_{\hat{\gamma}_{2SLS}})'(y - Z_{\hat{\gamma}_{2SLS}})/n$.

The application of instrumental variables to the spatial lag model was outlined in Anselin (1980, 1988b, pp. 82–6), where some ad hoc suggestions were made for the selection of the instruments (see also Land and Deane, 1992, for an early discussion). Specifically, the choice of a spatial lag of the predicted values of the y (using only the exogenous variables) or of spatially lagged exogenous variables was considered.

In Kelejian and Robinson (1993), the consistency of $\hat{y}_{2SLS}$ is derived formally and the selection of instruments is couched in terms of the reduced form (26.44). From this, it follows that:

$$E[Wy|X] = W(I - \rho W)^{-1}X\beta, \tag{26.86}$$

or, using the expansion (26.19):

$$E[Wy|X] = WX\beta + \rho W^2 X\beta + \rho^2 W^3 X\beta + \dots. \tag{26.87}$$

Based on this expansion, Kelejian and Robinson (1993) suggest the use of a subset of columns from $\{X, WX, W^2X, W^3X, \dots\}$ as the instruments (see also Kelejian and Prucha, 1998).

In the context of a model with both a spatial lag and spatial error dependence, recent work has focused on the selection of "optimal" instruments (see also section 26.5.3.3). First consider this for the simpler specification of the pure spatial lag model without error dependence. Lee (2003) suggested using the optimal instrument matrix:

$$Q = [X, W(I - \hat{\rho} W)^{-1}X\hat{\beta}], \tag{26.88}$$

where the values for $\hat{\rho}$ and $\hat{\beta}$ are obtained in a first-round estimation, using WX as the instrument (possibly augmented with W^2X).[19]

To avoid the inverse matrix operation, Kelejian et al. (2004) introduce a series approximation, with the instrument matrix (for the pure spatial lag case) as:

$$Q = \left[X, \sum_{s=0}^{r} \hat{\rho}^s W^{s+1} X\hat{\beta}\right], \tag{26.89}$$

and the values for $\hat{\rho}$ and $\hat{\beta}$ from a first-round estimation, as in the Lee (2003) approach. The highest power in the approximation is related to the sample size, with $r = o(n^{1/2})$.[20]

Recent extensions of the instrumental variables approach to systems of simultaneous equations are considered in Rey and Boarnet (2004) and Kelejian and Prucha (2004). In Pinkse et al. (2002), an instrumental variable estimator is applied to a semiparametric spatial lag model. Instead of using a spatial weights matrix, the spatial dependence is specified in a generic way, as in equation (26.1). The function g is approximated by a polynomial series expansion in distance measures, the coefficients of which are estimated jointly with the other parameters in the model.

26.5.3.2   Spatial correlation as a nuisance parameter

A basic property of FGLS is that it suffices to obtain a consistent estimate for the parameters of the error variance–covariance matrix in order to obtain consistent estimates for the β in the second step, as in (26.71). This general approach refers to the error variance–covariance matrix parameters as *nuisance* parameters, in that they are not of interest in and of themselves, but are only useful in terms of improving the properties of the $\hat{\beta}$.

Kelejian and Prucha (1999) suggest a generalized moments approach to obtain a consistent estimate of the parameter λ in a spatial autoregressive error process $\varepsilon = \lambda W \varepsilon + u$. The idiosyncratic error term u is assumed to be i.i.d. with variance σ^2. Using the property that $trW = 0$, three moment conditions on the u and their spatial lags Wu follow as:

$$E[(1/n)u'u] = \sigma^2 \tag{26.90}$$

$$E[(1/n)u'W'Wu] = (1/n)\sigma^2 tr(W'W) \tag{26.91}$$

$$E[(1/n)u'W'u] = 0. \tag{26.92}$$

Since $u = \varepsilon - \lambda W \varepsilon$ and $Wu = W \varepsilon - \lambda WW \varepsilon$, these conditions can be expressed in terms of the regression errors ε. They are made operational by using the sample counterparts, i.e., the residuals e, their spatial lags We and double spatial lags WWe. After some algebra, this yields a system of three equations in the unknowns λ, λ^2 and σ^2.

$$\begin{bmatrix} (2/n)e'\bar{e} & (-1/n)\bar{e}'\bar{e} & 1 \\ (2/n)\bar{e}'\bar{\bar{e}} & (-1/n)\bar{\bar{e}}'\bar{\bar{e}} & (1/n)tr(W'W) \\ (1/n)(e'\bar{\bar{e}} + \bar{e}'\bar{e}) & (-1/n)\bar{e}'\bar{\bar{e}} & 0 \end{bmatrix} \begin{bmatrix} \lambda \\ \lambda^2 \\ \sigma^2 \end{bmatrix} = \begin{bmatrix} (1/n)e'e \\ (1/n)\bar{e}'\bar{e} \\ (1/n)e'\bar{e} \end{bmatrix} \tag{26.93}$$

with, for notational simplicity, $\bar{e} = We$ and $\bar{\bar{e}} = WWe$. This system can be solved for λ and σ^2 using nonlinear least squares. The resulting estimate $\hat{\lambda}$ is then plugged into the expression for the spatially weighted least squares estimator (26.75) (for technical details, see Kelejian and Prucha, 1999). Note that the nuisance parameter approach precludes inference about the coefficient λ, since there is no asymptotic variance for $\hat{\lambda}$.

26.5.3.3   Spatial lag with spatial SAR errors

The general moments estimator can also be applied to the residuals from a two-stage least squares regression. A special case consists of the specification with both a spatial lag and a spatial autoregressive error term (26.53), considered in Kelejian and Prucha (1998). This model can also be expressed as:

$$y = Z\gamma + (I - \lambda W_2)^{-1}u, \tag{26.94}$$

with $Z = [W_{1y}, X]$ and $\gamma = [\rho, \beta]$, as before. Removing the inverse term yields:

$$y - \lambda W_2 y = (Z - \lambda W_2 Z)\gamma + u, \tag{26.95}$$

or,

$$y_L = Z_L \gamma + u, \tag{26.96}$$

with y_L and Z_L as spatially filtered variables, analogous to the transformed variables in the spatially weighted least squares regression. Note how the first term in Z_L is $(W_1 y)_L = W_1 y - \lambda W_2 W_1 y$.

The generalized spatial two-stage least squares (GS2SLS) estimator developed in Kelejian and Prucha (1998) consists of three steps. The first step is a spatial two-stage least squares estimation, as in (26.84). The second step consists of substituting the residuals $e = y - Z\hat{\gamma}_{2SLS}$ into the system of equations (26.93), using the weights W_2 from the error process. The solution of the system by nonlinear least squares yields a consistent estimate $\hat{\lambda}$ for the autoregressive error parameter.

Next, the values for $\hat{\lambda}$ are substituted into the spatial filter to obtain y_L and Z_L. The final stage consists of a second two-stage least squares estimation, using the spatially filtered variables and the instruments:

$$\hat{Z}_L = Q(Q'Q)^{-1}Q'Z_L, \tag{26.97}$$

with the estimator as:

$$\hat{\gamma}_{GS2SLS} = [\hat{Z}_L'\hat{Z}_L]^{-1}\hat{Z}_L'y. \tag{26.98}$$

The estimation procedure can also be iterated, substituting the residuals from the GS2SLS estimation in the equation system (26.93) to yield a new value of $\hat{\lambda}$, etc. The asymptotic variance for the GS2SLS estimator follows in the usual fashion.

Note how the instruments boil down to replacing the $(W_1 y)_L$ in Z_L by the predicted values:

$$\widehat{(W_1 y)}_L = Q(Q'Q)^{-1}Q'(W_1 y - \hat{\lambda} W_2 W_1 y). \tag{26.99}$$

Initially, Kelejian and Prucha (1998, p. 104) suggested that the instruments be selected as a subset of $\{X, W_1 X, W_1^2 X, \ldots, W_2 X, W_2 W_1 X, W_2 W_1^2 X, \ldots\}$, such as $[X, W_1 X, W_2 X, W_2 W_1 X]$. More recently, optimal instruments have been considered, as discussed in section 26.5.3.1. Specifically, the optimal instruments (26.88) of Lee (2003) in this general model are:

$$Q = (I - \hat{\lambda} W_2)[X, W_1(I - \hat{\rho} W_1)^{-1}X\hat{\beta}]. \tag{26.100}$$

For the Kelejian *et al.* (2004) series estimator (26.89), this is:

$$Q = (I - \hat{\lambda} W_2)[X, \sum_{s=0}^{r} \hat{\rho}^s W_1^{s+1} X\hat{\beta}]. \tag{26.101}$$

Monte Carlo experiments to assess the finite sample properties of the GS2SLS estimator relative to ML are reported in Das *et al.* (2003). In general, very small differences are obtained. Interestingly, there does not seem to be a worthwhile payoff from iterating on the GS2SLS (Das *et al.*, 2003, p. 12). This finding does not transfer to the methods using the optimal instruments, evaluated in Monte Carlo experiments in Kelejian *et al.* (2004). There, a suggestion is made that iterating will tend to improve efficiency. Overall, the performances of the estimators with the three forms of instruments were found to be very similar.

26.5.3.4 Heteroskedastic and autocorrelation consistent estimators

Up to this point, the estimators considered pertain to models in which the spatial dependence is specified in parameterized form, typically as a SAR process. An alternative is to avoid such specification, and estimate the error variance–covariance matrix in non-parametric fashion. This follows along the lines of the White (1980) heteroskedastic-consistent approach and its extension to both heteroskedasticity and serial correlation by Newey and West (1987) and others.

For example, a ready extension of the S2SLS estimator in the spatial lag model is to allow for heteroskedasticity of unspecified form, as a direct application of the White approach. In a first step, a S2SLS estimation is carried out using instrument matrix Q (as before), followed by:

$$\hat{\beta}_{HS2SLS} = [Z'Q(\widehat{Q'\Sigma Q})^{-1}Q'Z]^{-1}Z'Q(\widehat{Q'\Sigma Q})^{-1}Q'y, \qquad (26.102)$$

with $(\widehat{Q'\Sigma Q})^{-1} = (Q'SQ)^{-1}$, where S is a diagonal matrix containing the squared S2SLS residuals. The asymptotic variance for $\hat{\beta}_{HS2SLS}$ is obtained in the usual fashion.

The incorporation of spatial dependence in this framework was first considered by Conley (1999) in the context of GMM estimation, and recently elaborated upon in Kelejian and Prucha (2003) (see also section 26.3.3).[21] Using a consistent estimate for $(Q'\Sigma Q)^{-1}$, along the lines of (26.30) or (26.31), yields a heteroskedastic and spatial autocorrelation consistent (HAC) estimator for the spatial lag model as in (26.102). Alternatively, this idea can be exploited to obtain robust inference in the standard linear regression model, using OLS to estimate the β, but a HAC estimator for the asymptotic variance:

$$AsyVar[\hat{\beta}_{OLS}] = (X'X)^{-1}\hat{V}(X'X)^{-1}, \qquad (26.103)$$

with $\hat{V}$ based on (26.30) or (26.31) (omitting the term n^{-1}).

The HAC approach is asymptotic and in finite samples a major practical problem is to ensure that the estimated variance–covariance matrix is positive semidefinite. A number of suggestions have been formulated, but considerable research remains to be done to obtain insight into finite sample properties (see Kelejian and Prucha, 2003, for some technical details).

26.6 Specification testing

In applied work, diagnostic tests against the presence of spatial correlation are arguably more relevant than estimation itself. Ignoring spatial correlation when it is present may lead to biased and inconsistent estimates of the model parameters (spatial lag model), or inefficient estimates and biased t-test statistics (spatial error model). Also, given the complexities associated with estimating models that include spatial dependence, it is important to be able to assess whether this is, in fact, necessary. It is therefore reasonable that some check for autocorrelation should be as common in cross-sectional regression work as are tests for serial correlation in the time domain. In these tests, the null hypothesis is the absence of spatial autocorrelation, or the standard regression model. Alternatives include the many spatial models reviewed in sections 26.3 and 26.4, as well as combinations of these spatial models with other sources of misspecification, such as hetero-skedasticity and non-linearity.

The literature on specification tests against spatial correlation in cross-sectional regression is by now quite extensive (for recent reviews, see Anselin and Bera, 1998; Anselin, 2001a; Florax and de Graaff, 2004). In the following sections, the main features of the most commonly used tests are outlined, organized as tests against spatial autocorrelation, tests based on the Maximum Likelihood principle, and tests against multiple sources of misspecification.[22] To close, a brief discussion is given of the specification search process.

26.6.1   Tests against spatial autocorrelation

Tests against spatial autocorrelation are so-called "diffuse" tests (Florax and de Graaff, 2004), in that the alternative is an unspecified form of spatial correlation. These test statistics are excellent tools as misspecification diagnostics. However, they offer little in terms of guiding a specification search, since they have power against multiple forms of spatial autocorrelation. Hence, it is not always clear which of these is the proper alternative.

26.6.1.1   *Moran's I test*

Perhaps the best-known test statistic against spatial autocorrelation is the application of Moran's I statistic (Moran, 1948) to regression residuals (Moran, 1950), popularized in the work of Cliff and Ord (Cliff and Ord, 1972, 1973, 1981).

Formally, Moran's I for regression residuals is:

$$I = \frac{e'We/S_0}{e'e/n},\qquad(26.104)$$

where e is an $n \times 1$ vector of OLS residuals $y - X\hat{\beta}$, W is a spatial weights matrix, and $S_0 = \sum_i \sum_j w_{ij}$, a normalizing factor.[23] Inference in a test against spatial autocorrelation is based on a normal approximation, using a standardized value, or z-value. This is obtained by subtracting the mean under the null and dividing by the square root of the variance. The first two moments were derived in Cliff and Ord (1972) as:

$$E[I] = tr(MW)/(n - k),\qquad(26.105)$$

and

$$\text{Var}[I] = \frac{tr(MWMW') + tr(MWMW) + [tr(MW)]^2}{(n-k)(n-k+2)} - (E[I])^2, \tag{26.106}$$

where $M = I - X(X'X)^{-1}X'$ The normality of the z-value is an approximation, which works well in large samples.

Exact inference for Moran's I can be carried out, under the assumption of normality for the error terms, by noting that, under the null, the statistic consists of a ratio of quadratic forms of independent normal random variables (see Tiefelsdorf and Boots, 1995). To obtain exact critical values for the statistic, it is necessary to compute the $n-k$ non-zero eigenvalues of MW, which is not practical in medium to large samples (see also Tiefelsdorf, 2002, for an alternative approximation).

Moran's I has been shown to have certain optimality properties, similar to the Durbin–Watson test against serial correlation in the time domain. For example, King (1981) demonstrated that the test is locally best invariant. Also, Moran's I turns out to be asymptotically equivalent to a Likelihood Ratio (LR) test, and to a Rao Score (RS) or Lagrange Multiplier (LM) test (Cliff and Ord, 1972; Burridge, 1980), and therefore shares the asymptotic properties of these statistics.

Moran's I is often interpreted as a test statistic against serial error correlation, but this is incorrect. The test has power against any alternative of spatial correlation, including spatial lag dependence, as demonstrated in a large number of Monte Carlo simulation experiments (see, for example, Anselin and Rey, 1991; Anselin and Florax, 1995b; Florax and de Graaff, 2004). In addition, not unlike the Durbin–Watson statistic, the test has power against heteroskedasticity as well (Anselin and Griffith, 1988).

Moran's I test statistic is very general and can be applied in many contexts other than the classic regression model. For example, in Anselin and Kelejian (1997) the test is applied to the residuals of a model with endogenous variables, estimated by two-stage least squares (2SLS). A distinction needs to be made between the case where the endogenous variables include a spatial lag and the standard non-spatial case. The general case can be written as:

$$y = Z\gamma + e, \tag{26.107}$$

with $Z = [Wy, Y, X]$ and $\gamma = [\rho, \delta, \beta]$, where Wy is the spatially lagged dependent variable, Y is a matrix of non-spatial endogenous variables, and X a matrix of exogenous variables.

The general result for the asymptotic distribution of Moran's I in this model is:

$$n^{1/2}I \xrightarrow{d} N(0, \phi^2), \tag{26.108}$$

with I as in (26.104), but using the 2SLS residuals from (26.107), and

$$\phi^2 = \frac{S_2}{2S_1^2} + \frac{4}{S_1^2\hat{\sigma}^2}A. \tag{26.109}$$

The terms in the expression for the asymptotic variance include the error variance estimated from 2SLS residuals, $\hat{\sigma}^2$, and functions of the elements of the weights matrix:

$$S_1 = (1/n)S_0 \tag{26.110}$$

$$S_2 = (1/n)tr[(W + W')(W + W')] \tag{26.111}$$

and

$$A = (e'WZ/n)(n[(Z'Q)(Q'Q)^{-1}Q'Z]^{-1})(Z'W'e/n), \tag{26.112}$$

with e as the 2SLS residuals, S_0 as in (26.104), Z as in (26.107), and Q as the matrix of instruments used in the 2SLS estimation (for details, see Anselin and Kelejian, 1997, pp. 162–4). When no spatially lagged dependent variable is included in the model, the second term in (26.109) becomes zero and the test statistic simplifies to the Lagrange Multiplier statistic for spatial error auto-correlation (see section 26.6.2.1).

A general framework for the asymptotic properties of Moran's I in a wide range of specifications is presented in Kelejian and Prucha (2001). This includes a spatial auto-correlation test in probit models, which is considered more closely in section 26.8.3.

26.6.1.2 Kelejian–Robinson test

A second test against an unspecified form of spatial correlation was suggested by Kelejian and Robinson (1992). The rationale for the test is intuitive: if the covar-iance between "neighboring" pairs of error terms shows a systematic variation, then the null hypothesis of no spatial autocorrelation should be rejected. For-mally, the spatial covariance is specified as:

$$Cov[\varepsilon_i \varepsilon_j] = \sigma_{ij} = v_{ij}\gamma \neq 0, \tag{26.113}$$

where v_{ij} is a $1 \times q$ vector of covariates related to the pair of locations i, j. For example, a given element h of v_{ij} can be specified as $v_{ijh} = x_{ih}x_{jh}$, the product of the explanatory variable x_h for the pair of locations i, j. Under the null hypothesis, there should be no covariance, hence $H_0 : \gamma = 0$. The test is made operational by selecting h_n pairs of cross-products of residuals, $\hat{C}_{ij} = e_i.e_j$, and regressing them on matching cross-products of the explanatory variables, v_{ij}. In matrix notation:

$$\hat{C} = V\gamma + u, \tag{26.114}$$

with u as an idiosyncratic error. The test statistic is a measure of goodness-of-fit in this auxiliary regression:

$$KR = \frac{\hat{\gamma}'V'V\hat{\gamma}}{\hat{\sigma}^4}, \tag{26.115}$$

which, under the null hypothesis, is distributed asymptotically as $\chi^2(q)$, with q as the number of explanatory variables in the auxiliary regression (i.e., the number of columns of V). The denominator term $\hat{\sigma}^4$ is any consistent estimator for σ^4, such as $\hat{\sigma}^4 = (\hat{C} - V\hat{\gamma})'(\hat{C} - V\hat{\gamma})/h_n$. Anselin and Bera (1998, p. 269) show how the test has an asymptotically equivalent expression in the form of the familiar NR^2 in an auxiliary regression:

$$KR = h_n \cdot \frac{\hat{C}'V(V'V)^{-1}V'\hat{C}}{\hat{C}'\hat{C}}, \qquad (26.116)$$

where h_n is the sample size of the auxiliary regression and R^2 is the uncentered coefficient of determination in a regression of $\hat{C}$ on V.

The properties of the test statistic are obtained without assuming normality, and they do not require the regression model to be linear. Kelejian and Robinson (1992) suggest that the test is not based on the use of spatial weights, but only the existence of a "spatial ordering," which determines the pairs i, j to be included in the auxiliary regression. In practice, this often boils down to the use of contiguity. This may be problematic, since it is well established that the spatial covariance (on which the test is based) only corresponds to the spatial weights for *local* patterns of spatial correlation. For example, this is the case for the spatial error components model covered in section 3.4 (see Kelejian and Robinson, 1995, p. 89), but not for a SAR alternative (for further discussion, see Anselin and Moreno, 2003, pp. 599–600).

The KR test is a large sample test, and its asymptotic properties are not well reflected in small sample situations. This is evidenced in a number of Monte Carlo simulation studies (for example, Anselin and Florax, 1995b; Anselin and Moreno, 2003; Florax and de Graaff, 2004).

26.6.2 Tests based on maximum likelihood

In contrast to diffuse spatial autocorrelation tests, "focused" tests are constructed with a specific alternative in mind. In general, they boil down to a test of restrictions on the parameters of a model that includes spatial dependence, such as a spatial error model or a spatial lag model. The most commonly used approach is based on the three classic test statistics obtained under maximum likelihood estimation: the Wald, Likelihood Ratio and Lagrange Multiplier (or Rao Score) tests.[24]

Both the Wald and Likelihood Ratio tests are standard, and require estimation of the unrestricted or spatial model (for technical details, see Anselin, 1988b, ch. 6). The Lagrange Multiplier tests, on the other hand, are based on estimation under the null, or restricted, model, i.e., the classic linear regression and its OLS residuals. In contrast to results in mainstream econometrics, the LM test statistics for spatial dependence cannot be obtained in an NR^2 form based on a simple auxiliary regression (for a recent comprehensive overview, see Anselin, 2001a).

26.6.2.1 Spatial error autocorrelation

The point of departure for a LM test for spatial error autocorrelation is the log-likelihood (26.72) for a specific data-generating process for the regression error terms, such as SAR or SMA. In the usual fashion, a LM test statistic is then obtained as:

$$LM = [d(\theta)]'[I(\theta)]^{-1}[d(\theta)], \qquad (26.117)$$

where $d(\theta)$ is the familiar score, $\partial L(\theta)/\partial\theta$, and $I(\theta)$ is the information matrix, $-E[\partial^2 L(\theta)/\partial\theta\partial\theta']$. Both score and information matrix are derived for the unrestricted (spatial) model, but evaluated under the null, i.e., with the restricted parameters. For the SAR and SMA alternatives, this is $\lambda = 0$ in (26.14), or $\gamma = 0$ in (26.24). Both restrictions lead to the same test statistic (Burridge, 1980; Anselin, 1988a):

$$LM_\lambda = \frac{[e'We/(e'e/n)]^2}{tr[W'W + WW]}, \qquad (26.118)$$

where e is an $n \times 1$ vector of OLS residuals. Apart from the scaling factor in the denominator, this statistic is essentially the square of Moran's I. It is asymptotically distributed as $\chi^2(1)$.

Since the LM test exploits the slope of the log-likelihood under the null, it is possible that different alternatives result in the same slope. This is the case for the SAR and SMA alternatives, which are termed "locally equivalent alternatives" or LEA (Godfrey, 1981). As a consequence, it is not possible to distinguish between these two alternatives using a LM test.

Traditionally, the asymptotic properties for the LM test are obtained for a complete specification of the log-likelihood, including an assumption of normality. This turns out to be overly restrictive, and the same asymptotic properties can also be derived, without assuming normality, by using the appropriate CLT (for technical details, see Anselin and Kelejian, 1997; Kelejian and Prucha, 2001).

The LM principle can also be applied to other one-directional spatial error alternatives, such as the error components model (26.32) or direct representation (26.28). The resulting test statistic for the error components model is (Anselin, 2001a; Anselin and Moreno, 2003):

$$LM_{SEC} = \left[\frac{e'WW'e}{e'e/n} - T_1\right]^2 \Big/ 2\left[T_2 - \frac{T_1^2}{n}\right] \qquad (26.119)$$

where $T_1 = tr(WW')$ and $T_2 = tr(WW'WW')$. The statistic is asymptotically distributed as $\chi^2(1)$.[25]

A test statistic for the direct representation model derived from ML principles is more complex since, under the null, the parameter value is on the boundary of the parameter space. Moreover, the nuisance parameters are only identified under the alternative hypothesis. These non-standard conditions invalidate the use of LR or Wald statistics. The LM statistic can still be employed, but it requires an approximation due to Davies (1977, 1987), applied to the direct representation model in Anselin (2001a, pp. 130–2).

An alternative strategy, still based on ML principles, applies the idea of double length artificial regressions (DLR, Davidson and MacKinnon, 1984, 1988) to the spatial models, as outlined in Baltagi and Li (2001a). The DLR approach consists of expressing the regression model as a function of standard normal error terms. In the spatial models, this follows as a simple standardization. Furthermore, Baltagi and Li (2001a) exploit the eigenvalue decomposition of the log-Jacobian term (26.79) to obtain the contribution of each observation to the log-likelihood as:

$$l_i(y_i, \phi) = -(1/2)\ln(2\pi) - (1/2)f_i^2(y_i, \phi) + k_i(y_i, \phi), \tag{26.120}$$

with $\phi = [\beta, \lambda, \sigma]'$ as a vector of parameters, f_i as the standard normal error term:

$$f_i(y_i, \phi) = (1/\sigma)[(y_i - x_i'\beta) - \lambda \sum_j w_{ij}(y_j - x_j'\beta)], \tag{26.121}$$

and k_i as the complete log-Jacobian (including the error variance):

$$k_i(y_i, \phi) = \ln(1 - \lambda\omega_i) - \ln\sigma, \tag{26.122}$$

where ω_i are the eigenvalues of the spatial weights matrix. The DLR consists of an artificial regression with $2n$ "observations":

$$\begin{bmatrix} f(y, \phi) \\ \iota_n \end{bmatrix} = \begin{bmatrix} -F(y, \phi) \\ K(y, \phi) \end{bmatrix} b + u, \tag{26.123}$$

in which the u are unspecified residuals, ι_n is an $n \times 1$ vector of ones, and F and K are $n \times (k+2)$ matrices of partial derivatives $F_{ij}(y_i, \phi) \equiv \partial f_i(y_i, \phi)/\partial \phi_j$, and $K_{ij}(y_i, \phi) \equiv \partial k_i(y_i, \phi)/\partial \phi_j$. Using the expressions (26.121) and (26.122) for the spatial SAR error model, this yields:

$$\begin{bmatrix} e/\hat{\sigma} \\ \iota_n \end{bmatrix} = \begin{bmatrix} (1/\hat{\sigma})X & (1/\hat{\sigma})We & e/\hat{\sigma}^2 \\ 0 & -\omega & -\iota_n/\hat{\sigma} \end{bmatrix} b + u \tag{26.124}$$

with e as the OLS residuals, $\hat{\sigma}$ as the OLS estimate for the disturbance standard error, and ω as an $n \times 1$ vector of the eigenvalues ω_i. The test statistic is computed as $2n$ less the residual sum of squares in the artificial regression. It is asymptotically distributed as $\chi^2(1)$. While the artificial regression is easy to carry out, in practice it suffers from the necessity to compute the eigenvalues of the spatial weights matrix, which is problematic in large samples (see section 26.5.2.3).

26.6.2.2 Spatial lag

Using the same principle as in (26.117) applied to the log-likelihood of the spatial lag model (26.61), and with the constraint $\rho = 0$, yields a LM test statistic for spatial lag dependence, as shown in Anselin (1988a):

$$LM_\rho = [e'Wy/(e'e/n)]^2/D, \tag{26.125}$$

with e as the OLS residuals and denominator term:

$$D = [(WX\hat{\beta})'[I - X(X'X)^{-1}X'](WX\hat{\beta})/\hat{\sigma}^2] + tr(W'W + WW), \quad (26.126)$$

where the estimates for $\hat{\beta}$ and $\hat{\sigma}^2$ are from OLS. The test statistic is asymptotically distributed as $\chi^2(1)$.

Similarly, the application of the DLR principle to the log-likelihood and log-Jacobian terms of the spatial lag model yields the artificial regression (Baltagi and Li, 2001a):

$$\begin{bmatrix} e/\hat{\sigma} \\ \iota_n \end{bmatrix} = \begin{bmatrix} (1/\hat{\sigma})X & (1/\hat{\sigma})Wy & e/\hat{\sigma}^2 \\ 0 & -\omega & -\iota_n/\hat{\sigma} \end{bmatrix} b + u, \quad (26.127)$$

where, again, all estimates are based on OLS. The test statistic ($2n$ less the residual sum of squares) is also asymptotically distributed as $\chi^2(1)$.

26.6.2.3 Higher-order models

So far, the tests considered are for one-directional alternatives. When the alternative is of a higher order, such as the models reviewed in section 26.4.2, different test strategies may be pursued. One is a so-called *marginal* test, which only focuses on one source of misspecification at a time, ignoring the other, such as the tests covered so far. A second perspective is that of a *joint* test, where the null hypothesis is to set all spatial parameters equal to zero. For example, for the spatial lag model with a SAR error term (26.53), $H_0 : \rho = \lambda = 0$.[26]

In contrast to standard results, the joint test statistic is not simply the sum of the marginal test statistics, i.e., $LM_{\lambda\rho} \neq LM_\lambda + LM_\rho$, but it takes on a far more complex form (Anselin, 1988a). To simplify notation, set $d_\rho = (e'Wy)/(e'e/n)$ and $d_\lambda = (e'We)/(e'e/n)$ and use D as in (26.126), but with W_1 as the spatial weights matrix pertaining to the lag model. As before, all estimates are from OLS. Further, using W_2 for the spatial weights in the error process, take $T_{ij} = tr[W_iW_j + W_i'W_j]$. The LM test statistic for the joint null hypothesis is given by:

$$LM_{\rho\lambda} = \frac{[d_\lambda^2 D + d_\rho^2 T_{22} - 2d_\lambda d_\rho T_{12}]}{DT_{22} - T_{12}^2}. \quad (26.128)$$

This test statistic is asymptotically distributed as $\chi^2(2)$. This will result in a loss of power relative to the proper one-directional test when only one source of misspecification is present. In the commonly used simplification, where $W_1 = W_2$, the test statistic becomes:

$$LM_{\rho\lambda} = \frac{d_\lambda^2}{T} + \frac{(d_\lambda - d_\rho)^2}{D - T}. \quad (26.129)$$

Extensions of these principles to joint tests in SARMA(p, q) models are straightforward, and can be found in Anselin (2001a).

Yet a third testing strategy for higher-order alternatives is to take a *conditional* approach, where a test on the null hypothesis $\rho = 0$ is carried out in a model with $\lambda \neq 0$, and vice versa. This can no longer be based on OLS estimates, but requires estimation of the proper spatial model by means of ML. For example, a test statistic for $H_0 : \lambda = 0$ in the spatial lag model is obtained as:

$$LM_{\lambda|\rho} = \frac{d_\rho^2}{T_{22} - (T_{21A}^2 \, \widehat{Var}(\hat\rho))}, \qquad (26.130)$$

where all the estimates are obtained using ML in the spatial lag model, $T_{21A} = tr[(W_2 W_1 + W_2' W_1)(I - \hat\rho W)^{-1}]$, and the other notation is as before. The test statistic is asymptotically distributed as $\chi^2(1)$. It forms the ML-based counterpart to the Moran's I for S2SLS residuals outlined in equations (26.108)–(26.109). A test statistic for $H_0 : \rho = 0$ in the spatial error model, $LM_{\rho|\lambda}$, can be developed along the same lines, but turns out to be quite complex (for technical details, see Anselin, 1988a; Anselin *et al.*, 1996; Anselin and Bera, 1998).

26.6.2.4 Robust tests

In a higher-order model, the parameter that is not of interest can be considered to be a nuisance parameter. Unfortunately, the one-directional test statistics LM_λ and LM_ρ become non-central χ^2 in the presence of local misspecification in the form of the other type of spatial dependence. In other words, in the presence of spatial lag dependence, the LM_λ test against error correlation becomes biased and, in the presence of spatial error dependence, the LM_ρ test against lag dependence becomes biased. Using a result of Bera and Yoon (1993), a robust version of these test statistics can be developed, as shown in Anselin *et al.* (1996) (see also Anselin and Bera, 1998, pp. 273–8).

Limiting attention to the case where $W_1 = W_2 = W$, the expression for the robustified test against spatial error dependence is:

$$LM_\lambda^* = \frac{(d_\lambda - TD^{-1} d_\rho)^2}{[T(1 - TD)]}, \qquad (26.131)$$

using the same notation as before, and with all estimates obtained from OLS in the classic regression. The essence of the robustification is to correct the LM_λ statistic for the covariance between d_λ and d_ρ. The new test statistic is asymptotically distributed as $\chi^2(1)$.

Similarly, a robustified test against a spatial lag alternative takes the form:

$$LM_\rho^* = \frac{(d_\rho - d_\lambda)^2}{(D - T)}, \qquad (26.132)$$

and is also asymptotically distributed as $\chi^2(1)$.

An interesting result is the decomposition of the two-directional test statistic (26.129). As pointed out, this is not the sum of the two one-directional tests, but instead:

$$LM_{\rho\lambda} = LM_\rho + LM_\lambda^* = LM_\lambda + LM_\rho^*, \tag{26.133}$$

or, the sum of the one-directional statistic for one source of misspecification and the robustified version of the test statistic for the second source (for technical details, see Anselin *et al.*, 1996).

26.6.3 Tests against multiple sources of misspecification

In sections 26.6.1 and 26.6.2, the misspecifications considered consisted of forms of spatial dependence only. In practice, cross-sectional data are also likely to be affected by other sources of misspecification, such as heteroskedasticity and non-linearity. Testing for heteroskedasticity in the presence of spatial dependence is straightforward. As shown in Anselin (1988b), a Breusch–Pagan (BP) type LM test statistic (Breusch and Pagan, 1979, 1980) readily extends to the ML-residuals in a spatial lag model, or to the spatially filtered residuals in the ML estimation of a spatial error model.[27]

A *joint* test for heteroskedasticity and spatial error dependence consists of the sum of a BP statistic and the LM_λ (26.118) (Anselin, 1988b). An alternative is the extended Kelejian–Robinson statistic outlined in Kelejian and Robinson (1998), which does not require an assumption of normality and applies equally to linear and nonlinear regressions. For notational simplicity, consider the scalar case only, in which the heteroskedasticity is modeled as $\sigma_i^2 = g(z_i)$, where z is one of the explanatory variables in the regression specification (this generalizes to z being a subset of the explanatory variables). The resulting test statistic is obtained as a joint test of significance on the slope coefficients in an auxiliary regression (Kelejian and Robinson, 1998, p. 393):

$$e_i e_j = a_0 \delta_{ij} + a_1(\delta_{ij} z_i) + a_2(z_i w_{ji} + z_j w_{ij}) + u, \tag{26.134}$$

with the terms $e_i e_j$ including all the squared residuals and all cross-products for $j > i$ and $(w_{ji} + w_{ij}) \neq 0$, $\delta_{ii} = 1$, and $\delta_{ij} = 0$ for $i \neq j$. The joint significance test on $a_1 = a_2 = 0$ uses a heteroskedastic-consistent (White) covariance estimator. The extension of the simple scalar case to a situation with multiple z variables requires nonlinear least squares (for details, see Kelejian and Robinson, 1998, pp. 394–5).

A *conditional* test for spatial error autocorrelation in a heteroskedastic regression model can be derived from the LM-test principles. With $\hat{\Omega}$ as the estimated (diagonal) heteroskedastic variance matrix, for example, with elements $\hat{\sigma}_i = g(\hat{\alpha}, z_i)$ (where the $\hat{\alpha}$ are consistent estimates, say obtained in a maximum likelihood estimation), the heteroskedastic LM statistic becomes (Anselin, 1988b, p. 107):

$$LM_{H\lambda} = \frac{(e'\hat{\Omega}^{-1} We)^2}{tr(WW + W'\hat{\Omega}^{-1} W\hat{\Omega})}, \tag{26.135}$$

with e as the residuals in the heteroskedastic regression. The $LM_{H\lambda}$ test statistic is asymptotically distributed as $\chi^2(1)$.[28]

The joint presence of spatial correlation and functional misspecification has also received some attention. In Baltagi and Li (2001b), the LM principle is applied to derive a test for a general Box–Cox alternative with spatial error dependence, as well as conditional tests for functional form given spatial error dependence and vice versa. The test statistics do not reduce to simple analytical forms, but require computing the expression (26.117) with the proper elements for the score and information matrix substituted in each special case. De Graaff *et al.* (2001) consider the extension of a general misspecification test from chaos theory in time series to the spatial domain in order to assess dependence, heterogeneity and nonlinearity.

26.6.4 Specification search

In practice, the sheer number of available test statistics can seem overwhelming and a strategy needs to be developed to move from the null model to a superior alternative (when appropriate). Given that tests may be based on marginal, joint or conditional approaches, the results of a specification search may be subject to the order in which tests are carried out, and whether or not adjustments are made for pre-testing (see, for example, Florax and Folmer, 1992; Anselin and Florax, 1995b; Florax and de Graaff, 2004).

Based on a large number of simulation results, an ad hoc decision rule was suggested in Anselin and Rey (1991) for the simple case of choosing between a spatial lag or spatial (SAR) error alternative. There is considerable evidence that the proper alternative is most likely the one with the largest significant *LM* test statistic value. This was later refined in light of the robust forms of the statistics in Anselin *et al.* (1996) to a sequence where, in the first step, the significance of the LM_λ and LM_ρ test statistics was assessed. The robust forms LM_λ^* and LM_ρ^* are only considered when *both LM_λ and LM_ρ* are significant. At that point, the largest, most significant, value of the robust statistics suggests the most likely alternative.

In a recent paper by Florax *et al.* (2003), this classic forward stepwise specification search is compared to a "general-to-simple" model selection rule. In the backward stepwise approach, the point of departure is the spatial common factor (or spatial Durbin) model (26.43). Failure to reject the factor constraints suggests a spatial error model. Alternatively, rejection of the factor constraints suggests a spatial lag model. If the autoregressive coefficient in the lag model is not significant, the final model selection is the standard regression specification. In simulation experiments, the forward and backward specification searches are compared and some evidence is provided of better performance by the forward strategy (for further discussion, see also Florax *et al.*, 2006; Hendry, 2006).

26.7 Spatial effects in panel data

Up to this point, the focus in this chapter has been on models for a single cross-section. Early efforts to incorporate spatial effects in a panel data setting, with observations over time as well as across space, were described in Anselin (1988b, chapter 10). More recently, this has received growing attention in the mainstream econometric literature. For example, the second edition of Baltagi's well-known panel data text now includes a brief discussion of *spatial panels* (Baltagi, 2001, pp. 195–7).

The topic of spatial panels is too broad ranging to be covered satisfactorily within a single chapter section, and by necessity the treatment here will be limited to a few salient issues (for a recent and extensive review, see Anselin *et al.*, 2006). First, the generic aspects of incorporating spatial effects in pooled cross-section and time series models will be considered. This is followed by a brief review of specification, estimation and diagnostic testing in two special models that have received considerable attention in empirical practice, the error components model with spatial effects and the spatial seemingly unrelated regression (SUR) model.[29]

26.7.1   Spatial effects in pooled cross-section and time series models

26.7.1.1   Model specification

The basic specification for a model containing observations in the time domain as well as across space can be given as:

$$y_{it} = x'_{it}\beta + \varepsilon_{it}, \tag{26.136}$$

where i is an index for the cross-sectional dimension, with $i = 1, \ldots, n$, and t is an index for the time dimenson, with $t = 1, \ldots, T$. Using customary notation, y_{it} is an observation on the dependent variable at i and t, x_{it} a $k \times 1$ vector of observations on the (exogenous) explanatory variables, β a matching $k \times 1$ vector of regression coefficients, and ε_{it} an error term. The setting considered here is where the cross-sectional dimension dominates, with $n \gg T$. Also, even though the basic design is referred to as "space" and "time," the second dimension could equally pertain to different cross-sections, such as in a study of industrial sectors or household types. In stacked matrix form, the simple pooled regression then becomes:

$$y = X\beta + \varepsilon, \tag{26.137}$$

with y as an $nT \times 1$ vector, X as an $nT \times k$ matrix and ε as an $nT \times 1$ vector. Note that, in order to incorporate spatial effects, the stacking is for a complete cross-section at a time, and not for each individual cross-section over time.

The models (26.136)–(26.137) refer to homogeneous panels, in that the intercept and slope coefficients are assumed to be constant over the cross-sectional units. In contrast, in a heterogeneous panel, these coefficients are specific to each cross-sectional unit:

$$y_{it} = \alpha_i + x'_{it}\beta_i + \varepsilon_{it}. \tag{26.138}$$

Common approaches to deal with the heterogeneity are fixed effects and random effects models, which are not considered in detail here (specific examples are covered in sections 26.7.2 and 26.7.3). For a technical discussion of spatial effects in fixed and random effects models, see, for example, Elhorst (2003) and Anselin *et al.* (2006).

Spatial effects can easily be introduced into the homogeneous panel by straightforward extension of the models considered in sections 26.3 and 26.4. This is readily accomplished by generalizing the notion of a cross-sectional n-dimensional spatial weights matrix, W_n, to the panel dimension nT. Typically, it is assumed that the weights remain constant over time. Consequently, the $nT \times nT$ dimension simplifies to:

$$W_{nT} = I_T \otimes W_n, \tag{26.139}$$

where the subscripts refer to the matrix dimension and $\otimes$ is the Kronecker product. A spatial lag model can then be expressed as:

$$y = \rho(I_T \otimes W_N)y + X\beta + \varepsilon, \tag{26.140}$$

where ρ is the spatial autoregressive parameter (constant over the time dimension), and the other notation is as before. Similarly, a model with spatial SAR error dependence results in an $nT \times nT$ non-spherical error variance–covariance matrix of the form:

$$\Sigma_{NT} = \sigma_u^2 [I_T \otimes (B_N' B_N)^{-1}], \tag{26.141}$$

where $B_n = I_n - \lambda W_n$, σ_u^2 is a common variance term, and the spatial autoregressive coefficient λ is assumed to be constant over the time dimension. More complex model specifications can be introduced in the same fashion (see Anselin *et al.*, 2005).

26.7.1.2 Estimation

Estimation of the spatial lag and spatial error specifications for homogeneous panels can be carried out by direct extension of the methods covered in sections 26.5.2 and 26.5.3.

For example, consider maximum likelihood estimation and the log-likelihood for the spatial lag model (26.61), as the point of departure. Its counterpart in the panel setting requires the generalization of the log-Jacobian term to $\ln |I_T \otimes (I_n - \rho W_N)| = T \ln |I_n - \rho W_n|$, which yields:

$$L = T \ln |I_n - \rho W_n| - \frac{1}{2} \ln |\Sigma_{nT}| - \frac{1}{2} \varepsilon' \Sigma_{nT}^{-1} \varepsilon, \tag{26.142}$$

with $\varepsilon = y - \rho(I_T \otimes W_N)y - X\beta$, and Σ_{nT} as a general $nT \times nT$ error variance–covariance matrix. A special case of particular interest in practice is the groupwise heteroskedasticity considered in section 26.5.2.1. This allows each time period to have a separate error variance. The extension of ML estimation for panel spatial error models follows in the same fashion: for example, using (26.141) as the expression for the error variance–covariance matrix (see Anselin *et al.*, 2006).

The principles of instrumental variables estimation and method of moments outlined in section 26.5.3 can be extended to the pooled case as well, taking advantage of the spatial weights $I_T \otimes W_n$. For example, the instruments in an IV estimation of the spatial lag model would be $(I_T \otimes W_n)X$ (with X as a stacked $nT \times (k-1)$ matrix, excluding the constant term). Similarly, the Kelejian–Prucha GM estimator (Kelejian and Prucha, 1999), considered in section 26.5.3.2, can be generalized by replacing the single equation spatial weights by their pooled counterparts. Specifically, consider a stacked vector of SAR errors:

$$\varepsilon = \lambda(I_T \otimes W_n)\varepsilon + u, \tag{26.143}$$

where both ε and u are $nT \times 1$ vectors, and $u \sim \text{IID}[0, \sigma_u^2 I_{nT}]$.

Extending the moment conditions for the idiosyncratic errors u from (26.90) to this case yields:

$$E\left[\frac{1}{nT}u'u\right] = \sigma_u^2 \tag{26.144}$$

$$E\left[\frac{1}{nT}u'(I_T \otimes W_n')(I_T \otimes Wn)u\right] = \frac{1}{N}\sigma_u^2 tr(W_n'W_n) \tag{26.145}$$

$$E\left[\frac{1}{nT}u'(I_T \otimes W_n)u\right] = 0, \tag{26.146}$$

where use is made of $tr(I_T \otimes W_n'W_n) = TtrW_n'W_n$ and $tr(I_T \otimes W_n) = 0$.

The estimator is made operational by substituting $u = \varepsilon - \lambda(I_t \otimes W_n)\varepsilon$, and replacing ε by the regression residuals. The result is a system of three equations in λ, λ^2 and σ_u^2, which can be solved in the same fashion as for the single cross-section case.

Extension to the estimation of spatial effects in heterogeneous panel models are outlined in Elhorst (2003) and Anselin *et al.* (2006).

26.7.1.3   Specification testing

Specification tests in pooled models also generalize directly from the single cross-section case. For example, the LM statistics against a spatial error and spatial lag alternative are readily obtained as:

$$LM_\lambda = \frac{[e'(I_T \otimes W_n)e/(e'e/nT)]^2}{Ttr(W_nW_n + W_n'W_n)}, \tag{26.147}$$

and

$$LM_\rho = \frac{[e'(I_T \otimes W_N)y/(e'e/nT)]^2}{[(W\hat{y})'M(W\hat{y})/\hat{\sigma}^2] + Ttr(W_nW_n + W_n'W_n)}, \tag{26.148}$$

with e as an $nT \times 1$ vector of OLS residuals, $W\hat{y} = (I_T \otimes W_n)X\hat{\beta}$ is the spatially lagged predicted values from the regression, and $M = I_{nT} - X(X'X)^{-1}X'$. Both statistics are asymptotically distributed as $\chi^2(1)$, since the spatial parameter is constrained to remain constant over time.

Extensions incorporating groupwise heteroskedasticity can be obtained using the principles outlined in section 26.6.3, and robustified versions can be derived using extensions of the results from section 26.6.2.4.

In heterogeneous panels, a test statistic that does not require the specification of a spatial weights matrix was recently suggested by Pesaran (2004). It consists of an average of cross-sectional residual correlations, based on the residuals of individual-specific regressions, $e_{it} = y_{it} - \hat{\alpha}_i - x'_{it}\hat{\beta}_i$. The test statistic is obtained as:

$$CD = \sqrt{\frac{2T}{n(n-1)}} \left(\sum_{i=1}^{n-1} \sum_{j=i+1}^{n} \hat{\gamma}_{ij} \right), \tag{26.149}$$

with the pairwise correlation coefficients defined as:

$$\hat{\gamma}_{ij} = \sum_{t=1}^{T} \frac{e_{it}e_{jt}}{(e'_i e_i)^{1/2} (e'_j e_j)^{1/2}}, \tag{26.150}$$

where e_i and e_j are $T \times 1$ residual vectors for each cross-sectional unit. The statistic is asymptotically distributed as standard normal. Extensions to "local" forms of cross-sectional dependence are given as well (see Pesaran, 2004, for details).

26.7.2 Spatial effects in error component models

In the textbook case of the two-way error component regression model, heterogeneity is introduced to the panel setup through random effects. The error term ε_{it} contains a cross-sectional unobserved random effect (α_i), a random time effect (ϕ_t), as well as an idiosyncratic component u_{it} (for example, Baltagi, 2001, p. 31):

$$\varepsilon_{it} = \alpha_i + \phi_t + u_{it}. \tag{26.151}$$

The cross-sectional component has variance σ_α^2, the time component has variance σ_ϕ^2, and the idiosyncratic error term is assumed to be $i.i.d$ with variance σ_u^2. Furthermore, the three random components are assumed to have zero means and to be uncorrelated with each other. The random components α_i are assumed to be uncorrelated across cross-sectional units, and the components ϕ_t are assumed to be uncorrelated across time periods. This model is standard, except that, in a spatial econometric context, the data are stacked as cross-sections for different time periods. For each time period $t = 1, \ldots, T$, the $n \times 1$ cross-sectional error vector ε_t is:

$$\varepsilon_t = \alpha + \phi_t \iota_n + u_t, \tag{26.152}$$

where α is an $n \times 1$ vector of cross-sectional error components, ϕ_t is the scalar time component for time t, ι_n is an $n \times 1$ vector of ones, and u_t is an $n \times 1$ vector of idiosyncratic errors. The common time component (but not the cross-sectional component) yields a particular type of cross-sectional correlation of the form $\sigma_\phi^2 \iota_n \iota_n'$. This equicorrelation across space is different from the usual spatial auto-correlation, since no distance decay is present. Stacking the error vectors by cross-section for each time period yields the complete $nT \times 1$ error vector as (see also Anselin, 1988b, p. 153):

$$\varepsilon = (\iota_T \otimes I_n)\alpha + (I_T \otimes \iota_n)\phi + u, \tag{26.153}$$

where the subscripts indicate the dimensions, ϕ is a $T \times 1$ vector of time error components, u is an $nT \times 1$ vector of idiosyncratic errors, and the other notation is as before. The overal error variance–covariance matrix then follows as:

$$\Sigma_{nT} = \sigma_\alpha^2(\iota_T \iota_T' \otimes I_n) + \sigma_\phi^2(I_T \otimes \iota_n \iota_n') + \sigma_u^2 I_{nT}. \tag{26.154}$$

This differs slightly from the standard textbook notation, due to the stacking of observations by cross-section.

A spatially lagged dependent variable can be added to the regression part of this model in the usual fashion. However, given possible identification problems between the spatial correlation induced by the lag term and the spatial correlation that results from the time random component, this is typically only considered for the one-way error component model:

$$\varepsilon = (\iota_T \otimes I_n)\alpha + u. \tag{26.155}$$

This model does not contain the time component ϕ_t and its error variance–covariance is a subset of (26.154), without the second term.

A one-way error component spatial lag model is a special case of the spatial lag specification for pooled data considered in section 26.7.1.1. Using the appropriate expression for the error variance–covariance matrix (and exploiting some standard results on matrix Kronecker products), the log likelihood for this model follows as (omitting constants):

$$L = T \ln |I_n - \rho W_n| - \tfrac{1}{2}\ln |\sigma_\alpha^2(\iota_T \iota_T' \otimes I_n) + \sigma_u^2 I_{nT}|$$
$$- \tfrac{1}{2}\varepsilon'[\sigma_\alpha^2(\iota_T \iota_T' \otimes I_n) + \sigma_u^2 I_{nT}]^{-1}\varepsilon. \tag{26.156}$$

Inference can be based on the maximum likelihood estimates.

Another way to introduce spatial dependence into the one-way error component specification is through the error term. Two different approaches have been suggested in the literature, each leading to a particular estimation strategy.

The first approach consists of the specification of a SAR process for the error component u_t in each cross-section, for $t = 1, \dots, T$ (Anselin, 1988b, p. 153):

$$u_t = \lambda W_n u_t + \xi_t, \tag{26.157}$$

with λ as the spatial autoregressive parameter (constant over time), W_n as the spatial weights matrix, and ξ_t as an *i.i.d.* idiosyncratic error term with variance σ_ξ^2.

Using the notation $B_n = I_n - \lambda W_n$ and $u_t = B_n^{-1}\xi_t$, the complete $nT \times 1$ error vector ε for the stacked observations is:

$$\varepsilon = (\iota_T \otimes I_n)\alpha + (I_T \otimes B_n^{-1})\xi. \tag{26.158}$$

The matching variance–covariance matrix for ε is then:

$$\Sigma_{nT} = \mathrm{E}[\varepsilon\varepsilon'] = \sigma_\alpha^2(\iota_T\iota_T' \otimes I_n) + \sigma_\xi^2[I_T \otimes (B_n'B_n)^{-1}]. \tag{26.159}$$

Note that the first component induces correlation in the time dimension, but not in the cross-sectional dimension, whereas the opposite holds for the second component (correlation only in the cross-sectional dimension).

Maximum likelihood estimation is again a special case of the linear model with a nonspherical variance–covariance matrix, which was treated in section 26.5.2.2. To operationalize this method, use is made of some matrix Kronecker product properties to simplify the complex structure of (26.159). Specifically, with $\eta = \sigma_\alpha^2/\sigma_\xi^2$, the error variance–covariance matrix can be rewritten as $\Sigma_{nT} = \sigma_\xi^2\Psi_{nT}$, where:

$$\Psi_{nT} = \iota_T\iota_T' \otimes \eta I_n + [I_T \otimes (B_n'B_n)^{-1}]. \tag{26.160}$$

This allows the determinant and inverse to be obtained as (see Anselin, 1988b, p. 154, for details):

$$|\Psi_{nT}| = |(B_n'B_n)^{-1} + (T\eta)I_n||B_n|^{-2(T-1)} \tag{26.161}$$

and

$$\Psi_{nT}^{-1} = \frac{\iota_T\iota_T'}{T} \otimes [(B_n'B_n)^{-1} + (T\eta)I_n]^{-1} + \left(I_T - \frac{\iota_T\iota_T'}{T}\right) \otimes (B_n'B_n). \tag{26.162}$$

The log-likelihood thus becomes:

$$\begin{aligned}
L = &-\frac{nT}{2}\ln\sigma_\xi^2 + (T-1)\ln|B_n| \\
&-\frac{1}{2}\ln|(B_n'B_n)^{-1} + (T\eta)I_n| \\
&-\frac{1}{2\sigma_\xi^2}\varepsilon'\left[\frac{\iota_T\iota_T'}{T} \otimes [(B_n'B_n)^{-1} + (T\eta)I_n]^{-1}\right]\varepsilon \\
&-\frac{1}{2\sigma_\xi^2}\varepsilon'\left[\left(I_T - \frac{\iota_T\iota_T'}{T}\right) \otimes (B_n'B_n)\right]\varepsilon,
\end{aligned} \tag{26.163}$$

with $\varepsilon = y - X\beta$. Note how, in contrast to the standard SAR error model, the log-likelihood involves the inverse $(B_n'B_n)^{-1}$, which constitutes a serious computational challenge.

The likelihood framework for the one-way error component model with spatial error autocorrelation can be exploited to derive LM tests for a range of mis-specifications (Anselin, 1988b; Baltagi *et al.*, 2003a, b). Taking, as a point of departure, the standard pooled specification (26.137), both the error component and the spatial parameter can be considered as part of the null hypothesis, thus allowing a number of interesting combinations to result. The corresponding tests can be classified as marginal, joint or conditional, depending on which combinations of parameters restrictions are considered (Baltagi *et al.*, 2003b).

Specifically, marginal tests would be on either $H_0 : \lambda = 0$ (the spatial parameter) or on $H_0 : \sigma_\alpha^2 = 0$ (the error component), in both based on the residuals of the pooled model. A joint test is on $H_0 : \lambda = \sigma_\alpha^2 = 0$ and conditional tests are for $H_0 : \lambda = 0$ (assuming $\sigma_\alpha^2 \geq 0$) or $H_0 : \sigma_\alpha^2 = 0$ (assuming λ may or may not be zero). Each case yields a LM statistic using the standard principles applied to the proper likelihood function (for details, see Baltagi *et al.*, 2003b). This rationale can be further extended to include a time-dependent process, as in Baltagi *et al.* (2003a). LM test statistics robust to local misspecification of one of the other forms can also be developed along these lines. The derivation and evaluation of effective diagnostics for spatial effects in error component models is still an area of active research.

A second approach to introducing spatial error autocorrelation into an error components model was recently suggested by Kapoor *et al.* (2003). Instead of specifying a spatial process for the idiosyncratic error u in (26.155), the error vector (in the pooled model) is first subject to a SAR process:

$$\varepsilon = \lambda(I_T \otimes W_n)\varepsilon + u, \tag{26.164}$$

or

$$\varepsilon = (I_T \otimes B_n^{-1})u, \tag{26.165}$$

where, as before, $B_n = I - \lambda W_n$. The error components are introduced into the error u as:

$$u = (\iota_T \otimes I_n)\alpha + v. \tag{26.166}$$

This results in an overall error variance–covariance matrix:

$$\Sigma_{nT} = \mathrm{E}[\varepsilon\varepsilon'] = (I_T \otimes B_n^{-1})[\sigma_\alpha^2(\iota_T\iota_T' \otimes I_n) + \sigma_v^2 I_{nT}](I_T \otimes B_n^{-1'}). \tag{26.167}$$

Again, this model combines both time, as well as cross-sectional, correlation. The middle term in (26.167) is the standard expression from the error components literature, which enables a simple solution to be employed to obtain the inverse of the matrix. This leads to a system of six moment conditions in three unknowns (the spatial parameter λ and the variance components) that can be solved to obtain consistent estimators for the parameters. This readily yields FGLS estimates for the model coefficients β (for technical details, see Kapoor *et al.*, 2003).

Further work is needed to compare the relative merits of the two spatial error component formulations in empirical practice.

26.7.3 Spatial seemingly unrelated regression models (SUR)

A special case of temporal heterogeneity (different parameter values over time, but constant values across space) that has received considerable attention in empirical work (for example, in regional economics, Rey and Montouri, 1999) consists of a system of cross-sectional equations connected through cross-equation error correlation. This is a special case of fixed effects, in that the number of cross-sections T is typically fixed. In the mainstream literature, such seemingly unrelated regressions are considered primarily for the case where $T \gg n$. In the spatial context, however, the more interesting design is where $n \gg T$ and the equations are stacked one cross-section at a time:

$$y_t = X_t \beta_t + \varepsilon_t, \quad \text{for } t = 1, \ldots, T, \quad (26.168)$$

where β_t is a time-specific $k \times 1$ vector of regression coefficients. In practice, interest centers on the null hypothesis of homogeneity, $H_0 : \beta_t = \beta$ for $t = 1, \ldots, T$. In each cross-section, the variance–covariance matrix is $\mathrm{E}[\varepsilon_t \varepsilon_t'] = \sigma_t^2 I_n$ for $t = 1, \ldots, T$. The temporal covariance matrix between the cross-section at t and the cross-section at s takes the general form:

$$\mathrm{E}[\varepsilon_t \varepsilon_s'] = \sigma_{ts} I_n, \quad \text{for } s \neq t, \quad (26.169)$$

where σ_{ts} is the temporal covariance between s and t (by convention, the variance terms are expressed as σ_t^2). In stacked form (T cross-sections), the model becomes:

$$y = X\beta + \varepsilon, \quad (26.170)$$

with

$$\mathrm{E}[\varepsilon \varepsilon'] = \Sigma_T \otimes I_n \quad (26.171)$$

and Σ_T is the $T \times T$ temporal covariance matrix with elements σ_{ts}.

A spatial lag SUR model is obtained by introducing a spatially lagged dependent variable with a time-specific autoregressive coefficient ρ_t for each period, with the cross-equation error covariance as in (26.171). Each individual cross-section for time period t follows the model:

$$y_t = \rho_t W_n y_t + X_t \beta_t + \varepsilon_t, \quad \text{for } t = 1, \ldots, T. \quad (26.172)$$

The full system can be expressed concisely in stacked form as:

$$y = (R_T \otimes W_n)y + X\beta + \varepsilon, \quad (26.173)$$

where R_T is a $T \times T$ diagonal matrix containing the time-specific autoregressive coefficients ρ_t on the diagonal, and β is a $kT \times 1$ vector of stacked time-specific coefficient vectors. The matrix X is an $nT \times kT$ block-diagonal matrix:

$$X = \begin{pmatrix} X_1 & 0 & \cdots & 0 \\ 0 & X_2 & \cdots & 0 \\ \cdots & \cdots & \cdots & \cdots \\ 0 & 0 & \cdots & X_T \end{pmatrix}. \tag{26.174}$$

In a spatial lag SUR model, there special interest in testing the null hypothesis $H_0 : \rho_t = \rho, \ \forall \ t = 1, \ldots, T$, i.e., whether the spatial process governing the cross-sectional dependence in each time period is stable over time.

Maximum likelihood estimation of the spatial lag SUR model can be considered to be special case of the general log-likelihood (26.61), but with a log-Jacobian of $\ln |I_{nT} - (R_T \otimes W_n)|$ and an error variance–covariance matrix of $\Sigma_T \otimes I_n$. The block diagonal structure of the Jacobian can be exploited to simplify this expression to $\Sigma_t \ln |I_n - \rho_t W_n|$ (with the sum over $t = 1, \ldots, T$). The log-likelihood then follows as (omitting the constant):

$$L = \sum_t \ln |I_n - \rho_t W_n| - \frac{n}{2} \ln |\Sigma_T| - \frac{1}{2} \varepsilon'(\Sigma_T^{-1} \otimes I_n)\varepsilon, \tag{26.175}$$

with $\varepsilon = [I_{nT} - (R_T \otimes W_n)]y - X\beta$ (for further details, see Anselin, 1988b, pp. 145–6). Instrumental variables estimation of this model is a special case of three-stage least squares (see Anselin *et al.*, 2005).

Spatial error autocorrelation is introduced into the SUR specification in each time period, with the $n \times 1$ error vector ε_t

$$\varepsilon_t = \lambda_t W_n \varepsilon_t + u_t, \quad \text{for } t = 1, \ldots, T, \tag{26.176}$$

or

$$\varepsilon_t = (I_n - \theta_t W_n)^{-1} u_t. \tag{26.177}$$

The cross-equation covariance is specified through the remainder error term u_t, with $E[uu'] = \Sigma_T \otimes I_N$, where Σ_T contains the elements σ_t^2 on the diagonal, and has σ_{ts} as off-diagonal entries. As a result, the overall error covariance becomes:

$$E[\varepsilon\varepsilon'] = B_{nT}^{-1}(\Sigma_T \otimes I_n)B_{nT}^{-1'} \tag{26.178}$$

with $B_{nT} = [I_{nT} - (\lambda_T \otimes W_N)]$ and λ_T a $T \times 1$ vector of time-specific spatial autoregressive coefficients λ_t.

Maximum likelihood estimation follows as a special case of a linear model with non-spherical error variance–covariance matrix, along the lines presented in section 26.5.2.2. Similarly, specification tests for the presence of spatial error autocorrelation in the SUR model can be based on the LM principle (Anselin, 1988c).

26.8 Spatial effects in models with limited dependent variables

In applied econometrics, interest often focuses on models where the dependent variable is not continuous, as considered so far in this chapter, but instead takes on a limited number of values, or is truncated or censored in some fashion. The extension of spatial effects to such models is not straightforward and is a very active area of research. In spatial econometrics, the main interest in this context has been in the *spatial probit* model, where the multivariate normal distribution provides a flexible framework in which to incorporate spatial correlation. This will be the focus of the current section, where specification, estimation and diagnostic testing in this model will be briefly reviewed in turn. Recent, more in-depth, treatment of spatial probit models can be found in Pinkse and Slade (1998), Novo (2001), Fleming (2004) and Beron and Vijverberg (2004). Illustrative applications are Holloway *et al.* (2002), Beron *et al.* (2003) and Murdoch *et al.* (2003).

Before proceeding with the spatial probit, it is worthwhile briefly pointing out some alternative approaches, mostly formulated in the statistical literature. The almost exclusive emphasis on the normal distribution as the stochastic framework within which to handle spatial correlation for discrete dependent variables is because most other distributions do not provide an analytical link between the marginal distribution (at each location) and the joint distribution, at least without impractical constraints on the correlation structure (Johnson and Kotz, 1969, chapter 11). Initially, some conditional models were suggested by Besag (1974), such as the auto-logistic and auto-Poisson, but these constrain the spatial range of the dependence as well as the parameter space. For example, the auto-Poisson model only allows negative spatial autocorrelation, thus precluding its use for modeling diffusion or contagion processes. Approaches that allow a relaxation of this requirement have only recently been developed (for a technical discussion and extensions, see Kaiser and Cressie, 1997, 2000).

Alternatives to the auto models that incorporate spatial correlation in specifications for limited dependent variables are based on generalized linear models (GLM) and generalized linear mixed models (GLMM). These utilize specialized estimators, such as quasi-likelihood and estimating equations (see, for example, Gotway and Stroup, 1997; Gotway and Wolfinger, 2003; Zhang, 2002). In addition, there is a growing literature on hierarchical random coefficient models from a Bayesian perspective, where spatial correlation is often introduced through a conditional autoregressive (CAR) prior on one of the model parameters (such as the mean in a Poisson count model). A detailed discussion of these methods is beyond the scope of the current chapter. Recent reviews can be found in Lawson (2001), Banerjee *et al.* (2004) and Waller and Gotway (2004), among others.

26.8.1 Spatial probit

The textbook model for a linear latent variable regression specifies an unobserved (latent) dependent variable y_i^* as a linear function of an "index function" and a random error term:

$$y_i^* = x_i'\beta + \varepsilon_i, \tag{26.179}$$

with $x_i\beta$ as the index function, and where x_i is a $k \times 1$ vector of observations on the explanatory variables and β is a matching vector of coefficients. The observed counterpart of y_i^*, the discrete dependent variable y_i, equals 1 for $y_i^* > 0$ and zero otherwise. Interest therefore centers on $P[y_i^* > 0] = P[x_i'\beta + \varepsilon_i > 0]$. By specifying a distribution for the random error term, estimates for β can be obtained. In the probit model, the standard normal distribution is used, which, due to its symmetry, yields the familiar result:

$$P[y_i = 1] = P[y_i^* > 0] = P[\varepsilon_i < x_i'\beta] = \Phi[x_i'\beta], \tag{26.180}$$

where Φ is the cumulative density function for a standard normal random variate.

Spatial dependence is introduced into this model either through the latent variable itself, with $\text{Cov}[y_i^* y_j^*] \neq 0$ for "neighboring" i, j, or through the error term, with $\text{Cov}[\varepsilon_i \varepsilon_j] \neq 0$ for "neighboring" i,j. Following standard practice, the neighbors are defined by means of a spatial weights matrix.

A spatial lag model in the latent variable becomes:

$$y_i^* = \rho \sum_j w_{ij} y_j^* + x_i'\beta + \varepsilon_i, \tag{26.181}$$

or, in matrix notation, and using the counterpart of the reduced form (26.40):

$$y^* = (I - \rho W)^{-1} X\beta + (I - \rho W)^{-1}\varepsilon. \tag{26.182}$$

In this *simultaneous* model, the latent variables are jointly determined, both by the values for x at their own location and by the values for x at all other locations, subject to a distance decay effect. This is quite distinct from a *conditional* specification, where the observed actions of the neighbors enter on the right-hand side, not the unobserved (and unobservable) latent values.

The conditional counterpart of (26.181) is:

$$y_i^* = \rho \sum_j w_{ij} E[y_j^* | X] + x_i'\beta + \varepsilon_i, \tag{26.183}$$

where $E[y_j^* | X]$ can be estimated by $y_i^L = \Sigma_j w_{ij} y_j$, the average of the observed decisions y_j at the neighboring locations. The new variable y_i^L can be included on the right-hand side of the model as an exogenous variable. Consequently, the neighboring observations cannot be jointly determined with the observations at i. While the standard probit model remains valid, coding methods must be employed to ensure that the sample does not contain these neighbors.

In contrast, the simultaneous model (26.182) causes two major complications. First, the error term is no longer independent and homoskedastic, since $u = (I - \rho W)^{-1}\varepsilon$ has variance–covariance matrix $[(I - \rho W)'(I - \rho W)]^{-1}$. The induced heteroskedasticity (when the number of neighbors is not constant across observations) will cause standard probit estimators to be inconsistent. A standardization must be carried out that takes into account the location-specific variance. The correlation structure means that to obtain the marginal cumulative density for each individual error term u_i, the remaining $n - 1$ dimensions need to be integrated out. Second, the inequality constraint on the random error does not pertain to $x_i\beta$, but to a series expansion, containing both ρ and β, as well as the spatially lagged x. With

$$G(X, W, \beta, \rho) = x_i'\beta + \rho[WX\beta]_i + \rho^2[W^2X\beta]_i + \cdots \qquad (26.184)$$

as the familiar series expansion, the censoring condition becomes:

$$P[y_i = 1] = P\left[u_i < \frac{G_i(X, W, \beta, \rho)}{\sigma_i}\right], \qquad (26.185)$$

where the cumulative density is for the marginal distribution of u_i, obtained by integrating out the $n - 1$ other dimensions in a multivariate normal density, and σ_i is the square root of the heteroskedastic variance at i.

The probit model with error terms that follow a SAR process is represented by the latent variable specification (26.179) with the error term as:

$$\varepsilon = \lambda W\varepsilon + u \qquad (26.186)$$

This also requires the marginal density for a multivariate error term in the censoring condition. However, unlike (185), this does not involve a function G, but instead:

$$P[y_i = 1] = P\left[u_i < \frac{x_i'\beta}{\sigma_i}\right], \qquad (26.187)$$

where the probability for u_i is for the marginal density from a multivariate normal distribution with variance–covariance matrix $[(I - \lambda W)'(I - \lambda W)]^{-1}$.

26.8.2 Estimation of the spatial probit

The textbook solution to estimation in the probit model consists of a straightforward application of the maximum likelihood principle. Each observation on the discrete dependent variable y_i can be considered to be an independent draw from a binomial random variable with probability $\Phi(x_i'\beta)$. The log-likelihood readily follows as:

$$\ln L = \sum_i [y_i \ln \Phi(x_i'\beta) + (1 - y_i) \ln(1 - \Phi(x_i'\beta))], \qquad (26.188)$$

with $y_i = 0$, 1. Since $1 - \Phi(x'_i\beta) = \Phi(-x'_i\beta)$, and using $q_i = 2y_i - 1$, this can be expressed succinctly as:

$$\ln L = \sum_i \ln \Phi(q_i x'_i \beta). \tag{26.189}$$

In the spatial case, the simple summation as in (26.189) is no longer appropriate and the full multivariate density must be evaluated to obtain the log-likelihood. Consider u as the $n \times 1$ vector of multivariate normal random variables with variance–covariance matrix Σ. In order to generalize the censoring conditions for both values of y_i, set Q as a diagonal matrix with diagonal elements q_i defined above. The multivariate censoring conditions (or the upper bounds on the integrals in the evaluation of the multivariate cumulative density) are:[30]

$$u < QX\beta \tag{26.190}$$

for the spatial error probit model, and:

$$u < Q(I - \rho W)^{-1} X\beta \tag{26.191}$$

for the spatial lag probit model. These must be evaluated in a multivariate normal distribution with Σ respectively as $[(I - \lambda W)'(I - \lambda W)]^{-1}$ or $[(I - \rho W)'(I - \rho W)]^{-1}$. The corresponding log-likelihood can be expressed as:

$$\ln L = \ln \Phi_n[QX\beta; 0, \Sigma_\lambda] \tag{26.192}$$

for the spatial error probit model, and:

$$\ln L = \ln \Phi_n[Q(I - \rho W)^{-1} X\beta; 0, \Sigma_\rho], \tag{26.193}$$

for the spatial lag probit model, where Φ_n stands for an n-dimensional multivariate normal cumulative distribution function with the upper bounds as the first term, mean 0, and variance–covariance matrix Σ. The evaluation of this log-likelihood involves the computation of n-dimensional integrals, which is infeasible in practice.

A crucial step in any numerical optimization of the log-likelihood is the evaluation of the probabilities involved. Beron and Vijverberg (2004) outline a simulation estimator for the spatial probit model based on the relative importance sampler (RIS) for an n-dimensional multivariate normal density (see also Vijverberg, 1997; Beron et al., 2003).[31]

The problem consists of evaluating the multivariate normal probability $P[u < V]$, with V as either $QX\beta$ or $Q(I - \rho W)^{-1} X\beta$, and $u \sim \text{MVN}(0, \Sigma)$. Since Σ is positive definite, there exists a Choleski decomposition $A'A = \Sigma^{-1}$, where A is an upper triangular matrix. This is particularly useful for SAR models, since Σ^{-1} does not involve an inverse operation. For example, in the spatial error probit, this requires a Choleski decomposition of $(I - \lambda W)'(I - \lambda W) = I + \lambda(W + W') + \lambda^2 WW'$.

The transformation $\eta = Au$ yields a vector of independent standard normal random variables, whose joint density can be computed as a simple product of the marginal densities. With $B = A^{-1}$ (an upper triangular matrix with positive diagonal elements), the random vector u can be replaced by $u = A^{-1}\eta = B\eta$. Since the matrix B is upper triangular and its diagonal elements are positive, the bounds on the random vector η can be written, starting from the bottom (i.e., for $i = n$), as:

$$\eta_n < b_{nn}^{-1} V_n \equiv v_n \tag{26.194}$$

$$\eta_{n-1} < b_{n-1\,n-1}^{-1}[V_{n-1} - b_{n-1\,n}\eta_n] \equiv v_{n-1}, \tag{26.195}$$

and, in general,

$$\eta_j < b_{jj}^{-1}\left[V_j - \sum_{i=j+1}^{n} b_{ji}\eta_i\right] \equiv v_j. \tag{26.196}$$

The values for V_j are based on the current value of the model parameters, including the spatial autoregressive parameter. For a given choice of a proper density function for the importance sampler, the simulator operates in a recursive fashion, by first drawing a random variable $\bar{\eta}_n$ that satisfies the condition $\bar{\eta}_n < v_n$. The value $\bar{\eta}_n$ is substituted in the expression for the bound v_{n-1} to obtain $\bar{v}_{n-1}$. A second random variable, $\bar{\eta}_{n-1}$, is then drawn satisfying this new bound. This is continued until an $n \times 1$ vector of bounds $\bar{v}$ is obtained. This vector is then used to evaluate the joint density as a product of the individual cumulative densities (technically, these are ratios of densities in the importance sampler). In the case of a normal sampler, this simplifies to $\Pi_{j=1}^{n}\Phi(\bar{v}_j)$. This process is repeated R times to obtain an estimate for the log-likelihood as the average of the sampled joint probabilities (for technical details, see Beron and Vijverberg, 2004, pp. 176–7):

$$\hat{p} = (1/R)\sum_{r=1}^{R}\left[\prod_{j=1}^{n}\Phi(\bar{v}_{j,r})\right]. \tag{26.197}$$

This is then used in a nonlinear optimization algorithm to obtain a new set of parameter values, and the process is repeated until convergence. Two important computational challenges in this procedure are the Choleski decomposition of the inverse variance matrix, and the need for the inverse $(I - \rho W)^{-1}$, which is required for the bounds in the spatial lag model. The RIS estimator for the spatial probit model was applied in empirical work by Beron et al. (2003) and Murdoch et al. (2003).

An alternative simulation estimator for the spatial probit model was formulated by LeSage (1999, 2000). This uses Markov Chain Monte Carlo (MCMC) simulation methods, such as the Gibbs sampler and the Metropolis–Hastings sampler, and is couched in a Bayesian context (see also Holloway et al., 2002). The basic principle of a Gibbs sampler is to generate draws for the joint posterior distribution of the parameters by sampling from the full conditional distributions. For example, in a model with two parameters, $[\theta_1, \theta_2]$, a sample from the joint density can be obtained by alternating repeated draws from $f(\theta_1|\theta_2)$ and $f(\theta_2|\theta_1)$, using the sampled variate at each iteration to condition.[32] In this process it is important to establish a proper posterior conditional density from which it easy to sample.

In the spatial probit model, two key aspects need to be considered. First, the analysis proceeds similar to the Bayesian framework for the standard spatial regression model, conditional upon the latent dependent variable y^*. The latter is obtained from its posterior conditional density, which can be shown to be a truncated normal distribution (given values for the other parameters in the model). Sampling from this distribution generates "observations" on the latent variable, which can then be conditioned on the remainder of the analysis.[33] A second aspect pertains to the conditional density for the spatial parameters. While the conditional densities for the β parameters (in a homoskedastic probit model, $\sigma^2 = 1$ to avoid identification problems) are the usual multivariate normal, the conditional density for the spatial parameters is of unknown form (see also LeSage, 1997). For example, in the spatial lag model (ignoring σ^2), this is:

$$f(\rho|\beta, y^*) \propto |I - \rho W| \exp[(y^* - \rho W y^* - X\beta)'(y^* - \rho W y^* - X\beta)]. \qquad (26.198)$$

Sampling from this conditional density requires a specialized approach, such as a Metropolitan–Hastings algorithm. This also involves the evaluation of the Jacobian term (for technical details, see LeSage, 1997, 1999, 2000).

Alternatives to these simulation estimators can be based on GMM, as in Pinkse and Slade (1998). However, these approaches only tackle the additional heteroskedasticity in the spatial models, but ignore the off-diagonal elements in the variance–covariance matrix. Specifically, the heteroskedasticity is a function of the spatial autoregressive parameters, which can be exploited to adjust the correction by σ_i in (26.185) and (26.187).[34]

To date, relatively little is known about the relative performance of these estimators in finite samples (some preliminary findings are given in Novo, 2001).

26.8.3   Specification tests in spatial probit

Testing for the presence of spatial effects in the probit model is hampered by the fact that neither the true residual, nor the dependent variable, in the latent variable model are observed. Instead of $e_i^* = y_i^* - x_i'\beta$, either a naive residual, $e_i = y_i - \Phi(x_i'\hat{\beta})$, or the notion of a generalized residual (Cox and Snell, 1968) must be used. The latter follows from the first-order conditions in the probit log-likelihood (26.188):

$$\partial L/\partial \beta = \sum_i \phi_i \left[\frac{y_i}{\Phi_i} - \frac{1 - y_i}{1 - \Phi_i} \right] x_i = 0, \qquad (26.199)$$

where Φ_i and ϕ_i are, respectively, the cumulative standard normal distribution and the standard normal density, evaluated at $x_i'\beta$. This takes on the general form of the familiar orthogonality condition $\Sigma_i \hat{\varepsilon}_i x_i = 0$, used as the basis for GMM estimation. After some algebra, the *generalized residual* can be expressed as:

$$\hat{\varepsilon}_i = \hat{\phi}_i \left[\frac{y_i - \hat{\Phi}_i}{\hat{\Phi}_i (1 - \hat{\Phi}_i)} \right], \tag{26.200}$$

with a consistent estimate $\hat{\beta}$ used to evaluate $\hat{\Phi}_i$ and $\hat{\phi}_i$.

The main results obtained so far are developed in papers by Pinkse and Slade (1998), Pinkse (1999, 2004), and Kelejian and Prucha (2001). A test statistic against spatial error correlation in the probit model takes the form of a generalized Moran's I statistic or a LM statistic, asymptotically distributed as, respectively, standard normal or $\chi^2(1)$:

$$I^* = e'We/\Gamma \xrightarrow{d} N(0,1), \tag{26.201}$$

or

$$LM_\lambda = [e'We]^2/\Gamma \xrightarrow{d} \chi^2(1), \tag{26.202}$$

where e is a vector of "residuals" and Γ is a standardization factor, containing weights matrix traces and variance terms.[35]

In Pinkse and Slade (1998), the residuals are standardized generalized residuals, so as to correct for the inherent heteroskedasticity in the model. Since the variance of the generalized residual $\hat{\varepsilon}_i$ is $\phi_i^2/[\Phi_i(1 - \Phi_i)]$, dividing (26.200) by the square root of this variance yields the standardized residual as:

$$\varepsilon_i^s = \frac{y_i - \hat{\Phi}_i}{\sqrt{\hat{\Phi}_i(1 - \hat{\Phi}_i)}}. \tag{26.203}$$

The Pinkse–Slade LM test statistic is then:

$$LM_{PS} = \frac{(\hat{\varepsilon}_i^{s'} W \hat{\varepsilon}_i^s)^2}{tr(WW + W'W)}. \tag{26.204}$$

The asymptotic distribution is not formally derived but, instead, a bootstrap procedure is suggested for carrying out inference (see Pinkse and Slade, 1998, p. 131). In contrast, both Pinkse (1999) and Kelejian and Prucha (2001) obtain formal asymptotic results, albeit under slightly different sets of assumptions.[36] Pinkse (1999) takes a LM perspective and demonstrates that:

$$LM_\lambda = \frac{(\hat{\varepsilon}_i' W \hat{\varepsilon}_i)^2}{\hat{\sigma}^4 tr(WW + W'W)} \xrightarrow{d} \chi^2(1), \tag{26.205}$$

where $\hat{\varepsilon}_i$ are the generalized residuals from (26.200), and

$$\hat{\sigma}^2 = \frac{1}{n} \sum_i \frac{\hat{\phi}_i^2}{\hat{\Phi}_i(1 - \hat{\Phi}_i)}. \tag{26.206}$$

Kelejian and Prucha (2001) derive the asymptotic properties of the generalized Moran's I statistic in a wide range of specifications. For the probit model, the corresponding test statistic is (Kelejian and Prucha, 2001, pp. 234–6):

$$I^* = \frac{e_i'We_i}{\sqrt{tr(W\Sigma W\Sigma + W'\Sigma W\Sigma)}} \xrightarrow{d} N(0,1), \qquad (26.207)$$

with $e_i = y_i - \hat{\Phi}_i$, and Σ being a diagonal matrix containing $\hat{\sigma}_i^2 = \hat{\Phi}_i(1 - \hat{\Phi}_i)$.

The I^* and LM_λ test statistics differ in the regularity conditions under which they are developed. There are operational distinctions as well, these being in the way in which the residuals are estimated (generalized vs naïve) and in the expression for the variance used in the standardization factor. Little is known about the relative performance of these test statistics in finite samples (for limited evidence, see Novo, 2001).

26.9   Future directions

The objective of this chapter was to review the current state of the art in spatial econometrics, while emphasizing recent results. There is now a solid body of results in the literature to deal with spatial effects in the linear regression model. However, considerable work remains to be done in the context of panel data and limited dependent variable models. To close the chapter, it may be useful to outline a number of directions where progress is most desired.

There is still no encompassing theoretical framework to handle asymptotics in the spatial domain that translates into readily verifiable conditions. Whereas several useful results have been obtained to date, they tend to be case-specific and to depend on particular views of the spatial sampling process. As a result, properties that hold for one conceptual framework do not readily translate into another.

There also seems to be considerable room for further integration of the insights obtained in the statistical literature on hierarchical Bayesian spatial models into spatial econometric formulations with random coefficients. Along the same lines, the simulation estimators that are crucial for obtaining results in these models require efficient computational algorithms. In order to become useful in the empirical (large data) context that is commonly encountered in applied economics, important computational issues remain to be tackled, especially in handling space-time dynamics.

Finally, the dissemination of theoretical results down to the empirical practice of econometricians crucially depends on the availability of software. While considerable progress has been made (see the review in Anselin *et al.*, 2004b, pp. 10–11), this has been primarily concerned with the linear regression setup, and much remains to be done to develop useful software tools to tackle panel data and limited dependent variable settings.

It is hoped that the current chapter will stimulate further work in both the theory and practice of spatial econometrics.

Acknowledgments

The research on which this chapter is based was supported in part by U.S. National Science Foundation grant BCS-9978058 to the Center for Spatially Integrated Social Science (CSISS) and through a Cooperative Agreement between the Center for Disease Control and Prevention (CDC) and the Association of Teachers of Preventive Medicine (ATPM), award number TS-1125. The contents of the chapter are the responsibility of the author and do not necessarily reflect the official views of NSF, CDC or ATPM.

Notes

1. For overviews of the salient issues, see, for example, Anselin (1988b, 1990), Jones and Casetti (1992), Casetti (1997), Fotheringham *et al.* (2002), as well as in the statistical literature, Gelfand *et al.* (2003) and Gamerman *et al.* (2003).
2. See also Hordijk and Paelinck (1976), Hordijk (1979).
3. A more extensive treatment of spatial weights is postponed until section 26.3.1.1.
4. Note that both global or local interaction can be implemented in this framework, by specifying y_{-i} either as a population mean or as the mean in a subset of the population.
5. See, for example, Johnson and Kotz (1969, chapter 9) for a formal discussion of contagious distributions.
6. For technical details, see Andrews (2005).
7. See also Manski (1995, 2000) and Brock and Durlauf (2001a,b) for technical details.
8. In what follows, the notation w_{ij} will be used to denote row-standardized weights.
9. See also Cressie (1993, pp. 405–7, 456–7) for further details.
10. For further technical details, see Haining (1990, pp. 81–3), Cressie (1993, pp. 405–7), Anselin and Bera (1998, pp. 248–9), and Anselin (2003a, pp. 155–6), among others.
11. For further details, see Mardia and Marshall (1984, p. 141) and Anselin (2001a, pp. 128–30).
12. Since $E[\varepsilon] = 0$, the usual deviations from the mean can be ignored in this example.
13. The estimator presented in Kelejian and Prucha (2003) is slightly more general than the illustration given here in that it pertains to instrumental variable estimation.
14. In Conley (1999), where the setting is a rectangular grid, the critical distance in each direction is $o(n^{1/3})$ in the dimension of that direction (see Assumption C1 in Conley, 1999, p. 12). In Kelejian and Prucha (2003, Assumption 4a), the constraint is through the maximum number of neighbors within the critical distance, $l_n = o(n^{1/3})$. This implies that, for a data set with $n = 100$, the distance criterion would result in no more than four spatially covarying neighbors allowed per observation, whereas with $n = 1,000$, the number of spatially correlated neighbors increases to 10.
15. An exception is the case where all observations in a "region" are considered to be neighbors, yielding weights of $1/(n_g - 1)$ for each (with n_g as the number of members in the group). In this case, OLS can be shown to yield consistent estimates (Lee, 2002; Kelejian and Prucha, 2002).
16. For example, this model is relevant when different subregions in the data are allowed to have a different error variance, or when pooling observations in space-time, see section 26.7.1.2.
17. In contrast to the time series literature, there is relatively little attention to unit root and cointegration issues in the spatial domain. An exception is the work of Fingleton (1999).
18. For example, a first order contiguity weights matrix for the 3,140 US counties contains only 0.19 per cent non-zero elements.
19. Since this optimal instrument involves the inverse of an $n \times n$ matrix, it will be computationally prohibitive in large samples. Lee (2003) suggests a workaround based on Cholesky decomposition.

20. In their simulation experiments, Kelejian *et al.* (2004) set $r = n^{\alpha}$, with $\alpha = .25$, $.35$ and $.45$.
21. A slightly different approach towards estimating the error covariance matrix non-parametrically is offered in Pinkse *et al.* (2002, pp. 1126–1128).
22. The focus is on parametric tests. For a general nonparametric approach to testing spatial error dependence, see Brett and Pinkse (1997).
23. Note that for row-standardized weights, $S_0 = \Sigma_i 1 = n$, such that the normalizing factors cancel out and $I = e'We/e'e$.
24. In the remainder, the LM/RS test statistics will be referred to as *LM* for notational simplicity, although they can equally be considered *RS* statistics.
25. An alternative test statistic against the SEC model can be based on an auxiliary regression and a significance test on the estimated variance component (see Kelejian and Robinson, 1993, p. 304).
26. Note that since the SAR error and SMA error are LEA, either alternative may be considered.
27. In Kelejian and Robinson (1998, p. 395) the estimated spatial autoregressive coefficient is included in a test statistic along the lines of the expression (26.114) in section 26.6.1.2 (see also Kelejian and Robinson, 2004).
28. A similar, heteroskedasticity robust version of Moran's I is derived in Kelejian and Robinson (2004, pp. 89–90).
29. More extensive reviews of the recent literature can also be found in Elhorst (2001, 2003).
30. The notation used is similar to the suggestion made in Beron and Vijverberg (2004).
31. The RIS estimator is a generalized version of the well-known GHK simulation estimator. For a review, see Stern (1997).
32. A technical discussion of the Gibbs sampler and other MCMC techniques is beyond the current scope. A classic reference is Geman and Geman (1984). For introductory overviews, see, for example, Casella and George (1992), Gilks *et al.* (1996) and Gelman *et al.* (2004, chapter 11). A basic reference for application to the probit model is Albert and Chib (1993).
33. This is similar in spirit to the EM algorithm (expectation-maximization), which was applied in the spatial probit context by McMillen (1992). See LeSage (2000) and Fleming (2004) for a critical assessment.
34. A GMM approach as a weighted nonlinear estimator of the linear probability model is outlined in Fleming (2004).
35. Tests against a spatial lag alternative have received much less attention. In Pinkse (1999), a statistic of the form $y^{*\prime}We/\Gamma$ is suggested, along the lines of the LM_ρ statistic in the linear regression. The latent dependent variable is estimated as $\hat{y}_i^* = x_i'\hat{\beta} + \hat{\varepsilon}_i$ with $\hat{\varepsilon}_i$ as in (26.200). The standardizing factor Γ is a complex expression in matrix traces and variance terms (see Pinkse 1999, p. 11). To date, this test statistic has seen little application.
36. For example, Pinkse (1999) assumes the explanatory variables to be independently distributed, whereas Kelejian and Prucha (2001) focus on moment conditions and constraints on the spatial weights.

References

Akerlof, G.A. (1997) Social distance and social decisions. *Econometrica* **65**, 1005–1027.

Albert, J.H. and S. Chib (1993) Bayesian analysis of binary and polychotomous response data. *Journal of the American Statistical Association* **88**, 669–79.

Andrews, D.W. (1991) Heteroscedasticity and autocorrelation consistent covariance matrix estimation. *Econometrica* **59**, 953–66.

Andrews, D.W. (2005) Cross-section regression with common shocks. *Econometrica* **73**, 1551–1585.

Anselin, L. (1980) *Estimation Methods for Spatial Autoregressive Structures*. Regional Science Dissertation and Monograph Series, Cornell University, Ithaca, NY.

Anselin, L. (1988a) Lagrange Multiplier test diagnostics for spatial dependence and spatial heterogeneity. *Geographical Analysis* **20**, 1–17.

Anselin, L. (1988b) *Spatial Econometrics: Methods and Models*. Dordrecht: Kluwer Academic Publishers.

Anselin, L. (1988c) A test for spatial autocorrelation in seemingly unrelated regressions. *Economics Letters* **28**, 335–41.

Anselin, L. (1990) Spatial dependence and spatial structural instability in applied regression analysis. *Journal of Regional Science* **30**, 185–207.

Anselin, L. (1992) Space and applied econometrics. Introduction. *Regional Science and Urban Economics* **22**, 307–16.

Anselin, L. (2001a) Rao's score test in spatial econometrics. *Journal of Statistical Planning and Inference* **97**, 113–39.

Anselin, L. (2001b) Spatial econometrics. In B. Baltagi (ed.), *A Companion to Theoretical Econometrics*. Oxford: Blackwell, pp. 310–30.

Anselin, L. (2001c) Spatial effects in econometric practice in environmental and resource economics. *American Journal of Agricultural Economics* **83**(3), 705–10.

Anselin, L. (2002) Under the hood. Issues in the specification and interpretation of spatial regression models. *Agricultural Economics* **27**(3), 247–67.

Anselin, L. (2003a) Spatial externalities. *International Regional Science Review* **26**(2), 147–52.

Anselin, L. (2003b) Spatial externalities, spatial multipliers and spatial econometrics. *International Regional Science Review* **26**(2), 153–66.

Anselin, L. and A. Bera (1998) Spatial dependence in linear regression models with an introduction to spatial econometrics. In A. Ullah and D.E. Giles (eds), *Handbook of Applied Economic Statistics*. New York: Marcel Dekker, pp. 237–89.

Anselin, L., A. Bera, R.J. Florax and M. Yoon (1996) Simple diagnostic tests for spatial dependence. *Regional Science and Urban Economics* **26**, 77–104.

Anselin, L. and R.J. Florax (1995a) *New Directions in Spatial Econometrics*. Berlin: Springer-Verlag.

Anselin, L. and R.J. Florax (1995b) Small sample properties of tests for spatial dependence in regression models: some further results. In L. Anselin and R.J. Florax (eds), *New Directions in Spatial Econometrics*. Berlin: Springer-Verlag, pp. 21–74.

Anselin, L., R.J. Florax and S.J. Rey (2004a) *Advances in Spatial Econometrics: Methodology, Tools and Applications*. Berlin: Springer-Verlag.

Anselin, L., R.J. Florax and S.J. Rey (2004b) Econometrics for spatial models, recent advances. In L. Anselin, R.J. Florax and S.J. Rey (eds), *Advances in Spatial Econometrics: Methodology, Tools and Applications*. Berlin: Springer-Verlag, pp. 1–25.

Anselin, L. and D.A. Griffith (1988) Do spatial effects really matter in regression analysis. *Papers, Regional Science Association* **65**, 11–34.

Anselin, L. and H.H. Kelejian (1997) Testing for spatial error autocorrelation in the presence of endogenous regressors. *International Regional Science Review* **20**, 153–82.

Anselin, L., J. Le Gallo and H. Jayet (2006). Spatial panel econometrics. In L. Matyas and P. Sevestre (eds), *The Econometrics of Panel Data: Fundamentals and Recent Developments in Theory and Practice*, 3rd edn. Dordrecht: Kluwer (in press).

Anselin, L. and R. Moreno (2003) Properties of tests for spatial error components. *Regional Science and Urban Economics* **33**(5), 595–618.

Anselin, L. and S.J. Rey (1991) Properties of tests for spatial dependence in linear regression models. *Geographical Analysis* **23**, 112–31.

Anselin, L. and O. Smirnov (1996) Efficient algorithms for constructing proper higher order spatial lag operators. *Journal of Regional Science* **36**, 67–89.

Baltagi, B.H. (2001) *Econometric Analysis of Panel Data*, 2nd edn. Chichester, UK: John Wiley & Sons.

Baltagi, B.H. and D. Li (2001a) Double length artificial regressions for testing spatial dependence. *Econometric Reviews* **20**(1), 31–40.

Baltagi, B.H. and D. Li (2001b) LM tests for functional form and spatial error correlation. *International Regional Science Review* **24**(2), 194–225.

Baltagi, B.H., S.H. Song, B.C. Jung and W. Koh (2003a) Testing for serial correlation, spatial autocorrelation and random effects using panel data. Working paper, Texas A&M University, College Station, TX.

Baltagi, B.H., S.H. Song and W. Koh (2003b) Testing panel data regression models with spatial error correlation. *Journal of Econometrics* **117**, 123–50.

Banerjee, S., B.P. Carlin and A.E. Gelfand (2004) *Hierarchical Modeling and Analysis for Spatial Data*. Boca Raton, FL: Chapman & Hall/CRC.

Barry, R.P. and R.K. Pace (1999) Monte Carlo estimates of the log determinant of large sparse matrices. *Linear Algebra and its Applications* **289**, 41–54.

Basu, S. and T.G. Thibodeau (1998) Analysis of spatial autocorrelation in housing prices. *The Journal of Real Estate Finance and Economics* **17**, 61–85.

Bera, A. and M.J. Yoon (1993) Specification testing with misspecified alternatives. *Econometric Theory* **9**, 649–58.

Beron, K.J., J.C. Murdoch and W.P. Vijverberg (2003) Why cooperate? Public goods, economic power, and the Montreal Protocol. *The Review of Economics and Statistics* **85**(2), 286–97.

Beron, K.J. and W.P. Vijverberg (2004) Probit in a spatial context, a Monte Carlo analysis. In L. Anselin, R.J. Florax and S.J. Rey (eds), *Advances in Spatial Econometrics*. Heidelberg: Springer-Verlag, pp. 169–95.

Besag, J. (1974) Spatial interaction and the statistical analysis of lattice systems. *Journal of the Royal Statistical Society B* **36**, 192–225.

Besley, T. and A. Case (1995) Incumbent behavior: vote-seeking, tax-setting and yardstick competition. *American Economic Review* **85**, 25–45.

Bivand, R. and S. Szymanski (1997) Spatial dependence through local yardstick competition: theory and testing. *Economics Letters* **55**, 257–65.

Blommestein, H. (1983) Specification and estimation of spatial econometric models: a discussion of alternative strategies for spatial economic modeling. *Regional Science and Urban Economics* **13**, 250–71.

Blommestein, H. (1985) Elimination of circular routes in spatial dynamic regression equations. *Regional Science and Urban Economics* **15**, 121–30.

Blommestein, H.J. and N.A. Koper (1998) The influence of sample size on the degree of redundancy in spatial lag operators. *Journal of Econometrics* **82**(2), 317–33.

Bolthausen, E. (1982) On the central limit theorem for stationary mixing random fields. *The Annals of Probability* **10**, 1047–1050.

Brandsma, A. and R.H. Ketellapper (1979) A biparametric approach to spatial autocorrelation. *Environment and Planning A* **11**, 51–8.

Brett, C. and J. Pinkse (1997) Those taxes all over the map! A test for spatial independence of municipal tax rates in British Columbia. *International Regional Science Review* **20**, 131–51.

Breusch, T. (1980). Useful invariance results for generalized regression models. *Journal of Econometrics* **13**, 327–40.

Breusch, T. and A. Pagan (1979) A simple test for heteroskedasticity and random coefficient variation. *Econometrica* **47**, 1287–1294.

Breusch, T. and A. Pagan (1980) The Lagrange Multiplier test and its applications to model specification in economics. *Review of Economic Studies* **67**, 239–53.

Brock, W. and S. Durlauf (2001a) Discrete choice with social interactions. *Review of Economic Studies* **59**, 235–60.

Brock, W.A. and S.N. Durlauf (2001b) Interactions-based models. In J.J. Heckman and E. Leamer (eds), *Handbook of Econometrics*, vol. 5. Amsterdam: North-Holland, pp. 3297–3380.

Brueckner, J.K. (1998) Testing for strategic interaction among local governments: the case of growth controls. *Journal of Urban Economics* **44**, 438–67.

Brueckner, J.K. (2003) Strategic interaction among governments: an overview of empirical studies. *International Regional Science Review* **26**(2), 175–88.

Brueckner, J.K. and L.A. Saavedra (2001) Do local governments engage in strategic tax competition? *National Tax Journal* **54**, 203–29.

Burridge, P. (1980) On the Cliff–Ord test for spatial autocorrelation. *Journal of the Royal Statistical Society B* **42**, 107–8.

Burridge, P. (1981) Testing for a common factor in a spatial autoregressive model. *Environment and Planning A* **13**, 795–800.

Case, A.C. (1991) Spatial patterns in household demand. *Econometrica* **59**, 953–65.

Case, A.C. (1992) Neighborhood influence and technological change. *Regional Science and Urban Economics* **22**, 491–508.

Case, A.C., H. Rosen and J.R. Hines (1993) Budget spillovers and fiscal policy interdependence: evidence from the states. *Journal of Public Economics* **52**, 285–307.

Casella, G. and E. George (1992). Explaining the Gibbs sampler. *American Statistician* **46**, 167–74.

Casetti, E. (1997) The expansion method, mathematical modeling, and spatial econometrics. *International Regional Science Review* **20**, 9–33.

Cliff, A. and J.K. Ord (1972) Testing for spatial autocorrelation among regression residuals. *Geographical Analysis* **4**, 267–84.

Cliff, A. and J.K. Ord (1973) *Spatial Autocorrelation*. London: Pion.

Cliff, A. and J.K. Ord (1981) *Spatial Processes: Models and Applications*. London: Pion.

Coakley, J., A.-M. Fuentes and R. Smith (2002) A principal components approach to cross-section dependence in panels. Working Paper, Department of Economics, Birkbeck College, University of London, London, United Kingdom.

Conley, T.G. (1999) GMM estimation with cross-sectional dependence. *Journal of Econometrics* **92**, 1–45.

Conley, T.G. and E. Ligon (2002) Economic distance, spillovers and cross country comparisons. *Journal of Economic Growth* **7**, 157–87.

Conley, T.G. and G. Topa (2002) Socio-economic distance and spatial patterns in unemployment. *Journal of Applied Econometrics* **17**, 303–27.

Cook, D. and S. Pocock (1983) Multiple regression in geographic mortality studies, with allowance for spatially correlated errors. *Biometrics* **39**, 361–71.

Cox, D.R. and E.J. Snell (1968) A general definition of residuals. *Journal of the Royal Statistical Society Series B* **39**, 248–75.

Cressie, N. (1993) *Statistics for Spatial Data*. New York: Wiley.

Das, D., H.H. Kelejian and I.R. Prucha (2003) Finite sample properties of estimators of spatial autoregressive models with autoregressive disturbances. *Papers in Regional Science* **82**, 1–27.

Davidson, R. and J.G. MacKinnon (1984) Model specification tests based on artificial regressions. *International Economic Review* **25**, 485–502.

Davidson, R. and J.G. MacKinnon (1988) Double-length artificial regression. *Oxford Bulletin of Economics and Statistics* **50**, 203–17.

Davies, R. (1977) Hypothesis testing when a nuisance parameter is present only under the alternative. *Biometrika* **64**, 247–54.

Davies, R. (1987) Hypothesis testing when a nuisance parameter is present only under the alternative. *Biometrika* **74**, 33–43.

de Graaff, T., R.J.G.M. Florax, P. Nijkamp and A. Reggiani (2001) A general misspecification test for spatial regression models: dependence, heterogeneity, and nonlinearity. *Journal of Regional Science* **41**(2), 255–76.

Dietz, R.D. (2002) The estimation of neighborhood effects in the social sciences: an interdisciplinary approach. *Social Science Research* **31**, 539–75.

Driscoll, J.C. and A.C. Kraay (1998) Consistent covariance matrix estimation with spatially dependent panel data. *The Review of Economics and Statistics* **80**, 549–60.

Dubin, R. (1988) Estimation of regression coefficients in the presence of spatially autocorrelated errors. *Review of Economics and Statistics* **70**, 466–74.

Dubin, R. (1992) Spatial autocorrelation and neighborhood quality. *Regional Science and Urban Economics* **22**, 433–52.

Dubin, R., R.K. Pace and T.G. Thibodeau (1999) Spatial autoregression techniques for real estate data. *Journal of Real Estate Literature* **7**, 79–95.

Durlauf, Steven N. (1997) Statistical mechanics approaches to socioeconomic behavior. In B.W. Arthur, S.N. Durlauf and D.A. Lane (eds), *The Economy as an Evolving Complex System II*. Reading, MA: Addison-Wesley, pp. 81–104.

Durlauf, Steven N. (2004) Neighborhood effects. In J. Henderson and J.-F. Thisse (eds), *Handbook of Regional and Urban Economics*, vol. 4. Amsterdam: North-Holland, pp. 2173–2242.

Elhorst, J.P. (2001) Dynamic models in space and time. *Geographical Analysis* **33**, 119–40.

Elhorst, J.P. (2003) Specification and estimation of spatial panel data models. *International Regional Science Review* **26**(3), 244–68.

Fazekas, I. and A.G. Kukush (2000) Infill asymptotics inside increasing domains for the least squares estimator in linear models. *Statistical Inference for Stochastic Processes* **3**, 199–223.

Ferrándiz, J., A. López, A. Llopis, M. Morales and M. Tejerizo (1995) Spatial interaction between neighbouring counties: Cancer mortality data in Valencia (Spain). *Biometrics* **51**, 665–78.

Ferrándiz, J., A. López and P. Sanmartín (1999) Spatial regression models in epidemiological studies. In A. Lawson, A. Biggeri, D. Böhning, E. Lesaffre, J.-F. Viel and R. Bertollini (eds), *Disease Mapping and Risk Assessment for Public Health*. New York: John Wiley, pp. 203–15.

Fingleton, B. (1999) Spurious spatial regression: some Monte Carlo results with spatial unit root and spatial cointegration. *Journal of Regional Science* **39**(1), 1–19.

Fleming, M. (2004) Techniques for estimating spatially dependent discrete choice models. In L. Anselin, R.J. Florax and S.J. Rey (eds), *Advances in Spatial Econometrics*. Heidelberg: Springer-Verlag, pp. 145–68.

Florax, R. and H. Folmer (1992) Specification and estimation of spatial linear regression models: Monte Carlo evaluation of pre-test estimators. *Regional Science and Urban Economics* **22**, 405–32.

Florax, R.J. and T. de Graaff (2004) The performance of diagnostic tests for spatial dependence in linear regression models: a meta-analysis of simulation studies. In L. Anselin, R.J. Florax and S.J. Rey (eds), *Advances in Spatial Econometrics: Methodology, Tools and Applications*. Berlin: Springer-Verlag, pp. 29–65.

Florax, R.J., H. Folmer and S.J. Rey (2003) Specification searches in spatial econometrics: The relevance of Hendry's methodology. *Regional Science and Urban Economics* **33**(5), 557–79.

Florax, R.J., H. Folmer and S.J. Rey (2006) A comment on specification searches in spatial econometrics: The relevance of Hendry's methodology: a reply. *Regional Science and Urban Economics* (forthcoming).

Florax, R.J. and S.J. Rey (1995) The impacts of misspecified spatial interaction in linear regression models. In L. Anselin and R.J. Florax (eds), *New Directions in Spatial Econometrics*. Berlin: Springer-Verlag, pp. 111–35.

Florax, R.J.G.M. and A. van der Vlist (2003) Spatial econometric data analysis: moving beyond traditional models. *International Regional Science Review* **26**(3), 223–43.

Fotheringham, A., C. Brunsdon and M. Charlton (2002) *Geographically Weighted Regression*. Chichester: John Wiley and Sons.

Gamerman, D., A.R. Moreira and H. Rue (2003) Space-varying regression models: Specifications and simulation. *Computational Statistics and Data Analysis* **42**(3), 513–33.

Gelfand, A.E., H.-J. Kim, C. Sirmans and S. Banerjee (2003). Spatial modeling with spatially varying coefficient processes. *Journal of the American Statistical Association* **98**, 387–96.

Gelman, A., J.B. Carlin, H.S. Stern and D.B. Rubin (2004) *Bayesian Data Analysis*, 2nd edn. Boca Raton, FL: Chapman and Hall.

Geman, S. and D. Geman (1984) Stochastic relaxation, Gibbs distributions, and the Bayesian restoration of images. *IEEE Transactions on Pattern Analysis and Machine Intelligence* 6, 721–41.

Getis, A., J. Mur and H.G. Zoller (2004) *Spatial Econometrics and Spatial Statistics*. Basingstoke: Palgrave Macmillan.

Gilks, W., S. Richardson and D. Spiegelhalter (1996) *Markov Chain Monte Carlo in Practice*. London: Chapman and Hall.

Glaeser, E.L., H. Kallal, J. Scheinkman and A. Schleifer (1992) Growth in cities. *Journal of Political Economy* 100, 1126–1152.

Glaeser, E.L., B. Sacerdote and J. Scheinkman (1996) Crime and social interactions. *Quarterly Journal of Economics* 111, 507–48.

Glaeser, E.L., B.I. Sacerdote and J.A. Scheinkman (2002) The social multiplier. Technical Report 9153, NBER, Cambridge, MA 02138.

Godfrey, L. (1981) On the invariance of the Lagrange Multiplier test with respect to certain changes in the alternative hypothesis. *Econometrica* 49, 1443–1455.

Gotway, C.A. and W.W. Stroup (1997) A generalized linear model approach to spatial data analysis and prediction. *Journal of Agricultural, Biological and Environmental Statistics* 2(2), 157–78.

Gotway, C.A. and R.D. Wolfinger (2003) Spatial prediction of counts and rates. *Statistics in Medicine* 22, 1415–1432.

Gotway, C.A. and L.J. Young (2002) Combining incompatible spatial data. *Journal of the American Statistical Association* 97, 632–48.

Greenland, S. (2002) A review of multilevel theory for ecologic analyses. *Statistics in Medicine* 21, 389–95.

Griffith, D.A. and A. Sone (1995) Trade-offs associated with normalizing constant computational simplications for estimating spatial statistical models. *Journal of Statistical Computation and Simulation* 51, 165–83.

Haining, R. (1988) Estimating spatial means with an application to remotely sensed data. *Communications in Statistics, Theory and Methods* 17, 573–97.

Haining, R. (1990) *Spatial Data Analysis in the Social and Environmental Sciences*. Cambridge: Cambridge University Press.

Hall, P. and P. Patil (1994) Properties of nonparametric estimators of autocovariance for stationary random fields. *Probability Theory and Related Fields* 99, 399–424.

Hendry, D.F. (2006) A comment on specification searches in spatial econometrics: the relevance of Hendry's methodology. *Regional Science and Urban Economics* (forthcoming).

Holloway, G., B. Shankar and S. Rahman (2002) Bayesian spatial probit estimation: A primer and an application to HYV rice adoption. *Agricultural Economics* 27(3), 383–402.

Hordijk, L. (1974) Spatial correlation in the disturbances of a linear interregional model. *Regional Science and Urban Economics* 4, 117–40.

Hordijk, L. (1979) Problems in estimating econometric relations in space. *Papers, Regional Science Association* 42, 99–115.

Hordijk, L. and J. Paelinck (1976) Some principles and results in spatial econometrics. *Recherches Économiques de Louvain* 42, 175–97.

Hsiao, C. and M.H. Pesaran (2004) Random coefficient panel data models. Working paper, University of Cambridge, Cambridge, United Kingdom.

Huang, J. (1984) The autoregressive moving average model for spatial analysis. *Australian Journal of Statistics* 26, 169–78.

Irwin, E.G. (2004) Identifying interaction effects among spatially distributed agents: An application to land use spillovers. Working paper, Department of Agricultural, Environmental and Development Economics, The Ohio State University, Columbus, OH.

Johnson, N. and S. Kotz (1969) *Distributions in Statistics: Discrete Distributions*. Boston, MA: Houghton Mifflin.

Jones, J.-P. and E. Casetti (1992) *Applications of the Expansion Method*. New York: Routledge.

Kaiser, M.S. and N. Cressie (1997) Modeling Poisson variables with positive spatial dependence. *Statistics and Probability Letters* **35**, 423–32.

Kaiser, M.S. and N. Cressie (2000) The construction of multivariate distributions from Markov random fields. *Journal of Multivariate Analysis* **73**, 199–220.

Kapoor, M., H.H. Kelejian and I.R. Prucha (2003) Panel data models with spatially correlated error components. Working paper, University of Maryland, College Park, MD.

Kelejian, H.H. and I. Prucha (1997) Estimation of spatial regression models with autoregressive errors by two stage least squares procedures: a serious problem. *International Regional Science Review* **20**, 103–11.

Kelejian, H.H. and I. Prucha (1998) A generalized spatial two stage least squares procedures for estimating a spatial autoregressive model with autoregressive disturbances. *Journal of Real Estate Finance and Economics* **17**, 99–121.

Kelejian, H.H. and I. Prucha (1999) A generalized moments estimator for the autoregressive parameter in a spatial model. *International Economic Review* **40**, 509–33.

Kelejian, H.H. and I. Prucha (2001) On the asymptotic distribution of the Moran I test statistic with applications. *Journal of Econometrics* **104**(2), 219–57.

Kelejian, H.H. and I.R. Prucha (2002) 2SLS and OLS in a spatial autoregressive model with equal spatial weights. *Regional Science and Urban Economics* **32**(6), 691–707.

Kelejian, H.H. and I.R. Prucha (2003) HAC estimation in a spatial framework. Working paper, Department of Economics, University of Maryland, College Park, MD.

Kelejian, H.H. and I.R. Prucha (2004) Estimation of simultaneous systems of spatially interrelated cross sectional equations. *Journal of Econometrics* **118**, 27–50.

Kelejian, H.H., I.R. Prucha and Y. Yuzefovich (2004) Instrumental variable estimation of a spatial autoregressive model with autoregressive disturbances: Large and small sample results. In J.P. LeSage and R.K. Pace (eds), *Advances in Econometrics: Spatial and Spatiotemporal Econometrics*. Oxford: Elsevier Science Ltd., pp. 163–98.

Kelejian, H.H. and D.P. Robinson (1992) Spatial autocorrelation: a new computationally simple test with an application to per capita country police expenditures. *Regional Science and Urban Economics* **22**, 317–33.

Kelejian, H.H. and D.P. Robinson (1993) A suggested method of estimation for spatial interdependent models with autocorrelated errors, and an application to a county expenditure model. *Papers in Regional Science* **72**, 297–312.

Kelejian, H.H. and D.P. Robinson (1995) Spatial correlation: a suggested alternative to the autoregressive model. In L. Anselin and R.J. Florax (eds), *New Directions in Spatial Econometrics*. Berlin: Springer-Verlag, pp. 75–95.

Kelejian, H.H. and D.P. Robinson (1998) A suggested test for spatial autocorrelation and/or heteroskedasticity and corresponding Monte Carlo results. *Regional Science and Urban Economics* **28**, 389–417.

Kelejian, H.H. and D.P. Robinson (2004) The influence of spatially correlated heteroskedasticity on tests for spatial correlation. In L. Anselin and R.J. Florax (eds), *Advances in Spatial Econometrics*. Heidelberg: Springer-Verlag, pp. 79–97.

Kim, C.-W., T.T. Phipps and L. Anselin (2003) Measuring the benefits of air quality improvement: A spatial hedonic approach. *Journal of Environmental Economics and Management* **45**, 24–39.

King, G. (1997) *A Solution to the Ecological Inference Problem: Reconstructing Individual Behavior from Aggregate Data*. Princeton, NJ: Princeton University Press.

King, M. (1981) A small sample property of the Cliff–Ord test for spatial correlation. *Journal of the Royal Statistical Association B* **43**, 263–4.

Lahiri, S. (1996) On the inconsistency of estimators under infill asymptotics for spatial data. *Sankhya A* **58**, 403–17.

Lahiri, S. and K. Mukherjee (2004) Asymptotic distributions of M-estimators in a spatial regression model under some fixed and stochastic spatial sampling designs. *Annals Institute of Statistical Mathematics* **56**, 225–50.

Land, K. and G. Deane (1992) On the large-sample estimation of regression models with spatial or network-effect terms: a two stage least squares approach. In P. Marsden (ed.), *Sociological Methodology*. San Francisco: Jossey-Bass, pp. 221–48.

Lawson, A.B. (2001) *Statistical Methods in Spatial Epidemiology*. New York: John Wiley & Sons.

Lee, L.-F. (2002) Consistency and efficiency of least squares estimation for mixed regressive, spatial autoregressive models. *Econometric Theory* **18**(2), 252–77.

Lee, L.-F. (2003) Best spatial two-stage least squares estimators for a spatial autoregressive model with autoregressive disturbances. *Econometric Reviews* **22**, 307–35.

Leenders, R.T.A.J. (2002) Modeling social influence through network autocorrelation: constructing the weights matrix. *Social Networks* **24**, 21–47.

LeSage, J.P. (1997) Bayesian estimation of spatial autoregressive models. *International Regional Science Review* **20**, 113–29.

LeSage, J.P. (1999) *Spatial Econometrics*. The Web Book of Regional Science, Regional Research Institute, West Virginia University, Morgantown, WV.

LeSage, J.P. (2000) Bayesian estimation of limited dependent variable spatial autoregressive models. *Geographical Analysis* **32**, 19–35.

LeSage, J.P. and R.K. Pace (2004) *Advances in Econometrics: Spatial and Spatiotemporal Econometrics*. Oxford: Elsevier Science Ltd.

LeSage, J.P., R.K. Pace and M. Tiefelsdorf (2004) Methodological developments in spatial econometrics and statistics. *Geographical Analysis* **36**, 87–9.

Magnus, J. (1978) Maximum likelihood estimation of the GLS model with unknown parameters in the disturbance covariance matrix. *Journal of Econometrics* **7**, 281–312. Corrigenda, *Journal of Econometrics* **10**, 261.

Mandy, D. and C. Martins-Filho (1994) A unified approach to asymptotic equivalence of Aitken and feasible Aitken instrumental variables estimators. *International Economic Review* **35**, 957–79.

Manski, C.F. (1993) Identification of endogenous social effects: the reflexion problem. *Review of Economic Studies* **60**, 531–42.

Manski, C.F. (1995) *Identification Problems in the Social Sciences*. Cambridge, MA: Harvard University Press.

Manski, C.F. (2000) Economic analysis of social interactions. *Journal of Economic Perspectives* **14**(3), 115–36.

Mardia, K. and R. Marshall (1984) Maximum likelihood estimation of models for residual covariance in spatial regression. *Biometrika* **71**, 135–46.

Mardia, K. and A. Watkins (1989) On multimodality of the likelihood for the spatial linear model. *Biometrika* **76**, 289–95.

Martin, R. (1993) Approximations to the determinant term in Gaussian maximum likelihood estimation of some spatial models. *Communications in Statistics: Theory and Methods* **22**, 189–205.

McMillen, D.P. (1992) Probit with spatial autocorrelation. *Journal of Regional Science* **32**, 335–48.

Moran, P. (1948) The interpretation of statistical maps. *Biometrika* **35**, 255–60.

Moran, P. (1950) A test for the serial dependence of residuals. *Biometrika* **37**, 178–81.

Murdoch, J.C., M. Rahmatian and M.A. Thayer (1993) A spatially autoregressive median voter model of recreational expenditures. *Public Finance Quarterly* **21**, 334–50.

Murdoch, J.C., T. Sandler and K. Sargent (1997) A tale of two collectives: sulfur versus nitrogen oxides emission reduction in Europe. *Economica* **64**, 281–301.

Murdoch, J.C., T. Sandler and W.P. Vijverberg (2003) The participation decision versus the level of participation in an environmental strategy: a Spatial Probit analysis. *Journal of Public Economics* **87**, 337–62.

Nelson, G.C. (2002) Introduction to the special issue on spatial analysis. *Agricultural Economics* **27**(3), 197–200.

Newey, W.K. and K.D. West (1987) A simple, positive semi-definite, heteroskedasticity and autocorrelation consistent covariance matrix. *Econometrica* **55**, 703–8.

Novo, A.A. (2001) *Spatial Probit Models: Statistical Inference and Estimation. Monte Carlo Simulations and an Application to Contagious Currency Crises.* PhD thesis, University of Illinois, Urbana-Champaign, Champaign, IL. Department of Economics.

Ord, J.K. (1975) Estimation methods for models of spatial interaction. *Journal of the American Statistical Association* **70**, 120–6.

Pace, R.K. and R. Barry (1997a) Quick computation of spatial autoregressive estimators. *Geographical Analysis* **29**, 232–46.

Pace, R.K. and R. Barry (1997b) Sparse spatial autoregressions. *Statistics and Probability Letters* **33**, 291–7.

Pace, R.K. and J.P. LeSage (2002) Semiparametric Maximum Likelihood estimates of spatial dependence. *Geographical Analysis* **34**, 76–90.

Pace, R.K. and J.P. LeSage (2004) Chebyshev approximation of logdeterminants of spatial weights matrices. *Computational Statistics and Data Analysis* **45**, 179–96.

Paelinck, J. and L. Klaassen (1979) *Spatial Econometrics.* Farnborough: Saxon House.

Pesaran, M.H. (2002) Estimation and inference in large heterogenous panels with cross section dependence. DAE Working Paper 0305 and CESifo Working Paper no. 869, University of Cambridge, Cambridge, United Kingdom.

Pesaran, M.H. (2004) General diagnostic tests for cross section dependence in panels. Working paper, University of Cambridge, Cambridge, United Kingdom.

Pinkse, J. (1999) Asymptotics of the Moran test and a test for spatial correlation in Probit models. Working paper, Department of Economics, University of British Columbia, Vancouver, BC.

Pinkse, J. (2004) Moran-flavored tests with nuisance parameter. In L. Anselin, R.J. Florax and S.J. Rey (eds), *Advances in Spatial Econometrics.* Heidelberg: Springer-Verlag, pp. 67–77.

Pinkse, J. and M.E. Slade (1998) Contracting in space: an application of spatial statistics to discrete-choice models. *Journal of Econometrics* **85**, 125–54.

Pinkse, J., M.E. Slade and C. Brett (2002) Spatial price competition: a semiparametric approach. *Econometrica* **70**(3), 1111–1153.

Rey, S.J. and M.G. Boarnet (2004) A taxonomy of spatial econometric models for simultaneous equations systems. In L. Anselin, R.J. Florax and S.J. Rey (eds), *Advances in Spatial Econometrics.* Heidelberg: Springer-Verlag, pp. 99–119.

Rey, S.J. and B.D. Montouri (1999) US regional income convergence: a spatial econometrics perspective. *Regional Studies* **33**, 143–56.

Ripley, B.D. (1981) *Spatial Statistics.* New York: Wiley.

Royle, J.A. and L.M. Berliner (1999) A hierarchical approach to multivariate spatial modeling and prediction. *Journal of Agricultural, Biological and Environmental Statistics* **4**(1), 29–56.

Saavedra, L.A. (2000) A model of welfare competition with evidence from AFDC. *Journal of Urban Economics* **47**, 248–79.

Smirnov, O. (2005) Computation of the information matrix for models with spatial interaction on a lattice. *Journal of Computational and Graphical Statistics* (forthcoming).

Smirnov, O. and L. Anselin (2001) Fast maximum likelihood estimation of very large spatial autoregressive models: a characteristic polynomial approach. *Computational Statistics and Data Analysis* **35**, 301–19.

Stein, M.L. (1999) *Interpolation of Spatial Data: Some Theory for Kriging.* New York: Springer-Verlag.

Stern, S. (1997) Simulation-based estimation. *Journal of Economic Literature* **35**, 2006–2039.

Stoker, T.M. (1993) Empirical approaches to the problem of aggregation over individuals. *Journal of Economic Literature* **33**, 1827–1874.

Tiefelsdorf, M. (2002) The saddlepoint approximation of Moran's *I* and local Moran's I_i's reference distribution and their numerical evaluation. *Geographical Analysis* **34**, 187–206.

Tiefelsdorf, M. and B. Boots (1995) The exact distribution of Moran's I. *Environment and Planning A* **27**, 985–99.

Upton, G.J. and B. Fingleton (1985) *Spatial Data Analysis by Example. Volume 1: Point Pattern and Quantitative Data.* New York: Wiley.

Vijverberg, W.P. (1997) Monte Carlo evaluation of multivariate normal probabilities. *Journal of Econometrics* **76**, 281–307.

Wall, M.M. (2004) A close look at the spatial structure implied by the CAR and SAR models. *Journal of Statistical Planning and Inference* **121**, 311–24.

Waller, L., B. Carlin and H. Xia (1997a) Structuring correlation within hierarchical spatio-temporal models for disease rates. In T. Grégoire, D. Brillinger, P. Russek-Cohen, W. Warren and R. Wolfinger (eds), *Modeling Longitudinal and Spatially Correlated Data.* New York: Springer-Verlag, pp. 309–19.

Waller, L., B. Carlin, H. Xia and A. Gelfand (1997b) Hierarchical spatiotemporal mapping of disease rates. *Journal of the American Statistical Association* **92**, 607–17.

Waller, L.A. and C.A. Gotway (2004) *Applied Spatial Statistics for Public Health Data.* Hoboken, NJ: John Wiley.

Warnes, J. and B.D. Ripley (1987) Problems with likelihood estimation of covariance functions of spatial Gaussian processes. *Biometrika* **74**, 640–2.

White, H. (1980) A heteroskedastic-consistent covariance matrix estimator and a direct test for heteroskedasticity. *Econometrica* **48**, 817–38.

Whittle, P. (1954) On stationary processes in the plane. *Biometrika* **41**, 434–49.

Wikle, C. K., L.M. Berliner and N. Cressie (1998) Hierarchical Bayesian space-time models. *Environmental and Ecological Statistics* **5**, 117–54.

Zhang, H. (2002) On estimation and prediction for spatial generalized linear mixed models. *Biometrics* **56**, 129–36.

27

Signal Extraction

Andrew Harvey and Giuliano De Rossi

Abstract

This chapter develops the theory of signal extraction, i.e., the estimation of the components of an unobserved components (UC) model for an observed time series. It begins by analysing linear time-invariant models, of which stationary processes are a special case, and introduces the classic Wiener–Kolmogorov signal extraction formula for estimating the components of structural time series models. The statistical treatment of UC models is best carried out by using the state space form and the associated algorithms of the Kalman filter and smoother, and these are then introduced and the methodology developed. Extensions to models formulated in continuous time are then considered, before the latest computational advances for dealing with signal extraction in nonlinear and non-Gaussian models are discussed.

27.1	Introduction		971
27.2	Time-invariant models		972
	27.2.1	Classical formulae for signal extraction	972
	27.2.2	Structural time series models	973
	27.2.3	Stochastic properties of auxiliary residuals	975
	27.2.4	Frequency domain analysis	976
	27.2.5	Correlated components	976
27.3	State space form		977
	27.3.1	Kalman filter	978
	27.3.2	Innovations	979
	27.3.3	Time-invariant models	980
	27.3.4	Maximum likelihood estimation and the prediction error decomposition	980
	27.3.5	Smoothing algorithms	980
	27.3.6	Missing observations, temporal aggregation and mixed frequency	982
	27.3.7	Bayesian treatment	983
27.4	Continuous time and irregular spacing		983
	27.4.1	Stochastic trends in continuous time	984
	27.4.2	Stocks	984
	27.4.3	Flows	984
	27.4.4	Irregular spacing	985
27.5	Nonlinear and non-Gaussian models		986
	27.5.1	General nonlinear state space model	986
	27.5.2	Count data and qualitative observations	988

      27.5.3   Heavy-tailed distributions and robustness   989
      27.5.4   Particle filtering   990
27.6   Conclusion   998

27.1   Introduction

A linear unobserved components (UC) model for a univariate time series can be written in matrix form as

$$\mathbf{y} = \boldsymbol{\mu} + \boldsymbol{v}, \tag{27.1.1}$$

where $\mathbf{y}$, $\boldsymbol{\mu}$ and $\boldsymbol{v}$ are $T \times 1$ vectors with zero means and covariance matrices $\mathbf{V}_y$, $\mathbf{V}_\mu$ and $\mathbf{V}_v$ respectively. Signal extraction, or *smoothing*, is concerned with the estimation of $\boldsymbol{\mu}$ given the observations $\mathbf{y}$. If $\boldsymbol{\mu}$ and $\boldsymbol{v}$, and hence $\mathbf{y}$, have multivariate normal distributions, it follows from a standard lemma on the multivariate normal distribution[1] that the distribution of $\boldsymbol{\mu}$ conditional on $\mathbf{y}$ is normal with mean and covariance matrix given by

$$E(\boldsymbol{\mu} \mid \mathbf{y}) = \mathbf{V}_{\mu y}\mathbf{V}_y^{-1}\mathbf{y} \quad \text{and} \quad Var(\boldsymbol{\mu} \mid \mathbf{y}) = \mathbf{V}_\mu - \mathbf{V}_{\mu y}\mathbf{V}_y^{-1}\mathbf{V}_{y\mu} \tag{27.1.2}$$

respectively, where $\mathbf{V}_{\mu y} = E(\boldsymbol{\mu}\mathbf{y}')$; if $\boldsymbol{\mu}$ and $\boldsymbol{v}$ are independent, $\mathbf{V}_{\mu y} = \mathbf{V}_\mu$. The conditional mean is the minimum mean square error estimate (MMSE) of $\boldsymbol{\mu}$. As such its MSE matrix is $Var(\boldsymbol{\mu} \mid \mathbf{y})$; this does not depend on the observations and so it is the unconditional as well as the conditional MSE. Thus it is the appropriate MSE matrix when the conditional mean is viewed as an estimator rather than an estimate. In the present context the estimator is called a *smoother*.

Since $E(\boldsymbol{\mu} \mid \mathbf{y})$ is a linear function of the observations, we will adopt the convention of denoting it by the corresponding Latin letter, $\mathbf{m}$. If the normality assumption is dropped, $\mathbf{m}$ is the minimum mean square error linear estimator (MMSLE) of $\boldsymbol{\mu}$. This can be shown by considering any linear estimator of $\boldsymbol{\mu}$, denoted $\mathbf{Wy}$, where $\mathbf{W}$ is a fixed $T \times T$ matrix. The MSE matrix of $\mathbf{Wy}$ is

$$MSE(\mathbf{Wy}) = E[(\mathbf{Wy} - \boldsymbol{\mu})(\mathbf{Wy} - \boldsymbol{\mu})']$$

and, on expanding and taking expectations, it is seen that $MSE(\mathbf{Wy})$ will exceed $MSE(\mathbf{m})$ by a positive semi-definite (p.s.d.) matrix; see Whittle (1983, p. 46). This result is sometimes known as the *extended Gauss–Markov theorem*.

The signal extraction expressions in (27.1.2) are exact, but computationally cumbersome since they require the inversion of the $T \times T$ matrix, $\mathbf{V}_y$. The state space smoother provides an efficient algorithm for computing $\mathbf{m}$ and the diagonal elements in its MSE matrix. It may be generalized so as to compute off-diagonal elements in the MSE matrix and to handle models with several unobserved components. However, like the matrix expressions, the state space smoother gives little insight into the structure of the estimator. Hence section 27.2 looks at linear time-invariant models, of which stationary processes are a special case, and describes the classical Wiener–Kolmogorov (WK) signal extraction formulae. Section 27.3 sets out the state space methods. Section 27.4 looks at models formulated in continuous time, while section 27.5 describes some of the latest computational advances for dealing with signal extraction in nonlinear and non-Gaussian models.

27.2 Time-invariant models

An *autoregressive-integrated-moving average* model of order (p, d, q) is one in which the observations follow a stationary and invertible $ARMA(p, q)$ process after they have been differenced d times. It is often denoted by writing $y_t \sim ARIMA(p, d, q)$. If a constant term, θ_0, is included we may write

$$\Delta^d y_t = \theta_0 + \phi_1 \Delta^d y_{t-1} + \cdots + \phi_p \Delta^d y_{t-p} + \xi_t + \theta_1 \xi_{t-1} + \cdots + \theta_q \xi_{t-q} \qquad (27.2.1)$$

where $\phi_1, \ldots, \phi_p$ are the autoregressive parameters, $\theta_1, \ldots, \theta_q$ are the moving average parameters and $\xi_t \sim NID(0, \sigma^2)$. By defining polynomials in the lag operator, L,

$$\phi(L) = 1 - \phi_1 L - \cdots - \phi_p L^p \quad \text{and} \quad \theta(L) = 1 + \theta_1 L + \cdots + \theta_q L^q \qquad (27.2.2)$$

the model can be written more compactly as

$$\phi(L)\Delta^d y_t = \theta_0 + \theta(L)\xi_t. \qquad (27.2.3)$$

A UC time series model normally contains several disturbance terms. Provided the model is linear, the components driven by these disturbances can be combined to give a model with a single disturbance. This is known as the *reduced form*. The reduced form is an ARIMA model, and the fact that it is derived from a structural form will typically imply restrictions on the parameter space.

27.2.1 Classical formulae for signal extraction

Consider a model consisting of two mutually uncorrelated stationary stochastic components, μ_t and v_t, that is

$$y_t = \mu_t + v_t. \qquad (27.2.4)$$

This is a special case of (27.1.1). The MMSLE of μ_t (MMSE in a Gaussian model), in a doubly infinite sample, is of the form

$$m_{t|\infty} = w(L)y_t = \sum_{j=-\infty}^{\infty} w_{-j}L^j y_t = \sum_{i=-\infty}^{\infty} w_i y_{t+i}. \qquad (27.2.5)$$

The Wiener–Kolmogorov (WK) formula for finding the weights is

$$w(L) = g_\mu(L)/g_y(L) \qquad (27.2.6)$$

where $g_\mu(L)$ is the autocovariance-generating function (ACGF) of μ_t and the ACGF of y_t is

$$g_y(L) = g_\mu(L) + g_v(L), \qquad (27.2.7)$$

where $g_v(L)$ is the ACGF of v_t. In terms of the reduced form parameters, $y_t = \phi^{-1}(L)\theta(L)\xi_t$, where ξ_t is white noise with variance σ^2,

$$g_y(L) = \{|\theta(L)|^2/|\phi(L)|^2\}\sigma^2, \qquad (27.2.8)$$

where we follow Whittle[2] in adopting the convention that $|\theta(L)|^2 = \theta(L)\theta(L^{-1})$ and similarly for $\phi(L)$.

The MSE of an estimated component may be derived from the ACGF of $m_{t|\infty} - \mu_t$, that is $g_\mu(L)g_v(L)/g_y(L)$, by evaluating the coefficient of L^0. If v_t is white noise, ε_t, this ACGF reduces to $\sigma_\varepsilon^2 w(L)$ and so, if expressions for the weights can be found, then so can the estimation MSE.

The weights for a semi-infinite sample, that is one in which an infinite number of past observations are available, and for a finite sample may be obtained by modifying the WK formula as described in Whittle (1983, chapters 6 and 7).

27.2.2 Structural time series models

Although formula (27.2.6) is only proved for stationary models in Whittle (1983, pp. 56–8), it is argued in Bell (1984) that it can still be used for models with unit roots even though expressions like (27.2.8) are no longer ACGFs. This is because nonstationary operators like first differences cancel out of the expression. The following models provide the basis for extracting trends from a series.

Local level Suppose that a random walk is observed with error, that is

$$y_t = \mu_t + \varepsilon_t, \quad t = 1, \ldots, T \qquad (27.2.9)$$

$$\mu_t = \mu_{t-1} + \eta_t \qquad (27.2.10)$$

where η_t and ε_t are mutually uncorrelated white noise disturbances with variances σ_η^2 and σ_ε^2 respectively. The reduced form is *ARIMA*(0,1,1). Equating the auto-correlations of first differences at lag one gives

$$\theta = \left[(q^2 + 4q)^{1/2} - 2 - q\right]/2 \qquad (27.2.11)$$

where $q = \sigma_\eta^2/\sigma_\varepsilon^2$. Provided $q > 0$, the WK formula for estimating μ_t yields

$$m_{t|\infty} = w(L)y_t = \frac{\sigma_\eta^2/|1 - L|^2}{\sigma^2|1 + \theta L|^2/|1 - L|^2} y_t = \frac{(1 + \theta)^2}{|1 + \theta L|^2} y_t, \qquad (27.2.12)$$

as $\sigma_\eta^2 = (1 + \theta)^2 \sigma^2$. On recognizing that $1/|1 + \theta L|^2$ is the ACGF of an $AR(1)$ model with parameter $-\theta$, it can be seen that the weights decline symmetrically and exponentially, that is

$$w_j = \{(1 + \theta)/(1 - \theta)\}(-\theta)^{|j|}, \quad j = 0, \pm 1, \pm 2, \ldots \tag{27.2.13}$$

On setting $L = 1$ in (27.2.12), it can immediately be seen that the weights sum to unity. The lower the signal–noise ratio, q, the closer is θ to minus one, and the more spread out are the weights.

The weights for the smoothed estimator of μ_t near the end of a semi-infinite sample are given in Whittle (1983, p. 69) as:

$$w_j = \{(1 + \theta)/(1 - \theta)\}[(-\theta)^{|-j|} + (-\theta)^{-j+2(T-t)+1}], \quad -\infty < j \leq T - t. \tag{27.2.14}$$

Setting $t = T$ gives the weights for the filtered estimator (27.2.15), that is

$$w_{-j} = (1 + \theta)(-\theta)^j, \quad j = 0, 1, 2, \ldots \tag{27.2.15}$$

while if $t \ll T$, the weights are as for a doubly infinite sample as given in (27.2.13).

The MSE may be obtained as described in subsection 27.2.1 and is

$$\mathrm{MSE}(m_{t|\infty}) = \sigma_\varepsilon^2[(1 + \theta)/(1 - \theta)]. \tag{27.2.16}$$

The formula may be adapted to semi-infinite samples. The MSE associated with (27.2.14) is shown by Whittle (1983, p. 70) to be

$$\sigma_\varepsilon^2[(1 + \theta)/(1 - \theta)][1 - \theta(-\theta)^{2(T-t)}], \quad t \leq T. \tag{27.2.17}$$

The MSE of the filtered estimator (27.2.15), is obtained when $t = T$, so it is $\sigma_\varepsilon^2(1 + \theta)$, while if $T - t$ is large we get the MSE of the smoother, namely (27.2.16) above. Note that (27.2.17) is bigger than (27.2.16) because, as can be seen from (27.2.11), θ is negative for positive q.

Local linear trend The local linear trend model is obtained by adding a slope component, β_t, to the local level model so that μ_t in (27.2.9) is

$$\begin{aligned} \mu_t &= \mu_{t-1} + \beta_{t-1} + \eta_t \\ \beta_t &= \beta_{t-1} + \zeta_t \end{aligned} \tag{27.2.18}$$

where ζ_t is a white noise disturbance, with variance σ_ζ^2, uncorrelated with η_t and ε_t. The weights may be found from the WK formula by noting that the reduced form is $ARIMA(0, 2, 2)$. For the smooth trend model, $\sigma_\eta^2 = 0$ (but $\sigma_\zeta^2 > 0$),

$$w(L) = \frac{\sigma_\zeta^2}{\sigma_\zeta^2 + |1 - L|^4 \sigma_\varepsilon^2} = \frac{\sigma_\zeta^2}{\sigma^2|1 + \theta_1 L + \theta_2 L^2|^2}. \tag{27.2.19}$$

By equating the autocovariances at lags one and two, it can be shown that the reduced form parameters satisfy $\theta_1 = -4\theta_2/(1 + \theta_2)$, with $0 \leq \theta_2 < 1$ and

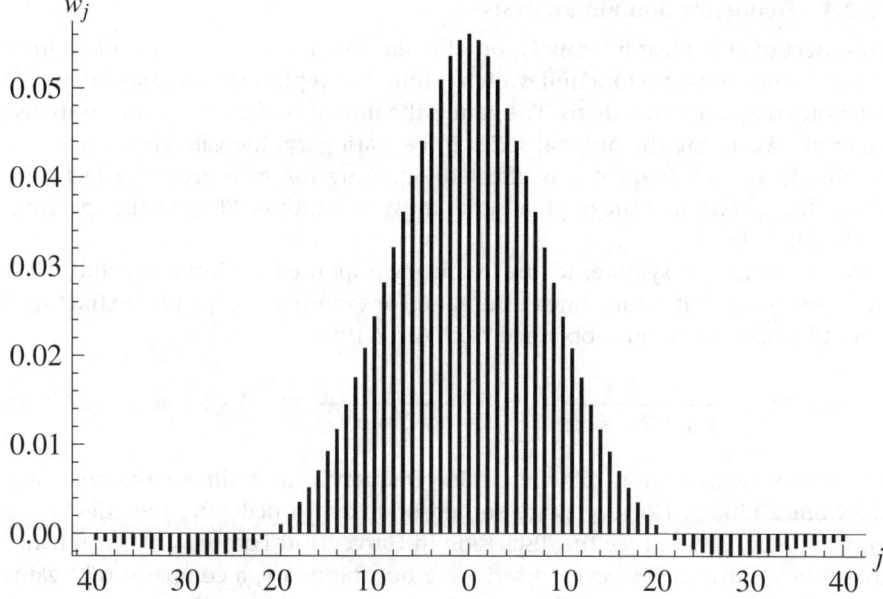

Figure 27.1 Weights for Hodrick–Prescott filter

$-2 < \theta_1 \leq 0$. The roots of the polynomial $1 + \theta_1 L + \theta_2 L^2$ are complex. Since $1/|1 + \theta_1 L + \theta_2 L^2|^2$ is the ACGF of an $AR(2)$ process, it follows that the weights decay according to a damped sine wave with frequency $\cos^{-1}[-\theta_1/2\sqrt{\theta_2}]$; Harvey and Koopman (2000) plot the weights for various values of the signal–noise ratio $q_\zeta = \sigma_\zeta^2/\sigma_\varepsilon^2$ and illustrate how they become more spread out as q_ζ decreases. The value of $q_\zeta = 0.000625$, that is $1/q_\zeta = 1600$, corresponds to the filter proposed by Hodrick and Prescott (1997) for quarterly observations and is shown in Figure 27.1. The initial slow decline of the weights contrasts with the exponential decline of the weights in (27.2.13) for extracting a random walk trend: hence the smooth trend.

27.2.3 Stochastic properties of auxiliary residuals

The Wiener–Kolmogorov formula can be used to obtain the specification of the processes followed by the estimators of the various disturbances in a UC model. These will typically be serially correlated. For example, in the local level model, the process followed by e_t, the smoothed estimator of ε_t, is

$$e_t = -\theta e_{t+1} + \xi_t^* - \xi_{t+1}^*, \quad \xi_t^* = -\theta \xi_t,$$

where ξ_t is the reduced form disturbance term. This process is a backwards non-invertible $ARMA(1,1)$. Harvey and Koopman (1992) show how the standardized estimators, known as *auxiliary residuals*, can be used to detect outliers and structural breaks.

27.2.4   Frequency domain analysis

The effect of any linear filter, $w(L)$, on different frequencies can be obtained from the frequency response function, which is found by replacing L by $exp(-i\lambda)$, where λ denotes frequency in radians. The gain is the modulus of the frequency response function. Assuming the original series to be stationary, the gain shows how the amplitude at each frequency is affected. Squaring the gain gives the factor by which the spectrum of the original series must be multiplied to give the spectrum of the filtered series.

When the filter is symmetric, the frequency response function is real and if it is nowhere negative it is the same as the gain. For example, the gain for extracting a smooth stochastic trend is obtained from (27.2.19) as

$$w(e^{-i\lambda}) = \frac{1}{1 + q^{-1}(2 - 2\cos\lambda)^2} = \frac{1}{1 + q^{-1}2^4 \sin^4(\lambda/2)}, \quad 0 \leq \lambda \leq \pi. \quad (27.2.20)$$

It is interesting to see how this cuts out low frequencies according to the value of q; see Gomez (2001). However, care should be taken in deducing the effect on a nonstationary process; see the discussion in Harvey and Trimbur (2003) on band-pass filters. Nevertheless, even if series are nonstationary, a comparison of gains can still be used to give an indication of the closeness of two filters.

When filters are asymmetric, there is a phase shift at different frequencies and this can be deduced from $w(e^{-i\lambda})$.

27.2.5   Correlated components

If the parameters in the model are unknown, assumptions about the correlations between the disturbances in different components have to be made for reasons of identifiability. An important advantage of uncorrelated components is that the signal extraction filter in the middle of the sample is symmetric. Here we follow Harvey and Koopman (2000) in examining what happens when the disturbances are correlated, using the local level model as an illustration.

The future state form of the local-level model can be written as (27.2.9) with

$$\mu_{t+1} = \mu_t + \eta_t. \quad (27.2.21)$$

It is convenient to write $\sigma_\eta^2 = \alpha^2 \sigma_\varepsilon^2$. Then

$$E(\varepsilon_t \eta_t) = \rho\alpha\sigma_\varepsilon^2, \quad t = 1, \ldots, T, \quad E(\varepsilon_t \eta_s) = 0, \quad t \neq s, \quad (27.2.22)$$

with $|\rho| \leq 1$ and $\alpha \geq 0$. Of course, $\alpha^2 = q$, the signal–noise ratio. The contemporaneous state model has μ_t as in (27.2.10) with the covariance still as in (27.2.22). When the correlation, ρ, is zero the two models are essentially the same, but for non-zero ρ the signal extraction weighting patterns display an interesting asymmetry.

When the two components in (27.2.4) are correlated, the WK formula becomes

$$w(L) = \frac{g_{\mu y}(L)}{g_y(L)} = \frac{g_\mu(L) + g_{\mu v}(L)}{g_y(L)}, \quad (27.2.23)$$

where $g_{\mu y}(L)$ and $g_{\mu v}(L)$ are the cross-covariance-generating functions of μ_t and y_t, and μ_t and v_t, respectively. The ACGF of y_t is now

$$g_y(L) = g_\mu(L) + g_{\mu v}(L) + g_{v\mu}(L) + g_v(L). \tag{27.2.24}$$

For the future state model, the weights for $\theta \neq 0$ can be expressed as

$$w_j = \frac{1+\theta}{1-\theta}\left[1 - \frac{\rho}{\alpha}\left(1+\frac{1}{\theta}\right)\right](-\theta)^{-j}, \quad j \leq -1$$

$$w_j = \frac{1+\theta}{1-\theta}\left[1 - \frac{\rho}{\alpha}(1+\theta)\right](-\theta)^j, \quad j \geq 0 \tag{27.2.25}$$

For $\theta = 0$, $w_{-1} = \rho^2$, $w_0 = 1 - \rho^2$, and $w_j = 0, j \neq -1, 0$.

When $\rho = 1$ the smoothed estimator is exactly the same as the filtered estimator. The future state model corresponds to the single source of error model of Chatfield *et al.* (2001), while the contemporaneous form yields the Beveridge–Nelson filter; further discussion can be found in Harvey and Koopman (2000).

27.3 State space form

The statistical treatment of unobserved components models can be carried out efficiently and in great generality by using the state space form (SSF) and the associated algorithms of the Kalman filter and smoother. The general linear state space form applies to a multivariate time series, y_t, containing N elements. These observable variables are related to an $m \times 1$ vector, α_t, known as the *state vector*, through a *measurement equation*

$$y_t = Z_t\alpha_t + d_t + \varepsilon_t, \quad t = 1, \ldots, T \tag{27.3.1}$$

where Z_t is an $N \times m$ matrix, d_t is an $N \times 1$ vector and ε_t is an $N \times 1$ vector of serially uncorrelated disturbances with mean zero and covariance matrix H_t.

In general the elements of α_t are not observable. However, they are known to be generated by a first-order Markov process,

$$\alpha_t = T_t\alpha_{t-1} + c_t + R_t\eta_t, \quad t = 1, \ldots, T. \tag{27.3.2}$$

where T_t is an $m \times m$ matrix, c_t is an $m \times 1$ vector, R_t is an $m \times g$ matrix and η_t is a $g \times 1$ vector of serially uncorrelated disturbances with mean zero and covariance matrix, Q_t. Equation (27.3.2) is the *transition equation*.

The specification of the state space system is completed by assuming that the initial state vector, α_0, has a mean of a_0 and a covariance matrix P_0, where P_0 is positive semi-definite, and that the disturbances ε_t and η_t are uncorrelated with the initial state for all t. In what follows it will be assumed that the disturbances are uncorrelated with each other in all time periods, that is $E(\varepsilon_t\eta_s') = 0$ for all $s, t = 1, \ldots, T$, though this assumption may be relaxed, the consequence being a slight complication in some of the filtering formulae.

It is sometimes convenient to use the future form of the transition equation,

$$\alpha_{t+1} = T_t\alpha_t + c_t + R_t\eta_t, \quad t = 1, \ldots, T, \tag{27.3.3}$$

as opposed to the contemporaneous form (27.3.2). The orresponding filters are the same unless ε_t and η_t are correlated.

UC models like those in section 27.2 are easily put into state space form. Thus, for the local linear trend model:

$$y_t = [1 \ 0]\alpha_t + \varepsilon_t, \quad t = 1, \ldots, T, \tag{27.3.4}$$

$$\alpha_t = \begin{bmatrix} \mu_t \\ \beta_t \end{bmatrix} = \begin{bmatrix} 1 & 1 \\ 0 & 1 \end{bmatrix} \begin{bmatrix} \mu_{t-1} \\ \beta_{t-1} \end{bmatrix} + \begin{bmatrix} \eta_t \\ \zeta_t \end{bmatrix} \tag{27.3.5}.$$

27.3.1   Kalman filter

The Kalman filter is a recursive procedure for computing the optimal estimator of the state vector at time t, based on the information available at time t. This information consists of the observations up to and including y_t. The system matrices, together with a_0 and P_0, are assumed to be known in all time periods and so do not need to be explicitly included in the information set.

Consider the Gaussian state space model with observations available up to and including time $t - 1$. Given this information set, let α_{t-1} be normally distributed with known mean, a_{t-1}, and $m \times m$ covariance matrix, P_{t-1}. Then it follows from (27.3.2) that α_t is normal with mean

$$a_{t|t-1} = T_t a_{t-1} + c_t \tag{27.3.6}$$

and covariance matrix

$$P_{t|t-1} = T_t P_{t-1} T_t' + R_t Q_t R_t', \quad t = 1, \ldots, T.$$

These two equations are known as the *prediction equations*. The predictive distribution of the next observation, y_t, is normal with mean

$$\tilde{y}_{t|t-1} = Z_t a_{t|t-1} + d_t \tag{27.3.7}$$

and covariance matrix

$$F_t = Z_t P_{t|t-1} Z_t' + H_t, \quad t = 1, \ldots, T. \tag{27.3.8}$$

Once the new observation becomes available, the standard result on the multivariate normal distribution yields the *updating equations*,

$$a_t = a_{t|t-1} + P_{t|t-1} Z_t' F_t^{-1} (y_t - Z_t a_{t|t-1} - d_t) \tag{27.3.9}$$

and

$$P_t = P_{t|t-1} - P_{t|t-1} Z_t' F_t^{-1} Z_t P_{t|t-1},$$

as the mean and variance of the conditional distribution of $\boldsymbol{\alpha}_t$; see Harvey (1989, p. 109).

Taken together, (27.3.6) and (27.3.9) make up the Kalman filter. If desired, they can be written as a single set of recursions going directly from $\mathbf{a}_{t-1}$ to $\mathbf{a}_t$ or, alternatively, from $\mathbf{a}_{t|t-1}$ to $\mathbf{a}_{t+1|t}$. We might refer to these as, respectively, the *contemporaneous* and *predictive filter*. In the latter case

$$\mathbf{a}_{t+1|t} = \mathbf{T}_{t+1}\mathbf{a}_{t|t-1} + \mathbf{c}_{t+1} + \mathbf{K}_t\boldsymbol{\nu}_t \tag{27.3.10}$$

or

$$\mathbf{a}_{t+1|t} = (\mathbf{T}_{t+1} - \mathbf{K}_t\mathbf{Z}_t)\mathbf{a}_{t|t-1} + \mathbf{K}_t\mathbf{y}_t + (\mathbf{c}_{t+1} - \mathbf{K}_t\mathbf{d}_t) \tag{27.3.11}$$

where the gain matrix, $\mathbf{K}_t$, is given by

$$\mathbf{K}_t = \mathbf{T}_{t+1}\mathbf{P}_{t|t-1}\mathbf{Z}_t'\mathbf{F}_t^{-1}, \quad t = 1, \ldots, T. \tag{27.3.12}$$

The recursion for the covariance matrix,

$$\mathbf{P}_{t+1|t} = \mathbf{T}_{t+1}(\mathbf{P}_{t|t-1} - \mathbf{P}_{t|t-1}\mathbf{Z}_t'\mathbf{F}_t^{-1}\mathbf{Z}_t\mathbf{P}_{t|t-1})\mathbf{T}_{t+1}' + \mathbf{R}_{t+1}\mathbf{Q}_{t+1}\mathbf{R}_{t+1}', \tag{27.3.13}$$

is a *Riccati equation*.

The starting values for the Kalman filter may be specified in terms of $\mathbf{a}_0$ and $\mathbf{P}_0$ or $\mathbf{a}_{1|0}$ and $\mathbf{P}_{1|0}$. Given these initial conditions, the Kalman filter delivers the MMSE of the state vector as each new observation becomes available. When all T observations have been processed, the filter yields the MMSE of the current state vector, and/or the state vector in the next time period, based on the full information set; see Anderson and Moore (1979, pp. 29–32) and the discussion surrounding (27.1.2). A diffuse prior corresponds to setting $\mathbf{P}_0 = \kappa\mathbf{I}$, and letting the scalar κ go to infinity.

27.3.2 Innovations

The joint density function for the T sets of observations, $\mathbf{y}_1, \ldots, \mathbf{y}_T$, is

$$p(\mathbf{y}_1, \ldots, \mathbf{y}_T; \boldsymbol{\psi}) = \prod_{t=1}^{T} p(\mathbf{y}_t|\mathbf{Y}_{t-1}) \tag{27.3.14}$$

where $p(\mathbf{y}_t|\mathbf{Y}_{t-1})$ denotes the distribution of $\mathbf{y}_t$ conditional on the information set at time $t - 1$, that is $\mathbf{Y}_{t-1} = \{\mathbf{y}_{t-1}, \mathbf{y}_{t-2}, \ldots, \mathbf{y}_1\}$, and $\boldsymbol{\psi}$ is the vector of parameters, or hyperparameters, that enter into the system matrices. In the Gaussian state space model, the conditional distribution of $\mathbf{y}_t$ is normal with mean $\tilde{\mathbf{y}}_{t|t-1}$ and covariance matrix $\mathbf{F}_t$. Hence the $N \times 1$ vector of prediction errors or *innovations*,

$$\boldsymbol{\nu}_t = \mathbf{y}_t - \tilde{\mathbf{y}}_{t|t-1}, \quad t = 1, \ldots, T, \tag{27.3.15}$$

is serially independent with mean zero and covariance matrix $\mathbf{F}_t$, that is $\boldsymbol{\nu}_t \sim NID(\mathbf{0}, \mathbf{F}_t)$.

27.3.3   Time-invariant models

In many applications the system matrices Z_t, H_t, T_t, R_t and Q_t are all independent of time and so can be written without a subscript. The Kalman filter applied to such models is in a steady state if the error covariance matrix is time-invariant, that is $P_{t+1|t} = P$. The recursion for the error covariance matrix is redundant in the steady state, while the recursion for the state becomes

$$\mathbf{a}_{t+1|t} = \mathbf{La}_{t|t-1} + \mathbf{Ky}_t + (\mathbf{c}_{t+1} - \mathbf{Kd}_t) \qquad (27.3.16)$$

where $\mathbf{L} = \mathbf{T} - \mathbf{KZ}$ and $\mathbf{K} = \mathbf{TPZ'F}^{-1}$. The conditions for convergence to a steady-state are discussed in Burridge and Wallis (1988).

27.3.4   Maximum likelihood estimation and the prediction error decomposition

Once the observations are available, the joint density in (27.3.14) can be reinterpreted as a likelihood function and written $L(\boldsymbol{\psi})$. The ML estimator of $\boldsymbol{\psi}$ is then found by maximizing $L(\boldsymbol{\psi})$. This will normally be carried out by some kind of numerical optimization procedure. It follows from the discussion below (27.3.14) that the Gaussian likelihood function can be written in terms of the innovations, that is

$$\log L(\psi) = -\frac{NT}{2} \log 2\pi - \frac{1}{2} \sum_{t=1}^{T} \log |\mathbf{F}_t| - \frac{1}{2} \sum_{t=1}^{T} \boldsymbol{v}_t' \mathbf{F}_t^{-1} \boldsymbol{v}_t. \qquad (27.3.17)$$

This is sometimes known as the *prediction error decomposition* form of the likelihood. The modifications needed to deal with nonstationary components can be found in Durbin and Koopman (2001).

27.3.5   Smoothing algorithms

The aim of filtering is to find the expected value of the state vector, $\boldsymbol{\alpha}_t$, conditional on the information available at time t. The aim of smoothing is to take account of the information made available after time t. The mean of the distribution of $\boldsymbol{\alpha}_t$, conditional on all the sample, that is $E(\boldsymbol{\alpha}_t \mid \mathbf{Y}_T)$, is known as the smoothed estimate and in a linear Gaussian model it is denoted by $\mathbf{a}_{t|T}$. The covariance matrix of $\boldsymbol{\alpha}_t$ conditional on all T observations is denoted by $\mathbf{P}_{t|T}$. When $\mathbf{a}_{t|T}$ is viewed as an estimator, it is called a smoother. It is the MMSE of $\boldsymbol{\alpha}_t$ and $\mathbf{P}_{t|T}$ is its MSE matrix. Since $\mathbf{P}_{t|T}$ is independent of the observations, it is unconditional; see the discussion below (27.1.2). If the Gaussian assumption is dropped, $\mathbf{a}_{t|T}$ is the MMSLE of $\boldsymbol{\alpha}_t$.

There are basically three smoothing algorithms in a linear model. *Fixed-point* smoothing is concerned with computing smoothed estimates of the state vector at some fixed point in time. Thus it gives $\mathbf{a}_{\tau|t}$ for particular values of τ at all time periods $t > \tau$. *Fixed-lag* smoothing computes smoothed estimates for a fixed delay, that is $\mathbf{a}_{t-j|t}$ for $j = 0, 1, \ldots, M$, where M is the lag length and t is the latest time period. Both of these algorithms can be applied in an *on-line* situation. *Fixed-interval* smoothing, on the other hand, is concerned with computing the full set of smoothed estimates for a fixed span of data. Hence it is an *off-line* technique which yields $\mathbf{a}_{t|T}, t = 1, \ldots, T$. It therefore tends to be the most widely used algorithm for economic and social data.

All three smoothing algorithms are recursive and are linked closely to the Kalman filter. The fixed-point algorithm runs in parallel with the Kalman filter, while the fixed-interval algorithm is a backward recursion which starts at time T, and produces the smoothed estimates in the order $T, \ldots, 1$. Fixed-lag smoothing also runs in parallel with the Kalman filter. Only the fixed interval smoother will be described here. Full details of the fixed-point and fixed-lag algorithms can be found in Anderson and Moore (1979, ch. 7) and de Jong (1989).

The smoothing algorithms all yield MSE matrices corresponding to the estimators that they compute. Since a smoothed estimator is based on at least as much information as the corresponding filtered estimator, it follows that the MSE matrix of the filtered estimator exceeds the MSE matrix of the smoothed estimator by a p.s.d. matrix, that is $\mathbf{P}_{t|T} \le \mathbf{P}_t, t = 1, \ldots, T$. When parameters are estimated, $\mathbf{P}_{t|T}$ will underestimate the true MSE because it does not take into account the extra variation, of $O(T^{-1})$, due to estimating $\boldsymbol{\psi}$. Methods of approximating this additional variation are discussed in Ansley and Kohn (1986) and Quenneville and Singh (2000). Using the bootstrap is also a possibility; see Stoffer and Wall (2004).

The *classical fixed interval smoother* is given by the backward recursions

$$\mathbf{a}_{t|T} = \mathbf{a}_t + \mathbf{P}_t^*(\mathbf{a}_{t+1|T} - \mathbf{T}_{t+1}\mathbf{a}_t - \mathbf{c}_{t+1}), \quad t = T, T-1, \ldots, 1, \qquad (27.3.18)$$

and

$$\mathbf{P}_{t|T} = \mathbf{P}_t + \mathbf{P}_t^*(\mathbf{P}_{t+1|T} - \mathbf{P}_{t+1|t})\mathbf{P}_t^{*\prime}, \quad \text{where } \mathbf{P}_t^* = \mathbf{P}_t \mathbf{T}_{t+1}\mathbf{P}_{t+1|t}^{-1}.$$

A more efficient smoother, as in de Jong (1989), uses the recursion

$$\mathbf{r}_{t-1} = \mathbf{L}_t'\mathbf{r}_t + \mathbf{Z}_t'\mathbf{F}_t^{-1}\boldsymbol{\nu}_t, \quad \mathbf{N}_{t-1} = \mathbf{L}_t'\mathbf{N}_t\mathbf{L}_t + \mathbf{Z}_t'\mathbf{F}_t^{-1}\mathbf{Z}_t, \quad t = T, \ldots, 1, \qquad (27.3.19)$$

where $\mathbf{L}_t = \mathbf{T}_t - \mathbf{K}_t\mathbf{Z}_t$, with initialization $\mathbf{r}_T = 0$ and $\mathbf{N}_T = 0$. The Kalman filter output of $\boldsymbol{\nu}_t, \mathbf{F}_t^{-1}$ and $\mathbf{K}_t$ must be stored for $t = 1, \ldots, T$, but $\mathbf{P}_{t+1|t}$ does not need to be stored and inverted. The recursions have a similar form to the Kalman filtering equations, with $\mathbf{r}_t$ playing an analogous role to the estimated state vector. Instead of being driven by the innovation vector, the recursion for $\mathbf{r}_t$ can be driven by the *smoothing error vector*, which is defined by

$$\mathbf{u}_t = \mathbf{F}_t^{-1}\boldsymbol{\nu}_t - \mathbf{K}_t'\mathbf{r}_t. \qquad (27.3.20)$$

Then $\mathbf{r}_{t-1} = \mathbf{T}_t'\mathbf{r}_t + \mathbf{Z}_t'\mathbf{u}_t, t = T, \ldots, 1$, and this is sometimes advantageous in that $\mathbf{T}_t$ is typically sparse and this can be exploited in programming. The smoothed state vector and its MSE matrix can be evaluated by

$$\mathbf{a}_{t|T} = \mathbf{a}_{t|t-1} + \mathbf{c}_t + \mathbf{P}_{t|t-1}\mathbf{r}_{t-1}, \quad \mathbf{P}_{t|T} = \mathbf{P}_{t|t-1} - \mathbf{P}_{t|t-1}\mathbf{N}_{t-1}\mathbf{P}_{t|t-1}, \quad t = T, \ldots, 1.$$
$$(27.3.21)$$

The additional memory space required to store $\mathbf{a}_{t|t-1}$ and $\mathbf{P}_{t|t-1}$ of the Kalman filter can be avoided if the MSE is not required by computing $\mathbf{a}_{t|T}$ using the forward recursion

$$\mathbf{a}_{t+1|T} = \mathbf{T}_t \mathbf{a}_{t|T} + \mathbf{c}_{t+1} + \mathbf{R}_t \mathbf{Q}_t \mathbf{R}'_t \mathbf{r}_t, \quad t = 1, \ldots, T,$$

with $\mathbf{a}_{1|T} = \mathbf{a}_1 + \mathbf{P}_1 \mathbf{r}_0$. The derivation of (27.3.19) and (27.3.21) follows by noting that $\mathbf{a}_{t|T}$ is constructed from $\mathbf{a}_{t|t-1}$, which depends on $\mathbf{Y}_{t-1}$, and the innovations $\mathbf{v}_j, j = t, .., T$, which contain all the new information on the subsequent observations; see Durbin and Koopman (2001, pp. 70–3).

The estimators of the disturbances $\boldsymbol{\varepsilon}_t$ and $\boldsymbol{\eta}_t$ are obtained from the two vectors, $\mathbf{u}_t$ and $\mathbf{r}_t$. Specifically, the estimators and their unconditional covariance matrices[3] are

$$
\begin{aligned}
\mathbf{e}_{t|T} &= \mathbf{H}_t \mathbf{u}_t, & Var(\mathbf{e}_{t|T}) &= \mathbf{H}_t(\mathbf{F}_t^{-1} + \mathbf{K}'_t \mathbf{N}_t \mathbf{K}_t)\mathbf{H}_t \\
\mathbf{n}_{t|T} &= \mathbf{Q}_t \mathbf{R}'_t \mathbf{r}_t, & Var(\mathbf{n}_{t|T}) &= \mathbf{Q}_t \mathbf{R}'_t \mathbf{N}_t \mathbf{R}_t \mathbf{Q}_t.
\end{aligned}
\tag{27.3.22}
$$

These are the auxiliary residuals introduced earlier in subsection 27.2.4.

In a time-invariant system with a stable steady-state, that is one in which the roots of $\mathbf{L}$ have modulus less than one, the disturbance smoother implies a backward autoregressive representation for the $\mathbf{r}'_t s$ driven by the innovations, that is

$$\mathbf{r}_{t-1} = \mathbf{L}' \mathbf{r}_t + \mathbf{Z}' \mathbf{F}^{-1} \mathbf{v}_t, \quad t = T, \ldots, 1, \tag{27.3.23}$$

with $\mathbf{r}_T = 0$. Thus $\mathbf{r}_t$ depends on future innovations. The process becomes stationary once the effect of the starting condition on $\mathbf{r}_T$ has worked itself out. The dynamic properties of $\mathbf{r}_t$, and therefore $\mathbf{n}_{t|T}$, may be derived using standard results on VAR(1) processes. The properties of $\mathbf{u}_t$ and $\mathbf{e}_{t|T}$ may be obtained by substituting in (27.3.20). Burridge and Wallis (1988) show that the classical fixed interval smoother implies the classical WK formulae for stationary models.

Koopman and Harvey (2003) give an algorithm for computing the weights implicitly used to extract components in general state space models at any point in time. This is available as a subroutine in the SsfPack package of Koopman *et al.* (1999). The gain and phase can be calculated directly if a frequency domain analysis is required.

27.3.6 Missing observations, temporal aggregation and mixed frequency

Missing observations are easily handled in the SSF simply by omitting the updating equations while retaining the prediction equations. Filtering and smoothing then go through automatically and the likelihood function is constructed using prediction errors corresponding to actual observations. When dealing with flow variables, such as income, the issue is one of temporal aggregation. This may be dealt with by the introduction of a cumulator variable into the state as described in Harvey (1989, subsection 27.6.3). The ability to handle missing and temporally aggregated observations offers enormous flexibility, for example in dealing with observations at mixed frequencies.

27.3.7 Bayesian treatment

Since the state vector is a vector of random variables, a Bayesian interpretation of the Kalman filter as a way of updating a Gaussian prior distribution on the state to give a posterior is quite natural. The mechanics of filtering, smoothing and prediction are the same irrespective of whether the overall framework is Bayesian or classical. Smoothing gives the mean and variance of the state, conditional on all the observations. For the classical statistician, the conditional mean is the MMSE, while for the Bayesian it minimizes the expected loss for a symmetric loss function. With a quadratic loss function, the expected loss is given by the conditional variance.

The real differences in classical and Bayesian treatments arise when the parameters are unknown. In the classical framework these are estimated by maximum likelihood. Inferences about the state observations are then usually made conditional on the estimated values of the hyperparameters, though some approximation to the effect of parameter uncertainty can be made as noted in subsection 27.3.5. In a Bayesian set-up, on the other hand, the hyperparameters, as they are often called, are random variables. The development of simulation techniques based on Markov chain Monte Carlo (MCMC) has now made a full Bayesian treatment a feasible proposition. This means that it is possible to simulate a distribution for the state that takes account of hyperparameter uncertainty. The computations may be speeded up considerably by using the *simulation smoother* introduced by de Jong and Shephard (1995) and further developed by Durbin and Koopman (2002).

Prior distributions of variance parameters are often specified as inverted gamma distributions. This distribution allows a non-informative prior to be adopted as in Frühwirth-Schnatter (1994, p. 196). As regards informative priors, any knowledge we might have is most likely to be on signal–noise ratios rather than on the variances themselves. Koop and van Dijk (2000) adopt an approach in which the signal–noise ratio in a local-level model is transformed so as to lie between zero and one. Harvey, Trimbur and van Dijk (2003) use non-informative priors on variances together with informative priors on the frequency and damping factor parameters in the stochastic cycle.

27.4 Continuous time and irregular spacing

Now suppose observations are generated by a stochastic trend model, but are observed every δ time periods, where δ is an integer. For a stock variable, this leads to a model for the observations in which the level and slope disturbances are correlated. For variables observed as a flow, that is aggregated over the δ time periods, the level, slope and irregular disturbances are all correlated with each other; see Harvey (1989, pp. 309–26). The implications are best explored by working with models set up in continuous time. If the observations are irregularly spaced, δ need no longer be an integer.

27.4.1 Stochastic trends in continuous time

The local-level component, $\mu(t)$, is defined by $d\mu(t) = \sigma_\eta dW_\eta(t)$, where $W_\eta(t)$ is a standard Wiener process. Thus the increment $d\mu(t)$ has mean zero and variance $\sigma_\eta^2 dt$.

The linear trend component is

$$\begin{bmatrix} d\mu(t) \\ d\beta(t) \end{bmatrix} = \begin{bmatrix} 0 & 1 \\ 0 & 0 \end{bmatrix} \begin{bmatrix} \mu(t)dt \\ \beta(t)dt \end{bmatrix} + \begin{bmatrix} \sigma_\eta dW_\eta(t) \\ \sigma_\zeta dW_\zeta(t) \end{bmatrix} \tag{27.4.1}$$

where $W_\eta(t)$ and $W_\zeta(t)$ are mutually independent Wiener processes.

We suppose that observations, $y_\tau, \tau = 1, \ldots, T$, are made at intervals δ apart. Let t_τ denote the time at which the τth observation is made and let μ_τ and β_τ denote $\mu(t_\tau)$ and $\beta(t_\tau)$ respectively.

27.4.2 Stocks

For the local-level model it follows almost immediately that

$$\mu_\tau = \mu_{\tau-1} + \eta_\tau, \quad Var(\eta_\tau) = \delta\sigma_\eta^2 \tag{27.4.2}$$

since

$$\eta_\tau = \mu(t_\tau) - \mu(t_{\tau-1}) = \sigma_\eta \int_{t_{\tau-1}}^{t_\tau} dW_\eta(t) = \sigma_\eta(W_\eta(t_\tau) - W_\eta(t_{\tau-1})).$$

The discrete model is therefore a random walk for equally spaced observations. If the observation at time τ is made up of $\mu(t_\tau)$ plus a white noise disturbance term, ε_τ, uncorrelated with η_τ in all time periods, the discrete time measurement equation can be written

$$y_\tau = \mu_\tau + \varepsilon_\tau, \quad Var(\varepsilon_\tau) = \sigma_\varepsilon^2, \quad \tau = 1, \ldots, T \tag{27.4.3}$$

and the set-up corresponds exactly to the familiar random walk plus noise model with signal–noise ratio $q_\delta = \delta\sigma_\eta^2/\sigma_\varepsilon^2 = \delta q$.

The local linear trend model may be handled in similar fashion. When $\sigma_\eta^2 = 0$, signal extraction yields a cubic spline; see Wecker and Ansley (1983).

27.4.3 Flows

For a flow, the irregular is assumed to be aggregated over the observation interval in the same way as the trend. Thus

$$y_\tau = \int_{t_{\tau-1}}^{t_\tau} \mu(t)dt + \sigma_\varepsilon \int_{t_{\tau-1}}^{t_\tau} dW_\varepsilon(t)$$

where $W_\varepsilon(t)$ is a Wiener process, independent of $W_\eta(t)$.

If the level is redefined as $\mu_\tau^* = \delta\mu(t_{\tau-1})$, it follows from (9.3.15) of Harvey (1989, p. 495) that the local-level model can be cast in the standard future state form

$$y_\tau = \mu_\tau^* + \varepsilon_\tau^*$$
$$\mu_{\tau+1}^* = \mu_\tau^* + \eta_\tau^* \qquad (27.4.4)$$

with covariance matrix

$$Var\begin{bmatrix} \eta_\tau^* \\ \varepsilon_\tau^* \end{bmatrix} = \begin{bmatrix} \delta^3 \sigma_\eta^2 & \frac{1}{2}\delta^3 \sigma_\eta^2 \\ \frac{1}{2}\delta^3 \sigma_\eta^2 & \frac{1}{3}\delta^3 \sigma_\eta^2 + \delta\sigma_\varepsilon^2 \end{bmatrix}.$$

A similar formulation is possible for the local linear trend.

Signal extraction can be carried out by setting up a state space model in which the state vector is augmented by a cumulator variable as described in Harvey (1989, ch. 9). Chambers and McGarry (2002, p. 396) show that the continuous time flow model can be represented by a state space model in which the disturbance driving the level is an MA(1) process with variance $2\delta^3\sigma_\eta^2/3$ and first-order autocovariance $\delta^3\sigma_\eta^2/6$. Thus

$$\mu_t = \mu_{t-1} + \eta_t + \theta^\dagger \eta_{t-1}, \qquad \eta_t \sim NID(0, \sigma_\eta^2) \qquad (27.4.5)$$

with $\theta^\dagger = 0.268$. The canonical decomposition of Pierce (1979) and Tiao and Hillmer (1978) yields (27.4.5) with $\theta^\dagger = 1$ when applied to an ARIMA(0,1,1) model.

27.4.4 Irregular spacing

The SSF can be adapted to handle irregular spacing in UC models; see Harvey (1989, ch. 9). This is particularly straightforward for STMs. An important case is the continuous time local linear trend model based on (27.4.1), with $\sigma_\eta = 0$, for which the implied discrete time model is a variant of (27.18) in which, with τ replacing t,

$$Var(\eta_\tau) = \sigma_\zeta^2 q \delta_\tau^3/3, \qquad Var(\zeta_\tau) = \sigma_\zeta^2 q \delta_\tau, \qquad E(\eta_\tau \zeta_\tau) = \sigma_\zeta^2 q \delta_\tau^2/2, \qquad (27.4.6)$$

where $q = \sigma_\zeta^2/\sigma_\varepsilon^2$ and δ_τ is the time between observations at times t_τ and $t_{\tau-1}$. As noted earlier, this is equivalent to a cubic spline. The fact that irregularly spaced data may be handled means that the model can be used to fit a nonlinear function to cross-sectional data. Setting up a UC model for a cubic spline enables the smoothness parameter to be estimated by maximum likelihood and the spline to be computed by a smoothing algorithm. The model can easily be extended, for example to include other components, and it can be compared with alternative models using standard statistical criteria. Harvey and Koopman (2000) apply this method to an example in Green and Silverman (1994) and find that the implied weighting pattern is *not* symmetric. This is in contrast to the nonparametric approach where the weighting pattern is symmetric in that observations which are at the same "distance" from the time point in question receive the same weight. The reason the optimal weights, obtained from the model, are not symmetric is that the number of data points observed around a particular observation is taken into account. An observation at a time point where relatively many observations are concentrated receives relatively less weight because it has less impact.

It is curious that the cubic spline-fitting methodology, as expounded in Green and Silverman (1994) and elsewhere, makes little or no reference to the time series literature.

27.5   Nonlinear and non-Gaussian models

Nonlinearities can be introduced into state space models in a variety of ways. A general formulation is laid out in the first subsection below, but more tractable classes of models are obtained by focusing on different sources of nonlinearity. In the first place, the time-variation in the system matrices may be endogenous. This opens up a wide range of possibilities for modeling, with the stochastic system matrices incorporating *feedback* in that they depend on past observations. The Kalman filter can still be applied when the models are conditionally Gaussian. A second source of nonlinearity arises in an obvious way when the measurement and/or transition equations have a *nonlinear functional form*. Finally, the model may be *non-Gaussian*. The state space system may still be linear as, for example, when the measurement equation has disturbances generated by a *t*-distribution. More fundamentally, nonnormality may be intrinsic to the data. Thus the observations may be count data, in which the number of events occurring in each time period is recorded. A more extreme example is when the data are dichotomous and can take one of only two values, zero and one. The structural approach to time series model-building attempts to take such data characteristics into account and a brief account of how this is done is given in subsection 27.5.2. The robust treatment of outliers and structural breaks by heavy-tailed distributions is described in subsection 27.5.3.

In recent years the availability of cheap computational power has triggered a proliferation of simulation-based methods to obtain filtering and smoothing densities in situations where analytical solutions cannot be found. These include MCMC and importance sampling; recent examples can be found in Stroud *et al.* (2003), Eraker (2001) and Durbin and Koopman (2000). Section 27.5.4 is devoted to one of the most recent and successful techniques, particle filtering.

27.5.1   General nonlinear state space model

The general formulation of a state space model is specified by the distribution of the observations conditional on the current state and past observations, that is

$$p(\mathbf{y}_t|\boldsymbol{\alpha}_t, \mathbf{Y}_{t-1}), \tag{27.5.1}$$

where $\mathbf{Y}_{t-1} = \{\mathbf{y}_{t-1}, \mathbf{y}_{t-2}, \ldots\}$, the distribution of the current state conditional on the previous state and observations, that is

$$p(\boldsymbol{\alpha}_t|\boldsymbol{\alpha}_{t-1}, \mathbf{Y}_{t-1}) \tag{27.5.2}$$

and the initial distribution of the state, $p(\boldsymbol{\alpha}_0)$. In a Gaussian model (27.5.1) and (27.5.2) are specified by the measurement and transition equations.

Filtering requires us to derive a recursion for $p(\boldsymbol{\alpha}_t|\mathbf{Y}_t)$, the distribution of the state vector conditional on the information at time t. Suppose this is given at time t-1. The distribution of $\boldsymbol{\alpha}_t$ conditional on $\mathbf{Y}_{t-1}$ is

$$p(\boldsymbol{\alpha}_t|\mathbf{Y}_{t-1}) = \int p(\boldsymbol{\alpha}_t, \boldsymbol{\alpha}_{t-1}|\mathbf{Y}_{t-1})d\boldsymbol{\alpha}_{t-1}$$

but the right-hand side may be rearranged as

$$p(\boldsymbol{\alpha}_t|\mathbf{Y}_{t-1}) = \int p(\boldsymbol{\alpha}_t|\boldsymbol{\alpha}_{t-1}, \mathbf{Y}_{t-1})p(\boldsymbol{\alpha}_{t-1}|\mathbf{Y}_{t-1})d\boldsymbol{\alpha}_{t-1}. \qquad (27.5.3)$$

The conditional distribution $p(\boldsymbol{\alpha}_t|\boldsymbol{\alpha}_{t-1})$ is given by the specification of the transition equation and so $p(\boldsymbol{\alpha}_t|\mathbf{Y}_{t-1})$ may, in principle, be obtained from $p(\boldsymbol{\alpha}_{t-1}|\mathbf{Y}_{t-1})$. In the case of a linear Gaussian model, these conditional distributions are characterized by their first two moments and the operation implied by (27.5.3) is carried out by means of the Kalman filter prediction equations.

As regards updating,

$$\begin{aligned} p(\boldsymbol{\alpha}_t|\mathbf{Y}_t) &= p(\boldsymbol{\alpha}_t|\mathbf{y}_t, \mathbf{Y}_{t-1}) = p(\boldsymbol{\alpha}_t, \mathbf{y}_t|\mathbf{Y}_{t-1})/p(\mathbf{y}_t|\mathbf{Y}_{t-1}) \\ &= p(\mathbf{y}_t|\boldsymbol{\alpha}_t, \mathbf{Y}_{t-1})p(\boldsymbol{\alpha}_t|\mathbf{Y}_{t-1})/p(\mathbf{y}_t|\mathbf{Y}_{t-1}) \end{aligned} \qquad (27.5.4)$$

where

$$p(\mathbf{y}_t|\mathbf{Y}_{t-1}) = \int p(\mathbf{y}_t|\boldsymbol{\alpha}_t, \mathbf{Y}_{t-1})p(\boldsymbol{\alpha}_t|\mathbf{Y}_{t-1})d\boldsymbol{\alpha}_t \qquad (27.5.5)$$

and $p(\mathbf{y}_t|\boldsymbol{\alpha}_t)$ is given from the assumed distribution of the measurement equation disturbance term, $\boldsymbol{\varepsilon}_t$. The likelihood function may be constructed as the product of the predictive distributions (27.5.5), as in (27.3.14).

On noting that

$$\begin{aligned} p(\boldsymbol{\alpha}_t, \boldsymbol{\alpha}_{t+1}|\mathbf{Y}_T) &= p(\boldsymbol{\alpha}_{t+1}|\mathbf{Y}_T)p(\boldsymbol{\alpha}_t|\boldsymbol{\alpha}_{t+1}, \mathbf{Y}_T) \\ &= p(\boldsymbol{\alpha}_{t+1}|\mathbf{Y}_T)p(\boldsymbol{\alpha}_t|\boldsymbol{\alpha}_{t+1}, \mathbf{Y}_t) \\ &= p(\boldsymbol{\alpha}_{t+1}|\mathbf{Y}_T)p(\boldsymbol{\alpha}_t, \boldsymbol{\alpha}_{t+1}|\mathbf{Y}_t)/p(\boldsymbol{\alpha}_{t+1}|\mathbf{Y}_t) \\ &= p(\boldsymbol{\alpha}_{t+1}|\mathbf{Y}_T)p(\boldsymbol{\alpha}_{t+1}|\boldsymbol{\alpha}_t)p(\boldsymbol{\alpha}_t|\mathbf{Y}_t)/p(\boldsymbol{\alpha}_{t+1}|\mathbf{Y}_t) \end{aligned}$$

the formula for smoothing is

$$\begin{aligned} p(\boldsymbol{\alpha}_t|\mathbf{Y}_T) &= \int p(\boldsymbol{\alpha}_t, \boldsymbol{\alpha}_{t+1}|\mathbf{Y}_T)d\boldsymbol{\alpha}_{t+1} \\ &= p(\boldsymbol{\alpha}_t|\mathbf{Y}_t)\int [p(\boldsymbol{\alpha}_{t+1}|\mathbf{Y}_T)p(\boldsymbol{\alpha}_{t+1}|\boldsymbol{\alpha}_t)/p(\boldsymbol{\alpha}_{t+1}|\mathbf{Y}_t)]d\boldsymbol{\alpha}_{t+1}. \end{aligned} \qquad (27.5.6)$$

In the linear Gaussian case, this is equivalent to the fixed-interval smoothing algorithm.

Point estimates may be obtained from the relevant conditional distributions. Thus the conditional mean

$$E(\alpha_t|\mathbf{Y}_T) = \int \alpha_t \, p(\alpha_t|\mathbf{Y}_T) d\alpha_t$$

is the MMSE of α_t. Other point estimates may be constructed. In particular, the maximum *a posteriori* estimate is the mode of the relevant conditional distribution. However, once we move away from normality, there is a case for using the whole conditional distribution.

The general filtering and smoothing expressions may be difficult to solve analytically. Linear Gaussian models are an obvious exception and tractable solutions are possible in a number of other cases. Where an analytic solution is not available, Kitagawa (1987) has suggested using numerical methods to evaluate the various densities. The main drawback with this approach is the computational requirement: this can be considerable if a reasonable degree of accuracy is to be achieved.

27.5.2   Count data and qualitative observations

Count data models are usually based on distributions such as the Poisson or negative binomial. If the means of these distributions are constant, or can be modeled in terms of observable variables, then estimation is relatively easy. The essence of a time series model, however, is that the mean of a series cannot be modeled in terms of observable variables and so has to be captured by some stochastic mechanism. The structural approach explicitly takes into account the notion that there may be two sources of randomness, one affecting the underlying level and the other coming from the distribution of the observations around that level. Thus one can consider setting up a model in which the distribution of an observation conditional on the mean is Poisson or negative binomial, while the mean itself evolves as a stochastic process that is always positive. The same ideas can be used to handle qualitative variables.

There are a number of ways of proceeding. Here we focus on the exponential family with explicit transition equations. The exponential family of distributions contains many of the distributions used for modeling count and quantitative data. For a multivariate series

$$p(\mathbf{y}_t|\boldsymbol{\theta}_t) = \exp\{\mathbf{y}_t'\boldsymbol{\theta}_t - b_t(\boldsymbol{\theta}_t) + c(\mathbf{y}_t)\}, \quad t = 1, \ldots, T$$

where $\boldsymbol{\theta}_t$ is an $N \times 1$ vector of "signals," $b_t(\boldsymbol{\theta}_t)$ is a twice-differentiable function of $\boldsymbol{\theta}_t$ and $c(\mathbf{y}_t)$ is a function of $\mathbf{y}_t$ only. The $\boldsymbol{\theta}_t$ vector is related to the mean of the distribution by a link function. For example, when the observations are supposed to come from a univariate Poisson distribution with mean λ_t, we set $\exp(\theta_t) = \lambda_t$. By letting $\boldsymbol{\theta}_t$ depend on a state vector that changes over time, it is possible to allow the distribution of the observations to depend on stochastic components other than the level. The simplest option is to let $\boldsymbol{\theta}_t = \mathbf{Z}_t\boldsymbol{\alpha}_t$ and have $\boldsymbol{\alpha}_t$ generated by a linear transition equation. Explanatory variables could also be included.

The statistical treatment is by simulation methods. Carter and Kohn (1996) and Shephard and Pitt (1997) base their approach on MCMC, while Durbin and Koopman (2001) use importance sampling and antithetic variables. Both techniques can also be applied in a Bayesian framework. A full discussion can be found in Durbin and Koopman (2001).

27.5.3 Heavy-tailed distributions and robustness

Simulation techniques of the kind alluded to in the previous subsection are relatively easy to use when the measurement and transition equations are linear but the disturbances are non-Gaussian. Allowing the disturbances to have heavy-tailed distributions provides a robust method of dealing with outliers and structural breaks.

27.5.3.1 Outliers

If the disturbance term in the measurement equation has a heavy-tailed distribution, such as Student's *t*, observations that would be very unlikely to occur with a Gaussian distribution are no longer seen as outliers and the model responds in an appropriate way. This robust approach is to be contrasted with one where the aim is to try to detect outliers and then to remove them by treating them as missing or modeling them by an intervention. Proceeding in this way effectively says that outliers contain no useful information and this is rarely the case except, perhaps, when an observation has been recorded incorrectly.

An example is given in Durbin and Koopman (2001, pp. 233–5) based on a series for gas consumption in the UK. Estimating a Gaussian model made up of trend, seasonal and irregular components produces a rather unappealing wobble in the seasonal component at the time North Sea gas was introduced in 1970. Allowing the irregular to follow a *t*-distribution produces a more satisfactory seasonal pattern around that time.

Another example of the application of robust methods is the seasonal adjustment paper of Bruce and Jurke (1996).

27.5.3.2 Structural breaks

The argument for modeling breaks by dummy variables is at its most extreme in the advocacy of piecewise linear trends, that is, deterministic trends subject to changes in slope. This is to be contrasted with a stochastic trend where there are small random breaks at all points in time. Of course, stochastic trends can easily be combined with deterministic structural breaks. However, if the presence and location of potential breaks not known beforehand, there is a strong argument for using heavy-tailed distributions in the transition equation to accommodate them. Such breaks are not deterministic and their size is a matter of degree rather than kind. From the forecasting point of view this makes much more sense: a future break is virtually never deterministic – indeed, the idea that we might know its location and size in advance is rather optimistic. A robust model, on the other hand, takes account of the possibility of future breaks in its computation of MSEs and in the way it adapts to new observations.

27.5.4   Particle filtering

The particle filter is able to overcome one of the difficulties with standard MCMC, which is that convergence of the chain to its target distribution can be very slow when there is a high degree of nonlinearity and/or nonnormality. The idea is to approximate the filtering and smoothing densities by discrete distributions whose support is made up of points drawn recursively from a suitable density. In many cases this approach yields very flexible and computationally efficient algorithms that, combining importance sampling and resampling steps, approximate the target densities recursively. A survey of the literature can be found in Doucet *et al.* (2001). The aim of this subsection is to give a brief account of the methodology and describe some applications in economics and finance.

27.5.4.1   *Monte Carlo filter and smoother*

This subsection describes a general Monte Carlo filter and smoother proposed by Berzuini *et al.* (1997) and Doucet *et al.* (2000). Slightly different algorithms can be found in Kitagawa (1996) and Hürzeler and Künsch (1998). The parameters in the densities $p(\mathbf{y}_t|\boldsymbol{\alpha}_t)$ and $p(\boldsymbol{\alpha}_t|\boldsymbol{\alpha}_{t-1})$ are assumed to be known, although the algorithm can be used in the context of maximum likelihood estimation, as in Hürzeler and Künsch (2001), or Bayesian estimation of fixed parameters, as in Kitagawa (1998).

Consider the general state space model characterized by the densities (27.5.1) and (27.5.2). We will also assume that an importance density $q(\boldsymbol{\alpha}_t|\boldsymbol{\alpha}_{t-1}, \mathbf{Y}_t)$ has been chosen, in such a way that it is easy to draw from and it has the same support as $p(\boldsymbol{\alpha}_t|\boldsymbol{\alpha}_{t-1}, \mathbf{Y}_t)$. The notation stresses the fact that the importance density could be a function of the observations up to and including time t.

Filter A particle filter approximates the filtering density $p(\boldsymbol{\alpha}_t|\mathbf{Y}_t)$, which is not available in closed form, by a density with discrete support, as in the example shown in Figure 27.2. Its support and probability mass are obtained recursively from the formulae (27.5.3)–(27.5.5) as follows.

Suppose an approximation to the filtering density for time $t-1$, $p(\boldsymbol{\alpha}_{t-1}|\mathbf{Y}_{t-1})$, is available: we have obtained a density with a discrete support consisting of N points $\tilde{\boldsymbol{\alpha}}_{t-1}^{(1)}, \ldots, \tilde{\boldsymbol{\alpha}}_{t-1}^{(N)}$ and N corresponding probability masses $w_{t-1|t-1}^{(1)}, \ldots, w_{t-1|t-1}^{(N)}$. Formally, this could be written

$$p(d\boldsymbol{\alpha}_{t-1}|\mathbf{Y}_{t-1}) \simeq \sum_{i=1}^{N} w_{t-1|t-1}^{(i)} \delta_{\{\tilde{\boldsymbol{\alpha}}_{t-1}^{(i)}\}}(d\boldsymbol{\alpha}_{t-1})$$

where $\delta_{\{\}}()$ is the Dirac delta function. N new values $\hat{\boldsymbol{\alpha}}_t^{(1)}, \ldots, \hat{\boldsymbol{\alpha}}_t^{(N)}$ are drawn from $q()$ using the old ones, $\tilde{\boldsymbol{\alpha}}_{t-1}^{(1)}, \ldots, \tilde{\boldsymbol{\alpha}}_{t-1}^{(N)}$, as starting points:

$$\hat{\boldsymbol{\alpha}}_t^{(i)} \sim q\left(\cdot|\hat{\boldsymbol{\alpha}}_{t-1}^{(i)}, \mathbf{Y}_t\right), \quad i = 1, \ldots, N.$$

Applying formulae (27.5.3)–(27.5.5) and marginalizing $\boldsymbol{\alpha}_{t-1}$ yields an approximation to the filtering density for time t:

$$p(d\boldsymbol{\alpha}_t|\mathbf{Y}_t) \simeq \sum_{i=1}^{N} \hat{w}_{t|t}^{(i)} \delta_{\{\hat{\boldsymbol{\alpha}}_t^{(i)}\}}(d\boldsymbol{\alpha}_t)$$

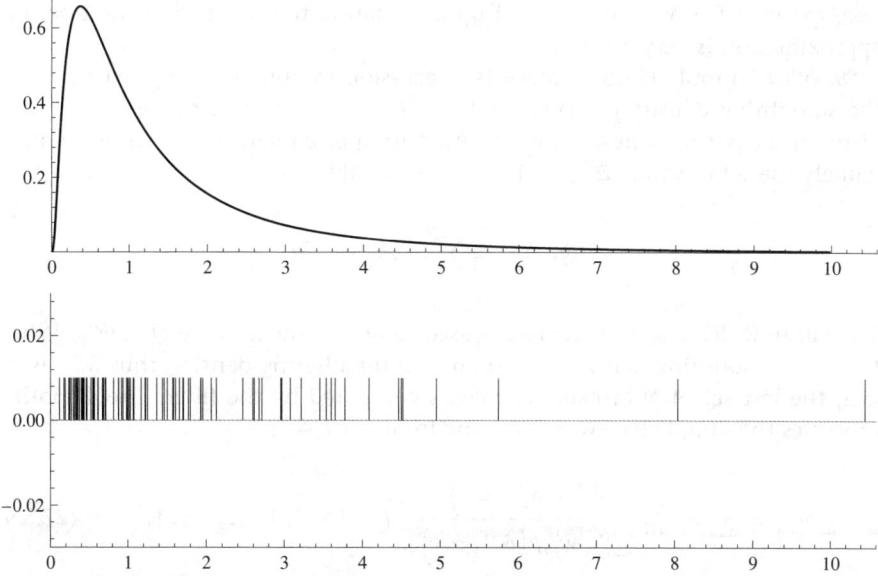

Figure 27.2 Example of true density (top) and particle approximation (bottom)

where

$$\hat{w}_{t|t}^{(i)} = \frac{\check{w}_{t|t}^{(i)}}{\sum_{i=1}^{N} \check{w}_{t|t}^{(i)}}$$ (27.5.7)

and

$$\check{w}_{t|t}^{(i)} = w_{t-1|t-1}^{(i)} \frac{p\left(\mathbf{y}_t | \hat{\boldsymbol{\alpha}}_t^{(i)}\right) p\left(\hat{\boldsymbol{\alpha}}_t^{(i)} | \tilde{\boldsymbol{\alpha}}_{t-1}^{(i)}\right)}{q\left(\hat{\boldsymbol{\alpha}}_t^{(i)} | \tilde{\boldsymbol{\alpha}}_{t-1}^{(i)}, \mathbf{y}_t\right)}.$$ (27.5.8)

In words, the filtering density is approximated by a density with discrete support consisting of the points we have drawn from q (), i.e., $\hat{\boldsymbol{\alpha}}_t^{(1)}, \ldots, \hat{\boldsymbol{\alpha}}_t^{(N)}$, with probability masses $\hat{w}_{t|t}^{(1)}, \ldots, \hat{w}_{t|t}^{(N)}$. Expression (27.5.8), the unnormalized weights, can be easily evaluated since it only depends on $p(\mathbf{y}_t | \boldsymbol{\alpha}_t), p(\boldsymbol{\alpha}_t | \boldsymbol{\alpha}_{t-1})$ and $q(\boldsymbol{\alpha}_t | \boldsymbol{\alpha}_{t-1}, \mathbf{y}_t)$. Given the unnormalized weights, it is straightforward to obtain the weights $\hat{w}_{t|t}^{(1)}, \ldots, \hat{w}_{t|t}^{(N)}$ from (27.5.7). The recursion can be initialized with a set of N draws from $q(\boldsymbol{\alpha}_1 | \mathbf{y}_1)$, say $\hat{\boldsymbol{\alpha}}_1^{(1)}, \ldots, \hat{\boldsymbol{\alpha}}_1^{(N)}$.

Once an approximation to the filtering density $p(\boldsymbol{\alpha}_t | \mathbf{y}_t)$ has been obtained, resampling is performed in order to obtain the draws $\tilde{\boldsymbol{\alpha}}_t^{(1)}, \ldots, \tilde{\boldsymbol{\alpha}}_t^{(N)}$ and weights $w_{t|t}^{(1)}, \ldots, w_{t|t}^{(N)}$ that will be used in the next recursion. The values $\tilde{\boldsymbol{\alpha}}_t^{(i)}, i = 1, \ldots, N$, are drawn (with replacement) from a discrete distribution with support $\hat{\boldsymbol{\alpha}}_t^{(1)}, \ldots, \hat{\boldsymbol{\alpha}}_t^{(N)}$ and probability masses $\hat{w}_{t|t}^{(1)}, \ldots, \hat{w}_{t|t}^{(N)}$. The corresponding weights $w_{t|t}^{(i)}, i = 1, \ldots, N$, are set equal to $1/N$. The aim of the resampling step is to avoid the degeneracy of the algorithm that typically appears after a few recursions. Without resampling, a few weights $w_{t|t}^{(i)}$ end up dominating the others and the resulting approximation is very poor.

Smoother Formula (27.5.6) suggests a recursion to obtain an approximation to the smoothing density $p(\alpha_t|Y_T), t = 1, \ldots, T$. The support of the approximating distribution is the same as the one used to approximate the filtering density, namely the set of values $\hat{\alpha}_t^{(i)}, i = 1, \ldots, N$. Formally

$$p\,(d\alpha_t|Y_T) \simeq \sum_{i=1}^{N} \hat{w}_{t|T}^{(i)} \delta_{\{\hat{\alpha}_t^{(i)}\}}(d\alpha_t).$$

We will now describe the recursions used to obtain the new weights $\hat{w}_{t|T}^{(i)}$. When $t = T$ the smoothing density corresponds to the filtering density, thus $\hat{w}_{T|T}^{(i)}$ is, in fact, the last set of N probability masses computed by the filter. The smoother processes the sample backwards starting from $t = T - 1$:

$$\hat{w}_{t|T}^{(i)} = \sum_{j=1}^{N} \hat{w}_{t+1|T}^{(j)} \frac{\hat{w}_{t|t}^{(i)} p\left(\hat{\alpha}_{t+1}^{(j)}|\hat{\alpha}_t^{(i)}\right)}{\sum_{l=1}^{N} \hat{w}_{t|t}^{(l)} p\left(\hat{\alpha}_{t+1}^{(j)}|\hat{\alpha}_t^{(l)}\right)} \qquad t = T - 1, T - 2, \ldots, 1. \qquad (27.5.9)$$

Example: The Constantinides model. We have applied the methodology described above to a simple nonlinear one-factor model of the term structure of interest rates. In the discrete state space model, the state variable follows an AR(1) process with zero mean. Call $\alpha_t, t = 1, 2, \ldots$, the position of the state at evenly spaced points in time $s = \Delta, 2\Delta, \ldots$ Then we have the transition equation

$$\alpha_t = e^{-\kappa\Delta}\alpha_{t-1} + \eta_t, \quad \eta_t \sim N\left(0, \frac{1 - e^{-2\kappa\Delta}}{2\kappa}\sigma^2\right)$$

where κ and σ are constants that represent respectively the mean reversion speed and the instantaneous standard deviation in continuous time. Under the assumptions of Constantinides (1992), observed yields can be shown to be quadratic functions of the latent factor α_t. Call $y(t, t + \tau)$ the yield to maturity at time t of a discount bond with maturity $t + \tau$. Then in equilibrium we have

$$y(t, t + \tau) = A(\tau) + B(\tau)\alpha_t + C(\tau)\alpha_t^2 \qquad (27.5.10)$$

where the functions A, B and C depend on κ, σ and τ. We have set $\kappa = 0.1, \sigma = 0.15$ and $\Delta = 0.25$ (which implies that the observations are sampled at a quarterly frequency). The model is closed by setting the long term interest rate $g = 0.06$ and the position parameter $\alpha = 0.5858.$[4] We have generated a time series of three-month yields by evaluating A, B and C in (27.5.10) and adding a normally distributed measurement error ε_t with a standard deviation of 30 basis points:

$$y_t = 0.0227 - 0.0650\alpha_t + 0.153\alpha_t^2 + \varepsilon_t, \quad \varepsilon_t \sim N(0, 0.003^2).$$

The trajectory of the state and the observations y_t are plotted in Figure 27.3.

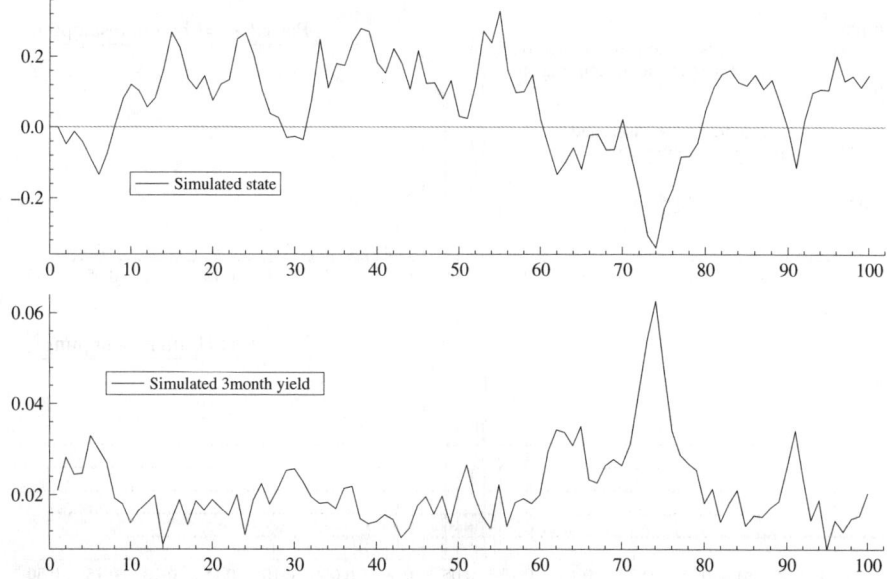

Figure 27.3 Simulated realization of the state (top) and simulated three-month interest rate (bottom) in the Constantinides model. The nonlinear measurement equation prevents interest rates from becoming negative

In order to set up a particle filter for this problem, one needs to specify an importance density. To keep the example simple, we have used the transition density $p(\alpha_t|\alpha_{t-1})$ as an importance density, thereby ignoring the information available at time t from the observation y_t. Thus $q(\alpha_t|\alpha_{t-1}, Y_t) = p(\alpha_t|\alpha_{t-1})$ and $q(\alpha_1|y_1) = p(\alpha_1)$. We have then drawn $N = 100$ values, $\hat{\alpha}_1^{(1)}, \ldots, \hat{\alpha}_1^{(N)}$, from $q(\alpha_1|y_1)$ and calculated the corresponding weights $\hat{w}_1^{(1)}, \ldots, \hat{w}_1^{(N)}$, which in this case are simply proportional to the density $p(y_1|\alpha_1)$.

We then set $w_{1|1}^{(i)} = \hat{w}_{1|1}^{(i)}$ and $\tilde{\alpha}_1^{(i)} = \hat{\alpha}_1^{(i)} \forall i$ (resampling is not performed after the first step) and started the filter recursions. For every $t = 2, \ldots, T$ and every $i = 1, \ldots, N$, we drew N times from $q(\hat{\alpha}_t^{(i)}|\tilde{\alpha}_{t-1}^{(i)}, y_t)$ and calculated new weights

$$\hat{w}_{t|t}^{(i)} \propto w_{t-1|t-1}^{(i)} p\left(y_t|\hat{\alpha}_t^{(i)}\right)$$

noting that $q(\hat{\alpha}_t^{(i)}|\tilde{\alpha}_{t-1}^{(i)}, y_t)$ and $p(\hat{\alpha}_t^{(i)}|\tilde{\alpha}_{t-1}^{(i)})$ cancel out in (27.5.8). The results for $t = 2$ are shown in Figure 27.4.

At the end of the resampling step the new weights are all equal to $1/N$. Some of the values $\hat{\alpha}_1^{(i)}$ that made up the support of the approximating density in the top panel have disappeared in the bottom panel because they have been discarded. Some others appear more than once because they have been repeatedly drawn during the resampling procedure. This is indicated by a vertical bar whose height is proportional to the number of times the same draw is obtained (i.e., $2/N$, $3/N$ and so on).

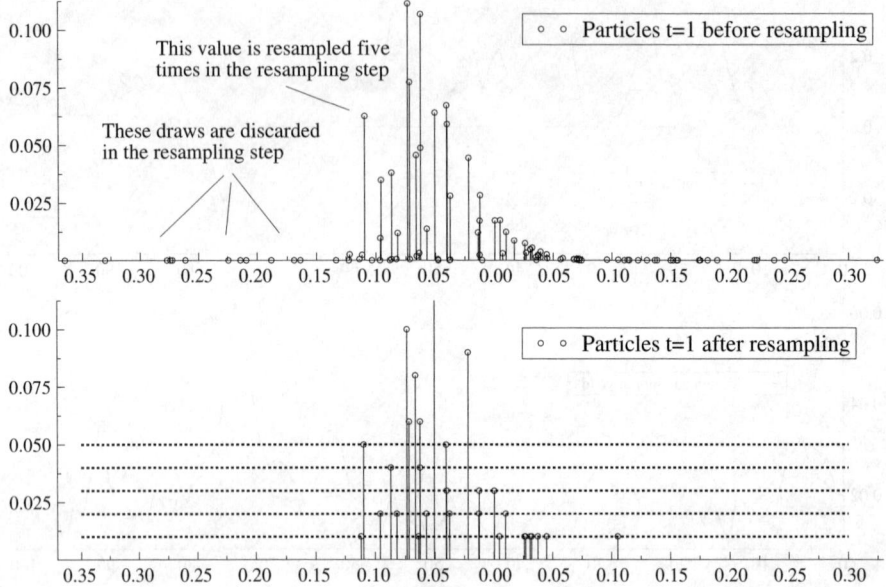

Figure 27.4 Particles before (top panel) and after (bottom panel) the resampling step

Once all the filtering recursions have been performed, it is possible to obtain estimates of the moments or quantiles of the filtering and smoothing distributions. We have estimated 15 and 85 percent quantiles for the relevant distributions. The results are shown in Figure 27.5. The signal falls almost always between the 15 and the 85 percent quantiles of the estimated filtering density. The smoothing density reconstructs the trajectory of the state much more accurately between the observations 55 and 80. Both densities show a symmetric shape between time 10 and time 55, which reflects the bimodality of the conditional state distribution.

27.5.4.2   Properties and extensions

Properties   It is worth noting that the approximating distributions obtained through the filter and smoother in the previous section *do not* converge pointwise to the true filtering and smoothing densities, i.e., $p(\alpha_t|Y_t)$ and $p(\alpha_t|Y_T)$. Derivations of asymptotic distributions and proofs of consistency for the Monte Carlo filter in the existing literature refer to the expected value of an arbitrary function $g()$ of the state α. Berzuini *et al.* (1997) show that, under regularity conditions,

$$\frac{1}{N}\sum_{i=1}^{N} g\left(\tilde{\alpha}_t^{(i)}\right) w_{t|t}^{(i)} \xrightarrow{P} \int g(\alpha_t)p(\alpha_t|Y_t)d\alpha_t \qquad (27.5.11)$$

and

$$\frac{1}{N}\sum_{i=1}^{N} g\left(\tilde{\alpha}_t^{(i)}\right) w_{t|T}^{(i)} \xrightarrow{P} \int g(\alpha_t)p(\alpha_t|Y_T)d\alpha_t. \qquad (27.5.12)$$

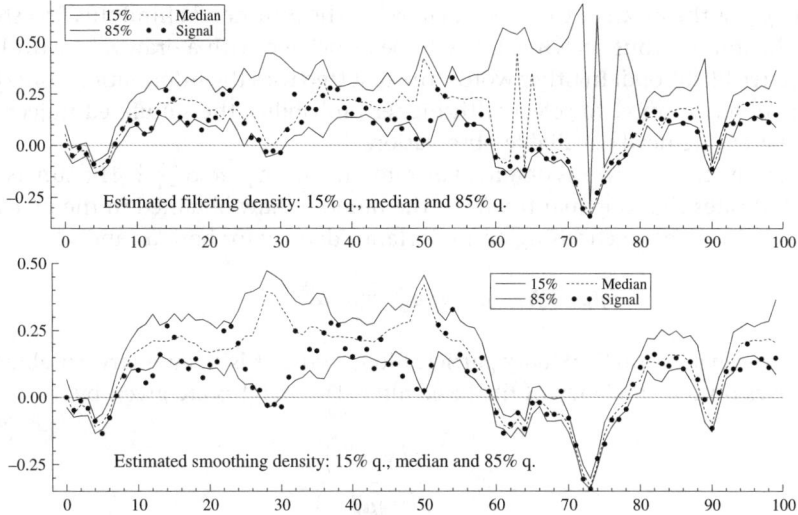

Figure 27.5 Estimated 15, 50, and 85 percent quantiles, filtering (top) and smoothing distribution (bottom), plotted against the state trajectory

Obvious special cases of the above results are $g(\alpha_t) = \alpha_t$, which gives the quantities referred to as *the* filter and *the* smoother in sections 27.3.1 and 27.3.5, and $g(\alpha_t) = 1(\alpha_t \leq z)$, which gives $\Pr(\alpha_t \leq z)$ and can be used to estimate quantiles of the filtering and smoothing distributions. The elegant measure-theoretical approach set forth by Crisan (2001) can be used to obtain proofs for more sophisticated versions of the filtering algorithm; see, for example, Godsill *et al.* (2004).

The crucial issue for obtaining good approximations by means of the Monte Carlo filter is the choice of the importance density q. In fact, while the convergence results (27.5.11)–(27.5.12) can be established under fairly weak conditions, it turns out that only if the importance density is carefully chosen will the estimator have good properties in terms of rate of convergence. A good strategy involves choosing the conditional importance density as similar as possible to the true conditional density $p(\boldsymbol{\alpha}|\mathbf{y})$; see Durbin and Koopman (2000), Doucet *et al.* (2000). Clearly, if we knew $p(\boldsymbol{\alpha}|\mathbf{y})$ the likelihood could simply be obtained as $p(\mathbf{y}) = p(\mathbf{y}, \boldsymbol{\alpha})/p(\boldsymbol{\alpha}|\mathbf{y})$ at any point $\boldsymbol{\alpha}$ and no simulation would be needed.

The auxiliary particle filter   Among the many strategies proposed in the literature to improve on the efficiency of the simple Monte Carlo filter, the auxiliary particle filter of Pitt and Shephard (1999) is often regarded as the most successful.[5] Their algorithm differs from the one described in the previous section in that draws from the importance density, $\hat{\boldsymbol{\alpha}}_t^{(i)}, i = 1, \ldots, N$, are obtained for each recursion as the result of a two-stage procedure. Firstly, an index $k \in \{1, \ldots, N\}$ is drawn from a multinomial distribution with probabilities

$$\Pr(k = n) \propto w_{t-1|t-1}^{(n)} p\left(\mathbf{y}_t | \boldsymbol{\alpha}_t = \boldsymbol{\mu}_t^{(n)}\right)$$

where $\mu_t^{(k)}$ is the mean or the mode of $\alpha_t|\alpha_{t-1}^{(k)}$. The intuition behind this first step is that the index k thus drawn is likely to be associated with a draw $\alpha_{t-1}^{(k)}$ with large predictive likelihood. In other words, the first step uses the information contained in the observation $\mathbf{y}_t$ to select with higher probability the simulated trajectories that match the newly available observation.

Secondly, the draw $\hat{\alpha}_t^{(i)}$ is obtained by sampling from $p\left(\alpha_t|\alpha_{t-1}^{(k^{(i)})}\right)$. The superscript on k indicates that the quantity $k^{(i)}$ is the random draw obtained in the first step. This is equivalent to choosing an importance density for both α_t and k:

$$q(\alpha_t, k|\mathbf{Y}_t) \propto p(\mathbf{y}_t|\mu_t^{(k)})p(\alpha_t|\alpha_{t-1}^{(k)})w_{t-1|t-1}^{(k)}.$$

Hence the expression "auxiliary particle filter," where k is an auxiliary variable that improves on the efficiency of the basic filter. The weights are given by

$$\hat{w}_{t|t}^{(i)} \propto \frac{p\left(\mathbf{y}_t|\hat{\alpha}_t^{(i)}\right)}{p\left(\mathbf{y}_t|\mu_t^{(k^{(i)})}\right)}.$$

Once the draws and the corresponding weights have been obtained, resampling is performed.

Extensions of the algorithm include the use of rejection sampling instead of importance sampling and the introduction of MCMC moves. The method has been applied to the estimation of an ARCH(1) plus noise model and a stochastic volatility model in Pitt and Shephard (1999). For the latter model, Pitt and Shephard show how to specify $q(\alpha_t, k|\mathbf{Y}_t)$ based on a first-order expansion of $p(\mathbf{y}_t|\alpha_t)$ and improve the efficiency of the algorithm further. Smith and Santos (2003) propose an alternative choice of $q(\alpha_t, k|\mathbf{Y}_t)$ based on a second-order Taylor expansion.

Smoothing algorithms   The main drawbacks of the smoothing algorithm presented in the previous section are its large computational complexity and the focus on the marginal smoothing density only. Firstly, to evaluate expression (27.5.9) one needs to perform a number of operations of order TN^2, which becomes unfeasible if N is large. Secondly, the smoothing algorithm is designed to approximate $p(\alpha_t|\mathbf{Y}_T)$, but in many applications we may be interested in the joint density of the values of the state at several points in time, for example, $p(\alpha_t, \ldots, \alpha_{t+h}|\mathbf{Y}_T)$. A natural solution to the latter problem can be found by keeping track of the whole trajectory $\alpha_1^{(i)}, \ldots, \alpha_T^{(i)}$ in the filtering procedure, so that for each i the trajectory $\alpha_1^{(i)}, \ldots, \alpha_T^{(i)}$ (referred to as *particle i*) may be viewed as a draw from $p(\alpha_1, \ldots, \alpha_T|\mathbf{Y}_T)$. To this end, the resampling step must be interpreted as a procedure that resamples the whole particle, rather than a single value for α_t.

Formally, the resampling step described above is substituted by the following: for $i = 1, \ldots, N$, draw an index $j(i)$ from a multinomial with probabilities $\hat{w}_{t|t}^{(1)}, \ldots, \hat{w}_{t|t}^{(N)}$ and set $\left(\tilde{\alpha}_1^{(i)}, \ldots, \tilde{\alpha}_T^{(i)}\right) = \left(\hat{\alpha}_1^{(j)}, \ldots, \hat{\alpha}_T^{(j)}\right)$. However, in the initial portion of the sample this approximation is typically very poor, because the resampling steps tend to generate sample impoverishment. In other words, the initial parts of the trajectories will, in many cases, be equal across different particles i because those with higher weights are selected more often. Thus the idea of marginalizing the approximated joint smoothing density of the whole trajectory (given by $\left(\tilde{\boldsymbol{\alpha}}_1^{(i)}, \ldots, \tilde{\boldsymbol{\alpha}}_T^{(i)}\right), i = 1, \ldots, N$, with weights $1/N$) to find the joint smoothing density for a given set of points in time is not viable.

A simple smoothing algorithm based on a refinement of this idea has been proposed by Kitagawa (1998) and Kitagawa and Sato (2001), who use the fixed-lag smoother as an approximation to the fixed interval smoother. For a fixed arbitrary integer L, they first obtain an approximation to the joint filtering distribution $p(\boldsymbol{\alpha}_1, \ldots, \boldsymbol{\alpha}_{t+L}|\mathbf{Y}_{t+L})$ of the form

$$p(d(\boldsymbol{\alpha}_1, \ldots, \boldsymbol{\alpha}_{t+L})|\mathbf{Y}_{t+L}) \simeq \sum_{i=1}^{N} w_{t+L|t+L}^{(i)} \delta_{\{\tilde{\boldsymbol{\alpha}}_1^{(i)}, \ldots, \tilde{\boldsymbol{\alpha}}_{t+L}^{(i)}\}} (d(\boldsymbol{\alpha}_1, \ldots, \boldsymbol{\alpha}_{t+L})).$$

Then an approximation to the marginal fixed-lag smoothing density is obtained by marginalization, i.e., it is taken to be

$$p(d\boldsymbol{\alpha}_t|\mathbf{Y}_{t+L}) \simeq \sum_{i=1}^{N} w_{t+L|t+L}^{(i)} \delta_{\{\tilde{\boldsymbol{\alpha}}_t^{(i)}\}} (d\boldsymbol{\alpha}_t).$$

Kitagawa and Sato argue that, since the first few observations ($\mathbf{y}_{t+1}, \mathbf{y}_{t+2}$ and so on) arriving after time t have a predominant effect on the density $p(\boldsymbol{\alpha}_t|\mathbf{Y}_T)$, if L is carefully chosen, then the above density approximates well the fixed interval smoothing density $p(\boldsymbol{\alpha}_t|\mathbf{Y}_T)$. This approach is much less computationally demanding than the one described in the previous section. Applications to nonlinear seasonality modeling and stochastic volatility are presented in Kitagawa (1998) and Kitagawa and Sato (2001) respectively.

The task of obtaining draws from $p(\boldsymbol{\alpha}_1, \ldots, \boldsymbol{\alpha}_T|\mathbf{Y}_T)$ that avoid the lack of diversity in the initial part of the simulated trajectories is undertaken by Godsill et al. (2004). They start with the trajectories obtained through the filter, $\left(\tilde{\boldsymbol{\alpha}}_1^{(i)}, \ldots, \tilde{\boldsymbol{\alpha}}_T^{(i)}\right), i = 1, \ldots,$ N, and perform backward simulation. An index j is drawn from a multinomial distribution with probabilities $w_{T|T}^{(1)}, \ldots, w_{T|T}^{(N)}$. Then $\dot{\boldsymbol{\alpha}}_T$ is set equal to $\tilde{\boldsymbol{\alpha}}_T^{(j)}$. Going backward, from $t = T - 1$ to 1, new weights $w_{t|t+1}^{(i)}, i = 1, \ldots, N$, are calculated as

$$w_{t|t+1}^{(i)} \propto w_t^{(i)} p(\dot{\boldsymbol{\alpha}}_{t+1}|\boldsymbol{\alpha}_t^{(i)}).$$

An index j is drawn from a multinomial distribution with probabilities $w_{t|t+1}^{(1)}, \ldots, w_{t|t+1}^{(N)}$. Then $\dot{\boldsymbol{\alpha}}_t$ is set equal to $\tilde{\boldsymbol{\alpha}}_t^{(j)}$. The trajectory $(\dot{\boldsymbol{\alpha}}_1, \ldots, \dot{\boldsymbol{\alpha}}_T)$ is an approximate draw from $p(\boldsymbol{\alpha}_1, \ldots, \boldsymbol{\alpha}_T|\mathbf{Y}_T)$.

This algorithm can be used repeatedly to draw independently from the joint smoothing distribution $p(\boldsymbol{\alpha}_1, \ldots, \boldsymbol{\alpha}_T|\mathbf{Y}_T)$. Since it does not suffer from the sample impoverishment that characterizes the other procedures described here, it can be used to find marginal smoothing densities or joint smoothing densities of only a few points in time by marginalization. For example, if one is interested in the joint density of the values of the state at two subsequent points in time t and $t + 1$, one can draw a large number R of trajectories $\left(\dot{\boldsymbol{\alpha}}_1^{(1)}, \ldots, \dot{\boldsymbol{\alpha}}_T^{(1)}\right), \ldots, \left(\dot{\boldsymbol{\alpha}}_1^{(R)}, \ldots, \dot{\boldsymbol{\alpha}}_T^{(R)}\right)$ and use

$$p(d(\boldsymbol{\alpha}_t, \boldsymbol{\alpha}_{t+1})|\mathbf{Y}_T) \simeq \frac{1}{R} \sum_{i=1}^{R} \delta_{\{\dot{\boldsymbol{\alpha}}_t^{(i)}, \dot{\boldsymbol{\alpha}}_{t+1}^{(i)}\}} (d(\boldsymbol{\alpha}_t, \boldsymbol{\alpha}_{t+1})).$$

It is worth noting that the computational complexity per realization of the algorithm grows with NT, a considerable improvement on the Monte Carlo smoother described in the previous section.

27.6 Conclusion

The smoothing weights for a stationary UC model may be obtained by the Wiener–Kolmogorov formulae. These formulae may also be adapted for use when unit roots are present and the resulting expressions often give an interesting insight into the nature of signal extraction. The state space approach, however, is more general, since it applies to models that are not time invariant and, as Burridge and Wallis (1988) point out, it offers a more satisfactory treatment of the theory underlying signal extraction in nonstationary models. The smoothing recursions yield the estimates at all points in time together with their MSEs and so there seems to be no case for basing computations on a Wiener-Kolmogorov approach. If the state space signal extraction weights are to be made explicit, then this is easily done using the algorithm in Koopman and Harvey (2003).

Continuous time state space models allow irregularly spaced observations to be handled. They also provide the basis for fitting cubic splines to cross-sectional data. Recent work on signal extraction in nonlinear models has focused on the development of particle filtering. This appears to offer a viable simulation based approach in many situations.

Notes

1. See, for example, Harvey (1989, p. 165) or Durbin and Koopman (2001, p. 37).
2. Whittle (1983, p. 12) writes "Our arguments so often concern real γ_j, and z on $|z| = 1$, that we are scarcely guilty of inconsistency if we use ... $|\gamma(z)|^2$ to denote $\gamma(z)\gamma(z^{-1})$."
3. These should be distinguished from the covariance matrices of the estimation error; see Durbin and Koopman (2001, pp. 20, 76).
4. These parameters only affect the measurement equation; their role is described in Constantinides (1992).
5. See, for example, Godsill *et al.* (2004), Liu and West (2001) and Smith and Santos (2003).

References

Anderson, B.D.O. and J.B. Moore (1979) *Optimal Filtering*. Englewood Cliffs, NJ: Prentice-Hall.
Ansley, C.F. and R. Kohn (1986) Prediction mean square error for state space models with estimated parameters. *Biometrika* **73**, 467–74.
Bell, W.R. (1984) Signal extraction for nonstationary time series. *Annals of Statistics* **12**, 646–64.

Berzuini, C., N.G. Best, W. Gilks and C. Larizza (1997) Dynamic conditional independence models and Markov chain Monte Carlo methods. *Journal of the American Statistical Association* 92, 1403–1412.

Bruce, A.G. and S.R. Jurke (1996) Non-Gaussian seasonal adjustment: X-12–ARIMA versus robust structural models. *Journal of Forecasting* 15, 305–28.

Burridge, P. and K.F. Wallis (1988) Prediction theory for autoregressive-moving average processes. *Econometric Reviews* 7, 65–9.

Carter, C.K. and R. Kohn (1996) Markov chain Monte Carlo in conditionally Gaussian state space models. *Biometrika* 83, 589–601.

Chambers, M.J. and J. McGarry (2002) Modeling cyclical behaviour with differential-difference equations in an unobserved components framework. *Econometric Theory* 18, 387–419.

Chatfield, C., A.B. Koehler, J.K. Ord and R.D. Snyder (2001) A new look at models for exponential smoothing. *The Statistician* 50, 147–59.

Constantinides, G.M. (1992) A theory of the nominal term structure of interest rates. *Review of Financial Studies* 5, 531–52.

Crisan, D. (2001) Particle filters – a theoretical perspective. In A. Doucet, N. de Freitas and N. Gordon (eds) *Sequential Monte Carlo Methods in Practice*. New York: Springer, pp. 17–42.

de Jong, P. (1989) Smoothing and interpolation with the state-space model. *Journal of the American Statistical Association* 84, 1085–1088.

de Jong, P. and N. Shephard (1995) The simulation smoother for time series models. *Biometrika* 82, 339–50.

Doucet, A., N. de Freitas and N. Gordon (2001) An introduction to sequential Monte Carlo methods. In A. Doucet, N. de Freitas and N. Gordon (eds), *Sequential Monte Carlo Methods in Practice*. New York: Springer, pp. 3–14.

Doucet, A., S.J. Godsill and C. Andrieu (2000) On sequential Monte Carlo sampling methods for Bayesian filtering. *Statistics and Computing* 10, 197–208.

Durbin, J. and S.J. Koopman (1997) Monte Carlo maximum likelihood estimation for non-Gaussian state space models. *Biometrika* 84, 669–84.

Durbin, J. and S.J. Koopman (2000) Time series analysis of non-Gaussian observations based on state space models from both classical and Bayesian perspectives. *Journal of the Royal Statistical Society* B 62, 3–56.

Durbin, J. and S.J. Koopman (2001) *Time Series Analysis by State Space Methods*. Oxford: Oxford University Press.

Durbin, J. and S.J. Koopman (2002) A simple and efficient simulation smoother for state space time series analysis. *Biometrika* 89, 603–16.

Eraker, B. (2001) MCMC analysis of diffusion models with application to finance. *Journal of Business and Economic Statistics* 19, 177–91.

Frühwirth-Schnatter, S. (1994) Data augmentation and dynamic linear models. *Journal of Time Series Analysis* 15, 183–202.

Godsill, S.J., A. Doucet and M. West (2004) Monte Carlo smoothing for nonlinear time series. *Journal of the American Statistical Association* 99, 156–68.

Gomez, V. (2001) The use of Butterworth filters for trend and cycle estimation in economic time series. *Journal of Business and Economic Statistics* 19, 365–73.

Green, P.G. and B.W. Silverman (1994) *Nonparametric Regression and Generalized Linear Models*. London: Chapman and Hall.

Harvey, A.C. (1989) *Forecasting, Structural Time Series Models and the Kalman Filter*. Cambridge: Cambridge University Press.

Harvey, A.C. and S.J. Koopman, (1992) Diagnostic checking of unobserved components time series models. *Journal of Business and Economic Statistics* 10, 377–89.

Harvey, A.C. and S.J. Koopman (2000) Signal extraction and the formulation of unobserved components models. *Econometrics Journal* 3, 84–107.

Harvey, A.C. and T. Trimbur (2003) General model-based filters for extracting cycles and trends in economic time series. *Review of Economics and Statistics* **85**, 244–55.

Harvey, A.C., T. Trimbur and H. van Dijk (2003) Cyclical components in economic time series: a Bayesian approach. Discussion paper, Cambridge.

Hodrick, R.J. and E.C. Prescott (1997) Postwar US business cycles: an empirical investigation. *Journal of Money, Credit and Banking* **24**, 1–16.

Hürzeler, M. and H.R. Künsch (1998) Monte Carlo approximations for general state-space models. *Journal of Computational and Graphical Statistics* **7**, 175–93.

Hürzeler, M. and H.R. Künsch (2001) Approximating and maximising the likelihood for a general state-space model. In A. Doucet, N. de Freitas, and N. Gordon (eds) *Sequential Monte Carlo Methods in Practice*. New York: Springer, pp. 159–76.

Kitagawa, G. (1987) Non-Gaussian state-space modelling of nonstationary time series. *Journal of the American Statistical Association* **82**, 1032–1063.

Kitagawa, G. (1996) Monte Carlo filter and smoother for non-Gaussian nonlinear state space models. *Journal of Computational and Graphical Statistics* **5**, 1–25.

Kitagawa, G. (1998) A self-organizing state-space model. *Journal of the American Statistical Association* **93**, 1203–1215.

Kitagawa, G. and S. Sato (2001) Monte Carlo smoothing and self-organising state-space model. In A. Doucet, N. de Freitas and N. Gordon (eds) *Sequential Monte Carlo Methods in Practice*. New York: Springer, pp. 177–96.

Koop, G. and H.K. van Dijk (2000) Testing for integration using evolving trend and seasonals models: a Bayesian approach. *Journal of Econometrics* **97**, 261–91.

Koopman, S.J. and A.C. Harvey (2003) Computing observation weights for signal extraction and filtering. *Journal of Economic Dynamics and Control* **27**, 1317–1333.

Koopman, S.J., N. Shephard and J.A. Doornik (1999) Statistical algorithms for models in state space using SsfPack 2.2. *Econometrics Journal* **2**, 113–66.

Liu, J. and M. West (2001) Combined parameter and state estimation in simulation-based filtering. In A. Doucet, N. de Freitas and N. Gordon (eds) *Sequential Monte Carlo Methods in Practice*. New York: Springer, pp. 197–224.

Pierce, D.A. (1979) Signal extraction error in nonstationary time series. *Annals of Statistics* **7**, 1303–1320.

Pitt, M.K. and N. Shephard (1999) Filtering via simulation: auxiliary particle filter. *Journal of the American Statistical Association* **94**, 590–9.

Quenneville, B. and A.C. Singh (2000) Bayesian prediction MSE for state space models with estimated parameters. *Journal of Time Series Analysis* **21**, 219–36.

Shephard, N. and M.K. Pitt (1997) Likelihood analysis of non-Gaussian measurement time series. *Biometrika* **84**, 653–67.

Smith, J.Q. and A.A.F. Santos (2003) Second order filter distribution approximations for financial time series with extreme outliers. *Estudos do Grupo de Estudos Monetários e Financeiros*, Coimbra, No. 3.

Stoffer, D. and K. Wall (2004) Resampling in state space models. In A.C. Harvey, S.J. Koopman and N. Shephard (eds) *State Space and Unobserved Component Models*. Cambridge: Cambridge University Press, pp. 171–202.

Stroud, J.R., P. Müller and N. Polson (2003) Nonlinear state-space models with state-dependent variances. *Journal of the American Statistical Association* **98**, 377–86.

Tiao, G.C. and S.C. Hillmer (1978) Some consideration of decomposition of a time series. *Biometrika* **65**, 497–502.

Wecker, W.E. and C.F. Ansley (1983) The signal extraction approach to nonlinear regression and spline smoothing. *Journal of the American Statistical Association* **78**, 81–9.

Whittle, P. (1983) *Prediction and Regulation*, 2nd edition. Oxford: Blackwell.

28

Nonparametric Econometrics

Jeff Racine and Aman Ullah

Abstract

Nonparametric methods provide a variety of advanced techniques for analysing economic data. Great strides have been made since the pioneering work of the 1950s, and the appeal of nonparametric methods, stemming from their potential to reveal data structure that may be missed by parametric specifications, has become increasingly appreciated by econometricians. This chapter outlines some of the recent developments in nonparametric kernel estimation, emphasizing those issues of estimation and inference that arise in the course of modern regression analysis. It begins by surveying nonparametric regression and testing of hypotheses and then moves on to consider a variety of estimation issues: how to deal with a mix of discrete and continuous data, how to deal with time series, and how to estimate cumulative distribution functions. There then follows an overview of semiparametric regression models, before the discussion broadens out to consider nonparametric estimation of limited dependent variable models and panel data models.

28.1	Introduction	1002
28.2	Nonparametric regression	1003
	28.2.1 Local polynomial regression	1003
	28.2.2 Combined estimation	1006
	28.2.3 Additive regression	1007
	28.2.4 Nonparametric nonadditive random functions	1008
	28.2.5 Structural nonparametric models	1008
	28.2.6 Window width selection	1009
28.3	Testing of hypotheses	1011
	28.3.1 Consistent testing for correct parametric functional form	1011
	28.3.2 Consistent significance testing for nonparametric regression	1012
28.4	Nonparametric estimation with discrete and mixed continuous and discrete variables	1014
	28.4.1 Regression	1014
	28.4.2 Conditional density estimation with irrelevant variables	1015
28.5	Time series nonparametric regression	1016
	28.5.1 Regression, volatility (variance), and correlation	1016
	28.5.2 Estimation of long-range dependence	1019
28.6	Cumulative distribution estimation	1020
28.7	Semiparametric models	1021

28.8   Limited dependent variable models   1021
    28.8.1   Semiparametric binary choice models   1021
    28.8.2   Censored parametric regression models with nonparametric
               heteroskedasticity   1022
    28.8.3   Nonparametric censored and truncated regression   1022
    28.8.4   Nonparametric multinomial choice models   1023
    28.8.5   Nonparametric censored density and hazard rate estimation 1024
28.9   Panel data models   1024
28.10   Conclusion   1025

28.1   Introduction

Local modeling is a data-based approach for studying the relationships between explanatory variables and a response (dependent) variable. In a regression framework this approach is also called "nonparametric regression" or "nonparametric smoothing." Nonparametric kernel[1] methods are becoming increasingly popular for applied data analysis; they are best suited to situations involving large data sets for which the number of variables involved is manageable. Researchers gravitate toward local nonparametric methods when common global parametric specifications of the model are deemed inadequate for a problem at hand, particularly when formal rejection of a parametric model yields no clues as to the direction in which to search for an improved parametric model. The growing popularity of nonparametric methods stems from the fact that they relax the assumptions on the functional form of an unknown model and let the data determine a function tailored to the data at hand.

The number of books devoted to the subject continues to multiply, including Prakasa Rao (1983), Devroye and Györfi (1985), Silverman (1986), Härdle (1990), Scott (1992), Bickel, Klaassen, Ritov and Wellner (1993), Wand and Jones (1995), Fan and Gijbels (1996), Simonoff (1996), Azzalini and Bowman (1997), Hart (1997), Horowitz (1998), Efromovich (1999), Eubank (1999), Pagan and Ullah (1999), Ruppert, Carroll and Wand (2003), Härdle, Müller, Sperlich and Werwatz (2004), and Li and Racine (forthcoming).

Nonparametric kernel methods share one defining feature, namely "local averaging." In a regression context, we may compute a consistent estimate of a conditional mean by locally averaging those values of the dependent variable which are "close" in terms of the values taken on by the regressors. By controling the amount of local information used to construct the estimate (the "local sample size") and allowing the amount of local averaging to become more informative as the sample size increases, while also decreasing the neighborhood in which the averaging occurs, we can ensure that our estimates are consistent under standard regularity conditions. The amount of local information used to construct the average is controlled by a window width, also called a "bandwidth" or "smoothing parameter."

There are other ways to do local modeling in the literature, for example, see Eubank (1999) for spline methods, Gallant (1982) and Newey (1997) for series methods, Yatchew (2003) for differencing methods, and Kuan and White (1994) for neural network methods. However, in what follows, we restrict our attention to kernel smoothing procedures because of their vast applicability, simplicity, and their well developed theoretical underpinnings for both time series and cross section data.

In this chapter we outline some of the recent developments in nonparametric kernel estimation, with an emphasis on estimation and inference issues that arise in the course of modern regression analysis. In section 28.2 we survey nonparametric regression. Section 28.3 considers nonparametric testing of hypotheses. Section 28.4 outlines recent developments in kernel estimation when faced with a mix of discrete and continuous data types. Section 28.5 surveys advances in nonparametric estimation of time series models. Section 28.6 outlines advances in kernel estimation of cumulative distribution function estimation. Section 28.7 contains an overview of semiparametric regression models. Section 28.8 outlines nonparametric estimation of limited dependent variable models. Section 28.9 outlines nonparametric estimation of panel data models, and section 28.10 presents some brief concluding thoughts.

28.2 Nonparametric regression

28.2.1 Local polynomial regression

Suppose our aim is to analyze a regression function $g(x)$, which represents a relationship between the dependent variable y and a $q \times 1$ vector of regressors x, i.e., the conditional mean of y given $x, E(y|x) = g(x)$. The regression model is then written as $y = g(x) + \varepsilon$, where ε is the error in the model. The parametric approach toward regression involves fitting a parametric regression model through the data via, say, the linear model

$$y = a + x'b + \varepsilon \qquad (28.1)$$

or, more generally, a parametric model of the form $y = g(x, \theta) + \varepsilon$. This "global" modeling method can produce a smooth low variance fit to the data, but may possess high bias when the parametric regression model is misspecified. Furthermore, the global modeling method is usually not flexible enough for highly nonlinear relationships.

A better alternative is to model the regression function locally. For notational simplicity, we assume for the remainder of this section that $q = 1$. To obtain the regression function at a given point x, we can apply the linear regression method to an interval of data around x. That is, model the data in a "window width" of size h by the linear model

$$y_i = a(x) + b(x)(x_i - x) + \varepsilon_i \qquad (28.2)$$

for x_i in $(x - h/2, x + h/2)$, $i = 1, \ldots, n$.

The local linear method is based on the following minimization problem,

$$\min_{a,b} \sum_{i=1}^{n}(y_i - a(x) - b(x)(x_i - x))^2 K\left(\frac{x_i - x}{h}\right), \tag{28.3}$$

where $K(\cdot)$ is a nonnegative weight function, which is a decreasing function of distances of x_i from the point x, and h is a window width that determines how rapidly the weights decrease as the distance of x_i from x increases. We note that fitting a local linear model $y_i - a(x) - b(x)(x_i - x)$ in (28.2), by rewriting, is the same as fitting $y_i - c(x) - b(x)x_i$ where $c(x) = a(x) - b(x)x$.

Let $\hat{a} = \hat{a}(x)$ and $\hat{b} = \hat{b}(x)$ be solutions to (28.3). It is straightforward to demonstrate that $\hat{a}(x)$ is a consistent estimator of $g(x)$ and $\hat{b}(x)$ is a consistent estimator of $g^{(1)}(x) \overset{def}{=} \partial g(x)/\partial x = b(x)$ (both $b(x)$ and $g^{(1)}(x)$ are $q \times 1$ vectors). The local linear regression approach given in (28.3) is easily understood and it provides a "local linear least squares" estimator. Hence, the slope estimator $\hat{b}$ estimates the local slope $g^{(1)}(x)$ while $\hat{a} = \hat{g}(x)$ estimates the local value of $g(x)$. Furthermore, evaluating $\hat{g}(x)$ over a range of x yields a nonparametric regression model.

The local linear regression approach in (28.2) amounts to considering a linear Taylor series expansion of $g(x_i)$ around x in the model $y_i = g(x_i) + \varepsilon_i$. This approach can be extended to a local polynomial regression by representing the unknown regression function $g(x_i)$ locally by a polynomial of order p. Assuming $q = 1$, and assuming the existence of the $(p+1)$-th derivative of $g(x)$ at the point x, we can write

$$g(x_i) \approx g(x) + g^{(1)}(x)(x_i - x) + \cdots + \frac{g^{(p)}(x)}{p!}(x_i - x)^p \tag{28.4}$$
$$= a(x) + b_1(x)(x_i - x) \cdots + b_p(x)(x_i - x)^p.$$

Then the local polynomial least squares estimators are obtained as a solution to

$$\min_{a,b_1,\ldots,b_p} \sum_{i=1}^{n}\left(y_i - a(x) - \sum_{j=1}^{p} b_j(x_i - x)^j\right)^2 K\left(\frac{x_i - x}{h}\right). \tag{28.5}$$

When $p = 0$, the resulting estimator is the Nadaraya (1965) and Watson (1964) kernel regression estimator, which is also called the "local constant" least squares estimator. When $p = 1$, we obtain the "local linear" least squares estimators given by (28.3). Local polynomial fitting has been systematically studied by Stone (1977), Cleveland (1979), Cleveland and Devlin (1988), and Cleveland, Devlin and Grosse (1988). Also see the books by Fan and Gijbels (1996) and Li and Racine (forthcoming). The advantages of using local polynomial estimators ($p \geq 1$) over the Nadaraya–Watson estimator ($p=0$) have been analyzed by Fan (1992) and Hastie and Loader (1993), among others. Advantages include bias reduction and the absence of boundary effects. When conducting local polynomial fitting, p is usually small and the flexibility of the fit is influenced by the window width h (see Figure 28.1 in section 28.2.6). When h is small, the resulting fit is the most complex model. When $h=\infty$, we observe that $K((x_i - x)/h) = K(0)$ is a constant, and the resulting fit is the global polynomial model. For example, when $p=1$ and $h=\infty$, the local least squares estimator from (28.3) is the same as the global parametric linear least squares estimator from (28.1). For details on choosing p and h, see Fan and Gijbels (1995), Chu and Marron (1991), Ruppert and Wand (1994), Ruppert, Sheather and Wand (1995), Hurvich, Simonoff and Tsai (1998), and Li and Racine (2004).

The local polynomial estimators with $p \geq 1$ often suffer singularity problems in applied settings. This well-known problem can often frustrate first-time users. Ridging has been proposed by a number of authors to overcome these problems. See Seifert and Gasser (2000) for rules of thumb for the ridge parameters in one and two dimensions.

Local polynomial regression estimators can be seen as fitting a parametric polynomial regression model in the neighborhood of data points around x, which is achieved by considering the minimization of weighted squared errors with weights given by a kernel. This principle can easily be generalized to other parametric regression settings, such as local logit and probit, local proportional hazards, local quantile, robust regression, and nonlinear time series models. For example, if we let $g(x_i, \theta)$ be a parametric model and $L_i(x_i, y_i, g(x_i, \theta))$ be the discrepancy loss or the log-likelihood of the i-th observation, then we can minimize (if a loss) or maximize (if a likelihood) the objective function given by

$$L(\theta) = \sum_{i=1}^{n} L_i(x_i, y_i, g(x_i, \theta)) K\left(\frac{x_i - x}{h}\right). \tag{28.6}$$

The function $g(x_i, \theta)$ is now locally estimated by $g(x_i \hat{\theta}(x))$. For example, when $g(x_i, \theta) = a + bx_i$, then $g(x_i, \hat{\theta}(x)) = \hat{a}(x) + \hat{b}(x)x_i$, where $\hat{a}(x)$ and $\hat{b}(x)$ minimize (28.6) with $L_i(x_i, y_i, g(x_i, \theta)) = (y_i - a - bx_i)^2$, or maximize $L(\theta)$ with L_i written presuming normality of errors. Similarly, in a single index econometric model, where the dependent variable y_i takes values 1 or 0 and the probability of $y_i = 1$ depends on the cumulative distribution function of the index βx_i, denoted by $F(\beta x_i)$,

$$L_i(x_i, y_i, g(x_i, \theta)) = \log[F(\beta x_i)^{y_i}(1 - F(\beta x_i))^{1-y_i}]. \tag{28.7}$$

The local least squares estimators are based on the quadratic loss function, which is sensitive to outliers and large variability. To obtain a more robust estimator one can replace quadratic loss by absolute deviation loss. A generalization of this leads to a loss function which provides the α-quantile (percentile) regression estimators of the conditional distribution of y given x. This is obtained by considering

$$L_i(x_i, y_i, g(\beta x_i)) = \varepsilon_i(\alpha - I(\varepsilon_i < 0)), \tag{28.8}$$

where $\varepsilon_i = y_i - a(x) - \Sigma_{j=1}^p b_j(x_i - x), 0 < \alpha < 1$, and $I(\cdot)$ is the usual indicator function.

In particular, when $\alpha = 0.5$, the estimator defined via (28.8) estimates a conditional median (50th percentile) or second quantile. For another class of loss functions that provide robust estimators, see Cleveland (1979), Härdle and Gasser (1984), Tsybakov (1982), and Fan, Hu and Truong (1994), among others. See Chaudhuri (1992), Yu and Jones (1998), Cai (2002), and Hansen (2004) for asymptotic theory in a special case of this model. For semiparametric approaches to quantile estimation, see Koenker and Zhao (1996), Engle and Manganelli (1999), and Lee (2003). When h goes to ∞, the nonparametric local polynomial conditional quantile estimators reduce to those of parametric quantile estimators given in the seminal work of Koenker and Bassett (1978); also see the works of Kim and White (2003) and Komunjer (2003).

The local polynomial estimators provide the local (pointwise) estimates of $b_j(x)$, which vary with x. In many situations one may be interested in studying the local estimators of $b_j(z)$, where the vector of z variables are not in the model but are assumed to affect the local parameters. The local polynomial estimators of $b_j(z)$ are then obtained from (28.5) with $K((x_i - x)/h)$ replaced by $K((z_i - z)/h)$. For examples and applications of these models, see Robinson (1989) and Lee and Ullah (2003).

The asymptotic properties of the local polynomial estimators are analyzed in Masry (1996a,b); also see Li and Racine (2004) and Fan and Gijbels (1996). The implication of these results is that the rate of convergence of the pointwise estimator of the r-th derivative of $g(x)$, $\hat{g}^{(r)}(x)/r! = b_r(x), 0 \leq r \leq p$, is the inverse of $(nh^{q+2r})^{1/2}$, which is slower than the parametric rate of $\sqrt{n}$. In fact, as the dimension of the regressors q and/or r increase the rates become worse, which is the well known "curse of dimensionality" problem. To improve the rate of convergence, one can calculate the average of the pointwise estimators (global estimators) of these derivatives. For example, Rilstone (1991) estimated $\Sigma_{i=1}^n \hat{g}^{(1)}(x_i)/n$, where $\hat{g}^{(1)}(x)$ is the first derivative of the Nadaraya–Watson estimator ($p = 0$); also see Härdle and Stoker (1989) for an alternative estimator based on the Nadaraya–Watson estimator. Li, Lu and Ullah (2003) provide the average first derivative estimator based on the polynomial estimator and demonstrate improved performance of their estimator in small samples. All of these average derivative estimators have a $\sqrt{n}$ rate of convergence.

28.2.2　Combined estimation

As noted above, although data-based nonparametric regression techniques may trace irregular patterns in the data quite well (low bias), they may be quite variable (high variance). On the other hand, the application of misspecified parametric regression models will yield a parametric fit that is biased, though it may be less variable than the nonparametric fit. By combining these two modeling techniques, it is possible to obtain a model having a smaller MSE than either of the nonparametric or parametric approaches separately (see Eubank and Spiegelman, 1990; Fan and Ullah, 1999; and Glad, 1998). Suppose an econometrician starts with a parametric model

$$y = g(x, \beta) + u = g(x, \beta) + g_u(x) + v, \tag{28.9}$$

where $g_u(x) = E(u|x)$ and $v = u - E(u|x)$ such that $E(v|x) = 0$. If the parametric model is correctly specified then $g_u(x) = 0$, otherwise $g_u(x) \neq 0$, and it is obtained by nonparametric local polynomial estimation. The combined estimator of $g(x)$ is given by $\hat{g}(x) = g(x, \hat{\beta}) + \hat{g}_{\hat{u}}(x)$, where $\hat{g}_{\hat{u}}$ is obtained by the local polynomial estimation of $\hat{u} = y - g(x, \hat{\beta})$ with respect to x. Fan and Ullah (1999) consider a model where $g(x, \beta)$ in (28.9) is adjusted by $\lambda \times g(x)$, where λ is the adjustment parameter. Instead of additive adjustments, Glad (1998) considers a multiplicative adjustment to the parametric model given by

$$g(x) = g(x, \beta) \frac{g(x)}{g(x, \beta)} = g(x, \beta) g_u(x), \tag{28.10}$$

where $u = y/g(x, \beta)$ is now an error in a multiplicative model $y = g(x, \beta)u$. The combined estimator is now $\hat{g}(x) = g(x, \hat{\beta})\hat{g}_{\hat{u}}(x)$, where $\hat{u} = y/g(x, \hat{\beta})$ is the standardized residual. The correction term $g_u(x)$ in both (28.9) and (28.10) provides a correction to the bias of the misspecified parametric model $g(x, \beta)$. In this sense, the combined estimator is also called a "bias-corrected estimator". See Rahman and Ullah (2002) for its small sample properties.

A general class of combined estimators can also be developed by defining $g(x) = g(x, \beta)c(x)$, where $c(x)$ is a correction term to be determined; similarly $g(x) = g(x, \beta) + c(x)$ for an additive combined estimator. The choice of $c(x)$ can be developed along the lines of Naito (2004), who develops a general class of correction factor for density estimation. Another idea for combined estimation is to combine a nonparametric model with the nonparametric model of the residual of this nonparametric model, that is $\tilde{g}(x) = \hat{g}(x)\hat{g}_{\hat{u}}(x)$, where $\hat{u} = y/\hat{g}(x)$ and $\hat{g}(x)$ is a nonparametric estimator of $g(x)$. Such a combined estimator can be regarded as an iterative or updated nonparametric estimator.

Hypothesis testing for a specific parametric model $g(x, \beta)$ can also be developed by testing for $g_u(x) = 0$ in the additive case and for $g_u(x) = 1$ in the multiplicative case. This will essentially provide the test of Li and Wang (1998) outlined in section 28.3.1.

28.2.3 Additive regression

The curse of dimensionality limits the application of nonparametric methods to low-dimension settings. The rate of convergence of many nonparametric estimators worsens rather dramatically as the number of covariates increases (i.e., the dimension of the regressor space). There have been many methods designed for mitigating this curse. One of the most popular is to presume that the underlying DGP is additive in its terms; however, each regressor is permitted to enter the additive structure in a nonparametric fashion. That is, rather than presume a parametric additive structure of the form $\beta_0 + \sum_{j=1}^{q} x_{ji}\beta_j$ for the conditional mean function, one presumes a structure of the form $\beta_0 + \sum_{j=1}^{q} f(x_{ji})$. Imposing additivity results in an estimator having the one-dimensional nonparametric rate of convergence. Given the central role additivity plays in the specification of production and demand relationships, it may be reasonable to presume such a structure in certain economic settings. Such models are collectively known as *generalized additive models* (Hastie and Tibshirani, 1990; see also Linton and Nielsen, 1995; Linton and Härdle, 1996; Linton, 1997, 2000; Li, 2000; and Fan and Li, 2003 for nonparametric kernel estimation of such models). Linton and Gozalo (2001) and Chen, Liu and Tsay (1995) also provide tests for additivity for the nonparametric model.

Horowitz and Mammen (2004) have pointed out that some of these approaches, for example, Linton and Härdle (1996), provide an estimator of the additive components that is based on marginal integration. Their estimator is asymptotically normal at the rate $n^{-2/5}$, but it requires a component to have an increasing number of derivatives as the dimension of x increases. Thus, it suffers from the curse of dimensionality. Horowitz and Mammen (2004) provide a new estimator that avoids this dimensionality problem. Further, their estimator has an "oracle" property: the asymptotic distribution of each component is the same as it would be if the other components were known.

28.2.4　Nonparametric nonadditive random functions

Often economists presume a model of the form $y = g(x) + \varepsilon$, in which ε is typically interpreted as the difference between the observed y and its conditional expectation $g(x)$. When beginning from a formal behavioral economic model, however, ε could denote a productivity shock or heterogeneity parameter in a utility function, and often the function by which the values of y are determined from x and ε is nonadditive in ε. That is, the model to be studied is of the form $y = g(x, \varepsilon)$.

Presuming that $g(\cdot)$ is strictly increasing in ε and that ε is distributed independently of x, Matzkin (2003) considers identification and estimation of such models in a nonparametric setting in which the function $g(\cdot)$ and the distribution of ε are of unknown form. Estimation proceeds by expressing the unknown function $g(\cdot)$ and the distribution of ε in terms of the distribution of y and x, and then substituting the nonparametric estimator of the distribution of the observable variables y and x into such expressions. The resulting estimators are therefore nonlinear functionals of a kernel estimator for the distribution of the observable variables. Conditions under which the estimator is consistent and asymptotically normal are given in Matzkin (2003).

28.2.5　Structural nonparametric models

Often in economic applications it is the so-called "structural relationship" among endogenous (dependent) variables that is of interest. Direct application of the standard local constant or local polynomial estimator is inappropriate in such settings. Newey and Powell (2003) consider conditions under which the relationship between the structural and reduced forms can be relied upon to yield a solution, while they also propose a computational solution. Their approach is a nonparametric counterpart to the standard two-stage least squares estimator for linear parametric models. Consider a model of the form

$$y = g(x, z_1) + \varepsilon, \quad E(\varepsilon|z) = 0, \quad z = (z_1, z_2), \quad x = h(z) + u, \quad (28.11)$$

where z_1 and z_2 are $d_1 \times 1$ and $d_2 \times 1$ vectors of instrumental variables, x is a $q \times 1$ vector of explanatory variables, h is a $q \times 1$ vector of functions of the instruments z, and u and ε are disturbances. We are interested in estimating $g(\cdot)$ and its derivatives. The conditional expectation of (28.11) is given by

$$\pi(z) \equiv E(y|z) = E(g(x, z_1)|z) = \int_{-\infty}^{\infty} g(x, z_1) \, dF(x|z), \quad (28.12)$$

where F is the conditional cumulative distribution function of x given z. π and F are nonparametric generalizations of reduced forms for y and x, and since they are functionals of the distribution function for (y, x, z), they are identified, while identification of $g(\cdot)$ depends on the existence of a unique solution to (28.12).

Newey, Powell and Vella (1999) show that $g(\cdot)$ is identified up to an additive constant if there is no functional relationship between (x, z_1) and u; also see Pinske (2000), Roehrig (1988) and Newey *et al.* (1999) on identification conditions. Newey *et al.* (1999) use series approximations that exploit the additive structure of the model and provide a two-stage estimator of $g(\cdot)$. Pinske (2000) provides an alternative series estimator by assuming independence between the instrumental variable and the error terms in both the structural and reduced form models. In contrast, Newey and Powell (2003) analyze the estimation of $g(\cdot)$ under the restrictions that $E(\varepsilon|z) = 0$ and $E(u|z) = 0$ and give identification results. Using sieve approximations, they propose a nonparametric analog of the conventional two-stage least squares estimator for linear parametric models and prove a consistency result for their estimator. All of these works are based upon series approximations. Su and Ullah (2003), under the assumption that $E(\varepsilon|z, u) = E(\varepsilon|u)$, observe that $E(y|x, z, u) = g(x, z) + E(\varepsilon|u)$, which is simply an additive model. They first generate u as a residual in the first stage nonparametric estimation of x on z, and then estimate $g(\cdot)$ by using a procedure for estimating additive regression outlined in section 28.2.3. They show the asymptotic normality of their proposed estimator, and their simulation results suggest improved performance of their estimator in small samples. For other related work in this area, see Das (2004), Brown and Matzkin (1996), Darolles, Florens and Renault (2001), Imbens and Newey (2001), Li and Wooldridge (2002), and Su and Ullah (2004).

28.2.6 Window width selection

Window width selection is by far the most important aspect of nonparametric estimation. It is directly analogous to choosing the functional specification underlying parametric models. Furthermore, the consequence of using an overly large window width is the same as using an overly parsimonious parametric specification, i.e., they will both tend to produce biased estimates. Conversely, an overly small window width, just like an overly parameterized parametric model, will tend to produce estimates that are too variable though having low bias. Therefore, it is necessary to pay careful attention to the manner in which window widths are chosen. Most methods of window width selection can be viewed as attempts to balance this classic bias–variance trade-off.

Window width selection rules fall into roughly three broad categories: (1) Reference rules. (2) Plug-in, penalizing, and cross-validation methods. (3) Bootstrap methods.

Reference rules use a window width that would be optimal for a reference data-generating process (DGP), say, the normal linear model. Though reference rule approaches enjoy widespread application in density estimation, mainly due to their computational simplicity, they are not suited to nonparametric regression for two simple reasons: (i) the appropriate window width depends on the unknown distribution of the data, while (ii) the window width also depends on whether the variable in question is relevant or not (see Hall, Racine and Li, 2004). It is known that, for the local linear estimator, if the underlying DGP is in fact linear, then the appropriate window width is $h = \infty$, which will deliver a globally linear fit. Of course, reference rules are incapable of adapting to the underlying DGP and will, in general, either undersmooth or oversmooth relative to the optimal window width. Therefore, what may be appropriate for one dataset may be totally inappropriate for another, and such approaches are best left for *exploratory data analysis*.

The most popular applied methods are perhaps data-driven methods such as plug-in, penalization, and cross-validation approaches. The relative merits of these approaches have been discussed extensively. As yet there is no dominant consensus and each enjoys widespread application. See Loader (1999) and the references therein for a critical comparison of plug-in and cross-validation methods: see also Pagan and Ullah (1999, chapter 3). Bootstrap window width selection has been proposed by a number of authors and is based upon minimizing a bootstrap estimate of error loss with respect to the window width; see Marron (1992).

By way of illustration, consider the following example using data from Fox's (2002) car library in R (R Development Core Team, 2003). The data set consists of 102 observations, each corresponding to a particular occupation. The dependent variable is the prestige of Canadian occupations, measured by the Pineo–Porter prestige score for occupation taken from a social survey conducted in the mid-1960s. The explanatory variable is average income for each occupation measured in 1971 Canadian dollars. Figure 28.1 plots the data and five local linear regression estimates (see section 28.2.1), each differing in their window widths, the window widths being undersmoothed, oversmoothed, Ruppert *et al.*'s (1995) direct plug-in, Hurvich *et al.*'s (1998) corrected AIC ("AIC$_c$"), and cross-validation (CV) (Li and Racine, 2004). A second-order Gaussian kernel was used throughout.

It can be seen that the oversmoothed local linear estimate is globally linear and, in fact, is exactly a simple linear regression of *y* on *x* as expected (see section 28.2.1),

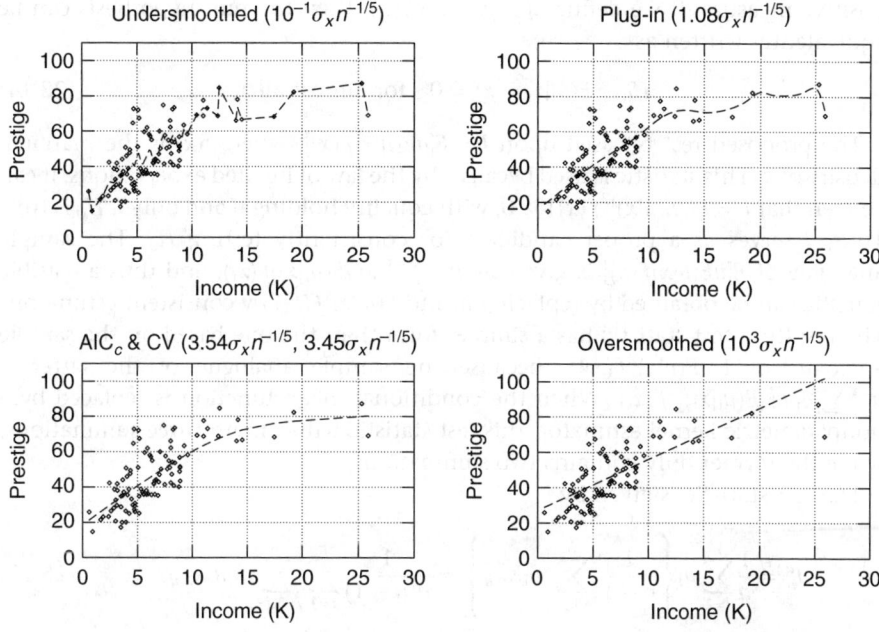

Figure 28.1 Local linear kernel estimates with varying window widths

while the AIC_c and CV criterion appears to provide the most reasonable fit to this data.

28.3 Testing of hypotheses

Nonparametric methods can deliver test statistics which can be consistent for unspecified forms of the alternative hypothesis. Given that parametric tests are generally inconsistent under a misspecified parametric alternative hypothesis, nonparametric methods have obvious appeal. We outline a variety of nonparametric tests that appear in the literature.

28.3.1 Consistent testing for correct parametric functional form

Li and Wang (1998) consider testing the correctness of a parametric regression model defined by $g(x, \gamma_0)$. The null hypothesis is

$$H_0 : E(y|x) = g(x, \gamma_0) \quad \text{for almost all } x \text{ and for some } \gamma_0 \in \mathcal{B} \subset \mathbb{R}^p, \qquad (28.13)$$

where $g(x, \gamma)$ is a known function with γ being a $p \times 1$ unknown parameter vector (which clearly includes a linear regression model as a special case) and $\mathcal{B}$ is a compact subset of $\mathbb{R}^p$, a p-dimensional real space. The alternative hypothesis is the negation of H_0, i.e., $H_1 : E(y|x) \equiv g(x) \neq g(x, \gamma)$ for all $\gamma \in \mathbb{B}$ on a set (of x) with positive measure. If we define $u_i = y_i - g(x_i, \gamma_0)$, then the null hypothesis can be equivalently written as

$$H_0: \quad E(u_i|x_i = x) = 0 \quad \text{for almost all } x. \tag{28.14}$$

The proposed test is based upon $I = E[uE(u|x)f(x)]$, where $f(x)$ is the marginal density of x. This statistic is used because, by the law of iterated expectations, it can be seen that $I = E\{[E(u|x)]^2 f(x)\} \geq 0$, with equality holding if and only if H_0 is true. Thus, I serves as a proper candidate for consistently testing H_0. The sample analogue of $E[uE(u|x)f(x)]$ is given by $n^{-1}\sum_{i=1}^{n} u_i E(u_i|x_i)f(x_i)$, and thus a feasible statistic can be obtained by replacing u_i and $E(u_i|x_i)f(x_i)$ by consistent estimators. The resulting test statistic has a simpler form than the one based on the sample analogue of $E\{[E(u|x)]^2 f(x)]\}$, because the sample analogue of the latter is $n^{-1}\sum_{i=1}^{n} u_i^2 [E(u_i|x_i)]^2 f(x_i)$. When the conditional mean function is replaced by a nonparametric kernel estimator, this test statistic will contain three summations, while the former only contains two summations.

The test statistic is given by

$$I_n^a \stackrel{def}{=} \frac{1}{n}\sum_{i=1}^{n} \hat{u}_i \left\{ \frac{1}{n-1} \sum_{j=1,j\neq i}^{n} \hat{u}_j K_{h,ij} \right\} = \frac{1}{n(n-1)} \sum_{i=1}^{n} \sum_{j=1,j\neq i}^{n} \hat{u}_i \hat{u}_j K_{h,ij}, \tag{28.15}$$

where $\hat{u}_i = y_i - g(x_i, \hat{\gamma})$ is the residual obtained from the parametric null model and $K_{h,ij}$ is a generalized product kernel capable of handling a mix of discrete and continuous variables (see section 28.4). Li and Wang (1998) derive the limiting normal distribution of the statistic, and advocate using the wild bootstrap procedure in practice. For the finite sample properties of this and other related nonparametric tests, see Lee and Ullah (2003).

28.3.2 Consistent significance testing for nonparametric regression

Often it is desirable to test the significance of a regressor or group of regressors. For notational simplicity, partition the vector x into two parts, the variables whose significance is to be tested $x_{(j)}$, and all other conditioning variables $x_{(-j)}$ excluding $x_{(j)}$. Let $x = (x_{(-j)}, x_{(j)})$, where $x_{(j)} \in \mathbb{R}^j$ and $x_{(-j)} \in \mathbb{R}^{p-j}$. If the conditional mean $E(y|x)$ is independent of a variable or group of variables in question, $x_{(j)}$, then the true, but unknown, vector of partial derivatives of the conditional mean of the dependent variable with respect to these variables is zero. We state this condition for independence of $E(y|x)$ and $x_{(j)}$ as

$$E(y|x) \perp x_{(j)} \Leftrightarrow \frac{\partial E(y|x)}{\partial x_{(j)}} = 0, \tag{28.16}$$

where $\partial E(y|x)/\partial x_{(j)} \in \mathbb{R}^j$ and $\perp$ denotes orthogonality or independence.

Nonparametric estimation techniques yield partial derivatives that are permitted to vary over their domain. Contrast this with parametric multivariate linear regression techniques in which the partial derivative is typically restricted to be constant over their domain. This has implications for the type of test statistic used in a nonparametric context. In particular, tests must be formulated to detect whether a partial derivative equals zero over the entire domain of each variable in question.

Noting explicitly that the partial derivatives will, in general, vary over its domain, the null hypothesis can be stated in terms of the vector of partial derivatives of the conditional mean as

$$H_0: \quad \frac{\partial E(y|x)}{\partial x_{(j)}} = 0 \quad \text{for all } x \in \mathbb{R}^j$$

$$H_A: \quad \frac{\partial E(y|x)}{\partial x_{(j)}} \neq 0 \quad \text{for some } x \in \mathbb{R}^j.$$

(28.17)

Since a test statistic in this context must necessarily involve some aggregate measure of the derivative over its domain, we consider an aggregate involving the L_2 norm. Using this aggregate based on the unknown derivatives, we can now state the null and alternative hypotheses as

$$H_0: \quad \lambda = E\iota' \left[\frac{\partial E(y|x)}{\partial x_{(j)}} \right]^2 = 0$$

$$H_A: \quad \lambda = E\iota' \left[\frac{\partial E(y|x)}{\partial x_{(j)}} \right]^2 > 0,$$

(28.18)

where ι denotes a unit vector of length j. If the null hypothesis is true, λ will be identically equal to zero. Otherwise, λ will exceed zero.

The proposed test statistic can be obtained by forming a sample average of equation (28.18), replacing the unknown derivatives with their nonparametric estimates $\hat{\beta}(x_i) \in \mathbb{R}^j$. There is one minor modification of equation (28.18) that will be employed for more efficient bootstrap simulations. This modification involves scaling the derivatives by an asymptotically pivotal quantity for improved bootstrapping. This so-called "pre-pivoting" will be achieved by scaling the partial derivatives by their estimated asymptotic standard errors. Calling the resulting test statistic $\hat{\lambda}$, we have

$$\hat{\lambda} = n^{-1} \sum_{i=1}^{n} \sum_{h=j}^{q} \left[\frac{\hat{\beta}_h(x_i)}{SE\left(\hat{\beta}_h(x_i)\right)} \right]^2,$$

where $SE(\hat{\beta}_h(x_i))$ denotes the estimated asymptotic standard error of $\hat{\beta}_h(x_i)$.

Nested bootstrapping is used to obtain the sampling distribution of $\hat{\lambda}$ under the null. Both the value of the test statistic and the critical value under the null are calculated. For a treatment of this approach, see Racine (1997). See Fan and Li (1996), Chen and Fan (1999), Lavergne and Vuong (2000) and Delgado and Manteiga (2001) for alternative nonparametric tests of significance of continuous variables in nonparametric regression models. See Lavergne (2001) and the references therein for a non-smoothing nonparametric test of regression constancy over subsamples, and Racine, Hart and Li (2004) for a smoothing nonparametric test of significance for discrete regressors.

In addition to using the test statistic given above for the hypothesis in (28.17), one can also get useful information about the derivatives by forming their asymptotic or bootstrap confidence intervals and also examining the regions of data for which the null hypothesis is verified. Another test often conducted in regression analysis is to know if the residuals follow a specific distribution function, for example, normal. A nonparametric test of this follows from the work of Fan (1994), whose test is essentially looking at the Euclidean distance of a nonparametric kernel density function of the data from the assumed density function of the data (see section 28.4).

28.4   Nonparametric estimation with discrete and mixed continuous and discrete variables

28.4.1   Regression

Traditional (i.e., fully nonparametric) kernel methods presume that the underlying data types are continuous in nature. Semiparametric methods have been proposed to deal with the existence of discrete regressors (e.g., Robinson, 1988). Recently, nonparametric methods for estimating unconditional distributions, conditional distributions, and regression functions have been proposed that allow for a mix of continuous and discrete variables in a fully nonparametric framework (see Li and Racine, 2003, 2004, forthcoming; Hall *et al.*, 2004; and Racine and Li, 2004). We briefly outline this approach, which builds on the work of Aitchison and Aitken (1976), who propose a kernel method for multivariate binary discriminant analysis. The idea is based upon the notion of *generalized product kernels* that seamlessly admit a mix of continuous and categorical data (both *nominal* and *ordinal*).

Recall that, for continuous data, a popular kernel function is the so-called product kernel formed by taking the product of univariate kernel functions. Call such kernel functions $K^c((x_i - x)/h)$; for example, $K^c(\cdot)$ could be the Epanechnikov kernel (Epanechnikov, 1969) given by

$$K^c(x_i, x, h) = \begin{cases} \frac{3}{4\sqrt{5}}\left(1 - \frac{1}{5}\left(\frac{x_i-x}{h}\right)^2\right) & \text{if } \left|\frac{x_i-x}{h}\right| < \sqrt{5} \\ 0 & \text{otherwise} \end{cases}, \tag{28.19}$$

where h is a window width restricted to lie in the range $(0, \infty)$.

Following Aitchison and Aitken (1976), for an unordered discrete variable ("nominal categorical variable") $x^d \in \{0, 1, \ldots, c-1\}$, define a univariate kernel function

$$K^u(x_i^d, x^d, \lambda) = \begin{cases} 1 - \lambda & \text{if } x_i^d = x^d, \\ \lambda/(c-1) & \text{if } x_i^d \neq x^d. \end{cases} \tag{28.20}$$

Note that when $\lambda = 0, K^u(x_i^d, x^d, 0) = 1(x_i^d = x^d)$ becomes an indicator function, and if $\lambda = (c-1)/c, K^u(x_i^d, x^d, (c-1)/c) = 1/c$ is a constant for *all* x_i^d and x^d. The range of λ is $[0, (c-1)/c]$.

Assuming that x^d can assume c different ordered values ("ordinal categorical variable"), $\{0, 1, \ldots, c-1\}$, Racine and Li (2004) suggest the use of the following alternative kernel function,

$$K^o(x_i^d, x^d, \lambda) = \lambda^{|x_i^d - x^d|}. \tag{28.21}$$

The range of λ is $[0, 1]$. Again, when λ assumes its extreme upper bound value ($\lambda = 1$), we see that $K^o(x_i^d, x^d, 1) \equiv 1$ for all $x^d \in \{0, 1, \ldots, c-1\}$.

A generalized product kernel could be formed using products of the kernels defined in (28.19), (28.20), and (28.21), where one uses the appropriate kernel for the appropriate data type. In this manner, one is able to apply the local constant estimator or the local polynomial estimator seamlessly, where the regressors can be a mix of data types, without having to resort to semiparametric methods in which one presumes parametric structure for the discrete components. The convergence rates for the cross-validated local constant and local linear cross-validated window widths, based upon second order continuous kernels, are $\hat{h} = O_p(n^{-1/(4+q)})$ and $\hat{\lambda} = O_p(n^{-2/(4+q)})$, where q is the number of continuous regressors (see Racine and Li, 2004; Li and Racine, 2004).

28.4.2 Conditional density estimation with irrelevant variables

Hall *et al.* 2004, consider estimation of a conditional density function defined over a mix of discrete and continuous variables wherein some of the conditioning variables are, in fact, irrelevant. They demonstrate that cross-validation automatically determines which components are relevant and which are not, through assigning large window widths to the latter and consequently shrinking them toward the uniform distribution on the respective marginals. This effectively removes irrelevant components from contention by suppressing their contribution to the estimator variance; they already have a very small bias, a consequence of their independence of y. Cross-validation also provides important information about which components are relevant: the relevant components are precisely those which cross-validation has chosen to smooth in a traditional way, by assigning them window widths of conventional size. Indeed, cross-validation produces asymptotically optimal smoothing for relevant components while eliminating irrelevant components by oversmoothing.

An interesting application of the mixed data methods is to problems involving an outcome that is a count (e.g., number of successful patent applications, as in Hausman, Hall and Griliches, 1984). In such situations, one can model the outcome using the estimator of Hall *et al.* (2004), treating the outcome as a count by using the kernel function (28.21), thereby explicitly recognizing the natural ordering of the count.

For a treatment of irrelevant variables in a regression framework, see Hall, Li and Racine (2004).

28.5   Time series nonparametric regression

28.5.1   Regression, volatility (variance), and correlation

In this section we consider nonparametric methods for estimating the function $g(x) \in y = g(x) + \varepsilon$ for dependent time series observations, in which the q-dimensional x_t is a stationary process and ε_t is a series of innovations that are independent of $x_t, t = 1, \ldots, n$. When $x_t = (y_{t-1}, y_{t-2}, \ldots, y_{t-q})$, the regression model is referred to as an autoregressive model. There is an extensive literature on linear and nonlinear parametric time series models; see, for example, Hamilton (1994) and Tong (1990). Robinson (1983) first developed the Nadaraya–Watson estimation of $g(x)$ and showed its asymptotic normality; also see Györfi, Härdle, Sarda and Vieu (1989) and Masry and Tjøstheim (1995). The local polynomial least squares estimators in (28.5) also apply to time series data. For details of the properties of local polynomial estimators in time series settings, see the important work of Masry (1996a, b). We note that the estimation of $g(x)$ in the time series case can also be used for future forecasts. For these, see Auestad and Tjøstheim (1994), Chung and Zhou (1996) and Hong and Lee (2003a, 2003b), among others. Collomb, Härdle and Hassani (1987) also propose forecasting future observations based on the mode function $g(x) = \arg\max_x h(y|x)$, where $h(y|x)$ represents the conditional density function of y given x. We note that tests to help decide whether to use a nonparametric model rather than a parametric model are given by Hjellvik and Tjøstheim (1995) and Li (1999); the test by the latter is essentially the test in (28.15) with time series data. See Lee and Ullah (2001, 2003) for the properties of these tests.

Hong and Lee (2003a) propose a diagnostic test for linear and nonlinear time series models using a generalized spectral approach. This test is consistent for any type of serial dependence in the model's standardized residuals, permitting choice of lag order among others. Their approach is based on kernel estimates of a generalized spectral density of a model's residuals $\{\varepsilon_t\}$, denoted $f(\omega, u, v)$. When the residuals are *i.i.d.*, $f(\omega, u, v)$ has a particularly simple form, denoted as $f_0(\omega, u, v)$; hence their test is based on the standardized integrated deviation of $f(\omega, u, v)$ from $f_0(\omega, u, v)$.

For the implementation of time series nonparametric regression, the selection of the window-width is extremely important, especially since the MSE of the estimators are affected by the dependence among observations. Härdle and Vieu (1992) propose using leave-one-out cross-validation involving minimization of $CV(h) = T^{-1} \sum_{t=1}^{T} \{y_t - \hat{g}_{-t}(x_t)\}^2 w(x_t)$, where $\hat{g}_{-t}(x_t)$ is a leave-one-out Nadaraya–Watson estimator of $g(x)$ and $w(x_t)$ is a weight function. They show that $\hat{h} = \min_h CV(h)$ so obtained converges to the optimal h under an α-mixing condition. Similar results for density estimation with time series observations were obtained by Hart and Vieu (1990). For details on window width selection and related references in the *i.i.d.* case, see Pagan and Ullah (1999). For their implementation in practice, see Härdle, Klinke and Turlach (1995) and Racine (2002a).

Another important issue when implementing the nonparametric estimator of $g(x)$ is how best to choose the lag length and number of exogenous variables. For linear parametric models, these are often done by using information criteria such as FPE, AIC, and BIC (Akaike, 1970; Schwarz, 1978), and also by performing residual analysis. In the nonparametric analysis of time series, Auestad and Tjøstheim (1990, 1994) provide the FPE procedure, and Cheng and Tong (1992) and Gao and Tong (2004) propose cross-validation methods.

The nonparametric time series analysis described above has expanded recently in various directions. For example, Xiao, Linton, Carroll Mammen 2003 show that if the autocorrelation function of the error process is ignored, then the nonparametric local polynomial least squares estimator of $g(x)$ becomes inefficient. They consider the estimation of $g(x)$ when the error ε is stationary and has an invertible linear parametric process (Wold decomposition theorem) representation: $\varepsilon_t = \sum_{j=0}^{\infty} c_j u_{t-j}$, where u_t is *i.i.d.* $(0, \sigma_u^2)$. They show that the nonparametric estimator of $g(x)$ under this correlation structure has a smaller asymptotic variance than the nonparametric estimator of $g(x)$ obtained without it, that is, by assuming ε_t to be *i.i.d.* Su and Ullah (2003) extend the model of Xiao *et al.* (2003) by considering a nonparametric model of finite-order lags: $\varepsilon_t = g_1(\varepsilon_{t-1}, \ldots, \varepsilon_{t-d}) + u_t$, which incorporates nonlinear structures of errors, such as cycles and jumps. They propose a local polynomial-based procedure for estimating $g(x)$ by defining an additive structure for the nonparametric model as $y_t = g(x_t) + g_1(\varepsilon_{t-1}, \ldots, \varepsilon_{t-d}) + u_t$, and show that their estimator is more efficient compared to the conventional local polynomial estimator, ignoring serial correlation. In contrast to Xiao *et al.* (2003) and Su and Ullah (2003), Hidalgo (1992) considers the case in which $g(x) = a + x'b$ is a parametric model and ε follows a nonparametric structure.

Time series nonparametric approaches also suffer from the "curse of dimensionality," unless the autoregressive order q is very small. The nonparametric additive model described in section 28.2.3 is again useful for taking care of this problem; see the works of Jones (1978), Chen and Tsay (1993), Linton and Nielsen (1995), Auestad and Tjøstheim (1994), Masry and Tjøstheim (1995), Wong and Kohn (1996) and Li (2000), among others. Chen *et al.* (1995) also provide tests for additivity in a time series nonparametric model.

A functional coefficient nonparametric autoregressive model, say for $q = 1$, $g(x_t) \simeq a(z) + \sum_{j=1}^{b} b_j(z)(x_t - x)^j$, is also of interest in time series settings, such as the nonparametric local AR model, in which the coefficients change according to a threshold lag variable $z = x_{t-12}$; also see section 28.2. Such a local functional coefficient autoregressive model provides a nonparametric model corresponding to various parametric functional coefficient autoregressive models in the literature, such as the threshold AR models of Tong (1978, 1983) and Tsay (1989), the exponential AR models of Haggan and Ozaki (1981), and the Star models of Granger and Teräsvirta (1993). For nonparametric and parametric estimation and testing of these models, see Lee and Ullah (2001, 2003).

The nonparametric time series regression techniques described above deal with the estimation of $g(x)$, the conditional mean of y given x, $E(y|x)$. Similar techniques have been extended recently to study higher-order conditional moments. For example, there is an extensive parametric literature on the volatility function, the conditional variance of y given a set x consisting of past information $(V(y|x) = \sigma_t^2)$; see Engle (1982) and Bollerslev, Engle and Nelson (1994) for the GARCH family of models. This literature considers models of the form

$$y_t = g(x_t, \theta) + \varepsilon_t, \quad t = 1, \ldots, n,$$

where ε_t satisfies $E(\varepsilon_t|I_{t-1}) = 0, E(\varepsilon_t^2|, I_{t-1}) = \sigma_t^2, I_{t-1}$, is the information set at time $t-1$, and σ_t^2 follows a GARCH-type model specification. However, if the parametric model σ_t^2 is misspecified then its parametric estimates are inconsistent. In view of this, Ziegelmann (2002) proposes a local polynomial estimator of σ_t^2, being a solution to

$$\min_{a, b_1, \ldots, b_b} \sum_{t=1}^{n} \left[\hat{\varepsilon}_t^2 - \Psi\left(a(x) - \sum_{j=1}^{p} b_j(x)(x_{tj}^* - x_j^*) \right) \right]^2 K\left(\frac{x_t^* - x^*}{h} \right),$$

where x_t^* is a scalar variable belonging to the information set I_{t-1}, $\hat{\varepsilon}_t = y_{t-g}(x_{t-g}\hat{\theta})$ or $\hat{\varepsilon}_t = y_t - \hat{g}(x_t)$ if $g(x_t)$ is an unknown nonparametric function. If $\Psi(\cdot)$ is a function such that when $\Psi(z) = z$, we have the local linear estimator for the conditional variance (see Häardle and Tsybakov, 1997; Tjøstheim and Auestad, 1994a,b; also see Fan and Yao, 1998). When $\Psi(z) = \exp(z)$, we have the local exponential estimator of the conditional variance, as in Ziegelmann 2002. One obvious advantage of the local exponential approach over the conventional local linear estimator is that it ensures the nonnegativity of the estimator of the conditional variance. Mishra, Su and Ullah (2003) extend Ziegelmann's (2002) estimator to the case where the volatility function may depend on all the past information and they also provide a combined estimator of σ_t^2 by writing $\sigma_t^2 = \sigma_{p,t}^2 E(\varepsilon_t^*|I_{t-1})$, where $\varepsilon_t^* = \varepsilon_t|\sigma_{p,t}$ is a standardized error and $\sigma_{p,t}^2$ represents a parametric volatility function. This is analogous to the combined mean regression estimator in section 28.2.2. Mishra *et al.*'s (2003) results indicate that this combined estimator is essentially a bias-corrected estimator, where the correction to a parametric specification $\sigma_{p,t}^2$ is done by a nonparametric correction factor $E(\varepsilon_t^{*2}|I_{t-1})$. Such a combined estimator traces the asymmetric impact of the conditional variance well, and statistically it performs better than a purely nonparametric estimator or misspecified parametric model. Hsiao and Li (2001) provide a consistent test for conditional versus unconditional variance that is helpful when deciding whether or not a nonparametric approach should be employed.

An extension of the model to nonparametric vector autoregression with conditional variances is presented in Härdle, Lütkepohl and Chen (1996), who consider the model

$$y_t = g(x_t) + D_T^{-1}\varepsilon_t,$$

where y_t is an $r \times 1$ vector, $x_t = (y_{t-1}, \ldots, y_{t-q})$, D_t is a diagonal matrix with diagonal elements equal to the square root of the conditional variance for y_t, and ε_t is *i.i.d.* (0, *I*). This model considers conditional correlations in the system to be zero. However, for asset allocation, risk management, hedging, and asset pricing, conditional correlations are very important because they measure the comovement of different assets in the same or in different markets. In view of this, a recent parametric literature has developed for estimating the above models, where D_t is a matrix with the off-diagonal elements as conditional correlations; see Bera and Higgins (1993), Engle and Kroner (1995), Tsse and Tsui (2002), Engle (2002), Engle and Sheppard (2001) and Pelletiery (2003), among others. A nonparametric estimate of the conditional correlation can be obtained by using procedures similar to those of the conditional mean $(g(x_t))$ and conditional variance (σ_t^2). A combined estimator is developed in Long and Ullah (2001).

The above nonparametric analysis is developed under the assumption of stationarity of the time series observations. Phillips and Park (1998) consider the estimation of density functions and regression functions for the case of time series data with unit roots; also see Hoogstrate (1994). For further work on nonparametric testing for unit roots and cointegration, see Breitung (2002) and Park and Whang (1999). Many existing tests for unit roots and cointegration are based on a parametric model, for example using a linear autoregressive representation of the time series. Breitung (2002) provides variance ratio-based nonparametric test statistics for unit roots and cointegration which are robust to misspecification and structural breaks and can be used to test a wide range of nonlinear models. On the other hand, Park and Whang (1999) developed Kolmogrov–Smirnov and Cramer–Von Mises type nonparametric tests for testing a null hypothesis of $g(y_{t-1}) = y_{t-1}$ against an alternative where $g(y_{t-1})$ is an unspecified nonparametric function. For the nonparametric estimation of continuous time models, see Ait-Sahalia (1996); on detecting jumps in time series, see Pawlak, Rafajlowicz and Steland (2004).

28.5.2 Estimation of long-range dependence

Often economists are interested in estimating the long-memory parameter d_0 for some stationary process, say $\{x_t\}$, where the spectral density $f(\lambda)$ of $\{x_t\}$ is of the form

$$f(\lambda) = |\lambda|^{-2d_0} \varphi(\lambda), \tag{28.22}$$

where $d_0 \in [d_1, d_2]$, $-1/2 < d_1 < d_2 < 1/2$, and $0 < \varphi(0) < \infty$, with d_0 determining the long-memory properties of $\{x_t\}$ and $\varphi(\lambda)$ determining its short-run dynamics.

Instead of parameterizing $\varphi(\lambda)$, one could pursue a semiparametric approach by approximating it via nonparametric methods. Andrews and Sun (2004) consider one such generalization of the Gaussian semiparametric estimator of $\varphi(\lambda)$ ("local Whittle" estimator) proposed by Künsch (1987). Rather than approximating the short-run component of the spectrum by a constant in a shrinking neighborhood of frequency zero, they approximate its logarithm via a constant (G) minus an even polynomial of degree $2r(\log G - \sum_{k=1}^r \theta_k \lambda^{2k})$, leading to their "local polynomial Whittle" (LPW) estimator. Andrews and Sun's (2004) approach is motivated by the work of Cleveland (1979). The choice of r serves the role of the window width.

Andrews and Sun (2004) demonstrate that, for sufficiently smooth $\varphi(\lambda)$, their method can approach the parametric rate, being $\sqrt{n}$ consistent, a property shared by local polynomial approximations in general.

While Andrews and Sun (2004) consider estimating the long-memory parameter d_0 for stationary processes, Phillips and Shimotsu (2004) consider the asymptotic properties of the local Whittle estimator of the memory parameter d_0 when the process $\{x_t\}$ is nonstationary or possesses a unit root $(1/2 < d_0 \leq 1)$. In particular, they demonstrate consistency, while both the limit distribution and rate of convergence depend on the value of d_0.

28.6 Cumulative distribution estimation

Consider the unconditional kernel estimator of a cumulative distribution function (CDF), where the kernel estimator of a probability density function (PDF) is given by

$$\hat{f}(x) = \frac{1}{nh}\sum_{i=1}^{n} k\left(\frac{x - x_i}{h}\right) \tag{28.23}$$

and that for the kernel estimator of a CDF is given by

$$\hat{F}(x) = \int_{-\infty}^{x} \hat{f}(t)\, dt = \frac{1}{n}\sum_{i=1}^{n} K\left(\frac{x - x_i}{h}\right) \tag{28.24}$$

where $K((x - x_i)/h) = \int_{-\infty}^{x} k((t - x_i)/h)\, dt$. This estimator, like its parametric counterpart, has a $\sqrt{n}$ rate of convergence.

Data-driven methods of window width selection for kernel estimators of unconditional CDFs have been studied by a number of authors, notably Bowman, Hall and Prvan (1998), who studied cross-validation methods, and Polansky and Baker (2000), who examined plug-in methods. These methods produce IMSE-optimal window widths, that is, window widths that globally minimize the MSE of the resulting estimator. It can readily be shown that the globally-optimal reference window width, assuming an underlying normal distribution when using a Gaussian kernel, is $h = 1.587\sigma(x)n^{-1/3}$. This differs substantially from the reference window width that is optimal for kernel estimation of a PDF, which is $h = 1.059\sigma(x)n^{-1/5}$. See also also Bashtannyk and Hyndman (2001) for some rule-of-thumb and reference window width selection rules.

Estimation of conditional CDFs has recently been considered by Hansen (2004) and Hall, Wolff and Yao (1999). A defining feature of these approaches is that they smooth both y and x, which makes window width selection more involved. Hansen (2004) considers plug-in rules for estimating a conditional distribution function having one conditioning and one conditioned variable. His approach is based on minimizing IMSE and he considers both a local constant and a modified local linear approach. Hall et al. (1999) propose two novel methods for conditional CDF estimation with multivariate x, one based on locally fitting a logistic model and the other based on a biased bootstrap method applied to a local constant estimator. They provide rates of convergence as well as asymptotic distribution properties of the proposed estimators. However, window width selection is accomplished through an approximate parametric method. Data-driven methods of window width selection for conditional CDF estimation remains a topic of active research.

Su and White (2003) consider testing the conditional independence hypothesis, $\Pr[F(\tau|x,z) = F(\tau|x)] = 1$ for all $\tau \in \mathbb{R}$, using a class of smooth empirical likelihood-based tests formed from a local constant estimator of the conditional CDF. Their test statistic is an integrated weighted smoothed empirical likelihood ratio. After appropriate centering and rescaling, the resulting test statistic is shown to have a limiting $N(0, 1)$ distribution. They demonstrate weak optimality (maximum average local power) with respect to a certain space of local alternatives. Furthermore, their test is applicable to time series data.

28.7 Semiparametric models

Semiparametric models generally consist of a combination of parametric and nonparametric models. Such models are useful when the fully nonparametric models may not perform well, for example when there is a curse of dimensionality or when the mean regression is parametric but the functional forms of the heteroskedasticity, serial correlation, or density of the errors are not known. We can also have situations (Engle, Granger, Rice and Weiss, 1986) in which some regressors may appear as a linear function but the functional form with respect to the other variables is not known, or the regression function is nonparametric but the structure of the error is parametrically specified.

To see some of these semiparametric models more explicitly, suppose $y = x'\beta + g(z) + \varepsilon$, which is the partially linear model proposed by Robinson (1988) and Speckman (1988), where x is unobserved and generated by $x = h(z) + u$ (Li and Wooldridge, 2002). A further model is $y = g(x, \beta) + \varepsilon$, where $E(\varepsilon|x) = 0$ and $V(\varepsilon|x) = \sigma^2(x)$ is of unknown functional form (see Carroll, 1982; Robinson, 1987; and Delgado, 1992); see Hidalgo (1992) when ε has serial correlation of unknown form, and see Engle and González-Rivera (1991) when ε has a density function of unknown form in the likelihood estimation of β. In addition, there is an extensive application of semiparametric models in econometric models with limited dependent variables; see section 28.8. For further details on semiparametric models, see Bickel *et al.* (1993), Robinson (1988), Newey (1990), Linton (1995), and Horowitz and Lee (2002).

28.8 Limited dependent variable models

28.8.1 Semiparametric binary choice models
A semiparametric single index model is of the form

$$y = g(x'\beta_0) + u, \tag{28.25}$$

where y is the dependent variable, $x \in \mathbb{R}^q$ is a $q \times 1$ vector of explanatory variables, β_0 is the $q \times 1$ vector of unknown parameters, and u is the error satisfying $E(u \mid x) = 0$. This model is semiparametric in nature since one must specify the functional form of the index, while $g(\cdot)$ is estimated nonparametrically. Such models naturally arise in binary choice settings. When considering the relationship between a binary dependent variable (y) and some other economic covariates (x), one might model this relationship as follows:

$$y_i = \begin{cases} 1, & \text{if } \alpha + x_i'\beta + \varepsilon_i > 0, \\ 0, & \text{if } \alpha + x_i'\beta + \varepsilon_i \le 0. \end{cases} \tag{28.26}$$

Rather than specify the unknown distribution $g(\cdot)$, one could instead use a semi-parametric approach where $g(\cdot)$ is estimated nonparametrically.

Ichimura (1993), Manski (1988) and Horowitz (1998, pp. 14–20) provide excellent intuitive explanations of the identifiability conditions underlying semiparametric single index models (i.e., the set of conditions under which the unknown parameter vector β_0 and the unknown function $g(\cdot)$ can be sensibly estimated). Ichimura (1993) obtains results for consistency and asymptotic normality of this semiparametric estimator. For details on estimation techniques, see Pagan and Ullah (1999).

28.8.2 Censored parametric regression models with nonparametric heteroskedasticity

Chen and Khan (2000) consider estimation procedures for heteroskedastic censored linear regression models that have weaker requirements for identification than Powell's (1984) censored least absolute deviations (CLAD) estimator, and that allow for various degrees of censoring. Powell's estimator is defined as the minimizer of

$$S_n(\beta) = \frac{1}{n} \sum_{i=1}^{n} |y_i - \max(x_i'\beta, 0)|, \tag{28.27}$$

and he demonstrates $\sqrt{n}$ consistency under conditional heteroskedasticity and non-normality of the error distribution. However, an empirical problem arises when the matrix $E[I(x_i'\beta_0 > 0)x_i x_i']$ is not of full rank and hence β_0 cannot be identified. This arises typically in cases where the index $x_i'\beta_0$ is negative with high probability, as often occurs under heavy censoring of the data. Chen and Khan (2000), by restricting the conditional heteroskedasticity to be multiplicative, allow for less stringent identification conditions than those required by Powell's (1984) CLAD estimator.

28.8.3 Nonparametric censored and truncated regression

Often economists must deal with censored regression models of the form $y = \max[c, g(x) - \varepsilon]$. One could write the model as $g(x) + \varepsilon$ without loss of generality, and if $E(\varepsilon) = 0$, then the function $g(x)$ equals the regression function of the uncensored population. The censoring point c is presumed to be a known constant. Examples include observed purchases that are censored below by zero if consumers can only purchase (but not sell) a product.

Lewbel and Linton (2002) consider nonparametric estimation of the function $g(x)$ and the distribution of ε, F, both of which are assumed to be unknown. Conditions are given under which $g(x)$ can be consistently estimated, where $g(x)$ is the conditional expectation for the uncensored population, while F can be estimated given $g(x)$.

The estimation proceeds as follows. First, estimate the regression function $E(y \mid x)$ using a local polynomial estimator, and call this $\hat{r}(x)$. Next, let $\hat{q}(r)$ be the one-dimensional nonparametric regression of $I(y > 0)$ on the generated regressor $\hat{r}(x)$. Then let

$$\hat{g}(x) = \lambda_0 - \int_{\hat{r}(x)}^{\lambda_0} \frac{1}{\hat{q}(r)} \, dr. \tag{28.28}$$

Lewbel and Linton (2002) demonstrate that $\hat{g}(x)$ is a consistent and asymptotically normal estimator of $g(x)$.

Motivated by classes of problems in which interest lies in the estimation of a location function in regions where it is *less* than the censoring point, Chen, Dahl and Khan (2005) propose an extension of the nonparametric location-scale model to handle censored data with a model of the form

$$y_i^* = \mu(x_i) + \sigma_0(x_i)\varepsilon_i,$$
$$y_i = \max(y_i^*, 0), \tag{28.29}$$

where y_i^* is an unobserved latent dependent variable, y_i is the observed dependent variable, equal to y_i^* if it exceeds the fixed censoring point, zero otherwise, x_i is an observed d-dimensional random vector, $\sigma_0(x_i)$ is a heteroskedastic scale term, and ε_i is a mean zero *i.i.d.* random disturbance distributed independently of x_i.

Chen *et al.* (2005) present conditions under which $\mu(x_i)$ can be identified and estimated after imposing a location restriction that the median of ε_i is zero, and they are able to identify $\mu(x_i)$ on the entire support of x_i, not just the region exceeding the censoring point. Their approach is based on a structural relationship between the conditional mean and upper quantiles holding for those x_i for which $\mu(x_i) \geq 0$, and uses the condition $P_X(x_i : \mu(x_i) \geq 0) \geq 0$, $P_X(\cdot)$ being the probability measure of x_i.

28.8.4 Nonparametric multinomial choice models

Hall *et al.* (2004) propose a cross-validated kernel estimator of a conditional probability function. Their estimator employs generalized kernels and is designed to admit a mix of continuous and discrete data. Their estimator can be directly applied to the estimation of multinomial choice models in which the choices may be unordered or ordered. See Racine (2002b,c) for parametric and semiparametric density-based approaches to modeling multinomial choice and associated marginal effects. See Racine, Li and Zhu (2004) for an extension of the approach of Hall *et al.* (2004) to the multivariate conditional density case.

28.8.5   Nonparametric censored density and hazard rate estimation

Economists often deal with long-term studies in which a series of dependent and possibly censored failure times are observed. Under the assumption that the failure times have a common marginal distribution function, Cai (1998) has proposed a nonparametric estimator of the density and hazard rate for a censored dependent model.

Consider a sequence of true survival times $\{t_i\}$ for n individuals having a common unknown continuous marginal distribution function $F(t) = P(t_i \leq t)$ with PDF $f(t) = F'(t)$. Let the random variable t_i be right censored by the random variable y_i, so that one observes $Z_i = \min[t_i, y_i]$, and let $\delta_i = I(t_i \leq y_i)$ denote the usual indicator function. It is assumed that the censoring times $\{y_i\}$ are i.i.d. and independent of $\{t_i\}$. Interest lies in estimation of the unknown density f and hazard function $\lambda(t) = f(t)/(1 - F(t))$ based on the censored observations $\{(Z_i, \delta_i)\}$. Letting $N_n(t)$ be the number of uncensored observations less than or equal to t and $Y_n(t)$ the number greater than or equal to t, the Kaplan–Meier estimator for $1 - F(t)$ based on the censored data is given by

$$1 - \tilde{F}_n(t) = \prod_{s \leq t}\left(1 - \frac{dN_n(s)}{Y_n(s)}\right) = \prod_{i:Z_{(i)} \leq t}\left(\frac{n-1}{n-1+1}\right)_i^{\delta}, \quad \text{for } t \leq Z_{(n)}, \tag{28.30}$$

where $Z_{(i)}$ are the order statistics of Z_i, $\delta_{(i)}$ the concomitant of $Z_{(i)}$, and $dN_n(s) = N_n(s) - N_n(s-1)$.

Defining $q_1 = \tilde{F}_n(Z_{(1)})$ and $q_i = \tilde{F}_n(Z_{(i)}) - \tilde{F}_n(Z_{(i-1)})$, the proposed kernel estimators of f and λ are given by

$$\hat{f}(t) = \frac{1}{h}\sum_{i=1}^{n}K\left(\frac{t-Z_i}{h}\right)q_i,$$

$$\hat{\lambda}(t) = \frac{1}{h}\sum_{i=1}^{n}K\left(\frac{t-Z_i}{h}\right)\frac{\delta_i}{n-1+1}. \tag{28.31}$$

Cai (1998) demonstrates consistency and asymptotic normality when $\{t_i\}$ is α-mixing, and demonstrates that the optimal window width is of order $n^{-1/5}$.

28.9   Panel data models

The panel data economic models are formulated for data where the same cross-sectional units are observed over time. These can be written, for $i = 1, \ldots, n$ and $t = 1, \ldots, T$, as

$$y_{it} = g(x_{it}) + v_i + u_{it}$$

where u_{it} is the usual equation error and v_i represents the cross-sectional hetero-geneity parameters. When v_i is treated as random we have the random effect (error component) model, and when v_i is treated as fixed we get the fixed effect model. There is an extensive literature on parametric estimation of these models where $g(x_{it})$ has a parametric specification, say $g(x_{it}, \beta) = x_{it}\beta$; see Hsiao (2003) and Baltagi (2001). In the nonparametric literature the developments are as follows. Considering first the case of random effect models, where the combined error has the usual covariance matrix Ω under the *i.i.d* assumptions on v and u, Henderson and Ullah (2003) propose a local linear generalized least squares estimator that has an improved performance compared to the conventional local least squares estimator (section 28.2), which considers the covariance matrix of the combined error as an identity matrix; also see Lin and Carroll (2000) and Ruckstuhl, Welsh and Carroll (2000). The above model can be extended to the case of a semiparametric random effect model $y_{it} = z_{it}\beta + g(x_{it}) + v_i + u_{it}$, where z_{it} is a vector of observed variables including a lagged dependent variable. This model has been studied in Li and Ullah (1998) and Berg, Li and Ullah (2000), who propose a $\sqrt{n}$ consistent instrumental variable estimator of β; see also Li and Stengos (1994), Li and Kniesner (2002), Khanna, Mundra and Ullah (1999), Kumar and Ullah (2000), Das (2004), Honore (1992), and Zegar and Diggle (1994), among others. You and Zhou (2003) provide a law of iterated logarithms for the estimators of β and variances of u, v, and they obtain the optimal nonparametric convergence rate of the estimator of $g(\cdot)$. You and Zhou (2004) have examined the semiparametric model above, where they consider u_{it} to be serially correlated, and You, Zhou and Zhou (2004) consider the case of conditional heteroskedasticity of u_{it}. However, the estimation of the fixed effect model is not fully developed, although Porter (1996) attempts series estimation and Mukherjee (2002) attempts kernel estimation.

28.10 Conclusion

Nonparametric methods provide a variety of advanced techniques for applied data analysis. Great strides have been made since the pioneering work that began in the 1950s, and more are certain to follow. The appeal of nonparametric methods relative to parametric ones stems from the fact that they have the potential to reveal structure in the data (functional form) that may be missed by common parametric specifications. Given that nonparametric kernel estimation is local in nature, it can provide varying estimates of economic parameters as opposed to the single global estimate typically presumed in parametric models. Furthermore, nonparametric estimation is useful for developing semiparametric models, in which a parametric model is combined with a nonparametric component. In addition, nonparametric methods can provide test statistics which can be consistent for unspecified forms of the alternative hypothesis, since parametric tests are generally inconsistent under a misspecified parametric alternative hypothesis.

The adoption of kernel methods has, however, been slowed somewhat by two factors: (i) the lack of a unified approach toward data-driven window width selection; and (ii) the lack of a software paradigm that permits fast computation of kernel-based objects for large datasets in a desktop environment (see Racine, 2002a and the references therein). We are confident that these issues will be overcome in the near future.

Acknowledgments

The authors are grateful to Terry Mills and an associate editor for their valuable comments and suggestions. Racine gratefully acknowledges financial support from the National Science Foundation. Ullah gratefully acknowledges financial support from the Academic Senate, UCR.

Note

1. A "kernel" is simply a weighting function.

References

Ait-Sahalia, Y. (1996) Testing continuous-time models of the spot interest rate. *The Review of Financial Studies* 9, 385–426.

Aitchison, J. and C.G.G. Aitken (1976) Multivariate binary discrimination by the kernel method. *Biometrika* 63(3), 413–20.

Akaike, H. (1970) Statistical predictor identification. *Annals of the Institute of Statistics and Mathematics* 22, 203–17.

Andrews, D. and Y. Sun (2004) Adaptive local polynomial whittle estimation of long-range dependence. *Econometrica* 72(2), 569–614.

Auestad, B. and D. Tjøstheim (1990) Identification of nonlinear time series: first order characterization and order estimation. *Biometrika* 77, 669–87.

Auestad, B. and D. Tjøstheim (1994) Nonparametric identification of non-linear time series: selecting significant lags. *Journal of the American Statistical Association* 89, 1410–1419.

Azzalini, A. and A.W. Bowman (1997) *Applied Smoothing Techniques for Data Analysis: The Kernel Approach with S-Plus Illustrations.* New York: Oxford University Press.

Baltagi, B. (2001) *Econometric analysis of panel data,* 2nd edn. New York: John Wiley.

Bashtannyk, D.M. and R.J. Hyndman (2001) Bandwidth selection for kernel conditional density estimation. *Computational Statistics and Data Analysis* 36, 279–98.

Bera, A. and M. Higgins (1993) ARCH models: properties, estimation, and testing. *Journal of Economic Surveys* 7, 305–66.

Berg, M.D., Q. Li and A. Ullah (2000) Instrumental variable estimation of semiparametric dynamic panel data models: Monte carlo results on several new and existing estimators. *Advances in Econometrics* 15, 297–315.

Bickel, P.J., C.A.J. Klaassen, Y. Ritov and J.A. Wellner (1993) *Efficient and Adaptive Estimation for Semi-parametric Models.* Baltimore: Johns Hopkins University Press.

Bollerslev, T., R. Engle and D. Nelson (1994) ARCH models. *Handbook of Econometrics* 4.

Bowman, A., P. Hall and T. Prvan (1998) Bandwidth selection for the smoothing of distribution functions. *Biometrika* 85, 799–808.

Breitung, J. (2002) Nonparametric tests for unit roots and cointegration. *Journal of Econometrics* 108, 343–63.

Brown, D. and R. Matzkin (1996) Estimation of nonparametric functions in simultaneous equations models, with an application to consumer demand. Technical report, Northwestern University.

Cai, Z. (1998) Kernel density and hazard rate estimation for censored dependent data. *Journal of Multivariate Analysis* 67, 23–34.

Cai, Z. (2002) Regression quantiles for time series data. *Econometric Theory* 18, 169–92.

Carroll, R.J. (1982) Adapting for heteroskedasticity in linear models. *Annals of Statistics* 10, 1224–1233.

Chaudhuri, P. (1992) Multivariate location estimation using extension of R-estimates through U-statistics type approach. *The Annals of Statistics* 20, 897–916.

Chen, R., J.S. Liu and R.S. Tsay (1995) Additivity tests for nonlinear autoregressive models. *Biometrika* 82, 369–83.

Chen, R. and R. Tsay (1993) Nonlinear additive arx models. *Journal of the American Statistical Association* 88, 955–67.

Chen, S., G.B. Dahl and S. Khan (2005) Nonparametric identification and estimation of a censored location-scale regression model. *Journal of the American Statistical Association* 100(469), 212–21.

Chen, S. and S. Khan (2000) Estimating censored regression models in the presence of nonparametric multiplicative heteroskedasticity. *Journal of Econometrics* 98, 283–316.

Chen, X. and Y. Fan (1999) Consistent hypothesis testing in semiparametric and nonparametric models for econometric time series. *Journal of Econometrics* 91, 373–401.

Cheng, B. and H. Tong (1992) On consist non-parametric order determination and chaos (with discussion). *Journal of the Royal Statistical Society, Series B* 54, 427–74.

Chu, C.I. and J.S. Marron (1991) Choosing a kernel regression estimator (with discussions). *Statistical Science* 6, 404–36.

Chung, Y.P. and Z. Zhou (1996) The predictability of stock returns: a nonparametric approach. *Econometric Reviews* 15, 299–330.

Cleveland, W.S. (1979) Robust locally weighted regression and smoothing scatterplots. *Journal of the American Statistical Association* 74, 829–36.

Cleveland, W.S. and S.J. Devlin (1988) Locally weighted regression: an approach to regression analysis by local fitting. *Journal of the American Statistical Association* 83, 596–610.

Cleveland, W.S., S.J. Devlin and E. Grosse (1988) *Regression by local fitting. Journal of Econometrics* 37, 87–114.

Collomb, G., W. Härdle, and S. Hassani (1987) A note on prediction via estimation of the conditional mode function. *Journal of Statistical Planning and Inference* 15, 227–36.

Darolles, S., J.P. Florens and E. Renault (2001) Nonparametric instrumental regression. Technical report, Universitè de Montreal.

Das, M. (2004) Instrumental variables estimators for nonparametric models with discrete endogenous regressors. *Journal of Econometrics* 124, 335–61.

Delgado, M. (1992) Semiparametric generalised least squares in the multivariate nonlinear regression model. *Econometric Theory* 8, 203–22.

Delgado, M. and W. Manteiga (2001) Significance testing in nonparametric regression based on the bootstrap. *Annals of Statistics* 29, 1469–1507.

Devroye, L. and L. Györfi (1985) *Nonparametric Density Estimation: The L^1 View*. New York: Wiley.

Efromovich, S. (1999) *Nonparametric Curve Estimation: Methods, Theory and Applications*. New York: Springer Verlag.

Engle, R. (1982) Autoregressive conditional heteroscedasticity with estimates of the variance of UK inflation. *Econometrica* 50, 987–1008.

Engle, R. (2002) Dynamic conditional correlation: a simple class of multivariate generalized autoregressive conditional heteroskedasticity models. *Journal of Business and Economic Statistics*, 339–350.

Engle, R. and G. Gonzàlez-Rivera (1991) Semiparametric ARCH models. *Journal of Business and Economic Statistics* 9, 345–59.

Engle, R., C.W.J. Granger, J. Rice and A. Weiss (1986) Semiparametric estimates of the relation between weather and electricity demand. *Journal of the American Statistical Association* 81, 310–20.

Engle, R. and K. Kroner (1995) Multivariate simultaneous generalized ARCH. *Econometric Theory* **11**, 122–50.

Engle, R. and S. Manganelli (1999) CAVaR: conditional autoregressive value at risk by regression quantiles. Technical report, University of California San Diego, Manuscript.

Engle, R. and K. Sheppard (2001) Theoretical and empirical properties of dynamic conditional correlation multivariate GARCH. Technical Report 2001-15, University of California San Diego Economics Discussion Papers.

Epanechnikov, V.A. (1969) Nonparametric estimation of a multidimensional probability density. *Theory of Applied Probability* **14**, 153–8.

Eubank, R.L. (1999) *Nonparametric Regression and Spline Smoothing*, vol. 157 of *Statistics, Textbooks and Monographs*. New York: Marcel Dekker.

Eubank, R. and C. Spiegelman (1990) Testing the goodness of fit of a linear model via nonparametric regression techniques. *Journal of the American Statistical Association* **85**, 387–92.

Fan, J. (1992) Design-adaptive nonparametric regression. *Journal of the American Statistical Association* **87**, 998–1004.

Fan, J. and I. Gijbels (1995) Data-driven bandwidth selection in local polynomial fitting: variable bandwidth and spatial adaptation. *Journal of the Royal Statistical Society, Series B* **57**, 371–94.

Fan, J. and I. Gijbels (1996) *Local Polynomial Modelling and Its Applications*. London: Chapman and Hall.

Fan, J., I.C. Hu and Y.K. Truong (1994) Robust nonparametric function estimation. *Scandinavian Journal of Statistics* **21**, 433–46.

Fan, J. and Q. Li (2003) A kernel based method for estimating additive partially linear models. *Statistica Sinica* **13**, 739–62.

Fan, J. and Q. Yao (1998) Efficient estimation of conditional variance functions in stochastic regression. *Biometrika* **85**, 645–60.

Fan, Y. (1994) Testing the goodness-of-fit of a parametric density function by kernel method. *Econometric Theory* **64**, 865–90.

Fan, Y. and Q. Li (1996) Consistent model specification tests: omitted variables and semiparametric functional forms. *Econometrica* **64**, 865–90.

Fan, Y. and A. Ullah (1999) On goodness-of-fit tests for weakly dependent processes using kernel method. *Journal of Nonparametric Statistics* **11**, 337–60.

Fox, J. (2002) *An R and S-PLUS Companion to Applied Regression*. Sage.

Gallant, A. (1982) Unbiased determination of production technologies. *Journal of Econometrics* **20**, 285–323.

Gao, J. and H. Tong (2004) Semiparametric non-linear time series model selection. *Journal of the Royal Statistical Society, Series B* **66**, 321–36.

Glad, I.K. (1998) Parametrically guided nonparametric regression. *Scandinavian Journal of Statistics* **25**, 649–68.

Granger, C. and T. Teräsvirta (1993) *Modelling Nonlinear Economic Relationships*. Oxford: Oxford University Press.

Györfi, L., W. Härdle, P. Sarda and P. Vieu (1989) *Nonparametric Curve Estimation from Time Series*. New York: Springer-Verlag.

Haggan, V. and T. Ozaki (1981) Modeling nonlinear vibrations using an amplitude-dependent autoregressive time series model. *Biometrika* **68**, 189–96.

Hall, P., Q. Li and J.S. Racine (2004) Nonparametric estimation of regression functions in the presence of irrelevant regressors. Technical report, Manuscript.

Hall, P., J. Racine and Q. Li (2004) Cross-validation and the estimation of conditional probability densities. *Journal of the American Statistical Association* **99**(2), 1015–1026.

Hall, P., R.C.L. Wolff and Q. Yao (1999) Methods for estimating a conditional distribution function. *Journal of the American Statistical Association* **94**, 154–63.

Hamilton, J.D. (1994) *Time Series Analysis*. Princeton, NJ: Princeton University Press.

Hansen, B.E. (2004) Nonparametric estimation of smooth conditional distributions. Technical report, manuscript.

Härdle, W. (1990) *Applied Nonparametric Regression*. Cambridge, New Rochelle.

Härdle, W. and T. Gasser (1984) Robust nonparametric function fitting. *Journal of the Royal Statistical Society, Series B* **46**(1), 42–51.

Härdle, W., S. Klinke and B. Turlach (1995) *XploRe: an Interactive Statistical Computing Environment*. New York: Springer-Verlag.

Härdle, W., H. Lütkepohl and R. Chen (1996) A review of nonparametric time series analysis. Technical report, Centre de Recherche en Economie et Statistique Working Paper.

Härdle, W., M. Müller, S. Sperlich and A. Werwatz (2004) *Nonparametric and Semiparametric Models*, Springer Series in Statistics. Berlin: Springer-Verlag.

Härdle, W. and T. Stoker (1989) Investigating smooth multiple regression by the method of average derivatives. *Journal of the American Statistical Association* **84**, 986–95.

Härdle, W. and A. Tsybakov (1997) Locally polynomial estimators of the volatility function. *Journal of Econometrics* **81**, 223–42.

Härdle, W. and P. Vieu (1992) Kernel regression smoothing of time series. *Journal of Time Series Analysis* **13**, 209–32.

Hart, J.D. (1997) *Nonparametric Smoothing and Lack-of-Fit Tests*. New York: Springer-Verlag.

Hart, J. and P. Vieu (1990) Data-driven bandwidth choice for density estimation based on dependent data. *Annals of Statistics* **18**.

Hastie, T. and C. Loader (1993) Local regression: automatic kernel carpentry (with discussion). *Statistical Science* **8**, 120–43.

Hastie, T. and R. Tibshirani (1990) *Generalized Additive Models*. London: Chapman and Hall.

Hausman, J., B.H. Hall and Z. Griliches (1984) Econometric models for count data with an application of the patents–R&D relationship, *Econometrica* **52**(4), 909–38.

Henderson, D. and A. Ullah (2003) A nonparametric random effects estimator. Technical report, University of California, Riverside.

Hidalgo, J. (1992) Adaptive estimation in the presence of autocorrelation of unknown form. *Journal of Time Series Analysis* **13**, 47–78.

Hjellvik, V. and D. Tjøstheim (1995) Nonparametric tests for linearity for time series. *Biometrika* **82**, 351–68.

Hong, Y. and T.-H. Lee (2003a) Diagnostic checking for the adequacy of nonlinear time series models. *Econometric Theory* **19**, 1065–1121.

Hong, Y. and T.-H. Lee (2003b) Inference on predictability of foreign exchange rates via generalized spectrum and nonlinear time series models. *Review of Economics and Statistics*. **85**, 1048–1062.

Honore, B. (1992) Trimmed lad and least squares estimation of truncated and censored regression models with fixed effects. *Econometrica* **60**, 533–65.

Hoogstrate, A.J. (1994) Nonparametric regression with integrated processes. Technical report, University of Maastricht.

Horowitz, J.L. (1998) *Semiparametric Methods in Econometrics*, Lecture notes in statistics. New York: Springer-Verlag.

Horowitz, J. and S. Lee (2002) Semiparametric methods in applied econometrics: do the models fit the data? *Statistical Modelling* **2**, 3–22.

Horowitz, J. and E. Mammen (2004) Nonparametric estimation of an additive model with a link function. *Annals of Statistics* **32**(6), 2412–2443.

Hsiao, C. (2003) *Analysis of Panel Data*, 2nd edn. Cambridge: Cambridge University Press.

Hsiao, C. and Q. Li (2001) A consistent test for conditional heteroskedasticity in time-series regression models. *Econometric Theory* **17**, 188–221.

Hurvich, C.M., J.S. Simonoff and C.L. Tsai (1998) Smoothing parameter selection in nonparametric regression using an improved akaike information criterion. *Journal of the Royal Statistical Society B* **60**, 271–93.

Ichimura, H. (1993) Semiparametric least squares (SLS) and weighted SLS estimation of single-index models. *Journal of Econometrics* **58**, 71–120.

Imbens, G. and W. Newey (2001) Identification and estimation of triangular simultaneous equations models without additivity.

Jones, D. (1978) Non-linear autoregressive processes. *Journal of the Royal Statistical Society, Series A* **360**, 71–95.

Khanna, M., K. Mundra and A. Ullah (1999) Parametric and semi-parametric estimation of the effect of firm attributes on efficiency: the electricity generating sector in India. *Journal of International Trade and Economic Development* **8**, 419–36.

Kim, T. and H. White (2003) Estimation, inference, and specification testing for possibly misspecified quantile regressions. In T. Fomby and R. Hill (eds), *Maximum Likelihood Estimation of Misspecified Models: Twenty Years Later*. Amsterdam: Elsevier, pp. 107–32.

Koenker, R. and G. Bassett (1978) Regression quantiles. *Econometrica* **46**, 33–50.

Koenker, R. and Q. Zhao (1996) Conditional quantile estimation and inference for arch models. *Econometric Theory* **12**, 793–813.

Komunjer, I. (2003) Quasi-maximum likelihood estimation for conditional quantiles. Manuscript, Caltech.

Kuan, C. and H. White (1994) Artificial neural networks: an econometric perspective. *Econometric Reviews* **13**, 1–91.

Kumar, S. and A. Ullah (2000) Semiparametric varying parameter panel data models: an application to estimation of speed of convergence. *Advance in Econometrics* **14**, 109–128.

Küunsch, H.R. (1987) Statistical aspects of self-similar processes. In *Proceedings of the First World Congress of the Bernoulli Society*. VNU Science Press, pp. 67–74.

Lavergne, P. (2001) An equality test across nonparametric regressions. *Journal of Econometrics* **103**, 307–44.

Lavergne, P. and Q. Vuong (2000) Nonparametric significance testing. *Econometric Theory* **16**, 576–601.

Lee, S. (2003) Efficient semiparametric estimation of partially linear quantile regression models. *Econometric Theory* **19**, 1–31.

Lee, T.H. and A. Ullah (2001) Nonparametric bootstrap tests for neglected nonlinearity in time series regression models. *Journal of Nonparametric Statistics* **13**, 425–51.

Lee, T. and A. Ullah (2003) Nonparametric bootstrap specification testing in econometric models. In D. Giles (ed), *Computer-Aided Econometrics*. New York: Marcel Dekker, pp. 451–77.

Lewbel, A. and O. Linton (2002) Nonparametric censored and truncated regression. *Econometrica* **70**(2), 765–79.

Li, Q. (1999) Consistent model specification tests for time series econometric models. *Journal of Econometrics* **92**, 101–47.

Li, Q. (2000) Efficient estimation of additive partially linear models. *International Economic Review* **41**, 1073–1092.

Li, Q. and T. Kniesner (2002) Semiparametric panel data models with heterogeneous dynamic adjustment: theoretical consideration and an application to labor supply. *Empirical Economics* **27**, 131–48.

Li, Q., X. Lu and A. Ullah (2003) Multivariate local polynomial regression for estimating average derivatives. *Journal of Nonparametric Statistics* **15**, 607–24.

Li, Q. and J.S. Racine (2003) Nonparametric estimation of distributions with categorical and continuous data. *Journal of Multivariate Analysis* **86**(2), 266–92.

Li, Q. and J.S. Racine (2004) Cross-validated local linear nonparametric regression. *Statistica Sinica* **14**(2), 485–512.

Li, Q. and J.S. Racine (forthcoming) *Nonparametric Econometrics: Theory and Practice*. Princeton, NJ: Princeton University Press.

Li, Q. and T. Stengos (1994) Adaptive estimation in the panel data error component model with heteroscedasticity of unknown form. *International Economic Review* **35**, 981–1000.

Li, Q. and A. Ullah (1998) Estimating partially linear panel data models with one-way error components. *Econometric Reviews* **17**, 145–66.

Li, Q. and S. Wang (1998) A simple consistent bootstrap test for a parametric regression functional form. *Journal of Econometrics* **87**, 145–65.

Li, Q. and J.M. Wooldridge (2002) Semiparametric estimation of partially linear models for dependent data with generated regressors. *Econometric Theory* **18**(3), 625–45.

Lin, X.H. and R. Carroll (2000) Nonparametric function estimation for clustered data when the predictor is measured without/with error. *Journal of the American Statistical Association* **95**, 520–34.

Linton, O. (1995) Estimation in semiparametric models: a review. In P.C.B. Phillips and G.S. Maddala (eds), *A Volume in Honor of C. R. Rao*. Oxford: Blackwell.

Linton, O. (1997) Efficient estimation of additive nonparametric regression models. *Biometrika* **84**, 469–74.

Linton, O. (2000) Efficient estimation of generalized additive nonparametric regression models. *Econometric Theory* **16**, 502–23.

Linton, O.B. and P. Gozalo (2001) Testing additivity in generalized nonparametric regression models with estimated parameters. *Journal of Econometrics* **104**, 1–48.

Linton, O. and W. Härdle (1996) Estimating additive regression with known links. *Biometrika* **83**, 529–40.

Linton, O. and J. Nielsen (1995) A kernel method of estimating structured nonparametric regression based on marginal integration. *Biometrika* **82**, 93–100.

Loader, C.R. (1999) Bandwidth selection: classical or plug-in? *The Annals of Statistics* **27**(2), 415–38.

Long, X.D. and A. Ullah (2004) Theoretical properties and empirical application of semiparametric conditional correlation model. Technical report, University of California, Riverside.

Manski, C.F. (1988) Identification of binary response models. *Journal of the American Statistical Association* **83**(403), 729–38.

Marron, S. (1992) Bootstrap bandwidth selection. In R. LePage and L. Billard (eds), *Exploring the Limits of Bootstrap*. New York: Wiley, pp. 249–62.

Masry, E. (1996a) Multivariate local polynomial regression estimation for time series: uniform strong consistency and rates. *Journal of Time Series Analysis* **17**, 517–99.

Masry, E. (1996b) Multivariate regression estimation local polynomial fitting for time series. *Stochastic Processes Application* **65**, 81–101.

Masry, E. and D. Tjøstheim (1995) Non-parametric estimation and identification of ARCH and ARX nonlinear time series: convergence properties and rates. *Econometric Theory* **11**, 259–89.

Matzkin, R.L. (2003) Nonparametric estimation of nonadditive random functions. *Econometrica* **71**(5), 1339–1375.

Mishra, S., L. Su and A. Ullah (2003) Combined estimator of time series conditional heteroskedasticity. Manuscript, University of California, Riverside.

Mukherjee, D. (2002) Nonparametric and semiparametric generalized panel data analysis of convergence and growth. PhD thesis, University of California, Riverside.

Nadaraya, E.A. (1965) On nonparametric estimates of density functions and regression curves. *Theory of Applied Probability* **10**, 186–90.

Naito, K. (2004) Semiparametric density estimation by local L2-fitting. *Annals of Statistics* **3**, 1162–1192.

Newey, W. (1990) Semiparametric efficiency bounds. *Journal of Applied Econometrics* **5**, 99–135.

Newey, W. (1997) Convergence rates and asymptotic normality of series estimators. *Journal of Econometrics* **29**, 147–68.

Newey, W.K. and J.L. Powell (2003) Instrumental variables estimation of nonparametric models. *Econometrica* **71**(5), 1565–1578.

Newey, W., J. Powell and F. Vella (1999) Nonparametric estimation of triangular simultaneous equations models, *Econometrica* **67**, 565–603.

Pagan, A. and A. Ullah (1999) *Nonparametric Econometrics*, Cambridge University Press.

Park, J. and Y.J. Whang (1999) Testing for martingale hypothesis, Technical report, Rice University.

Pawlak, M., E. Rafajlowicz and A. Steland (2004) On detecting jumps in time series: nonparametric setting. *Journal of Nonparametric Statistics* **16**, 329–47.

Pelletiery, D. (2003) Regime switching for dynamic correlations, Technical report, North Carolina State University and Université de Montréal.

Phillips, P.C.B. and J.Y. Park (1998) Nonstationary density estimation and kernel autoregression, Technical Report 1181, Cowles Foundation Discussion Paper.

Phillips, P.C.B. and K. Shimotsu (2004) Local whittle estimation in nonstationary and unit root cases, *The Annals of Statistics* **32**(1), 656–92.

Pinkse, J. (2000) Nonparametric two-step regression functions when regressors and error are dependent, *Canadian Journal of Statistics* **28**, 289–300.

Polansky, A.M. and E.R. Baker (2000) Multistage plug-in bandwidth selection for kernel distribution function estimates, *Journal of Statistical Computation and Simulation* **65**, 63–80.

Porter, J. (1996) Essays in econometrics, PhD thesis, Harvard University.

Powell, J.L. (1984) Least absolute deviations estimation for the censored regression model, *Journal of Econometrics* **25**, 303–25.

Prakasa Rao, B.L.S. (1983) *Nonparametric Functional Estimation*, Academic Press.

R Development Core Team (2003) *R: A language and environment for statistical computing*, R Foundation for Statistical Computing, Vienna, Austria. ISBN 3-900051-00-3. URL: *http://www.R-project.org*.

Racine, J.S. (1997) Consistent significance testing for nonparametric regression, *Journal of Business and Economic Statistics* **15**(3), 369–79.

Racine, J.S. (2002a) Parallel distributed kernel estimation, *Computational Statistics and Data Analysis* **40**, 293–302.

Racine, J.S. (2002b) New and improved direct marketing: A nonparametric approach, In A. Montgomery and P.H. Franses (eds) *Advances in Econometrics: Econometric Models in Marketing*, Vol. 16, Elsevier Science, pp. 139–62.

Racine, J.S. (2002c) Index-free, density-based multinomial choice. In A. Ullah, A. Wan and A. Chaturvedi (eds) *Handbook of Applied Econometrics and Statistical Inference*, New York: Marcel Dekker, pp. 115–42.

Racine, J.S., J. Hart and Q. Li (2004) Testing the significance of categorical predictor variables in nonparametric regression models, Unpublished manuscript, Department of Economics, Texas A&M University.

Racine, J.S. and Q. Li (2004) Nonparametric estimation of regression functions with both categorical and continuous data, *Journal of Econometrics* **119**(1), 99–130.

Racine, J.S., Q. Li and X. Zhu (2004) Kernel estimation of multivariate conditional distributions, *Annals of Economics and Finance* **5**(2), 211–35.

Rahman, M. and A. Ullah (2002) Improved combined parametric and nonparametric regressions: Estimation and hypothesis testing. In *Handbook of Applied Econometrics and Statistical Inference*, New York: Marcel Dekker Inc., pp. 159–76.

Rilstone, P. (1991) Nonparametric hypothesis testing with parametric rates of convergence, *International Economic Review* **32**, 209–27.

Robinson, P.M. (1983) Nonparametric estimators for time series, *Journal of Time Series Analysis* **4**, 185–207.

Robinson, P.M. (1987) Asymptotically efficient estimation in the presence of heteroscedasticity of unknown form, *Econometrica* **56**, 875–91.

Robinson, P.M. (1988) Root-n consistent semiparametric regression, *Econometrica* **56**, 931–54.

Robinson, P.M. (1989) Hypothesis testing in semiparametric and nonparametric models for econometric time series, *Review of Economic Studies* **56**, 511–34.

Roehrig, C. (1988) Conditions for identification in nonparametric and parametric models, *Econometrica* **55**, 875–91.

Ruckstuhl, A., A. Welsh and R. Carroll (2000) Nonparametric function estimation of the relationship between two repeatedly measured variables, *Statistic Sinica* **10**, 51–71.

Ruppert, D., R.J. Carroll and M.P. Wand (2003) *Semiparametric Regression Modeling*. Cambridge University Press.

Ruppert, D., S.J. Sheather and M.P. Wand (1995) An effective bandwidth selector for local least squares regression. *Journal of the American Statistical Association* **90**, 1257–1270.

Ruppert, D. and M.P. Wand (1994) Multivariate weighted least squares regression. *Annals of Statistics* **22**, 1346–1370.

Schwarz, G. (1978) Estimating the dimension of a model. *The Annals of Statistics* **6**, 461–4.

Scott, D.W. (1992) *Multivariate Density Estimation: Theory, Practice, and Visualization*. New York: Wiley.

Seifert, B. and T. Gasser (2000) Data adaptive ridging in local polynomial regression. *Journal of Computational and Graphical Statistics* **9**(2), 338–60.

Silverman, B.W. (1986) *Density Estimation for Statistics and Data Analysis*. New York: Chapman and Hall.

Simonoff, J.S. (1996) *Smoothing Methods in Statistics*. New York: Springer.

Speckman, P. (1988) Kernel smoothing in partial linear models. *Journal of the Royal Statistical Society, Series B* **50**, 413–36.

Stone, C.J. (1977) Consistent nonparametric regression. *Annals of Statistics* **5**, 267–84.

Su, L. and A. Ullah (2003) More efficient estimation of nonparametric regression with nonparametric errors. Technical report, Department of Economics, University of California San Diego.

Su, L. and A. Ullah (2004) Local polynomial estimation of nonparametric simultaneous equations models. Technical report, Department of Economics, University of California San Diego.

Su, L. and H. White (2003) Testing conditional independence via empirical likelihood. Technical Report 2003–14, Department of Economics, University of California San Diego.

Tjøstheim, D. and B. Auestad (1994a) Non-parametric identification of non-linear time series: projection. *Journal of the American Statistical Association* **89**, 1398–1409.

Tjøstheim, D. and B. Auestad (1994b) Non-parametric identification of non-linear time series: selecting significant lags. *Journal of the American Statistical Association* **89**, 1410–1419.

Tong, H. (1978) On a threshold model. In *Pattern Recognition and Signal Processing*, Sijhoff and Noordhoff.

Tong, H. (1983) *Threshold Models in Nonlinear Time Series Analysis*, Lecture Notes in Statistics. Berlin: Springer-Verlag.

Tong, H. (1990) *Non-Linear Time Series: a Dynamical System Approach*. Oxford: Oxford University Press.

Tsay, R. (1989) Testing and modeling threshold autoregressive processes. *Journal of the American Statistical Association* **84**, 231–40.

Tse, Y. and A. Tsui (2002) A multivariate generalize autoregressive conditional heteroscedasticity model with time-varying correlations. *Journal of Business and Economic Statistics* 351–62.

Tsybakov, A.B. (1982) Robust estimates of a function. *Problems of Information Transmission* **18**, 190–201.

Wand, M.P. and M.C. Jones (1995) *Kernel Smoothing*. London: Chapman and Hall.

Watson, G.S. (1964) Smooth regression analysis. *Sankhya* **26**(15), 175–84.

Wong, C.M. and R. Kohn (1996) A Bayesian approach to estimating and forecasting additive nonparametric autoregressive models. *Journal of Time Series Analysis* **17**, 203–20.

Xiao, Z., O. Linton, R. Carroll and E. Mammen (2003) More efficient local polynomial estimation in nonparametric regression with autocorrelated errors. *Journal of the American Statistical Association* **98**, 980–92.

Yatchew, A. (2003) *Semiparametric Regression for the Applied Econometrician*. Cambridge: Cambridge University Press.

You, J. and X. Zhou (2003) Asymptotic properties of estimators for semiparametric partially linear panel data models. Technical report, University of Hong Kong Polytechnic University.

You, J. and X. Zhou (2004) Statistical inference in a panel data semiparametric regression model with serially correlated errors. Technical report, University of Hong Kong Polytechnic University.

You, J., X. Zhou and Y. Zhou (2004) Statistical inference for panel data semiparametric partially linear regression models with heteroscedastic errors. Technical report, University of Hong Kong Polytechnic University.

Yu, K. and M. Jones (1998) Local linear quantile regression. *Journal of the American Statistical Association* **93**, 228–37.

Zeger, S. and P. Diggle (1994) Semiparametric model for longitudinal data with application to cd4 cell numbers in HIV seroconverters. *Biometrics* **50**, 689–99.

Ziegelmann, F. (2002) Nonparametric estimation of volatility functions: the local exponential estimator. *Econometric Reviews* **18**(4), 985–91.

29

Performance of Seasonal Adjustment Procedures: Simulation and Empirical Results

Dennis Fok, Philip Hans Franses and Richard Paap

Abstract

In this chapter we use a simulation experiment to examine whether the seasonal adjustment methods Census X12-ARIMA and TRAMO/SEATS effectively remove seasonality properties from time series data, while preserving other features like the stochastic trend. As data-generating processes we use a variety of processes that are actually found in practice. These processes include constant seasonality, changing seasonal patterns due to seasonal unit roots and processes with periodically varying parameters. To check for seasonality, we consider tests for seasonal unit roots, for deterministic seasonality, for seasonality in the variance, and for periodicity in the parameters. Our simulation results show that both adjustment methods are able to remove stochastic seasonal patterns from the data with the exception of changing seasonal patterns due to periodicity in the parameters. On average, the two methods perform equally well.

29.1	Introduction	1036
29.2	Seasonal adjustment procedures	1037
	29.2.1 Census X12-ARIMA	1038
	29.2.2 TRAMO/SEATS	1039
29.3	Diagnostic tests	1040
	29.3.1 HEGY test	1040
	29.3.2 Canova–Hansen test	1041
	29.3.3 Test for equal seasonal dummies	1042
	29.3.4 Test for correlation at the seasonal lag	1042
	29.3.5 Test for periodicity in AR parameters	1042
	29.3.6 Test for seasonality in the variance	1043
29.4	Data-generating processes	1043
	29.4.1 DGP1: constant annual growth	1044
	29.4.2 DGP2: deterministic seasonality	1044
	29.4.3 DGP3: stochastic seasonality	1046
	29.4.4 DGP4: airline model	1046
	29.4.5 DGP5: periodic autoregressive process	1048
29.5	Simulation results	1048
	29.5.1 DPG1	1048
	29.5.2 DPG2	1051

29.5.3   DPG3   1051
29.5.4   DPG4   1052
29.5.5   DPG5   1052
29.6   Concluding remarks   1053

29.1   Introduction

Many quarterly observed macroeconomic time series, such as gross domestic product, private consumption, and industrial production, often display (i) an upward trend, (ii) substantial intra-year seasonal variation, (iii) several aberrant observations, and (iv) nonlinearity. Macroeconomists and policymakers tend to be interested mainly in the trend and in variable-specific business-cycle variation.

Some macroeconomists tend to feel that seasonal variation is likely to blur their view on the trend and the business cycle movements in macroeconomic time series and therefore they want this variation to be removed from the data before any business cycle analysis. Indeed, a first glance at almost any graph of a quarterly macroeconomic time series immediately indicates that seasonal variation can be quite dominant. Rough calculations, based on regressing the growth rates of such variables on quarterly seasonal dummies, show that almost 80 to 90 percent of the variation may be attributable to seasonality: see, for example, Miron (1996). Whether this is the best way of summarizing the data is not beyond discussion (see Hylleberg, 1994, among others), but it does indicate that business-cycle variation is not immediately and visually obvious in the presence of such substantial seasonality.

There are two main criticisms on (the use of) seasonally adjusted data. The first states that seasonal variation can be important to study in its own right, and it might, for example, be informative concerning which variables lead others into or out of a recession: see Miron (1996), Hylleberg (1994), Ghysels (1994), Franses and Paap (1999) and Matas-Mir and Osborn (2003), among many others. Of course, the analysis of unadjusted data is more involved, as one needs to include specific parameters and variables in the model to capture seasonality. However, recent advances in the area of modelling seasonality show that this analysis need not be that difficult: see Ghysels and Osborn (2001) and Franses and Paap (2004).

The second criticism is that the process of seasonal adjustment may change (dynamic) correlations between macroeconomic variables. Long-run relationships and short-run dynamics in multivariate models tend to differ across models calibrated with unadjusted and with adjusted data. Only if the seasonal adjustment filter is linear and common to all variables is there is no conflicting inference: see Sims (1974) and Wallis (1974) for early references, and Ghysels and Perron (1993) and Ericsson *et al.* (1994) for more recent evidence. Ghysels *et al.* (1996), however, challenge the linearity of the Census X-11 filter.

In this chapter we abstain from a discussion on whether one should seasonally adjust data or not. As our starting point, we will assume that one is simply interested in seasonally adjusted data and that an automatic adjustment method is needed to remove seasonality from many time series. For this purpose, there are two popular methods for seasonal adjustment. The first is the Census X12-ARIMA method (see Findley *et al.*, 1998). This method is data-based and consists of several steps, including outlier correction, trading-day correction and various sequences of moving average filters. The second method, TRAMO/SEATS, is more model-based (see Gómez and Maravall, 1997). In this, a reasonably adequate univariate time series model for the data is specified, and the seasonal adjustment filter is derived from the model's properties.

To judge the quality of both adjustment methods, in this chapter we consider a simulation experiment. Instead of comparing the adjusted series with the raw series, our main focus is to analyze whether seasonal adjustment methods are able to remove the seasonal patterns in time series in an adequate way while leaving the possible stochastic trend properties of the series untouched. To stay close to reality, we use data-generating processes which are likely to be found in practice. These processes display either constant seasonality or changing seasonal patterns due to seasonal unit roots, and processes with periodically varying parameters. Plausible parameter values are obtained by estimating the corresponding time series models for 14 US industrial production series. To search for seasonal patterns before and after correction, we consider tests for seasonal unit roots, for deterministic seasonality, for seasonality in the variance, and for periodicity in the parameters.

The outline of the remainder of this chapter is as follows. In section 29.2 we briefly discuss the two seasonal adjustment procedures that we apply in this chapter. In section 29.3 we discuss several diagnostic and specification tests that we use to evaluate the quality of both seasonal adjustment filters. Section 29.4 discusses the data-generating processes for our simulation experiment. The outcomes of our simulation study are given in section 29.5 and we conclude in section 29.6.

29.2 Seasonal adjustment procedures

In this section we briefly discuss the two seasonal adjustment methods under scrutiny. We have no intention to be complete and we strongly suggest readers to consult other studies, like Hylleberg (1986), Findley *et al.* (1998), Maravall (1985, 1995) and Harvey (1989), for more details.

The main assumption of seasonal adjustment is that a seasonally observed time series $y_t, t = 1, \ldots, T$, can be decomposed into two unobserved components, that is,

$$y_t = y_t^{ns} + y_t^s \tag{29.1}$$

(or $y_t = y_t^{ns} y_t^s$ in the case of multiplicative seasonality), with y_t^{ns} denoting the nonseasonal component containing the trend, cycle and all kinds of other features, and y_t^s denoting the seasonal component.

When seasonality is purely deterministic, y_t^s is assumed to be a function of sine and cosine functions. When seasonality is not constant over time, one can consider certain moving average filters to characterize changing seasonality. Preferably, these filters are linear, symmetric and centered around the current observation: see Grether and Nerlove (1970). Denoting the backward shift operator as L, defined by $L^k y_t = y_{t-k}, k = 0, \pm 1, \pm 2, \ldots$, such a linear moving average filter is given by

$$C_m(L) = c_0 + \sum_{i=1}^{m} c_i(L^i + L^{-i}), \qquad (29.2)$$

where $c_0, c_1, \ldots, c_m$ are the weights. A simple example is the $C_1(L)$ filter with $c_0 = 1/2$ and $c_1 = -1/4$, which equals $-1/4(L^2 - 2L + 1)L^{-1}$, where we use $LL^{-1} = 1$. This filter assumes two unit roots at the nonseasonal frequency because $(L^2 - 2L + 1) = (1 - L)^2$. Hence it removes the stochastic trend (in fact, it removes two such trends). Generally, when the aim is to remove stochastic trends, it holds that $C_m(1) = c_0 + 2\sum_{i=1}^{m} c_i = 0$ Notice that the commonly applied differencing filter $(1 - L)$ is not a symmetric filter.

Following the same line of thought, to remove changing seasonality in quarterly data, one may opt for a filter like

$$4C_3(L) = (1 + L + L^2 + L^3)(1 + L^{-1} + L^{-2} + L^{-3}). \qquad (29.3)$$

This $C_3(L)$ filter has two times three seasonal unit roots, that is, two times -1 and two times $\pm i$ (see Hylleberg *et al.*, 1990). Writing (29.3) as (29.2), we have that $4c_0 = 4, 4c_1 = 3, 4c_2 = 2$ and $4c_3 = 1$. Generally, for filters that remove changing seasonality, it holds that $c_0 + 2\sum_{i=1}^{m} c_i = 1$ (which also holds for (29.3) after scaling). More details of the use of linear moving average filters are given in Maravall (1995) and Grether and Nerlove (1970), where it is shown that filters like (29.3) have certain optimal properties.

29.2.1 Census X12-ARIMA

The X12-ARIMA method is one of the most popular seasonal adjustment procedures in use. The key references for this approach are Shiskin and Eisenpress (1957) and Shiskin *et al.* (1967). A recent extensive documentation of this method appears in Findley *et al.* (1998). Apart from the treatment of holiday, trading-day and calendar effects, the additive version of the X12-ARIMA method concerns two main actions. The first is the sequential application of a set of linear moving average filters, as in (29.2), to characterize the trend and seasonal fluctuations. The filters have to be selected by the practitioner: that is, one has to select the value of m, where often m equals 5, 7 or 9 for quarterly data. The second and very important action is the removal of outlying observations in several rounds of moving average filtering, and the replacement of these observations by data points that are somehow weighted. Again, this involves decisions that should be made by the practitioner and will vary across the time series at hand. The outlier weighting part makes the overall procedure an intrinsically nonlinear method, in the sense that the weights will depend on the choice of moving average filters. Indeed, Ghysels *et al.* (1996) show that after seasonally adjustment nonlinear features may appear in linear time series.

Neglecting the outlier removal part of the official Census method, it is possible to give a linear symmetric moving average approximation to an often applied sequence of moving average filters in the Census X-11 program. For quarterly time series, the weights in this $C_{28}(L)$ filter are given in Laroque (1977). An approximate version of the $C_{28}(L)$ filter is given in Ghysels and Perron (1993), and a detailed version in Franses (1996, table 4.1). In Laroque (1977, table 3) it is shown that the linear $C_{28}(L)$ filter approximately contains the component

$$(1 + L + L^2 + L^3)^2 = (1 + L)^2(1 - iL)^2(1 + iL)^2, \tag{29.4}$$

see also Bell and Kramer (1996). Hence, the resulting seasonal adjustment filter from the Census program approximately encompasses the $C_3(L)$ filter in (29.3)

In order to seasonally adjust observations at time t with the $C_{28}(L)$ filter, one needs the observations over the sample $y_{t-28}, \ldots, y_{t+28}$. Since such observations are not available at the beginning and at the end of a sample, one needs to obtain backcasts and forecasts of y_t. One approach is now to estimate seasonal ARIMA models for $y_t, t = 1, 2, \ldots, T$, and to generate $\hat{y}_{-27}, \ldots, \hat{y}_0, \hat{y}_{T+1}, \ldots, \hat{y}_{T+28}$ (see Dagum, 1980 for details). The ARIMA estimation routine is known as regARIMA. This routine also allows for additional regressors to capture, for example, calendar effects, and allows for outlier correction.

In our simulation study below, we use the X12-ARIMA procedure with all the default settings. In accordance with the data-generating processes we consider, we impose an additive seasonal pattern (so, no natural logs are taken). As regressor variables we only use an intercept. The ARIMA model selection is done using the automatic procedure. We let X12 select the best ARIMA specification out of a (default) set of options.

29.2.2 TRAMO/SEATS

In response to the possible ambiguities involved in the application and evaluation of the Census X-11 procedure, Hillmer and Tiao (1982) proposed the so-called ARIMA-model-based approach to seasonal adjustment (see also Burman, 1980, and Gómez and Maravall, 1994). A lucid exposition of the model-based method is given in Maravall and Pierce (1987). The most popular seasonal adjustment method in this area is the TRAMO/SEATS (Time Series Regression with ARIMA Noise, Missing Observations, and Outliers/Signal Extraction in ARIMA Time Series) method of Gómez and Maravall (1997). The adjustment method consists of two steps. In the first step (TRAMO), a time series model is estimated. The second part (SEATS) deals with the extraction of the seasonal pattern from the selected ARIMA model.

In a very simple version, it is assumed that a time series can be decomposed as (29.1). The seasonal component in (29.1) is described by a seasonal ARIMA model, as proposed by Box and Jenkins (1970) and Box *et al.* (1994); for example,

$$(1 + L + L^2 + L^3)y_t^s = \psi(L)\eta_t \tag{29.5}$$

and the nonseasonal part by a nonseasonal ARIMA model like

$$(1 - L)^d y_t^{ns} = \theta(L)\xi_t, \qquad (29.6)$$

where $\psi(L)$ and $\theta(L)$ are polynomials in L. The two components are assumed to be orthogonal. This routine also allows for outlier correction and for additional regressors to capture, for example, calendar effects. After model selection by TRAMO, in the SEATS part the Wiener–Kolmogorov filter is used to extract the seasonal component from the series.

In our simulation study below, we apply the TRAMO and SEATS procedures with the default settings. To fit the data, we do not use the standard data transformation to logs. With the default settings the TRAMO/SEATS procedure uses an Airline model (see section 29.4.4 below) to estimate the seasonal component of a series.

29.3   Diagnostic tests

There are several criteria that can be used to evaluate the quality of seasonally adjusted data obtained from the above procedures. An extensive discussion of several such criteria is given in Hylleberg (1986, chapter 3) and Bell and Hillmer (1984). In this chapter we judge the quality of a seasonal adjustment procedure by applying a number of diagnostic and specification tests concerning the presence of seasonal patterns before and after correction. Each test focuses on a property that should (or should not) be present in seasonally adjusted data. We consider tests for the presence of seasonal unit roots, the presence of changing seasonal means, the presence of deterministic seasonality, the presence of correlation at the seasonal lag, the presence of periodicity in the autoregressive parameters and the presence of seasonality in the variance of the series. In this section we consider tests for quarterly data but the tests can easily be extended to monthly data.

29.3.1   HEGY test

The unit roots in seasonal data, which can be associated with changing seasonality, are the so-called seasonal unit roots (see Hylleberg *et al.*, 1990). For quarterly data, these roots are -1, i, and $-i$. For example, data generated from the model $y_t = -y_{t-1} + \varepsilon_t$ would display seasonality. Similar observations hold for the model $y_t = -y_{t-2} + \varepsilon_t$ which can be written as $(1 + L^2)y_t = \varepsilon t$, where the autoregressive polynomial $1 + L^2$ corresponds to the seasonal unit roots i and $-i$, as these two values solve the equation $1 + z^2 = 0$. Hence, when a model for y_t contains an autoregressive polynomial with roots -1 and/or i, $-i$, the data are said to have seasonal unit roots.

To test for the presence of seasonal unit roots, we consider the approach of Hylleberg *et al.* (1990), henceforth abbreviated as HEGY. The HEGY method amounts to a regression of $\Delta_4 y_t = y_t - y_{t-4}$ on deterministic terms, like seasonal dummies and a trend, and on $x_{1t} = (1 + L + L^2 + L^3)y_{t-1}$, $x_{2t} = (-1 + L - L^2 + L^3)y_{t-1}$,

$x_{3t} = -(1 + L^2)y_{t-1}, x_{4t} = -(1 + L^2)y_{t-2}$, and on lags of $\Delta_4 y_t$, where $\Delta_i y_t = y_t - y_{t-i}$. The test regression reads

$$\Delta_4 y_t = \sum_{s=1}^{4} \beta_s D_{s,t} + \gamma t + \pi_1 x_{1t} + \pi_2 x_{2t} + \pi_3 x_{3t} + \pi_4 x_{4t} + \sum_{i=1}^{p} \phi_i \Delta_4 y_{t-i} + \varepsilon_t, \qquad (29.7)$$

where $D_{s,t} = 1$ if t corresponds to season s and 0 otherwise. The t-test for the significance of the parameter for x_{1t} (π_1) is denoted by t_1, the t-test for π_2 by t_2, and the joint significance test for π_3 and π_4 is denoted by F_{34}. If the π parameters are equal to 0, this corresponds to the presence of the associated root(s), which are 1, -1, and the pair i, $-$i, respectively. Critical values of these test statistics are given in Hylleberg et al. (1990, table 1).

We argue that, in a properly seasonally adjusted times series, the seasonal unit roots -1, i and $-$i should not be present. Ideally, the finding of the unit root 1 should not be altered if it is present, as this root is associated with the stochastic trend in the series. The value of p can be determined using an information criterion such as the Bayesian Information Criterion (BIC).

29.3.2   Canova–Hansen test

The test developed by Canova and Hansen (1995) takes as the null hypothesis that the seasonal pattern is deterministic. To explain the test, consider the process

$$y_t = \sum_{s=1}^{4} \delta_{st} D_{s,t} + \varepsilon_t \qquad (29.8)$$

with

$$\delta_{1t} = \mu_t + \alpha_{1t} - \alpha_{3t} \qquad \delta_{2t} = \mu_t - \alpha_{2t} + \alpha_{3t}$$
$$\delta_{3t} = \mu_t - \alpha_{1t} - \alpha_{3t} \qquad \delta_{4t} = \mu_t + \alpha_{2t} + \alpha_{3t}, \qquad (29.9)$$

where the stochastic trend is defined as

$$\mu_t = \mu + \mu_{t-1} + \xi_t \qquad (29.10)$$

with $\xi_t \sim N(0, \sigma_\xi^2)$, and the stochastic seasonal terms are given by

$$\alpha_{jt} = \beta_j + \alpha_{j,t-1} + \eta_{jt} \qquad (29.11)$$

with $\eta_{jt} \sim N(0, \sigma_j^2)$ for $j = 1, \ldots, 3$. The process has a stochastic seasonal pattern if one or more $\sigma_j^2 > 0$. If $\sigma_j^2 = 0$ for all j, we have deterministic seasonality. The Canova–Hansen test corresponds to jointly testing $\sigma_1^2 = \sigma_2^2 = \sigma_3^2 = 0$. The asymptotical critical values are given in Canova and Hansen (1995). For the quarterly case and a significance level of 5 percent, the critical value is 1.010. We will denote this test by CH in the remainder of this chapter.

The CH test also allows for testing for the stationarity of the process itself, that is, testing for $\sigma_\xi^2 = 0$. However, this is not considered here as we only focus on the seasonal properties of the data. In fact, given our data-generating process, we apply in our simulation experiment the CH test to the first difference of the series to circumvent possible size distortions in the test for the seasonal part: see, for example, Taylor (2003) and Busetti and Taylor (2003).

The null hypothesis in the CH test is rejected if the seasonality of a series is not constant. After seasonal adjustment the CH test therefore should not reject the null hypothesis. Note that having no seasonal pattern at all also implies constant seasonality.

29.3.3   Test for equal seasonal dummies

A basic test for the presence of seasonality in a time series is to regress the time series on four seasonal dummies. If there is no seasonality in the series, the four coefficients associated with these dummies should be equal. This property can easily be tested with a standard F-test. The test regression equals

$$\Delta_1 y_t = \sum_{s=1}^{4} \beta_s D_{s,t} + \varepsilon_t, \tag{29.12}$$

where $\Delta_1 y_t = y_t - y_{t-1}$ and $D_{s,t} = 1$ if t corresponds to season s and 0 otherwise. If seasonal adjustment is properly done, and hence there is no seasonality, the F-test for $\beta_1 = \beta_2 = \beta_3 = \beta_4$ should not reject the null hypothesis.

29.3.4   Test for correlation at the seasonal lag

Seasonal time series typically display autocorrelation at seasonal lags. To test for significant autocorrelation at the seasonal lag we consider the following regression model

$$\Delta_1 y_t = \mu + \phi_1 \Delta_1 y_{t-1} + \phi_2 \Delta_1 y_{t-2} + \phi_3 \Delta_1 y_{t-3} + \phi_4 \Delta_1 y_{t-4} + \varepsilon_t \tag{29.13}$$

and we test for $\phi_4 = 0$ using a t-test. Insignificant values of the t-test statistic mark the absence of correlation at the seasonal lag. One has to be a little cautious with this approach. Autocorrelation at the seasonal lag does not have to imply seasonality as the true lag-order of the series may be 4 or higher. Note that we do not include seasonal dummies in the test regression as we want to focus on testing for correlation at the seasonal lag. The previous test in (29.12) should already indicate the presence of unequal seasonal means.

29.3.5   Test for periodicity in AR parameters

Another property which may indicate the presence of seasonality in time series concerns different autoregressive parameters across the seasons (see Franses and Paap, 2004). To investigate this periodicity we consider the PAR(p) model

$$\Delta_1 y_t = \mu + \sum_{i=1}^{p} \phi_{is} D_{s,t} \Delta_1 y_{t-i} + \varepsilon_t. \tag{29.14}$$

Absence of periodicity corresponds with the restriction $\phi_{i1} = \phi_{i2} = \phi_{i3} = \phi_{i4}$ for $i = 1, \ldots, p$. This can be tested with a standard F-test. If the F-statistic is not significant, there is no statistical evidence for periodicity in the autoregressive parameters. The value of p can be determined using an information criterion such as the BIC. Again, the test regression does not contain seasonal dummies as we focus on periodicity in the autoregressive structure. Given the linear and not seasonal-specific structure of the seasonal adjustment procedures, we expect that both procedures are not fully capable of removing periodicity from the parameters.

29.3.6 Test for seasonality in the variance

The previous tests mainly consider the presence of seasonality in the mean of the series. To test for the presence of seasonality in the variance of the series we consider the estimated residuals $\hat{\varepsilon}_t$ of an AR(p) model for $\Delta_1 y_t$

$$\Delta_1 y_t = \mu + \sum_{i=1}^{p} \phi_i \Delta_1 y_{t-i} + \varepsilon_t. \tag{29.15}$$

The LM-test for seasonality in the residuals amounts to testing for $\beta_1 = \beta_2 = \beta_3 = \beta_4$ in the auxiliary regression

$$\hat{\varepsilon}_t^2 = \sum_{s=1}^{4} \beta_s D_{s,t} + \sum_{i=1}^{p} \rho_i \Delta_1 y_{t-i} + \eta_t \tag{29.16}$$

using a standard F-test, where $\hat{\varepsilon}_t$ denotes the estimated residuals of (29.15) (see Franses and Paap, 2004, p. 40). A significant value of of the F-statistic indicates the presence of seasonality in the variance. The value of p can again be determined using BIC. In the ideal case, seasonal adjustment methods should remove any seasonality in the variance.

The above diagnostic tests will now be used to analyze the quality of the two seasonal adjustment methods in a simulation experiment. In the next section we discuss the data-generating processes we will use in this experiment.

29.4 Data-generating processes

To analyze whether seasonal adjustment methods are capable of removing seasonal properties from seasonal time series, we perform a simulation experiment. In this section we discuss the five data-generating processes we consider. The DGPs are chosen such that they mimic series which are frequently encountered in reality. Plausible values of parameters are obtained by applying the model corresponding to each DGP to the logarithm of 14 quarterly observed US industrial production series for different industry codes. These are given in Table 29.1. The series can be downloaded from http://www.economagic.com. A thorough analysis of the seasonal properties of these series can be found in Franses and Paap (2004). All artificial series are generated with standard normal innovations, that is, $\varepsilon_t \sim N(0, 1)$.

Table 29.1   US industrial production series

Series	Industry code	Sample
Total index	1	1919.1–2000.4
Final products	2	1939.1–2000.4
Total products	30	1939.1–2000.4
Consumer goods	1000	1939.1–2000.4
Automotive products	1001	1947.1–2000.4
Auto parts & allied goods	1002	1947.1–2000.4
Other durable goods	1006	1947.1–2000.4
Clothing	1012	1947.1–2000.4
Chemical products	1016	1954.1–2000.4
Paper products	1017	1954.1–2000.4
Energy products	1018	1954.1–2000.4
Fuels	1019	1954.1–2000.4
Durable consumer goods	1020	1947.1–2000.4
Foods & tobacco	1022	1947.1–2000.4

29.4.1   DGP1: constant annual growth

The first data-generating process assumes a constant unconditional yearly growth rate for each quarter. It is an autoregressive [AR] process of order 5 for the annual growth rate, that is,

$$(\Delta_4 y_t - \mu) = \sum_{i=1}^{5} \phi_i (\Delta_4 y_{t-i} - \mu) + \sigma \varepsilon_t. \tag{29.17}$$

Table 29.2 displays the parameter settings we use for this DGP, which are based on the true parameter estimates of the 14 US industrial production series.

This model assumes the presence of three seasonal unit roots, that is, -1 and $\pm i$ and hence it allows for a changing seasonal pattern. We expect that both X12-ARIMA and TRAMO/SEATS are capable of removing the changing seasonal pattern from these series.

29.4.2   DGP2: deterministic seasonality

The second process we consider is a seasonal autoregressive moving average [SARMA] process for the first difference of the series with different but constant unconditional growth rates per quarter. The exact specification is

$$(1 - \phi_4 L^4)(\Delta_1 y_t - \mu - \delta_1 D_{1,t} - \delta_2 D_{2,t} - \delta_3 D_{3,t}) = (1 + \psi_1 L + \psi_4 L^4)\sigma \varepsilon_t. \tag{29.18}$$

Table 29.3 displays the values of the parameters which are used to generate the data. The values corresponds to the parameter estimates of (29.18) for the 14 US industrial production series.

This particular specification allows for a nonzero expected growth over an entire year. Nonzero values of the δ_s parameters imply different growth rates in

Table 29.2 Parameter values for DGP1

Parameter	Industry code													
	1	2	30	1000	1001	1002	1006	1012	1016	1017	1018	1019	1020	1022
100μ	4.06	3.51	3.45	3.31	3.57	3.95	4.23	0.63	4.94	2.49	3.04	1.69	3.98	2.36
ϕ_1	1.22	1.43	1.46	1.08	0.75	0.93	1.26	1.14	0.78	0.98	0.45	0.55	1.04	0.63
ϕ_2	−0.47	−0.64	−0.73	−0.32	−0.04	−0.02	−0.57	−0.39	−0.08	−0.21	0.03	0.21	−0.29	0.08
ϕ_3	0.38	0.19	0.27	0.18	0.04	−0.05	0.26	0.11	0.15	0.09	0.07	−0.01	0.11	0.12
ϕ_4	−0.77	−0.38	−0.42	−0.59	−0.50	−0.48	−0.57	−0.51	−0.42	−0.36	−0.18	−0.31	−0.49	−0.40
ϕ_5	0.44	0.25	0.26	0.32	0.28	0.32	0.29	0.39	0.38	0.23	0.25	0.24	0.24	0.17
$\ln(\sigma)$	−3.05	−3.57	−3.66	−3.63	−2.23	−3.04	−3.19	−3.58	−3.65	−3.87	−3.29	−3.60	−2.84	−4.22

Note: The DGP is given in (29.17).

Table 29.3 Parameter values for DGP2

Parameter	Industry code													
	1	2	30	1000	1001	1002	1006	1012	1016	1017	1018	1019	1020	1022
100μ	0.78	0.80	0.37	−0.96	14.27	0.01	5.43	−3.87	−6.57	−3.51	2.38	−0.20	8.10	−5.01
$100\delta_1$	−0.41	−0.16	−0.36	1.54	−10.10	0.94	−7.56	0.99	3.39	2.35	12.00	−3.80	−7.24	2.09
$100\delta_2$	0.97	0.10	1.31	1.56	−10.55	1.67	−4.37	9.57	12.58	5.18	−24.91	3.24	−5.23	9.39
$100\delta_3$	−0.12	0.90	1.48	3.34	−32.89	1.82	−5.81	3.36	14.31	8.59	5.39	2.51	−16.10	10.95
ϕ_4	−0.53	0.03	0.06	0.92	0.81	0.75	0.16	0.95	0.86	0.89	0.88	0.89	0.86	0.85
ψ_1	0.40	0.45	0.47	−0.03	−0.26	0.02	0.58	0.16	−0.28	0.01	−0.75	−0.27	−0.08	−0.36
ψ_4	0.58	0.21	0.23	−0.83	−0.71	−0.79	0.08	−0.83	−0.46	−0.36	−0.14	−0.72	−0.80	−0.47
$\ln(\sigma)$	−1.39	−1.58	−1.61	−1.59	−1.01	−1.37	−1.37	−1.59	−1.59	−1.67	−1.44	−1.60	−1.25	−1.84

Note: The DGP is given in (29.18).

each quarter. The seasonal pattern in these series is, however, constant over time. Also for this DGP, we expect all seasonal adjustment procedures to perform well, although the methods impose seasonal unit roots which should appear as moving average seasonal unit roots in the adjusted series.

29.4.3   DGP3: stochastic seasonality

For some economic series the seasonal pattern changes over time. The third DGP in our simulation experiment mimics this feature through stochastic seasonality. We consider a structural time series process with a random walk with drift and trigonometric seasonality, that is

$$
\begin{aligned}
y_t &= \mu_t + \delta_{2t} + \delta_{3t} + \sigma\varepsilon_t \\
\mu_t &= \mu + \mu_{t-1} + \sigma_\mu\eta_t \\
\delta_{1t} &= \delta_{2,t-1} + \sigma_1\xi_{1t} \\
\delta_{2t} &= \delta_{1,t-1} + \sigma_2\xi_{2t} \\
\delta_{3t} &= -\delta_{3,t-1} + \sigma_3\xi_{3t},
\end{aligned}
\tag{29.19}
$$

where $\eta_t, \xi_{1t}, \xi_{2t}, \xi_{3t} \sim NID(0, 1)$: see, for example, Harvey (1989, p. 41) for a discussion. This DGP is close to the process in DGP1, although now seasonality does not change as quickly. Table 29.4 displays the parameter values used to generate the series based on the fourteen industrial production series.

DGP3 does not assume seasonal unit roots in the series, but it does assume random walk like patterns in the parameters. When the variances of the error terms are large, it is quite likely that the data from this process can be approximated by a model with seasonal unit roots. When the variances are zero, this process collapses to DGP2. When the variances are very small, the data from this process can display slowly changing seasonal patterns.

29.4.4   DGP4: airline model

The fourth data-generating process in our simulation experiment is exactly the model underlying the TRAMO/SEATS method, that is, the airline model. This process is specified as

$$
\Delta_1\Delta_4 y_t = (1 + \psi_1 L)(1 + \psi_4 L^4)\sigma\varepsilon_t.
\tag{29.20}
$$

DGP4 assumes three seasonal unit roots. Bell (1987) shows that when the MA(4) parameter gets close to -1, the model generates data that are close to those of DGP2. In principle, the airline model can describe data that show varying patterns of changing seasonality over time.

It is to be expected that TRAMO/SEATS will yield the best seasonally adjusted series for this DGP. The parameter values, based on parameter estimates for the 14 industrial production series, are given in Table 29.5.

Table 29.4 Parameter values for DGP3

	Industry code													
Parameter	1	2	30	1000	1001	1002	1006	1012	1016	1017	1018	1019	1020	1022
$\ln(\sigma)$	-20.00	-20.00	-20.00	-20.00	-7.33	-20.00	-20.00	-20.00	-20.00	-20.00	-8.57	-8.85	-20.00	-10.32
100μ	0.92	1.04	1.01	0.88	0.86	0.87	1.03	0.17	1.33	0.65	0.84	0.48	0.98	0.56
$\ln(\sigma_\mu)$	-1.98	-7.08	-7.22	-7.46	-5.10	-6.30	-6.32	-7.41	-7.86	-8.38	-8.05	-8.27	-5.92	-9.43
$\ln(\sigma_1)$	-4.71	-15.60	-15.19	-13.41	-9.28	-12.47	-12.73	-12.12	-10.78	-11.26	-9.54	-12.94	-11.84	-12.06
$\ln(\sigma_2)$	-4.71	-15.60	-15.19	-14.46	-10.59	-14.38	-12.73	-13.77	-13.16	-13.33	-12.07	-13.22	-12.68	-15.72

Note: The DGP is given in (29.18). In some cases σ converges to a very small value in which case we put σ equal to $\exp(-20)$, and for some series we need to impose that $\sigma_1 = \sigma_2$.

Table 29.5 Parameter values for DGP4

	Industry code													
Parameter	1	2	30	1000	1001	1002	1006	1012	1016	1017	1018	1019	1020	1022
ψ_1	0.36	0.45	0.47	0.18	-0.15	0.09	0.50	0.29	-0.33	0.10	-0.80	-0.38	0.17	-0.41
ψ_4	-0.98	-0.84	-0.83	-0.82	-0.73	-0.93	-0.82	-0.69	-0.52	-0.41	-0.42	-0.78	-0.82	-0.61
$\ln(\sigma)$	-3.14	-3.63	-3.702	-3.65	-2.25	-3.08	-3.19	-3.60	-3.63	-3.84	-3.34	-3.68	-2.86	-4.21

Note: The DGP is given in (29.20).

29.4.5   DGP5: periodic autoregressive process

The final DGP we consider is a periodic autoregressive process of order 2, that is,

$$y_t = \sum_{s=1}^{4} (\delta_s D_{s,t} + \tau_s D_{s,t} T_t + \sum_{i=1}^{2} \phi_{is} D_{s,t} y_{t-i}) + \sigma \varepsilon_t, \qquad (29.21)$$

where $T_t = [(t-1)/4] + 1$, where $[\cdot]$ is the integer function: see Franses and Paap (2004) for a survey on periodic models. The values of the autoregressive parameters are different across the seasons. In fact, test results in Franses and Paap (2004, table 3.2) show that this feature cannot be rejected for any of the 14 industrial production series. The values of the parameters are displayed in Table 29.6 and are based on parameter estimates of a periodic autoregression of order 2 for the 14 series.

This DGP displays a slowly changing seasonal pattern. As the seasonal adjustment filters do not use periodic filters, we expect that the seasonal adjustment methods are not able to fully remove this seasonal pattern from the series.

29.5   Simulation results

In this section we discuss the results of our simulation experiment. The set-up of our experiment is as follows. For each DGP in section 29.4 we simulate 1,000 time series with the 14 different parameter settings and hence we obtain 5 times 14,000 seasonal time series with different properties. Each time series contains 60 years of quarterly data. The first ten years are discarded to initialize the data-generating process. The analysis below is based on the remaining 50 years. All series are seasonally adjusted using X12-ARIMA and TRAMO/SEATS using default options. We apply the diagnostic tests discussed in section 29.3 to the raw series and both seasonally adjusted series.

The results of our simulation experiment are presented in Table 29.7.[1] The table displays the rejection frequencies of the diagnostic tests for the raw data and the seasonally adjusted data using X12-ARIMA and TRAMO/SEATS for the five DGPs. All tests are performed with a 5 percent level of significance. To ease the interpretation of Table 29.7, Table 29.8 displays the desired outcomes of the diagnostic tests after seasonal adjustment.

29.5.1   DPG1

The first panel of Table 29.7 displays the simulation results of DGP1. Columns 4–6 show the results of the HEGY tests. The rejection frequency of the test for the root at the zero frequency is 5 percent for the unadjusted series as expected. For the seasonally adjusted series they are about 5 percent and hence both seasonal adjustment methods do not seem to affect the unit root in the series. The rejection frequencies for the roots -1 and $\pm i$ are about 10 percent. The slight size distortion is due to the fact that we select the lag-order of the test regression using BIC to mimic reality. If we fix the lag-order at the true value the size is 5 percent.

Table 29.6 Parameter values for DGP5

Parameter	Industry code														
	1	2	30	1000	1001	1002	1006	1012	1016	1017	1018	1019	1020	1022
$100\delta_1$	3.16	7.73	6.53	1.04	66.82	15.68	-19.61	17.21	6.71	-20.44	4.15	34.72	15.96	-59.58
$100\delta_2$	13.37	0.08	1.79	-12.56	44.49	28.59	3.34	-71.13	-1.57	-6.04	11.72	1.40	15.17	10.41
$100\delta_3$	15.98	28.45	26.27	25.95	38.65	16.34	35.41	75.20	-6.20	-8.07	-17.74	-9.25	39.78	80.57
$100\delta_4$	0.42	11.90	11.56	18.07	39.76	-12.30	42.41	14.60	22.73	65.06	27.14	27.71	31.69	5.65
$100\tau_1$	0.06	0.14	0.12	0.13	1.19	0.53	0.16	-0.30	0.43	-0.09	0.39	-0.09	0.65	-0.31
$100\tau_2$	0.21	0.00	0.01	-0.19	0.69	0.51	0.30	0.17	-0.23	-0.11	-0.37	0.18	0.44	-0.03
$100\tau_3$	0.35	0.47	0.46	0.34	0.95	0.20	0.57	0.07	0.04	-0.14	-0.03	-0.15	0.79	0.53
$100\tau_4$	0.00	0.08	0.03	0.11	0.54	-0.13	0.46	-0.05	0.30	0.50	0.58	0.08	0.19	0.02
ϕ_{11}	1.35	1.34	1.33	1.40	0.80	1.42	1.66	1.22	1.03	1.24	1.24	0.74	1.23	0.85
ϕ_{12}	1.13	1.25	1.20	1.10	0.78	0.85	1.00	1.17	0.57	0.73	-0.21	0.41	0.92	0.98
ϕ_{13}	1.28	1.39	1.33	1.09	1.10	0.93	1.52	1.23	1.33	2.12	1.27	0.88	1.18	0.79
ϕ_{14}	1.40	1.64	1.71	0.74	0.00	1.22	0.95	1.34	0.02	0.16	0.09	0.63	0.62	0.54
ϕ_{21}	-0.37	-0.37	-0.36	-0.42	-0.12	-0.53	-0.65	-0.22	-0.11	-0.18	-0.28	0.19	-0.37	0.32
ϕ_{22}	-0.19	-0.25	-0.21	-0.04	0.03	0.01	-0.05	-0.03	0.48	0.30	1.23	0.56	-0.02	0.01
ϕ_{23}	-0.37	-0.52	-0.46	-0.19	-0.37	0.01	-0.69	-0.41	-0.30	-1.07	-0.20	0.17	-0.41	-0.04
ϕ_{24}	-0.40	-0.69	-0.75	0.21	0.82	-0.18	-0.10	-0.38	0.88	0.62	0.79	0.30	0.29	0.44
$\ln(\sigma)$	-3.14	-3.71	-3.78	-3.69	-2.32	-3.14	-3.24	-3.71	-3.68	-3.76	-3.45	-3.77	-2.93	-4.10

Note: The DGP is given in (29.21).

Table 29.7 Rejection frequencies of diagnostic tests

| DGP | Series | HEGY | | | CH | Seasonality in mean | Seasonal lag | Periodicity in AR | Seasonality in variance |
		root 1 (%)	root − 1 (%)	roots ±i (%)	(%)	(%)	(%)	(%)	(%)
DGP1 (29.17)	Unadjusted data	5	9	11	89	100	100	13	6
	X12-ARIMA	6	100	100	0	0	63	8	4
	TRAMO/SEATS	4	100	100	0	0	97	5	6
DGP2 (29.18)	Unadjusted data	6	88	95	14	84	79	32	8
	X12-ARIMA	6	100	100	0	0	37	7	5
	TRAMO/SEATS	6	100	100	0	0	15	5	5
DGP3 (29.19)	Unadjusted data	7	78	74	60	97	90	30	8
	X12-ARIMA	6	100	100	0	0	57	7	5
	TRAMO/SEATS	6	100	100	0	0	36	4	6
DGP4 (29.20)	Unadjusted data	6	10	11	89	100	100	31	9
	X12-ARIMA	6	100	100	0	0	100	20	9
	TRAMO/SEATS	12	100	100	8	0	78	9	10
DGP5 (29.21)	Unadjusted data	36	78	86	54	90	81	72	13
	X12-ARIMA	38	100	100	0	0	55	65	23
	TRAMO/SEATS	39	100	100	0	0	28	61	27

Note: The diagnostic tests are discussed in section 29.3.

Table 29.8 Null hypotheses of tests and favorable outcomes after seasonal adjustment

Test	H_0	Favorable rejection frequency
HEGY (zero frequency, 1)	presence of unit root	unchanged
HEGY (seasonal frequency, -1, $\pm i$)	presence of seasonal unit root	high
CH	stationary seasonal process	low
Seasonality in mean	equal seasonal dummies	low
Seasonal lag	absence of correlation	low
Periodicity in AR parameters	absence of periodicity	low
Seasonality in variance	absence of seasonality	low

Both seasonal adjustment methods remove the seasonal unit roots from the series leading to 100 percent rejection frequencies. The CH test rejects constant seasonality in 89 percent of the cases for the unadjusted series. After seasonal adjustment, constant seasonality (if present) cannot be rejected and hence this suggests that both seasonal adjustment methods remove the seasonal unit roots in an adequate way. The seventh column shows that the presence of different seasonal means is rejected after applying both seasonal adjustment methods. X12-ARIMA seems to remove fourth-order correlation from the series in a better way than TRAMO/SEATS, where in 97 percent of the cases a zero coefficient for the seasonal lag is rejected. The absence of periodicity in the AR parameters and the absence of seasonality in the variance is rejected in about 5 percent of the cases for the adjusted and unadjusted data. Note that there is a slight size distortion in the test for periodicity for the raw series which is again due to the fact that we select the lag-order of the test regression using BIC.

29.5.2 DPG2

The second panel of Table 29.7 displays the results for DGP2. Again we reject the presence of the root 1 in about 5 percent of the cases for the unadjusted and adjusted data. The presence of seasonal unit roots -1 and $\pm i$ is rejected in more than 88 percent of the cases for the unadjusted series and always rejected after correction. The CH tests for constant seasonality is rejected in 14 percent of the cases for the unadjusted series. The small size distortion is due to the fact that we have a large MA component which is not completely captured by the nonparametric estimate of the serial correlation in the series. After seasonal correction the rejection frequency is zero. The pattern of the outcomes of the remaining tests corresponds to the results for DGP1. However, the rejection frequency for a zero parameter at the seasonal lag is now higher for the X12-ARIMA than for the TRAMO/SEATS corrected series. Hence, TRAMO/SEATS performs slightly better.

29.5.3 DPG3

The HEGY procedure rejects the presence of seasonal unit roots in about 75 percent of the cases as can be seen from the third panel of Table 29.7. This rejection frequency is 100 percent for the adjusted series. The presence of the nonseasonal unit root is rejected in about 6 percent of the cases for both the unadjusted and adjusted series. Constant seasonality is rejected in 60 percent for the raw series and never rejected for the adjusted series. The outcomes of the remaining tests correspond to the results for DGP2. Hence, the performance of both seasonal adjustment methods is about the same.

29.5.4 DPG4

TRAMO/SEATS uses the airline model to remove seasonality from a series. Hence, we expect that this correction should perform best for this DGP, see the fourth panel of Table 29.7. Remarkably, the presence of a unit root at the zero frequency is rejected in 12 percent of the cases after applying TRAMO/SEATS, while X12-ARIMA reports a rejection frequency of about 5 percent. Seasonal unit roots are removed properly as the rejection frequencies after seasonal adjustment are 100 percent. Note that we have a little size distortion for the seasonal unit roots tests for the raw series which is again due to the fact that we select the lag order of the test regression using BIC. The CH test rejects constant seasonality in 8 percent of the cases after applying TRAMO/SEATS, while X12-ARIMA never rejects constant seasonality. The parameter belonging to the seasonal lag remains significant after seasonal correction with X12-ARIMA. For TRAMO/SEATS, however, we reject in 78 percent of the cases. Hence, TRAMO/SEATS seems to perform a little better. The outcomes of the remaining test are as expected.

29.5.5 DPG5

The final panel of Table 29.7 displays the results for DGP5. The presence of a unit root is rejected in about 38 percent of the cases for the adjusted and unadjusted series. This is due to the fact that many of the parameter settings correspond to processes which are close to unit root type behavior. Seasonal unit roots are rejected in about 80 percent of the cases for the raw series and in 100 percent of the cases for the adjusted data. The CH test reports constant seasonality after seasonal correction. A clear difference with the previous DGPs is that the test for equal autoregressive parameters is rejected in more than 60 percent of the cases. This holds for both the unadjusted and the adjusted series. Hence, both adjustment filters do not remove this type of seasonality from the series. After seasonal adjustment there also seems to be more seasonality in the variance. This is not a surprise, as periodic time series with constant variance of the error term may have different variances across the season: see, for example, Franses and Paap (2004, pp. 31–3). Finally, although DGP5 is a second-order autoregressive model, we reject in about 80 percent of the cases a zero parameter at the seasonal lag. After seasonal adjustment this percentage is reduced for both seasonal adjustment methods but TRAMO/SEATS performs better.

In sum, we conclude that both seasonal adjustment methods remove stochastic seasonal patterns due to seasonal unit roots or stochastic trigonometric seasonality in an adequate way. Rejection frequencies of seasonal unit roots are 100 percent after applying the seasonal adjustment filters. The CH test for constant seasonality is never rejected after applying the seasonal adjustment filter except for DGP4, where we reject constant seasonality in 8 percent of the cases after applying TRAMO/SEATS. Both adjustment methods do not seem to affect the presence of a unit root, although for DGP4 there is a slight increase in the rejection frequency after applying TRAMO/SEATS. Different means across the seasons are fully captured by both methods. We detect significant correlation at the seasonal lag after applying TRAMO/SEATS in fewer cases than after applying X12-ARIMA. Applying TRAMO/SEATS also leads to less periodicity in the autoregressive parameters but the differences with X12-ARIMA are relatively small.

29.6   Concluding remarks

In this chapter we have demonstrated that, when averaged over many realistic DGPs and large samples, the CENSUS X12-ARIMA and TRAMO/SEATS methods seem to perform about equally well. We acknowledge the possibility that for specific series the adjusted series may well be different across methods, but on average our simulations do not indicate a preference for either one of the two methods.

Hence, in the end, our results suggest that a preference for one of the methods merely amounts to a matter of taste. We must say, though, that an advantage of the TRAMO/SEATS method is that it easily allows for the construction of confidence bounds around seasonally adjusted data (see Koopman and Franses, 2002). This feature seems to do justice to the fact that, after all, seasonally adjusted data are estimates which are based on real data.

Note

1. All simulations were done in Ox 3.4 (Doornik, 1999). The actual seasonal adjustment was done through calls to the original procedures of CENSUS X12-ARIMA and TRAMO/SEATS which are shipped with EViews 5.

References

Bell, W.R. (1987) A note on overdifferencing and the equivalence of seasonal time series models with monthly means and models with $(0, 1, 1)_{12}$ seasonal parts when $\theta = 1$. *Journal of Business & Economic Statistics* 5, 383–7.

Bell, W.R. and S.C. Hillmer (1984) Issues involved with the seasonal adjustment of economic time series (with discussion). *Journal of Business & Economic Statistics* 2, 291–320.

Bell, W.R. and M. Kramer (1996) Towards variances for X-11 seasonal adjustments. Tech. Rep. 96/07, Statistical Research Division, Bureau of the Census.

Box, G.E.P. and G.M. Jenkins (1970) *Time Series Analysis: Forecasting and Control*. San Francisco: Holden-Day.

Box, G.E.P., G.M. Jenkins and G.C. Reinsel (1994) *Time Series Analysis, Forecasting and Control*, 3rd edn. Englewood Cliffs, NJ: Prentice Hall.

Burman, J.P. (1980) Seasonal adjustment by signal extraction. *Journal of the Royal Statistical Society A* 143, 321–37.

Busetti, F. and A.M.R. Taylor (2003) Testing against stochastic trend and seasonality in the presence of unattended breaks and unit roots. *Journal of Econometrics* 117, 21–53.

Canova, F. and B.E. Hansen (1995) Are seasonal patterns constant over time? A test for seasonal stability. *Journal of Business & Economic Statistics* 13, 237–52.

Dagum, E.B. (1980) The X-11-ARIMA seasonal adjustment method. Tech. Rep. 12-564E, Statistics Canada, Ottawa.

Doornik, J.A. (1999) *Object-Oriented Matrix Programming Using Ox*, 3rd edn. London: Timberlake Consultants Press and Oxford: www.nuff.ox.ac.uk/Users/Doornik.

Ericsson, N.R., D.F. Hendry, and H.A. Tran (1994) Cointegration, seasonality, encompassing, and the demand for money in the United Kingdom. In C.P. Hargreaves (ed.), *Nonstationary Time Series Analysis and Cointegration*. Oxford: Oxford University Press.

Findley, D.F., B.C. Monsell, W.R. Bell, M.C. Otto and B.-C. Chen (1998) New capabilities and methods of the X-12-ARIMA seasonal-adjustment program. *Journal of Business & Economic Statistics* **16**, 127–77.

Franses, P.H. (1996) *Periodicity and Stochastic Trends in Economic Time Series*. Oxford: Oxford University Press.

Franses, P.H. and R. Paap (1999) Does seasonality influence the dating of business cycle turning points? *Journal of Macroeconomics* **21**, 79–92.

Franses, P.H. and R. Paap (2004) *Periodic Time Series Models*. Oxford: Oxford University Press.

Ghysels, E. (1994) On the periodic structure of the business cycle. *Journal of Business & Economic Statistics* **12**, 289–98.

Ghysels, E., C.W.J. Granger and P.L. Siklos (1996) Is seasonal adjustment a linear or nonlinear data filtering process? *Journal of Business & Economic Statistics* **14**, 374–86.

Ghysels, E. and D.R. Osborn (2001) *The Econometric Analysis of Seasonal Time Series*. Cambridge: Cambridge University Press.

Ghysels, E. and P. Perron (1993) The effect of seasonal adjustment filters on tests for a unit root. *Journal of Econometrics* **55**, 57–98.

Gómez, V. and A. Maravall (1994) Program SEATS signal extraction in ARIMA time series: instructions for the user. Tech. Rep. ECO 94/28, European University Institute, Florence, Italy.

Gómez, V. and A. Maravall (1997) Programs TRAMO and SEATS, instructions for the user. Beta version: November.

Grether, D.M. and M. Nerlove (1970) Some properties of optimal seasonal adjustment. *Econometrica* **38**, 682–703.

Harvey, A.C. (1989) *Forecasting, Structural Time Series Models and the Kalman Filter*. Cambridge: Cambridge University Press.

Hillmer, S.C. and G.C. Tiao (1982) An ARIMA-model-based approach to seasonal adjustment. *Journal of the American Statistical Association* **77**, 63–70.

Hylleberg, S. (1986) *Seasonality in Regression*. Orlando, FL: Academic Press.

Hylleberg, S. (1994) Modelling seasonal variation. In C. Hargreaves (ed.), *Nonstationary Time Series Analysis and Cointegration*. Oxford: Oxford University Press.

Hylleberg, S., R.F. Engle, C.W.J. Granger and B.S. Yoo (1990) Seasonal integration and cointegration. *Journal of Econometrics* **44**, 215–38.

Koopman, S.J. and P.H. Franses (2002) Constructing seasonally adjusted data with time-varying confidence intervals. *Oxford Bulletin of Economics and Statistics* **64**, 509–26.

Laroque, G. (1977) Analyse d'une Méthode de Désaisonnalisation: Le Programme X-11 du Bureau of Census, Version Trimestrielle, *Annales de l'INSEE* **28**, 105–27.

Maravall, A. (1985) On structural time series models and the characterization of components. *Journal of Business & Economic Statistics* **3**, 350–5.

Maravall, A. (1995) Unobserved components in economic time series. In H. Pesaran, P. Schmidt and M. Wickens (eds), *The Handbook of Applied Econometrics*, vol. 1. Oxford: Basil Blackwell, pp. 12–72.

Maravall, A. and D.A. Pierce (1987), A prototypical seasonal adjustment model. *Journal of Time Series Analysis* **8**, 177–93.

Matas-Mir, A. and D.R. Osborn (2003) Seasonal adjustment and the detection of business cycle phases. The School of Economics Discussion Paper Series 0304, School of Economics, The University of Manchester.

Miron, J.A. (1996) *The Economics of Seasonal Cycles.* Cambridge, MA: MIT Press.

Shiskin, J. and H. Eisenpress (1957) Seasonal adjustment by electronic computer methods. *Journal of the American Statistical Association* **52**, 415–49.

Shiskin, J., A.H. Young and J. Musgrave (1967) The X-11 variant of the census method II seasonal adjustment program. Technical report, Bureau of the Census, US Department of Commerce, Washington DC, USA.

Sims, C.A. (1974) Seasonality in regression. *Journal of the American Statistical Association* **69**, 618–27.

Taylor, A.M.R. (2003) Robust stationarity tests in seasonal time series processes. *Journal of Business & Economic Statistics* **21**, 156–63.

Wallis, K.F. (1974) Seasonal adjustment and relations between variables. *Journal of the American Statistical Association* **69**, 18–31.

Author Index

Abadir, K., 12
Abraham, B., 460–1
Abrevaya, J., 717
Adentstedt, R., 355
Agiakloglou, C., 233, 235, 253, 257
Ahn, B. C., 526
Ahn, S. K., 492, 498, 542, 569, 650, 653
Ainkaran, P., 462–3
Aitchison, J., 142, 1014
Aitken, A. C., 31, 110, 136
Aitken, C. G. G., 1014
Akaike, H., 240, 489, 1017
Akerlof, G. A., 905
Albert, J., 856, 867
Aldrich, F. T., 857
Aldrich, J., 63, 72, 90, 108, 110
Alexander, C., 775
Almon, S., 146
Alonso-Borrego, C., 654
Al-Osh, M. A., 246
Alt, P. L., 147
Alt, R., 297, 495
Altissimo, F., 299, 308
Alvarez, J., 655
Alzaid, A. A., 246
Amemiya, T., 648, 704
Amisano, G., 502
Amsler, C., 326
An, H.-Z., 235
Andel, J., 377
Anders, U., 418
Andersen, A. P., 397, 406
Andersen, E., 717
Andersen, L. C., 144
Andersen, T. G., 386, 759–61
Anderson, A. P., 463
Anderson, B. D. O., 979, 981
Anderson, H. M., 402, 614–15, 617, 622, 626
Anderson, R. L., 227
Anderson, T. W., 129–30, 132, 136, 234, 239, 282–4, 557–8, 565, 570, 617, 650
Andrade, P., 338
Andreou, E., 49

Andrews, D. W. K., 192, 268, 274, 299–304, 306, 315, 317, 327–9, 336, 342, 365–8, 411, 586–8, 656, 831, 907, 914, 916, 921, 1019–20
Andrieu, C., 990, 995
Angrist, J., 80, 500, 641, 715
Anselin, L., 466, 902–4, 907–10, 913, 917–19, 923–7, 932–44, 946–8, 950, 958
Ansley, C. F., 232, 981, 984
Antoch, J., 283
Arai, Y., 289, 334–5, 593
Arango, L. E., 400
Arellano, M., 49, 634, 637, 641, 649–55, 657, 659
Arora, S. S., 638
Arteche, J., 374, 377, 386
Athreya, K. B., 835
Auestad, B. H., 416, 1016–18
Azzalini, A., 1002

Bachelier, L. J., 739
Backhouse, R. E., 13
Bacon, D. W., 400–1
Bai, J., 285, 287–8, 290–5, 305–9, 311, 329, 341, 399, 522, 525–6, 623, 629
Bailey, D. H., 790
Baillie, R. T., 253, 340, 385, 498, 749, 751–2, 754–4, 757
Baker, E. R., 1020
Balakrishnan, N., 798
Balestra, P., 644
Balke, N. S., 399, 571, 580–1, 593
Baltagi, B. H., 48, 512, 535, 633–4, 637, 639, 643–4, 653, 659, 937–8, 941–2, 945, 948, 1025
Banerjee, A., 316, 327–8, 333, 389, 480, 512, 544
Banerjee, S., 903, 912, 951
Bardet, J.-M., 360
Barkoulas, J. T., 581
Barnard, G. A., 436, 449
Barndorff-Nielsen, O. E., 209
Barry, R. P., 926
Barsky, R. B., 317

Bartel, H., 505
Bartlett, M. S., 21, 100, 102–3, 109,
    216, 228
Bartley, W. A., 334–5
Basawa, I. V., 430, 471
Bashtannyk, D. M., 1020
Basmann, R. L., 108–9, 134
Bassett, G., 469, 1006
Basu, A. K., 498
Basu, S., 914
Bates, D. M., 402
Battese, G. E., 638
Baum, C. F., 581
Bauwens, 51
Bauwens, L., 766, 771, 774–5, 778, 780,
    864, 874, 876, 885–7
Baxter, M., 612
Beaudry, P., 579
Bec, F., 571–2, 580, 593
Bell, W. R., 973, 1037–40, 1046
Bellhouse, D. R., 441–2
Bellman, R., 290
Beltrao, K. I., 369
Belz, M. H., 124
Benini, R., 105, 109
Benkwitz, A., 504
Bennett, J. H., 25
Ben-Salem, M., 580
Bentzel, R., 134
Bera, A. K., 430, 444, 446, 453, 460–1,
    463–4, 466, 494, 668, 692, 708,
    772, 903, 909, 923, 932, 935,
    939–41, 1019
Beran, J., 340–1
Beran, R., 819
Berg, M. D., 1025
Berger, J. O., 843, 849–50, 889
Berk, K. N., 256, 259
Berkes, I., 751, 756
Berkowitz, J., 488, 490, 831
Berliner, L. M., 903
Bernanke, B., 502
Bernard, J.-T., 664, 817
Bernardo, J. M., 842, 849–50, 864–5
Beron, K. J., 951, 954–5
Berzuini, C., 990, 994
Besag, J., 467, 903, 912, 921, 951
Besley, T., 906
Best, N. G., 990, 994
Beveridge, S., 190, 321, 611, 616
Bhansali, R. J., 229, 241, 369, 498
Bhapkar, V. P., 438, 445, 448–9
Bhargava, A., 234, 260, 269, 535

Bhat, B. R., 430, 471
Bhat, C., 709
Bhattacharya, P. K., 281, 292
Bhattacharya, R. N., 284
Bickel, P. J., 1002, 1021
Bilias, Y., 430, 444, 446, 453, 725
Billingsley, P., 170, 175, 181, 184,
    208, 274
Binder, M., 513, 529
Bivand, R., 906
Bjerkholt, O., 123, 127, 146
Black, F., 753, 766
Blanchard, O., 502
Blaug, M., 13, 62, 66, 68, 70
Bleaney, M., 512
Blommestein, H., 918–19
Blundell, R., 653–4, 657
Boarnet, M. G., 928
Bodkin, R. G., 141, 146
Boivin, J., 625
Bollerslev, T., 385–8, 464, 744,
    749–52, 754–7, 759–61, 766,
    768, 771–3, 775, 779, 1018
Bolthausen, E., 921
Bond, S., 649–54, 657
Boots, B., 933
Borenstein, S. A., 579
Borsch-Supan, A., 663, 670, 674
Bos, C., 389
Boschan, C., 626
Bose, S. S., 100, 102
Boswijk, H. P., 808
Boswijk, P. H., 34, 49, 561, 571, 877
Boumans, M., 71
Bover, O., 653–4, 657
Bowley, A. L., 21, 101, 119
Bowman, A., 1002, 1020
Bowsher, C. G., 652
Box, G. E. P., 34, 143, 216–17, 221, 225,
    229–30, 235–8, 322, 416,
    797, 1039
Brailsford, T. J., 491
Brandsma, A., 918
Brännäs, K., 246, 407
Bray, T. A., 798
Breidt, F. J., 385–6
Breiman, L., 205–6
Breitung, J., 284, 339, 502–3, 513,
    524, 619, 1019
Brett, C., 928
Breunig, R., 417
Breusch, T. S., 639, 646, 648, 925, 940
Brock, W. A., 397, 905

Brockett, P. L., 415
Brockwell, P. J., 217, 219, 221, 229,
    241, 243
Brodsky, J., 357–8, 364, 369
Brooks, C., 766–7, 773–4, 780
Brooks, S. P., 412, 866
Brown, D., 1009
Brown, E. H. P., 132
Brown, J. A. C., 142
Brown, R. L., 297
Bruce, A. G., 989
Brueckner, J. K., 905
Brüggemann, R., 491–3, 502–3
Bruneau, C., 338
Bry, G., 626
Bühlmann, P., 830–1
Burda, M. M., 500
Burdekin, R. C. K., 317
Burke, S. P., 773–4, 780
Burman, J. P., 1039
Burridge, P., 917, 933, 936, 980, 982, 998
Busetti, F., 318–19, 330, 1042
Butler, J. S., 719, 757, 857

Caglayan, M., 581
Cai, Z., 1006, 1024
Caldwell, B. J., 66
Calvo, E., 325
Camacho, M., 420
Cameron, A. C., 579
Campbell, J. Y., 329, 568, 748
Campos, J., 334
Candelon, B., 619
Canepa, A., 239
Caner, M., 412, 579, 586, 604
Canova, F., 1041
Cao, C. Q., 745
Carlin, B. P., 903, 912, 951
Carlin, J. B., 851–2, 864, 866–7
Carlson, K. M., 144
Carnap, 23
Carrasco, M., 580, 751
Carrion-i-Silvestre, J. L., 325, 328, 334–5
Carroll, R. J., 1002, 1017, 1021, 1025
Carter, R. A. L., 245, 989
Cartwright, N., 29, 63–4, 71–2
Carvalho, V. M., 626
Case, A. C., 906, 910
Casella, G., 852
Chalmers, A. F., 11, 19
Chamberlain, G., 459, 622, 634, 641
Chambers, E. A., 798
Chambers, M. J., 985

Champernowne, D. A., 136
Chan, K. S., 399, 401, 579, 586
Chan, N. H., 209, 273
Chandra, A. S., 460, 464
Chandrasekhar, B., 449
Chang, Y., 256, 273, 524, 830
Chao, H.-K., 70
Chao, J. C., 597, 888
Charnes, A., 101
Chatfield, C., 228–9, 977
Chatterjee, S., 397
Chaudhuri, P., 1006
Chay, K., 725
Chen, B.-C., 512, 1037–8
Chen, J., 430
Chen, M.-H., 852, 867
Chen, R., 402, 1008, 1017–18
Chen, S., 725, 1022–3
Chen, W. W., 372–3, 379, 383
Chen, X., 751, 1013
Chen, Z.-G., 235
Cheng, B., 1017
Chernoff, H., 282
Chernozhukov, V., 667
Chesher, A., 708
Cheung, C., 699
Cheung, Y.-W., 388
Chiang, M.-H., 512, 526–8
Chib, S., 663, 667, 704, 759, 770,
    780, 852, 856, 859, 867, 887–8
Chibumba, A., 775
Choi, B. S., 216, 235, 247
Choi, E., 830
Choi, I., 253, 513, 518–20, 524–6,
    528–9, 531, 535, 592–3
Choi, K., 389
Chong, T. T. L., 287, 294, 317
Chou, R., 766
Chow, G. C., 217
Christ, C. F., 8, 18, 26, 126, 132, 134, 146
Christensen, B. J., 387
Christiano, L. J., 326, 328, 612
Christie, A. A., 753
Chu, C. I., 1005
Chu, C.-S. J., 253, 298, 513, 535
Chue, T. K., 525–6, 529, 531
Chung, C. F., 377
Chung, H., 749, 757
Chung, Y. P., 1016
Claessen, H., 505
Clark, C., 121
Clemente, J., 329
Clements, M. P., 281, 498

Cleveland, W. S., 228, 1003, 1006, 1019
Cliff, A., 903, 909, 912, 923, 932–3
Coakley, J., 512, 916
Coase, R. H., 120
Cochrane, D., 31, 136
Coddington, P. D., 795
Collomb, G., 1016
Conley, T. G., 905, 910, 914–15, 921, 931
Constantinides, G. M., 990, 998
Cook, D., 914
Cook, S., 334
Cooley, T., 75
Cooper, R. L., 35
Cooper, W. W., 101
Corander, J., 888
Cornwell, C., 644
Corradi, V., 299, 308
Cowden, D. J., 96
Cowles, M. C., 866–7
Cox, D. R., 144, 798, 956
Cragg, J. G., 597, 705
Crainiceanu, C. M., 299
Cramér, H., 216, 441
Cramer, J. S., 142
Crandall, R. E., 790
Crato, N., 385–6
Cressie, N., 903, 912–13, 921, 951
Crisan, D., 995
Crowder, M., 446, 458, 471
Croxton, F. E., 96
Crum, W. L., 146
Csörgő, M., 281
Cubadda, G., 569, 617–18
Culver, S. E., 512
Curnow, R. N., 294
Cybenko, G., 404

D'Agostino, R. B., 52
Dacorogna, M. M., 759
Dagum, E. B., 1039
Dahl, G. B., 1023
Dahlquist, G., 100, 103
Dale, A. I., 90
Dale, S., 714
Danielsson, J., 663, 769, 780
Darling, D. A., 282–4
Darnell, A. C., 63
Darolles, S., 1009
Das Gupta, S., 237, 239
Das, D., 920, 930–1
Das, M., 1009, 1025
Das, S., 524
David, F. N., 110

Davidson, J. E. H., 137, 161, 166–7,
    170, 181, 185, 192–5, 198, 203,
    209, 234, 755
Davidson, R., 108, 217, 245, 253, 441,
    459, 789, 806, 815, 818–19, 823–4,
    834–5, 937
Davies, N., 237
Davies, R. B., 274, 299, 410, 586, 936
Davis, G. C., 70
Davis, H. T., 28, 89–90, 94, 97–9, 111
Davis, R. A., 217, 219, 221, 229, 233–4,
    241, 243
Davison, A. C., 826, 831, 833, 835
Davydov, 198
Dawid, A. P., 866
De Freitas, N., 990
De Gooijer, J. G., 407
De Graaff, T., 932–3, 935, 941
De Jong, P., 981, 983
De Jong, R. M., 195, 198, 203, 209
De Lima, P., 385–6
De Marchi, N., 70
Deane, G., 928
Deely, J. J., 849
Deistler, M., 505
DeJong, D. J., 253, 257, 873–4
Delgado, M. A., 369, 1013, 1021
DeLong, J. B., 317
DeMaris, A., 696, 701
Dempster, A. P., 403, 666, 704
Deng, A., 287, 293, 299, 320
Dennis, J. G., 557
Deo, R. S., 357–8, 364, 386–7
Deshayes, J., 281, 298–300
Desmond, A. F., 430, 432, 439, 446, 471
Devlin, S. J., 1004
Devroye, L., 798, 1002
Dey, D., 867
Dhrymes, P., 144, 696
DiCiccio, T. J., 833
Dickey, D. A., 33, 49, 217, 253–6, 264,
    267, 269, 274, 323–4, 329, 563
Diebold, F. X., 285, 340, 388–9,
    760–1, 770
Diebolt, J., 604
Dietz, R. D., 910
Diggle, P., 1025
DiNardo, J., 50
Ding, A. A., 404
Ding, Z., 340, 385, 754, 775
Dionne, G., 703
Dirks, F. C., 121
Dittmann, I., 380, 387

Dolado, J. J., 333, 480, 500, 544
Domencich, T. A., 143
Donald, S. G., 597
Donsker, M. D., 176
Doob, J. L., 27, 37
Doornik, J. A., 494–5, 505, 789, 795–6,
   799–800, 803, 808, 982, 1053
Dorfman, J., 873
Douc, R., 572
Doucet, A., 990, 995, 997–8
Downham, D. Y., 241
Drèze, J. H., 140, 885, 894
Driscoll, J. C., 916
Dubin, R., 914
Dudley, R. M., 170
Duffie, D., 759
Dufour, J.-M., 267, 269, 297, 499–500,
   664, 817
Duhem, P., 69
Duncan, G., 707
Dunsmuir, W. T. M., 233–4
Durbin, J., 31, 100, 103, 109, 136, 230,
   235–6, 243, 297, 429–30, 438–9,
   441–2, 456, 980, 982–3, 986, 989,
   995, 998
Durlauf, S. N., 579, 603, 905
Dustman, C., 726
Dwass, M., 814

Edgerton, D., 493
Edgeworth, F. Y., 101, 110, 430–1, 441–2
Edmond, C., 512
Efromovich, S., 1002
Efron, B., 43, 273, 820, 825, 833
Eisenpress, H., 1038
Elhorst, J. P., 943–4
Elliott, G., 254, 261–2, 264–5, 267–9,
   272, 274, 291, 293, 304, 319–20,
   326, 329, 519
Elster, J., 82
Embens, H., 760
Enders, W., 398, 571, 580–1
Engle, R. F., 34, 49, 76, 144, 220, 253,
   340, 356, 385, 410, 461, 464, 479,
   498, 541, 548, 554, 569, 571, 573,
   580, 616, 612, 614, 618, 626,
   742–4, 747–9, 752, 754, 757, 766,
   771–6, 779, 872, 891, 1006,
   1018–19, 1021, 1038, 1040–1
Epanechnikov, V. A., 1014
Epstein, R. J., 8, 25–6, 29, 63, 126–7,
   129, 133–5, 142, 146
Eraker, B., 986

Ericsson, N. R., 33, 334, 789, 1036
Escobar, M., 894
Escribano, A., 417, 572
Estrin, S., 512
Eubank, R. L., 1002, 1007
Evans, J. L., 63
Evans, J. M., 297
Evans, M., 147
Ezekiel, M., 106–7, 124, 146

Fachin, S., 566
Fair, R., 704, 709, 729
Falk, B., 317, 581
Fan, J., 397, 418, 1002, 1004–6, 1018
Fan, Y., 1007–8, 1013–14
Farebrother, R. W., 90–1, 101, 104, 108,
   110, 145
Farrell, M. J., 142
Faust, J., 77
Fazekas, I., 922
Feder, P. I., 292
Feigl, H., 81
Feller, W., 170, 205
Ferger, W. F., 125
Ferguson, R. O., 101
Fernández, C., 888
Ferrándiz, J., 910
Filardo, A. J., 403
Filon, L. N. G., 90
Fin, T., 705
Findley, D. F., 497, 1037–8
Fine, T. L., 403, 418
Fingleton, B., 903, 909
Fisher, I., 62, 147
Fisher, L. A., 502
Fisher, R. A., 15–16, 20–3, 65, 71, 110,
   134, 428–30, 432–6, 439, 441–3,
   451, 471, 556
Fisher, W. D., 290, 894
Fishman, G. S., 793
Fitzgerald, T. J., 612
Fitzmaurice, G. M., 469
Flachaire, E., 823–4, 826
Flannery, B. P., 791
Fleissig, A. R., 512
Fleming, M., 951
Florax, R. J. G., 903, 918, 920, 932–3,
   935, 939–41, 958
Florens, J. P., 1009
Folmer, H., 918, 941
Fomby, T. B., 399, 571, 580–1, 593
Forni, M., 612, 622, 624–6, 629
Fowler, R. F., 120

Fox, J., 1010
Fox, K. A., 8, 18, 133–4
Frankel, J. A., 512
Franses, P. H., 253, 260, 281, 389, 397,
    414, 418, 420, 1036, 1039,
    1042–3, 1048, 1052–3
Frantzen, D., 512
Freedman, D. A., 822, 832
Freeland, K., 246–7
French, K. R., 741, 747
Friedman, M., 19, 111, 136, 144
Frisch, R., 5, 24, 63, 108, 110, 122–6,
    129, 134, 146, 220
Frühwirth-Schnatter, S., 983
Fu, Y.-X., 294
Fuentes, A.-M., 916
Fuertes, A. M., 512
Fuller, W. A., 33, 49, 217, 253, 255–6,
    264, 267, 269, 274, 317, 323–4,
    329, 563, 638
Funahashi, K., 404
Funk, M., 512

Gabr, M. M., 406
Gagne, R., 703
Galbraith, J. W., 480, 544
Galí, J., 502
Gallant, A. R., 192, 759, 769, 1002
Gao, J., 1017
Garcia, R., 302, 305, 417
Gardner, L. A., 282, 304, 311, 318,
    333–4, 339–40
Garratt, A., 891
Gasser, T., 1005–6
Gauss, C. F., 90–1
Geary, R. C., 108, 146
Geisser, S., 850
Gelfand, A. E., 856, 861, 866–7, 903,
    912, 951
Gelman, A., 851–2, 864, 866–7
Genest, I., 664, 817
Gentle, J. E., 793
George, E. I., 852
Gerdtham, U. G., 512
Getis, A., 903
Geweke, J., 225, 356, 663, 667, 670,
    674, 744, 852–4, 866, 874–6,
    886–7, 894
Ghosh, M., 845
Ghysels, E., 253, 664, 766, 1036, 1038–9
Giannini, C., 499, 502
Gibson, W. M., 102–3
Giere, R. N., 71

Gijbels, I., 1002–3, 1005–6
Gil-Alana, L. A., 341
Gilbert, C. L., 31, 135–9, 146–7
Gilbert, R., 579
Gilboy, E. W., 106–7
Gilks, W. R., 852, 894, 990, 994
Gini, C., 105, 107, 122
Giot, A., 876, 887
Giraitis, L., 340, 368, 378, 385
Glad, I. K., 1007
Glaeser, E. L., 905, 916
Glosten, L. R., 753, 757, 770, 773
Godambe, V. P., 430, 438–42, 446,
    450–2, 454–9, 469, 471
Godfrey, L. G., 229, 238–9, 824, 835, 936
Godsill, S. J., 990, 995, 997–8
Goering, G. E., 579
Goldberger, A. S., 29–30, 109, 133, 138,
    145–6, 699
Goldfeld, S. M., 399, 402
Golub, G., 879
Gómez, V., 976, 1037, 1039
Gonçalves, S., 822, 824, 831
González, A., 400, 412
Gonzalez, M., 579–80
González-Rivera, G., 1021
Gonzalo, J., 416, 502, 579–80, 582,
    591, 594, 597–8, 600–1, 612
Goodhart, C. A. E., 759
Gordon, N., 990
Gordon, R. J., 147
Gotway, C. A., 903, 907, 951
Gourieroux, C., 245, 285, 340, 389, 618,
    663, 668, 689–90, 692
Gozalo, P., 1008
Granger, C. W. J., 33–5, 49, 63, 81, 144,
    147, 217, 253, 285, 340–1, 354–6,
    385, 387, 389, 397–8, 406, 413,
    415, 418, 420, 460, 462–3, 478–9,
    495, 498, 500, 541, 548, 554, 569,
    572–3, 580–2, 594, 600–1, 616,
    754, 872, 1017, 1021, 1036, 1038,
    1040–1
Gray, H. L., 377
Green, P. G., 985–6
Greenberg, E., 780, 852, 887
Greene, W. H., 32, 49–50, 697–9, 703,
    707, 710, 712, 714–15, 717, 719, 729
Greenland, S., 908
Greenstein, B., 146
Gregoir, S., 338
Gregory, A. W., 78, 311, 334, 336
Grether, D. M., 1037–8

Grier, D. A., 109
Griffith, D. A., 926, 933
Grigoletto, M., 497
Griliches, Z., 144, 147, 1015
Groen, J. J. J., 512, 533–4, 573
Gronau, R., 143
Grosse, E., 1004
Grunwald, G. K., 220
Guay, A., 664
Guégan, D., 397
Guest, P. G., 99–100, 103, 109
Guggenberger, P., 365, 368
Gupta, V. K., 284
Gurmu, S., 726
Guthery, S. B., 290
Gutierrez, L., 512, 531
Gutierrez, M. M., 512
Györfi, L., 1002, 1016

Häardle, W., 1018
Haavelmo, T., 6, 26–8, 30, 61, 63, 71–2, 90, 111, 124, 127, 129, 131–4, 139
Haberler, G., 120
Hacking, I., 22, 66
Hackl, P., 281
Hadri, K., 520, 526
Haggan, V., 400, 1017
Hahn, F., 62
Hahn, J., 654, 657–8
Haining, R., 903, 913, 921
Hájek, J., 288
Hajivassiliou, V., 663, 670, 674, 692
Hakkio, C. S., 317
Hald, A., 23, 90, 101, 110–11, 430
Haldrup, N., 253, 260, 273
Hall, A. R., 246, 281
Hall, P., 356, 830–1, 833, 915, 1010, 1014–15, 1020, 1023–4
Hall, W. J., 471
Hallin, M., 612, 622, 624–5, 629
Hamilton, J. D., 49, 217–18, 225, 229, 232–5, 403, 417, 419, 480, 544, 572, 1016
Hammersley, J. M., 805
Hamori, S., 330
Hands, D. W., 70, 83
Handscomb, D. C., 805
Hannan, E. J., 217, 228, 235, 241, 243, 379, 489, 505
Hansen, B. E., 204, 209, 271–2, 284, 299, 310–12, 334–6, 411, 414, 416–17, 526–7, 531, 542, 571, 579, 581–2, 586–7, 593, 602, 604, 757, 833, 1006, 1020, 1041

Hansen, E., 557
Hansen, H., 312, 494–5, 558
Hansen, L. P., 7, 78, 93, 108, 568
Hansen, P. R., 294, 342, 512
Hao, K., 312–13
Harbo, I., 563
Harding, D., 612, 626–7
Härdle, W., 831, 1002, 1006, 1008, 1016, 1018
Harris, R. D. F., 513
Harrod, R. F., 4
Hart, J. D., 1002, 1014, 1016
Hartley, J. E., 78
Harvey, A. C., 217, 232, 284, 297, 319, 330, 385, 542, 611–12, 619, 626, 628, 766–71, 975–7, 979, 982–3, 985, 998, 1037, 1046
Harvey, D. I., 318, 330–1
Hassani, S., 1016
Hassler, U., 380, 388
Hastie, T., 1005, 1008
Hatanaka, M., 144, 281, 331–2, 480
Hausman, D. M., 65–6
Hausman, J., 380, 634, 640, 646, 648, 657, 697, 721, 1015
Hawkins, D. L., 299
Hawkins, D. M., 290, 296
Hayashi, F., 48, 480
Haykin, S., 403
He, C., 750–1
Heckman, J. J., 8, 64, 133, 143, 500, 676, 697–8, 713–14, 729
Hecq, A., 325, 617–19
Hellström, J., 246
Henderson, D., 1025
Hendry, D. F., 8, 18, 29, 33, 35, 41, 49, 63, 72, 74, 76–7, 80, 88, 90, 108, 122–5, 134, 145–6, 217, 281, 333–4, 480, 491, 495, 498, 505, 544, 663, 692, 789, 795–6, 804–5, 808, 891, 941, 1036
Hendry, D. G., 137
Henry, M., 354, 366–7, 385
Henry, O. T., 767
Hentschel, L., 748
Herwartz, H., 512
Heyde, C. C., 375, 430, 446, 449, 459–60, 469, 471
Hickman, B. G., 147
Hidalgo, F. J., 378, 382, 388
Hidalgo, J., 341, 377–8, 1017, 1021
Higgins, M. L., 461, 463–4, 1019
Hildreth, C., 146

Hillier, G. H., 267
Hillmer, S. C., 985, 1039–40
Hills, S. E., 856, 866
Hines, J. R., 906, 910
Hinich, M. J., 415
Hinkley, D. V., 292, 826, 831, 833, 835
Hjellvik, V., 415, 1016
Hodrick, R. J., 975
Hoeting, J. A., 848
Hogue, A., 498
Holloway, G., 951, 955
Holly, A., 138–9
Holmes, M. J., 512
Holt, C. C., 141
Hong, H., 667
Hong, S., 593
Hong, Y., 1016
Honoré, B., 634, 725–7, 1025
Hood, W. C., 29, 63, 74, 110, 127
Hoogerheide, L. F., 894
Hoogstrate, A. J., 1019
Hooper, J. W., 103
Hoover, K. D., 13, 62–4, 67, 70, 73–4,
    77–9, 81, 500
Hopkins, S., 512
Hordijk, L., 903
Hornik, K., 298, 404
Horowitz, J. L., 48, 692, 831, 1002,
    1008, 1021–2
Horváth, L., 281, 299, 751, 756
Horvath, M. T. K., 563
Hosking, J. R. M., 354–5, 492, 778
Hosoya, Y., 386
Hotelling, H., 97, 99, 122
Hsiao, C., 513, 529, 535, 633, 650, 659,
    916, 1018, 1025
Hsieh, D. A., 749, 759, 769
Hsu, C.-C., 341
Hu, F., 836
Hu, I. C., 1006
Hualde, J., 388
Huang, C. J., 324, 330
Huang, J., 919
Hughes Hallett, A., 147
Huh, H., 502
Hull, J., 766
Hume, D., 66–7
Huntington, E. V., 93
Hurst, H., 284, 356
Hurvich, C. M., 357–9, 364, 369–73,
    379, 383, 386–7, 1005, 1010
Hürzeler, M., 990
Hušková, M., 283

Hutchison, T. W., 19
Hwang, J. T. G., 404
Hylleberg, S., 253, 569, 1036–8, 1040–1
Hyndman, R. J., 220, 1020
Hyung, N., 285, 340–1, 389

Iacone, F., 379
Ibragimov, I. A., 205
Ibrahim, J. G., 852
Ichimura, H., 1022
Im, K. S., 253
Imbens, G. W., 500, 1009
Imhof, J. P., 282
Inder, B., 313, 878, 880–4, 886, 888–9
Inoue, A., 285, 336, 340, 389, 828
Inoue, T., 594
Irish, M., 708
Irwin, E. G., 908
Issler, J. V., 612, 617–18, 626

Jacod, J., 170
Jacquier, E., 759, 769
Jagannathan, R., 753, 757, 770, 773
James, A. T., 882–3, 888
James, B., 299
James, K. L., 299
Jandhyala, V. K., 283–4
Jansson, M., 253, 270, 272–4
Jarque, C. M., 494, 668, 692, 708
Jasiak, J., 285, 340, 389
Jayet, H., 942–4
Jeffreys, H., 23, 849
Jeganathan, P., 270, 273
Jeliazkov, I., 867
Jenkins, G. M., 34, 143, 216–17, 221,
    225, 229–30, 235, 416, 1039
Jensen, M. J., 360
Jevons, W. S., 5, 14
Jewell, T., 512
Jiang, G. J., 770
Jin, S., 534
Jing, B.-Y., 831
Jöckel, K.-H., 815
Johansen, S., 34, 49, 144, 312, 336–7,
    479–80, 495, 531, 535, 542, 544,
    551, 558, 563–71, 583, 591, 872,
    875, 884, 891
Johnson, N. L., 675, 798, 951
Johnson, P. A., 579
Johnston, J., 30, 32, 50, 136, 138–9
Jones, A., 706
Jones, D., 1002, 1006, 1017
Jordá, O., 417

Jørgensen, C., 571
Jowett, G. H., 102–3
Joyeux, R., 253, 354
Jubinski, P. D., 388
Judge, G. G., 441, 469
Judson, R. A., 649
Juhl, T., 299
Jung, B. C., 948
Jung, R. C., 246–7
Jung, S. H., 469
Juréen, L., 130
Jurke, S. R., 989
Juselius, K., 75, 544

Kabaila, P., 497
Kadane, J. B., 848, 894
Kaiser, M. S., 912, 951
Kalbfleisch, J. D., 836
Kale, B. K., 430, 438, 444, 446, 449, 471
Kallal, H., 905
Kander, Z., 282
Kao, C., 512, 526–8, 530–1
Kapetanios, G., 329, 625
Kapoor, M., 948
Kapteyn, A., 637
Karakus, M. C., 512
Karanasos, M., 224, 244, 751
Karatzas, I., 199
Kass, R. E., 849–50, 865–6
Kauppi, H., 528
Keane, M. P., 653, 663, 667, 670, 674,
    721, 852
Keenan, J. M., 414
Kelejian, H. H., 905, 910, 914–15, 917,
    920–1, 928–31, 933–6, 940, 944,
    948, 957–8
Kemp, G. C. R., 498
Kendall, M. G., 437, 675
Kennan, 711
Kennedy, P. E., 10, 32, 146
Ketellapper, R. H., 918
Keuzenkamp, H. A., 63, 68, 80–3
Keynes, J. M., 5, 14, 23, 25, 65, 125
Khalaf, L., 664, 817
Khan, S., 725, 1022–3
Khanna, M., 1025
Kiefer, N., 710
Kilian, L., 488, 490, 504, 822, 824, 828, 831
Kim, C.-W., 375, 918
Kim, D., 332
Kim, H.-J., 296, 299
Kim, I. M., 253, 281

Kim, J. H., 497
Kim, J. Y., 318
Kim, K., 273
Kim, M., 360
Kim, S., 759, 770, 772
Kim, T.-H., 319–20, 330, 334, 342, 512, 1006
Kimball, B. F., 430, 436–9, 444
King, A., 512
King, G., 908
King, M. L., 264, 267, 269, 299, 770, 933
King, R. G., 502, 612, 891
Kitagawa, G., 988, 990, 997
Kiviet, J. F., 239, 297, 649, 657
Klaassen, C. A. J., 1002, 1021
Klaassen, L., 902
Kleibergen, F. R., 533–4, 573, 873–4,
    876–80, 885–8
Klein, 739
Klein, L. R., 29, 133, 136, 138–9, 142–3
Klein, R., 726
Klinke, S., 1016
Kloek, T., 853, 887
Knaap, T., 656
Kniesner, T., 1025
Knight, F. H., 19
Knuth, D. E., 791, 793, 798
Koehler, A. B., 977
Koenker, R., 469, 1006
Koh, W., 948
Kohn, R., 981, 989, 1017
Kokoszka, P., 340, 369, 385, 751, 756
Kolmogorov, A. N., 27, 216
Komunjer, I., 1006
Kongsted, H. C., 571
Kontrus, K., 298, 312, 341
Koop, G., 504, 557, 579, 852, 864,
    867, 873, 983
Koopman, S. J., 619, 628, 975–7, 980,
    982–3, 985–6, 989, 995, 998, 1053
Koopmans, T. C., 25–6, 29, 63, 74, 110,
    122, 124, 127–8, 130–1, 134, 141, 146
Koper, N. A., 919
Korn, O., 418
Kotz, S., 675, 798, 951
Koul, H. L., 356
Koyck, L. M., 136
Kozicki, S., 612, 614
Kraay, A. C., 916
Kramer, M., 1039
Krämer, W., 281, 297–8, 312, 341, 495
Krätzig, M., 480, 505
Kreiss, J.-P., 831

Krishnaiah, P. R., 281
Krolzig, H.-M., 77, 491
Kroner, K., 766, 772–3, 1019
Krueger, A., 80, 714
Kshirsagar, A. M., 617
Kuan, C.-M., 287, 298, 313, 331, 341, 1003
Kuersteiner, G., 657
Kuhn, T., 66
Kukush, A. G., 922
Kulperger, R. J., 283
Kumar, S., 1025
Kunitomo, N., 326
Künsch, H. R., 360, 830, 990, 1019
Kuo, B.-S., 311
Kurozumi, E., 289, 320, 330, 334–5
Kurtz, T. G., 209
Kuznets, S. S., 12, 94
Kwan, A. C. C., 237
Kwiatkowski, D., 253, 283–4, 330, 520–2, 525
Kydland, F. E., 63, 78
Kyriazidou, E., 726–7

L'Ecuyer, P., 791–4, 800
Labys, P., 760–1
Lahiri, P., 836
Lahiri, S. N., 830, 922
Laib, N., 604
Laird, N. M., 403, 469, 666, 704
Lakatos, I., 69
Lamoureux, C. G., 747–8
Lancaster, T., 636, 851–2, 864, 867
Land, K., 928
Lang, G., 360
Lange, O., 125–6, 146
Lanne, M., 326, 330, 535
Larizza, C., 990, 994
Laroque, G., 663, 1039
Larsson, R., 531–4, 573, 892
Lastrapes, W. D., 747–8
Latsis, S. J., 69
Laurent, S., 767, 771, 774–5, 778, 780
Lavergne, P., 1013
Lavielle, M., 287–8, 341
Lawless, J., 471
Lawson, A. B., 951
Lawson, T., 63, 82
Lazarová, S., 341
Le Cam, L., 266, 270, 273
Le Gallo, J., 942–4
Leamer, E. E., 34, 63, 73, 75, 81, 141, 144, 146, 848, 864
Leaven, D. H., 146

Lee, D., 388
Lee, H. S., 569
Lee, H. Y., 512
Lee, J., 303–4, 306, 324, 326, 330–1, 334–5, 512
Lee, K. C., 504, 891
Lee, L. F., 663, 668, 670, 675, 677, 680, 682, 685, 691–2, 726, 730, 910, 920, 928, 930
Lee, M., 707, 726–7, 730
Lee, S., 460–1, 757, 1006, 1021
Lee, T. H., 1012, 1016–17
Leenders, R. T. A., 910
Lehfeldt, R. A., 104, 106, 120
Lehmann, E. L., 21–2, 24, 38, 43, 263, 266, 273–4
Leipus, R., 340, 385
Leisch, F., 404
Lele, S. R., 466, 836
Lenoir, M., 104
Leon, L. M. A., 512
Leonard, H. B., 34
Leontief, W. W., 5, 6, 146
LeRoy, S. F., 75
LeSage, J. P., 903, 921, 926, 956
Levin, A., 253, 512–13, 535
Levy, D., 381
Lewbel, A., 1023
Lewis, A. L., 498
Lewis, H. G., 143
Lewis, R., 498
Ley, E., 888
Leybourne, S. J., 234, 318–20, 324, 330–1, 334, 342, 512, 522
Li, D., 464, 937–8, 941
Li, H., 488, 490, 831
Li, K., 724
Li, M., 724
Li, Q., 1002–3, 1005–18, 1021, 1023–5
Li, W. K., 236, 492, 778
Liang, K. Y., 430, 452, 468–9
Liesenfeld, R., 769–70
Ligon, E., 910, 914–15
Lilien, D. M., 748
Lim, K. S., 398, 579
Lin, C.-F., 253, 401, 415, 512–13, 535
Lin, J.-L., 418
Lin, X. H., 1025
Lindgren, G., 402
Lindholdt, P. M., 377
Lindley, D. V., 849
Lindsay, B. G., 451–2
Ling, S., 778

Linnik, Y., 205
Linton, O. B., 1008, 1017, 1021, 1023
Lippi, M., 612–13, 622, 624–5, 629
Litterman, R., 883
Liu, J. S., 308, 998, 1008, 1017
Liu, R. Y., 823
Liu, T. C., 74, 130, 134, 142, 146
Ljung, G. M., 237–8
Llopis, A., 910
Lo, A., 284, 388
Lo, M. C., 579, 581
Loader, C. R., 1005, 1010
Lobato, I. N., 285, 340, 361–4, 372, 387–8
Lomnicki, Z. A., 494
Long, S., 696, 701
Long, X. D., 1019
López, A., 910
Loretan, M., 204, 528, 531
Los, B., 512
Löthgren, M., 512, 531–4, 573
Lothian, J. R., 512
Louis, T. A., 852
Lovell, M. C., 77, 108
Lu, B., 656
Lu, X., 1006
Lu, Y., 387
Lubrano, M., 864, 874, 876, 885–7
Lucas, A., 414
Lucas, R. E., 34, 142
Luintel, K. B., 512
Lumsdaine, R. L., 287, 294–5, 309, 311, 316, 327–9, 756–7
Lundbergh, S., 419
Lütkepohl, H., 326, 329–30, 336–8, 480–1, 486, 488, 490–6, 498–505, 544, 1018
Luukkonen, R., 253, 413–14, 877
Lyhagen, J., 531–4, 573

MacDonald, R., 512
Machlup, F., 19
MacKinnon, J. G., 108, 217, 245, 253, 441, 459, 789, 806, 815, 818–19, 823–4, 826, 828, 834–5, 937
MacNeill, I. B., 282–4
MaCurdy, T. W., 648, 729
Maddala, D. S., 401
Maddala, G. S., 253, 281, 488, 490, 513, 518–19, 522, 634, 639, 663, 668, 696, 700–1, 831
Maddock, R., 147
Madigan, D., 848
Magnello, M. E., 110

Magnus, J. R., 63, 68, 80, 146, 498, 924
Mäkeläinen, T., 284
Maki, U., 13
Malinvaud, E., 129, 138
Mammen, E., 823–4, 1008, 1017
Mandelbrot, B. B., 176, 197, 209, 284, 355–6, 739
Mandy, D., 910
Manganelli, S., 1006
Mankiw, N. G., 317
Mann, H. B., 128–9
Manski, C. F., 470, 692, 726, 905, 907–8, 1022
Mansur, A., 78
Manteiga, W., 1013
Maravall, A., 406, 1037–9
Marcellino, M., 407, 625
Mardia, K., 914, 922, 925
Marinucci, D., 198, 364, 374–5, 379–80
Maritz, J. S., 849
Mark, N., 512, 526, 529
Marmol, F., 375, 380, 383–4, 388
Marriott, F. H. C., 231
Marriott, J. M., 242, 330
Marron, S., 1005, 1010
Marsaglia, G., 792–3, 798–800, 803
Marschak, J., 125–6, 129, 131, 140, 146
Marshall, A. W., 5, 14, 789
Marshall, R., 914, 922, 925
Martin, G., 878, 893–4
Martin, R., 926
Martin, V., 893
Martins-Filho, C., 910
Masarotto, G., 497
Mascagni, M., 795
Masry, E., 1006, 1016–17
Matas-Mir, A., 1036
Mathiason, D. J., 471
Matsumoto, M., 793–4
Mátyás, L., 46, 48, 634
Matzkin, R. L., 1008–9
Mayo, D. G., 10–12, 20, 22, 40, 43, 52
McAleer, M., 63, 81, 83
McCabe, B. P. M., 166, 234, 247, 522
McCallum, B. T., 144
McCoskey, S. K., 512, 531
McDonald, G., 512
McFadden, D., 143, 606, 663, 670, 692
McGarry, J., 985
McGuirk, A., 10, 47, 49
McKenzie, E., 246
McLeish, D. L., 430, 438, 446, 471
McLeod, A. I., 224, 492

Medeiros, M. C., 405, 418
Meiselman, D., 144
Melenberg, B., 707–8
Metcalf, G. E., 648
Meyer, W., 513
Miao, B. Q., 281
Michael, P., 579
Michelacci, C., 388
Mikkelsen, H. O., 385, 754–5, 757
Milhoj, A., 750
Mill, J. S., 14
Miller, D. J., 441
Miller, J., 233, 235
Miller, K. W., 791
Miller, P. J., 147
Mills, F. C., 96, 15
Mills, T. C., 324, 330, 49
Minogue, C. D., 283
Mira, S., 572
Miron, J. A., 317, 1036
Mises, L. v., 67
Mishra, S., 1018
Mitchell, W. C., 19, 123
Mittelhammer, R. C., 441, 469
Mizon, G. E., 33, 75–7, 137, 646, 648
Modigliani, F., 141
Moffitt, R., 719, 721
Monfort, A., 245, 663, 668, 689–90, 692
Monsell, B. C., 1037–8
Montañés, A., 273, 323–5, 329
Montesinos, R., 579
Montouri, B. D., 949
Moon, C., 725, 727
Moon, H. R., 512, 519, 522, 526–7, 529,
    534–5, 573
Moore, H. L., 5, 16–18, 36, 43, 106–7,
    119–20, 122, 124
Moore, J. B., 979, 981
Moore, L. R., 793
Morales, M., 910
Moran, P., 932
Moreno, R., 935–6
Morgan, B. J. T., 412
Morgan, M. S., 8, 18, 23, 25–6, 28, 63,
    71–2, 74, 88, 90, 104–9, 111, 120,
    122–6, 134, 145–6
Morgenstern, O., 12, 123, 147
Morin, N., 594
Morley, J. C., 611
Morris, C., 849
Morrison, M., 71
Mosconi, R., 337, 499, 563
Mosteller, F., 43

Moulines, E., 287–8, 341, 359–60, 369,
    372–3, 387, 572
Mount, T. D., 639
Mukerjee, R., 845
Mukherjee, D., 1025
Mukherjee, K., 922
Mukhopadhyay, P., 430
Muller, M. E., 797
Müller, M., 1002
Müller, P., 986
Muller, U. A., 759
Müller, U. K., 254, 268–9, 291, 293,
    304, 326
Mundlak, Y., 645–6, 716
Mundra, K., 1025
Munnell, A. H., 147
Mur, J., 903
Murdoch, J. C., 906, 951, 954–5
Murphy, K., 714
Musgrave, J., 1038
Muth, J. F., 141, 568

Nabeya, S., 269, 284
Nadaraya, E. A., 1003
Nadler, J., 284
Nagler, R. J., 759
Naik-Nimbalkar, U. V., 430, 466
Nair, K. R., 97, 100, 102–3
Naito, K., 1007
Najarian, S., 417
Nandram, B., 867
Nankervis, J., 253, 257
Nardari, F., 769–70
Nason, J. M., 311, 334
Nataf, A., 142
Neale, A. J., 789, 808
Nelson, C. R., 147, 190, 217, 321, 327,
    611, 616, 872
Nelson, D., 461, 464, 745, 753, 766,
    773, 1018
Nelson, F., 708
Nelson, G. C., 903
Nerlove, M., 136, 770, 1037–8
Neumann, M., 504
Newbold, P., 35, 49, 217, 228, 233, 235,
    237–8, 253, 257, 287, 313, 319–20,
    324, 330–1, 334, 341–2, 402, 478, 512
Newey, W. K., 49, 258, 274, 459, 606,
    641, 707, 777, 914, 931, 1002, 1009,
    1021
Newton-Smith, W., 66, 68
Neyman, J., 21–2, 110, 438, 449,
    451–3, 717

Ng, S., 254, 257–62, 267, 273, 324, 489, 502, 522, 525–6, 623, 629
Ng, V. K., 773–6
Nicholls, D. F., 222, 245, 407, 460 462
Nickell, S., 649
Nielsen, B., 337, 563, 570
Nielsen, J., 1008, 1017
Nielson, M. O., 383, 387
Nijkamp, P., 941
Nijman, T., 721, 723
Nishimura, T., 793
Nobay, A. R., 579
Noh, J., 334
Novo, A. A., 951, 956, 958
Nunes, L. C., 287, 313, 331, 341
Nyblom, J., 284, 407, 542

O'Connell, P. G. J., 512, 522, 524, 579, 581
O'Hagan, A., 864, 888
O'Hara, M., 759
Obstfeld, M., 579
Öcal, N., 402
Ogaki, M., 529
Oh, K.-Y., 512
Ohara, H. I., 329
Okuma, A., 443
Okunade, A. A., 512
Oliver, F. R., 94, 99
Olloqui, I., 325
Olsen, R. B., 699, 704, 759
Omtzigt, P., 490, 566
Ooms, M., 389
Oppenheim, G., 377
Orcutt, G. H., 29, 31, 130, 136, 142, 147
Ord, J. K., 467, 903, 909, 912, 923, 926, 932–3, 977
Ortuño, M. A., 325, 328
Osborn, D. R., 253, 402, 1036
Otto, M. C., 1037–8
Ould Haye, M., 377
Ouliaris, S., 258, 333, 531
Owen, A. B., 471
Owen, A. L., 650
Ozaki, T., 400, 1017

Paap, R., 878–9, 886–8, 891, 894, 1036, 1042–3, 1048, 1052
Pace, R. K., 903, 914, 926
Paelinck, J., 902
Pagan, A. R., 33–4, 48, 63, 81, 141, 217, 222, 245, 408, 417, 502, 612, 626–7, 639, 663, 708, 940, 1002, 1010, 1016, 1022
Page, E. S., 282, 284
Pakes, A., 104, 670
Palm, F. C., 617, 619
Panneton, F., 793–4
Pantula, S. G., 253
Paparoditis, E., 253
Papell, D. H., 329, 512
Park, J. Y., 253, 256, 273, 335, 500, 542, 830, 1019
Park, S. K., 791
Paruolo, P., 563, 570–1, 619
Pascual, L., 497
Patil, P., 915
Patterson, D., 415
Patterson, K., 49
Paulsen, J., 231, 490
Pawlak, M., 1019
Pearl, J., 500
Pearl, R., 94, 96–9
Pearson, E., 438
Pearson, K., 15, 22, 52, 90, 92, 95–6, 109–110, 429–430, 471
Peaucelle, I., 618
Pedroni, P., 526–7, 530–1
Peel, D. A., 399, 579
Peirce, C. S., 23
Peiris, S., 462
Pelletiery, D., 1019
Peltzman, S., 579
Penm, J. H. W., 491
Perez, S. J., 77, 81
Pericchi, L. R., 850
Perlman, M. D., 237, 239
Perron, P., 253–4, 256–62, 267, 273, 281, 283–91, 293–6, 298–9, 302, 305–10, 313–7, 320–32, 340, 342, 489, 519, 522, 529, 1036, 1039
Persand, G., 767, 773–4, 780
Persons, W. M., 119
Pesaran, B., 498
Pesaran, M. H., 144, 147, 253, 281, 504, 513, 522, 529, 535, 557, 563, 573, 891, 916, 945
Pesavento, E., 274
Phillips, A. W., 137
Phillips, P. C. B., 33, 49, 138–9, 144, 190, 204, 225, 242, 253–4, 256, 258, 273, 283–4, 311, 324, 330, 333, 335, 358, 374–6, 386, 441, 500, 512, 519–22, 525–8, 531, 534–5, 542, 573, 597, 603, 886, 889, 893, 1019–20

Phipps, T. T., 918
Picard, D., 281, 292, 298–300
Pictet, O. V., 759
Pierce, D. A., 236–8, 985, 1039
Pierse, R. G., 504
Pinkse, J., 928, 951, 956–7, 1009
Pippenger, M. K., 579
Pitarakis, J.-Y., 302, 310, 416, 579, 591,
    594, 597–8, 601, 612
Pitt, M. K., 770–1, 989, 995–6
Ploberger, W., 268, 274, 297–9, 302–4,
    306, 312, 315, 341, 411, 495,
    519, 889
Plosser, C. I., 217, 321, 327, 502, 872, 891
Pocock, S., 914
Poirier, D. J., 724, 859, 864, 866, 894
Polansky, A. M., 1020
Politis, D. N., 43, 253, 830–1
Pollard, D., 161, 170, 209, 670
Polson, N., 759, 769, 986
Pope, J. A., 231
Popper, K., 68
Porter, J., 1025
Porter-Hudak, S., 356
Poskitt, D. S., 235, 238–9, 242, 500, 505
Potter, S. M., 397, 399, 557, 579
Powell, J. L., 470, 707, 725, 1009, 1022
Prakasa Rao, B. L. S., 1002
Prášková, Z., 283
Prescott, E. C., 63, 78, 81, 975
Press, S. J., 865
Press, W. H., 791
Prest, A. R., 135, 147
Priestley, M. B., 415
Proietti, T., 551, 611
Protter, P., 209
Provine, W. B., 109
Prucha, I. R., 910, 914–15, 917, 920–1,
    928–31, 934, 936, 944, 948, 957–8
Prvan, T., 1020

Qin, D., 8, 90, 122, 124–5, 130, 134,
    141, 146–7
Qin, J., 471
Qu, Z., 284–6, 289–90, 294–6, 308–10,
    339–40
Quah, D., 502, 535
Quandt, R. E., 282, 299, 399, 402
Quenneville, B., 981
Quenouille, M. H., 227
Quine, W. V. O., 69
Quinn, B. G., 241, 407, 460, 462, 489
Quintos, C. E., 311–12

Racine, J., 1002–3, 1005–6, 1010, 1013–16,
    1023–4, 1026
Racine-Poon, A., 856, 866
Rafajlowicz, E., 1019
Raftery, A. E., 848, 865
Rahbek, A. C., 557, 563, 570–2, 593
Rahman, M., 1007
Rahman, S., 951, 955
Rahmatian, M., 906
Ramsey, J. B., 144, 414
Rao, C. R., 15, 21–2, 43, 238, 437, 441
Rappoport, P., 284, 321
Ray, B. K., 370–1, 387
Raymond, J., 757
Rech, G., 418
Reddaway, S. F., 795
Redman, D. A., 5, 8
Reed, L. J., 94, 98–9
Reggiani, A., 941
Reichlin, L., 284, 321, 612–13, 622,
    624–6, 629
Reiersøl, O., 108, 130, 146
Reimers, H.-E., 502, 512
Reinsel, G. C., 217, 221, 229–30, 498,
    542, 569, 1039
Renault, E., 245, 499–500, 663, 668,
    689–90, 692, 766, 1009
Rényi, A., 288
Rey, S. J., 903, 920, 928, 933, 941,
    949, 958
Reyes, M., 323–4, 329
Rhodes, E. C., 97, 101
Rice, J., 1021
Rich, R., 757
Richard, J.-F., 41, 76, 217, 554, 663, 692,
    769–70, 864, 887, 891
Richardson, S., 852, 894
Ridder, G., 723
Rilstone, P., 828, 1006
Ripatti, A., 877
Ripley, B. D., 791, 798, 806, 903, 914, 925
Rissanen, J., 228, 241, 243, 489
Ritov, Y., 1002, 1021
Robbins, L., 19, 65
Robbins, N. B., 284
Robins, R. P., 748
Robinson, D. P., 905, 915, 928, 934–5, 940
Robinson, P. M., 198, 340–1, 356–64,
    366–9, 371, 373–80, 382, 385–6,
    388, 668, 1006, 1014, 1016, 1021
Rochina-Barrachina, M., 726
Rodríguez, G. H., 329
Roehrig, C., 1009

Roll, R., 747
Romano, J. P., 43, 830
Rombouts, J. V. K., 767, 771, 775, 778, 780
Romo, J., 497
Ronning, G., 246
Roos, C. F., 28, 122, 146
Rose, A. K., 512
Rosen, H., 906, 910
Rosenberg, A., 63
Rosenblatt, M., 24
Rossi, P. G., 759, 769
Roth, R., 290
Rothenberg, T. J., 140–1, 254, 261–2,
    264–5, 267, 270, 274, 319–20, 326,
    329, 519
Rothman, P., 420
Rothschild, M., 622, 774–5
Rotnitzky, A. G., 469
Rousseeuw, P. J., 101
Roy, A., 317
Royle, J. A., 903
Rubin, D. B., 403, 500, 666, 704, 851–2,
    864, 866–7
Rubin, H., 129–30, 132
Ruckstuhl, A., 1025
Rudebush, G., 388
Ruiz, E., 497, 767–71
Runkle, D. E., 653, 663, 721, 753, 757,
    770, 773
Rünstler, G., 621
Ruppert, D., 1002, 1005, 1010
Rush, M., 317
Ruud, P., 663, 666
Rydén, T., 572

Saavedra, L. A., 906
Sacerdote, B., 905, 916
Said, S. E., 254, 256
Saikkonen, P., 243, 253, 326, 329–30,
    333, 336–8, 413–14, 486, 492–3, 500,
    526, 528, 531, 535, 592–3, 877
Salanie, B., 663
Salmon, W., 15
Salyer, K. D., 78
Samarov, A., 368
Samorodnitsky, G., 205
Sampson, M., 498
Samuelson, P. A., 119
Sandler, T., 951, 955
Sanmartin, P., 910
Sanso, A., 260, 273, 334–5
Sansó-i-Rossello, A. S., 325, 328
Santos, A. A. F., 996, 998

Sarda, P., 1016
Sargan, J. D., 33, 137, 234, 260, 535, 806
Sargent, T. J., 34, 78, 142, 568
Sarno, L., 400, 512, 524, 535
Sato, S., 326, 997
Savage, L. J., 23
Savin, N. E., 253, 257, 285, 340, 388
SCAN, 795
Schaumburg, E., 569
Scheffe, H., 24
Scheinkman, J., 905, 916
Schleifer, A., 905
Schmidt, P., 253, 273, 283–4, 330, 520–2,
    525, 644, 646, 648, 650, 653, 705
Scholes, M., 753, 766
Schuermann, T., 573
Schultz, H., 91, 98–9, 107–8, 122, 125
Schwarz, G., 241, 489, 867, 889, 1017
Schwert, G. W., 253, 257, 740–1
Scott, D. M., 795
Scott, D. W., 1002
Scott, E. L., 449, 451–2, 717
Scruggs, J. T., 769–70
Seber, G. A. F., 402
Secrist, H., 111
Seifert, B., 1005
Selden, T. M., 512
Sen Roy, S., 498
Sen, P. K., 297
Sent, E.-M., 147
Sentana, E., 770
Seo, B., 312, 558, 571, 581–3, 593
Sevestre, P., 634
Shaban, S. A., 281
Shankar, B., 951, 955
Shao, J., 836, 852
Shaw, D., 700
Sheather, S. J., 1005, 1010
Sheffrin, S. M., 147
Shephard, N., 209, 234, 572, 663, 666–7,
    759, 982–3, 989, 995–6, 766–71,
    795–6
Sheppard, K., 1019
Shibata, R., 241
Shiller, R. J., 568, 741
Shimotsu, K., 358, 362, 375–6, 383,
    388, 1020
Shin, S., 513
Shin, Y., 253, 283–4, 324, 330, 333, 335,
    504, 520–2, 525, 563, 891
Shiryaev, A. N., 170
Shiskin, J., 1038
Shively, T. S., 299

Shreve, S. E., 199
Shrivastava, M. P., 100, 102–3
Shukur, G., 493
Sibbertsen, P., 341
Siegfried, J. J., 857
Siegmund, D., 291, 296, 299
Siklos, P. L., 317, 571, 581, 1036, 1038
Silverman, B. W., 867, 985–6, 1002
Silvey, S. D., 238
Sim, A.-B., 237
Simard, R., 793–4, 800
Simon, H. A., 74, 130, 141
Simonoff, J. S., 24, 43, 1002, 1005, 1010
Sims, C. A., 33, 35, 63, 74–5, 142, 478,
    486, 500, 502, 504, 1036
Sinai, Y. G., 354
Singh, A. C., 981
Singleton, K. J., 759
Sjöberg, B., 100, 103
Skalin, J., 402
Skeels, C., 708
Skorokhod, A. V., 175
Slade, M. E., 928, 951, 956–7
Slutsky, E., 23, 123, 216
Small, C. G., 430, 438, 471
Smirnov, O., 919, 926
Smith, A. A., 245, 826
Smith, A. D., 340
Smith, A. F. M., 842, 856, 861, 864–5, 866
Smith, B. B., 125
Smith, G. W., 78, 333
Smith, J. Q., 996, 998
Smith, K. A., 795
Smith, L. V., 512
Smith, R., 281, 563, 675, 916
Smith, V., 319–20
Smyth, R., 512
Snell, E. J., 956
Snyder, R. D., 977
Solo, V., 190
Solow, R. W., 136
Sone, A., 926
Song, F. M., 512
Song, S. H., 948
Sonnberger, H., 281
Sørensen, M., 446, 471
Soulier, P., 359–60, 369, 372–3, 377–8,
    386–7
Sowell, F., 304
Spady, R., 726
Spanos, A., 7, 10–11, 15, 17–19, 21–3, 28–9,
    33, 36, 38–43, 45–50, 52, 63, 73,
    80, 217

Speckman, P., 1021
Speigelhalter, D. J., 852, 894
Speight, A. E. H., 399
Sperlich, S., 1002
Spiegelman, C., 1007
Srinivasan, A., 795
Staehle, H., 121
Stambaugh, R. F., 741
Steel, M. F. J., 888
Stein, M. L., 921
Steland, A., 1019
Stengos, T., 1025
Stern, H. S., 851–2, 864, 867
Steutel, F. W., 246
Stigler, G. J., 8, 16, 105
Stigler, S. M., 18, 65, 73, 90, 99, 101,
    110–11, 788
Stigum, B. P., 13, 26, 63, 70
Stinchombe, M., 404
Stock, J. H., 253–4, 259–62, 264–5, 267,
    270, 272–4, 281, 287, 294–5, 309, 311,
    316, 319–20, 326–9, 333, 405, 486,
    498, 500, 502, 519, 528, 531, 542,
    624, 626, 891
Stockmeyer, P. K., 791
Stoffer, D., 981
Stoker, T. M., 908, 1006
Stone, C. J., 1003
Stone, J. R. N., 31, 121–2, 133, 135–6,
    139, 147
Stone, M., 866
Stone, W. M., 121
Strachan, R., 877–8, 880–4, 886–9, 891
Strauss, J., 512
Strazicich, M. C., 330–1, 334–5, 512
Strikholm, B., 416
Stroud, J. R., 986
Stroup, W. W., 951
Stuart, A., 675
Student, 788
Su, L., 1009, 1017–18, 1021
Subba Rao, T., 406
Sugita, K., 894
Sul, D., 512, 522, 526, 529
Summers, L. H., 7, 68, 80, 317
Summers, R., 807
Sun, Y. X., 366–8, 386, 1019–20
Suppe, F., 70
Suppes, P., 70
Surgailis, D., 385
Svenssen, S., 100, 103
Swamy, P. A. V. B., 638
Swanson, N. R., 397, 418

Swensen, A. R., 568
Szymanski, S., 906

Tahmiscioglu, A. K., 529
Takemura, A., 234
Talmain, G., 12
Tanaka, K., 269, 284
Tang, S. M., 283
Taniguchi, M., 460, 464
Tanner, M. A., 666, 856
Tanur, J. M., 865
Taqqu, M. S., 205, 284, 340, 359
Tauchen, G., 49, 759, 769
Tay, A. S., 497
Taylor, A. M. R., 318–19, 579, 1042
Taylor, L. D., 101
Taylor, M. P., 400, 512, 524, 535
Taylor, R. L., 430
Taylor, S. J., 754, 766
Taylor, W. E., 634, 639–40, 646, 648
Tedesco, L., 220
Teichrow, D., 788
Tejerizo, M., 910
Teräsvirta, T., 281, 389, 397, 400–2, 405,
    412–19, 459–60, 495, 572, 750–1, 1017
Terrell, R. D., 222, 245, 491
Terrin, N., 341
Terza, J., 709, 715
Teukolsky, S. A., 791
Teverosovky, V., 340
Teyssière, G., 340, 385
Thavaneswaran, A., 460–2, 471
Thayer, M. A., 906
Theil, H., 103, 109, 132, 134, 142, 147
Thibodeau, T. G., 914
Thiele, T. N., 100–2, 106, 109
Thomas, J. J., 145
Thompson, M. E., 442, 450–1, 454, 457–8
Thompson, T. S., 692
Tiao, G. C., 140, 322, 399, 985, 1039
Tibshirani, R., 43, 1008
Tiefelsdorf, M., 903, 933
Tierney, L., 852
Tieslau, M. A., 512, 749
Tinbergen, J., 25, 28, 65, 109, 120–6, 128,
    132, 146–7
Tintner, G., 28, 97–9, 111
Tjøstheim, D., 231, 397, 402, 415,
    1016–18
Tobias, J. L., 724, 864, 867
Tobin, J., 142, 702, 729
Tocher, K. D., 790
Toda, H. Y., 500

Tokihisa, A., 330
Tompa, H., 887
Tong, H., 281, 397–401, 418, 462, 579,
    1016–17
Topa, G., 905, 910, 914–15
Topel, R., 714
Train, K. E., 663
Tran, H. A., 1036
Trapletti, A., 404
Tremayne, A. R., 166, 229, 235, 238–9,
    242, 246–7, 824
Trenkler, C., 337–8
Trimbur, T., 976, 983
Trivedi, P. K., 805
Trognon, A., 663, 668, 689–90, 692
Truong, Y. K., 1006
Tsai, C. L., 1005, 1010
Tsang, W. W., 799, 803
Tsay, R. S., 397, 399, 402, 414, 416, 420,
    460, 579, 581, 1008, 1017
Tse, Y. K., 772, 1019
Tsui, A., 1019
Tsybakov, A. B., 1006, 1018
Tukey, J. W., 43
Turlach, B. A., 356, 1016
Turnbull, H. W., 110
Turtle, H. J., 464
Tweedie, R. L., 220
Twefik, A. H., 360
Tyssedal, J. S., 402
Tzavalis, E., 513

Uhlig, H., 504
Ullah, A., 48, 1002, 1006–7, 1009–10,
    1012, 1016–19, 1022, 1025
Upton, G. J., 903, 909
Urbain, J. P., 325, 617, 619, 891
Urga, G., 389, 512

Vahid, F., 612, 614–15, 617–18, 622, 626
Valavanis, S., 31
van der Sluis, P. J., 770
Van der Vaart, A. W., 266, 270
Van der Vlist, A., 903
van der Weide, R., 775
Van Dijk, D., 281, 397, 405, 414, 418, 420
Van Dijk, H. K., 853, 873–4, 876–9,
    883–8, 891, 894, 983
Van Harn, K., 246
Van Loan, C., 879
Van Ness, J. W., 197, 209, 355
Van Soest, A., 707–8
Van Yzeren, J., 102

Vanesse, C., 703
Varadharajan-Krishnakumar, J., 644
Veall, M. R., 828
Velasco, C., 253, 359, 371–5, 380–4, 387–8
Vella, F., 663, 708, 722–3, 726, 729, 1009
Verbeek, M., 721–2, 723
Verdinelli, I., 861, 888
Verspagen, B., 512
Vetterling, W. T., 791
Viano, M. C., 377
Vieu, P., 1016
Vijverberg, W. P., 951, 954–5
Villani, M., 878, 880, 883, 885, 887–92
Vining, R., 30, 131
Vinod, H. D., 430
Vogelsang, T. J., 260, 273, 298–9, 301, 304, 315–16, 318, 325–6, 328–9, 331, 342
Volcker, P. A., 63, 81
Volinsky, C. T., 848
Von Neumann, J., 136
Vougas, D., 402
Vuong, Q., 1013

Wada, T., 322
Wadhwani, S., 770
Wald, A., 100, 102–3, 108–9, 123, 128–9, 436–7, 845
Walker, G., 226
Walker, J., 707
Wall, K., 981
Wall, M. M., 913
Wallace, C. S., 799
Waller, L. A., 903, 951
Wallis, J. R., 356
Wallis, K. F., 227, 497, 980, 982, 998, 1036
Walters, A. A., 142
Wand, M. P., 1002, 1005, 1010
Wandji, J., 604
Wang, J., 330
Wang, S., 1007, 1011–12
Wansbeek, T. J., 637, 656
Warnes, J., 914, 925
Wasserman, L., 849–50, 861, 866, 888
Waterman, R. P., 452
Watkins, A., 914, 925
Watson, G. S., 31, 136, 544, 563, 1003
Watson, M. W., 333, 405, 480, 486, 500, 502, 528, 531, 611, 624, 626, 891
Watt, D. G., 311, 334
Watts, D. G., 400–2
Waugh, F. V., 108, 110, 122, 125, 134
Waymire, E., 284
Wecker, W. E., 407, 984

Wedderburn, R. W. M., 445–6, 468–9
Wei, C. Z., 209, 273
Wei, S., 579, 581
Weil, D. N., 317
Weiner, S., 573
Weintraub, R. E., 141
Weiss, A. A., 463, 757, 1021
Wellner, J. A., 1002, 1021
Welsh, A., 1025
Werwatz, A., 1002
West, K. D., 258, 274, 914, 931
West, M., 894, 995, 997–8
Westlund, A. H., 281
Whalley, J., 78
Whang, Y. J., 1019
White, H., 77, 166, 192, 195, 298, 404–7, 418, 644, 766, 822, 931, 1003, 1006, 1021
White, J. S., 255
Whiteman, C. H., 77, 253, 257
Whitman, R. H., 106
Whittle, P., 903, 910, 971, 973–4, 998
Wiener, N., 176
Wild, C. J., 402
Wilke, C. K., 903
Wilks, S. S., 435–6
Winkelmann, R., 709, 719, 727
Winkler, R. L., 845
Wise, D., 697, 721
Wohar, M. E., 581
Wold, H. O. A., 23, 26, 123, 130, 134, 146, 190, 216, 218, 224
Wolf, M., 43
Wolff, R. C. L., 1020
Wolfinger, R. D., 951
Wolfson, L. J., 848
Wolpert, R. L., 843
Wolters, J., 388, 504
Wong, C. M., 856, 1017
Woodward, W. A., 377
Wooldridge, J. M., 48, 50, 195, 410, 414, 659, 699, 702, 718–19, 723, 727, 729, 756, 771–3, 1009, 1021
Working, E. J., 124
Working, H., 119
Worsley, K. J., 299
Wouk, H., 729
Wright, J. H., 341
Wright, J. W., 387
Wright, P. G., 106, 108, 121–2
Wright, S., 109
Wu, C. F. J., 666, 823
Wu, J. L., 512

Wu, S., 308, 512–13, 518–20, 522
Wu, Y., 237, 512
Wulwick, N. J., 137
Wyhowski, D., 644

Xia, H., 903
Xiao, Z., 253, 299, 1017

Yabu, T., 316–17, 332
Yajima, Y., 355, 378, 382
Yamada, K., 281, 331–2
Yamamoto, E., 439, 498
Yanagimoto, T., 439
Yang, G. L., 266, 270
Yang, Y., 375
Yao, Q., 397, 418, 1018, 1020
Yao, Y.-C., 292, 308
Yasui, Y., 466
Yatchew, A., 1003
Yeo, S., 281
Yilmaz, M. R., 397
Yin, Y., 520, 522
Ying, Z., 725
Yoo, B. S., 253, 498, 569, 571, 1038, 1040–1
Yoon, M., 939–41
You, J., 1025
Young, A. H., 1038
Young, G. A., 833, 835

Young, L. J., 907
Yu, K., 1006
Yule, G. U., 23, 31, 49, 65, 94–7, 109–10, 123, 126, 136, 147, 216, 219, 226, 430, 788
Yuzefovich, Y., 920, 928, 930–1

Zabel, J., 721
Zacks, S., 281–2
Zaffaroni, P., 354, 388
Zeger, S. L., 430, 452, 468–9, 1025
Zellner, A. A., 23, 51, 63, 81, 83, 140, 245, 864, 874, 886
Zha, T., 504
Zhang, H., 512, 951
Zhang, N. F., 377
Zhang, W., 677
Zhao, Q., 1006
Zhou, X., 1025
Zhou, Y., 1025
Zhou, Z., 1016
Zhu, X., 287, 332, 1024
Zhurbenko, I. G., 372
Zidek, J. V., 308
Ziegelmann, F., 1018
Ziliak, J. P., 653
Zivot, E., 61, 274, 327–30, 336, 342, 389, 579, 581, 880
Zoller, H. G., 903

Subject Index

a priori validity, 17
AB-model, 502–3
accelerated failure time models, 711
additive model, 1009
adjustment coefficients, 571–2, 883
aggregation, 142–3
Akaike Information Criterion (AIC), 38,
    240–1, 257, 416, 489–90, 597, 829,
    1010–11, 1017
antipersistence, 355
    see also negative memory, 355
antithetic
    variables, 989
    variates, 804–6
arbitrage pricing theory (APT) model, 770
ARCH, 32, 189, 385, 460–1, 463–6, 739,
    742, 824
    asymmetric model, 461
    effects, 747, 751, 757
    errors, 465, 824
    exponential GARCH (EGARCH): model,
        755, 773; process, 753
    fractionally integrated GARCH
        (FIGARCH), 385, 754–5: martingale,
        755; model, 755, 757
    fractionally integrated exponential
        GARCH (FIEARCH), 385, 387:
        modified model, 755
    generalized autoregressive conditional
        heteroskedasticity (GARCH), 189,
        385, 464–5, 754, 758, 766, 770, 772,
        775–7, 779–80, 824: asymmetric,
        753; errors, 465; innovations, 749,
        751; martingale model, 750; model,
        681, 689, 738, 747, 750–2, 757–8,
        760–1, 766–7, 774–5, 1018;
        parameters, 824; process, 679–680,
        744–7, 749–752, 756, 775, 824–5;
        simultaneous equation model, 748;
        symmetric model, 776
    innovations, 742, 749, 757
    integrated GARCH (IGARCH), 752, 778:
        model, 752; process, 753, 757
    long memory, 754

model, 681, 738, 743–4, 747, 749–50,
    752, 754–6, 761, 766, 770
    multivariate GARCH (MGARCH), 773:
        asymmetric, 773; models, 767–8,
        771–2, 775, 778–80; seasonal, 774
    orthogonal GARCH (OGARCH) model,
        775
    parameters, 465, 744
    plus noise model, 996
    process, 679, 741, 743, 745, 749, 756
    representation, 746
ARCH in Mean (ARCH-M)
    model, 748–9, 751
    parameter, 748
ARFIMA
    fractional model, 370
    model, 32, 354, 358, 369, 761
    process, 755
ARIMA, 972–4
    approach, 33
    estimation (regARIMA), 1039
    model, 42, 416, 611, 740–1, 747, 752,
        972, 985: nonseasonal, 1040;
        seasonal, 1039
ARMA
    backwards noninvertible, 975
    cycle, 620–1
    disturbances, 751
    integer (INARMA) model, 246
    linear component, 463
    mixed process, 228, 231, 234
    model, 23, 32, 216, 224–5, 228–9,
        231–40, 242–4, 246, 406,
        741, 747
    processes, 190, 219, 245–6, 256, 354,
        370, 377, 668, 676, 745–6, 972:
        GARMA, 377
    representation, 747
artificial neural network (ANN) model,
    403, 405
Arzelà-Ascoli
    conditions, 181
    theorem, 180
asymmetry tests, 776

asymptotic
  approach, 161, 288–90, 293, 310,
    562, 574
  bias, 365–7, 379, 648, 655
  conditional variance, 566
  covariance matrix, 700, 714
  distribution, 312, 364, 378, 382, 414,
    485–6, 504, 517, 562, 565–6,
    571, 617, 655, 806–8, 812–13,
    818, 1021
  efficiency, 485
  MSE, 366, 369
  normality, 471
  P value, 818
  theory, 570
  variance, 387
attrition, 703, 721
autocorrelation, 138
  first-order, 741
  function (ACF), 219, 221, 223–4, 226–8,
    354, 750–1: inverse (IACF), 228–9;
    partial (PACF), 221–7, 229; sample
    (SPACF), 227–8, 230; sample (SACF),
    227–8, 230; residual, 236
  local, 913
autocovariance-generating function
    (ACGF), 223–4, 973–5, 977
auto-logistic model, 951
auto-Poisson model, 951
autoregression
  pure, 223–4, 227–8, 231, 234, 239, 244
autoregressive
  coefficient, 298, 323, 805
  operator, 234, 243
  parameters, 1042–3, 1048, 1051–3
  polynomial, 238
  process, 23, 192, 220, 225–7, 230, 237,
    242, 414, 572, 599, 668, 757, 768, 804,
    828, 830, 911, 992, 1044
  representation, 224, 232, 244
  specification, 590
autoregressive (AR) model, 49, 216, 219,
    221–3, 227, 229–33, 239–41, 254–6,
    267, 410, 416, 429, 498, 513, 523, 544,
    548, 579, 583, 650, 655, 657, 740, 742,
    766, 805, 828, 974
  additive nonlinear, 408, 410
  asymmetric moving average
    (ARasMA), 407
  autoregressive errors (ARAR), 245
  conditionally linear autoregressive
    (CLAR), 220, 246–7
  exponential (EAR), 400

exponential smooth transition (ESTAR),
    400, 402, 416
  integer (INAR), 246–7
  known-variance, zero-mean Gaussian,
    262, 265, 267–8
  linear, 400–1, 408
  logistic smooth transition (LSTAR),
    401–2, 413, 416
  Markov-switching (AR-MS or MS-AR)
    model, 402–3, 408, 410, 417–19
  neural network (AR-NN), 404–5, 415,
    417–19
  order, 518, 524
  periodic (PAR), 1042, 1048
  random coefficient, 406–7, 460
  self-exciting threshold (SETAR), 398–9,
    401–3, 412, 416–20
  "single hidden layer", 404
  smooth transition (STAR), 401–4, 408,
    410, 414, 416–20
  spatial, 466
  suddenly changing (SCAR), 402–3
  threshold (TAR), 398, 408, 410, 412,
    414, 462, 571, 584: momentum-,
    398; self-exciting models, 586;
    two-regime, 398; vector, 420
  time series, 438
  time-varying (TV-AR), 401
  vector smooth transition
    (VSTAR), 420
auxiliary residuals, 975, 982
averaged periodogram (AP), 363
  estimate, 364, 369
  estimation, 385
  matrix, 383
  statistic, 379
averaged t-test, 513, 517
  see also IPS test

back-propagation, 405
backward stepwise approach, 941
Balanced Growth Hypothesis, 891
bandwidth, 299, 386–8, 1002
  auxiliary, 365
  choice, 388
  conditions, 365
  optimal, 366–9
Bartlett corrections, 490
Bartlett's paradox, 887–8
Bayes
  empirical analysis, 849
  factor, 847, 850, 861, 888
  fractional approach, 888

Bayes – *continued*
  rule, 849
  Theorem, 843–4, 846, 850, 852
Bayesian
  approach, 23, 34, 708, 724, 744, 759,
      842, 848–9, 852, 864, 955–6, 989–90
  cointegration, 872–3, 876: analysis,
      872–3, 880, 885; methods, 872
  computation, 852, 873
  critical value, 847
  estimators, 845
  hierarchical spatial modelling, 912, 958
  inductive inference, 23
  inference, 842, 873–4, 876, 893, 983
  Information Criterion (BIC), 241, 243,
      257, 416, 418, 597–8, 1017, 1041,
      1043, 1048, 1051–2
  interval estimation, 845
  MCMC: estimator, 704, 706, 725;
      method, 769–70
  model averaging (BMA), 848, 890–1
  models, 789
  paradigm, 841–2
  perspective, 844, 846
  point estimates, 845, 848
  predictive density, 847
  reasoning, 864
  statistics, 842
  techniques, 51, 90, 140, 330, 504, 724,
      872, 874, 892
  VAR methods, 873–4
BEKK
  formulation, 773
  model, 772
best linear unbiased estimator (BLUE), 32,
      636, 640, 646
best quadratic unbiased (BQU)
      estimators, 638
Between
  estimators, 646
  regression, 638
Beveridge–Nelson
  cycles, 611, 617, 619, 621, 627
  decomposition, 190, 193, 611:
      multivariate, 618; univariate, 618
  filter, 977
  framework, 628
  trend-cycle representation, 616
  trends, 611, 617, 619
bias-corrected estimator, 1007
bilinear
  model, 463–4
  processes, 463

Billingsley's theorem, 181–2
binary choice
  estimators, 717
  model, 702, 707, 709, 717–18, 817
bivariate
  cointegrated process, 545
  model, 499
  process, 499, 546, 566, 592
  system, 583–4
blocking step, 858
bootstrap
  biased method, 1021
  block, 830–1, 835
  block-of-blocks, 822, 831
  confidence intervals, 813, 822, 832–4
  covariance matrices, 825
  data-generating process (DGP), 813, 815,
      817–30, 832, 834–5: parametric,
      821, 826–7; semiparametric, 820,
      822, 825–7
  distribution, 832–3
  ERP, 819
  errors, 824–7, 829
  failure, 835
  grid, 833
  inference, 835
  method, 789, 795, 812, 817, 831, 835,
      957, 981, 1010
  moving block, 830
  nested, 1013
  P value, 814, 816–19
  pairs, 822–5, 828, 831–2, 835
  parametric, 817–20, 825, 828–9, 834–5
  resampled error terms, 821
  samples, 813, 816, 818, 820, 822, 825,
      828–30
  semiparametric, 828
  sieve, 828, 830, 835
  simulations, 1013
  stationary, 830
  t method, 833–4: *see also* percentile
      t method
  technique, 43, 239, 419, 490, 497, 504,
      524, 566, 664, 725
  test statistic, 813, 816, 818–19,
      822, 832
  testing, 789, 814, 819–20, 826, 835
  wild, 823–4, 835, 1012:
      recursive-design, 824
Borel
  field, 162, 171, 174–6
  sets, 173
Box–Cox transformation, 368

Box–Jenkins strategy, 33–5, 41–2, 143–4,
    217, 236
Box–Muller method, 797–8
break
    dates, 280, 282, 285–91, 293–5,
        299–300, 302–3, 305, 307, 311–13,
        317–18, 320, 325–32, 334–9
    points, 285–6
Breusch–Godfrey test, 492–3
Breusch–Pagan LM
    statistic, 940
    test, 940
Brownian
    bridge, 188, 282–3, 297, 308, 586
    motion (BM), 176, 178–9, 182, 184–5,
        187–90, 193, 195–6, 198, 200–1,
        204, 207–8, 255, 261, 515, 526,
        563, 565, 569, 571–2, 586–7,
        603, 808: de-meaned, 187, 517;
        de-trended, 187, 517; fractional
        (fBM), 197–8, 375, 380
    sheet, 587, 604
Bry–Boschan
    algorithm, 626
    requirements, 627
bunch maps, 135
    analysis, 122, 135
    exploding, 135
business cycle, 626–8
    analysis, 119, 122–3, 612, 628, 1036
    econometric model, 65
    frequencies, 612
    modeling, 130
    real (RBC) model, 891
    theories, 120
    variation, 1036: variable-specific, 1036

cadlag functions, 174, 179, 181, 185
calibration methodology, 78
Canova–Hansen (CH) test, 1041–2, 1051–2
capital asset pricing model (CAPM), 738–9
    conditional (CCAPM), 767, 774
categorical data, 1014
Cauchy
    distribution, 164, 205
    form, 886
    prior, 883
    sequence, 173–5, 180, 185
    tails, 886
Cauchy–Schwartz inequality, 453, 455
causal
    asymmetry, 130
    ordering, 130
causality, 81, 130, 498, 500

censored
    data, 696, 709, 720: interval, 709;
        models, 704, 710
    least absolute deviations estimator
        (CLAD), 725, 1022
    normal model, 707
    observation, 711–12, 718, 951
    regression model, 712, 727, 1022
censoring, 695–7, 700–3, 708, 710, 712,
    715, 718, 720, 728, 818
    condition, 953–4
    model, 708: two-tailed, 703
    point, 1023
    times, 1024
Census
    X11-procedure, 1039
    X12-ARIMA method, 1038–9, 1044,
        1048, 1051–3
central limit theorem (CLT), 164–9, 176,
    178–9, 182–3, 186, 188–9, 193, 195,
    205–6, 235, 291, 386, 516, 529, 570,
    602–3, 757, 854, 921, 936
    dependent, 207
    functional (FCLT), 166, 174, 177–9, 181,
        184–90, 192–3, 195–6, 199, 201,
        203–4, 207, 279, 288, 292, 585
    martingale, 188
change of support problem (COSP), 907
characteristic
    function (ch.f.), 165, 173, 178, 205
    polynomial approach, 926
Chebyshev criterion, 101
    see also method of minimax
Choleski decomposition, 75, 494, 502, 557,
    829, 926, 954–5
Chow test, 637
classical linear regression (CLR), 696
    model, 9, 30–2, 47, 698, 701, 709,
        815–17, 831, 935
co-breaking, 338
Cochrane–Orcutt (CORC)
    estimator, 136
    transformation, 73
codependence, 618
coding approach, 920
cofeature
    combination, 614
    restrictions, 617
    space, 615
    vector, 614
cointegrated
    process, 546–7, 549
    system, 605
    variables, 479

cointegrating
  coefficient, 566
  panel regressions, 526
  rank, 313, 336, 339, 483–4, 488, 490,
    541–2, 545, 552–3, 560, 562–3,
    593, 612, 619, 888
  regression model, 593
  relationship, 335, 338, 533, 593–5,
    621, 873: nonlinear, 593
  residuals, 581
  space, 878, 880–5, 887–93
  vector, 333–6, 338–40, 545–7, 553–4,
    581–3, 593, 601, 611, 617, 874,
    876–82, 885, 889–93
cointegration
  analysis, 556, 872, 876–8
  inference, 874
  model, 544, 558, 562, 568, 572, 885:
    fractional, 878
  multicointegration parameter, 571
  multivariate models, 611
  nonlinear, 544, 593, 595
  panel data, 574
  properties, 481–2
  relation, 479, 483, 486, 490, 496–7, 542,
    549, 551–6, 561–3, 568, 571, 890–1
  residual-based tests, 542
  seasonal, 544, 568, 574
  Space Approach, 893
  tests, 530
combination tests, 513, 518, 520, 522–3,
  525, 532
common shocks, 907
compactness, 179–80
completeness, 173
computer technology, 139
conditional
  autoregressive (CAR): model, 912–13;
    prior, 951; process, 912
  covariance, 748, 771–2, 774–5,
    778, 780
  density, 756–8
  distribution, 51, 161, 697
  heteroskedasticity, 378, 385, 1022, 1025
  likelihood function, 233
  mean, 738–9, 741–3, 747, 749, 751, 755,
    766, 971, 983, 1003, 1012–13:
    equation, 771, 773, 775; function,
    702–3, 710, 725, 1008, 1012; model,
    752; vector, 774
  moment tests, 708
  moments, 459–60, 467
  probabilities, 696, 862

  probability function, 1023
  variance, 742–8, 752–5, 757, 759, 766–8,
    770–3, 775–6, 778, 780, 983
conditionally conjugate models, 855
confidence intervals, 22, 291, 293, 436,
  504, 664, 751, 804, 813, 824, 831–5
  equal-tailed, 832
  symmetric, 832
confluence analysis, 24, 26
  approach, 134–5
congruous measurement, 52
conjugate gradient approach, 926
connection strengths, 404
consistency, 428–9, 436, 439, 457, 469,
  471, 534, 590, 652, 655, 756, 808
  modulus of, 180
  theorem, 172–4
continuity thesis, 62
continuous
  almost sure, 176, 182, 195
  data, 1014
  mapping theorem (CMT), 166, 169,
    185–8, 196, 199, 204
continuously compounded rate of
  return, 739
control variables, 805–6
convergence, 177
  almost sure, 163
  in distribution, 163, 202, 255, 481
  in mean square, 163
  in probability, 163, 202–3, 436, 485,
    564, 606
  joint, 201, 203
  pointwise, 178, 182
  rate of, 287, 290, 292, 294–5, 311, 314,
    332, 338, 341, 356, 369, 378, 380,
    383, 387, 389, 402, 486, 819, 995,
    1006–8, 1020–1, 1025
  stochastic, 163
  weak, 177–8, 193, 516
corner solution, 705
  model, 702, 705
count
  data model, 709, 728, 818, 988:
    Poisson, 951
  response variable, 726
covariance
  asymmetry, 774
  matrix, 597, 767–8, 773, 776:
    conditional, 774; sample, 825;
    stationary, 829–830
  stationary, 591–2, 595–6, 599, 606–7,
    744, 751–2: system, 592, 599

covering-law model of explanation, 67
  see also received view
Cowles Commission, 26, 28–32, 42, 44,
  126–33, 145
  methodology, 74–5, 79–81
  research, 131
  structural modeling paradigm, 140–1,
    143–5
Cramér's
  rule, 226
  Theorem, 166–7, 806
Cramer–Rao lower bound (CRLB), 432,
  438–40, 442, 444–5, 639
Cramér–Wold theorem, 166–7, 184
critical values, 588
cross-validation (CV)
  kernel estimator, 1023
  methods, 1010–11, 1015–17, 1020
crush test, 794, 800–1
cubic spline, 985–6, 998
cumulative distribution function
  (c.d.f.), 162, 173, 796–7, 817, 819,
  952, 1020
  conditional, 1020–1
curse of dimensionality, 1006, 1008, 1017,
  1021
curve-fitting, 5, 24, 26, 28, 30, 32, 51
CUSUM test, 280, 297, 299, 313,
  341, 495
cut-off property, 224, 227–9
cycle, 611, 614, 616, 627, 1037
  common, 612–22, 626–8
  innovations, 620
  reference, 626–7
  test, 617
  UC common, 621
  unobserved, 612
cyclical variations, 614
cylinder sets, 174
  finite dimensional, 171–2

data gathering mechanism, 696–7
data generating
  mechanism (DGM), 20, 27, 36, 702, 728
  process (DGP), 71–2, 740, 788–9, 803–4,
    807, 814–15, 817–19, 821, 824, 834,
    935, 1008, 1010, 1043–4, 1046,
    1048, 1052
data mining, 43, 72, 77, 144, 327
data-led modeling approach, 143–4
Davies problem, 586
decision space, 846
deductive-nomological form, 67

definitions
  external, 123
  internal, 123
dependence
  long range, 354, 359, 375
  near-epoch (NED), 192–3, 572
  nonlinear, 463
  positive, 807
  spatial parameter, 466
  weak, 189–90, 355, 375, 378
determinants
  direct analysis, 110
  Jacobian, 129
  theory of, 110
deterministic components, 260–2,
  266–7, 272
detrended data, 320
diagnostic checks, 34, 689, 851
Dickey–Fuller
  coefficient, 530
  covariate augmented (CADF)
    test, 272
  distributions, 255, 523, 544, 562–3,
    569, 571
  GLS test, 519
  regressions, 261
  statistic, 186
  test, 189, 264–5, 267, 269, 332, 517,
    524, 531, 564, 579
DIEHARD tests, 793–4
difference stationary variable, 610
diffuse tests, 932
direct representation, 913–4, 925
  model, 922, 936
directing process, 921
disequilibrium market model, 681
Donsker's theorem, 184
double length artificial regressions (DLR)
  approach, 937–8
double maximum tests, 306–7
double threshold, 462
dummy variable coefficients, 717, 721
duration
  data, 709, 711
  dependence: negative, 711; positive, 711
  models, 710
Durbin's algebraic procedure, 103
Durbin–Watson
  statistic, 9, 136, 227, 441, 816
  test, 31, 778, 933
dynamic
  conditional correlation (DCC)
    specification, 779

dynamic – *continued*
  models, 668, 672, 677, 679, 689, 822,
    830–1: behavioral, 141; factor, 612;
    multinormal, 684

econometric
  experiments, 792
  inference, 122
  methodology, 8
  model, 851
  modeling, 4, 7–8, 10, 12
economic model, 851
effects
  contextual, 908
  correlated, 908
  endogenous, 908
efficiency, 428–9, 436, 449, 457, 460, 469–70
  asymptotic, 429–30
efficient
  importance sampling (EIS), 769
  Method of Moments (EMM)
    estimator, 759
  score test, 664, 667–8: *see also* Lagrange
    Multiplier tests
eigenvalues, 312, 337, 382–3, 558–60,
    592, 598, 622, 624–5, 771, 775, 788,
    890, 926, 937
eigenvectors, 312, 383, 558–9, 624–5,
    775, 890
EM algorithm, 403
embedding
  approach, 878–80, 893
  model, 878–9
  specification, 880
empirical
  distribution function (EDF), 820
  economics, 138
  evidence, 6–7, 9, 25, 47, 49
  likelihood (EL) approach, 471
  modeling, 8–9, 12, 16, 26–7, 29–31, 42,
    44, 51
  regularities, 19
encompassing, 76
endogeneity, 641–2, 645, 655
equicontinuous,
  requirement, 183
  stochastic, 180–1, 194, 198
  uniform, 180
ergodicity, 399
error component regression model, 639,
    642, 948, 1025
  dynamic, 650
  one-way, 635, 645, 649, 946, 948
  two-way, 945

error correction
  mechanism (ECM), 137, 334, 338–9, 546,
    550, 555–6, 568, 569–70, 594–5,
    601, 872–4, 878–9, 883, 885–6, 888:
    cointegrated, 873, 875–7, 879,
    890–1, 893–4; reduced rank, 888;
    multivariate, 593, 601; nonlinear,
    571; parameters, 894;
    representation, 873
  model, 33–4, 49, 333, 580–1: *see also*
    error correction mechanism
  multivariate framework, 593
  term, 583
error in rejection probability (ERP), 813,
    819, 823, 833
error statistical account, 10
error-fixing strategy, 10
errors-in-equations models, 6, 104, 108, 135
  see also simultaneous equations models
errors-in-variables models, 6, 103–4, 108,
    122, 130, 134, 437
estimating
  equation (EE), 429–30, 433, 445–6, 464,
    470: generalized (GEE); approach,
    468; estimator, 469; linear unbiased,
    429; optimal, 457
  function (EF), 430, 432, 434, 436–44,
    449, 451, 453–4, 456–8, 461, 464,
    468–9, 471: approach, 429–30, 432,
    438–9, 442, 448, 450, 452, 458–60,
    464–5, 470–2; biased, 452;
    elementary, 454–5, 459, 469–70;
    minimum variance unbiased (MVU),
    429, 443; optimal, 437, 439, 441,
    443–8, 450–3, 455–6, 458–468, 470;
    orthogonal, 458, 467; quadratic,
    458; quasi-score, 468; regular, 439,
    445, 454; stable, 437; statistical,
    437; sufficient (SEF), 437–8, 444;
    unbiased, 439, 443–5, 448, 450, 454–5
Euclidean
  distance, 172
  norm, 178
exact score, 668, 670
excess kurtosis, 749–50, 756, 758
exchangeability, 842
expectation and maximization (EM)
  algorithm approach, 666, 704
  estimate, 666
expected posterior loss, 844, 846
experimental
  economics, 65: experimental-design
    approach, 71–3
  method, 14, 24

experiments, 11–12
exploratory data analysis (EDA), 34, 43, 1010
explosive
  behavior, 591
  process, 548, 569, 585
  roots, 544, 546, 568–9, 574
exponential smoothing process, 740, 752, 779
extended
  Gauss–Markov theorem, 971
  inequality, 444
extension theorem, 162
external invalidity, 13, 36, 40–1, 44–5
extreme bounds analysis, 848

factor
  analysis models, 122
  loading, 916
failure times, 1024
falsificationism, 67–9, 80
family of densities
  conjugate, 843
  exponential, 843
feature, 614–15
  common, 614–15, 622, 628: tests, 622
feedback, 986
filter, 976, 978–9, 992, 1038
  contemporaneous, 979
  particle, 990, 993, 998: auxiliary, 995–6
  periodic, 1048
  predictive, 979
  recursions, 993–4
filtered estimator, 974, 977, 981
filtering, 457, 980, 982–3, 986–8, 990, 994
  density, 990–2, 994
  distribution, 995: joint, 997
finite dimensional distributions (fidis), 171, 174, 182, 184, 188, 198, 207
  multivariate Gaussian, 184
first difference (FD) transformation, 650
Fisher's test, 522, 524
  modified, 526
Fisher–Neyman probabilistic perspective, 37, 43–4, 50–1
fixed effects (FE), 655–6, 716–17, 721, 725, 949
  estimates, 641
  estimator, 636, 646, 649, 657, 717: *see also* Within estimator
  least squares, 636: *see also* least squares dummy variable (LSDV)
  linear regression, 724
  model, 636–7, 716–18, 721, 723, 726, 942–3, 1025

flexible
  conditioning method, 454, 457
  Fourier Form (FFF) filter, 759
fluctuations tests approach, 341
forecast
  error, 496–8, 501, 504: impulse responses, 501–3; shocks, 501; variance, 504–5; vector, 504
  horizon, 498, 505
  intervals, 497
forward prediction error, 240
Fourier
  discrete transform (DFT), 356, 360, 371–3, 375: tapered, 371–3
  frequencies, 357, 364, 371–4, 382
  transform, 625
FPE, 1017
fractals, 176
fractional
  autoregressive (FAR) estimate, 369
  cointegration, 380, 383–4
  difference integration filters, 355
  differencing, 355, 375–6
  exponential (FEXP): estimate, 369; model, 369
  Gaussian noise, 354
  truncated filter, 374
fractionally cointegrated systems, 378
frequency
  domain, 123, 359: estimates, 356; least squares (FDLS) coefficients, 379–380; method, 124, 144
  response function, 976
frequentist, 843–5
  approach, 844
  methods, 852
  reasoning, 864
Frisch's
  macrodynamic model, 123
  structural approach, 123, 125–6, 129, 131–2
F-statistic, 654
  adjusted, 384
  customary, 384
F-test, 1042–3
Fully Modified estimator, 335
functionals
  Exp, 318–19
  Mean, 318–19, 341
  Sup, 318–19, 341

Gaussian
  distribution, 165, 176, 565–6
  errors, 554, 557, 564, 750

Gaussian – *continued*
 function, 170
 kernel, 1010
 likelihood function, 543, 557, 559, 980
 linear model, 987–8
 maximum likelihood, 557
 mixed distribution, 204
 multivariate process, 293
 semiparametric estimate, 360
Gauss–Hermite quadrature, 719
Gauss–Markov (G-M)
 assumptions, 31
 perspective, 30–1, 48, 51
 theorem, 32, 46–7
generalized
 additive models, 1008
 least squares (GLS), 9, 32, 481, 485, 642–3,
  645, 650–1, 925: detrending, 262,
  329: local, 261; procedure, 295, 326,
  329, 336–7; EGLS estimator, 487;
  estimate, 359; estimator, 487,
  637–40, 646; dynamic, 529; feasible
  (FGLS), 9, 32, 639–40, 829, 924–5,
  929, 948; estimator, 925;
  Swamy-Arora feasible
  estimator, 639
 linear: mixed models (GLMM), 951;
  models (GLM), 951
 method of moments (GMM), 7, 46, 48,
  108, 245, 304, 458–9, 471, 534, 650,
  652–3, 655–6, 727, 757, 759, 769,
  920, 931, 956–7: estimator, 530, 617,
  651–3, 657; extended system, 654;
  first difference, 654, 658;
  symmetrically normalised (SNM),
  654–5; inferences, 46; orthogonality
  conditions, 656; tests, 615
 product kernel, 1014–5
 residual, 708, 957
 spectral density, 1016
general-to-simple model selection
 rule, 941
general-to-specific modeling strategy, 33,
 35, 76, 123, 236
generators
 congruential, 791: linear (LCG), 790–1,
  794–6, 798, 801–2, 809;
  multiplicative, 791
 high-period, 792–3, 809
 linear feedback shift register (LFSR),
  792–6, 801
 multiplicative, 791

multiply-with-carry (MWC), 792, 794,
  796, 800–3, 809
 random number (RNG), 790–3, 796, 800,
  803: pseudo, 790; uniform, 790, 794,
  796–7, 801
 WELL, 793–5, 801
GHK
 sampler, 674–5, 678, 680–1
 simulation, 676, 678
 simulator, 670, 673–4, 677, 684
Gibbs sampler, 667, 724, 854–6, 858, 861,
 875–6, 885–7, 955
 griddy-Gibbs, 876, 887
global
 modeling method, 1003
 polynomial model, 1005
Gompertz function, 93, 96
Granger
 causal, 498–9
 causality, 144, 495, 499–500, 505
 noncausal, 498–500
 Representation Theorem, 543–4, 546–8,
  551–2, 556, 563, 569, 572, 616
Grassman manifold, 883–5, 889
Gumbel distribution, 684, 686

Haavelmo
 bias, 128, 131, 134
 distribution, 131
 methodology, 142
Hadamard matrix product, 362
Hadri test, 520–2
Hammersley–Clifford theorem, 912
Hannan–Quinn criterion (HQ), 489–90
Hansen's generalized method of
  moments, 93
 see also method of moments
hard core propositions, 69
Harvard ABC barometers, 119
Hausman test, 641, 646, 708, 721
 statistic, 640
hazard
 function, 711: models, 711
 models, 710
 rate, 710
Heckman two step estimator, 715
 see also two step least squares
HEGY
 method, 1040, 1051
 tests, 1048
hermitian matrix, 361, 381
heterogeneous panels, 944–5

heteroskedasticity, 706–7, 725, 745, 778, 817–18, 821–5, 834, 912, 914, 919, 922–3, 931, 933, 940, 945, 953, 956–7
 time-dependent, 751
heteroskedasticity-consistent covariance matrix estimate (HCCME), 822, 826
 test, 407
hidden
 Markov model, 402: *see also* autoregressive Markov-switching model
 units, 417–18
high frequency, 759, 761
 returns, 760
highest posterior density (HPD)
 intervals, 845
 region, 845
Hodrick–Prescott filter, 617
homogeneous panels, 942–3
Hotelling's method, 98
Huber–White sandwich estimator, 706
hurdle model, 705–6, 712, 726
Hurst effect, 754
Hyperbolic tangent function, 401, 404
hypothesis, 814, 817, 851
 testing, 22, 119, 132, 143, 240, 438, 573, 663, 812–13, 825, 834, 846, 850: *see also* Neyman-Pearson methodology
hypothetical-deductive method, 5, 13–14, 19, 67
 see also received view
hypothetical infinite population, 15, 20

idempotent matrix, 635
identification, 129, 130, 140, 143, 876–7, 882
 conditions, 1009
 global, 873, 875, 880
 local, 873, 878–9
 problem, 72, 74, 129, 142, 411–14, 873, 878–80, 893, 906–7, 919, 946, 956
identity matrix, 635
idiosyncratic errors, 946, 948
importance
 density, 990, 993, 995–6: conditional, 995
 function, 853–4
 sampler, 955: relative (RIS), 954–5
 sampling, 853, 986, 989, 996: estimator, 853–4
impulse
 response: analysis, 478, 505, 557; coefficients, 503; function, 556–7, 886–7

responses, 501–5: orthogonal, 502; structural, 505
 shocks, 123
incidental parameters (IP) problem, 717, 719
incongruous measurement, 12–13, 36, 40, 44–5
increasing domain, 921–2
independent and identically distributed (IID), 820, 822, 828
 errors, 835
 process, 15, 23
indicator function, 814
individual
 dummies, 636–7
 effects, 637, 641, 645–6, 649–50, 656: invariant, 639–40; specific, 634
inductive
 behavior, 22
 inference, 7, 17–18, 22–3, 30, 36, 44–5, 51
 logic, 20
 procedure, 21
 reasoning, 22, 52
inductive-statistical explanation, 67
inference functions, 471
information
 criterion (IC), 239, 829, 1017, 1041, 1043
 matrix, 849, 923–6, 936, 941
innovation dummy, 550, 563
innovations, 979, 982
 see also prediction errors
instrumental variables (IV), 9, 29, 32, 46–7, 644, 654, 656, 827, 927–8, 944, 950, 1009
 estimator, 48, 108, 529, 654, 657, 827: IV-GLS, 529; Within-IV-GLS, 529; Within-IV-OLS, 529
 method, 108, 121, 528, 641–2, 650–1, 757
 regression, 654, 894
 weak problem, 657–8
instruments, 642–8, 650–1, 655, 658, 748, 1009
 optimal, 930–1
 redundant, 644
integrated variables, 544
interaction
 global, 905
 local, 905
 social, 905, 907–8
 strategic, 905: model, 906
invariance
 principle, 186, 266, 268, 279
 properties, 332, 372, 442–3

invariant test, 267, 269, 272
inverse
  chi-square test, 518: *see also* Fisher's test
  Mills ratio, 698, 713, 715
  normal test, 518, 523
  problem, 906
inversion principle, 796
inverted Wishart
  distribution, 886
  form, 875
  priors, 876
invertibility conditions, 223–4, 406–7
IPS
  statistic, 517
  test, 517, 520, 523, 525, 531
iterated expectations, 744
Itô integrals, 199–201

Jacobian, 922, 926
  term, 922
Jeffreys'
  rule, 849–50
  prior approach, 877–8, 880, 886, 888, 893
Jensen's inequality, 749

Kalman
  filter, 232, 235, 542, 620, 769, 977–83,
    986: prediction equations, 987
  smoother, 977
k-class estimator, 9, 29, 32
kernel, 915, 1005
  density estimation, 862
  estimates, 260, 1016, 1025
  estimators, 258, 915, 1008, 1024:
    Bartlett, 259; regression, 1004;
    unconditional, 1020
  function, 367, 726, 862, 915, 1015:
    univariate, 1014
  generalized, 1023
  smoothing methods, 24, 43, 1003
Kiefer process, 587
Kolmogorov's
  consistency theorem, 27, 37, 171:
    see also consistency theorem
  inequality, 182, 188
KPSS test, 283, 330
Kronecker product, 481, 585, 635

lag order selection, 488–9
Lagrange Multiplier (LM), 283, 363, 408,
    411, 481, 704, 708
  linearity tests, 408, 414
  principle, 320
  procedure, 238

statistic, 303, 363, 409, 411–12, 414, 493,
    639, 666, 707, 817, 934–9, 941, 944,
    948, 957–8
test, 238–9, 301, 303–4, 311, 313, 319,
    326, 363, 385, 407, 409–10, 414,
    416–17, 492–3, 520–1, 639, 664, 705,
    708, 757, 772, 933, 935–6, 948,
    1043: Exp-LM test, 312; Mean-LM test,
    304, 311–12; Sup-LM test, 311–12
Laplace methods, 889
latent
  data, 708, 858
  dynamic models, 689–90
  regime indicator, 681
  variables, 682–3, 690, 709, 857, 952–3,
    956, 1023: model, 689, 856
law of
  dynamic equilibrium, 119
  iterated expectations, 200, 743, 1012
  large numbers (LLN), 165, 169, 189, 288,
    291–2, 446, 515, 523, 529, 921:
    strong (SLLN), 164, 853; weak
    (WLLN), 164, 167, 177, 451
least squares (LS), 5, 481, 485, 602, 696,
    704, 720, 829
  concentrated, 584
  conditional (CLS), 230–2
  direct least squares, 109
  dummy variable (LSDV), 636, 639:
    regression, 637
  equation, 447
  estimator, 459, 461, 485, 503, 582, 584–5,
    700, 714
  indirect least squares (ILS), 109,
    121–2, 128
  linear regression, 698
  method of estimation, 91, 95–102, 127,
    134, 286, 429–30, 448, 460, 589
  nonlinear (NLS) estimator, 699, 725
  residuals, 486
  three-stage least squares (3SLS), 9, 29,
    32, 950
  two-stage least squares (2SLS), 9, 29, 32,
    134–6, 642–5, 647–8, 654, 657–8,
    927, 929, 933–4, 939, 1009: Between
    (B2SLS), 643–4; error component
    (EC2SLS), 643–5; Fixed effects, 642;
    forward filter estimator, 653;
    generalized (G2SLS), 644–5; spatial,
    927, 931; generalized (GS2SLS),
    930–1; Within (W2SLS), 642, 644
  two-step least squares, 714, 724
  weighted, 125, 127, 446, 467, 470, 726,
    922: regression, 638

Lévy
  motion, 207–8
  process, 207
likelihood
  approach, 543
  function, 433, 567, 620, 674, 676,
    679–80, 682, 817, 843, 873, 980,
    982, 987: multinormal, 684
  principle, 843, 850
  ratio (LR): principle, 239, 363, 410, 704;
    statistic, 303–4, 417, 598, 705, 707,
    817, 833, 936; test, 238–9, 265, 282,
    299–302, 304, 307, 313, 326, 329,
    412, 438, 488, 532, 534, 542, 552,
    559–61, 564–6, 571, 598, 617, 668,
    926, 933, 935
limit
  cycles, 398, 400, 462
  distribution, 283, 286–7, 289, 291–7, 300,
    306–11, 314–15, 317–19, 325–6, 329,
    331, 334, 337, 339–41, 557, 563–4,
    570: non-degenerate, 316, 318, 335
limiting distribution, 169, 236, 294, 485,
    494, 521–5, 527–8, 531–2, 585–7, 591,
    603, 757, 806
  of normalized sums, 199
Lindeberg condition, 165
linear
  process, 216, 545
  trend, 481–3, 486, 526
linearity, 439
  hypothesis, 412–13
  tests, 408, 416
link relatives, 107
linking function, 245
Ljung–Box test, 778
LLC test, 513–14, 516–17, 525
local
  averaging, 1002
  constant least squares estimator, 1004
  least squares estimator, 1005
  level model, 975–6, 983–5
  linear: estimate, 1010, 1018; least squares
    estimator, 1004, 1025; model, 1004;
    regression approach, 1004
  modeling, 1002
  polynomial: estimators, 1005–7; fitting,
    1004–5; least squares estimators,
    1004; regression, 1004–5; Whittle
    (LPW); estimate, 366;
    likelihood, 366
  Whittle (LW): estimate, 360, 362, 366–9,
    371, 374–7, 380–1, 386–7: ELW, 376,
    383, 388; nonlinear (NLW), 387;

tapered, 374; estimation, 361, 385,
  388; residual-based, 383; frequency
  domain, 360; likelihood, 361;
  log-likelihood, 376; memory
  estimate, 382
locally
  best invariant (LBI) test, 283–4, 319
  equivalent alternatives (LEA), 936
logical positivism, 66–7, 80
logistic function, 93–4, 96–9, 104
logit model, 142, 1020
  binary, 717, 798
log-Jacobian, 922, 925–6, 937–8, 943, 950
log-likelihood, 925, 935–8, 943, 946–7,
    950, 953–6
  function, 699, 701, 706, 714–15, 717:
    conditional, 719; unconditional, 719
log-periodogram (LP)
  estimate, 357, 361, 363–5, 368–9, 371,
    373–4, 377–8, 380, 386, 389:
    nonlinear (NLP), 386
  estimation, 360, 386, 388
  inference, 375
  memory estimate, 382
  polynomial (PLP), 366: estimate, 365–8
  regression, 358–61, 369, 373–4, 381,
    386, 389: augmented, 364–5;
    modified, 368; nonlinear (NLP), 386
  regression coefficients, 359
  residuals, 373
long memory
  parameter, 1019–20
  volatility parameter, 754
long-run
  relations, 541–3, 551, 553, 556
  value, 551
loss function, 846, 849, 889
  absolute deviation, 1006
  all-or-nothing, 844, 849
  asymmetric linear, 844
  predictive, 847
  quadratic, 844, 1005–6
lost dimensions, 129
LSE approach, 33, 35, 41, 75–8, 137
Lucas critique, 142, 296
Lucas–Sargent approach, 34–5, 41

marginal likelihood, 843, 846, 856, 861
Markov
  Chain: reducible, 886; samplers, 667
  Chain Monte Carlo (MCMC): estimator,
    802; method, 667, 724, 759, 886–7,
    889, 893, 921, 955, 983, 986,
    989–90, 996; output, 888

Markov – *continued*
  process, 37, 977
  switching model, 572, 894
martingale
  difference (m.d.), 188–9: assumption, 166,
     193; sequence, 739, 742; stationary,
     188, 190
  model, 739
  process, 747, 749
maximally-equidistributed sequences, 793
maximum likelihood (ML), 26, 231, 234–5,
    242–3, 481, 487, 503, 559–60, 569–71,
    699, 704, 706, 712, 714–15, 717, 722–3,
    766, 769, 772, 776, 778–80, 817, 819,
    829, 834, 920–2, 924, 927, 930, 932, 937,
    939–40, 943, 947, 950, 953, 983, 990
  conditional, 402, 451
  equation, 433, 435, 445–7, 560
  estimate, 292, 432, 438, 720, 849, 875, 923
  estimating equations (EE), 434
  estimator (MLE), 20, 128, 230, 232, 234,
    240, 243, 312, 409, 429, 436, 442,
    449, 451–2, 454, 466, 470, 487,
    503, 534, 559, 561, 566, 571–2,
    657, 668, 696, 699, 705, 708, 715,
    717–18, 721, 725, 756–8, 761, 886,
    924, 980: bias-corrected, 657;
    conditional (CMLE), 232–4; exact
    (EMLE), 232–3, 235; quasi- (QMLE),
    232, 294–5, 310, 503, 756–7, 761,
    769, 773; restricted, 721; simulated
    (SMLE), 667, 685–6, 689, 769
  full information estimator (FIML), 9, 29,
    32, 128, 721, 723: *see also* maximum
    likelihood estimator
  limited information estimator (LIML), 9,
    29, 32, 128–9, 133–5, 654–6
  principle, 90, 122, 128, 134, 337, 403,
    428–30, 433, 436–7, 441, 447–9,
    451, 460, 464, 470–1
  quasi maximum likelihood estimator
    (QMLE), 529: fixed effects, 530
  statistic, 707
maximum score estimator, 726
Mean Square Error (MSE), 364, 366, 369,
    481, 496, 638, 973–4, 982, 989, 998
  conditional, 971
  forecast, 498
  matrix, 496, 971, 980–1
  minimum (MMSE), 495–6, 751, 971–2,
    979–80, 983, 988
  minimum linear estimator (MMSLE),
    971–2, 980

  optimal bandwidth, 364–5
  optimal rate, 364
  reduction, 368
measurement
  equation, 977
  error, 634, 641, 907
memory
  conditions, 189
  estimates, 370, 373–4, 384
  estimation, 359
  long, 197–8, 280, 284, 340–1, 354–5,
    360, 370, 377, 385–6, 388–9, 749:
    Seasonal or Cyclical Long Memory
    (SCLM), 377: processes, 377: negative,
    355, 375
  parameter, 354, 356–8, 361, 370, 375,
    377–8, 380, 383, 385, 388
  semi-parametric estimate, 364
  short, 191–2, 204, 217, 221, 227, 284,
    290, 340–1, 371
Mersenne
  prime, 791, 793
  twister, 793–4
M-estimate, 367–8
method of
  averages, 92, 95–6, 99–103, 105, 109
  composition, 859
  elemental sets, 92: *see also* selected points
  least absolute deviations, 100–1
  least absolute errors, 92: *see also* least
    absolute deviation
  minimax, 92, 100–1
  moments, 92, 95–6, 109, 229–30,
    429–30, 470–1, 769, 927, 944:
    estimator, 454
  normal places, 100, 106, 109: *see also*
    least squares
  orthogonal least squares, 105, 107
  Rousseeuw's least median of squared
    errors, 101
  selected points, 92, 94, 96
  subsets, 92: *see also* selected points
methodological framework, 5–6, 8, 36, 51
methodology
  econometric, 62–3, 141–2, 217
  forecasting, 143
  model-theoretic, 71
  scientific, 65–6
  scientific research programs, 69
  statistical, 10, 543
Metropolis–Hastings Algorithm, 854–6, 859,
    887–8, 955–6
Metropolis-within-Gibbs step, 856

minimization problem, 301
minimum chi-squared method, 641
misspecification, 12, 46–7, 49, 52, 771,
    940–1
  errors, 39, 663, 686
  test, 10, 17, 21, 38–41, 43, 45, 47,
    49–51, 780
mixed data methods, 1015
mixing
  assumption, 193
  strong, 191–2
  uniform, 191
model
  adequacy, 236–7
  selection, 850, 856: approach, 597–9, 601;
    criteria, 240–1, 243, 489–91,
    617, 623
  specification procedures, 130–1
model-based expectations, 568
  rational, 568
modified exponential function, 93, 96
Monte Carlo, 655, 769, 805–6
  confidence intervals, 832, 834
  design variables, 804
  direct estimator, 854
  estimates, 804, 808
  experiments, 652–3, 656, 684, 689,
    788–9, 795, 803–4, 806–7, 930–1, 933
  filter, 990, 994–5
  integration, 719, 874–5: direct, 853–5
  mean, 652–3
  method, 788–90, 805, 834–5
  parameter space, 807
  recursive, 808–9
  replications, 656–7
  results, 657–8, 718
  sample size, 804
  smoother, 990, 998
  studies, 707–8, 717, 721, 787, 935
  test, 813–17, 834
  variance, 652–3
  variance reduction techniques, 789
Moran's I statistic, 932–3, 936, 939, 957–8
mover stayer model, 723–4
moving average (MA), 228, 230, 232–4,
    237–40, 242, 245–6, 257, 481, 651,
    768, 1046, 1051
  asymmetric (asMA) model, 407
  exponentially weighted (EWMA) model,
    778
  filter, 1037–9
  integer (INMA) model, 246
  model, 216, 223, 233–4, 244, 579: random
    errors, 123

nonlinear model, 407
  operator, 234, 243
  polynomial, 238, 621
  process, 222–4, 228, 244, 830, 985
  pure, 223–4, 227–8, 231, 234, 244
  representation, 23, 245, 501, 545,
    547–8, 569
  root, 235, 257
M-test, 259, 261–2
  see also Phillips–Perron tests
multinomial choice, 1024
  models, 1023
Multivariate Linear Regression (MLR)
    model, 48
Mundlak correction, 716, 721

Nadaraya–Watson estimator, 1005–6, 1016
naïve distribution theory, 169
narrow band
  coefficients, 379: *see also* frequency
    domain least squares (FDLS)
    coefficients, 379
  estimates, 356
natural experiments, 80
naturalistic turn, 62
near-efficiency property, 267, 272
neighborhood, 905, 909
neighboring
  locations, 904, 921, 952
  terms, 934
neighbors, 904, 909–12, 915–16, 952–3
nested structure, 144
neural networks, 404–5
Neyman–Pearson (N–P)
  hypothesis testing framework, 11, 22, 26
  lemma, 263, 265, 267–71
  methodology, 120, 132, 134
  tests, 40, 43
nomological machine, 64, 72
nonidentification
  global, 880, 885, 893
  local, 877–8, 880, 885, 893
nonlinear
  adjustment processes, 582
  functional form, 986
  panel data analysis, 534
  regression, 698
  univariate models, 397, 459
nonnormality tests, 491, 494
nonparametric
  additive model, 1017
  analysis, 1019
  autoregressive model, 1017

nonparametric – *continued*
  estimation, 1009, 1012–13, 1023, 1025:
    local polynomial, 1007
  estimator, 1007–8
  kernel: density function, 1014; estimation
    methods, 1002–3, 1012, 1025
  location-scale model, 1023
  methods, 1002, 1007, 1011, 1025
  model, 1007–8
  non-smoothing test, 1014
  regression, 1002–4, 1010, 1013
  smoothing, 1002: test, 1014
  tests, 1011–12, 1019
  time series: analysis, 1017; regression,
    1016–17
  vector autoregression, 1018
nonresponse, 634
nonsense
  correlation, 788
  regressions, 65, 126
nonstationary
  fractionally integrated (NFI) vector, 383
  panel regressions, 534
  panels, 512
  time series, 512
normality test, 675, 678–9, 681, 683–6, 689
nuisance parameters, 144, 255–6, 258, 263,
    266, 268, 291, 299, 331, 339, 341, 361,
    410, 416, 440, 442, 449–53, 456, 460,
    469, 524–5, 586, 843, 847, 850, 929, 939

Olsen transformation, 699, 715, 717, 727
omitted variables, 47–8, 503
  bias, 636–7
  test, 675, 678, 680, 683
optimality
  determinant, 449
  local, 264
  matrix, 448
  point, 264
  trace, 449
options pricing framework, 766, 780
ordinary least squares (OLS), 9, 29, 46, 230,
    243, 523, 636–8, 641, 652, 655–6, 704,
    714, 760, 804, 820, 831, 931, 938
  coefficient, 358, 365, 383–4
  estimate, 365, 379, 383, 641, 720, 829, 937
  estimator, 32, 47, 204, 231, 517, 526–7,
    636, 649, 804–5, 807: fully modified
    (FM-OLS), 527–8; pooled, 527–8;
    pooled, 515, 527–8
  method, 105, 120, 125, 127, 133–5, 325,
    359, 380

regression, 357, 523, 525, 623, 825
residuals, 297, 313, 359, 384, 639, 815,
    935, 937–8
Ornstein–Uhlenbeck (OU) process,
    195–6, 264
orthogonal polynomials, 99–100
orthogonality conditions, 530, 653, 655–6,
    663, 957
outlier model
  additive (AO), 322, 326, 328–9, 331–2, 336
  innovational (IO), 322–3, 325–9,
    331–2, 336
outliers, 989

panel
  cointegration, 512
  data: models, 639, 685, 689, 725–8, 915;
    autoregressive, 653, 657; dynamic,
    649–50, 653–4, 656; regression,
    634; dynamic, 649; sets, 633,
    715, 723
  IV estimator, 528
  regressions, 512, 529
  stationary tests, 522
  tests, 512, 522
  unit root tests, 513–14, 522–5, 529: *see also*
    unit root tests for independent panels
  VAR model, 529
parameter
  chain, 855
  redundancy problem, 243–4
parameterization, 795
parametric
  approach, 1002–3
  global linear least squares estimator, 1005
  model, 1007, 1009, 1017, 1025
  regression model, 1003, 1005, 1011
  tests, 1011, 1025
  time series models: linear, 1016;
    nonlinear, 1016
  volatility function, 1018
participation equation, 705–6
path
  analysis, 109, 122
  coefficient, 109
Pearl–Reed method, 98
penalizing methods, 1010
percentile t method, 833
periodogram, 23, 371–3, 375–9
  analysis, 16
  bias, 371
  residual, 384
  tapered, 371–4

Phillips Curve, 137
Phillips–Perron tests, 258–9, 261
  modified, 260
piecewise
  autoregressive model, 398
  linear: function, 173–4, 462; model,
    401; processes, 579; vector
    autoregression, 583
Pinkse–Slade LM test statistic, 957
pivot, 814–15, 832
  asymptotic, 833
pivotal test statistic, 814–16, 831, 834
  asymptotically, 818–19, 826, 831
plug-in methods, 1010, 1020
Poincaré's separation theorem, 888–9
point
  estimate, 844–5, 847, 862, 889, 988
  estimation, 843, 845, 889
Poisson regression model, 700–1, 709,
  715, 717
  censored, 710
polar-Marsaglia method, 798–801
policy analysis, 126, 140, 142
  model-based, 140
pooled t-test, 513
  see also LLC test
portmanteau
  procedures, 238
  statistic Q, 237
  test, 237–9, 492: modified, 237
posterior
  conditional density, 855
  covariance matrix, 854
  density, 856: joint, 858, 875
  distribution, 887, 892: augmented, 858;
    conditional, 875, 877; marginal, 876
  inference, 874
  information criterion (PIC), 889
  marginal, 861
  mean, 852–3, 855, 860, 862, 889
  odds, 847
  probability, 862
  simulation, 856, 872, 885
  standard deviation, 853, 855, 860, 889
Powell's consistent estimator, 725, 1022
power
  asymptotic, 261, 298, 301, 320, 337
  envelopes, 262–5, 267, 269–70, 272,
    519–20: asymptotic, 261, 263–9,
    271–2, 329, 519–20; Gaussian
    local, 320
  functions, 298, 316, 320, 340
  local asymptotic functions, 289

monotonic, 304, 316
non-monotonic, 280, 298, 301, 304, 307,
  313, 330, 340
pre-data error probabilities, 22
prediction, 983
  equations, 978, 982
  error, 979, 982: decomposition, 232, 980
predictive density
  conditional, 848
  marginal, 848
pre-pivoting, 1013
principal component
  estimator, 624
  method, 523
prior
  covariance matrix, 857
  density, 843
  distribution, 849, 983
  dogmatic, 884
  embedding, 888
  improper, 850, 888
  informative, 877, 884, 893, 983
  intrinsic, 850
  marginal, 861
  non-informative, 877, 893, 983
  non-subjective, 849–50
  normal, 874, 876
  odds, 847
  probability function, 846
  proper, 850
  reference, 850
  uniform, 849, 874, 878, 881, 883, 885,
    887–8, 891
probabilistic-reduction (PR) approach, 27,
  36–40, 42–3, 45, 48, 73
probability, 842, 845, 864
  approach, 131–3
  density function (PDF), 1020
  measure, 162, 172
  model, 71, 139
  space, 162: derived, 162; fundamental, 162
  theory, 16
probit
  equation, 721
  model, 142, 702, 706–7, 723, 725, 817,
    952–3, 956–8: binary, 705, 713–14,
    717, 798; habit persistent, 684;
    multinormal, 673–4, 689; ordered,
    709, 857–8; specification, 857; spatial,
    921, 951, 954–6; error, 954; lag, 954
product
  kernel, 1014
  topology, 184

progressive program, 69
projective Frobenius
  linear subspace distance, 889–90
  loss, 890
propagation mechanism, 123
proposal density, 856, 859
  symmetric, 856
protective belt, 69

Q statistic, 335
Q test, 296, 311, 318–19, 333,
    335, 339–40
quantification, 9, 31–2
quasi-demeaning, 650
quasi-differencing, 136
quasi-likelihood, 468
  approach, 447, 457
  equation, 446
  estimate, 685
  estimator, 470
quasi-score, 448, 459
  function, 446

Rademacher distribution, 824
random
  components, 945
  effects, 655, 716, 719, 721, 723, 945:
      estimator, 638, 646, 721; GLS
      estimator, 650; MLE, 655; model,
      469, 637, 646, 716, 719, 721, 728,
      942–3, 1025; unobserved, 719
  numbers: common, 806–8; generation,
      789, 798, 809; generator (RNG), 790;
      see also generators; pseudo, 790;
      quasi-, 790; tests, 793; uniform, 792,
      797, 801–3
  sequence, 170
  walk, 49, 546, 553, 580, 592, 594, 611,
      615–16, 619, 752, 984: plus noise
      model, 520, 984; processes, 311, 321,
      872; trends, 611–12; with drift, 1046
rank
  condition, 130, 554, 556, 595
  configuration, 595–6, 599
  statistics, 43
  test, 560, 562, 564, 574
Rao Score (RS) test, 933, 935
rational
  economic policy, 127
  expectations (RE) hypothesis, 141, 144:
      Muth's model, 141
received view, 67, 70
recursions, 991–2

recursive residuals, 297
  demeaned, 297
reduced
  form (RF), 28–9, 128–9, 972: approach,
      144; regression, 641
  rank, 877–9, 894: algorithm, 560–1;
      estimates, 559; model, 880, 888;
      regression, 557–61, 568–70, 617;
      restrictions, 873, 876
reference
  DGP, 1010
  rules, 1010
reflection problem, 907–8
regime-switching, 397, 583
regression
  augmented, 365–6
  band-spectrum, 379
  classical errors-in-equations model, 134:
      see also errors-in-equations models
  classical model (CRM), 160
  cointegrating, 203–4, 335
  diagonal mean, 122
  equation, 706
  feasible GLS, 317
  infeasible GLS, 316–17
  least squares, 133, 143, 541: panel, 530
  linear model, 145, 341, 357, 470
  median model, 459, 469–70
  multiple linear, 285
  spatial model, 459, 466
  switching model, 399
  time series, 514, 523
  weighted, 122
Regression Specification Error Test
    (RESET), 414
regularity conditions, 958
rejection
  algorithm, 798, 800
  frequency, 1048, 1051–3
  method, 797–802
  probability function (RPF), 818
relative numerical efficiency (RNE), 854
repartition, 294
replication, 795–6, 804, 806
Representation Theorem, 842
resampling, 820, 991–3, 996
rescaled range
  procedure, 284, 359
  test, 340
residual
  autocorrelation, 10: tests, 491–2
  serial correlation, 135–6
  sum of squares (RSS), 777: restricted
      (RRSS), 637; unrestricted (URSS), 637

residual-based tests, 530–1
conditional moment, 776–7
resource flow, 906
respecification, 10, 38–9, 41, 43, 49–50, 52
response surfaces, 807
Riccati equation, 979
risk function, 844
robust-estimation approach, 73

Said–Dickey
regressions, 261: *see also* Dickey–Fuller
regressions
test, 257–8
sample selection model, 721, 724–5,
727–8, 818
sampling theory, 21
Sargan test, 652–3
Schwarz criterion (SC), 489–90
score
conditional function, 452
effective, 452–3
partial likelihood function, 456
pseudo function, 457
vector, 690–1
seasonal
adjustment, 1036, 1039–40, 1042–3,
1046, 1052–3: filter, 1036–7, 1039,
1048, 1052; methods, 1037–8,
1051–3
autoregressive moving average (SARMA)
process, 1044
dummies, 1042–3
lags, 1042, 1052–3
stochastic terms, 1041, 1046, 1052
unit roots, 1040–1, 1044, 1046, 1051–2
variation, 1036
seasonals, 613
seemingly unrelated regression (SUR), 949
approach, 524, 529, 950
equations, 828
semantic approach to scientific
theories, 70–2
semi-orthogonal
matrix, 886
specification, 886
semi-parametric
approach, 726
estimator, 725–6: Gaussian, 1019
models, 1021, 1025: random effects,
1025; single index, 1021–2
sensitivity analysis, 848–50
separable space, 173
sequence splitting, 795

sequential
asymptotics, 514, 517
elimination, 491
testing procedure, 308, 488–9
shock,
permanent, 557
structural, 556–7
transitory, 557
σ-field, 162, 171, 174, 188, 191, 199
projection, 172, 175–6
sign and size bias tests, 766
negative sign bias, 766
signal extraction, 971, 985, 998
filter, 976
signal–noise ratio, 976, 983–4
simulated
annealing, 412
data, 834
EM (SEM), 670: approach, 666–7, 672,
689; estimation, 668
estimating functions, 670
likelihood function, 686
log likelihood function, 685
normality test, 684
score (SSC), 667–70, 675, 678, 680–1,
683–4: statistic, 667–8, 672, 685–6,
688–9; test, 668; vector, 671
specification test, 667, 688
trajectories, 997
simulation, 788, 803, 807, 815, 998
estimation, 795
experiment, 788–90, 800, 1037, 1043,
1046, 1048
methods, 663, 787, 983, 989
results, 808
simultaneity
bias, 29
problem, 121–2, 136–7, 139
simultaneous
equations: bias, 714; model (SEM), 28–30,
32, 104, 110, 122, 127–9, 131–2,
134–5, 140–3, 478, 642, 894;
system, 828
model, 952
Skorokhod
processes, 202
representation theorem, 201
topology, 175–6, 185, 208
Slutsky's Theorem, 166–7
smoothed estimator, 974–5, 977, 980–1
smoother, 971
classical fixed interval, 981–2
simulation, 983

smoothing, 971, 980, 982–3, 986, 988,
    990, 994
  algorithms, 980–1, 985, 996–7
  density, 992, 994, 997: fixed-interval,
      997; fixed-lag, 997; joint, 997;
      marginal, 997
  distribution, 995: joint, 997
  error vector, 981
  fixed-interval, 980–1, 987, 997
  fixed-lag, 980–1, 997
  fixed-point, 980–1
  parameter, 862, 1002
  recursions, 998
smoothness, 801–2
social engineering, 127
  see also rational economic policy
spatial
  autocorrelation, 909, 914–15, 932, 934–5,
      946: consistent (HAC) estimator,
      931; global, 912
  autocovariance, 915
  autoregressive (SAR): error, 917, 925, 929,
      937–8, 941, 943–4, 947; model,
      904, 910, 913, 916, 918, 927, 954;
      moving average (SARMA) model, 919,
      938; parameter, 904, 943, 955–6;
      process, 912, 914, 917, 921, 931,
      935–6, 946, 948, 953
  common factor model, 917
  correlation, 908, 915, 931, 933, 946:
      local, 916; matrix, 914
  covariance, 904, 913, 920, 934–5
  dependence, 902, 920, 931–2, 935, 940
  Durbin model, 917
  econometrics, 902–3, 958
  error, 907, 957: autocorrelation, 904, 934,
      948, 950; components; model, 916,
      935; process, 915; dependence, 928,
      939–41; models, 904, 917, 920, 924,
      941; process, 925
  filter, 930
  heterogeneity, 902, 906
  lag, 904, 906, 908–9, 919, 941:
      dependence, 933, 939; model, 905,
      907–8, 916–18, 923, 925, 927–8, 931,
      938–41, 943–4, 952; SUR model,
      949–50
  methods, 903
  modeling, 903, 932
  moving average (SMA): error terms, 919;
      process, 913–14, 919, 921, 925, 936;
      variance, 916
  multiplier, 917: effects, 916, 918

ordering, 905, 935
panels, 942
parameter, 956
random field, 909: *see also* spatial
    stochastic process
reaction function, 905
regression model, 920, 922, 925, 956
sampling, 921, 958
scale, 907
seemingly unrelated regression (SUR)
    model, 942
statistics, 903
stochastic process, 909, 913
structure, 902, 905
variance, 915
weights, 910, 918–21, 926, 935, 944:
    matrix, 904, 908–9, 911, 926, 928,
    937–8, 945
spatially
  correlated errors, 907
  lagged dependent variable, 904
  weighted least squares, 925, 929–30
specification, 130–1, 135, 140, 143
  see also model specification procedures
  dynamic, 136–7
  Ramsey RESET test, 144
  search, 131
  test, 633–4, 666, 668, 675, 818, 822,
      923, 944, 950, 1040: statistic,
      666, 689
spectral
  decomposition representation, 638
  density, 354, 356, 358, 360, 366, 368,
      370, 372, 375–7, 382, 384, 386–7:
      autoregressive estimator, 259;
      function, 298, 370; matrix, 358,
      361, 381, 624–5
  representation theorem, 624
spillover, 905–6, 915
split population models, 697
squashing function, 404
stability
  analysis, 495
  tests, 491
stable
  convergence laws, 205–7
  distribution, 205, 207
  process, 482
state
  space: form (SSF), 977–8, 982, 985; model,
      982, 985–6, 992; Gaussian, 978–9;
      signal extraction weights, 998;
      system, 977; vector, 977

stationarity, 330, 399
stationary distribution, 821
statistical
    adequacy, 18, 44–5, 50, 52
    description, 15
    induction, 14–15, 19–21
    inference, 6–7, 16, 23–4, 26, 32, 44, 842
    misspecification, 17, 36, 40
    model, 37, 41–5, 48–9, 51
    regularity, 18, 43–4
statistically adequate model, 42–5, 48
Stiefel manifold, 882–3
stochastic
    convergence, 161
    integral convergence theorem
        (SICT), 203–4
    recurrence, 606–7
stock market
    return, 741
    volatility, 740–1
structural
    breaks, 989: tests, 389
    change, 279–82, 284–5, 287, 289,
        294, 296, 299, 302, 305–7, 309, 313,
        317, 320, 326, 333–4, 337, 340–1:
        models, 308; partial, 285, 289, 295;
        pure, 285, 290, 302
    form (SF), 28, 484
    model, 29, 41–4
    relationship, 1008
Student t distribution, 774, 801, 989
sufficiency, 428, 436, 438–9
summability, 194
    absolute, 194
    square, 194
Sup F test, 282
support, 746
switching
    algorithm, 569–71
    cointegrating vector, 594
    equilibria, 593

tapering, 376–7, 380, 382, 388
tapers, 372–3
    type-1, 372–4
    type-2, 372–4
    Zhurbenko's, 372
target density, 855
textbook approach, 30–5, 37, 41–3
theory-of-errors approach, 72–3
threshold
    autoregressive class of models, 579: *see also*
        autoregressive models

cointegration, 399, 581–2, 595–6, 600
    distance, 627
    effects, 579–85, 587–9, 591, 595–6, 600–1
    models, 579–580
    nonlinearities, 601
    parameter, 582–3, 585–6, 589–91, 599,
        606, 709
    permanent-transitory decomposition,
        600–1
    switching, 601
    unit root model, 580
    VAR, 607
    variable, 582–3, 585, 587–8, 590
tightness, 179, 207
    uniform, 179, 181–2, 184, 198, 208
time series
    analysis, 217
    methods, 217
tobit model, 142, 702, 704, 706–9, 716–18,
    720–1, 723, 725, 727–8
    dynamic, 679–680
    GARCH, 679
top coding, 709, 720
trace test, 560
TRAMO/SEATS, 1037, 1039–40, 1044,
    1046, 1048, 1051–3
transfer function, 218–19, 224, 235, 242, 245
transition
    density, 993
    equation, 977–8, 987–9, 992
treatment effects model, 714, 724
trend, 611, 613–14, 616, 627, 1036–7
    common, 612–13, 615–19, 621–2
    function, 322–3, 333–4, 336, 341
    innovations, 611, 620
    model: local linear, 974, 978, 984–5;
        smooth, 974; stochastic, 983
    random walk, 975
    ratios, 107
    smooth, 975: stochastic, 976
    stochastic, 478–9, 481–2, 872, 1038, 1041
    unobserved, 612
truncated
    filter, 625
    normal ordinates, 859
    normal proposal density, 859
    random variable, 699, 951
    regression model, 700, 703–5, 713,
        717–18, 720, 725
truncation, 695–8, 700–2, 718, 728, 818
    direct, 701
    incidental, 713
    mechanism, 698

truncation – *continued*
    model, 700, 703, 715
    point, 698
two step
    estimators, 723
    procedures, 722
Type-1 error, 813, 815

unbiased linear estimators, 102
unbiasedness, 429, 434, 437–40, 442
unconditional moments, 459, 463
uniform
    distribution, 882–3, 885
    integrability, 165
    metric, 172–4
uniformly most powerful (UMP) test, 263–4
unit
    circle, 168, 221, 233–5, 239, 245, 322, 404,
        513, 585, 591, 595–6, 658, 745, 753
    root, 33, 49, 217, 223, 234, 252–3, 255,
        260, 266, 268, 270, 280, 283–4, 287,
        312–13, 318, 320, 327–9, 340–1, 355,
        370, 380, 412, 414, 479, 482, 498,
        519, 521, 524, 528–9, 545, 573,
        579–80, 585, 601, 657, 747, 872:
        autoregressive, 234, 253, 314, 412;
        MA processes, 234; models, 279;
        test, 49, 253–4, 256–8, 262–5,
        267–72, 311, 316, 319, 322–4,
        326–7, 329, 331, 333–4, 337, 341,
        512, 518–19, 522, 524, 529–30,
        580, 634; tests for independent
        panels, 513
unobserved
    components (UC) model, 619, 621–2,
        625, 971, 975, 977–8, 985: stationary,
        998; time series, 972
    heterogeneity, 707, 721, 726
unreliability, 36, 47
updating equations, 978, 982

variables
    observational, 27
    theoretical, 27
    true, 27
variance-reduction techniques, 788,
    804–5, 808
variate parameters, 129
VECH model, 771–3
    diagonal, 772–3
    unrestricted, 772
vector
    autoregression (VAR), 34–5, 49, 75,
        143–4, 167, 336–8, 480–4, 490,
        494–5, 497–9, 529, 561, 563, 573,
        581, 601, 779, 872–4, 876, 883,
        887, 982: analysis, 480, 484, 489,
        492, 503, 505; bivariate, 588;
        coefficients, 486, 492, 500, 504, 874;
        cointegrated, 876; model, 568, 574;
        system, 312; levels form, 487, 503;
        linear models, 500; models, 32, 38–9,
        142, 294, 295, 478, 480, 482, 484–6,
        488–9, 491, 500–1, 505, 543–4, 546,
        552, 557, 568, 573–4, 618–19, 874;
        moving average (VARMA) model,
        505, 612, 622, 625, 779; unrestricted,
        627; parameters, 485; reduced form
        models, 484; structural VAR (SVAR),
        478, 481, 501–2, 556, 613; subset
        models, 488; unrestricted model,
        488, 888
    error correction model (VECM), 479–84,
        487–8, 490, 492, 494–5, 499, 505,
        543, 580–2, 586–7, 591–5, 600–1,
        611, 616, 618–19, 627: heterogeneous,
        531; linear, 583, 589, 591–2, 595;
        reduced rank, 617–19; stacked, 531
    moving average (VMA) representation,
        873
volatility, 737, 739–40, 744, 747–9,
    751–3, 755, 757–61, 765–6
    clustering, 766
    excess, 741
    feedback hypothesis, 748
    latent, 769, 779
    model, 739
    process, 743
    realized (RV), 738, 760–1: series, 761
    stochastic (SV), 385, 738, 765–7, 770–1,
        780: models, 738, 757–61, 766, 768,
        770, 777; factor, 770; independent
        (ISV), 771; long memory (LMSV),
        385–7; multivariate (MSV), 767–71,
        774, 778–80; univariate, 769–70
von Neumann ratio, 136

Wald
    principle, 410, 704
    statistic, 303–5, 384, 411, 500, 585–8,
        601–5, 707, 777, 817, 936
    test, 300–5, 313, 317, 341, 359, 363,
        411, 488, 500, 565, 567, 582, 584–5,
        589, 640, 668, 833–4, 935: Exp-Wald
        test, 303–5, 315–17; Mean-Wald test,
        303–5, 311, 315–17; modified, 382;
        Sup-Wald test, 303–5, 310–11,
        315–17, 341

Walrasian general equilibrium system, 127, 131
wavelet
  analysis, 359
  coefficients, 359–60
weak exogeneity, 554–5, 561–2
Weiner process, 293, 297, 300, 309, 325
white noise, 30, 222, 235, 481–2, 484, 487, 494–7, 522, 621, 761
  disturbances, 973–4, 984
  error, 9, 36, 50, 219, 229
  MA, 618
  process, 217, 624, 745–6, 761
  unobservable input, 235
White's
  estimator, 826
  theorem, 77
Whittle
  estimate, 385, 387
  local estimator, 1019–20
  local polynomial (LPW) estimator, 1019
Wiener
  measure, 176, 255, 264, 270–1: *see also* Brownian motion
  process, 984
Wiener–Kolmogorov (WK)
  filter, 1040
  signal extraction formula, 972–6, 982, 998

window, 851
  Bartlett, 372
  Parzen, 372
  width, 1003–5, 1010, 1014–16, 1019: optimal, 1024; selection, 1009–10, 1020–1, 1025
within
  estimator, 639, 646, 649–50
  regression, 638
  residuals, 647
  (Q) transformation, 637, 640, 647, 649
Wold
  decomposition, 216, 218–22, 237, 245, 738, 746, 751–2, 1017
  MA representation, 501
  representation, 615
  Theorem, 190
working covariance matrix, 468–9

Yule–Walker
  equations, 226, 229, 829
  estimates, 229, 231

zero restrictions, 488, 490
ziggurat
  implementation, 803
  method, 799–800
zymosis, 2